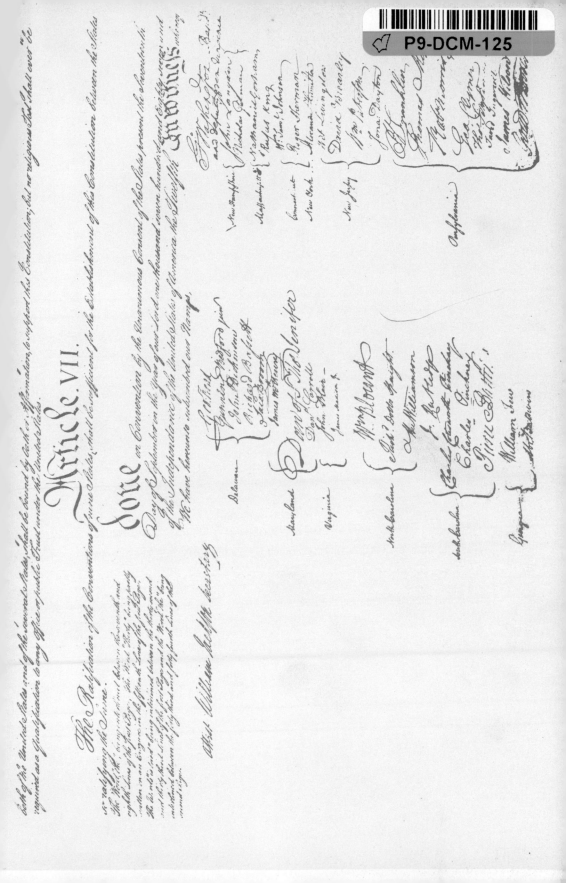

the Congress of the United States, and of the several States, shall be bound by Oath or Affirmation, to support this Constitution; but no religious Test shall ever be required as a Qualification to any Office or public Trust under the United States.

Article. VII.

The Ratification of the Conventions of nine States, shall be sufficient for the Establishment of this Constitution between the States so ratifying the Same.

Done in Convention by the Unanimous Consent of the States present the Seventeenth Day of September in the Year of our Lord one thousand seven hundred and Eighty seven and of the Independence of the United States of America the Twelfth In Witness whereof We have hereunto subscribed our Names,

G⁰. Washington—Presid. and deputy from Virginia

Attest William Jackson Secretary

New Hampshire { John Langdon, Nicholas Gilman

Massachusetts { Nathaniel Gorham, Rufus King

Connecticut { W⁰. Saml. Johnson, Roger Sherman

New York . . Alexander Hamilton

New Jersey { Wil: Livingston, David Brearley, Wm. Paterson, Jona: Dayton

Pennsylvania { B Franklin, Thomas Mifflin, Rob⁰ Morris, Geo. Clymer, Tho⁵ FitzSimons, Jared Ingersoll, James Wilson, Gouv Morris

Delaware { Geo: Read, Gunning Bedford jun, John Dickinson, Richard Bassett, Jaco: Broom

Maryland { James M⁹Henry, Dan of St Thos. Jenifer, Danl Carroll

Virginia { John Blair—, James Madison Jr.

North Carolina { Wm. Blount, Rich⁴. Dobbs Spaight, Hu Williamson

South Carolina { J. Rutledge, Charles Cotesworth Pinckney, Charles Pinckney, Pierce Butler

Georgia { William Few, Abr Baldwin

ENCYCLOPEDIA OF AMERICAN HISTORY

BICENTENNIAL EDITION

CONSULTING EDITORS

ENCYCLOPEDIA OF

American History

BICENTENNIAL EDITION

EDITED BY **RICHARD B. MORRIS**
GOUVERNEUR MORRIS PROFESSOR OF HISTORY
COLUMBIA UNIVERSITY

ASSOCIATE EDITOR **JEFFREY B. MORRIS**
SPECIAL ASSISTANT TO THE EXECUTIVE VICE
PRESIDENT FOR ACADEMIC AFFAIRS,
COLUMBIA UNIVERSITY

HARPER & ROW, PUBLISHERS

1817

NEW YORK, EVANSTON, SAN FRANCISCO, LONDON

Five maps—Cold War Alliances; American Overseas Expansion to 1917; Western Indian Reservations, 1875; Immigration to the U.S. 1890–1917; and Triangular Trade Routes—are used with the kind permission of Rand McNally & Co., copyright by Rand McNally & Co., R.L. 74-S-38.

Designed by Sidney Feinberg

Library of Congress Cataloging in Publication Data

Morris, Richard Brandon, 1904–   ed.
   Encyclopedia of American history.
   Includes index.
   1. United States—History—Chronology.   2. United States—History—Dictionaries.   I. Morris, Jeffrey Brandon, 1941–   joint ed.   II. Title.
   E174.5.M847 1976   973'.03   74-15839
   ISBN 0-06-013081-4

76 77 78 79 10 9 8 7 6 5 4 3 2 1

CONTENTS

2. Topical Chronology

3. Five Hundred Notable Americans

MAPS and CHARTS

HOW TO USE THIS BOOK
Foreword to the Bicentennial Edition

★ ★
★

The nation's Bicentenary provides a fitting occasion to reexamine the American past and reassess our changing values and institutions. To make such a reassessment one needs to know the facts about the past. Accordingly, it is the aim of this *Encyclopedia* to provide in a single handy volume the essential historical facts about American life and institutions. The organization is both chronological and topical. *Dates, events, achievements,* and *persons* stand out, but the text is designed to be read as a narrative.

The *Encyclopedia* is comprehensive in its coverage. There are three main divisions. Part I (Basic Chronology) presents the major political and military events in the history of the United States, introduced by an account of explorations, settlement, and colonial and Revolutionary problems. After reviewing the main political and constitutional developments in the original Thirteen Colonies, the focus is widened to encompass imperial and intercolonial issues. Thereafter the emphasis is upon national, federal, or major sectional problems rather than on localized and isolated occurrences—on the President, Congress, the Supreme Court, and the issues of war and peace.

Events are arranged in time sequence, with annual coverage beginning with the year 1763. For the purpose of clarity, however, as well as compression, many subjects are arbitrarily treated under the year in which they came to national attention; but, where feasible, the entire story is told only once even though it may be necessary to spread the net over more than one year. For instance, the removal of the federal government's deposits from the 2d Bank of the U.S. is treated under the year 1833 when it took place, but the censuring resolution of 1834 is thereunder included as well as the final expunging of that resolution in 1837. If, then, you do not find the entry under the year in which the event occurred, consult the Index.

The nonpolitical aspects of American life are examined in Part II (Topical Chronology), which organizes the facts about constitutional developments, American expansion, and demographic, economic, scientific, technological, and cultural trends. Much of this information has never been presented before in a general chronological framework. Needless to say, social and cultural events and contributions often do not lend themselves to close dating.

A special feature of the *Encyclopedia* is Part III (Biographical Section), which furnishes data on 500 notable Americans chosen for their outstanding achievements in major fields of activity. Elsewhere, the names of significant persons not included in this section are followed (the first time cited) by the dates of birth and death and in many cases by brief biographical information.

Events Before 1752. The old Julian Calendar, in force in Great Britain and her colonies until 1752, overestimated the solar year by 11 minutes 14 seconds a year. Under that calendar the year technically began on 25 Mar. The New Style Calendar, which went into effect in 1752 (based upon the calendar ordained by Pope Gregory XIII in 1582), adjusted the errors in the old chronology by adding 10 days down through the year 1699 and 11 days beginning with 1700, and leaving 11 days out of the calendar in 1752 (3 Sept. became 14 Sept.). In addition, the new year once more began on 1 Jan. This chronology follows New Style usage for all dates prior to 1752. Thus, the Mayflower Compact, bearing the date of 11 Nov. 1620, was actually signed on 21 Nov. Under the Julian Calendar (Old Style), George Washington was born 11 Feb. 1731/2, but this book lists it as 22 Feb. 1732 (New Style).

Presidential Elections. Presidential and congressional elections were originally held on varying days. For convenience the day when the electors cast their ballots has been designated election day (the first Wed. in Dec. under the Act of 1 Mar. 1792; the Tues. following the first Mon. in Nov. under Act of 23 Jan. 1845).

Acts of Congress bear the date when they were signed by the president, although the dates of actual passage are indicated when deemed significant, as well as the division of the votes in Senate and House.

Bicentennial Edition. This completely revised, enlarged, and updated edition covers American historical events from the era of discovery and exploration to 1 January 1974. Where, as in the Watergate scandals, no resolution of an issue had occurred by that date, every effort has been made to update events to press time. Some significant changes have been made in this edition. Headnotes to each subsection aim to organize and assimilate the discrete facts that follow and to furnish some sense of pattern and significance. Much more space is allotted to minorities, ethnic groups, and the role of women than in previous editions. The domestic and foreign affairs chronologies have been completely reorganized for the period since 1945 and the content reassessed in terms of recent interpretive scholarship. Extensive changes are found throughout the Topical Chronology, including under "Expansion of the Nation" sections on "Land, Natural Resources, and the Environment" and on "Indian Land Policy and Reform Since the Civil War." The section on "Population, Immigration, and

Ethnic Stocks" includes a conspectus of black Americans since the Civil War. "The American Economy" section has been extensively enlarged and reorganized, subsections on Film and Dance have been added to "Thought and Culture," and a new section, "Mass Media," covering the press, radio, and TV has been incorporated in this edition. Finally, the Biographical Section now provides compact accounts of 500 notable Americans, 100 more than previously, a compilation based on an extensive poll among historians and specialists in a variety of fields. As a result of these considerable revisions, the updated supplement and its index in the previous "Enlarged and Updated" edition have been incorporated in their appropriate locations.

A concluding word about historical facts. The *Encyclopedia* endeavors to incorporate the results of the latest research. This often involves revisions of previously accepted data. For example, radiocarbon tests support very different datings for the crossing of the Bering Strait and the southward penetration into the Americas than had prevailed a generation ago, but one should be cautioned that much of the nonorganic objects uncovered lack evidence either of being man-made or of any links to human occupation. The extensive current publication programs of the writings of American statesmen are providing massive documentation of the authorship and dates of state papers, in some cases correcting previous information. We now know that John Jay wrote a first draft of the "Olive Branch Petition," whose final version has been correctly attributed to John Dickinson, while the latter's authorship of the "Declaration of the Causes and Necessities of Taking Up Arms" must now be shared with Jefferson, as Dr. Julian P. Boyd has conclusively demonstrated. Long-accepted birth dates for persons born in such different centuries as Peter Stuyvesant, Alexander Hamilton, and George Washington Carver have been revised on the basis of recent discoveries. This Bicentennial Edition incorporates the latest findings of *Historical Statistics of the United States: Colonial Times to 1957* (1960) and the *Continuation to 1962*, brought up to date by the annual *Statistical Abstracts*, including census figures for 1970.

For historians there is no quicksand more treacherous than a "first." In most cases "firsts" might more prudently be phrased as "earliest known." Particularly in the field of science and technology must the researcher seeking to establish priority of discovery and invention be on guard against pitfalls. Priority is often a matter of definition. Whether one accepts 1636 or 1786 as the year of the earliest known strike depends on what kind of work stoppage constitutes a "strike." With this problem in mind the *Encyclopedia* attempts to define terms with some degree of precision. Thus, Royall Tyler's *The Contrast* was the first *American comedy* to be produced by a *professional company*, but it was not the first native play. That distinction must be awarded to Thomas Godfrey's tragedy *The Prince of Parthia*. However, amateur performances of English plays had been given in the colonies as far back as 1665, more than 100 years earlier. Last, where the facts remain in the realm of conjecture (as in the Viking explorations and Polynesian contacts with South America), the *Encyclopedia* indicates how scholars still differ in interpreting the available evidence.

In the years that have elapsed since the preparation of the first edition of the *Encyclopedia*, which appeared in 1953, and in the preparation of four subsequent editions, this enterprise has incurred numerous debts to scholars and librarians, above all to Cass Canfield, who conceived the project. The editor has constantly enlisted his sagacious judgment and been sustained by his unfailing encouragement. Many others at Harper & Row have cooperated beyond the call of duty in the preparation of earlier editions, among them Daniel F. Bradley and Beulah W. Hagen (the latter for this edition also), as well as Corona Machemer and Nancy K. MacKenzie. The list of the editor's obligations in the preparation of the various revised editions and this Bicentennial Edition is extensive, starting with Henry Steele Commager and the other consulting editors. In the revisions of the opening section, "Original Peopling of the Americas," the editor enlisted the scholarship of Professor Helmut de Terra, formerly of Columbia University. In selections for biographical subjects in the categories of science, invention, and technology, the editor leaned heavily upon the sagacious counsel of Professor I. I. Rabi of Columbia University, and in the previous editions Arthur Dreifuss of Hollywood, Calif., was indispensable in revising and updating the subsections on theater, film, radio, and TV.

1
Basic
Chronology

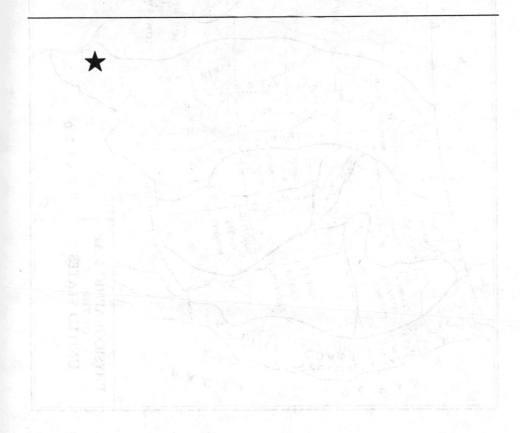

★

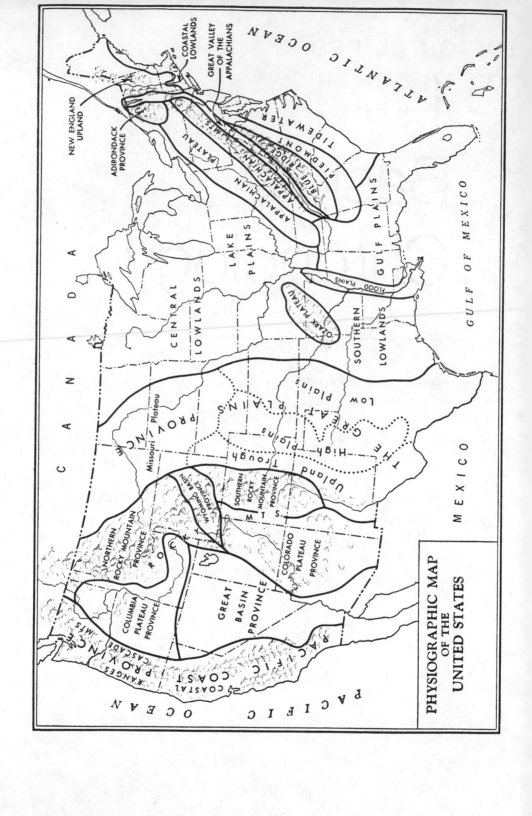

PHYSIOGRAPHIC MAP
OF THE
UNITED STATES

ORIGINAL PEOPLING
OF THE AMERICAS

★ ★
★

As geologic time is counted, man is a latecomer to the New World, but as we record human events his arrival reaches back into remote antiquity, indubitably 10,000 years ago, and possibly as far back as 35,000 B.C. The aborigines of America, truly the first discoverers, came from northeast Asia and moved southward from Alaska to populate both continents. Since the waves of migration that brought the original settlers covered an enormous time span and since their settlements were widely scattered, the aborigines varied considerably in physical and cultural characteristics, speaking many different, often unrelated, languages. These cultural variances were most striking at the time of the Spanish occupation. Thus, the Aztecs in Mexico and the Incas in Peru had, by the time of Columbus, attained a cultural level of sophistication far higher than the North American Indian tribes.

In North America, notably the area that is now the United States, the European settlers and the Indians quickly came into cultural conflict. The white man spurned amalgamation with the Indians, and his farming practices and expansionist proclivities led to the expulsion or annihilation of great numbers of them. Until fairly recent times, when the Indian population has enjoyed some numerical recovery, the susceptibility of the Indians to epidemic diseases, notably smallpox and measles, brought by Europeans, compounded by military defeat and mass transplantation, led to an astonishing rate of depopulation of the native races in North America, extraordinary however disputed the population estimates may be. What happened after 1492 in Meso-America and North America was a demographic disaster with no known parallel in world history. Displaced, defeated, bypassed, and largely ignored, the Indian shared not at all in the affluence of white America.

c.50,000–8000 B.C. **ASIATIC ORIGINS.** The first human explorers entered this unpopulated region from northern Asia. Russian excavations since 1956 on the Chukchi peninsula at the easterly tip of Asia confirm the migration of man into America from that point over an ancient land bridge of what is now the Bering Strait. Despite differences among scholars over the exact date, it now appears that the bulk of the early migration occurred during the last stages of the **Pleistocene glaciation** (the last **Ice Age**). Physical tests based on the half cycle of Carbon 14, which is present in all organic matter and disappears at a known rate, indicate that the centers of population around the edges of the Arctic Ocean, then a warm, open sea, began shifting south in relatively heavy waves, when c.11,000 years ago the Arctic froze over, the Atlantic warmed, and the Ice Age ended (Haynes, 1964). The crossing of Bering Strait and the southward penetration of the Western Hemisphere introduced into this region Mongoloids, traced to southeast and west-central Asia. By 1492 this stock was dominant from Cape Horn to Point Barrow. The very early human remains found in archaeological deposits in the New World all belong to the modern human species, *Homo sapiens,* although physical anthropologists disagree on nomenclature. It is widely agreed that man did not evolve in the New World and that no pre-*Homo sapiens* ever existed here.

LINGUISTIC STOCKS OF AMERICAN INDIANS are highly varied. Their diversity is due to considerable variety in stock and language among the original immigrants for at least several millennia, and to increasing differentiation once the American Indians were in the New World. By conservative estimate some 10 to 12 unrelated linguistic stocks or families have been listed north of the Rio Grande. A few links have been postulated between Eskimo and Chukchee, and the Athapascan and Sino-Tibetan, but in general few linkages between Old and New World linguistic stocks have so far been fully demonstrated, indicating a considerable period of isolation.

c.35,000–8000 B.C. EARLIEST SETTLEMENT. Carbon 14 tests indicate early-man sites in the Americas even prior to the ending of the **Ice Age**, and

range in date from 35,000 to 8000 B.C. The Folsom culture of the Lindenmeier site in Colorado flourished c.8820 B.C. (Haynes and Agogino, 1960) and a similar age is suggested for Tepexpan Man from the Valley of Mexico (de Terra, 1958). Responsible opinion does not support the hypothesis of a considerably earlier date for man's migration to the Americas and casts doubt upon radiocarbon dates obtained for a Clovis-type fluted projectile point near Dallas, Tex. (Haynes, 1964); the basin-shaped hearths on Santa Rosa Island off the southern California coast and the Calico site in California (Leakey, 1968) as being truly man-made; and the occurrence near Pueblo, Mex., of fossil bone fragments bearing engravings of animals, possibly both discoveries c.30,000 years old. Despite current scientific controversy over early datings, no doubt exists concerning the widespread dispersal of early man in both Americas 10,000 years ago, as suggested by radiocarbon dates obtained from sites in Chile and southern Argentina. Tools fashioned either of stone or bone and clearly recognizable types were found in direct association with extinct animals such as the mammoth, ground sloth, camel, and other forms which have long since disappeared.

HUMAN REMAINS OF EARLY MIGRATION. Great faunal interchanges took place between northern Asia and North America in the closing stage of the Pleistocene glaciation. Man was only one of the many animals which moved either west into Asia or east into North America during such periods. Accurately recorded ancient skeletal remains of these early migrants are scarce and disputed. The fossil-man discoveries include the bones of the **Minnesota Woman** from the dried-up bed of glacial Lake Agassiz; the **Punin Calvarium** from fossil deposits near Quito, Ecuador; the **Lagoa Santo** skulls from coastal Brazil; the **Vero** and

Melbourne finds in Florida; the **Midland Man** (Midland, Tex., c.12,000–20,000 years old); and the **Tepexpan Man** from the Valley of Mexico. Racial admixture is indicated by the variety of the skulls.

c.9000–1500 B.C. EARLY KNOWN HUNTING AND GATHERING CULTURES. Archaeological research has demonstrated that these early human immigrants were in a simple hunting, fishing, and gathering stage of culture. Their formidable prowess as hunters is indicated by the fact that they killed great animals like the mammoth, mastodon, and large extinct species of bison. Cultural remains in the form of camps, hearths, stone and bone tools, and slain-animal remains indicate that they had no knowledge of horticulture. The earliest widespread pointed weapon is the "clovis projectile," found near the town of Clovis, N.M., at the Blackwater Draw No. 1 site. The site also contains blades, scrapers, hammerstones, bone shafts, and flakes as well as the bones of camels, horses, bison, and mammoths. The Folsom Fluted Points (8000 B.C.) developed from the Clovis form. The points were found underlying those of the Folsom culture (Sandia Cave, New Mex.) and even more prominently in the Lindenmeier location in Colorado. The people of the Folsom culture were hunters who used grooved, chipped darts with which they killed mammoth and bison. Remains of this culture have been found from Alaska south beyond the Great Plains. To the south, in Arizona and New Mexico, there were equally ancient peoples of the Cochise culture. Though the Cochise used grinding stones, remains of mammoths, horses, pronghorn antelopes, prairie wolves, and bison have been found, indicating the Cochise were both farmers and hunters. Traces of early hunters and gatherers have been found in Texas, the deserts of California, Oregon, Nevada, Utah,

Washington, Iowa, Nebraska, and in Mexico, Peru, Chile, and Argentina. This prehorticultural period persisted through many millennia. In marginal or other regions unfavorable to farming, it survived up to and beyond the time of the European invasion. However, in the nuclear or heart regions of native American culture, primarily from Mexico south to Peru, it was gradually superseded by another mode of life.

c.3000–1000 B.C. EARLIEST AMERICAN FARMERS. The earliest evidences of extensive New World horticulture are based on recent discoveries. The **Huaca Prieta horizon,** 1946, revealed people who lived on seafood, simple farming, and gathering. They grew and twined or wove cotton and bast; cultivated beans and gourds, but did not grow maize (Indian corn) or manufacture pottery. Their stone industry was rudimentary. Farther north in **Chiapas** (S.E. Mexico), **Honduras,** and **Tamaulipas** (N.E. Mexico) evidences suggesting preceramic cultivators have since come to light. At Chiapas maize was grown even in this early period. The Chiapas area dates stratigraphically and with the aid of radiocarbon from 1500 B.C. to 1000 B.C. At Tamaulipas, a tiny primitive corn was first grown between 3000 to 2200 B.C., and pottery first produced about 1400 B.C. Still farther north, at **Bat Cave,** in central New Mexico, very primitive types of pod corn have been found in association with chipped stone tools, both below and intermixed with the remains of pottery. Carbon 14 tests at Huaca Prieta give estimates of dates back to 2307 B.C., at Bat Cave perhaps back to between 3000 and 2000 B.C., but such Carbon 14 datings may still require more adequate materials and further checking.

c.1000 B.C. FORMATIVE EPOCH. Based on this incipient farm pattern there developed in the Andean and Mesoamerican regions a series of Forma-

tive cultures sharing in common the expansion of horticulture (including cultivation of maize, squash, beans, and other
plants), and in the later stages of this
epoch developing large settlements, irri-
gating systems, and, in the Andean region, metallurgy based on gold, copper,
and other minerals (save iron, which was
never smelted in the aboriginal New
World). Unlike the Old World, domesti-
cated animals were few (dogs, turkeys
in N. America, plus muscovy ducks in
Mexico; in S. America, dogs, guinea pigs,
and llamas), and neither utilitarian
wheel traction nor the potter's wheel was
known in these or later native American
cultures. Many of these long-flourishing
Formative cultures have now been identified in Peru, Honduras, and Mexico.

c.1 A.D.–900 A.D. FLORESCENT, OR
CLASSIC EPOCH IN MEXICO AND
PERU. In Meso-America and Peru this
culture dates around 1 A.D.; in the Maya
region of the Petén and Yucatán, stone
stelae carved with the glyphs of an accurate calendrical system date the most
elaborate of the Mayan temples, sculp-
tures, and art forms from c.300–900 A.D.
Teotihuacán, near Mexico City, the dead
religious center with its huge pyramids
and impressive mural paintings, belongs
to this epoch as does the finest period
Monte Albán III, in the vast ceremonial
ruin in Oaxaca. The Monte Albán III
period has exhibited evidences of monu-
ment art, hieroglyphics, numbers, and a
calendar. Marked by great population,
tremendous construction, and wide trade,
this epoch constitutes the apogee of native American cultural progress and is
comparable to that of the Bronze Age in
the Old World which had flourished
more than 3,000 years earlier in the
Near East. On the northern coast of Peru
the people of the Mochica kingdom built
vast adobe-brick structures, made un-
surpassed pictorial or modeled pottery,
and practiced metallurgy; but unlike

Teotihuacán, the Peruvians did not have
a system of writing or a calendar, but did
have an art form absorbed in depicting
warlike activity and rigid priestly and
other class distinctions.

c.900 A.D.–1400 A.D. EPOCH OF NA-
TIVE EMPIRES. In this period Meso-
America and the central Andean region
remained the major centers of cultural
progress and military and political activity. Known as the Militaristic or Epoch
of Fusion, this period in Mexico was
marked by the Toltec rule at Tula
(11th–12th centuries) and the Mexicani-
zation of the Maya regions of Yucatán
beginning in the 10th century, when
Chichén Itzá was probably invaded by
Mexican Toltecs. Following came the
little-understood barbarian Chichimec invasion from the north, and then the rise
of the short-lived but barbarically pic-
turesque Aztec Empire (c.1325–1521).
Similar conflict in Peru wiped out the
Florescent Mochica, Nazca, and kindred
cultures to be replaced by the so-called
Tiahuanaco and related military conquerors. Finally, there emerged the far-
flung Inca Empire, one of the most
closely integrated totalitarian regimes of
the pre-Columbian world. Zenith of Inca
power: 11th to 15th centuries. After
1492 Spain pitted the small but desperately effective armies of Cortés and
Pizarro against the more or less well organized native empires of the Aztecs
(1518–21) and the Incas (1531–35),
respectively, the latter then in the throes
of bitter civil war.

c.1492. CULTURES AND POPU-
LATIONS OF NATIVE AMERICA
NORTH OF MEXICO. The regions
north of the Rio Grande were occupied
by largely unregimented native peoples,
with strongly individualistic, if less complex, cultural patterns than the natives of
the southern empires. On the basis of
environmental and cultural similarities,
the area now included within the United

res and Canada can, in late pre-
columbian times, be broken up into five
major cultural and ecological areas:
Southwest (in U.S.), Intermediate,
Northwest coast, Arctic coast, Eastern-
Northern. Estimates of the total population for this area vary between 1,025,950
for the late pre-Columbian period (Kroeber, 1939) to a figure between 9,800,000
and 12,250,000 for c.1492 (Debyns,
1966). The latter is based on a depopulation ratio of 20 to 1 for the lower figure,
25 to 1 for the higher total, both from
the time of conquest to the beginning of
population recovery.

1. SOUTHWESTERN CULTURE
AREA is an arid and elevated region
where farming tribes lived in close jux-
taposition to hunters (a northern advance of Mexicanlike cultures) and gatherers (a southward extension of simpler
hunting and gathering patterns to the
north). In the northeastern plateau, a
region of summer rains, farming is possible in selected areas, as the long
archaeological record of the Anasazi or
Basket Maker–Pueblo sequence clearly
indicates. In the southwestern desert lowland farming was possible only in the
flood plains of a few rivers or where irrigation was practiced. This region was
the center of another ancient subcultural
province known, archaeologically, as the
Hohokam. Between these farming peoples were some other scattered tribes
which eked out a living through gathering and hunting, much like the Intermediate area, below.

First to attract the notice of the Spanish explorers when they pushed north
from Mexico were the Pueblo, or town-
dwelling and farming peoples of the
Anasazi province. In 1540 the Pueblos
occupied some 70 towns scattered in the
region of the present states of Arizona
and New Mexico. Various linguistic
stocks occupied this area, but, among
the Pueblos, the Shoshonean-speaking

Hopi to the north, the central Zuni, and
the Keresan-speaking and other Pueblos
of the Rio Grande valley were outstanding. The mythical riches of the Zuni
towns, under the name of the "Seven
Cities of Cibola," lured Coronado.

Pueblo Culture Pattern. The "Three
Sisters," corn, beans, and squash, were
the basic commodities of these skilled
farmers, whose life was oriented around
cultivating. Elaborate rituals were employed to bring the summer rains. Differing locally, Pueblo settlement patterns
ranged from the contiguous stone ma-
sonry house of the Hopi, perched on top
of high mesas, to the scattered adobe
houses of the Rio Grande Pueblos. All
were essentially town-minded, built no
temples, but had underground Kivas or
ceremonial rooms for their various clans
and societies. The contiguous and sometimes several-storied buildings with roof
entrances formed fortifications, further
protected by their positions on high
mesas or cliffs. The Pueblo government
was theocratic; only the priests ruled.
Each Pueblo group was a rule unto itself; no large tribal groups or confederacies existed. In the west the social unit
was the maternal clan; in the Rio Grande
region a dual organization was dominant.
Religious rites included rain-making rites
in both east and west, curing ceremonies
in the east, and throughout the region
procreative rites. Although unwarlike,
the Pueblos through their town organization and fortifications strove to hold
off the nomadic tribes, such as the
Apache, which surrounded them. Archae-
ology indicates that their territory had
been drastically cut down long before
the arrival of the white man. Intensely
conservative, the twenty-odd surviving
pueblos today constitute the most viable
and truly native culture pattern to be
observed in the territory of the U.S.
Their neighbors, the Athapascan-speak-
ing Navajo, originally scattered nomads,

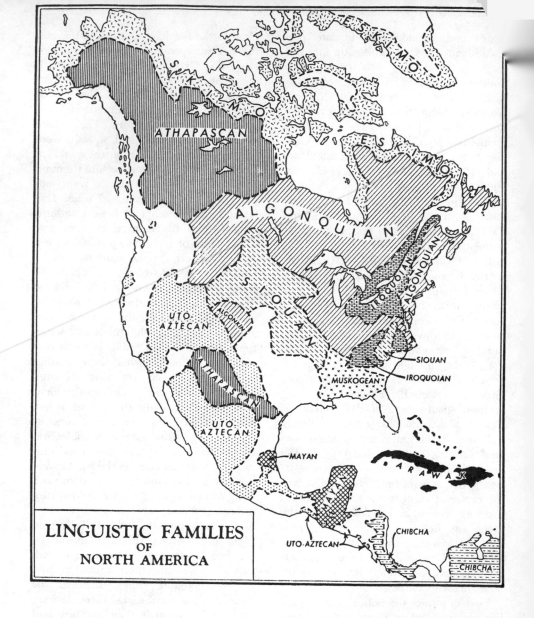

LINGUISTIC FAMILIES
OF
NORTH AMERICA

far surpass all present North American tribes in numbers, but the basic Navajo economic patterns, farming and sheep-herding, represent their respective debts, first to their Pueblo neighbor, and then to the white man.

2. **INTERMEDIATE CULTURE AREA.** North of the Southwestern area extends the arid intermontane Great Basin, and, to the north, the rugged Columbia and Fraser Plateau. These two regions, with that of central California across the Sierra Nevada range, represent a varied topographic but an essentially similar pre-Columbian culture pattern (Kroeber). (1) The **isolated**

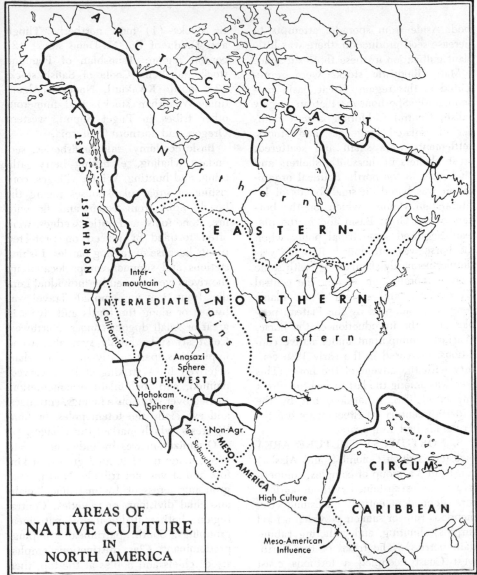

AREAS OF
NATIVE CULTURE
IN
NORTH AMERICA

These two maps are adapted from A. L. Kroeber, *Anthropology,*
rev. ed., 1948, Harcourt, Brace and Co., Inc.

Great Basin proved one of the most unfavorable regions in North America for native culture; life based on intensive gathering of weed seeds, piñon nuts, insects, and small game; little leisure for activities unrelated to subsistence. (2) The **northern Plateau region** provided salmon runs that came up the great rivers which drained it, game, and access to the buffalo herds of the Great Plains after the white man brought the horse. (3) **Central California** abounded in a variety of oaks bearing acorns. The native, a balanophagist (acorn eater), supplemented his basic diet with deer and other game and locally abundant seafood. Aside from sporadic attempts to increase seed production, there was little plant cultivation in these three subareas.

Many **linguistic stocks** were represented in this region: Great Basin predominantly Shoshonean; Plateau largely Salish; Central California, a vast number of isolated languages and stocks. **Settlements** were small and scattered, brush shelters in the south, shelters and pit houses in the north. **Political organization** was based on small bands of bilateral family units, which, on the borders of the Great Basin and in the plateau, acquired some tribal polity when the horse was introduced. **Religion** was simple, primarily shamanistic, with some more elaborate cults among the central Californians, and certain Great Plains ceremonies adopted by the Plateau peoples after the introduction of the horse. **Warfare**, unimportant under native conditions, increased in the early 19th century with the advent of the horse. This area was among the last to feel the direct impact of U.S. expansion, but by the mid-19th century its effects were drastic. Tribal life had disappeared.

3. NORTHWEST CULTURE AREA (western British Columbia and Alaska) constituted a group of complex, competitive societies sustained without agriculture, dependent entirely on fishing (tremendous runs of salmon provided a food surplus), hunting, and gathering (abundant berries). The tribes of the Northwest Coast occupied a tortuous coast backed by the steep coast range located in a coniferous forest saturated but warmed by the Japan Current. Facing the sea, all life focused on the beach. ("When the tide is out the table is set," Nootka expression.) **Northern regions** (despite lack of plant domestication) were the most complex culturally just prior to the white invasion, with perhaps the greatest population density in native North America. At least **3 major linguistic stocks**—(1) most northerly: **Tlingit** and **Haida** of the Na-Dene stock; (2) central region: **Tsimshian** of Penutian stock and **Bella Coola** of Salish stock; (3) south: **Kwakiutl, Nootka** (Algonquian-Wakashan stock), and numerous other tribes in Puget Sound, western Oregon, and northern California.

Basic economy: salmon fisheries; secondary, whaling, sea fishing, berry gathering, and hunting. **Winter villages,** consisting of great plankhouses facing the beach, split from cedar and fir with fire, stone tools, and antler wedges, were often fortified or placed on protected points because of raiding parties. **Fishing stations** and **summer camps** located up the rivers were owned by individual families from time immemorial. Travel was by sea or along the fjords and rivers in great or small dugout canoes. **Northwest Coast art style,** highly symbolic: wood implements, particularly of cedar, characterized by a striking style of carved, painted, and shell-inlaid ornamentation, carried over into house facings, entrances, and especially the **totem poles,** or family crests, which marked the villages.

Organization was by independent villages, made up of graded groups of kinfolk and slaves, not tribally. North: local groupings crosscut by matrilineal clans and dual divisions, or moieties; Central region: both matrilineal and patrilineal groupings; South: patrilineal groupings predominant. **Class distinctions** emphasized: chiefs and nobles at the top; then commoners; last, slaves who were war captives or debtors. All rank rested on wealth, with an endless variation and shifting of grades. A comprehensive system of **private ownership** (embracing land, fishing stations, houses, masks, crests, names, etc.) carried prestige, and was acquired by inheritance, purchase, and sometimes warfare. At **potlatches** (ceremonies or feasts) rival chiefs, supported by their respective kinsmen and slaves of all degrees, competed in ostentatious display of wealth and property exchanges. "Gifts" between rival chiefs had to be returned with interest, default leading to social degradation. In the later periods the white fur trade made this society even more highly competitive by producing greater surpluses of exchangeable goods. With its class stratification resting upon validated wealth and ostentatious exchange and destruction of property, the Northwest Coast economy was **capitalist** in form, with a trading acumen which matched the Yankees who in the late 18th century traded along its coast for sea-otter fur.

Religion ranged from the belief in a supreme deity to pure shamanism; rich in display, complex in masks and other equipment, and sexual in character. The winter season was taken up with elaborate ceremonies held by the graded societies, of which the **hamatsa**, or cannibal society, and the animal societies were the most numerous. Like the potlatch, these society affairs were competitive, each trying to outdo the other in richness of costume and ferocity of act and aspect. **Warfare,** sporadic, chiefly for purposes of revenge, to secure slaves, and, occasionally, crests or property. As a result of the impact upon this culture of the Russians coming from the north (after 1741), the Spanish from the south (1774), and the Anglo-Americans from the east (1786), tribal life has been largely shattered.

4.   ARCTIC   COAST   CULTURE AREA: THE ESKIMO. A relatively small population speaking related languages, the Eskimo-Aleut, occupied the long northern coast from the Aleutians all the way east to Greenland and southern Labrador. Present archaeological evidence indicates that the early Eskimoan groups entered western Alaska shortly before 1 A.D., with the last eastward migration reaching Greenland about the

same time as the Norsemen arrived from the east (c.1000 A.D.). In **physical type** the Eskimo share most basic Mongoloid characteristics with the main Indian population, with certain minor, but distinctive, features. The Eskimo-Aleut language family falls into 2 divisions: the Eskimo and the Aleut. The Eskimoan **language** has two divisions: Western (Yupik) with perhaps two languages and Eastern (Ihupik), one language spoken from the Bering Strait to and including Greenland. **Occupations:** primarily hunters and fishermen, with numerous variations based on differences in water, temperature, and ice conditions along their extended coastal terrain. **Open, western Pacific:** Eskimos hunted large sea mammals in skin-covered **kayaks** and open boats, seasonally going inland after the caribou, but also eating fish, birds, foxes, and polar bear. Similar open-water conditions prevailed in Greenland and Labrador. **Central region** (where the sea freezes all winter, typically Eskimoan): Eskimos are ice hunters, living in block-built snow **igloos**, traveling by dog sledge, and securing the seal through the ice and the walrus along the floe edges; in summer moving to caribou-skin tents and hunting caribou and fishing salmon in the interior. **Settlement pattern:** villages attaining considerable size in western Alaska and southern Greenland, but composed of small, shifting family groups in the north-central regions. Tailored fur and leather clothing, elaborate hunting gear including toggle harpoons, floats, sleds, and dog traction in winter and **kayaks** in summer, all speak of long and skillful adaptation to Arctic conditions. Hence, the most successful Arctic explorers like Peary not only were accompanied by Eskimos but employed clothing, food, equipment, and methods of transportation of Eskimo origin. **Political organization:** loose; shifting family groupings dominant. **Religion:**

based in large part on fear of a hostile universe wherein many spirits dwell who must be propitiated. Contact with the supernatural is often attained through the **shaman,** who knows the speech of animals, and sends his soul away to treat with the recalcitrant spirits. The more elaborate ceremonies in western Alaska involve the use of masks, carvings, and equipment reminiscent of Northwest Coast culture. **Organized warfare:** rare or absent, although Indian-Eskimo conflicts were noted (by Samuel Hearne, 1771). Early European explorers, like Frobisher (1576–78) and John Davis (1585), were attacked by the Eskimos of Baffin Land. Today, a somewhat mixed Eskimo population of less than half the numbers estimated for the first contact period still survives in all but the southern limits of their former range. In the central Arctic, the old basic hunting pattern of life still continues in a few isolated places, but in general the Greenland, Canadian, and Alaskan Eskimos have today come under the influence of Euro-American culture although much of the native language, economy, and culture still persist.

5. **EASTERN-NORTHERN CULTURE AREA** comprises a great terrain which slopes east from the Rocky Mountains to the Atlantic Ocean. Variant but without drastic environmental or abrupt cultural breaks, this ecological area falls into 3 major subdivisions: (1) **Southeast,** (2) **Great Plains,** and (3) **Northeastern–Great Lakes** cultural provinces. From the palms of southern Florida to the dwarf-willow scrub of northern Labrador there is a gradual transition from tropical to subarctic conditions. Similarly, on the cultural plane, there is a gradual gradient from the elaborately class-structured society of the **Natchez** (Mississippi) to the wandering, classless **Naskapi** hunters (northern Labrador). The Great Plains to the west, due to the

introduction of the horse and firearms in post-Columbian times (c.1540–1880), became for a time somewhat unique, but the original cultural pattern was of the same fabric. **Ecologically,** the entire area is mainly woodland, deciduous trees predominating, with the addition of pine and spruce. Dominating the main regions were the hardwoods, thinning out into river-valley cover in the **tall-grass-prairie** regions from Illinois west, and, eventually, disappearing in the **short-grass** region of the **High Plains west of the 100th meridian** (westward from the 20-in.-rainfall line to the Rockies, an area of scanty rainfall which later offered greater inducements to cattlemen than to farmers). In the central regions the bison was important for food; to the north, deer, moose, and caribou. Native means of navigation over the great rivers and lake systems served as a means of intercommunication: the birchbark canoe, best developed in the Great Lakes region, like the dugout canoes and rafts on the lower rivers, and the "bullboats" of the Missouri, reminiscent of but not historically related to the Welsh coracle. Owing to the preoccupation with war, the natives failed to exploit the rich agricultural potential of this region.

Linguistically, the northeastern and Great Lakes regions were dominated by **Algonquian**-speaking tribes extending north to Labrador and as far south as the Carolinas. Splitting this distribution, from the Cherokee of Georgia north along the Great Lakes to the St. Lawrence, were a number of **Iroquoian**-speaking groups, most famous being the powerful **League of the Iroquois (Mohawk, Onondaga, Oneida, Cayuga, Seneca,** and, later, **Tuscarora**) in upper New York State. The southeastern subarea was dominated by **Muskogean**-speaking peoples, including the **Choctaw, Chickasaw, Creek, Seminole,** and the **Cherokee** (Iroquoian-speaking)—later known as the

"Five Civilized Nations"—and many others. Interspersed were peoples of **Siouan** and other smaller linguistic stocks. On the Great Plains to the west, tribes of the **Caddoan** linguistic stock stretched from Arkansas to the Dakotas, with many Siouan tribes along the west bank of the Mississippi and on both sides of the Missouri in both the tall-grass prairie and short-grass plains. Algonquian-speaking and other tribes were also interspersed throughout the Great Plains area. Most of these seem to have been latecomers, mainly after the advent of the horse, but some, like the **Blackfoot** (Algonquian), **Mandan** (Siouan), and **Pawnee** (Caddoan), appear to have been old residents. **Timetable of European settlement:** Southeast, by the French and Spaniards, beginning **1565**; the Northeastern Great Lakes and eastern Great Plains, by the French, beginning **1634** (Nicolet); the eastern maritime regions by the English, principally beginning **1607**. As in Meso-America, the Spanish encountered the most culturally advanced tribes.

Basic Economy. The aboriginal Southeast depended on the cultivation of **corn, beans,** and **squash,** supplemented by gathering, hunting, and fishing. Native farming by slash and burn methods soon exhausted the deciduous forest soil, causing villages to move frequently. Maize cultivation extended with lessening productivity north as far as the St. Lawrence River, and west along the river valleys of the Prairie-Plains. North and west of this area early frosts and drought prevented native farming. The extreme northern regions were dependent mainly on hunting the moose and caribou or fishing; the short-grass plains, primarily on the bison herds. The Great Lakes region had both farming and hunting, supplemented (in Wisconsin and Minnesota) by gathering "wild rice," which grows abundantly in shallow lakes. Because of farming, the

southeastern subregion supported the larger population, while the forest and tundra of the northern subarea had a lower population density. Considering its rich agricultural food potential, even the eastern subarea seems underpopulated. Crude methods of cultivation, warfare, diseases, and disruption spread by the Europeans, limited population (Borah, Dobyns).

The **settlement** pattern in the Southeast, and north to the St. Lawrence river, at the time of first European penetration seems mainly to have been one of **villages** (generally larger in the south) often surrounded with **stockades. Architecture:** in the southeast with its Meso-American cultural cast, round, semi-subterranean "**hothouses**" for winter; loosely constructed, rectangular bark or "**shake**" **houses** for summer were the rule. These family units were arranged in a square ground pattern with an open plaza in the center often surrounded by artificial mounds of earth within which the ceremonial "**Chunkey**" game was played. To the north, the Iroquois and many of their Algonquian neighbors made "**longhouses**" out of bark and poles to house many families. To the west, arborlike houses of bark, matting, and poles were used. On the Great Plains even the earth lodge and the graceful skin **tipi** were employed. North of the St. Lawrence the conical **wigwam** covered with birchbark or caribou hide was most common. In the Southeast, the eastern prairies, and again north to the St. Lawrence, stockades, bastions, and firing platforms protected the villages. In the south-central area quite elaborate temple mound structures were in use, flourishing in the period 700 A.D.–1700 A.D., often located on top of large artificial earth mounds with ramps leading up to them. Some 100,000 mounds are estimated to exist in the U.S. The so-called ancient Indian "**Mound builders**" of the

Ohio region left remains of just such mound structures, often forming burial chambers, as De Soto, Bartram, and other white explorers found actually in use in what is now the southeastern U.S.

Political Organization: Confederacy. Beginning with the **matrilineal** system, family, or clan, political organization evolved into the **moiety** or dual division, then to the **tribal** group, and finally, to the **Confederacy,** or loose grouping of tribes, embodying certain concepts of the "state." In the south between **1836–40,** the **Creek Confederacy** included numerous tribes speaking a number of distinct languages in some 50 towns; the dominant one was Muskogee (Creek). Others, like the **Powhatan Confederacy** (c.1607) in Virginia—more like an incipient state —were smaller. One of the most famous was the **League of the Iroquois** (beg. c.1559–70) in New York. Founded for peace, the Iroquois Confederacy became a deadly instrument for war in the northeast. The unusual power exercised by the women in the latter tribes actually made or broke **sachems,** or chiefs. The northern peoples had a less complex political and social organization. Beyond the St. Lawrence it was based upon shifting family bands. To the west confederacies existed among the Caddoan peoples, matrilineal clans among certain Siouan peoples, and patrilineal and bilateral organizations among the bordering Plains tribes. Among some tribes on the lower Mississippi a true class system evolved; most celebrated was that of the **Natchez,** where by an imperative class-intermarriage system lineages passed from the top role of relatives of the sun to the lowest class of **"Stinkards"** within four generations.

Introduction of Horse. Archaeological research clearly indicates that the basic patterns of the eastern, or tall-grass-prairie, plains were horticultural and of a Southeastern semisedentary type (pre-1540). With the advent of the European horse (post-1540), the pattern changed to equestrian, bison-hunting. Many border tribes then first entered the plains from north, east, and west, to overrun the older, more settled Caddoan and Siouan peoples such as the Arikara, Pawnee, and the Mandan respectively. The early Spanish pioneers from the south encountered the semisedentary native peoples; the later modern American westward migration met the equestrian bison hunters in their militaristic prime.

Religious and Ceremonial Activities were varied and complex (see J. R. Swanton, *Indians of the Southeastern U.S.,* Bur. Amer. Ethnology, *Bull. 137,* 1946). **Southeast:** temples and idols widely distributed, with a definite priesthood. Cultural climax attained by the **Natchez,** with their deified ruler representing the sun, living in a temple with sacred fetishes on top of a mound complex. Alongside supreme deities, a vast number of other deities, spirits, and sacred places were worshiped among the various tribes. Notable ceremonies: the **"busk"** or green-corn dance; and the **"new fire"** ceremony with its aim of "life renewal" and accompanying drinking of the "black drink," an emetic which led to purification. Ceremonies for both war and peace existed side by side. Evidence of a probable Meso-American cast to Southeastern culture exists in the pottery, special cemeteries, low conical or domed earthen mounds for burial, the cultivation of tobacco, and the use of tubular pipe. The 4-footed vessels seen early in Tchefuncte in the Southeast indicate more than any other form of pottery, possible Mexican influence (Jennings). **West:** basic in the religion of the Caddoan tribes were sacred bundles dedicated to agricultural pursuits. **North:** religion simpler and more shamanistic; great importance given to dreams in guiding all activity; the individual soul was iden-

tified with the breath. Among the most
northeasterly Algonquians, the **Naskapi**
combined an animalistic mythology, a
shamanistic belief, with a native concept
of a supreme deity associated with the
caribou, the most important food animal.
**WARFARE: SUBJUGATION OF
TRIBES IN U.S.** Warfare played a destructive role in the aboriginal Southeast, in the later phases of native life in
the Iroquois region, and in the Great
Plains, but to a much lesser extent in
the northern areas. The fact that the
eastern Indians cultivated less than 1% of
the arable land available and achieved
a population density of only 9 Indians
per township in a region which today
supports 400 persons per township is attributed by Kroeber to the "insane, at-
tritional type of war" waged throughout
the area, carried on incessantly by individuals for revenge, by small parties,
towns, tribes, and confederacies. Warfare was highly ceremonialized, accompanied by elaborate torture rites (reaching a peak among the Iroquois), with
war honors essential to almost every
youth and the warpath the primary road
to fame and honor. Aggressive behavior
was somewhat canalized off in such ceremonial games as lacrosse. In addition,
peace towns, moieties, and leagues were
organized to maintain peace, but the
eastern war pattern persisted to the end,
latterly becoming blended with European war practices and weapons brought
in by the new invaders. As a result of
military defeat and white penetration
native life as such has ended in most of
the Eastern-Northern cultural provinces.
The "Five Civilized Nations" were by
1838 moved over the "Trail of Tears"
to the Indian Territory (Oklahoma); the
Seminoles, after prolonged warfare with
the U.S., suffered heavy losses while being deported to Indian Territory in 1842.
Other eastern groups, like the Iroquois,
were confined to reservations or else have
blended with the modern white and
Negro populations of the area. Only in
the far north do the old hunting and fishing patterns still persist, along with fur
trapping, which is post-Caucasian, but
even these faint marginal manifestations
decrease from year to year. In addition
to the Oklahoma Reservation for the Five
Civilized Tribes, various reservations in
the Dakotas and elsewhere were assigned
to the Sioux and other tribes. Resisting
the advancing mining frontier and the
federal government's reservation policy,
the Indians of the West were finally over-
whelmed by superior numbers and technology in a series of wars, 1861–68,
1875–90 (**Cheyenne-Arapaho War, 1861–
64; Red River War, 1874; Sioux Wars,
1862–67 and 1875–76; Nez Percé War,
1877; Apache War, 1871–87; Ghost
Dance Uprising, 1890,** also pp. 611, 613–
615). For 20th-century issues and problems, see pp. 643–646.

THE ERA OF EXPLORATION

★ ★
★

Pre-Columbian Exploration

Out of the mists of forgery and fact there is now emerging a somewhat clearer picture of when the Vikings came to America, where they made their landfalls, and why they discontinued their explorations. The Vikings lacked both the firepower of the later European invaders of North America and the manpower to defend themselves against the Indians, or Eskimos, in an area so far removed from the home base of Greenland, which in turn was abandoned after several centuries of occupation. With the freeze-over of the Arctic Ocean by the end of the fourteenth century, drift ice about Greenland, or between Greenland and Vinland, forced the abandonment of the old sea routes.

It remained for Columbus and Spanish and Portuguese navigators to inaugurate a whole new era for exploration and conquest. The first explorers for Spain were followed by the conquistadores, whose subjugation of the Aztecs in Mexico and of the Incas in Peru opened up vast treasures, brought Spanish and Roman Catholic culture to Central and South America and the borderlands that now form part of the United States, transformed Western society by vastly increasing the quantity of money in circulation, thereby unwittingly undermining the feudal structure and shaking the underpinnings of status, spurring capitalist activity, and arousing the cupidity of the have-not nations, notably of France, England, and Holland. In the late sixteenth and early seventeenth centuries the three latecomers staked out claims to largely unexplored and unsettled sections along the North Atlantic seaboard.

800–986. VIKING SETTLEMENT AND EXPLORATION. After occupying the Shetlands, the Faroes, and the Orkneys (by 800), the Vikings settled Iceland (874). **Eric the Red,** in exile from Iceland, after 3 years spent exploring the coasts of Greenland (982–85), led a group of settlers to the southwestern coast of that island, where the first Norse colony was planted (986). The discovery of the Narssaq Farm at the foot of Mt. Qagarsung in Greenland in 1953 confirms Eric's settlement in Greenland. **Bjarni Herjulfson** is credited with sighting the mainland of North America in 986 when blown off his course while seeking the new colony.

c.1000. LEIF ERICSON, the son of Eric the Red, either by accident (in 1000, according to the **Karlsevni Saga**) or with forethought (in 1002, according to the **Greenland Saga**), explored the North American coast, naming the regions, as he voyaged southward, **Helluland** (land of flat rocks), **Markland** (forest land), and **Vinland** (wineland). Experts differ as to the identity of Vinland: Newfoundland (Hovgaard), mouth of the St. Lawrence (Steensby), Nova Scotia (Storm), northern New England (Thorvarson), Cape Cod (F. J. Pohl), Rhode Island (Rafn), New York (Gathorne-Hardy), middle Atlantic coast (Haugen), Virginia (Mjeldi). **Thorvald Ericson,** Leif's brother, explored the coast of the continent (1004–07), using Leif's headquarters in Vinland. A second brother, **Thorstein,** tried unsuccessfully to find Vinland (1008).

1010–13. Thorfinn Karlsevni, a trader from Iceland, with 3 ships and 160 men, mostly Greenlanders, sailed on an exploratory trip to the North American mainland. Despite similarity between the names used to designate the regions Karlsevni visited and those explored by the sons of Eric, enough differences in their geographical descriptions exist to raise some doubt that they were in the same area. The operations of the Ericsons, according to the prevailing view, were confined to the east coast of North America; but the possibility exists that Karlsevni, instead of coasting along Labrador or Newfoundland, sailed into Hudson's Bay. **Freydis,** Eric's daughter, believed to be a member of Karlsevni's group, is credited with making the last trip to the mainland described in the Sagas (1014–15).

Confirmation of Norse Voyages and Settlement. Discovery of the Vinland Map, executed before 1440, announced by Yale Univ. Press (1965), seemed to furnish circumstantial confirmation of Norse voyages. The map shows a large insular land mass west and southwest of Greenland, extending from c.47° N to c.67° N. An inscription attributes the discovery of the island (named Vinland) to Leif and Bjarni. Ink tests disclosed the map to be a forgery (1974). Recent archaeological discoveries by Helge Ingstad, 1961–68, confirm the Norse settlement of Vinland in the early 11th century as having occurred at L'Anse aux Meadows in Newfoundland. Most important among the artifacts found in excavation were: 8 house sites of a longhouse type similar to findings in Norway, Iceland, and Greenland; fireplaces, ember pits, a smithy, and boathouses, all with Norse characteristics; a stone lamp of old Icelandic type, a Norse-type spindle whorl of soapstone and a Viking-era type bronze ringheaded pin; 16 radiocarbon datings have confirmed the date of the house as c.1000 (Ashe). In addition, the North American mainland has yielded scores of Norse relics, most of which were either so patently spurious or found under such unverifiable circumstances that they have been dismissed by the majority of scholars. These repudiated findings include the **Newport Tower** (a round stone structure in Rhode Island, more likely built in the 17th than the 11th–12th centuries), the **Kensington Stone,** a slab with runic inscriptions dated 1362 (found in Minnesota, 1898), chiseled out apparently with a modern chisel and with runes and grammatical forms unknown to the 14th century; recent discoveries at Beardmore, in western Ontario, of a sword, axhead, and shield grip, definitely from the 11th century, but believed to have been brought to America in 1923 (Wallace).

1014–1415. DURATION OF NORSE SETTLEMENT. The Greenland Colony continued at least until the second decade of the 15th century, although its connection with Europe weakened during the 14th century. Its active role as a colony ceased with the sailing of the last royal ship to that island (1367). A party of Icelanders visited the colony, 1408, and a churchman appears to have sailed there in the second decade of the 15th century, but no further contacts are known.

1447–98. PORTUGUESE EXPLORATION. Under the impetus of **Prince Henry the Navigator** (1394–1460), third son of John I, expeditions were sent down the west African coast, and the Azores, the Canaries, and Madeira were occupied. **Bartolomeu Dias** reached the Cape of Good Hope, 1488, and **Vasco da Gama** completed a voyage around Africa to India and return, 1498. Portuguese claims to the discovery of the New World are based on a number of westward explorations. On the basis of a map of the Venetian Andrea Biancho (1448), in which a large island, **Ixola Otinticha** (authentic island), is shown lying a good distance southwest of Cape Verde, it has been suggested that the Portuguese already knew of the existence of South America. In 1452 Diogo de Teive and Pedro Vasquez sailed to the Azores, where they discovered two additional islands of that group (Corvo and Flores). After these discoveries they were blown northward, and the Portuguese scholars (particularly Cortesão) believe that they reached the Grand Bank of Newfoundland before returning to Portugal. Sometime before 1460 a Portuguese ship is said to have reached Antillia, identified by the Portuguese with the legendary **Ilha das Sete Cidades** (Island of the Seven Cities). A Portuguese document credits João Vaz Corte-Real and Álvaro Martins Homem with the discovery of **Tiera de los Bacalaos** (1472), a name applied to Newfoundland shortly after the voyages of Columbus. Lack of supporting data compels one scholar (Jansen) to place these explorers on a known Danish expedition as observers for the Portuguese Crown. In 1476 Fernão Teles sailed west in

search of Antillia. Fernão Dulmo received a patent from the King (3 Mar. 1486) to explore islands or the mainland of Ilha das Sete Cidades. After entering into partnership with João Alfonso de Estreito, he had his plans approved by the king (24 July and 4 Aug. 1486), but there is no mention of this expedition. Admitting the possibility that Portugal may have wished to keep her territorial discoveries secret, scholars are hesitant about accepting claims to New World exploration put forth in behalf of the explorers of that nation.

1473–81. DANISH AND ENGLISH ACTIVITIES. Diderik Pining and Hans Pothorst, German mariners, allegedly sailed on an exploratory trip to Greenland for King Christian of Denmark, 1472. Cartographical sources indicating that Scolvus, possibly a Pole, sailed to the northwest at this time point to the probability that he went on this Danish voyage as a pilot. Possibly Corte-Real and Homem were also in the party. In 1480 Thomas Lloyd of Bristol, England, sailed in search of the island Antillia. Further exploratory trips were made annually in Bristol ships both to this island and to Brasil, another small island shown on contemporary maps beginning in 1481 (Quinn).

OTHER POSSIBLE PRE-COLUMBIAN CONTACTS. African contacts with the New World, based on the alleged presence of Negroes in pre-Columbian America, have been postulated by Leo Weiner, but widely discredited. Claims have also been advanced that fishermen from the west coast of France sailed to the fishing waters off Newfoundland prior to 1492. Even had such trips been made, they failed to contribute to making Europeans aware of the existence of the New World. In fact, after the translation of Ptolemy's *Geography* (1410), and perhaps even before that date, such a possibility was suggested by available scientific knowledge. A connection between Inca and South Seas cultures has been argued by Thor Heyerdahl, who in 1947 sailed in an Inca-style raft in 101 days from the Peruvian port of Callao to one of the Tuamotu islands. Heyerdahl's thesis of a South American origin for Polynesian culture is disputed by Alfred Métraux (1957) and by Thomas S. Barthel's decipherment of the writing on the Easter Island statues, revealing that the people who made the mysterious statues spoke a Polynesian language. Hence, the evidence suggests rather a South Pacific westward cultural migration with the likelihood that contacts came after the development of Formative cultures on both sides of the Pacific. In short, there is no hard evidence for any pre-Columbian human introduction of a single plant or animal from the Old World to the New or vice versa (Riley).

Columbus and Subsequent Exploration

Improvements in navigation which gave impulse to exploration included (1) the **magnetic compass;** (2) the **astrolabe,** a device for determining latitude; (3) the use of **portolani,** the first practical hydrographic charts; and (4) the construction of the fast Portuguese **caravel,** a small vessel with broad bows, high narrow poop, and usually triangular lateen sails, which could sail against the wind more efficiently than earlier ships. The early explorations to the New World were largely shaped by geographical factors—winds and ocean currents determined the landfalls and guided the interior exploration. Since chronometers and watches were not in common use, it was difficult to determine longitude at sea. Mariners would first strike the desired latitude and continue on the course until their goal was reached. Thus, Columbus, sailing for the latitude of Japan and then heading west, was helped along by the **northeast trade winds** and by ocean currents. On his return trip he was aided by the **westerly winds.** Once North America was reached, penetration and occupation were determined by opportunities for profitable exploitation and by natural advantages for travel.

Thus, the accumulated wealth of Mexico and Central America repaid costly and laborious inroads and settlement, whereas similar expeditions from Florida and Mexico which ranged the lower half of the Mississippi Valley yielded nothing. The other two natural entries to the interior, the St. Lawrence–Great Lakes (with a branch by way of the Hudson River) and Hudson Bay, were first explored in vain as routes to Asia or to rich kingdoms, but remained unused until the North Atlantic fisheries stimulated a fur trade whose rapid drain of the supply drew traders along the waterways into the continent.

1451, c.25 AUG.–31 OCT. CHRISTO-PHER COLUMBUS (It., **Cristoforo Colombo;** Span., **Cristóbal Colón**) was born in or near Genoa of a family of wool weavers. The fact that he could write only one modern language, Spanish, even before he went to Spain, combined with vagueness and inconsistencies in his earliest biographies (his 2d son Fernando's *Historie* and Bartolomé de Las Casas' *Historia de las Indias*), have cast some doubt on his Genoese birth. On the other hand, the records of that city present a wealth of substantiating evidence which no other location can offer, including references to his family as well as several to Columbus himself in various notarial papers (31 Oct. 1470; 20, 26 Mar. 1472; 7 Aug. 1473). Fernando's assertion that his father attended the Univ. of Pavia is not borne out by that institution's records. Columbus may have gone to sea in the service of René d'Anjou (1470–73), and made one or more trips to the island of Chios for the Centurione interests (1474–75).

1476–80. Following a naval battle off Cape St. Vincent between a Genoese fleet on which he was shipping and a Franco-Portuguese flotilla, Columbus arrived in Portugal (1476). Shortly thereafter (Feb. 1477) he made a trip to northern waters (possibly Iceland, but more likely England). Returning to Lisbon, he sailed (1478) once more for the Centurione, this time to Madeira. He married (1479 or 1480) Doña Felipa de Perestrello é Moñiz, daughter of the captain of Porto Santo, to which he moved (1480), the year in which his son Diego was born. Probably (1481–82) he made a trip to the Guinea Coast.

1484. Columbus asked King João II of Portugal to sponsor a western voyage to the island of Cipangu (Marco Polo's Japan). The plan was rejected (1485) either because of lack of confidence in Columbus' geographical knowledge or because the crown was licensing self-financed voyages with similar objectives (Fernão Dulmo, 1486–87). Columbus' stay at Lisbon is believed to have furnished him with opportunities for acquiring knowledge of geography and navigation. Portugal was the home of the most advanced geographers, including José Vizinho and Diogo Ortiz de Vilhegas; was visited by the great Nuremberg cosmographer, Martin Behaim. The court corresponded with the Italian geographer Toscanelli (1474), as did Columbus (c.1481).

1485–86. Columbus left Lisbon with his son Diego (his wife had died) and landed at Palos, Spain, where he was befriended by a Franciscan friar, Antonio de Marchena. After unsuccessful negotiations with Don Enrique de Guzmán, Duke of Medina Sidonia, Columbus turned to Don Luis de la Cerda, Count of Medina Celi, who arranged a meeting between Columbus and Queen Isabella (c.1 May 1486). The result was inconclusive. For the next two years Columbus received a small yearly stipend from the crown.

1488. Columbus attempted to reopen negotiations with King João II, and was in Lisbon to witness the triumphant return of Bartolomeu Dias. With India apparently within its grasp, Portugal was disinclined to back Columbus, who returned to Spain.

1490–92. Columbus' plan was twice rejected by the Castilian commission, but at the insistence of **Luis de Santangel,** Marrano treasurer of Aragon, the court, following the fall of Granada (2 Jan. 1492), marking the end of the reconquest of Spain from the Moors, agreed to sponsor his expedition. His voyage was financed by both the royal treasury and private sources. By the Capitulations of 17 Apr. and the Title of 30 Apr. 1492 Columbus was appointed Admiral of the Ocean Sea, Viceroy, and governor of whatever territory he might discover.

1492, 3 Aug.–1493, 15 Mar. 1ST VOYAGE. The 3 ships of Columbus' fleet (the *Niña,* commanded by Vincente Yáñez Pinzón; the *Pinta* by Martín Alonso Pinzón; and the *Santa Maria,* by Columbus), with a crew of 90, sailed from Palos. They arrived at the Canaries (12 Aug.), sailed west (6 Sept.), and during the first stage of the ocean crossing (9–19 Sept.) enjoyed favorable winds. With the next stage (20–30 Sept.) marked by unfavorable winds and calms morale dropped, with the crews at the point of

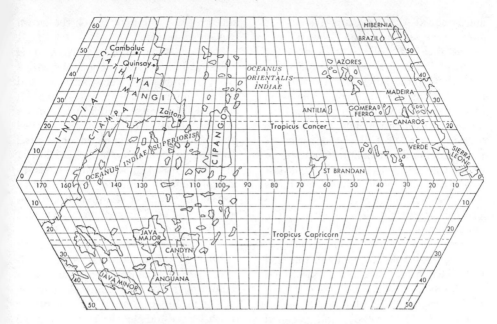

Reconstruction of alleged Toscanelli map (1474?)
reputedly used by Columbus on his first voyage

mutiny 2 days before land was actually sighted. Columbus first sighted (12 Oct.) **Guanahani** (probably **Watlings Island**) in the Bahamas, which he named San Salvador. He explored the Bahamas (14–26 Oct.), discovered and explored the northeastern coast of **Cuba** (27 Oct.–5 Dec.), then (6 Dec. 1492–15 Jan. 1493) the northern coast of **Hispaniola** (Santo Domingo), where the *Santa Maria* was wrecked (25 Dec.) and a post established (**La Navidad**). On the homeward journey (16 Jan.–15 Mar.) stops were made at the Azores (18–24 Feb.) and Lisbon (4–13 Mar.). News of the voyage had already reached the court in a letter written by Columbus off the Canaries (15 Feb.), addressed to Luis de Santangel, a substantial backer of the expedition. This was printed at Barcelona in the original Spanish shortly after its receipt; reprinted, Valladolid, with slight corrections.

1493–94. DIPLOMATIC CONSEQUENCES OF THE DISCOVERY. At the urging of the Spanish rulers Pope Alexander VI (Rodrigo Borgia) issued (3–4 May) two bulls, **Inter Caetera** (granting Spain all lands not under Christian rule) and **Inter Caetera II** (setting a demarcation line at 100 leagues west of the Azores and Cape Verde Islands, beyond which all future discoveries not held by a Christian prince on 25 Dec. 1492 would belong to Spain). By the **Treaty of Tordesillas** (7 June 1494) between Portugal and Spain the line of demarcation was moved to 370 leagues west of the Cape Verde Islands, Portugal to have exclusive rights to all land east of the line.

1493, 25 SEPT.–1496, 11 JUNE. 2ND VOYAGE. Columbus sailed from Cádiz with 17 ships and some 1,200 men (including his brother Diego). The fleet stopped at the Canaries (2–7 or 10 Oct.)

and reached the **Leeward Islands** (4 Nov.). After exploring the Leewards and **Puerto Rico,** Columbus anchored off La Navidad (28 Nov.), where he found his post destroyed. Columbus planted (2 Jan. 1494) **Isabela,** a second colony on Santo Domingo, which served as a base for inland exploration, and explored the southern coast of Cuba, the coasts of Jamaica, and the remaining coastline of Hispaniola (29 Apr.–29 Sept.). The Isabela settlement faced serious difficulties from the start owing to its unsuitable location, sparse gold resources, and the resentment of the natives to enslavement by the conquerors. It was abandoned, and the city of **Santo Domingo** founded 1496. Leaving in command of the island his brother, Bartholomeu, who had joined him in 1494, Columbus sailed for Spain (10 Mar. 1496) and reached Cádiz (11 June).

1498, 30 MAY–1500, 25 Nov. 3RD VOYAGE. Columbus, with a fleet of 7 ships, left the mouth of the Guadalquivir, touched at Madeira (7 June) and the Canaries (19 June), whence 3 ships proceeded directly to Santo Domingo and the remainder, with Columbus, took a more southerly route, touching the Cape Verde Islands (27 June–4 July) and reaching **Trinidad** (31 July). Columbus sighted South America (1 Aug.) at **Punta Bombeador,** explored the **Gulf of Paria** (1–13 Aug.), and sailed for **Santo Domingo,** where he arrived (31 Aug.) to find the colony in a state of rebellion. Some improvement in administration followed the granting of immunity to the rebel leaders (Sept. 1499), but news of unrest convinced the court of the need for a change in administration. The new governor, Francisco de Bobadilla, arrived 23 Aug. 1500, and the three brothers Columbus were sent home in chains (Oct.). They were ultimately restored to their honors but never to their old

authority in the Indies, which the crown henceforth retained.

1502, 11 MAY–1504, 7 Nov. 4TH AND LAST VOYAGE. Columbus with a fleet of 4 ships sailed from Cádiz, stopped at the Canaries (20–25 May), and hit land at **Martinique** (15 June). After stopping at Hispaniola Columbus sailed past Cuba to the mainland of Central America on the **Honduran coast** (31 July) and explored southward as far as **central Panama** (31 July 1502–15 Apr. 1503). En route to Hispaniola he was shipwrecked and marooned in Jamaica (25 June 1503–29 June 1504), and returned to Spain 7 Nov. 1504.

1506, 20 MAY. DEATH AND BURIAL PLACE. Columbus died in Valladolid after spending his final days trying to regain his old privileges. Until his death he insisted that he had skirted the shores of Asia. However, recognition that the territory he had charted was in fact a New World was already gaining ground. His remains were sent to Santo Domingo some time after 5 Nov. 1540 along with those of his son Diego (d.1526), and placed in the cathedral. As a result of the Treaty of Basel (22 July 1795), under which the Spanish part of Santo Domingo was ceded to France, the Spanish authorities removed certain remains from the cathedral in an unmarked lead casket and installed them in the cathedral at Havana. Bones were later removed to Seville and deposited at the cathedral in that city (1898). Meantime (10 Sept. 1877), a cask discovered on the Gospel side of the sanctuary of the Santo Domingo cathedral bore markings indicating that it held the Discoverer's remains. Authorities are divided on the authenticity of the find. Hence, two Columbus shrines at the present day—one at Seville, the other at Santo Domingo.

1497, 2 MAY–6 AUG. 1ST CABOT VOYAGE. John Cabot (b.c.1455, probably in Genoa), a resident (1461) and citizen (1472) of Venice, migrated to England (c.1484–90), where he lived chiefly in Bristol as a merchant or mariner. Henry VII issued (5 Mar. 1497) to the Cabots (John and his 3 sons, Lewis, Sebastian, and Sancio) a patent to discover for England regions to the east, west, and north (avoiding Portuguese claims). In return for a trade monopoly and customs exemptions the Cabots were to turn over to the crown 20% of all trading profits. John Cabot sailed from Bristol (c.20 May 1497) with a crew of 18, including some prominent Bristol merchants and possibly his son **Sebastian,** on a voyage of general reconnaissance. He sighted land (24 June), probably the northernmost tip of **Newfoundland,** took possession of the area for Henry VII, and then sailed southwest far enough to ascertain the direction of the coast, possibly reaching Maine before sailing for England (c.15 July), arriving at Bristol 6 Aug.

1498, EARLY MAY. 2D CABOT VOYAGE. Under new letters patent (3 Feb. 1498) Cabot left Bristol for Cipangu (Japan) and the Spice Islands via Newfoundland. From available evidence (La Cosa map, 1500, and the Hajeda patent, 8 June 1501), it appears that Cabot's company explored the coast of North America as far south as the Delaware or Chesapeake Bay.

1499–1501. SPANISH EXPLORATION AFTER COLUMBUS. Amerigo **Vespucci** (b.Mar. 1454 in Florence and employed by the Pier Francesco branch of the Medici, first in Italy, 1484–92, and then in Spain, 1492–99) sailed on an expedition commanded by **Alonso de Hajeda** (Ojeda), on which Juan de la Cosa, a member of Columbus' first and second expeditions, also participated. Before sighting land the party separated. Vespucci's company probably sighted land

south of **Cape Cassipore** (c.27 June), journeyed down the South American coast, possibly exploring the mouth of the Amazon and the Pará, thence southeastward, passing "Cabo de la Vela" (19 Sept., possibly near Camocim, Brazil). Meantime, the Hajeda–La Cosa group had already arrived at Hispaniola (5 Sept.). Vespucci returned (end of Nov.), and, after sailing around the Bahamas and visiting the Azores, he reached Spain (mid-June 1500) several months after Hajeda and La Cosa. Two other expeditions sailing under the Spanish flag left in 1499 for the New World: (1) Peralonso Niño (former pilot of the *Santa Maria* and *Niña*) and Cristóbal Guerra went on an expedition to the Pearl Coast (Venezuela) in June and returned to Spain (Apr. 1500) laden with pearls. Vincente Yáñez Pinzón (captain of the *Niña* on Columbus' first voyage) sailed in Nov. or Dec. and reached the coast of Brazil (20 Jan. 1500) at about 8°S and explored either the Amazon or the Marañón before returning to Spain (30 Sept. 1500). In 1500–01 Rodrigo de Bastidas explored the northern coast of South America from Maracaibo to the Gulf of Darien, and, possibly, Juan de la Cosa made another trip in 1501 (perhaps with Vespucci), in which he explored the Gulf of Darien and the Atrato River, where he found traces of gold.

1499–1501. PORTUGUESE VOYAGES TO NEW WORLD. João Fernandes, a small landowner of the rank of **Llavrador,** i.e., peasant, and a seaman of the Azores, under a patent from King Manoel of Portugal (28 Oct. 1499) reached Greenland, initially called by his rank (Labrador). Under a patent from King Manoel (12 May 1500) **Gaspar Corte-Real** sailed (June 1500) to the east coast of Greenland, down and around its southern tip, and up the west coast until he encountered icebergs. On a second trip (15 May 1501) to Greenland he crossed Davis Strait to present Labrador, coasted south to Newfoundland, dispatched 2 boats home, continued southward in a third, and was never heard from again. His brother, **Miguel,** sailed (10 May 1502) to Newfoundland, but was also lost. A Portuguese expedition to locate the missing brothers (1503) presumably visited Newfoundland, and out of these voyages the Portuguese fishery developed there. In addition to their activity in northern waters, the Portuguese made voyages to South America. Pedro Alvarez Cabral reached the coast of Brazil (1500). **Amerigo Vespucci,** having switched flags, sailed west for the Portuguese (13 May 1501). He made his landfall a short distance south of **Cape São Roque** (16 Aug.) and, after sailing to the cape, he coasted southward as far as **Porto di San Giulian** (Puerto San Julián, Feb. 1502) in **Argentina.** Upon his return to Lisbon he wrote a letter (1502) to **Lorenzo di Pier Francesco de' Medici,** his former employer and patron, setting forth his conviction that what he had seen was a new land and a continent. This letter, along with 2 others to de' Medici, are generally accepted as authentic. Two others, the first called **Mundus Novus** (Aug. 1504) and addressed to de' Medici, and the second, called the **Four Voyages** (Sept. 1504) and addressed to Piero Soderini, are held to be forgeries, spiced-up versions of authentic letters, but not without evidential value. On the basis of these dubious letters 4 voyages are ascribed to Vespucci. On the first (1497) he purportedly explored the Gulf of Mexico and voyaged north and eastward from Campeche, even reaching the Atlantic coast of the present U.S. The fourth voyage (1503) supposedly ended near Baía, Brazil. In 1507 Martin Waldseemüller, the geographer, proposed that the newly

discovered world should be called "America, because Americus discovered it."

1501–04.   ANGLO-PORTUGUESE VOYAGES FROM BRISTOL. Under letters patent of Henry VII (19 Mar. 1501) a mixed group of 3 merchants from Bristol and 3 men from the Azores, including João Fernandes, are presumed to have made 2 transatlantic voyages. Under a patent (9 Dec. 1502) to an Anglo-Portuguese group known as the "Company of Adventurers to the New Found Lands," trips were made annually to the New World (1502–05), possibly as far south as the Middle Atlantic states.

1503–04. Binot Paulmier de Gonneville, a merchant of Normandy, left Honfleur (June 1503) for a voyage around Africa to the Indies, was blown off his course, and arrived off the coast of Brazil, where he stayed for 6 months before sailing (3 July 1504) for home.

1509. SEBASTIAN CABOT (b.Venice, c.1483) sailed north and west from England (c.1509), and then southwest, returning to England (after 21 Apr. 1509). In later years he claimed to have reached Hudson Bay.

1508–13. SPANISH EXPLORATION FROM CARIBBEAN. Hispaniola was the center from which the Spaniards directed their explorations. By 1512 that colony was sending annually to Spain almost $1 million in gold and was raising sugar cane (introduced by the Spaniards from the Canaries), cotton, and cattle. In 1508 Sebastián de Ocampo circumnavigated Cuba, proving that it was not part of the mainland. Vincente Yáñez Pinzón and Juan Díaz de Solís explored the coasts of Honduras and Yucatán (1508–09). The conquest of the Caribbean Islands was the first military problem. Puerto Rico (1508–09), Jamaica (1510), and then Cuba (1511) were subjugated. **Juan Ponce de León,** conqueror of Puerto Rico, sailed (3 Mar.

1513) to explore lands north of Cuba. Passing the Bahamas, he sighted **Florida** somewhere between St. Augustine and the St. Johns River, remaining a short time (2–8 Apr.). Thence he sailed north and, reversing his course, explored the entire eastern coast of Florida as well as the western shore as far north as Charlotte Harbor (23 May). In addition, he visited the Florida Keys and the Bahamas, and returned to Puerto Rico (21 Sept.). The Spanish set up temporary trading posts in present Venezuela and Colombia (at Santa Marta and Cartagena). From a third post, Santa Maria de la Antigua on the Gulf of Darien, **Vasco Nuñez de Balboa** pushed across the **Isthmus of Panama** to discover the **Pacific Ocean** (25 Sept. 1513). This discovery stimulated efforts to get around or through America.

1515–19. FURTHER SPANISH EFFORTS. Juan Díaz de Solís sailed from Spain (1515) and reached South America near present Rio de Janeiro, then sailed south to the mouth of the Río de la Plata (Jan. 1516). Francisco Hernández Cordoba and Antón de Alaminos explored Yucatán (Sept. 1517), while Juan de Grijalva explored the Mexican coast from Yucatán to the Panuco River (Tampico, 1518). Alvárez Pineda explored the Gulf of Mexico from Florida to Vera Cruz (1519).

1519–22. MAGELLAN'S CIRCUMNAVIGATION. Fernando Magellan (Port. Fernão Magalhães), a Portuguese, sailed under the Spanish flag from St. Lucar (20 Sept. 1519), skirted the coast of South America (29 Nov. 1519–end of Mar. 1520), and wintered at Puerto San Julián (Apr.–Aug. 1520). Sailing through the strait that now bears his name and thence north and westward, he reached the Ladrones (Marianas) and **Philippines**, where he was killed (27 Apr. 1521). After many vicissitudes the rem-

nants of his expedition returned to Spain (6 Sept. 1522). Permanent Spanish occupation of the Philippine Islands began with the expedition of Miguel López de Legaspi (1564).

1519–21. CONQUEST OF MEXICO. Hernando Cortés headed an expedition into the province of Tabasco, Mexico (Mar. 1519), defeated the Tabascan (25 Mar.) and Tlascala Indians (5 Sept.), but was amicably received by **Montezuma** (Moctezuma) in the Aztec capital of Tenochtitlán (Mexico City, 8 Nov.). After the death of Montezuma (30 June 1520), whom Cortés had imprisoned, the latter crushed an Aztec revolt at Otumba (7 July) and ended resistance by 13 Aug. 1521. This conquest opened to Spain the treasures of Mexico.

1521–30. SPANISH VOYAGES in these years include explorations of Francisco de Gordillo, along the Atlantic coast from Florida to South Carolina (1521); of Estcban Gómez, a Portuguese in Spanish service, from Nova Scotia to Florida (1524); of Pedro de Quexos as far north as 40°N (1524–25); and of Sebastian Cabot, sailing under the Spanish flag, to the Río de la Plata, exploring the Paraná and Paraguay rivers (1526–30).

1521–74. COLONIZING EFFORTS IN FLORIDA (see pp. 59–61).

1523, Dec.–1524, July. FRENCH EXPLORATION. French fishing vessels proceeded as far as Newfoundland (1504, p. 70). Efforts to find a route to the Indies through North America persisted.

GIOVANNI DE VERRAZANO (Fr. Jehan de Varrasanne), b. near Florence, was dispatched by Francis I of France as pilot on a ship commanded by Antoine de Conflans to find a route to the Indies. After leaving Dieppe (Dec. 1523) he sailed west from Madeira (17 Jan. 1524) and reached North America, probably the Carolina coast (c.19 Mar.), thence proceeding southward "fifty leagues" before reversing his course and coasting north, reaching **New York Harbor** (c.17 Apr.) and **Narragansett Bay** (c.21 Apr.–6 May), and continuing northward as far as **Nova Scotia** before returning to Dieppe. Copies of Verrazano's report to Francis I (8 July 1524) constitute the chief source of information about this voyage.

1527, 10 June. The English crown dispatched two ships from Plymouth, the *Samson* and the *Mary Guildford*. The former probably foundered, but the latter explored the North Atlantic coast from Labrador south and arrived in the West Indies (19–26 Nov.).

1528–36. NARVÁEZ EXPEDITION. Pánfilo de Narváez sailed from Spain (1527) and landed near Tampa Bay, Florida (14 Apr. 1528) with a group of 400 colonists. They marched north and reached the village of Apalachee (25 June) near present Tallahassee. Unsuccessful in their quest for gold, they embarked, probably at Apalachee Bay, and sailed for Mexico (22 Sept.). As a result of shipwreck only 2 survived to reach Mexico City, Apr. 1536, one of whom was **Cabeza de Vaca**, whose account of the expedition popularized the notion that New Mexico (specifically, the Seven Cities of Cibola) was fabulously rich.

1534–43. INTERIOR EXPLORATION OF NORTH AMERICA: FRENCH. Jacques Cartier (b. St. Malo, Normandy, 1491), believed to have been on the Verrazano expedition, was granted (Mar. 1534) 6,000 livres by Francis I to proceed to Newfoundland in search of islands and countries where it was hoped to find gold and "other riches." After sailing from St. Malo to the **Strait of Belle Isle** (20 Apr.–10 June 1534), he continued down the west coast of Newfoundland and passed Prince Edward Island, Chaleur Bay, and Gaspé Bay, and returned to St. Malo (5 Sept.). On his

second voyage he sailed to Pillage Bay in the estuary of the St. Lawrence (19 May–9 Aug. 1535) and then proceeded up the river to **Quebec** (7 Sept.), where he left his ships and some men and went in small boats as far as **Montreal.** After wintering in Quebec, he returned home (6 May–16 July 1536). His last trip was organized for the conquest of the kingdom of Saguenay, which Indians had led him to believe possessed great treasure. He left St. Malo (23 May 1541), reached Quebec (end of Aug.), set up a post at nearby Cap Rouge. En route home he stopped off at St. Johns, Newfoundland, where a few days before (8 June 1542) **Jean François de la Rocque, Sieur de Roberval,** commissioned (15 Jan. 1541) by Francis I to direct the conquest of Saguenay, had already arrived. Cartier brought back to France a shipload of iron pyrites (fool's gold) and some quartz crystals he believed to be diamonds. Roberval led one, apparently fruitless, expedition up the St. Lawrence (6 June 1543) toward the kingdom of Saguenay, but he was back in France in the fall of that year.

1539, May 28–1543, 10 Sept. INTERIOR EXPLORATION: SPANISH. Hernando de Soto, newly appointed governor of Cuba, landed with 600 soldiers on the Florida coast, either at Tampa Bay or Charlotte Harbor (28 May 1539), and, after exploring the western part of the peninsula, he wintered in Apalachee. The following spring he marched north to the vicinity of the Savannah River, thence west to the Blue Ridge Mountains, and southwest almost to the Gulf of Mexico near Mobile (17 Nov.), wintered (1540–41) probably in the Yazoo Delta country, and, proceeding north in the spring, crossed the **Mississippi** (May 1541) south of Memphis. He continued west through the Ozarks, wintered near the junction of the Arkansas and Canadian rivers in eastern Oklahoma, and returned to the Mississippi where he died of fever (1542). With Luís Moscoso de Alvarado as their leader, the survivors journeyed west to the upper reaches of the Brazos River, but returned to spend a last winter (1542–43) at the mouth of the Arkansas. They sailed down the Mississippi (July 1543) and reached Panuco (10 Sept.).

1539–42. NEW MEXICO. The Franciscan **Fray Marcos de Niza** headed an expedition from Mexico into the Zuni country, accompanied by Esteban, a Moorish or Negro companion of Cabeza de Vaca. Their discovery of a Zuni pueblo at Hawikuh in western New Mexico was magnified in Mexico. **Francisco Vásquez de Coronado** led a force into New Mexico to conquer the Seven Cities of Cibola. He left Compostela (23 Feb. 1540) and captured the first city (Hawikuh, named Granada Cibola, 7 July), which served as a base for further expeditions. Don Garcia López de Cárdenas, proceeded westward and discovered the Grand Canyon; Hernando de Alvarado, going east, reached the Rio Grande around Albuquerque (region called Tiguex) and, continuing past the upper reaches of the Pecos, pushed into the Texas Panhandle in search of Quivera, a mythical kingdom of gold. After wintering at Tiguex, Coronado marched to the upper Brazos River (26 May 1541) where, separating from his main force, he moved north and northwest across the Arkansas River near Ford, Kan. (29 June), into the district of the Wichita Indians, returning to Tiguez (20 Oct.), which he finally abandoned (Apr. 1542), and returned to Mexico City (before 13 Oct.).

1539–43. SPANISH WEST COAST EXPLORATION. Francisco de Ulloa sailed from Acapulco (8 July) into the Gulf of California, circled the southern tip of Lower California, and sailed up its western shore possibly as far north as 30°N, thereby establishing its peninsularity. Hernando de Alarcón, heading an expedition from Acapulco to support Coronado, sailed up the Gulf of California and into the Colorado River (c.25 Aug. 1540), proceeding to some point between the junctions of the Gila and Williams with the Colorado, but left shortly before a Coronado searching party, headed by Melchior Díaz, reached the same area. In an exploration of the west coast **Juan Rodriguez Cabrillo** sailed (27 June 1542) up the California coast to Drake's Bay and took possession of the country for Spain. He died on San Miguel Island (3 Jan. 1543), and his successor in command, **Bartolomé Ferrelo**, sailed north, possibly to the California-Oregon border (1 Mar. 1543). Permanent Spanish settlement of the California coast did not start until a system of presidios and missions (Franciscan) was established at San Diego (1769), Monterey (1770), and San Francisco (1776).

1577, 13 Dec.–1580, 26 Sept. DRAKE'S CIRCUMNAVIGATION. Ostensibly on a voyage to Alexandria, Egypt, but actually to prey upon Spanish shipping in the Pacific (considerable following the conquest of Peru, 1530–32, by **Francisco Pizarro**), **Francis Drake** sailed through the Strait of Magellan and reached the Pacific (6 Sept. 1578). Raiding the west coast of South America—Valparaiso (5 Dec.), Tarapacá and Arica (4 and 5 Feb. 1579)—and capturing a rich treasure ship between Callao and Panama (1 Mar.), he continued north possibly to 40°N, then reversed his course, anchoring probably at **San Francisco Bay** (17 June). Upon taking possession of this territory in behalf of Queen Elizabeth he had a plaque struck commemorating the event. (A brass plate answering its description was uncovered [1936] in the San Francisco Bay district, but its authenticity is not definitely established.) On leaving California (July 1579), Drake sailed north apparently to 48°N in search of the western end of the Northwest Passage; then, heading westward across the Pacific, he completed his circumnavigation (26 Sept. 1580).

1576–1606. ENGLISH SEARCH FOR NORTHWEST PASSAGE. (1) **Martin Frobisher** sailed from England (June 1576) and pressed northwest after sighting Greenland until, at 62°N, he reached **Baffin Land** and entered **Frobisher Bay,** believing it to be a strait between America and Asia. To exploit his discovery (including ore [mistakenly believed to have gold content] brought back to England) the Company of Cathay was organized and Frobisher sailed under its auspices (May, 1577) both for further exploration and for mining operations, which he conducted in Baffin Land. He returned to Bristol (15 Oct.) with 200 tons of ore. On his third voyage (1578) for the purpose of shipping ore Frobisher reached **Hudson Strait,** which he now considered a more likely passage to Asia. His ore proved worthless. (2) **John Davis** made 3 trips in search of the Northwest Passage (1585–87). The first led him to Baffin Land via the west coast of Greenland and the strait now bearing his name; on the second he followed the north coast of Labrador but missed Hudson Strait, and on the third he reached 73°N in Baffin Bay. (3) **George Waymouth,** backed by the East India Co., sailed from Radcliffe, England (2 May 1602), reached Baffin Land, sailed south past Frobisher Bay and into Hudson Strait, where the mutiny of his crew forced him to return to England (autumn). (4) **John Knight,** sponsored by both the East India and Muscovy companies, explored the shores of Newfoundland and Labrador (1606).

1598–1610. SPANISH SETTLEMENT OF SOUTHWEST was begun in New Mexico by **Juan de Oñate** (1598), who dispatched an expedition which explored from Kansas to the Gulf of California. **Santa Fe** was founded (1609–10).

1608–11. VOYAGES OF HUDSON. In 1608 **Henry Hudson** made a voyage for the Muscovy Co. in search of the Northwest Passage, reaching the Kara Sea. With the same goal in view he sailed from Amsterdam for the Dutch East India Co. (25 Mar. 1609), reached Nova Zembla (Novaya Zemlya), where he was forced back by calms and mutiny. Sailing westward, he passed Newfoundland (3 July), continued south to the Carolina coast, reversed his course, entered **Delaware Bay** (28 Aug.), and the **Hudson River** (13 Sept.), up which he sailed as far as **Albany** (19 Sept.). Hudson's last voyage (begun 27 Apr. 1610) was under private English auspices and to locate the Northwest Passage. He reached Resolution Island (end of June), but was forced south by ice. Proceeding through Hudson Strait, he entered **Hudson Bay** (3 Aug.) and coasted along its eastern shore to **James Bay,** where he wintered. On the homeward journey he was set adrift by his own men (23 June 1611).

1603–35. CHAMPLAIN'S VOYAGES. After having sailed with a Spanish convoy to the West Indies (3 Feb. 1599–2 July 1601), **Samuel de Champlain** (b.c.1567) made 11 trips to eastern Canada. On the first, sailing from Honfleur (15 Mar. 1603) as a geographer on an expedition sponsored by Aymar de Chastes, he reached **Tadoussac** on the St. Lawrence, already a trading station for furs and fish. He then explored the St. Lawrence as far as **Lachine Rapids.** On his return to France (20 Sept.), he wrote his first book, *Des Sauvages,* reporting his voyage. On his second trip (early June 1604–06) he sailed in the same capacity in an expedition to set up a fur-trading post for Pierre du Guast, Sieur de Monts, who had received the trading patent previously held by Aymar de Chastes. Unsuccessful attempts were made to establish a post at New Brunswick and Annapolis Basin in Nova Scotia, but Champlain made 2 trips as far south as Nauset Harbor on Cape Cod (20 July 1605) and Vineyard Sound (20 Oct. 1606). On his third voyage (13 Apr. 1608–15 Oct. 1609) he sailed in the service of de Monts, holder of a new monopoly. After erecting a fort at Quebec (8 July) and cementing friendly relations with the Indians (Algonquins of the lower St. Lawrence and Hurons and Algonquins of the Ottawa River), he voyaged up the Richelieu River into **Lake Champlain** (30 July 1609). On his fourth and fifth voyages (7 Mar.–27 Sept. 1610 and 1 Mar.–26 Sept. 1611) he devoted himself to the fur trade and Indian relations. On his sixth trip (6 Mar.–26 Sept. 1613) he pushed up the Ottawa River in quest of Hudson Bay (Northern Sea) above Waltham (7 June). On his seventh trip (24 Apr. 1615–3 Aug. 1616) he reached Georgian Bay via the Ottawa and Mattawa rivers and Lake Nipissing. **Étienne Brûle,** who had accompanied Champlain on the 1608–09 trip and had traveled in the Huron region, and **Le Caron,** a Recollect (Franciscan) missionary, preceded Champlain by a week. Champlain joined the Hurons in raiding the Iroquois and, crossing Lake Ontario, penetrated south to Lake Oneida. After unsuccessfully besieging an Iroquois stronghold (probably on Lake Onondaga), 10–16 Oct. 1615, he wintered with the Hurons. In a trip growing out of this campaign, Brûle traveled (Sept.–Oct. 1615) down the Susquehanna as far as Chesapeake Bay.

THE FOUNDING OF THE ENGLISH COLONIES, 1578-1732

The English colonization of America was a phenomenon of extraordinary magnitude. Prompted by hunger, overpopulation, religious vision, mercantilist ambitions, and nationalist aspirations—drives that varied from colony to colony —the colonization movement shaped the future of a large part of the New World and affected the balance of power among the great nations of the Old. It involved both the transplantation from England and the European continent of many thousands of individuals and families as well as the grafting on the Atlantic beachhead of the institutions of local self-government of the mother country and the setting up of representative legislatures for each colony modeled after the Parliament of England. Some of the colonies, such as Virginia and Massachusetts Bay, were initiated by joint stock companies; others like Maryland, Pennsylvania, Delaware, and New York, for a short time after the conquest of the Dutch colony, were governed by proprietors, but the remainder were either from the start or in the course of time directly under royal control. In all the Thirteen Colonies governmental systems emerged without parallel among the contemporary colonies of other nations.

Settlement of the Tobacco Provinces

Virginia

1578–83. SIR HUMPHREY GILBERT obtained a patent (11 June) from Queen Elizabeth for discovery and colonization in northwest America. He made a voyage to the New World (1578–79), but his plan to establish a colony as a base against Spain had to await financial support. With meager funds raised in Bristol and Southampton, he sailed (June 1583) with 5 ships and 260 men, reached Newfoundland, and made exploratory trips, but his vessel was lost (Sept.) on the homeward journey.

1584–1602. RALEIGH'S COLONY. Sir Walter Raleigh, half brother of Gilbert and a member of his last expedition, was granted a virtual renewal of the Gilbert patent (25 Mar.). With the aid of Walsingham, Drake, Sidney, and the elder and younger Richard Hakluyt, he equipped an expedition which sailed (27 Apr. 1584) under the command of **Sir Richard Grenville** and **Ralph Lane,** both to explore the North American mainland and reconnoiter Spanish Caribbean defenses. After accomplishing the latter mission, the expedition entered Albemarle Sound on the North Carolina coast, landed on Roanoke Island (July), and returned to England (mid-Sept.). Raleigh named his discovery **Virginia** and dispatched a colonizing expedition (9 Apr. 1585) under the same commanders, which landed at Roanoke Island (27 July). Grenville left Lane in charge of settlement. As a result of Indian troubles and Spanish tension the colony was abandoned (June 1586) when Drake, stopping by after a raid on the Spanish West Indies, offered the settlers passage home. Returning with supplies a few weeks later, Grenville left 15 men at the deserted colony. A fourth expedition under **John White** (probably the painter whose watercolors of Indian life served as the conventional representation of the aborigines) sailed (8 May 1587), arrived at Roanoke Island (22 July), found no survivors of the Grenville expedition, but left a group of colonists. White sailed home to obtain supplies (25 Aug.) only a week after the birth of his grandchild, **Virginia Dare** (18 Aug.), the first English child born in the present U.S. His return to the colony was delayed by the threat and then the actuality of the Spanish Armada until 17 Aug. 1590, when he found no trace of the colonists, but noted the cryptic letters, CRO, cut in a tree and the word CROTOAN carved on a doorpost—apparently references to an island off the coast held by friendly Indians. Coincidental with the 350th anniversary of the colony's founding, a quartz stone was discovered in Chowan Co., N.C. (Sept., 1937), carved with

what purported to be a message from Eleanore White Dare, Virginia's mother, describing the slaughter of the entire colony save 7, presumably saved by friendly natives. This "find" was followed by 48 others, all seeming to corroborate the first (1937–39), but they were exposed as forgeries (by Boyden Sparkes, 1941). Raleigh dispatched a final expedition (Mar. 1602) in a futile search for survivors.

1605, 5 MAR.–1606, 18 JULY. GEORGE WEYMOUTH sailed under the auspices of the Earl of Southampton and the latter's Roman Catholic son-in-law, Sir Thomas Arundel, ostensibly to establish a colony for Catholics who found their position in England insecure (Catholic priests banished, 1604; Guy Fawkes' arrest, 4 Nov. 1605). The account of his voyage to Nantucket and the Marine coast, as narrated in James Rosier's *Relation,* prompted two interrelated groups of merchants, from London and Plymouth, to petition the crown (c.Sept. 1605) for a patent, which was conferred (20 Apr. 1606). Under its terms two **Virginia companies**—the **London** (or South Virginia) **Co.** and the **Plymouth** (or North Virginia) **Co.** were established. The former was authorized to settle in a region between 34°N and 41°N (present New York City); the latter between 45°N and 38°N (present Washington, D.C.), but neither was to settle within 100 miles of the other, in effect creating a neutral zone between the two colonies. Each was to receive all lands 50 miles north and south of the first settlement and 100 miles into the interior.

1606, 20 DEC.–1609, 23 MAY. SETTLEMENT OF JAMESTOWN. The London Co. dispatched 3 vessels, which reached Virginia (26 Apr. 1607), entered Chesapeake Bay, and disembarked at **Jamestown** (24 May). During the first 7 months famine and disease cut the number of settlers from the original

105 to 32 as the councilors chosen before sailing proved unable to cope with the situation. The arrival of 2 supply ships (Jan. and Apr., 1608), the compulsory work program instituted by Capt. **John Smith** (p. 1154) upon his election as president of the council (Sept.), and the emphasis upon self-sustaining agriculture, notably maize (1609), marked a turning point. Smith's capture by Powhatan, giving rise to the legend of Pocahontas' intercession, occurred when he left Jamestown (10 Dec. 1607) and ascended the Chickahominy to obtain provisions. He explored Chesapeake Bay (24 July–7 Sept. 1608). A new charter granted to Virginia (2 June 1609) vested control in a council to be selected by the company and extended the colony's boundaries north and south from Old Point Comfort 200 miles in each direction and from "sea to sea."

1609–19. Dissension marked the period preceding the delayed arrival of **Thomas Lord De La Warr** (16 June 1610). Smith refused to yield authority, but left the colony (5 Oct. 1609). The "starving time" ran through the winter of 1609–10. **Sir Thomas Dale** assumed control (23 May 1611) as deputy for De La Warr, whom sickness had forced from Virginia. The "Dale Code" (**Laws Divine, Morall, and Martiall**, London, 1612) imposed severe penalties to check internal disorder. Dale began construction of a fort at Henrico, 50 miles up the James, and a system of stockades. Both projects were completed under **Sir Thomas Gates** (governor from Aug. 1611 to early 1614). A third charter to the Virginia Co. (22 Mar. 1612) placed Bermuda under its authority. During the administrations of Gates, Dale (early 1614–Apr. 1616), and **George Yeardley** (acting governor, 1616–17), except for the misrule of **Sir Samuel Argall** (deputy governor, 1617–Nov. 1618), such constructive developments occurred as the introduction of tobacco cultivation (credited to John Rolfe, 1612; first shipment to England, Mar. 1614; married Pocahontas, 14 Apr. 1614), individual allotments to tenant farmers (1613–14) supplementing the prevailing system of community labor, and fee simple grants (beg. c.1617).

1619–24. FINAL PERIOD OF COMPANY CONTROL. When, in 1618, **Sir Edwin Sandys** and the Earl of Southampton gained control of the company, reforms were introduced through **George Yeardley**, newly appointed governor (arrived Virginia 29 Apr. 1619). The harsh legal code was repealed. A **General Assembly**, comprising 22 burgesses (2 chosen by the planters from each town, hundred, or plantation) and the governor and council, met in Jamestown (9–14 Aug. 1619), constituting the first colonial legislature in the New World, although it also served in a judicial capacity. In this period a previously inaugurated system of granting land to subordinate corporations (Society of Smith's Hundred, 1617; Martin's Brandon, 1617; Martin's Hundred, 1618) was extended, with 44 patents issued between 1619 and 1623. Heavy mortality from disease continued. An Indian massacre (22 Mar. 1622) provoked a series of retaliatory raids. A break in 1619 between the Sandys-Southampton group and that of Sir Thomas Smith, previous treasurer, was followed by several years of unprofitable operations, to which the suspension (8 Mar. 1622) by the Privy Council of the lottery, authorized in the charter of 1612 as a fund-raising device, contributed. The company went into receivership and was placed under the management of the Privy Council (July 1623). The charter was revoked 24 May 1624, and Virginia became a **Royal Colony.**

1624–42. SIR FRANCIS WYATT, who had been company governor, 1621–

24, was appointed governor by James I (24 Aug. 1624). He in turn was superseded by **George Yeardley** (14 Mar. 1626). His successor, **Francis West** (Nov. 1627–5 Mar. 1629), was instructed to call a General Assembly, which convened at the end of March, 1628. Pending the arrival of his successor, **John Harvey**, Dr. **John Pott** controlled affairs down to the spring of 1630, acting thereafter as opposition leader. Harvey was finally replaced (Jan. 1639) by **Sir Francis Wyatt** (1639–41), who was instructed to convene the burgesses "once a year or oftener."

1642–52. BERKELEY'S FIRST ADMINISTRATION. Wyatt's successor, **Sir William Berkeley** (1606–77), introduced a number of reforms, including the abolition of the poll tax. An Indian uprising (18 Mar. 1644) by Opechancanough was suppressed. The Indians ceded all lands between the York and the James from the falls to Kecoughton, but retained territory north of the York. Peace lasted until 1675. On 30 Jan. 1649 Virginia announced its allegiance to the Stuart house after the execution of Charles I and gave refuge to prominent Cavaliers. In retaliation, Parliament passed an act (Oct. 1650) imposing a blockade on Virginia and subsequently dispatched 2 armed vessels with commissioners who received the submission of Berkeley and the council (12 Mar. 1652) upon liberal terms. Following a new election, the burgesses chose as governor **Richard Bennett**, one of the parliamentary commissioners. When the succeeding governor, **Samuel Matthews**, threatened to dissolve the burgesses (1658), he was temporarily removed as an object lesson, then reelected. With the collapse of the Protectorate and the death of Matthews (close of 1659) the burgesses asserted "supreme power" until lawful authority might be forth-

coming from England, and elected the royalist **Berkeley** governor (12 Mar. 1660). Upon the Restoration in England (29 May), Berkeley was commissioned by Charles II (31 July).

1660–75. DETERIORATING CONDITIONS. As a result of the Navigation Acts (p. 698) tobacco prices declined from 3d per lb. previously paid by the Dutch to ½d. (1667). To meet the crisis attempts were made to limit tobacco acreage and establish clothworks in each county. The Dutch Wars (1664 and 1672) caused severe losses to the tobacco fleet. The crisis was deepened by a cattle epidemic (1672–73), the reintroduction of the poll tax, and a number of servant uprisings (p. 760). Additional unrest was provoked by implementing the grant made by Charles II (1649) to Lord Hopton of a tract of more than 5 million acres between the Rappahannock and Potomac rivers (assigned to Lord Culpeper, 1689, on whose death proprietary rights descended to his grandson, **Thomas Fairfax**, 1693–1781, 6th Baron Fairfax of Cameron, who settled in Virginia, 1747), and by a grant of all Virginia (25 Feb. 1673) to Lords Arlington and Culpeper for 31 years. This claim was reduced to quitrents and escheats and ultimately assigned to the king in payment to Culpeper of £600 for 20 years (1684). Despite growing discontent, Berkeley had stubbornly refused to call another election since the last one (1662).

1675–76. BACON'S REBELLION: PRELIMINARIES. Bands of Susquehannock Indians fleeing more powerful tribes to the north crossed the Potomac and committed atrocities. A joint force of Marylanders (under Thomas Trueman) and Virginians (under John Washington) failed at Piscataway Creek (27 Sept.) to destroy the Indians, who now stepped up their attacks, killing in one

January (1676) raid 36 Virginians on a single day. Frontier settlers deserted their homes, but Berkeley, who was accused of protecting the fur trade in which he was personally involved, refused to allow a force under Sir Henry Chicherley to march against the Indians.

1676, 10 MAY–18 OCT. BACON'S REBELLION. Nathaniel Bacon (p. 977), a recent settler in Henrico Co. and a member of the council, marched without commission at the head of a force of frontiersmen to the Roanoke River, where he destroyed a body of Susquehannocks. Declared a traitor (26 May), he was arrested when he tried to take his seat in the burgesses, to which he had been elected, but was freed (5 June) on acknowledging his offense and pardoned by Berkeley. Returning to Henrico, he raised a force of 500 which he led unopposed into Jamestown (23 June), forcing Berkeley to sign his commission. The assembly now enacted a number of democratic reforms. Again Berkeley proclaimed Bacon a rebel (29 July), but, failing to raise a force against him, fled to the Eastern Shore. Meeting at the Middle Plantation (3 Aug.), the large planters took oath to support Bacon. Returning (13 Sept.) from an expedition against the Indians on the upper reaches of the Potomac and Rappahannock, Bacon drove Berkeley's force out of Jamestown (18 Sept.), which he burned the next day. He died suddenly (18 Oct.)

1676, OCT–1677, MAY. RESTORATION OF ORDER. The loss of its commander reduced the rebel army to a series of bands which were captured by treachery or surrendered piecemeal to Berkeley (Nov.–Dec.) under promise of amnesty. Commissioners John Berry and Francis Moryson arrived 29 Jan. 1677 to investigate the uprising, preceding by a few days Col. **Herbert Jeffreys**, sent to

restore order. Jeffreys brought with him royal pardons for the rebels which Berkeley (10 Feb.) nullified. Executions totaling 23 continued until Jeffreys formally took over the government (27 Apr.) just prior to Berkeley's departure (5 May).

1677–89. REVOLUTION OF 1689 IN VIRGINIA. Jeffreys and his successors, Sir **Henry Chicherley** (9 Nov. 1678–May, 1680) and **Lord Culpeper** (10 May 1680–28 Sept. 1683), enjoyed comparatively peaceful administrations, but that of **Lord Howard of Effingham** (1683–89) was marked by a struggle between the governor and the legislature. A list of popular grievances was presented to James II (Sept. 1688), but before it could be acted upon William and Mary had landed in England. Their accession (13 Feb. 1689) and Howard's subsequent removal were hailed in Virginia.

Maryland

1620–32. PRELIMINARIES OF SETTLEMENT. George Calvert (c.1580–1632) became principal Secretary of State (1619), which office he resigned upon entering the Roman Catholic church (1625). By this act he did not lose favor with James I, who created him 1st **Lord Baltimore.** A member of the Virginia Co. (1609–20) and of the Council for New England (1622), Calvert bought from Sir William Vaughan (1620) the southeastern peninsula of Newfoundland, which he named Avalon. Because of the severity of the climate this colony did not prosper. After visiting Virginia (1628), Baltimore induced Charles I to grant him (1632) territory north of the Potomac River. The Maryland charter was granted (30 June) after his death. His son, Cecilius Calvert, 2d **Lord Baltimore** (c.1605–75), became its first proprietor. The charter recognized Calvert as **proprietor;** conferred upon him the authority of the county Palatine of Durham, subject to the limitations that laws be made with the consent of the freemen and agreeable to the laws of England. The charter did not forbid the establishment of churches other than Protestant, and Baltimore took advantage of this to settle his coreligionists. The northern boundary was finally settled at 40°N, the southern at the Potomac River (conflicting with Virginia's claims), with a line drawn east of the mouth of the Potomac constituting the southern boundary on the Eastern Shore.

1634–40. EARLY PROBLEMS. The first group of some 200 colonists, including 2 Jesuits and many other Catholics, sailed from Portsmouth (22 Nov. 1633), arrived in Virginia (27 Feb. 1634), and went up Chesapeake Bay to Blakiston's Island, erecting a cross and celebrating mass (26 Mar.) before finally settling at **St. Mary's** (Yoacomaco). The 2d Lord Baltimore never visited the colony himself, but governed by deputy. His brother, the first governor, **Leonard Calvert,** established the manorial government authorized by the charter, maintained friendly relations with the Indians, but came into conflict with Virginia. **William Claiborne** (c.1587–c.1677), a member of the Virginia Council, had established a trading post on Kent Island under royal license soon after the return of the 1st Lord Baltimore to England. Although this territory lay within Baltimore's patent, Claiborne refused to recognize his overlordship. His community sent representatives to the Virginia assembly, which supported his claim. The controversy culminated in sea fights between Claiborne's and Baltimore's vessels (23 Apr. and 10 May 1635). Claiborne visited England (1637) in a vain attempt to substantiate his claims, was attainted by the Maryland assembly (3 Apr. 1638), the crown finally ruled against him (4 Apr.)

1640–60. UNDER LONG PARLIAMENT AND COMMONWEALTH. Baltimore's position in England grew increasingly insecure as Maryland suffered troubled times (1644–46). Claiborne proceeded to retake Kent Island and Capt. **Richard Ingle** (1609–c.1653), a Protestant tobacco trader, captured St. Mary's and plundered the colony, forcing Calvert to flee to Virginia. With the aid of Berkeley he recaptured the province, but Ingle, on return to England, almost succeeded (1647) in having the charter revoked. During the administration of **William Stone,** a Protestant, as deputy governor (1648–52) a **Toleration Act** was passed (21 Apr. 1649), granting religious freedom to all Trinitarians. When Stone left the colony (Nov. 1651) he designated **Thomas Greene,** a Roman Catholic royalist, as his deputy. The latter, by recognizing Charles II as lawful heir to the throne (15 Nov.), precipitated an investigation in England and the dispatch to the province of parliamentary commissioners, among whom was Claiborne. The commissioners ousted Stone (29 Mar. 1652), who still asserted his authority. William Fuller, designated governor by the commissioners, called an assembly (30 Oct. 1654), which repudiated the proprietor's authority, repealed the Toleration Act, and denied Catholics the protection of law. In the ensuing brief **Civil War** the Puritans were victors (25 Mar. 1655), Stone was wounded and imprisoned, and 4 of his supporters executed. Baltimore persuaded the Committee of Trade to restore his privileges (Jan. 1656) subject to the condition that **Josias Fendall** (who was actually chosen, 10 July) be governor in Stone's place. The new assembly (10 Mar. 1660) declared itself free of proprietary control. On accepting his commission from that body, Fendall was promptly ousted and **Philip Calvert** appointed in his place (Nov.). In turn, he was succeeded by **Charles Calvert** (1637–1715), who, upon his father's death (1675), became proprietor and 3d **Lord Baltimore.**

1661–81. INCREASING TENSION. The proprietary regime became increasingly unpopular as a result of the decline in tobacco prices, the restriction of the suffrage to freeholders (18 Dec. 1670), Indian raids, absentee proprietorship and official nepotism, and continued anti-Catholic sentiment. A short-lived uprising under William Davyes and John Pate (Sept. 1676) was crushed and the two leaders hanged, but in Apr. 1681, Fendall, enemy of the proprietary party, staged an unsuccessful "rebellion" and was fined and banished.

1684–95. REVOLUTION OF 1689 IN MARYLAND. Baltimore returned to England (May 1684) to settle boundary disputes with William Penn and the colony of Virginia and to answer charges of favoring Roman Catholics and interfering with the royal customs collectors. He was also called to account for the murder of Christopher Rousby (31 Oct. 1684), a collector, by the proprietor's nephew, **George Talbot,** acting governor in his absence. The charges of pro-Catholicism were dropped, Baltimore was fined £2,500 for obstructing the customs, and Talbot was taken to Virginia and sentenced to death (24 Apr. 1686), only to have this sentence commuted by the king to five years' banishment (9 Sept.). While the Maryland-Virginia Eastern Shore boundary had been settled (1668, 1671), Baltimore's claim to the entire Potomac was not settled for 200 years (1878), and the complicated border dispute with Penn also remained unsettled, until 1769, when the crown ratified the line defining the southern

boundary of Pennsylvania. A demarcation of the 2 colonies' boundaries, begun in 1763, was completed 4 years later by 2 English surveyors, Charles Mason and Jeremiah Dixon. Extended in 1784, the **Mason and Dixon Line** came to be known as the dividing line between slavery and free soil, as to its south lay Delaware, Maryland, and Virginia (incl. present W. Va.). During the absence of Baltimore (1684–89) and the disgrace of his lieutenant, Talbot, antiproprietary sentiment mounted. When Baltimore finally dispatched (1688) **William Joseph,** an advocate of divine right, to act as his deputy, the assembly (24 Nov.) voiced its disapproval, but took the oath (27 Nov.). Joseph then prorogued that body to meet in Apr. 1689, and again prorogued it until Oct. During the feverish period preceding the Glorious Revolution rumors were spread that the colony was to be turned over to the Roman Catholics. After the accession of William and Mary and the declaration of war with France (May 1689), an uprising led by **John Coode** (d.1709), with 250 recruits chiefly from Charles Co., marched on St. Mary's, where a surrender was signed by Joseph and 4 of his lieutenants (1 Aug.). The insurgent leaders (**Protestant Association**) called the assembly into session (22 Aug.). That body petitioned the crown to take over the province, and proceeded to elect **Nehemiah Blakiston** its president. The Lords of Trade made Maryland a **Royal Province** (27 June 1691), with Sir **Lionel Copley** as first royal governor, although Baltimore retained his property rights. In 1692 the Church of England was established, and in 1695 the capital moved from Catholic St. Mary's to Protestant Annapolis. With the death of Benedict Leonard Calvert (who had become a convert to the Church of England, 1713, and reared his children in his new faith) in 1715, leaving Charles, 4th

Lord Baltimore (1699–1751), as his heir, the government was restored to the proprietor (May 1715) and the charter of 1632 again put into force.

Settlement of New England

Plymouth

1606–20. EARLY ACTIVITIES OF PLYMOUTH COMPANY. The first expedition of the Plymouth Co. (dispatched Aug. 1606) was captured by the Spaniards in the West Indies. A second (Oct.) sponsored by Sir **John Popham** explored the coast from Maine southward and returned with extensive data on the coastal areas. Sir **Ferdinando Gorges** fitted out the *Gift of God* (under George Popham) and the *Mary and John* (under Raleigh Gilbert), which sailed separately (1 May and 1 June 1607) and dropped anchor off the Maine coast north of Monhegan (7 Aug.), then sailed to Popham Beach (14 Aug.) on the Sagadahoc River (lower Kennebec). There a fort was erected, within which were constructed other buildings. The colony failed owing to idleness and factionalism. After George Popham's death (5 Feb. 1608), the venture was abandoned (Sept.). Sir Francis Popham, son of Sir John, sent trading and fishing expeditions to the mainland and islands off Maine (1608–14) as did Dutch, French, and Spanish traders and fishermen, with fairly permanent posts established on the islands of Damariscove and Monhegan, and at Pemaquid Point. Capt. **John Smith** sailed for the New England coast (3 Mar. 1614). On his return (c.Sept. 1614) he pointed out to Gorges settlement possibilities of the area. Richard Vines, a former Gorges' agent, spent a winter at the mouth of the Saco (1616–17). The richness of the cod fishery in these waters revived the interest of the Plymouth Co. Through Gorges the company petitioned James I (3 Mar. 1620) for a charter according it privileges already granted the Virginia Co. A new charter, granted 13 Nov. to a **Council for New England** all land lying between 40°N and 48°N and from sea to sea.

1606–20.   PILGRIM   PRELIMINARIES. A group of separatists from the Church of England who had established a congregation at Scrooby, Nottinghamshire, emigrated to Amsterdam (Aug. 1608) and then removed to Leyden (1 May 1609). Although they enjoyed religious freedom in Holland, they found their children losing contact with English culture, were excluded from the local guilds, and feared the expiration of the 12 years' truce between Spain and the Netherlands (1609–21) would imperil their position and subject them to the rigors of the Inquisition. Leaders of the Leyden group—their pastor, John Robinson, and **William Brewster** (1567–1644)—sent agents to England (1616–19) to negotiate with the Virginia Co. for the right to plant a colony within its borders. Through the intervention of Sir Edwin Sandys they received a patent (19 June 1619) in the name of **John Wyncop,** an English clergyman. Pending royal approval, the Leyden group rejected an offer by the Dutch to settle under the States General (Feb. 1620). Meantime, **Thomas Weston,** a London ironmonger, in association with **John Peirce,** a London clothmaker, had received a patent from the Virginia Co. (20 Feb. 1620) and persuaded the Leyden group to join with them (July). Three groups were set up: (1) adventurers in England (70 in all) at £10 per share; (2) adventurer-planters, given 2 shares for each £10 in consideration of their settling; (3) planters, given 1 share each for their labor. Both capital and profits were to belong to the joint-stock for 7 years, at the end of which period they were to be divided proportionately.

1620, 22 July–9 Nov. VOYAGE OF THE PILGRIMS. Thirty-five members of Leyden group (known henceforth as **Pilgrims**), under the leadership of Brewster, left the Netherlands on the *Speedwell* (22 July) for England. When that ship proved unseaworthy, it was abandoned at Plymouth and the entire company crowded aboard the *Mayflower*, 180 tons burden, a ship provided by the adventurers. Sailing (16 Sept.), she carried, besides officers and crew, 101 persons (a majority non-Pilgrims, including Capt. **Miles Standish** [c.1584–1656], hired as their military leader), with 14 indentured servants and hired artisans. There were 35 from Leyden, 66 from Southampton and London. After Cape Cod was sighted (9 Nov.), decision was reached to land nearby despite the fact that this was outside the territory of the Virginia Co. This decision may have been inspired by a suggestion of Weston, who had reason to doubt the legality of their patent.

1620, 21 Nov. MAYFLOWER COMPACT. Fearing that the rebellious members of their company might prove even more untractable ashore, the Pilgrim leaders ("Saints") drafted an agreement which was signed in the cabin of the *Mayflower* by 41 adults. This preliminary plan of government, based on the social compact idea found in separatist church covenants, set up "a civil body politic" to frame "just and equal laws."

1620–24. PLYMOUTH, first sighted 11 Dec., was chosen as the site for the new settlement 25 Dec. The first winter

(1620–21) was mild, but disease carried off half the settlers the first year. The Indians, decimated by a plague (1616–17), proved peaceful. Deacon **John Carver** (c. 1576–1621), the first governor, was succeeded on his death (Apr. 1621) by **William Bradford** (p. 990), who held that office, with the exception of 5 years, down to 1656. A second **Peirce Patent,** obtained (1 June) from the newly organized Council for New England, vested title to land jointly in the adventurers and planters (100 acres for each person transported and 1,500 for public use) at a yearly quitrent of 2s. per 100 acres, but the colony's boundaries remained undefined. A party of some 50 men under **Andrew Weston** landed at Plymouth in June, moved to Wessagusset to establish a fishing and trading post, but failed because of Indian troubles and poor management (1623). Another colony was established (1623) by Capt. Wollaston at Passonagessit (Quincy). On Wollaston's departure within the year **Thomas Morton** assumed control at Mount Wollaston (Merrymount). The Pilgrims, outraged equally by his uninhibited life and his success at Indian trading, dispatched Miles Standish (June, 1628) to destroy the settlement and sent Morton back to England. **Robert Gorges,** son of Sir Ferdinando, sent out an expedition which moved into Weston's abandoned settlement at Wessagusset (end of Sept. 1623). Gorges abandoned the project (1624), but some settlers remained. In 1624 communal planting was modified and individual garden plots assigned. Meadow and pasture allotments were made (1632).

1626, 15 Nov. LIQUIDATION OF LONDON ADVENTURERS. Strengthened by a steady influx of settlers (since Aug. 1623), the Pilgrims were encouraged to make an agreement to buy out the London investors for £1,800 and assume the company's debt of

£ 600. Eight colonists underwrote the agreement in return for a monopoly of trade and a tax of 3 bu. of corn or 6 lbs. of tobacco per shareholder until the debt was paid (July 1627). This group established a trading post on the Kennebec (1628) and another on the Penobscot (c.1631).

1630, 23 JAN. NEW PLYMOUTH PATENT ("OLD CHARTER") granted by the Council for New England defined the colony's boundaries and confirmed title to land on the Kennebec.

1636. Adoption of a code, "Great Fundamentals," drawn up for the government of the colony established a General Court, comprising 2 deputies from each town chosen by the freemen together with the governor and assistants sitting as a single house.

Maine and New Hampshire

1622–31. On 10 Aug. 1622 the Council for New England granted **John Mason** and **Sir Ferdinando Gorges** all land lying between the Merrimack and Kennebec rivers. Special grants of 6,000 acres apiece were made to David Thomson (1622), who founded a plantation at the mouth of Piscataqua (Rye, 1623), and Christopher Levett (1623), who settled probably on an island at the mouth of Casco River (end of 1623). John Oldham and Richard Vines settled on the south side of the Saco (present Biddeford, 1623–24). In 1629 Mason and Gorges divided their northern holdings. Gorges received all land north of the Piscataqua; Mason all land to its south. A trading grant was conferred on Mason and Gorges (17 Nov.) of an indefinite area extending to Lake Champlain and the St. Lawrence. Under Walter Neale, settlements were made at present Portsmouth, c.1631, and present South Berwick, c.1632. After receiving a grant (2 Dec. 1631) of 24,000 acres on the Aga-

menticus (York) River, Gorges focused his colonizing activity in this area.

Massachusetts Bay

1624–26. DORCHESTER COMPANY planted a colony of Dorsetshire men on Cape Ann (present Gloucester). Proving ill-suited to both fishing and agriculture, most of the settlers returned to England, but the remainder (30–40) under Roger Conant removed to Naumkeag (Salem, 1626), where they set up a trading post.

1628, 19 MAR. NEW ENGLAND COMPANY. Rev. **John White,** a Dorsetshire nonconformist who had been active in the first Dorchester Co., formed a new association, the New England Co., which received a patent to land extending from 3 miles north of the Merrimack River to 3 miles south of the Charles River. The company's 90 members (largely but not entirely Puritan) included 6 from the old Dorchester group.

1628, 20 JUNE. JOHN ENDECOTT (c.1589–1665) sailed with a small group of colonists to Naumkeag (Salem). On arrival (6 Sept.) he served as governor (1628–30), handing over the administration to John Winthrop.

1629, 14 MAR. MASSACHUSETTS BAY COMPANY, successor to the New England Co., received a royal charter which specified no location for its annual meeting. This oversight made it possible to transfer the government to New England and transform the company into a self-governing commonwealth. The company dispatched its first fleet (Apr.), followed by 2 other ships (25 Apr. and mid-May). The Salem church was organized along separatist lines, and 2 freemen were sent home (Aug.) when they insisted on conforming to the Anglican ritual.

1629, 5 SEPT. CAMBRIDGE AGREEMENT. The position of the Puritans was becoming increasingly insecure after the dissolution of Parliament (10 Mar. 1629) and the growing influence of **William Laud** (Bishop of London, 1628), a zealous defender of conformity. In addition, the Thirty Years' War disrupted trade with the Continent and depressed the cloth industry. Twelve Puritan members of the Massachusetts Bay Co. signed the Cambridge Agreement, whereby they undertook to emigrate to America provided the charter and government were transferred thither. The company ratified the agreement (8 Sept.).

1630–40. EARLY COLONIZATION. The first 4 of 11 ships outfitted at Southampton sailed (29 Mar. 1630) with **John Winthrop** (p. 1187), the newly elected governor. The remaining 7 sailed a month later; other emigrants embarked at Bristol and Plymouth (Feb. and Mar. 1630). The *Arbella,* first of the Southampton ships, entered Salem Harbor (12 June). The population settled along the Massachusetts coast north of Plymouth. Endecott moved to Mishawum (Charlestown); others went to Shawmut (Boston), Mystic (Medford), Watertown, Roxbury, and Dorchester. The elevation of Laud to the primacy in England, combined with the increasing economic difficulties, led to an influx of new settlers, beginning 1633, including such notable clergymen as **John Cotton** (p. 1007) from St. Botolph's Church, Boston in Lincolnshire (4 Sept.), and **Thomas Hooker** (1586–1647). In the first decade some 20,000 settlers emigrated to New England.

1630–34. CIVIL GOVERNMENT was rapidly established. The first meeting of the governor and assistants was held 2 Sept. 1630; the first General Court, 29 Oct. In addition to the 12 original freemen-settlers, 118 others were admitted to the freemanship (28 May 1631), but the freemanship was restricted to church members (in force until 1664), in viola-

tion of the charter. On 13 Feb. 1632 Watertown protested a tax levied by the Court of Assistants, and on 19 May the General Court regained the right of electing the governor and deputy governor. The freemen of each town were authorized to send deputies to the General Court (1634). Deputies and assistants (the latter elected by the freemen in a court of election) sat in one house until 1644, when, as a result of the "Sow Case" (*Shearman* v. *Keayne,* 1642–43), the legislature became bicameral.

1635. BANISHMENT OF ROGER WILLIAMS. Williams (p. 1185) arrived in New England (5 Feb. 1631), served in the Salem and Plymouth churches, and became pastor of the former (early 1635). He attacked the validity of the charter, questioned the right of the civil authorities to legislate in matters of conscience, and urged the Salem church to separate from the rest. The General Court (12 Sept. 1635) expelled the Salem deputies, seating them only when they had repudiated Williams. The court banished him (13 Sept.), but permitted him to remain over the winter. Fearing seizure and deportation to England, he fled from Salem (Jan. 1636) and wintered among the Indians. Joined by others in the spring, he first sought to settle at Plymouth, was warned off, and purchased land from the Indians at the site of the present Providence, which he founded (June 1636).

1635 MAY–1638, APR. ATTEMPTS TO REVOKE CHARTER. Thomas Morton, who went back to New England (1629), was arested by Endecott, had his house burned down, and was then deported, allied himself with Sir Ferdinando Gorges to secure revocation of the Massachusetts charter. On Gorges' complaint, the case came before the Privy Council (19 Jan. 1633). A Privy Council committee ("Lords Commissioners for the Plantations in General," known as "Laud Commission") ordered the recall of the charter on the ground that it had been surreptitiously obtained and unwarrantably overstepped (May 1635). Gorges was ordered to serve a writ of quo warranto on the Massachusetts officials, and the King's Bench ordered the charter canceled (3 May 1637). Meantime, Gorges' ship had broken in the launching, and he failed to secure the charter. Winthrop ignored a Privy Council order (4 Apr. 1638), but the outbreak of revolt in Scotland (signing of the Solemn League and Covenant, 28 Feb.) prevented the crown from taking further action.

1636–38. ANNE HUTCHINSON SEDITION TRIAL. Young Sir Henry Vane (1613–62), an aristocratic Puritan, elected governor (25 May 1636), the year after his arrival, came under the influence of **Anne Hutchinson** (p. 1065), along with most members of the Boston church including John Cotton. Her views, loosely called **"Antinomianism,"** stressed "grace" rather than "works," and her emphasis on personal revelation minimized the role of the orthodox clergy. When Rev. **John Wheelwright** (c.1592–1679), her brother-in-law, in a sermon in Boston (20 Jan. 1637) denounced the doctrine of works, he was tried for sedition and contempt, convicted, but his sentencing was postponed. On election day (27 May 1637) Winthrop's faction had the voting transferred from pro-Hutchinson Boston to Newtown (Cambridge). Winthrop defeated Vane, who returned to England (3 Aug.). A synod of 25 ministers convened at Newtown (30 Aug.) defined orthodox Puritan doctrine. On 12 Nov. the General Court banished Wheelwright and ordered Anne Hutchinson to stand trial for sedition and contempt. She was sentenced to be banished (17 Nov.). After an ecclesiastical trial (Mar. 1638), in which she was excommunicated, the sentence was put into effect. With her husband and children she journeyed to Roger Williams' new settlement on Narragansett Bay. In cooperation with another Boston exile, William Coddington, she founded the town of Pocasset (Portsmouth, 7 Mar.). Upon her husband's death she removed to Long Island (1642) and later to the vicinity of Eastchester, where she and her entire household (except one daughter ransomed by the Dutch, 1651) were murdered by Indians (Aug. or Sept. 1643).

Expansion of New England, 1631–60

1631–60. FOUNDING OF CONNECTICUT. In the fall of 1632 Edward Winslow of Plymouth explored the Connecticut Valley probably as far north as Windsor. In support of their claim to the region the Dutch at New Amsterdam sent a ship up the Connecticut River (June 1633) and erected a small fort and trading post (Fort Good Hope, later Hartford). Although Winslow and Bradford sought unsuccessfully to organize a joint Plymouth-Massachusetts expedition to the Connecticut River (July), John Oldham of the Bay Colony took a small party overland (Sept.) and spent the winter (1634–35) at Pyquag (Wethersfield). Also in Sept. Lt. William Holmes, commissioned by Winslow, set up a trading post at Windsor above Hartford. Restlessness in Massachusetts seacoast towns where pasture lands were already proving inadequate caused a group from Dorchester (with perhaps a few from Newtown and Watertown) to settle in Windsor in defiance of Plymouth's claims (spring 1635) and a group from Newtown (Oct.) to settle around Hartford. Meantime, on 7 July a group headed by Lord Saye and Sele, who claimed rights to settle the region on the basis of a patent from the Council for

New England assigned by the Earl of Warwick (1631), authorized **John Winthrop the Younger** (1606–76), son of the Bay Colony's governor, to take control at the mouth of the Connecticut River. The settlers accepted Winthrop as governor (before Mar. 1636) and the Massachusetts General Court laid down a plan of government (13 Mar.) and placed final authority in the hands of the "inhabitants." After the arrival (Oct. 1635) of Rev. Thomas Shepard, who settled his followers at Newtown, Rev. **Thomas Hooker** departed with the remainder of his Newtown followers, and reached Hartford (31 May 1636). Hooker's democratic views were reflected in a sermon (31 May 1638), in which he declared that authority should rest upon the free consent of the "people." His views, as well as those of his associates, **John Haynes** and **Roger Ludlow** (founded Fairfield and Stratford, 1638), were reflected in the **Fundamental Orders** (24 Jan. 1639), a frame of government adopted by Hartford, Windsor, and Wethersfield. (Springfield under **William Pynchon** refused to join, and by 1649 deputies from that town sat regularly in the Massachusetts General Court.) The governor, who was to be of an approved congregation, and the magistrates were to be elected "by the vote of the country"; by this was meant the freemen, who were "admitted inhabitants" who had been selected for freemanship either by the General Court or by one or more of the magistrates. Voting in town affairs was open to "admitted inhabitants," i.e., Trinitarian male householders (after 1657 possessor of a £30 estate). In operation the franchise was as restricted as that of the Bay Colony. By 1662 (before the absorption of New Haven) 15 towns had been settled.

1636–56. RHODE ISLAND SETTLEMENTS. Roger Williams established his colony at Seekonk (**Providence**) on Narragansett Bay (June 1636) solely on the basis of an Indian deed. He was joined (Apr. 1638) by a band of Boston exiles under William Coddington, who bought the island of Aquidneck (**Rhode Island**) from the Indians, and, in collaboration with Anne Hutchinson, founded Pocasset (**Portsmouth**). Splitting with Mrs. Hutchinson, Coddington founded **Newport** (8 May 1639). These 2 Rhode Island colonies were joined (12 Mar. 1640). A fourth town, **Warwick,** was founded by Samuel Gorton (1643). Imperiled by the hostile New England Confederacy, Roger Williams left for England via New Amsterdam (Mar. 1643) to obtain a charter, which was granted him (24 Mar. 1644). Under its authority a general assembly composed of freemen from the 4 towns (Providence, Portsmouth, Newport, and Warwick) convened at Portsmouth (29–31 May 1647) and drafted a constitutional structure establishing freedom of conscience, separating church and state, providing for town referenda on laws passed by the assembly, and giving to towns as well as the assembly the right to initiate laws. William Coddington opposed the union, went to England (Oct. 1649), and obtained a separate charter for the island of Aquidneck (Mar. 1651), which Williams was able to have the Council of State revoke (Oct. 1652). Coddington finally accepted the authority of Providence Plantations (Mar. 1656).

1637–43. FOUNDING OF NEW HAVEN. Rev. **John Davenport** (1597–1670), a friend of John Cotton, sailed from England (Apr. 1636) with a group of followers, notably **Theophilus Eaton** (c.1590–1658), a London merchant, and, after stopping at Boston (26 June), established Quinnipiac (**New Haven**) as a colony and trading post. Land was purchased from the Indians, a town laid out on a modified grid pattern, and a government established which restricted the franchise to church members. In 1641 **Stamford** was founded and in 1643 the independent settlements of **Guilford** (6 July) and **Milford** (23 Oct.) joined New Haven colony. A General Court, comprising 2 deputies from each of the 4 towns, adopted (6 Nov.) a Frame of Government, established the Mosaic law as the basis of its legal system, and made no provision for trial by jury.

1636–37. PEQUOT WAR. A punitive expedition (24 Aug., led by John Endecott of Mass.) against the Pequots (who dominated the area between the Pequot [Thames] River and the present western boundary of Rhode Island, as well as eastern Long Island and Long Island Sound) in reprisal for the murder of a New England trader, John Oldham (20 July 1636), led to reprisals the following spring. A Connecticut force under Capt. John Mason destroyed the main Pequot stronghold near the present village of Stonington (5 June). The fleeing remnants were slaughtered near New Haven (28 July) by a combined force from Plymouth, Massachusetts, and Connecticut.

1638–43. NEW HAMPSHIRE. After John Mason's death (Dec. 1635) his lands and buildings were appropriated by his colonists. In Apr. 1638 **John Wheelwright,** banished from Massachusetts Bay, established the town of **Exeter.** His settlers signed (14 July 1639) the **Exeter Compact** (based on the Mayflower Compact). Portsmouth and Dover conceded the authority of Massachusetts (1641), and Hampton (1642) and Exeter (1643) followed, causing Wheelwright to withdraw to Maine rather than submit. Merrimack, Salisbury, and Haverhill were then united with the Piscataqua settlements.

1640–51. MAINE. Despite the attempt of Gorges to govern Maine through his cousin, Thomas Gorges, and the establishment of a provincial court at York (25 June 1640), Massachusetts persisted in its expansionist aims. Despite an appeal by the Maine government to Parliament (5 Dec. 1651), the Massachusetts General Court held that Maine was legally included within the boundaries of the Bay Colony (31 May 1652). Ligonia was annexed (4 July); Kittery (20 Nov.) and York (22 Nov.) capitulated.

1641–60. MASSACHUSETTS AS AN INDEPENDENT COMMONWEALTH. In response to criticism that too much discretionary authority was lodged in the magistrates, the General Court adopted (Dec. 1641) the **Body of Liberties,** a code drawn up by **Nathaniel Ward,** in preference to an earlier proposed draft by John Cotton, "Moses his Judicialls" (1636), which was published in England inaccurately as *An Abstract of the Lawes of New England* (1641). While less wholly drawn upon Mosaic law, the Body of Liberties based its criminal code on the Pentateuch. On 14 Nov. 1646 **Robert Child** and other remonstrants attacked the Bay Colony for its civil and religious discrimination against non-Puritans and for not observing the laws of England. Winthrop and other magistrates framed a reply, and the General Court declared: "Our allegiance binds us not to the laws of England any longer than while we live in England." A more extensive code was adopted in 1648, which was influential throughout the northern colonies with the exception of Rhode Island, whose code of 1647 adhered to the English common law. On 7 June 1652 the General Court set up a mint, and the "pine-tree shilling" was minted (down to 1684). On 29 Oct. Massachusetts, in defiance of Parliament, declared itself an independent commonwealth.

1643, 19 MAY. NEW ENGLAND CONFEDERATION. As a result of experience in the Pequot War, in which military action was not well coordinated, and the threat of Dutch expansion, representatives from Massachusetts, Plymouth, Connecticut, and New Haven, meeting at Boston, drew up 12 articles of confederation, which were ratified ·by the 4 colonies. The **United Colonies of New England** represented a union of the 4 colonies, each of whose territorial integrity was guaranteed. The government was a board of 8 commissioners, 2 from each colony, chosen annually by their respective general courts. The commissioners were empowered to declare both offensive and defensive war, the expenses for which were to be borne by the colonies in proportion to the number of their male inhabitants between 16 and 60. In addition, the commissioners were given jurisdiction over interstate quarrels, fugitive servants, fugitives from justice, and Indian affairs. Six votes were required for a decision. Annual sessions were held until 1664, occasional meetings prior to King Philip's War, which served as a basis for renewed activity. Thereafter operations virtually ceased, and the union was terminated in 1684.

1644–52. CONVERSION OF INDIANS. As a result of orders of the Massachusetts General Court (29 Nov. 1644 and 14 Nov. 1646), Rev. **John Eliot** (1604–90), pastor at Roxbury, who learned the Indian dialects and began to preach to the Indians at Nonantum (Newton), settled a group of converts at Natick (1651), followed by 13 other colonies of "Praying Indians," comprising more than 1,000 in numbers. His efforts resulted in the founding in London (19 July 1649) of the **Society for Propagating the Gospel in New England.** His work was largely destroyed by King Philip's War (1675).

1649–60. TREATMENT OF RELIGIOUS MINORITIES. The independent government of Maine, organized after the death of Sir Ferdinando Gorges (July 1649), passed an act (16 Oct.) granting all Christians the right to form churches provided "they be orthodox in judgment and not scandalous in life." On 18 July 1651 the Massachusetts authorities heavily fined and banished 3 Baptists. The first Quakers to arrive in Boston (July–Aug. 1656) were imprisoned, brutally treated, and expelled, a step which was ratified by the Federal Commissioners (17 Sept.). The Massachusetts General Court imposed penalties on Quakers entering the colony (24 Oct.), forbade Quaker meetings (29 May 1658), and imposed the death penalty for Quakers who returned in defiance of expulsion (Oct. 1658). Two returning Quakers (William Robinson and Marmaduke Stevenson) were hanged (27 Oct. 1659), and thereafter Mary Dyer, one-time follower of Anne Hutchinson (1 June 1660), and William Leddra (24 Mar. 1661) suffered the same penalty. Similar laws in Plymouth (1657–58) and New Haven (1658) were not as ruthlessly enforced.

New England Under the Restoration, 1660–75

1660–61. CHARLES II PROCLAIMED. The Restoration imperiled the position of the New England colonies. The Puritans were sympathetic with the cause of the Commonwealth, and New Haven harbored the regicide judges, Whalley and Goffe (1661). First to proclaim Charles II was Rhode Island (18 Oct. 1660), followed by Connecticut (14 Mar. 1661), New Haven (5 June), and Massachusetts (7 Aug.).

1661, SEPT.–1662, 18 OCT. SUSPENSION OF QUAKER PERSECUTION. A royal order which reached Boston 9 Sept. 1661 commanded that all Quakers under sentence of death or corporal punishment be remanded to England for trial. Massachusetts released all imprisoned Quakers, permitting them to leave the colony rather than sending them to England for trial, and suspended (7 Dec.) the corporal punishment act of 1 June; but within a year (18 Oct. 1662) that penalty was revived.

1661–63. CONNECTICUT AND RHODE ISLAND CHARTERS. The Restoration threatened the independent existence of Connecticut (which had no charter) and Rhode Island (whose charter, 1644, now had no legality). Through the influence of Lord Saye and Sele, **John Winthrop, Jr.** (governor since 1657), obtained a royal charter for Connecticut (3 May 1662), whose boundaries were defined as Massachusetts on the north, Long Island Sound on the south, Narragansett Bay on the east, and the South Sea on the west. Since this grant included Providence, an agreement was entered into between Winthrop and John Clark, Rhode Island agent, to confine Connecticut's eastern limits to the Pawcatuck. The charter granted Rhode Island (18 July 1663) guaranteed religious freedom regardless of "differences in opinion in matters of religion." In implementing the charter provisions, the General Assembly (Mar. 1664) repealed the law requiring approval by the towns of laws of the General Court.

1662, Oct.–1665, 5 Jan. CONNECTICUT ANNEXES NEW HAVEN. Connecticut demanded that New Haven be incorporated within her territory in accordance with the Charter of 1662. Despite a vote of the freemen to maintain independence (4 Nov.), Southold voted to join Connecticut. Rather than come under the jurisdiction of the Duke of York, whose grant (12 Mar. 1664) included all land lying between the Connecticut and Delaware rivers, Stamford, Guilford, and part of Milford joined Connecticut (14 Dec.). New Haven formally submitted (5 Jan. 1665). Rather

than yield, a group in Branford left for Newark in East Jersey.

1664–66. KING'S COMMISSIONERS. The crown dispatched four commissioners to New England to secure aid in the war against the Dutch, investigate the governments of the colonies, settle boundary disputes, and see that the Navigation Acts were enforced. They laid down 4 conditions of compliance: (1) that all householders take an oath of allegiance to the crown, (2) that all men of competent estates be freemen, (3) that all of orthodox belief be admitted to existing churches or churches of their own choosing, and (4) that all laws derogatory to the crown be expunged. Plymouth (17 Feb. 1665), Connecticut (20 Apr.), and Rhode Island (3 May) agreed to comply, but Massachusetts, which had made a pretense of admitting nonchurch members to the franchise by qualifying all ratable at 10s (23 July 1664), refused further compliance (19–24 May 1665). Three out of the 4 commissioners recommended the cancellation of the Massachusetts charter. When, in 1666, the king commanded the Bay Colony to send representatives to England to answer charges, the General Court refused to comply.

1665–69. MASSACHUSETTS ANNEXES MAINE. The king's commissioners (following a regime set up, 1661, by commissioners of the Gorges' heirs) established a government in Maine which lasted from Oct. 1665 to May 1668. At a special convention at York the authority of Massachusetts was recognized (6 July 1668), and in May 1669 3 Maine deputies were seated in the Massachusetts General Court.

1674, 29 June. A patent was issued to the Duke of York confirming his title to all lands between the Connecticut and Delaware rivers and (in Maine) between the St. Croix and the Kennebec. He proceeded to designate **Sir Edmund**

Andros (1637–1714) his governor general.

King Philip's War, 1675–76

1671, 10 APR.–1675, 14 JUNE. PRELIMINARIES. Five tribes which increasingly felt the pressure of the New England settlers' expansionist activities were (1) the **Wampanoags,** who had been pushed from the east coast to the eastern shores of Narragansett Bay; (2) the **Narragansetts,** whose lands between the Thames River and Narragansett Bay were threatened by a large land company, the Atherton Co. (organized 1659), which was attempting to foreclose a mortgage on most of this area (1662–76); (3) the **Mohegans,** occupying the hill country between the Connecticut and Thames rivers; (4) the **Podunks** to their north; and (5) the **Nipmucks,** who hunted in the country along the northern watersheds of the Thames and Pawtucket rivers. **Philip** (c.1639–76) son of the friendly sachem Massasoit, became chief of the Wampanoags on his brother Alexander's death (1662). At the request of the Plymouth authorities that he yield his arms, he made a token delivery (10 Apr. 1671). Accusations of conspiracy against the colonists brought against Philip resulted in the murder of the accuser and, in turn, the trial and execution of 3 Indians (8 June 1675).

1675, 20 JUNE–6 SEPT. START OF HOSTILITIES. When Philip attacked Swansea (20–25 June) a combined force of Plymouth and Boston troops attacked Mt. Hope, the Wampanoag stronghold on the Taunton River (28 June), but failed to destroy Indian forces. Philip now attacked the entire southern frontier, joined by the Nipmucks, who attacked Mendon (14 July) and Brookfield (2–4 Aug.). In turn, Lancaster (19 Aug.), Deerfield and Hadley (1 Sept.),

and Northfield (2 Sept.) were attacked. The last was abandoned (6 Sept.).

1675, 9 SEPT. NEW ENGLAND CONFEDERATION DECLARES WAR. Massachusetts was assigned a quota of 527 men; Connecticut, 315; Plymouth, 158. Indian victories at **Bloody Brook** near Hadley (18 Sept.) and attacks on Springfield (5 Oct.), Hatfield (16 Oct.), and other settlements followed.

1675, 2 NOV.–1676, JAN. NARRAGANSETT CAMPAIGN. A combined force under **Josiah Winslow** of Plymouth stormed the principal fort of the Narragansetts (present South Kingston, R.I.) on 19 Nov. Some 300 women and children were killed, but most of the warriors escaped. By the end of Jan. 1677 most of the tribe's women, children, and old men had been killed, while the warriors fled to the Nipmucks.

1676, 10 FEB.–30 MAR. INDIANS COUNTERATTACK. Driven by hunger the Indians attacked Lancaster (10 Feb. 1676), sacked the town, and took many captives, including **Mrs. Mary Rowlandson,** whose *True History* describing her captivity (ransomed, 2 May 1676) reveals the extent of Indian starvation. Attacks on Sudbury, Chelmsford, Medford, and Weymouth followed. Even Plymouth (12 Mar.) and Providence (29–30 Mar.) were attacked, as were Groton, Warwick, Marlboro, Sudbury, Rehoboth (all in Mar.), and Wrentham, Seekonk, Andover, Chelmsford, Scituate, and Bridgewater (Apr. and May).

1676, 18 MAY–28 AUG. COLLAPSE OF INDIAN RESISTANCE. A force of 180 under Capt. William Turner attacked a large body of Indians in the Connecticut Valley, near Deerfield, and destroyed many men and supplies, but subsequently were ambushed and annihilated. But the war of attrition stripped the Indians of offensive power. After Capt. John Talcott with 250 men from the Connecticut Valley and 200 Mohegans, defeated the Indians at Hadley (12 June), chased the Valley tribes into the New Hampshire hills, and then, turning eastward, destroyed 250 Indians near Marlboro, Indians started surrendering in large numbers (410 from 16 June to 6 July). Philip, betrayed, was run down in the Assowamset Swamp and shot (12 Aug.), his wife and 9-year-old child were sold into West Indian captivity, and the last sizable surrender took place 28 Aug.

1675, 5 SEPT.–1678, 12 AUG. WAR IN THE NORTH. Following a raid on Falmouth (12 Sept.), 80 Maine settlers were killed by 10 Dec. The resumption of warfare (11 Aug. 1676) caused the abandonment of the region between Casco Bay and the Penobscot. Indian raids were renewed in the spring of 1677. Sir Edmund Andros constructed a fort at Pemaquid (Aug. 1677), negotiated for a release of prisoners, and concluded peace with the Indians (12 Apr. 1678), by which they were to receive one peck of corn yearly for each family settled in Maine.

COST OF WAR. Some 600 English colonials were killed, £150,000 expended in prosecuting the war, 1,200 houses burned (including 12 towns completely destroyed and half of the New England towns suffering damage), and a probable 3,000 Indians were killed. With the exception of the tribes of Maine, the independent power of the Indians of New England was ended.

New England to the Glorious Revolution, 1676–89

1676, JUNE. EDWARD RANDOLPH (c.1632–1703) arrived in Boston as special agent of the crown to convey royal instructions and check on the enforcement of the Navigation Acts. On return to England he submitted 2 reports (20 Sept. and 12 Oct.) charging Massachusetts with failing to enforce the Naviga-

tion Acts, putting English citizens to death for their religious views, denying the right of appeal to the Privy Council, and refusing the oath of allegiance.

1677. MASSACHUSETTS BUYS OUT GORGES HEIRS. The Lords of Trade upheld the title to Maine of the heirs of Sir Ferdinando Gorges. Through its agent, John Usher, Massachusetts proceeded to buy out the heirs for £1,250 (13 Mar.). Maine remained incorporated in Massachusetts until 1820 (p. 190–191).

1680, 4 FEB.–1686. ROYAL GOVERNMENT IN NEW HAMPSHIRE. By royal commission (Sept. 1680) New Hampshire was separated from Massachusetts. The administration of Governor John Cutt (1680–82) was comparatively peaceful except for the attempt of Robert Mason, John Mason's heir, to collect quitrents. Cutt's successor, Edward Cranfield (1682–85), ruled without an assembly when that body refused to pass his revenue bills (1683). Walter Barefoote, his deputy governor, succeeded him, pending arrival of the Dudley Commission. New Hampshire was part of the Dominion of New England (1686–89); its royal authority was reestablished (1692), after which date it had no connection with Massachusetts except that from 1698–1741 both provinces had the same governor.

1684, 21 JUNE. ABROGATION OF MASSACHUSETTS CHARTER. Edward Randolph, appointed collector and surveyor of customs (1678), wrote a series of hostile reports to the home authorities (11 Apr., 7 Aug. 1682) and returned to England to aid in the prosecution against the Bay Colony (13 June 1683). The Court of Chancery annulled the charter (21 June 1684; final decree, 18 Oct.).

1685–88. DOMINION OF NEW ENGLAND AND ANDROS REGIME. Joseph Dudley (1647–1720), who had been sent to England to protest the threatened loss of the charter (1682), was appointed by James II (Sept. 1685) governor of Massachusetts, Maine, and New Hampshire. He was succeeded by **Sir Edmund Andros,** who arrived in Boston, 20 Dec. 1686, to assume the government of all the New England colonies (save Connecticut and Rhode Island) and to organize a Dominion of New England, to include New York, New Jersey, and Pennsylvania, for more effective military operations in the event of war with France and better enforcement of the Navigation Acts. Rhode Island was incorporated on 30 Dec., and Connecticut's government taken over (1 Nov. 1687), although the charter was successfully concealed in the **Charter Oak.** Other actions increasing his unpopularity were (1) his demand that Anglicans be permitted to share the Old South Meeting House (21 Dec. 1686), which he converted into an Anglican church (25 Mar. 1687); (2) his insistence that all land titles be reexamined and that the payment of a quitrent be a condition of regrants; (3) his imposition of assessments, which were resisted by an Ipswich town meeting (23 Aug. 1687), under the leadership of Rev. **John Wise** (1652–1725), arrested, tried, and fined £10 and costs; 4 others fined and disqualified from holding office; (4) an order limiting town meetings to one annually (17 Mar. 1688); (5) the placing of the militia under the direct control of the governor (24 Mar.). Rev. **Increase Mather** (1639–1723), president of Harvard, eluding detection, sailed for England to place the grievances of New Englanders before the Lords of Trade (10 Aug.).

1689, 10 JAN.–25 JULY. GLORIOUS REVOLUTION IN NEW ENGLAND. Andros received news of the impending landing of William of Orange while he was at Pemaquid, Me. (10 Jan. 1689), and returned to Boston in the middle of March. On 18 Apr. an armed uprising in Boston forced Andros to take refuge in the fort. A manifesto (largely the work of Rev. **Cotton Mather** [p. 1099]), excoriating the Andros regime and justifying the uprising on the grounds of fear of a French alliance and a Popish plot, was read to the populace. At the end of the day Andros surrendered and was lodged in jail. Also jailed were Randolph and Dudley. A "Council for the Safety and the Conservation of the Peace" was set up (20 Apr.). Deputies to a General Court were elected (6 June) before receipt of an order in council (25 July) for the return of Andros and his councilors to stand trial.

1691, 17 OCT. ROYAL CHARTER. Efforts to have the old charter restored proved unavailing; a royal charter was issued which formally incorporated Maine and Plymouth within Massachusetts' boundaries, provided for a governor to be appointed by the crown, a council elected by the General Court subject to the governor's veto, the substitution of a property for the religious qualification for voting, royal review of legislation, and appeals to the king in council. As a result of opinions of the attorney general (for Connecticut, 2 Aug. 1690; for Rhode Island, 7 Dec. 1693) that neither colony had been legally deprived of its charter, both colonies operated under their old charters until 1818 and 1842 respectively.

Settlement of the Middle Colonies

New Netherland

1610–18. INDEPENDENT VOY-AGES. Following the voyage of Henry Hudson for the Dutch East India Co. (25 Mar.–4 Nov. 1609), several exploring and trading voyages under Dutch auspices were made to the area (1610, 1611, 1613–14). **Adriaen Block** (d.1624) sailed to Manhattan (1613), braving the perilous passage named by him "Hellegat" (Hell Gate), discovered the Housatonic and Connecticut rivers, Rhode Island, and Block Island (named for him). His map was the first to show Manhattan and Long Island as separate islands. A fort (Fort Nassau, later Orange) erected up the Hudson around this time (at Castle Island) was transferred (1617) to the west side of the river (present Albany). The 13 shipowners engaged in trade with the New World organized the New Netherland Co. (1614), with a 3-year trading monopoly between 40° and 45°N. At expiration date the charter was not renewed.

1621, 3 June. FOUNDING OF DUTCH WEST INDIA CO. Under the leadership of Willem Usselinx, a prominent merchant, the Dutch West India Co. was chartered by the States General, which participated in its financing. The charter conferred a trading monopoly and the right to colonize in the New World and along the west coast of Africa below the Tropic of Cancer. The company was organized into 5 chambers. The most important, that of Amsterdam, had immediate control of New Netherland (which province played a minor role in the vast trading activities of the company). The director-general of the colony, while chosen by the company, had to be confirmed by the States General. The Council of Nineteen (the company's executive body) adopted a resolution (3 Nov. 1623) authorizing the Amsterdam Chamber to dispatch 5 or 6 families to start a settlement and approved a **Provisional Order** (28 Mar. 1624), the first plan of government of the colony, based in large measure on the *Artikelbrief*, rules governing life aboard ship. Colonists were divided into 2 classes: (1) private colonists (*colonen*) who received transportation, seeds, cattle, and necessities of life for the first 2 years and free use of as much farmland as they could cultivate, upon agreeing to remain for six years; (2) *bouwmasters*, or head farmers, *bouwlieden*, or farmers, and *bouwknechten*, or farm laborers, who were required to work for a stipulated term on the company's own farms (*bouweries*) or on those of company officials. Trading with outsiders was prohibited, and the export trade confined to the company.

1624. FIRST PERMANENT SETTLEMENT. Some 30 families, mostly Walloons, sailed from Amsterdam (after 30 Mar. 1624) under the leadership of **Cornelis Jacobsen May**, a sea captain, named first director of the colony. On arrival in New York Bay, a small group was left at a fort on Nut (Governor's) Island, several families sent to the Delaware, where they established Ft. Nassau (now Gloucester, N.J.), and 18 families proceeded up the Hudson to the older Ft. Nassau. It is conjectured, but not established, that some members of this third group settled on Manhattan Island

and that other Walloons (at this time or somewhat later) crossed the East River to Long Island, settling at Wallabout (Walloon's Cove).

1625, JAN.–1626, SEPT. EARLY GOVERNMENT. Willem Verhulst, sent out as supercargo, became second director, with a council made up of available Dutch sea captains, a vice-director, and a vice-commissioner. As a result of his mismanagement the council ousted him (c.Sept. 1626), appointing in his place **Peter Minuit** (Pierre Minuyt, c.1580–1638), born Wesel on the Rhine of Dutch or Walloon ancestry. Minuit had arrived, 4 May 1626, on the *Sea-mew*, with a new group of emigrants who proceeded that summer to erect on Manhattan Island 30 houses. The same year he purchased Manhattan from native Indian chiefs for 60 guilders (c.$24) paid in trading goods, and changed its name to **New Amsterdam.** Settlement was reinforced by withdrawing settlers from Ft. Orange (leaving 16 men) and from the Delaware (completely abandoned by 14 June 1627).

1629, 7 JUNE. ESTABLISHMENT OF PATROONSHIPS. To promote farm settlement with a view to making the colony self-sufficient as well as a supply base for the expanding merchant marine of the company both in Brazil and the West Indies, the States General confirmed the **Charter of Freedoms and Exemptions,** under which the company was empowered to grant to those transporting 50 settlers estates fronting 16 miles along navigable rivers, and extending inland as far as settlement would permit. The grantees (*patroons*) were given feudal rights, including the right to hold courts as well as exemption from taxation for 8 years. By the end of Jan. 1630 5 patroonships had been granted along the Hudson, Connecticut, and Delaware rivers to directors of the company. Three were settled: **Pavonia,** across the North River from Manhattan, incl. Staten Island; **Swaanendael,** on the west side of Delaware Bay; and **Rensselaerswyck,** near Ft. Orange, the patroonship of **Kiliaen Van Rensselaer** (1595–1644), Amsterdam diamond and gold merchant, who ruled as an absentee proprietor. Rensselaerswyck was the only patroonship that succeeded. Its tenants held perpetual leaseholds. It was not until 1638 that Article 21 of the Freedoms and Exemptions, offering land to homesteaders, was implemented, and then to counter expansion of neighboring English settlements.

1629–37. UNDER MINUIT AND VAN TWILLER. Despite a generally constructive administration, Minuit was recalled by the company (1631) for being too liberal in granting trading privileges to the patroons. He was succeeded, temporarily, by Bastiaen Janseen Krol (Mar. 1632–Apr. 1633), who, in turn, was followed by **Wouter Van Twiller** (1633–38), nephew of Van Rensselaer, who was elevated from a clerkship in Amsterdam. Trade expansion was promoted by the construction of Ft. Good Hope (present Hartford), 8 June 1633, and by the ouster of a party of Virginians who had occupied the abandoned Ft. Nassau (Aug. 1635). A garrison was placed on the Delaware and the settlement of Long Island begun by grants of patents (1636) to Jacobus Van Curler, Wolfert Gerritsen, Director Van Twiller, and others in Flatlands and vicinity following purchase from the Indians. Although exports increased during his regime (45,000 guilders, 1626; 91,375 gldrs., 1634; 134,924 gldrs., 1635), Van Twiller was charged with illegal trading, incompetence, and hostility toward the Dutch Reformed Church, and was replaced (2 Sept. 1637) by **Willem Kieft** (1597–1647), an Amsterdam merchant.

New Netherland and Its Neighbors, 1638–64

1638–40. FOUNDING OF NEW SWEDEN. The New Sweden or New South Co. was organized (1633) as successor to a series of trading companies of which Willem Usselinx was the guiding spirit. The capital for the company was supplied by Dutch and Swedish investors in equal parts. Through the influence of Samuel Blommaert, who had a substantial interest in the patroonship of Swaanendael (destroyed by the Indians before 6 Dec. 1632), and Peter Minuit, who had now entered the Swedish service, the company was granted a charter for settlement on the Delaware (c.1637). Its first expedition sailed (31 Dec. 1637) under Minuit, arrived at the Delaware (mid-Mar. 1638), and, despite Dutch protests, built Ft. Christina (present Wilmington). Minuit was lost at sea on a return trip to Sweden (June), but the leaderless colony managed to survive until the arrival of a new expedition (spring 1640), bringing Peter Hollender Ridder, as governor; Rev. Reorus Torkillus, a Lutheran minister; and much-needed livestock. A group of Dutch settlers from Utrecht were planted 20 miles north of Ft. Christina (Nov. 1640).

1640, 19 JULY. NEW CHARTER OF FREEDOMS AND EXEMPTIONS, granted to promote peopling of New Netherland, reduced the size of patroonships, provided grants of 200 acres to those transporting 5 persons, liberalized commercial privileges, and provided for local self-government.

1640–45. DUTCH EXPANSION. New settlements were established at Vriesendael on Tappan Zee, Hackensack, and at Staten Island (1641). The movement of English colonists into Westchester (the Hutchinson, Throgmorton, and Cornell plantations) and on Long Island (Maspeth and Lady Moody's settlement at Gravesend) impelled Kieft to appoint a special English secretary (11 Dec. 1642). Confronted with expanding European settlements in the southern part of the province and Iroquois ascendancy in the north, the Indians of the lower Hudson Valley raided Staten Island and Manhattan (summer 1641). Kieft, who had levied tribute from the tribes, was accused by the settlers of provoking war. Twelve representatives of heads of families (**The Twelve**), called together by Kieft (21 Jan. 1642), agreed to a campaign against the Indians, which proved ineffectual (Mar.). A year's truce was arranged by Jonas Bronck, a settler on the Bronx River. The Twelve were dismissed (18 Feb.) when they requested representation on the council and courts to prevent taxes being levied without their consent. In Feb. 1643 the Mohawks, armed by traders at Rensselaerswyck and Ft. Orange, attacked the Indians of the lower Hudson, forcing them to seek refuge among the Dutch at Pavonia (New Jersey) and Manhattan. They were slaughtered by Kieft's men (25–26 Feb.), with resultant Indian reprisals throughout the area; Kieft was now (Sept.) forced to seek counsel from 8 men (**The Eight**). Despite reinforcements by a small English force under John Underhill of Connecticut (29 Sept.), the Dutch failed to prevent English plantations in Westchester (the Hutchinson, Throgmorton, and Cornell settlements) and Long Island from being destroyed (Lady Moody's at Gravesend was spared) as well as settlements on the west bank of the Hudson (17 Sept.–1 Oct.). Kieft's disastrous policy brought him into conflict with The Eight, who refused approval of excises (18 June 1644) and appealed to the Amsterdam Chamber for relief (Oct.). Peace with the Indians was finally established (9 Aug. 1645) through the intervention of the Mohawks, but only after most settlers south of Ft. Orange and Rensselaerswyck had retired behind the walls of Ft. New Amsterdam, on the southern tip of Manhattan (1644).

1644, 16 Nov.–1646. RESETTLEMENT OF LONG ISLAND. After Kieft purchased the western portion of Long Island (Coney Island to Gowanus), settlements were begun (Breukelen [northwest Brooklyn], 1646; Lady Moody's at Gravesend, chartered, 19 Dec. 1646), as well as English settlements at Heemstede (Hempstead, 16 Nov. 1644, and Flushing, 19 Oct. 1645). Meantime, the Dutch position on the Connecticut deteriorated with the expansion of English settlement in that area.

1646, 28 JULY–1664, 19 MAR. STUYVESANT'S REGIME. Kieft was succeeded by **Peter Stuyvesant** (p. 1162), commissioner in Brazil (1635) and governor of Curaçao (1643–44). On arrival at New Amsterdam (11 May 1647) he consented to an election (25 Sept.) by the Dutch householders of Manhattan, Pavonia (Jersey City), and Long Island of 18 men, from whom he and the council chose 9 (**The Nine**) to advise the governor and council and serve in a judicial capacity. The Nine soon complained to the States General (13 Oct. 1649), charging neglect by the company, and proposed reforms, including the establishment of local self-government. Stuyvesant was ordered by the Amsterdam Chamber to grant New Amsterdam a city government (Apr. 1652). The director-general proclaimed New Amsterdam a municipality, appointed the municipal officials, and retained the right to enact ordinances (2 Feb. 1653). By Dec. 1661 5 Dutch and 6 English villages were incorporated on western Long Island, as were the villages of Bergen and Esopus. After establishing municipal government for New Amsterdam, The Nine were disbanded, and most of their duties transferred to the

magistrates of New Amsterdam. Stuyvesant called 5 assemblies of delegates from towns adjacent to New Amsterdam, 2 (Dec. 1653 and May 1654) during the Anglo-Dutch War; the other 3 while the colony was in its last crisis (July, Nov. 1663, Apr. 1664).

1647–63. END OF SWEDISH RULE ON THE DELAWARE. The Dutch members of the New Sweden Co. were bought out (1641) and the company reorganized (1642), with an increase of capital and an extension of control by the Swedish crown. **Johan Björnsson Printz** (1592–1663), a Swedish soldier of fortune, served as governor of New Sweden (1643–53). He erected a series of blockhouses at Varkens Kill (Salem Creek), Upland, New Gothenburg on Tinicum Island, 1643, and Ft. New Krisholm near the mouth of the Schuylkill (1647). Stuyvesant countered by building Ft. Beversrede across the river (at present Philadelphia, 27 Apr. 1648). Although the Swedes twice burned the post (May, Nov. 1648), the Dutch held the site until the establishment of Ft. Casimir (Newcastle, 5 Nov. 1651), controlling the approaches to New Sweden. This fort was captured by **Johan Classon Rising,** the newly appointed governor of New Sweden (1654), but Stuyvesant proceeded to retake the fort (26 Sept. 1655), thereby ending Swedish rule in North America. In payment of debts incurred as a result of this campaign, the Dutch West India Co. transferred to the city of Amsterdam all lands west of the Delaware from Cristina Kill to Boomtje's (Bombay) Hook. The city sent out 167 settlers, who, on arrival at Ft. Casimir (21 Apr. 1657), reorganized the settlement as **New Amstel,** under Jacob Alrichs as vice-director (succeeded, 1659, by Alexander d'Hinoyossa). As a result of the transfer to the city of Amsterdam by the company of all remaining lands on the west bank of the Delaware, as well as a tract 3 miles broad along the east bank (8 Feb. 1683), all authority in the area passed into the hands of d'Hinoyossa.

1650–64. ANGLO-DUTCH RELATIONS. Fearful of the encroachments of New Haven upon Westchester, Connecticut on Ft. Good Hope, and both colonies on Long Island, Stuyvesant at Hartford negotiated a boundary settlement (23–29 Sept. 1650) with the commissioners of the New England Confederacy whereby Long Island was divided by a line running north and south through Oyster Bay, and the mainland by a line 10 miles east of the Hudson (Ft. Good Hope to remain in Dutch hands). Although the English government never recognized this treaty, the boundaries were respected until shortly before the fall of New Netherland. During the **Anglo-Dutch War** (July 1652–Apr. 1654) the Confederacy refrained from declaring war on New Netherland, although Ft. Good Hope was seized (5 July 1653) by Connecticut and formally sequestered (Apr. 1654). In the spring of 1663 Connecticut dispatched Capt. John Talcott into Westchester and James Christie into Long Island. The former dismissed the magistrates and took an oath of allegiance from the settlers; the latter forced Stuyvesant to recognize English suzerainty over the English towns on Long Island (3 Mar. 1664) pending negotiations between England and the Netherlands.

1658, 31 MAY–1664, 16 MAY. INDIAN RELATIONS. Increasing hostility of the Hudson Valley Indians (beginning 1657) culminated in an attack on Wiltwyck, the village on the Esopus (7 June 1663). In 3 Dutch retaliatory expeditions (July, Sept., Oct.) 2 Indian forts were destroyed as well as most of their standing corn. On 16 May 1664 the Indians surrendered the whole of the Esopus Valley. Generally amicable relations with the Five Nations of the Iroquois, upon whom the Dutch were chiefly dependent for their furs, were marred by the activities of the *bosch loopers,* runners who intercepted Indians going to Ft. Orange to trade. Ordinances and prosecutions (June 1660) were instituted to end such illegal activities.

Establishment of English Rule

1661–64. CONQUEST OF NEW NETHERLAND. The English regarded the Dutch settlement as blocking westward expansion and interfering with the enforcement of the Navigation Acts through clandestine trade in tobacco. An open clash of national trading interests resulted from the chartering (1660) of "The Company of Royal Adventurers to Africa," with a monopoly of the African slave trade (reincorporated as the **Royal African Co.,** 1663; lost its monopoly, 1698). On 22 Mar. 1664 Charles II granted his brother, James, Duke of York, all of Maine between the St. Croix and Kennebec rivers and from the coast to the St. Lawrence, all islands between Cape Cod and the Narrows, and all land from the western boundary of Connecticut (Connecticut's claims west of the Connecticut River were recognized, 30 Nov. 1667) to the eastern shore of Delaware Bay, with power to govern, subject to the reservation that judicial appeals might be taken to the crown. On 2 Apr. the duke appointed Col. **Richard Nicolls** (1624–72) as chief of a commission to capture New Netherland and settle disputes in the New England colonies. A task force of 4 frigates reached New York Harbor (29 Aug.), and on 7 Sept. Stuyvesant, lacking support from the inhabitants, capitulated to Nicolls. Under the liberal surrender terms the Dutch were granted liberty of conscience, property and inheritance rights, and direct trade with Holland for 6 months (extended briefly, 1667; but canceled, 1668). Col.

George Cartwright, another commissioner, took the surrender of Ft. Orange without incident (20 Sept.) and the British assumed the place of the Dutch as allies of the Five Nations of the Iroquois (24 Sept.). But Delaware did not yield until Sir Robert Carr had stormed Ft. Casimir (10 Oct.).

1664, Oct.–1668, 21 Apr. ESTABLISHMENT OF ENGLISH RULE. Nicolls renamed New Amsterdam New York in honor of the Duke of York, but permitted the Dutch municipal officers to continue to function and even to name their own successors (2 Feb. 1665). Long Island, Staten Island, and Westchester were constituted as "Yorkshire," with three ridings (East, Suffolk Co.; West, Staten Island, Brooklyn, and northwest Queens; and North, Westchester and central Long Island). A meeting at Hempstead (11 Mar. 1665) of 34 deputies from 17 towns from Westchester and Long Island (13 English and 4 Dutch) approved the **Duke's Laws** (a compilation by **Matthias Nicolls**), which contained a civil and criminal code, based in part on New England codes, provided for the election of overseers and a constable in each town, set up a general provincial organization of the courts and the militia, and assured freedom of conscience. Initially, the code applied only to "Yorkshire," but it was later extended to the Delaware (21 Apr. 1668). In June, 1665, the offices of mayor, alderman, and sheriff in New York City, all appointed for 1 year by the governor, replaced the schout, burgomasters, and schepens. As a result of the **Second Anglo-Dutch War** (Dec. 1664–July 1667) Nicolls confiscated all property of the Dutch West India Co. (23 Feb. 1665) as well as the property of Dutch owners who had not taken the oath of allegiance to the British crown (10 Oct.). The **Peace of Breda** (21 July 1667) ending the war confirmed the English possession of New Netherland. Pursuing the same general policy of conciliation, Nicolls' successor, Col. **Francis Lovelace** (1668–73), refrained from extending the Duke's Law to the predominantly Dutch areas of Kingston (Esopus, Wiltwyck), Albany, and Schenectady (settled 1661).

1673, 30 July–1674, 31 Oct. DUTCH REOCCUPATION OF NEW YORK. Following the outbreak of the **Third Anglo-Dutch War** (Mar. 1672), a Dutch fleet arrived at New York Harbor (7 Aug.), and after a brief exchange of fire (8 Aug.) the fort surrendered to the Dutch land force under Capt. **Anthony Clove,** designated governor general (12 Aug.). Esopus and Albany were speedily occupied (15 Aug.) and Dutch officials appointed for both the province and city of **New Orange** (New York, 17 Aug.). Western Long Island and settlements in New Jersey submitted, but the 5 towns of the East Riding (Suffolk) resisted. The province was restored to England by the **Treaty of Westminster** (19 Feb. 1674) and formally surrendered (10 Nov.) to **Sir Edmund Andros,** the deputy of the Duke of York to whom the province had been regranted by the king (9 July).

1674–87. STRUGGLE FOR REPRESENTATIVE GOVERNMENT. Andros confirmed the Duke's Laws, reappointed the previously ousted English officials, confirmed previous land grants, and secured the submission of towns on eastern Long Island which had claimed to be under Connecticut's jurisdiction. Despite popular demands for an assembly (as early as 1670), the duke (Jan. 1676) indicated his opposition on the ground that such a body would "prove destructive . . . to the peace of the government." By the "Bolting Act" (1678) New York City was given a monopoly on flour milling for export and its position was reaffirmed by Andros as the sole port of entry. Although exonerated of charges of illegal trading with the Dutch and corruption in office, Andros was supplanted by Col. **Thomas Dongan** (1634–1715), an Irish Catholic, who arrived in New York, 28 Aug. 1683. Pursuant to instructions from the duke he called a general assembly of delegates from each of the three ridings of Yorkshire and from New York and Harlem, Albany, Schenectady, Esopus, Martha's Vineyard, Nantucket, anad Pemaquid (eastern Maine), which proceeded to enact the **Charter of Liberties** (30 Oct. 1683), largely the work of the speaker, **Matthias Nicolls**. The charter, providing for a meeting at least once in 3 years of an assembly whose consent was necessary for the imposition of taxes, was approved by the duke, but after his accession as James II (6 Feb. 1685) he disallowed the legislation of the assembly (29 May 1686) and expressly empowered the royal governor to exercise full legislative as well as executive power in conjunction with the council. The assembly was dissolved (Jan. 1687), never to meet again. Dongan granted municipal charters to New York City and Albany (1683), taking the latter out of the hands of the patroon.

1689, 31 MAY–1691, 20 MAY. LEISLER'S REBELLION. Andros' commission as governor of the Dominion of New England included New York (7 Apr. 1687). His 42-man council appointed by the king included 8 New Yorkers (16 Apr.). Andros went to Boston (1 Oct.), leaving his lieutenant governor, Capt. **Francis Nicholson**, in charge of affairs. When news of the Boston rising and the outbreak of war between England and France reached New York (26–27 Apr. 1689), Suffolk, Queens, and Westchester ousted their officials and elected others in their place. Dongan, retired to Hempstead, was rumored to be the center of a Catholic plot, which included Nicholson as well. **Jacob Leisler** (1649–91) a trader who had come from Germany,

1660, in the employ of the Dutch West India Co., seized Ft. James (31 May 1689), and was left in control of the city when Nicholson fled (11 June). Leisler called upon representatives from counties and towns to join the government in New York (12 June), proclaimed William and Mary (22 June), and formed a Committee of Public Safety (26 June). Suffolk, Ulster, and Albany counties and a few isolated towns refused to participate in Leisler's first assembly (27 July– 15 Aug.), and Albany elected its own officials (14 Oct.). A letter from William III's secretary of state addressed to Nicholson (20 July 1689), or "in his absence to such as for the time being take care for preserving the peace and administering the laws," was intercepted by Leisler and interpreted as applying to himself. The burning of Schenectady by a mixed force of French and Indians (9 Feb. 1690) impelled Albany to accept Leisler. Representatives from Massachusetts, Plymouth, Connecticut, and New York convened at Albany (1 May) voted to prosecute an invasion of Canada by 2 land forces (from New York and New England), and to dispatch a naval force up the St. Lawrence. The expedition proved a fiasco (summer 1690). Meantime, the Lords of Trade had recommended sending a new governor (31 Aug. 1689). Col. **Henry Sloughter** was commissioned (24 Nov.), but admiralty red tape and shipwreck delayed his arrival in the colony until 29 Mar. 1691. He was preceded by Maj. **Robert Ingoldesby**, who reached New York City with an English regiment (8 Feb.). Leisler refused Ingoldesby's request for the surrender of the fort on the ground that he lacked a royal commission as commander in chief or instructions from Sloughter to act as his deputy. Ingoldesby seized City Hall, and hostilities broke out (27 Mar.) just 2 days before the arrival of Sloughter. Leisler surrendered to Sloughter (30 Mar.). He was tried, along with 9 of his supporters (10–27 Apr. 1691), and with 7 others sentenced to death. Leisler and Jacob Milborne, his lieutenant, were hanged (26 May), while the 6 others were reprieved and eventually pardoned by the crown (15 Mar. 1694). Sloughter's commission had empowered him to call an assembly. Such a call was issued, 30 Mar. 1691, a date which marked the beginning of representative government in New York.

New Jersey

1664, 4 July–1665, 20 Feb. PROPRIETARY GRANT. The Duke of York granted to **John Lord Berkeley** and **Sir George Carteret** the region between the Hudson and Delaware rivers, bounded on the north by a line running from 41°N on the Hudson to the northernmost point of the Delaware. Technically, no governmental rights were conveyed, but the proprietors proceeded to issue their **Concessions and Agreements** (20 Feb. 1665), modeled on the Carolina Concessions, granting freedom of conscience, land on generous terms subject to quitrents, and the right of the freeholders to send deputies to a general assembly (first session 4 June 1668; last legal assembly until 1675 was held Nov. 1671). **Philip Carteret,** a distant relative of the proprietor (appointed governor 10 Feb. 1665), was accepted by the Dutch in the northern section (around present Bergen), but his authority was contested by English settlers under grants from Gov. Nicolls of New York.

1674–87. DEVOLUTION OF PROPRIETARY RIGHTS. Lord Berkeley sold his proprietary rights for £1,000 to **John Fenwick** (1618–83) and **Edward Byllinge,** fellow Quakers. On 8 Aug. 1674 the Duke of York then granted Sir George Carteret that part of New Jersey

lying north of a line running from Barnegat Creek on the Atlantic to the mouth of Rankokus Kill on the Delaware. The province was divided (11 July 1676) between **East** and **West Jersey** by the **Quintipartite Deed** (between Carteret on one hand and Byllinge, William Penn, and two other Quakers on the other). The duke recognized the new proprietors of West Jersey, but substituted as a boundary between the two sections a line running from Little Egg Harbor (in the Barnegat region) to the northernmost branch of the Delaware (16 Aug. 1680). After Byllinge's death (1685) his heirs sold his share to Dr. **Daniel Coxe** of London. On the death of Sir George Carteret (1680), the trustee for his heir sold his rights in East Jersey (1 Feb. 1681) to William Penn and 11 associates, for the most part highly connected Quakers (who enlarged their numbers, 1682, to 24; confirmed by the duke, 14 Mar. 1683).

1674–88 GOVERNMENT OF EAST JERSEY. Philip Carteret, recommissioned governor (13 June 1674), resumed his post in the colony, but his authority was challenged by Gov. Andros of New York, who insisted on collecting duties on goods entering Jersey ports (5 Apr. 1679). Carteret was seized (30 Apr. 1680), tried in New York for illegally exercising governmental powers, but acquitted by a jury (May). Undeterred, Andros attended a session of the East Jersey assembly (2 June), which he dissolved when it refused to do his bidding, and continued in the exercise of executive powers (July–Aug.). Although Dongan's commission did not give him jurisdiction over East Jersey, he banned Jersey vessels from the Hudson (Aug. 1686) and proposed to the home authorities that the province be annexed to New York (19 Feb. 1688). James II had writs of quo warranto issued against the Jersey proprietors and secured the surrender of both Jersey charters (Mar.

1688), incorporating the area in the Dominion of New England. In the fall of 1692 the proprietors resumed control. **Andrew Hamilton,** a Scot, served as governor until his death (Apr. 1703), save for a period in 1698 when Jeremiah Basse, one of the proprietors, acted in that capacity.

1675–1701. GOVERNMENT OF WEST JERSEY. The first English settlement in the western portion of the province was established by Fenwick at Salem (1675). On charges of illegally assuming governmental functions Fenwick was arrested (8 Nov. 1676), brought to New York (Jan. 1677), fined £40, and released on parole. Despite warnings to desist (3 June 1678) he attempted to function as governor until Andros appointed his own officials (26 Oct.). Fenwick continued to make land grants until he had deeded most of his holdings to William Penn (1 Mar. 1682). On 13 Mar. 1677 the 4 proprietors of West Jersey issued the **Laws, Concessions, and Agreements,** largely the work of William Penn, providing for liberty of conscience, civil rights including trial by jury, and no taxation save with the consent of the representatives of the voters (proprietors, freeholders, and inhabitants). Byllinge, designated governor (1680), dispatched Samuel Jennings to serve as his deputy. The assembly, with its first session, 1681, continued to meet at **Burlington** until 1701. In 1683 that body challenged the proprietors' right to govern and chose Jennings as governor and its own councilors. On Byllinge's death Daniel Coxe, who had purchased his rights, including the title of hereditary governor, proceeded to function through deputies. Coxe sold his interest (1692) to a group of 48 (West Jersey Society, largely Anglicans).

1701–38. NEW JERSEY AS ROYAL PROVINCE. In 1701 the Board of Trade recommended that the crown resume control of private colonies. On 26 Apr. 1702 the proprietors of both Jerseys surrendered governmental authority to the crown. Until 1738 the governor of New York was also governor of New Jersey, but under a separate commission. Thereafter, beginning with **Lewis Morris** (1671–1746), New Jersey had its own royal governor. Despite the loss of governmental rights the proprietors retained their property interest. A Board of Proprietors of East Jersey (est. 1684, headquarters Perth Amboy) and a similar organization for West Jersey (est. 1688, headquarters Burlington) have continued in existence to the present day.

Pennsylvania

1680, 1 JUNE–1682, AUG. GRANTS TO PENN. William Penn (p. 1125), son of Admiral Sir William Penn, who had joined the Society of Friends, studied in France, then at Lincoln's Inn, received a charter from Charles II on 14 Mar. 1681, possibly in lieu of his father's claim against the exchequer for £16,000. Under its terms he was made absolute proprietor of an area between 43°N and 40°N, running west from the Delaware through five degrees in longitude. The ambiguity of the description left the lower Delaware undecided. The charter included specific limitations on his governmental powers: (1) laws had to receive the approval of an assembly; (2) the Navigation Acts were to be obeyed; (3) the Privy Council had the right to disallow all legislation within five years after passage; (4) the crown reserved the right to hear appeals from the courts of the province; (5) an ambiguous clause recognized the right of the king to impose taxes "by act of Parliament," an issue which remained academic until 1765.

1682–1704. PENN TAKES OVER DELAWARE. On 24 Aug. 1682 a grant to Penn of the region on the western shore of Delaware Bay, from New Castle to Cape Henlopen, was made by the Duke of York, who in fact lacked legal title to the area. These grants contained no rights of government. Hence, Penn's control over Delaware was of dubious legality. By the Charter of 1701 Delaware was empowered to have a government separate from Pennsylvania. On 22 Nov. 1704 the first independent assembly met at New Castle. Down to the Revolution both provinces were under the same governor, save that the king had to approve for Delaware.

1682–88. EARLY CONSTITUTIONAL DEVELOPMENTS IN PENNSYLVANIA. Penn's **Frame of Government** (5 May 1682) provided for a governor (proprietor or his deputy), council (in which proprietor had a treble vote; 72 members, later reduced to 18; one third elected each year), and assembly (200–500 members; reduced in 1683 to 32), elected by the freeholders. The council was to initiate laws, act in an administrative and judicial capacity, and try officials impeached by the assembly, which could merely ratify or reject legislation. The assembly's right to initiate legislation was recognized in 1696. The right to amend and alter (exercised by 1688) was the subject of controversy for many years. William Markham, dispatched (10 Apr. 1681) to inform the inhabitants (c.500 Dutch and Swedes) of the Penn proprietorship, was succeeded by 4 commissioners (Sept. 1681), and, in turn, by Thomas Holme, who (early 1682) laid out the site for Philadelphia. Penn arrived on the Delaware (27 Oct. 1682), received the territory from the Duke of York's agent (28 Oct.), and proclaimed in assembly (2 Nov.) that the Duke's Laws were to be in force until the people decided otherwise. At Upland Penn called a general court (8 Nov.) to consist of representatives from 6 counties (3 from present

Pennsylvania; 3 from present Delaware). The assembly (17 Dec. 1682) passed a declaration of liberty of conscience and placed the 3 lower counties under one administration. A new **Frame of Government,** reducing the size of council and assembly, was approved by a second assembly (12 Apr. 1683). Penn returned to England (16 Aug. 1684) to defend his southern boundary against Lord Baltimore, governing by deputy in his absence.

1682–83. EARLY SETTLEMENT. As the result of extensively publicizing his colonial venture in the British Isles, Holland, and Germany, immigration was sizable from the start. The first large contingent, Welshmen, arrived 13 Aug. 1682, settling on lands purchased from the Indians north and west of Philadelphia. Quakers from the Rhineland and lower Palatinate settled Germantown (fall, 1683), and groups of Irish and English Quakers established scattered settlements. Land grants were carelessly made; title quarrels were common. It remained for Penn's second son, **Thomas** (1702–75), on his arrival in the province, 1732, to organize the land system and straighten out the claims.

1688–94. GLORIOUS REVOLUTION IN PENNSYLVANIA. Because of the friendship between Penn and James II and the passive stand of the Pennsylvania Quakers toward participating in the war against France, the crown appointed Gov. Benjamin Fletcher of New York as governor of Pennsylvania (18 Mar. 1692). **Royal rule** lasted until 20 Aug. 1694, when the proprietary government was restored. Penn returned to the colony as a resident governor (1699).

1701, 8 Nov. CHARTER OF LIBERTIES, granted by Penn, remained the constitution of Pennsylvania down to the Revolution. Under its terms the legislature became **unicameral,** laws being passed by the governor with the consent of the assembly alone. Except in the appointment of a governor, proprietary rule, from a political point of view, virtually ceased. Penn returned to England (1701), leaving James Logan (1674–

1751) as his agent. All but ruined by the chicanery of Philip Ford, a steward, Penn landed in the Fleet for debt, and had to mortgage the province to trustees (1708).

Settlement of Florida, the Carolinas, and Georgia

Early Spanish Colonizing Efforts

1521. PONCE DE LEÓN'S ATTEMPT. After a previous exploration of the Florida coast (1513, pp. 24–25), Ponce de León received a patent from the crown of Spain (27 Sept. 1514) to settle the "islands of Bimini and Florida." Sailing from Puerto Rico (20 Feb.) with 200 men, he landed, probably at Charlotte Harbor, where he was attacked by the natives, wounded, and forced to withdraw to Cuba, dying in May or June.

1526–27. DE AYLLÓN'S ATTEMPT. Lucas Vásquez de Ayllón received a patent similar to de León's (12 June 1523), sailed from Hispaniola (July 1526) with some 500 settlers for the Cape Fear region, whence he coasted south probably to the Pedee River to establish a settlement. He died shortly thereafter (18 Oct.) and the remnant of 150 who survived a difficult winter (1526–27) abandoned the site and returned to Hispaniola.

1528. NARVÁEZ EXPEDITION (p. 26).

1539. DE SOTO IN FLORIDA. Under a grant to settle the entire region north of the Gulf of Mexico, Hernando de Soto landed at Tampa Bay (May), and headed north (1 Aug.) for his long march into the interior (pp. 26–27).

1549. PIONEER MISSIONARY EFFORT. Fray Luis Cancer de Babastro, a Dominican, who had seen service in

Guatemala (1535–38, 1542–46), sailed from Vera Cruz (spring) to convert the Florida Indians, coasted northward from Tampa Bay, then returned to that region where he was killed by the natives (26 June).

1558–61. SETTLEMENT FAILURES. In quest of Spanish treasure in the holds of ships wrecked along the Florida coast as well as for the conversion of the natives, **Don Tristán de Luna y Arellano** sailed from Vera Cruz (11 June 1559) with a party of 1,500 colonists with the immediate objectives of settling at Santa Elena and on the Gulf. Entering Pensacola Bay (14 Aug.), they failed to establish a permanent foothold, but explored the interior (northwest Alabama). Command passed to **Angel de Villafañe,** who made an unsuccessful voyage, possibly as far north as Cape Hatteras (27 May–9 July 1561) to establish a settlement. The entire project was abandoned that year. On 23 Sept. Philip II issued a cedula barring further colonizing efforts in Florida.

Struggle Between France and Spain for Control

1562–65. EARLY FRENCH ATTEMPTS AT SETTLEMENT. Gaspard de Coligny, Admiral of France, who had previously sent an unsuccessful expedition to Brazil (1555), dispatched 5 ships (16 Feb. 1562) under **Jean Ribaut of**

Dieppe to establish a Huguenot colony. Landing on the north Florida coast (30 Apr.), they settled in present South Carolina at Santa Elena, whose name they changed to **Port Royal**. Failing to receive supplies, the colonists abandoned settlement early in 1564. A second expedition of Huguenots under **René de Laudonnière** was established at Ft. Caroline (1564) near the mouth of the St. Johns River (commanding the homeward route of the Spanish treasure ships) and was reinforced by supplies and settlers brought by Ribaut (spring 1565).

1565–67. FOUNDING OF ST. AUGUSTINE AND OUSTING OF THE FRENCH. The new French threat impelled Spain to reverse its policy toward Florida and to dispatch **Pedro Menéndez de Avilés** (20 Mar. 1565) both to settle Florida and to expel the French. Sailing from Cádiz (28 July 1565) with a party of 1,500, he arrived at St. Augustine Harbor (28 Aug.), which he named, inspected the approaches to the St. Johns River (4 Sept.), returned to St. Augustine, where he disembarked the colonists (7–8 Sept.). To destroy the Spanish colony Ribaut left 240 men at Ft. Caroline and sailed (10 Sept.) with the major part of his force for St. Augustine, but a storm (13 Sept.) wrecked his fleet. Menéndez countered with a march to Ft. Caroline (17–19 Sept.), which he captured (20 Sept.), killing 132 French defenders in the first hour of the attack and massacring those taken prisoner save for a few who managed to escape to some French vessels anchored in the river. Renaming the fort San Mateo, Menéndez established a garrison, hunted down French survivors of the Ribaut expedition, set up forts on the Indian River (Nov.; removed to Santa Lucia, Feb. or early Mar. 1566) and at Santa Elena (San Felipe, Apr. 1566) and blockhouses at San Pedro and at the headwaters of the Broad River, as well as posts on the

west coast at San Antonio (Charlotte Harbor, 1566) and Tocobago (Tampa Bay, 1567) and to the south at Tegesta near Miami (early 1567).

1567, 22 Aug.–1568, 2 June. FRENCH RETALIATION. Dominique de Gourgues sailed to the West Indies from France with 3 vessels (crew of 80 and 100 arquebusiers), finally landed on an island near San Mateo (c.Apr. 1568), enlisted Indian aid, marched on 2 blockhouses at the mouth of the St. Johns, which he captured (12 Apr.), then advanced upon San Mateo, which fell to him (16 Apr.), and massacred his prisoners, taking similar revenge on crews from captured Spanish vessels (6 June).

1566–72. JESUIT ACTIVITIES. Efforts of the Jesuits at converting the Florida Indians were launched (1566–68). Under **Fray Batista Segura** another group of Jesuits sailed from Santa Elena (5 Aug. 1570) to Axacan (Chesapeake Bay region), where all were murdered (in present Virginia, 14–18 Feb. 1571). As a result, all Jesuits were removed from Florida by the summer of 1572.

1576–81. FURTHER INDIAN AND FRENCH CONFLICTS. Indian unrest following the death of Avilés (1574) forced abandonment of the garrisons on the west coast of Florida, including San Felipe. **Pedro Menéndez Marqués,** acting governor, rebuilt the fort at Santa Elena (July 1577), burned a large Indian village (Cocopay, c.Apr. 1578), taking many captives, whom he traded for 12 Frenchmen previously captured by the Indians. In addition, French corsairs, including Nicolas Estrozi, were captured and killed (by early 1580). In a naval battle with a French force under **Gilberto Gil** at San Mateo (17 July), Marqués was the victor and Gil was killed. Another Indian uprising (4 Oct.) was quelled (by Jan. 1581).

1586, June–July. SIR FRANCIS DRAKE attacked and destroyed the fort and other buildings at St. Augustine and looted the settlement at Santa Elena.

Development of Spanish Florida

1577–1655. SPANISH MISSIONARY EFFORTS. Franciscan missionary activity under **Fray Alonso de Reynoso,** with the support of the crown, was attempted (1577–92) with conspicuous success. A more intensive effort was begun under **Fray Juan de Silva** (23 Sept. 1595) with the establishment of mission provinces: Timucua (north-central Florida), Apalachee (northwest Florida), Guale (Georgia coast), Orista (South Carolina coast), and Tama (interior Georgia). Despite Indian hostility in the Guale district 1,500 natives were converted (1595–96) and chapels were erected at San Pedro (Cumberland Island), Santiago de Ocone (Jekyll Island), Asao (St. Simon's Island), Tolomato (on the mainland above the mouth of the Altamaha River), and Tupique (north of Tolomato). As a result of attacks by the Guale Indians (1597–1600), all missions north of Saint Augustine were abandoned except Santa Elena. A punitive expedition out of St. Augustine (10 Oct.) destroyed Indian villages and supplies and forced the Indians to sue for peace (spring 1600). Thereafter (1603–06) Franciscan missions were established at San Juan and Santa Maria (below the St. Marys River), at San Pedro, Macoma, Talaxe (south bank of the Altamaha), and at Santa Catalina de Guale (on St. Catherine Island). In the period 1606–80 a chain of missions were pushed northward along the coast to Chatuache (Satuache, between the Combahee and Edisto rivers, by 1650), with subsequent activity among the Tamali (in the area between the junction of the Ocmulgee and Oconee rivers and the Guale, 1680). A second line of advance went west from St. Augustine across the northern neck of the Florida peninsula. Itinerant missionaries were active in Potano (1606–07), east of the Ocilla River, and at Apalachee (Oct. 1633), where (by 1655) 9 missions were established. Activity spread westward to the Chatot country around the Apalachicola River, where two missions (San Carlos de los Chacatos and San Nicolas de Tolentino) were established by 1674. Despite an Indian uprising (1647) 38 missions were established and some 26,000 Indians at least partly converted by 1655.

English in the Carolinas

1629–39. EARLY PATENTS. In 1629 Sir **Robert Heath** was granted a patent to settle the area between 31° and 36°N ("New Carolana"). On the basis of a conveyance from Heath (1630), **Samuel Vassal** and others made ineffectual efforts to explore and settle the area. In 1632 **Henry Lord Maltravers** is reputed to have been granted the "province of Carolana" by Heath, and by the Harvey Patent (1638), issued by Governor Sir John Harvey of Virginia, laid claim to land south of the James River to be called Norfolk County. But in neither area did did he effect a settlement.

1653–54. ALBEMARLE COLONY. Settlers from Virginia began to move across the Nansemond Valley and the Dismal Swamp into present North Carolina, settling (by 1653) north of Albemarle Sound between the Chowan River and the sea. This movement was encouraged by the Virginia assembly for the protection of its southern frontier with offers of land grants to the first settlers between the Chowan and Roanoke rivers (July) and by the expenditures of 2 Virginians, Francis and Argall Yeardley.

1655. FALL OF JAMAICA to England encouraged the belief that the Spaniards could be ousted from North

America and promoted English expansion along the southern frontier.

c.1660–63. CAPE FEAR COLONY. A group of New Englanders in association with London merchants organized the Cape Fear Co. and sent settlers from New England to the region around the Cape Fear River (c.1662), but the settlement was abandoned before the fall of 1663.

1663, 3 APR.–1665, 10 JULY. CHARTERS OF THE CAROLINAS. As a result of a project formulated by Sir John Colleton, a Barbadian planter, Sir William Berkeley, former governor of Virginia, and **Sir Anthony Ashley Cooper** (later, 1672, **Earl of Shaftesbury**), an outstanding colonial promoter, Charles II granted to 8 proprietors—the 3 aforementioned prime movers as well as such high-ranking personages as the **Earl of Clarendon** (the king's chief minister), the **Duke of Albemarle** (General Monck), **John Lord Berkeley** (brother of Sir William and a high-ranking naval officer), the **Earl of Craven,** and **Sir George Carteret**—the area lying between 31° and 36°N and extending westward to the "south seas." Maltravers' heir, the Duke of Norfolk, and Samuel Vassal both countered by filing claims to this territory (10 June) and the Cape Fear Co. likewise challenged the validity of the charter (6 Aug.). However, the Privy Council declared all previous patents void (22 Aug. 1665), but claims continued to be urged until 1768, when the descendants of Daniel Coxe of New Jersey, to whom the Heath patent had been transferred in 1696, received from the crown a grant of 100,000 acres in New York in satisfaction of their claim. By a second charter (10 July 1665) the bounds were extended to include the northern end of Currituck Inlet (31° 30′N) and pushed south to 29°N to include the entire settled part of Florida.

1663, 23 MAY–1665. PRELUDE TO SETTLEMENT. From their first meeting the proprietors sought to promote settlement from New England and Barbados (considered overpopulated) and were encouraged by the favorable report (6 Feb. 1664) from Capt. William Hilton, who had recently explored the area. Sir William Berkeley, authorized to name a governor for the Chowan River settlement, designated (Oct. 1664) William Drummond as governor of the province of **Albemarle** (later North Carolina). For the government of the entire chartered area the proprietors drew up the **Concessions and Agreements** (1665)— the same as those adopted by Berkeley and Carteret for New Jersey 6 weeks later—granting freedom of conscience, generous terms of land distribution subject to a quitrent (½d. per acre), and an assembly of freeholders' representatives.

1669–70. FUNDAMENTAL CONSTITUTIONS. To supplant the inadequate Concessions and Agreements the proprietors issued (11 Mar. 1669) the Fundamental Constitutions, generally attributed to **John Locke** in collaboration with Sir Anthony Ashley Cooper. This elaborate scheme of government blended advanced concepts with an artificially contrived aristocratic society. Religious freedom was guaranteed, but, under the revision of 1 Mar. 1670, the Church of England was established. A popular, as opposed to a standing, army was authorized. At the apex of Carolina society was a hereditary nobility: the **proprietors** (each with a seignory of 12,000 acres in each county); next came the **landgraves** (with 4 baronies apiece, 48,000 acres in all), followed by the **caciques** (Spanish for Indian chief, 2 baronies, 24,000 acres). Below them stood **lords of manors** (3,000 to 12,000 acres) and **freeholders** (with 50-acre minimum requirement for voting). Land and rank were synonymous; the loss of one meant the loss of the other. The 8 proprietors in England constituted a **Palatine Court** which appointed the governor, disallowed laws, and heard appeals from the colony. The provincial assembly was to comprise the governor, hereditary nobility, and the deputies (holders of 500-acre freeholds), but ultimately that body became bicameral (by 1693). The governor's council came to be called the Grand Council. In all, 26 landgraves and 13 caciques were created. In a few cases the title descended to the second and third generations; in most they expired with the original holder. In fact, no seignory or barony above 12,000 acres was ever set up and no manors erected. The proprietors revised the Fundamental Constitutions (12 Jan. 1682); declared inoperative (1693); again revised in abridged form (1698); but they were never accepted by the assembly.

1669–80. FOUNDING OF CHARLESTON. A party of settlers under Joseph West left England (Aug. 1669), and finally settled at Port Royal Sound (by the end of Mar. 1670). Fear of the Spaniards caused them to move north to the Ashley, where at Albemarle Point their first settlement (Charles Town) was established (Apr. 1670, later called Old Charles Town). Subsequently (1680) this settlement was relocated at the junction of the Ashley and Cooper rivers, present site of Charleston.

1670, 18 July. TREATY OF MADRID between England and Spain, temporarily recognizing the principle of effective occupation in the New World, served as a basis for future boundary discussions involving the Carolina-Florida border area.

1671–74. EARLY GROWTH AND FACTIONALISM. As a result of arrivals from Barbados (including Sir John Yeamans), England, and New York the population of Charles Town colony was

close to 400 (by 1672). The first governor, William Sayle, was succeeded on his death (4 Mar. 1671) by Joseph West, who summoned the first assembly (25 Aug.). On 14 Dec. Sir John Yeamans claimed the right as sole landgrave resident in the province to be governor in place of West, a cacique whom he outranked. Yeamans, commissioned, reached the province Apr. 1672. He was supplanted by West (1674).

1671–83. INDIAN TRADE AND CONFLICT. A war against the Coosa, a tribe in the vicinity of Charles Town, who were believed to be conspiring with the Spaniards, resulted in their complete defeat (1671). Numerous captives were enslaved, marking the beginning of the experiment with Indian slavery. In May 1674 Dr. Henry Woodward was commissioned Indian agent to open trade with the Westos east of the lower Savannah in furs, deer hides, and slaves. Trade was also opened with the Kiowa to the north. A **Westo** uprising (Apr. 1680) was smashed by the end of that year and the natives along the Savannah persuaded to cooperate in trade with the western tribes.

1677–80. CULPEPER'S REBELLION. In protest against the arbitrary acts of Gov. John Jenkins at Albemarle, Thomas Miller, a leader of the "proprietary faction," undertook to combine the functions of governor and customs collector. The antiproprietary party set up a revolutionary government (3 Dec. 1677), and imprisoned Miller, who escaped to England and laid his case before the Privy Council. The rebels were defended before the proprietors by one of their leaders, **John Culpeper.** Through the conciliatory influence of Shaftesbury the proprietors decided that Miller had exceeded his authority and Culpeper, who was tried for treason before the king's bench, was acquitted.

1679, 10 Oct. An act passed in Vir-

ginia prohibiting the importation of Carolina tobacco made Carolinians increasingly dependent upon Massachusetts and
Rhode Island sea captains and traders
who carried their tobacco to New England and reshipped it to Europe in evasion of the Navigation Acts.

1682–86. PORT ROYAL COLONY.
Under a patent from the Carolina proprietors (1682) a settlement of Scotsmen
under Henry Erskine, Lord Cardross, was
established (fall of 1684) at Port Royal
on a site named Stuart's Town, despite
the hostility of the Spaniards, who
viewed this incursion as violating the
Treaty of Madrid, and the antagonism
of Charleston settlers, unwilling to divide
their lucrative Indian trade with the
Scotch Covenanters. As a result of the
Westo War (1680) the Spanish authorities withdrew from their most northerly
missions and sought to pull back their
Indian allies. Rather than move south
the Yamassees sought refuge among the
English and Scots (the first Yamassee
refugees arrived at Stuart's Town, Feb.
1685) and settled on former Westo lands.
The Charleston authorities, who had ordered the arrest of Lord Cardross (5
May 1685) because of his refusal to submit to their control, now failed to heed
appeals from Stuart's Town for aid
against impending Spanish attack. The
Spaniards, threatened in Guale, which
they finally abandoned (1684–85), and
outflanked by Carolina traders (who had
reached the Lower Creeks on the middle
Chatahoochee River by 1685), had previously erected a new mission at the junction of the Flint and Chatahoochee
(1681) and engaged in raiding coastal
settlements in southern Carolina. Stuart's
Town was completely destroyed (Sept.
1686). Only a storm saved Charleston.

**1683–96. POLITICAL UNREST IN
THE CAROLINAS.** The colonists of
Berkeley Co. (Charleston area) rejected the revised Fundamental Constitutions of 1682. On orders from the proprietors Gov. Joseph Morton dissolved
the assembly (20 Sept. 1685) and Gov.
James Colleton (arrived Feb. 1687) refused to call an assembly (on orders,
1689). Under constant threat of Spanish
invasion the colonists in this area made
common cause with the corsairs who
preyed on Spanish shipping, and juries
acquitted those charged with violating
the Navigation Acts. In the north Albemarle ousted (1689) its governor, Seth
Southel (arrived c.1683), who went to
Charleston and proceeded to oust Colleton, take over the government (Oct.
1690), and call an assembly. In Nov.
1691 he was suspended by the Palatine
Court and charged with high treason.
His death (1694) ended the controversy.
The next three governors (Philip Lud-
well, 1691–93; Thomas Smith, 1693–94;
and John Archdale, 1694–96) attempted
to restore harmony.

**1706–29. SOUTH CAROLINA AS A
ROYAL COLONY.** After 1706 proprietary control steadily weakened, ac-
centuated by the crises of the French
and Spanish attack (1706) and the Yamassee War (p. 75). In Nov. 1719 the
colonists set up a revolutionary government, ousted the last proprietary governor, Robert Johnson, and replaced him
with James Moore as temporary governor. The crown then appointed **Francis
Nicholson** (1655–1728), who had been
governor or deputy governor of 3 other
colonies (proclaimed 29 May 1721),
thus formally incorporating South Carolina as a **royal colony.** The proprietary
charter was surrendered (1729), and 7
out of the 8 proprietors sold their claims
for £ 2,500 apiece. The eighth, Lord
Carteret, exchanged his portion (1743)
for a tract south of Virginia's southern
boundary, which he retained until the
Revolution.

1691–1729. NORTH CAROLINA AS A ROYAL COLONY. Albemarle, known after 1691 as North Carolina and governed by a deputy, was torn by sectionalism and unrest. The passage of the Vestry Act (1701), making the Church of England the established church, aroused intense opposition on the part

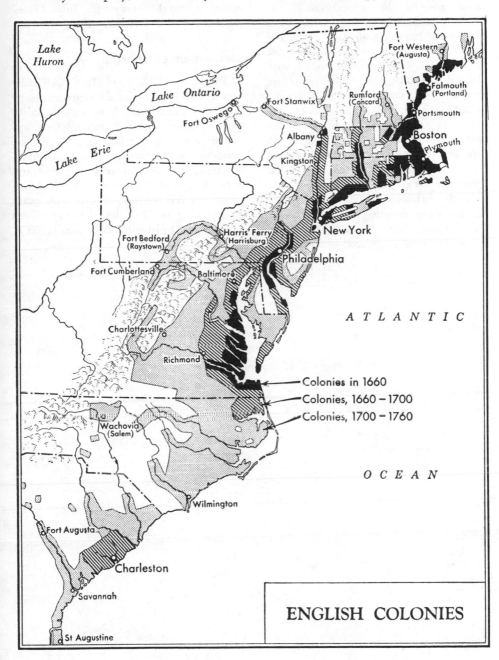

Colonies in 1660
Colonies, 1660 – 1700
Colonies, 1700 – 1760

ENGLISH COLONIES

of the Quakers and other dissenters. Though disallowed, a second Vestry Act (1704) was passed. In attempting to enforce the act, **Thomas Cary,** deputy governor, aroused the antagonism of the Quakers (now barred from office by a related act imposing an oath), who obtained from the proprietors an order for his removal. Cary refused to be supplanted by William Glover, chosen acting governor, rebelled, and was convicted of high crimes and misdemeanors. Escaping to Virginia, Cary was seized, dispatched to England, but allowed to return home. The crisis in the northern colony was further intensified by the **Tuscarora War** (1711–12), in which, after the massacre of 200 settlers, the Indians were defeated with the aid of Virginia and South Carolina. Remnants of the Tuscaroras removed to New York and joined the Iroquois as a sixth nation. In 1712 a separate governor was set up for North Carolina, with **Edward Hyde** the first incumbent. North Carolina became a **royal colony,** 25 July 1729, with the formal surrender of the charter.

Settlement of Georgia

20 June 1732. ROYAL CHARTER granted to trustees for 21 years territory south of the Savannah River originally part of South Carolina, but retained by the crown when the Carolinas were surrendered by the proprietors in 1729, plus a one-eighth interest retained by Carteret at time of surrender, which he conveyed to the trustees. The charter was surrendered in 1752, when Georgia became a royal province. (See also p. 76.)

THE COLONIES AND THE EMPIRE, 1624-1775

It seemed an extraordinary paradox that the first British Empire, hailed by Englishmen both in the mother country and in the American colonies as a palladium of liberty, should have been dissolved in the acid bath of revolution. In an age of enlightened monarchs England was the only nation whose monarchy rested on a firm constitutional base, the only one where there seemed to be an effective check upon royal absolutism, the only one which had a functioning representative government in which monarchical, aristocratic, and democratic roles were blended.

The plan of government by which England ruled her empire had evolved empirically and unsystematically. Parliament always exercised some role in colonial rule, but during the century following 1660, that body confined its interest in the colonies largely to trade regulation, and refrained from imposing direct taxes on the colonists. With the Restoration the crown had assumed the main burdens of administering an empire numbering by the middle of the eighteenth century thirty-one colonies, extending from Hudson Bay to Borneo, from the Honduran logwood coast to the Bay of Bengal, acquired in bits and pieces over 150 years. Different mechanisms were improvised to meet special governmental problems as they arose, but by the middle of the eighteenth century a clear trend toward the setting up of royal provinces had emerged, colony after colony having been brought under the direct control of the crown, with a considerable measure of centralization achieved by 1696, when the Board of Trade was established. Authority over the colonies was divided among other departments and agencies as well, while the Privy Council reviewed legislation from the colonies and acted as the highest court of appeals for colonial lawsuits. The royal governors' authority came to be increasingly impaired by the colonial assemblies, which voted taxes, paid out or withheld salaries, and had by the middle of the eighteenth century exercised in fact much of the appointing power which the royal governor in theory possessed. The Second Hundred Years' War, waged between England and France, 1689–1763, eliminated France as a power in the New World and caused Great Britain to reshape her imperial policy, laying as much stress on strategic and military considerations as on direct benefits, while at the same time the expulsion of the French from North America liberated the colonists from fear of foreign aggression and loosened their sense of dependency upon the mother country.

Centralized Administration

1624, 24 MAY. REVOCATION OF VIRGINIA CO. CHARTER, making Virginia a royal colony (p. 32).

1634, 28 APR.–1641, AUG. LAUD COMMISSION. Under James I the Privy Council rather than Parliament had exercised control over trade and colonies. A Commission of Trade set up by Charles I (1625), subordinate to the Privy Council, considered the Gorges patent, and a special committee on New England Plantations (1632) served temporarily. On 28 Apr. 1634 there was set up as a subdivision of the Privy Council the **Commission for Foreign Plantations** ("Laud Commission" after its chairman, the primate, William Laud). Despite its broad powers, its 7 years of activity were marked by few achievements. Most supervisory activities were carried on by special Privy Council committees or occasional outside groups.

1643–59. PARLIAMENTARY COMMISSION FOR PLANTATIONS, comprising 18 members, assumed the functions of the Privy Council in colonial affairs. Save for the appointment of one governor, Sir Thomas Warner, for the Caribbean islands (1643) and the granting of the charter of Providence Plantations (1644), it was virtually inactive, and its functions assumed by the **Council of State** (14 Feb. 1649), which set up a standing committee to handle trade (17 Dec. 1651) and plantations (4 May 1652). The **Protector's Council** (16 Dec. 1653) directed plantation affairs, assisted by the Committee for Foreign Plantations (10 May 1655) and the Committee for America (15 July 1656). It was replaced by the **Council of State** (May 1659).

1660, 4 JULY–1695, 15 MAY. LORDS OF TRADE. The king in council appointed a Committee for Trade and Plantations of the Privy Council (Lords of Trade) to report to the council as a whole. A Council of Trade (7 Nov.) and a Council for Foreign Plantations (1 Dec.) were also subordinate to the Privy Council. When they ceased to function (1665), the Privy Council reappointed its own plantation committee (7 Dec. 1666), and on 31 Jan. 1668 a new standing committee was created similar to the Lords of Trade of 1660. It was assisted (1668) by a special Council of Trade and Plantations combining the functions of the two councils of 1660. These functions were again separated upon the revival (20 July 1670) of the **Council for Foreign Plantations,** but after considerable activity its commission was withdrawn (1674) and its functions assigned to the Lords of Trade (1675).

1696–1782. THE BOARD OF TRADE, commissioned by William III, comprised 15 members (7 high officials including Privy Councilors, 8 paid members, including a first Lord of Trade, president of the board), was empowered to supervise (1) trade and the fisheries, (2) care of the poor, (3) plantation affairs, (4) recommend appointments of colonial officials, and (5) review colonial legislation and report to the Privy Council. Its first 20 years were marked by exceptional activity, although its powers were curbed as early as 1704 when the Secretary of State for the Southern Dept. assumed the right to appoint governors (1704). With the accession of George I and the ascendancy of Newcastle the board declined, reaching its nadir during the presidency of Baron Monson (1737–48). It was revived under **George Mon-**

tagu Dunk, **Earl of Halifax** (11 Nov. 1748). Under an order in council (11 Mar. 1752) nominations to colonial offices were to be made by the board and transmitted (in the case of high officials) to the Privy Council or (in the case of lesser ones) to the Secretary of State. Nevertheless, the Seven Years' War marked a renewed decline of the board's activity. With Halifax's resignation (Mar. 1761) the board soon lost its right of nomination (22 May). The board's powers were subsequently curtailed by an order in council (8 Aug. 1766), and correspondence was henceforth channeled through the Secretary of State. With the appointment of Hillsborough as both Secretary of State and president of the Board of Trade (20 Jan. 1768), both offices were held by the same person until 1782.

1673–76. THE TREASURY BOARD'S colonial functions were greatly expanded as a result of the Navigation Laws (particularly the Act of 1673). Immediately subordinate to that body were the **commissioners of customs** with jurisdiction over the collectors, searchers, and surveyors of customs in the colonies. Naval officers to enter and clear vessels were appointed (as early as 1676 for Jamaica) to enforce the Acts of Trade, eventually 6 for each colony.

1697. ESTABLISHMENT OF VICE-ADMIRALTY COURTS. Under the Navigation Act of 1696 the Privy Council directed the Board of Trade to establish vice-admiralty courts in the colonies. Acting under commission the governors of New York, Massachusetts, Maryland, Pennsylvania, and Virginia designated judges and other officers of such courts. The vice-admiralty courts had jurisdiction over the Acts of Trade and ordinary maritime cases as well as prize (by act of 1708). In addition, the act of 1722 conferred jurisdiction over infringements on conserving timber—"broad-arrow pol-

icy" (p. 699). At first appeals lay to the High Court of Admiralty; after 1748 it shared appellate jurisdiction with the Privy Council, which assumed sole appellate jurisdiction (11 July 1766). But the new admiralty courts set up under the Townshend Acts (1767, p. 90) centered final control in America.

ROYAL DISALLOWANCE. The Board of Trade reviewed colonial legislation and made recommendations for disallowance where laws conflicted with imperial policy, were prejudicial to trade, or were in conflict with the law of England. Out of 8,563 acts submitted by the continental colonies (not including Pennsylvania prior to 1700 nor Maryland, 1691–1715), 469 were disallowed, with the highest percentage from Pennsylvania, 15.5 (E. B. Russell). Its application was more general in the first 2 decades (beginning 1691) than at any later time. The existence of such machinery of review undoubtedly affected the course of later legislation and prompted colonial evasion by passage of temporary acts.

1696–1783. JUDICIAL APPEALS TO THE PRIVY COUNCIL were taken from all the colonies in some 1,500 cases. Civil cases were chiefly taken from Rhode Island, Virginia, and Massachusetts (among the continental colonies); criminal appeals were largely restricted to the early years (chiefly from Barbados); and Chancery appeals to the British West Indies.

THE ROYAL GOVERNOR, chief representative of the crown in the royal colonies and executive head of the provincial government, was guided by **instructions** generally formulated by the Board of Trade and transmitted by the Secretary of State for the Southern Dept. His authority came in the course of time to be undermined both by the home government and by the colonial assemblies. By the middle of the 18th century the Secretary of State came to appoint an increasing number of provincial officials, including the naval officer responsible for enforcement of the Navigation Acts. In the conflict with the assemblies the governors gradually lost control over expenditures. The New York assembly forced the governor, Lord Cornbury (1701–08), to accept its own treasurer (1706). Under George Clarke, acting governor (1736–43), the assembly, by securing the right to pay salaries by name and amount, gained increasing control over all appointments. Both governors Jonathan Belcher of Massachusetts (1730–41) and Lewis Morris of New Jersey (1738–46) failed to secure from the legislature other than temporary appropriations. In 1752 the Board of Trade instructed the governors to demand a **fixed civil list** (obtained nowhere except Jamaica) and in 1761 to appoint judges **during the pleasure of the crown** (a policy which aroused colonial antagonism reflected in the Declaration of Independence).

Anglo-French Colonial Rivalry to 1763

1497–1604. RIVALRY OVER FISH-ERIES. John Cabot (p. 22) and his English crew, first Europeans definitely known to have visited the Newfoundland coast since the Vikings, reported its waters as "swarming with fish." The French, who fished these waters as early as 1504, were in a dominant position by 1540, although after 1560 Portuguese and Spanish fishermen entered the area. Until 1578 England was dependent upon the Iceland fisheries. To free themselves of dependence on France and Portugal for their solar salt used in "green fishing" (i.e., salting fish aboard ship without drying), English fishermen introduced "dry fishing" (i.e., drying fish on land with a minimum amount of salt) in the Newfoundland area. Such fish found a ready market in Mediterranean ports (c.1580–1604). To compete, the French now sought land bases on which to dry their catch. Since the English had already preempted some of the best bases in Newfoundland, they chose Cape Breton and the Gaspé Peninsula.

1534–99. START OF FUR TRADE. Trade in furs developed virtually with the first contacts between the French and the Indians (as far back as Cartier's voyage of discovery, 1534). As the French fishermen increased their land bases, the fur trade was expanded, notably at Tadoussac on the St. Lawrence (by the 1580s). European weapons hastened the extinction of the beaver, in immense demand for hatmaking, and drew the fur trade into the interior.

1598–1613. BACKGROUND OF FRENCH SETTLEMENT. Despite two unsuccessful attempts at settlement (under Baron de Léry, 1518, and Roberval, 1542–43, p. 26), the French crown granted (12 Jan. 1598) Troïlus du Mesgouez, Marquis de la Roche, a monopoly of the fur trade and settlement rights in Canada, Newfoundland, and adjacent lands. La Roche transported 2 shiploads of jailbirds (mostly beggars and vagabonds) to **Sable Island** off the coast of Nova Scotia and dominating Newfoundland, Acadia, and the Gulf of St. Lawrence, but, after an uprising, the settlement was abandoned. Another monopoly finally was assigned (1603) to **Pierre du Guast, Sieur de Monts,** who established a settlement at the mouth of the St. Croix River (June, 1604). This colony was moved across the Bay of Fundy to **Port Royal** (Annapolis Royal, Nova Scotia, Aug. 1607), but was abandoned when Monts' patent was canceled (1607), then reestablished (1610) with two subsequent stations set up on the west bank of the Bay of Fundy (by 1613).

1608–27. SETTLEMENT OF ST. LAWRENCE VALLEY. His monopoly restored for 1 year (7 Jan. 1608), Monts dispatched **François du Pontgravé** (5 Apr.) and **Samuel de Champlain** (c.1567–1635) (13 Apr.) to Canada. Champlain founded **Quebec** (3 July) and remained in charge of the new colony as lieutenant for a chain of successors of Monts as viceroys. However, stress on the fur trade discouraged permanent settlement and left the colony vulnerable to attack. With the outbreak of war between England and France (Mar. 1627), control was vested (25 Apr.) in **The Company of New France** (**The Hundred Associates**), a joint-stock company, which, in return for undertaking settlement, was given the fur monopoly.

1609–27. FRENCH-INDIAN RELATIONS. The entry of the French into the St. Lawrence challenged control of the area by the Five Nations of the **Iroquois.** The Montagnais (Saguenay Valley), the Algonquins of the Ottawa, and the Hurons (between the Ottawa and Georgia Bay) assured the French a steady flow of furs from the interior and sought to oust the Iroquois from the area. Before Champlain's arrival the Iroquois had been ousted from the St. Lawrence Valley, and Champlain undertook 2 expeditions (1609, with the Algonquins to Lake Champlain; 1615, with the Hurons into the Onondaga country), designed to push the Five Nations southward and protect the link with the friendly Indians. The arrivals of the Recollect friars (1615) and the Jesuits

(1625) served as another link between France and her Indian allies. Missions were established as far west as Georgian Bay (by 1616), while further campaigns against the Five Nations (1618, 1627 guarded the trade route from the west (Georgian Bay–Lake Nipissing–Ottawa River–St. Lawrence–Quebec).

1613–29. EARLY ENGLISH ATTACKS. After the French settlements on either side of the Bay of Fundy had been totally destroyed in a raid conducted by Capt. Samuel Argall (1613), the English crown granted the region (1621) to **Sir William Alexander,** who, in the course of the war between France and England (1627–29), was given a monopoly of the St. Lawrence fur trade. On 20 July 1629 Sir David Kirke, who had joined forces with Alexander, captured Quebec, unaware that peace had already been established (24 Apr.) by the Treaty of Susa. By the Treaty of St. Germain-en-Laye (29 Mar. 1632) England restored Acadia and the St. Lawrence to France.

New France to King William's War

1632–70. ACADIAN DEVELOPMENTS. Settlement of Acadia by the French began in earnest after the appointment of Isaac de Razilly as governor (10 May 1632), but was halted by factionalism and civil war. A small force collected in Boston under Maj. Robert Sedgwick, originally intended to attack New Netherland but diverted to Acadia to eliminate French competition with New England in fish and furs, easily reduced the area (c.1 July 1654). The English held the province for 16 years until its return to France (1670) under provisions of the Treaty of Breda (July 1667).

1632–35. NEW FRANCE UNDER CHAMPLAIN. Champlain's return to

Canada (22 May 1633), this time both as royal governor and company governor, inaugurated a period of expansion, with settlements founded at Beauport (near Quebec, 1634), Three Rivers (1634), and **Montreal** (14 Oct. 1641). Recollect and Jesuit missions were re-established among the Hurons (1634) and as far west as the Algonquin tribes at Sault Ste. Marie (by 1641). Exploration of the interior was pressed, notably by **Jean Nicolet,** who journeyed as far west as Green Bay and the Fox River Valley, possibly even reaching the Mississippi (1634–35).

1642–53. IROQUOIS WAR. The Five Nations, armed by the Dutch, who sought to divert the northern and interior fur trade of the Huron and Algonquin to their own posts, with the Iroquois as intermediaries, attacked the Hurons on the Richelieu (3 Aug. 1642) and even raided Montreal (30 Mar. 1644). A short truce (14 July 1645–18 Oct. 1646) was broken by the Iroquois, Ft. Richelieu (erected by the French at the mouth of the Richelieu River, 1642) was burned (1647), with raids deep into the Huron country which forced the Jesuits to abandon their last Huron mission (1650) and the Hurons to retreat as far west as Wisconsin, where they were joined by other fugitive tribes from the Ottawa Valley, the Ohio, and southern Michigan. Raids along the St. Lawrence penetrated to the Saguenay-Rupert River country (1652). Victorious, though dangerously overextended, the Iroquois signed a peace with the French (5 Nov. 1653).

1654–72. RENEWED FRENCH EXPANSION. Revival of the fur trade by the Algonquins began in 1654. **Médard Chouart, Sieur des Grosseilliers,** and his brother-in-law, **Pierre-Esprit Radisson,** set forth (Aug. 1659) for a journey into the interior to the western and southern shores of Lake Superior and into north-

western Wisconsin. On Mazarin's death (1661) Louis XIV assumed personal rule. His finance minister **Colbert** pressed French colonization. A base and settlement were established at Placentia, Newfoundland (1662–63), and a resident governor appointed (1668). The government of Canada was placed under a governor, appointed council, and an intendant (the king's personal representative). During his terms in office (1663–68, 1670–72) **Jean Baptiste Talon** (1625–91), the "great intendant," dominated the government of New France. To guard the old Iroquois route to the St. Lawrence, forts were erected on the Richelieu River and at the head of Lake Champlain (1665–66). Renewed war against the Five Nations, now in alliance with England, was prosecuted, and the tribes were forced to sue for peace (1666). Despite the gradual return to their original homes of tribes dispossessed by the Five Nations, the French now continued direct trade with the Indians of Lake Superior and Michigan. To establish more permanent relations with the interior tribes, Talon sent Nicolas Perrot to the Wisconsin region (1668–69) and François Daumont, Sieur de St. Lusson, to Sault Ste. Marie. Missions were founded on the upper Michigan peninsula (c.1668) and on Green Bay and the Fox River (1670–72). **René Robert Cavelier, Sieur de La Salle** (1643–87), temporarily established amicable relations with the Iroquois and penetrated south of Lake Erie to present Ohio (1669–70).

1673–83. EXPANSION IN THE MISSISSIPPI VALLEY. When the English established trading posts on Hudson Bay (1670–83), tapping the continent's richest fur area, the French accepted the challenge, notably during the governorships of **Louis de Buade, Comte de Frontenac** (1620–98, gov. 1672–82) and Jacques René de Brisay, Marquis de Denonville (gov. 1682–88). Frontenac favored the Recollects (allied in France with the king in the struggle for temporal power) to check the Jesuits, supported by the papacy. In the beaver trade and the founding of missions the former outdistanced the latter in this period. **Père Jacques Marquette** (1637–75), a Jesuit missionary, and **Louis Joliet** (1648–1700), trader and explorer, set out from Mackinac Straits (17 May 1673), voyaged down Lake Michigan through Green Bay, up the Fox River, and, after a long portage, down the Wisconsin to the Mississippi (17 June), which river they paddled down as far as the Arkansas (17 July). Convinced that the Mississippi flowed into the Gulf of Mexico rather than the Pacific, they returned to Mackinac Straits by way of the Illinois River and Lake Michigan. La Salle, who wished to erect a government in the Mississippi Valley free of Jesuit control, sailed across the Great Lakes with **Father Louis Hennepin** (1640–1701?), who was the first to describe Niagara Falls, which they passed (Dec. 1678), for Green Bay, Wis., continuing by way of Mackinaw to the Illinois River, where he built Ft. Crèvecoeur (15 Jan. 1680). Hennepin, detached to accompany an expedition to explore the upper Mississippi, discovered St. Anthony's Falls (present Minneapolis, 1680). On a later expedition La Salle descended the Illinois to its mouth, embarked upon the Mississippi, paddling to its mouth (9 Apr. 1682), and took possession of the entire region, which he named **Louisiana.**

1668–88. EARLY STRUGGLE FOR HUDSON BAY. Radisson and Grosseilliers secured the backing of an English syndicate headed by **Prince Rupert,** cousin of the king, for a voyage to Hudson Bay (June 1668–Oct. 1669). The syndicate, now enlarged, was chartered by the crown (2 May 1670) as the **Governor and Company of Adventurers of England into Hudson's Bay.** To divert the fur trade from the St. Lawrence posts were erected at the mouths of the Rupert, Moose, and Albany rivers on James Bay and at the mouth of the Hayes River on the west side of Hudson Bay. After returning to French allegiance and capturing the governor of the Hudson's Bay Co. (1682), Radisson switched back to the company (1684). A French force under **Pierre le Moyne, Sieur d'Iberville** (1661–1706), captured the three James Bay posts (1686), leaving the English with lone posts at the mouth of the Hayes and the Severn. The French followed up their success with the setting up of two posts to the north, on Lake Abitibi (1686) and Lake Nipigon (1684).

1684–87. LA SALLE'S ATTEMPT TO SETTLE ON THE GULF. With a view to reaching the Spanish mines and establishing a base of operations against the Spaniards on the Gulf of Mexico (Spain and France were at war, Oct. 1683–Aug. 1684), La Salle sailed from France (July 1684) with a small fleet to the Gulf, failed to find the mouth of the Mississippi, landed at Matagorda Bay, Tex. (Jan. 1685), continued on foot in an attempt to reach Canada, and was murdered by his rebellious men on the banks of the Brazos (1687).

1684–89. RENEWED IROQUOIS HOSTILITIES. Encouraged by Gov. Thomas Dongan of New York, the Iroquois raided as far west as the Mississippi and across Lakes Erie and Ontario into the Huron country (1684), breaking the chain of trade that stretched along the lakes (by 1686). Nicolas Perrot conducted an ineffectual campaign against them (1687). In retaliation the Iroquois raided the St. Lawrence Valley (1688–89), slaughtering 200 at Lachine (Aug. 1689) and taking 90 prisoners.

The First Two Intercolonial Wars

FRENCH ADVANTAGES. (1) Centralized control, contrasted with colonial decentralization and lack of unity; (2) strategically placed forts; (3) an army considered the most formidable on the European continent; (4) Indian alliances, extending from the Abenakis in Maine to the Algonquin in Wisconsin and north toward Hudson Bay; (5) *coureurs du bois* familiar with forests and trails in the area of conflict.

ENGLISH ADVANTAGES. (1) Overwhelming numerical superiority (over 100,000 in New England alone contrasted with 12,000 in New France, 1688); (2) the Iroquois alliance; (3) marked naval superiority in combination with the Dutch; (4) trading and financial superiority.

1689, 12 MAY–1697, 20 SEPT. KING WILLIAM'S WAR (WAR OF THE LEAGUE OF AUGSBURG). The European phase of the war broke out first when William III joined the League of Augsburg and the Netherlands (Grand Alliance, 12 May 1689) to resist Louis XIV's invasion of the Rhenish Palatinate (25 Sept. 1688). In America hostilities broke out between the English and French on Hudson Bay and between the Iroquois and the French in the area from the Mohawk to the St. Lawrence. The French under Frontenac (returned as governor, Oct. 1689) struck with their Indian allies along the northern frontier, with raids on Schenectady (9 Feb. 1690), Salmon Falls, N.H. (27 Mar.), and Falmouth (Portland, Me., 31 July), followed by Abenaki raids on Wells, Me. (21 June 1692), Durham, N.H. (23 June 1694), and Haverhill, Mass. (15 Mar. 1697). On the western frontier Frontenac attacked the Iroquois (1693–

96). On the part of the English the only successful colonial operation was the seizure of **Port Royal** (11 May 1690) by an expedition of Massachusetts troops under **Sir William Phips** (1651–95), recaptured a year later by the French. The 3-pronged attack on the St. Lawrence projected at the Albany Conference (p. 55) failed (3 Aug.–23 Oct. 1690). Iberville ousted the English from their Hudson Bay posts at the mouths of the Severn (1690) and the Hayes (1694), but the English recaptured the James Bay area (1693). The inconclusive **Treaty of Ryswick** (30 Sept. 1697) restored the *status quo ante* in the colonies and turned the Hudson Bay dispute over to commissioners, who reached no agreement (1699).

1698–1702. FRENCH SETTLEMENT OF LOUISIANA. Fearing an influx of English traders into the West following a French order (1696) closing the western posts (owing to a glutted fur market; rescinded, 1699), the French were determined to secure the Mississippi Valley. A Sulpician mission was established at **Cahokia** (near present East St. Louis, 1699) and a Jesuit post at the mouth of the junction of the **Kaskaskia** and the Mississippi (1703). To protect the route to this region forts were built at Mackinac (1700) and Detroit (1701). Iberville established Ft. Maurepas on Biloxi Bay (1699), but the colony was moved (1702) to Ft. Louis on the Mobile River.

1702, 4 MAY–1713, 11 APR. QUEEN ANNE'S WAR (WAR OF THE SPANISH SUCCESSION). To prevent the close cooperation, if not the amalgamation, of France and Spain on the death of Charles II of Spain (1 Nov. 1700), the Grand Alliance (7 Sept. 1701) declared war on France (4 May 1702). In **New England** the war followed the pattern of the previous conflict. The Abenakis raided Maine settlements (10 Aug. 1703), destroyed Deerfield, Mass. (28–29 Feb. 1704), and attacked Winter Harbor, Me. (21 Sept. 1707). To eliminate the source of Abenaki supplies and seize control of the Acadian fisheries, a force of 500 New Englanders under Col. Benjamin Church destroyed the French villages of Minas and Beaubassin (1, 28 July 1704). After 2 unsuccessful sieges of Port Royal (1704, 1707), a third expedition under Col. **Francis Nicholson** and **Sir Charles Hobby** reduced that stronghold (16 Oct. 1710). In **Newfoundland,** a mixed force of French and Indians operating out of Placentia destroyed an English settlement at Bonavista (18–29 Aug. 1704), and as a result of the capture of St. Johns (21 Dec. 1708) brought the eastern shore under French control. In the **South** the Carolina assembly authorized (10 Sept. 1702) an expedition to seize St. Augustine before it could be reinforced by the French. A mixed force of 500 colonists and Indians seized, burned, and pillaged the town (Dec.) after failing to capture the fort. Another mixed force under former Gov. James Moore destroyed all but one of the 14 missions in the Apalachee country (1704), opening the road to Louisiana. But the Carolinians were unable to penetrate the Choctaw screen protecting French Gulf settlements. By the **Treaty of Utrecht** (11 Apr. 1713) Newfoundland, Acadia, and Hudson Bay were ceded to Great Britain, but France retained Cape Breton Island and the islands of the St. Lawrence. The failure to define the boundaries of Acadia, Hudson Bay, and the interior of the continent left the door open to later conflict. Great Britain was also accorded (26 Mar.) the **Assiento,** a contract allowing the South Sea Co. (formed 1711) to import into the Spanish colonies 4,800 Negroes a year for 30 years and to send 1 trading ship a year to the Spanish colonies.

Interlude Between Wars, 1713–39

1718–29. FRENCH EXPANSION ON MISSISSIPPI. Prosperity in Louisiana was supported by the profits of John Law's Company of the Indies given royal permission to develop the Mississippi Valley. The founding of **New Orleans** (Nov. 1718) by **Jean Baptiste le Moyne, Sieur de Bienville,** brother of Iberville, marked intensive French expansion. Forts were erected at the mouths of the Kaskaskia and the Illinois (1720, 1726) and on the north bank of the Missouri (1723), and settlers from Canada relocated in the Illinois country (c.1735). Following initial success with the Indians in the South (Ft. Toulouse erected among the Creeks on the Alabama River), the French were on the defensive as the result of being outbid by Carolina traders. The Yazoo and Natchez joined the Chickasaws in attacking French settlements (1729), ultimately confining the French to the Louisiana Valley area.

1715–28. THE CAROLINA FRONTIER: THE YAMASSEE WAR. Pressed by South Carolina settlers given large coastal grants for cattle ranches, the Yamassees joined the Lower Creeks, resentful of Carolinian trading practices, and raided the area northwest of Port

Royal, ultimately ousting the Carolina traders from the entire area west of the Savannah. With the aid of the Cherokee located at the headwaters of the Savannah, the Carolinians defeated the Yamassees (Jan. 1716) and by spring had almost eliminated the Creeks from their frontier. Forts were built at present Columbia and Port Royal (1718) and, as a defense against the French and Spaniards, on the Altamaha, the Savannah, and the Santee (1716–21) despite Spanish protests. A brief **Anglo-Spanish War** (Feb. 1727–Mar. 1728) served as a pretext for the Carolinians to stage a deep march into Florida to destroy a Yamassee village near St. Augustine (9 Mar. 1728).

1732–52. FOUNDING OF GEORGIA. James Edward Oglethorpe (p. 1117), a Tory member of Parliament (since 1722), concerned with the problems of pauperism, relief for imprisoned debtors, imperial trade, and naval supremacy, received, along with 19 associates, including John, Viscount Perceval (first Earl of Egmont), a charter (20 June 1732), conferring upon them as **trustees** for 21 years the right to settle the area between the Savannah and Altamaha rivers, originally part of South Carolina, but retained by the crown when the Carolinas were surrendered by the proprietors (1729). The charter granted liberty of conscience to all except Catholics and limited individual grants to 500 acres. Sailing with the first group of settlers, Oglethorpe founded **Savannah** (12 Feb. 1733). During the first year the trustees prohibited the importation or use of rum or brandy as well as slaves. Gradually the landholding restrictions were relaxed. Seven-year tenancies were permitted on new land, size of holdings increased from 500 to 2,000 acres (1740), original grants in tail male (inalienable and restricted to male heirs) to serve as military fiefs were enlarged

to fee simple (1750), rum importation permitted (1742), and, as a result of pressure from Carolinians settling in the province, the prohibition on slavery was repealed (1749). With the last meeting of the trustees (4 July 1752) control of the colony passed to the crown. In support of the project, which combined humanitarian and imperialist features, Parliament had by 1752 appropriated £ 136,608.

1733–39.   MILITARY   PREPARATIONS IN GEORGIA. Oglethorpe set about fortifying the southern frontier, erecting forts on St. Simon's, St. Andrew's, Cumberland, and Amelia islands (by 1739), and founding Augusta on the Savannah and Ft. Okfuskee on the Talapoosa (present Alabama, 1735). A notable achievement was his establishment of peace with the interior tribes, particularly the Creeks (1739).

1719–41.   RIVAL   PREPARATIONS IN THE NORTH. The powerful fortress of Louisbourg on Cape Breton Island (constructed 1720) secured the St. Lawrence approaches, guarded from the south by a new fort at Crown Point on Lake Champlain (1731). To protect the route to the Mississippi (Lake Erie–Maumee–Wabash) the French built Ft. Miami (1704) at the portage, Ft. Ouiataon on the Wabash (c.1719), and Ft. Vincennes (c.1724) on the lower Wabash. Ft. Niagara was built (1720) to secure the lower Great Lakes and serve as a base of operations against the Iroquois. The British countered by establishing Ft. Oswego on Lake Ontario (1725), and New Englanders built forts on the northern frontier against the Abenakis, who, as a result of Jesuit activities, remained loyal to France. In the West, **Pierre Gaultier de Varennes, Sieur de la Vérendrye,** French commander at Lake Nipigon, together with his 3 sons, readied both the Saskatchewan (1734) and the Missouri valleys (1738) for defense.

War of Jenkins' Ear and King George's War

1739–42. WAR OF JENKINS' EAR. Great Britain, aroused by tales of mistreatment of her merchant seamen (notably Robert Jenkins) and other hostile acts (provoked by British abuses of the Assiento and activities of her logwooders on the Honduran coast as well as by the unsettled Florida border), declared war on Spain (19 Oct. 1739). His western flank protected by the friendly Creeks, Cherokee, and Chickasaw, Oglethorpe invaded Florida, captured forts San Francisco de Pupo and Picolata on the San Juan River (Jan. 1740), and besieged St. Augustine (May–July), breaking off when his rear was threatened. A Spanish counterattack was crushed at the **Battle of Bloody Swamp** on St. Simon's Island (1742).

1740–48. KING GEORGE'S WAR (WAR OF THE AUSTRIAN SUCCESSION). The invasion of Silesia by Frederick II of Prussia (16 Dec. 1740) following the death of Emperor Charles VI (20 Oct.) touched off a series of continental wars with France, now allied with Prussia (5 June 1741), invading south-ern Germany. With the signing of the **Second Family Compact** (25 Oct. 1743) between France and Spain, France joined the war against England (15 Mar. 1744). Neither side prosecuted the war in America vigorously. The French made an unsuccessful assault on Annapolis Royal (Port Royal, Nova Scotia, 1744), and an expedition of New Englanders under **William Pepperrell** (1696–1759, Bt., 1746) in cooperation with a fleet under Sir Peter Warren captured Ft. Louisbourg (16 June 1745). The Maine towns were raided by the French and Indians (from Aug. 1745). In New York **William Johnson** (p. 1072), Mohawk Valley Indian trader and commissary of New York for Indian affairs (1746), succeeded in getting the Iroquois on the warpath, with resultant French retaliatory raids on Saratoga (burned, 28–29 Nov. 1745) and Albany. The inconclusive **Treaty of Aix-la-Chapelle** (18 Oct. 1748) restored the *status quo ante* in the colonies and returned Louisbourg to France.

Prelude to the Last War

1748–50. Although their area of effective control was confined to Nova Scotia the British claimed that Acadia included, in addition, present New Brunswick and the Gaspé Peninsula. To strengthen their hold on Nova Scotia Lord Halifax sent out 2,500 settlers (1749) to found the town of **Halifax.**

1744–54. WESTWARD MOVEMENT OF PENNSYLVANIANS AND VIRGINIANS. Ohio Valley traders from Pennsylvania, led by **George Croghan** (c.1718–82) and **Conrad Weiser** (1696–1760), rapidly expanded their posts in the Ohio area and as agents for the Pennsylvania legislature secured the alle-

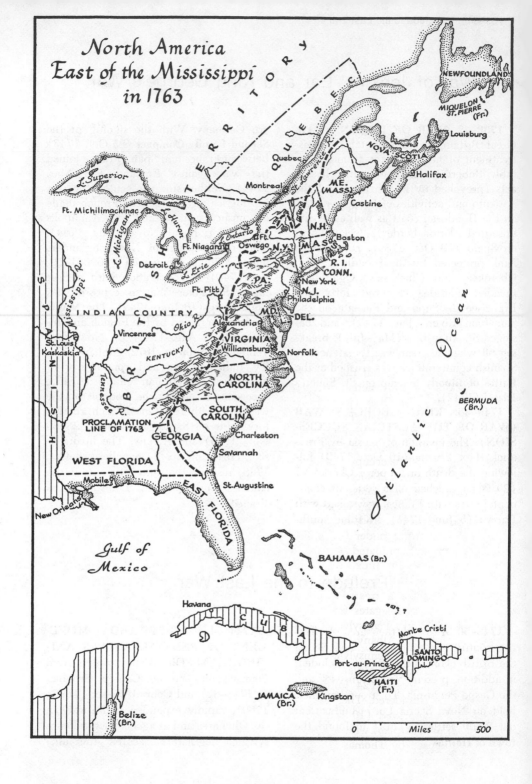

North America
East of the Mississippi
in 1763

giance of the Indians of the area (Aug. 1748). Virginians were equally interested in the area. The Ohio Co. (p. 590) obtained a huge grant on the upper Ohio and sent out **Christopher Gist** (1750) to explore the region. Erection of a trading house at present Cumberland, Md., and trail-blazing activities aroused the French to fortify present Toronto (1749), to divert trade from Oswego, to locate a post at Niagara portage, strengthen Detroit, and dispatch **Céloron de Bienville** to seize the Ohio Valley (1749). In the summer of 1752 the French attacked the trading post of Pickawillany and killed its defenders, and erected Ft. Presque Isle (Erie, Pa.) and Ft. Le Boeuf at the portage to French Creek (spring 1753), and Ft. Venango at the junction of French Creek and the Allegheny. Lt. Gov. **Robert Dinwiddie** (?1693–1770) of Virginia dispatched 21-year-old **George Washington** (p. 1177) to protest these moves and to ascertain French intentions. He visited Ft. Venango and Ft. Le Boeuf (1753), reporting on his return (Jan. 1754) that the French planned to occupy the entire Ohio and could not be removed except by force.

The French and Indian War (Seven Years' War)

1754, 17 APR.–3 JULY. HOSTILITIES BEGIN. To forestall the French, Dinwiddie ordered construction of a fort at the Forks of the Ohio (junction of Allegheny and Monongahela, Feb. 1754), but the French seized the site and erected Ft. Duquesne. Dispatched with an advance party of 150 to occupy that post, Washington, following a successful skirmish with a French reconnaissance party (28 May), constructed Ft. Necessity at Great Meadows. Reinforced, he resisted a larger French force under Coulon de Villiers, but finally capitulated.

1754, 19 JUNE–10 JULY. ALBANY CONGRESS. Advised by the British authorities to make a treaty with the wavering Iroquois, delegates from New England, New York, Pennsylvania, and Maryland met at Albany. **Benjamin Franklin** (p. 1033), a Pennsylvania delegate, who had drawn up a plan of union (Mar. 1751), proposed (24 June) that the subject be considered. The "Plan of Union" finally approved (10 July) was based on Franklin's plan, with additions probably proposed by **Thomas Hutchin-** son (p. 1065), a Massachusetts delegate. The plan called for a union of all the colonies (except Georgia and Nova Scotia) under a president general appointed and paid by the crown. A grand council elected by the colonial assemblies (each colony to have from 2 to 7 delegates, depending on its contribution to the general treasury) was to have legislative power subject to approval by the president general and the crown. President general and grand council were to have jurisdiction over Indian affairs, including new land purchases "not now within the bounds of particular colonies." The plan was rejected both by the colonies and the home government. The Board of Trade countered with a proposal (9 Aug.) for a single commander in chief and a commissary of Indian affairs.

1755, 14 APR.–9 Nov. CAMPAIGNS OF BRADDOCK AND SHIRLEY. Gen. **Edward Braddock** (?1695–1755) arrived in Virginia (14 Apr. 1755) as commander in chief of the British forces in America. At the head of 1,400 British regulars and 450 colonials under Lt. Col. Washington, he headed for Ft. Duquesne. On the Monongahela, about 8 miles below the fort, he was met by a mixed force of 900 French and Indians, surrounded, and defeated at the **Battle of the Wilderness** (9 July). With Braddock mortally wounded, Washington led the remnant back to Ft. Cumberland. Gov. **William Shirley** (1694–1771) of Massachusetts, replacing Braddock in command, was forced to postpone his campaign against Ft. Niagara owing to reinforcements which reached the French when their fleet slipped through a blockade established by Adm. Edward Boscawen (6–13 June). On 19 June Ft. Beauséjour was captured by a force of 2,000 New Englanders and a few British regulars under Colonels Robert Monckton (1726–62) and John Winslow (1703–74). By 30 June the Bay of Fundy area was completely in British hands. William Johnson, commanding a mixed force of 3,500 colonials, chiefly New Englanders, and 400 Indians, began constructing Ft. William Henry on Lake George in anticipation of a French attack. At the **Battle of Lake George** (8 Sept.) he defeated Baron Dieskau's mixed force of 1,400 French and Indian troops. But bad morale among the New England troops prevented Johnson from moving on Crown Point.

1755, JULY–8 OCT. EXPULSION OF THE ACADIANS. Fearing that a French attack would be supported by the Acadians acting as a fifth column, Col. Charles Lawrence, governor of Nova Scotia, announced that all who refused to take the oath of loyalty to the British crown would be expelled (5 Sept.). Embarkation began (8 Oct.). In all some 6,000 Acadians were exiled and distributed among the Thirteen Colonies. Villages at the head of the Bay of Fundy were burned to the ground, but many of the inhabitants escaped to the woods. A

sizable number eventually returned to Nova Scotia.

1756, 16 JAN.–29 AUG. WAR SPREADS TO EUROPE. The European phase of the war began following a new alliance between Britain and Prussia, on the one hand (16 Jan. 1756), and France and Austria, on the other (1 May), with a declaration of war by Great Britain on France (15 May). A British setback at Minorca, which fell 28 June, was matched by continued reversals in America.

1757–58. FURTHER BRITISH SETBACKS IN AMERICA. To command French forces in America **Louis Joseph, Marquis de Montcalm** (1712–59), arrived in Canada with reinforcements (11 May 1756). He was opposed by **John Campbell, Earl of Loudoun,** who arrived in America on 23 July. Montcalm took and destroyed forts Oswego and George (Aug.) and on 9 Aug. 1757 took and demolished Ft. William Henry, whose outnumbered defender, Lt. Col. George Monro, surrendered only to have his force treacherously set upon by the Indians. With 1,400 survivors he reached Ft. Edward. Under orders from Pitt to attack Louisbourg rather than Quebec, Loudoun assembled a large force at Halifax (30 June), but abandoned the attack on learning that the French navy had reached Louisbourg. Rear Adm. Francis Holborne proceeded to bottle up the French in Louisbourg Harbor, but a hurricane smashed the British fleet (24 Sept.). Loudoun's preparations had been hampered by failure to receive wholehearted cooperation from colonial assemblies.

1757. PITT'S WAR LEADERSHIP. French success in Europe continued, with Hanover overrun and three armies converging on Frederick II. With his advent to power in the **Pitt-Newcastle ministry** (29 June) **William Pitt** (1708–78, Earl of Chatham in 1766) committed the government to unlimited warfare, reinforcements in America, and subsidies to the continental allies, necessitating higher taxes and war loans.

1757, 30 DEC.–1758, 18 SEPT. ABERCROMBY IN COMMAND. James Abercromby (1706–81) supplanted Loudoun in command, and assembled about 12,000 troops at Lake George (1 July 1758) for a march on **Ticonderoga.** Electing to defend a low ridge outside the fort, Montcalm, with a greatly outnumbered force of 3,000, threw up breastworks. Abercromby's frontal attack (8 July) was routed by withering fire. The British withdrew with great casualties (464 killed, 29 missing, 1,117 wounded). This disaster was counterbalanced by Maj. Gen. **Jeffrey Amherst** (1717–97), who, with Brig. Gen. **James Wolfe** (1727–59), a fleet of 40 ships, and a force of 9,000 British regulars and 500 colonials, took **Louisbourg** (26 July). Col. **John Bradstreet** (1711–74) took Ft. Frontenac (27 Aug.), and Brig. Gen. **John Forbes** (1710–59), marching along a new road he constructed southwest from Raystown, forced the French to blow up Ft. Duquesne (25 Nov.). With the turn of the tide, Abercromby was relieved of his command (18 Sept.) and Amherst named his successor.

1759. YEAR OF FRENCH DISASTER. Pitt outlined a 3-pronged campaign: (1) to capture Ft. Niagara and reinforce Oswego in order to sever the West from the St. Lawrence; (2) to strike through the Lake Champlain waterway to the St. Lawrence Valley; (3) to launch an amphibious attack against Quebec. **Ft. Niagara** fell (25 July) to a force of 2,000 regulars under Brig. Gen. John Prideaux (killed prior to the capitulation) and 100 Iroquois under Sir William Johnson. Meantime, Col. Frederick Haldimand had reinforced Oswego. Outnumbered by British attackers under Amherst the French blew up Ft. Carillon (**Ticonderoga,** 26 July) and Ft. St. Fred-

eric (**Crown Point,** 31 July)—both refortified by Amherst—and retreated down the Richelieu. A combined force of 9,000 troops under Wolfe and a fleet under Rear Adm. Charles Saunders sailed up the St. Lawrence (16 June), anchoring off Bic and St. Barnabé, where Rear Adm. Durell landed a detachment of troops on the Île-aux-Coudres (28 May) and advanced to the Île d'Orléans to await the main force (25 June). Wolfe landed troops on Île d'Orléans (27 June); sent Monckton to occupy Pointe Lévis opposite Quebec, and Brig. Gen. George Townshend (1724–1807) to the north shore (9 July). After the failure of attempts by Montcalm to burn the British fleet (27 July) and by the British to storm the enemy position (31 July), Wolfe dispatched a force under Brig. Gen. James Murray (1719–94) to engage troops above Quebec. On their return (25 Aug.) he decided to attack. While the French were led to expect a major attack from the St. Lawrence, Wolfe moved his troops on the night of 12–13 Sept. upstream in small boats, landing before dawn on the north shore, and made a surprise ascent of the **Plains of Abraham,** a plateau about the city. Unwilling to await reinforcements by a force of 3,000 in the Cap Rouge area, Montcalm engaged the British with 4,500 troops. Superior discipline and arms won the day for the British, who lost only 60 killed and 600 wounded as against 200 killed and 1,200 wounded for the French. But these fatalities included both Wolfe and Montcalm. **Quebec** soon capitulated (18 Sept.).

1760. SURRENDER OF CANADA. Converging on Montreal, Amherst, striking from Lake Ontario, landed at Lachine (6 Sept.); William Haviland, marching north from Crown Point, captured Chambly (1 Sept.); and Gov. James Murray, pressing down from Quebec, made a junction with the others massed before Montreal, forcing Pierre François de Rigaud, Marquis de Vaudreuil, Governor of Canada, to surrender the entire province (8 Sept.). Maj. **Robert Rogers** (1731–95) took possession of Detroit and other Great Lakes posts (1760–61).

1761–62. INVOLVEMENT OF SPAIN. Apprehensive that a British victory would upset the balance of colonial power, Spain prepared to throw her weight on the side of France and Austria. Anticipating attack, Great Britain declared war (2 Jan. 1762). Martinique, principal French base in the lesser Antilles, fell to the British (15 Feb. 1762), followed by St. Lucia and Grenada, and, after a 2-month siege, Havana capitulated (12 Aug.). Manila fell (5 Oct.) to a second fleet operating in the Far East. To compensate Spain for her loss, France, anxious to end the war, ceded to her ally, by the secret **Treaty of Fontainebleau** (3 Nov. 1762), all her territory west of the Mississippi as well as the Isle of Orleans (ratified 13 Nov. 1762).

1763, 10 Feb. TREATY OF PARIS ended the west European and colonial phases of the Seven Years' War and the Treaty of Hubertusburg (15 Feb.) concluded its German phase. France ceded to Great Britain all claim to Acadia, Cape Breton, Canada, and the islands of the St. Lawrence, but retained fishing rights on Newfoundland's banks and was given the islands of St. Pierre and Miquelon. France further yielded all territory east of the Mississippi (including the port of Mobile) except the city of New Orleans. Pitt, preferring Canada to the French West Indies for reasons of military security as well as trade, returned to France Martinique, Guadeloupe, and St. Lucia, while St. Vincent, Dominica, and Tobago were restored to Great Britain. France agreed to evacuate her positions in Hanover, restore Minorca to the British, and to the *status quo ante* in India. Cuba was restored to Spain in exchange for East and West Florida, and the British agreed to demolish fortifications on the Honduran coast, but the rights of her logwooders to operate in that area were specifically recognized by Spain.

THE ERA OF THE AMERICAN REVOLUTION, 1763-89

The issue of autonomous rule, articulated by the Albany Congress in 1754, for example, anticipated the rapid upsurge of antimonarchical sentiment on the very eve of the Revolution, sentiment which climaxed in the Declaration of Independence. When it came, the American Revolution was a movement of a colonial people for independence, a forerunner of the anticolonial movements in Latin America, Asia, and Africa. Second, it was a revolt against monarchy, which led to the establishment of a republic. Finally, it was a civil war, fought in each state, county, and village. Unlike later revolutions it was not fought along strictly class lines, as both Patriots and Loyalists recruited support from the landed aristocrats, the merchants engaged in transatlantic and Caribbean trade, the local shopkeepers, the professional people, the mechanics, and the laboring classes, while, in addition, the Loyalists had a following among tenant farmers and in certain frontier areas. The fact that the leadership of the American Revolution was upper class and moderate served to prevent conditions deteriorating to a state of terror, such as would blemish the subsequent revolution in France.

The American Revolution created a new nation conceived on republican principles, formulating new tenets governing the relation of men to government under the broad rubric of constitutionalism, inaugurating far-reaching democratic reforms, effective self-government, and acting as a spur to social and economic equality. It tested the establishment of a durable union spread out over a large extent of territory and governed along republican lines, one which would preserve to the states the powers of internal police but concede to the Congress the powers over war and peace and foreign affairs. The first formal constitution, the Articles of Confederation, attempted to define the relation of the whole and the parts in the new federal system. Its deficiencies spawned the movement for greater centralization of powers, without sacrificing the federal principle or jeopardizing the inherent rights of the people.

1763

7 Oct. PROCLAMATION OF 1763.
The French and Indian War had revealed the insecurity of the frontiers
against Indian raids. The first step in
placating the Indians was the appointment by Gen. Braddock of **Sir William
Johnson** as Indian Commissioner (Apr.
1755) and his reappointment as Commissioner for the North (spring 1756).
Since land frauds were believed to lie
at the root of Indian unrest Johnson's
secretary, Peter Wraxall, urged (9 Jan.
1756) that henceforth land cessions require the approval of the Indian commissioners. By the **Treaty of Easton**
(Oct. 1758) with its western Indians
Pennsylvania agreed to make no settlements west of the Alleghenies. However,
the abandonment of Ft. Duquesne (24
Nov.) and its occupation by the British
resulted in an influx of settlers, compelling Col. **Henry Bouquet** (1719–65) to
forbid settlement west of the mountains
(13 Oct. 1761). The Earl of Egremont
as Secretary of State for the Southern
Dept. required royal approval for land
grants in or adjacent to Indian territory
(2 Dec.). To **William Petty, Lord Shelburne,** head of the Board of Trade in
the Halifax-Grenville-Egremont ministry,
was assigned the formulation of a policy
for the newly acquired territory in North
America resulting from the Treaty of
Paris. Shelburne recommended (8 June
1763) that the Appalachians constitute
the dividing line between the settlers
and an Indian reservation save for a
projected colonial settlement in the upper Ohio and some provision for Indian
settlement east of that line. Out of the
newly acquired territory 3 new provinces were to be created: (1) Quebec;
(2) East Florida; (3) West Florida, with
boundaries confined within modest limits
in no way encroaching upon the Thirteen Colonies. News of an Indian crisis
reached the British ministry in August.
Before the plan was put into effect Shelburne was replaced (2 Sept.) by the
less-experienced **Earl of Hillsborough,** a
close associate of Halifax, who prepared
a proclamation which modified Shelburne's proposal by omitting provision
for upper Ohio settlement and ordering
colonists already settled in that area
"forthwith to remove themselves." Purchases of land from the Indians east of
the line were forbidden. Indian territory
west of the line was placed under the
control of the military commander in
chief in America. English law was established in Quebec, a provision deemed
unfair and anti-Catholic by French settlers. The proclamation was rushed
through the cabinet and Privy Council
and signed by the king (7 Oct.).

7 May–28 Nov. PONTIAC'S REBEL-
LION. Following the surrender of Detroit to the English under Maj. Robert
Rogers (29 Nov. 1760), the Indians demanded that the British authorities lower
prices on trade goods and furnish them
with ammunition. When these demands
were not met at a conference at Detroit
(9 Sept. 1761) the Indians grew increasingly restive, stirred up by the Delaware
Prophet, a visionary living in the upper
Ohio, and by his disciple, **Pontiac**
(c.1720–69), chief of the Ottawa. After
his plan to take Detroit by a surprise
attack was betrayed (May), Pontiac took
to open warfare. Within a few weeks
every British post west of Niagara was
destroyed (Sandusky, 16 May; Ft. St.
Joseph, 25 May; Ft. Miami, 27 May; Ft.
Ouiatenon, 1 June; Ft. Venango, c.16
June; Ft. Le Boeuf, 18 June; Ft.
Presque Isle, 20 June), save for Detroit,
which, under Maj. Henry Gladwin, resisted a 5-month siege, and Ft. Pitt,
under Capt. Simeon Ecuyer. In retaliation Amherst proposed to Bouquet that
"Small pox" be sent among the disaffected tribes, and the latter replied that

he would try to distribute germ-laden blankets among them, but, because of the danger of exposure to British troops, preferred hunting the Indians "with English dogs" (13 July). As a result of reinforcements which reached Detroit (29 July), Gladwin made a sortie against Pontiac and was repulsed at **Bloody Ridge** (31 July). Marching to the relief of Ft. Pitt, Bouquet defeated (with heavy British losses) and routed the Indians at **Bushy Run,** east of present Pittsburgh (2–6 Aug.), and relieved the fort (10 Aug.). In Nov. Pontiac raised his siege of Detroit. A number of tribes had already signed treaties with Col. John Bradstreet at Presque Isle (12 Aug. 1764). Pontiac finally submitted, concluding a peace treaty with Sir William Johnson at Oswego (24 July 1766). Subsequently he remained loyal to the British, but was murdered (1769) in Cahokia (Ill.), according to Parkman's version, by a Kaskaskia Indian bribed by an English trader.

5 Nov.–1 Dec. PARSON'S CAUSE. This case was the result of legislation in Virginia regulating salaries of Anglican ministers, which, from 1662, had by law been paid in tobacco, varying with the market value of that commodity. Owing to failure of the tobacco crop as a result of drought, the legislature (Oct. 1755) commuted such pay into currency at the rate of 2d. per lb.; reenacted, 1758. Acting on memorials from the Virginia clergy the Privy Council disallowed the act (10 Aug. 1759). As a result the clergy proceeded to sue for back salary even though the act had not been declared null and void *ab initio.* Most publicized was the case brought by Rev. **James Maury** in Hanover Co. Court. The bench held that the 1758 act was "no law," but a jury (swayed by the rhetoric of young **Patrick Henry** [p. 1057], who declared that by disallowing the act the king had broken the compact

between the governed and the ruler, thereby forfeiting "all rights to his subjects' obedience") returned a verdict of 1d. for plaintiff. The action of the General Court (10 Apr. 1764) in giving judgment against the clergy was affirmed by the Privy Council (3 Dec. 1766).

13–27 Dec. FRONTIER DISORDER IN PENNSYLVANIA: THE PAXTON BOYS. As a result of the insecurity of the frontier against Indian attacks (1754–63), a mob from Paxton and Donegal attacked the peaceful Conestoga Indians in Lancaster Co. The assembly, which had failed to respond to the demand of frontiersmen for protection, ordered that the "Paxton Boys" be arrested and brought to Philadelphia for trial. Instead, the frontiersmen marched east, but were persuaded by Franklin to forego battle, and issued a formal protest by which they obtained greater representation in the legislature.

1764

5 Apr. REVENUE FROM AMERICA. Faced by a large postwar debt, heavy taxes at home, and the necessity of supporting an army in America, the ministry of the Earl of Bute sought revenue from the colonies. When the debate on the 1764 budget opened in the House of Commons (9 Mar.), the Chancellor of the Exchequer, George Grenville, presented an American Revenue Act (generally known as the **Sugar Act**) to become the first law ever passed by Parliament for the specific purpose of raising moneys in the colonies for the crown. The act (1) extended the Molasses Act of 1733 but reduced the 6d.-per-gallon duty upon foreign molasses to 3d., the old rate on raw sugar was continued, and an increased duty levied on foreign refined sugar; (2) placed new or higher import duties on non-British textiles, coffee, and indigo, and on Madeira and Canary wines imported directly; (3) doubled the duties on foreign goods reshipped in England to the colonies; (4) added iron, hides, whale fins, raw silk, potash, and pearl ash to the enumerated list; (5) banned the import into the colonies of foreign rum and French wines. Grenville estimated that the act, if efficiently administered, would return c. £ 45,000 annually.

ENDING SALUTARY NEGLECT. More significant was Grenville's determination to enforce the trade laws by revitalizing the customs service (at that time the American customs returned little more than one fourth [£ 2,000] the cost of collecting them). A companion measure provided for tighter enforcement by (1) establishing a vice-admiralty court at Halifax with jurisdiction over all the American colonies and enabling prosecutors and informers to bring suit there at their option rather than in local colonial courts; (2) annulling the right of an accused to sue for illegal seizure; (3) placing the burden of proof upon the accused and obliging him to post bond for the cost of the trial; and (4) establishing stricter registration and bonding procedures for ships carrying nonenumerated as well as enumerated cargoes. Grenville ended the practice under which American customs officials were permitted to live in England and entrust their duties to a deputy in the colonies.

CURRENCY ACT widened the scope of colonial opposition as it affected the plantation as well as the commercial provinces. Aimed principally at Virginia, which had issued £ 250,000 of legal-tender paper money during the war, the act prohibited after 1 Sept. issues of legal-tender currency in all the American colonies (thereby extending the ban already operative in New England since 1751), as well as any extension of the recall date for outstanding issues. To

guard against evasion, the act nullified all acts of colonial assemblies contrary to its terms and provided for a fine of £ 1,000 and dismissal from office (with ineligibility for any government position in the future) of any colonial governor who assented to legislative acts in defiance of the law.

COLONIAL OPPOSITION. To Americans already distressed by a marked postwar business decline, the Grenville program, by combining higher imposts and strict enforcement with the severe deflationary shock of the Currency Act, seemed calculated to ruin the colonial economy. Massachusetts led the way in protest. A Boston town meeting (24 May) denounced taxation without representation and proposed united action by the colonies in protest. The House of Representatives authorized a Committee of Correspondence (13 June) to contact the other provinces. In Aug. Boston merchants agreed to do without English lace and ruffles, an example which the town's mechanics followed (Sept.) in pledging to wear no leather work clothes not of Massachusetts make. By the end of the year **nonimportation** had spread to other colonies, notably New York.

1765

QUARTERING ACT. Requested by Gen. Thomas Gage, commander of the British forces in America, and not an integral part of the Grenville program, the Quartering Act added fuel to the rising fire of American resentment. Effective 24 Mar. for a 2-year term, the act required the civil authorities in the colonies to supply barracks and supplies for the British troops. A second act (1766) provided for quartering and billeting in inns, alehouses, and unoccupied dwellings.

22 Mar. STAMP ACT, the first direct tax ever levied by Parliament upon

America, was designed to raise £60,000 annually, which, together with the return from the 1764 imposts, would produce an American return equal to about one third the £300,000 upkeep of the colonial military establishment. The act (passed the Commons, 27 Feb., the Lords, 8 Mar., to become effective 1 Nov.) placed a tax upon newspapers, almanacs, pamphlets and broadsides, legal documents of all types, insurance policies, ship's papers, licenses, and even dice and playing cards. The receipts were to be paid into the royal exchequer for the defense of the colonies. With the sensibilities of the colonists in mind Grenville appointed Americans to be the stamp agents. Penalties for infringements could be imposed by courts of vice-admiralty (which had no jury) as well as by colonial common-law courts.

STAMP ACT CRISIS. Factors underlying the virtually unanimous opposition to the act were (1) the novelty of direct taxation by Parliament and the fear that this tax was to be but the first of many; (2) its all-inclusive character transcended sectionalism; (3) by affecting groups which carried great weight throughout the colonies (lawyers, printers, tavern owners, and land speculators as well as merchants and shipowners) the act broadened the base of the opposition; (4) the grant of jurisdiction to vice-admiralty courts raised fears of an assault upon the right to trial by jury; and (5) the imposition of the tax at a time of economic stagnation and currency stringency convinced many that Britain was deliberately aiming to weaken the colonies.

NEW POLITICAL THEORIES. In 1764 James Otis (p. 1120) had raised the issue of no taxation without representation. But the Stamp Act impelled other American writers to draw distinctions aimed at establishing the measure's illegality. Widely read and quoted was the argument advanced (*Considerations*) by Daniel Dulany, a Maryland attorney, conceding the right of Parliament to regulate trade, even when such acts produced a revenue, but denying its authority to impose internal taxes for revenue upon the colonists inasmuch as the Americans were not and by their situation could not be represented in Parliament. The same distinction was expressed more militantly in the Virginia Resolutions (29 May) introduced before the House of Burgesses by **Patrick Henry** with the "Treason" speech in which he warned George III to note the fate of Cæsar and Charles I. Asserting that the right of Virginia to govern its internal affairs had always been recognized by the crown, the resolutions claimed for the province's general assembly the sole power to tax Virginians. Upon further deliberation (30–31 May) the House rejected the more radical of these claims, contenting itself with stating that Virginians in the past had legislated respecting their own internal polity and approving the principle of no taxation without representation. Henry's complete set of resolutions were, however, published in the colonial newspapers.

SONS OF LIBERTY. During the summer of 1765 secret organizations known as the Sons of Liberty (the term had been used by Colonel Isaac Barré in a speech against the Stamp Act in the House of Commons) were formed in the provincial towns to organize the opposition to the Stamp Act. Often organized, sometimes personally led (as in New York City) by men of wealth and high position, these groups did not hesitate to resort to violence to force stamp agents to resign their posts and merchants to cancel orders for British goods. A notorious instance occurred in Boston on 26 Aug., when the records of the vice-admiralty court were burned, the home of the comptroller of the currency ransacked, and the elegant home and library of Chief Justice Thomas Hutchinson looted. The Boston stamp agent, Andrew Oliver (Hutchinson's brother-in-law), had been forced by mob violence to resign 15 Aug. Before the effective date of the Stamp Act (1 Nov.) all the stamp agents in the colonies had resigned.

7–25 OCT. STAMP ACT CONGRESS. Upon the motion of James Otis, the Massachusetts assembly resolved (6 June) to propose an intercolonial meeting to seek relief from the Stamp Act. A circular letter was dispatched to each colonial assembly (8 June) suggesting that a congress meet at New York City in Oct. South Carolina endorsed the proposal promptly (2 Aug.), followed by Rhode Island, Connecticut, Pennsylvania, and Maryland. The assemblies of New Jersey, Delaware, and New York failed to take formal action, but were represented by delegates chosen informally. The other 4 provinces failed to act, and were not represented when the Congress opened.

The moderate character of the Stamp Act Congress was clearly reflected in the "Declaration of Rights and Grievances" (19 Oct.), chiefly the work of **John Dickinson** (p. 1013). In 14 resolutions the delegates claimed all the rights and liberties of the king's subjects in Great Britain, stated that taxation without consent expressed personally or through representatives was a violation of these rights, pointed out that the colonists were not and could not be represented in the House of Commons, and concluded that no taxes could be constitutionally imposed on them but by their own legislatures. Specifically condemned was the provision in the Stamp Act giving jurisdiction to admiralty courts.

Separate petitions embracing these resolutions and demanding repeal of the Stamp Act and the measures of 1764 were prepared for submission to the king, the House of Commons, and the House of Lords before the 27 delegates disbanded. On 11 Feb. 1766 the Northampton, Va., County Court declared the Stamp Act unconstitutional.

ECONOMIC SANCTIONS. The passage of the Stamp Act gave a new impetus to **nonimportation.** In New York City leading citizens signed an agreement (28 Oct.) banning the purchase of European goods until the Stamp Act was repealed and the trade regulations of 1764 modified. Following suit were 200 merchants (31 Oct.), some 400 Philadelphia merchants (Nov.), and 250 Boston merchants (9 Dec.). Business throughout the colonies was generally suspended when the Stamp Act went into effect (1 Nov.), owing to the practically universal refusal to use the stamps. Except in Rhode Island, where Gov. Stephen Hopkins refused to execute the act, the courts also closed rather than use the stamps as the law required. Before the end of the year, however, business was renewed without the stamps in open violation of the act.

BRITISH DEMANDS FOR REPEAL. When the Stamp Act became operative a movement in Britain for its repeal was already well along. Grenville's ministry, which had fallen from power in a crisis over a regency bill (10 July), was succeeded by a government under the Marquis of Rockingham. The decline in British exports to America (from £2,-249,710 in 1764 to £1,944,108 in 1765) spoke more eloquently than colonial resolutions. A committee of merchants, organized to work for the Stamp Act's repeal, called upon some 30 towns in Britain to petition Parliament for repeal. The petition of the London merchants

(17 Jan. 1766) cited several bankruptcies resulting from shrunken American
markets.

1766

**18 MAR. REPEAL OF THE STAMP
ACT.** Parliament met on 14 Jan. and
immediately debated the Stamp Act.
Grenville demanded that the army be
used to enforce it, while William Pitt,
calling for repeal, commended the Americans for disobeying a tax framed by a
body in which they were not represented.
The colonial agents were called before
the Commons sitting as a committee of
the whole (beginning 3 Feb.) to give
their views. The most telling testimony
was given (13 Feb.) by **Benjamin Franklin** (p. 1033), agent for Pennsylvania. He
stressed the heavy expenditures voted
by the colonial assemblies during the
French and Indian War (Pennsylvania
spent £500,000, with a rebate of only
£60,000 from the crown), pointed to
the continuing expenses borne for prosecution of Indian wars, and declared that
the Thirteen Colonies lacked sufficient
specie to pay the stamp taxes for a
single year. He warned that an attempt
to carry out the Stamp Act by the use of
troops might bring on rebellion, endorsed Dulany's distinction between internal and external taxes, and called
for outright repeal.

A bill for full repeal was brought before the Commons by a vote of 275–167
(22 Feb.), passed the House (4 Mar.),
and, as a result of pressure from the
king, passed the Lords (17 Mar.). The
repeal bill, effective 1 May, received the
royal assent 18 Mar. America received
the news (word reached New York 26
Apr.) with rejoicing. Nonimportation
was immediately abandoned; the New
York assembly voted statues to honor
the king and Pitt (30 June).

18 MAR. DECLARATORY ACT. Generally overlooked in the rejoicing over
the Stamp Act's repeal was a statement
of Parliament's authority over America
enacted into law on the same day as the
repeal measure (couched in the same
terms as the Irish Declaratory Act of
1719), and asserting that Parliament
had full authority to make laws binding
the American colonists **"in all cases
whatsoever."**

1. Nov. TRADE LAWS MODIFIED.
The repeal of the Stamp Act was followed by another retreat on the government's part. The 3d. duty on foreign
molasses imported by the colonists was
now withdrawn (effective 1 Nov.) in
favor of a uniform 1d.-per-gallon duty
on all molasses, British as well as foreign,
coming into the continental colonies. Export duties on British West Indian sugar
were removed, thereby reducing its price
on the American mainland. The act contained one notably unfavorable provision: all colonial products shipped to
northern Europe henceforth had to clear
through ports in Great Britain en route.

**NEW YORK AND THE QUARTER-
ING ACT CRISIS.** Through Gov. Sir
Henry Moore (1713–69) Gen. Gage requested (13 Dec. 1765) that the New
York assembly make provision for quartering and supplying his troops in accord
with the Quartering Act. The assembly,
contending that his act weighed heaviest
upon their province (New York was
Gage's headquarters), refused full compliance (Jan. 1766). Tension mounted
through the spring and summer. The
destruction of a liberty pole by British
soldiers (10 Aug.) led to a clash on the
following day between citizens and
bayonet-wielding redcoats in which
Isaac Sears (c.1730–86), a leader of the
Sons of Liberty, was wounded. On 15
Dec. the assembly refused any appropriations for Gage's forces and was pro-

rogued (19 Dec.). Not until 6 June 1767 did the assembly vote £ 3,000. Ignorant of this step, Parliament suspended the assembly's legislative powers (effective 1 Oct. 1767), but due to the grant of 6 June the suspension was not carried out by the governor. On 7 May 1768 the Board of Trade sustained his decision by declaring invalid acts of the assembly after 1 Oct. 1767.

1767

29 June. TOWNSHEND ACTS. When the Chatham ministry came into office (Aug. 1766) Charles Townshend became Chancellor of the Exchequer. By the beginning of 1767, due to Lord Chatham's illness, Townshend was the actual leader of the government. In Jan., he attacked the distinction Americans (and Chatham himself, then William Pitt) had made between external and internal taxation and revealed that he was preparing a new revenue measure to free the administration of government in America from dependence on colonial assemblies. A reduction in the British land tax, carried in defiance of the ministry (27 Feb.), made it imperative to carry out this pledge, for that revision involved a cut of £ 500,000 in home revenue.

The Townshend Acts conformed to the American position of 1765–66: the taxes were all **external**: import duties on glass, lead, paints, paper, and tea. The estimated annual return of £ 40,000 could be used (according to the bill's preamble) not only for the defense of the colonies but also for "defraying the charge of the administration of justice, and the support of civil government" in America. To provide for efficient collection of the new duties this bill and a companion measure (1) clearly affirmed the power of superior or supreme court justices to issue writs of assistance; (2)

established new vice-admiralty courts; and (3) an American Board of Commissioners of the Customs at Boston, directly responsible to the British Treasury Board. The acts received the royal assent on 29 June and became effective 20 Nov.

28 Oct. REVIVAL OF NONIMPORTATION. Once more the colonists turned to nonimportation to force Parliament to retreat again. A Boston town meeting (28 Oct.) drew up a list of British products, chiefly luxury goods, which were not to be purchased after 31 Dec. In Providence a stringent nonimportation agreement was signed (2 Dec.) to become effective 1 Jan. 1768; Newport followed suit (4 Dec.); and a mass meeting in New York City (29 Dec.) appointed a committee to draw up a plan to promote domestic industry and employment.

5. Nov. FARMER'S LETTERS. The most significant statement of the constitutional basis for the opposition to the Townshend Acts was written by John Dickinson. First appearing in the *Pennsylvania Chronicle* (5 Nov. 1767–Jan. 1768), his 14 essays, entitled "Letters From a Farmer in Pennsylvania to the Inhabitants of the British Colonies," were widely reprinted in pamphlet form both in Britain and America during 1768. Dickinson conceded Parliament's authority to regulate trade, even if revenue was incidentally produced, but denied its right to tax in order to raise a revenue in America, declared the Townshend duties unconstitutional, and assailed the suspension of the New York assembly as a blow to the liberties of all the colonies.

1768

11 Feb. MASSACHUSETTS CIRCULAR LETTER, drawn up by **Samuel Adams** (p. 972) and approved by the Massachusetts House of Representatives, informed the assemblies of the other 12 colonies of the steps taken by the Massachusetts General Court, denounced the Townshend Acts as violating the principle of no taxation without representation, reasserted the impossibility of representing America adequately in the British Parliament, attacked any move by the crown to make colonial governors and judges independent of the people, and concluded by soliciting proposals for united action. Gov. Francis Bernard (1712–79) condemned the circular letter as seditious and on 4 Mar. dissolved the General Court. This view was shared by the Secretary of State for the Colonies, Lord Hillsborough, who, in a dispatch to the colonial governors (21 Apr.), denounced the letter and ordered that their respective assemblies be prevented, by dissolution if necessary, from endorsing it. This order came too late. By May the assemblies of New Hampshire, New Jersey, and Connecticut had commended the stand of Massachusetts, and Virginia had drafted its own circular letter advising support of Massachusetts. On 22 Apr. Hillsborough ordered Gov. Bernard to dissolve the new General Court should the House of Representatives refuse to rescind the circular letter. Bernard ordered the House to expunge the resolution embodying the letter from its journal (21 June), but after a protracted debate the representatives voted 92–17 (30 June) to defy this command. The court was then dissolved (1 July). The 17 "Rescinders" came under heavy attack by the Sons of Liberty; 7 lost their seats in the election of May 1769.

10 June. SEIZURE OF THE "LIBERTY." Meanwhile, the obstructionist tactics of the people of Boston had led the customs commissioners there to request an armed force to protect them in carrying out their duties (Feb.); repeated in a memorial to the ministry 28 Mar. From Halifax the frigate *Romney*, 50 guns, was dispatched to Boston. Its arrival (17 May) made the customs officials overconfident. When they were informed (9 June) that a wharf official had been locked in a cabin of John Hancock's sloop *Liberty* while Madeira wine was landed without payment of duty, they ordered the seizure of Hancock's vessel (10 June). The *Liberty* was towed from her wharf and anchored close to the *Romney*. A crowd assaulted the customs officials on the dock and demonstrated before their homes. The next day (11 June) the customs officials fled to Castle William on an island in the harbor and again (15 June) appealed for troops.

1 Oct. BRITISH TROOPS IN BOSTON. On 12 Sept. the Boston town meeting, on the alleged ground of an imminent war with France, called upon the people to arm and requested the governor to call the General Court into session. When he refused, 96 Massachusetts towns sent delegates to an informal provincial convention (23–28 Sept.), which broke up the very day British troopships arrived in the harbor. Despite threats of armed resistance made by the Sons of Liberty, 2 regiments of infantry with artillery landed without opposition (1 Oct.) and stationed in the town.

PROGRESS OF NONIMPORTATION. Boston merchants adopted (Mar.) a more stringent nonimportation agreement contingent upon similar action by New York and Philadelphia. In New York such an agreement was signed in Apr. (effective 1 Oct.), but meetings in Philadelphia (Mar.-June) failed to yield a similar compact. Thereupon the Boston merchants drew up their own plan (1 Aug.) barring the importation of the items bearing the Townshend duties from 1 Jan. 1769 until the duties were repealed, and of all but a brief list of British goods (mostly supplies for the

was averted only when Lt. Gov. Hutchinson bowed to a demand by Sam Adams and withdrew the troops from the town to islands in the harbor. Preston and 8 of his men were arrested for murder by the civil authorities (6 Mar.). Two outstanding Patriot lawyers, **John Adams** (p. 971) and **Josiah Quincy** (1744–75), agreed to undertake the defense. At the trial (24–30 Oct.) Preston and 6 soldiers were acquitted, while 2 of the guard, found guilty of manslaughter, pleaded their clergy (were branded on the hand) and were released.

1771

LULL IN AGITATION. Despite exploitation of the "Boston Massacre" by Sam Adams as well as Paul Revere's engraving of the incident, tension relaxed between colonies and mother country. Compacts against the importation and use of dutied tea remained the sole significant vestiges of conflict.

16 MAY. BATTLE OF ALAMANCE. In interior North Carolina a group known as the **Regulators,** active as an organized body since 1768 (under the leadership of **Herman Husbands** [1724–95]), had taken the law into their own hands, protesting lack of representation for the Piedmont areas in the assembly and charging extortion and oppression by the eastern part of the province. Increasing disorders led to the passage of the Johnston Bill (the "Bloody Act"), which made rioters guilty of treason (15 Jan. 1771). Early in May Gov. **William Tryon** (1729–88) led a force of 1,200 militiamen into the heart of the Regulator country. On 16 May he met and crushed some 2,000 Regulators (many of whom had no firearms) at Alamance Creek near Hillsboro. One insurgent leader, James Few, was executed on the battlefield (17 May); 12 others were found guilty of treason (17 June) and

6 executed. The other 6 as well as some 6,500 Piedmont settlers were obliged to take an oath of allegiance to the government. The incident revealed deep-seated sectional differences, also reflected in South Carolina, where the grievances of a vigilante movement, also called Regulators, who had protested lawlessness on the frontier, were largely met in 1769 when courts were set up in the back country.

1772

9 JUNE. BURNING OF THE "GAS-PEE." On the afternoon of 9 June the customs schooner *Gaspee* ran aground on Namquit Point, 7 miles below Providence, while pursuing another vessel. After nightfall 8 boatloads of men from Providence led by merchant **John Brown** (1736–1803) attacked the schooner. Lt. William Duddingston, in command, was wounded. After the officer and crew were set ashore, the attackers set the *Gaspee* afire. A royal proclamation (26 Aug.) offered a £500 reward for the discovery of the culprits. On 2 Sept. Gov. Joseph Wanton (R.I.), the vice-admiralty judge at Boston, and the chief justices of Massachusetts, New York, and New Jersey were named as Commissioners of Inquiry. Those identified by the commissioners were to be sent to England for trial. Two sessions were held at Newport (Jan. and May 1773) but, in the face of open hostility by Rhode Islanders, neither turned up any tangible evidence. The commission finally adjourned June 1773.

13 JUNE. CRIPPLING THE POWER OF THE PURSE. The proposal to try the case of the *Gaspee* in England alarmed even the moderates. More threatening to local self-rule was the announcement by Gov. Hutchinson of Massachusetts (13 June) that henceforth he would receive his salary from the crown, followed in Sept. by a similar an-

nouncement relative to the Massachusetts judges. Thus executive and judiciary were at a stroke rendered practically independent of the General Court's power of the purse.

2 Nov. NEW COMMITTEES OF CORRESPONDENCE. Sam Adams issued a call (5 Oct.) to the towns to form associations to discuss this new threat. Over considerable opposition (led by John Hancock) within the Patriot circle, he succeeded (28 Oct.) in having a call issued for a Boston town meeting, at which (2 Nov.) he secured the appointment of a 21-man standing Committee of Correspondence to communicate Boston's position to the other towns in the province and "to the World" with the request that the other towns reciprocate. James Otis was made chairman of the Boston committee. On 20 Nov. 3 radical statements were reported from the committee to the town meeting, endorsed, and sent on to the other towns: Sam Adams' "State of the Rights of the Colonists," a "List of Infringements and Violations of those Rights" by **Joseph Warren** (1741–75), and a "Letter of Correspondence" by Dr. **Benjamin Church** (1734–76), later proved to be a British informer. The appointment of town Committees of Correspondence continued into 1773.

1773

EXPANSION OF COMMITTEES OF CORRESPONDENCE. Radicals elsewhere hastened to adopt the Massachusetts system. The Virginia House of Burgesses (12 Mar.) appointed an 11-man standing committee for intercolonial correspondence, including Patrick Henry, **Thomas Jefferson** (p. 1070), and Richard Henry Lee. By 8 July Rhode Island, Connecticut, New Hampshire, and South Carolina, in addition, had formed provincial committees, and by Feb. 1774 all but

North Carolina and Pennsylvania had taken action.

10 MAY. TEA ACT. By early 1773 the East India Co. was on the verge of bankruptcy, its stock down from 280 to 160 on the London exchange. With a vast surplus of 17 million lbs. of tea on hand in England, the company sought relief from a government predisposed to save it because of its valuable hold on India. A bill passed by the Commons (27 Apr.) provided for full remission (after 10 May) of all British duties on teas exported to the American colonies. The import tax of 3d. per lb. in America was retained, however. More important was the provision giving the company (obliged up to this time to sell its tea at public auction in England) the right to sell tea directly to agents or consignees in the colonies. With the drawbacks on the British duties enabling it to cut the price of its tea the company was now in a position, even with the handicap of the 3d. duty in America, to undersell there both the law-abiding colonial merchant who had bought tea through middlemen at higher prices and the colonial smuggler who bought his tea in Holland. The company, authorized (Sept.) to send half a million lbs. of tea to Boston, New York, Philadelphia, and Charleston, consigned the tea to a picked group of merchants.

TERRORIZING THE TEA CONSIGNEES. The American opposition to the Tea Act centered not upon the duty (now 6 years old) but upon the threat of monopoly. A mass meeting in Philadelphia (16 Oct.) condemned the act and appointed a committee to demand resignation of the Philadelphia consignees. The latter bowed to this demand. A Boston town meeting (5–6 Nov.) endorsed the Philadelphia resolves but was unable to secure the resignation of the Boston consignees, among whom were 2 sons and a nephew of Gov.

Hutchinson. In New York City, a broadside (10 Nov.) warned harbor pilots against guiding any tea ship up the harbor. A meeting of the Sons of Liberty (29 Nov.) branded tea importers enemies of America and pledged a boycott. The New York consignees resigned their commissions (1 Dec.).

16 DEC. BOSTON TEA PARTY. The *Dartmouth*, first of 3 tea ships, arrived in Boston harbor 27 Nov. Two mass meetings (29–30 Nov.) resolved that the tea must be sent back to England without payment of any duty. This Hutchinson refused to permit. He gave orders to the harbor authorities to allow the tea ships to pass outward only upon presentation of a permit certifying that the tea duties had been paid, a position he reiterated on 16 Dec. On the next day, in keeping with a 20-day waiting period under customs regulations, the tea aboard the *Dartmouth* became liable to seizure for nonpayment of customs duties. On the evening of the 16th some 8,000 people assembled in and near Boston's Old South Church heard Francis Rotch, the *Dartmouth*'s owner's son, inform Sam Adams, chairman of the meeting, of the governor's final refusal. Thereupon, at a signal from Adams, a disciplined group of men disguised as Mohawk Indians rushed to Griffin's Wharf, boarded the tea ships, and, working through the night, dumped all the tea (342 chests) into the harbor. No other property aboard was damaged.

22 DEC. TEA LANDED AT CHARLESTON. Charleston's tea ship, the *London*, arrived 2 Dec. A mass meeting held the next day demanded and secured the resignations of the tea consignees. After the lapse of the 20-day period the customs officials, without opposition, landed the tea for nonpayment of the duties upon it. The tea was stored in government warehouses and remained there until the revolutionary government auctioned it off to raise funds (July 1776).

DEC. HUTCHINSON LETTERS SCANDAL. Late in 1772 Benjamin Franklin, as London agent for the Massachusetts House of Representatives, sent Speaker Thomas Cushing the originals of 6 letters written (1767–69) by Thomas Hutchinson (then chief justice) and 4 by Andrew Oliver (province secretary) to Thomas Whately, a member of the Grenville and North ministries. The letters were given to Franklin to show him that false advice from America went far toward explaining the obnoxious acts of the British government. Franklin sent the letters to Cushing, warning him that they were not to be copied or published but merely shown in the original to individuals in the province. But in June 1773 Samuel Adams read the letters before a secret session of the House of Representatives and later had the letters copied and printed. The House petitioned the king for the removal of Hutchinson and Oliver from office. When this petition reached London the affair of the letters became a scandal. Whately was now dead, but his brother William accused a John Temple of having stolen and released the letters. The pair fought a duel (11 Dec.), and when that was inconclusive plans were made for another encounter. Learning of this, Franklin announced (25 Dec.) that he alone was responsible for sending the letters to Boston.

1774

30 JAN. FRANKLIN DISCIPLINED. On 11 Jan. a committee of the Privy Council began hearings on the Massachusetts petition. Franklin was granted a postponement. Questioning was resumed on 29 Jan., by which date the news of the Boston Tea Party had reached London. Franklin disdained replying to a virulent attack by Solicitor General Alexander Wedderburn, who denounced Franklin as a man without honor and a thief. The committee's report to the Privy Council that the petition was based on false charges was approved (7 Feb.). On 30 Jan. Franklin was informed that he had been dismissed from his office of Deputy Postmaster General for America. In Massachusetts the House voted in Feb., 92-8, to impeach Oliver for accepting a salary from the crown, but before the case was tried Hutchinson prorogued (30 Mar.), and then dissolved the General Court.

MAR.–DEC. FURTHER TEA DISORDERS. March saw further Boston disorders. When a reckless private consignee elected to land a cargo of tea secretly in New York, Sons of Liberty disguised as Indians dumped the tea into the harbor (22 Apr.). A tea cargo brought into Annapolis aboard the *Peggy Stewart* (14 Oct.) was destroyed by fire along with the ship (19 Oct.). Flames consumed a shipment of tea (22 Dec.) temporarily stored at Greenwich, N.J.

31 MAR., 20 MAY. COERCIVE ACTS. Parliament met (7 Mar.) in an angry mood. Chatham and Edmund Burke failed to dissuade it from endorsing the king's personal wish that Massachusetts be punished for the Tea Party in particular and for its long intransigence in general. The first of the "Coercive" measures, the **Boston Port Bill**, passed the Commons 25 Mar. and received the royal assent 31 Mar. Effective 1 June, this act prohibited the loading or unloading of ships in any part of Boston Harbor. Exceptions were made for military stores and for shipments of food and fuel which obtained clearance from the customs officials henceforth to sit at Salem rather than Boston. The king was authorized to reopen the port to trade when the East India Co. and the customs had been compensated for the losses incurred by the Tea Party.

Two months later more comprehensive measures were enacted. The **Administration of Justice Act** (20 May) was designed to encourage crown officials in Massachusetts by protecting them from major suits before hostile provincial courts. Upon the sworn statement of the governor that the act upon which an indictment for a capital offense was based had been committed in putting down a riot or in collecting revenue, and that a fair trial could not be obtained in Massachusetts, the trial could be transferred to Britain (the provincial council's assent to the move was stipulated).

Massachusetts Government Act (20 May) worked even more drastic changes, virtually annulling the Massachusetts charter. Effective 1 Aug., members of the Council, heretofore elected by the House of Representatives, were to be appointed by the king and hold office at royal pleasure. Effective 1 July, the attorney general, inferior judges, sheriffs, and justices of the peace became appointable and removable by the governor. The governor was also empowered to nominate the chief justice and superior judges for appointment by the king. Juries were to be summoned by the sheriff rather than elected by the people of the towns. Finally, in a move designed to deprive the radicals of their most effective medium, the town meeting, the act provided that meetings in addition to the annual election session could not be held without the prior written consent of the governor and, if approved, must be confined to the agenda which he approved.

20 MAY. QUEBEC ACT, though not a part of the coercive program, was regarded by the colonists as one of the "Intolerable" measures. The act provided a permanent civil government for Can-

ada, ruled since 1763 by makeshift means. In keeping with the French tradition of the inhabitants the administration was made highly centralized. Legislative authority was vested in a council appointed by the crown. Its acts were subject to the royal veto and all but purely local taxation was specifically reserved to the British Parliament. Civil cases were to be tried without benefit of a jury. Catholics were granted religious toleration and civil rights; their church's privileges confirmed. American colonists looked askance at all these features so opposed to their own traditions. But perhaps the most objectionable feature of the Quebec Act in their eyes was the extension of Canada's boundaries to the Ohio River, an area in which Virginia, Connecticut, and Massachusetts had claims.

2 JUNE. QUARTERING ACT applied to *all* the colonies. It legalized the quartering of troops not only in taverns and deserted buildings (as had the 1765–6 acts) but also in **occupied dwellings**.

COLONIAL PROTEST. On 13 May Gen. Thomas Gage arrived in Boston to supplant Hutchinson as governor. On the same day a Boston town meeting called for new economic sanctions against Britain to force repeal of the Coercive Acts. The first of many public calls for an intercolonial congress came from Providence (17 May). Philadelphia (21 May) and New York City (23 May) sidestepped Boston's appeal for immediate nonimportation in favor of a congress at which common measures binding all the colonies might be framed. Massachusetts yielded. On 17 June the House of Representatives suggested that a congress be held in Sept. at Philadelphia. Boston's Committee of Correspondence, nevertheless, drew up a Solemn League and Covenant (5 June) which bound its subscribers to end all business dealings with Britain and stop consumption of British imports after 1 Oct. In the other colonies provincial congresses or county conventions proceeded to name delegates to Congress (15 June–25 Aug.). Only in Georgia was the attempt (10 Aug.) to name delegates defeated.

5 SEPT.–26 OCT. 1ST CONTINENTAL CONGRESS. Twelve colonies (excepting Georgia) sent 56 delegates to the Congress, which opened in Carpenters' Hall. Among them were conservatives, such as **Joseph Galloway** (Pa., c.1731–1803), **James Duane** (N.Y., 1733–97), and **George Read** (Del., 1733–98), and radicals like the two Adamses (Mass.), **Christopher Gadsden** (S.C., 1724–1805) and **Patrick Henry** and **Richard Henry Lee** (Va.). **Peyton Randolph** (Va., c.1721–75) was elected president, and a nondelegate, **Charles Thomson** (Pa., 1729–1824), named secretary. The delegates decided to vote by provincial units, each having one vote, and pledged themselves to secrecy. On 17 Sept. the radical delegates succeeded in having the **Suffolk Resolves** endorsed by the Congress. These resolutions, the work of Joseph Warren, had been adopted by a convention in Suffolk Co., Mass. (9 Sept.), and carried posthaste to Philadelphia by Paul Revere. The resolutions (1) declared the Coercive Acts unconstitutional and hence not to be obeyed; (2) urged the people of Massachusetts to form a government to collect taxes and withhold them from the royal government until the repeal of the Coercive Acts; (3) advised the people to arm and form their own militia; and (4) recommended stringent economic sanctions against Britain.

28 SEPT. GALLOWAY'S PLAN OF UNION. The conservatives attempted to offset the endorsement of the Suffolk Resolves by uniting behind Joseph Galloway's "Plan of a Proposed Union between Great Britain and the Colonies" to regulate the "general affairs of America," each colony continuing to govern its internal affairs. The central administration would consist of (1) a president-general appointed by the king and holding office at the king's pleasure with a veto over the acts of (2) a grand council, whose members were to be chosen for 3-year terms by the assemblies of each province. The president and council would constitute an "inferior and distinct branch of the British legislature." Measures dealing with America might originate either with this body or the British Parliament, the consent of the other being required for a measure to become law. By a vote of 6–5 this plan was defeated, and subsequently (22 Oct.) expunged from the minutes of Congress.

14 Oct. DECLARATION AND RESOLVES adopted by the Congress denounced the Coercive Acts and the Quebec Act as unjust, cruel, and unconstitutional, and criticized the revenue measures imposed since 1763, the extension of vice-admiralty jurisdiction, the dissolution of colonial assemblies, and the keeping of a standing army in the colonial towns in peacetime. Ten resolutions set forth the rights of the colonists, among them to "life, liberty and property," and, of the provincial legislatures, to the exclusive power of lawmaking "in all cases of taxation and internal polity," subject only to the royal veto. Thirteen parliamentary acts since 1763 were declared to violate American rights and economic sanctions pledged until they were repealed.

18 Oct. CONTINENTAL ASSOCIATION, closely modeled upon a Virginia Association framed 1–6 Aug., constituted a pledge by the delegates that their provinces would (1) cease all importation from Britain effective 1 Dec.; (2) totally discontinue the slave trade 1 Dec.; (3) institute nonconsumption of British products and various foreign luxury products (1 Mar. 1775); (4) embargo all exports to Britain, Ireland, and the West Indies effective 1 Sept. 1775. Notable were those clauses establishing extralegal machinery for enforcement. A committee was to be elected in each county, town, and city to execute the Association. Violators were to be punished by publicity and boycott. On the higher level, any province which failed to keep the Association was to be boycotted. By Apr. 1775 the Association was in operation in 12 colonies; even Georgia adopted a modified version (23 Jan. 1775).

26 Oct. ADJOURNMENT OF CONGRESS. After preparing an address to the king and to the British and American peoples, Congress adjourned, but (22 Oct.) resolved to meet again 10 May 1775 if by that date American grievances had not been redressed.

DOMINION THEORY. The delegates at Philadelphia had been influenced by the constitutional viewpoints of **James Wilson** (Pa., p. 1186) and young **Thomas Jefferson.** Wilson's *Considerations on the Nature and Extent of the Legislative Authority of the British Parliament* (17 Aug.) rejected Parliament's authority over the colonies in favor of allegiance to the king alone. Jefferson expressed a similar view in his *Summary View of the Rights of British America* (July), an appeal to George III to heed "liberal and expanded thought." After Congress adjourned John Adams expressed the "dominion theory" in his **Novanglus** letters (Dec. 1774–Apr. 1775) written to answer the Tory viewpoint of "Massachusettensis" (Daniel Leonard, p. 849). The colonies, Adams contended, were not part of the British realm and hence not subject to Parliament, for "Massachusetts is a realm, New York is a realm . . ." over which the king is sovereign.

WAR PREPARATIONS IN NEW ENGLAND. On 1 Sept. British troops from Boston marched out to Charles-town and Cambridge and seized cannon and powder belonging to the province. Thousands of militiamen flocked to Cambridge but hostilities did not break out. Gen. Gage set about fortifying Boston Neck (Sept.). On 7 Oct. the Massachusetts House, meeting in Salem in defiance of Gage, constituted itself a Provincial Congress, and named John Hancock to head a Committee of Safety empowered to call out the militia. Special groups within the militia (minutemen) were to be ready for instant call. On 14 Dec., warned on the 13th by Paul Revere of a plan to garrison British troops at Portsmouth, N.H., a band led by **John Sullivan** (1740–95) broke into Ft. William and Mary in Portsmouth, overpowered the small garrison without inflicting or suffering casualties, and carried away arms and gunpowder.

1775

27 FEB. LORD NORTH'S CONCILIATION PLAN. The petitions and Declaration of Congress were laid before Parliament on 19 Jan. The next day Chatham moved an address from the Lords to the king requesting immediate removal of the troops in Boston but was defeated by a 3–1 margin. Later (1 Feb.) he introduced a plan of reconciliation which embraced (1) a recognition of the Continental Congress, (2) a pledge by Parliament that no revenue measures would be levied upon America without the consent of the provincial assemblies, (3) American recognition of the "supreme legislative authority and superintending power" of Parliament, and (4) a plan by which the Continental Congress would vote a revenue for the crown. This measure was also rejected by the Lords. A declaration by both houses (9 Feb.) termed Massachusetts to be in rebellion. On 20 Feb. Lord

North presented the ministerial plan for reconciliation which had George III's grudging consent. By its terms Parliament, with royal approval, would "forbear" to lay any but regulatory taxes upon any American colony which, through its own assembly, taxed itself to provide for the common defense and for the support of the civil government and judiciary within its own province. The Commons endorsed the plan 27 Feb.

30 MAR. NEW ENGLAND RESTRAINING ACT. On the same day (27 Feb.) a bill was introduced forbidding the New England colonies to trade with any nation but Britain and the British West Indies after 1 July and barring New Englanders from the North Atlantic fisheries after 20 July. Despite a brilliant speech by Burke (22 Mar.) the bill was passed and received the royal assent (30 Mar.). Soon afterward (13 Apr.) the provisions of the act were made to apply to New Jersey, Pennsylvania, Maryland, Virginia, and South Carolina, news of their ratification of the Continental Association having reached London.

CRISIS IN NEW ENGLAND. A second Massachusetts Provincial Congress met at Cambridge (1 Feb.), and under the leadership of Hancock and Joseph Warren framed measures to prepare the colony for war. On 26 Feb. British troops landed at Salem to seize military supplies, but were turned back without violence. On 23 Mar. Patrick Henry predicted in his famous "Liberty or Death" speech before the Virginia House of Burgesses that news of the outbreak of hostilities in New England could be expected momentarily. He proved to be a good prophet. On 14 Apr. Gen. Gage received a letter of 27 Jan. from Lord Dartmouth, Secretary of State for the Colonies, ordering him to use force if necessary to execute the Coercive and other acts, to strike at once, even if that meant bringing on hostilities, rather than permit the rebellious faction time to perfect their organization.

19 Apr. LEXINGTON AND CONCORD. Aware that Concord (21 miles from Boston by road) was a major supply depot for the militia organized by the Provincial Congress, Gage decided to strike quickly. On 14 Apr. he relieved the Light Infantry and Grenadiers from guard duty and had boats brought ashore from the transports (15 Apr.). On 18 Apr. Lt. Col. Francis Smith received secret orders to lead a force of some 700 men to Concord and destroy the supplies there the next morning. About 10 P.M. the troops marched to the edge of the Common and began embarking in boats for the short row across the Charles River to Cambridge. The Boston Committee of Safety, learning of their destination, sent **Paul Revere** and **William Dawes** (1745–99) to alert the countryside. Revere reached Lexington (5 miles from Concord) at midnight and warned Sam Adams and John Hancock, who were staying there. About 1 A.M. (19 Apr.) Revere, joined by Dawes and Dr. Samuel Prescott, left Lexington for Concord. On the way a British mounted patrol surprised them. Prescott escaped and got through to Concord; Dawes eluded the British but had to turn back; Revere was captured and brought back to Lexington before being released.

Smith's forces reached Lexington at dawn and found 70 armed Minute Men under Capt. **John Parker** (1729–75) drawn up on the Common. Upon the repeated commands of Maj. John Pitcairn, commanding the British advance units, the Americans had begun to file off (though without dropping their weapons as ordered) when a report from an unidentified firearm brought, without a command by Pitcairn, a series of volleys from the British platoons. Only a few shots were returned from the American ranks where 8 lay dead and 10

were wounded. Only one British soldier was wounded. Smith re-formed his men and marched on to Concord, where he destroyed some gun carriages, entrenching tools, flour, and a liberty pole. Late in the morning the steadily swelling American forces attacked a British platoon at Concord's North Bridge, inflicting 14 casualties. Smith left Concord for the return march to Boston shortly after noon and soon found the countryside swarming with militiamen who assailed his column from all sides. Only the arrival of reinforcements when he reached Lexington saved him from complete disaster. The relentless attacks continued until the expeditionary force reached Charlestown and the protection of the guns of the men-of-war in the harbor. Total British casualties for the day: 73 killed, 174 wounded, 26 missing. Almost 4,000 American militia saw action during that day; of these 93 were dead, wounded, or missing. The provincial forces closed in on Boston and began a siege which was to last until Mar. 1776. On 23 Apr. the Provincial Congress authorized the raising of 13,600 men, made **Artemas Ward** (1727–1800) commander in chief, and appealed to the other colonies for aid. By 20 May Rhode Island, Connecticut, and New Hampshire had voted to send 9,500 men to Cambridge, Ward's headquarters.

10 May. CAPTURE OF FT. TICONDEROGA. Late in Apr. the Massachusetts Committee of Safety authorized **Benedict Arnold** (p. 975) to raise 400 men in western Massachusetts and attack Ft. Ticonderoga on Lake Champlain, a strategic post rich in artillery and other military supplies. On 6 May Arnold learned that **Ethan Allen** (1738–89) was raising a force at Castleton, Vt., for an attack on Ticonderoga. Arnold hurried to Castleton and claimed command but without success. Nevertheless he accompanied Allen and was

up the hill only to be turned back by a murderous fire. Reinforced by Clinton for a third assault, Howe had his men drop their packs and ordered a bayonet charge. This time the fire from the redoubt slackened as the supply of powder gave out and the British seized the hill. Bunker Hill was then rapidly assaulted and won as the American retreat became a near rout. Howe decided against pressing on toward Cambridge and stopped the pursuit at the base of the peninsula. The British had won the field but at a cost of 1,054 casualties, a high proportion of them officers. The American losses, almost all of which were suffered after the fall of the redoubt, numbered 100 dead (including Joseph Warren), 267 wounded, 30 taken prisoner. Two weeks after the battle Washington reached Cambridge and took formal command of an army of 14,500 on 3 July.

5 July. OLIVE BRANCH PETITION, adopted by Congress and written by **John Dickinson** (largely discarding an earlier draft by John Jay), professed the attachment of the American people to George III, expressed their hope for the restoration of harmony, and begged the king to prevent further hostile actions against the colonies until a reconciliation was worked out. On 6 July Congress adopted another important resolution, written jointly by Jefferson and Dickinson, a "Declaration of the Causes and Necessities of Taking Up Arms," which rejected independence but asserted that Americans were ready to die rather than be enslaved. A significant phrase touched upon the possibility of receiving foreign aid against Britain. On 15 July Congress voted to waive the provisions of the Continental Association where war supplies were concerned and on 31 July rejected Lord North's plan for reconciliation. Before adjourning (2 Aug.) Congress assumed 2 additional functions of an independent government: the appointment of commissioners to negotiate treaties of peace with the Indian tribes (19 July), and the establishment of a Post Office Department with Benjamin Franklin as Postmaster General (26 July).

28 Aug.–31 Dec. MONTGOMERY'S EXPEDITION AGAINST QUEBEC. On 27 June, having received word that Sir Guy Carleton, British commander in Canada, was recruiting a Canadian force for an invasion of New York, Congress authorized Gen. Philip Schuyler to seize any points in Canada vital to the security of the colonies. Schuyler assembled an expeditionary force at Ticonderoga and began his advance from there (28 Aug.) with about 1,000 men. Crossing into Canada, he laid siege to St. John's (6 Sept.), garrisoned by about 600 British and Canadian troops. Ill health forced Schuyler to leave the army (13 Sept.) in the command of Brig. Gen. **Richard Montgomery** (1738–75), to whom the garrison of St. John's capitulated (2 Nov.). Carleton withdrew the remnants of his small force toward Quebec, thereby uncovering Montreal, which the Americans occupied 13 Nov. Carleton was almost captured when his flotilla of 11 small ships surrendered (19 Nov.), but managed to escape to Quebec.

12 Sept.–31 Dec. ARNOLD'S EXPEDITION AGAINST QUEBEC. Benedict Arnold recruited a force of about 1,100 volunteers at Cambridge with Washington's permission and set out for Maine (12 Sept.). From Gardiner he moved inland to Ft. Western (Augusta), from which base the main trek began (24 Sept.) through country few white men had seen. The difficult terrain and shortness of provisions led one of the expedition's 4 divisions to turn back (25 Oct.). With 650 men Arnold reached the St. Lawrence opposite Quebec (8 Nov.) and crossed the river on the 13th. On 3 Dec. he was joined by Montgomery with 300 men from Montreal. At 5 A.M., 31 Dec., a combined assault was launched against Quebec but ended in disaster. Montgomery was killed, Arnold wounded, almost 100 men killed or wounded, over 300 taken prisoner. With the remnants of his force Arnold maintained a weak cordon around the city throughout the winter.

12 SEPT. CONGRESS RECONVENES. The presence of a delegation from Georgia made Congress for the first time representative of all 13 colonies. On 9 Nov. news arrived that George III had refused to receive the Olive Branch Petition and had (23 Aug.) proclaimed the American colonies to be in open rebellion. (On 7 Nov. the House of Commons received the petition but a motion that it constitute a basis for reconciliation was defeated 83–33.) Congress answered the royal proclamation on 6 Dec., disclaiming any intention to deny the sovereignty of the king, but disavowing allegiance to Parliament. The breach was further widened on 23 Dec. when a royal proclamation was issued closing the colonies to all commerce effective 1 Mar. 1776.

13 OCT. CONGRESS AUTHORIZES A NAVY. On 2 Sept. Washington authorized Col. **John Glover** (Mass., 1732–97) to convert fishing vessels into armed ships. In Congress a committee was appointed (5 Oct.) to prepare a plan for intercepting 2 British ships known to have military stores aboard, and another (13 Oct.) authorized to fit out 2 ships of 10 guns each, an authorization increased to 4 ships (30 Oct.). Congress resolved to raise 2 battalions of marines (10 Nov.) and on 25 Nov. formally declared British vessels open to capture in retaliation for British raids on American coastal towns. "Rules for the Regulation of the Navy of the United Colonies" were adopted 28 Nov. and a marine committee appointed (14 Dec.) to carry

them out. On 22 Dec. Congress commissioned officers for the 4 Continental ships, naming **Esek Hopkins** (R.I., 1718–1802) commodore. Congress authorized privateering (19 Mar. 1776) and issued letters of marque and reprisal (23 Mar.).

29 Nov. CONGRESS LOOKS ABROAD. Congress appointed a 5-man Committee of Secret Correspondence with wide discretionary powers to get in contact with "our friends" abroad. An appropriation of $3,000 for the use of agents was voted 11 Dec. On the 12th the committee wrote to **Arthur Lee** (1740–92), agent for Massachusetts in London, requesting him to ascertain the attitude of the European powers toward America. Later that month a French agent, Achard de Bonvouloir, communicated with the Secret Committee and gave informal assurances that France would welcome American ships and might offer material aid to the colonies.

11 DEC. HOSTILITIES IN THE SOUTH. On 7 Nov. Gov. Dunmore (Va.) placed his colony under martial law, established a base at Norfolk, and began recruiting a Loyalist army. By a promise of freedom to those slaves who deserted their masters (17 Nov.) he raised a Negro regiment, but forfeited the support of almost the entire planter class. On 11 Dec. Dunmore was decisively defeated by a mixed force of 900 Virginians and North Carolinians at Great Bridge. He evacuated Norfolk, but on 1 Jan. 1776 landed there again and destroyed much of the town by fire. In Feb. the Americans reoccupied and completed the destruction of the town, rendering it practically useless as a base of operations.

1776

MILITARY BALANCE SHEET. The Patriots were favored by (1) campaigning on their own ground, (2) widespread acquaintance with firearms, (3) a great leader in George Washington, (4) the superiority (in both range and accuracy) of the American rifle over the British smoothbore musket, and (5) a significant number of officers and men with military experience gained against the French or Indians. Grave disadvantages: (1) lack of training and discipline; (2) short-term enlistments; (3) shortage of ammunition, food, clothing, and medical supplies; (4) the hostility or active opposition of perhaps one third of the colonial populace; and (5) the lack of an efficient naval arm.

British commanders in America possessed the advantages of (1) a well-equipped, trained, and disciplined force; (2) support of the British navy in landing and transporting troops and guarding communication and supply lines at sea; (3) a rich war chest which permitted the hiring of foreign troops to supplement their own forces; and (4) the cooperation of American Loyalists. Weighing against these advantages were (1) the distance of the theater of war from Britain; (2) its vast extent and varied nature; (3) a reluctance to adapt tactics to American conditions; (4) a disinclination to mobilize the Loyalists as an effective force; and (5) a tendency on the part of military and political leaders to underestimate the opponent.

9 JAN. "COMMON SENSE." The first clarion call for independence was voiced by **Thomas Paine** (p. 1120) in *Common Sense,* a pamphlet which appeared in Philadelphia. Paine attacked George III (the "Royal Brute") as chiefly responsible for the obnoxious measures against the colonies and flayed the monarchical form of government. His simple yet electric presentation converted thousands to the cause of independence.

FEB.–JUNE. HOSTILITIES IN THE SOUTH. Gen. **Henry Clinton** arrived off Cape Fear, N.C. (Mar.), with a British expeditionary force. Clinton had originally planned to land in North Carolina and join forces with a Loyalist army, but scrapped these plans when he learned that the Loyalists had been crushed at the Battle of Moore's Creek Bridge near Wilmington (27 Feb.). After being joined by troops from Britain under Gen. **Cornwallis** (3 May) Clinton decided to attack Charleston, S.C., where defense preparations were well under way when the British appeared on 1 June. On 4 June Gen. **Charles Lee** arrived from New York to take command of the defense. On 28 June, the wind finally being favorable, the British warships under Sir Peter Parker moved against the main point of the American defenses, a palmetto log fort (later named **Ft. Moultrie** for its defender) on Sullivan's Island. Parker's fire was returned by the defenders with great effect, forcing him to abandon the attack at nightfall, with all his ships damaged and over 200 casualties. In the fort 10 were dead, 21 wounded. Clinton's troops likewise failed to achieve their objectives on the 28th and had to be withdrawn. The British failure at Charleston ended active operations by them in that theater for over 2 years.

17 MAR. BRITISH EVACUATE BOSTON. On 24 Jan. Gen. **Henry Knox** (1750–1806) reached Cambridge with 43 cannon and 16 mortars hauled laboriously overland from Ft. Ticonderoga. On 16 Feb. a council of war drew up plans for the seizure of Dorchester Heights, from which point Boston and most of its harbor would be within range of Knox's artillery. Under cover of a heavy cannonade the occupation was carried out by 2,000 men under Gen. **John Thomas** (1724–76) during the night of 4–5 Mar. Gen. Howe, who had succeeded Gage as British commander (10 Oct. 1775), gathered 2,400 men for an assault on the unfinished works on the 5th but heavy rains that day and the next forestalled the attack. On 7 Mar. Howe decided to evacuate Boston. By the 17th all his troops, plus some 1,000 Loyalists, were embarked on the troopships in the harbor. On 26 Mar. the fleet left for Halifax.

MAR.–MAY. FRANCE DECIDES TO AID AMERICA. On 1 Mar. the French foreign minister, Comte de Vergennes, wrote to the foreign minister of Spain, Grimaldi, asking his reaction to joint secret measures to provide help for Britain's rebellious colonists. Spain showed herself receptive. Thereupon Louis XVI ordered (2 May) that 1 million livres' worth of munitions be supplied the Americans through a fictitious company, Roderigue Hortalez et Cie., actually administered by secret agent **Pierre de Beaumarchais.** Charles III of Spain made a similar arrangement shortly afterward. From these sources the American armies were to receive over 80% of their gunpowder, to mention but one type of military supplies, throughout 1776–77. Meanwhile Congress, ignorant of these developments, voted (3 Mar.) to send **Silas Deane** (1737–89) to Europe to purchase war matériel. This action made inevitable the resolution of 6 Apr., an important forerunner of the Declaration of Independence, opening the ports of the colonies to the trade of all nations but Britain. Deane arrived in Paris 7 July.

APR.–JULY. RETREAT FROM CANADA. On 1 Apr. Gen. **David Wooster** (1711–77) arrived at Quebec with reinforcements for the Northern Army and to take over command from Arnold, but gave way to Gen. John Thomas on 1 May. Thomas had already decided to abandon the siege of Quebec when British reinforcements reached Carleton (6 May) and enabled the latter to turn an orderly American retreat into a rout. Thomas retreated to Chambly and died there of smallpox (2 June). Gen. Sullivan, who succeeded him, attempted a counterattack against **Three Rivers** (7 June) but was defeated. He then retreated to St. John's, was joined there by Arnold and the Montreal garrison, and continued his retreat to Ticonderoga early in July. With command of Lake Champlain the key to all strategy, both Arnold and Carleton set to work to collect and build ships for a fleet.

APR.–JULY. MOVEMENT TOWARD INDEPENDENCE. By the spring of 1776 sentiment for a break with Britain was clearly in the ascendant. On 12 Apr. the North Carolina Convention empowered its delegates in Congress to vote for a declaration of independence. Virginia followed suit (15 May). With this authorization Richard Henry Lee offered a resolution (7 June) that the United Colonies "are, and of right ought to be, free and independent States." While after some debate (7–10 June) it was decided to postpone a decision on the resolution until 1 July, a committee consisting of **Jefferson, Franklin, John Adams, Robert R. Livingston,** and **Roger Sherman** (p. 1151) was appointed (11 June) to prepare a declaration of independence. Within the committee it was decided that Jefferson should write the draft of the declaration. With a few changes by Adams and Franklin it was this draft which was presented to Congress on 28 June. Jefferson said he "turned to neither book nor pamphlet" in preparing the paper. He drew upon the prevalent "natural rights" political philosophy and compiled a long list of despotic "abuses and usurpations" by George III (Parliament received no direct mention) in asserting the right and the duty of the American people to dissolve their tie to Britain and declare the United Colonies free and independent States.

2 JULY. CONGRESS VOTES INDEPENDENCE. On 1 July Congress sat as a committee to debate the Lee resolution. When brought to a vote in committee the motion was carried, though Pennsylvania and South Carolina were in the negative and Delaware's vote was divided. On 2 July Congress, now sitting in formal session rather than as a committee, took the final vote for independence (12 for, none against). South Carolina shifted her vote, the arrival of a third delegate from Delaware (Caesar Rodney) threw the vote of that colony for independence, and Pennsylvania swung to the affirmative when John Dickinson and Robert Morris purposely absented themselves on the 2nd. The New York delegation, advised (11 June) by the New York Provincial Congress to take no action for or against independence, abstained from voting.

Congress next debated the form and content of the declaration prepared by Jefferson (2–3 July), making several changes. On 4 July the amended Declaration of Independence was approved without dissent (New York again abstained) and signed by Hancock (president) and Thomson (secretary). Copies were prepared (5–6 July) to be dispatched to all the states. The declaration was first publicly proclaimed in Philadelphia (8 July) and was read before Washington and his troops in New York City the next day. On 9 July also the Provincial Congress of New York voted to endorse the declaration, a decision of which Congress was informed 15 July. Congress then resolved (19 July) to have the "Unanimous Declaration" engrossed on parchment for the signature of the delegates. On 2 Aug. most of the 55 signatures were affixed. One "Signer," Matthew Thornton of New Hampshire (not a member of Congress when the declaration was adopted), added his name as late as Nov.

27 Aug. BATTLE OF LONG ISLAND. After evacuating Boston, Howe planned to use strategic New York City as his base of operations. Anticipating Howe's movement, Washington shifted his army from Boston (21 Mar.–13 Apr.). On 2 July Howe landed unopposed on Staten Island with about 10,-000 men. His brother, Adm. **Lord Richard Howe,** arrived with a strong fleet and 150 transports 12 July. Other reinforcements reached Staten Island throughout July and early August until Gen. Howe had a command of 32,000 men, about 9,000 of whom were German mercenaries. Between 22–25 Aug. he landed about 20,000 troops on Long Island. On the evening of the 26th he led a wide flanking movement around the left of the forces under Gen. Putnam on Brooklyn Heights. On the morning of the 27th Howe fell upon the rear of Sullivan's position, routed his forces, and took the general prisoner. Gen. **William Alexander** (1726–83, who claimed the title "Lord Stirling") fought a gallant delaying action to protect the escape route of the American forces, but finally surrendered to the Hessian general, De Heister. Howe cautiously halted the pursuit at the breastworks on Brooklyn Heights after inflicting 1,500 casualties upon an American force of about 5,000 at a cost of less than 400 of his own men. On the 28th Howe began constructing siege-works. Having decided against making a stand in Brooklyn, Washington during the night of 29–30 Aug. skillfully withdrew Putnam's entire force to Manhattan Island unknown to the British.

11 Sept. STATEN ISLAND PEACE CONFERENCE. On 3 May Gen. and Adm. Howe had been appointed peace commissioners by the king with powers to pardon and protect those Americans who returned to their true allegiance, but without authority to negotiate with any colony until all extralegal congresses and conventions had been dissolved.

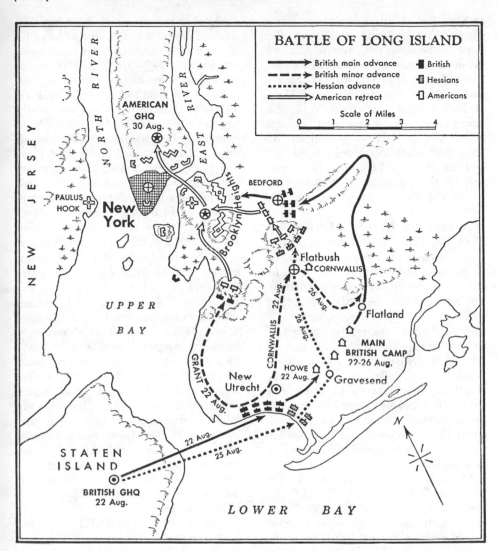

BATTLE OF LONG ISLAND

→ British main advance   ◼ British
- -→ British minor advance   ◈ Hessians
····→ Hessian advance   ◻ Americans
⇒ American retreat

Scale of Miles
0   1   2   3   4

After the Battle of Long Island the Howes sent their prisoner, Gen. Sullivan, to Congress with a proposal that an informal peace conference be held. On 6 Sept. Congress appointed Franklin, John Adams, and Edmund Rutledge to confer with Lord Howe. The meeting took place on Staten Island and, although cordial, was fruitless. Howe's demand for a revocation of the Declaration of Independence as a necessary preliminary to negotiations for peace left no ground for further conversations.

15 Sept. BRITISH OCCUPY NEW YORK CITY. On 12 Sept. Washington decided to evacuate New York City rather than risk being trapped on lower Manhattan Island. The movement of his troops to hilly northern Manhattan was still under way when the British landed at Kip's Bay on the eastern side of the island (15 Sept.) and almost cut off a large section of the American army. Washington retreated to Harlem Heights, repulsed the British there (16 Sept.), and prepared new fortifications. Howe decided against an assault upon the American works and the next 3 weeks saw a lull in activity, marred by the great fire which destroyed almost 300 buildings in New York City (21 Sept.) and by the execution of **Nathan Hale** (1755–76) as an American spy (22 Sept.).

26 SEPT. CONGRESS APPOINTS A DIPLOMATIC COMMISSION. On 12 June Congress appointed a committee to prepare plans for treaties of commerce and amity with foreign nations. The report of this committee (17 Sept.) was, after some alteration, adopted. On 26 Sept. 3 commissioners were appointed to negotiate treaties with European nations: **Silas Deane** (already in Europe), **Franklin,** and **Jefferson.** Jefferson declined the appointment and **Arthur Lee** (also in Europe) was named in his place. Franklin joined Deane and Lee in Paris on 21 Dec. Two days later Congress authorized the commission to borrow up to £2 million.

11 OCT. BATTLE OF VALCOUR BAY. The fleets which Arnold and Carleton had been gathering on Lake Champlain finally came to grips on 11 Oct. Arnold had placed his 83-gun fleet in the channel between Valcour Island and the western shore of Lake Champlain. Carleton's 87-gun fleet, manned by experienced sailors in contrast to Arnold's motley crews, attacked, and in a 7-hour battle crippled most of the American flotilla. That night Arnold's remaining ships slipped by the British. Another engagement at **Split Rock** (13 Oct.) resulted in the complete destruction of the American flotilla as a fighting force.

Carleton occupied Crown Point but then decided winter was too near at hand for a siege of Ticonderoga. He abandoned Crown Point (3 Nov.) and drew his forces back into Canada.

28 OCT. BATTLE OF WHITE PLAINS. In an effort to outflank Washington's strong position in northern Manhattan, Howe embarked the bulk of his army (12 Oct.), sailed up the East River and Long Island Sound, and landed on the mainland (13 Oct.) at Pell's Point. To meet this threat to his rear Washington evacuated his main force from Manhattan (23 Oct.) and moved northward to White Plains, leaving a strong garrison at Ft. Washington on the island. Howe moved against Washington (28 Oct.) and, in a sharp battle in which he suffered over 300 casualties and inflicted about 200, captured a key hill position. While Howe awaited reinforcements, Washington again slipped away (1 Nov.) to a new line 5 miles north at North Castle. On 16 Nov. Howe sent 13,000 troops against Ft. Washington, which capitulated. The British lost 458 in killed or wounded but took 2,818 prisoners. On 19 Nov. Howe sent Cornwallis across the Hudson with 4,500 men for an assault upon Ft. Lee. Gen. **Nathanael Greene** (p. 1046) evacuated the fort but was forced to abandon badly needed military supplies.

18 Nov.–20 DEC. RETREAT ACROSS NEW JERSEY. Greene and Washington joined forces at Hackensack and, with Cornwallis at their heels, retreated toward the Delaware River. After repeated commands from Washington, Gen. Charles Lee led the troops at North Castle across the Hudson (2 Dec.) and into Jersey. Washington crossed the Delaware into Pennsylvania 11 Dec. and 2 days later Lee was captured at Basking Ridge, N.J., by a British patrol. Sullivan took command of his troops and on 20

Dec. joined Washington in Pennsylvania. Congress, fearing a British attack on Philadelphia, fled from that city to Baltimore (12 Dec.) after vesting Washington with virtually dictatorial powers.

26 Dec. COUP AT TRENTON. Howe sent the bulk of his army back to winter quarters in New York (13 Dec.) but left garrisons at Trenton, Princeton, Bordentown, Perth Amboy, and New Brunswick. Informed that the Hessian garrison (c.1,400) at Trenton under Col. Johann Rall was ill-prepared to meet attack, Washington decided on an assault by 3 forces, only one of which—the main body of 2,400 under Washington himself—succeeded in crossing the ice-choked Delaware. Washington crossed 9 miles north of the town, split his force into 2 divisions, and at 8 A.M. drove into Trenton from the north and northeast. The surprise was complete. After an hour of confused street fighting in which Rall was mortally wounded, the garrison surrendered. Of the Hessians 918 were captured, 30 killed; while Washington suffered only 5 casualties. Washington recrossed into Pennsylvania with his prisoners and then once again crossed to the Jersey side and reoccupied Trenton (30–31 Dec.).

1777

3 Jan. COUP AT PRINCETON. Howe reacted to the news of the Trenton disaster with unusual celerity. On 1 Jan. he sent Gen. James Grant from New Brunswick toward Trenton and from New York dispatched a large force under Cornwallis to join Grant at Princeton. On 2 Jan. the British made contact with Washington's army of 5,200 men east of Trenton, but Cornwallis elected to wait until the next day for the attack which would "bag the fox." Leaving behind only enough men to give the illusion of an occupied camp, Washington stole around Cornwallis' flank that night and by dawn (3 Jan.) was close to Princeton. Near the town Patriot units under Gen. **Hugh Mercer** (c.1725–77) clashed with a British column under Col. Charles Mawhood marching to join Cornwallis. Mercer was killed and the American vanguard routed. Then Washington appeared with the main body and drove the British back with heavy losses toward New Brunswick. Cornwallis, hearing the sounds of battle to his rear, also fell back to protect the supply depot there. Washington drew his tired troops off to the northeast and soon established winter quarters in the hills around Morristown (6 Jan.). His victories had cleared all but easternmost New Jersey of the enemy and had an incalculable effect in restoring the shattered Patriot morale.

12 Mar. CONGRESS RECONVENES IN PHILADELPHIA. Congress returned to Philadelphia (4 Mar.), where it considered measures to obtain foreign aid. While at Baltimore Congress had resolved (30 Dec. 1776) to send commissioners to Austria, Prussia, Spain, and Tuscany. The commissioner to Spain was to be authorized to offer British-held Pensacola in Florida in return for a declaration of war by Spain against Britain. Similarly, the commissioners already in France were authorized to offer access to the Newfoundland fishing grounds and territorial gains as well if France would enter the war. On 1 Jan. Franklin was appointed to the Spanish, in addition to the French, mission, but on 1 May **Arthur Lee** was named to represent the U.S. at the Spanish court in his place. On 7 May **Ralph Izard** (1742–1804) was appointed commissioner to the Grand Duke of Tuscany, and on 9 May the Vienna and Berlin posts were assigned to **William Lee** (1739–95). Meanwhile, the Committee of Secret

Correspondence had been reconstituted by Congress as the Committee for Foreign Affairs (17 Apr.).

14 JUNE. STARS AND STRIPES. Congress resolved that the flag of the U.S. be "thirteen stripes alternate red and white, that the Union be thirteen stars white in a blue field. . . ."

RECRUITING FOREIGN OFFICERS. Congress had authorized Silas Deane to secure several European military experts for service in America, and by Mar. was swamped by applicants appearing in Philadelphia to claim commissions. On 13 Mar. Congress ordered that its agents send in the future only persons with the highest qualifications, including a knowledge of English. On 27 July two of the most famous foreign officers of the Revolution reached Philadelphia, 20-year-old **Marquis de Lafayette** (1757–1834) and veteran "Baron" **Johann de Kalb** (1721–80). Lafayette, who volunteered to serve without pay, was commissioned major general (31 July), as was De Kalb (15 Sept.). Foremost among the other foreign officers were **Thaddeus Kosciusko** (1746–1817), commissioned colonel of engineers (18 Oct. 1776), and **Baron Friedrich Wilhelm von Steuben** (1730–94), appointed inspector general 5 May 1778.

BRITISH PLAN KNOCKOUT BLOW. On 28 Feb. Gen. John Burgoyne, back in England, submitted to Lord George Germain, Secretary of State for the Colonies, his plan for a 3-pronged attack to isolate New England: (1) a main army of not less than 8,000 regulars to push southward down Lake Champlain and the upper Hudson; (2) an auxiliary force to operate from Oswego through the Mohawk Valley; (3) a strong force under Howe to move up the Hudson. Germain approved the plan; Burgoyne was given command of the main army to move from Canada; but Germain also approved (3 Mar.) Howe's plan for an attack on Philadelphia (by sea according to Howe's plan of 2 Apr.), hoping Howe could be finished in time to help Burgoyne.

23 JULY–26 SEPT. HOWE'S CAMPAIGN AGAINST PHILADELPHIA. On 23 July Howe embarked from New York with 15,000 troops, sailed up Chesapeake Bay, and landed at Head of Elk on 25 Aug. Washington, with about 10,500 men, took up a defensive position barring the way to Philadelphia on the eastern side of **Brandywine Creek.** Howe attacked on 11 Sept., using a carefully planned flanking movement. The Germans under Gen. William von Knyphausen attacked the American center at Chad's Ford; Cornwallis routed Sullivan on the American right. Greene managed to turn the flight into an orderly if hard-pressed retreat, but the whole American army was forced back toward Philadelphia. Casualties: American, c.1,000; British, 576. The British scored again (21 Sept.), when a bayonet attack in the early hours of the morning routed a force under Gen. **Anthony Wayne** (1745–96) at Paoli. On 26 Sept. Howe occupied Philadelphia. Congress fled (19 Sept.) to Lancaster and then to York (30 Sept.).

4 OCT. BATTLE OF GERMANTOWN. On the night of 3 Oct. Washington began an intricate movement toward Howe's main encampment at Germantown. The battle began before dawn on the 4th with the Americans winning important initial successes. But the coordinated attack which Washington had planned did not materialize. Detachments became lost in a heavy fog and at one point American troops fired on each other. A retreat by several brigades forced the American detachments which had penetrated into the streets of Germantown to fall back. Again Greene distinguished himself in directing a stubborn retreat. Washington suffered almost

700 casualties and had 400 of his men taken prisoner against British losses of 534. The 400-man garrison of Ft. Mercer (on the Delaware below Philadelphia) repelled an attack by 1,600 Hessians (22 Oct.), but was forced to evacuate (20 Nov.) in the face of an assault by 5,000 men under Cornwallis. By 23 Nov. the Delaware as far north as Philadelphia was clear for British vessels. Washington meanwhile had withdrawn northwestward from Germantown and took up winter quarters at **Valley Forge** (mid-Dec.).

17 JUNE–17 OCT. NORTHERN CAMPAIGN: BURGOYNE AND ST. LEGER. On 17 June, with a force of about 7,700 British and German troops, Canadians and Indians, Burgoyne left St. John's with a huge baggage train and 138 pieces of artillery. By 30 June his army had reached Ft. Ticonderoga commanded by Gen. **Arthur St. Clair** (1736–1818). On 2 July the British seized Mt. Defiance, a strategic height south of the fort which the Americans had carelessly left unfortified and by 5 July had hauled cannon to the top, rendering the fort untenable. That night St. Clair evacuated, abandoning substantial supplies. Burgoyne, in pursuit, took Skenesborough and Ft. Anne, 6–7 July. Thereafter, his advance was slowed by the forested terrain and trees felled by Schuyler's forces. On 4 Aug. Schuyler was replaced in command by Gen. **Horatio Gates** (1727–1806).

Meanwhile a British force of 1,800, mostly Loyalists and Indians, advanced eastward from Oswego on Lake Ontario under the command of Col. **Barry St. Leger.** On 3 Aug. St. Leger reached and besieged Ft. Stanwix on the Mohawk River, garrisoned by 750 men under Col. **Peter Gansevoort** (1749–1812). On 6 Aug. 800 militiamen marching to the fort's relief under Gen. **Nicholas Herkimer** (1728–77) were caught in ambush at **Oriskany** by a force of Indians and Loyalists led by the Mohawk chief **Joseph Brant** (1742–1807). Herkimer, badly wounded at the outset of the battle, drew his men together on high ground and fought back fiercely. The Indians, alarmed by firing from Stanwix, where the garrison made a sortie against the British camp, broke off the engagement. Herkimer retreated eastward with less than half his original strength. Schuyler now sent Arnold with a force of 1,000 volunteers to Gansevoort's aid. By a ruse the Indians were frightened off, and St. Leger abandoned the siege of Stanwix and retreated to Oswego (22 Aug.).

By early Aug. Burgoyne's supply problem became alarming. Learning that the Americans had quantities of military stores at Bennington, he detached some 700 men under the command of Lt. Col. Friedrich Baum to capture them (11 Aug.). At **Bennington** were some 2,600 American troops under Gen. **John Stark** (1728–1822), most of them raw militiamen now taking up arms in increasing numbers as news of atrocities by Burgoyne's Indians (particularly the murder of Jane McCrea on 27 July) spread through New England. Stark launched an attack on Baum on 16 Aug. Baum was mortally wounded and, except for the Indians (most of whom fled), almost his entire force killed or taken prisoner. The reinforcements for Baum under Lt. Col. Heinrich C. Breymann arrived too late and were in turn attacked by Stark, now reinforced by Col. Seth Warner (1743–84) leading 400 veteran Massachusetts troops. Breymann, with the loss of a third of his 650 men, was forced to fall back on Burgoyne.

Burgoyne resolved to press on to Albany, crossed to the west side of the Hudson (13 Sept.), and moved against the entrenched position Gates had prepared on Bemis Heights. Gates, reinforced, now had over 6,000 men, with

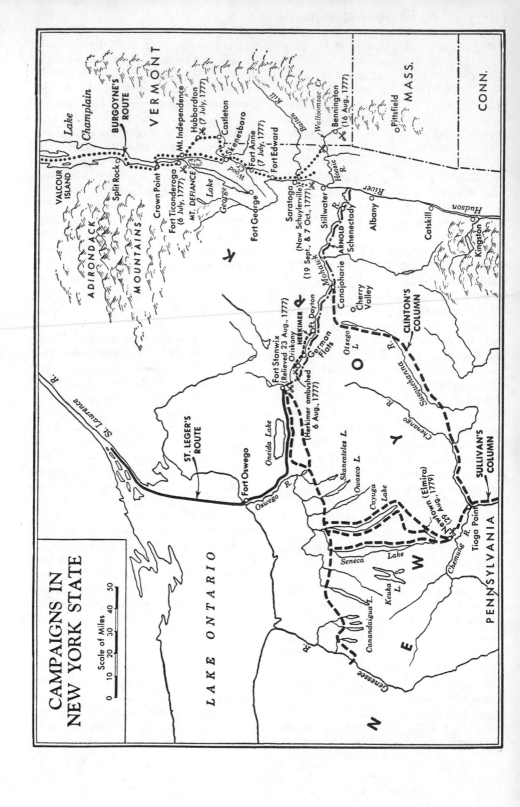

CAMPAIGNS IN
NEW YORK STATE

Scale of Miles
0 10 20 30 40 50

LAKE ONTARIO

St. Lawrence R.

Fort Oswego
Oswego

ST. LEGER'S ROUTE

Oneida Lake

Fort Stanwix
(Relieved 23 Aug., 1777)
Oriskany
Herkimer ambushed
6 Aug., 1777

HERKIMER
Ft. Dayton
German Flats

Skaneateles L.
Owasco L.
Cayuga Lake
Seneca Lake
Keuka L.
Canandaigua L.
Genesee R.

Newtown (Elmira)
(29 Aug., 1779)

SULLIVAN'S COLUMN

Chemung R.
Tioga Point

PENNSYLVANIA

N E W

Y O R K

Otsego L.
Canajoharie
Cherry Valley

Susquehanna R.
Chenango R.

CLINTON'S COLUMN

ADIRONDACK
MOUNTAINS

VALCOUR ISLAND
Split Rock

Lake Champlain

BURGOYNE'S ROUTE

Crown Point
Fort Ticonderoga
(6 July, 1777)
MT. DEFIANCE
Lake George

Fort George

Mt. Independence
Hubbardton
(7 July, 1777)
Castleton
Skenesboro
Fort Anne
(7 July, 1777)
Fort Edward

VERMONT

Wood Cr.

Batten Kil

Battenkill

Walloomsac Cr.
Bennington
(16 Aug., 1777)

Hoosic R.
Pittsfield

MASS.

CONN.

Saratoga
(Now Schuylerville)
(19 Sept., & 7 Oct., 1777)
Stillwater
ARNOLD
Schenectady
Mohawk R.

Albany

Catskill

Hudson River

Kingston

militiamen arriving daily. On 19 Sept. Burgoyne attempted to gain high ground on the American left but was checked short of his goal at **Freeman's Farm** by Gen. **Daniel Morgan** (p. 1106) and Col. **Henry Dearborn.** British casualties, c.600; American, 300. On 3 Oct. Gen. Clinton, commanding British troops in New York City, moved up the Hudson, taking Fts. Clinton and Montgomery on the 6th. Receiving an urgent appeal for help from Burgoyne on the 9th, he sent the fleet farther up the Hudson to Esopus (Kingston), which the British burned (16 Oct.), but felt too insecure to push on to Albany, and returned to New York for reinforcements.

Meanwhile Burgoyne had become desperate. On 7 Oct. he again ventured out of his lines toward the American left with 1,650 troops. A countermove by Gates, led by Morgan and Gen. Ebenezer Learned, repulsed the British. Then Benedict Arnold, though without a command that day, led a fierce assault which threw Burgoyne back upon **Bemis Heights.** The Americans continued to press on and carried the Breymann redoubt. That night, weakened by the day's toll of close to 600 (American casualties, c.150), Burgoyne withdrew northeastward about 1 mile and on 8 Oct. retreated to Saratoga. On 13 Oct., surrounded by a force now 3 times his own, he asked for a cessation of hostilities. On 17 Oct., by the terms of the "Convention of Saratoga," the 5,700 men constituting the remnants of Burgoyne's army laid down their arms. They were to be marched to Boston, shipped back to England, and pledged not to serve again in the war against America.

25 SEPT.–23 DEC. "CONWAY CABAL." As a result of congressional antagonism to the military direction of the war **Gates** was named (27 Nov.) president of the Board of War and **Thomas Conway,** previously an Irish colonel in the French army, inspector general (14 Dec.). Earlier Conway had written Congress (25 Sept.) disparaging his own commanding officer, Lord Stirling, and on 11 Oct. had sent Gates a letter attacking Washington. The rebuke by Washington (9 Nov.) forced Gates to disavow any connection with the affair. Doubt exists whether there was in fact any organized plot to supplant Washington. Conway, who resigned from the army, was wounded in the summer of 1778 in a duel with Gen. John Cadwalader, and later apologized to Washington.

15 Nov. ARTICLES OF CONFEDERATION. When Richard Henry Lee offered his resolution for independence (7 June 1776), he also proposed that "a plan of confederation be prepared and transmitted to the respective colonies for their consideration and approbation." Congress appointed a committee headed by John Dickinson (12 June). On 12 July 1776 the committee's report, "Articles of Confederation and Perpetual Union," was presented to Congress. For over a year the Articles were debated intermittently. On 7 Oct. 1777 a vote was finally taken on the question of voting in the Congress under the Articles, 1 vote for each state winning acceptance. On 14 Oct. the apportionment of the expenses of the central government was settled on a basis of surveyed land in each state. Finally, on 15 Nov., the 13 Articles were formally adopted and on 17 Nov. sent to each state for prompt ratification. Complete ratification did not occur until 1 Mar. 1781.

17 DEC. FRANCE AND U.S. INDEPENDENCE. When Lord North heard the news of Burgoyne's surrender (early Dec.) he began preparing a new offer of reconciliation. A British agent, Paul Wentworth, was sent to Paris to confer with Deane and Franklin, but found they stood squarely for full independence (15 Dec.–6 Jan. 1778). Fearful that the Americans might come to terms with the British, the French informed the American envoys (17 Dec.) that the king's council had decided to recognize the independence of the U.S.

1778

6 Feb. FRANCO-AMERICAN ALLIANCE. After an unsuccessful attempt by the French to induce Spain to join in a tripartite pact against Britain, Comte de Vergennes informed the American commissioners (8 Jan.) that France was prepared to enter into an alliance with the U.S. Two treaties resulted from the negotiations of the next 4 weeks: (1) a treaty of amity and commerce, under which each nation was granted most-favored-nation status by the other; and (2) a treaty of alliance to become effective if and when war broke out between France and Britain. Article II of the latter declared its aim was to "maintain effectually the liberty, Sovereignty, and independence" of the U.S. The U.S. was given a free hand to conquer Canada and Bermuda; France, to seize the British West Indies, with mutual territorial guarantees and an agreement that neither would conclude a truce or peace with Britain without the other's consent. On 20 Mar. Franklin, Deane, and Lee were officially received by Louis XVI and within the week Conrad Gérard was named minister to the U.S. Congress received the news on 2 May, ratified the treaties unanimously on the 4th, voted (11 Sept.) to replace the commission in France by a minister, and elected (14 Sept.) Franklin to that post. Meanwhile, on 17 June a clash between French and British naval forces occurred; the two nations were at war.

12 Apr. CARLISLE PEACE COMMISSION. To forestall U.S. ratification of the French alliance, Lord North introduced (17 Feb.) in Commons a series of bills for effecting reconciliation with America, proposing (1) repeal of the Tea and Coercive Acts; (2) a pledge that Parliament would impose no revenue taxes upon the American colonies; (3) appointment of a peace commission with powers to negotiate with Congress, and, if necessary, to agree to suspension of all acts passed since 1763. The bills passed the Commons 16 Mar. The Earl of Carlisle was appointed to head the commissioners (22 Feb.). William Eden, a member of the Board of Trade; George Johnstone, former governor of West Florida; and the Howe brothers, already in America, were the other members of the group (commissioned 12 Apr.). When Carlisle, Eden, and Johnstone reached Philadelphia (6 June), they learned Congress was cold to conciliation and had resolved (22 Apr.) that any man or group who came to terms with the commission was to be branded an enemy of the U.S. To a request (9 June) for a conference, Congress replied (17 June) that the only negotiations it would undertake would be for the withdrawal of British forces and the recognition of U.S. independence. The British evacuation of Philadelphia by Clinton (who succeeded Howe 8 May) forced the commissioners to move to New York. Before leaving Philadelphia, however, George Johnstone tried to bribe congressmen **Joseph Reed** (1741–85), **Robert Morris** (p. 1108), and **Francis Dana** (1743–1811). His attempt failed and its revelation led him to resign from the commission (26 Aug.). On 3 Oct. Carlisle and Eden appealed to the people over the head of Congress in a Manifesto and Proclamation which threatened a war of great destructiveness if the Americans did not abandon their French allies and make peace with Britain. On 27 Nov. the commissioners left New York for England, their mission a complete failure.

23 Apr. JOHN PAUL JONES' RAIDS. The little squadron which Congress had put under Esek Hopkins' command late in 1775 was too weak to operate as a fleet. A successful raid was carried out by Hopkins on Nassau (Mar. 1776), but thereafter the Continental Navy generally operated in single units whenever a captain could slip out to sea through the British cordon off the American coast. American privateers proved much more vexing to the British. The House of Commons was informed (Feb. 1778) that they had taken 733 prizes, but even their numbers declined from 143 in 1775 to a low of 73 in 1777. The revival of American naval operations in 1778 (115 privateers were in action in that year) was highlighted by the exploits of Capt. **John Paul Jones** (p. 1073) aboard the *Ranger*. Jones left Portsmouth, N.H., 2 Nov. 1777 and, after refitting at Nantes and Brest, sailed into the Irish Sea in Apr. He took 2 prizes (14–17 Apr.) and then on 23 Apr. landed at Whitehaven, England, spiked the guns of the fort, and set fire to a ship at anchor. That same evening he sailed to St. Mary's Island in Solway Firth, landing with the intention of kidnaping the Earl of Selkirk, who, in fact, was not on the island. Jones then crossed to the coast of northern Ireland, where, at Carrickfergus, he forced the British sloop *Drake* to strike after an hour's battle (24 Apr.) and took it to Brest (8 May).

28 JUNE. BATTLE OF MONMOUTH. The agony at Valley Forge ended for Washington on 19 June. Though the shrinking American army, desperately short of food, clothing, and military supplies, was but 20 miles from Philadelphia, Howe made no effort to disperse it during the winter. He was relieved by Clinton (8 May), who, concerned over reports of a French fleet heading for America, evacuated Philadelphia (18 June) and set out across New Jersey toward New York City. Washington broke camp at Valley Forge

on 19 June and started in pursuit. Gen. Charles Lee (who had been exchanged and had returned to the army 20 May) was given command of a strong advance corps (26 June) with orders to press home at the first opportunity an attack on Clinton's extended column. On the 28th Lee attacked near Monmouth Court House. His orders to Lafayette and Wayne were vague and contradictory and early advantages were not followed up. As British reinforcements arrived, Lee suddenly ordered a retreat, a move which encouraged Clinton to engage his main army. Washington's arrival checked the flight of Lee's command and the discipline which Von Steuben had instilled at Valley Forge showed its worth when the Americans beat back Clinton's repeated attacks. The British, who stole away during the night, marched to Sandy Hook and boarded transports which took them to New York. Both sides had suffered about 350 casualties at Monmouth. After a court-martial suspended Lee from the service for disobedience and misbehavior (4 July), Washington led his army northward, crossed the Hudson, and on 30 July took up a position at White Plains above New York City.

3 JULY AND 11 Nov. WYOMING AND CHERRY VALLEY MASSACRES. On 3 July Sir John Butler led Loyalists and Indians in a sweep through Pennsylvania's Wyoming Valley. In New York a series of raids planned by Sir John Johnson and Guy Johnson and executed by Butler's Rangers and Bryant's Indians terrorized the outlying settlements from May through the culminating attack on Cherry Valley (11 Nov.) in which some 40 survivors were massacred after they had surrendered.

4 JULY. CLARK'S CAPTURE OF KASKASKIA. In the fall of 1777 **George Rogers Clark** (p. 1001), a militia leader at Harrodsburg, Ky., proposed to the Virginia authorities an expedition against the British, Indians, and Loyalists who, under the command of Col. Henry Hamilton (the "Hair Buyer"), lieutenant governor at Detroit, were raiding western settlements. Commissioned lieutenant colonel by Gov. Patrick Henry, Clark with 175 men moved (May) to the Ohio River, sailed down it almost to the Mississippi, and then struck northwestward. On 4 July he occupied Kaskaskia and, with the support of the French inhabitants, the other posts in the area within the next 6 weeks, organizing the territory as part of Virginia. On 17 Dec. Hamilton recaptured Vincennes with a force, more than half of which were Indians, numbering over 500. Clark gathered about 150 men at Kaskaskia, set out (6 Feb. 1779) across inundated plains for Vincennes, reached there 23 Feb., and by various ruses caused Hamilton's Indians to desert and Hamilton himself to surrender (25 Feb.).

29 JULY–29 AUG. FRANCO-AMERICAN ATTACK ON NEWPORT. On 11 July a French fleet of 17 ships under the **Comte d'Estaing** arrived off New York harbor, but the size of his ships made a crossing of the bar so hazardous that the plan of a sea-land assault on New York was abandoned (22 July) in favor of a joint operation against a British garrison of 3,000 men at Newport, R.I. D'Estaing arrived off that town on 29 July but it was 8 Aug. before the American land forces under Gen. Sullivan were grouped before Newport in sufficient numbers to begin the operation, by which date Howe's reinforced fleet was on its way to aid the garrison. D'Estaing moved out to meet Howe on the 10th and a decisive battle loomed when a fierce storm (11 Aug.) scattered both fleets. Without naval support Sullivan had to withdraw from Newport after an attack on the

garrison (29 Aug.) in which each side suffered about 250 casualties. D'Estaing left Boston (where he had gone for repairs) for the West Indies (4 Nov.).

29 DEC. FALL OF SAVANNAH. Clinton now shifted British operations to the South, anticipating aid from large numbers of Loyalists. On 25 Nov. a detachment of 3,500 men embarked for Georgia under the command of Lt. Col. Archibald Campbell, landed near Savannah (29 Dec.), crushed 1,000 militia under Gen. **Robert Howe** (1732–86), and occupied the town.

1779

6 JAN.–19 JUNE. BRITISH PROGRESS IN THE SOUTH. On 6 Jan. Ft. Sunbury fell to a force under Gen. Augustine Prevost which pushed northward from Florida; Augusta was seized by Campbell 29 Jan. The Americans were heartened by Moultrie's successful defense of **Port Royal**, S.C., (3 Feb.) and by Col. **Andrew Pickens'** victory over a Loyalist brigade at Kettle Creek, Ga. (14 Feb.). However, an attempt to recapture Augusta from the British failed when Gen. **John Ashe** (c.1720–81) lost over 350 men and inflicted fewer than 20 casualties at **Briar Creek** (3 Mar.). When Gen. **Benjamin Lincoln** (1733–1810) with a corps of Continental troops detached by Washington moved inland for another attempt against Augusta (23 Apr.), Prevost struck northward along the coast and reached Charleston (12 May), but pulled back. Lincoln attacked the British rear at **Stono Ferry** (19 June), but lost 300 men to 130 enemy casualties and failed to prevent Prevost from regaining Savannah. In isolated actions in the South during the spring a force of North Carolina and Virginia troops led by Col. **Evan Shelby** (1719–94) struck successfully at Chickamauga Indian villages in Tennessee (Apr.), while the British captured and set fire to Portsmouth and Norfolk, Va. (10 May).

31 MAY–15 SEPT. WAR IN THE NORTH. On 31 May Clinton led 6,000 men up the Hudson and seized (1 June) 2 uncompleted American forts at Stony Point and Verplanck's Point. Another force under William Tryon, royal governor of New York, was sent to ravage (5–11 July) the Connecticut shore of Long Island Sound. On 15 July Gen. **Anthony Wayne** led 1,200 men in a night bayonet attack on **Stony Point** which bagged all but 1 man of the garrison of almost 700 at a cost of 15 killed, 83 wounded. Wayne dismantled the fort and evacuated it 18 July. While Clinton's attention was thus turned northward, Maj. **Harry Lee** (1756–1818) drove the British from their last major outpost in New Jersey, **Paulus Hook,** and took over 150 prisoners (19 Aug.).

More significant was the expedition led by Gens. **John Sullivan** and **James Clinton** (1736–1812) against the Loyalists and Indians who were ravaging the frontier settlements of Pennsylvania and New York. At Newtown (Elmira) a force of 1,500 Loyalists and Indians led by Sir **John Johnson** and **Joseph Brant** were defeated (29 Aug.). From Newtown, Sullivan moved northwestward meeting but scattered resistance. He destroyed 40 Seneca and Cayuga villages with their orchards and food plots and some 160,000 bushels of beans and maize. Sullivan turned back (15 Sept.) after penetrating as far as Geneseo (without pressing on to Ft. Niagara). His expedition had materially reduced the offensive threat from the Iroquois.

21 JUNE. SPAIN ENTERS THE WAR. Fearful for her American possessions, Spain opposed American independence. When Britain refused to cede Gibraltar to her as the price of her neutrality or mediation, Spain delivered an ultimatum (3 Apr. 1779), which, if accepted, would have sacrificed U.S. interests. On 12 April the secret **Convention of Aranjuez** between France and Spain provided for the entrance of the latter into the war if the ultimatum was rejected. When the British turned it down, Spanish and French fleets began joint operations in May. On 21 June Spain formally declared war on Great Britain, but refused to recognize U.S. independence or to pledge herself to fight on, as the French had, until that independence was secured. On 27 Sept. Congress appointed its president, **John Jay** (p. 1069), as minister to Spain, but he failed to obtain recognition, an alliance, or a substantial loan (he was able to borrow only $174,011) during his stay (Jan. 1780–May 1782).

14 AUG. CONGRESSIONAL PEACE TERMS. On 15 Feb. a report of a committee of Congress to propose peace terms (presented 23 Feb.) set forth as ultimata: independence, certain minimum boundaries, complete British evacuation of U.S. territory, rights to the fisheries, and free navigation of the Mississippi. Most of these terms were quickly approved by Congress, but those relating to the fisheries and the Mississippi occasioned long debate along sectional lines. Finally, on 14 Aug., Congress agreed on the instructions which were to guide the U.S. peace negotiator (still to be appointed). In these instructions the fisheries claim was removed from the list of ultimata, but that concerning the navigation of the Mississippi retained (4 Oct.). On 27 Sept., **John Adams,** who had replaced Silas Deane as one of the commissioners in Paris (8 Apr. 1778), was named to negotiate the peace treaty with Britain.

23 SEPT. "BONHOMME RICHARD" AND "SERAPIS." In Jan. Jones (in France) was given command of a decrepit French ship, the *Duc de Duras*.

He refitted it, crowded 42 guns aboard, and renamed it the *Bonhomme Richard* in Franklin's honor. On 14 Aug. he sailed from L'Orient with 1 other American ship and 4 French ships. Two of the French ships soon turned back. On 23 Sept. Jones sighted a fleet of 39 merchant ships convoyed by the *Serapis* (44 guns) and the *Countess of Scarborough* (22 guns) off the east coast of England. Jones bore down on the *Serapis* and began action at close range. The early exchanges went heavily in favor of the *Serapis,* but a query as to surrender brought "I have not yet begun to fight" as Jones' reply. American marksmen in the rigging took a heavy toll on the enemy's deck, an American grenade touched off a powder explosion on the gun deck of the *Serapis,* and when its mainmast fell Capt. Pearson struck his flag. With the *Richard* in flames (it sank on the 24th) Jones transferred his 237-man crew, half of them casualties, to the *Serapis* and brought it to port 6 Oct. One of the French ships in Jones' squadron, the *Pallas,* took the *Countess of Scarborough* during the *Richard-Serapis* engagement.

3 Sept.–28 Oct. FAILURE AT SAVANNAH. On 3 Sept., off Savannah, Adm. d'Estaing returned to the American coast with a French fleet of 35 ships and 4,000 troops. He captured 2 British frigates and 2 supply ships and then moved against Prevost's 3,000-man garrison in Savannah (15 Sept.). On the 23rd 1,400 American troops under Gen. Lincoln joined the French in besieging the city. The siege proceeded too slowly for d'Estaing's timetable; assault was pressed on 9 Oct. D'Estaing was wounded, Count **Casimir Pulaski** (1749–79) killed, and the Allies suffered over 800 casualties to 155 of Prevost's. With the withdrawal of d'Estaing's fleet (28 Oct.) the initiative again passed to the British. Clinton evacuated Rhode Island (11 Oct.) to permit an increased effort in the South and on 26 Dec. left New York with nearly 8,000 troops with Charleston as his target.

1780

11 Feb.–12 May. FALL OF CHARLESTON. Clinton arrived off the Carolina coast on 1 Feb. By 11 Apr. he had completed the investment of the city with 14,000 attackers. On 6 May Ft. Moultrie fell; Lincoln capitulated on the 12th. At a cost of only 255 casualties Clinton captured the 5,400-man garrison and 4 American ships, making this the heaviest American defeat of the war. On 29 May a force of cavalry under Col. **Banastre Tarleton** destroyed a Virginia regiment at **Waxhaw Creek.** On 5 June Clinton left for New York, satisfied that South Carolina was rewon for the crown, leaving Cornwallis with about 8,000 men to maintain, and if possible extend, control.

28 Feb. RUSSIA'S ARMED NEUTRALITY. The declaration of Catherine II that the Russian navy would be used against all belligerents to protect neutral Russian trade was a blow to British blockade efforts against France and Spain, for Russia refused to recognize naval stores (required by the Allies) as contraband. More significant was Catherine's invitation to other European neutrals to join in a **League of Armed Neutrality.** Denmark (9 July) and Sweden (1 Aug.) promptly accepted; the Netherlands, Prussia, Portugal, Austria, and the Kingdom of the Two Sicilies joined in the next 2 years. Britain went to war with the Netherlands (20 Dec.) and was able to shut off the clandestine trade between the U.S. and the Dutch island of St. Eustatius in the West Indies, center of contraband trade with the U.S. Although the League failed to aid the Dutch, its existence hampered

British naval measures against the Allies. On 19 Dec. Congress appointed Francis Dana as minister to Russia, but he was ignored at St. Petersburg.

25 MAY. MUTINY AT WASHINGTON'S CAMP. The condition of Washington's army during the winter of 1779–80 at Morristown, N.J., was even more critical than at Valley Forge, as supplies failed to arrive (Mar.) owing to the drop in value of Continental currency (40 [Continental] to 1 [Specie]). Rations were cut to one eighth of normal quantity during the next 6 weeks. On 25 May 2 Connecticut regiments paraded under arms to demand a full ration and immediate payment of their salaries, then 5 months in arrears, but were curbed by Pennsylvania troops.

11 JULY. FRENCH ARMY AT NEWPORT. Under the **Comte de Rochambeau** (1725–1807) 5,000 troops with a strong naval escort sailed from France on 2 May and arrived at Newport, R.I., 11 July. Washington planned to combine this army with his own for an attack on New York, but lacked adequate naval support. A British fleet under Adms. Marriot Arbuthnot and George Rodney blockaded Newport within a few weeks of Rochambeau's arrival.

16 AUG. BATTLE OF CAMDEN. The British hold on Georgia and South Carolina was not seriously challenged (guerrilla bands led by **Andrew Pickens** [1739–1817], **Francis Marion** [p. 1097], and **Thomas Sumter** [1734–1832] prevented consolidating British strength until Gates was commissioned by Congress [13 June] to lead a Southern Army with a core of Continental troops detached by Washington). Gates took over his command at Coxe's Mill, N.C. (25 July), and began a slow march against the British post and supply base at Camden, S.C. Cornwallis, with about 2,400 men, made contact with the Americans early on 16 Aug. north of that town. American troops

broke when Tarleton's dragoons came crashing down upon their rear. Estimated U.S. losses: 800–900 killed (including Kalb) and 1,000 captured. Gates fell back to Hillsboro, N.C., 160 miles from Camden.

Defeat by Tarleton of an American force under Sumter at Fishing Creek, S.C. (18 Aug.), opened the way for a British invasion of North Carolina, begun by Cornwallis 8 Sept. On 7 Oct. a Loyalist force of about 1,100 led by Maj. Patrick Ferguson, screening Cornwallis' left flank, was caught atop **King's Mountain** on the border between the Carolinas by a 900-man force of American frontiersmen under Col. **Isaac Shelby** (1750–1826) and Col. **William Campbell** (1745–81). The marksmanship of the backwoodsmen prevailed over Ferguson's bayonet charges. The Americans lost 28 killed, 62 wounded in killing or capturing the entire enemy force. Cornwallis retreated back into South Carolina and established winter quarters at Winnsborough (14 Oct.). On the same day capable **Nathanael Greene** was named to succeed Gates in the southern command.

c.SEPT. 1780–JUNE 1781. RUSSO-AUSTRIAN COMEDIATION PROPOSALS. As the war spread without decisive results, neutral nations pressed for a negotiated peace. Count Nikita Panin, the Russian chancellor, proposed a general armistice to be followed by a peace conference to which delegates from the 13 separate American states rather than the Continental Congress would be invited. Austrian chancellor Prince Wenzel Anton von Kaunitz propelled himself by April 1781 into the role of comediator. While recognizing that the Panin-Kaunitz formula would mean the partition of America, Vergennes was prepared to accept it. However, in July 1781 John Adams reminded him that the authority to negotiate with foreign powers was the exclusive province of the Congress under the Articles of Confederation. Adams' timely intervention ended the comediation efforts.

21 Sept. TREASON OF ARNOLD. As early as May 1779 Benedict Arnold, then under fire for his administration as military commander of Philadelphia, opened negotiations with Gen. Sir Henry Clinton in New York and by 23 May was sending him information on Washington's movements. Relations were broken off for a time when Clinton refused (late July) to pay £10,000 to Arnold for his services and indemnify him as well for any losses he might suffer if detected. But after a court-martial found Arnold guilty on 2 charges of misusing his powers at Philadelphia (26 Jan. 1780) and after Washington, in keeping with the decision of the court, reprimanded Arnold officially (6 Apr.), Arnold reopened negotiations with the British in May. On 15 June he informed them that he expected to be put in command of West Point and on 12 July wrote Maj. John André, Clinton's adjutant, that he desired a conference with a British officer to plan the "disposal" of that key fortress. Arnold took up command at West Point 5 Aug. and on 21 Sept. met André on the west bank of the Hudson near Haverstraw to deliver plans of the fort and inform the British of its weak points. On his way back to the British lines André doffed his uniform in favor of civilian clothes against Clinton's specific orders. On 23 Sept. he was captured by 3 New York militiamen near Tarrytown and the incriminating papers discovered. His captors, not suspecting Arnold's part in the affair, sent word of André's apprehension to him at West Point. When Arnold received this information (25 Sept.) he fled to the *Vulture,* a British warship in the Hudson. On 29 Sept. André was convicted as a spy, and executed on 2 Oct. For his treachery Arnold was commissioned a brigadier general in the British army and

received £6,315 in cash, an annual pension of £500 for his wife Peggy (Shippen), army commissions for 3 sons by a previous marriage, and, beginning in 1783, pensions of £100 a year each for Peggy's 5 young children. Arnold led British raids against Virginia (Dec. 1780–Apr. 1781) and New London, Conn. (6 Sept. 1781).

1781

1 Jan. MUTINY OF THE PENNSYLVANIA LINE. The appearance of recruiting agents who paid $25 in coin to new enlistees provoked 1,500 out of 2,400 veterans of the Pennsylvania division to quit their quarters, seize arms and artillery, kill one and wound several officers who tried to stop them, and march off under their sergeants toward Philadelphia. On 3 Jan. they made camp at Princeton and elected negotiators to treat with the officials of their state. Joseph Reed, president of Pennsylvania's Executive Council, who opened negotiations (7 Jan.), made concessions which ended the mutiny, though over half the line left the service. When, on 20 Jan., troops of the New Jersey Line mutinied at Pompton, Washington dispatched Gen. Robert Howe with 600 men, some from West Point, others from Pompton vicinity, to put down the mutiny. Howe surprised the mutineers' camp (27 Jan.), forced them to parade unarmed, restored the officers to their commands, and had 2 men executed. Another outbreak among the Pennsylvania troops in May was similarly nipped by several executions.

20 Feb. ROBERT MORRIS MADE SUPERINTENDENT OF FINANCE. On 6 Feb. Congress resolved to establish a department of finance under a superintendent responsible to Congress. On 20 Feb. **Robert Morris** (p. 1108) was named. He took office on 14 May at a critical time. Despite subsidies and loans from France and Spain (totaling for the entire period of the war almost $9 million), American finances were close to collapse after 1779. By the beginning of 1780 Congress had issued $191,500,000 in paper money ("Continentals"). Additional millions were outstanding in quartermaster certificates (receipts given in payment by the army for supplies it requisitioned), close to $50 million in loan-office certificates, most paying 6% interest, and more debits in the form of certificates given soldiers for their back pay. An attempt had been made (Jan. 1779) to retire some of the paper money, but when the failure of the states to provide for the current expenses of the war resulted in new issues exceeding the amount retired by over $35 million Continental currency dropped precipitately. On 14 Jan. 1779 it stood at 8–1 with specie but by the end of the year was down to 40–1. On 18 Mar. 1780 Congress resolved to retire the bills in circulation by accepting them in payments due it from the states at one fortieth their face value. About $120 million in Continental bills was thus retired while the remaining $71 million was worthless by the end of 1780. When Morris took office his first proposal (21 May) was for a national bank, which Congress approved (26 May), but did not actually charter the Bank of North America until 31 Dec. In June Morris received authorization to supply the army by contract rather than by the inefficient and expensive system of requisition from the states. A timely subsidy from France (May) and French backing for a large loan from the Netherlands (5 Nov.) enabled Morris to make some progress toward returning the country to a specie basis by the end of the year.

1 MAR. RATIFICATION OF THE ARTICLES OF CONFEDERATION, before the states ever since November 1777, was delayed by Maryland's refusal to ratify until the states claiming western lands ceded them to the U.S. With the cession by Virginia (2 Jan. 1781, and p. 596), Maryland signed the Articles, 27 Feb. Congress then set 1 Mar. for final ratification and on 2 Mar. assumed a new title, "The United States in Congress Assembled." The president of the old Congress, **Samuel Huntington** (Conn., 1731–96), continued in office.

WAR IN THE CAROLINAS. After assuming command of the army in the South in Dec. 1780, Gen. Greene moved from North Carolina to Cheraw, S.C. Too weak to attack Cornwallis' main camp at Winnsborough, he detached Gen. **Daniel Morgan** with about 800 men for a sweep to the west and **Henry Lee** for guerrilla activity between Cornwallis and Charleston. Cornwallis ordered Tarleton to drive Morgan back against the main British force. But Morgan selected a position near **Cowpens**, disposed his force (now grown to 1,000) with great care, and met Tarleton's assault there on 17 Jan. By skillful handling of his militia and assisted by cavalry under Col. **William Washington** (1752–1810), Morgan won a smashing victory over the 1,000-man enemy force, suffering less than 75 casualties to Tarleton's 329, and capturing 600. Cornwallis now pursued Morgan into North Carolina. At Guilford Courthouse Greene and Morgan joined forces (9 Feb.) and retreated across the Dan River into Virginia. Lacking boats and supplies, Cornwallis was forced to discontinue the pursuit and withdrew into North Carolina. When reinforcements brought Greene's command up to 4,400 men he followed the British and offered battle at **Guilford Courthouse** (15 Mar.), where Cornwallis won the field but at a cost of almost 100 killed and over 400 wounded. Too weakened by these losses to continue the campaign, he retreated (18 Mar.) to

Wilmington to receive reinforcements by sea.

Greene now marched into South Carolina, and though defeated at **Hobkirk's Hill** (25 Apr.), failed in his siege of the British post at **Ninety-Six** (22 May–19 June), and lost again at **Eutaw Springs** (8 Sept.), he managed (aided by successes scored by Marion, Lee, and Sumter in capturing the smaller British posts in the state) by fall to narrow British control in South Carolina to Charleston and its immediate vicinity.

2 APR. "MARS" AND "MINERVA." In Apr. Capt. **John Barry** (1745–1803), returning from France on the *Alliance,* was attacked by 2 British privateers, the *Mars* and the *Minerva,* but soon had forced both to surrender (2 Apr.). On 29 May, while becalmed, 2 British men-of-war, the *Atalanta* and the *Trepassy,* attacked. Barry was badly wounded but held his rebellious crew to their guns until a breeze enabled him to drive between his attackers and force each to surrender. 1781 also saw a new high in the number of American privateers in action: 449. By the end of the war American privateers had accounted for about 600 British ships, worth, with their cargoes, over $18 million. The Continental Navy captured or destroyed 196 enemy ships during the war.

14 JUNE. U.S. PEACE COMMISSION. On 11 June Congress decided to entrust the peace negotiations to a commission rather than to John Adams alone. **John Jay** (13 June), **Benjamin Franklin, Henry Laurens** (1724–92), and **Thomas Jefferson** (14 June) were named in addition to **Adams.** On 15 June Congress modified the 1779 peace instructions. Only U.S. independence and sovereignty were deemed essential. Other matters were to be handled by the commissioners at their discretion without definite binding instructions. This change was made largely on the advice of the Chevalier de la Luzerne, French minister to the U.S., who was also responsible for that section of the instructions which directed the commission to take no action without the "knowledge and concurrence" of the French ministry and which bound them to "ultimately govern yourselves by their advice and opinion."

10 MAY–1 AUG. CORNWALLIS' CAMPAIGN IN VIRGINIA. Convinced that British control could not be restored in the Carolinas while Virginia remained as a supply and training base for the Americans, Cornwallis left Wilmington 25 Apr. with 1,500 men and marched northward into Virginia. At Petersburg (20 May) he joined his small force to a body of over 4,000 British troops which had followed up Arnold's expedition. Further reinforcements brought his strength to about 7,500, much superior to the small American forces under Lafayette and Von Steuben. He raided deep into Virginia (Tarleton almost captured Gov. Jefferson and the members of the legislature at Charlottesville, 4 June). But as Lafayette was reinforced by Anthony Wayne (10 June) and then joined by Von Steuben (19 June), Cornwallis turned back to the coast to establish a base from which he could maintain communication by sea with Clinton's force in New York. He picked Yorktown, where he arrived 1 Aug.

21 MAY. MEETING OF WASHINGTON AND ROCHAMBEAU. At a conference at Wethersfield, Conn., Washington secured Rochambeau's reluctant consent for a joint attack against New York supported by the French West Indian fleet under Comte de Grasse. Rochambeau left de Grasse free either to sail to New York or to operate against the British in Virginia. Meanwhile the French army moved from Rhode Island and joined Washington's above New York (5 July). Before a large-scale at-

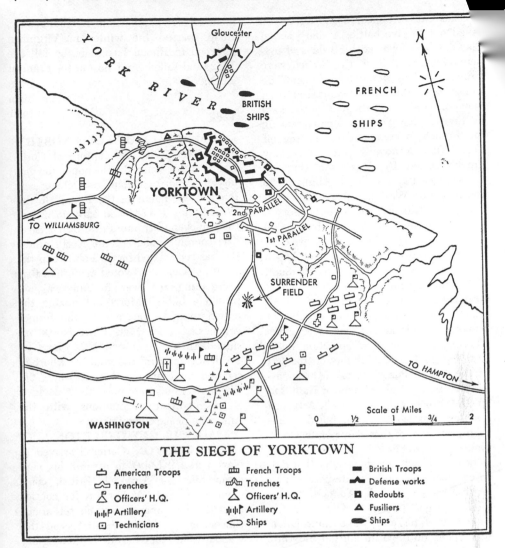

THE SIEGE OF YORKTOWN

	American Troops		French Troops		British Troops
	Trenches		Trenches		Defense works
	Officers' H.Q.		Officers' H.Q.		Redoubts
	Artillery		Artillery		Fusiliers
	Technicians		Ships		Ships

tack could be mounted, a letter from de Grasse reached Washington (14 Aug.) with news that he would leave the West Indies for Chesapeake Bay on 13 Aug. with 3,000 French troops and his entire fleet and would be available for operations in that area until mid-Oct. Washington immediately prepared to march both his and Rochambeau's troops to Virginia. Preserving the appearance of a movement against New York, the two armies crossed the Hudson (20–26 Aug.), feinted toward Staten Island, and then struck out southward across New Jersey.

30 Aug.–19 Oct. YORKTOWN CAMPAIGN. On 30 Aug. de Grasse arrived off Yorktown, set up a naval blockade of the garrison with his fleet, and landed (31 Aug.) his troops to join Lafayette's forces hemming in Cornwallis by land. On 5 Sept. the British fleet under Adm.

...omas Graves appeared and de Grasse ...iled out to give battle. A sharp action ...hat day was followed by 3 days of maneuvering. On 9 Sept. the French were strengthened by the arrival of Comte de Barras with the French squadron from Newport and on 10 Sept. Graves drew off toward New York for repairs, leaving the French in command of the sea off Yorktown. Cornwallis' fate was now quickly sealed. De Grasse sent ships up Chesapeake Bay to bring the bulk of the forces under Washington and Rochambeau to Williamsburg (14–24 Sept.). From there the Allied army (about 9,000 American and 7,800 French troops) moved forward (28 Sept.) and began the siege of Yorktown. On 30 Sept. Cornwallis abandoned his outer line of fortifications, thereby permitting the Allies to bring up siege guns capable of hammering all parts of his inner line. These guns went into operation on 9 Oct. On 14 Oct. 2 redoubts on the left of the British line were taken in an assault in which Col. **Alexander Hamilton** (p. 1048) distinguished himself. A British counterattack on the 16th failed to regain possession of these key points. Cornwallis now regarded his position as hopeless and when a storm later that day forced him to abandon a desperate plan for escaping across the York River, he opened negotiations (17 Oct.) for the surrender of his army. The capitulation was signed on the 18th and on the 19th the British force of almost 8,000 men laid down their arms. Total Allied casualties were 262, against 552 British casualties (excluding prisoners). On 24 Oct. Clinton arrived off Chesapeake Bay with 7,000 reinforcements for Cornwallis, but put back to New York when he learned of the surrender. Washington now urged an attack on New York, but de Grasse, now overdue in the West Indies, refused to participate. Washington marched his army northward to resume the envelopment of New York while Rochambeau's troops passed the winter in Virginia, returned to Rhode Island in the fall of 1782, and sailed from Boston for France 24 Dec.

1782

20 Mar. **FALL OF LORD NORTH'S MINISTRY.** With the capture of Cornwallis' entire army British hopes for victory in America collapsed. Defeats suffered at the hands of the French in the West Indies in 1781 and early 1782 further quickened Britain's desire for peace. The coercive policy of the North ministry was repudiated on 27 Feb. when the House of Commons voted against further prosecuting the war in America and passed a bill (5 Mar.) authorizing the crown to make peace with the former colonies. On 20 Mar. Lord North resigned. He was succeeded (22 Mar.) by Lord Rockingham, the minister who had secured the Stamp Act's repeal in 1766. The new ministry immediately decided to open direct negotiations with the American peace commissioners.

4 Apr. **SIR GUY CARLETON SUCCEEDS CLINTON.** Carleton arrived in New York (9 May) to assume his new commission (4 Apr.) as British commander in chief. With plans for continuing the war abandoned, he set about concentrating all British forces on the seaboard at New York. Wilmington, N.C., had been evacuated (Jan.), Savannah (11 July), and finally Charleston (14 Dec.). A skirmish at Combahee River, S.C. (27 Aug.), was the last land action of the war on the seaboard.

12 Apr. **PEACE TALKS BEGIN IN PARIS. Richard Oswald,** named by the Rockingham ministry to open peace negotiations with the American commissioners, began talks with Franklin (12 Apr.), at that time the only commissioner present in Paris. The British re-

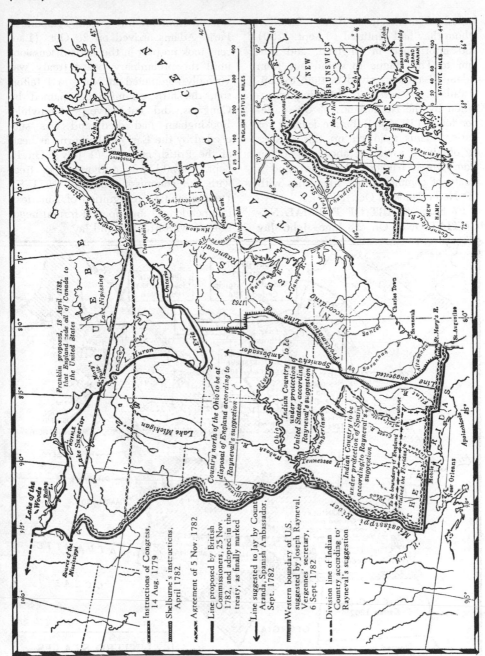

Boundaries proposed in the peace negotiations of 1782
between the United States and England

leased Commissioner Henry Laurens, whom they had captured (3 Sept. 1780) and imprisoned in England, and sent him to The Hague to sound out John Adams. Laurens arrived in time to congratulate the latter on obtaining recognition by the Netherlands of U.S. independence (19 Apr.). Before leaving for Paris, Adams followed up this success by obtaining a loan of about $2 million from Dutch bankers (11 June) and a treaty of commerce and friendship with the Netherlands (8 Oct.).

27 Sept. START OF FORMAL NEGOTIATIONS. On 23 June, John Jay arrived from Madrid to join Franklin in Paris. Adams arrived on 26 Oct. (Laurens took no part in the Paris discussions until the preliminary peace treaty was virtually completed in Nov., and Jefferson, the fifth commissioner named by Congress, did not serve.) Meanwhile, Rockingham had died and was succeeded by the **Earl of Shelburne** as head of the British ministry (1 July). On 19 Sept. Oswald was authorized to treat with the commission of the "13 U.S." (tantamount to recognition of American independence) and opened formal negotiations with Franklin and Jay.

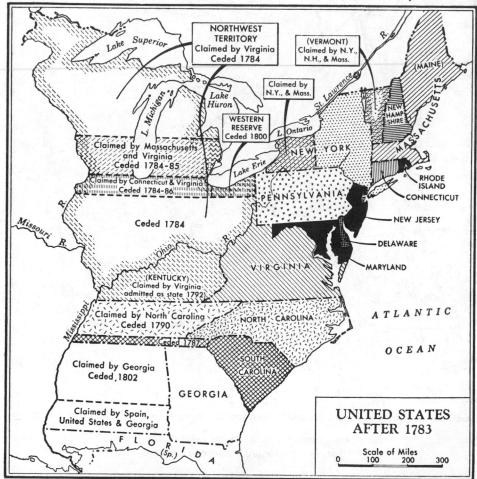

UNITED STATES AFTER 1783

30 Nov. SIGNING OF PRELIMINARY ARTICLES OF PEACE. Jay's fears that France, in support of Spain, was determined to confine the U.S. within severe territorial limits and curtail her fishing rights were touched off by news (9 Sept.) that French undersecretary Gérard de Rayneval had gone on a secret mission to Shelburne. To counter this move, Jay dispatched to England a pro-American Englishman, Benjamin Vaughan, to press upon Shelburne the urgency of acknowledging U.S. independence as a precondition to any settlement. On 18 Sept. Shelburne persuaded the British cabinet to revise Oswald's commission in the manner Jay had requested. On Oswald's return to Paris, 27 Sept., with the new commission, negotiations moved forward rapidly. On 5 Oct. Jay presented Oswald with the draft of a preliminary treaty, to become effective when a similar treaty was signed by Britain and France. Upon the basis of these preliminary articles (which did not include an earlier demand by Franklin that Canada be ceded to the U.S.) negotiations continued. Oswald was joined by Henry Strachey (28 Oct.), Undersecretary of State in the Home Office. About 1 Nov. the 3 U.S. commissioners (Adams was now on the scene) decided to disobey Congress' instructions concerning full consultation with the French and to proceed on their own initiative. A new set of articles was agreed to on 5 Nov. With a few last-minute changes these constituted the preliminary treaty of peace signed by Oswald for the British and by Adams, Franklin, Jay, and Laurens for the U.S. Without a single change these articles became the definitive peace treaty signed 3 Sept. 1783. Its most important provisions: (1) Britain recognized U.S. independence; (2) boundaries: the St. Croix River dividing Maine and Nova Scotia; the St. Lawrence-Atlantic watershed divide, the 45th parallel, a line through the Great Lakes and their connecting waterways, and a line from Lake Superior to the Mississippi dividing Canada and the U.S.; a line through the middle of the Mississippi River south to the 31st parallel to be the boundary with Spanish Louisiana; and the 31st parallel and the Apalachicola and St. Mary's rivers as the boundary with Spanish Florida (Spain obtained Florida from Britain in the final peace treaty); (3) U.S. given the "right" to fish in their accustomed grounds off Newfoundland and Nova Scotia, and the "liberty" to dry and cure fish on any unsettled shore in Labrador, the Magdalen Islands, and Nova Scotia; (4) all debts due creditors of either country by citizens of the other were validated; (5) Congress was pledged to "earnestly recommend" to the legislatures of the states a full restoration of the rights and property of the Loyalists; and (6) hostilities were to cease and all British land and sea forces evacuated "with all convenient speed."

Vergennes, taken aback by the extremely favorable terms obtained for the U.S., criticized the commissioners (15 Dec.) for signing without consulting him. However, his own desire for a speedy settlement of the war and a tactful reply by Franklin (17 Dec.) prevented serious discord.

1783

20 Jan. EFFECTIVE DATE OF ARTICLES OF PEACE. The Anglo-American preliminary treaty was not to go into effect until Britain reached a settlement with France. On 20 Jan. preliminary articles of peace were signed between Britain and France and by Britain and Spain. Provisions were then made for a general armistice and on 4 Feb. Britain proclaimed a cessation of hostilities.

10, 12 Mar. NEWBURGH ADDRESSES. Early in Jan. a delegation of army officers memorialized Congress regarding grounds of their discontent: arrears in pay, unsettled food and clothing accounts, and Congress' failure to make provision for the life pension of half pay from the time of their discharge promised them 21 Oct. 1780. Their failure to obtain assurances of payment of sums owed officers and to secure a commutation of the pension for 6 years' full pay (rejected 25 Jan. by Congress) led to the first anonymous address to the officers of the army circulated at Washington's main camp near Newburgh, N.Y. Written by Maj. **John Armstrong** (1758–1843), the address attacked the "coldness and severity" shown by Congress, advised the officers to assume a bold tone and "suspect the man who would advise to more moderation and longer forbearance," and called upon them to meet the next day (11 Mar.) and draw up a "last remonstrance" which, if not well received by Congress, would justify the army in defying that body. Armstrong's call for pressure on Congress had the backing of Gen. Gates, Gouverneur Morris (1752–1816), and other civilian leaders who hoped to coerce the states into yielding more power to Congress. The address was well received by many of the officers, but Washington, with skill and tact, soon blunted the movement's force. On 11 Mar. he issued an order forbidding the unauthorized meeting called for by the anonymous address on that day, but went on to propose a regular meeting of the officers for the discussion of grievances on 15 Mar. A second anonymous address (also written by Armstrong) was issued on 12 Mar., expressing the opinion that Washington's action in calling for a meeting proved that he "sanctified" the claims of the officers. To the consternation of the plotters, Washington addressed the 15 Mar.

meeting in person, denounced the resort to immoderate measures, while promising quick redress for the officers' grievances. After Washington withdrew, the officers adopted resolutions, without dissent, affirming their patriotism, their confidence in Congress, and their disdain for the "infamous propositions . . . in a late anonymous address." Congress a week later granted the officers a sum equal to 5 years' full pay. Washington's stand is a historic precedent for the subordination of the military to civilian government.

15 Apr. ARTICLES OF PEACE RATIFIED. On 13 Mar. Congress received the text of the provisional treaty from Paris. On 11 Apr. it issued a similar proclamation of the cessation of the war and on 15 Apr. ratified the provisional treaty after a debate in which the action of the commissioners in proceeding without consulting the French came in for considerable criticism. The treaty was signed in Paris 3 Sept., ratified by Congress 14 Jan. 1784, ratifications exchanged 12 May 1784.

26 Apr. 7,000 LOYALISTS SAIL FROM NEW YORK, their departure made necessary by the impending embarkation of the British army. This group was among the last of the total of almost 100,000 Loyalists who left the U.S. for Europe or Canada. The early "test acts" passed by the revolutionary state governments in 1776–77 requiring a repudiation of loyalty to George III had been followed by more severe repressive measures. Nine states had passed acts exiling prominent Tories, 5 had disfranchised all Loyalists, and in most of the states Loyalists were expelled from all offices, barred from the professions, and forced to pay double or treble taxes. On 27 Nov. 1777 Congress recommended to the states that they appropriate the property of residents who had forfeited "the right to protection." By 1782 all the states had passed confiscation acts, some, in fact, antedating Congress' recommendation. New York obtained over $3,600,000 and Maryland over $2 million from the sale of Loyalist property. The British government established a commission (July) to which the Loyalists might present claims to cover their damages. The commission functioned until 1790, examined 4,118 claims, and authorized payment of a generous total of £3,292,452 in compensation.

13 June. ARMY DISBANDS. Congress voted (26 May) to give furloughs to soldiers who had enlisted for the duration until the signing of the peace treaty should permit their full discharge. Certificates for 3 months' pay were authorized for those furloughed. On 13 June, without waiting for these certificates to reach camp, most of Washington's army departed for their homes from the camps in the Hudson Highlands. On 18 Oct. Congress discharged all previously furloughed and on 3 Nov. discharged all other troops enlisted for the duration of the war. Only a small force of men serving time enlistments remained with Washington to await the evacuation of New York City by the British.

24 June. CONGRESS FLEES PHILADELPHIA. On 17 June about 80 soldiers began a march from Lancaster to Philadelphia to obtain justice from the state government and from Congress; they were joined (21 June) by an additional 200 from regiments in Philadelphia, and demonstrated before Independence Hall, where both the executive council of Pennsylvania and Congress were meeting. When the state authorities proved unwilling or unable to deal with the mutineers, President **Elias Boudinot** (1740–1821) changed the meeting place of Congress from Philadelphia to Princeton (24 June). Congress met there until 3 Nov., when it adjourned to meet 26 Nov. at Annapolis, Md., under a plan (adopted 21 Oct.) calling for alternate sessions there and at Trenton until dual permanent seats for the government (authorized 7 and 17 Oct.) were established on the Delaware and Potomac rivers.

25 Nov. BRITISH EVACUATE NEW YORK CITY. On 21 Nov. the British drew back from northern Manhattan Island and from eastern Long Island into New York City and Brooklyn. Washington moved to Manhattan, taking up a position at Harlem Heights. Early in the afternoon of the 25th the last British troops left the docks of New York and Washington, accompanied by Gov. **George Clinton** (p. 1003), entered the city. By 4 Dec. the British had completed the evacuation of Staten Island and Long Island and were putting out to sea in their transports. On that same day Washington took leave of his officers at Fraunces' Tavern. After a triumphal tour to Annapolis where the Congress was in session, he appeared before that body (23 Dec.) to resign his commission as commander in chief and "take . . . leave of all the employments of public life."

SIGNIFICANT RESULTS OF THE REVOLUTION: (1) The 13 colonies became independent states and united under the Confederation of the U.S.; (2) the U.S. obtained title to a vast empire from the seaboard settlements to the Mississippi; (3) royal and proprietary colonial governments were replaced by republican state governments; (4) the overthrow of the royal and proprietary ruling class and the participation of men of all social levels in the Revolution brought a broader popular base to political life; (5) the confiscation of royal lands, proprietary estates, and Loyalist property, though chiefly designed as revenue-raising measures, brought, ultimately, a somewhat more democratic redistribution of property; (6) quitrents formerly collected by the crown and by colonial proprietors were abolished by the states; (7) entail and primogeniture, twin pillars of aristocratic land holding, were virtually abolished by state legislation, 1776–91; (8) the Anglican Church was disestablished in all colonies in which it had been tax-supported, 1776–86; (9) the slave trade was prohibited or heavily taxed in 11 states (1776–86), slavery abolished in Massachusetts (1780), in New Hampshire (1784), and gradual emancipation adopted by Pennsylvania (1780), Connecticut (1784), and Rhode Island (1784); (10) the reform of penal codes and prisons was advanced as well as the secularization and democratization of education.

1784

STATE CONSTITUTIONS. During the Revolution 11 of the 13 states drew up new constitutions. (Connecticut and Rhode Island continued to use the colonial charters of 1662 and 1663, merely deleting all references to the British crown.) Except in the case of Massachusetts, where a constitutional convention was called (1779) and its handiwork submitted to the people for ratification (1780), these new constitutions were the work of revolutionary congresses or conventions. Constitutions were adopted by New Hampshire, New Jersey, Pennsylvania, Delaware, Maryland, Virginia, North Carolina, and South Carolina in 1776; by New York and Georgia in 1777.

Main features: (1) **Bicameral legislature** (exceptions: Pennsylvania, with a unicameral legislature and plural executive—executive council of 13; and New Hampshire, with an executive council under 1776 constitution). (2) **Weak chief executive:** in 9 of 13 states his term was for 1 year; in 7 his reeligibility was variously limited; in 9 a veto power denied him. In 9 out of 11 the executive shared appointing power with the legislature; governors with greatest power were found in Massachusetts and New York, elected by the people rather than by the legislature. (3) **Strong legislature:** elected executive in 8 states; shared appointing power in 6; lower house originated all money bills in 9. (4) **Frequent elections:** in every state except South Carolina (where both houses had 2-year terms) the lower house was elected annually, or semiannually (Rhode Island and Connecticut); upper house elected annually in 8 states for terms of 2 years (South Carolina), 3 years (Delaware), and 4 years (New York and Virginia). (5) **Property qualifications for office-holding** ranged as high as £10,000 for governor (South Carolina); £2,000 (North Carolina); £1,000 (New Jersey and Maryland) for the upper house; £500 (New Jersey and Maryland) for the lower. (6) **Property qualifications for voting** ranged from payment of a low poll tax (New Hampshire and Pennsylvania, where sons of freeholders were eligible to vote without payment of taxes) to Virginia's requirement of 25 acres of settled or 500 acres of unsettled land, with a shift from a freehold to a taxpaying qualification in evidence in numerous states. (7) **An appointive judiciary with tenure for good behavior** (8 states; annual appointment, Connecticut and Rhode Island; for 5 years, New Hampshire; for 7 years, New Jersey and Pennsylvania).

Innovations: (1) **Bills of Rights** (beginning with Virginia, 12 June 1776, drafted by **George Mason,** p. 1098) included in many constitutions; (2) **Council of Appointment** in New York, chosen annually from senate and assembly, exercised (with the governor, who had but one vote) appointive power; (3) **Council of Censors** in Pennsylvania, elected by the people every seventh year and empowered to investigate actions of the assembly and executive council and summon a convention to consider constitutional amendments.

23 Apr. JEFFERSON'S 1ST TERRITORIAL ORDINANCE. On 1 Mar., the day Congress accepted a revised version of Virginia's cession of her western lands, a committee headed by Jefferson proposed a plan for temporary government in the West, the division of the domain into states to enter the Confederacy on equality with the original members. Jefferson's proposal prohibiting slavery after 1800 in all parts was narrowly defeated. After amendments, the report was adopted 23 Apr. and, though never put into effect, served as the basis for the Northwest Ordinance (1787).

7 May. SECRETARY FOR FOREIGN AFFAIRS. In Dec. 1783 Robert R. Livingston (p. 1087) resigned as first Secretary for Foreign Affairs (named 10 Aug. 1781). After long delay **John Jay**, then about to return to America from Europe, was named to succeed him.

May–July. WYOMING VALLEY VIOLENCE. On 30 Dec. 1782 a 5-man court appointed by Congress (Aug.) held unanimously that the disputed title to the Wyoming Valley claimed by both Pennsylvania and Connecticut should be awarded the former, whose territory was contiguous. Without awaiting settlement of individual claims, the Pennsylvania Assembly approved a plan to oust the Connecticut settlers (1783). Militia actions against settlers were denounced by the Pennsylvania Council of Censors, which forced the assembly to enact measures (15 Sept.) restoring settlers to their lands under protection of a new commission (9 Sept.). After further violence in 1787, a Pennsylvania act of that year brought an equitable and conclusive settlement.

28 May. TREASURY BOARD. At his own request Robert Morris was replaced as Superintendent of Finance by a board of 3 commissioners—**Samuel Osgood** (1748–1813), **Walter Livingston** (1740–97), named 25 Jan., and **Arthur Lee** (27 July). The central government was still dependent upon requisitions on the states. Of an $8 million requisition (Oct. 1781) only $1,486,512 had been paid by 1 Jan. 1784. Late in 1783 Morris had been forced to overdraw his account in Europe to provide for the army's demobilization pay. Negotiation of loans by John Adams in Holland (1784) enabled Morris to pay off $230,000 in notes (outstanding 1 Jan.) and leave office (1 Nov.) with a surplus of $21,000.

30 Aug. OPENING OF CHINA TRADE. Independence brought freedom from the British Navigation Acts but also the closing to the U.S. of the British West Indies. A British order in council (2 July 1783) banned importation of meats, fish, and dairy products from the U.S. into the West Indies and closed the trade in all other products to all but British ships. As a result, American businessmen looked to new markets, notably to the Orient. On 22 Feb. the *Empress of China*, Capt. John Greene, sailed from New York by way of Cape Horn and reached Canton 30 Aug. The profit from the cargo of tea and silks which it brought back (May 1785) prompted merchants of Philadelphia, Boston, and Providence to fit out ships for China. Despite gains in trade with France and Holland, Britain was still the best customer of the U.S., in part the result of an order in council (26 Dec. 1783) permitting the importation of American manufactured goods (with a few exceptions) into Britain on the same favorable terms as in colonial days.

British exports to the U.S. amounted (1784) to £3,679,467 as against imports from the U.S. of only £749,345. The unbalance increased specie scarcity in the U.S. and led to overextension of inventories and credit.

23 Dec. NEW YORK TEMPORARY CAPITAL. Congress met in Trenton (1 Nov.) and voted (10 Dec.) to move from Trenton; on the 23rd it appointed commissioners to lay out a federal district on the banks of the Delaware and to move to New York until the federal city was ready.

1785

16 Feb. CONGRESS AND THE COMMERCE POWER. The weakness of the central government under the Articles of Confederation made it difficult to obtain commercial concessions from foreign nations. The British ambassador in Paris told Franklin, Adams, and Jefferson (26 Mar.) that Britain could hardly enter into a treaty with Congress when one state could render "totally fruitless and ineffectual" any such agreement, and proposed that they obtain authorizations from the individual states as well. Congress unsuccessfully appealed in 1784 for a 15-year grant of power to regulate foreign commerce. On 24 Jan. a committee headed by **James Monroe** (p. 1105) was appointed to consider a new appeal to the states. Its report called for an amendment to the 9th Article, which forbade Congress to enter into any treaty of commerce that deprived any state of its individual right to impose duties. No action was taken.

24 Feb., 10 Mar. MINISTERS TO BRITAIN AND FRANCE. On 31 July 1784, Jefferson reached Paris to serve with Franklin and Adams as commissioners to negotiate commercial treaties. On 24 Feb. Congress appointed John Adams minister to the Court of St. James

and granted Franklin's request to be replaced as minister to France, appointing (10 Mar.) Jefferson to succeed him. Jefferson was received by Louis XVI on 17 May and Adams by George III on 1 June.

8 Mar. HENRY KNOX SECRETARY OF WAR. In 1781 Congress replaced the cumbersome Board of War by a Secretary heading a War Department. Gen. Lincoln held that office until 1783. After a 2-year vacancy Knox was chosen to succeed him.

28 Mar. MT. VERNON CONFERENCE. Late in March 4 commissioners from Virginia, including Madison and Mason, met at Alexandria with 4 Maryland commissioners, including Samuel Chase (1741–1811), to consider problems relating to the navigation of Chesapeake Bay and Potomac River. On 28 Mar. the negotiators adjourned to **Mt. Vernon,** where Washington acted as their host but apparently took no direct part in the discussions. Swift agreement was reached concerning the jurisdiction of the Potomac and the apportionment of expenses for marking the channel through Chesapeake Bay. The commissioners then drafted an agreement recommending to their respective legislatures uniform commercial regulations and imposts, a uniform currency, and annual conferences on common commercial problems. A request was also drawn up that Pennsylvania be invited to join Virginia and Maryland in a pact to establish water communication between the Chesapeake and the Ohio River. The Maryland legislature not only endorsed this plan (5 Dec.) but proposed the addition of Delaware. At Madison's behest, the Virginia legislature invited (21 Jan. 1786) all the states to discuss commercial problems at a convention to be held at Annapolis (Sept.).

20 May. BASIC LAND ORDINANCE provided for rectangular surveys dividing the land into townships of 6 miles square. Townships were to be divided into 36 lots of 640 acres each (1 lot set aside for maintaining public schools; but an attempt to include another lot for the support of the religion of the majority of resident adult males narrowly missed passage) and sale of minimum lots (640 acres) authorized at $1 an acre.

23 JUNE–11 JULY. MASSACHUSETTS AND FOREIGN COMMERCE. As early as 1783 Maryland laid discriminatory rates and port fees on British shipping and South Carolina imposed a general duty of 2½% on foreign goods, with higher rates on specified articles. Pennsylvania, New York, and North Carolina acted in 1784. On 23 June Massachusetts banned the export of U.S. products in British ships and doubled the tonnage duty on all goods imported in other than American ships. New Hampshire took similar steps the same day. Earlier in June Rhode Island passed a high protective tariff to encourage domestic industry. On 11 July the Massachusetts legislature passed a resolution favoring a convention to revise the Articles of Confederation, but her delegates at New York failed to offer this resolution. Pennsylvania (20 Sept.) placed a discriminatory tonnage duty on ships of foreign nations which had no treaties with the U.S. U.S. imports from Britain totaled £2,308,023, a drop of £1,371,444 from the abnormally high figure of 1784, but exports to Britain rose from £749,345 (1784) to £893,594.

20 JULY. JAY-GARDOQUI NEGOTIATIONS. Spain refused to be bound by that part of the Anglo-American treaty which set the 31st parallel as the boundary between Spanish Florida and the U.S., claiming the territory 100 miles northward as far as the junction of the Yazoo River with the Mississippi (at 32°22′), and in 1784 refused to permit American shipping to pass freely through the lower Mississippi. On 15 May 1785 Don Diego de Gardoqui arrived as Spanish minister to the U.S. with specific instructions to make no concession on the navigation of the Mississippi. Congress authorized John Jay to negotiate with Gardoqui (20 July) and instructed him (24 Aug.) "particularly to stipulate the right of the United States to . . . the free navigation of the Mississippi. . . ." A year of fruitless negotiation followed. Finally, on 29 Aug. 1786, Congress authorized Jay to "forbear" American navigation rights for 25 or 30 years in return for a favorable commercial treaty with Spain. But the bitter debate on this authorization and the close vote (7–5) indicated the unlikelihood that 9 states (required by the Articles) would ratify the treaty. Hence, negotiations broke down, and the issues remained unsettled until the Pinckney Treaty of 1795.

10 SEPT. TREATY WITH PRUSSIA. John Adams negotiated (1784) with Baron Thulemeier, Prussian minister at The Hague, but was called to his English post before completing the treaty. Jefferson then sent his secretary, William Short, to complete negotiations. The treaty outlawed privateering and endorsed the principle of free ships-free goods.

30 Nov. NEGOTIATIONS WITH BRITAIN. In Britain Adams found that the inability of the U.S. to force the states to abide by those terms of the Treaty of Paris concerning the treatment of Loyalists and the removal of impediments to collection of debts to English creditors made it virtually impossible for him to obtain commercial concessions or British compliance with the treaty terms requiring them to evacuate Oswego, Niagara, Detroit, Michilimackinac, and other garrisons on U.S. soil. Adams' formal demand (30 Nov.) for the evacuation of the western posts brought the blunt reply (28 Feb. 1786) that the posts would be held until British creditors obtained payment from America. After 3 years, during which he pressed U.S. claims tenaciously but without success, Adams resigned and left for the U.S. (Apr. 1788).

1786

16 JAN. ADOPTION OF THE VIRGINIA STATUTE FOR RELIGIOUS FREEDOM. In 1779 an Ordinance of Religious Freedom written by Jefferson was proposed in the Virginia legislature and failed of adoption, but in Dec. 1785, virtually the same measure, now brought forward by James Madison, passed the House of Burgesses. Model for the 1st Amendment of the U.S. Constitution, the statute declared that no man could be compelled to attend or support any church nor suffer any discrimination because of his religious beliefs. Jefferson ranked his authorship of this act with the drafting of the Declaration of Independence and the founding of the Univ. of Virginia as his most significant accomplishments. Some months earlier Madison had drafted (June, 1785) his "**Memorial and Remonstrance**" against religious assessments, which successfully propagandized against a bill to have a general assessment levied for the support of religion and argued the inalienable right of individual freedom of conscience.

28. JUNE. TREATY WITH MOROCCO. With the removal of the protection of the British fleet, American commerce in the Mediterranean and off the coasts of Spain and Portugal suffered substantial losses from pirates from Algiers, Tripoli, Tunis, and Morocco. On 22 Feb. John Adams had an interview in London with the Tripolitine ambassador, Abdrahaman, who demanded £200,000 for the protection of U.S. commerce. Negotiations broke down.

Jefferson proposed a plan for an international expedition against the Barbary states, but Congress balked at contributing a frigate. On 28 June, Thomas Barclay, in direct negotiations with the Emperor of Morocco, obtained a treaty in exchange for gifts worth about $10,000. With Algiers, Tripoli, and Tunis, however, the U.S. was unable to reach agreements until 1795, 1796, and 1797 respectively.

JUNE–SEPT. LOW POINT OF DEPRESSION (p. 746). Imports from and exports to Great Britain dropped to £1,603,465 and £843,119 respectively compared to £2,308,023 and £893,594 (1785). Farm wages showed a decline of as much as 20% from the 1780 level. The combination of a money shortage, high taxes, and insistent creditors brought demands for relief through stay laws and paper money. The paper-money advocates succeeded in obtaining issues totaling £800,000 in Pennsylvania (Mar. 1785), South Carolina (Oct. 1785), North Carolina (Nov. 1785), New York (Apr.), Rhode Island (May), New Jersey (May), and Georgia (Aug.). In the remaining 6 states the pressure for similar action was greatest in Massachusetts. In Rhode Island the paper-money issue provided the background for the case of *Trevett* v. *Weeden,* in which the state's supreme court upheld the doctrine of judicial review propounded by counsel James Varnum in ruling (25 Sept.) that an act forcing a creditor to accept the paper money was unconstitutional.

7 AUG. PROPOSALS TO REVISE THE ARTICLES. On 26 June Congress debated a motion (3 May) by **Charles Pinckney** (S.C., 1757–1824) for a reorganization of the government. The debates and the proposed amendments submitted 7 Aug. by a special committee reveal the delegates' awareness of the weaknesses of the Articles of Confedera

tion. One proposal would have set up a federal court of 7 judges with appeal jurisdiction from the state courts in cases involving foreign nations and federal matters; another would have given Congress power over foreign and domestic commerce; 2 others attempted to strengthen the requisition system to ensure payment of the state quotas. (The need for such measures had been highlighted when New Jersey flatly refused, 20 Feb., to pay the requisition voted by Congress in Sept. 1785.) Congress, apparently despairing of winning that unanimous approval necessary under the Articles for adoption of an amendment, never submitted these proposals to the states.

11–14 Sept. ANNAPOLIS CONVENTION. Virginia's invitation to an interstate commercial convention at Annapolis (issued on 21 Jan.) was accepted by 9 states. Georgia, South Carolina, Connecticut, and, oddly enough, Maryland took no action. The delegates named by New Hampshire, Massachusetts, Rhode Island, and North Carolina failed to reach Annapolis in time to participate. Hence, only New York, New Jersey, Delaware, Pennsylvania, and Virginia were represented. When the convention opened on the 11th John Dickinson, now a resident of Delaware, was elected chairman. The slim attendance convinced the 12 delegates that it would be useless to proceed to a study of interstate commercial problems. A committee was appointed, however, on 13 Sept. to prepare an address to the states, which the convention adopted 14 Sept. Drafted by **Alexander Hamilton,** a leading force at the meeting, the report called upon the states to send commissioners to a new convention at Philadelphia on the 2d Monday in May 1787, to discuss not only commercial problems but *all* matters necessary "to render the constitu-

tion of the Federal Government adequate to the exigencies of the Union." Congress referred this invitation to committee 11 Oct. Not until 21 Feb. 1787 was a cautious endorsement of the plan adopted. On that day Congress described as "expedient" a convention "for the sole and express purpose of revising the Articles of Confederation and reporting to Congress and the several legislatures such alterations and provisions therein." Five states (Virginia, New Jersey, Pennsylvania, Delaware, and North Carolina) had already named delegates to the Philadelphia convention.

Aug.–Dec. SHAYS' REBELLION. When the Massachusetts legislature adjourned on 8 July without heeding the petitions of the debt-ridden farmers for a paper-money issue or laws to stay the mounting number of farm and home foreclosures, discontent mounted. A town meeting of protest at Worcester (15 Aug.) was followed by a Hampshire Co. convention of some 50 towns at Hatfield (22–25 Aug.) The delegates condemned the Massachusetts senate, lawyers, the high costs of justice, and the tax system, and called for an issue of paper money. They also advised against violence, but mob action followed. On 31 Aug. armed men prevented the sitting of the court at Northampton and on 5 Sept. the court at Worcester was broken up. When similar mob actions occurred at Concord and Great Barrington, Gov. **James Bowdoin** (1726–90) sent 600 militiamen under Gen. **William Shepherd** (1737–1817) to protect the supreme court sitting at Springfield. About 500 insurgents gathered there under the leadership of **Daniel Shays** (1747–1825), a destitute farmer who had risen to the rank of captain during the Revolution, confronted the militia (26 Sept.), and obliged the court to adjourn. Shays' presence in Springfield, site of a federal arsenal, prompted Congress to authorize Gen. Knox to raise 1,340 men, mostly in Massachusetts and Connecticut, ostensibly for service against the Indians (20 Oct.). Actually, the federal forces never had to be used. The insurrection in eastern Massachusetts collapsed with the capture of Job Shattuck on 30 Nov. A greater threat to public order was posed in the western part of the state. At Worcester Shays gathered a force of about 1,200 men during Nov. and early Dec. On 26 Dec. he marched to Springfield to join forces with other insurgents led by Luke Day and threaten Shepherd's smaller force guarding the arsenal. The governor called for 4,400 men, enlisted for one month, to assemble at Boston and Springfield on 18–19 Jan. Command was given to Gen. **Benjamin Lincoln.**

1787

4 Feb. SHAYSITES ROUTED AT PETERSHAM. Shays and Day, their forces separated by the Connecticut River, planned to scatter Shepherd's force and seize the arsenal before Lincoln reached Springfield. On 24 Jan. Shays proposed a combined assault the next day. Day's reply that he could not attack until the 26th was intercepted, with the result that Shays went ahead confident of Day's cooperation. About 4 P.M. he led some 1,200 men toward the arsenal. When the insurgents approached to within 100 yards of the building (despite warnings), Shepherd opened fire with artillery. The Shaysites quickly broke and fled, leaving 4 dead. On 27 Jan. Lincoln arrived at Springfield and on the 28th moved on to Amherst, pushing Shays before him to Pelham and isolating Day, who fled to New Hampshire. On 3 Feb., in the midst of negotiations, Shays marched eastward to Petersham. Lincoln followed in a punishing night march and early on 4 Feb. surprised the insurgents, captured 150, scattered the rest, and sent Shays fleeing to Vermont. The uprising was completely crushed by the end of Feb. In Mar. the legislature offered a pardon to all Shaysites except Shays, Day, and 2 other leaders. Shays was finally pardoned 13 June 1788. The uprising had the effect of inducing the legislature not to impose a direct tax in 1787 and to enact laws lowering court fees and exempting clothing, household goods, and tools of one's trade from debt process.

Feb.–May. DELEGATES NAMED TO PHILADELPHIA CONVENTION. In addition to the 5 states that had already acted, 6 others (Massachusetts, New York, Georgia, South Carolina, Maryland, and Connecticut) named delegates. New Hampshire and Rhode Island were the only states that failed to act by the date set (14 May) for the opening of the convention. New Hampshire finally fell into line in June (its delegates reached Philadelphia 23 July) but Rhode Island ignored the convention.

25 May. OPENING OF CONSTITUTIONAL CONVENTION. On 14 May only the delegates from Virginia and Pennsylvania were on hand at Philadelphia's State House (Independence Hall). Not until 25 May was a quorum of 7 states obtained. From 81-year-old Franklin to 26-year-old Jonathan Dayton (New Jersey, 1760–1824) the delegates included outstanding public figures. Most respected and influential men were Washington and Franklin, while the actual leaders in the floor debates proved to be **Madison** and **George Mason** (Virginia), **Gouverneur Morris** and **James Wilson** (Pennsylvania), **Roger Sherman** (Conn.) and **Elbridge Gerry** (Massachusetts, 1744–1814). Of the 55 delegates 29 were college trained, over half were lawyers, while planters and merchants together with a few physicians and college professors made up the rest. When the convention opened Robert Morris nominated **Washington** as president; this won unanimous approval. **William Jackson** (Ga., 1759–1828) was elected secretary. (The journal kept by Jackson was meager; knowledge of the debates is derived very largely from notes taken each day by Madison. In keeping with the pledge of secrecy [29 May] these were not published until 1840, 4 years after his death.)

29 MAY. VIRGINIA PLAN. Edmund Randolph (Virginia, 1753–1813) proposed 15 resolutions comprising the "Virginia Plan" of Union, which went beyond revision of the Articles and favored a new national government. Outstanding features: (1) a bicameral national legislature, representing the states proportionally, with the lower house elected by the people, and the upper house by the lower house from nominees proposed by the state legislatures; (2) an executive chosen by the legislature; (3) a judiciary including a supreme court and inferior courts elected by the legislature; (4) a council of revision consisting of the executive and several members of the judiciary, with a veto over the legislature's acts. On 30 May the convention resolved itself into a committee of the whole and debated the Virginia Plan until 13 June. On that date 19 resolutions based on Randolph's proposals were reported to the convention.

15 JUNE. NEW JERSEY PLAN. Opposition to the Virginia Plan came chiefly from the small states and centered upon the provision for proportional rather than equal representation of the states in both houses of the proposed legislature. On 15 June **William Paterson** (New Jersey, 1745–1806) introduced 9 resolutions which stressed retention of the confederation but conferred upon Congress the powers to tax and regulate foreign and interstate com-

merce and to name a plural executive (without a veto) and a supreme court. U.S. treaties and acts of Congress were to be the supreme law in the states. The issue before the convention: whether to content themselves with amendments to the Articles or to draw up the framework of a new national government. After 3 days of debate (16–19 June) the convention voted 7–3 to work toward a national government as visualized in the Virginia Plan. The committee of the whole now debated the issue of equal versus proportional representation in the legislature.

13 JULY. NORTHWEST ORDINANCE. While the convention was debating a plan to supplant the Articles, the Congress of the Confederation registered its greatest achievement, the ordinance for the government of the territory north of the Ohio River. Based in part upon Jefferson's plan of 1784 and in part upon a committee report of 19 Sept. 1786, the Northwest Ordinance, largely written by Nathan Dane (Mass.), provided: (1) the territory to be governed initially by a governor, a secretary, and 3 judges appointed by Congress; (2) when there were 5,000 free adult males in the territory a bicameral legislature to be established; (3) ultimately, from 3 to 5 states to be created (a population of 60,000 free inhabitants was requisite for admission to the Union); (4) the new states to be "on an equal footing with the original states in all respects whatsoever"; (5) freedom of worship, right of trial by jury, and public support of education provided; and (6) involuntary servitude, save in punishment for crime, prohibited. On 5 Oct. **Arthur St. Clair** was elected first governor of the territory and **Winthrop Sargent** (1753–1820) named secretary.

16 JULY. CONNECTICUT COMPROMISE. A committee (appointed 2 July) reconsidered and rejected a pro-

opposition was considerable. In the convention, which met 21 Nov., the Federalist representatives from Philadelphia and the commercial towns defeated the Antifederalist moves for amendments and delays, and finally won on 12 Dec. by 46–23. In New Jersey, where Antifederalism was weak, the state convention required only a week's time to vote unanimously for ratification (18 Dec.).

1788

2 Jan.–6 Feb. FURTHER RATIFICATIONS. On 2 Jan., Georgia became the fourth state to ratify the Constitution and the third to do so unanimously. Connecticut was next to act favorably. Its convention met 4 Jan. and voted (9 Jan.) 128–40 for ratification. On that same day the Massachusetts convention met. Early estimates of Antifederalist strength gave opponents 192 votes against 144 for the Federalists, who reduced this opposition 30 Jan. by proposing that amendments to the Constitution be recommended along with ratification, a move which won over Sam Adams, and swung the convention for ratification. The Constitution was approved unconditionally (187–168) on 6 Feb. along with 9 recommended amendments, most significant, the reservation to the states of all powers not "expressly delegated" by the Constitution to the central government.

24 Mar. REJECTION BY RHODE ISLAND. Despite the failure of Rhode Island to send a delegation to the Philadelphia convention, the commercial and professional groups of the state made a determined effort to have the legislature call a state convention, but the rural legislators rejected a convention and proposed instead (Feb.) a popular referendum (held 24 Mar.), in which the Federalists refused to participate. Out of 2,945 of the more than 6,000 eligible to vote, only 237 voted in favor of the

Constitution. Not until Jan. 1790 was a state convention called. On 29 May 1790 Rhode Island finally ratified (34–32).

21 June. NINTH STATE RATIFIES. On 28 Apr. the Maryland convention ratified (63–11); South Carolina was next to act. Though the resolution for a convention passed by only one vote in the legislature (12 May), in the convention Antifederalist sentiment was much weaker, and ratification passed (23 May) by a large majority (149–73). With 8 states having ratified, one more was necessary for adoption of the Constitution. A New Hampshire convention, meeting 13 Feb., adjourned after a week until 18 June. The Federalists overcame an early majority against them and won by 57–47 on 21 June. Twelve amendments were proposed.

25 June, 26 July. RATIFICATION IN VIRGINIA AND NEW YORK. Virginia's convention met on 2 June with Patrick Henry leading the foes of the Constitution and Madison in the vanguard of its supporters. The latter's logical arguments counteracted Henry's eloquence; the vote on 25 June showed 89 for, 79 against. Virginia attached to ratification proposals for a bill of rights of 20 articles as well as 20 other changes. In New York the convention met at Poughkeepsie on 17 June with Gov. George Clinton's Antifederalists holding a clear majority. Hamilton worked for delay, counting on the effect of news of affirmative action by New Hampshire and Virginia. His strategy turned the tide. A plan for conditional ratification was rejected (25 July) and on 26 July ratification was carried, 30–27.

2 Aug. RATIFICATION IN NORTH CAROLINA. In the North Carolina convention, which met on 21 July, despite strong Federalist sentiment, the view prevailed that ratification should be withheld until the incorporation of certain amendments, particularly a bill of rights. The submission of 12 proposed amendments to the states by the new Congress on 25 Sept. 1789 led to a second convention (16–23 Nov. 1789) at which ratification was carried (194–77) 21 Nov.

13 SEPT. CONGRESS PREPARES FOR THE NEW GOVERNMENT. On 2 July the president of Congress, Cyrus Griffin (Virginia, 1748–1810), announced that the Constitution had been ratified by the requisite 9 states. A committee, appointed to prepare the details for the change in government, reported (8 July), but not until 13 Sept. did Congress adopt an ordinance which set the site of the new government as New York and

fixed the dates in 1789 for the appointment of presidential electors (7 Jan.), for the balloting by the electors (4 Feb.), and for the meeting of the first Congress under the Constitution (4 Mar.). On 2 Oct. the last Congress under the Articles was unceremoniously moved from its rooms in New York's City Hall in order that the edifice might be renovated as the capitol for the incoming government. On 10 Oct. Congress transacted its last official business. The only significant political action thereafter was the cession by Maryland (23 Dec.) of 10 square miles to Congress for a federal town, future site of the District of Columbia.

THE EARLY NATIONAL AND ANTEBELLUM PERIODS, 1789-1860

★ ★
★

In a scant dozen years of Federalist rule the Constitution was demonstrated to be a workable instrument of government. The chief executive determined the powers and traditions of the presidency, the cabinet system evolved, a federal judiciary was established, the taxing power was wielded audaciously and effectively, a national debt was created to strengthen the national authority and stimulate the economy. American credit was fixed at home and abroad on a firm foundation, and American territory cleared of British and Spanish interlopers. The coming of the French Revolution precipitated the rise of a two-party system, unanticipated by the founding fathers. Holding national survival as the central objective of foreign policy, the first two presidents prudently steered a neutral course.

In his old age Jefferson retrospectively hailed his election to the presidency in 1800 as a "revolution," but his eight years as president fell far short of accomplishing a root-and-branch change in the governmental system inherited from the Federalists. Much the same observation might be made of the next twenty years of Republican rule. Despite their rhetoric, the Republicans neither opposed private property nor sought to turn the country into a "mobocracy." Jefferson's aristocratic inclinations notwithstanding, he had the vision to identify himself with the cause of the common man, and if the substance of the Republican administration was not too different from its predecessors, the style sharply diverged. The sense of American nationality which emerged in this era was buttressed by great nationalist decisions of the Supreme Court, by huge territorial acquisitions—Louisiana Territory and Florida—by an inconclusive second war with Britain, and by the inauguration of extensive internal improvements.

With the accession of Andrew Jackson to the presidency the pace of change swiftened. It was a time of political ferment, when the elective franchise was broadened, popular participation in politics intensified, the spirit of reform was in the air, the railroads introduced a transportation revolution, and such issues as labor, banking, the tariff, and slavery impinged on national and local politics. It was a time of manifest destiny, in which the acquisition of Texas, the war

1

with Mexico, and the settlement of the conflict over Oregon gave the United States in substance its present continental domain.

In the decades before the Civil War the movement to abolish or restrict slavery became the central national issue. By 1840 abolitionism was a political movement, touching off a vigorous response from the slaveholding states both ideologically and politically. While great unifying forces were at work, sectional differences, both economically and culturally, were if anything intensified, and these sectional tensions were strained to the breaking point by the issue of the extension of slavery to the territories. Neither the compromises of 1820 or 1850 nor the Kansas-Nebraska Act effected a durable resolution between the sections. "Bleeding Kansas," the Dred Scott decision, John Brown's raid, and the election of 1860 created an unbridgeable chasm between North and South, with the Southern states moving in a seemingly irreversible course toward secession.

1789

7 JAN. FIRST PRESIDENTIAL ELECTION. Presidential electors, chosen in all of the ratifying states with the exception of New York, were named either by the state legislatures or directly by the people. On 4 Feb., as elections of senators and representatives progressed in the various states, the presidential electors cast their ballots.

4 MAR. FIRST CONGRESS under the Constitution met in New York without a quorum (8 senators and 13 representatives present, the remainder still en route); 54 of the members of the first Congress had been members of the Federal Convention or state ratifying conventions; all but 7 had advocated ratification.

1 APR. HOUSE OF REPRESENTATIVES organized, with 30 of its 59 members present. Frederick A. Muhlenberg (Pa.) was elected speaker, and on 8 Apr. the House began its deliberations.

6 APR. THE SENATE, with 9 of its 22 members present, elected as temporary presiding officer John Langdon (N.H.), who counted the ballots cast by the presidential electors. **George Washington,** with 69 votes, was unanimously elected president; **John Adams,** receiving 34 votes, was chosen vice-president.

30 APR. FIRST INAUGURAL. On 16 Apr. Washington set out from Mount Vernon for New York City, arriving there on 23 Apr. Adams, meanwhile, had taken his seat as vice-president on 21 Apr. In a ceremony held on the balcony of Federal Hall, at the corner of Wall and Broad streets, Washington was inaugurated as the first president of the U.S. The oath of office was administered by Robert R. Livingston, chancellor of the state of New York. The first inaugural address was delivered in the Senate chamber housed in Federal Hall.

9 SEPT.–22 DEC. BILL OF RIGHTS. The Constitution, already ratified by 11 states, was ratified by North Carolina (21 Nov.) and Rhode Island (29 May 1790), whose delay pointed to the active strength of the Antifederalists. Five state ratifying conventions had stressed the need for immediate amendments to the Constitution; Federalist leaders had pledged themselves to changes in the Constitution; and in his inaugural address Washington had alluded to such alteration. Moreover, the Federalists wanted to forestall action on demands for a second constitutional convention.

Chiefly at the instigation of James Madison, the House of Representatives decided (9 Sept.) to recommend for adoption by the various states 12 amendments originally suggested by the state ratifying conventions (submitted to states 25 Sept.). Of these amendments, 10 were ratified by the states, and comprised a specific Bill of Rights. New Jersey was the first state to ratify these amendments (20 Nov.); Maryland followed on 19 Dec. and North Carolina on 22 Dec. On 15 Dec. 1791 the Bill of Rights became part of the Constitution.

EXECUTIVE DEPARTMENTS. The first executive department created under the new government was that of Foreign Affairs. Established on 27 July, it was officially redesignated (15 Sept.) as the Department of State. **Thomas Jefferson** was appointed (26 Sept.) to head the department, but did not take office until 22 March 1790. During the interim, John Jay handled the affairs of the State Department.

The War Department was set up on 7 Aug.; **Henry Knox** was named Secretary of War (12 Sept.). The Treasury Department was established on 2 Sept.; **Alexander Hamilton** was appointed Secretary of the Treasury (11 Sept.). The office of Postmaster General was created by Congress (22 Sept.); **Samuel Osgood** appointed to that office 26 Sept. The Post Office Department was established by Congress 8 May 1795.

24 SEPT. FEDERAL JUDICIARY ACT made provision for the organization of the Supreme Court to consist of a chief justice and 5 associates, as well as 13 district and 3 circuit courts; and established the office of attorney general. On 26 Sept. **John Jay** became chief justice of the U.S. and Edmund Randolph became attorney general.

1790

HAMILTON'S FISCAL PROGRAM. The chief issue of Washington's first term was the fiscal program devised by Alexander Hamilton and submitted to the House of Representatives in a series of reports on the national and state debt, an excise tax, and a national bank. Controversy over these proposals ultimately led to the party cleavage between Federalists and Republicans.

14 JAN. FIRST REPORT ON THE PUBLIC CREDIT. Hamilton dealt with the debt inherited from the Confederation. The foreign debt, held chiefly by the French and Dutch, was set at $11,710,-379; the domestic debt, including arrears of interest and unliquidated claims and currency, was fixed at $40,414,086; state debts were estimated at $25 million. Hamilton recommended (1) funding of the foreign and domestic debt at par, enabling creditors to exchange depreciated securities for new interest-bearing bonds at face value; and (2) assumption by the federal government, to the extent of $21,500,000, of debts incurred by the states during the Revolution.

These measures had a double purpose: (1) to establish and maintain the public credit and thereby revive confidence in the government at home and abroad; (2) to strengthen and stabilize the central government by fostering a consciousness of national solidarity of interest among those business and commercial groups holding the greater part of the domestic debt.

While the proposal concerning the foreign debt was virtually unopposed, the plan to fund the domestic debt was bitterly attacked by debtor and agrarian groups compelled by necessity to sell their securities at a steep discount. James Madison's proposal to discriminate between original holders and subsequent purchasers was rejected (22 Feb.) by the House by almost 3 to 1.

Arousing even heavier opposition was the assumption scheme, which resulted in an approximately sectional alignment. The New England states, with the largest unpaid debts, generally favored assumption. But the Southern states, most of whom had made arrangements for discharging their indebtedness, were hostile to an immense increase in the national debt for which their inhabitants would be taxed. In addition, they feared that assumption would tend to aggrandize federal power at the expense of the states.

Virginia led the opposition to the plan, and her leading congressional spokesman, Madison, broke with the administration on this score. The assumption proposal was defeated in the House (12 Apr.) by a vote of 31 to 29.

SECTIONAL COMPROMISE. Hamilton's resourceful negotiations kept the assumption measure alive, and differences were finally settled by a compromise on the location of the permanent seat of the national government hammered out between congressmen from Pennsylvania and Virginia even before Hamilton, consulting with Madison at a dinner party (c.20 June) arranged by Jefferson, had agreed to exert his influence to secure enough Northern votes to assure location of the national capital along the Potomac (instead of Philadelphia) in return for Madison's pledge to obtain a sufficient number of Southern votes to effect passage of assumption.

The House, 32–29 (10 July), fixed the site of the projected national capital in a district 10 miles square along the Potomac, the precise area to be selected by the president. Philadelphia, where Congress assembled on 6 Dec., was named temporary capital until 1800. By 34–28 (26 July) the House adopted the assumption plan, and the funding provision for the debt became law on 4 Aug.

SOUTHERN FEARS. Despite the compromise, Southern apprehensions still remained, and found their voice in the Virginia resolutions (16 Dec.) framed by Patrick Henry. The Virginians protested that the assumption scheme established and perpetuated a moneyed interest, subordinated agricultural to commercial interests, and was inimical to republican institutions and the federal form of government, and that they could "find no clause in the constitution authorizing Congress to assume the debts of states!" Wrote Hamilton, privately: "This is the first symptom of a spirit which must either be killed, or will kill the Constitution."

1791

25 Feb. BANK OF THE U.S. On 13 Dec. 1790 Hamilton submitted to the House his report on a national bank. Before signing (25 Feb.) the bill chartering the Bank of the U.S., President Washington requested members of his cabinet to submit written opinions on the constitutionality of the measure.

Jefferson's opinion (15 Feb.) maintaining that the bill was unconstitutional advanced the doctrine commonly known as "strict constructionist." Jefferson took as his main ground the 10th Amendment (not yet adopted). The incorporation of a bank, he argued, was not among the powers specifically delegated to Congress.

Hamilton's opinion (23 Feb.) elaborated the doctrine of "implied powers" (the so-called "loose constructionist" view of the Constitution). He contended that the proposed bank was related to congressional power to collect taxes and regulate trade: a delegated power implied the employment of such means as were proper for its execution. He declared: "If the *end* be clearly comprehended within any of the specified powers, and if the measure have an obvious relation to that *end,* and is not forbidden by any particular provision of the Constitution, it may safely be deemed to come within the compass of the national authority."

Although Washington was not fully convinced of the weight of argument on either side, he favored Hamilton's view on the ground that in such instances presidential support should go to the cabinet officer whose department was immediately and directly involved.

3 Mar. WHISKY TAX. Hamilton's second report on the public credit (13 Dec. 1790) recommended an excise tax on the manufacture of distilled liquors as a means of supplementing revenue yielded by the traiff. This levy, imposing a heavy burden on backwoods farmers for whom distilling was the chief mode of disposing of surplus grain (owing to poor roads and high shipment costs), stirred keen discontent among those affected by it.

EMERGING POLITICAL ALIGNMENTS. Dissatisfied with the administration's fiscal policies, Jefferson and Madison made a tour (May–June) of New York state, with excursions into New England, where they appear to have sounded out Antifederalist sentiment (particularly among the Clinton-Livingston-Burr faction in New York) for the purpose of forming a coalition on national lines. The political breach was widened with the establishment (31 Oct.) of the *National Gazette,* an anti-administration organ under the editorship of Philip Freneau, which soon crossed swords with the Federalist *Gazette of the United States* edited by John Fenno (begun 15 Apr. 1789).

The emerging **Jefferson-Hamilton feud** later became a personal quarrel, but its essential significance lay in its origin: a conflict of principle over the nature and ends of society and government. Jeffersonian principles embraced (1) a democratic agrarian order based on the individual freeholder; (2) a broad diffusion of wealth; (3) relative freedom from industrialism, urbanism, and organized finance; (4) sympathy for debtor interests; (5) distrust of centralized government; (6) belief in the perfectibility of man; and (7) confidence in the view that the people, acting through representative institutions, could be left to govern themselves. Hamiltonian principles included (1) a balanced and diversified economic order; (2) active governmental encouragement of finance, industry, commerce, and shipping; (3) sympathy for creditor interests; (4) advocacy of a strong national government under executive leadership; (5) distrust of the people's capacity to govern; and (6) a belief that the best government was that of an elite.

These views generally reflected the doctrines associated with the two national parties (in each case a larger grouping of local coalitions) formed during this period: the Republicans, also known as the Democratic-Republicans, under the leadership of Jefferson; and the Federalists, under the leadership of Hamilton. Competent latter-day authorities differ over the approximate date of origin of these parties. Among the dates indicated for their definite emergence are 1787–88 (C. A. Beard), 1791–92 (J. S. Bassett; D. Malone), 1792–93 (N. Cunningham), and 1798 (O. G. Libby).

26 Nov. ORIGINS OF THE CABINET. As early as Oct. 1789 Washington consulted heads of departments on the advisability of his making a tour of the U.S. He continued to consult them individually on matters of policy. On 26 Nov. and 28 Dec. 1791 he met with department heads to consider foreign and military matters. At least 3 such meetings occurred in 1792. By the time Adams became president the practice of cabinet meetings was well established.

5 Dec. REPORT ON MANUFAC-TURES submitted by Hamilton proposed a system of tariffs for industry, bounties for agriculture, and a network of internal improvements under federal sponsorship. Hamilton's argument for encouraging manufactures made no marked impression at this time.

1792

21 Feb. PRESIDENTIAL SUCCESSION ACT (passed the House, 31–24, after passing the Senate 27–24) provided that in case of the removal, death, resignation, or disability of both president and vice-president, the president pro tempore of the Senate would succeed; if there was no Senate president, then the speaker of the House. The Federalists defeated Jefferson's effort to have the Secretary of State made next in line of succession, a proposal finally put into effect by the Act of 1886.

8 May. MILITIA ACT. To cope with the growing Indian menace in the Northwest Territory (Gen. Arthur St. Clair had been defeated by Ohio Indians 4 Nov. 1791; Gen. Anthony Wayne was commissioned Apr. commander in chief of army to move against Ohio Indians), the Militia Act authorized state enrollment and organization of all able-bodied free white citizens between the ages of 18 and 45.

21 Aug.–15 Sept. RESISTANCE TO THE EXCISE TAX was manifested in the South (especially in the central counties of North Carolina) and in the 4 Pennsylvania counties west of the Alleghenies. At a Pittsburgh convention (21 Aug.) a series of resolutions drawn up by a committee of which **Albert Gallatin** (p. 1037) was a member de-

nounced the excise tax and declared that legal measures would be used to obstruct collections of the tax. Washington issued a proclamation (29 Sept.) warning against unlawful combinations and stating that the excise provision would be enforced.

JEFFERSON-HAMILTON FEUD. Violent attacks upon Hamilton's fiscal policies appearing in the *National Gazette* provoked Hamilton to rejoinder with a series of anonymous articles (July–Dec.) in the *Gazette of the United States*. Hamilton asserted that Jefferson had been opposed to the Constitution and its adoption, that he did not support the program of the administration, and was responsible for political intrigue disparaging the government.

Letters written by Jefferson (13 May) and Hamilton (30 July) to Washington, prevailing upon him to serve as president for a 2d term, revealed the mutual animosity and distrust of the 2 cabinet officers. Washington intervened, and in letters to Jefferson (23 Aug.) and Hamilton (26 Aug.) sought to heal their differences. Their replies (9 Sept.) indicated that the quarrel was still in progress. Jefferson intimated his intention to retire after the close of Washington's 1st term. During a meeting with Jefferson at Mount Vernon (2 Oct.), Washington's attempt to mediate failed again.

5 Dec. PRESIDENTIAL ELECTION. Presidential electors cast their ballots. **Washington,** receiving 132 votes (with 3 abstentions), was reelected president; **John Adams,** with 77 votes, re-elected vice-president. The Antifederalist opposition gave 50 votes to George Clinton (N.Y.) for vice-president.

1793

ATTACK ON HAMILTON. Rep. William Branch Giles (Va.) proposed a series of resolutions (23 Jan.) inquiring into the condition of the Treasury. The move climaxed the loose charges of corruption and mismanagement that had been made against Hamilton. In reports to the House (4, 13 Feb.) Hamilton made a detailed and factual defense of his official conduct. Giles and others submitted 9 resolutions (28 Feb.) censuring Hamilton's course, but none passed the House.

John Taylor of Caroline (Va., 1753–1824) published *An Examination of the Late Proceedings in Congress Respecting the Official Conduct of the Secretary of the Treasury*. An attack on the administration's fiscal measures, this pamphlet claimed that moneyed interests dominated Congress, and asked for a return to "genuine republicanism." Taylor wrote another pamphlet in a similar vein, *An Enquiry into the Principles and Tendency of Certain Public Measures* (1794).

IMPACT OF THE FRENCH REVOLUTION widened the cleavage between the Federalists and their antagonists, making party lines more definite. At its outset, the French Revolution had enlisted the sympathy of most Americans; but with the proclamation of the French Republic (21 Sept. 1792) and the execution of Louis XVI (21 Jan.), American opinion began to divide sharply. The French issue was injected into domestic affairs after France declared war (1 Feb.) on Great Britain, Spain, and Holland.

22 APR. WASHINGTON'S NEUTRALITY PROCLAMATION. While both Hamilton and Jefferson desired to keep America neutral, Hamilton, unlike Jefferson, thought the occasion a good opportunity to repeal the treaties concluded with France in 1778. Hamilton's sympathies lay with Great Britain, those of Jefferson with France. Washington, however, steered an independent course. On 22 April he issued the Neutrality Proclamation (in which the word "neutrality" was not used) declaring that the U.S. was at peace with Great Britain and France and urging citizens to abstain from acts of hostility against any of the belligerent powers. Washington preferred Attorney General Randolph's draft to that of Chief Justice Jay, which used as a test for the recognition of new, revolutionary governments the extent to which they rested upon a popular mandate. Madison questioned the President's right to issue such a proclamation without Congressional concurrence.

CITIZEN GENÊT AFFAIR. On 8 Apr. **Citizen Genêt** (Edmond Charles Genêt), minister of the French Republic to the U.S., landed at Charleston, S.C., under instructions from the Girondist regime to win U.S. amity and negotiate a new treaty of commerce. Even before presenting his credentials, he commissioned 4 privateers and dispatched them to prey upon British vessels along the U.S. coast. He also took steps to organize on American soil expeditions against Spanish and British territories.

En route (18 Apr.–16 May) from Charleston to Philadelphia, Genêt received a warm ovation. President Washington, however, received him (18 May) with cool formality; and on 5 June Jefferson presented Genêt with a communication from the president stating that Genêt's grants of military commissions on American soil constituted an infringement of U.S. national sovereignty. Genêt was also notified that the privateers commissioned by him would have to leave American waters and could not send their prizes to U.S. ports.

Genêt promised to comply, but soon afterward authorized the arming of *The Little Sarah*, a prize that had been brought in by a French vessel and was being refitted as *La Petite Démocrate*. When Genêt was warned against dispatching the vessel, he threatened to appeal over the president to the people. In violation of a promise made to Jefferson, Genêt ordered the French privateer out to sea.

The newly established Democratic societies (from which the Democratic-Republican party took its name) and Antifederalist newspapers attacked Washington's neutrality policy. Hamilton, writing a series of articles under the pseudonym "Pacificus," defended the Neutrality Proclamation and the president's right to decide the matter. He was answered by Madison, who wrote under the signature of "Helvidius." But both Jefferson and Madison agreed that Genêt's conduct and poor judgment had harmed the Antifederalist cause.

The cabinet decided (2 Aug.) to demand Genêt's recall. Washington sent to Congress his full correspondence with the French minister, pointing out that Genêt's conduct had tended to involve the U.S. "in war abroad, and discord and anarchy at home." By this time the Jacobins had come to power in France. Genêt's successor, Joseph Fauchet, who arrived in 1794, carried orders for Genêt's arrest. Washington refused to extradite Genêt, who became an American citizen and married a daughter of Gov. George Clinton.

31 Dec. JEFFERSON'S RESIGNATION. President Washington, who had originally favored maintaining friendship with France, now veered toward the Federalists and henceforth tended to lean more heavily upon Hamilton for advice on foreign affairs. Jefferson submitted his resignation (31 July) as Secretary of State, but his withdrawal did not become effective until 31 Dec. He was succeeded (2 Jan. 1794) by Edmund Randolph.

POLITICAL OPINION split on the French issue. Most Federalists supported the British cause, regarding it as a bulwark against French anarchy and atheism. Most Republicans were in sympathy with the French, not so much from principle as from long-standing antagonism to the British.

1794

5 Mar. 11TH AMENDMENT, proposed by Congress to the states following protests from the legislatures of Georgia and other states against the Supreme Court decision in *Chisholm* v. *Georgia* (1793, p. 664), provided in effect that a state was not suable by a citizen of another state. It was declared ratified on 8 Jan. 1798.

5 June. NEUTRALITY ACT forbade U.S. citizens to enlist in the service of a foreign power and prohibited the fitting out of foreign armed vessels in U.S. ports. This reinforcement of the Neutrality Proclamation, however, did not entirely ease tension between the U.S. and Great Britain.

July–Nov. WHISKY INSURRECTION, the result of discontent over enforcement of the excise tax, broke out among the backwoods farmers of the Monongahela Valley in western Pennsylvania. President Washington issued a proclamation (7 Aug.) ordering the insurgents to return to their homes, and called for 12,900 militia from Virginia, Maryland, New Jersey, and Pennsylvania. Negotiations with the leaders of the insurrection proving fruitless, Washington issued a second proclamation (24 Sept.) ordering the suppression of the rebellion. Government forces under the command of Henry Lee, who was accompanied by Hamilton and President Washington (the latter going as far as Bedford, Pa., before returning to Philadelphia, marking the only occasion when a president took the field with his troops), quelled the demonstrations, as none of the "Whisky Boys" came forth to do battle. Of the insurgents tried for treason (May 1795), 2 were convicted, and were pardoned by Washington.

19 Nov. JAY'S TREATY. An old source of American grievance against England was the British refusal, despite the provisions of the peace treaty of 1783, to evacuate the Northwest military posts. The British justified their maintenance of garrisons on the ground that legal obstacles had been raised against the recovery of pre-Revolutionary debts owed to British merchants and Loyalist property confiscated by the states. Retention of the posts retarded Western settlement and kept the lucrative fur trade in the hands of the British. To assure their control of the posts and the fur trade, the British had encouraged the establishment of an Indian barrier state. American settlers in the Ohio country believed that Indian massacres of pioneers were instigated by the British.

Anglo-U.S. friction was intensified when the British issued orders in council (8 June, 6 Nov., 1793) interfering with neutral shipping. The enforcement of these orders resulted in the seizure of American vessels and the impressment and imprisonment of American crews. The two nations verged on war.

One of the leading motives behind the U.S. desire for a settlement was the maintenance of the fiscal structure. British exports to the U.S. were the chief source of tariff revenue, the main prop of Hamilton's fiscal system. For the negotiation of outstanding differences, President Washington named **John Jay,** chief justice of the U.S., as special envoy to Great Britain. Jay, whose nomination was confirmed in the Senate on 19 Apr., arrived in England in June. He was under instructions to make no commitment in violation of the treaties with France.

Jay's Treaty was signed on 19 Nov. The outstanding concession gained by the U.S. was the British withdrawal from the Northwest posts on or before 1 June 1796. The treaty also provided for (1) admission of U.S. vessels to British East Indian ports on a nondiscriminatory basis; (2) opening of the West Indian trade to U.S. vessels not exceeding 70 tons burden, on condition that Americans renounce their carrying trade in such staples as cotton, sugar, and molasses; (3) referral to joint commissions of the payment of the pre-Revolutionary debts (British claims settled at $2,664,000, 8 Jan. 1802), the northeast boundary question, and compensation for illegal maritime seizures; and (4) placing of British trade with the U.S. on a most-favored-nation basis. No provisions were made for impressment, the Indian question, the slaves removed by the British, or Loyalist claims.

When the terms of the treaty were made known (March 1795), the Republicans took the lead in whipping up popular opposition. Southern planters were chagrined by the treaty's provision for settlement of the debt (much of which was owed by Virginia) and its silence concerning the stolen slaves. Northern shipping and commercial interests as well as Southern Federalists attacked the treaty; even Washington and some Federalist legislators thought the treaty unsatisfactory. Hamilton entered the controversy with the publication (22 July 1795 *et seq.*) of his "Camillus" papers in support of the treaty.

The Senate ratified the treaty (24 June 1795) only after long debate and after suspension of that portion of Article XII pertaining to the West Indian trade. The Republicans in the House attempted to block the treaty by denying the appropriation for enforcing its provisions. The House request (24 Mar. 1796) for papers relating to Jay's Treaty was refused by Washington because the concurrence of the two Houses was not required to give validity to a treaty and "because of the necessity of maintaining the boundaries fixed by the Constitution." By asserting his executive prerogative, Washington thereby set an important precedent. The appropriation was approved on 30 Apr. 1796 by one vote, following a supporting speech (28 Apr.) by **Fisher Ames** (1758–1808).

1795

CABINET REORGANIZATION. Timothy Pickering (Mass.) was named (2 Jan.) Secretary of War. Hamilton resigned (31 Jan.) as Secretary of the Treasury and was succeeded by Oliver Wolcott, Jr., but continued as unofficial adviser on major policy decisions. Secretary of State Edmund Randolph resigned (19 Aug.) on suspicion of corruption, a charge for which he was never tried. Washington believed that Randolph had intrigued with the French minister, Joseph Fauchet, to block the ratification of Jay's Treaty. Some held that Randolph had been in the pay of the French (vindication of Randolph's conduct in Irving Brant's *Madison*, v. 3, 1950). Washington, although fearful that disclosure of letters and conversations with Randolph would damage relations with Britain and France, permitted Randolph to publish in his own defense "any and every private and confidential letter I ever wrote you; nay more: every word I have ever uttered in your presence." Randolph was succeeded by Pickering, and James McHenry became (27 Jan. 1796) Secretary of War. The cabinet as reorganized by Washington included only Federalists. After Adams took office as president, he retained Washington's cabinet. Pickering, McHenry, and Wolcott continued to be influenced by Hamilton.

29 JAN. NATURALIZATION ACT required 5 years' residence.

27 OCT. TREATY OF SAN LORENZO (PINCKNEY'S TREATY), signed at Madrid, 27 Oct. The failure of the Jay-Gardoqui negotiations (1785–86) to adjust differences between the U.S. and Spain left open the questions of the southern and western boundaries of the U.S. and the free navigation by Americans of the Mississippi from its source to its mouth. Negotiations for the U.S. were undertaken by **Thomas Pinckney** (1750–1828), U.S. minister to Great Britain. Spain recognized the boundary claims of the U.S. under the Treaty of 1783 (the Mississippi at the west, the 31st parallel at the south) and gave to Americans free navigation of the Mississippi and the right of deposit for their goods at New Orleans for 3 years and thereafter, if need be, at another point to be designated.

1796

8 MAR. *Hylton* v. *U.S.* (3 Dallas 171), a case involving the carriage tax imposed in 1794, in which the Supreme Court for the first time upheld the constitutionality of a congressional act.

17 SEPT. WASHINGTON'S FAREWELL ADDRESS. Dated 17 Sept., it was first published (19 Sept.) in the Philadelphia *Daily American Advertiser*. Written with the aid of Madison (1792) and Hamilton (1796), it was never orally delivered before the public. The address (1) presented Washington's reasons for declining to stand for a 3d term; (2) deplored the dangers of a party system, particularly a division along geographical lines; (3) counseled that the public credit be cherished; (4) advised the nation to steer clear of *permanent* alliances with foreign nations and trust to "temporary alliances for extraordinary emergencies." Nowhere did it contain the phrase "entangling alliances" (used by Jefferson in his 1st inaugural).

7 DEC. PRESIDENTIAL ELECTION indicated the rising strength of the Democratic-Republican party, much of it due to dissatisfaction with Jay's Treaty. **John Adams,** Federalist candidate, received 71 votes and was elected president; **Thomas Jefferson,** Democratic-Republican, with 68 votes, vice-president. Among the other candidates were Thomas Pinckney (Federalist, 59 votes) and Aaron Burr (Democratic-Republican, 30 votes).

1797–1800

31 MAY. RELATIONS WITH FRANCE. The French Directory, angered by Jay's Treaty, interfered with American shipping and refused to receive **Charles Cotesworth Pinckney** (1746–1825) as U.S. minister to France when he arrived in Dec. 1796. President Adams appointed (31 May) a commission to France consisting of Pinckney and **John Marshall** (both Federalists) and **Elbridge Gerry** (Republican), who were instructed to secure a treaty of commerce and amity with France.

18 OCT. XYZ AFFAIR. The commissioners arrived at Paris (4 Oct.) and were unofficially received (8 Oct.) by the French foreign minister, Talleyrand, who found a pretext for delaying the opening of official discussions. The commissioners were visited (18 Oct.) by three agents of Talleyrand (Hottinguer, Hauteval, and Bellamy; later designated in the mission's dispatches as X, Y, and Z) who suggested a U.S. loan to France and a bribe of $240,000. The Americans refused to make concessions; Marshall replied firmly (17 Jan. 1798); and on 19 Mar. President Adams reported to Congress the failure of negotiations. Only Gerry remained at Paris, Talleyrand having intimated that if he departed, a French declaration of war against the U.S. would ensue. On 3 Apr. 1798 Adams submitted to Congress the XYZ correspondence, which aroused American public opinion regardless of party.

UNDECLARED NAVAL WAR WITH FRANCE, 1798–1800. The prowar faction of the Federalists, headed in the cabinet by Pickering, wanted an immediate declaration of war against France. Adams, however, favored a peaceful course while strengthening national defenses: if war were to come, France would have to take the initiative. **Defense measures:** 20 Acts of Congress (passed 27 Mar.–16 July 1798) provided for consolidating the national defense. Washington was named (2 July 1798) commanding general; Hamilton, second in command, inspector general. On 3 May the Navy Department was established, and on 21 May Benjamin Stoddert named Secretary of the Navy. Congress repealed (7 July 1798) the treaties with France, and thus terminated the alliance. An undeclared naval war began with the capture of the schooner *Retaliation* by the French off Guadeloupe (20 Nov. 1798) and the engagement (9 Feb. 1799) between the *Constellation* (Capt. Thomas Truxtun, commander) and *L'Insurgente,* in which the latter was captured. On 1 Feb. 1800 the *Constellation* fought a drawn battle with *La Vengeance,* and on 12 Oct. Capt. George Little in the *Boston* captured the French ship *Le Berceau.*

CONVENTION OF 1800. A complete surprise to Hamilton's prowar faction was Adams' nomination (18 Feb. 1799) of **William Vans Murray** as minister to France, followed by publication of Talleyrand's assurance that a U.S. minister would be received with respect. Federalist pressure upon Adams to change his course failed, and the president appointed a commission to France consisting of Vans Murray, Chief Justice Oliver Ellsworth, and William R. Davie, governor of North Carolina (replacing Patrick Henry, who declined because of age). The negotiations bore fruit in the **Treaty of Morfontaine** (30 Sept. 1800, commonly known as the **Convention of 1800**), which superseded the treaties of 1778 and thus formally released the U.S. from its defensive alliance with France. The Senate ratified the convention on condition that the treaties of 1778 be not merely suspended but abrogated. The convention became effective on 21 Dec. 1801.

Adams' handling of the French crisis created a schism in the Federalist party. Adams finally concluded that he was the victim of a cabinet conspiracy, and that Pickering and McHenry, in conjunction with Hamilton, were working for his defeat in the presidential election of 1800. On 6 May 1800 he requested the resignation of McHenry (effective 31 May); on 10 May he asked for the resignation of Pickering (dismissed from office, 12 May). Pickering was succeeded in the State Department by John Marshall of Virginia (13 May).

1798

ALIEN AND SEDITION ACTS. Several of the leading Republican publicists were European refugees. The threat of war with France sharpened hostility to aliens and gave the Federalists an opportunity to impose severe restrictions:

18 JUNE. Naturalization Act changed from 5 to 14 years the period of residence required for admission to full citizenship. It was repealed in 1802, when the naturalization law of 1795 was reenacted.

25 JUNE. Alien Act authorized the president to order out of the U.S. all aliens regarded as dangerous to the public peace and safety, or suspected of "treasonable or secret" inclinations. It expired in 1800.

6 JULY. Alien Enemies Act authorized the president, in time of declared war, to arrest, imprison, or banish aliens subject to an enemy power.

14 JULY. Sedition Act made it a high misdemeanor, punishable by fine and imprisonment, for citizens or aliens to enter into unlawful combinations opposing execution of the national laws; to prevent a federal officer from performing his duties; and to aid or attempt "any insurrection, riot, unlawful assembly, or combination." A fine of not more than $2,000 and imprisonment not exceeding 2 years were provided for persons convicted of publishing "any false, scandalous and malicious writing" bringing into disrepute the U.S. government, Congress, or the president; in force until 3 March 1801.

The Sedition Act was aimed at repressing political opposition, and its enforcement, carried out in a partisan manner, resulted in the prosecution of 25 persons and the conviction of 10, all of them Republican editors and printers. (Most notable: **James Thomas Callender,** tried before Judge Samuel Chase, fined $200 and sentenced to 9 months' imprisonment; **Matthew Lyon,** imprisoned and fined $1,000; and Dr. **Thomas Cooper,** imprisoned for 6 months. When Jefferson became president he pardoned all those convicted under the act. Congress restored the fines with interest.) The Republicans attacked the Alien and Sedition Acts as unnecessary, despotic, and unconstitutional.

KENTUCKY AND VIRGINIA RESOLUTIONS. The Kentucky resolutions (in 2 sets, passed by the state legislature on 16 Nov. 1798 and 22 Nov. 1799) were drafted by Jefferson. The Virginia resolutions (passed by the state legislature 24 Dec. 1798) were framed by Madison. Both invoked the compact theory of the Constitution and maintained that the Alien and Sedition Acts were unconstitutional. The Kentucky resolutions, the more forthright of the 2, held that where the national government exercised powers not specifically delegated to it, each state "has an equal right to judge for itself, as well of infractions as of the mode and measure of redress." The Virginia resolutions pointed out that in such cases the states "have the right and are in duty bound to interpose for arresting the progress of the evil." The second set of Kentucky resolutions was enacted after several Northern states repudiated the doctrines set forth by Kentucky and Virginia and indicated that the federal judiciary was the exclusive arbiter of constitutionality. It was on this occasion that the Kentucky legislature added, as it restated the view that the states had the right to judge infractions of the Constitution: "That a nullification of those sovereignties, of all unauthorized acts done under color of that instrument, is the rightful remedy." Both states, however, declared their firm attachment to the Union and took no steps to nullify or obstruct the Alien and Sedition Acts.

14 Dec. 1799. DEATH OF WASHINGTON at Mt. Vernon; eulogized in Congress (26 Dec.) by Henry Lee as "first in war, first in peace, first in the hearts of his countrymen."

1799

30 Jan. LOGAN ACT made it a high misdemeanor subject to fine and imprisonment for any citizen to carry on correspondence with a foreign government in any controversy in which the U.S. was engaged. The act was prompted by a visit to France (June–Nov. 1798) by Dr. George Logan (1753–1821), a Philadelphia Quaker, who had gone abroad in an effort to preserve peace

between the 2 nations. The act is still on the statute books.

Feb. FRIES UPRISING. John Fries (c.1750–1818) raised several hundred men in Northampton, Bucks, and Montgomery counties, Pa., in opposition to the direct federal property tax established by acts of 9 and 14 July 1798 in anticipation of war with France. At Bethlehem he resisted the U.S. marshal. Convicted of treason, he was retried before Justice Samuel Chase, again convicted and sentenced to death, but pardoned by President Adams.

1800

4 Apr. FIRST FEDERAL BANKRUPTCY LAW enacted, extended only to merchants and traders; made possible the release of Robert Morris from prison; repealed 19 Dec. 1803.

17 Nov. Congress convened in Washington for first time.

3 Dec. PRESIDENTIAL ELECTION. Major campaign issues: (1) Alien and Sedition Acts, (2) increase by the Federalists of direct taxes occasioned by heavy defense expenditures, (3) reduction of trade with France, and (4) growth of anti-British sentiment over the impressment of American seamen. Federalist candidates: **John Adams** (Mass.) and **Charles Cotesworth Pinckney** (S.C.). Democratic-Republican: **Thomas Jefferson** (Va.) and **Aaron Burr** (N.Y.).

1801

20 Jan. One of Adams' last official acts was his appointment of **John Marshall** (p. 1097) as chief justice of the Supreme Court after John Jay had declined nomination and confirmation for a 2d term.

11–17 Feb. ELECTORAL TIE. When the ballot count (11 Feb.) in the electoral college resulted in a Jefferson-Burr tie (73 votes each; 65 for Adams, 64 for Pinckney, 1 for John Jay), the election was thrown into the Federalist-dominated House of Representatives. A deadlock followed; the Federalist caucus decided to back Burr; Hamilton, however, regarded Jefferson as the lesser evil, and used his influence to break the deadlock. It has been supposed that Jefferson made certain commitments to the Federalists, but there is no reliable evidence supporting this view. On the 36th ballot (17 Feb.) **Jefferson** was chosen president by 10 states (each state having 1 vote). **Burr** was elected vice-president.

The election demonstrated the inadequacy of the machinery provided by the Constitution for selecting the president. To prevent a similar situation in the electoral college, the **12th Amendment** was proposed by Congress (9 Dec. 1803) and was declared ratified on 25 Sept. 1804. It provided for separate balloting for president and vice-president.

13 Feb. JUDICIARY ACT reduced to 5 the number of Supreme Court justices, created 16 circuit courts (establishing a judgeship for each), and added to the number of marshals, attorneys, and clerks. In principle, the measure was justified, but it was exploited by Adams for political purposes, making under this law the so-called "midnight appointments" (3 Mar. until 9 P.M.) of Federalist judges and court officials.

4 Mar. Jefferson's inaugural was the first held at Washington, where the permanent capital had been officially established in the summer of 1800 (Congress assumed jurisdiction over District of Columbia 27 Feb. 1801; incorporation as a city 3 May 1802, its mayor to be appointed by the president). In his conciliatory inaugural address Jefferson stressed the need for a government of limited powers, economy in the national administration, support of state governments in all their rights, acquiescence in majority decisions, the preservation of civil liberties, and "peace, commerce, and honest friendship with all nations, entangling alliances with none."

8 Dec. Jefferson's first annual message to Congress broke the precedent, established by Washington and continued by Adams, of addressing Congress in person. Jefferson forwarded a written version to each house. This remained the custom until Woodrow Wilson reverted (1913) to the original practice.

TRIPOLITAN WAR, 1801–05. In order to buy immunity from interference with American commerce along the North African coast, Washington and Adams continued the custom, established by the British, of paying tribute to the pirates of the Barbary States (Algiers, Morocco, Tripoli, and Tunis). When the Pasha of Tripoli increased his demands for tribute and declared war (14 May 1801) against the U.S., Jefferson, although favoring economy and peace and opposed to a navy, decided to resist and dispatched warcraft to Mediterranean waters. In 1803 Commodore Edward Preble was named commander of the Mediterranean squadron, and on his orders Lieut. **Stephen Decatur** performed the most notable exploit of the war: the destruction (16 Feb. 1804) of the frigate *Philadelphia,* which had been captured and converted by the Tripolitans. A vigorous blockade brought the war to an end. A treaty of peace favorable to the U.S. was signed on 4 June 1805 (but the payment of tribute to other Barbary States continued until 1816).

1802

8 Jan.–29 Apr. REPEAL OF THE JUDICIARY ACT OF 1801 was moved (8 Jan.) in the Senate at Jefferson's insistence; upon a deadlock, an adverse vote by Burr blocked the measure temporarily; but it was repealed 8 Mar. A new Judiciary Act, passed 29 April, restored to 6 the number of Supreme Court justices, fixed 1 term annually for the high court, and set up 6 circuit courts, each headed by a Supreme Court justice.

NEW FINANCIAL POLICY framed by Secretary of the Treasury Gallatin carried out Jefferson's pledge of retrenchment. It called for reduction of the national debt, repeal of all internal taxes (with a corollary cut in expenditures by the War and Navy departments), and a congressional system of appropriations for specific purposes. Between 1801–09 the national debt was reduced from $83 million to $57 million, notwithstanding the acquisition of Louisiana and the Tripolitan War.

16 Mar. U.S. Military Academy established by Act of Congress. On 4 July the academy was formally opened at West Point, N.Y.

1803

24 Feb. MARBURY v. MADISON (1 Cranch 137). The conflict between president and judiciary was brought to a head after Jefferson ordered Secretary of State Madison to withhold from William Marbury the signed and sealed commission of his appointment (2 Mar. 1801) by President Adams under the Judiciary Act of 1801 as justice of the peace of the District of Columbia. Marbury was joined in his suit for a writ of mandamus compelling delivery of the commission by 3 other Federalists, Robert T. Hooe, William Harper, and Dennis Ramsay, in the same situation. In dismissing Marbury's suit on the ground that the court lacked jurisdiction, Chief Justice Marshall employed a strategy calculated to avoid an open struggle with the executive branch responsible for enforcement of the writ. The case is remembered, however, as the first occasion

on which the high court held an Act of Congress unconstitutional: Marshall declared that Section 13 of the Judiciary Act of 1789, empowering the court to issue such a writ, was contrary to the Constitution and therefore invalid. This is the first case in which the Supreme Court held a law of Congress void; it did not do so again until the Dred Scott decision (pp. 263–264).

LOUISIANA PURCHASE. By the Treaty of Fontainebleu (1762) France ceded Louisiana to Spain, but by the secret Treaty of San Ildefonso (1 Oct. 1800) the province was returned to France. The transfer was made at the behest of Napoleon, who projected the revival of a French colonial empire in North America. The retrocession was confirmed (21 Mar. 1801) by the Treaty of Madrid; shortly afterward, Jefferson learned of the secret arrangement.

Jefferson was profoundly concerned over (1) the threat posed to American security by a neighboring imperial and aggressive power; (2) the possibility that the French possession of New Orleans would close the Mississippi to Western commerce. On 16 Oct. 1802, the Spanish intendant at New Orleans interdicted the right of deposit (restored 19 Apr. 1803). This action caused consternation in the West. In a letter (18 Apr. 1802) to the American minister at Paris, Robert R. Livingston, Jefferson declared: "The day that France takes New Orleans . . . we must marry ourselves to the British fleet and nation."

The president instructed Livingston to negotiate for a tract of land on the lower Mississippi for use as a port or, failing this, to obtain an irrevocable guarantee of free navigation and the right of deposit. On 12 Jan. 1803 James Monroe was named minister plenipotentiary to France and was given specific instructions for the purchase of New Orleans and West Florida with the $2 million provided by a congressional appropriation; if need be, he was to offer as much as $10 million. Even before Monroe arrived at Paris (12 April), Napoleon abandoned his scheme for a colonial empire. His decision to sell Louisiana and confine his sphere to the Old World was influenced by the costly French failure to suppress the slave revolt in Haiti (1794–1804), and by the impending resumption of hostilities with Great Britain. On 11 Apr. Talleyrand asked Livingston how much the U.S. was prepared to pay for the whole of Louisiana. With Barbé-Marbois, Napoleon's finance minister, acting for the French, Livingston and Monroe closed the negotiations. In sealing the bargain, the American envoys exceeded their instructions.

By the treaty of cession (signed 2 May, but antedated 30 Apr.), Louisiana was purchased by the U.S. for 60 million francs (approximately $15 million). The price for the territory itself was $11,250,000; the remainder covered the debts, owed by France to U.S. citizens, which the U.S. government assumed.

The purchase of Louisiana doubled the area of the U.S. by the acquisition of a tract of some 828,000 square miles lying between the Mississippi and the Rocky Mountains. The treaty, however, did not define exact boundaries. While the Gulf of Mexico was fixed as the line to the south and the Mississippi as that to the east, there was no clear understanding as to whether the cession included West Florida and Texas.

The Constitution made no provision for the purchase and assimilation of foreign territory, and the constitutional aspect of the purchase perplexed Jefferson, who, although in principle committed to strict construction, took a broad constructionist view on this issue, while the Federalists took an equally inconsistent strict constructionist stand. The substance of the Republican position—that the power to govern territory flows from the right to acquire it—was upheld (1828) by Chief Justice Marshall in *American Insurance Co.* v. *Canter* (1 Peters 511).

The Senate approved the treaty (20 Oct.) 24–7. On 20 Dec. the U.S. took formal possession of Louisiana. William C. C. Claiborne was formally installed (1 Oct. 1804) as territorial governor. In 1812 the state of Louisiana became the first to be admitted from the territory.

NORTHERN   CONFEDERACY SCHEME, 1803–04. Behind the constitutional controversy over Louisiana lay Federalist fears that the states carved out of the Western territories would inevitably change the political balance of power in Congress, with the agrarian and frontier interests of the South and West gaining ascendancy over the commercial and industrial interests of the Northeast.

ESSEX JUNTO, a name first applied by John Hancock in 1781 to a group in Essex Co., Mass., who opposed the 1778 draft of the state constitution; later a propertied elite of anti-French Federalist extremists, some of whom under the leadership of Sen. **Timothy Pickering** (Mass.) considered establishment of a Northern Confederacy including the 5 New England states, New York, and New Jersey, but such extremists as George Cabot and Theophilus Parsons refused to associate themselves with the plan, which had considerable popular support. Hamilton's opposition to Pickering's scheme intensified when it became apparent that the disunionists were counting on Burr's election as governor of New York, a state held essential to the formation of the confederacy.

11 July 1804. BURR-HAMILTON DUEL. Hamilton, who played a decisive role in securing Burr's defeat in the New York election (25 Apr. 1804), was reported to have said (16 Feb. 1804) that Burr was "a dangerous man, and one who ought not to be trusted with the reins of government." Burr's demand for an explanation led to the Burr-Hamilton duel (Weehawken, N.J., 11 July 1804), in which Hamilton was fatally wounded. With Hamilton's death (12 July), the Burr-Pickering coalition disintegrated completely.

LEWIS AND CLARK EXPEDITION, 1803–06. In his message to Congress (Jan.) Jefferson asked for an appropriation for an expedition for the purpose of cultivating friendly relations with the Indians and extending the internal commerce of the U.S. Congress lent its approval. **Meriwether Lewis** and **William Clark** (p. 1084) were chosen to lead the expedition. On 31 Aug. the party began descent of the Ohio and on 14 May 1804 began ascent of the Missouri. They spent the following winter in a Mandan village, near present-day Bismarck, N.D. On 7 Apr. 1805, they began their ascent of a Missouri River fork which they named the Jefferson (others named Madison and Gallatin), crossed the Rockies, and came within sight of the Pacific Ocean on 7 Nov. 1805. The expedition, which returned to St. Louis on 23 Sept. 1806, proved the feasibility of an overland route to the Far West, added to scientific knowledge, and ultimately stimulated Western settlement and commerce.

1804

12 MAR. IMPEACHMENT OF PICKERING AND CHASE. Jefferson's conflict with the Federalist judiciary was carried forward by the impeachment as unfit of Judge John Pickering, federal district judge in New Hampshire, who was adjudged guilty by the Senate and removed from his post (12 Mar.), despite evidence at the trial establishing

that he was insane and hence not culpable of high crimes or misdemeanors. Contrariwise, **Samuel Chase** (Md., 1741–1811), associate justice of the Supreme Court, was impeached for his biased conduct in the trials of Fries and Callender and for an inflammatory anti-Republican charge to a Baltimore grand jury. His acquittal (1 Mar. 1805) discouraged subsequent administrations from using the impeachment device to remove politically obnoxious judges, while bringing to a close the Republican campaign against the Federalist bench.

5 DEC. PRESIDENTIAL ELECTION. The first regular caucus of members of Congress for the nomination of presidential candidates had (25 Feb.) unanimously nominated **Jefferson** for reelection and **George Clinton** as his running mate. **Thomas Jefferson,** opposed by the Federalist candidate **Charles Cotesworth Pinckney,** was reelected president, with 162 out of 176 electoral votes. Jefferson carried all the New England states except Connecticut. In the first election with separate ballots for president and vice-president, **George Clinton** was elected vice-president, 162 to 14 for Rufus King. The Republican party won undisputed control of Congress.

1805

9 AUG. PIKE'S EXPEDITIONS. Lieut. Zebulon M. Pike (p. 1128) was dispatched by Gen. James Wilkinson to explore (1805–06) the sources of the Mississippi. In a second expedition (1806–07) he explored Colorado and New Mexico. Named after him was Pikes Peak, Colo., which he sighted 15 Nov. 1806.

1806

25 JAN.–21 Nov. COMMERCE AND NEUTRAL RIGHTS. With the resumption (1803) of the Napoleonic wars, American neutrality faced new tests. Great Britain and France clamped further restrictions on the neutral carrying trade in order to deprive each other of the means of war. The overwhelming superiority of British over French naval power made its interference with American commerce the more serious invasion of neutral rights. There followed a renewal of the controversies with England over neutral trade, impressment, and blockade.

In a series of acts and orders (1804–05) the British evolved a West Indian trade policy calculated to destroy neutral commerce with French and Spanish colonies in America that furnished staples to Napoleon's armies. The "Rule of 1756," laid down by British courts during the Seven Years' War, to the effect that where a European nation has forbidden trade with its colonies in time of peace it shall not open it to neutrals in time of war, was enforced against U.S. neutral carriers (1793) after the outbreak of war between England and France. The latter had evaded this restriction by landing cargo at a U.S. port, passing it through the customs, and securing fresh clearance for a belligerent port. This principle of the "broken voyage" was upheld in British admiralty decisions in the cases of the *Immanuel* (1799) and the *Polly* (1800). Thereafter the large number of American vessels plying between the French West Indies and France enjoyed relative freedom. British policy was abruptly reversed by the decision (23 July 1805) in the *Essex* case, when the British judge, Sir William Scott, declared that American cargo was subject to seizure and condemnation unless the shipper could prove that he had originally intended to terminate the voyage in an American port. Failing that, the voyage could be regarded as a **continuous** one between enemy ports. As a

result of this decision, the seizures of American vessels increased sharply.

Madison's report (25 Jan.) on the British infringement of the rights of neutral commerce and the impressment of American seamen was followed (12 Feb.) by a Senate resolution attacking British seizures as "an unprovoked aggression" and a "violation of neutral rights." Great Britain took no heed. In retaliation, Congress passed the **Nicholson** (or first) **Non-Importation Act** (18 Apr.) prohibiting the importation from England of a long list of articles (including hemp, flax, tin, brass, and some classes of woolens) which could be produced in the U.S. or imported from other countries. It was to become effective 15 Nov.; upon the advice of Jefferson it was suspended (19 Dec.) and was not again operative until 22 Dec. 1808. On 16 May British foreign minister Charles James Fox declared a blockade of the European coast from Brest to the river Elbe. Napoleon answered with the **Berlin Decree** (21 Nov.) declaring the British Isles in a state of blockade, forbidding all commerce and communication with them, and authorizing the seizure and confiscation of vessels and cargo.

31 DEC. MONROE-PINKNEY TREATY. At the instigation of Congress, Jefferson dispatched (May) William Pinkney (Md.) as special envoy to London to join James Monroe in negotiating a treaty with Great Britain. His instructions called for (1) British abandonment of the impressment of American seamen, (2) restoration of the West Indian trade on the basis of the "broken voyage," (3) indemnity payments for seizures made after the *Essex* decision. Prolonged discussions with Lord Holland began 27 Aug.; as a bargaining point, the U.S. envoys used the threat of enforcing the Non-Importation Act. British refusal to make concessions finally moved

Monroe and Pinkney to violate their instructions. The treaty was a defeat for U.S. diplomacy. It made no reference to impressment or indemnities and constituted a slight compromise on the West Indian trade. Jefferson received the treaty in Mar. 1807. Deeply embarrassed over its terms, he never submitted it to the Senate, but instructed the U.S. envoys (20 May 1807) that the treaty serve as a basis for reopening discussions.

1807–09

7 Jan.–17 Dec. BRITISH AND FRENCH COUNTERMEASURES. The British retaliated against the Berlin Decree with an order in council (7 Jan.) barring all shipping from the coastal trade of France and her allies. The enforcement of Napoleon's Continental system nevertheless became more effective after his Tilsit agreement (25 June) with Czar Alexander I of Russia. The British struck back with new orders in council (11 Nov.) prohibiting commerce with Continental ports from which the British flag was excluded; only vessels which had first passed through a British port, and there paid customs duties and secured new clearances, were permitted to call at open ports on the Continent. Napoleon's **Milan Decree** (17 Dec.) declared that all vessels searched by the British or obeying the orders in council would be regarded as "denationalized" and subject to seizure and confiscation as British property.

19 Feb.–1 Sept. AARON BURR "CONSPIRACY" AND TRIAL, 1804–07. Shortly after slaying Hamilton, Burr, his political career now at an end, asked money of Anthony Merry, British minister to the U.S., supposedly for the purpose of organizing a movement for separating the Western states from the U.S. The British never gave him funds; from the Spanish minister, whom he subse-

quently approached, Burr received a small sum. Whether Burr's aim was treasonable, or whether he was planning to lead a filibustering expedition against the Spanish dominions, is still a matter of dispute (Henry Adams, 1890, held that Burr plotted disunion; W. F. McCaleb, 1903, maintained that Burr, far from conspiring to commit treason, sought to build a Western empire through annexation of Spanish territories in the Southwest and Mexico). Burr is known to have conferred with Gen. James Wilkinson, commander of U.S. forces in the Mississippi Valley, during a tour (May–Sept. 1805) of that region. At the end of Aug. 1806, Burr went to Blennerhassett's Island, in the Ohio River, the home of Harman Blennerhassett, one of his chief associates. Here he made preparations for a military expedition, his force consisting of some 60 to 80 men and about 10 boats, and then left for Tennessee. Wilkinson and others warned President Jefferson, who issued a proclamation (27 Nov. 1806) warning citizens against participating in an illegal expedition against Spanish territory. Burr was apparently unaware of the proclamation by the time he rejoined his followers for the journey down the Mississippi. The expedition passed several American forts without interference; when the party reached a point some 30 miles above Natchez, Burr learned that Wilkinson, at New Orleans, had betrayed him. Burr fled toward Spanish Florida, but was arrested in Alabama (19 Feb.) and taken to Richmond, Va., where he was brought (30 Mar. 1807) before Chief Justice Marshall, presiding over the U.S. circuit court. Originally held for a misdemeanor in forming an expedition against Spanish territory, Burr was indicted (24 June) for treason. The trial (3 Aug.–1 Sept.), which ended in the acquittal of Burr and his associates, settled the U.S. law of treason, which Marshall strictly construed. In the course of the trial Marshall issued a subpoena duces tecum to President Jefferson for evidence in his hands. The president, while ignoring the subpoena, did in fact make the information in his possession available. Burr went into European exile to escape further prosecutions (for murder of Hamilton in New York and New Jersey and for treason in Ohio, Kentucky, Mississippi, and Louisiana).

22 JUNE. CHESAPEAKE-LEOPARD AFFAIR. The U.S. frigate *Chesapeake*, commanded by Commodore James Barron, was hailed by the British frigate *Leopard* outside the 3-mile limit off Norfolk Roads. The British commander claimed that 4 men aboard the *Chesapeake* were British deserters, and demanded their surrender. When Barron refused to permit search of his vessel, the *Leopard* opened fire, killing 3 and wounding 18, and removed the 4 alleged deserters. The crippled *Chesapeake* returned to Norfolk. News of the incident aroused anti-British feeling. Jefferson issued (2 July) a proclamation ordering British warships to leave U.S. territorial waters. A British proclamation (17 Oct.) ordered a more vigorous prosecution of impressment of British subjects from neutral vessels. Discussions concerning reparations for the attack on the *Chesapeake* lasted until 1808, but satisfaction was blocked by the British demanding as a condition the withdrawal of Jefferson's proclamation. Not until 1 Nov. 1811 did the British present an offer of settlement which Secretary Monroe accepted (12 Nov.).

1807–09, EMBARGO. Jefferson decided to rely upon economic pressure to bring the belligerent powers to terms. While the Non-Importation Act had again become effective (14 Dec. 1807), its threatened use had already failed to move the British. Jefferson sent (18 Dec.) a message to Congress recommending an embargo. Federalist opposition failed to block speedy action on the measure. The bill was passed in the Senate (18 Dec.), 22–6; passage in the House (21 Dec.), 82–44, was supported chiefly by the South and West. The embargo became law on 22 Dec.

The **Embargo Act** interdicted virtually all land and seaborne commerce with foreign nations. It forbade all U.S. vessels to leave for foreign ports. U.S. ships in the coastal trade were required to post bond double the value of craft and cargo as a guarantee that the goods would be relanded at a U.S. port. While importation in foreign bottoms was not prohibited, it was almost outlawed by the provision that foreign vessels could not carry goods out of an American port. The law was supplemented by the **Embargo Acts** of 9 Jan. and 12 Mar. 1808.

Means were soon found for evading its provisions. A brisk smuggling trade was carried out by land and water, particularly across the Canadian border. U.S. ships which had been at sea when the act went into operation remained in foreign waters and continued their trade with the warring nations. The British government cooperated with merchants who violated the law. The effect upon the British economy was minor, as British shippers gained by the wholesale removal of U.S. competition, while their government was able to draw upon South America as a fresh source of supply. The French used the embargo to their own advantage. Under the pretext of aiding the U.S. to enforce the law, Napoleon issued the **Bayonne Decree** (17 Apr. 1808) ordering the seizure of all U.S. vessels entering the ports of France, Italy, and the Hanseatic towns. Napoleon justified this move by accepting the embargo as effective and declaring that any U.S. shipping in those ports must obviously be British vessels furnished with false papers. The strict enforcement of the Bayonne Decree resulted in French confiscation (1808–09) of some $10 million worth of U.S. goods and shipping.

Domestic opposition to the embargo was strongest in the mercantile areas of New England and New York, where Eastern Republicans made common cause with Federalists on this issue. Although the embargo stimulated New England industry, the benefits were outweighed by the heavy losses sustained by the carrying trade. Widespread economic distress brought the Federalists into power in the New England state governments after the elections of 1808. Popular hostility to the embargo was increased by the **Enforcement Act** (9 Jan. 1809), which provided for strict enforcement and authorized severe penalties for evasions of the act. Numerous town meetings attacked the embargo as a pro-French, anti-British measure, and state legislatures challenged its constitutionality. Resolutions drawn up by the Massachusetts legislature (Jan., Feb., 1809) characterized it as unjust and arbitrary. In his address to the Connecticut legislature (23 Feb. 1809) Gov. Jonathan Trumbull asserted that whenever Congress exceeded its constitutional powers, the state legislatures were in duty bound "to interpose their protecting shield between the rights and liberties of the people and the assumed power of the general government." Governors refused to furnish militia officers requested by collectors for enforcing the embargo. Timothy Pickering proposed a New England convention for nullifying the embargo.

Amid this flurry of states'-rights views, Chief Justice Marshall handed down his opinion (20 Feb. 1809) in *U.S. v. Peters* (5 Cranch 115). Although the case was not related to the embargo (it involved the annulment of a federal court order by the state of Pennsylvania), it was memorable for Marshall's pronouncement sustaining the power of the national over state authority. The embargo itself was upheld (1808) by a Federalist Judge John Davis in U.S. district court in Massachusetts, but appeal on the decision was never taken to the Supreme Court.

In Congress opposition came from (1) the Federalists, (2) the dissident "Quids," including a faction led by **John Randolph** of Roanoke (p. 1134), as well as other dissidents. Jefferson signed the **Non-Intercourse Act** (1 Mar. 1809) repealing the embargo effective 15 Mar. 1809, reopening trade with all nations except France and Great Britain, and authorizing the president to proclaim resumption of trade with France or Great Britain in the event either power should cease violating neutral rights. The British minister to the U.S., David M. Erskine, gave assurances to Secretary of State Robert Smith that the orders in council of 1807, as applicable to the U.S., would be revoked 10 June 1809. Unaware that Erskine had not been authorized to speak for his government, President Madison issued a proclamation (19 Apr. 1809) legalizing trade with Great Britain. British Foreign Secretary George Canning disavowed (30 May 1809) Erskine's arrangement and ordered him back to England. President Madison in turn issued a proclamation (9 Aug. 1809) reviving the Non-Intercourse Act against Great Britain.

1808

1 JAN. AFRICAN SLAVE TRADE. Congressional interference with the foreign slave trade before 1808 was forbidden under Art. I, Sect. 9 of the Constitution. In keeping with Jefferson's recommendation (2 Dec. 1806), Congress forbade (2 Mar. 1807) slave importations into U.S. on and after 1 Jan.

1808. The law provided a penalty of forfeiture of vessel and cargo, with disposal of the seized slaves to be left to the state in which the ship was condemned.

7 DEC. PRESIDENTIAL ELECTION. Confirming the precedent established by Washington, Jefferson refused to stand for a 3d term. As his successor in the "Virginia dynasty" he supported **James Madison,** who was nominated by a congressional caucus. Madison's nomination was opposed by 2 insurgent wings of the Republican party. The Southern "Old Republicans" (John Randolph–John Taylor of Caroline group) chose **James Monroe** (Va., who withdrew from the contest). The Eastern Republicans, smarting under the embargo, nominated Vice-President **George Clinton** (N.Y.). The Federalist candidates were **Charles Cotesworth Pinckney** (S.C.) and **Rufus King** (N.Y.). **Madison** received 122 electoral votes to 47 for Pinckney and 6 for George Clinton. **Clinton** received 113 for vice-president to 47 for Rufus King. The Federalists gained in the House, but did not secure a majority.

1810

1 MAY. MACON'S BILL NO. 2. Congress took its own course after the collapse of the Erskine agreement. Since the Non-Intercourse Act was due to expire at the close of the second session of the 11th Congress in 1810, a substitute measure introduced by Nathaniel Macon (N.C.), chairman of the Foreign Affairs Committee, authorized the president to reopen commerce with Great Britain and France, adding that in the event either nation should before 3 Mar. 1811 modify or revoke its edicts so as to cease violations of American shipping, the president could prohibit trade with the other. If at the end of 3 months the other power failed to withdraw its edicts,

the president was empowered to revive non-intercourse against it. The bill, which also excluded British and French naval craft from American territorial waters, passed the House 64–27, the Federalists voting solidly against it. The French regarded the act as discrimination in favor of Great Britain, whose naval power closed the sea routes to French shipping.

5 AUG.–2 Nov. NAPOLEON'S DECEPTION. Acting on the pretense of making reprisals against the Non-Intercourse Act, Napoleon issued (23 Mar.) the **Rambouillet Decree** ordering seizure and confiscation of all U.S. vessels entering any French port. The decree, published 14 May, was made retroactive to 20 May 1809. When Napoleon learned of Macon's Bill No. 2, he instructed (5 Aug.) his foreign minister, the Duc de Cadore, to notify John Armstrong, U.S. minister at Paris, that the Berlin and Milan decrees would be revoked after 1 Nov. on condition that the U.S. declare non-intercourse against the British unless the orders in council were withdrawn. Yet on the same day Napoleon signed the **Decree of Trianon** ordering sequestration of U.S. vessels that had called at French ports between 20 May 1809 and 1 May 1810.

In communicating Napoleon's order to Armstrong, the Duc de Cadore took liberty with his phrasing and declared that the Berlin and Milan decrees had been actually canceled. President Madison unsuspectingly accepted the French communication at face value and issued (2 Nov.) a proclamation reopening trade with France and declaring that commerce with Great Britain would come to a halt on 2 Feb. 1811. Non-intercourse against the British was sanctioned (2 Mar. 1811) by Congress. More than a year elapsed before the British revoked the orders in council. The delay proved costly. The immediate British response to the move was a renewal of the blockade of New York and a more vigorous impressment of American seamen.

Napoleon's duplicity was revealed after Joel Barlow, whom Madison had named minister to France, arrived at Paris (19 Sept. 1811) in order to seek clarification of the Berlin and Milan decrees. The Duc de Bassano, Napoleon's foreign minister, showed Barlow the Decree of St. Cloud, supposedly signed by Napoleon 28 Apr. 1811. It stated that his earlier decrees had been declared nonexistent in regard to U.S. vessels since 1 Nov. 1810. The decree had never been published and, despite French assurances, had never been communicated to the U.S. government. Barlow's death (24 Dec. 1812) in Poland, where he had gone to confer with Napoleon, brought his mission to an end. By this time, however, Napoleon's involvement in the Russian campaign had terminated his influence in American affairs, and the U.S. was at war with Great Britain.

27 Oct. ANNEXATION OF WEST FLORIDA. The Louisiana treaty of 1803 made no reference to the status of Spanish-ruled East and West Florida. Jefferson supported the view that Louisiana included that portion of Florida between the Mississippi River to the west and the Perdido River to the east. In 1810 Southern expansionists led a revolt in the Spanish dominion, captured the fort at Baton Rouge, and proclaimed (26 Sept.) the independent state of the Republic of West Florida. Madison issued a proclamation (27 Oct.) announcing U.S. possession of West Florida from the Mississippi to the Perdido and authorizing its military occupation as part of the Orleans Territory. Congress assembled in secret session and adopted a resolution (15 Jan. 1811) authorizing extension of U.S. rule over East Florida as well in the event local authority consented or a foreign power took steps to occupy it. On

14 May 1812 West Florida was incorporated by Congress into the Mississippi Territory. After the outbreak of the War of 1812, Gen. James Wilkinson took the Spanish fort at Mobile (15 Apr. 1813) and occupied the Mobile district of West Florida to the Perdido River. This was the sole territorial conquest retained by the U.S. after the War of 1812.

YAZOO LAND FRAUD. The Georgia legislature (7 Jan. 1795) sold to 4 land companies (whose shareholders were discovered to include Georgia legislators) 35 million acres in the Yazoo River country (Mississippi and Alabama) for $500,000. A new legislature rescinded (1796) this sale. When Georgia ceded (1802) to the U.S. her Western claims, the national government sought a final settlement by awarding 5 million acres to holders of Yazoo land warrants. With the support of other "Quids" John Randolph, who had already split with the administration over Louisiana, succeeded in blocking the bill (1804–05), which was not passed until 1814, when the claimants were awarded $4.2 million. Randolph's opposition precipitated a party schism and led to his removal as leader of the majority. The Yazoo affair was the subject of Chief Justice Marshall's opinion (1810) in *Fletcher* v. *Peck* (6 Cranch 87), in which he maintained that the judiciary could not inquire into the motives of legislators who made the original grant and construed the grant as a contract within the meaning of the Constitution and the rescinding law as impairing the obligation of the contract; hence void.

1811

24 Jan.–20 Feb. BANK DEBATE. The charter of the first U.S. Bank was due to expire 4 Mar. Petitions for extension of the charter had been made in 1808 and 1810, but congressional consideration was postponed because of the pressure of foreign affairs. Secretary of the Treasury Gallatin, lauding the management of the bank, endorsed renewal of the charter. Opposed to renewal were (1) "Old Republicans" who viewed the bank as the last survival of Federalist power, denounced it on constitutional grounds, and desired to drive Gallatin from office on the issue; (2) Anglophobes who pointed to the fact that two thirds of the bank stock was held by Britons and insisted that the measure would aid a potential enemy; (3) interests favoring the growth of state-chartered banks, which had increased rapidly, expanded their note issues, and were eager to share the profits of the bank. The recharter bill died in the House (24 Jan.). In the Senate, where William Henry Crawford (Ga.) led the fight for the administration bill and William Branch Giles (Va.) opposed it, the tie (17 to 17) was broken by Vice-President Clinton, who voted (20 Feb.) against renewal. The bank wound up its business and expired. Failure to recharter the bank deprived the government of urgently needed financial resources during the War of 1812.

16 MAY. "LITTLE BELT" AFFAIR. In May, British cruisers off New York Harbor resumed more freely their impressment of American seamen. The British 38-gun frigate *Guerrière* overhauled (1 May) off Sandy Hook the American brig *Spitfire* and impressed a native-born American. Capt. John Rodgers, commanding the U.S. 44-gun frigate *President,* was ordered (6 May) to cruise off Sandy Hook to give protection to American vessels. En route Rodgers sighted a ship he mistook for the *Guerrière* (actually the craft was the British 20-gun corvette *Little Belt*). Rodgers gave chase; the *Little Belt* refused to identify herself; and the pursuit ended in an evening engagement (16 May) off

Cape Charles. The broadsides of the *President* disabled the *Little Belt,* killing 9 and wounding 23 of her crew. On 1 Nov. the U.S. government informed the British minister, Augustus John Foster, that it was willing to settle the matter amicably, provided the orders in council were revoked.

31 JULY–8 Nov. TECUMSEH AND THE NORTHWEST. Along the frontiers of the Old Northwest the Shawnee chief **Tecumseh** (p. 1167) undertook the organization of a defensive tribal confederacy to resist the westward sweep of white settlement. The British governor in Canada, as well as the fur traders, were reputedly backing Tecumseh and his brother, the Prophet. When extensive Indian activity during the summer of 1811 created fear among frontier settlers, the people of Vincennes adopted resolutions (31 July) calling for the destruction of the Indian capital on Tippecanoe Creek. The settlers finally induced Gen. **William Henry Harrison** (p. 1053) governor of the Indiana Territory, to take the initiative against Tecumseh (who meanwhile had gone to the Southwest to seek support for his plan). Leading a force of some 1,000 men, Harrison set out (26 Sept.) from Vincennes for the Indian capital 150 miles to the north, near the confluence of the Tippecanoe and the Wabash. Ft. Harrison, about 65 miles above Vincennes, was established; on 28 Oct. the force resumed its march and encamped (6 Nov.) about a mile from the Indian village. In a surprise dawn attack (7 Nov.) the Indians descended upon the Americans. After a day-long battle, Harrison's men, despite heavy losses, beat back the Indians and razed the village (8 Nov.). The Americans then withdrew to Ft. Harrison. Westerners acclaimed the **Battle of Tippecanoe** as a great victory. Although the British authorities in Canada subsequently took steps to cut off aid to the Indians, the event increased anti-British sentiment along the frontier and resulted in louder demands for expelling the British from Canada. Indian raids broke out again (Apr. 1812) along the frontier, but Tecumseh chose to remain on the defensive. It was generally recognized that open war with the Indians would necessarily be part of a declared war against the British.

4 Nov. "WAR HAWKS." The prowar feeling that swept the country in 1810-11 left its mark on the congressional elections. The 12th Congress numbered even fewer Federalists and, in place of many of the cautious legislators who had enacted Macon's Bill No. 2, brought to the fore a new type of Republican who espoused nationalism and expansionism. Upon these war Republicans John Randolph bestowed the epithet: "war hawks." Among them were **Henry Clay** (p. 1002), **Richard M. Johnson** (Ky., 1780-1850), **John C. Calhoun** (p. 996), **William Lowndes** (S.C., 1782-1822), **Langdon Cheves** (S.C., 1776-1857), **Felix Grundy** (Tenn., 1777-1840), **Peter B. Porter** (1773-1844) from western New York. Notwithstanding their numerical minority the "war hawks" achieved a commanding position in the House. Clay was elected speaker; the Foreign Relations Committee came under the control of Calhoun, Grundy, and Porter; Cheves was named chairman of the Naval Committee.

Most of the "war hawks" came from the agrarian areas of the South and West whose people were hardly affected by maritime issues (although some Westerners claimed that the orders in council had crippled their markets for agricultural produce); yet they chose to view maritime seizure and impressment as outrages upon national rights and honor. Northern and Southern "war hawks" found common ground in expansionism (J. W. Pratt, 1925). Those from the Northwest, eager to destroy the frontier

Indian menace they attributed to British intrigue and incitement, equated security with land hunger and demanded the conquest of Canada. The Southerners wanted to wrest Florida from Spain, Britain's ally.

5 Nov. Despite expansionist pressures, the U.S. would not have been involved in war had it not been for maritime and commercial issues. Madison was no tool of the war party (see Theodore Clarke Smith, 1931), although he ultimately supported its program. The president's message to Congress attacked Great Britain, had no friendly words for France, but made no express reference to impressment. The president requested preparations for the national defense, pointing to the "evidence of hostile inflexibility in trampling on rights which no independent nation can relinquish."

1812

1-10 Apr. WAR PREPARATIONS. Madison's message to Congress (1 Apr.) recommending an immediate and general embargo for 60 days was regarded by the "war hawks" as a prelude to armed conflict. The bill passed in the House (70-41). In the Senate, where the vote was 20-13, moderate Republicans, anxious to prolong negotiations with Great Britain, amended the bill to extend the embargo to 90 days. The embargo became law on 4 Apr. On 10 Apr. the president was empowered to call up for 6 months' service 100,000 militia from the states and territories.

10 Apr.-16 June. FAILURE OF DIPLOMACY. Madison's persistence in maintaining that the Berlin and Milan decrees were not in force against the U.S. was countered by British denial that Napoleon had unconditionally revoked them. Refusing to annul the orders in council, the British affirmed their view in a note (10 April) sent by Foreign

Secretary Lord Castlereagh. Madison interpreted it as final notice of Britain's unyielding position, and toward the close of May drafted a message calling for an immediate declaration of war.

Under the impact of economic distress at home, the British government had begun to give way gradually, if reluctantly. The revival of non-intercourse, combined with the increased effectiveness of the Continental system, created severe hardships for English commercial and industrial interests. In 1810–11 factories and mills shut down; unemployment rose; the price of foodstuffs soared; and in one year alone (1811) British exports fell off by a third. Employers and workers joined in petitioning Parliament to consider repeal of the orders. Prime Minister Spencer Perceval stood in danger of losing his office on the issue when he was assassinated (11 May) by a deranged malcontent. The consequent delay in taking up the question was crucial. Lord Castlereagh announced (16 June) suspension of the orders in coun-cil (formally suspended 23 June). Across the Atlantic the U.S. Congress, unaware of the British concession, had already moved for war.

18 June. DECLARATION OF WAR ON GREAT BRITAIN. Madison's message to Congress (1 June) listed 4 major grounds for war: (1) impressment of American seamen, (2) violation of U.S. neutral rights and territorial waters, (3) the blockade of U.S. ports, and (4) refusal to revoke the orders in council. The House (4 June) supported the declaration of war 79–49. In the Senate, where action was delayed by Federalist and "Old Republican" opposition, the vote (18 June) in favor of war was 19–13. The New England states (with the exception of inland Vermont) and other maritime and commercial states, such as New York, New Jersey, and Delaware, voted for peace. The vote of the Southern and Western states assured a declaration of war. On 19 June Madison proclaimed a state of war with Great Britain.

War of 1812 (1812–14)

THE BALANCE SHEET. U.S. advantages: (1) Great Britain's involvement in the Napoleonic wars prevented her from devoting her main resources to the war against the U.S.; (2) the U.S. had an initial advantage of proximity to the theater of war; (3) the U.S. population was overwhelmingly superior in numbers to that of Canada, the chief target of U.S. land operations; (4) the U.S. Navy, although numerically inferior to the British (it had but 16 seagoing craft), was manned by efficient and well-trained officers and crews. U.S. disadvantages: (1) a small and badly ad-ministered regular army composed of volunteers and raw militia with few experienced and capable commanders, and poorly equipped and supplied; (2) lack of united popular support, particularly in New England and New York, where the people spoke of "Mr. Madison's war" and accused the president of being a tool of the French; (3) lack of a national bank, which deprived the government of centralized financial machinery and compelled dependence upon borrowing by public subscription (a move that evoked a feeble response in the financial centers of the disaffected Northeast).

1812

MILITARY SETBACKS. The impro-
vised U.S. plan of operations called for a
3-pronged drive into Canada. In the east,
a force under Gen. **Henry Dearborn**
(1751–1829) was to use the Lake Champlain route for an assault on Montreal.
In the center, troops under Gen. **Stephen
Van Rensselaer** (1764–1839) were to
attack the Canadians along the Niagara
River frontier. In the west, an expedition
under Gen. **William Hull** (1753–1825)
was to launch from Detroit an attack
against Upper Canada. The U.S. forces
were composed mainly of ill-trained militia.

16 Aug. Hull's Surrender. The Canadian campaign began with a series of
disasters. The surrender (17 July) of the
U.S. post on Michilimackinac Island, in
the Strait of Mackinaw joining Lakes
Huron and Michigan, led the Northwest
Indians under Tecumseh to align themselves definitely with the British. The
British gained valuable intelligence when
Hull's personal baggage (containing
official papers and plans) was seized
(1 July) as it was being conveyed to
Detroit. With a force of 2,200 men, Hull
crossed the Detroit River into Canada
(12 July) and occupied Sandwich, but
withdrew to Detroit (8 Aug.), apprehensive that the Indians would cut his
line of communication with Ohio and
of the Canadian force of some 2,000
under Gen. Isaac Brock. Fearing an Indian massacre of women and children,
Hull surrendered Detroit (16 Aug.) to
Brock without firing a shot. The garrison
of Ft. Dearborn (at the site of Chicago)
was massacred (15 Aug.) as it evacuated
the post, which was burned the next day.
Hull's surrender left the British in control of Lake Erie and the Michigan country. A court-martial sentenced Hull to
death for cowardice and neglect of duty
(26 March 1814). The penalty was remitted because of Hull's Revolutionary
War record but his name was dropped
from the army roll.

13 Oct.–28 Nov. Niagara Campaign.
Brock reached Ft. George on the Canadian side of the Niagara River (23
Aug.), where, facing the U.S. line under
Van Rensselaer in New York state, he
established a strong defense. Van Rensselaer took the offensive (13 Oct.) with
the occupation of Queenston Heights
(Gen. Brock was killed in the engagement). Opposed by a British force of
1,000, the 600 Americans on the heights
were crushed when New York state
militia failed to reinforce them on the
ground that their military service did
not require them to leave the state. Van
Rensselaer retired from his command
and was succeeded by Gen. Alexander
Smyth, an indecisive regular army officer who made a feeble attempt (28
Nov.) to cross the Niagara River. As a
result of his failure, Smyth was relieved
of his command and his name dropped
from the army roll.

19 Nov. Montreal Fiasco. Stationed
at Plattsburg, under the command of
Gen. Dearborn, was the largest force of
Americans under arms. Projecting a syn-
chronized movement with Smyth's operation at Niagara, Dearborn led his army
(19 Nov.) to the Canadian frontier, at
which point the militia refused to proceed further. On 23 Nov. Dearborn returned his army to Plattsburg.

The military disasters of 1812 revealed the need for well-trained regular
troops and an overhauling of the army
command. Madison's dissatisfaction with
the War Department led to the replacement (13 Jan. 1813) of Secretary William Eustis by John Armstrong (N.Y.).
Although he succeeded in invigorating
the army command, Armstrong was tact-
less; upon his retirement in 1814, Monroe took charge of the War Department,
remaining in that post until the appoint-

ment of William Henry Crawford (Ga.) in 1815.

NAVAL SUCCESSES. The skill and valor of U.S. seamanship were demonstrated in the engagement (19 Aug.) off Nova Scotia between the U.S. 44-gun frigate *Constitution,* Capt. **Isaac Hull** (1773–1843) commanding, and the British 38-gun frigate *Guerrière.* After a duel lasting about a half-hour, the *Guerrière* was so badly riddled and disabled that Hull had to abandon taking her as a prize and instead blew her up. The U.S. casualties numbered 14; the British, 79. News of the victory, coming hard upon reports of the fall of Detroit, helped to bolster sagging morale. The 18-gun sloop-of-war *Wasp,* Capt. Jacob Jones commanding, bested the British 18-gun brig *Frolic* in an encounter (17 Oct.) 600 miles off the Virginia coast. The U.S. losses, 10 killed or wounded; British, c.90. The 44-gun frigate *United States,* Capt. **Stephen Decatur** (p. 1011) commanding, subdued (25 Oct.) the British 38-gun frigate *Macedonian* off the Madeira Islands and brought her into New London as a prize. The *Constitution,* under her new commander, Capt. **William Bainbridge** (1774–1833), destroyed (29 Dec.) the British 38-gun frigate *Java* in a duel off the coast of Brazil (American loss, 12 killed, 22 wounded; British loss, 48 dead, 102 wounded). Her performance on this occasion earned for the *Constitution* the sobriquet "Old Ironsides."

PEACE FEELERS. At the instruction of Secretary of State Monroe, the U.S. chargé at London, Jonathan Russell, informed Lord Castlereagh (24 Aug.) that the U.S. was willing to negotiate an armistice provided the British would abandon impressment and paper blockades and agree to indemnities for maritime spoliations. On his own initiative, Russell added informally that the U.S. would renounce the practice of naturalizing Brit-

ish seamen. Castlereagh rejected (29 Aug.) both proposals. From Halifax, Adm. Sir John Borlase Warren sent to Washington an offer of armistice and negotiation (30 Sept.). Monroe replied (27 Oct.) that the U.S. would accept only on condition that the British suspend impressment. This peace overture also bore no result.

NEW ENGLAND DISAFFECTION. The declaration of war provoked sharp remonstrances in the Federalist stronghold. Gov. Caleb Strong (Mass.) issued a proclamation (26 June) declaring a public fast in view of the war "against the nation from which we are descended." The Massachusetts House of Representatives issued an "Address to the People" (26 June) terming the war as one against the public interest and asserting that "there be no volunteers except for defensive war." The General Assembly of Connecticut condemned the war (25 Aug.). The governors of Connecticut (2 July) and Massachusetts (5 Aug.) refused to furnish militia to the federal government. In New Hampshire the Rockingham memorial (5 Aug.) protested against "hasty, rash, and ruinous measures" and made veiled hints of disunion.

2 DEC. PRESIDENTIAL ELECTION. At a congressional caucus (18 May) where Southern Republican insurgents put aside their differences, **Madison** was renominated by unanimous vote. Vice-President **Clinton** having died in office (20 Apr.), **Elbridge Gerry** (Mass.) was chosen as vice-presidential candidate. The Federalist charge that Madison won renomination by truckling to **Henry Clay** (p. 1002) and the war Republicans appears to be without foundation. In New York state the antiwar Republicans nominated (29 May) **De Witt Clinton** (p. 1003) for the presidency. At a secret meeting (Sept.) in New York, the Federalists threw their support to Clinton, and both groups endorsed Clin-

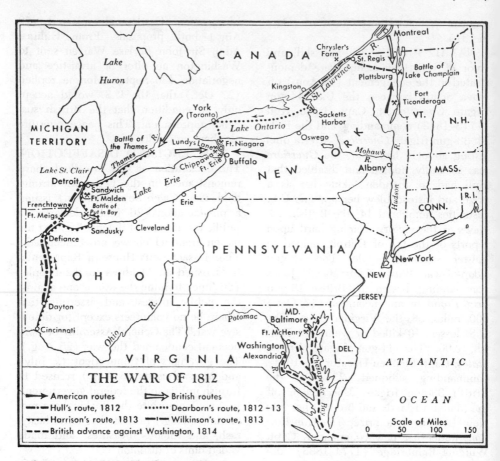

THE WAR OF 1812

➤ American routes ⟹ British routes
•—•— Hull's route, 1812 •••••• Dearborn's route, 1812–13
ᵛᵛᵛᵛ Harrison's route, 1813 •—ᴵ— Wilkinson's route, 1813
–––– British advance against Washington, 1814

ton's running mate, **Charles Jared Ingersoll** (Pa.), a moderate Federalist. The electoral vote: for president—**Madison,** 128; Clinton, 89. For vice-president—**Gerry,** 131; Ingersoll, 86. Madison carried the Southern and Western states. Clinton carried all of New England and the Middle States to the Potomac, with the exception of Vermont and Pennsylvania. The sweeping Federalist victory in the Northeast doubled the party's strength in the new Congress.

1813

BRITISH BLOCKADE. The blockade of Chesapeake and Delaware bays (announced 26 Dec. 1812) shut off commerce from those waters and was marked by British raids along the shores of the upper Chesapeake by a naval force under Rear Adm. Sir George Cockburn. The blockade was extended (26 May) to the mouth of the Mississippi and to the ports and harbors of New York, Charleston, Port Royal, and Savannah. Chesapeake Bay was used as a British naval station, and from the early months of 1813 until the end of the war the southern coast down to Georgia was kept in a constant state of panic. After the announcement (16 Nov.) of the blockade of Long Island Sound, only the ports along the New England coast north of New London remained open to neutral trade. The British hoped to exploit New

England disaffection. When the Northeast failed to fulfill expectations of disunion, and when the British decided to use a complete blockade as a support for general offensive operations in 1814, the blockade was extended to New England (25 Apr. 1814).

Despite many individual exploits by U.S. naval vessels, the blockade was highly effective. It created a scarcity of goods that stimulated domestic manufactures and led to widespread speculation and price inflation, with consequent hardships on farmers. The sharp reduction in customs receipts weakened the Treasury, helping to bring the government to near bankruptcy in 1814.

The Americans retaliated by dispatching cruisers to prey on merchant convoys. Until its capture (28 Mar. 1814) off Valparaiso, the 32-gun frigate *Essex,* Capt. David Porter (1780–1843) commanding, captured or destroyed more than twoscore merchant ships or whalers in the Atlantic and South Pacific. But such individual ship actions did little to lessen British naval superiority. The Americans also resorted to privateering. Ineffective in 1813, privateering did not become a powerful weapon until 1814, when the U.S. blockade of British coasts made it unsafe for enemy shipping to sail without convoy from the English to the Irish Channel. By the summer of 1814 Lloyd's listed 825 vessels as captured by Americans. But even these inroads did not affect the tight British blockade of the U.S. coast.

HARRISON IN THE WEST. The fall of Detroit and Ft. Dearborn (Aug. 1812) compelled the Americans to fall back to the Wabash-Maumee line. Westerners took alarm. Shortly after learning of Hull's defeat, a group of Kentucky officials and citizens (including Henry Clay) commissioned William Henry Harrison a major general of militia and appointed him to head an expedition to Detroit.

The move revived confidence along the frontier. When Madison and Secretary of War Eustis learned of Kentucky's action, they commissioned Harrison a brigadier general (17 Sept. 1812) and gave him command of the northwestern army (Harrison was nominated a major general on 27 Feb.). Harrison's orders were simply to retake Detroit. At his disposal he had 10,000 men. The first battle, at **Frenchtown** on the Raisin River, at the western end of Lake Erie, resulted in defeat (22 Jan.) for the Kentucky force led by Gen. James Winchester. Some 500 Americans were taken prisoner; another 400 were killed in action or massacred by the Indians. The British and Tecumseh failed in their siege (1–9 May) of **Ft. Meigs,** at the mouth of the Maumee, where Harrison commanded the defense. The British assault (2 Aug.) on **Ft. Stephenson,** on the Sandusky River, was repulsed by a stout defense led by Maj. George Croghan. Harrison could not move on Detroit as long as the British remained in control of Lake Erie.

1 JUNE. DESTRUCTION OF THE "CHESAPEAKE." The gloom that hung over the American cause in 1813 was darkened by news of the encounter between the U.S. 38-gun frigate *Chesapeake* and the British 38-gun frigate *Shannon,* 30 miles off Boston harbor. Acting against his better judgment, the commander of the *Chesapeake,* **James Lawrence** (1781–1813), accepted a challenge from Capt. P. B. V. Broke of the *Shannon.* Lawrence's sole advantage lay in the number of his crew (379) as against that of the *Shannon* (330), but the recently acquired American crew was ill-trained and poorly disciplined. Powerful broadsides raked the *Chesapeake* from stem to stern with unerring effect. A British boarding party of 50 men captured the disabled *Chesapeake* and brought her into Halifax as prize. The British suffered 83 casualties; the Americans, 146. It is said that the last order of the dying Capt. Lawrence was, "Don't give up the ship!" His words became the rallying cry of the U.S. navy.

10 Sept. BATTLE OF LAKE ERIE. Lawrence's last order was inscribed on the battleflag of the *Lawrence,* flagship of the 28-year-old Capt. **Oliver Hazard Perry** (p. 1127) in the Battle of Lake Erie, the most important naval engagement on the Great Lakes during the war. Ordered from Newport (17 Feb.) to the Great Lakes, Perry reached Presque Isle (27 Mar.), where a flotilla of 2 brigs, a schooner, and 3 gunboats was under construction from materials (with the exception of timber) transported over land and water from Philadelphia by way of Pittsburgh. With the British evacuation of Ft. Niagara and Ft. Erie (27 May), Perry was able to remove 5 vessels from the navy yard at Black Rock (near Buffalo) and bring them to Presque Isle (5 June). During the temporary absence of the British blockading squadron (4 Aug.), Perry floated his heavier vessels over the harbor bar and brought them into deep water. He anchored off the island of Put in Bay, north of the mouth of the Sandusky River. The British squadron under Capt. Robert H. Barclay, consisting of 6 vessels (mounting a total of 65 guns), sailed for Perry's force (9 Sept.). Perry had at his disposal 10 vessels (mounting a total of 55 guns), improvised over the winter of 1812–13, but superior in tonnage and heavy armament. The engagement (10 Sept.), lasting more than 3 hours, was one of the bloodiest naval actions of the war, and resulted in a decisive defeat for the British. Perry's flagship was riddled to pieces, and 80% of her crew were casualties. British casualties: 41 killed, 94 wounded. Perry sent to Gen. Harrison, at Seneca on the Sandusky River, the message (dispatched 10 Sept., received 12 Sept.) containing the words:

"We have met the enemy and they are ours." Perry's victory placed Lake Erie under U.S. control and renewed the threat to Canada. It forced the British to evacuate Malden and Detroit and to fall back to a defensive line along the Niagara frontier.

5 Oct. BATTLE OF THE THAMES. Perry's triumph enabled Harrison to move his main force of about 4,500 infantry across Lake Erie to Middle Sister Island (20 Sept.) and to disembark them (27 Sept.) near Malden in Upper Canada. Meanwhile, against the protests of Tecumseh, Gen. Henry A. Proctor had evacuated Detroit (18 Sept.). The British, with Harrison in pursuit, withdrew from Malden (24 Sept.) and retreated northward by way of Sandwich. Harrison overtook the British and Indians at Moravian Town on the north bank of the Thames River, defeating them in a battle marked by the prowess of a Kentucky mounted regiment under Col. **Richard Mentor Johnson** (1780–1850). U.S. losses: 15 killed, 30 wounded; British: 12 killed, 36 wounded, 477 taken prisoner. The results of the battle were far-reaching. Tecumseh's death in this encounter brought about the collapse of the Indian confederacy and led the Indians to desert the British cause. The U.S. military frontier in the Northwest was made secure, and British power swept from that region (except at Ft. Michilimackinac, which the British occupied until the end of the war).

DRIVE ON UPPER CANADA. Despite their loss of Lake Erie, the British still maintained control of Lake Ontario. Their position was challenged by a combined military and naval action under Gen. **Henry Dearborn** and Capt. Isaac Chauncey, naval commander on Lake Ontario. Their plan was to gain U.S. control by seizing British naval craft at York (Toronto), capital of upper Canada. About 1,600 troops embarked (22

Apr.) from Sackett's Harbor and raided York (27 Apr.), garrisoned by about 600 British troops. The U.S. descent upon York resulted in its surrender and the destruction of 1 ship and capture of another. But 320 Americans (including Gen. Zebulon M. Pike) were killed or wounded by the explosion of a powder magazine; the bypassing of Kingston wrecked the plan to gain control of the lake; and the burning of the public buildings at York (including the assembly houses and the residence of the governor), put to the torch against Dearborn's orders, later gave the British their pretext for burning Washington in 1814.

The raiding force returned to Niagara (8 May), where, during Dearborn's illness, the troops came under the immediate command of Col. **Winfield Scott** (p. 1148), the general's chief of staff. Employing Chauncey's fleet, Scott moved a force of 4,000 men and attacked from the rear (27 May) the British force of 1,600 men stationed at Ft. George under command of Gen. John Vincent. Although the Americans failed to destroy the enemy body, the evacuation of Ft. George compelled the simultaneous withdrawal of the British from Ft. Erie to the south (opposite Buffalo), thus enabling Perry to liberate the vessels at the Black Rock navy yard.

A force of 2,000 Americans pursued Vincent. With only 700 men, Vincent attacked (6 June) at **Stony Creek**, 10 miles from Hamilton, compelling the Americans to fall back on Ft. George. Two American generals, William H. Winder and John Chandler, were captured by the British. The U.S. force at Ft. Erie withdrew (9 June), and that post was occupied by the British over the following winter.

The outstanding action in this sector was the **Battle of Sackett's Harbor** (28–29 May), in which Gen. **Jacob J. Brown** (1775–1828) repulsed a British landing force commanded by Sir George Prevost, governor general of Canada.

2D ATTEMPT TO TAKE MONTREAL. Dearborn was removed from his command (6 July) and replaced by Gen. **James Wilkinson** (1757–1825). The reorganization of the U.S. command also placed (3 July) Gen. **Wade Hampton** at the head of the force on Lake Champlain. Secretary of War John Armstrong, who arrived (5 Sept.) at Sackett's Harbor and established headquarters in the field, projected a combined attack on Montreal by Wilkinson and Hampton by way of the St. Lawrence. The strong Montreal position was supported by some 15,000 British troops in and around the city. Wilkinson's troops were to start from Sackett's Harbor and make the descent of the St. Lawrence; Hampton's force was to march northward from Plattsburg and effect a junction with them. The mutual dislike existing between the 2 generals made cooperation difficult.

Wilkinson left Sackett's Harbor (17 Oct.) at the head of 8,000 men and began (5 Nov.) the descent of the St. Lawrence. The flotilla stopped (10 Nov.) at Chrysler's Farm on the north bank of the river, about 90 miles from Montreal. Learning of an enemy force advancing from the rear, Wilkinson ordered Gen. John Parke Boyd to take the offensive. Boyd's 3 brigades of regulars (about 2,000 men) were virtually routed (11 Nov.) by a British force of 800 led by Col. J. W. Morrison. U.S. casualties: 102 killed, 237 wounded, more than 100 taken prisoner; British: 22 killed, 48 wounded, 12 missing. Informed (12 Nov.) that Hampton had abandoned the attack on Montreal, Wilkinson went into winter quarters (13 Nov.) at French Mills, along the Salmon River.

Hampton had marched his force of about 4,000 men to the Canadian line (19 Sept.) and, instead of proceeding north, had moved west (26 Sept.) to the Chateaugay River, where he awaited news of Wilkinson's progress. Ordered by Armstrong (16 Oct.) to move down the Chateaugay, Hampton established his force about 15 miles from the mouth of the river (22 Oct.). Although he theoretically menaced Montreal and British communications with upper Canada, Hampton had a numerically inferior force and lacked water transportation. His position was untenable. After attacking a smaller British force (**Battle of the Chateaugay**, 25 Oct.), Hampton, without consulting Wilkinson, abandoned the drive on Montreal and fell back on Plattsburg. His decision may have been influenced by his receipt (25 Oct.) of Armstrong's order indicating that the army was going into winter quarters on the American side. Before resigning from the army (Mar. 1814), Hampton presided over the court-martial of Gen. Hull.

29–30 Dec. BURNING OF BUFFALO. When Gen. Vincent dispatched a British force to retake Ft. George, that post was evacuated (10 Dec.) by George McClure, a brigadier general of New York militia. Before withdrawing, McClure burned the village of Newark and part of Queenston. In retaliation, a British force under Col. John Murray captured Ft. Niagara (18 Dec.), killing 67, wounding 11, and taking 350 prisoners. Then the British set loose the Indians, who ravaged Lewiston and the surrounding countryside. Leading a British force of 1,500 men, Gen. Gordon Drummond burned Buffalo and Black Rock (29–30 Dec.), destroying ships and supplies. Ft. Niagara remained in British hands until the end of the war.

RUSSIAN MEDIATION. The diplomatic mission of **John Quincy Adams** (p. 971), named minister to Russia (27 June 1809), benefited from the widening

gulf between Napoleon and Czar Alexander I. The Czar courted French hostility by interfering on behalf of U.S. commerce in Denmark, giving orders to release U.S. ships at Archangel, and issuing an imperial ukase (19 Dec. 1811) admitting U.S. goods to Russian ports. Following Napoleon's declaration of war on Russia (22 June 1812) the Czar learned (6 Aug. 1812) of the U.S. declaration of war on Great Britain, now Russia's ally, and took steps to end Anglo-U.S. differences in order to strengthen the Allied effort against Napoleon. Adams was notified (21 Sept. 1812) of the Czar's offer to mediate between the U.S. and Great Britain. Receiving Adams' communication (8 Mar.), Madison dispatched as peace commissioners James A. Bayard (Del.), a Federalist, and Secretary of the Treasury Gallatin. Bayard and Gallatin reached St. Petersburg on 21 July. In the meantime, however, Lord Castlereagh had declined mediation (5 July).

CASTLEREAGH'S PROPOSAL. Despite his resentment of the Czar's personal interference, Lord Castlereagh was becoming increasingly lukewarm toward the war with the U.S. British victories at Vittoria (21 June) and Leipzig (18–19 Oct.) were counterbalanced by reports of British defeats in the Lake Erie region. He sent (4 Nov.) an official letter to Monroe offering direct negotiation. The proposal was immediately accepted by Madison, who acted upon news of British victories on the Continent and the deteriorating U.S. military situation along the Niagara frontier and in the Lake Champlain region. The Senate confirmed (18 Jan. 1814) Madison's nomination of **J. Q. Adams, J. A. Bayard, Henry Clay,** and **Jonathan Russell** as peace commissioners. The addition of **Gallatin** to the commission was confirmed on 8 Feb. 1814 (Gallatin being replaced as Secretary of the Treasury by George W.

Campbell, Tenn., 9 Feb. 1814). The Flemish town of Ghent was designated as the meeting place, and discussions began 8 Aug. 1814. The British were represented by Lord Gambier, Henry Goulburn, and William Adams.

1814

WAR EMBARGO. New England and New York contractors supplied beef, flour, and other provisions to the British armies in Canada and to enemy vessels off the East Coast. In a special message to Congress (9 Dec. 1813), President Madison recommended an embargo to interdict trade with the enemy. The measure passed in the House 85–57; in the Senate, 20–14; and became law on 17 Dec. 1813. It was modified (25 Jan.) when its strict enforcement along the coast resulted in the near starvation of the people of Nantucket. But the border trade with Canada persisted. Madison gradually recognized that his entire system of commercial restriction had failed in its aim both at home and abroad. His message to Congress (31 Mar.) recommended repeal of the Embargo and Non-Importation Acts. The only significant protest against repeal came from Rep. Elisha Potter (R.I.), who spoke for newly developed manufacturing interests thriving under the exclusion of imports and for commercial interests profiting from the high prices created by scarcity. New England as a whole, however, supported repeal. As a protective measure for U.S. manufactures, the repeal bill guaranteed war duties for 2 years after peace. The bill passed in the House (7 Apr.) 115–37; the Senate (12 Apr.), 26–4; and with Madison's approval (14 Apr.) commercial restriction came to an end. On 1 Sept. the British landed at the mouth of the Castine River in Maine, captured Castine, and advanced to Bangor. To the end of the war U.S. ships trading with the British paid out £ 13,-000 in duties to the royal customs officials at Castine.

CREEK WAR. In 1811 Tecumseh had visited the Creek Indians in the Alabama country, apparently attempting to enlist Creek support for his confederacy. A year after the outbreak of the War of 1812, a war faction of the Creeks known as the "Red Sticks," numbering some 2,000 warriors from the upper Creek country, took part in a general uprising along the frontier. A party of U.S. settlers clashed (27 July 1813) with some Indians at Burnt Corn, about 80 miles north of Pensacola. This led directly to the Creek War, which was opened by the Creek attack (30 Aug. 1813) on Ft. Mims, on the east bank of the Alabama River about 35 miles above Mobile. Of the 550 persons in the fort, 250 were massacred and many others burned to death. News of the affair reached **Andrew Jackson** (p. 1068) at Nashville. As major general of Tennessee militia, he called out 2,000 volunteers. Frontier armies were organized also in Georgia and in what later became the state of Mississippi, but the major engagements against the Creeks were fought by the Tennesseans under Jackson.

Tennessee militia under Gen. John Coffee, Jackson's chief subordinate, destroyed the Indian village of **Talishatchee** (3 Nov. 1813). Jackson surrounded and destroyed (9 Nov. 1813) **Talladega,** killing more than 500 Indian warriors. The Tennesseans were repulsed at **Emuckfaw** (22 Jan.) and **Enotachopco Creek** (24 Jan.), and suffered heavy casualties at **Calibee Creek** (27 Jan.). Jackson's major effort came in the early spring of 1814, when he penetrated to the heart of the upper Creek country. At the head of 3,000 men, Jackson and

Coffee attacked (27 Mar.) the fortified position built by the Creeks and their Cherokee allies at the **Horseshoe Bend** of the Tallapoosa River. An estimated 850 to 900 warriors were killed, some 500 Indian women and children were taken prisoner; U.S. casualties: 51 killed, 148 wounded. The campaign was brought to a close by the capitulation of the Creeks. Under the **Treaty of Ft. Jackson** (9 Aug.), signed by only part of the Creeks, two thirds of the Creek lands were ceded to the U.S. and the Indians agreed to withdraw from the southern and western part of Alabama. At almost the same time the Northwest Indians signed the **Treaty of Greenville** (22 July) restoring peace with the U.S. and requiring the Delaware, Miami, Seneca, Shawnee, and Wyandot Indians to declare war on the British. The treaty was signed for the U.S. by William Henry Harrison and Gen. Lewis Cass. Harrison had already resigned his army commission (11 May) and Jackson had been promoted to major general of the regular army (22 May).

BRITISH TAKE THE OFFENSIVE. The overthrow of Napoleon (6 Apr.) enabled the British to concentrate their resources on the war in North America. During the summer of 1814 some 14,000 British troops, veterans of the Duke of Wellington's Peninsular campaign, were sent across the Atlantic. The British planned concerted land and naval operations based on a triple thrust against Lake Champlain, Chesapeake Bay, and New Orleans. To support the general offensive, the blockade along the U.S. coast was enforced more rigorously.

U.S. MILITARY RESOURCES. While the U.S. military establishment was authorized at 58,254, the effective strength of the regular army (Jan.) stood at about 11,000. Under the law of 27 Jan., the army strength was authorized at 62,773; yet by 1 Oct. the regular army

had only 34,000 men. The administration's proposal to raise 100,000 men by conscription was never accepted by Congress. Whenever possible, the government used the militia only as a last resort. In other respects, the military establishment had been improved. Secretary of War Armstrong divided the country into 9 military districts and revamped (Jan.–Feb.) the army command. Incompetent generals were removed from active sectors. Wilkinson, who was relieved from his command (24 March) and acquitted by a court of inquiry, was replaced by Maj. Gen. **Jacob Brown,** who, with the newly promoted Brig. Gen. **Winfield Scott,** was responsible for operations in the Niagara sector. Also promoted to major general was George Izard (S.C.), who replaced Hampton at Plattsburg (1 May).

NORTHERN CAMPAIGN: Niagara. Between Long Point on Lake Erie and York on Lake Ontario the British Gen. Gordon Drummond had under him in the spring of 1814 less than 4,000 troops. The first considerable body of British reinforcements did not begin to arrive in that sector until late in July. In the meantime, Brown and Scott took the offensive and invaded Canada.

5 JULY. Battle of Chippewa. The U.S. army under Brown, consisting of about 3,500 effectives, crossed the Niagara River and seized Ft. Erie (3 July). Gen. Sir Phineas Riall established a British force along a defensive line on the north bank of the Chippewa River, 16 miles north of Ft. Erie, then, after routing the brigade under Gen. Peter B. Porter, he drew up his main force of 1,500 men on the Chippewa Plain about a mile from the river. He was engaged by Gen. Winfield Scott's brigade, called into action by General Brown as its 1,300 men were belatedly celebrating the 4th of July with a dinner and parade. The outnumbered Americans inflicted a severe defeat upon the British, whose lines crumbled after an action lasting a half hour. Scott's brigade lost 48 killed and 227 wounded; Riall's force lost 137 killed and 375 wounded. The Battle of Chippewa was the only one of the war in which approximately equal numbers of regular troops, neither enjoying the advantage of position, engaged in close combat in extended order. After Chippewa, no force of U.S. regulars was defeated by its British counterpart.

25 July. Battle of Lundy's Lane. In pursuit of Riall, Brown went as far north as Queenston (10 July). He requested (13 July) Commodore Isaac Chauncey, naval commander on Lake Ontario, to leave Sackett's Harbor and join his fleet with the army on the lake shore west of Ft. George, in order to work out a plan of operations for the conquest of upper Canada. Chauncey's failure to cooperate was a decisive factor in the subsequent U.S. retreat from the Canadian side of the Niagara frontier.

With 2,600 effectives at his disposal, Brown moved on the village of **Lundy's Lane,** near Niagara Falls. In the most sharply contested land action of the war, he engaged 3,000 British troops under Riall and Drummond in a 5-hour battle ending in a draw (although the Americans retired, leaving the British in possession of the field). U.S. losses: 171 killed, 572 wounded, 110 missing; British: 84 killed, 559 wounded, 193 missing, 42 taken prisoner.

2 Aug.–1 Sept. Siege of Ft. Erie. The U.S. army fell back on Ft. Erie. A British force of 3,500 under Drummond entrenched before Ft. Erie (2 Aug.) and brought up 6 siege guns from which they laid down a heavy fire (13 Aug.) before assaulting the fort. The attack was repulsed (15 Aug.) by Gen. Edmund Pendleton Gaines, causing heavy losses to the enemy. The British continued their bombardment of the fort, which held

about 2,000 Americans. Gen. Peter B. Porter led 1,600 men in a sortie (17 Sept.) that destroyed the enemy batteries and compelled Drummond to withdraw (21 Sept.). British losses: 609 killed, wounded, and missing; U.S.: 511 killed, wounded, and missing. Later in the year Ft. Erie was evacuated and destroyed by the Americans (5 Nov.) in final abandonment of the drive on Canada.

11 Sept. Lake Champlain and Plattsburg. The British offensive from Canada was planned as a joint land and water operation along the Lake Champlain route. The campaign was committed to Gen. Sir George Prevost, who had under him an army of 11,000 British veterans supported by a fleet of 4 ships and 12 gunboats (mounting a total of 90 guns and carrying about 800 men) commanded by Capt. George Downie. The Americans had at Plattsburg a mixed force of only 3,300 regulars and militia under Gen. Alexander Macomb, who took immediate command after Gen. Izard, with 4,000 troops, marched off for Buffalo (29 Aug.).

In order to meet the British attack, the U.S. required control of Lake Champlain. The naval commander on the lake was 30-year-old Capt. **Thomas Macdonough** (1783–1825), who had taken his post on 12 Sept. 1812, and by the spring of 1814 had at his command a flotilla of 4 ships and 10 gunboats (mounting a total of 86 guns and carrying about 850 men). Macdonough sought to use to full advantage his powerful short-range guns against the long-range pieces of the British. Choosing his position carefully, he anchored his fleet in the narrow channel between Crab Island and Cumberland Head, across the bay from Plattsburg. His vessels were so deployed that the enemy fleet would be obliged to enter a narrow stretch of water under a raking fire and meet him at close range.

Meanwhile, Sir George Prevost, leaving the St. Lawrence frontier (31 Aug.), marched along the western edge of Lake Champlain, driving Macomb's army to a heavily defended position south of the Saranac River, just below Plattsburg. Prevost halted his army (6 Sept.) and waited for his naval support to appear. Downie's fleet rounded Cumberland Head (11 Sept.) and deployed his vessels within 300 yards of Macdonough's fleet. The **Battle of Lake Champlain** lasted 2 hours, 20 minutes. For 2 hours the battle favored the British, but Macdonough won the victory by hauling about his flagship, the *Saratoga*, and bearing down with broadsides on the enemy flagship, the *Confiance*, which struck her flag. The British fleet received no support from Prevost's shore batteries at Plattsburg, at Macdonough's rear. The encounter resulted in the seizure or destruction of all of the British vessels except the gunboats. U.S. losses: 52 killed, 58 wounded; British: 57 killed, 72 wounded. The victory gave the U.S. undisputed control of Lake Champlain and compelled Prevost's army to retreat to Canada. Prevost left behind great quantities of supplies; many of his troops deserted. He was recalled to Canada and was replaced by Sir George Murray.

19–22 Aug. MARCH ON WASHINGTON AND BALTIMORE. A British force of 4,000 veterans commanded by Gen. Robert Ross left France (27 June) under instructions "to effect a diversion" on the U.S. coasts in support of the army in Canada. The instructions authorized quick descents upon selected points for the purpose of destroying naval and military property. The operation, as finally planned by Sir Alexander Cochrane, was in retaliation for York and for the unauthorized U.S. raid on Long Point on Lake Erie (15 May). Cochrane issued orders (18 July) directing his blockading squadron in Southern waters "to destroy and lay waste such towns and districts upon the coast as you may find assailable." This order was still in effect when Cochrane's squadron and the transports bearing Ross' troops moved up Chesapeake Bay to the mouth of the Patuxent River (Md.) and were landed at Benedict (19 Aug.). The British expedition had 3 aims: to seize or destroy the flotilla of gunboats under Commodore Joshua Barney that had taken shelter in the Patuxent, to descend on Baltimore, and to raid Washington and Alexandria. At the approach of Rear Adm. Sir George Cockburn's fleet, Barney blew up his gunboats (22 Aug.) in order to prevent their seizure by the British.

24 Aug. Battle of Bladensburg. Without encountering resistance, Ross marched to Marlboro (22 Aug.). Meanwhile, hasty preparations were being made at the poorly defended capital, where the incompetent Gen. **William H. Winder** held the command of the Potomac District. From nearby states Winder received militia reinforcements and Commodore Barney brought his 400 sailors to Washington. At the head of a mixed force of about 7,000 men, of whom only several hundred were regulars, Winder took up his position at Old Fields, about 8 miles from Bladensburg, through which the British would inevitably pass. Learning that the British were advancing on Bladensburg (24 Aug.), Winder hastened there, followed by President Madison and most of the cabinet. The Americans, despite the advantage of position, were routed by 3,000 of the enemy and withdrew to Georgetown. Barney, with his 400 sailors and 5 24-pound guns, was left to cover the road about a mile from the village, on the District of Columbia line. The sailors offered stout opposition, holding their ground for a half hour against 4,000 invaders. U.S. losses: 26 killed,

51 wounded; British: 64 killed, 185 wounded.

24–25 Aug. Capture and Burning of Washington. The British marched unopposed to Washington (the panic-stricken U.S. army, together with government officers, had fled to Virginia) and encamped a quarter of a mile from the national capital. Detachments under Ross and Cockburn entered the town and set fire to the Capitol, the White House, all of the department buildings (with the exception of the Patent Office), several private homes, and the office of the *National Intelligencer*. The navy yard was destroyed by Americans at the order of Secretary of the Navy William Jones. The destruction (later estimated at more than $1,500,000) was completed on the morning of 25 Aug. A storm compelled the enemy to retire from the town. The British broke up their camp on the night of 25 Aug. and boarded their transports on the Patuxent. President Madison and some of his cabinet officers returned to Washington on 27 Aug. Denounced by an irate citizenry and militia, Secretary of War Armstrong announced (3 Sept.) his resignation. He had already been replaced by Monroe, who was named (27 Aug.) ad interim Secretary of War.

12–14 Sept. Attack on Baltimore. The British fleet under Cochrane sailed from the Potomac (6 Sept.) and reached the mouth of the Patapsco River, about 16 miles from Baltimore. During the British march on Washington, Baltimore had prepared a formidable system of defense works. Gen. Samuel Smith had under him about 13,000 regulars and militia. A mixed force of about 1,000 men held Ft. McHenry, where a line of sunken hulks barred enemy vessels from the harbor. Ross' army disembarked (12 Sept.) at North Point, about 14 miles from Baltimore, while the fleet moved up the river toward Ft. McHenry. The en-

emy land advance was opposed by 3,200 militia under Gen. John Stricker. The Americans fell back, but not before inflicting severe casualties on the British (Gen. Ross being mortally wounded), who were delayed until 13 Sept. When the enemy drew up within sight of the heavily defended heights, they halted. The British fleet's bombardment (13–14 Sept.) of Ft. McHenry was unsuccessful (inspiring a witness, Francis Scott Key, to write the verses of "The Star-Spangled Banner"). The invaders abandoned their attempt to capture the town and its shipping and made a rapid withdrawal to their transports. On 14 Oct. the British army left Chesapeake Bay and sailed for Jamaica.

8 Jan. 1815. BATTLE OF NEW ORLEANS. In May, Gen. **Andrew Jackson** was named commander of Military District No. 7, embracing the Mobile-New Orleans area and the U.S. army in the Southwest. He prepared an invasion of Spanish Florida and, disobeying Monroe's orders, seized Pensacola (7 Nov.). He then left Mobile (22 Nov.) for New Orleans, arriving there on 1 Dec. Jackson was unaware that a large British fleet carrying 7,500 veterans under Sir Edward Pakenham had sailed from Jamaica (26 Nov.) and was moving through the Gulf of Mexico for an assault on New Orleans. The British aim was to secure control of the Mississippi and its strategic river valley.

When he learned of the British move, Jackson established his main defense at Baton Rouge, 120 miles away, with a view to opposing an enemy attack by way of the Mississippi. But instead the British fleet of more than 50 craft entered Lake Borgne (13 Dec.), about 40 miles east of New Orleans. Jackson ordered (15 Dec.) his forces at Baton Rouge to speed to New Orleans, and proclaimed martial law in the city. Pakenham spent an entire week disembarking his troops. Without being detected, a British advance guard marched to 7 miles below New Orleans, where the U.S. had no troops or defense works.

Acting swiftly, Jackson led 5,000 troops, supported by the 14-gun war schooner *Carolina*, in a night attack upon the enemy force (23–24 Dec.), checking the British advance. During the delay in enemy operations, Jackson withdrew to a point 5 miles from New Orleans, where he utilized a dry, shallow canal to construct a line of breastworks between a cypress swamp and the east bank of the Mississippi. A furious artillery battle occurred on 1 Jan. 1815, in which the Americans outgunned the enemy. Pakenham waited for reinforcements and, on the morning of 8 Jan. 1815, attacked with his main force of 5,300 men. Behind Jackson's entrenchments were about 4,500 troops, many of them expert Tennessee and Kentucky marksmen armed with long rifles, and followers of French freebooter **Jean Laffite** (c.1780–c.1821). The British regulars, in close ranks, made 2 direct assaults in the face of a withering rifle and artillery fire. The British were cut down and driven back. The battle lasted about a half hour. Gen. Pakenham and 2 other British generals were killed. In this action, and in a tributary engagement on the west bank of the river, British losses: 2,036 men killed and wounded; U.S.: 8 killed, 13 wounded. The surviving British senior officer, Gen. John Lambert, withdrew his troops and reembarked them on 27 Jan.

The Battle of New Orleans, the last major engagement of the war, was fought 2 weeks after the signing of the peace at Ghent (24 Dec.). The greatest American land victory of the war, it had no effect upon its outcome, but acted as a powerful restorative to national pride and created Andrew Jackson a military hero.

MILITARY LOSSES. U.S.: 1,877 killed in action, 4,000 wounded. The total number of enlistments was 531,622 (a misleading figure, for numerous militiamen served or reenlisted as many as 10 times).

24 Dec. PEACE OF GHENT. The peace negotiations opened with the envoys of both nations firmly insisting on leading demands. The U.S. commissioners were under instructions to obtain satisfaction on impressment, blockades, and other maritime grievances (although Monroe's instructions of 27 July sanctioned the withdrawal of the impressment issue if such a concession became necessary). The British demanded the establishment of a neutral Indian buffer state in the Northwest and territorial cessions along the line from Maine to west of Lake Superior (amounting to about one third of the territory held by the U.S.). Neither nation pressed for the other to carry out disarmament on the Great Lakes.

The attitude of the British was governed by reports of the prevailing military situation. When the British learned (27 Sept.) of the burning of Washington, they affirmed the principle of *uti possidetis* (retention of territories held in actual possession). The U.S. supported the principle of *status quo ante bellum* (restoration of prewar territorial conditions). The U.S. commissioners rejected the British terms after receiving news (21 Oct.) of Macdonough's victory on Lake Champlain. The Duke of Wellington, proffered the Canadian command, replied to his government that their waning military fortunes on the Great Lakes did not entitle the British to demand a cession of territory. This consideration, combined with the depletion of the British treasury and Castlereagh's diplomatic embarrassments at the Congress of Vienna, led the British envoys to concede (26 Nov.) to the U.S. view.

The treaty restored the peace, but was silent on the issues over which Great Britain and the U.S. had clashed. No reference was made to impressment, blockades, indemnities, the right of search and visit, and other maritime differences. Nor did its clauses advert to military control of the Great Lakes or a neutral Indian barrier state. The treaty provided for the release of prisoners, a restoration of all conquered territory (although West Florida, taken from the Spanish, remained in U.S. hands), and for the appointment of an arbitral commission to settle the disputed northeastern boundary between the U.S. and Canada. By mutual understanding, the questions of the Great Lakes and the fisheries were left open for future negotiation.

News of the signing reached New York on 11 Feb. 1815. The treaty was unanimously ratified by the Senate (17 Feb. 1815) and was proclaimed by President Madison on the same day.

15 DEC.–5 JAN. 1815. HARTFORD CONVENTION. Early in 1814 numerous Massachusetts towns sent memorials to the state legislature calling for a convention of the New England states to discuss their "public grievances and concerns" and to propose amendments to the Constitution. The convention, called by invitation of the Massachusetts legislature (17 Oct.), assembled in secret session at Hartford, Conn., and was attended by Federalist delegates (26) from Connecticut, Rhode Island, Massachusetts, New Hampshire, and Vermont. Except for delegates from the last 2 states, chosen by local conventions, all were elected by their respective state legislatures.

The convention's proceedings and measures did not reflect the views of the extremist wing of the Federalist party. The Massachusetts delegation was headed by **George Cabot** (1752–1823), leader of the moderate element among the Federalists in the state. Cabot presided over the convention, and an influential role was played by his fellow delegate, **Harrison Gray Otis** (1765–1848). The report issued by the convention included a statement (echoing the states'-rights doctrine of the Kentucky and Virginia resolutions) that "in cases of deliberate, dangerous and palpable infractions of the Constitution, affecting the sovereignty of a State and liberties of the people; it is not only the right but the duty of such a State to interpose its authority for their protection, in the manner best calculated to secure that end."

The convention adopted a set of resolutions calling for (1) protection of the citizens of their states against military conscription unauthorized by the Constitution; (2) use of federal revenue collected within these states to provide for the defense of their territory; (3) an interstate defense machinery, independent of federal provisions, for repelling enemy invasion; (4) a series of amendments to the Constitution, including apportionment of direct taxes and representation among the states according to the number of free persons in each; (5) prohibition of all embargoes lasting more than 60 days; requirement of a two-thirds vote of both houses for declarations of war, restrictions on foreign commerce, and admissions of new states; (6) prohibition of the holding by naturalized citizens of civil office under federal authority; and (7) limitation of presidential tenure to one term. A committee of 3, headed by Otis, was appointed by the Massachusetts legislature to negotiate with the national government. News of Jackson's victory at New Orleans and the signing of the Treaty of Ghent brought an abrupt end to the work of the committee and made the Hartford Convention the butt of popular ridicule. That the convention had been conducted in secrecy gave its opponents a handle which they used for accusing the Hartford gathering of conspiracy, sedition, and treason (although there is no evidence supporting the charge).

1815

PEACETIME MILITARY ESTABLISHMENT. President Madison recommended a standing army of 20,000 men, but the House, by a vote of 70 to 38 (3 March), fixed the army strength at 10,-000. Congress ordered (27 Feb.) the navy's gunboat flotilla to be put up for sale, and the armed vessels on the lakes were stripped of their equipment and laid up. No further reduction was made in the naval establishment; henceforth most of its vessels consisted of cruisers. A 3-man Board of Navy Commissioners was authorized (7 Feb.) to carry out, under the Secretary of the Navy, general supervision of the department.

3 MAR.–30 JUNE. DECATUR'S ALGERINE EXPEDITION. During the War of 1812 the Dey of Algiers renewed his plunder of American Mediterranean commerce. He dismissed the U.S. consul, declared war, seized American vessels, and enslaved U.S. nationals on the pretext that he was not receiving sufficient tribute. An act of Congress (approved 3 Mar.) authorized hostilities against the Dey. Capt. Stephen Decatur sailed from New York (10 May) with 10 vessels, seized the Algerine 44-gun frigate *Mashouda* (17 June), captured the 22-gun brig *Estido* (19 June), and sailed into the harbor of Algiers. He exacted a treaty (30 June) whereby the Dey renounced molestation of U.S. commerce and tribute, and agreed to release all U.S. prisoners without ransom. Decatur received similar guarantees from Tunis (26 July) and Tripoli (5 Aug.), both states making compensation for U.S. vessels which they had permitted Great Britain to seize as prizes. Decatur's action brought to a close the troubles with the Barbary States.

3 JULY. COMMERCIAL CONVENTION WITH BRITAIN ended discriminatory duties and admitted U.S. commerce to the East Indies without making specific concessions regarding the West Indies.

1816

10 APR. 2D U.S. BANK. The wartime disorganization of the currency, bringing in its train a general suspension of specie payments, emphasized anew the need for a national bank. Secretary of the Treasury **Alexander J. Dallas** recommended (17 Oct. 1814) the creation of a bank capitalized at $50 million, under which the president would be empowered to suspend specie payments. His scheme was approved in principle by the House (24 Oct. 1814) by a vote of 66 to 40, but an emasculated compromise measure provided for a capitalization of $30 million and did not grant the bank authority to suspend specie payments and to lend up to 60% of its capital to the government. The bill passed in the House (7 Jan. 1815), 120–38; and the Senate (20 Jan. 1815), 20–14. Madison vetoed the bill (20 Jan.), basing his objection on practical considerations, but conceding the constitutional authority of Congress to enact such legislation.

Madison's annual message (5 Dec. 1815) noted that if state banks could not restore a uniform national currency, "the probable operation of a national bank will merit consideration." Congressional debate witnessed a Republican reversal of objections to the measure on constitutional grounds. The debate was also noteworthy for the leading role played by the triumvirate of **John C. Calhoun, Henry Clay** and **Daniel Webster** (p. 1179), to dominate House and

Senate proceedings until the decade before the Civil War.

The bill introduced by Calhoun (8 Jan.) followed in substance the recommendations of Dallas, and was supported by Clay, who in 1811 had maintained that the measure was unconstitutional. Calhoun backed the bill on the ground that it was necessary for the restoration of a sound and uniform circulating medium; for its constitutional sanction, he pointed to the power of Congress to regulate the currency. Clay, explaining his reversal, left the speaker's chair to assert that a change in circumstances made the bank an indispensable necessity, and that Congress had the "constructive power" to authorize the bank. Webster opposed the bill, arguing that no currency reform was required in view of the constitutional and statutory provisions for gold and silver currency. He maintained that the currency problem could be solved by congressional action against the note issues of suspended banks.

The bill, which passed in the House (14 Mar.) 80–71 (with 33 Republicans and 38 Federalists voting against it), and the Senate 22–12, created the 2d Bank of the U.S. with an authorized capitalization of $35 million, of which the government was to subscribe one fifth. In return for its charter privileges, the bank was to pay the government a bonus of $1,500,000. The president was empowered to name 5 of its 25 directors. The bank was authorized to act as a depository for government funds without paying interest for their use. In most other respects, the provisions followed the 1st Bank charter (1791). The central office remained at Philadelphia, and in time had 25 branches throughout the country. The bank began its operations on 1 Jan. 1817. Its first president was William Jones, whose inept management brought a congressional threat to repeal the charter (Jan. 1819). The bank management was reorganized and performed capably under Langdon Cheves, who was named president in 1819. Cheves was succeeded (1823) by **Nicholas Biddle** (p. 986), who served until the expiration of the charter in 1836.

A bill introduced by Webster and adopted by Congress stipulated that after 20 Feb. 1817 the payment of public dues would be collected in either legal currency or in bank notes redeemable in specie. This measure virtually compelled the resumption of specie payments by state banks and resulted in a contracted note issue.

4 Dec. PRESIDENTIAL ELECTION. At the Republican congressional caucus (16 Mar.) the younger element in the party supported William H. Crawford against **James Monroe.** Monroe won by a vote of 65 to 54, thus assuring the continuation of the "Virginia dynasty." **Daniel D. Tompkins** (N.Y., 1774–1825) was nominated for the vice-presidency. In the national elections, Monroe was opposed by the Federalist candidate, **Rufus King** (N.Y.). The waning strength of the Federalists, coupled with their popular discredit during the war years, gave **Monroe** an overwhelming victory. With 4 abstentions in the electoral college, he received 183 electoral votes, King 34. Monroe carried all of the states except Massachusetts, Connecticut, and Delaware. **Tompkins** was elected vice-president.

1817

3 Mar. BONUS BILL VETO. The rapid development of the West and the South created a need for adequate transportation facilities to link the outlying agricultural regions with the markets of the eastern seaboard, a need underscored by the military operations of the War of 1812. In his last annual message (3 Dec.

1816) President Madison recommended a federally subsidized network of roads and canals, but his misgivings about its constitutionality led him to indicate the necessity for a constitutional amendment.

Calhoun reported a bill (23 Dec. 1816) to create a permanent fund for internal improvements by setting aside the $1,500,000 bonus paid by the Bank of the U.S. and all future dividends from bank stock held by the government. Introducing the measure on 4 Feb., he declared that while the Constitution did not specifically authorize internal improvements, sanction could be drawn from the "general welfare" clause and from the power to establish post roads. Although Calhoun regarded the constituitional question as subsidiary to the value of internal improvements as a military necessity and a cement of national union, his argument showed the extent to which the Republican party had accepted the Hamiltonian doctrine of implied powers.

The bill passed in the House (8 Feb.), 86–84, and in the Senate, 20–15. Opposition to the bill was based on sectional rather than constitutional grounds. In the House, 34 opposing votes came from New England Federalists fearful of Western expansion; the South divided, 23 for, 25 against; the Middle States, 42 for, 6 against.

Performing his last act of office, President Madison vetoed the bill on constitutional grounds, stating that to draw authority from the "general welfare" clause for such a purpose "would be contrary to the established and consistent rules of interpretation, as rendering the special and careful enumeration of powers which follow the clause nugatory and improper."

4 MAR. Monroe's inaugural address revealed the Republican party's adoption of Federalist nationalist principles, including support of a standing army and an adequate naval establishment, and "the systematic and fostering care of the government for our manufactures."

ERA OF GOOD FEELINGS. During May–Sept. President Monroe toured the eastern seaboard north of Baltimore and visited the West as far as Detroit. The journey, undertaken ostensibly as an official tour of duty, soon became a popular symbol of the triumph of national feeling over party animosity. Enthusiasm, particularly marked in New England, where Federalists extended a warm welcome to the president, moved the Boston *Columbian Centinel* (12 July) to bestow upon the times the epithet "era of good feelings," a phrase commonly used to describe the state of the nation during Monroe's 2 terms in office (1817–25). The description is superficial and misleading. Although no formal political opposition existed during this period, new political factions and contenders were rising, as indicated by intra-cabinet controversies and by the circumstances attending the presidential election of 1824. During the same era, underlying sectional and economic issues were working basic transformations in the national life.

28–29 APR. RUSH-BAGOT AGREE-MENT. Among the sequels to the Treaty of Ghent was the arrangement for mutual disarmament on the Great Lakes effected by an exchange of notes between the British minister to the U.S., Charles Bagot, and Acting Secretary of State Richard Rush, although the agreement was almost wholly the work of Monroe and Castlereagh, and was the direct outcome of a threatened naval armaments race on the Great Lakes. The British and U.S. agreed to limit their naval forces on inland waters to 1 vessel each on Lake Champlain and Lake Ontario and 2 vessels each on the upper Lakes, none to exceed 100 tons or to have more than 1 18-pound gun. To allay British suspicion that succeeding U.S. administrations might not consider the arrangement binding, the Rush-Bagot agreement was submitted to the Senate, which gave it unanimous approval (16 Apr. 1818). The demilitarization of the Great Lakes, and the supposed extension of the principle to the land frontier, was thereafter regarded as an outstanding example of mutual disarmament. In reality, demilitarization of border fortifications and the equally important seaboard naval defenses was a lengthy and gradual process that did not produce genuine mutual disarmament until after the Treaty of Washington (1871).

1818

JACKSON AND THE FIRST SEMINOLE WAR. Ft. Apalachicola, on the river of that name in Spanish-held East Florida, had been built by the British during the War of 1812. After the war, the fort and the surrounding countryside occupied by Seminole Indians became a refuge for runaway slaves and hostile Indians. The threat to the Georgia border caused the U.S. government to dispatch an expedition which destroyed the fort (27 July 1816) and touched off armed conflict with the Negroes and Indians. A force led by Gen. Edmund P. Gaines was instructed to pursue hostile elements across the Florida boundary to the limits of the Spanish posts. On 26 Dec. 1817 command was transferred to Gen. Andrew Jackson, given similar orders. Upon receiving his instructions, Jackson wrote (6 Jan.) his **"Rhea letter"** to President Monroe, stating: "Let it be signified to me through any channel (say Mr. [congressman] J. Rhea) that the possession of the Floridas would be desirable to the United States and in sixty days it will be accomplished." No immediate action on the letter was taken at Washington by President Monroe and Secretary of War Calhoun. Jackson chose to regard their official silence as tantamount to approval of his subsequent course in Florida. The letter was revived during the political controversies of 1831 when Calhoun, during his break with Jackson, published the Seminole correspondence.

Jackson marched into Florida and seized St. Marks (7 Apr.) and Pensacola (24 May), even as Secretary of State Adams was conducting discussions with the Spanish minister, Luis de Onís, concerning a settlement of the Florida question. During the campaign Jackson captured and court-martialed 2 British traders, **Alexander Arbuthnot** and **Robert Ambrister,** both of whom were accused of aiding the enemy. Arbuthnot was hanged and Ambrister was shot. British public opinion was incensed, but Great Britain took no action. Jackson's raid also had domestic repercussions. His course met the disapproval of all cabinet members except Adams. Two of its members, Calhoun and Crawford, believed Jackson merited stern disciplinary action. A House report (12 Jan. 1819) condemned Jackson's conduct. Anti-Jackson forces in the House, with Henry Clay at their head, proposed a resolution of censure during a debate (18 Jan.–8 Feb. 1819) on the question, and a Senate committee submitted a report (24 Feb. 1819) unfavorable to Jackson. No proceedings were taken against him.

Popular approval of Jackson's Seminole campaign, which brought all of East Florida under U.S. military control, influenced Monroe's decision not to punish Jackson. Actually, Jackson's raid strengthened the administration's hand in foreign affairs. Adams' firm instructions (28 Nov.) to the U.S. minister at Madrid was virtually an ultimatum to the Spanish government. Accusing Spain of aiding and abetting hostilities against the U.S., Adams declared that the U.S. government had acted in self-defense. He defended Jackson's conduct and informed the Spanish government that it faced the alternatives of protecting and controlling Florida or ceding it to the U.S.

20 OCT. CONVENTION OF 1818. Another sequel to the Treaty of Ghent was the Convention of 1818, signed at London by Richard Rush, minister to Great Britain, and Albert Gallatin, minister to France. Under its terms, the northwest boundary between the U.S. and British North America was fixed along the 49th parallel from the Lake of the Woods to the crest of the Rocky Mountains (thus recognizing the northern line of the Louisiana Purchase). No boundary was established for the region west of the mountains, but the 2 powers agreed that the Oregon country was to be open to their subjects for 10 years, stipulating that such joint occupation would not be considered prejudicial to the territorial claims of either power in the Pacific Northwest. The convention gave U.S. nationals fishing privileges off sections of the coasts of Labrador and Newfoundland, and renewed the commercial treaty of 1815.

1819

PANIC OF 1819 was caused by commodity inflation, wild speculation in Western lands, overextended investments in manufacturing, mismanagement of the 2d Bank of the U.S., collapse of foreign markets, and contraction of credit. The last factor was a result of the congressional order (1817) for the resumption of specie payments, a move that strained the resources of state banks, caused many failures, and created hardships for debtors. The most severe effects of the panic were felt in the Southern and Western states. Many of the Western states, among them Missouri and Illinois, enacted legislation for the relief of debtors; in Kentucky such legislation led to the "relief war" (1823–26), a contest between the state legislature and judiciary over the constitutionality of replevin and stay laws. A more general result of the panic was widespread resentment against the national bank in rural areas, where it became known as "The Monster," an epithet originated by **Thomas Hart Benton** (Mo., p. 983).

CESSION OF EAST FLORIDA. The Spanish posts seized by Andrew Jackson in East Florida were returned to Spain, but Adams' vigorous instructions, coupled with Spanish colonial difficulties in South America, led the Madrid government to accede to the U.S. demands. The extended negotiations which Adams had conducted with the Spanish minister resulted in the **Adams-Onís Treaty** (signed at Washington, 22 Feb.) whereby Spain renounced all claims to West Florida and ceded East Florida to the U.S. The U.S. renounced its claims to Texas and assumed the claims of its own citizens against Spain to the maximum amount of $5 million. The treaty also defined the western limits of the Louisiana Purchase. The boundary was established from the mouth of the Sabine River on the Gulf of Mexico, proceeding in a broken northwesterly line along the Red and Arkansas rivers and the 42d parallel, from which it was drawn due west to the Pacific Ocean. In effect, the Spanish claims to the Pacific Northwest were surrendered to the U.S. It was stipulated that the Treaty of San Lorenzo (1795) was to remain in force, except as altered by the Adams-Onís Treaty. The Senate ratified the treaty (24 Feb.); because of delays created by the Spanish government, the Senate again ratified on 19 Feb. 1821. The exchange of ratifications became final on 22 Feb. 1821.

2 FEB. DARTMOUTH COLLEGE CASE. In 1816 the Republican-dominated New Hampshire legislature altered the royal charter (1769) of Dartmouth College under which the college had been established, and vested the administration of the institution in a board of trustees appointed by the state. The old board of trustees, asserting that the legislative act was unconstitutional because it impaired the obligation of contracts, sued William H. Woodward, secretary of the university, for recovery of the seal, the charter, and other documents. The state court upheld the action of the legislature, declaring that the body established under the Dartmouth charter of 1769 was a public, not a private, corporation; and that as such its charter was not a contract within the meaning of the Constitution.

The case was appealed to the Supreme Court (*Trustees of Dartmouth College v. Woodward*, 4 Wheaton 518), with Daniel Webster as counsel for the college. Chief Justice Marshall, for the court, held that a charter to a private corporation constituted a contract and was therefore protected under the contract clause of the Constitution against impairment by state legislatures and declared the New Hampshire law invalid.

The decision appeared to place charters of existing private corporations outside the scope of control by the states that had chartered them. While it encouraged business growth, it also led to abuses of corporate privileges. Important modifications of Marshall's opinion in this case were made in *Charles River Bridge v. Warren Bridge* (p. 667) in 1837, and in *Munn v. Illinois* (p. 671) in 1877.

6 MAR. M'CULLOCH v. MARYLAND. During the postwar period of financial disorganization, state banks took advantage of popular feeling against the 2d Bank of the U.S. to encourage legislation restricting its operations. A Maryland law provided that all banks not created by authority of the state were required to comply with restrictions concerning note issues or, in lieu of that, to pay an annual tax of $15,000. When the Baltimore branch of the National Bank ignored these provisions on the ground that the act was unconstitutional, the cashier of the branch, James W. M'Culloch, was sued by the state.

The case was appealed to the Supreme Court (*M'Culloch v. Maryland*, 4 Wheaton 316). The 2 leading points immediately at issue were the constitutionality of the act of Congress establishing the bank, and the constitutionality of the tax imposed by the state legislature. Daniel Webster was among counsel representing the bank, and the proceedings before the court included a notable 3-day argument by William Pinkney, senior counsel for the bank.

The opinion, delivered by Chief Justice Marshall for a unanimous court, ranks among Marshall's most important pronouncements, and is commonly regarded as his most vigorous and detailed exposition of the Constitution. Drawing liberally upon the Hamiltonian doctrine of implied powers, Marshall expounded the origin and nature of the federal union. The powers of the national government are derived from the people and are exercised directly on them, said Marshall; although the national government is limited in its powers, it is supreme within its sphere of action; and a government must be equipped with suitable and effective means to execute the powers conferred on it. He then proceeded to state the doctrine of "loose construction" based on Hamilton's opinion (1791) on the constitutionality of the 1st Bank of the U.S. "Let the end be legitimate," declared Marshall, "let it be within the scope of the constitution, and all means which are appropriate, which are plainly adapted to that end, which are not prohibited, but consist with the letter and spirit of the constitution, are constitutional." The act incorporating the bank was therefore constitutional. As for the power of the Maryland legislature to tax the branch bank, Marshall declared that no state possessed that right, denying it on the ground that "the power to tax involves the power to destroy." Accordingly, he held the act of the Maryland legislature unconstitutional and void.

Of all his other opinions, only that pronounced (1821) in *Cohens* v. *Virginia* (p. 665) compares with this forthright assertion of nationalist doctrine. *M'Culloch* v. *Maryland* set off a nationwide controversy, with declarations by several states against inroads on state power. Marshall himself entered the argument with a series of anonymously published articles answering the criticisms of Judge Spencer Roane of Virginia.

1820

3 Mar. MISSOURI COMPROMISE. At the close of 1819, when the applications of Missouri and Maine for admission to statehood were before Congress, there were 22 states in the Union, 11 slave and 11 free. The slave states: Virginia, Maryland, Delaware, Kentucky, Tennessee, North Carolina, South Carolina, Georgia, Alabama, Mississippi, and Louisiana. The free states: Massachusetts, Connecticut, Rhode Island, Vermont, New Hampshire, New York, New Jersey, Pennsylvania, Ohio, Indiana, and Illinois. The political balance between North and South had been maintained by admitting alternately (1802–19) slave and free states. But even with the three-fifths ratio operating in their favor, the slave states had only 81 votes in the House of Representatives as against 105 votes held by the free states. In addition, the population of the North was growing at a more rapid pace (free states: 5,152,-000; slave states: 4,485,000). To preserve the sectional balance, the South looked to its equal vote in the Senate.

Late in 1819, the Missouri Territory embraced all of the Louisiana Purchase with the exception of the segments organized as the state of Louisiana (1812) and the Arkansas Territory (1819). The application of the Missouri Territorial Assembly (which had originally petitioned for statehood in 1817) raised the question of the legal status of slavery in Missouri and in the rest of the territory west of the Mississippi. In 1818 there were an estimated 2,000–3,000 slaves in the upper Louisiana country (where slavery went back to Spanish and French rule).

13 Feb. 1819. Tallmadge Amendment. When the enabling legislation for Missouri came before Congress at the outset of 1819, Rep. James Tallmadge (N.Y.) introduced an amendment (13 Feb. 1819) prohibiting the further introduction of slaves into Missouri and providing that all children born of slaves in Missouri after its admission should become free at the age of 25. The amendment set off a fierce debate. In the House, the first clause of the amendment was carried by 87–76 (16 Feb.) and the second clause 82–78 (17 Feb.); but the amendment was lost in the Senate (27 Feb.), 22–16 (1st cl.), 31–7 (2d cl.).

26 Jan. 1819. Taylor Amendment. When the organization of Arkansas Territory came before Congress, Rep. John W. Taylor (N.Y.) moved a proviso forbidding the further introduction of slavery. It was defeated (18 Feb. 1819), and Congress organized Arkansas as a territory (2 Mar. 1819) with its northern boundary at 36°30′ and with no restriction on slavery.

8 Dec. 1819–20 Mar. 1820. Missouri Debate. Sen. Rufus King (N.Y.) maintained that Congress was empowered to forbid slavery in Missouri and to make the prohibition of slavery a prerequisite for admission. Sen. William Pinkney (Md.) in reply asserted that the Union was composed of equal states and that Congress could not restrict Missouri's freedom of action.

17 Feb. 1820. Thomas Amendment. The 16th Congress, convened 6 Dec. 1819, faced the sectional issue with the presentation to Congress (8 Dec. 1819) of a memorial from the people of Maine petitioning for admission to statehood and the adoption (14 Dec. 1819) of a joint congressional resolution admitting Alabama as the 22nd state. A proposition to combine the bill for the admission of Maine with that of Missouri (without restriction on slavery) was passed in the Senate, 23–21 (16 Feb.). Sen. Jesse B. Thomas (Ill.) introduced a compromise amendment providing for the admission of Missouri as a slave state and for the prohibition of slavery in the Louisiana Purchase north of the line 36°30′. The Thomas amendment passed in the Senate (17 Feb.) 34–10. On 18 Feb. the Senate agreed to admit Maine to statehood on condition that Missouri enter as a slave state.

The Senate bill was rejected by the House (28 Feb.). By 91–82, the House passed its own bill prohibiting slavery (1 Mar.), a measure incorporating the restrictive amendment proposed (26 Jan.) by Rep. Taylor (N.Y.). Compromise elements arranged a conference and broke the deadlock. As a result, the Senate received the House bill, eliminated the Taylor amendment, and inserted the Thomas amendment. The Missouri bill was returned to the House, which passed the compromise measure, 90–87 (2 Mar.). The compromise became final 3 Mar., when by a House vote, 134–42, Maine was admitted as a free state, Missouri as a slave state, and slavery excluded from the Louisiana Purchase north of the line 36°30′. The decisive vote was made possible only by the defection of Northern representatives (whom John Randolph described as **"doughfaces"**). The admission of Maine as the 23rd state became effective 15 Mar.

19 July. Missouri Constitution. On 6 Mar. Congress authorized the people of Missouri to adopt a constitution. The Missouri convention at St. Louis (12 June) incorporated in the constitution (19 July) a provision excluding free Negroes and mulattoes from the state. This clause provoked antislavery sentiment in Congress when the Missouri constitution was presented to the Senate (14 Nov.) and the House (16 Nov.). A compromise formulated by Henry Clay resulted in the so-called second Missouri Compromise (2 Mar. 1821) providing that the state of Missouri should not gain admission to the Union until the legislature gave assurance that the offending clause would never be construed as sanctioning the passage of any law abridging the privileges and immunities of U.S. citizens. This condition was accepted by the Missouri legislature (26 June 1821), which qualified its pledge by insisting that it had no power to bind the people of the state. On 10 Aug. 1821 President Monroe proclaimed the admission of Missouri as the 24th state.

15 May. AFRICAN SLAVE TRADE. Under the act of 3 Mar. 1819, a $50 bounty was granted to informers for every illegally imported Negro slave seized in the U.S. or at sea, and the president empowered to return to Africa slaves captured under such circumstances. Under the 1820 act the foreign slave trade was declared piracy. In addition to the forfeiture of vessels authorized by the act of 1807, the death penalty was provided for all U.S. citizens engaging in the importation of slaves.

6 Dec. PRESIDENTIAL ELECTION. Because of the poor attendance at the Republican congressional caucus called at Washington in Apr., no formal nominations were made. In the absence of old party distinctions, **Monroe's** candidacy for a 2d term went unopposed. Out of 235 electoral votes (with 3 abstentions), **Monroe** received 231. One dissenting vote by a New Hampshire elector went to John Quincy Adams. **Daniel D. Tompkins** was reelected vice-president, with 218 votes.

1821

5 Mar. The 4th of Mar. falling on a Sunday, Monroe postponed the inaugural exercises until the 5th, thereby setting a precedent.

28 Aug.–10 Nov. EXTENSION OF THE SUFFRAGE. The proposal to abolish the property qualification for voting in New York state, strenuously resisted at the New York Constitutional Convention by such conservatives as Chancellor James Kent (p. 1075) and Chief Justice Ambrose Spencer, carried the day. For extension elsewhere, see p. 762.

1822

4 May. CUMBERLAND ROAD BILL VETO. Construction of the Cumberland Road, more commonly known as the National Road or Turnpike, came to a halt with the panic of 1819. The road extended from Cumberland, Md., to Wheeling, on the Ohio River. A bill for the repair of the road, authorizing establishment of toll gates and collection of tolls, passed in the House (29 Apr.), 87–68, and the Senate, 29–7. In his veto

of the bill Monroe held that Congress did not have the right of jurisdiction and construction, but recommended a national system of internal improvements sanctioned by an appropriate constitutional amendment.

LATIN-AMERICAN   REPUBLICS. The success of the independence movements in Spanish America after 1817 led Henry Clay to advocate (1818) recognition of the revolutionary governments. In 1821, at Clay's instigation, the House of Representatives adopted a resolution expressing sympathy with the Latin-American republics and indicating the willingness of the House to support the president whenever he should decide to recognize the republics. It was clear that such a move would antagonize the Spanish government, but this consideration became a minor one after the final exchange of ratifications (1821) of the Florida treaty. President Monroe sent to Congress (8 Mar.) a special message proposing recognition of the Latin-American republics. A House resolution (28 Mar.) called for recognition, and the Act of 4 May provided for establishment of diplomatic intercourse with those nations. The Republic of Colombia was formally recognized on 19 June and Mexico on 12 Dec. Chile and Argentina were recognized on 27 Jan. 1823, Brazil on 26 May 1824, the Federation of Central American States on 4 Aug. 1824, and Peru on 2 May 1826.

1823

RUSSIAN CLAIMS. The Czar issued an imperial ukase (4 Sept. 1821) extending Russian claims along the Pacific coast to north of the 51st parallel (which lay within the Oregon country) and closing the surrounding waters (of which the most important was Bering Strait) to the commercial shipping of other powers. The Russian claim was challenged by

Secretary of State Adams, who informed the Russian minister to the U.S. (17 July) "that we should contest the right of Russia to any territorial establishment on this continent, and that we should assume distinctly the principle that the American continents are no longer subjects for any new European colonial establishments." This principle regarding future European colonization in the New World was to become more familiar after its incorporation in the Monroe Doctrine. Under the treaty signed on 17 Apr. 1824, Russia agreed to a 54°40′ line and withdrew the maritime restriction. The U.S. renounced all claims to territory north of that line.

2 DEC. MONROE DOCTRINE. Great Britain was not sympathetic to the revolutionary governments in the former Spanish provinces; yet she was anxious to prevent the revival or extension of Spanish and French power in the New World, primarily in order to keep open to British commerce the rich markets of Latin America. This policy assumed a definite shape after George Canning became British foreign secretary (Sept. 1822).

At the Congress of Verona (Nov. 1822) the Quadruple Alliance (France, Austria, Russia, and Prussia) agreed to act to restore the authority of King Ferdinand VII of Spain, who in 1820 had been forced to accept a constitutional monarchy. The French were authorized to invade Spain, but no action was taken on the French request to intervene in South America. Canning protested against the Holy Alliance program of intervention and broke with the concert of European powers. Early in 1823, Canning attempted to obtain from France a promise barring the acquisition, either by cession or conquest, of any territory in Spanish America. France refused to make the pledge. (Authorities differ over the nature of the French

threat to the Spanish colonies: H. W. V. Temperley, 1925, holds it serious; Dexter Perkins, 1927, no genuine peril; C. K. Webster, 1938, holds that the French failed to formulate specific plans.)

Canning's break with the Holy Alliance was followed by a move to come to an understanding with the U.S., with whom Great Britain had experienced difficulties (1822–23) concerning Cuba. Canning followed up an informal proposal (16 Aug.) to Richard Rush, U.S. minister at London, with a note (20 Aug.) regarding the possibility of joint Anglo-U.S. action against intervention of the Holy Alliance in the New World. Rush was not authorized to commit the U.S., but he indicated (23, 26 Aug.) that this proposition might meet with the favor of his government if the British recognized the Latin-American republics. Rush referred the matter to Monroe, who turned to his unofficial advisers, Jefferson and Madison. Both voiced support of close cooperation with the British.

Secretary of State Adams took a different view. Adams believed that the U.S. should assert its strength and independence by acting alone, in order to create an "American system" in the Western Hemisphere, because (1) he was skeptical of Canning's apparently disinterested motives; (2) viewed the British proposal as a preliminary to exacting from the U.S. a pledge renouncing American designs on Cuba; and (3) felt that so long as the British maintained naval supremacy in the Atlantic, Russia's claims in the Pacific Northwest constituted a greater danger than possible French intervention in South America. Adams stated his position (7 Nov.): "It would be more candid, as well as more dignified, to avow our principles explicitly to Russia and France, than to come in as a cock-boat in the wake of the British man-of-war."

The U.S. government took no action on Canning's proposal. In the meantime, Canning secured his object in the **Polignac Agreement** (9 Oct.), whereby France renounced all intentions to conquer or annex the Spanish-American colonies. He did not resume his efforts to obtain a joint Anglo-American declaration.

The substance of Adams' views was adopted by Monroe and the cabinet. In preparing an announcement of U.S. policy, Monroe acceded to Adams' suggestion that the formulation of views concerning European affairs (such as Greek independence) should be toned down. Adams held that the declaration of policy would be stronger were it based on wholly American interest. However, Monroe rejected Adams' recommendation that the declaration should be embodied in diplomatic communications to the various governments. With the support of Calhoun, Monroe decided to make the announcement in his annual message to Congress (2 Dec.). That portion of the message relating to foreign affairs was largely the work of John Quincy Adams (on the question of substantive authorship, see W. C. Ford, 1902, and S. F. Bemis, 1949, both of whom attribute it to Adams; W. A. MacCorkle, 1923, Dexter Perkins, 1927, and A. P. Whitaker, 1941, ascribe it to Monroe).

The Monroe Doctrine contained 4 major points: (1) the American continents were no longer to be considered as subjects for future colonization by European powers; (2) there existed in the Americas a political system essentially different and separate from that of Europe; (3) the U.S. would consider dangerous to its peace and safety any attempt on the part of European powers to extend their system to any point in the Western Hemisphere; (4) the U.S. would not interfere with existing colonies or dependencies of European powers in the New World; she would not interfere in the internal affairs of European nations; nor would she take part in European wars of solely foreign interest.

At the time of its announcement the Monroe Doctrine drew scant attention from the great powers. In Commons Canning, defending his Latin-American policy, declared (12 Dec. 1826): "I called the New World into existence to redress the balance of the Old." Although the Monroe Doctrine had no standing in international law until the Senate ratified the Act of Havana in 1940, that pronouncement served as the classic definition of the U.S. role in international affairs. But its major significance emerged only after the middle of the 19th century. Over the course of the years, it was modified and extended to meet changing circumstances.

1824

30–31 Mar. "AMERICAN SYSTEM." In a speech defending the protective features of the Tariff of 1824, Henry Clay applied the phrase "American system" to a combination of the protective tariff and a national system of internal improvements as a means of expanding the domestic market and lessening U.S. dependence upon overseas sources.

30 Apr. INTERNAL IMPROVEMENTS. In 1818, William Lowndes (S.C.) submitted to the House 4 resolutions on internal improvements. The House (89–75) declared that Congress had authority to appropriate money for building military roads and other land routes, canals, and improved natural waterways. But following a debate on the constitutionality of these propositions, the House rejected all of them. Monroe's veto (1822) of the Cumberland Road Bill was sustained by both houses. The widespread demand, particularly from the West, for more and improved internal routes resulted in the introduction of the General Survey Bill empowering the president to initiate surveys and estimates of roads and canals required for national military, commercial, or postal purposes. By 115–86 (10 Feb.) the House passed the bill. The vote by sections: New England, 12 for, 26 against; the West, 43 for, none against; the South, 23 for, 34 against; the Middle States, 37 for, 26 against. The Senate passed the bill 24–18.

CABINET INTRIGUES. Between 1820 and 1822 political factionalism linked to presidential ambitions caused dissension within the cabinet. When the supporters of Secretary of War John C. Calhoun obtained his permission (28 Dec. 1821) to announce his presidential candidacy, Calhoun was attacked by the adherents of Secretary of the Treasury William H. Crawford. The political rivalry between Calhoun and Crawford extended even to the administration of government business. The Senate, dominated by Crawford's followers, called for retrenchment in Calhoun's War Department expenditures and refused to approve nominations of military officers made by President Monroe at the recommendation of Calhoun.

Suspecting that Crawford was intriguing against the administration and was also attempting to establish a new political party, Monroe asked Crawford for an explanation. Crawford denied that he opposed the administration program, and assured the president of his loyalty. Monroe sought to remain neutral during the contest for power within the cabinet, but the realization that he would soon be leaving office reduced his influence.

A direct outcome of factionalism at high levels was the "A.B." plot. Under the signature "A.B.," Sen. Ninian Edwards (Ill.) published a series of articles (1823) in the Washington *Republican,* the organ of the Calhoun forces. The articles attacked Crawford for malfeasance in office. It was widely believed that Edwards' object in accusing Crawford was to injure the latter's standing as a presidential candidate. Edwards, who was appointed minister to Mexico 4 Mar., was recalled to Washington to testify before a House investigating committee. On 19 Apr. Edwards preferred charges against Crawford, but the Secretary of the Treasury was exonerated (25 May) by the House committee.

PRESIDENTIAL CAMPAIGN. The dissolution of the old party distinctions, and a rising opposition to the congressional caucus as a means of choosing the presidential candidate, left most of the nominations to the state legislatures. **John C. Calhoun** announced his candidacy in 1821. The Tennessee legislature nominated **Andrew Jackson** (20 July 1822), who was also chosen (4 Mar.) by a state nominating convention at Harrisburg, Pa. The action of the Tennessee legislature, which followed its move by a formal protest against the caucus procedure (1823), was the signal for other state and local resolves. The Kentucky legislature nominated **Henry Clay** (18 Nov. 1822); **John Quincy Adams** was nominated by a meeting (15 Feb.) at Boston. The rump congressional caucus (attended by only 66 out of the 216 Republican representatives) that nominated (14 Feb.) **William H. Crawford** (1772–1834) was the last one to nominate a presidential candidate.

A paralytic stroke virtually eliminated Crawford (Sept. 1823). Calhoun withdrew and became vice-presidential candidate on the Jackson and Adams tickets. Adams held the strongest position; although he did not take part in trading for votes, he was to profit by the dissensions among the candidates from the

South and West. In addition, his support of the "American system" brought him close to Clay, who had strong differences with Jackson. Most of the candidates supported a protective tariff and internal improvements. To these issues, Jackson added his attacks upon "King Caucus," and supported the right of the people to choose their own president.

1 DEC. PRESIDENTIAL ELECTION. Jackson received 99 electoral votes; Adams, 84; Crawford, 41; and Clay, 37. **Calhoun,** receiving 182 electoral votes, was chosen vice-president. As no candidate had a majority (popular vote cast: Jackson, 152,933; Adams, 115,696; Clay, 47,136; Crawford, 46,979 [in 6 states the legislature cast the electoral vote]) the choice of the president was submitted to the House, which considered only the 3 leading candidates. Clay, eliminated, advised his friends (8 Jan. 1825) to vote for Adams; and the Kentucky representatives, acting under Clay's influence, disobeyed the instructions of their state legislature to vote for Jackson and instead cast their ballots for Adams. In the House vote (9 Feb. 1825), **Adams** received the votes of 13 states to 7 for Jackson and 4 for Crawford.

The charge that Clay had made a "corrupt bargain" by supporting Adams in return for the promise of the Secretaryship of State was made (Jan. 1825) by Rep. George Kremer (Pa.) in an unsigned letter to a newspaper. Clay demanded a congressional inquiry, but his accuser declined to appear. The charge received popular credence after Clay was appointed Secretary of State in the Adams cabinet, and was repeated by Jackson in 1827. Although no persuasive evidence exists in support of the charge, the accusation clung to Clay's name until the end of his career.

The election of Adams ended the succession of the "Virginia dynasty." Over the winter of 1824–25, the Republican party divided into two groups. The Adams-Clay wing became known as the **National Republicans,** while the "Jackson men" emerged as the **Democratic Republicans.**

1825

CIVIL SERVICE POLICY. In keeping with his declared aim to lend a nonpolitical character to his administration, Adams refused to employ against his opponents the principle of political rotation in federal appointive offices. He asserted that he would renominate any officeholder who did not warrant removal for official misconduct or incompetence (only 12 removals were made during his single term in office). Many of the incumbents were appointees of Crawford or John McLean (Jackson-Calhoun supporter) and used their influence against the president. Adams' deliberate refusal to have any connection with patronage cost him an essential means of building a political party.

AN OPPOSITION EMERGES. When the 19th Congress convened (5 Dec.) it soon became apparent that the forces opposed to Adams were beginning to coalesce. Adams' first annual message to Congress (6 Dec.) crystallized the opposition. Taking a broad nationalist view of constitutional powers, Adams recommended construction of roads and canals, a national university, an astronomical observatory, standardization of weights and measures, the exploration of the U.S. interior and the Pacific Northwest coast, and the passage of laws for the promotion of agriculture, commerce, and manufacturing and the encouragement of the arts, sciences, and literature. These proposals antagonized Southern adherents of states' rights.

There were other signs of opposition to the president. Calhoun, using the recently granted powers of the vice-president to appoint Senate committees, filled half of the important posts with senators who did not support the administration program. Adams, however, could count on the alliance of New England and the West based on common loyalty to the "American system"; so long as factionalism was rife in Southern politics, Adams still held the initiative.

1826

6 Jan. The first number of the *United States Telegraph* appeared at Washington, edited by Duff Green, a close friend of Calhoun and supported by senators and representatives opposed to the Adams administration.

PANAMA DEBATE. The first organized test of the Adams administration arose over the question of the mission to the Panama Congress. That assembly had been called for 1826 by Simon Bolívar, whose original invitation to the Latin-American republics (1824) had been extended by Colombia and Mexico to include the U.S. (1825). While not fully aware of the aims of the congress, President Adams, with the support of Secretary of State Clay, believed that the dominant position of the U.S. in the Western Hemisphere demanded representation at the congress. It was later revealed that the program of the congress looked to a union of the Latin-American republics against Spain or other unfriendly nations and the establishment of a general assembly equipped with full war powers binding upon the member countries, neither of which were actually provided. Following his reference to the congress in his annual message (6 Dec. 1825), Adams sent a special message to the Senate (26 Dec. 1825). He nominated 2 delegates to the Panama Congress and stressed the limited and consultative nature of U.S. participation.

The opposing coalition in the Senate, brought together on this issue by Calhoun and Sen. Martin Van Buren (N.Y.), attacked the message on the ground (1) that since the Panama Congress would have the status of a government, U.S. participation would sharply diverge from traditional concepts of national independence and neutrality; (2) that Adams had accepted the invitation without consulting the Senate. On this score, Sen. John Branch (N.C.) submitted a resolution affirming the authority of the Senate to pass upon appointments of ambassadors or other public ministers. Southern animosity was aroused on the slavery question. Adams' message had made no reference to slavery, but it was commonly known that the subject would enter into the proceedings at the Panama Congress, where some republics under the control of Negroes would be represented.

The Senate Committee on Foreign Relations reported unfavorably (11 Jan.) on the proposal, but the Senate approved the mission, 24–19 (14 Mar.), and the House approved the appropriation for it, 134–60 (25 Mar.). The U.S. was never represented at the congress. Of the 2 delegates, Richard C. Anderson died en route (24 July) and John Sergeant had not gone farther than Mexico City when the congress adjourned.

During the Panama debate John Randolph made his famous charge against the Adams-Clay "corrupt bargain." Randolph declared from the Senate floor (30 Mar.) that the administration was "the coalition of Blifil and Black George," the combination "of the puritan with the black-leg." Randolph's accusation was followed by a challenge from Clay. The duel, fought on the Virginia bank of the Potomac (8 Apr.), left both contenders unharmed.

4 July. Death of Thomas Jefferson at Monticello and of John Adams at Quincy,

Mass. on the 50th anniversary of the adoption of the Declaration of Independence (p. 107). Jefferson's death occurred a few hours before that of Adams. Shortly before he died, Adams is reported to have exclaimed: "Thomas Jefferson still survives."

1827

BROADENING OF DEMOCRACY. The movement against property-holding and taxpaying qualifications for voting was initiated before the War of 1812, with the abolition of those requirements in New Jersey (1807) and Maryland (1810), but even greater progress was made after 1815, with the admission of new Western states. The constitutions of Indiana (1816), Illinois (1818), and Alabama (1819) provided for white manhood suffrage; Maine, in 1820, made the same provision. The era of state constitutional revision between 1816 and 1830 saw a liberalizing of the constitutions of Connecticut (1818), Massachusetts (by amendments, 1821), and New York (1821), all of which abolished property qualifications. Religious qualifications for voting and officeholding were removed, as in Maryland (by constitutional amendment, 1826). There was also a trend toward apportionment on the basis of population rather than taxpayers, and an increase in popular elective offices. The selection of presidential electors was gradually transferred from the state legislatures to the people. By 1828 only 2 of the 24 states in the Union (S.C. and Del.) still chose electors through their legislatures.

REVIVAL OF THE TARIFF QUESTION. Dissatisfied with the Tariff of 1824 because it failed to eliminate British competition, the wool-growing and woolen textile interests of the Northeast attempted to obtain higher duties. A bill introduced 10 Jan. incorporated 3 minimum valuations for woolen goods and made the importation of those articles virtually prohibitive. The bill was passed in the House (10 Feb.), but was lost in the Senate when Vice-President Calhoun, aligning himself with the antitariff forces, cast the decisive vote.

The rejection of this bill touched off a move for higher duties generally. At the call of the advocates of protection, a convention, dominated by the woolen interests, met at Harrisburg, Pa. (30 July–3 Aug.), with 100 delegates from 13 states in attendance. It called for the establishment of the minimum-valuation principle on textiles and proposed additional duties on hemp, flax, hammered bar iron and steel, and other goods. The memorial of the Harrisburg Convention was presented to Congress (24 Dec.). Dependent upon a world market for the disposal of its agricultural commodities, the South opposed a protective tariff which meant higher prices for manufactured goods.

South Carolina, whose economy had suffered gravely under the exhaustion of cotton lands (in general the effects of the Panic of 1819 lingered in the South longer than the North), took the lead against protectionism. In a speech made at Columbia, S.C. (2 July), **Thomas Cooper** (1759–1839), speaking for a small minority, condemned the economic ambitions of the North as a menace to Southern equality within the Union, and declared that the South would have to calculate the value of the federal Union, for the "question is fast approaching the alternative of submission or separation."

1828

19 May. TARIFF OF ABOMINATIONS. The 20th Congress that convened on 3 Dec. 1827 witnessed the transfer of leadership from the administration forces to the "Jackson men." The protectionist scheme of the Harrisburg Convention having been rejected, the

Jacksonians decided to exploit the tariff issue to discredit Adams. Crucial in the impending national elections were the Middle States. Jackson supporters reasoned that in any case the vote of New England would go to Adams and the vote of the South to Jackson. The Jacksonians who dominated the House Committee on Manufactures planned their tactics accordingly. They would report a bill with such excessively high duties (particularly at the cost of New England interests) that no section would vote for it; the responsibility for the defeat would be attributed to Adams; and the protectionist interests of the Middle States would be alienated from Adams. The Jacksonians, without offending Southern free-trade adherents, would then assure the Pennsylvanians that they favored protection of their iron interests.

The House committee framed a bill imposing very high duties on raw materials, iron, hemp, and flax, and eliminated some of the protective features pertaining to woolen goods. The bill was introduced in the House on 31 Jan., and discussion began on 4 Mar. The alliance of the Middle States and the South engineered by Martin Van Buren and Calhoun voted down every attempt by the New Englanders to amend the bill, and confidently awaited its defeat. To the surprise of the Jacksonians, New England voted for the bill despite its deficiencies, supporting it on the ground that it embodied the protective principle. The bill passed in the House, 105–94 (23 Apr.); the Senate, 26–21 (13 May). The Jacksonians of the West and the Middle States voted for the tariff, thereby depriving the Adams-Clay forces of a campaign issue. John Randolph asserted that "the bill referred to manufactures of no sort or kind, but the manufacture of a President of the United States."

19 Dec. Resolves of South Carolina Legislature. The South Carolina legislature promptly adopted a set of 8 resolutions (19 Dec.) terming the tariff unconstitutional, oppressive, and unjust. The Georgia legislature also protested (30 Dec.), as did Mississippi (5 Feb. 1829) and Virginia (4 Feb.). The Carolina resolutions were accompanied by the *South Carolina Exposition and Protest,* written (but not signed) by Calhoun. A lengthy essay on the theory of state sovereignty and minority rights, the *Exposition* expounded the doctrine of nullification by a single state. With it, Calhoun formally abandoned nationalism and identified himself with the particularist views of his state and section.

PRESIDENTIAL CAMPAIGN. Nominated for the presidency by the Tennessee legislature (Oct. 1825), **Jackson** resigned from the U.S. Senate and began to build his political following for the election of 1828. His campaign was managed by a group of able editors and politicians including Amos Kendall, William B. Lewis, Duff Green, James Buchanan, and John H. Eaton. Jackson could count on the Southern vote, while in much of the West "Old Hickory" was acclaimed as a frontier military hero, a symbol of the common man, and a supporter of the "American system." **John C. Calhoun** was vice-presidential candidate on the Jackson ticket.

The National Republican Convention at Harrisburg, Pa., nominated **Adams** for a 2d term with **Richard Rush** (Pa.) as his running mate. The Jacksonians, now called Democrats, based their campaign on personal grounds, and their opponents retaliated in kind. The "corrupt bargain" charge was used against Adams and Clay with telling effect.

3 Dec. PRESIDENTIAL ELECTION. Jackson received 647,231 popular votes and 178 electoral votes; Adams 509,097 popular votes, 83 electoral votes. **Calhoun,** with 171 electoral votes, was reelected vice-president. The crucial states of Pennsylvania and New York went for Jackson. The vote in New York was close: 140,763 votes (20 electoral) for Jackson; 135,413 votes (16 electoral) for Adams. New York had been swung into the Jackson ranks by Martin Van Buren and William L. Marcy, leaders of the powerful "Albany Regency" that had succeeded the old Republican machine in the state and maintained its power by exercising the "spoils system."

1829

4 MAR. In his inaugural address, Jackson pledged himself to economy in government, a proper regard for states' rights, a "just and liberal policy" toward the Indians, and a revamping of the federal civil service. The address contained no clear statement of policy on the tariff, internal improvements, the currency, or the Bank of the U.S. The boisterous reception at the White House, where Western frontiersmen mingled with Washington society, became a symbol of the common people's arrival at political power.

"**KITCHEN CABINET.**" Shortly after taking office, Jackson suspended the practice of holding cabinet meetings. For advice on policy he drew upon a small group of unofficial political confidants whom his opponents called the "Kitchen Cabinet" (also known as the "Lower Cabinet"). Among them were **Amos Kendall, Isaac Hill, William B. Lewis, Andrew J. Donelson,** and **Duff Green.** Some of them held minor government posts: Kendall was fourth auditor of the Treasury, while Lewis served as second auditor. The "Kitchen Cabinet" was at the height of its influence between 1829 and 1831. With the reorganization of the cabinet (1831), Jackson relied upon the members of that body for counsel.

"**SPOILS SYSTEM.**" The phrase, "to the victor belongs the spoils," was used (1831) by Sen. William Learned Marcy (N.Y.) during the course of a congressional debate. The "spoils system" refers to the use of patronage for party purposes. First president to use the system was Jefferson, who employed it with restraint. By 1829, it was entrenched in the political machines of several states, including New York and Pennsylvania. Although Jackson introduced the system into national politics on a scale hitherto unmatched, he did not make wholesale political removals. The peak of Jackson's so-called "clean sweep" was reached during his first year in office, when only about 9% of the officeholders were replaced. During Jackson's 2 terms (1829–37) not more than 20% of the officeholders were removed on political grounds.

WORKINGMEN'S PARTY (also p. 762) was organized in Philadelphia (1828). Its candidates were defeated, but the party continued to agitate for free public education and for the protection of mechanics against competition from prison contract labor. In New York the Workingmen's party was formed in 1829, under the leadership of Robert Dale Owen, Thomas Skidmore, Fanny Wright, and George H. Evans. The Jacksonians attempted to exploit the party for their own ends. Erastus Root, speaker of the assembly and an adherent of Van Buren, sought to win the Workingmen's nomination (16 Apr. 1830) for governor. In turn, Fanny Wright and Robert Dale Owen split the party and nominated (14 Sept. 1830) Ezekiel Williams for governor.

1830

19–27 JAN. WEBSTER-HAYNE DEBATE had its inception when Sen. **Samuel A. Foot** (Conn.) proposed a resolution (29 Dec. 1829) inquiring into the expediency of temporarily restricting the sale of public lands. The resolution, taken up on 13 Jan., came at a time when Jackson had not yet made any public announcement on the nullification stand taken by South Carolina. **Thomas Hart Benton** (Mo.) charged (18 Jan.) that Northeastern interests were attempting to check the settlement and prosperity of the West and was supported in this by **Robert Y. Hayne** (S.C.). In a speech (19 Jan.) invoking strict constructionist and states'-rights views against federal interference, Hayne asserted that "the very life of our system is the independence of the States, and that there is no evil more to be deprecated than the consolidation of this government." Hayne was answered (20 Jan.) by Daniel Webster (Mass.), who deplored the tendency of some Southerners to "habitually speak of the Union in terms of indifference, or even of disparagement."

From this point onward the debate became a contest between Webster and Hayne, and was eventually confined to the origin and nature of the Constitution and the Union. Hayne's first reply (21, 25 Jan.) advanced the doctrine of state sovereignty and nullification. Webster's reply to Hayne (26, 27 Jan.) was one of the most eloquent orations ever delivered in the Senate. Passing over the Southerner's expression of economic grievances, Webster denied the validity of the constitutional doctrines advanced by Hayne, and expounded the nature of the Union. The states are sovereign only so far as their power is not qualified by the Constitution, said Webster, but only the Constitution and the national government are sovereign over the people. In the event of disagreement between the states and the national government, the settlement of the dispute rested with the agencies provided for that purpose in the Constitution: the federal courts, the amending power, and regular elections. Attacking disunionist tendencies, Webster closed his oration with an eloquent peroration celebrating "Liberty *and* Union, now and forever, one and inseparable!"

Hayne's second reply to Webster (27 Jan.) included the statement that the federal government resulted from the compact between the states, and that each party to the compact was the rightful judge of infringements upon its rights. Questions of sovereignty, said Hayne, are not subject to judicial consideration; therefore the right of state interposition is "as full and complete as it was before the Constitution was formed." In his rebuttal (27 Jan.) Webster opposed Hayne's historical theory of the Constitution by attempting to show that the Constitution was not the result of a compact, but was established as a popular government with a distribution of powers binding upon the national government and the states.

13 APR. "OUR UNION—" The Jefferson Day Dinner, held at Brown's Indian Queen Hotel in Washington, was arranged by Senators Benton and Hayne, ostensibly to align the Democratic party with Jeffersonian principles and to signify the alliance between the West and the South. Jackson gave much thought to the phrasing of his volunteer toast, given after he had heard 24 prepared toasts, many of them alluding to the propriety of state sovereignty and nullification. Jackson offered his toast: "Our Union: It must be preserved." Calhoun responded· "The Union, next to our liberty, most dear. May we always remember that it can only be preserved by distributing equally the benefits and burdens of the Union." At the request of Hayne, Jackson agreed to amend his toast for publication, to read: "Our Federal Union—." But the nullifiers could find only small comfort in this concession.

27 MAY. MAYSVILLE ROAD VETO. In his first annual message to Congress (8 Dec. 1829) Jackson referred to the constitutional objections that had been raised against internal improvements. He recommended the distribution of the surplus revenue among the states according to their congressional apportionment, the states to use the funds at their own discretion. Meanwhile, he had been heeding Van Buren's advice to put an end to congressional logrolling that resulted in the construction of internal improvements at federal expense. Van Buren had a political object: to strike at the Clay party.

The opportunity arose when Congress passed a bill authorizing a government subscription of stock to the amount of $150,000 in the Maysville, Washington, Paris, and Lexington Turnpike Road Co., for the construction of a 60-mile road in Kentucky. In his first veto, on expediency and strict constructionist grounds, Jackson declared that as the road lay within the limits of a single state and had no connection with any established system of improvements, it was not embraced by national jurisdiction. If federally subsidized roads and canals were thought desirable, said Jackson, they should be sanctioned by a constitutional amendment.

Jackson's concession to Southern states' rights was made without withdrawing his general support of internal improvements. Thus Jackson kept his Southern political support and did not antagonize the North and the West. His subsequent policy on internal improvements terminated sizable federal expenditures on roads and canals, although it did not materially affect the improvement of harbors and rivers. The only large land-route project he approved was the Cumberland Road Bill (31 May).

7 DEC. Publication of the first number of the *Washington Globe*. The growing gulf between Jackson and Calhoun led the president and the "Kitchen Cabinet" to arrange for the establishment of an administration newspaper. Francis P. Blair, Sr., of Kentucky, was chosen to edit the *Globe*. After the formal break between Jackson and Calhoun, Duff Green's *United States Telegraph* (with the aid of a loan from the Bank of the U.S.) became an antiadministration organ.

1831

JACKSON'S BREAK WITH CALHOUN. In the spring of 1830 Jackson learned that in 1818 Calhoun, as Secretary of War, had favored punishing Jackson for his conduct in the Seminole War. The letter containing this charge was written by William H. Crawford and was made known by William L. Lewis and others for the purpose of discrediting Calhoun. Jackson, who hitherto believed that Calhoun had supported him in 1818, requested an explanation. Calhoun's defense of his position did not satisfy the president. "Understanding you now," wrote Jackson, "no further communication with you on this subject is necessary" (30 May 1830). At Calhoun's direction, a pamphlet containing the correspondence on the Seminole affair was published (15 Feb.). It angered Jackson, completed the breach between him and Calhoun, and helped to confirm Jackson in his choice of Van Buren as presidential successor.

EATON AFFAIR. The split in Jackson's cabinet between the supporters of Calhoun and those of Van Buren as heir apparent to the presidency impinged upon a Washington social feud waged against Peggy O'Neale, a barmaid who had become (1829) the second wife of Secretary of War John H. Eaton. Jackson supported Mrs. Eaton, whose status in society soon became a political issue. Mrs. Calhoun and the wives of other members of the cabinet refused to receive Mrs. Eaton. Jackson's stubborn efforts to compel recognition met with little success; he encountered resistance even in the White House, where Mrs. Andrew J. Donelson withdrew as hostess rather than call on Mrs. Eaton. When he raised the issue at a cabinet meeting, the only cabinet member to support Mrs. Eaton was the widower Martin Van Buren, who thereby increased Jackson's favor for him.

Van Buren, who saw the Eaton affair as a liability to the administration, submitted his resignation, aware that this would precipitate a reorganization of the cabinet. When Eaton learned that Van Buren's resignation was impending, he offered his own.

CABINET REORGANIZATION. The resignations of Eaton (7 Apr.) and Van Buren (11 Apr.) were accepted by Jackson, who then requested and received those of Secretary of the Treasury Samuel D. Ingham (19 Apr.), Secretary of the Navy Branch (19 Apr.), and Attorney General John M. Berrien (15 June). Van Buren was named minister to England, and Jackson ended the Washington social war by appointing Eaton governor of Florida. A reorganized cabinet was formed with an eye to harmony: Levi Woodbury of New Hampshire, Secretary of the Navy (23 May); Edward Livingston of Louisiana, Secretary of State (24 May); Roger B. Taney of Maryland, Attorney General (20 July); Lewis Cass of Ohio, Secretary of War (1 Aug.); and Louis McLane of Delaware, Secretary of the Treasury (8 Aug.). The only cabinet member retained was Postmaster General William T. Barry.

JACKSONIAN DIPLOMACY. West Indian Trade. U.S. shipping interests suffered under the severe British restrictions on direct trade with the West Indies. The unsatisfactory results of the halfway measures adopted (1822–25) by the U.S. and Great Britain led both governments to make provisions (1826–27) for closing West Indian ports to direct trade. After taking office, Jackson adopted a moderate approach on the issue, basing his application for a reopening of trade on the grounds of a new administration, a change in public opinion, and the restoration of privileges rather than rights. Congress authorized Jackson (29 May 1830) to take reciprocal action in the event British colonial ports were reopened. After some months of negotiation Jackson announced by proclamation (5 Oct.) that trade was reopened with the West Indian ports on the basis of reciprocal privileges.

French Spoliation Claims. Claims against the French for depredations on U.S. commerce during the Napoleonic wars had been pending since 1815. The negotiations lagged because of French counterclaims based on alleged U.S. violations of a commercial clause in the Louisiana Treaty. Jackson instructed William C. Rives, minister to France, to secure a satisfactory adjustment. A treaty was concluded (4 July) whereby France agreed to pay 25 million francs and the U.S. 1,500,000 francs for spoliations committed against the subjects of either nation in 6 annual installments. Delay in the French payment of the first installment caused Jackson to recommend (annual message, 2 Dec. 1834) reprisals on French property in the event no provision was made for payment. The French voted an appropriation (25 Apr. 1835) on condition that Jackson apologize for certain expressions in his message. Jackson replied in his annual message (7 Dec. 1835): "The honor of my country shall never be stained by an apology from me for the statement of truth and the performance of duty." In a special message to Congress (15 Jan. 1836) Jackson again recommended reprisals and an expansion of naval and coastal defenses, but at the same time made an adroitly phrased offer of conciliation. Great Britain's offer of mediation (27

Jan. 1836) was accepted, and on 10 May 1836 Jackson announced that the French had paid 4 installments. Other spoliation claims to the amount of $5 million based on depredations committed before 1800 were incorporated in a bill that passed the Senate (28 Jan. 1835), but did not receive House action.

ANTI-MASONIC PARTY. The mysterious disappearance in western New York of William Morgan (Sept. 1826), who had prepared an exposé of Freemasonry, led to a series of official inquiries and court trials (1827–31) that threw no light on the fate of Morgan but revealed that virtually all of the officeholders in New York State were members of the order. During the subsequent popular reaction against Freemasonry opponents of Jackson (who was a Mason) exploited the issue. In mid-1830 the Anti-Masons appeared in New York State as a political party opposed to Jackson. Anti-Masonry and antipathy to all kinds of secret societies spread to other states, and a national convention of Anti-Masons assembled at Baltimore (26 Sept.), nominating William Wirt (Md., 1772–1834) for president and Amos Ellmaker (Pa.) for vice-president. The Anti-Masonic party was the first third party in the U.S., the first to hold a national nominating convention, and the first to announce a platform. The party declined after the election of 1836 and was eventually absorbed by the Whigs.

ABOLITION MOVEMENT (p. 757).

13–23 Aug. NAT TURNER INSURRECTION (p. 757).

1832

INDIAN POLICY. Jackson's Indian policy was based mainly on the prospect of voluntary emigration to tracts west of the Mississippi set aside for permanent occupancy. Under the act of 28 May 1830 Congress made provision for removal; the act of 30 June 1834 established a special Indian territory in the Arkansas country.

Under a series of treaties (1791 *et seq.*) concluded with the U.S., the Cherokee inhabiting the state of Georgia were recognized as a nation with their own laws and customs. However, Georgia settlers encroached upon the Cherokee as well as the neighboring Creek Indians. Alabama and Mississippi likewise violated federal treaties in annexing the lands of the Choctaw and the Chickasaw. Under a state law of 20 Dec. 1828, Georgia pronounced the laws of the Cherokee Nation null and void after 1 June 1830. After gold was discovered on the Cherokee lands (July 1829), the Cherokee sought relief in the Supreme Court. In an opinion delivered by Chief Justice Marshall (1831), an injunction against Georgia was denied on the ground that the court lacked jurisdiction because the Cherokee comprised a "domestic dependent" nation rather than a foreign state within the meaning of the Constitution (*Cherokee Nation* v. *Georgia*, 5 Peters 1).

A Georgia law (1830) ordered white residents in Cherokee country to secure a license from the governor and to take an oath of allegiance to the state. Samuel A. Worcester and Elizur Butler, both New England missionaries, refused to obey the law and were convicted and sentenced to 4 years at hard labor. On appeal to the Supreme Court Chief Justice Marshall (3 Mar. 1832) held that Indian nations were capable of making treaties, that under the constitution treaties are the supreme law of the land, that the national government had exclusive jurisdiction in the territory of the Cherokee nation, and that the law was unconstitutional because the Cherokee nation had territorial boundaries within which the laws of Georgia "can have no force." (*Worcester* v. *Georgia*, 6 Peters

515). Georgia defied the court and was supported by Jackson, who is reported to have said: "John Marshall has made his decision, now let him enforce it!"

Jackson pursued a broad policy of extinguishing Indian land titles in states and in removing the Indian population. During his 2 terms 94 Indian treaties were concluded under coercion. In the Old Southwest, the Creeks, Choctaw, and Chickasaw signed treaties of evacuation. By the end of 1833 only the Cherokee insisted on retaining their lands. Finally, under the treaty of 29 Dec. 1835 the Cherokee surrendered to the U.S. all their lands east of the Mississippi in return for $5 million, transportation costs, and land in Indian territory. A **Bureau of Indian Affairs** was established in 1836. Some Indians resorted to armed resistance. Seeking to reoccupy their ceded lands in Wisconsin Territory and Illinois, the Sac and Fox Indians fought the **Black Hawk War** (6 Apr.–2 Aug. 1832) along the upper Mississippi. They were beaten back. In Florida, the **Second Seminole War** broke out in Nov. 1835 and lasted until 14 Aug. 1842.

NULLIFICATION CONTROVERSY.

In his annual message of 1830 Jackson affirmed the constitutionality of the Tariff of 1828 and protectionism. But to conciliate the South, he recommended tariff revision in his subsequent message.

During 1830–31, the nullification forces in South Carolina enlarged their following; but Union sentiment in the state was strong enough to prevent the calling of a convention. The Tariff of 1832, while somewhat milder than that of 1828, retained the protective principle. Its passage (14 July) encouraged the South Carolina nullifiers, who, under the leadership of Gov. James Hamilton, Jr., and Robert Barnwell Rhett, took a belligerent stand. The state elections (Oct.) resulted in a decisive victory for the nullification party.

Ordinance of Nullification. Meanwhile, Calhoun had reaffirmed and elaborated the doctrine of nullification in 2 important papers: the **Fort Hill Address** (26 July 1831), which contained the principle of the concurrent majority, and in a letter to Gov. James Hamilton, Jr. (28 Aug.) which defended nullification as a constitutional, conservative, and legitimate means of redress for acts deemed injurious to the state.

Gov. Hamilton called an extraordinary session of the legislature (22 Oct.), which promptly called for a state convention. The convention which assembled at Columbia (19 Nov.), attended by only a handful of Unionists, adopted (136–26) an ordinance nullifying the tariff acts of 1828 and 1832 (24 Nov.). The ordinance prohibited the collection of duties within the state, beginning 1 Feb. 1833; required a test oath for all state officeholders except members of the legislature; forbade appeal to the U.S. Supreme Court of any case in law or equity arising under the ordinance; and asserted that the use of force by the federal government would be cause for secession. The legislature (27 Nov.) passed laws for the enforcement of the ordinance. Among them were provisions authorizing the raising of a military force and appropriations for arms.

Jackson ordered the Secretary of War (29 Oct.) to alert the forts in Charleston Harbor. Maj. Gen. Winfield Scott was given the command of the army forces in South Carolina. Jackson's message to Congress (4 Dec.) again recommended downward revision of the tariff. On 10 Dec. he issued his **Proclamation to the People of South Carolina**, which was drafted by Edward Livingston and ranks as Jackson's most important state paper. The proclamation characterized nullification as an "impractical absurdity" and asserted the supremacy of a sovereign and indivisible federal government. No state, said Jackson, could refuse to obey the laws of the land, and no state could leave the Union. "Disunion by armed force is **treason**," Jackson concluded.

The South Carolina legislature adopted a series of resolutions (17 Dec.) replying to the Nullification Proclamation, and the newly installed governor, Robert Y. Hayne, issued a counterproclamation (20 Dec.). Calhoun resigned the vice-presidency (28 Dec.), having been elected (12 Dec.) U.S. senator in place of Hayne (121–28). A call by South Carolina for a general convention of the states to consider relations between the federal and state governments elicited a series of replies by various state legislatures unequivocally condemning nullification and secession.

Force Bill. Jackson asked Congress (16 Jan. 1833) for authority to enforce the revenue laws by the use of the military if necessary. The congressional battle against the so-called Force Bill was led by Calhoun, who was engaged by Webster in a notable debate on nationalism and states' rights. Meanwhile, Henry Clay had formulated a compromise tariff. Introduced on 12 Feb. 1833, it passed the House, 119–85 (26 Feb. 1833), and the Senate, 29–16 (1 Mar.). The Force Bill was passed in the Senate, 32–1 (20 Feb. 1833; Calhoun, Clay, and others abstained from voting), and passed the House, 149–47 (1 Mar.). The compromise tariff of 1833 and the Force Bill were approved by Jackson on 2 Mar.

Upon learning that a compromise tariff was in the making, South Carolina suspended the ordinance of nullification (21 Jan. 1833). Calhoun supported the compromise, although he did not participate in the proceedings of the state convention which met on 11 Mar. and adopted (153–4) a rescinding ordinance (15 Mar.). As a face-saving gesture the convention (132–19) adopted (18 Mar.) an ordinance declaring the Force Bill null and void, and adjourned on the same day. The nullification episode was closed, with both sides claiming victory.

10 JULY. BANK VETO. The charter of the 2d Bank of the U.S. was due to expire in 1836. Under the conservative management (1823 *et seq.*) of **Nicholas Biddle** the bank had prospered and expanded. It aided business operations and reduced the threat of inflation posed by a disorganized currency. But there was a many-sided opposition to the bank. Biddle's policy of branch drafts, which compelled state and local banks to contract their note issues, made the bank unpopular among debtor groups, particularly in the South and West. Southern states'-rights groups questioned its constitutionality. State banks sought government deposits. Van Buren and his New York supporters disputed Philadelphia's financial leadership. Biddle's personal domination of the bank's policies, and his identification with conservative interests, ultimately made him a target for popular resentment against monopolies, corporations, and a moneyed aristocracy.

Jackson's first annual message (1829) questioned the bank's constitutionality and expediency, and asserted that the bank had failed to establish a sound and uniform currency. Jackson favored a government-owned institution with severely limited operations confined chiefly to deposit. When it became clear that Jackson was intent upon eliminating the bank, Biddle embarked upon a policy of opposition. Until early in 1832, however, he planned to defer his application for renewal of the bank charter until after the presidential elections.

Sen. Thomas Hart Benton launched an attack upon the bank in a speech (Feb. 1831). Biddle, alarmed, and at Clay's advice, decided to make immediate application for renewal of the charter, thereby forcing the bank issue upon Jackson.

A bill for recharter of the bank was reported in the House (10 Feb.) and in the Senate (13 Mar.). The measure passed the Senate, 28–20 (11 June), and the House, 107–86 (3 July). Jackson vetoed the bill (10 July). Although his message showed no firm grasp of banking and finance, it was an indictment of monopoly and special privilege, and accepted the challenge of the opposition to make the bank the major issue of the campaign of 1832. In referring to the Supreme Court's views on the constitutionality of the bank, Jackson made a notable definition of the character of the presidential office: "The Congress, the Executive, and the Court must each for itself be guided by its own opinion of the Constitution. Each public officer who takes an oath to support the Constitution swears that he will support it as he understands it, and not as it is understood by others. . . . The opinion of the judges has no more authority over Congress than the opinion of Congress has over the judges, and on that point the President is independent of both." The Senate vote of 22–19 (13 July) failed to override the veto.

PRESIDENTIAL CAMPAIGN. A National Republican Convention assembled at Baltimore (12 Dec. 1831), where its delegates nominated **Henry Clay** for president and **John Sergeant** (Pa.) for vice-president. The Anti-Masonic party had already nominated (26 Sept. 1831) **William Wirt** (Md.) for president and **Amos Ellmaker** (Pa.) for vice-president. The campaign of 1832 witnessed the adoption of the **national nominating convention** by the 3 parties in the field. The first platforms ever adopted by national conventions were by the Anti-Masons (Sept. 1831) and by a group of young National Republicans convened at Washington in May.

The first national nominating convention of the Democratic party (as it was now formally called) was held at Baltimore (21–22 May). It unanimously endorsed **Jackson** for a second term and named **Martin Van Buren** for the vice-presidency. Van Buren's nomination as minister to England had been rejected in the Senate 24–23 (25 Jan.). Calhoun, who had cast the deciding vote, thought the rejection would end Van Buren's political career; the move had an opposite effect. The convention adopted the **"two-thirds rule"** (which remained in force until 1936) requiring that "two-thirds of the whole number of votes in the convention shall be necessary to constitute a choice." No platform was adopted. The principal campaign issue was the bank question, which struck a wide response from agrarian and frontier prejudice against the bank and from Eastern feeling against privileged corporations. The National Republicans were identified with the conservative interests. Biddle printed and circulated campaign literature supporting Clay.

5 Dec. PRESIDENTIAL ELECTION was an overwhelming Democratic victory. **Jackson** won the electoral votes of 16 of the 24 states with 219 electoral votes (687,502 popular votes); Clay received 49 electoral votes (530,189 popular votes). William Wirt carried only Vermont (7 electoral votes). The South Carolina legislature cast 11 votes for John Floyd (Va.) and Henry Lee (Mass.). **Van Buren**, with 189 electoral votes, was elected vice-president (Pennsylvania having thrown its 30 electoral votes to Sen. William Wilkins, a native son).

1833

REMOVAL OF DEPOSITS. The Calhoun and Clay forces in the House united in adopting a resolution (2 Mar.).

stating that government deposits might be safely continued in the Bank of the U.S. Jackson, however, interpreted his reelection as a popular mandate to proceed against the bank. Biddle had already embarked upon a policy of tightening credit to bring the administration to terms.

Jackson asked (19 Mar.) the opinion of the cabinet on the regulation of deposits and the establishment of a new bank. **Attorney General Taney** (3 Apr.) supported removal of the deposits and their distribution among selected state banks (a policy which Amos Kendall and Francis P. Blair, Sr., had already recommended). Secretary of the Treasury McLane (20 May) opposed removal and supported the formation of a new bank. Jackson then reorganized the cabinet, appointing McLane Secretary of State (1 June) and William J. Duane (Pa.) Secretary of the Treasury. Upon receiving Jackson's instructions for removing the deposits, Duane replied with a letter (10 July) opposing the step.

On 10 Sept. Jackson submitted to the cabinet a report by Kendall indicating the availability of state banks, and announced that on 1 Oct. the government would discontinue the Bank of the U.S. as a depository. Taney and Woodbury supported Jackson; McLane, Cass, and Duane were opposed. Jackson read to the cabinet (18 Sept.) a paper drafted by Taney listing the reasons for removal. The document illuminated Jackson's concept of the role of the cabinet: namely, that it was the personal organ of the president.

When Duane persisted in his refusal to carry out the removal, he was replaced (23 Sept.) by Taney as Secretary of the Treasury. Taney announced (26 Sept.) that the public funds would no longer be deposited in the Bank of the U.S., and issued the first order for removal (effected by transferring the funds). The Girard Bank of Philadelphia was the first state bank designated as a place of deposit. By the end of 1833, 23 state banks (popularly known as "pet banks") had been selected as depositories. By that time, too, Biddle's restrictions on credit had induced financial distress.

In his annual message (3 Dec.) Jackson assumed complete responsibility for removing the deposits, defending his action with the argument that the bank was attempting to influence elections. The Senate issued a call (11 Dec.) for a copy of the paper which Jackson had read to the cabinet. Jackson refused the request, declaring that "the executive is a co-ordinate and independent branch of the Government equally with the Senate, and I have yet to learn under what constitutional authority that branch of the Legislature has a right to require of me an account of any communication, either verbally or in writing, made to the heads of Departments acting as a Cabinet council."

Henry Clay introduced 2 **censuring resolutions** in the Senate (26 Dec.): The first, criticizing the action of the Treasury, was adopted 28 Mar. 1834, 28–18; the second, stating that "the President, in the late Executive proceedings in relation to the public revenue, has assumed upon himself authority and power not conferred by the constitution and laws, but in derogation of both," was adopted the same day, 26–20.

The Jackson supporters in the House pushed through 4 resolutions sustaining the administration's bank policy (4 Apr. 1834). Jackson made a formal protest (15 Apr. 1834), asserting that he had been charged with an impeachable offense but had been denied an opportunity to defend himself. On 21 Apr. 1834 he forwarded a supplementary message aimed at conciliating the Senate. By 27–16 (7 May 1834) the Senate rejected Jackson's power to question its authority and declined to enter the president's protest and message in the official record of its proceedings. In another move against Jackson, the Senate (24 June 1834) refused to approve Taney's nomination as Secretary of the Treasury. Through the repeated efforts of Sen. Benton, the resolution of censure was finally expunged from the Senate journal (16 Jan. 1837).

The Bank of the U.S., having failed to secure a new charter, obtained a state charter (Feb. 1836) and, upon the expiration of its national charter (1 Mar. 1836), became the Bank of the U.S. of Pennsylvania. Under the **Deposit Act** (23 June 1836) the Secretary of the Treasury was required to designate at least one bank in each state and territory as a place of public deposit, and the banks were assigned the general services previously rendered to the national government by the Bank of the U.S. The act also provided for the distribution of the surplus revenue in excess of $5 million among the states, as a loan subject to recall by the Secretary of the Treasury. It was never recalled.

1834

RISE OF THE WHIG PARTY. The union of the National Republican and Calhoun forces which secured the passage of the Senate censuring resolutions was the genesis of the Whig coalition on a national scale. The name "Whig" was formally adopted in 1834, after Clay mentioned it approvingly in a Senate speech (14 Apr.), but it had been in use for at least 2 years before that time. Gatherings of Northern and Southern opponents of the Jackson administration were held in the spring of 1834, apparently for the purpose of merging forces. By mid-1834 the Whig label was generally understood to refer to the coalition

of the political groups led by Clay, Webster, and Calhoun, even though Calhoun preferred an independent course and acted with the Whigs when expedient. Included in this loose coalition: (1) National Republican supporters of Clay, Adams, and the "American system"; (2) states'-rights groups opposed to Jackson's stand on nullification; (3) former administration supporters alienated by Jackson's bank policy; (4) Southern planters and Northern industrialists; and, after 1836, (5) the remnants of the Anti-Masonic party.

1835

30 JAN. Attempted assassination of President Jackson. The assailant, Richard Lawrence, fired 2 pistols (both of which misfired) at the president as he was leaving the House chamber. Jackson was unharmed. Lawrence was adjudged insane and committed to a lunatic asylum.

ABOLITIONIST PROPAGANDA. The Southern states met abolitionist propaganda with regulatory or prohibitory laws. A Georgia code (1835) provided the death penalty for the publication of material tending to incite slave insurrections. Northern abolitionist editors and agents were expelled from the South. To the South Carolina legislature (1835) Gov. George McDuffie declared that "the laws of every community should punish this species of interference by death without benefit of clergy." At Charleston (29 July), a boatload of abolitionist tracts from New York impounded by the postmaster was seized by a mob and publicly burned. The Charleston postmaster, Alfred Huger, requested antislavery societies to discontinue their use of the mails; his appeal was rejected. When Huger's report reached Postmaster General Kendall, the latter replied that he had no official authority to bar abolitionist propaganda from the mails; unofficially he advised Southern postmasters to intercept such material, having already declared, "We owe an obligation to the laws, but a higher one to the communities in which we live."

In his annual message (2 Dec.) Jackson recommended a law to prohibit the circulation of antislavery publications through the mails. A Senate committee headed by Calhoun presented (4 Feb. 1836) a minority report on abolitionist publications, which supported Jackson's opposition to the dissemination of antislavery literature but took objection on states'-rights grounds to the recommended federal law barring circulation through the mails and offered a bill for the interception by postmasters of any publication prohibited by the laws of a particular state. The bill was defeated in the Senate, 25–19 (8 June 1836).

29 Oct. LOCO-FOCOS. The radical wing of Jacksonian Democracy, an urban faction that inherited the mantle of the Workingmen's party in New York, emerged (1834–35) as the Equal Rights party. Its followers, dividing with the Democratic regulars chiefly over banking and currency questions, regarded Jackson's banking policy as inflationary. Called the "Loco-Focos," this faction fought those financial interests which, with the aid of the regular Democratic party in the state, applied for bank and corporation charters from the legislature, and advocated abolition of monopolies and special privileges, hard money, elections by direct popular vote, direct taxes, free trade, and Jeffersonian strict construction. The radical wing found a voice in the New York *Evening Post*. The origin of the name "Loco-Focos" dates from a primary meeting (29 Oct.) at Tammany Hall when the regulars, over the protests of the Equal Rights men, declared the ticket carried and the meeting adjourned. The dissidents remained in the hall. To oust them, the Tammany stalwarts turned out the gas lights, whereupon the Equal Rights men furnished candles which they lit with the new self-igniting friction matches known as loco-focos, and proceeded to formulate their platform and nominate their own ticket.

1836

REPUBLIC OF TEXAS. The American settlement of Texas began when **Moses Austin** secured a charter (17 Jan. 1821) granting lands for colonization by 200 American families. The charter was obtained from the moribund government of New Spain, which soon became the independent state of Mexico. Upon Austin's death in Missouri (10 June 1821), his settlement scheme was carried forward by his son, **Stephen F. Austin** (p. 977), who arrived at Bexar, Tex. (12 Aug. 1821), to take possession of the land grants. In 1822–23 Austin visited Mexico, where by a decree of the Emperor Iturbide he secured confirmation of his concession. Renewal was made during the subsequent revolutions in Mexico and the establishment of a federal republic under the constitution of 1824. A law (7 May 1824) made Texas part of a state (Coahuila) in the Mexican republic, and a colonization law (24 Mar. 1825) threw Texas open to colonization. The success of Austin's venture attracted other *empresarios* who obtained charters or grants and brought in settlers to develop the rich lands. Both J. Q. Adams and Jackson negotiated unsuccessfully for the purchase of Texas.

A procession of revolutionary governments in Mexico finally resulted in restrictions on Texan colonization and a violation of what the settlers held to be their local rights. The Mexican Congress (8 Apr. 1830) enacted a law prohibiting the introduction of more slaves and the further settlement of Texas by immigrants from the U.S. The Texans remonstrated in petitions and memorials adopted (1 Oct. 1832) by a convention held at San Felipe; another convention held there (1–13 Apr. 1833) resolved to separate from Mexico. When Austin visited Mexico City to present the resolves to the new Mexican government under the Federalist party headed by **Santa Anna,** he was arrested (3 Jan. 1834) and imprisoned for 8 months. Santa Anna, who had used his Federalist connection only to secure office, turned rapidly toward the Centralist position of absolute rule over all Mexicans, including Texans, worsening relations between the settlers and the government.

A group of Texan colonists led by William B. Travis seized the Mexican garrison at Anahuac (30 June 1835), and in the fall of that year other armed clashes occurred. At conventions (Oct.–Nov. 1835) Texans endorsed the Federalist party's position opposing overcentralized authority, drafted plans for an army to resist Santa Anna, and named commissioners to solicit aid from the U.S.

23 FEB.–6 MAR. The Alamo. Santa Anna replied by establishing a unitary state (15 Dec. 1835) which abolished all local rights. Then raising an army of about 6,000 men he marched against the Texans. A convention assembled at Washington, Tex. (1 Mar.), adopted (2 Mar.) a declaration of independence and drew up a constitution based upon that of the U.S. A provisional government was established, and **Sam Houston** (p. 1062) was named commander of the army (4 Mar.). Santa Anna began (23 Feb.) his **Siege of the Alamo** at San Antonio. The assaulting force of 3,000 Mexicans was held off by 187 Texans until 6 Mar., when the garrison commanded by William B. Travis (and including Davy Crockett) was massacred. Santa Anna also massacred (27 Mar.) more

than 300 of the defenders of Goliad led by Capt. James Fannin. By mid-April the Mexicans had swept through many of the American settlements and reached Galveston Bay.

21 APR. Battle of San Jacinto, fought on the western bank of the San Jacinto River at its junction with Buffalo Bayou, near Galveston Bay. The Texans under Sam Houston went into battle with the cry "Remember the Alamo!," defeated about 1,200 Mexicans, and captured Santa Anna. A treaty (14 May) pledging Santa Anna to secure the recognition of Texas was repudiated by the Mexican Congress. Sam Houston was installed (22 Oct.) as president of the independent republic of Texas.

Resolutions calling for the U.S. recognition of Texas were adopted by the Senate (1 July) and the House (4 July). While Jackson was sympathetic to the Texans, he believed that the U.S. must honor its obligations to Mexico and maintain a strict neutrality. He feared that recognition might disrupt the Democratic party and involve the U.S. in a war with Mexico. He finally yielded, however, by nominating (3 Mar. 1837) Alcée La Branche (La.) as chargé d'affaires to the Texas republic. Texas petitioned for annexation to the U.S. (4 Aug. 1837), but her formal offer was refused (25 Aug. 1837).

28 JUNE. Death of James Madison at Montpelier, his Virginia estate.

11 JULY. SPECIE CIRCULAR. Inflation and land speculation were fed by the expanded issue of paper money accepted as legal tender (also p. 747). The use of "land-office money" (currency based on speculators' notes) pyramided land sales from $2,623,000 in 1832 to $24,877,000 in 1836. The financial disorder was abetted by the employment of federal deposits by the "pet" banks.

President Jackson ordered Secretary of the Treasury Levi Woodbury to issue the

Specie Circular (11 July, after Congress adjourned) that had been drafted by Sen. Thomas Hart Benton (whose resolution embodying the basic purpose of the circular had been rejected in the Senate on 22 Apr.). It provided that after 15 Aug. only gold, silver, and, in some cases, Virginia land scrip would be accepted by the government in payment for public lands, but permitted the receipt of paper money until 15 Dec. for parcels of land up to 320 acres purchased by actual settlers or bona fide residents of the state in which the sale was made. The circular declared that it was aimed at repressing "alleged frauds," withholding government approval or support "from the monopoly of the public lands in the hands of speculators and capitalists," and discouraging the "ruinous extension" of bank notes and credit.

The circular succeeded in reducing public-land sales in the West but taxed the inadequate resources of the "pet" banks, drained specie from the East, led to hoarding, and weakened public confidence in the state banks. The pressure on the deposit banks was increased by the scheduled payment (1 Jan. 1837) to the states of the first installment of the surplus revenue under the distribution provisions of the Deposit Act.

Jackson defended the circular in his annual message (5 Dec.), maintaining that it had "produced many salutary consequences" and strengthened the Western banks against the rising financial distress. He recommended that public land sales should be limited in quantity and confined to actual settlers. A Whig resolution for repeal of the circular was introduced in the Senate (12 Dec.). A House bill (reported 18 Jan. 1837) provided for government acceptance of the notes of specie-paying banks discontinuing note issues of less than $10 denominations. The bill was amended by Sen. William C. Rives (Va.) to

provide for rescinding of the Specie Circular. The measure passed the Senate, 41–5 (10 Feb. 1837), and the House (1 Mar. 1837), but was pocket-vetoed by Jackson. The Specie Circular was finally repealed by a joint resolution (21 May 1838).

PRESIDENTIAL CAMPAIGN. The Democratic Nominating Convention met at Baltimore (20 May 1835) and unanimously chose **Martin Van Buren** as presidential candidate and **Richard M. Johnson** (Ky.) as the vice-presidential. No formal platform was adopted, but an address formulated by a committee and published in the Washington *Globe* (26 Aug. 1835) was the equivalent of the party's first platform. In his letter of acceptance Van Buren pledged himself to "tread generally in the footsteps of President Jackson."

The Whig coalition, unable to agree upon a single candidate, adopted the strategy of nominating candidates with strong local followings in the hope of throwing the election into the House. In Jan. 1835, **Daniel Webster** was nominated by a Massachusetts legislative caucus. In the same month **Hugh L. White** was chosen by anti-Jacksonian Democrats in the Tennessee legislature; the nomination was supported by Illinois and Alabama. Supreme Court Justice John McLean was nominated by an Ohio legislative caucus, but withdrew in Aug. 1836. The Anti-Masonic party met at Harrisburg, Pa. (16 Dec. 1835), and nominated **William Henry Harrison** (Ohio) for president and Francis Granger (N.Y.) for vice-president.

7 DEC. PRESIDENTIAL ELECTION. Van Buren received 761,549 votes. The Whig candidates received 736,250 votes (Harrison, 549,567; White, 145,396; Webster, 41,287). **Van Buren** carried 15 of the 26 states, receiving 170 electoral votes, including 3 disputed Michigan votes; Harrison, 73; White, 26; Webster,

14; and South Carolina gave its 11 electoral votes to Willie P. Mangum (N.C.). Van Buren retired as vice-president (28 Jan. 1837) and Sen. William R. King of Alabama was chosen president *pro tempore* of the Senate. None of the 4 vice-presidential candidates received a majority of the electoral votes. The election, for the first and only time, was thrown into the Senate, which chose **Richard M. Johnson** by a vote of 33 to 16 (8 Feb. 1837).

1837

4 MAR. Jackson published his *Farewell Address* (drafted by Taney), a review of his 2 terms, which appealed for loyalty to the Union, condemned sectionalism, monopolies, paper currency, and speculation.

PANIC OF 1837 (also p. 747) resulted from reckless speculation. In the South the price of cotton fell by almost one half on the New Orleans market (Mar.). In New York there were demonstrations (Feb.–Mar.) by the unemployed. Protesting against high rents and the inflated prices of foodstuffs and fuel, a mob broke into the city's flour warehouses and sacked the supplies (12 Feb.). The New York banks suspended specie payments (10 May), and were followed by banks at Baltimore, Philadelphia, and Boston. The sale of public lands fell from 20 million acres (1836) to 3,500,000 (1838). The effects of the panic persisted until 1842–43, particularly in the Southern and Western states.

In a message to a special session of Congress (5 Sept.) Van Buren advocated a specie currency, criticized state-chartered banks, and alluded to a scheme to establish Treasury depositories independent of state banks. In every year between 1837 and 1841 (with the exception of 1839), the government had a deficit. Numerous bank failures aroused dissatis-

faction with the use of state banks as depositories for public funds and helped to develop sentiment for the Independent Treasury (1840). In 1841 Congress authorized the establishment of a bonded debt.

ABOLITIONIST CONTROVERSY IN CONGRESS. The steady flow of petitions to Congress requesting the abolition of slavery and the slave trade in the District of Columbia reached a crest in 1836. Up to that time such petitions were customarily referred to the standing Committee on the District of Columbia, and did not create serious dissension in either house of Congress. By 1836 the mounting apprehensions of the slave states had hardened the conviction of many Southerners that congressional discussion of slavery was inimical both to the slave system and to the comity of the Union.

The Gag Rule. The Senate adopted a relatively workable formula for disposing of the petitions. When Thomas Morris of Ohio (7 Jan. 1836) and James Buchanan (Pa.) presented (11 Jan. 1836) abolitionist petitions, Calhoun made a bitter attack upon the abolitionists and recommended the barring of future petitions. Calhoun's motion was defeated, 36–10 (9 Mar. 1836); but on the motion of Buchanan, the Senate, 34–6 (11 Mar. 1836), rejected the prayer of the petitioners. Thereafter the Senate adopted this as a regular practice. It enabled the abolitionists to exercise their constitutional right of petition, and at the same time gave the foes of the antislavery agitators an opportunity to register their firm disapproval.

The issue was more complicated in the House, where former president **John Quincy Adams** ardently defended the right of petition from the very outset of his 8 successive terms (1831–48) as representative from the Plymouth District, Mass. Adams held antislavery opinions, but was not sympathetic to the abolitionist cause. His view was that Congress had no authority to interfere with the institution in the slaveholding states, although he declared in a House speech (25 May 1836) that in the event those states ever became a theater of war, "the war powers of Congress [would] extend to interference with the institution of slavery in every way." His persistence in supporting the right of petition earned for him the sobriquet "Old Man Eloquent."

Adams' stubborn intention was one of the factors that led the House to establish (8 Feb. 1836) a special committee under chairman Henry L. Pinckney (S.C.) to consider the question. Pinckney recommended the so-called "gag resolution" (18 May 1836), providing that "all petitions, memorials, resolutions, propositions or papers relating in any way or to any extent whatever to the subject of slavery or the abolition of slavery shall, without being printed or referred, be laid upon the table and that no further action whatever shall be had thereon."

The resolution was 1 of 3. The "gag resolution" itself was adopted (26 May 1836), 117–68. The resolution stating that Congress had no power over slavery in the states was adopted, 182–9; the one holding that interference with slavery in the District of Columbia was inexpedient was adopted, 132–45. When Adams' name was called on the roll, he withheld his vote with the response: "I hold the resolution to be a direct violation of the Constitution of the United States, of the rules of this House, and of the rights of my constituents."

When the 2d session of the 25th Congress convened (4 Dec.), the "gag rule" was not immediately renewed (House rules required its renewal at each session). At this time Northern abolitionist feeling was inflamed by the murder (7 Nov.) of the abolitionist editor **Elijah P. Lovejoy** at Alton, Ill. Rep. William Slade (Vt.) took advantage of the temporary lull in the "gag rule" and presented abolitionist petitions. The move culminated in an angry debate and led Southern representatives to consider an amendment for protecting the institution of slavery or, failing to gain that, to declare the expediency of dissolving the Union. Nothing came of this gesture. In reply to the abolitionists, a combination of Southern and Northern Democrats adopted a stricter "gag resolution," 122–74 (19 Dec.).

In the Senate, Benjamin Swift (Vt.) presented (19 Dec.) the resolutions of his state legislature opposing the annexation of Texas or the admission of any new slave state to the Union, upholding the constitutional authority of Congress to abolish slavery in the District of Columbia and to prohibit the interstate slave trade, and requesting Vermont representatives and senators to use their influence to promote these ends.

Calhoun responded by introducing into the Senate a set of 6 resolutions (27 Dec.). They reaffirmed the compact theory of the Union, the reserved-powers doctrine as it pertained to Southern action against abolitionist propaganda, and the theory that the federal government, as the agent of the states, was bound "to resist all attempts by one portion of the Union to use it as an instrument to attack the domestic institutions of another"; declared that the institution of slavery was not to be attacked or interfered with; that the efforts to abolish slavery in the District of Columbia or the territories was a "direct and dangerous attack on the institutions of all the slave-holding States"; and denounced as detrimental to the Union interference with annexation which might expand slave territory. During the course of the discussion in the Senate (3–12 Jan.

1838) the first 3 of Calhoun's resolutions were adopted; the 4th and 5th were altered and adopted; the 6th tabled.

The House "gag rule" was renewed at each session of Congress between 1836 and 1844 over the opposition of Adams, Joshua Giddings (Ohio), and a small group of other Northern legislators. The "gag rule," by depriving the abolitionists of one of their civil rights, enabled the antislavery agitators to add this charge to their arsenal of indictments against the South. Finally, when Northern Democratic support was lessened, the "gag resolution" was rescinded (3 Dec. 1844) on the motion of Adams.

During the course of Senate debates on the slavery question, Henry Clay, with an eye to the presidential nomination in 1840, attempted to placate Northern and Southern conservatives who tended to identify the Whig party with abolitionism. In a speech delivered on 7 Feb. 1839 he condemned the abolitionist agitators, accused them of being ready to risk a civil war, and denied congressional authority to interfere with the institution of slavery where it was already established. It was in reference to this speech that Clay remarked to Sen. William C. Preston (S.C.), when the latter suggested that the speech might injure Clay's following among Northern Whigs: "I trust the sentiments and opinions are correct; I had rather be right than be President."

1838

ANGLO-U.S. TENSIONS. In the wake of the Panic of 1837, the default of American state governments and corporations on debts owed to British creditors revived Anglo-American differences, aggravated by numerous British travel accounts presenting the U.S. as a nation of boors and blusterers. A powerful voice was added by many of the 56 British authors whose memorial (1 Feb. 1836) asking for copyright protection in the U.S. had been ignored by Congress, and the literary war found the Americans replying in kind. The controversy was heightened by the addition of incidents involving disputed boundary claims and violations of neutrality.

Caroline Affair. With the failure of the insurrection led by William Lyon Mackenzie in upper Canada in the autumn of 1837, the rebel leader and some of his followers, aided by American sympathizers, took refuge on Navy Island on the Canadian side of the Niagara River. Furnished with recruits, provisions, and arms by their Anglophobe U.S. supporters, the insurrectionists proclaimed a provisional government and launched attacks against the Canadian frontier. A small American steamboat, the Caroline, was employed to transport supplies from the U.S. side to Navy Island. On the night of 29 Dec. 1837 a party of Canadian militia crossed the river to the American side, boarded the Caroline, set it afire, and then turned the vessel adrift. In the course of overpowering the crew, the Canadians killed Amos Durfee, a U.S. citizen.

The Caroline affair touched off patriotic indignation and violent Anglophobe sentiment in the U.S. President Van Buren issued a neutrality proclamation (5 Jan.) warning Americans to desist from hostile acts against Great Britain. Militia called out by the president were posted along the Canadian frontier, where Gen. Winfield Scott took immediate command of the U.S. forces. The Canadian rebels abandoned Navy Island (13 Jan.) and surrendered their arms to U.S. militia.

The British Foreign Office ignored the protests made by the State Department concerning the violation of U.S. neutrality. A number of incidents during the course of 1838 kept anti-British feeling at a high pitch. A group of Americans boarded and burned the Canadian steamer *Sir Robert Peel* on the American side of the St. Lawrence (29 May). Along the frontier Americans organized secret Hunters' Lodges for the purpose of overthrowing the British regime in Canada. The U.S. government adopted measures to prevent violation of the frontier. A few parties dispatched by the Lodges penetrated Canada (Nov.–Dec.), but were quickly repulsed or captured. President Van Buren issued a second neutrality proclamation (21 Nov.) and ordered swift action against Americans violating the neutrality laws.

Anglo-U.S. tension lessened during 1839–40, but was renewed by the **McLeod case.** In Nov. 1840, Alexander McLeod, a Canadian deputy sheriff, was arrested in New York state on the charge of having murdered Amos Durfee and participated in the burning of the *Caroline*. He was jailed at Lockport, N.Y., to await trial. The British minister to the U.S. asked (13 Dec. 1840) for McLeod's immediate release. Secretary of State John Forsyth replied (26 Dec. 1840) that the New York courts had exclusive jurisdiction over McLeod. Brought to trial at Utica, N.Y., McLeod was acquitted (12 Oct. 1841). Had he been found guilty, Gov. **William H. Seward** (p. 1149) was prepared to pardon him in order to forestall international complications.

Aroostook "War." The disputed northeastern boundary (between New Brunswick and Maine) had loomed as an Anglo-American issue since 1783, when the peace treaty incorporated a complicated and unsatisfactory provision. The Peace of Ghent did not touch on the question. Shortly after Maine became a state (1820), its legislature, together with that of Massachusetts, disregarded British claims in making land grants to settlers along the Aroostook River. The

U.S. and Great Britain submitted the boundary differences to arbitration by the King of the Netherlands (29 Sept. 1827). His compromise award (10 Jan. 1831) was accepted by Great Britain, but was rejected by the Senate, 21–20 (23 June 1832).

During the winter of 1838–39 Canadian lumberjacks entered the disputed Aroostook region and began lumbering operations. Gov. John Fairfield of Maine requested the legislature (Jan. 1839) to name a land agent and to provide a force for breaking up the Canadian camps. Rufus McIntire, who was appointed land agent with authority to expel the lumberjacks, was seized by the Canadians (12 Feb. 1839). His arrest, and the refusal of the Canadians to leave, marked the beginning of the so-called Aroostook war, an undeclared conflict without bloodshed. Maine and New Brunswick called out their militia. The Nova Scotia legislature made war appropriations. Congress authorized a force of 50,000 men and voted $10 million for a possible emergency.

President Van Buren dispatched Gen. Winfield Scott to the trouble zone. War might have broken out had it not been for the truce (Mar. 1839) Scott arranged between the governor of Maine and the lieutenant governor of New Brunswick. The British agreed to refer the dispute to a boundary commission, and the question was settled by the Webster-Ashburton Treaty (1842).

18 Aug. WILKES EXPEDITION (p. 1184).

1839

13 Nov. LIBERTY PARTY. The entry of the antislavery forces into politics was signalized by the establishment of the Liberty party, which held its founding convention at Warsaw, N.Y., and nominated **James G. Birney,** a native of Kentucky and a former slaveholder, for president, and Thomas Earle (Pa.) for vice-president. These nominations were confirmed at the party's first national convention at Albany (1 Apr. 1840). Liberty party conventions were subsequently held in Ohio and other states in the Northwest. The party was composed of moderate abolitionists who did not share Garrison's opposition to political action. Unlike Garrison, they professed loyalty to the Constitution and did not advocate secession or dissolution of the Union. By virtue of holding the balance of power, the party played an important part in the presidential election of 1844, when it was responsible for the defeat of Clay. In 1848 it combined with the Free-Soil party and helped to defeat the Democratic candidate, Lewis Cass. The party's chief political issue was its stand against the annexation of Texas. Among its leaders were Gerrit Smith (N.Y.) and Salmon P. Chase (Ohio).

1840

4 July. INDEPENDENT TREASURY ACT. Van Buren's scheme to establish federal depositories independent of state banks and private business, set forth in his message (5 Sept. 1837) to a special session of Congress, had the support of the cabinet and of his congressional managers, Sen. Silas Wright and Rep. Churchill C. Cambreleng, both of New York. The plan aroused the bitter opposition of the Whigs under the congressional leadership of Henry Clay and Daniel Webster. While Calhoun and his followers still remained aloof from the Democratic party, they were in agreement with the administration on the Treasury issue, out of fear of the nationalist tendencies of the Whigs.

The independent treasury bill (also known as the subtreasury or divorce bill) was introduced in the Senate, where it passed, 26–20 (4 Oct. 1837), with incorporation of Calhoun's legal-tender amendment. This proviso called for a gradual reduction in the acceptance of notes of specie-paying banks in payment of government dues until 1841, when all payments should be made in legal tender. The amendment was later dropped, and the Senate (with Calhoun voting against the measure) passed the bill, 27–25. The bill was tabled in the House, 120–107 (14 Oct. 1837), and was rejected by that chamber, 125–11 (25 June 1838). Its defeat was caused largely by the split in the Democratic ranks: the conservative Democrats united with the Whig opposition, while the Loco-Focos supported the Van Buren plan.

A technicality that enabled the Democrats to organize the 26th Congress virtually assured its passage. Its enactment witnessed the reunion of the Calhoun wing with the Democratic party. The bill passed the Senate, 24–18 (23 Jan.), and the House, 124–107 (30 June), with Southern states'-rights men joining Northern hard-money Democrats to effect its passage.

The Independent Treasury Act entrusted the government with the exclusive care of its own funds and required the progressive enforcement of the legal-tender clause until all government payments and disbursements should be made in hard money after 30 June 1843. Subtreasuries were established at New York, Boston, Philadelphia, St. Louis, New Orleans, Washington, and Charleston. The act was repealed in 1841.

PRESIDENTIAL CAMPAIGN. When the Whig National Nominating Convention met at Harrisburg, Pa. (4 Dec. 1839), the Whig leaders, under the guidance of Thurlow Weed of New York, were determined to unite on a single candidate. Henry Clay was the leading contender, but his position on some issues, notably the protective tariff, impaired his availability. **William Henry Harrison** of Ohio had no substantial qualifications as a public servant, but he had no important political enemies, enjoyed a reputation as a military hero, and had received an encouraging vote in 1836. Clay had already indicated that in the interest of "union and harmony" he would if necessary defer to another candidate, and it was as the "union and harmony" convention that the Whig gathering went down in history. The convention adopted a rough equivalent of the **"unit rule"** by which the vote of the majority of each delegation was reported as the state's vote. Although Clay led on the 1st ballot, the convention finally nominated Harrison for president and **John Tyler** (Va.) for vice-president. Tyler was a states'-rights adherent who had turned against Jackson during the nullification episode. No platform was adopted. The Whigs, still a coalition rather than an organized political party, counted upon common opposition to the Democrats for their basic appeal.

The Democratic Convention at Baltimore (5 May) agreed on **Van Buren's** renomination, but failed to unite on a candidate for the vice-presidency. Because of strong opposition to the incumbent, Richard M. Johnson, the choice of a vice-presidential candidate was left to the state electors. The Democratic platform declared adherence to strict constructionist doctrine, opposed congressional interference with slavery (thus formally introducing the slavery question into the platform of a major political party), opposed a national bank and internal improvements at federal expense, and affirmed the principles of the Declaration of Independence (as no succeeding Democratic national convention during the pre-Civil War era would do).

Eschewing clear declarations on all leading issues, the Whigs waged their campaign on the basis of personalities. Ammunition for the Whig camp was unwittingly provided by a Democratic newspaper, the Baltimore *Republican*, which derisively remarked (23 Mar.) "that upon condition of his receiving a pension of $2,000 and a barrel of cider, General Harrison would no doubt consent to withdraw his pretensions, and spend his days in a log cabin on the banks of the Ohio." The Whigs turned this remark against their opponents, using the cider and log cabin symbols to present the hero of Tippecanoe as a sturdy son of the frontier and a simple man of the people.

In the rollicking **"Log Cabin and Hard Cider"** campaign that followed, the Whigs cleverly utilized many of the devices that later election contests featured as familiar means of stimulating popular enthusiasm: placards, emblems, campaign hats, effigies, floats, huge rallies, and transportable log cabins with the latchstring hanging out and furnished with coonskins and barrels of cider. The campaign slogan came into use ("Matty's policy, 50 cts. a day and soup; our policy, $2 a day and roast beef"), as well as newspaper advertisements with a political slant. ("The subscriber will pay $5 a hundred for pork if Harrison is elected, and $2.50 if Van Buren is.") The Whigs sang their way through the campaign to the words of "Tippecanoe and Tyler too," with its refrain of "Van, Van is a used up man."

In contrast to the studied simplicity of Harrison, the Whigs pictured Van Buren as an aristocrat of extravagant taste living amid the luxury of "the Palace" (as the Whigs called the White House) and supping with gold spoons. The campaign quickly degenerated into an exhibition of abuse, evasion, misrepresentation, and irrelevancies on a scale unparalleled in U.S. history up to that time. Its special significance, however, lay in its signaling the maturation of the **second party system** in U.S. history.

2 DEC. PRESIDENTIAL ELECTION. Van Buren received 1,128,702 popular votes; **Harrison,** 1,275,017; and the 7,059 votes received by the Liberty party candidate, James G. Birney, were drawn from all of the free states except Indiana. Carrying 19 of the 26 states, **Harrison** won 234 electoral votes, as did **Tyler,** Van Buren, 60. The elections gave the Whigs a congressional majority. The Whig victory was the first time since 1800 that a diffuse coalition defeated an organized political party holding power.

1841

4 MAR. Inauguration of William Henry Harrison, 9th president; John Tyler, vice-president. Harrison's platitudinous inaugural address made it clear that the executive would defer to congressional leadership.

CABINET APPOINTMENTS. Named to office 5 Mar. were Daniel Webster, Secretary of State (a post that had been refused by Henry Clay); Thomas Ewing (Ohio), Secretary of the Treasury; John Bell (Tenn.), Secretary of War; George E. Badger (N.C.), Secretary of the Navy; and John J. Crittenden (Ky.), Attorney General. Francis Granger (N.Y.) was appointed Postmaster General (6 Mar.). All of the cabinet members except Webster and Granger were supporters of Clay.

4 APR. Death of President Harrison, caused by pneumonia. John Tyler became the 10th president, the first vice-president to succeed to that office. A Virginia Democrat of the "old Republican" school, Tyler differed with the Whigs on constitutional principles and practical measures. In the quarrel between president and Congress that ensued, the mi-nority of Whigs that supported Tyler was contemptuously termed "the Corporal's Guard." Tyler issued (9 Apr.) an address to the people indicating his intention of securing changes in the government fiscal structure compatible with the principles of "the fathers of the great Republican school."

7 JUNE. Clay introduced a set of resolutions embodying the essentials of Whig policy. He called for repeal of the Independent Treasury Act, the incorporation of a bank, customs duties designed to provide adequate revenue, and the distribution of the proceeds from the sale of public lands.

9 MAR. AMISTAD CASE. The Supreme Court sustained the lower courts and freed Negroes who in the course of being transported as slaves in Spanish ships mutinied and were captured by a U.S. warship (1839) off Long Island and carried to New London (15 Peters 518).

13 AUG. REPEAL OF THE INDE-PENDENT TREASURY ACT. In order to clear the way for the incorporation of a national bank, the Whigs repealed the Independent Treasury Act. For 5 years thereafter a Whig majority in Congress defeated efforts of Democrats to reestablish the subtreasury system. During this period the management of the public funds was left to the discretion of the Secretary of the Treasury, who used the state banks as depositories. Until 1846 the deposit system of the government was not regulated by law.

16 AUG., 9 SEPT. FISCAL BANK VE-TOES. The Whig program was launched with a bill for incorporating a fiscal agency in the District of Columbia under the name of the Fiscal Bank of the U.S. The projected institution was tantamount to a revival of the 2d Bank of the U.S. Introduced in the Senate (12 June), **the** bill called for a bank capitalized at $30 million and authorized to set up state branches with deposit and discount functions, but only after obtaining the consent of the individual states in which branches were established (to satisfy Tyler's strict constructionist views). But this provision was eliminated, and a substitute measure stipulated that the consent of any state would be assumed unless its legislature registered explicit disapproval. The bill passed the Senate, 26–23 (28 July), and the House, 128–97 (6 Aug.). Tyler vetoed the bill on the grounds of constitutionality and expediency. The Senate (19 Aug.) failed to override the veto.

A second bank bill was formulated to which Tyler, in an interview with Rep. A. H. H. Stuart, a Virginia Whig, lent his apparent approval on condition of certain changes. The bill which was introduced provided for a fiscal corporation capitalized at $21 million. The provision for the establishment of offices only with state consent (one of the conditions Tyler had supposedly indicated as essential) was not included in the bill that passed the House, 125–94 (23 Aug.) and the Senate 27–22 (3 Sept.). The measure was vetoed by Tyler on substantially the same grounds as his veto of the first bill. The Senate (10 Sept.) failed to override his veto.

19 Aug. 2D FEDERAL BANKRUPTCY LAW permitted, with few exceptions, any person to become a voluntary bankrupt, but allowed creditors to proceed against traders; repealed 3 Mar. 1843. During its brief life 33,739 debtors availed themselves of the law; $441 million in debt canceled, while less than $47 million was surrendered by debtors.

11 Sept. CABINET RESIGNATIONS. Angry over what they regarded as a betrayal of faith, all the members of the cabinet except Webster resigned (11 Sept.). All of the departing members (with the exception of Granger) made public statements charging that Tyler had committed himself to support the bank bill. The evidence on the circumstances attending Tyler's second veto is conflicting, but it tends to clear Tyler of charges of duplicity.

Named to the cabinet on 13 Sept. were Walter Forward (Pa.), Secretary of the Treasury; Abel P. Upshur (Va.), Secretary of the Navy; Hugh Swinton Legaré (S.C.), Attorney General; and Charles A. Wickliffe (Ky.), Postmaster General. Upon the death of Legaré (20 June 1843), John Nelson (Md.) was named Attorney General (1 July 1943). On 12 Oct. John C. Spencer (N.Y.) was appointed Secretary of War.

Tyler's administration witnessed frequent cabinet shifts. Spencer was replaced in the War Department by James M. Porter (Pa., 8 Mar. 1843), who in turn was replaced (15 Feb. 1844) by William Wilkins (Pa.). Webster retired as Secretary of State (8 May 1843) and was replaced (24 July 1843) by Abel P. Upshur (Va.), who was succeeded as Secretary of the Navy by David Henshaw (Mass., 24 July 1843). Henshaw was replaced by Thomas W. Gilmer (Va., 15 Feb. 1844). Upshur and Gilmer were killed (28 Feb. 1844) by the explosion of a gun on the warship *Princeton*. John C. Calhoun was appointed Secretary of State (6 Mar. 1844) and John Y. Mason (Va.) was named Secretary of the Navy (14 Mar. 1844). Calhoun's entry into the cabinet marked his final *rapprochement* with the Democratic party, and the rise of Southern influence in shaping Democratic policy.

1842

21–23 Mar. "CREOLE" CASE AND GIDDINGS RESOLUTIONS. The *Creole*, an American brig carying a cargo of slaves, sailed from Hampton Roads,

Va. (27 Oct. 1841), for New Orleans. During the voyage the slaves mutinied, killed a white crew member in taking possession of the ship, and forced the mate to proceed to Nassau in the Bahama Islands. The British authorities at Nassau freed all slaves except actual participants in the revolt, who were held on criminal charges. Secretary of State Webster protested and demanded the return of the slaves as "mutineers and murderers and the recognized property" of U.S. citizens. The British took no immediate steps to satisfy the demand, and the matter was not adjusted until 1855, with an award of $110,330 to the U.S.

Rep. Joshua R. Giddings, a Whig from the Western Reserve district of Ohio, offered a series of resolutions (21–22 Mar.) based on the *Creole* case and directed against slavery and the coastal trade in slaves. The resolutions angered Southern representatives. When a censuring resolution against Giddings was adopted by a substantial House majority (23 Mar.), he resigned from Congress. A majority of more than 3,000 voters returned him to his seat in a special election (Apr.).

9 Aug. WEBSTER-ASHBURTON TREATY. Soon after taking office as Secretary of State, Webster initiated resumption of negotiations with Great Britain for settlement of the northeastern boundary question. A conciliatory atmosphere was created by the replacement (Sept. 1841) of the British government under Lord Melbourne by that headed by Sir Robert Peel. As special minister, Alexander Baring, 1st Lord Ashburton, arrived at Washington in the spring of 1842 and began his informal discussions with Webster on 13 June. Commissioners from the states of Maine and Massachusetts, and, at one critical point, President Tyler, took part in negotiations eventuating in the Webster-Ashburton Treaty.

Under its terms, the controversial northeastern boundary provisions of the Treaty of 1783 were scrapped and the Maine-New Brunswick boundary was fixed along its present line. The U.S. received about 7,000 of the 12,000 square miles of disputed territory, somewhat less than the award made by the King of the Netherlands in 1831. The compromise enabled the British to retain their military route between New Brunswick and Quebec. The claims of Maine and Massachusetts were satisfied in part by a U.S. payment of $150,000 to each state. The boundary line along the northern frontiers of Vermont and New York and thence westward to the Lake of the Woods was based on pre-1774 surveys and adjusted about a half mile north of the 45th parallel, thus leaving the U.S. in possession of its military works under construction at the northern head of Lake Champlain. Provision was made for a boundary commission to survey and mark the line.

Other articles gave the U.S. navigation rights on the St. John River (important for Maine's economy); provided for mutual extradition in cases involving 7 specified nonpolitical crimes; for a cruising convention authorizing the maintenance of joint squadrons for suppressing the slave trade along the African coast. The British without any reciprocal concession agreed to a line between Lake Superior and the Lake of the Woods (which gave the U.S. the Mesabi iron deposits, not discovered until 1866). Through an exchange of notes, Lord Ashburton made an unofficial and carefully guarded apology that disposed of the *Caroline* affair and the McLeod case.

The treaty was approved by the Senate, 39–9 (20 Aug.), and promulgated in Nov. The acceptance of the treaty was accompanied in both the U.S. and Great Britain by the so-called battle of the maps, in which each government answered domestic opposition by pointing to separate and conflicting maps indicating that the concessions were more than fair.

DORR REBELLION. The popular movement within the states to abolish limitations upon the suffrage resulted in serious disturbances in Rhode Island, where the charter granted (1663) by Charles II that served as the state constitution restricted suffrage to freeholders and their eldest sons. This provision deprived more than half of the adult males of voting privileges. When petitions proved ineffective, a committee of the disfranchised called a convention at Providence (Oct. 1841) that framed the "People's Constitution" providing for white manhood suffrage. The instrument was ratified by a majority of the adult male citizens who voted on it (Dec. 1841). In a countermove, the state legislature called a convention at Newport for revising the constitution (Nov. 1841), but the convention's decision to extend the franchise was defeated when the "Landholders' Constitution" was submitted to the vote of the freeholders (Mar.).

Both factions conducted separate elections for the legislature and state officers in the spring of 1842. The opponents of the old constitution chose **Thomas W. Dorr** as governor (18 Apr.). Dorr and his supporters, who controlled northwestern Rhode Island, established a state government basing its authority on the power residing in the people. Dorr was inaugurated at Providence. The old charter party reelected Gov. **Samuel W. King,** inaugurated at Newport. The conservative legislature of the King regime declared the Dorr party in a state of insurrection, imposed martial law, and called out the state militia to sustain its authority.

With Rhode Island under a dual government, both Dorr and King called upon President Tyler for help. Tyler replied in a letter to King which, despite its conciliatory tenor, made it clear that the national government would intervene if necessary on behalf of the old charter government to enforce Art. IV, Sect. 4 of the federal Constitution.

When the Dorr party undertook military preparations, President Tyler issued instructions for the employment of federal troops in support of state militia if circumstances required such action. The rebellion crumbled after the Dorrites made an unsuccessful attempt (18 May) to seize the Rhode Island state arsenal. After fleeing the state, Dorr returned and gave himself up to the authorities. He was tried and sentenced (25 June 1844) to life imprisonment, but amnestied and released in 1845. Meanwhile, a new constitution incorporating liberalized suffrage provisions was adopted (Apr. 1843). The suit arising from the contest of the 2 governments within the state led to the Supreme Court opinion (1849) in *Luther* v. *Borden* (p. 668).

31 Mar. CLAY'S RESIGNATION. The defeat of the Whigs in the midterm congressional elections enabled the Democrats to take control of the House. With the failure of the Whig program in Congress, Henry Clay, the chief proponent of party policy, resigned from the Senate to devote himself to consolidating the Whig party in preparation for the campaign of 1844. Clay took leave of the Senate in a speech that ranks among his most memorable. He was succeeded by John J. Crittenden.

1843

BEGINNINGS OF POLITICAL NATIVISM (also p. 827). The **Native American Association** was formed at

Washington in 1837. In the 1840s a variety of causes, including intensified anti-Catholic feeling and the influx of Irish immigrants, led to the establishment (June) of the **American Republican** party at New York. Its platform stressed opposition to voting and officeholding privileges for Catholics and foreigners. Nativist elements in New York and elsewhere frequently combined with the Whigs against the Democrats. The controversy was heightened by the public-school issue in New York state, where the Catholic demand for public funds to aid their parochial schools resulted in a movement to restrict voting privileges. Protestant resentment was also stirred by Catholic opposition to the reading of the King James version of the Bible in the public schools. In the local elections in New York City (1844), the American Republican party formed a coalition with the Whigs and succeeded in electing a nativist mayor.

The culmination of nativist agitation during the 1840s came at Philadelphia, where an American Republican Association was formed in Apr. 1844. A series of violent armed clashes between Protestants and Catholics (6–8 May, 5–8 July 1844) resulted in the death of about 20 persons and the injury of about 100. State militia were called out to suppress the disorders. The nativists called their first national convention at Philadelphia (5–7 July 1845) and adopted the name **Native American** party. Its platform called for changes in the naturalization laws. Nativist agitation was revived in the 1850s, which saw the rise of the **Know-Nothing (American)** party.

1844

OREGON DISPUTE. The Anglo-American Convention of 1818, which established a 10-year joint occupation of the disputed Oregon country, was renewed (6 Aug. 1827) for an indefinite term with the stipulation that on a year's notice the occupation agreement might be unilaterally terminated. The Oregon country lay between the Rocky Mountains and the Pacific Ocean, and between the 42nd parallel and 54°40'. The treaties which the U.S. concluded with Spain (1819) and Russia (1824) narrowed the Oregon controversy to 2 parties: the U.S. and Great Britain. The disputed area was the region north of the Columbia River and south of the 49th parallel.

U.S. Claims were based on (1) explorations of Capt. Robert Gray, who in 1792 discovered and entered the mouth of the Columbia River, which was named for his vessel; (2) Lewis and Clark expedition (1803–06); (3) rights to the Pacific coast north of the 42nd parallel, under the treaty with Spain, and to the coast south of 54°40', under the treaty with Russia; (4) the fur-trading post of Astoria, established (1811) at the mouth of the Columbia by **John Jacob Astor** (p. 976), head of the Pacific Fur Co., as the first permanent settlement along the lower Columbia; and (5) actual occupation by American settlers (including Methodist and Presbyterian missionaries), who after 1841 came to Oregon in growing numbers, establishing settlements in the Willamette Valley south of the Columbia River. By 1845 5,000 Americans were in the region below the Columbia River.

British Claims were based on (1) Nootka Sound Treaty (1790), under which Spain relinquished some of her claims; (2) voyage of Capt. Cook (1778); (3) explorations of Capt. George Vancouver (1792), who ascended part of the Columbia River shortly after its discovery by Gray, and of Sir Alexander Mackenzie (1793), who ascended part of the Fraser River; (4) fur-trading activities of the Hudson's Bay Co., which consolidated its power by absorbing (1821) the North West Co., an organization that earlier had amalgamated all British and Canadian fur-trading operations; and (5) establishment (1805) by the North West Co. of Ft. McLeod, the first settlement in the Oregon interior.

Beginning with the administration of John Quincy Adams, the U.S. government made repeated offers to fix the Oregon boundary along the 49th parallel. British refusal stemmed from unwillingness to sacrifice the trade of the Columbia River basin, access to a port on the Strait of Juan de Fuca, and the navigation of Puget Sound. The question did not cause serious controversy until the American population in Oregon began to increase rapidly.

A Senate bill introduced (16 Dec. 1841) by Lewis F. Linn (Mo.) provided for the militarization of the overland route from Missouri to Oregon and for land grants to male immigrants over 18 years of age. The measure, which was before Congress, 1841–43, never became law, but encouraged immigration to Oregon and increased British apprehensions. Petitions for the establishment of a territorial government were submitted to Congress by the people of Oregon and by state legislatures. A meeting of Oregon settlers at Champoeg (5 July 1843) adopted a constitution for a **provisional government** to serve until the U.S. extended its jurisdiction over Oregon. In the same month a Cincinnati convention held on the Oregon issue adopted a resolution calling for 54°40′ as the American line.

Great Britain responded to U.S. offers by indicating her readiness to make a boundary adjustment along the Columbia River line. By the close of 1844 the development of serious Anglo-U.S. friction was intensified by the injection of the Oregon question into the presidential campaign. Great Britain, rebuffed by the U.S. on an offer to reopen negotiations, took a more determined stand.

TEXAS QUESTION. Largely because of the opposition of the antislavery forces, the ambition of the Texas Republic under President Sam Houston for immediate annexation to the U.S. was not fulfilled. The abolitionists viewed the Texas settlements and revolution as a conspiracy of slaveholders. Northern Whigs opposed annexation from fear that several slave states would be carved from Texas territory. Resolutions calling for annexation adopted by Southern state legislatures were answered by opposing resolutions from Northern legislatures.

Rebuffed by the U.S., Texas formally withdrew its offer of annexation (12 Oct. 1838) and under **Mirabeau B. Lamar,** who succeeded Houston as president (Dec. 1838), proceeded to shape a foreign policy designed to assure its complete and permanent independence. Texas dispatched diplomatic agents to Europe, concluded treaties with France (1839), Holland and Belgium (1840), and Great Britain (1840), and secured loans for a program of commercial development. The British favored an independent Texas as a balance of power in North America, a buffer state against U.S. expansion, a valuable source of cotton production, and a duty-free market for British manufactured goods. In the lead of British public opinion supporting Texan independence were the abolitionists, who believed that Texas might accede to the abolition of slavery in return for a sizable loan and thus become a base of operations against the institution of slavery in the U.S. South.

Texas, however, never abandoned its willingness to become a part of the U.S. Its ends were furthered by British moves and American alarm after Houston returned to power (Dec. 1841). The Mexicans invaded Texas in 1842. In mid-

1843 the British and French ministers to Mexico arranged a truce between that country and Texas. Shortly afterward, Isaac Van Zandt, Texan minister at Washington, was instructed to inform the U.S. authorities that the Texans were no longer interested in discussing annexation. The prospect of a close understanding between Texas and the 2 European powers caused anxiety at Washington and stirred fresh interest in annexation. Southern misgivings were increased by the circulation of reports that the British intended to use their influence to abolish slavery in Texas.

On 23 Aug. 1843, President Santa Anna notified the U.S. that the Mexican government would "consider equivalent to a declaration of war against the Mexican Republic the passage of an act of the incorporation of Texas in the territory of the United States; the certainty of the fact being sufficient for the immediate proclamation of war. . . ." On 16 Oct. 1843 Secretary of State Upshur informed Van Zandt that the U.S. was prepared to reopen negotiations for the annexation of Texas. Houston proceeded with caution, aware that if the treaty met rejection by the U.S. Senate, Texas would risk losing the support of Great Britain. He accordingly declined Upshur's proposal, thereby spurring the Secretary of State to make further efforts. On 16 Jan. Upshur informed William S. Murphy, the U.S. chargé in Texas, that "a clear constitutional majority of two-thirds" of the Senate favored the measure, and instructed Murphy to convey this information to Houston.

ANNEXATION OF TEXAS. On the basis of such assurance, Houston decided to accept the U.S. offer on condition that after the signing of the treaty but before its ratification the U.S. would take steps to furnish military and naval protection along the Gulf of Mexico and the south-western border as a safeguard against a Mexican attack. With the death of Secretary Upshur, his successor, John C. Calhoun, successfully completed the negotiations. The treaty, signed 12 Apr., provided for the annexation of Texas "subject to the same constitutional provision" as other U.S. territories, the surrender by Texas of its public lands to the U.S., and the assumption by the U.S. of the Texan debt to a maximum of $10 million.

The treaty was submitted to the Senate (22 Apr.), accompanied by a message from President Tyler urging annexation on the ground of broad national interest. Tyler made brief reference to the security of the Southern states and to the abolitionist danger posed by British interference in Texas. These remarks, coupled with Calhoun's note (18 Apr.) to the British minister vigorously defending the institution of slavery, strengthened the forces opposed to annexation. The abolitionists pointed to Calhoun's letter as proof of a slaveholders' conspiracy and succeeded in arousing Northerners who had been indifferent to annexation. The Senate rejected the treaty, 35–16 (8 June). Tyler then made a move to incorporate Texas in the Union by a joint resolution of both houses of Congress, but the measure failed to come to a vote by the time Congress adjourned (17 June). Meanwhile, Tyler carried out his pledge to send naval vessels to the Gulf of Mexico and troops to the Texas border. On 12 Dec. **Anson Jones** succeeded Houston as president of Texas.

Texas annexation, together with the Oregon dispute, became the leading issue in the presidential campaign. The British continued to use their diplomatic resources to keep Texas out of the Union. But British success (May 1845) in winning Mexican recognition of Texan independence came too late, for by then the U.S. Congress had acted and the Texans had decided to enter the Union.

27 Apr. CLAY–VAN BUREN LETTERS. Tyler's alienation of the Democratic party and his firm opposition to the Whig program made him a president without a party, leaving him without vital political support for renomination. Van Buren, still the political heir of Jackson, loomed as almost certain choice for the Democratic nomination in 1844. In May 1842, Van Buren visited Clay at Ashland, Ky. It was generally surmised that the 2 rivals reached an agreement to bar the Texas annexation issue from the next presidential campaign.

Van Buren's Southern opponents, aware of his hostility to annexation, obtained a letter from Jackson (12 Feb. 1843) favoring the acquisition of Texas. The letter, published in the Richmond *Enquirer* (22 Mar.), posed an immediate and crucial test for Van Buren on the eve of the Democratic National Convention. Approval of annexation would cost him his Democratic following in the key state of New York, where a party schism had begun to develop over the slavery question; rejection of the policy would lose him the Southern vote.

On 27 Apr. Van Buren and Clay published separate letters opposing the immediate annexation of Texas. Van Buren's letter (dated 20 Apr.), which appeared in the Washington *Globe*, maintained that annexation would probably involve the U.S. in an unjustifiable war with Mexico. His declaration, which incensed Southerners and alienated Jackson, was instrumental in depriving Van Buren of the Democratic nomination. When Jackson learned of the letter, he indicated that the candidate "should be an annexation man" and should be "from the Southwest," and finally threw his support to James K. Polk.

Clay's **"Raleigh letter"** (dated 17 April) was published in the *National Intelligencer*. It declared that the annexation of Texas without the consent of Mexico would lead to war with that nation, and was "dangerous to the integrity of the Union . . . and not called for by any general expression of public opinion." After winning the Whig nomination for the presidency, Clay publicly qualified his position in the **"Alabama letters"** addressed to Stephen F. Miller of Tuscaloosa, Ala. In the first letter (1 July), Clay stated that while he was not opposed to annexation, he believed that the unyielding attitude of the abolitionists made the integrity of the Union the paramount consideration. His second letter (27 July) asserted that "far from having any personal objection to the annexation of Texas, I should be glad to see it, without dishonor, without war, with the common consent of the Union, and upon just and fair terms. I do not think that the subject of slavery ought to affect the question, one way or the other." His explanation further embittered Northern antislavery sentiment and, derisively quoted out of context, was used by the Democrats to picture Clay as an opportunist.

3 July. TREATY OF WANG HIYA negotiated by **Caleb Cushing** (p. 1008) with Commissioner Extraordinary Tsiyeng, representing the Emperor of China, opened 5 Chinese ports to American merchants, insured extraterritorial legal rights for Americans living in China, and gave U.S. most-favored-nation treatment.

PRESIDENTIAL CAMPAIGN. The national convention of the Liberty party met at Buffalo, N.Y. (30 Aug. 1843), and unanimously nominated **James G. Birney** for president and **Thomas Morris** (Ohio) for vice-president. Its platform, consisting of 21 planks based almost entirely on the salvery question, made no direct reference to the annexation of Texas, but denounced the extension of slave territory.

The Whig National Convention met at Baltimore (1 May) and unanimously nominated **Henry Clay** for president; **Theodore Frelinghuysen** (N.J.) was chosen for vice-president. The Whig platform, a general statement of party principles, advocated a single term for the presidency, made no reference to the Texas issue, and was silent on the question of a national bank.

The Democratic National Convention, which assembled at Baltimore (27 May), was the first convention whose proceedings were reported by telegraph (over a line connecting Baltimore and Washington). Van Buren led on the 1st ballot, but Southern insistence on the application of the "two-thirds rule" disposed of his bid. On the 9th ballot (29 May), and on the 2nd ballot after his name had been placed before the convention, **James K. Polk** (Tenn., p. 1130) was unanimously chosen as the presidential candidate. Silas Wright (N.Y.), a Van Burenite and antislavery man, was chosen for vice-president. He declined the nomination, and the convention chose instead **George M. Dallas** (Pa.). Polk, first "dark horse" nominee in the history of the presidency, had the support of Andrew Jackson. The suggestion for his nomination came from the historian George Bancroft, a member of the Massachusetts delegation, in consultation with Gideon J. Pillow (Tenn.).

Robert J. Walker (Miss.), chairman of the executive committee of the Democratic party, formulated an expansionist platform designed to appeal to Northerners and Southerners alike. Its main plank declared that "our title to the whole of the Territory of Oregon is clear or unquestionable; that no portion of the same ought to be ceded . . . exation of any other power; an . . . tion of Oregon

Texas at the earliest practicable period are great American measures, which this Convention recommends to the cordial support of the Democracy of the Union." The Democratic slogan of "54°40′ or Fight" (variously attributed to Sen. William Allen [Ohio] and Samuel Medary, editor of the *Ohio Statesman*) was used to court Northern voters on the Oregon issue and to offset the Whigs' scornful query, "Who is James K. Polk?"

The Tyler Democrats also assembled at Baltimore on 27 May, to the rallying cry of "Tyler and Texas." Although the delegates represented every state in the Union, they had an estimated total following of only 150,000. **Tyler,** who had unsuccessfully attempted to establish a third party by the use of patronage, accepted (30 May) the nomination. When it became clear that he could not hope to win over the annexationist element, he withdrew (20 Aug.) after reaching an understanding with Robert J. Walker, and brought his supporters into the Democratic fold. Tyler thus became the first president who failed to stand for a 2d term.

4 Dec. PRESIDENTIAL ELECTION resulted in a close popular vote: **Polk,** 1,337,243; Clay, 1,299,068; Birney, 62,300. Polk's victory hinged upon the electoral vote (36) of New York, which Clay lost by 5,080 votes, and where Birney, by an accession of antislavery Whig strength in the western counties, received 15,812 votes. **Polk** received 170 electoral votes, carrying 15 of the 26 states; Clay 105 votes. Had Clay carried New York, he would . . . al votes. . . . been elected president by 7 . . .

. . . 45

23 Jan. By act of Congress, the Tuesday following the first Monday in Nov. was designated the uniform election day for future presidential elections.

1 MAR. ANNEXATION OF TEXAS. When the 2d session of the 28th Congress convened (2 Dec. 1844), Tyler recommended that the Texas treaty be accepted by **joint resolution** of Congress. He made his plea on the grounds that (1) the presidential election had demonstrated that "a controlling majority of the States have declared in favor of immediate annexation," and (2) that strained relations between Texas and Mexico weakened both powers, to the advantage of interested foreign nations (i.e., Great Britain).

A joint resolution (demanding a simple majority in both houses and the signature of the president) obviated the necessity of the two-thirds Senate vote required for ratification. The annexation resolution was passed by the House (25 Jan.), 120–98 (112 Democrats and 8 Southern Whigs in favor, 70 Whigs and 28 Northern Democrats opposed). In the Senate, Thomas Hart Benton posed the constitutional objection that Congress was not authorized to admit a state carved from foreign territory. An amendment offered by Robert J. Walker (Miss.) empowered the president to negotiate a new treaty which might either be ratified by the Senate or adopted by a joint resolution. In this form the measure, which made no reference to securing the consent of Mexico, was passed by the Senate by 27–25 (27 Feb.) and the House (28 Feb.), 132–76, indicating a restoration of party lines. It was the first time that a joint resolution had been employed to appr[..] a treaty or to acquire territory. The [a]ction provided that Texas was to be [ad]mitted to statehood without a prelimina[ry] to state-territorial status; that, with th[e a]d of of Texas, not more than 4 add[..]t states might be formed from its territo[..] that Texas was to retain her public lands, but pay her own debt; and that the

Missouri Compromise line of 36°30' was to be extended to Texas territory.

Great Britain and France succeeded (Mar.–May) in inducing Texas and Mexico to sign the preliminaries of a treaty whereby Mexico would recognize the independence of Texas if the latter should promise to relinquish annexation. These negotiations were quickly abandoned by Texas after the Lone Star Republic received news of the congressional action. A special session of the Texan Congress voted for annexation (23 June); a convention (4 July) called by President Jones accepted the terms; and the act of the convention was ratified by the people of Texas (13 Oct.). Texas was admitted to the Union (29 Dec.). A state government was formally installed at Austin on 19 Feb. 1846.

3 MAR. President Tyler vetoed (20 Feb.) a bill that prohibited payment for some naval craft that he had ordered built. The Senate and the House passed the measure over his veto on the last day of his administration, the first time a presidential veto was overriden.

4 MAR. In his inaugural address, Polk reaffirmed the Democratic platform's declaration that the U.S. title to Oregon was "clear and unquestionable" and asserted that the question of Texas annexation belonged "exclusively to the United States and Texas" as the prerogative of 2 independent powers.

10 OCT. Formal opening of the "Naval School" at Ft. Severn, Annapolis, Md. Founded by Secretary of the Navy Bancroft, it became known (1850) as the U.S. Naval Academy.

"BARNBURNERS" AND "HUNKERS" were 2 factions (c.1843 *et seq.*) in the Democratic party in New York state whose electoral vote played a pivotal role [in] the presidential election of 1844. In [..] with the Loco-Focos of the cities, [..]rners" were the radical and reform wing of the party. Leaders: Martin Van Buren and his son, John; Silas Wright; Benjamin F. Butler (1795–1858); and Azariah C. Flagg. Because of their uncompromising determination, the "Barnburners" were thus characterized by their opponents after the Dutch farmer who burned his barn in order to destroy the rats. The conservative "Hunkers" were so called by their antagonists after a corruption of the Dutch word *hunkerer*, meaning a self-seeking person, with particular application to politicians who "hunkered," i.e., "hungered" or "hankered" after office. Leaders: William L. Marcy and Daniel S. Dickinson.

Their initial differences stemmed from local issues, such as internal improvements and the chartering of state banks (both favored by the Hunkers) and the distribution of patronage. After the election of Polk, these disagreements were colored by national issues. The Barnburners opposed the annexation of Texas and the extension of slavery into the territories.

An open political contest between the 2 wings occurred in 1845, when they ran separate candidates for the state legislature in many districts. In Sept. 1847, the Barnburners withdrew from the Democratic state convention at Syracuse after the Hunkers defeated their resolution declaring "uncompromising hostility to the extension of slavery into territory now free." In 1848 the Barnburners seceded from the Democratic national convention and joined the Free-Soilers, whose vote held the balance of power in the presidential election of 1848. The Barnburners later rejoined the Democratic fold, but their antislavery views led them into the Republican party in the mid-1850s.

ANTIRENT WAR, 1839–46, a culmination of agrarian unrest in upstate New York against the perpetual leases dating from the period of Dutch and English rule. The earliest serious disturbances connected with the Antirent War broke out (1839–40) in the manor of Rensselaerswyck in the Albany region when the heirs of Stephen Van Rensselaer precipitated tenant resistance by attempting to collect $400,000 in back rents. The ensuing "**Helderberg War,**" directed against the system of patroonships, was suppressed by militia called out by Gov. William H. Seward. Other revolts occurred in the area south of Albany, where farmers organized secret societies and, disguised as Indians, interfered with or attacked law-enforcement officers (a situation portrayed by James Fenimore Cooper in his novels *Satanstoe* [1845], *The Chainbearer* [1846], and *The Redskins* [1846]). The murder of a deputy sheriff (Aug.) caused Delaware Co. to be placed under martial law. Impact on state politics: Gov. Silas Wright called for legislation (1846) restricting the duration of farm leases and abolishing distress for rent in all new leases. The disturbances led to the adoption of the more liberal constitution of 1846. Perpetual leases were gradually replaced by fee-simple tenure.

2 Dec. "POLK DOCTRINE." In his first annual message to Congress, Polk recommended tariff revision, the restoration of the Independent Treasury, urged Congress to take measures to protect the U.S. claim to the whole of the Oregon country, and proposed abrogation of the convention for joint occupation. Especially significant was his elaboration of the Monroe Doctrine: (1) "The people of *this continent* alone have the right to decide their own destiny." (2) "We can never consent that European powers shall interfere to prevent such a union [of an independent state with the U.S.] because it might disturb the 'balance of power' which they may desire to maintain upon this continent." (3) "No future European colony or dominion shall with our consent be planted or established on any part of the North American continent."

"MANIFEST DESTINY." The earliest known appearance of the phrase occurred in an unsigned editorial article published in the expansionist organ, *The United States Magazine and Democratic Review* (July–Aug.). The article, subsequently attributed to the magazine's founder and editor, **John L. O'Sullivan,** declared that foreign governments were attempting to obstruct the annexation of Texas in order to check "the fulfillment of our manifest destiny to overspread the continent allotted by Providence for the free development of our yearly multiplying millions." The phrase came into vogue after use in an editorial in the New York *Morning News* (27 Dec.) on the Oregon dispute. Its first use in Congress supposedly dates from the speech (3 Jan. 1846) made by Rep. Robert C. Winthrop (Mass.). During the debate on the resolution for terminating the joint occupation of Oregon, Winthrop referred to "the right of our manifest destiny to spread over this whole continent."

BREAK WITH MEXICO. On 28 Mar., soon after the passage of the joint resolution for the annexation of Texas, Mexico broke off diplomatic relations with the U.S. and took steps (June) to increase its armed forces in order to resist annexation. Major grievances: (1) **Boundary disagreements** stemmed from Mexican insistence on the Nueces River as the southwestern line of Texas. Under the treaty of 12 May 1836, which had been rejected by the Mexican government, the Texans laid claim to the Rio Grande as their lower frontier. The view of the U.S. government, as shaped by Secretary of State Buchanan, was that the annexation of Texas had revived legitimate territorial claims west of the Sabine River held by the U.S. before the signing of the Adams-Onís Treaty (1819). (2) **Halting by Mexico of payments** (1843) of more than $2 million in **adjusted damages to U.S. nationals** authorized by the claims conventions of 1839 and 1843 and the commission award of 1840. (3) **Status of California,** where the Mexican government had issued orders for expulsion of U.S. settlers and exclusion of further immigrants. The U.S. government believed that the British were actively engaged in intrigues to take California. For its part Mexico regarded the U.S. annexation of Texas as evidence of insatiable land- and power-hunger, and regarded the Nueces, the Texas boundary when it was part of Coahuila province, as the correct boundary.

Gen. **Zachary Taylor,** in command of the U.S. forces in the Southwest, with headquarters at Ft. Jesup, La., was ordered (28 May) to maintain his troops (known as the "Army of Observation") in a state of readiness for an advance into Texas to be made upon his receipt of official information that it had been invaded after consenting to annexation. On 15 June he was ordered to occupy a point "on or near the Rio Grande" for the defense of the territory of Texas. Taylor advanced into Texas (26 July); established his base (31 July) on the south bank of the Nueces, near Corpus Christi, about 150 miles from the Rio Grande; and suggested (4 Oct.) that if the U.S. contemplated fixing the boundary line along the Rio Grande, an advantage would be secured by advancing to Point Isabel, on the Gulf of Mexico near the mouth of the Rio Grande. By mid-Oct. Taylor had under his command about 3,500 troops, approximately one half the U.S. army.

Taylor was ordered (13 Jan. 1846) to

advance from the Nueces to "positions on or near the left bank" of the Rio Grande, but did not receive his instructions until 3 Feb. and did not begin his advance until 8 Mar. Point Isabel was burned by the Mexicans before Taylor arrived there (24 Mar.). His second in command, Gen. William J. Worth, proceeded to the left (or north) bank of the Rio Grande, opposite Matamoros, where the Mexicans had about 5,700 men. Both sides spent the following month building fortifications. On 12 Apr. 1846, Gen. Pedro de Ampudia, in command of the forces at Matamoros, warned Taylor to retire beyond the Nueces; otherwise, "arms and arms alone must decide the question." Taylor refused to comply, and requested U.S. naval forces to blockade the mouth of the Rio Grande.

SLIDELL MISSION. In Aug. the U.S. received confidential information that the Mexican government was apparently willing to resume diplomatic relations. At the recommendation of Secretary of State Buchanan, President Polk appointed **John Slidell** (La., 1793–1871) to undertake a secret mission to Mexico for the purpose of purchasing Upper California and New Mexico, and adjusting the boundary line to run along the Rio Grande from its mouth to the 32nd parallel and thence westward to the Pacific. Polk, with the unanimous support of his cabinet, was prepared to pay from $15 to $40 million.

John Black, U.S. consul at Mexico City, reported (17 Oct.) that Manuel de Peña y Peña, foreign minister of the Mexican government under President José J. Herrera, had agreed (15 Oct.) to receive a "commissioner" authorized to discuss the Texas boundary issue, on condition that the U.S. squadron off Vera Cruz should be removed. The recall of the naval force was ordered by Commodore David Conner immediately after

he learned that the Mexicans had consented to negotiation.

President Polk and Secretary Buchanan agreed (7 Nov.) to dispatch Slidell at once. Despite the Mexican government's insistence on confining the discussions to the disputed Texas boundary, Slidell received amended instructions (10 Nov.) authorizing the purchase of New Mexico for $5 million and of California for $25 million, in return for Mexican approval of the Rio Grande as the Texas boundary. In addition, the U.S. would assume the claims of its nationals against Mexico. Slidell was accredited as envoy extraordinary and minister plenipotentiary. Meanwhile, Thomas O. Larkin, U.S. consul at Monterey, Calif., was appointed confidential agent (17 Oct.) with instructions to block the attempt by any foreign power to secure California. He was also informed that the U.S. policy envisaged the peaceful acquisition of California with the active support of the settlers, but in a manner that would not give the Mexicans cause for grievance.

When Slidell reached Mexico City (6 Dec.), the nature of his mission had already become known. After some delay caused by Herrera and his cabinet, who refused to accept responsibility in the face of a hostile public opinion, Slidell was informed (16 Dec.) that the Mexican government could not receive him for the following reasons: his mission apparently lacked the consent of Congress; his appointment had not been confirmed by the Senate; and the Mexicans had agreed to receive a commissioner authorized to negotiate the Texas question rather than a minister plenipotentiary empowered to discuss extraneous issues. When Slidell's report reached Washington (12 Jan. 1846), Gen. Taylor was ordered (13 Jan. 1846) to proceed to the Rio Grande.

Slidell's appointment was confirmed by the Senate (20 Jan. 1846). The Mexican government, however, persisted in its refusal to discuss any question other than the Texas boundary. Meanwhile, the Herrera government was overthrown (31 Dec.) by Gen. Mariano Paredes, who assumed the presidency (4 Jan. 1846) with a reaffirmation of Mexico's claim to Texas up to the Sabine River and a declaration of his purpose to defend all territory regarded by him as Mexican. Slidell informed Washington (6 Feb. 1846) that the inflexible attitude of the Mexicans was reinforced by their belief that the U.S. would become involved in war with Great Britain over the Oregon dispute. Upon Slidell's final inquiry (1 Mar. 1846), the Paredes government refused to receive him (12 Mar.), and late in Mar. he requested his passports and left Mexico.

1846

15 JUNE. OREGON SETTLEMENT. In his first annual message to Congress (2 Dec. 1845) Polk claimed the whole of Oregon; recommended ending the Anglo-U.S. convention for joint occupation; called for extension of U.S. jurisdiction over the Oregon settlers, military protection of the Oregon Trail, and the establishment of an Indian agency beyond the Rocky Mountains. His unyielding attitude toward Great Britain was greeted by expansionist cries of "54°40′ or fight!" Strong support of his position came from the states of the Old Northwest, whose prominent Democratic voices in Congress included Sen. **Lewis Cass** (Mich., p. 999) and Rep. **Stephen A. Douglas** (Ill., p. 1015).

The resolution for terminating joint occupation was introduced in the House (5 Jan.) and, after lengthy debate (including a Senate filibuster), was passed

(23 Apr.) in the Senate, 42–10, and in the House, 142–46. The resolution, signed by Polk on 27 Apr., authorized the president to give the required year's notice at his discretion. Polk served notice on 21 May.

Meanwhile, Richard Pakenham, British minister to the U.S., requested (27 Dec. 1845) renewal of the U.S. offer of the 49th parallel as the boundary of Oregon and asked that the question be submitted to arbitration. Polk refused to renew the proposal. Secretary Buchanan (26 Feb.) then informed Louis McLane, U.S. minister at London, that discussions would be reopened if the British took the initiative. There was strong resistance in Great Britain to concession on this score, but a truce in British party politics enabled the new ministry under Lord Russell to adopt a conciliatory approach toward the U.S. Not less important in influencing the British attitude toward the U.S. was consideration of the economic ties between the 2 nations (British Corn Laws repealed 26 June). Lord Aberdeen, British foreign secretary, submitted his proposal in the form of a draft treaty that reached Washington 6 June. Almost at the same time, Aberdeen informed the British minister to Mexico that Great Britain was unwilling to interfere between the U.S. and Mexico.

Because of the uncompromising stand he had taken on the Oregon question, Polk deemed it proper (at the suggestion of the cabinet) to take the unprecedented course of laying the British proposal before the Senate (10 June) for its advice on the matter. The Senate, 37–12 (12 June), advised its acceptance, and ratified it, 41–14 (15 June). Opposition came from expansionist elements in the Old Northwest, who accused Polk of deception and betrayal.

The treaty provided (1) that the

THE OREGON BOUNDARY DISPUTE

boundary between U.S. and British territory in Oregon should be an extension of the existing continental line along the 49th parallel to the middle of the channel between Vancouver Island and the mainland, and thence along a line running southward through Juan de Fuca Strait to the Pacific; (2) for free navigation of the channel and strait by both parties; and (3) free navigation by the British of the Columbia River below the 49th parallel. The water boundary, however, was not finally defined until the arbitration award of 1873.

6 Aug. INDEPENDENT TREASURY ACT. With the defeat of the Whigs in the election of 1844, the Congress organized by the Democrats proceeded to revive the Independent Treasury Act that had been repealed by the Whigs in 1841. The bill was in substance the act of 4 July 1840. Except for changes in the banking structure made during the Civil War, the act served without important change as the basis of the U.S. fiscal system until passage of the Federal Reserve Act (1913). The subtreasuries were not abolished until after the act of 1920.

24 APR.–3 MAY. OPENING SKIR-MISH. Gen. Mariano Arista succeeded Ampudia (24 Apr.) as commander of the Mexican forces at Matamoros, where the Mexicans had established Ft. Paredes. On the opposite bank of the river, Taylor's troops had erected Ft. Texas. Arista had orders (4 Apr.) from the Mexican minister of war authorizing him to attack. Arista notified Taylor (24 Apr.) that he considered hostilities as already begun. Pointing out that he had not committed any actions that could be construed as hostile, Taylor replied that "the responsibility must rest with them who actually commence them."

Arista dispatched a force of 1,600 cavalry under Gen. Anastasio Torrejón to cross the Rio Grande above Matamoros (24 Apr.). A reconnoitering party of 63 dragoons under Capt. Seth Thornton sent out by Taylor on the evening of the same day was surrounded and attacked (25 Apr.). Eleven Americans were killed, 5 wounded, the remainder captured. Upon receiving news of the Mexican attack, Taylor reported to Washington (26 Apr.) that "hostilities may now be considered as commenced." He immediately called upon the governors of Texas and Louisiana for a total of 5,000 volunteers. Taylor marched (1 May) to the relief of his supply base at Point Isabel. The Mexicans crossed the Rio Grande in force (30 Apr.–1 May) and on 3 May laid Ft. Texas (Maj. Jacob Brown commander) under siege.

The War with Mexico, 1846–48

11 MAY. POLK'S WAR MESSAGE. Slidell, reporting to Polk, 8 May, urged prompt action by the U.S. Taylor's report of the skirmish near Matamoros reached Washington Saturday, 9 May. The cabinet, in an evening session, unanimously supported the adoption of war measures. President Polk prepared his war message on Sunday and delivered it at noon on Monday, 11 May. Asserting that the U.S. held legitimate title to the disputed territory beyond the Nueces, Polk declared: "Mexico has . . . shed American blood upon the American soil."

13 MAY. DECLARATION OF WAR ON MEXICO. By 174–14 (11 May) the House of Representatives (29th Congress, 1st sess.) declared that "by the act of the Republic of Mexico, a state of war exists between that government and the United States." All of the opposing votes were cast by Northern representatives. An amendment stating that nothing in the measure should be construed as approval of Polk's course in ordering the military occupation of the disputed territory between the Nueces and the Rio Grande was defeated, 97–27. The House authorized a call for accepting 50,000 volunteers and voted a $10 million appropriation. Voting against this measure were 67 Whigs, foreshadowing the opposition to the administration that would increase as the war progressed. During the discussion of the war measures, an outspoken Whig, Garrett Davis (Ky.), asserted: "It is our own President who began this war."

In the Senate, Calhoun took exception to the preamble of the war declaration. He maintained that while armed clashes had occurred, Congress had not yet recognized a state of war, and so war did not exist "according to the sense of our Constitution." The war declaration, including the preamble, passed the Senate (12 May), 40–2 (both Whigs), with 3 abstentions, including Calhoun.

8–9 MAY. FIRST BATTLES. Battle of Palo Alto. After hastening construction of the defense works at Point Isabel, Taylor, at the head of about 2,300 troops and 200 supply wagons, began (7 May) his return march to Ft. Texas to relieve the besieged force. Midway on the road to Matamoros, near the water hole of Palo Alto, he encountered (8 May) an enemy force of 6,000 placed across the route of march. The engagement began at 2 P.M. and lasted about 5 hours. U.S. infantry broke up a Mexican cavalry attack across the prairie, and the Mexicans were finally repulsed by the superior fire of the U.S. guns, which easily won an artillery duel against the antiquated Mexican pieces. The U.S. losses: 9 killed, 45 wounded; Mexican losses: estimated 300–400. The Mexicans retreated southward, to a natural strong point above Matamoros, in a sunken riverbed or ravine called the Resaca de Guerrero, where a dense growth of chaparral afforded an excellent defensive position.

Battle of Resaca de la Palma. Instead of waiting for reinforcements, Taylor decided to pursue Arista's numerically superior force. At about 2 P.M. on 9 May, U.S. troops advanced to the edge of the Mexican position and occupied a ravine called the Resaca de la Palma.

About 1,700 Americans faced some 5,700 Mexicans in this engagement. Late in the afternoon, the Mexican army collapsed, fleeing across the Rio Grande with the Americans in close pursuit. U.S. losses: 39 killed, 83 wounded; estimated Mexican: 262 killed, 355 wounded, and about 150 captured or missing (in addition to many others lost by drowning during the crossing of the river). News of the battle made "Old Rough and Ready" Taylor a popular hero.

On the evening of 9 May, the siege of Ft. Texas was raised. The position was renamed Ft. Brown in honor of the officer who had commanded its defense. The Mexicans under Arista evacuated Matamoros (17–18 May), Taylor crossed the Rio Grande (18 May) and occupied the town.

MILITARY BALANCE SHEET. Mexican. At the outset of the war, the Mexican army had an initial numerical superiority. Its forces consisted of about 32,000 men, but the troops were defective in training, discipline, and equipment (most of its artillery pieces were obsolete and unreliable). It is estimated that during the war the peak strength of the Mexican army never exceeded 36,000 men. The officers were of a generally low quality (except for the engineers, who showed great skill in building entrenchments and fortifications), with a superabundance of high-ranking officers. The Mexicans had the advantage of fighting on familiar ground where the great distances involved afforded them a high degree of mobility.

U.S. At the outset of the war, the authorized U.S. regular army strength was 8,613, but the actual strength was 7,365 (8 regiments of infantry, 4 of artillery, 2 of dragoons). To fill the ranks, the government relied chiefly on short-term enlistments by volunteers (highly undependable). Six- and 12-month volunteers were the rule, and not until 12 Jan. 1847 did Congress enact legislation authorizing 5-year enlistments. Total U.S. force employed during the war, including about 31,000 regulars and marines: c.104,000. Chief U.S. disadvantages: (1) inadequate transportation and communication (telegraph not yet applied to military purposes); (2) poor provisions for health and sanitation (percentage of deaths caused by disease was more than 10% of total enrollment); (3) friction among the generals, and between them and the administration. Both Taylor and Gen. Winfield Scott were Whigs, and did not have the full confidence of a Democratic president and his cabinet. Scott was commanding general of the army, but because of strained relations with Polk and Marcy, was not permitted to depart for Mexico until late in 1846.

The Mexican campaigns gave U.S. officers who had never handled units larger than companies or battalions an opportunity to work with regiments and brigades. The war was valuable for its schooling of junior officers who later saw service as army or corps commanders with either side during the Civil War. Among those who later held commands in the Union armies were Lt. Ulysses S. Grant, Lt. William T. Sherman, Lt. George G. Meade, Lt. Joseph Hooker, Lt. George B. McClellan, Lt. John Pope, Lt. George H. Thomas, Lt. William B. Franklin, and Capt. Samuel P. Heintzelman. Those who afterward served with the Confederate forces included Capt. Robert E. Lee, Lt. Thomas Jonathan Jackson, Lt. Pierre G. Beauregard, Col. Albert Sidney Johnston, Lt. Col. Joseph E. Johnston, Lt. James Longstreet, Lt. Braxton Bragg, Lt. Richard S. Ewell, Lt. Daniel H. Hill, and Capt. William J. Hardee.

CAMPAIGN PLANS. Despite months of tension preceding the outbreak of hostilities, no military plans had been drawn up by the War Department. Within 2 days after declaration of war, Col. (later Gen.) **Stephen Watts Kearny** (1794–1848), commanding a cavalry regiment at Ft. Leavenworth, was ordered to lead the "Army of the West" (consisting of his regular force and a body of Missouri volunteers) on an expedition to New Mexico and to occupy its capital, Santa Fe. Commodore **David Conner** was ordered to blockade the enemy ports on the Gulf of Mexico, while Commodore

John D. Sloat was ordered to blockade the Mexican ports on the Pacific and to seize and hold San Francisco Bay. Additional instructions (3 June) authorized Kearny to take possession of California in conjunction with anticipated naval support from Sloat.

President Polk, in conference (14 May) with Secretary of War Marcy and Gen. Scott, formulated a plan of campaign, with the first major blow to be struck against the sparsely populated northern provinces of Mexico. At the urging of Scott, and after delays caused by friction between him and the administration, agreement was reached (20 Oct.–18 Nov.) on a joint army-navy expedition against Vera Cruz as the chief military objective. Gen. Scott was placed in command of the operation, which called for a landing at Vera Cruz, a march through the Mexican interior, and the seizure of Mexico City.

7 JULY–6 DEC. MISSION TO SANTA ANNA. Col. A. J. Atocha, a U.S. citizen of Spanish birth and a friend of Santa Anna (in exile in Cuba), advised Polk (Feb.) that in return for $30 million Santa Anna would arrange that the U.S. would get the Rio Grande as the southwestern boundary of Texas and that the boundary line of California would run through San Francisco Bay. Santa Anna advised Commander Alexander Slidell Mackenzie (7 July) that he would cooperate with the U.S., even give military advice. Accordingly, he was permitted to pass through the blockade, arrived at Vera Cruz (16 Aug.), and then proceeded to denounce the treachery of former President Herrera in attempting to negotiate with the U.S. He replied (19 Sept.) unsatisfactorily to Secretary Buchanan's peace feeler (19 Sept.). On 6 Aug. Paredes was deposed, Gen. Mariano Salas became acting president, and Santa Anna led (28 Sept.) an expeditionary force northward from Mexico City to

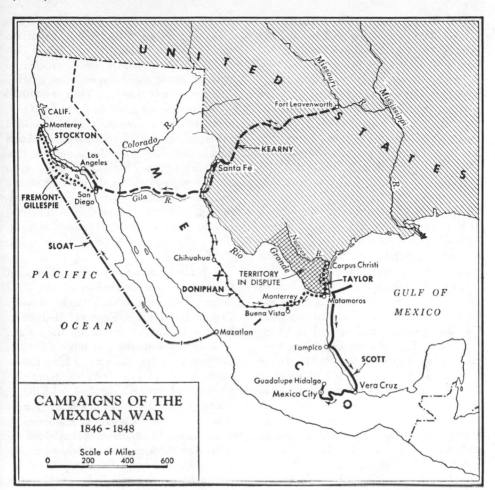

CAMPAIGNS OF THE
MEXICAN WAR
1846 - 1848

Scale of Miles
0   200   400   600

oppose Taylor. His election as president
by the Mexican Congress (6 Dec.) ended
hopes of early peace.

CONQUEST OF CALIFORNIA. Earlier History. Not until after 1840 did
the American settlement of the Mexican
province of California become numerically significant. The first important increase came with the colonization (1843)
of the San Joaquin Valley. By the outset
of 1846 there were approximately 500
American traders and settlers along the
500 miles of coast from Sonoma to San
Diego, c.8,000–12,000 Mexicans of
Spanish descent, and c.24,000 Indians.

The weak government of the province
was made even more vulnerable by the
conflict of authority between Pío Pico,
provincial governor at Los Angeles, and
Gen. José Castro, military commandant
at Monterey. Acting on the mistaken
belief that the U.S. and Mexico were at
war, and that a British fleet was threatening to take possession of California,
Commodore **Thomas ap Catesby Jones**
proceeded from the Peruvian coast and
landed a U.S. naval force at Monterey,
where he seized the public buildings and
raised the U.S. flag (20 Oct. 1842).
Informed by Thomas O. Larkin, U.S.

consul at Monterey, that relations between Mexico and the U.S. were still
normal, Jones hauled down the flag (21
Oct. 1842). His act was disavowed by
President Tyler, and reparation and
apologies were made to the Mexican
government. On 17 Oct. 1845 Polk appointed Larkin confidential agent to
induce the California settlers to enter the
Union or establish an independent state
under U.S. protection. He learned of the
appointment 17 Apr. 1846.

10 JUNE–5 JULY. Bear Flag Revolt.
Leading his third surveying expedition
to the West (May 1845 *et seq.*), Capt.
John Charles Frémont (p. 1033) reached
Monterey (27 Jan.). With the apparent
permission of Castro, he established his
camp in the Salinas Valley. When Castro
warned him (3 Mar.) to quit the area,
his expedition erected breastworks atop
Gavilan Mountain and hoisted the U.S.
flag. In the face of a superior force, Frémont decided to withdraw (9 Mar.) and
marched to the north. He had reached
the edge of Klamath Lake, on the Oregon frontier, when he was overtaken (9
May) by Marine Lt. Archibald H. Gillespie, who conveyed to him dispatches
and correspondence. Whether Frémont
received from Gillespie secret verbal instructions to precipitate a revolt of the
American settlers against Mexican authority has not been established, but he
returned south and helped provoke resistance, at a time when the Pico-Castro
feud was brought to a head by news of
the revolution in Mexico (Dec. 1845)
that deposed Herrera and installed
Paredes as head of the government.
Castro announced (April) his support
of Paredes; Pico called a general convention (scheduled for 15 June at Santa
Barbara) to establish California as an
independent state under the protection of
a foreign nation. Castro retaliated by
dispatching an armed expedition to Los
Angeles, seat of the Pico regime.

A party of U.S. settlers in the Sacra-

mento Valley attacked a section of Castro's expedition (10 June). Another
group, led by William B. Ide, seized Sonoma (14 June) and issued a proclamation declaring the independence of the
American settlements. This so-called
Bear Flag Revolt takes its name from the
standard of the "Republic of California"
raised at Sonama. Designed by William
Todd, this flag bore the name of the
republic, a grizzly bear, and a star, on a
field of white cloth. On 25 June, Frémont
arrived at Sonoma, where he identified
himself with the insurrection. A meeting
of the settlers (5 July) chose him to
direct the affairs of the "Republic of
California."

**7 JULY–17 AUG. Naval Expedition to
California.** The commander of the U.S.
naval force along the Pacific Coast,
Commodore **John D. Sloat** (1781–1867),
learned (17 May) of the opening skirmish of the war along the Rio Grande,
but took no action because of his written
instructions (24 June 1845) to avoid aggressive action and the lack of official
confirmation. When informed (7 June)
that Commodore Conner had blockaded
Vera Cruz, Sloat sailed for California
from the Mexican port of Mazatlán (8
June). He reached Monterey (2 July),
sent a force ashore (7 July), raised the
U.S. flag, and proclaimed California to
be a part of the U.S. On 9 July, under
Sloat's orders, Commander John B.
Montgomery seized San Francisco and
Lt. James W. Revere occupied Sonoma.
The Stars and Stripes replaced the Bear
Flag. Shortly afterward, a U.S. naval
party took possession of Sutter's Fort on
the Sacramento River.

In face of the common enemy, Castro
and Pico submerged their differences and
prepared their combined forces for a
stand at Los Angeles. Sloat, who was in
ill health, was replaced (23 July) by
Commodore **Robert F. Stockton** (1795–
1866), who issued a proclamation condemning Mexican resistance. The Cali-

fornia Battalion was organized (24 July) under Frémont, given the rank of major. Stockton's naval and military force occupied Santa Barbara and took Los Angeles (13 Aug.). Stockton issued a proclamation (17 Aug.) declaring the annexation of California by the U.S. and establishing a new regime with himself as governor. Frémont was named military commandant in the north and Gillespie in the south.

22–30 SEPT. Mexican Revolt. Immediately after Stockton reported to the Navy Department (22 Aug.) that "peace and harmony" had been restored in California, a Mexican revolt against the U.S. authorities broke out (22–30 Sept.), and the insurgents, under the leadership of Capt. José Maria Flores, drove the Americans from Los Angeles, Santa Barbara, San Diego, and other points. By 29 Oct., when Flores was installed as governor and military commandant, all of California south of San Luis Obispo was in the hands of the Mexicans. Meanwhile, the expeditionary force under Kearny, which had been reduced in the belief that the conquest of California had been consolidated, was headed toward San Diego.

2 AUG.–13 JAN. 1847. Kearny's Expedition. After a month's march from Ft. Leavenworth, the "Army of the West" under Kearny with a force of 1,700 reached Bent's Ft. (22–25 July) at the junction of the Arkansas River and the Santa Fe Trail, and he issued a proclamation (31 July) to the people of New Mexico declaring that he was entering the province "for the purpose of seeking union with and ameliorating the conditions of its inhabitants," and on 1 Aug. dispatched a letter to Gov. Manuel Armijo warning against resistance and pledging protection to those who cooperated.

Kearny's force began (2 Aug.) its march through the desert country, proceeding along the Arkansas to the mouth of the Timpas and thence southwest to the mountains, where the troops negotiated the Raton Pass (elevation, 8,560 ft.). Kearny reached Las Vegas (15 Aug.) and proclaimed New Mexico to be part of the U.S. The estimated 4,000 Mexican troops assembled at the Apache Canyon dispersed without offering battle, thus terminating all enemy resistance in the province (an uprising by the Mexicans during the winter of 1846–47 was suppressed by troops commanded by Col. Sterling Price, who ended all organized resistance by investing Taos, 4 Feb. 1847). On 18 Aug., after marching 29 miles in less than a day, Kearny's troops occupied Santa Fe. Kearny issued a proclamation absolving the inhabitants of their allegiance to Mexico. After establishing a temporary territorial government under Gov. Charles Bent, Kearny left for California (25 Sept.) with 300 dragoons.

En route he encountered (6 Oct.) Kit Carson, bound for Washington with a dispatch from Frémont announcing the occupation of California. Kearny sent back 200 of his men. With the remaining 100 he crossed the Colorado (25 Nov.); entered Southern California, where the Flores insurrection against the U.S. occupation was in progress; and defeated (6 Dec.) a Mexican force at the village of **San Pascual.** U.S. losses: 18 dead, 13 wounded. Kearny reached San Diego 12 Dec. His subsequent operations under the command of Stockton secured the reconquest of California. Stockton and Kearny left San Diego (29 Dec.) with a mixed force of 559 dragoons, sailors, marines, and volunteers, and advanced northward across the plain to Los Angeles, which was taken (10 Jan. 1847) after 2 brief clashes with the enemy along and above the San Gabriel River (8, 9 Jan. 1847). These were the concluding hostilities of the war in California. The remnants of the Mexican forces, under Andres Pico in the San Fernando Valley, capitulated to Frémont and signed (13 Jan. 1847) the **Treaty of Cahuenga,** which gave them generous terms.

KEARNY-STOCKTON AFFAIR grew out of a conflict of instructions concerning the establishment of a civil government in California. Stockton, following to the letter the Navy Department orders to Sloat, contested Kearny's right to organize a new territorial government, suspended Kearny from all command other than that over his small force of dragoons, and appointed Frémont governor (16 Jan. 1847). Kearny, after warning Frémont that he was guilty of disobedience to his superior officer, returned to San Diego. The arrival of fresh instructions (13 Feb. 1847) gave Kearny the duty of establishing a new government. He issued a proclamation setting up a provisional government with its capital at Monterey. At Los Angeles, however, Frémont persisted in executing his authority as governor and refused to carry out orders from Gen. Kearny. The controversy was prolonged until Kearny named Col. Richard B. Mason governor of California and, together with Stockton and Frémont, started out (31 May 1847) for Washington.

Frémont was tried by a court-martial (Nov. 1847–Jan. 1848) on charges of mutiny, disobedience, and prejudicial conduct; found guilty on all counts; and sentenced to dismissal from the service. President Polk approved the sentence (except for the charge of mutiny) and remitted the penalty with instructions to restore Frémont to duty. Frémont, however, resigned from the army. The affair precipitated open opposition between the Polk administration and Frémont's father-in-law, Sen. Thomas Hart Benton.

8 AUG. WILMOT PROVISO. The prospect of acquiring additional territory as a result of the Mexican War precipi-

tated a far-reaching congressional debate occasioned by the Wilmot Proviso, introduced in the House as an amendment to the administration bill for a $2 million appropriation to facilitate negotiations with Mexico for territorial adjustments. Polk's request (known as the "Two Million Bill") was encouraged by the discussions with Santa Anna, which at that time seemingly augured a speedy peace settlement.

The Wilmot Proviso stated that "as an express and fundamental condition" to the acquisition of any territory from Mexico by the U.S. "by virtue of any treaty which may be negotiated between them, and to the use by the Executive of the moneys herein appropriated, neither slavery nor involuntary servitude shall ever exist in any part of said territory, except for crime, whereof the party shall first be duly convicted."

The proviso was drafted and introduced by **David Wilmot** (1814–68), a Democrat from northeastern Pennsylvania, previously a Polk supporter (some authorities credit the original proposal to Jacob Brinkerhoff [Ohio], a Van Buren Democrat).

Administration forces tried to amend the Wilmot Proviso by limiting its operation to territory north of the Missouri Compromise line. This attempt was defeated by a House vote, 89–54, and the proviso was adopted (8 Aug.), 87–64. The bill was lost in the Senate (10 Aug.) when discussion was terminated by the adjournment of the 1st session of the 29th Congress.

Polk's supporters in the House introduced a similar appropriation measure (8 Feb. 1847) raising the sum to $3 million. The more pronounced slavery-exclusion clause of a previous bill moved (3 Jan. 1847) by Preston King, a New York Democrat, was adopted and introduced by Wilmot in place of his original proposal. In this form, the Wilmot Proviso was passed as an amendment to the "Three Million Bill," 115–106, and the amended bill passed, 115–105 (15 Feb. 1847). In the Senate, which drew up its own bill, an attempt to add the Wilmot Proviso was defeated, 31–21, and the measure passed, 29–24 (1 Mar. 1847). The Senate bill was taken up in the House in committee of the whole, and was passed, 115–81 (3 Mar.).

In the heated debate in both houses Democrats defended the war as a just one; Whigs attacked it as an expansionist drive for territorial spoils, and accused the president of having initiated the war in violation of the Constitution.

19 Feb. 1847. Calhoun Resolutions. Southern Democrats and their Northern allies united in opposing the proviso as an unnecessary agitation of the slavery question and a threat to Southern rights. The defense of the Southern position was set forth by Calhoun in 4 resolutions on the slavery question (19 Feb. 1847). He asserted that the territories of the U.S. were the joint and common property of the states; that Congress, as the agent of the states, had no right to make any law discriminating between the states of the Union and depriving any of them of its full and equal right in any territory acquired or to be acquired by the U.S.; that the enactment of any law interfering with slavery would be a violation of the Constitution and states' rights, and inimical to the equality of the states within the Union; and that the people had an unconditional right to form and adopt their state governments as they chose, no condition being imposed by the Constitution for the admission of a state except that its government should be republican. Calhoun's remarks (19–20 Feb. 1847) forecast the position of the South: insistence on a positive protection of slavery; appeal to states' rights and constitutional-compact theory; the view of the section as the bulwark of conserva-

tism within the Union; attack upon the "aggressive measures" of the nonslaveholding states. Pointing out that the South was already becoming a political minority in the national councils, Calhoun warned that were the balance between North and South destroyed, it would herald the approach of "political revolution, anarchy, civil war, and widespread disaster." The South, he said, was acting defensively and restricting itself to "repelling attacks . . . all we ask is to be let alone; but if trampled upon, it will be idle to expect that we will not resist it."

The fundamental principle of the Wilmot Proviso reappeared in later congressional debates, and became a vital plank in the platforms of the Free-Soil and Republican parties.

25 Sept. CAPTURE OF MONTEREY. Taylor's army, increased (May–June) from 5,000 to 14,500 men, many being 3- and 6-month volunteers, and handicapped by lack of supplies and faulty transportation, began (6 July) its ascent of the Rio Grande from the advance base of Reynosa to Camargo, using a small fleet of river steamboats. Camargo, which the first troops reached 14 July, lay on the San Juan River, a branch of the Rio Grande, c.1,000 miles north of Mexico City. It became Taylor's base for his march on Monterey. With a force of 3,080 regulars and 3,150 volunteers, Taylor began (19 Aug.) his advance on Monterey, reaching its outskirts on 19 Sept. The major fortification in the city was the Citadel (or Black Ft.). To the west of Monterey, the Mexicans had well-fortified defenses on Independence Hill and Federation Hill. Taylor took immediate command of the troops attacking from the east, and dispatched a force under Gen. William J. Worth to make the assault from the west. The attack on Monterey began 20 Sept.

Worth advanced along the Monterey-

Saltillo road, took the redoubt on Federation Hill (21 Sept.), and seized Independence Hill (22 Sept.), thus securing control of the western approaches. In the east, the U.S. troops penetrated the town (21 Sept.), meeting heavy resistance in the fortified streets and houses. After a 4-day siege, during which the enemy fell back on the Citadel, the Mexicans capitulated (24 Sept.), the surrender being carried out 25 Sept. Estimated losses: U.S., 120 killed, 368 wounded; Mexican, 367 killed and wounded.

Taylor consented to an 8-week armistice, pledging that the U.S. forces would not penetrate southward beyond the mountains unless the armistice was disclaimed by either government. The armistice brought the disapproval of Polk, eager to press the war in order to exert pressure on the Mexican congress. The War Department's notification (13 Oct.) did not reach Taylor until 2 Nov. The disapproval of the armistice increased Taylor's suspicion that the administration was engaged in intrigues against him because he had been mentioned in June by the Whig leader, Thurlow Weed, as that party's presidential possibility.

Taylor informed Santa Anna (5 Nov.), who had reached San Luis Potosí (8 Oct.), that the armistice would be terminated effective 13 Nov. Taylor occupied Saltillo, capital of Coahuila (16 Nov.). Meanwhile, a force of about 3,000 troops under Gen. John E. Wool left San Antonio (23–28 Sept.) on an expedition against Chihuahua. Wool occupied Monclova (29 Oct.), but abandoned his march on Chihuahua under orders from the War Department approved by Taylor. Wool took Parras (5 Dec.), to the west of Monterey, and reinforced Taylor at Saltillo (21 Dec.).

12 DEC. TREATY OF NEW GRANADA. U.S. concern about Central America was revived by a growing interest in an isthmian transit route between the Atlantic and the Pacific, and by suspicion of British designs on the Caribbean area. The Republic of New Granada (Colombia) feared that Great Britain or some other foreign nation might take possession of the Isthmus of Panama. At the initiative of the New Granada government, Benjamin A. Bidlack, the U.S. minister, signed (12 Dec.) a commercial treaty which conveyed to the U.S. the right of way across the isthmus. In return, the U.S. guaranteed the neutrality of the isthmus and the sovereignty of New Granada. The Senate approved the treaty (3 June 1848); ratifications exchanged 12 July 1848.

WHIG GAINS. State and congressional elections indicated loss of support for Polk. In the state contests (Oct.–Nov.) the Whigs carried New York, New Jersey, Ohio, Maryland, Georgia, and Florida, with strong gains in Pennsylvania. In the congressional elections (Nov.) the Whigs made capital of the war (although Polk's opposition to internal improvements and a high protective tariff were also under fire). The new House had a slim Whig majority.

7 DEC. NEW SESSION. The attack on Polk was resumed, with Whigs, notably Senators Robert Toombs (Ga., 8 Jan. 1847) and Thomas Corwin (Ohio, 11 Feb.), and antislavery Democrats joining forces. Nevertheless $5 million in war appropriations were voted (15 Feb., 3 Mar.) and Treasury notes to $23 million authorized (28 Jan.).

1847

OCT. 1846–1 MAR. 1847. DONIPHAN'S EXPEDITION. Before leaving New Mexico, Kearny ordered (23 Sept. 1846) Col. **Alexander W. Doniphan** (1808–87), commander of the 1st Regiment of Missouri Mounted Volunteers, to lead an expedition to the province of Chihuahua in support of Gen. Wool. Late in

Oct. 1846, Doniphan's troops departed from Santa Fe on a march that was to take them through 3,000 miles of mountain and desert country. After signing (22 Nov. 1846) a treaty of peace with the Navajo chiefs assembled at Bear Springs, he left Valverde (14 Dec.) for El Paso, 90 miles to the south, marched through virtually waterless country, and defeated the enemy in the **Battle of El Brazito** (25 Dec. 1846). U.S. loss: 7 wounded; Mexican, 43 killed. Occupying El Paso (27 Dec. 1846), Doniphan left the town (8 Feb.) on a march across desert wastes toward the provincial capital of Chihuahua. After defeating a defending Mexican force in the **Battle of the Sacramento** (28 Feb.)—U.S. loss: 1 killed, and 11 wounded; estimated Mexican: 300 killed, 300 wounded—he entered Chihuahua (1 Mar.).

22–23 Feb. BATTLE OF BUENA VISTA. In the late fall of 1846 Polk, convinced that Taylor could not bring the war to a successful conclusion, agreed to Gen. Winfield Scott's plan for an expedition to Vera Cruz. When Taylor learned (14 Jan.) that Scott had ordered (3 Jan.) the transfer of 9,000 of Taylor's troops to the Vera Cruz expedition and instructed him to remain on a "strict defensive" on the line of Monterey, Taylor's suspicions of political and military intrigue against him were again aroused. Most of Taylor's troops joined the expeditionary force at Tampico after Taylor withdrew from Victoria (12 Jan.), the capital of Tamaulipas, which had been occupied on 29 Dec. 1846. The friction between Taylor and the administration was intensified with the publication (22 Jan.) in the New York *Morning Express* of Taylor's letter to Gen. Edmund P. Gaines, in which he defended his agreement to the 8-week armistice, criticized the administration, and discussed military matters.

Taylor disobeyed orders (dated 20 Dec.) to communicate with Scott, and took the offensive, advancing (5–14 Feb.) to Agua Nueva, 18 miles west of Saltillo. Meanwhile, Santa Anna massed about 20,000 troops at San Luis Potosí, with the aim of striking a decisive blow at Taylor's army. On 20 Feb., Santa Anna reached La Encarnación, 35 miles from Taylor's encampment. Because of his poor defensive position at Agua Nueva, Taylor withdrew (21 Feb.) to La Angostura, a mountain defile along the Saltillo–San Luis Potosí road, in a valley 6,000 ft. above sea level. Here, 3 miles north of the hacienda of Buena Vista, the U.S. forces (c.4,800 men, mostly untried volunteer infantry) entrenched along deep gullies and ravines.

Santa Anna, after leading more than 15,000 ill-trained men on an exhausting march, sent Taylor a demand for unconditional surrender. Taylor refused, and the ensuing battle ended in a hard-won U.S. victory, the retirement of Santa Anna's forces (23–24 Feb.), and termination of the war in northern Mexico. U.S. loss: 267 killed, 456 wounded, 23 missing; Mexican: estimated at 1,500, of whom at least 500 killed. Santa Anna returned to Mexico City, where he took the oath of office as president (21 Mar.).

Shortly after the battle, Taylor received from Secretary Marcy a reprimand (dated 27 Jan.) for the Gaines letter. For the next 9 months Taylor remained in command of the U.S. forces in northern Mexico. Relieved at his own request, he left for the U.S. on 26 Nov. and received a hero's welcome.

21 Feb.–29 Mar. SCOTT'S VERA CRUZ EXPEDITION. Influenced by the favorable progress of events in California, and finally yielding to repeated proposals made by Scott, Polk placed Scott at the head of an expedition to take Vera Cruz, at that time the most powerful fortress in the Western Hemisphere. From this point on the east coast of Mexico, Scott was to proceed along a direct but mountainous inland route to Mexico City. After a reconciliation with Polk (19 Nov. 1846), Scott was ordered (23 Nov. 1846) to take command of a force whose projected strength of 20,000 actually never exceeded 10,000. Scott left Washington (24 Nov. 1846) and reached Camargo (3 Jan.), where his progress was hindered by bad weather and inadequate water transportation.

Scott established headquarters at Tampico (18 Feb.) and, without express approval of the administration, issued **General Order No. 20** (19 Feb.). The order, which set up a system for dealing with crimes not defined in the Articles of War, was aimed at preventing the atrocities committed by some of Taylor's volunteer troops and at securing the cooperation of the native population along Scott's lines of communication. To an extent compatible with military necessity, local government was left to Mexican officials acting under army supervision. The order and the machinery for its execution constituted the **first civil affairs administration** of enemy territory occupied by U.S. military forces.

Scott massed an invasion armada and 10,000 troops at the Lobos Islands, where he arrived 21 Feb. From this point, 50 miles below Tampico, the fleet under Commodore Conner sailed (2–5 Mar.) to the final rendezvous at Antón Lizardo, 12 miles south of Vera Cruz. Here Scott's operation was delayed by a serious outbreak of smallpox among the troops. At the advice of naval officers, Scott decided to abandon his plan to take the fortress city by direct assault from the sea. The Mexicans had 5,000 soldiers in the city.

The landings (9 Mar.), made on the beaches south of Vera Cruz, were virtually unopposed. The first large-scale amphibious operation in U.S. military history was carried out with special landing craft assembled at Sacrificios Island. Two weeks were spent in securing and building up the position on the beach. The Mexicans rejected a demand for surrender (22 Mar.). After a siege from U.S. land and naval batteries that began 22 Mar., Vera Cruz, with its strongly fortified seaward castle of San Juan de Ulúa, surrendered to Scott (27 Mar.) and was formally occupied (29 Mar.). U.S. losses: 82, of whom 19 were killed; Mexican losses: c.80 soldiers, 100 civilians.

18 APR.–20 AUG. CERRO GORDO TO CHURUBUSCO. The route of Scott's march through the interior lay across an initial 55 miles of lowland, which at the mountain pass of Cerro Gordo rises precipitously to slopes ultimately reaching a height of about 8,000 ft., and then cross a heavily populated plateau between Perote and Mexico City. Scott's immediate objective was Jalapa, 75 miles northwest of Vera Cruz and 4,250 ft. above sea level.

Battle of Cerro Gordo. Leaving Vera Cruz 8 Apr., Scott's force of about 9,000 men marched along the National Road. On 13 Apr. they encountered the outlying enemy defenses at Plan del Rio, just below Cerro Gordo. Santa Anna, leaving the Mexican capital (2 Apr.), had reached Cerro Gordo (9 Apr.) and designated it as the point for containing the U.S. advance. The Mexican force numbered about 13,000 men. A skillful reconnaissance of enemy positions along the canyon near Cerro Gordo was made by U.S. engineer officers (including Capts. **Robert E. Lee** and **George B. McClellan**), but its value was partly vitiated by a premature action (17 Apr.). In an enveloping operation that witnessed much hand-to-hand combat, the U.S. forces carried Cerro Gordo by assault (18 Apr.), routing Santa Anna and his staff officers, capturing 204 enemy officers and 2,837 men, and seizing 43 artillery pieces and 4,000 small arms. U.S. losses: 63 killed, 337 wounded.

Scott's troops occupied Jalapa (19 Apr.), Perote (22 Apr.), and reached Puebla (15 May), 80 miles from Mexico City. During this period Scott lost about one third of his effectives whose short-term enlistments had expired (7 regiments and 2 companies of volunteers). He was left with about 7,000 men, of whom some 1,000 were stricken with disease. Scott lacked money, supplies, and transportation; reinforcements from New Orleans were slow in arriving. Yet during a 3-month pause at Puebla, while the navy carried out operations along the southeastern coast of Mexico, Scott built up his force to 10,783 effectives. On 6 Aug. Gen. Franklin Pierce arrived at Puebla with 3,000 reinforcements.

Battles of Contreras and Churubusco. Scott began (7 Aug.) his advance from Puebla, cutting through the mountains and entering the Valley of Mexico at Ayotla, where he established his headquarters (11 Aug.). Santa Anna, who had again taken office as president (22 May) after some changes in the Mexican government, had about 20,000 men in the valley, concentrated in the vicinity of Contreras and Churubusco, along the roads leading to Mexico City. An American force of about 3,300 men stormed the Contreras position (19–20 Aug.) and routed the enemy, killing 700 and capturing 800 at a cost of 60 U.S. killed and wounded The fighting at Churubusco (20 Aug.), where the enemy had converted a church and a convent into powerful defensive positions, also resulted in a U.S. victory, but at a heavy price. U.S. losses in both battles: 133 killed, 865 wounded, 40 missing (about one seventh of force engaged). Santa Anna lost more than 7,000 killed, wounded, or captured (about one third of his army). Santa

Anna withdrew to Mexico City, now within 5 miles of U.S. lines, and requested an armistice. Negotiations were conducted (22–23 Aug.), and the armistice of Tacubaya went into effect (24 Aug.) to enable the Mexican government to consider the peace proposals that had been entrusted to **Nicholas P. Trist** (1800–74), confidential commissioner accompanying Scott's army.

26 Aug.–6 Sept. TRIST MISSION. With the fall of Vera Cruz, Polk renewed his efforts for a peace settlement. He decided, with the agreement of his cabinet, to dispatch a peace commissioner to Mexico. Chosen for the secret mission was Nicholas P. Trist, chief clerk of the State Department, who received his instructions from Polk and Buchanan (15 Apr.). The terms of the offer were essentially those that Mackenzie had made to Santa Anna, except that Trist was also authorized to negotiate for Lower California and the right of transit across the Isthmus of Tehuantepec. Trist's "confidential" mission became publicly known 4 days after he left Washington (16 Apr.).

Traveling under an assumed name, Trist reached Vera Cruz on 6 May. He was authorized, with certain reservations, "to enter into arrangements with the government of Mexico for the suspension of hostilities." There immediately ensued a controversy over Trist's authority, Scott regarding it as an invasion of his own and holding that an armistice was exclusively a military question. Relations between Trist and Scott were aggravated by an exchange of hostile correspondence. With the aid of the British legation in Mexico, a reconciliation was effected (25 June), and the armistice of Tacubaya was arranged by Scott. The negotiations (27 Aug.–6 Sept.) between Trist and the Mexican commission headed by former President Herrera ended with a

Mexican rejection of the peace offer. The armistice was terminated 7 Sept.

8–14 Sept. MARCH ON THE MEXICAN CAPITAL. Battle of Molino del Rey. Scott resumed his march at once. A force of 3,447 men under Gen. William J. Worth was ordered to carry out a diversionary raid on the gun foundry of Molino del Rey, just outside the gates of the city, where the enemy was supposedly casting church bells into cannon. Here, and at the adjoining Casa Mata and the walled park of Chapultepec, an estimated 12,000 Mexicans were entrenched behind massive fortifications. The U.S. attack opened 8 Sept., and what had been conceived as a minor raid developed into a serious day-long battle. Although the Americans took the position, they withdrew to Tacubaya at the day's end. U.S. losses: 117 killed, 653 wounded, 18 missing; Mexican: c.2,000 men killed and wounded, c.700 captured.

Battle of Chapultepec. For the final assault on the capital, Scott had 7,180 men as against an estimated 15,000 enemy troops in the city. Scott decided to storm the fortified hill of Chapultepec (c.200 ft. high) commanding the causeways leading to the San Cosmé and Belén gates at the western outskirts of the capital. On Chapultepec there were some 1,000 troops, supported by 4,000 in the immediate area. Following an artillery bombardment (12 Sept.), the divisions commanded by Gens. John A. Quitman and Gideon J. Pillow began their assault at 8:00 A.M. on the morning of 13 Sept. The storming parties scaled the rocky slopes with ladders and pickaxes. The summit was taken at 9:30 A.M. Gallant resistance was offered by "Los Ninos," about 100 boy cadets who defended the Mexican Military College on the crest of the hill. The Belén gate was taken at 1:30 P.M., and the San Cosmé gate by 6 P.M. U.S. losses: 130 killed, 703 wounded, 29 missing.

Capture of Mexico City. Scott immediately pressed on the capital (pop.: 200,000) with less than 6,000 effectives. Using picks and crowbars, the U.S. infantry hacked through the city walls and entered the capital during the night and early morning (13–14 Sept.). The U.S. flag was raised above the National Palace, where a battalion of U.S. Marines (authorized by Congress 10 Nov. 1775; formed into a corps by act of 11 July 1798) took guard over the "halls of Montezuma." After several days of disorder, the hostile population was brought under control. Gen. Scott reissued (16 Sept.) General Order No. 20; henceforth, military government became the chief function of his army. Scott remained in command until 18 Feb. 1848.

Even before the Americans occupied the capital, Santa Anna fled to the suburb of Gaudalupe Hidalgo, where he renounced the presidency (16 Sept.). At the head of about 8,000 men, he marched to Puebla, where the Mexicans under Gen. Joaquin Rea had begun a siege (14 Sept.) of the U.S. garrison (about 2,300 troops, mostly wounded and convalescent) under Col. Thomas Childs, who rejected a demand for surrender. Santa Anna left Puebla (1 Oct.) and the siege was raised (12 Oct.) by a relief expedition under Gen. Joseph Lane from Vera Cruz. Deposed as head of the army (7 Oct.), Santa Anna fled the country.

Pedro María Anaya was elected (11 Nov.) *ad interim* president of Mexico. The Anaya government informed Trist (22 Nov.) that it had named commissioners to negotiate peace on the basis of the original terms. Trist had received (16 Nov.) an order for his recall, but when the Mexicans pointed out that they had not received official notification of the withdrawal of his authority, Trist decided (4 Dec.) to remain in Mexico and negotiate a treaty.

1848

24 Jan. DISCOVERY OF GOLD in California by James W. Marshall, a New Jersey mechanic who was erecting a sawmill for **Johann Augustus Sutter** (1803–80) on a branch of the American River in Eldorado County, in the lower Sacramento Valley, about 40 miles from present-day Sacramento. The news, announced by Marshall to Sutter (28 Jan.), soon spread and stimulated the great California gold rush. Impetus was lent by Polk's confirmation of the discovery in his annual message to Congress (5 Dec.). Adventurers came from all parts of the U.S. and from overseas places as distant as China and Australia. By the end of 1849, it is estimated, the California population had been swelled by 100,000. The influx of the "Forty-niners" continued for the next 2 years. In 1851 the annual output of gold rose to $55 million.

2 Feb. TREATY OF GUADALUPE HIDALGO resulted from the unauthorized negotiations between Trist and the Mexican commissioners begun formally 2 Jan., and the treaty was signed at the village just outside Mexico City. By that time, Peña y Peña had become (8 Jan.) acting president of Mexico. **Terms:** Mexico relinquished all claims to Texas above the Rio Grande and ceded New Mexico and California to the U.S. The territory (including the present states of Arizona, Nevada, California, and Utah, and parts of New Mexico, Colorado, and Wyoming) added with Texas 1,193,061 square miles to the national domain. In return for the territory, the U.S. agreed to pay $15 million and assume the adjusted claims of its citizens ($3,250,000) against the Mexican government. The U.S.-Mexican boundary was fixed along the Rio Grande to the southern line of New Mexico, thence westward and northward along the Gila and Colorado rivers, and thence along the line between Upper and Lower California to the Pacific.

The treaty arrived at Washington on 19 Feb. Polk, doubtful and hesitant because the treaty was unauthorized, submitted it to the Senate (23 Feb.), which ratified the treaty, 38–14 (10 Mar.). For: 26 Democrats, 12 Whigs; against: 7 Democrats, 7 Whigs. A motion to add the Wilmot Proviso was defeated, 38–15. The opposition to the treaty stemmed from Secretary Buchanan and those senators who, supported by a growing expansionist demand, wanted to annex all of Mexico. The Mexican congress ratified the treaty (25 May), ratifications were formally exchanged (30 May), and Polk proclaimed the treaty in effect (4 July). The final territorial adjustment under the treaty was made with the **Gadsden Purchase** (1853, p. 257).

A military armistice suspending hostilities had been declared on 29 Feb., and the last action of the war was fought at Todos Santos in Lower California (30 Mar.). The U.S. forces evacuated Mexico City (12 June) and the last U.S. troops left Vera Cruz 2 Aug.

WAR COST. U.S. casualties: 1,721 killed or died of wounds; 11,155 died of disease; 4,102 wounded. Military and naval expenditures amounted to more than $97,500,000.

19 July. SENECA FALLS CONVENTION, held at the Wesleyan Chapel, Seneca Falls, N.Y., under the leadership of **Lucretia Mott** (1793–1880) and **Elizabeth Cady Stanton** (p. 1156), adopted a group of women's-rights resolutions, including a demand for woman suffrage, and a diminution of discrimination in employment and education. A few months earlier the 2 feminist leaders had worked successfully for the passage of the New York Married Women's Property Act, modifying the common law by recognizing a married woman's right to her separate property.

14 AUG. OREGON BILL. In his annual messages (1846–48) Polk urged the establishment of a territorial government for Oregon, whose provisional laws excluded slavery. The ensuing debates raised the issue of the constitutional power of Congress to prohibit slavery in the territories. The Senate tabled a bill passed by the House (16 Jan. 1847) applying the restrictions of the Northwest Ordinance. Sen. Stephen A. Douglas (Ill.) offered a bill (10 Jan.) providing that the Oregon laws should remain valid until the territorial legislature should change them.

The House (9 Feb.) reintroduced its Oregon bill. Sen. Jesse D. Bright (Ind.), acting chairman of the committee on territories, introduced an amendment (27 June) extending the Missouri Compromise line through all newly acquired territory to the Pacific. Thus the Oregon bill raised anew the problem of the status of slavery in California and New Mexico. Under the Mexican laws of 1829 and 1837 slavery had been forbidden in those areas. Calhoun opposed Bright's amendment, denied (27 June) both the validity of Mexican laws in the conquered territories and congressional authority over slavery in the territories, and insisted that slavery was not subject to congressional or local action.

The Senate (12 July) referred the question of slavery extension to a committee headed by John M. Clayton (Del.). The "Clayton Compromise," adopted by the Senate, 33–22 (27 July), validated the provisional laws of Oregon insofar as they were compatible with the Constitution, but forbade the territorial legislatures of New Mexico and California to pass laws on slavery. The question of the status of slavery in those territories was referred to appeals from the territorial courts to the Supreme Court.

The Senate bill was tabled by the House (28 July), which by 129–71

passed its own bill (2 Aug.) for organizing Oregon with restrictions on slavery. The Senate amendment to the bill extended the Missouri Compromise line to the Pacific. The House refused to concur, and its bill incorporating the prohibition of slavery in Oregon was adopted by the Senate (13 Aug.). Despite Calhoun's view that the measure merited a veto on constitutional grounds, Polk signed the bill (14 Aug.) on the ground that it did not conflict with the Missouri Compromise because the territory in question lay north of 36°30′.

PRESIDENTIAL CAMPAIGN. The slavery issue was injected into the Democratic National Convention at Baltimore (22 May) when the 2 factions of Barnburners (also known as the "Softs") and Hunkers (also known as the "Hards") from the key state of New York sent separate delegations. The anti-administration Barnburners were firm supporters of the Wilmot Proviso. When a compromise on seating the delegations failed, neither one took part in the convention; but the Hunkers, unlike their opponents, pledged their support to the nominees.

Polk, who in accepting the nomination in 1844 had pledged himself to a single term, declined to run for office. Gen. **Lewis Cass** (Mich.) was nominated for president and Gen. **William O. Butler** (Ky.) for vice-president. Cass, a conservative and an expansionist, had approved the doctrine of "squatter sovereignty" (local determination of the status of slavery) in a letter (29 Dec. 1847) to A. O. P. Nicholson of Nashville. While his selection indicated the Democratic party's desire to win the Western vote and promote sectional harmony, the principle of "squatter sovereignty" was not incorporated in the Democratic platform. The platform, in substance that of 1844, denied the power of Congress to interfere with slavery in the states and criticized all efforts to bring the slavery question before Congress. In a move to quell the agitation of the slavery issue, the convention voted down a minority resolution of the Southern delegates favoring noninterference with slavery in the territories.

When the Whig National Convention met at Philadelphia (7 June), the 3 contenders for the nomination were Henry Clay, Gen. Zachary Taylor, and Gen. Winfield Scott. **Taylor,** whose political following grew rapidly after the battle of Buena Vista, was chosen presidential candidate; **Millard Fillmore** (N.Y.), the vice-presidential nominee. A resolution affirming the power of Congress to control slavery in the territories was proposed by the antislavery Ohio delegation and voted down. Taylor's nomination was opposed by the antislavery delegations from New England and Ohio. The Whig platform was a recital of Taylor's military character and reputation.

The Barnburners, seceding from the Democratic convention, held their own convention at Utica, N.Y. (22 June), nominating **Martin Van Buren** for president and **Henry Dodge** (Wis.) for vice-president. Soon afterward the antislavery Democrats and Liberty party supporters joined with dissident New England Whigs (known as "Conscience Whigs" because of their opposition to slavery) in holding a national convention of the **Free-Soil party** at Buffalo (9 Aug.). It was attended by 465 delegates from 18 states (including the 3 slave states of Virginia, Maryland, and Delaware). The Free-Soil opposition to Cass and Taylor united on the common basis of the Wilmot Proviso. In return for Barnburner support of a "thorough Liberty platform," John P. Hale (N.H.), who had been nominated for president by the Liberty party convention at New York City (Jan. 1848), withdrew in favor of **Van Buren,** who was nominated for president. **Charles Francis Adams** (Mass., p. 970)

was nominated for vice-president. Among the prominent members of the party were **Charles Sumner** (Mass., p. 1164) and **Salmon P. Chase** (Ohio, p. 1001). The Free-Soil party was pledged to a "national platform of freedom in opposition to the sectional platform of slavery." It attacked the "aggressions of the slave power," upheld the substance of the Wilmot Proviso, and favored river and harbor improvements and free homesteads to actual settlers. For its slogan the party adopted "Free soil, free speech, free labor, and free men."

7 Nov. PRESIDENTIAL ELECTION (the first conducted on a uniform election day, in accord with the congressional act of 1845). Popular vote: **Taylor,** 1,360,101; Cass, 1,220,544; Van Buren, 291,263. Electoral vote: Taylor, 163 (carrying 8 slave and 7 free states); Cass, 127 (carrying 8 free and 7 slave states). While Van Buren failed to carry a single state, the Free-Soil party was instrumental in winning the election for Taylor by depriving Cass of New York's 36 electoral votes. In that state, Van Buren received 120,510 votes to 114,318 for Cass, thus splitting the Democratic ranks.

1849

22 JAN. "ADDRESS OF THE SOUTHERN DELEGATES." A caucus (22 Dec. 1848) of 69 Southerners in Congress considered steps to oppose legislation prohibiting the slave trade in the District of Columbia. Spokesman for the caucus was Calhoun, whose "Address" listed the "acts of aggression" committed by the North against Southern rights—including (1) exclusion of slaves from the territories, (2) impediments to the return of fugitive slaves—and reaffirmed the right of slaveholders to take their property into the territories. Two additional meetings of the caucus (15, 22 Jan.) were attended by about 80 members, but owing to Whig opposition only 48 signed the "Address" (2 of them Whigs).

3 MAR. DEPT. OF THE INTERIOR created as the sixth with cabinet status. Established at the recommendation of Secretary of the Treasury Robert J. Walker, it was originally called the Home Department, and brought under a single head diverse government bureaus, including the Office of the Census, the Office of Indian Affairs, and the General Land Office.

NEW CONGRESS. In the House of Representatives (31st Cong., 1st sess.) that convened on 3 Dec., there were 112 Democrats, 109 Whigs, and 13 Free-Soilers. The last group held the balance of power. The Democrats had a Senate majority of 10. The organization of the House revealed the bitter factionalism produced by sectional controversy. Southern Whigs under the leadership of Alexander Stephens and Robert Toombs opposed the Whig candidate for speaker, Robert C. Winthrop (Mass.), because the Whig caucus had refused to pledge opposition to the Wilmot Proviso. The Free-Soilers refused to support Winthrop on the ground that he had not given adequate recognition to antislavery spokesmen during his previous service as speaker. It took 3 weeks and 63 ballots before Howell Cobb (Ga.) was elected speaker (22 Dec.). The debates, marked by threats of disunion, widened the breach between the Northern and Southern wings of the Whig party.

CALIFORNIA AND NEW MEXICO. Polk's efforts to secure territorial organization for California and New Mexico failed. The stumbling block was the status of slavery in the newly acquired regions. With the influx of settlers into California after the discovery of gold, territorial organization became a pressing need.

It was Taylor's view that Congress ought not to pass on the question of slavery in California and New Mexico. The people of these territories, he held, had the right to adopt their own constitution and form of government without congressional authorization before applying for admission to the Union. The final decision would rest with Congress. Accordingly, he dispatched special messengers to California and New Mexico to inform the people that it was not necessary to await congressional action before establishing a government.

The Californians took steps even before Taylor's special agent arrived. A convention met at Monterey (1 Sept.–13 Oct.) and adopted a constitution prohibiting slavery. The constitution was ratified by the people (13 Nov.) and a state government went into operation on 20 Dec. Taylor recommended in his annual message (4 Dec.) the immediate admission of California, and urged that Congress "should abstain from the introduction of those exciting topics of sectional character which have hitherto produced painful apprehensions in the public mind." Referring to threats of dissolution that had been freely made during the year, Taylor asserted that whatever dangers menaced the Union, "I shall stand by it and maintain it in its integrity to the full extent of the obligations imposed and the powers conferred upon me by the Constitution." Southerners at once attacked Taylor's proposal. (In the Union at this time there were 15 free and 15 slave states, and the admission of California would upset the balance.) On 12 Mar. 1850 California applied to Congress for statehood.

1850

29 JAN.–20 SEPT. COMPROMISE OF 1850. Clay's Resolutions. Mounting sectional antagonism over territorial accessions alarmed moderates and conserv-

Clay's compromise. The "Compromise of 1850" is a collective term of later origin applied to the 5 laws enacted (9–20 Sept.) after Clay and Douglas succeeded in coalescing Union sentiment in Congress. With the exception of California, the territory won from Mexico was divided at the 37th parallel into a northern half (Utah) and a southern half (New Mexico). The compromise included the following measures:

9 Sept. (1) Admission of California as a Free State. The bill passed the Senate, 34–18 (13 Aug.); the House, 150–56 (7 Sept.).

9 Sept. (2) Texas and New Mexico Act, which organized New Mexico as a territory without restriction on slavery, adjusted the Texas-New Mexico boundary, and provided for the payment by the U.S. to Texas of $10 million in return for the abandonment by Texas of all claims to New Mexico territory. It included the "popular sovereignty" provision that was the substance of the compromise: "That, when admitted as a State, the said territory, or any portion of the same, shall be received into the Union, with or without slavery, as their constitution may prescribe at the time of their admission." The bill passed the Senate, 27–10 (15 Aug.); the House, 108–97 (6 Sept.).

9 Sept. (3) Utah Act, which established a territorial government with identical provisions.

18 Sept. (4) Fugitive Slave Act amended the original law of 1793; placed fugitive slave cases under exclusive federal jurisdiction; provided for special U.S. commissioners who were authorized, following a summary hearing, to issue warrants for the arrest of fugitives and certificates for returning them to their masters. An affidavit by the claimant was accepted as sufficient proof of ownership. A feature of the law that abolitionists regarded as especially prejudicial was the authorization of a $10 fee for commissioners when such a certificate was granted, and of only $5 when it was refused. The commissioners were authorized to call to their aid bystanders, or to summon a *posse comitatus,* when deemed necessary for enforcing the law. Fugitives claiming to be freemen were denied the right of trial by jury, and their testimony was not to be admitted as evidence at any of the proceedings under the law. Heavy penalties were provided for evasion or obstruction. Marshals and deputies refusing to execute warrants were liable to a $1,000 fine; and in cases where the fugitives escaped through official negligence, the marshal might be sued for the value of the slave. Citizens preventing the arrest of a fugitive, or aiding in his concealment or rescue, were subject to a fine of $1,000, imprisonment up to 6 months, and civil damages of $1,000 for each fugitive so lost. The bill passed the Senate, 27–12 (23 Aug.); the House, 109–76 (12 Sept.).

20 Sept. (5) An Act Abolishing the Slave Trade in the District of Columbia after 1 Jan. 1851, passed the Senate, 33–19 (16 Sept.); the House, 124–47 (17 Sept.).

Both North and South hailed the "finality" of the measures, although acceptance was in reality conditional. Most Northern Whigs and Democrats viewed it as a permanent settlement of the slavery question. Northern radicals, however, condemned the Fugitive Slave Act and hinted at their intention to obstruct its enforcement. That a majority of Southern voters regarded the compromise as a welcome alternative to disunion was indicated by the defeat of the secessionists in the Southern state elections of 1851, when the Unionists won by narrow margins over the Quitman-Davis faction (Miss.), the Rhett wing (S.C.), and the Yancey radicals (Ala.). Northern radicals, however, gained a signal triumph with the election (1851) of Charles Sumner (Mass.) to the U.S. Senate. The chief political effect of the compromise was its hastening of the breakup of the Whig party.

19 APR. CLAYTON-BULWER TREATY. U.S. interest in an interoceanic canal across the isthmian routes in Central America influenced Polk's foreign policy. Polk sent a special envoy, Elijah Hise, to Nicaragua to investigate British encroachments. The British, acting on the petition (1835) of the settlers of Belize (British Honduras), established a protectorate over the Mosquito Coast territory claimed by Nicaragua, drove the Nicaraguans from Mosquitia, and forced them (Jan. 1848) to renounce the area in the vicinity of the San Juan River, at the eastern terminus of the canal projected by the U.S.

Hise concluded with the Nicaraguans an unauthorized treaty granting the U.S. the exclusive right of way across the isthmus and the right to fortify the route, in return for the U.S. guarantee of the neutrality of the isthmus and the protection of Nicaraguan sovereignty. Polk never submitted the treaty to the Senate. A similar treaty was negotiated (1849) by E. G. Squier, an envoy sent by Taylor. Squier also obtained Tigre Island in the Gulf of Fonseca, at the western terminus of the projected canal. The island was seized (Oct., 1849) by British forces, who refused to leave despite Squier's contention that it belonged to the U.S.

Although the Taylor administration was anxious to reach an understanding with Great Britain, Secretary of State Clayton informed the British foreign secretary, Lord Palmerston, that the U.S. would not recognize the British protectorate over Mosquitia or its hold on the San Juan River. Clayton initiated discussions with the British minister to the U.S., Sir Henry Lytton Bulwer. The

treaty was ratified by the Senate, 42–10, and ratifications were exchanged on 5 July. Terms: both nations (1) agreed never to obtain or exercise exclusive control over an isthmian ship canal, or to fortify it; (2) guaranteed the neutrality and security of the canal; (3) agreed to keep any future canal open to their nationals on terms of equality; and (4) pledged not to colonize, occupy, or exercise dominion over any part of Central America.

The British made the major concessions, but the treaty, unpopular in the U.S. with Anglophobes and expansionists, remained in effect until abrogated by the Hay-Pauncefote Treaty (1901). Anglo-U.S. friction was further allayed by cession (22 Nov. 1859) by Britain of the Bay Islands to Honduras.

10 JUNE. NASHVILLE CONVENTION. Early in 1850 Southern advocates of a separatist program took steps to consider their position on Clay's compromise and the larger question of Southern rights. At the instigation of Calhoun, a Mississippi convention (1 Oct. 1849) and the state legislature (6 Mar.) adopted resolutions calling a convention of the slave states, to meet at Nashville, Tenn., 3 June. The extremists, led by **Robert Barnwell Rhett** (S.C.), saw an opportunity to broaden their support for secession. Nine slave states were represented, but the moderates were in control. The convention adopted (10 June) a resolution calling for the extension of the Missouri Compromise line westward to the Pacific. A second convention, attended by a handful of delegates (11–18 Nov.), denounced the Compromise and asserted the right of secession.

9 JULY. Death of President Taylor at Washington, D.C., of cholera morbus. **Millard Fillmore** became the 13th president, taking the oath of office on 10 July.

13–14 Dec. GEORGIA PLATFORM.
Indicative of Unionist sentiment among conservative Southerners was the Georgia Platform drawn up by Charles J. Jenkins and adopted by a state convention (10 Dec.) at Milledgeville. The resolutions stated that while Georgia did not wholly approve of the Compromise of 1850, it would "abide by it as a permanent adjustment of this sectional controversy"; however, they warned that Georgia "will and ought to resist, even (as a last resort) to a disruption of every tie which binds her to the Union," any future act of Congress that would repeal or substantially modify the fugitive slave laws, the suppression of the interstate slave trade, and the abolition of slavery in the District of Columbia. The Georgia Platform constituted the basis on which **Robert A. Toombs** (1810–85) and his colleagues, including the conservative Democrat **Howell Cobb** (1815–68), formerly established the Union Rights party.

"SILVER GRAY" WHIGS. The impact of the Compromise of 1850 upon the Whig party in the North was immediately reflected in the New York State Whig convention that met at Syracuse (Sept.). When the convention adopted resolutions approving Sen. Seward's radical position, 40 conservative delegates of the Fillmore wing left the hall. They were led by Francis Granger, whose gray hair lent the name "Silver Gray" to the faction. The seceders held their own convention at Utica (Oct.), condemned Seward's policies and supported those of Fillmore, and shortly after backed a fusion ticket that included Horatio Seymour, the Democratic candidate for governor. The "Silver Grays" lost their influence in the state Whig party and later seized control of the American (Know-Nothing) organization in New York.

FUGITIVE SLAVE RESCUES. Most controversial aspect of the Compromise of 1850 was the adoption and subsequent enforcement of the Fugitive Slave Law. Although the number of runaway slaves was small (estimated, 1850, by the census of 1860 as only 1,000 out of c.3 million slaves, most of whom were ultimately returned to their masters), the South regarded Northern interference with the rendition of fugitive slaves as a violation of a constitutional guarantee. Sectional strife was increased by the further enactment of more stringent **"personal liberty"** laws in Vermont (1850) and other free states during the decade. Southern slaveholders who entered free states to seize runaway slaves risked being mobbed, sued for false imprisonment, or prosecuted for kidnapping. Outstanding rescues or attempted rescues of fugitive slaves (some leading to riots and loss of life): **James Hamlet** at New York City (1850), **Rachel Parker** at Baltimore, **Shadrach** and **Thomas Sims** at Boston (1851), **"Jerry"** at Syracuse (1851), the **Christiana** (Pa.) **affair** (1851), **Anthony Burns** at Boston (1854), and the **Oberlin** rescue (1858).

21 Dec. HÜLSEMANN LETTER. While the Hungarian revolution of 1848 was still in progress, the Taylor administration instructed (1849) its special agent, A. Dudley Mann, to give the revolutionary regime discretionary assurance of U.S. recognition. Mann never entered Hungary, but the offended Austrian government instructed Chevalier Hülsemann, its chargé d'affaires in the U.S., to register a firm protest against interference in its affairs. Secretary Webster's reply to Hülsemann's letter defended the U.S. right to take an interest in the European revolutions and asserted that these "events appeared to have their origin in those great ideas of responsible and popular governments on which the American constitutions themselves are founded. . . . The power of this republic, at the present moment, is spread over a region, one of the richest and most fertile on the globe, and of an extent in comparison with which the possession of the House of Hapsburg are but as a patch on the earth's surface." Webster's letter received support in the U.S. Senate and was endorsed by both parties. U.S. sympathy with the revolutions of 1848 reached its height with the public reception (5 Dec. 1851) accorded **Louis Kossuth,** the Hungarian partiot.

1851

LOPEZ FILIBUSTERING EXPEDITIONS. Southern annexationists were involved in the armed expeditions undertaken against Cuba by the adventurer Gen. Narciso Lopez, a leader of Spanish refugees in the U.S. who claimed that Cuba was ripe for revolt against Spanish oppression. His first filibustering venture collapsed after President Taylor issued a proclamation (11 Aug. 1849) and federal authorities intervened. His second, manned by many Southern volunteers, failed after a landing was made at Cardenas, Cuba (19 May 1850). A proclamation by President Fillmore (25 Apr.) notwithstanding, Lopez sailed from New Orleans (3 Aug.) and landed (11–12 Aug.) about 60 miles from Havana. A Cuban uprising failed to materialize. Col. William L. Crittenden (Ky.) and 50 other Southern volunteers were captured (13 Aug.), tried and sentenced by a military court, and executed at Havana (16 Aug.). The news of the executions caused anti-Spanish riots at New Orleans (21 Aug.) and the wrecking of the Spanish consulate there. Lopez was captured (28 Aug.) and publicly garroted at Havana (1 Sept.). Nearly half his 162 supporters sent to Spain as prisoners were Americans. Their release was secured only after Congress voted a $25,000 indemnity for the damage at New Orleans.

1852

20 Mar. Publication in book form of *Uncle Tom's Cabin,* by **Harriet Beecher Stowe** (p. 1161), a work originally serialized in the antislavery newspaper, the *National Era* (Washington, D.C.). A sentimental novel directed against the brutality and injustice of slavery, it was inspired by the Fugitive Slave Act of 1850. By mid-1853 some 1,200,000 copies of the work had been published. As a stage play it was first presented 24 Aug. Mrs. Stowe wrote *Key to Uncle Tom's Cabin* (1853) in an attempt to show that she had relied on factual evidence.

"YOUNG AMERICA" was the name given to an amorphous movement that began in the mid-1840s identified with aggressive nationalism, manifest destiny, and sympathy with the European revolutions of 1848. The term is thought to have originated in an address (1845) made by Edwin de Leon. Most of its adherents were Democrats; most prominent, Stephen A. Douglas. Its chief spokesman was George N. Sanders (Ky.); its organ the *Democratic Review.* In 1852 the movement reached its high point when Sanders formulated a program of southward expansion, aid to republican elements in foreign countries, and free trade.

PRESIDENTIAL CAMPAIGN. The Democratic National Convention assembled at Baltimore (1 June) and nominated **Franklin Pierce** (N.H.) for president (49th ballot) and **William R. King** (Ala.) for vice-president on a platform accepting the finality of the Compromise of 1850, affirming opposition to attempts to renew congressional agitation of the slavery question, and endorsing the Kentucky and Virginia resolutions. The Whig National Convention met at Baltimore (16 June) and nominated Gen. **Winfield Scott** for president (53rd ballot) and **William A. Graham** (N.C.) for vice-president on a platform accepting the Compromise of 1850, condemning further agitation of the slavery question, affirming states' rights, and supporting river and harbor improvements. The Free-Soil convention met at Pittsburgh (11 Aug.) and nominated **John P. Hale** (N.H.) for president and **George W. Julian** (Ind.) for vice-president on a platform condemning slavery and the Compromise of 1850, and supporting free homesteads for "landless settlers" and unimpeded entry for immigrants.

2 Nov. PRESIDENTIAL ELECTION. Popular vote: **Pierce**, 1,601,474; Scott, 1,386,578; Hale, 156,149. Electoral vote: **Pierce**, 254 (27 states); Scott, 42 (4 states). The results indicated the further disintegration of the Whig party (the Unionists of the South having merged with the Democrats) and the decline of the Free-Soilers.

1853

4 Mar. Pierce's inaugural address (the first delivered by a president from memory) pledged full support to the Compromise of 1850 and favored new territorial acquisitions by peaceful means.

30 Dec. GADSDEN PURCHASE. James Gadsden (S.C., 1788–1858), named (19 May) to negotiate with Mexico a settlement of a boundary question arising from the Treaty of Guadalupe Hidalgo, signed a treaty whereby Mexico, for a payment of $15 million (later reduced to 10 million), ceded to the U.S. a rectangular strip of territory (area: about 29,640 sq. mi.) in the Mesilla Valley, south of the Gila River. The line established marks the existing boundary with Mexico. The region, which includes the southern part of present-day Arizona and New Mexico, was regarded as a desirable route for a

southern railroad to the Pacific. The treaty was ratified on June 1854.

1854

31 Mar. PERRY'S REOPENING OF JAPAN. Since the early 17th century Japan had been virtually isolated from the Western world. U.S. concern about its shipwrecked nationals, and interest in the commercial potentialities of Japan, led the Fillmore administration to authorize (Jan. 1852) a special expedition commanded by Commodore **Matthew C. Perry** (p. 1126). He sailed from Norfolk (24 Nov. 1852) and reached Yedo Bay (later Tokyo Bay) on 8 July 1853. In the face of considerable distrust he presented (14 July 1853) Fillmore's letter to representatives of the Japanese emperor and then withdrew to give the government time to reach a decision. To forestall Russian maneuvers he returned to Japan (Feb.) with a fleet of 7 ships, and at a conference near present-day Yokohama (8 Mar.) he gave the authorities American presents (including a miniature telegraph and railroad) which the Japanese accepted as impressive evidence of the civilized arts of the Western world. Perry signed a treaty of peace, friendship, and commerce (**Treaty of Kanagawa,** 31 Mar.) that opened the ports of Shimoda and Hakodate to U.S. trade and made provision for shipwrecked U.S. seamen. Officially promulgated 22 June 1855, the treaty laid the foundation for future U.S. demands, pressed shortly thereafter by **Townsend Harris** (p. 1052), appointed (4 Aug. 1855) consul general to Japan, and resulting in agreements signed 18 June 1857 and 29 July 1858. The first opened Nagasaki to U.S. commerce; the second opened additional ports, granted Americans residence rights, and established diplomatic representatives at the respective capitals.

30 MAY KANSAS-NEBRASKA ACT. The slavery extension issue was reopened with the introduction (23 Jan.) by Sen. **Stephen A. Douglas** (p. 1015) of a bill for organizing the territories of Kansas and Nebraska. (His first bill, introduced 4 Jan., provided for organizing the single territory of Nebraska; the second authorized its division at the 40th parallel.) The measure incorporated the "squatter" or "**popular sovereignty**" principle originated by Lewis Cass and permitted the admission of the territories with or without slavery. By implication, the bill repealed the Missouri Compromise (which was expressly repealed in the bill's final version) and thus formally established the doctrine of congressional nonintervention in the territories. Passed after 3 months of bitter debate, the bill also provided that in all cases involving slavery, there might be appeal to the territorial courts and the Supreme Court.

The "**Appeal of the Independent Democrats,**" published 24 Jan., condemned the measure as a "gross violation of a sacred pledge" and the work of slaveholders' "plot," and maintained that the Compromise of 1850 had specifically affirmed the Missouri Compromise. Signers included Sens. Charles Sumner and Salmon P. Chase. Widely reprinted, the Appeal was partly responsible for the organization of the Republican party.

Among the motives attributed to Douglas for sponsorship of the bill are (1) his belief in the principle of self-government; (2) his courting of Southern support for presidential ambitions; (3) his conviction that by force of geography and nature, the territories would remain free soil; (4) his interest in the building of a transcontinental railroad along a central route (as opposed to a southern one advocated by Pierce and Jefferson Davis) with Chicago as its eastern terminus, inpelling him to take steps to open to settlement the region west of Iowa.

The Kansas-Nebraska bill passed the Senate, 37–14 (3 Mar.), and the House, 113–100 (22 May). The Senate (25 May) approved the Clayton amendment denying voting and officeholding privileges to aliens.

26 APR. MASSACHUSETTS EMIGRANT AID SOCIETY organized by **Eli Thayer** (1819–99) of Worcester, Mass., an adherent of "popular sovereignty." Reincorporated (21 Feb. 1855) as the **New England Emigrant Aid Co.,** it promoted the settlement of antislavery groups in Kansas with the ultimate object of making it a free state. It founded Lawrence and other Free State communities and was active in Kansas until 1857, bringing some 2,000 settlers there. The activities of the company led in turn to the organization of secret societies in Missouri for the purpose of establishing slavery in Kansas.

5 JUNE. CANADIAN RECIPROCITY TREATY. The prolonged Anglo-U.S. dispute over fishing privileges granted by the Convention of 1818 was settled by the Reciprocity Treaty of 1854 signed at Washington. The negotiations were handled by Secretary Marcy and a special British delegation headed by Lord Elgin, governor general of Canada. The agreement gave the U.S. offshore seafishing privileges along the inlets of Canada, New Brunswick, Nova Scotia, Prince Edward Island, and several adjacent small islands. The British were granted fishing privileges along U.S. shores to the 36th parallel. The reciprocity arrangement provided for the duty-free entry of many articles, chiefly agricultural commodities. The treaty was to remain in force for 10 years, and thereafter until terminated by either country. It was abrogated by the U.S. on 17 Mar. 1866.

6–13 JULY. REPUBLICAN PARTY. Popular dissatisfaction with the Kansas-Nebraska Act caused realignment of political forces in the North and West. The immediate impact was felt in the Northwest, where "anti-Nebraska" men of all parties united on the common platform of opposing the extension of slavery into the territories. A coalition meeting of Whig, Free-Soilers, and antislavery Democrats held at Ripon, Wis. (28 Feb.), recommended the organization of a new party on this single principle and suggested the name "Republican." A state meeting of Michigan citizens held at Jackson (6 July) officially adopted the name. The Jackson platform called for the repeal of the Kansas-Nebraska Act and the Fugitive Slave Law and demanded the abolition of slavery in the District of Columbia. Similar meetings were held (13 July) in Ohio, Wisconsin, Indiana, and Vermont. By the end of the year the organization had begun to spread throughout the North. Among its leaders were radical antislavery men such as **Charles Sumner** and **George Julian;** Free-Soilers such as **Salmon P. Chase** and **Lyman Trumbull;** and conservative Whigs such as **Edward Bates** and **Orville H. Browning.**

KNOW-NOTHING PARTY. The anti-Catholic and anti-immigrant movement of the 1840s was revived on a national scale after the election of 1852, and by 1854 had emerged as an important political force. Officially called the American party, it was popularly known as the Know-Nothing party because of the password "I don't know" used by members of secret lodges that were active in nearly every state. These bodies stemmed from a clandestine organization, the Order of the Star Spangled Banner, established at New York in 1849. Its rise was symptomatic of the breakup of the 2 major parties over the slavery issue. The party program called for the exclusion o[f] Catholics and foreigners from public office and for a 21-year residence for immigrants as qualification for citizenship. Internal divisions over the slavery issue ultimately weakened the party, which reached its zenith in 1854–55. Its disruption came after the election of 1856. The Republicans drew accessions of strength from its ranks.

18 OCT. OSTEND MANIFESTO. When the U.S. merchant vessel *Black Warrior* was seized and condemned by authorities at Havana (28 Feb.) for an error in her manifest, a clamor for war with Spain broke out among expansionists in Congress. **Pierre Soulé** (1802–70), U.S. minister to Spain, presented a claim for damages (8 Apr.) followed by an ultimatum demanding immediate satisfaction. Secretary Marcy checked Soulé and in 1855 the U.S. accepted a Spanish apology and reparation.

Soulé was instructed by Marcy (16 Aug.) to meet at Ostend, Belgium, with **John Y. Mason** (1799–1859) and **James Buchanan,** U.S. minister to France and Great Britain, respectively, for the purpose of shaping a policy on the acquisition of Cuba. The meeting (9 Oct.), with the approval of President Pierce, resulted in the Ostend Manifesto, sent as a confidential diplomatic dispatch from Aix-la-Chapelle (its common designation was of later origin). Declaring Cuba indispensable for the security of slavery, the ministers recommended that the U.S. should make every effort to buy Cuba; should Spain refuse, "then by every law human and divine, we shall be justified in wresting it from Spain, if we possess the power." The aggressive pronouncement of the document was the work of Soulé. The document brought Marcy's disavowal, and Soulé resigned (17 Dec.). Publication (3 Mar. 1855) of the manifesto aroused Northern feeling and ntensified Spanish resentment of the administration's annexationist policy. The newly born Republican party pointed to the manifesto as proof that a Southern-dominated administration had surrendered to pressure for more slave territory; Buchanan's participation recommended him to Southern Democrats.

16 OCT. LINCOLN'S "PEORIA SPEECH." Speaking at Springfield, Ill. (4 Oct.), **Abraham Lincoln,** whose reputation as a politician and lawyer was still confined largely to Illinois, condemned the Kansas-Nebraska Act. The speech, delivered again at Peoria (16 Oct.), was Lincoln's first public denunciation of slavery. He denied that the Kansas-Nebraska Act was the result of a slaveholders' conspiracy. "I have no prejudice against the Southern people. . . . I surely will not blame them for not doing what I should not know how to do myself." He acknowledged the constitutional rights of the Southerners; with careful qualification favored gradual emancipation; and supported a fair and practical Fugitive Slave Law, but opposed slavery in free territory.

1855

"KANSAS QUESTION." The opening of Kansas to settlement under the "popular sovereignty" formula put that principle to a severe test. With congressional nonintervention a declared policy, control of the territorial government became a vital necessity. Armed contests between proslavery and antislavery settlers converted Kansas into a cockpit of civil war.

Proslavery Legislature. Andrew H. Reeder (Pa.), first territorial governor of Kansas, was appointed in June 1854. The election of **John W. Whitfield,** the proslavery candidate, as territorial delegate (29 Nov. 1854) was accompanied by fraud and violence, most of it the work

of about 1,700 armed men from western Missouri. Like methods were used by some 5,000 Missouri "Border Ruffians" in the election (30 Mar.) of a territorial legislature. Under armed intimidation, Reeder refused to declare the election fraudulent, and Kansas was organized with a proslavery legislature, which disregarded his conciliatory plea when it convened (2 July) at Pawnee and later (16 July) at Shawnee Mission, and enacted proslavery statutes providing severe penalties for antislavery agitation and authorizing a test oath for officeholders.

In convention at Big Springs (5 Sept.) the antislavery colonists repudiated the territorial legislature as illegal and asked admission to the Union under a free state constitution. Mass conventions (Sept.–Oct.) organized a Free State party. Arms poured in from the North. **James H. Lane** (Ind.) was appointed military commander of the Free State forces.

Antislavery Legislature. The **Topeka Constitution,** drawn up by a Free State convention (23 Oct.–2 Nov.), prohibited slavery. That the Free State colonists were not abolitionists was indicated by the ordinance prohibiting entry of Negroes which was submitted to popular vote together with the constitution. Both were adopted (15 Dec.) and a Free State governor and legislature were elected (15 Jan. 1856). Kansas now had dual government.

Meanwhile Reeder has been removed from office (31 July), ostensibly because of his implication in land speculation but actually because of his opposition to the proslavery legislature. He was succeeded by **Wilson Shannon** (Ohio), a proslavery man (arrived in Kansas 3 Sept.). On 9 Oct. Reeder was elected congressional delegate from Kansas Territory by the Free State men, while on 1 Oct. Whitfield had been reelected by proslavery men.

The so-called **"Wakarusa War"** (26

Nov.–7 Dec.), limited to a few shootings and brawls along the Wakarusa River near Lawrence, brought about 1,500 "Border Ruffians" into Kansas, who refrained from attacking Lawrence when they found that the town was heavily defended by Free State settlers. The "war" was terminated by the intervention of Gov. Shannon.

WALKER'S FILIBUSTERING EXPEDITIONS. American filibustering in the Caribbean region was climaxed by the expeditions against Nicaragua (1855–57) led by the military adventurer **William Walker** (1824–60). Although his incursions received some support in the South, they were widely misinterpreted in the North as part of a slaveholders' "plot" to extend slavery southward. Actually, Walker was backed by U.S. isthmian-transit interests (the Accessory Transit Co.).

Walker, who had led an unsuccessful filibustering expedition against Lower California (1853), exploited a civil war in Nicaragua to his own end, subjugated the divided country (June–Oct. 1855), and set himself up as dictator. Though President Pierce issued a proclamation (8 Dec.) against the invasion of Nicaragua, his reception of Walker's emissary (14 May 1856) amounted to virtual recognition. Walker became president (July 1856) and issued a decree opening Nicaragua to slavery. His downfall was brought about by **Cornelius Vanderbilt** (now in control of Accessory Transit Co.), who promoted the formation of a coalition of neighboring republics that ousted Walker, who surrendered 1 May 1857 to the U.S. naval commander.

Acclaimed in the South as a hero, Walker raised a new expedition and landed (25 Nov. 1857) at Greytown, at the mouth of the San Juan River. By this time Walker had seriously embarrassed U.S. isthmian policy. His expedition was broken up by the U.S. navy.

Again, in Aug. 1860, he landed at Honduras at the head of a filibustering expedition, was captured, court-martialed, and executed (12 Sept.).

1856

"BLEEDING KANSAS." In a special message to Congress (24 Jan.) Pierce condemned the Topeka government as an act of rebellion and in effect recognized the proslavery legislature. Although he issued (11 Feb.) a proclamation warning both Free State men and "Border Ruffians" to disperse, it was now clear that Pierce was committed to support of the proslavery element in Kansas.

21 MAY–15 SEPT. Civil War. Skirmishes began in the spring of 1856, often between land speculators and would-be settlers rather than forces of slavery and freedom, or were started by unruly plunderers, instead of idealists on either side, who hoped to profit from the turbulence. By this time the Free State party had received from the East fresh shipments of arms (the Sharps rifles popularly known as "Beecher's Bibles"). On 21 May, Lawrence was taken and sacked, as "Border Ruffians" joined Kansas proslavery men (including Col. Jefferson Buford's company and the Kickapoo Rangers) in burning down the Free State Hotel, pillaging many homes, and destroying the offices and presses of *The Herald of Freedom* and *The Kansas Free State*. One man was killed. Exaggerated accounts of the Lawrence affair inflamed Northern antislavery sentiment.

In retaliation for proslavery depredations, the fanatical **John Brown** (1800–59), with 6 companions (4 of them his sons), carried out the Pottawatomie massacre on the night of 24–25 May with midnight executions of 5 proslavery colonists who lived near Dutch Henry's Crossing at Pottawatomie Creek. Free State men disavowed this act of terror-

ism, but the incident raised feeling to a pitch that caused both parties to alert their military forces.

Gov. Shannon issued a proclamation (4 June) warning all irregular armed bodies to disperse. The Free State party sized Franklin (13 Aug.), a proslavery stronghold. About 300 proslavery men attacked the town of Osawatomie (30 Aug.), which was defended by John Brown and about 40 other Free State men, drove off their opponents, and pillaged the settlement. Guerrilla warfare was now raging throughout the territory. The total loss (Nov. 1855–Dec. 1856) was estimated at 200 killed and $2 million in property destroyed.

Shannon resigned as governor (18 Aug.) and was replaced by Daniel Woodson, a proslavery man who became acting governor. Woodson issued a proclamation (25 Aug.) declaring Kansas in a state of open insurrection and called out the proslavery militia. **John W. Geary** (Pa.), appointed territorial governor by Pierce, assumed his official duties on 11 Sept. With the aid of federal troops, Geary intercepted (15 Sept.) an army of 2,500 "Border Ruffians" who were marching on Lawrence and persuaded them to return to their homes. By his intervention, Geary brought temporary peace to Kansas.

Congressional Reaction. The Topeka Legislature adopted (4 Mar.) a memorial requesting statehood and elected Lane and Reeder U.S. senators. Douglas introduced (17 Mar.) an enabling act for Kansas, providing for the election of a constitutional convention and the formation of a state government. He denounced the Topeka government and the New England Emigrant Aid Co. as lawless bodies.

The congressional opposition to Pierce and Douglas supported the admission of Kansas under the Topeka constitution. An amendment to the Douglas bill was formulated by Robert Toombs (Ga.). Its substance provided for a free and open election for a constitutional convention. Introduced on 30 June, the Toombs amendment was approved in the Senate, 33–12 (2 July), but never considered in the House.

The House (19 Mar.) appointed a special 3-man committee to investigate the conduct of the Kansas elections. Its report, confirming the charges of fraud and violence, provided material for Republican electioneering. The House passed a bill (3 July) to admit Kansas under the Topeka constitution, but the measure was quashed in the Senate. The House (1 Aug.) refused to seat either the proslavery or Free State territorial delegate.

The Republicans held up an army appropriation bill (18 Aug.) by attaching a rider forbidding the use of the army in aid of the proslavery Kansas legislature. The bill was finally passed (30 Aug.) without the Kansas rider only after an extra session of Congress had been called. When Congress adjourned (30 Aug.), Kansas still had no settled government. The Democrats charged that the Republicans had deliberately left "Bleeding Kansas" to anarchy in order that they might exploit a catch phrase in the approaching elections.

19–20 MAY. "The Crime Against Kansas." During the congressional debates on Kansas, Sen. Charles Sumner delivered a speech that later became known by the title "The Crime Against Kansas." It was a bitter denunciation of the "Slave Oligarchy" and its "rape" of Kansas. Sumner's tirade included coarse and insulting aspersions upon the character of several senators, particularly the absent Andrew P. Butler (S.C.). In retaliation, Rep. Preston S. Brooks (S.C.), Butler's nephew, assaulted Sumner as the latter sat at his desk in the Senate chamber (22 May). Sumner collapsed under

the heavy blows of a cane. House attempts to expel or censure Brooks failed. His act brought general approval throughout the South. Brooks resigned his seat (14 July) and was unanimously reelected by his district. In the North, news of the assault created widespread indignation that became even more inflamed when it was reported that Lawrence had been pillaged. The Brooks-Sumner affair was condemned as a gross violation of liberty of speech. Except for a single day in Feb. 1857, Sumner did not again attend congressional sessions until Dec. 1859. During that time his empty chair in the Senate remained a symbol of Northern opinion of the attack upon him.

PRESIDENTIAL CAMPAIGN. The National Convention of the American (Know-Nothing) party met at Philadelphia (22 Feb.) and nominated **Millard Fillmore** (N.Y.) for president and **Andrew J. Donelson** (Tenn.) for vice-president on a nativist platform. These candidates were also nominated by the Whig National Convention that met at Baltimore (17 Sept.) and adopted a platform eschewing specific planks and warning against the sectionalization of parties.

The Democratic National Convention at Cincinnati (2 June) nominated **James Buchanan** (Pa.) for president on the 17th ballot (Pierce and Douglas being rejected because of their close association with the Kansas issue) and **John C. Breckinridge** (Ky.) for vice-president. The Democratic platform affirmed the Compromise of 1850 and supported the Kansas-Nebraska Act as "the only sound and safe solution of the slavery question."

The Republican National Convention met at Philadelphia (17 June) and unanimously nominated Col. **John C. Frémont** (Calif.) for president and **William L. Dayton** (N.J.) for vice-president on a platform upholding congressional authority to control slavery in the territories. Other planks condemned the Ostend Manifesto and favored a railroad to the Pacific and the admission of Kansas as a free state.

The chief campaign issue was "Bleeding Kansas," as Republican electioneers called it. The American party split on the slavery issue and in the Northeast supported the Republicans. The Democrats and Fillmore supporters attacked the "Black Republicans" as a sectional threat to the Union.

4 Nov. PRESIDENTIAL ELECTION. Popular vote: **Buchanan,** 1,838,169; Frémont, 1,335,264; Fillmore, 874,534. Electoral vote (counted 11 Feb. 1857): **Buchanan,** 174 (14 slave and 5 free states); Frémont, 114 (11 free states); Fillmore, 8 (1 slave state, Md.). The election results forecast the speedy demise of the Whig organization and the hardening of sectional lines.

1857

4 MAR. Buchanan's inaugural address condemned the slavery agitation and supported the policy of noninterference with slavery in the states and "popular sovereignty" in the territories.

6 MAR. DRED SCOTT DECISION. Dred Scott, a Negro slave and the household servant of Dr. John Emerson, an army surgeon, was taken (1834) by his master from St. Louis, Mo., to Rock Island, Ill. (where slavery had been forbidden by the Ordinance of 1787), and later to Ft. Snelling, in Wisconsin Territory (where slavery was prohibited by the Missouri Compromise). Scott remained on free soil during most of the period 1834–38.

In 1846 Scott sued for his liberty in the Missouri courts, holding that he had become free because of his stay in a free state and free territory. A lower court's judgment in favor of Scott was overruled (1852) by the state supreme court, which had previously ruled that under such circumstances a slave became free upon his return to Missouri. The case was maneuvered into the federal district court and finally to the Supreme Court of the U.S. (*Dred Scott* v. *Sandford,* 19 Howard 393). Scott's nominal owner at this time was John F. A. Sanford of New York (whose name is misspelled in the official reports).

The case involved 3 leading issues: (1) whether Scott was a citizen of the state of Missouri and thus entitled to sue in the federal courts; (2) whether his temporary stay on free soil had given him a title to freedom that was still valid upon his return to the slave state of Missouri; and (3) the constitutionality of the Missouri Compromise, whose prohibition of slavery applied to Wisconsin Territory.

Each of the justices handed down a separate opinion (that of Chief Justice Roger B. Taney is customarily cited for the majority). The majority held that Scott (and hence all Negro slaves or their descendants) was not a citizen of the U.S. or the state of Missouri, and thus was not entitled to sue in the federal courts (on this point, only 3 justices explicitly denied such citizenship, while only 2 affirmed it). Having refused jurisdiction, the majority passed on other issues: (1) Scott's temporary residence in free territory had not made him free upon his return to Missouri, since his status was determined by the laws of the state in which he resided when the question of his freedom was raised (on this point, the decision was 6 to 3); and (2) the Missouri Compromise was unconstitutional on the ground that under the 5th Amendment Congress was prohibited from depriving persons of their property without due process of law (on this point, the decision was 6 to 3), a principle first enunciated as regards a state

law in *Wynehamer* v. *The People,* 13 N.Y. 378 (1856).

The dissenting opinions of Justices John McLean and Benjamin R. Curtis, both of whom are generally held responsible for introducing the thorny issue of the Missouri Compromise, maintained that free Negroes were citizens of the U.S. and that Congress was constitutionally empowered (Art. IV, Sect. 3) to regulate slavery in the territories. Curtis' opinion was subsequently used by Republican and abolitionist elements as one of their chief grounds for attacking the court decision.

Northern denunciation of the decision included charges of "conspiracy." Opponents pointed to the fact that Buchanan's inaugural had predicted that the slavery controversy would be "speedily and finally settled" by the court. It has been established that Justices Robert C. Grier and John Catron violated judicial ethics in confidentially advising the president as to the intention of the court; there is no substance to the charge of collusion. The decision, first since *Marbury* v. *Madison* (1803) in which the court declared an act of Congress unconstitutional, lowered the court's prestige among Northerners and widened the sectional cleavage.

19 OCT.–21 DEC. LECOMPTON CONSTITUTION. In Kansas, Gov. Geary's recommendations for a thorough revamping of the laws to assure free elections and genuine self-government were ignored by the proslavery legislature. Meeting at Lecompton (12 Jan.– 14 Feb.), the legislature called for a census enumeration (Mar.) and an election (15 June) for delegates to a constitutional convention. No provision was made for submitting the constitution to a popular vote. Geary, whose sympathy with the proslavery party had been replaced by a desire for impartial justice, vetoed the bill, which was promptly passed over his objection. Geary's efforts to follow a nonpartisan course in Kansas failed to secure the support of the Pierce administration. He resigned (4 Mar.) and was succeeded (26 Mar.) by a Buchanan appointee, Robert J. Walker (Miss.).

Walker's inaugural address (26 May) made a plea for cooperation and pledged that any constitution adopted would be submitted to a fair vote. A Free State convention met at Topeka (15 July), but Walker finally persuaded its leaders to abandon their refusal to participate in the election of a new legislature. Walker's policy brought from the South demands that any constitution drawn up by the proslavery convention should go into force without being submitted to the people.

The territorial elections were held (5 Oct.) under fairly strict supervision. Walker and the territorial secretary, Frederick P. Stanton (Tenn.), threw out thousands of fraudulent votes cast by the proslavery party. The final results gave the Free State party a decisive majority in both houses of the legislature.

The Lecompton convention (19 Oct.– 8 Nov.) recognized that a proslavery constitution would be rejected if submitted to a fair vote. Instead of arranging to place the constitution as a whole before the people, the convention drafted a special article on slavery which alone was to be submitted to a popular vote. The article guaranteed the right of property in slaves. Should it be rejected (the "constitution without slavery"), slavery would exist "no longer," but the right of property in slaves already in the territory would not be abolished. This arrrangement gave the proslavery party an obvious advantage; in addition, the elections were to be conducted by officials named by the convention.

The Lecompton convention was denounced throughout the North. Walker, opposed to the Lecompton proposal, went to Washington to place the question before the president. Buchanan was anxious to preserve party unity and harmony; moreover, he was under the influence of his pro-Southern cabinet. He decided to reverse his earlier pledge to Walker, and upheld the Lecompton convention. Walker resigned (17 Dec.). Buchanan's fateful step precipitated a party crisis by placing Douglas (who had come out against the Lecompton constitution, 9 Dec.) in open opposition, and helped to bring on the disruption of the Democratic party.

The vote on the Lecompton constitution was held on 21 Dec. Free State men and others among its opponents refused to participate. Results: for the constitution with slavery, 6,226 (of these, 2,720 were later shown to be fraudulent); for the constitution without slavery, 569.

Rejection. The Free State party induced Stanton, now acting governor, to convene the territorial legislature on 7 Dec., in advance of its scheduled date. The legislature called another election, permitting unequivocal voting for or against the Lecompton constitution. The administration punished Stanton by removing him from office. The Kansas election was held on 4 Jan. 1858. Results: for the constitution with slavery, 138; for the constitution without slavery, 24; against the constitution, 10,226.

24 AUG. PANIC OF 1857 (also pp. 741, 748). The failure of the New York City branch of the Ohio Life Insurance and Trust Co. precipitated a commercial and financial panic.

"THE IMPENDING CRISIS." *The Impending Crisis of the South: How to Meet It*, by Hinton Rowan Helper (a native of N.C.), published at New York in mid-1857, sought to prove by statistics (drawn largely from the census of 1850) that slavery had degraded and impoverished broad sections of Southern whites. A compressed version of the book (the *Compedium*) was endorsed by 68 House Republicans (1859) and 100,000 copies distributed as electioneering material. The South banned the book on the ground that it was insurrectionary. In Dec. 1859, John Sherman (Ohio) was denied the House speakership because of his endorsement of the work. The Southern outcry against "Helperism" brought the publication of several rejoinders, among them *Helper's Impending Crisis Dissected,* by Samuel M. Wolfe.

1858

DOUGLAS AND LECOMPTON. In support of the Southern extremist position, President Buchanan submitted the Lecompton constitution to Congress (2 Feb.), recommending the admission of Kansas as a slave state. His policy stirred Douglas to open revolt. Taking his stand on principle, Douglas condemned the Lecompton constitution (3 Feb.) as a violation of "popular sovereignty" and a mockery of justice. The executive patronage was brought to bear against Douglas and his supporters. The Senate, 33–25 (23 Mar.), voted to admit Kansas under the Lecompton constitution.

1 APR. Crittenden-Montgomery Amendment, providing for resubmission of the constitution to popular vote, passed the House, 120–112.

4 MAY. English Bill, an administration compromise measure, sponsored by William H. English (Ind.), a moderate Democrat, was reported to both houses on 23 Apr. Designed to quell party upheaval, the English bill provided for a popular vote on the Lecompton constitution as a whole. In the event of ratification Kansas was assured of c.4 million acres of public land grants (Lecomptonites had requested 23½ million acres) and 5% of the net proceeds from about 2 million acres to be sold by the government in July. Rejection would delay admission to the Union until a census indictated that Kansas had a population (about 90,000) required for a congressional representative. By winning the votes of 9 anti-Lecompton Democrats, the compromise broke the House deadlock. In the Senate, Douglas wavered, but finally opposed the measure. On 30 Apr. the English bill passed the House, 112–103, and the Senate, 31–22.

16 JUNE. "A HOUSE DIVIDED." Abraham Lincoln (p. 1085), whose political reputation was still confined largely to the Northwest, in a speech before the Republican state convention at Springfield that nominated him for U.S. senator, took a radical stand on the institution of slavery, but scrupulously refrained from criticizing slaveholders. Lincoln asserted that under the Kansas-Nebraska Act the slavery agitation "has not only not ceased, but has constantly augmented. In my opinion, it will not cease until a crisis shall have been reached and passed. 'A house divided against itself cannot stand.' I believe this government cannot endure permanently half slave and half free. I do not expect the Union to be dissolved; I do not expect the house to fall; but I do expect it will cease to be divided. It will become all one thing, or all the other." Both as phrase and concept, the Biblical "house divided" passage was not new in the slavery controversy. It had been used, e.g., by Edmund Quincy, Theodore Parker, and the New York *Tribune*.

2 AUG. Lecompton Constitution rejected by Kansas voters (in favor, 1,926; against, 11,812). The decision to remain in territorial status brought the disturbances virtually to an end. Under the

Dred Scott decision slavery was legal in Kansas; practically, it was excluded because of Free Soil domination. Kansas did not enter the Union until 29 Jan. 1861, when it was admitted under the free-state **Wyandotte Constitution** (ratified 4 Oct. 1859). Political results of the Kansas controversy (1) gave the Republicans a powerful campaign issue; (2) encouraged Southern extremists; (3) lost Buchanan the support of Northern Democrats; and, by way of the Douglas-Buchanan feud, (4) disrupted the Democratic party.

21 AUG.–15 OCT. LINCOLN-DOUGLAS DEBATES. On 24 July Lincoln challenged Douglas, his opponent in the Illinois senatorial race, to a series of joint debates. Douglas accepted. Seven debates were held during the course of a state-wide campaign: Ottawa (21 Aug.), Freeport (27 Aug.), Jonesboro (15 Sept.), Charleston (18 Sept.), Galesburg (7 Oct.), Quincy (13 Oct.), and Alton (15 Oct.). The debates covered the ground of the slavery controversy and its impact on politics, law, and government. From them dates Lincoln's emergence as a national figure.

The most memorable debate was held at Freeport, where Lincoln asked Douglas how he could reconcile the doctrine of "popular sovereignty" with the Dred Scott decision. The question evoked from Douglas his formulation of what became known as the **"Freeport doctrine":** the people of a territory could, by lawful means, exclude slavery prior to the formation of a state constitution. The right to admit or bar slavery existed despite the Dred Scott decision, "for the reason that slavery cannot exist a day or an hour anywhere, unless it is supported by local police regulations," which could only be established by the local legislature. The "Freeport doctrine" provoked a storm of Southern criticism, and, along

with his opposition to the Lecompton constitution, was instrumental in depriving Douglas of Southern backing for the presidential nomination in 1860.

The debates as a whole illuminated the sharp difference between Lincoln and Douglas: where Lincoln regarded slavery as "a moral, a social, and a political wrong" (Quincy, 13 Oct., although he avoided a radical position, and at Charleston, 18 Sept., rejected Negro equality), Douglas evaded the moral issue. Lincoln lost the election by a narrow margin, winning the larger popular vote but failing to carry the legislature, where the vote was 54–41.

It was during this campaign, between the 2d and 3d debates, that Lincoln is supposed to have said at Clinton (2 Sept.): "You can fool all of the people some of the time, and some of the people all of the time, but you cannot fool all of the people all the time."

25 OCT. "IRREPRESSIBLE CONFLICT." Speaking at Rochester, N.Y., Sen. William H. Seward, at that time the leading contender for the Republican presidential nomination, delivered a radical pronouncement on the sectional controversy: "It is an irrepressible conflict between opposing and enduring forces, and it means that the United States must and will, sooner or later, become either entirely a slaveholding nation or entirely a free-labor nation."

REPUBLICAN SUCCESS. The results of the autumn elections indicated the rapidly growing strength of the Republican party. The chief campaign issue was the Lecompton constitution. In some areas the Republicans also stressed the protective tariff (Pennsylvania, New Jersey, and New England) and the homestead policy (Western states). Except for Illinois (where the prestige of Douglas was an important factor) and Indiana, every Northern state election was carried by the Republicans, even Buchanan's own state, Pennsylvania. In New York, the Republicans and antiadministration Democrats won 29 of the 33 congressional seats. In all, the Republicans gained 18 seats in the congressional elections. With a dozen anti-Lecompton Democrats in the House, the administration lost control of that body.

1859

16–18 Oct. JOHN BROWN'S RAID. Obtaining money from a number of New England and New York abolitionists (including Theodore Parker, Thomas W. Higginson, Samuel G. Howe, and Gerrit Smith), John Brown formulated a plan for instigating a slave insurrection in Virginia, establishing a free state in the southern Appalachians, and spreading a servile rebellion southward. Collecting arms and equipment at the Kennedy farm in Maryland, across the Potomac from Harpers Ferry, Va., he led 18 of the 21 men in his band (including 5 Negroes) in an attack on Harpers Ferry. They seized the federal arsenal and armory and held some of the local citizenry as hostages. No slaves came to the aid of the attackers. After 2 days of battle, Brown and his surviving followers were taken prisoner by a force of U.S. marines commanded by Col. Robert E. Lee.

25 Oct.–2 Dec. Treason Trial. Brown was indicted for treason against the state of Virginia and criminal conspiracy to incite a slave insurrection. He was tried (25–31 Oct.) at Charles Town, Va., convicted, and hanged (2 Dec.). Four of his band were hanged on 16 Dec.; 2 others on 16 Mar. 1860. Brown's raid spread alarm throughout the South, which fixed responsibility not only on the abolitionists but also on the "Black Republicans." Conservative Northerners deplored the raid, but antislavery groups mourned Brown as a hero and a martyr.

AFRICAN SLAVE TRADE. The **Southern Commercial Convention** at Vicksburg, Miss. (9–19 May), urged the repeal of all laws prohibiting the foreign slave trade. This move was in accord with the growing Southern view that the federal government's sole relation to slavery should be that of positive protection (on this score, Southern extremists were also demanding a federal slave code for the territories). Some Southerners, notably Jefferson Davis and William L. Yancey, condemned the slave importation act of 1820 as unconstitutional and called for its repeal.

The Buchanan administration was on the whole firmly opposed to the foreign slave trade. It increased the naval patrols off the African coast. In his message to Congress (19 Dec.), Buchanan declared that all lawful means would be employed to suppress the illicit traffic. But the administration also ordered that U.S. merchant ships were to be protected against detention or search, thus giving them immunity to the more effective British patrols. Under such circumstances, there was little recourse against non-American vessels which used the U.S. flag fraudulently.

1860

2 Feb. DAVIS RESOLUTIONS. The program of the Southern extremists was embodied in the set of resolutions introduced in the Senate by **Jefferson Davis** (p. 1010), asserted that (1) no state had a right to interfere with the domestic institutions of other states; (2) any attack on slavery within the slave states was a violation of the Constitution; (3) it was the duty of the Senate to oppose all discriminatory measures against persons or property in the territories; (4)

neither Congress nor a territorial legislature was in any way empowered to impair the right to hold slaves in the territories, and the federal government should extend all needful protection (i.e., a slave code) to slavery in the territories; (5) the territories might not decide on the question of slavery until admission to the Union; and (6) all state legislation interfering with the recovery of fugitive slaves was inimical to the constitutional compact. The resolutions, adopted 24 May, touched off an extensive Senate debate on the constitutional and political aspects of the slavery controversy, and widened the breach between the Northern and Southern wings of the Democratic party.

SECESSION THREATS. In the winter and spring of 1860 political leaders and state legislatures in the lower South openly avowed the right of secession and the idea of Southern solidarity. The more radical resolutions were adopted in South Carolina and Mississippi; in these states and a few others, the legislatures passed appropriations for raising military forces. Many of the states (e.g., Ala. and Fla.) asserted that the election of a "Black Republican" president would be considered just cause for dissolving the Union.

Prominent among the leaders who initiated an exchange of opinion on a course of future action was Gov. **William H. Gist** (S.C., 1807–74). However, the states of the upper South (notably Va.) did not support Gist's project for a convention on Southern rights. At this time public opinion in the upper South overwhelmingly believed that Southern grievances could be resolved within the Union. Even in the lower South (particularly Ga.) sentiment was divided.

27 FEB. LINCOLN'S COOPER UNION SPEECH. Appearing before a distinguished audience at Cooper Union in New York City, Abraham Lincoln, still a virtual stranger to Eastern audiences, delivered a carefully weighed speech refuting Douglas' "popular sovereignty" doctrine and examining Southern attitudes toward the North and the Republican party. Lincoln condemned Northern extremism and made an appeal for sectional understanding, but did not minimize the gravity of Southern disunionist threats and indicated that no compromise with principle on the slavery extension issue was possible.

PRESIDENTIAL CAMPAIGN. The disruption of the Democratic party was formalized at the national nominating convention at Charleston, S.C. (23 Apr.). The Southern Democrats, now under the dominant influence of the radicals, insisted on a platform supporting positive protection to slavery in the territories. The Douglas Democrats reaffirmed the party platform of 1856 approving congressional nonintervention, abiding by Supreme Court decisions, and acquiring Cuba. When the Douglas forces carried the convention, the delegations of 8 Southern states withdrew to meet in a separate convention. The Charleston convention adjourned (3 May), having failed to agree on a nominee after 57 ballots. The Democrats reassembled at Baltimore (18 June) and, following another session of Southern delegates, nominated **Stephen A. Douglas** (Ill.) for president (2nd ballot) and **Herschel V. Johnson** (Ga.) for vice-president.

The Charleston seceders, after meeting at Richmond (11 June), convened at Baltimore (28 June) and nominated **John C. Breckinridge** (Ky.) for president and **Joseph Lane** (Ore.) for vice-president on a platform supporting slavery in the territories, the admission of states into the Union on an equal footing with the rest, and the acquisition of Cuba.

The remnants of the Whig and American parties convened at Baltimore (9 May) and established the Constitutional

Union party, nominating **John Bell** (Tenn.) for president and **Edward Everett** (Mass.) for vice-president on a platform condemning sectional parties and upholding "the Constitution of the country, the Union of the States and the enforcement of the laws."

The Republican National Convention met at Chicago (16 May) and nominated **Abraham Lincoln** (Ill.) for president (3d ballot) after William H. Seward (N.Y.) had led on the first 2 ballots. Lincoln's "availability," as opposed to Seward's long political career and his identification with antislavery radicalism, was a prime factor in winning the nomination. **Hannibal Hamlin** (Me.) was chosen for vice-president.

The skillfully drawn Republican platform was calculated to win support in the East as well as the West, from conservatives as well as radicals. It reaffirmed the principles of the Declaration of Independence, the Wilmot Proviso, and the right of each state to control its domestic institutions. It supported internal improvements, a railroad to the Pacific, a homestead law, and a liberal immigration policy. Its reference to a tariff adjustment which would "encourage the development of the industrial interests of the whole country" was in-terpreted as support of a protective tariff (a leading issue in the doubtful states of Pa. and N.J.). The platform condemned attempts to reopen the African slave trade and denied the authority of Congress or a territorial legislature to give legal status to slavery in the territories.

6 Nov. PRESIDENTIAL ELECTION. The division among his opponents made Lincoln's election almost certain. The state elections (Sept.–Oct.), bringing Republican victories in Maine, Vermont, Indiana, and Pennsylvania, indicated the impending result. Popular vote: **Lincoln,** 1,866,352; Douglas, 1,375,157; Breckinridge, 847,953; Bell, 589,581. The electoral vote (Lincoln failing to secure a single Southern vote) demonstrated the sectional character of the contest: **Lincoln,** 180 (carrying 18 free states); Breckinridge, 72 (carrying 11 slave states); Bell, 39 (carrying 3 border slave states); Douglas, 12 (carrying Mo., and 3 N.J. votes). Had the Lincoln opposition combined on a fusion ticket (attempted unsuccessfully in several states), it would have changed the result only in New Jersey, California, and Oregon for a total of 11 electoral votes. Lincoln would still have had 169, a clear majority.

THE CIVIL WAR AND RECONSTRUCTION, 1861-77

★   ★
★

The Civil War established for all time the supremacy of the Union over the states and ended the institution of slavery. In his noblest utterance President Lincoln declared that the war was a contest to insure that "government of the people, by the people, and for the people shall not perish from the earth." In addition, the Civil War marked the triumph of the industrial North over the agricultural South and forecast, if it did not promote, the enormously rapid industrialization of the nation which followed in its wake. If the industrial potential of the victor determined the outcome of the war, the record hardly supports the view that the nation would have gone to war over the issue of a tariff, a national banking act, or special grants for railroads, as none of these issues had precipitated such a conflict in the past.

Decisive though the Civil War appeared to be, it failed to come to grips with the basic problem of race relations which underpinned the institution of slavery. It provided technical freedom for the slaves without genuine equality, and it was responsible for transforming the race problem from one that was largely sectional to one that became national in scope and intensity. Indeed, the return of the seceded states to the Union became involved in a political struggle that turned the Reconstruction era into a time of bitterness and hatred. The legacy of Reconstruction cast a long shadow, and many of its unsolved problems persist to haunt American society.

1860, 13 Nov.–24 Dec. SOUTH CAROLINA SECESSION CRISIS. On news of Lincoln's election the South Carolina legislature by unanimous vote called for a state convention, which met at Columbia and passed (20 Dec.) without a dissenting vote an ordinance declaring that "the union now subsisting between South Carolina and the other States, under the name of the 'United States of America,' is hereby dissolved." The convention then issued (24 Dec.) a "Declaration of Immediate Causes" reiterating the arguments for state sovereignty and justifying secession on grounds of the North's long attack on slavery, the accession to power of a sectional party, and the election of a president "whose opinions and purposes are hostile to slavery."

1861

9 JAN.–1 FEB. EXTENSION OF SECESSION. South Carolina was followed by the other 10 states which ultimately formed the Confederate States of America. The 7 states of the lower South (S.C., 20 Dec.; Miss., 9 Jan.; Fla., 10 Jan.; Ala., 11 Jan.; Ga., 19 Jan.; La., 26 Jan.; and Tex., 1 Feb.) grounded secession on Northern aggression against their "domestic institutions." The 4 states of the upper South (Va., Ark., Tenn., and N.C.), though not seceding at this time, warned they would oppose any attempt of the federal government to coerce a state. In only 3 states (Tex., Va., and Tenn.) were the ordinances of secession submitted to the voters for ratification; elsewhere public opinion was registered through the election of delegates to state conventions. The votes in these 3 states: Texas (23 Feb.), 34,794 for, 11,255 against; Virginia (23 May), 96,750 for, 32,134 against; Tennessee (8 June) 104,913 for, 47,238 against (on 9 Feb. a call to consider secession was rejected, 68,282 to 59,449), but in all cases the referenda were held after the state governments had already committed themselves to the Confederacy. Sizable Unionist minorities existed in some areas (notably N.C., Va., and Tenn.), and some outstanding Southern leaders opposed secession, including **Alexander H. Stephens** (p. 1157, in a speech as late as 14 Nov. 1860), **Benjamin H. Hill** (1823–82), and **Herschel V. Johnson** (1812–80) of Georgia; **Benjamin F. Perry** of South Carolina; and Gov. **Sam Houston** of Texas.

BUCHANAN'S LAST DAYS. President Buchanan in his message to Congress (3 Dec. 1860) recognized the grievances of the slave states, deprecated the disruption of the Union, but announced the impotence of the federal government to prevent secession by force (relying upon an opinion of Attorney General Jeremiah S. Black). On 18 Dec. Sen. **John J. Crittenden** (Ky., 1787–1863) introduced a peace resolution which would have recognized slavery in territories south of 36°30′. This was unacceptable to Lincoln, who, through Thurlow Weed, advised its rejection. A Senate committee of 13 (appointed 20 Dec. 1860 to consider the Crittenden proposal) disagreed 31 Dec.

4 FEB. MONTGOMERY CONVENTION AND CONFEDERATE CONSTITUTION. Motivated by Southern nationalism and the need for united action, the seceding states called a convention which met at Montgomery, Ala., framed a constitution, and set up a provisional government (8 Feb.). The Confederate Constitution resembled the U.S. Constitution, with significant differences. It stressed "the sovereign and independent character" of each state while establishing a federal government and obliging state officers to swear to support the new constitution, which, together with the laws and treaties, was declared "the supreme law of the land." No specific provision was included for state secession, but that right was implied. Several clauses recognized and protected slavery, but Art. 1, cl. 1, sect. 9 prohibited "the importation of negroes of the African race from any foreign country." This clause was inserted to conciliate British and French opinion. The president was empowered to disapprove of specific appropriations in a bill which he signed.

4 FEB. PEACE CONVENTION, called at the urging of the Virginia assembly, met in Washington behind closed doors, with ex-president John Tyler as its chairman. Border and Northern states were represented as well as the South. On 23 Feb. the delegates called on president-elect Lincoln for a frank exchange of views. The convention failed to agree upon an acceptable compromise to save the Union.

9 FEB. JEFFERSON DAVIS (p. 1010) elected provisional president of the Confederacy; **Alexander H. Stephens** provisional vice-president; inaugurated 18 Feb. **Confederate Cabinet:** *State:* Robert Toombs (Feb.–July 1861), R. M. T. Hunter (July 1861–Mar. 1862), Judah P. Benjamin (Mar. 1862–Apr. 1865); *War:* Leroy P. Walker (Feb.–Sept. 1861), Benjamin (Sept. 1861–Mar. 1862), George W. Randolph (Mar.–Nov. 1862), Gustavus W. Smith (Nov. 1862), James A. Seddon (Nov. 1862–Jan. 1865), John C. Breckinridge (Jan.–Apr. 1865); *Navy:* Stephen R. Mallory (Feb. 1861–Apr. 1865); *Treasury:* Christopher G. Memminger (Feb. 1861–June 1864), George A. Trenholm (June 1864–Apr. 1865); *Attorney General:* Benjamin (Feb. 1861–Sept. 1862), Thomas Bragg (September 1861–Mar. 1862), Thomas H. Watts (Mar. 1862–Jan. 1864), George Davis (Jan. 1864–Apr. 1865); *Postmaster General:* J. H. Reagan (Mar. 1861–Apr. 1865). Until regular elections were held (6 Nov. 1861) the Montgomery convention acted as a provisional congress.

SEIZURE OF FEDERAL FORTS AND ARSENALS. On 28 Dec. South Carolina commissioners presented demands on President Buchanan for removal of U.S. troops from Charleston Harbor and delivery of forts within the state. Buchanan refused (31 Dec.), but on 30 Dec. South Carolina troops seized the U.S. arsenal at Charleston. Other seizures: 3 Jan., Ft. Pulaski by Georgia state troops; 4 Jan., Mt. Vernon arsenal and 5 Jan., Ft. Morgan and Ft. Gaines by Alabama troops; 6 Jan., Apalachicola arsenal by Florida troops; 10 Jan., Baton Rouge arsenal and barracks by Louisiana troops; 24 Jan., Augusta arsenal by Georgia troops; 8 Feb., Little Rock arsenal by Arkansas troops; 16 Feb., San Antonio arsenal by Texas troops. On 18 Feb. Gen. David E. Twiggs surrendered to Texas U.S. military posts in that state.

Ft. Sumter. On 26 Dec. Maj. **Robert Anderson** (1805–71) commander of U.S. troops in Charleston Harbor, withdrew his garrison from Ft. Moultrie to the more formidable Ft. Sumter. On 5 Jan. President Buchanan ordered the dispatch to Sumter of the *Star of the West,* an unarmed ship with reinforcements and provisions. But on 9 Jan. the ship was repulsed with fire from South Carolina shore batteries and returned to New York. Buchanan's policy was to collect public revenues and protect public property "so far as . . . practicable under existing laws."

11–23 FEB. LINCOLN'S JOURNEY TO WASHINGTON. President-elect Lincoln took leave (11 Feb.) from his neighbors in Springfield, "not knowing when or whether I ever may return, with a task before me greater than that which rested upon Washington," and began his journey to the capital. In brief speeches en route (Indianapolis, Cincinnati, Columbus, Cleveland, Pittsburgh, Buffalo, Rochester, Syracuse, Albany, Troy, New York, Trenton, Philadelphia, Harrisburg) he avoided disclosure of plans and policies. Warned (22 Feb.) of an assassination plot in Baltimore, he was secretly put aboard a special train at night, arriving at Washington at 6 A.M., 23 Feb.

4 MAR. LINCOLN'S 1ST INAUGURAL was firm but conciliatory toward the South. He assured the South that the rights of that section would be protected and declared: "I have no purpose directly or indirectly to interfere with the institution of slavery in the States where it exists." On the other hand, secession would not be countenanced. "Physically speaking," he insisted, "we cannot separate. . . . No State, upon its own mere action, can lawfully get out of the Union." But there need be no violence "unless it be forced upon the national authority."

The Civil War, 1861–65

1–15 APR. FT. SUMTER AND THE CALL TO ARMS. Desirous of avoiding an overt act, Lincoln delayed a decision on Ft. Sumter. On 1 Apr. Secretary of State Seward proposed that Sumter be evacuated, but that the Gulf ports be reinforced and a strong stand adopted toward foreign nations in the interest of national unity. Lincoln, in reply, made clear that he intended to run his own administration. The president considered (4 Apr.) a proposal that Sumter be yielded in exchange for a loyalty pledge from Virginia, but rejected it as indicative of fatal weakness. When he decided to provision the fort he notified South Carolina (6 Apr.) that an expedition was on the way solely to provision the Sumter garrison. Fearing a ruse or prolonged federal occupation, South Carolina (11 Apr.) requested Maj. Anderson to surrender at once. Anderson's offer to surrender upon exhaustion of his supplies (a matter of a few days) was rejected by the state authorities, aware that provisions were on the way. At 4.30 A.M. 12 Apr. the shore batteries under command of Gen. **Pierre G. T. Beauregard** (1818–93) opened fire. The Civil War began. Anderson was forced to surrender at 2.30 P.M. 13 Apr., after 34 hours of intense but bloodless bombardment. **Lincoln's role:** Some historians (Masters, 1931; Ramsdell, 1937) charge that Lincoln deliberately maneuvered the South into the role of aggressor; others (Potter, 1942; Randall, 1945; Stampp, 1951) dispute the charge. The attack on Sumter galvanized the North to spring to defense of the Union. On 15 Apr. Lincoln declared that "insurrection" existed, and called for 75,000 3-month volunteers.

17 APR.–21 MAY. BORDER STATES. The outbreak of hostilities drove Virginia (17 Apr.), Arkansas (6 May), Tennessee (7 May), and North Carolina (20 May) over to the side of the Confederacy despite Unionist sentiment which had prevailed prior to the attempted reinforcement of Ft. Sumter. The declaration of Virginia's convention (17 Apr.) that the president's call for volunteers constituted a signal for the invasion of the South and its vote to secede (103–46) led to the resignation of some of the ablest officers in the U.S. army, including **Robert E. Lee** (p. 1082), who had been offered command of the federal forces, and **Joseph E. Johnston** (p. 1073). **Richmond** was chosen (21 May) as the new capital of the Confederacy; the government moved from Montgomery in early June.

West Virginia. The mountainous western section of Virginia, tied economically to the Ohio Valley and traditionally opposed to Tidewater and Piedmont, refused to recognize secession. A convention called at Wheeling (11 June) organized a Union government and elected Francis H. Pierpont governor (19 June). Ultimately the 50 western counties of Virginia were admitted into the Union as the state of West Virginia (20 June 1863), with a constitution providing for gradual emancipation of slaves.

3 June–11 Sept. Loyal Slave States: 4 slave states (Delaware, Maryland, Kentucky, and Missouri) remained loyal to the Union, but not without prolonged contests in the last 3. Delaware's legislature unanimously rejected secession (3 Jan.) and in Apr. raised troops to defend the Union.

Maryland, in a strategic position to cut the national capital off from the North, was divided. A majority opposed secession, but pro-Confederates were prominent, particularly in Baltimore, where a mob attacked the 6th Massachusetts Regiment 19 Apr. as it passed through the city en route to Washington (militia casualties: 4 killed, 36 wounded). To avoid repetition of the riot the Maryland authorities burned down the railroad bridges connecting Baltimore with Philadelphia and Harrisburg. Gov. Thomas Hicks, a Unionist, was opposed by a legislature ready to accept Southern independence or to remain "neutral" in the conflict (10 May). The federal government felt obliged to suspend habeas corpus in that state, followed, in the summer and fall of 1861, with arrest and imprisonment of numerous state and local officials. By the end of 1861 the state's position in the Union was assured. Maryland contributed 46,000 men to the Union army.

Kentucky, native state of both Lincoln and Jefferson Davis, was economically oriented to the South but strongly nationalistic. The legislature resolved (20 May) to be neutral. Lincoln gave assurances that no troops would be sent into Kentucky provided it remained peaceful, and pointed out that the war was fought to preserve the Union, not to free the slaves. When on 3 Sept. Confederate forces crossed from Tennessee into Kentucky and occupied Hickman and Columbus, Gen. **Ulysses S. Grant** (p. 1044) countered by occupying Paducah (6 Sept.). The legislature demanded (11 Sept.) the ouster of the Confederates, and on 18 Sept. took steps to expel them. Ultimately 75,000 Kentuckians served with the Union forces. In a convention held at Russellville (18 Nov.) the Kentucky soldiers in the Confederate army adopted an ordinance of secession.

Missouri became a theater of civil war. Attempts of Gov. Claiborne F. Jackson to lead the state out of the Union failed (22 Mar.). The state soon divided into opposed armed groups headed by Gen. Nathaniel Lyon, a Unionist, and Gov. Jackson, respectively. Two major battles were fought at **Wilson's Creek,** where Lyon was killed (10 Aug.), and at **Pea Ridge, Ark.** (6–8 Mar. 1862), a Union victory leading to Union control of the state. Guerrilla warfare thereafter necessitated the establishment of martial law. 109,000 Missourians joined the Union army; 30,000 fought for the Confederacy.

OPPOSING FORCES. The North was predominant in numbers and economic power. Population of 23 Northern and border states, 22 million, augmented by heavy foreign immigration during the war years (400,000 foreign-born served in the Union army). The North had the advantage of a **balanced economy** (advanced industrial development, prosperous agriculture, strong banking institutions), a **railroad grid** (an immense logistical advantage, with the Northeast closely bound to the Mississippi and Ohio valleys), a **merchant marine,** and **naval supremacy** which handicapped the South from the start of the war.

The South. The 11 seceded states numbered 9 million (with few immigrants), of whom 3,500,000 were Negro slaves. An **agricultural economy** (based on the staples: cotton, tobacco, rice, sugar cane, and naval stores), its industrial resources were stunted, in part due to lack of banking capital (one third that of the North) and in part to lack

of technological skills and equipment
(despite abundant resources in iron,
coal, and timber). An **inadequate railroad system,** despite expansion in the
1850s, progressively deteriorated during
the war. In addition, the Mississippi and
Tennessee rivers and the Great Valley
of Virginia offered invasion routes by the
Union armies. Its few good harbors
could be easily blockaded.

Calculated Risk. Despite preponder-
ant Northern strength the South risked
war as a result of underrating the North
and overestimating its own strength. Secessionists were convinced (1) that the
North would not fight to maintain the
Union; (2) if it did, Great Britain and
France, dependent on Southern staples,
would recognize Confederate independence and give material aid; (3) that the
South's control of the mouth of the Mississippi would swing the Great Valley to
the Confederacy (overlooking the new
East-West orientation resultant upon the
railroad building of the 1850s). Confederate optimism rested on (1) the fact
that it stood on the defensive; (2) it
could afford to lose battles and campaigns if only it could wear down the
Union in the process; (3) its men were
trained in arms and outdoor living and
predisposed toward military careers (182
general Confederate officers had begun
their careers in the U.S. army).

ENLISTMENTS (reduced to 3-years'
service equivalent and taking into
account desertions—Livermore): **Union,**
1,556,678; **Confederate,** 1,082,119, distributed as follows:

	Union	Confederate
July 1861	186,751	112,040
Jan. 1862	575,917	351,418
Mar. 1862	637,126	401,395
Jan. 1863	918,121	446,622
Jan. 1864	860,737	481,180
Jan. 1865	959,460	445,203

A relatively higher proportion of Southern than Northern men served in the
army. Considering the requirements of
offensive warfare, invasion, and maintaining long lines of communication, the
North had far less effective numerical
superiority than the figures would sug-
gest.

WAR AIMS: The North: Originally,
the restoration of the Union; after 1862
freeing of the slaves became a secondary
objective. President Lincoln insisted that
only *individuals* not *governments* had
taken up arms in rebellion and that the
Union army was in effect an enlarged
sheriff's posse. Yet in proclaiming a
blockade of the South (19, 27 Apr.)
and forbidding trade with the seceded
states (16 Aug.), Lincoln in fact recognized the existence of a state of war.
The conflict was conducted in accord
with the rules of war—captured Confederate soldiers and privateersmen were
treated as prisoners of war; prisoners
were exchanged. **The South:** Recognition
by the North of the independence and
sovereignty of the Confederacy.

STRATEGY. The **major military operations** took place in 2 theaters: (1) east
of the Appalachians, particularly in the
vicinity of the rival capitals of Washington and Richmond; (2) between the
western slope of the Appalachians and
the Mississippi. **Lesser operations:** (1)
isolated trans-Mississippi region; (2)
amphibious operations along the coasts
and inland waters; (3) war on the high
seas waged by cruisers, privateers, and
blockade runners. **Northern military
strategy** aimed at (1) starving the South
by blockading her coastline; (2) dispatching an army to seize Richmond in
the East; and (3) another force in the
West, aided by gunboats, to capture the
Mississippi and Tennessee rivers and
divide and subdivide the Confederacy.
Then the 2 armies would join and crush
the South. **Confederate strategy** proposed to seize Washington and move
northward into Maryland and central

Pennsylvania, thus cutting the Northeast off from the Northwest and forcing the federal government to sue for peace. A large part of the Confederate forces were to be employed for defense only.

15 APR.–20 JULY. EARLY SKIR-MISHING. Minor actions were fought in western Virginia, where 20,000 troops led by Maj. Gen. **George B. McClellan** (p. 1092), a West Pointer who had retired to railroad management in the 1850s but was recalled to service at the start of the war as commander of the Department of the Ohio, cleared the enemy from the Valley of the Kanawha, with a victory at Philippi (3 June).

21 JULY. 1ST BATTLE OF BULL RUN. Demand of press and politicians for a march on Richmond overruled the caution of General-in-Chief **Winfield Scott,** who wanted more time to train the green Union troops. Gen. **Irvin McDowell** (1818–85), in command of a force of 30,000, was ordered to advance from his position southwest of Washington against a Confederate force under Beauregard stationed at Manassas Junction, Va. Another federal force under Gen. Patterson was ordered to prevent Confederate general **Joseph E. Johnston** from bringing a force of 9,000 from the Shenandoah Valley. Patterson permitted Johnston to evade him and join Beauregard (20 July). Before dawn (21 July) McDowell attacked and by 3 P.M. seemed to have carried the day. Then the arrival of Confederate reinforcements and Gen. **Thomas J. Jackson's** (p. 1068) magnificent stand, which earned him the sobriquet of "Stonewall," turned an apparent Southern rout into victory. McDowell's men began an orderly retreat, which quickly became a confused, panicky stampede toward Washington.

24 JULY. McCLELLAN IN COMMAND. First Bull Run aroused the North to the peril to the capital and to the seriousness of the war and convinced Lincoln of the need for more thorough training for the army. McDowell was replaced by McClellan, who, upon retirement of Gen. Scott, became general-in-chief (1 Nov.).

NAVAL BLOCKADE. To enforce the blockade of the Confederate coast (proclaimed by Lincoln 19 Apr.) the Navy Department had to convert a small, and, for the main, obsolete, collection of ships into an effective force. Loss to the Virginia authorities of the Norfolk navy yard with its vast stores and the hull of the frigate *Merrimac* was a severe setback. A large naval construction program was launched (on 7 Aug. building of 7 ironclad gunboats by the engineer **James Buchanan Eads** [p. 1019] was authorized), but for immediate use ships of all types were purchased and assigned to blockade duty. By July the blockade of the 3,550 miles of Confederate coastline was well under way. The Confederates built numerous speedy ships to run the federal gauntlet, with Nassau in the Bahamas becoming a major supply port. About 800 vessels managed to evade the blockade in its first year of operation; by comparison, in 1860, last year of peace, 6,000 ships entered and cleared Southern ports. By Nov. 1861 the Union navy had set up bases on the Southern coast after the capture of Forts Clark and Hatteras, N.C. (28–29 Aug.), Ship Island on the Gulf (17 Sept.), and Port Royal, S.C. (7 Nov.). The Union gained control of Albemarle and Pamlico sounds when Gen. Burnside's naval and military expedition (Feb.–Mar. 1862) captured Roanoke Island (8 Feb.) and New Bern, N.C. (14 Mar.). With the fall of Ft. Pulaski (11 Apr.) commanding approaches to Savannah, Ft. Macon, N.C. (26 Apr.), and New Orleans (29 Apr.), the effectiveness of the blockade increased. Chances of capture were estimated as 1 in 10 (1861), later 1 in 3 (1864).

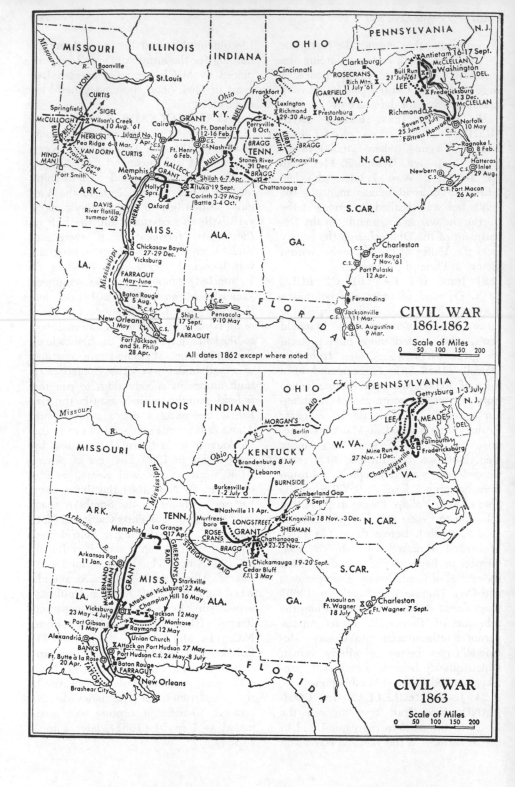

CIVIL WAR
1861-1862

Scale of Miles
0   50 100 150 200

All dates 1862 except where noted

CIVIL WAR
1863

Scale of Miles
0   50 100 150 200

KEY TO ALL MAPS
SYMBOLS INDICATE VICTOR

Federal		Confederate		Federal		Confederate	
——————	Major Advance	— ·— ·	O	Point taken by force	□
————	Minor Advance	— · — ·	ᴗ	Unsuccessful siege	ᐧᐧᐧ
▪▪▪▪▪	Major Retirement	●●●●●●	☐	Successful siege	☼
— — —	Minor Retirement	············	F.S.	Surrender	C.S.
✕	Battle	☓	P.E.	Evacuation	C.E.
▪	Point Occupied	▫	◄┫ Continuation of troop movement ☐►
▲	Point occupied, later yielded	△	Confederate names and dates in italics

EUROPE AND THE CIVIL WAR.
The war divided British opinion. The upper class favored the Confederacy; the commercial interests, irked at the new high tariffs imposed by the Union, looked to the opening of a vast free-trade market in the Confederacy; British manufacturers and shippers expected to benefit from the defeat of their Northern competitors. The working class, however, and a large proportion of the middle class, favored the Union. A British declaration of neutrality (13 May) aroused the North by its mention of the belligerent status of the Confederacy. On 21 May Secretary Seward instructed U.S. minister **Charles Francis Adams** (p. 970),

who arrived at Liverpool 12 May, that he should "desist from all intercourse whatever, unofficial as well as official, with the British Government, so long as it shall continue intercourse of either kind with the domestic enemies of this country." On representations to Lord John Russell, the latter replied that the British government had no intention of seeing the Confederate agents again (on 3 and 9 May Russell had received William L. Yancey and Pierre A. Rost, Confederate commissioners to Great Britain). On 1 June Great Britain forbade the armed ships of either side to bring their prizes to British ports, a heavy blow to Confederate privateering.

8 Nov.–25 Dec. "Trent" Affair. A second crisis with Britain arose when the U.S.S. *San Jacinto,* commanded by Capt. Charles Wilkes (p. 1184), stopped the British steamer *Trent* and removed James M. Mason and John Slidell, Confederate commissioners en route to England. News of the seizure provoked war fever in England, but war was abated when Secretary Seward ordered (26 Dec.) the release of Mason and Slidell on the ground that the 2 commissioners were "personal contraband" and, therefore, Wilkes had erred in not bringing the ship as well as the passengers to port for adjudication.

20 Dec. JOINT COMMITTEE ON CONDUCT OF THE WAR. As a result of growing dissatisfaction at the inactivity of the Union armies and a defeat at Ball's Bluff just above Washington (21 Oct.), a group of radical Republicans led by Sens. Benjamin F. Wade (Ohio, 1800–78) and Zachariah Chandler (Mich., 1813–79) and Rep. Thaddeus Stevens (Pa., p. 1158) pressed the administration for military action and emancipation of the slaves. Resentment at Lincoln's assumption of vast powers led Congress to set up the Joint Committee on the Conduct of the War, dominated by radical Republicans.

1862

15 Jan. STANTON AS WAR SECRETARY. The inefficiency and corruption of the War Department under Simon Cameron was ended when Edwin M. Stanton (1814–69) replaced him.

27 Jan. LINCOLN'S WAR ORDER NO. 1 set 22 Feb. for the launching of a general Union offensive. McClellan ignored this as well as subsequent orders.

WAR IN THE WEST. On 19–20 Jan. Union troops under Gen. George H. Thomas (p. 1168) decisively defeated the Confederates at the Battle of Mill Springs, Ky. A flanking movement by Union forces began in Feb. when Gen. Ulysses S. Grant, in conjunction with a gunboat flotilla under Commodore A. H. Foote, moved against Confederate positions on the Mississippi, Tennessee, and Cumberland. A joint attack captured Ft. Henry on the Tennessee (6 Feb.), but most of its garrison retreated to Ft. Donelson on the Cumberland, regarded by Confederate Gen. Albert S. Johnston (1803–62) as the major defense of Nashville. Another large Confederate force at Bowling Green, Ky., menaced by Gen. Don Carlos Buell from the north and by Grant from the south, retreated toward Tennessee to join the defense of Nashville and Ft. Donelson. After 4 days of siege Ft. Donelson surrendered to Grant (16 Feb.) with some 14,000 men. Johnston was forced to retreat from Kentucky and to evacuate Nashville, which fell 25 Feb.

6–7 Apr. SHILOH. Grant was prevented from striking a decisive blow against the main Confederate army of the East when his superior, Gen. Henry W. Halleck, given command of the armies in the West (11 Mar.), diverted part of the Union army under Pope to the task of expelling the enemy from the upper Mississippi. Pope, supported by Foote's fleet, besieged Island No. 10 in the Mississippi (16 Mar.–7 Apr.). The Confederates surrendered, giving Johnston time to draw up his forces at Corinth, Miss., together with Beauregard's and Polk's. Grant marched to Pittsburg Landing just over the Tennessee border from Corinth, where he planned his attack without preparing suitable defenses. The Confederates struck (6 Apr.), and after a day of confused fighting in which Gen. A. S. Johnston was killed, the Union forces were close to defeat. During the night of 6–7 Apr. reinforcements from Gen. Buell's Army of the Ohio as well as Gen. Lew Wallace's division arrived. With the resumption of battle at dawn the tide turned. By evening the Confederates withdrew to Corinth, with the Union army too exhausted for pursuit. Heavy losses sustained on both sides: 13,000 out of 63,000 Union troops engaged; 11,000 out of 40,000 Confederates.

26 APR. OCCUPATION OF NEW ORLEANS. Flag Officer (later Adm.) Farragut (p. 1026) ran the forts below New Orleans; bombarded the city (24–25 Apr.), which was occupied by Gen. **Benjamin F. Butler** (1818–93).

WAR IN THE EAST. Peninsula Campaign. Impatient with McClellan for his continued inactivity, Lincoln on 8 Mar. issued an order reorganizing the Army of Virginia into 4 corps. On 11 Mar. McClellan was relieved of supreme command except for the Army of the Potomac, and ordered to begin immediate operations against Richmond. McClellan preferred an advance by way of the peninsula between the James and York rivers instead of a frontal assault from Washington (Lincoln's preference). His opponents persuaded the president to withhold McDowell's corps in order to protect Washington.

9 MAR. "MONITOR" AND "MERRIMAC." The water route to Richmond up the James was guarded by the Confederate ironclad *Virginia* (formerly U.S.S. *Merrimac*), which on 8 Mar. had sunk the federal ship *Cumberland* and burned the *Congress* off Hampton Roads. The next day, when the *Virginia* sailed out to complete the destruction of the Union flagship *Minnesota*, which had run aground, she was met by the U.S.S. *Monitor*, another armored, raftlike craft with a revolving turret amidships. The ensuing 5-hour battle, the first naval engagement between ironclads, resulted in a draw, although the *Virginia* was driven back to Norfolk for repairs. The latter still closed the James and kept the federal fleet in Hampton Roads until burned by the Confederates to keep her from falling into Union hands when Norfolk fell 10 May.

17 MAR.–31 MAY. McCLELLAN'S ADVANCE. Embarkation of McClellan's army began from Alexandria, Va. On 5 Apr. McClellan began the siege of Yorktown, which he occupied 4 May. At a stubborn rear-guard action at **Williamsburg** (5 May) the Confederates frustrated McClellan's plans to come in contact with the main part of J. E. Johnston's army. By 14 May the Army of the Potomac had reached its advance base at White House on the Pamunkey River (20 miles from Richmond), where, despite overwhelming strength, McClellan awaited reinforcement by McDowell's corps.

23 MAR.–9 JUNE. JACKSON'S VALLEY CAMPAIGN. "Stonewall" Jackson, in command in the Shenandoah Valley with some 18,000 men, kept 2½ times that many Union troops engaged and pinned down by the forces of Gens. Banks and Frémont. In late Mar. his cavalry attacked at Winchester; his main force hit Banks at Kernstown, forcing the Union general to bring his full forces back into the Valley. On 23 May he struck Banks at **Front Royal**, forcing him to retreat to **Winchester**, where Jackson again struck (25 May), routing the Union forces, who were forced to retreat across the Potomac. Stanton that same day telegraphed Northern governors to send militia to defend the capital. From McDowell's command 20,000 men were detached and rushed to the Valley.

28 MAR. BATTLE OF GLORIETA PASS was fought near Albuquerque, N.M., between a volunteer army of miners and trappers from Colorado and Confederate forces under Brig. Gen. George H. Sibley that had been advancing westward. Confederates were forced to retreat, ending last serious threat to Far West.

31 MAY–1 JUNE. BATTLE OF SEVEN PINES (FAIR OAKS). McClellan's lines were extended along both sides of the Chickahominy River in a great V, the upper arm stretching out along the north bank to meet McDowell, the lower reaching out to within 5 miles of Richmond, just beyond Fair Oaks Station. On 31 May Johnston attacked the 2 Union corps on the south bank isolated by the flooded river from the main part of McClellan's army. Only the fortuitous arrival of another corps which managed to cross the river prevented a disastrous Union defeat. Heavy losses were sustained on both sides: Union, under 6,000; Confederate almost 8,000, including Johnston, who was severely wounded. **Robert E. Lee** was given command of the Army of Northern Virginia (1 June).

26 JUNE–2 JULY. 7 DAYS' BATTLES. In an offensive move to drive McClellan off the peninsula, Lee sent Jackson to attack the Union right flank while he himself struck at McClellan's center. The Union army was alerted by a cavalry raid by **James E. B. ("Jeb") Stuart** (p. 1162) which misfired. McClellan withdrew to protection of Union gunboats on the James River. On 26 June Lee struck at the Union's extreme right at **Mechanicsville** and for 6 days attacked the smaller Union forces. At Mechanicsville (26–27 June), Gaines' Mill (27 June), Savage's Station (29 June), and Frayser's Farm (30 June) McClellan inflicted heavy losses on the Confederates while withdrawing across the Chickahominy to a new base at Harrison's Landing on the James. At Malvern Hill (1 July), supported by Union gunboats on the James, he withstood Lee's last desperate attacks. The next day the Confederates withdrew toward Richmond, marking the end of the Peninsula Campaign. Casualties of 7

Days' Battles: Union, killed 1,734; wounded 8,062; missing 6,053. Confederate, killed 3,478; wounded 16,261; missing 875.

11 JULY. Maj. Gen. Halleck was named general-in-chief of the U.S. army.

29–30 AUG. 2D BULL RUN. Halleck consolidated the Armies of Virginia under Gen. **John Pope** (1822–92), ordered Burnside north from Fortress Monroe to Falmouth, and directed McClellan to bring his army to Alexandria and join Pope for an overland march on Richmond. Determined to strike quickly, Lee moved his army toward the Valley. Jackson defeated Banks at **Cedar Mountain** (9 Aug.) and struck at Pope's rear (26 Aug.), destroying his headquarters and supply base at Manassas Junction. When Pope moved to attack Jackson in the belief that he was isolated from the main Confederate army, he was drawn into a trap. Maj. Gen. **James Longstreet** (1821–1904) forced Thoroughfare Gap (left practically undefended by Pope), struck at Pope's flank, and sent the Union army reeling toward Bull Run. Gen. **Fitz-John Porter** (1822–1901), who failed to throw his corps into battle the first day was made the scapegoat of Pope's defeat (cashiered 21 Jan. 1863). McClellan also had failed to get substantial forces to Pope in time.

14–15 SEPT. MARYLAND INVADED. Pope withdrew (3 Aug.) to the defenses of Washington, and was supplanted (5 Aug.) by McClellan as commander of the Army of the Potomac. The latter reorganized the army and moved to meet Lee, who had begun a general invasion in the hope of cutting railroad lines and isolating Washington, with Harrisburg as his probable ultimate objective. Overestimating Confederate strength, McClellan proceeded with his customary caution. Federal victories over Lee at **South Mountain** and **Crampton's Gap** (14 Sept.) did not come in time to save **Harpers Ferry,** which fell to Jackson (15 Sept.), with its 11,000-man garrison and immense body of equipment.

17 SEPT. ANTIETAM. The Confederates (40,000) were caught by McClellan (70,000) near **Sharpsburg,** Md., the bloodiest day of the war. Union casualties, 2,108 killed, 9,549 wounded; Confederate, 2,700 killed, 9,029 wounded. McClellan failed to use his reserves, Lee held his lines, and the battle was a draw. But Lee pulled back to Virginia (18 Sept.), giving McClellan a technical victory. Although inconclusive from a military standpoint, Antietam had repercussions both at home and abroad. The British and French governments, on the verge of recognizing the Confederacy and intervening to force mediation (early Sept.), now held back. A crucial meeting of the British cabinet set for 23 Oct. was cancelled. French proposal (10 Nov.) for joint mediation including Russia was rejected (12 Nov.) by the British. The Union victory also enabled Lincoln to issue (22 Sept.) his **Preliminary Emancipation Proclamation,** freeing as of 1 Jan. 1863 all slaves in areas still in rebellion against the U.S. Lincoln had submitted the first draft of the proclamation to his cabinet on 22 July, but was persuaded to withhold it because of military reverses. On 1 Dec. the president appealed to Congress for passage of a constitutional amendment providing for **compensated emancipation,** but the border states opposed the plan.

8 DEC.–3 JAN. 1863. OPERATIONS IN THE WEST. Tied to Richmond by railroad, **Chattanooga** was the gateway to the nearer Southwest and a base to threaten Ohio and bar Union penetration of the lower South; while **Vicksburg** dominated the connections with the further Southwest and Texas, important supply sources. On 11 July Grant had been promoted to command the Army of West Tennessee. Gen. Braxton Bragg (successor to Beauregard), in an advance on Louisville from Chattanooga, was stopped by Gen. Buell's Army of the Ohio at **Perryville** (8 Oct.), but Bragg continued to dominate central Tennessee until forced to withdraw after the costly engagement with Rosecrans at **Murfreesboro** (31 Dec.–3 Jan. 1863). Casualties, Union, 1,677 killed, 7,543 wounded; Confederate, 1,294 killed, 7,945 wounded.

13 DEC. FREDERICKSBURG. The North, dismayed at Lee's escape at Antietam, was further shocked by McClellan's procrastination (Oct.), and by "Jeb" Stuart's daring cavalry raid around the Union army in Pennsylvania close to Gettysburg (10–12 Oct.). On 7 Nov. Lincoln replaced McClellan with Maj. Gen. **Ambrose E. Burnside** (1824–81). At Fredericksburg Burnside's overwhelming force (113,000 Union–75,000 Confederate) was shattered in a series of desperate attacks against the Confederate position, with losses of 1,284 killed, 9,600 wounded as against Confederate losses of 595 killed, 4,061 wounded. Burnside was replaced (25 Jan. 1863) by Gen. **Joseph Hooker** (1814–79).

17 DEC. CABINET CRISIS. A delegation of 7 Radical Republican senators demanded that Lincoln reorganize the cabinet, replace Seward by Chase, and fill the other cabinet posts with radicals. Lincoln confronted the committee with his whole cabinet (save Seward), who assured them that complete harmony existed. With the president declining the proffered resignations of Seward and Chase, the crisis was weathered.

1863

1 JAN. EMANCIPATION PROCLAMATION. To retain the loyalty of the border states Lincoln had resisted demands of the radical Republicans for abolition. **Military Action.** On 25 May 1861 Gen. B. F. Butler, in command of Fortress Monroe, Va., ruled that slaves escaping to his lines were "contraband of war" which he would not return to their masters. On 30 Aug. 1861 Gen. John C. Frémont issued a proclamation declaring that slaves of Missourians taking up arms against the U.S. were free. Lincoln modified this order (2 Sept.) to conform to existing law. On 9 May 1862 Gen. David Hunter proclaimed the emancipation of slaves in his Department (including Georgia, Florida, and South Carolina), but Lincoln disavowed this action 19 May. **Congressional Action.** The confiscation act of 6 Aug. 1861 provided for the emancipation of slaves employed in arms or labor against the U.S. A second confiscation act of 17 July 1862 liberated slaves of all persons who committed treason or supported the rebellion. Lincoln's plan of compensated emancipation was embraced by the act of 16 Apr. 1862 abolishing slavery in the District of Columbia, but no such compensation was provided in the act of 19 June 1862 abolishing slavery in the territories of the U.S. In vain Lincoln appealed to the loyal states to enact gradual and compensated emancipation. Aware of the public shift toward the radical position on slavery (as evidenced in Horace Greeley's signed editorial, "The Prayer of Twenty Millions," 20 Aug. 1862) and of the need to influence European opinion, Lincoln followed his Preliminary Emancipation Proclamation (22 Sept. 1862) with his Proclamation (1 Jan. 1863) declaring that all slaves in areas still in rebellion were "then, thenceforward, and forever free." The Proclamation actually freed no slaves; in fact, it went no further than Congress had already gone in legislation on the subject, for it applied *only* to areas over which the federal government exercised no control, specifically exempting all regions under federal military occupation.

RAISING THE ARMIES. Recruiting systems proved inefficient and inequitable. The state militia provided the bulk of the troops at the outbreak of war on a 3- to 9-month basis. Ill-trained and often poorly led by officers who were political appointees or elected by the men they commanded, the militia marched home when their terms expired, sometimes on the eve of important battles.

3 Mar. First Conscription Act made all men, 20–45, liable to military service, but service could be avoided by payment of $300 or procuring a substitute to enlist for 3 years. State quotas were fixed (proportionate to total population) and states given credit for previous enlistments. The draft was regarded as inequitable to the poor. The first drawings provoked serious riots in working-class quarters in New York City, culminating (13–16 July) in the **New York City Draft Riots,** 4 days of pillaging and Negro lynching, chiefly participated in by Irish-Americans, requiring the dispatch to New York of regiments detached from Meade's army sorely needed to pursue Lee after Gettysburg. Although there were 4 drafts in all, a very small proportion of the Union army was furnished through that means, although many "volunteered" under pressure (including **"bounty-jumpers"** who enlisted and deserted again and again).

Confederate Manpower Problems. The Confederacy first relied on enlistments; then, on 16 Apr. 1862, drafted into military service every white man (18–35) for 3 years. This first Confederate Conscription Act placed requisitions on the states but was administered and enforced by national authority. The lower classes denounced the long list of exempted occupations as well as the privilege of sending substitutes; many Southern lead-

after a siege begun in mid-May, captured **Port Hudson,** La. The entire Mississippi was now under Union control and the Confederacy split.

27 JUNE–4 JULY. GETTYSBURG CAMPAIGN. Partly in the hope of winning foreign recognition, partly to encourage dissension and appeasement in the North, Lee decided to carry the war to the enemy. Early in June the Army of Northern Virginia began a move up the Shenandoah Valley. Confederate Gen. Richard S. Ewell crushed the Union garrison at **Winchester** (13–15 June), crossed the Potomac (17 June), and by 23 June neared Chambersburg, Pa. Hooker, preferring to stage a counterblow against Richmond, was ordered instead to follow on Lee's flank. On 25 June he crossed the Potomac, coming between Lee and his cavalry chief, "Jeb" Stuart, who was off on one of his audacious but costly forays, as a result of which Lee was deprived for 3 days of information about enemy movements. Hooker established headquarters at Frederick (27 June) before Lee (at Chambersburg) learned his whereabouts. The next day Hooker, at odds with Halleck, resigned the command, and Lincoln appointed Maj. Gen. **George G. Meade** (1815–72) to command the Army of the Potomac. An aroused North responded promptly to Lincoln's call (15 June) for 100,000 volunteers for 6 months' service. Carlisle and York fell 27–28 June, and the next day Ewell's cavalry came within 10 miles of Harrisburg.

1–3 JULY. Gettysburg. Lee took up a strong defensive position along the eastern slope of South Mt., near Cashtown. Meade planned to take a defensive position behind Pipe Creek. On 30 June a chance contact at Gettysburg of a part of Confederate Gen. Ambrose P. Hill's force in search of boots and saddles with John Buford's cavalry division drew both

into that town, where the battle began. On the **1st day** (1 July), the Confederates drove the Union forces back through Gettysburg to strong defensive positions on Cemetery Hill and Culp's Hill. The Confederates occupied Seminary Ridge, a long, partially wooded rise running north and south parallel to the Union position. In the crucial battle that followed Meade enjoyed the advantage of a numerical superiority of 15,000, greater firepower, and a strong defensive position, with Cemetery Ridge and Culp's Hill heavily reinforced. Gettysburg was won and lost the **2nd day** (2 July). Lee attacked. Early was finally driven off Cemetery Ridge. Longstreet drove back Sickles' corps, but failed to take Little Round Top, which would have enabled him to enfilade the entire Union position. Ewell attacked Culp's Hill on the Union right; again on the **3rd day** (3 July), being repulsed. At Lee's insistence Longstreet reluctantly ordered a direct attack on the strongest part of the Union center, with Pickett's, Pettigrew's, and Trimble's divisions (15,000 strong). At 1 P.M. the Confederates opened up with an unprecedentedly heavy artillery barrage. As 3 gray lines of Confederate infantrymen approached Cemetery Ridge, they were mowed down by artillery fire and volleys of musketry. Less than a half company managed to reach the crest of Cemetery Ridge, only to be killed or captured. On 4 July Lee remained in position, but that afternoon retired to a position west of Hagerstown. There the flooded Potomac blocked his retreat. Lincoln and Halleck ordered Meade to attack, but rains stalled his reconnaissance; the river subsided, and Lee escaped into Virginia (13 July). Casualties: Union, 3,155 killed, c.20,000 wounded and missing; Confederate, 3,903 killed, c.24,000 wounded and missing. On 19 Nov. the cemetery at the Gettysburg battlefield was dedicated. The principal oration was delivered by Edward Everett, but Lincoln's brief remarks, in the course of which he referred to "a new birth of freedom," constituted the most memorable of all American addresses.

5 Sept. Diplomatic Fruits of Gettysburg. The Union victories at Vicksburg and Gettysburg decisively tipped the diplomatic balance in favor of the North. On 5 Sept. U.S. minister Adams warned Russell that the ironclads under construction in England for the Confederacy (the "Laird rams") meant "war." Russell ordered that the rams be not permitted to leave Liverpool, and in Oct. the British government took over the ships. Similarly, Napoleon III ordered 6 naval vessels under construction for the Confederacy to be sold to European governments. The close of 1863 saw Confederate hopes for foreign recognition and aid irretrievably shattered.

19–20 Sept. CHICKAMAUGA. Gen. William S. Rosecrans' Army of the Cumberland moved east from Murfreesboro at the end of June and maneuvered the unresourceful Braxton Bragg out of Chattanooga (9 Sept.), gateway to the East, without a battle. Alarmed at the loss of this key point, Davis rushed Longstreet and 11,000 troops from the East to reinforce Bragg. The armies clashed on the field of Chickamauga, northeast of Chattanooga, where the Union line cracked and broke, but Gen. **George H. Thomas,** who earned for himself the sobriquet "Rock of Chickamauga," used the bayonet to hurl back the Confederate attack until reserves saved the day. The Union forces retired into Chattanooga, and Bragg invested the city. Casualties: Union, 1,657 killed, almost 15,000 wounded and missing; Confederate, 2,312 killed, c.16,000 wounded and missing.

23–25 Nov. BATTLE OF CHATTANOOGA (LOOKOUT MOUNTAIN– MISSIONARY RIDGE). Grant, given command of the western armies (16 Oct.), replaced Rosecrans with Thomas; forced open communications with Chattanooga; and, reinforced by 2 corps under Hooker, prepared for the offensive. On 23 Nov. the armies came to grips. Hooker, Sherman, and Thomas drove Bragg off **Lookout Mountain** and the knolls south of Chattanooga, but Bragg concentrated his forces on **Missionary Ridge.** On 25 Nov. Thomas started a limited attack to clear the Confederates from the foot of the ridge, but continued to the crest, putting Bragg to rout. Casualties: Union, 753 killed, c.5,000 wounded and missing; Confederate, 361 killed, c.6,000 wounded and missing. The Union conquest of the Mississippi had split the Confederacy vertically. After Chattanooga, the Union armies of the West were poised to bisect the upper and lower South by marching across Georgia to the sea. On 3 Dec. Longstreet abandoned his siege of Knoxville, Tenn., and began a retreat.

1864

5–6 May. BATTLE OF THE WILDERNESS. Operations on the Virginia front bore little resemblance to the rapid movements of Sherman and Thomas. By comparison Grant's campaign before Richmond was slow and costly. Promoted (9 Mar.) to the newly revived rank of lieutenant general and given supreme command of the Union armies, Grant proposed to hammer away at Lee's army until it was decimated. The Army of the Potomac, over 100,000 strong, was assembled at Culpeper for its advance southward. Gen. Butler's Army of the James with some 36,000 men was to march up the south bank of the James and cut Lee off from the lower South. Maj. Gen. **Franz Sigel** (1824–1902) was to move up the Shenandoah Valley and seize Lynchburg. To meet Grant,

Lee had a force of 60,000, and was supported by Beauregard with 30,000 troops in the Richmond-Petersburg area. Grant and Meade crossed the Rapidan (4 May) and entered the Wilderness. Lee attacked Grant's right flank. In the ensuing indecisive 3-day battle Lee outmaneuvered his opponents, inflicting c.18,000 Union casualties (over 2,000 killed) to some 10,000 of his own men.

8–12 MAY. SPOTSYLVANIA. Disregarding losses, Grant futilely attempted to flank Lee at Spotsylvania Court House. Five bloody days of trench warfare followed. On 11 May Grant sent word to Halleck: "I propose to fight it out along this line if it takes all summer." Union losses, c.12,000, as Lee parried the Union blows. Heavy Confederate losses were never officially released.

1–3 JUNE. COLD HARBOR. At the Chickahominy, Grant again assaulted a well-entrenched foe, losing on 3 June alone 12,000 men. In one month ending 12 June Grant's losses amounted to nearly 60,000 (equal to Lee's total strength) as against Confederate casualties of c.25,000–30,000, but Lee's Army of Northern Virginia never really recovered from the heavy punishment.

15–18 JUNE. PETERSBURG. Grant decided to move his army south of the James to Petersburg, 20 miles below Richmond, approach the Confederate capital from the rear, and cut transportation connections with the South. Faulty generalship by Butler in his advance up the James prevented Grant from taking Petersburg, which withstood 4 days of battering and cost Grant 8,000 more men. Grant now dug in for a 9-month siege, longest of the war. On 30 July a huge mine was exploded in a costly but futile Union attempt to take the city.

2–13 JULY. EARLY'S RAIDS. Confederate Gen. **Jubal A. Early** (1816–94) who had defeated Sigel in the Shenandoah Valley (15 May) and driven Hunter, Sigel's successor, into West Virginia (16–18 June), suddenly struck north into Maryland. Moving from Winchester (2 July), he crossed the Potomac, exacted tribute from Hagerstown and Frederick; then swung southeast and reached the District of Columbia, within 5 miles of Washington on 11 July. A thrust by Lew Wallace at Monocacy, Md., 9 July, slowed up Early and gave Grant time to assemble troops to defend the capital. Two divisions hastily returned from the Petersburg front helped drive Early back to Virginia on 13 July. Given command of the Army of the Shenandoah (Aug.), Gen. **Philip H. Sheridan** (p. 1150) defeated Early at **Winchester** (19 Sept.) and **Fisher's Hill** (22 Sept.), and rallied his men at **Cedar Creek** (19 Oct.), turning defeat into victory. Sheridan then proceeded to scorch the Valley as thoroughly as Sherman laid waste Georgia.

7 MAY–2 SEPT. SHERMAN'S MARCH THROUGH GEORGIA. With 100,000 men Gen. **William T. Sherman** (p. 1151) set out from Chattanooga (May 1864) and began his invasion of Georgia. Joseph E. Johnston, who had replaced Bragg after Chattanooga, faced Sherman with some 60,000 men, but fought a skillful series of defensive actions at **Resaca** (13–16 May), **New Hope Church** (25–28 May), and **Kenesaw Mountain** (27 June), where, momentarily forsaking his flanking movements designed to cut the enemy's communications, Sherman assaulted Johnston and was repulsed with 2,000 killed and wounded, compared with 270 Confederate casualties. On 17 July the Union army crossed the Chattahoochee River, only 8 miles from Atlanta. Davis, impatient at Johnston's masterfully executed Fabian tactics, replaced him with **John Bell Hood** (1831–79), who attacked Sherman in 2 pitched battles (20, 22 July), but, after suffering heavy losses, pulled back into Atlanta's entrenchments. On 1 Sept. he was forced to evacuate Atlanta; the next day Sherman occupied the city. The fall of Atlanta lifted Northern morale, staggered by Grant's losses before Richmond, and contributed to the Republican success in the presidential campaign.

14 Nov.–2 Dec. MARCH TO THE SEA. Changing his strategy, Hood decided to strike at Sherman's long lines of communication stretching back to Tennessee. Dispatching Thomas to hold Hood and protect Tennessee, Sherman set out (14 Nov.) with 60,000 men in his march to the sea. Before leaving Atlanta he destroyed or confiscated all supplies useful to the enemy. On his march across Georgia his army cut a swath to the sea, 300 miles in length, 60 miles in width. Factories, cotton gins, warehouses, bridges, railroads, and some public buildings were systematically destroyed. His soldiers were ordered to "forage liberally on the country," and wild looting resulted. Sherman's advance was virtually unopposed. On 10 Dec. he reached Savannah, which fell (22 Dec.).

15–16 Dec. BATTLE OF NASHVILLE. In pursuit of Thomas, Hood made contact with part of the Union forces under Gen. John M. Schofield at **Franklin,** Tenn. (30 Nov.), and was repulsed with heavy Confederate losses (c.5,500 killed and wounded, as against c.1,200 Union killed and wounded). Schofield then joined Thomas at Nashville, where in a 2-day battle he all but destroyed Hood's army. Mopping up operations against Confederate forces in Tennessee were accomplished by Gen. James H. Wilson's cavalry.

PRESIDENTIAL CAMPAIGN. On 7 June the Republican or National Union Convention at Baltimore nominated **Lincoln,** with **Andrew Johnson** (Tenn.), a War Democrat, as his running mate. The Democratic National Convention at Chicago nominated (29 Aug.) Gen.

McClellan for president and **George H. Pendleton** (Ohio) for vice-president. Under Copperhead influence the Democrats adopted a platform calling for immediate cessation of hostilities and the restoration of peace "on the basis of the Federal Union of the States." McClellan repudiated the peace plank but sought to capitalize on Northern defeatism. Pacifism and defeatism in midsummer made the outlook for Lincoln's reelection seem dark. On 4 July the president pocket-vetoed the **Wade-Davis Bill,** a measure for the Radical Reconstruction of the South. A manifesto by the bill's authors denouncing him was published by **Horace Greeley** (p. 1045) in the N.Y. *Tribune* (5 Aug.). The Radicals covertly circulated a call for a new convention to replace Lincoln with another nominee. However, Sherman's success in Georgia in Sept. changed the election outlook and induced the Radicals to unite behind Lincoln.

8 Nov. PRESIDENTIAL ELECTION. Lincoln was reelected by 212–21 electoral votes, but with a popular majority of but 400,000 out of 4 million votes.

1865

LAST DAYS OF THE CONFEDERACY. The breakdown of transportation, the blockade (tightened by the capture of **Ft. Fisher,** N.C., 15 Jan., and the closing of the port of Wilmington, captured 22 Feb.), and federal occupation of important producing areas and devastation of others spread hunger throughout large sections of the South. Riots and demonstrations against the Confederate government or the food speculators broke out in Southern cities. Army morale was shattered by food and clothing shortages. Increasing desertions had forced Davis to admit (Sept. 1864) that "two-thirds of our men are absent . . . most of them absent without leave." In desper-

ation he approved the **arming of the slaves** (7 Nov. 1864), but the Confederate Congress failed to authorize such action until 20 Mar. 1865, too late to take effect before the close of the war. The Richmond government tightened its laws against conspiracy and suspended habeas corpus with increasing frequency. Disunion tendencies appeared. South Carolina virtually nullified (23 Dec. 1864) an act of the Confederate Congress which had authorized the central government to impress goods and services.

16 JAN.–21 MAR. SHERMAN'S DRIVE THROUGH THE CAROLINAS. Sherman's corps fanned northward through South Carolina, wreaking even greater destruction than in Georgia. More than a dozen towns were burned in whole or part, including (17 Feb.) a large part of **Columbia,** the state capital. Whether Union soldiers (with or without orders) set the blaze or, as Sherman later claimed, retreating Confederates were responsible, has never been definitely established. The fall of Columbia led to the evacuation of Charleston, which fell to the Union (18 Feb.). Sherman advanced into North Carolina, his progress somewhat slowed by Johnston, whom Lee, now commander in chief of all Confederate forces, had restored to command. At **Bentonville** (19–20 Mar.) Sherman and Johnston met in their last battle. The smaller Confederate force was pushed back, but not crushed. Sherman entered Goldsboro (21 Mar.), where he joined Gen. Schofield.

3 FEB. HAMPTON ROADS CONFERENCE. Jefferson Davis, while agreeing to send Vice-President Stephens, R. M. T. Hunter, and J. A. Campbell to confer with Lincoln and Seward aboard the Union transport *River Queen,* stubbornly insisted on recognition of Southern independence. This was, of course, unacceptable to Lincoln, and the conference broke up.

4 MAR. LINCOLN'S 2D INAUGURAL. The president appealed to the nation to forget vengeance. "With malice toward none; with charity for all . . . let us strive on to finish the work we are in; to bind up the nation's wounds . . . to do all which may achieve and cherish a just and lasting peace."

2 APR. PETERSBURG AND RICHMOND ABANDONED. On 25 Mar. Lee tried to break through Grant's besieging army by an attack on Ft. Steadman, east of Petersburg, but was badly beaten. Holding an advantage of 115,000 men to Lee's 54,000, Grant systematically battered the Confederate lines. On 1 Apr. Lee made his last assault of the war, hitting Grant's left flank at **Five Forks** near Petersburg, but was repelled by Sheridan, who arrived from the Valley. On 2 Apr. Lee evacuated Petersburg and Richmond and headed toward Lynchburg, whence he hoped to move by rail to North Carolina and join forces with Johnston.

9 APR. SURRENDER AT APPOMATTOX COURTHOUSE. With Grant in pursuit of Lee, Sheridan's force took Burkesville, a railway junction, preventing Lee from moving south toward Danville. He then blocked Lee's path westward, and the Confederates were virtually surrounded. Lee's forces had now shrunk to less than 30,000, with few rations remaining. On 7 Apr. Grant requested Lee to surrender. Lee asked for terms. On 9 Apr. he met Grant at Appomattox Courthouse and quickly came to terms, by which Lee's soldiers were paroled to return home, officers were permitted to retain side arms, and all soldiers allowed to retain private horses and mules. All equipment was to be surrendered. 25,000 rations were issued by the Union army to the Confederates.

14 APR. ASSASSINATION OF LIN-COLN. The president visited Richmond on 5 Apr., then returned to Washington (where news of Appomattox arrived by noon 9 Apr.) and worked on plans for restoration of peace. In his last public address (11 Apr.) and at his final cabinet meeting on the morning of 14 Apr. the president repeated his plea for conciliation. At 10:15 P.M. that evening, as he was sitting in his box at Ford's Theater in Washington, watching a performance of *Our American Cousin,* he was shot by **John Wilkes Booth** (1838–65), carried unconscious to a lodging house across the street, and died there just before 7:30 A.M.

15 APR. Vice-President Johnson took the oath of office as president 3 hours later. Simultaneously with the assassination of Lincoln, Secretary Seward was attacked and severely wounded at his home by Lewis Powell (alias Payne), a fellow conspirator of Booth. Booth escaped to Virginia, but was caught in a barn near Bowling Green. On his refusal to surrender, the barn was fired and (probably) he shot himself (26 Apr.). Of the 9 other persons implicated in the assassination 4 were hanged (7 July), 4 imprisoned, and a jury failed to convict the ninth suspect, John H. Surratt.

26 APR.–26 MAY. FINAL CAPITU-LATION. Sherman drew closer to Johnston's army when he occupied Raleigh on 13 Apr. Despite Davis' plea for continued resistance, Johnston surrendered to Sherman (18 Apr.), with 37,000 men, and was granted liberal terms, including unauthorized political concessions dis-avowed by President Johnson. Final surrender terms along the lines of the Appomattox capitulation were agreed upon (26 Apr.) near Durham Station, N.C. Gen. Taylor surrendered the remaining Confederate forces east of the Mississippi to Gen. Canby at Citronelle, Ala., 4 May. Resistance ended (26 May) with the capitulation of Gen. Kirby Smith to Gen. Canby at New Orleans. Jefferson Davis was captured in Georgia on 10 May. The legal termination of the war was held by the Supreme Court in the case of *The Protector* (12 Wall 700), 1871, to have ended with presidential proclamations of 2 Apr. 1866 and 20 Aug. 1866.

WAR LOSSES. In the proportion of casualties to participants the Civil War was the costliest U.S. war, with casualties totaling between 33% and 40% of the combined Union and Confederate forces. Union dead, 359,528 (including 110,070 killed in battle or died from wounds); wounded, 275,175. Confederate dead, 258,000 (94,000 in battle or from wounds); wounded, 100,000 minimum. These figures take no account of the sufferings on both sides from imprisonment. Most notorious of the military prisons was **Andersonville,** operated by the Confederacy in Georgia (Feb. 1864–Apr. 1865). Bad rations, unsanitary conditions, inadequate medical services accounted for the deaths of some 13,000 out of 32,000 Union prisoners. In a war crimes trial (Aug. 1865) the prison's commander, Capt. Henry Wirtz, was found guilty by a military commission and hanged 10 Nov. 1865.

Reconstruction, 1865–77

1863, 8 DEC.–1865, 4 DEC. PRESIDENTIAL RECONSTRUCTION. Two constitutional issues were involved: (1) Were the rebellious states in the Union? (2) Was the president or Congress responsible for direction of Reconstruction

(involving both the status of the freedmen and the restoration to the Union of the 11 Confederate states)? Lincoln consistently maintained that these states had never left the Union, but was little concerned with the "pernicious abstraction" of constitutional theory. In 1862 he appointed provisional military governors for Louisiana, North Carolina, and Tennessee. On 8 Dec. 1863 he announced his plan of Reconstruction: (1) amnesty, with certain exceptions, to Southerners taking a prescribed loyalty oath; (2) executive recognition of state governments in cases where 10% of the 1860 electorate had taken the oath and where the state agreed to emancipation. These steps were taken by Arkansas and Louisiana in 1864, but Congress refused to seat their representatives.

WADE-DAVIS BILL (4 July 1864), purporting to represent the congressional blueprint for Reconstruction, was enacted during absence of 5 key opponents of the measure. It required a majority of the electorate in each Confederate state to take an oath of past as well as future loyalty as a condition precedent to restoration. Lincoln pocket-vetoed the bill, and was excoriated by Radical Republicans, who considered him too lenient. Republicans of all shades feared a revived Democratic party. In addition, many in Congress resented the wartime expansion of the executive power.

JOHNSON'S POLICIES. Andrew Johnson quickly disabused the Radicals of any idea that he favored their program. In fact, he adopted Lincoln's Reconstruction plan with minor changes. During the recess of Congress he recognized the loyal governments of Arkansas, Louisiana, Tennessee, and Virginia set up by Lincoln.

29 May–13 July. RECONSTRUCTION PROCLAMATION. Johnson granted amnesty to Confederates who took the oath of allegiance, with several excepted classes (among them holders of taxable property exceeding $20,000) who could petition him for special pardons. These he granted liberally. He proceeded to organize provisional governments for the 7 remaining states. Provisional governors were empowered to convene conventions composed of delegates elected by "loyal" citizens (including those pardoned by the president) to amend the state constitutions, abolish slavery, and repudiate the state war debt. By Dec., every Confederate state except Texas had fulfilled these requirements. Texas conformed 6 Apr. 1866. In his first annual message to Congress (6 Dec.) Johnson announced that the Union was restored; the delegates of the ex-Confederate states awaited admission to Congress.

4 Dec. JOINT COMMITTEE OF 15. When the 39th Congress convened it refused to endorse Johnson's actions. Republicans secured the appointment of a joint committee of 6 senators and 9 representatives to examine the issues of suffrage and Southern representation in Congress. Controlled by the Radicals, this committee was dominated by **Thaddeus Stevens** (p. 1158), to whom, with some exaggeration, tradition has attributed the exercise of almost dictatorial powers both over the House and the Republican party.

RADICAL THEORIES OF RECONSTRUCTION. To Stevens the ex-Confederate states were "conquered provinces"; to Sen. Charles Sumner (Mass.) the seceding states had committed "suicide." Either interpretation put the South under the control of Congress. The joint committee declared that the South had no state governments and that Congress alone could restore them and impose such conditions for readmission as it deemed necessary.

18 DEC. 13TH AMENDMENT, abolishing slavery, ratified by 27 states, was formally proclaimed in effect.

1866

19 FEB. NEW FREEDMEN'S BUREAU BILL. Beginning with Mississippi (24 Nov. 1865), Southern state legislatures enacted **"Black Codes,"** a body of vagrancy and apprenticeship laws which bound the freedmen to the land. These codes varied in harshness; were notably lenient in Georgia, severe in Louisiana and Mississippi. To protect the Negro, Congress sought to enlarge the scope of the **Freedmen's Bureau** (est. 3 Mar. 1865) as a temporary bureau to care for the freedmen and the abandoned lands of the South. Congress sought to empower the bureau to try by military commission persons accused of depriving freedmen of civil rights. Johnson vetoed the bill on the ground that Congress had no power to legislate with 11 states unrepresented, and that the provisions for military trials violated the 5th Amendment. On 16 July the bill was passed over his veto.

9 APR. CIVIL RIGHTS ACT, bestowing citizenship upon the Negro (legislation necessitated by the Dred Scott decision) and granting the same civil rights to all persons born in the U.S. (except Indians), was passed by Congress over Johnson's veto, which had condemned the measure as an unwarranted invasion of states' rights. The act enumerated rights including the right to make and enforce contracts, to sue, give evidence, to inherit, purchase, lease, and convey real and personal property. It was specifically amended in the House to exclude any application to state segregation statutes.

16 JUNE. 14TH AMENDMENT was formulated by the joint committee of 15 because of widespread doubt as to the constitutionality of the Civil Rights Act. It passed Congress 13 June and was submitted to the states for ratification (16 June). Rejected by most of the Southern states, its ratification was made a condition of restoration to the Union (ratification announced 28 July 1868). The amendment for the first time defined national citizenship (to include Negroes) and threw the protection of the federal government around rights that might be invaded by the states. The charge has been made, with little support in fact, that the framers deliberately phrased the first section to protect property and the rights of corporations against state legislation. Subsequent judicial decisions did in fact so interpret the amendment. Section II abrogated the "three-fifths" clause, increasing Southern representation in the House by some 12 seats, but provided a proportionate reduction in representation when a state denied suffrage "except for participation in rebellion or other crime." This section has never been applied.

20 JUNE. REPORT OF THE JOINT COMMITTEE OF 15 recommended that the Confederate states were not entitled to representation, and maintained the authority of Congress rather than the executive over the process of Reconstruction. Tennessee, under Radical control, ratified the 14th Amendment (19 July) and was restored to the Union (24 July). The other Southern states rejected the amendment, counting upon the approaching congressional election to repudiate the Radical program.

CONGRESSIONAL ELECTIONS. Johnson's abortive attempt to join all moderates in a new party at a National Union Convention meeting in Philadelphia (14 Aug.) convinced many Northerners that his supporters were primarily ex-rebels and Copperheads. Republicans also capitalized upon the president's maladroit speaking tour (28 Aug.–15 Sept.).

In contrast, the Radicals' skillful campaign stressed the connection between the Republican party and the Union cause. Race riots in New Orleans (30 July) and Memphis supported the Radical contention that the South was unregenerate. While Johnson failed to capitalize on the discontent of Western farmers, the Republicans were more successful in persuading industrial interests that a Democratic victory would lead to a reversal of policies favoring business. In the fall elections the Republicans captured two thirds of each house, giving the Radicals effective control of Reconstruction.

1867–68

2 Mar. 1ST RECONSTRUCTION ACT, passed over Johnson's veto, divided the South into 5 military districts subject to martial law. To achieve restoration the Southern states were required to call new constitutional conventions, elected by universal manhood suffrage, which were to establish state governments guaranteeing Negro suffrage and ratifying the 14th Amendment. Excluded from voting were ex-Confederates disqualified under the proposed 14th Amendment. Congress reserved to itself the power to review each case, end military rule, and seat representatives.

2 Mar. 3d FEDERAL BANKRUPTCY ACT allowed both voluntary and involuntary bankruptcy; amended 22 June 1874 to provide for composition of debts over a period of years; repealed 7 June 1878.

23 Mar., 19 July 1867; 11 Mar. 1868. SUPPLEMENTARY RECONSTRUCTION ACTS. On failure of the South to call new constitutional conventions, Congress passed the first supplemental act requiring the military commanders to initiate the enrollment of voters; then a second act giving the commanders broad powers to discriminate between voters and officeholders; and lastly, a measure declaring that a majority of votes cast was sufficient to put a new state constitution into effect, regardless of the numbers participating.

MILITARY RECONSTRUCTION. Despite doubts as to their constitutionality, President Johnson executed these laws, as to how conscientiously, contemporaries as well as later historians differ. He appointed military commanders who led 20,000 troops (as well as Negro militia) into the South. The governments previously set up by Johnson were supplanted. A total of 703,000 Negroes and 627,000 whites were registered as voters. In 5 states (Ala., Fla., La., Miss., and S.C.) Negro voters were in the majority. In other states a Negro-white coalition constituted Radical majorities. Southern whites allying with Radicals were called "scalawags"; Northerners who went South to participate in Reconstruction, "carpetbaggers."

1867, 4 Dec. GRANGER MOVEMENT. The Patrons of Husbandry, popularly called the Grangers, a secret association devoted to the promotion of agricultural interests, was organized in Washington, D.C. Typical of its objectives were the resolutions adopted at the Springfield, Ill., Farmers' Convention (2 Apr. 1873) attacking "all chartered monopolies," and urging laws "fixing reasonable maximum rates" for freight and passengers. The Declaration of Purpose of the National Grange (1874) stressed (1) cooperation, (2) reduction of the number of middlemen, (3) opposition to monopoly, (4) establishment of agricultural and technical colleges. Associated with this movement was the rise of independent farmers' parties, which, by 1874, had been organized in 9 prairie states and in Oregon and California under the leadership of **Ingnatius**

Donnelly (Minn., 1831–1901) and Newton Booth (Kan.). Their most effective supporters were not farmers, who were too thinly spread to be politically effective, but town merchants and small businessmen who suffered most from railroad price practices. First Granger legislation was enacted in Illinois (7 Apr. 1871), setting up a railroad and warehouse commission to fix maximum rates. Intrastate railroad freight rates were regulated by law in Wisconsin (11 Mar. 1874) and Iowa (23 Mar. 1874). For the early validation of Grange laws by the courts, see p. 671.

NEW SOUTHERN STATE CONSTITUTIONS. In late 1867 the Southern states voted to call conventions, which met in 1868 and established new constitutions. These conventions were Radical-dominated. Negroes participated in every such convention and formed a majority in that of South Carolina. The new constitutions were similar to those in effect in the North except for guarantees of civil rights for Negroes, universal manhood suffrage, and the disqualification of ex-rebels.

1868, 22–25 JUNE. OMNIBUS ACT. Seven states (Ark. [22 June] and Ala., Fla., Ga., La., N.C., and S.C. [25 June]) satisfied the requirements of the Reconstruction Acts and were readmitted by Congress. On 26 Feb. 1869 Congress proposed the 15th Amendment forbidding any state from depriving a citizen of his vote because of race, color, or previous condition of servitude. By 1870 Mississippi, Texas, and Virginia, whose readmission had been held up by their refusal to approve the disfranchising clauses of the new constitutions, were restored to the Union following ratification of the 15th Amendment, proclaimed 30 Mar. 1870. Following restoration in 1868, Georgia was once more returned by Congress to military rule when, after withdrawal of federal military forces,

Negroes were expelled (Sept.) from the state legislature. With the return of troops, both the Reconstruction Acts and the 14th Amendment were enforced and the state (by act of Congress, 22 Dec. 1869) compelled to ratify the 15th Amendment and restore the expelled Negro members in order to gain readmission to the Union (15 July 1870).

1868

24 FEB.–26 MAY. IMPEACHMENT OF JOHNSON. The Radical sweep in the 1866 election resulted in their overriding Johnson's vetoes and enacting legislation curbing the power of the executive, who was prevented from appointing new Supreme Court justices (23 July 1866). Congress called itself into special session (22 Jan. 1867) and virtually deprived the president of Command of the army (Command of the Army Act, 2 Mar. 1867) by requiring that he issue all military orders through the General of the Army (U. S. Grant). An impeachment resolution was introduced (7 Jan. 1867) by Rep. James M. Ashley. The House Judiciary Committee reported 2 Mar. 1867 that further study of impeachment should continue in the 40th Congress, to begin 2 days later. The committee voted out a resolution of impeachment on 25 Nov., but the House of Representatives voted it down by a vote of 57–108 (7 Dec.). On 2 Mar. 1867 Congress passed the Tenure of Office Act, which prohibited the president from removing officials appointed by and with the advice of the Senate without senatorial approval. Johnson dismissed Secretary of War Stanton, 12 Aug., and named Grant Secretary of War ad interim. Johnson submitted his reasons for dismissing Stanton to the Senate when Congress reconvened (12 Dec.), but reinstated him (13 Jan.) after the Senate refused to concur with his action.

Challenging the Congress, he dismissed Stanton again (21 Feb. 1868). A resolution for impeachment, the **Covode Resolution,** was offered the same day, reported upon favorably by the Committee on Reconstruction 22 Feb., and the House impeached Johnson by a vote of 126–47 on 24 Feb. Subsequently the House drew up Articles of Impeachment encompassing 11 charges, including alleged violations of the Tenure of Office Act and Command of the Army Act and with attempting to bring disgrace and ridicule upon Congress.

4 MAR.–26 MAY. IMPEACHMENT TRIAL. The Managers of the House of Representatives presented the articles of impeachment to the Senate (4 Mar.). The president's attorneys filed an answer (23 Mar.) and the trial began with opening statements (30 Mar.). Chief Justice Chase presided over the Senate proceedings, and his insistence on the observance of legal procedure maintained some semblance of nonpartisanship. Johnson's counsel (Benjamin R. Curtis, William Maxwell Evarts [p. 1026], W. S. Groesbeck, and Henry Stanbery) disputed the evidence offered by the House managers (J. A. Bingham, G. S. Boutwell, B. F. Butler, J. A. Logan, T. Stevens, T. Williams, and J. F. Wilson). Voting (16 May) on the 11th article of impeachment as to whether the president was guilty of high misdemeanor as charged, the Senate voted 35 for conviction, 19 (including 7 Republicans and 12 Democrats) for acquittal, short by one vote of the two thirds necessary. On 26 May, 2 more ballots produced the same vote, and the Senate adjourned as a court of impeachment.

CAMPAIGN OF 1868. The Republican National Convention at Chicago nominated Gen. **U. S. Grant** for the presidency on the 1st ballot, with an Indiana Radical, **Schuyler Colfax** (1823–85) as his running mate (20–21 May).

The platform endorsed Radical Reconstruction, condemned Johnson and the Democrats, advocated payment of the national debt in gold, and equivocated on the tariff and Negro suffrage. The Democratic Convention, meeting in New York City (4 July), adopted a platform attacking Radical Reconstruction and endorsing Cong. **George H. Pendleton's** (1825–89) **"Ohio Idea"** (payment of the national debt in greenbacks). Their nominee for president on the 22nd ballot (9 July) was **Horatio Seymour** (1810–86), former governor of New York and a hard-money man. **Francis P. Blair** (Mo., 1821–1875) won second place. The Republicans made "the bloody shirt of the rebellion" their main campaign issue.

3 Nov. PRESIDENTIAL ELECTION. Grant captured 26 out of 34 states, with an electoral vote of 214–80, but a popular majority of only 306,000 out of 5,715,000 votes. A Negro vote exceeding 500,000 decided the election, in which 3 Southern states did not participate and 6 others were under Radical domination.

SUPREME COURT AND RECONSTRUCTION. In *ex parte Milligan* (Dec. 1866, p. 669) the court declared unconstitutional the resort to martial law where the civil courts were in operation. Nevertheless, the defiant Radicals made military tribunals a prominent feature of Reconstruction legislation. The court denied jurisdiction (*Georgia* v. *Stanton, Mississippi* v. *Johnson*) when 2 Southern states sought to enjoin executive enforcement of the Reconstruction Acts (Apr., May 1867). In Feb. 1868 the court agreed to consider *ex parte McCardle*. Fearing that a review of this case might invalidate Reconstruction measures Congress deprived the court of jurisdiction (27 Mar. 1868). In *Texas* v. *White* (1869) the court affirmed Lincoln's position that the Union was indissoluble, but at the same time upheld Congress' authority to reconstruct the states. In *ex parte Garland* and *Cummings* v. *Missouri* (1867) the court invalidated federal and state loyalty oaths which effectively barred ex-Confederates from pursuing their vocations.

1869

18 Mar. CURRENCY ISSUE. The Grant regime supported "hard" money. Congress, by the Public Credit Act, provided for payment of government obligations in gold, thus repudiating the "Ohio Idea." Bitter debate ensued over the question of whether the remaining $356 million in "greenbacks" still in circulation should be redeemed.

24 Sept. "BLACK FRIDAY." In an attempt to corner gold Jay Gould (1836–92) and James ("Jubilee Jim") Fisk (1834–72), stock manipulators, induced Abel Rathbone Corbin, lobbyist brother-in-law of President Grant, to exert himself to prevent the government from selling gold. Despite Grant's refusal to agree, they spread the rumor that the president opposed such sales. With Grant's approval, Secretary of the Treasury George S. Boutwell (1818–1905) ordered the sale of $4 million in gold, and the gold price plunged from 162 to 135, with the ruin of many speculators.

1870–71

KU KLUX KLAN was founded at Pulaski, Tenn. (1866); constitution adopted May 1867. Ex-Confederate Gen. Nathan Bedford Forrest (1821–77) was the first Grand Wizard. Aimed to destroy Radical political power and establish white supremacy, the order was used as a cloak for lawlessness and violence and formally disbanded (1869), although its activities continued for some time after that date. Congress took cognizance of the order and similar secret societies,

such as the Knights of the White Camelia, by passing the Ku Klux Klan Acts of 31 May 1870 and 20 Apr. 1871, to enforce the 15th and 14th Amendments, respectively. A congressional committee sat during the summer of 1871 and took 13 vols. of testimony on conditions in the South. Certain sections of the Act of 1870 were declared unconstitutional (*U.S.* v. *Reese; U.S.* v. *Cruikshank,* 1876). In *U.S.* v. *Harris* (1883) the Supreme Court held part of the act of 1871 unconstitutional.

1871

1 July 1871. DEPARTMENT OF JUSTICE ESTABLISHED, with attorney general (1789) designated head of new department.

3 Mar. CIVIL SERVICE REFORM. Spoils politics and corruption led to a demand for civil service reform voiced by such leaders as E. L. Godkin (p. 1042) of the *Nation,* Carl Schurz (p. 1147), Sumner, and Lyman Trumbull. Grant appointed (4 Mar.) George William Curtis (1824–92) to head the first Civil Service Commission, authorized by act of Congress, which failed to make an appropriation, but he resigned (1875) when his recommendations were ignored, and the commission was discontinued.

8 July. TWEED RING. George Jones of *The New York Times* initiated his exposé of the regime of Tammany Boss William Marcy Tweed (1823–78) in New York City, where, through a new city charter creating a Board of Audit, he had seized control of the municipal treasury, which was systematically plundered to the extent of from $75 million to $200 million through faked leases, padded bills, false vouchers, unnecessary repairs, and kickbacks. Tweed was arrested 27 Oct., convicted (5 Nov. 1872), and died in jail. Others spent their plunder abroad.

1872

22 MAY. GENERAL AMNESTY ACT removed the disability to hold office (contained in Section 3 of the 14th Amendment) from all but the most prominent (c.500) ex-Confederates.

LIBERAL REPUBLICAN MOVEMENT represented a reaction from the Radical Republican policy toward the South as well as from the corruption of the Grant administration. It had its genesis in Sumner's break with Grant over Santo Domingo (p. 334) and in party division in Missouri. Leaders included **Schurz, Gideon Welles** (1802–78), **Charles Francis Adams** (p. 970), **Godkin,** and **Horace Greeley.**

4 SEPT. CRÉDIT MOBILIER. A New York *Sun* exposé charged Vice-President Colfax, vice-presidential nominee Wilson, Rep. James A. Garfield (Ohio), and other prominent politicians with accepting stock of the Crédit Mobilier (a construction company, organized 1864 by the promoters of the Union Pacific Railway to divert to themselves the profits from building that line) in return for political influence. An investigation which followed resulted in the censure (27 Feb. 1873) of Reps. **Oakes Ames** (Mass.) and **James Brooks** (N.Y.). Colfax escaped formal censure when the House Judiciary Committee recommended against impeachment on the ground that his alleged misconduct had been committed before he became vice-president, but he was ruined politically.

CAMPAIGN OF 1872. Convening at Cincinnati (1 May) the Liberal Republicans nominated **Horace Greeley,** protectionist and reformer, for president and **B. Gratz Brown** (Mo.), for vice-president, and adopted a platform favoring civil service reform, return to specie payments, and reservation of the public domain for the actual settler. The Greeley-Brown slate was also picked by the Democratic National Convention at Baltimore (9 July) despite Greeley's tariff views and long association with the Republicans, and by the Liberal Colored Republicans at Louisville, Ky. (25 Sept.). A "Straight" Democratic National Convention, meeting at Louisville (3 Sept.), nominated **Charles O'Conor** (N.Y.) for president and **John Quincy Adams, II** (Mass.), for vice-president. The Republicans at Philadelphia (5 June) renominated **Grant** on the 1st ballot and named **Henry Wilson** (Mass.) as his running mate. The Prohibition party (org. 1869) held its first national convention at Columbus, Ohio, 22 Feb. 1872, naming **James Black** (Pa.) for president and **John Russell** (Mich.) for vice-president. Labor Reform ticket, p. 765.

5 Nov. PRESIDENTIAL ELECTION. Grant was the victor, with 286 electoral votes to 66 for Greeley, and a popular majority of 763,000. As Greeley died 29 Nov. his electoral votes were cast as follows: Thomas A. Hendricks, 42; B. Gratz Brown, 18; Charles J. Jenkins, 2; David Davis, 1.

1873

12 FEB. "THE CRIME OF '73," the **Coinage Act,** demonetized silver (omitting the standard silver dollar from the coinage) and made gold the sole monetary standard, despite the increase in U.S. silver production resultant upon new discoveries in the West (p. 611). The charge that this act was part of a "gold conspiracy" was without foundation, but was an article of faith of many Americans for 20 years. Gold-standard advocates had fears that silver presented at the Mint could feed inflation.

3 MAR. "SALARY GRAB" ACT doubled the president's salary to $50,000 a year and increased other government officials, including congressmen (from $5,000 to $7,500). Public indignation forced Congress to repeal the law (20 Jan. 1874) except for the increases voted the president and Supreme Court justices.

18 Sept. PANIC OF 1873. Unbridled railroad speculation, notably in the field of construction, combined with overexpansion in industry, agriculture, and commerce weakened the U.S. financial structure, further shaken by the contraction of European demand for U.S. farm products after 1871. The failure (18 Sept.) of the powerful banking firm of **Jay Cooke** (p. 1005) precipitated a fall in security prices, ultimately affecting national income and leading to substantial unemployment (p. 751). As a palliative the government released $26 million in greenbacks (20 Sept.–15 Jan. 1874).

1875

14 Jan. RESUMPTION OF SPECIE PAYMENTS was recommended by President Grant on 6 Dec. 1869 and 7 Dec. 1874. The financial stringency resulting from the Panic of 1873 led to passage of a bill (14 Apr. 1874) to increase the issuance of legal tender notes to $400 million, which Grant vetoed (22 Apr. 1874). Instead, Congress (20 June 1874) placed a ceiling of $382 million on greenbacks in circulation, and by the Specie Resumption Act provided for the resumption of specie payments (by 1 Jan. 1879) and the reduction of greenbacks in circulation to $300 million. (For the **Legal Tender Cases,** see p. 670.)

1 Mar. CIVIL RIGHTS ACT (Sumner's Bill) guaranteed equal rights in public places (inns, public conveyances, theaters, etc.) without distinction of color and forbade exclusion of Negroes from jury duty. An attempt to include a school integration clause was defeated. (For the 5 cases involving the validity of the act, see p. 671.)

1 May. WHISKY RING. A conspiracy of revenue officials (chief among them

John McDonald, a Grant appointee) and distillers, formed in St. Louis to defraud the government of the internal revenue tax, spread rapidly to other leading cities. As a result of an exposé by the *St. Louis Democrat,* Secretary of the Treasury **Benjamin H. Bristow** (1832–96) ordered an investigation, resulting in the indictment (10 May) of 238 persons, as well as Grant's private secretary, Gen. **O. E. Babcock** (indicted 9 Dec.), who was saved from conviction through the president's intervention.

1876

2 Mar. IMPEACHMENT OF BELKNAP. As a result of a House investigation disclosing that Secretary of War **William W. Belknap** (1829–90) had received bribes for the sale of trading posts in the Indian Territory, a resolution of impeachment passed the House. Belknap resigned the same day to avoid trial. Later (1 Aug.) he was aquitted by vote of the Senate, but 23 out of 25 senators who voted not guilty declared that they did so because they believed they had no jurisdiction over an official who had previously resigned.

PRESIDENTIAL CAMPAIGN. The Prohibition party meeting at Cleveland nominated Gen. Green Clay Smith (Ky.) for president and Gideon T. Stewart (Ohio) for vice-president. The National Greenback Convention at Indianapolis (18 May) nominated Peter Cooper (N.Y. p. 1006) for president and Samuel F. Carey (Ohio) for vice-president. The Republican National Convention at Cincinnati nominated (16 June) **Rutherford B. Hayes** (Ohio) for president on the 7th ballot and **William A. Wheeler** (N.Y.) for vice-president. Up to the final balloting the leading presidential candidate had been James G. Blaine, who had been discredited by testimony (31 May) before a House committee by James

Mulligan, a bookkeeper for Warren Fisher of Boston. Mulligan charged that Blaine had indirectly sold Little Rock and Fort Smith R.R. bonds to the Union Pacific and had borrowed from him and refused to return incriminating letters. On 5 June Blaine defended himself before the House, reading selected portions of the "Mulligan letters." The Democratic National Convention meeting at St. Louis (27–29 June) nominated **Samuel J. Tilden** (N.Y., 1814–86) for president and **Thomas A. Hendricks** (Ind.) for vice-president.

7 Nov.–6 Dec. DISPUTED ELECTION OF 1876. The presidential election gave Tilden a popular-vote margin of 250,000. More decisive, however, was the electoral vote. Tilden carried New York, New Jersey, Connecticut, Indiana, and, apparently, the South; but Republican headquarters refused to concede his election on the ground that the returns were in dispute in Florida, Louisiana, South Carolina, and Oregon (without these electoral votes Tilden, with 184, would be 1 short of the necessary majority). On 6 Dec. 2 sets of electoral returns were reported from the 4 disputed states (in the 3 Southern states Republican election boards threw out sufficient Tilden votes on the ground of irregularities to certify Hayes; in Oregon, which the Republicans had unquestionably carried, the Democratic governor, violating Oregon law, disqualified 1 Republican elector and certified a Democrat in his place).

1877

29 Jan. ELECTORAL COMMISSION. The Constitution offered no clear guide for the disputed election of 1876. It provided that "The President of the Senate shall, in the presence of the Senate and the House of Representatives, open all certificates and the votes shall then be counted." But counted by whom? If by the Senate (Republican), the Hayes electors would be sustained; if by the House (Democratic since 1875), the Tilden electors. To break an alarming deadlock Congress set up an **Electoral Commission** consisting of 5 members of the House, 5 of the Senate, and 5 justices of the Supreme Court. Four of the justices were designated in the bill: 2 Republicans, 2 Democrats. The House selected 3 Democrats and 2 Republicans; the Senate, 3 Republicans and 2 Democrats. The 15th member, the 5th justice, was to be selected by the other 4 justices, with the tacit understanding that Justice David Davis, an independent, would be chosen. But owing to his election by the Illinois state legislature to the U.S. Senate, Davis was replaced by Justice Bradley, a Republican.

9–28 Feb. COMMISSION AWARD. Under pressure from Republican politicians Bradley, who had first written an opinion favoring Tilden, switched to the Hayes side. Deciding by a vote of 8–7 (along straight party lines) not to "go behind the returns" and investigate the count in each disputed state, the commission (9 Feb.) awarded the vote in Florida to Hayes, and later (16, 23, 28 Feb.) gave similar decisions for the 3 remaining states.

2 Mar. HAYES DECLARED ELECTED (185–184). Support by Southern Democrats for the Electoral Commission's decision was the result of Republican promises (1) to withdraw federal troops from the South, (2) appoint at least 1 Southerner to the cabinet, and (3) make substantial appropriations for Southern internal improvements. A lobby headed by Thomas A. Scott, president of the Pennsylvania R.R., and Grenville M. Dodge, chief engineer of the Union Pacific (1866–70), persuaded many Southern congressmen that the construction of the proposed route of

the Texas & Pacific R.R. (chartered
1871) from East Texas to the Pacific
coast was dependent on Republican victory. Hayes was inaugurated 5 Mar.,
after having taken the oath privately
on 3 Mar. since 4 Mar. was a Sunday.
On 5 Mar. he appointed David M. Key
(Tenn.) Postmaster General, and in Apr.
withdrew the last federal troops from
the South.

**10–24 APR. END OF "BLACK RE-
CONSTRUCTION."** The period of Radical control of the ex-Confederate states
had been under attack for corruption, incompetence, and extravagance. Corrupt
financial practices were notorious in
South Carolina, where the public debt
rose from $7 million (1865) to $29 million (1873); but in other states extravagant governments had raised tax burdens and increased state debts (in Ark.,
from $3.5 million, 1868, to $15.7 million, 1875–$115 per voter; in La., from
$11 million to $50 million, 1875, and the
state tax rose almost 5-fold, treble the
N.Y. real property tax in 1870), while
property values declined sharply. But
maladministration and corruption were

not confined to the South in that period.
On the credit side, it should be pointed
out that large sums were needed for
rebuilding devastated areas and for essential public services in many cases
hitherto not adequately provided, such
as public education, hospitals, and asylums. By 1876 the constitution in nearly
every Southern state contained provisions making tax-supported free public
schools for both whites and Negroes
mandatory.

In reaction against Radical rule the
conservatives won control in Georgia,
North Carolina, Tennessee, and Virginia
(1869–71); and in Alabama, Arkansas,
Mississippi, and Texas (1874–75). By
the summer of 1876 only Florida, Louisiana, and South Carolina remained in
Radical hands. On 2 Jan. 1877 carpet-
bag rule ended in Florida with the inauguration of George F. Drew, Democratic
governor, and the Radicals also lost control in the 2 remaining states of the
South. Federal troops were withdrawn
from South Carolina (10 Apr.) and Louisiana (24 Apr.).

DOMESTIC ISSUES FROM HAYES TO WILSON, 1878-1918

Governmental leadership in the years immediately following Reconstruction was marked by timidity and complacency. Save for two nonconsecutive terms in the presidency of Grover Cleveland, a Democrat, the Republicans ruled the White House from 1869 down to the inauguration of Woodrow Wilson in 1913. The near monopoly of the office of the chief executive by the Republicans was countered by the fact that in Congress the two major parties were more or less evenly matched in strength, that until the presidency of Theodore Roosevelt, the initiative was retained by the Congress, and that trusts and monopolies expressed their will through the dominance of both political organizations and a relatively pliant Supreme Court. The trusts, hard currency, and high tariffs came to the fore as major issues, thus reflecting a pervasive grass-roots protest coupled with an awareness that the privileged constituted an ever-shrinking segment of the population. If the Populists alerted the nation to the perils of uncontrolled business leadership, the Progressives institutionalized the reform movement, gleaning a harvest of reform legislation in the states during the early years of the twentieth century and on the national level during the first Wilson administration, 1913–17.

1878

28 Feb. BLAND-ALLISON ACT. The demonetization of silver excited little controversy when adopted, but within a few years was characterized as the "Crime of '73" by Western silver-mine operators, among others. Chief factor in the agitation for resuming the unlimited coinage of silver was the discovery, during the middle 1870s, of new deposits in Nevada, Colorado, and Utah. The expansion of silver production coincided with a growing international trend toward adoption of the gold standard.

Declining market prices for silver bullion led Western mining interests to call for a return to bimetallism. The silverites found natural allies in inflationist-minded agrarian and labor groups who viewed an increase in the volume of circulating money as the best means of raising farm prices and industrial wages, while business interests were split over the issue. The House of Representatives, dominated by inflationist elements, passed a bill (13 Dec. 1876) sponsored by **Richard P. Bland** (Mo., 1835–99), providing for the free and unlimited coinage of silver at the ratio of 16 to 1. When the

Senate took no action, the House again passed the bill (5 Nov. 1877). Weakened by a Senate amendment introduced by Sen. **William B. Allison** (Iowa, 1829–1908), the bill was finally passed over President Hayes' veto.

The Bland-Allison Act required the Secretary of the Treasury to make monthly purchases of not less than $2 million and not more than $4 million worth of silver at the market price, such purchases to be converted into standard dollars. Thus, unlimited purchase and coinage, the original goal of the inflationists, was not attained. The act also provided for an international monetary conference (which met without achieving conclusive results).

The effect of the act was not inflationary because of the discretionary powers granted to the Secretary of the Treasury and his conservative use of them. Monthly purchases were made at the minimum amount authorized by law. A revival of prosperity beginning in 1879 staved off further agitation.

GREENBACK LABOR MOVEMENT. The labor unrest of 1877 helped to create labor support for the Greenback program. The Greenback Labor party, organized at the Toledo convention (22 Feb.) attended by some 800 delegates from 28 states, adopted a platform reflecting inflationist and labor viewpoints. The party denounced the resumption of specie payments, and called for the free coinage of silver on a parity with gold, the suppression of national bank notes, restrictions on the hours of industrial labor, and checks on Chinese immigration.

In the congressional elections of 1878, the Greenback party reached peak strength, with a total of 1,060,000 votes. Fourteen candidates won seats in Congress, where **James B. Weaver** (Iowa, (1833–1912) became the standard bearer

of the movement. In 1880 the party broadened its program by endorsing such issues as woman suffrage, federal regulation of interstate commerce, and a graduated income tax, but after that year declined in strength. In 1884 the Greenback Labor party ran its last independent presidential candidate, **Benjamin F. Butler** (Mass., 1818–93).

11 JULY. HAYES AND THE SPOILSMEN. By taking steps to separate the civil service from the domination of the Radical Republican machine leaders, President Hayes widened his differences with the Senate oligarchy. One of the most flagrant examples of corrupt patronage was the New York custom house, where appointments were controlled by the state political machine under Sen. **Roscoe Conkling** (1829–88). When Hayes asked for the resignations of **Chester A. Arthur** (p. 976), port collector of customs, and Alonzo B. Cornell (1832–1904), port naval officer, his request was ignored. The Tenure of Office Act prevented Hayes from removing them. Hayes' own nominations were blocked by the Senate Radicals (12 Dec. 1877), but soon after Congress adjourned in 1878, Hayes suspended Arthur and Cornell (11 July). Later, with Democratic support, Hayes secured confirmation of his appointments. This blow at the Conkling machine and the "Stalwart" faction within the Republican party weakened the Radical hold over the Senate and strengthened the executive, but it left Hayes without the support of a united party.

1879

1 JAN. RESUMPTION OF SPECIE PAYMENTS began, as authorized by the Act of 1875, with no wholesale attempt to reclaim greenbacks (now on a par with the national dollar). On 31 May

1878 Congress had enacted that the $346,681,000 outstanding in greenbacks should remain a permanent part of the currency. Because Secretary of the Treasury **John Sherman** (1823–1900) had accumulated a gold reserve of about $200 million, public confidence was restored in the government's ability to redeem the currency, reflected in the fact that on 17 Dec. 1878 greenbacks reached face value in gold, for the first time since 1862.

HAYES' "RIDER" VETOES. In 1879 the Democrats gained control of both houses of Congress. They attached to the Army Appropriation Act for 1880 a "rider" which in effect nullified the Force Acts of 1865 and 1874 authorizing the president to use federal troops in congressional elections. Hayes' veto (29 Apr.) invoked the constitutional principle of the equal independence of the various branches of the government. Hayes subsequently vetoed 4 other measures by which Congress attempted to repeal the Force Acts. In his avowal of the principle of military intervention in the South, Hayes drew the support of his party.

1880

PRESIDENTIAL CAMPAIGN. When the Republican National Convention met at Chicago (2 June), the field was open, for Hayes had earlier pledged not to run for a 2d term. There were 2 rival factions in the party—one headed by the supporters of James G. Blaine; the other by the "Stalwart" leader, Roscoe Conkling, who nominated Ulysses S. Grant. The Grant supporters failed in their effort to secure the adoption of the unit rule. Grant led on the 1st ballot, but **James A. Garfield** of Ohio, a "dark horse," was drafted on the 36th ballot (8 June) after the Blaine and Sherman

forces threw their support to him. The "Stalwart" faction was appeased with the nomination of **Chester A. Arthur** (N.Y.) for vice-president. The Republican platform advocated civil service reform, a protective tariff, veterans' legislation, and the restriction of Chinese immigration.

The Greenback Labor party met at Chicago (9 June) and nominated James B. Weaver (Iowa) for president and B. J. Chambers (Tex.) for vice-president. The Prohibition party met at Cleveland (17 June) and nominated Neal Dow (Me.) for president and A. M. Thompson (Ohio) for vice-president.

The Democratic National Convention met at Cincinnati (22 June) and nominated **Winfield Scott Hancock** (Pa., 1824–86) for president and **William H. English** (Ind.) for vice-president on a platform which, except for demanding a tariff for revenue purposes only, followed that of the Republican party.

The campaign indicated that the Republican tactic of "waving the bloody shirt" was losing its effectiveness, but the revival of prosperity favored the Republicans.

2 Nov. PRESIDENTIAL ELECTION. Popular vote: **Garfield,** 4,449,053; Hancock, 4,442,035; Weaver, 308,578; Dow, 10,305. Electoral vote: **Garfield,** 214; Hancock, 155. Victory in New York and Indiana decided the extremely close election for Garfield, whose plurality was under 10,000 out of over 9 million votes. The Republicans regained control of the House for the first time since 1874.

1881

23 MAR.–16 MAY. "HALF-BREEDS" AND "STALWARTS." Blaine's appointment to the cabinet as Secretary of State (5 Mar.) was regarded by the "Stalwarts" as a victory for the "Half-Breed" wing, and his prominent influence over the administration led to a reopening of political strife between the rival factions of the Republican party. The struggle, revolving about the spoils of office, came to a head when Garfield challenged Conkling's control of the New York patronage by naming (23 Mar.) a Conkling opponent, William H. Robertson, as collector of the port of New York over the protests of Conkling and Thomas Platt, junior senator from New York, who succeeded in blocking the appointment until May and then resigned (16 May) in protest. The New York legislature refused to reelect the pair. The result spelled Conkling's retirement from politics and the decline of the "Stalwart" faction. Garfield's determined stand was as much a victory for presidential power as it was for the "Half-Breeds."

2 July. ASSASSINATION OF GARFIELD. President Garfield was shot at the Washington railroad station by **Charles J. Guiteau,** a mentally unstable and disappointed office seeker who boasted that he was a "Stalwart" and wanted Arthur for president. Garfield died (19 Sept.) at Elberon, N.J. His assassin was tried (14 Nov.), convicted, and executed 30 June 1882. The murder of Garfield resulted in a strong wave of public opinion against "Stalwartism."

20 Sept. Vice-President **Chester A. Arthur** took oath of office as president; 21st occupant of the office.

CABINET CHANGES. With Arthur's accession to the presidency, the "Half-Breeds" and independents left the cabinet. Arthur's choices, however, showed surprising caution and independence of the "Stalwarts."

1882

15 May–4 Dec. TARIFF COMMISSION. Congress authorized appointment by the president of a 9-man Tariff Com-

mission, which on 4 Dec. recommended substantial tariff reductions. (For tariff of 1833, see p. 713.)

1883

16 Jan. PENDLETON ACT. Public reaction to Garfield's assassination, combined with Democratic victories in the fall elections of 1882, impelled the outgoing Republican Congress to adopt civil service reform legislation. The Pendleton Act, drafted by **Dorman B. Eaton** (1823–99), secretary of the Civil Service Reform Association, and sponsored by Sen. **George H. Pendleton** (Ohio, 1825–89), provided for a bipartisan 3-man Civil Service Commission (of which Eaton was named head) for drawing up and administering competitive examinations to determine on a merit basis the fitness of appointees to federal office. A limited classified civil service list was set up, which the president was empowered to extend at his discretion. The act forbade the levying of political campaign assessments on federal officeholders and protected the latter against ouster for failure to make such contributions. Appointments were to be made on the basis of an appointment among the states according to population. The act immediately affected only larger units and about one tenth of the total number of federal employees. In addition, it governed only future appointments. Despite its weaknesses, the Pendleton Act enabled the chief executive to broaden the merit system and provided the foundation for the federal civil service in its present form.

1884

RESURGENCE OF AGRARIAN DISCONTENT. Five years of farm prosperity (1879–84) were followed by a decline in the prices of agricultural commodities that was to continue steadily until 1896, the result of overproduction and rising competition of foreign wheat-growing countries. The long drought (1887 *et seq.*) caused heavy damage and losses. (For other factors, see p. 693.) When attempts to revive the cooperatives of the Granger era failed to alleviate their plight, farmers banded together in state and regional organizations such as the **Agricultural Wheel,** the **Farmers' Union,** the **Texas State Alliance,** the **Farmers' Mutual Benefit Association,** and the **National Colored Farmers' Alliance.** There finally emerged 2 great regional bodies, the **Southern Alliance** and the **National Farmers' Alliance of the Northwest.** The farmers aimed their attacks against Eastern moneyed interests, the middlemen, the railroads, industrial monopolies, and advocates of the gold standard.

BIG BUSINESS STRIKES BACK. Reacting to popular sentiment against monopoly and privileged wealth, business leaders invoked the philosophy of individualism and laissez-faire, reinforced and elaborated by the teachings of **social Darwinism,** as expounded by the Englishman Herbert Spencer, who portrayed consolidation and combination as the inevitable result of the "struggle for the survival of the fittest." Exponents of social Darwinism ranged from intellectuals like philosopher-historian **John Fiske** (1842–1901) and social scientist **William Graham Sumner** (p. 1164) to business tycoon **Andrew Carnegie** (p. 998). These evolutionary views also served to underpin racism and expansionism, and supported a laissez-faire interpretation of the Constitution by the courts.

6 Oct. U.S. Naval War College established at Newport, R.I., with Commodore Stephen B. Luce (1827–1917) as first president. The first institution of its kind, it was founded to provide naval officers with postgraduate training in advanced naval science and warfare, international law, and history.

PRESIDENTIAL CAMPAIGN. The National Greenback Labor party met at Indianapolis (28 May) and nominated Benjamin F. Butler (Mass.) for president and A. M. West (Miss.) for vice-president. The Republican National Convention met at Chicago (3 June) and on the 4th ballot (6 June) nominated **James G. Blaine** (Me.) for president. **John A. Logan** (Ill.) was nominated for vice-president. The Republican choice alienated the Independent Republicans, a reform group that regarded Blaine as inimical to the cause of good government. Among the Independents, who were shortly dubbed "Mugwumps," were George William Curtis, E. L. Godkin, Carl Schurz, and Charles F. Adams, Jr. Valuing civil service reform above party regularity, the Mugwumps backed the Democratic candidate. The Democratic National Convention, meeting at Chicago (8 July), nominated **Grover Cleveland,** governor of New York, on the 2d ballot (11 July) and chose **Thomas A. Hendricks** (Ind.) for vice-president. The Prohibition party national convention met at Pittsburgh (23 July) and nominated John P. St. John (Kan.) for president and William Daniel (Md.) for vice-president.

The campaign promptly degenerated into one of the most scurrilous in American political history. The "Mulligan letters" (1876), illuminating Blaine's corrupt dealings during his service as speaker of the House, were fully exploited by the Democrats. The Republicans in turn charged that Cleveland, as a young bachelor in Buffalo, had fathered an illegitimate child. With characteristic honesty, Cleveland acknowledged the truth of the accusation.

The key state in the election was New York, where the Tammany machine headed by John Kelly opposed Cleveland. Shortly before election day, Rev. **Samuel D. Burchard,** leader of a delegation of clergymen who called on Blaine at the Fifth Avenue Hotel in New York (29 Oct.), referred to the Democrats as the party of "Rum, Romanism, and Rebellion." Blaine's failure to disavow the remark or to rebuke Burchard cost him many votes in the Irish-American stronghold of New York. Blaine later said it cost him the election.

4 Nov. PRESIDENTIAL ELECTION. Popular vote: **Cleveland,** 4,911,017; Blaine, 4,848,334; Butler, 175,370; St. John, 150,369. Electoral vote: **Cleveland,** 219; Blaine, 182. The Democrats carried New York by 1,149 out of a total of 1,125,000 votes. Cleveland was the first Democratic candidate since Buchanan to win a presidential election. The Republicans gained 18 seats in the House, but that body still remained under Democratic control (since 1882).

1885

25 Nov. Death of vice-president Thomas A. Hendricks at Indianapolis, Ind.

1886

19 Jan. PRESIDENTIAL SUCCESSION ACT, which replaced the statute of 1792, provided that in the event of removal, death, resignation, or inability, of both the president and vice-president, the heads of the executive departments, in order of the creation of their offices, should succeed to the duties of the office of the president. This law remained in effect until 1947.

TREASURY SURPLUS. The accumulation of a large federal surplus, most of it the result of the continuance of internal revenue taxes levied to finance the Civil War, began to loom as a major

political question. The revival of national prosperity in 1879 swelled the surplus (see p. 735), now attacked for withdrawing large sums from general circulation and promoting extravagant government spending. Cleveland referred to the problem in his annual message to Congress in 1886, and looked to a reduction of tariff duties as a means of dealing with it. The Republicans were unwilling to modify protectionism.

WHITNEY AND THE "STEEL NAVY." After the Civil War the U.S. Navy, consisting of obsolescent wooden ships, fell into disrepair. In 1880 the U.S. stood 12th among the world's naval powers. In 1881 a naval advisory board recommended the construction of steel cruisers. On 3 Mar. 1883 Congress, taking initial steps toward the creation of a modern navy, authorized the building of 3 steel cruisers; further shipbuilding authorized 3 Aug. 1886. Constructive reforms and advances awaited the reorganization of the Navy Department by Secretary **William C. Whitney** (1841–1904). He coordinated the bureaus, rid the fleet of antiquated vessels, and embarked on the rapid construction of modern steel ships incorporating advances in naval armament (22 such vessels had been built or authorized by the time Whitney left office, 1889). By insisting upon naval armor of American manufacture, Whitney encouraged the development of domestic steelworks capable of producing heavy ship plates and huge naval guns, thereby eliminating American dependence upon European steelmakers. Whitney's naval policy was continued by succeeding administrations. By 1900 the U.S. ranked 3d among world naval powers.

1887

3 Feb. ELECTORAL COUNT ACT, designed to prevent a disputed national election (as in the instance of the Hayes-Tilden election of 1876), made each state the absolute judge over appointment or returns, specifying congressional acceptance of electoral returns certified by a state in accordance with its own electoral law. Congress can intervene only if the state itself is unable to decide or has decided irregularly. In such cases, a concurrent vote of Congress is decisive, but should the 2 houses disagree, the votes of those electors whose appointment is certified by the governor shall be counted.

4 Feb. INTERSTATE COMMERCE ACT. Public resentment of abuses in railway transportation led to numerous bills and resolutions being placed before Congress. In 1874 a special Senate Committee headed by **William Windom** (Minn., 1827–91) had advocated competitive routes to the seaboard, development of waterways, and establishment of a statistical bureau; but this report failed to satisfy the demand of agrarian groups and businessmen for government regulation. The McCrary Bill, introduced in 1874, provided for the establishment of a federal commission empowered to fix maximum rates, investigate complaints, and call witnesses. The measure passed the House by a narrow margin, but was never considered by the Senate. The Senate likewise failed to act on the Reagan Bill (1878), which called for the prohibition of railroad pools, rebates, drawbacks, and discriminatory rates.

In the absence of federal legislation, the movement for railroad regulation within the states gained momentum during the 70s with the passage of the so-called **Granger laws,** which received judicial approval in the Supreme Court decision in **Munn** v. **Illinois** (1877, p. 671). However, the states were virtually stripped of their restraining power over the railroads by the Supreme Court decision in the **Wabash Case** (1886, p.

671). Continuing public dissatisfaction made itself felt through the Cullom Committee headed by Sen. **Shelby M. Cullom** (Ill., 1829–1914), which in 1885 conducted hearings throughout the country and submitted a report recommending the federal regulation of interstate commerce.

The result was the Interstate Commerce Act, which passed the House, 219–41, and the Senate, 43–15. Applying only to railroads passing through more than one state, the act provided that all charges made by railway must be reasonable and just (but did not authorize rate-fixing); prohibited pooling operations, discriminatory rates, drawbacks, and rebates; and made it illegal to charge more for a short haul than for a long haul over the same line. Railroads were required to post their rates, and could not change them until after a 10-day public notice. The act created the **Interstate Commerce Commission,** the first regulatory commission in U.S. history. The commission was authorized to investigate the management of railroads, summon witnesses, and compel the production of company books and papers, but its orders did not have the binding force of a court decree. However, it could invoke the aid of equity proceedings in the federal courts. The commission was empowered to require railroads to file annual reports of operations and finances and to adopt a uniform system of accounting.

At the outset, the railroads conformed to the law, but after 1890 difficulties in interpretation and application made the practical results of the act feeble and disappointing. Railroad operators used a variety of devices for circumventing the provisions of the act. The decisions of the commission met serious reversals at the hands of the Supreme Court, as in the Maximum Freight Rate case (1897) and the Alabama Midlands case (1897).

By 1898 the commission had been reduced to virtual impotence, and was active chiefly as a body for the collection and publication of statistics.

11 Feb. CLEVELAND'S PENSION VETOES. By the middle 1880s Union veterans on the pension rolls constituted a heavy drain on the national treasury. Veterans' appropriations increased markedly after the passage of the Arrears of Pension Act (1879), enacted under pressure from the Grand Army of the Republic. Cleveland, insofar as pressure of duties permitted, followed a policy of investigating individual claims and vetoing those which appeared to be fraudulent. While he approved more special pension bills than did any of his predecessors, he also vetoed more. In 1885, annual expenditures for pensions stood at $56 million; by 1888, they had increased to $80 million. Cleveland's vetoes earned him the bitter antagonism of the organized "old soldier" interests.

The climax came when Sen. Henry W. Blair (N.H.) introduced the **Dependent Pension Bill,** passed by Congress in Jan. 1887. This measure provided a pension for all honorably discharged veterans with at least 90 days' service who were then unable to earn their support and depended on manual labor for a living. It established a precedent for pensioning without regard to service-connected disability. Cleveland vetoed the bill (11 Feb.), declaring it would make the pension list a refuge for frauds rather than a "roll of honor."

2 Mar. HATCH ACT for the promotion of agricultural science provided federal subsidies for the creation of state agricultural experiment stations.

5 Mar. TENURE OF OFFICE ACT (1867), as amended in 1869, was repealed after Cleveland's contest with the Senate over appointments and removals from office. Cleveland's message to the Senate (1 Mar. 1886) had insisted that

under the Constitution the president had the sole power of suspension or removal. By his action, Cleveland strengthened the independence of the executive.

7–15 June. CONFEDERATE BATTLE FLAGS. Cleveland again incurred the enmity of the organized Union veterans' interest when he approved a War Department order (7 June) for the return of captured Confederate battle flags to the South. Even though the order was by way of executive routine, and had been initiated at the behest of Adj. Gen. Richard C. Drum, a Republican and a member of the Grand Army of the Republic (G.A.R.), it brought angry protests from Republican politicians and leaders of the G.A.R. Cleveland revoked the order (15 June). The flags were finally returned in 1905 during the administration of Theodore Roosevelt.

6 Dec. After long deliberation, and without consulting the leaders of his party, Cleveland devoted his entire annual message to a plea for a lowered protective tariff, pointing out that the existing rates had encouraged the creation of trusts and the maintenance of high prices. His advocacy of tariff reform alienated protectionist elements within the Democratic party.

1888

PRESIDENTIAL CAMPAIGN. The Union Labor party convention met at Cincinnati (15 May) and nominated Alson J. Streeter (Ill.) for president and C. E. Cunningham (Ark.) for vice-president. The United Labor party, also meeting at Cincinnati (15 May), nominated Robert H. Cowdrey (Ill.) for president and W. H. T. Wakefield (Kan.) for vice-president. The national convention of the Prohibition party met at Indianapolis (30 May) and nominated Clinton B. Fisk (N.J.) for president and John A. Brooks (Mo.) for vice-president.

The Democratic National Convention met at St. Louis (5 June) and nominated President **Grover Cleveland** for reelection and **Allen G. Thurman** (Ohio) for vice-president. The Republican National Convention met at Chicago (19 June) and nominated **Benjamin Harrison** (Ind.) for president and **Levi P. Morton** (N.Y.) for vice-president.

The Republicans made the high protective tariff the chief plank in their platform, and the campaign thus became the first in U.S. history waged on this issue. The Republicans also included a promise of generous pensions for Civil War veterans. A huge Republican campaign fund, which found ready contributors among the enemies of tariff reform, was employed to denounce Cleveland's stand on the tariff, his pension vetoes, and the Confederate battle flag order. On the eve of the election the Democratic cause was dealt a severe blow by the "Murchison letter" involving the British minister to the U.S., Sackville-West. The letter was written ostensibly by "Charles F. Murchison," a naturalized Englishman (in reality George A. Osgoodby, a California Republican) seeking Sackville-West's counsel on how to vote in the approaching election. The British minister's reply (13 Sept.) intimated that "Murchison" should vote for Cleveland. The correspondence was published (24 Oct.) by the Republicans and aroused public indignation against foreign interference in internal affairs. Sackville-West was handed his passports (24 Oct.), but the damaging political blunder cost the Democrats many Irish-American votes.

6 Nov. PRESIDENTIAL ELECTION. Popular vote: Cleveland, 5,540,050; **Harrison,** 5,444,337; Fisk, 250,125; Streeter, 146,897; Cowdrey, 2,808. Electoral vote: **Harrison,** 233; Cleveland, 168. Harrison carried the key states of New York and Indiana.

1889

11 Feb. Department of Agriculture raised to cabinet status. Norman J. Coleman (Mo.) named first Secretary of Agriculture.

22 Feb. OMNIBUS BILL provided for the admission of North Dakota, South Dakota, Montana, and Washington.

1890

19 June. FORCE (or Federal Elections) BILL, reported in the House, provided for supervision of federal elections by the national government in order to protect Negro voters in the South against state measures designed to deprive them of the vote. It passed the House (2 July), but failed of adoption by the Senate.

27 June. DEPENDENT PENSION ACT. Upon taking office, Harrison appointed as Commissioner of Pensions James "Corporal" Tanner, a past commander of the G.A.R., who declared, "God help the surplus!" During his 6 months in office, Tanner pursued a liberal private pension policy. The administration's debt to the "old soldier" vote was discharged with the passage of the Dependent Pension Act, which granted pensions to veterans of the Union forces with at least 90 days' service who were then or thereafter disabled because of physical or mental reasons (without regard to origin) and were unable to earn a livelihood by manual labor. The act, which inaugurated the principle of the service pension, also provided that pensions of varying amounts were to be granted to minor children, dependent parents, and widows who had married veterans before the passage of the act and had to work for a living. Between 1891 and 1895 the number of pensioners rose from 676,000 to 970,000. By the time Harrison left office, the annual appropriation for pensions had increased from $81 million to $135 million.

2 JULY. SHERMAN ANTITRUST ACT. With the establishment of the first industrial combination, the Standard Oil Trust (1879), there followed in rapid succession other large combinations controlling such commodities as whisky, sugar, lead, beef, and linseed soil. In protest many Western and Southern states enacted antitrust laws, the first in Kansas in 1889. By 1893 similar legislation had been enacted in 15 other states and territories. Since such state laws were powerless to deal with trusts and monopolies engaged in interstate commerce, the demand for governmental regulation of national scope became insistent.

The result was the first federal measure that undertook to regulate trusts. Although the Sherman Antitrust Act was named for Sen. **John Sherman** (Ohio, 1823–1900), the bill was drafted by the Senate Judiciary Committee, the larger share of the work being credited to Sen. **George F. Hoar** (Mass., 1826–1904) and George F. Edmunds (Vt., 1828–1919). The act, consisting of 8 major provisions, declared: "Every contract, combination in the form of trust or otherwise, or conspiracy, in restraint of trade or commerce among the several states, or with foreign nations, is hereby declared to be illegal." The act authorized the federal government to proceed against a trust to obtain its dissolution, and invested federal circuit courts with jurisdiction to prevent and restrain violations of the law.

The most critical weakness of the act was its obscure and ambiguous phrasing, its failure clearly to define words like "trust," "combination," and "restraint." It was not clear whether the act was intended to apply to labor combinations and railroads as well as to combinations of capital. That its provisions embraced labor unions and railroads, respectively,

was the decision of the federal courts in *U.S.* v. *Debs* (1894) and in the Trans-Missouri Freight Association case (1897). In the case of *U.S.* v. *E. C. Knight Company* (1895), among the first in which the Supreme Court interpreted and applied the act, the effectiveness of the law was seriously limited. Between 1890 and 1901, the act was not vigorously enforced. During that period only 18 suits were instituted, 4 against labor unions. The existence of the statute did not prevent the continued growth of combinations and monopolies under other names. (See also p. 724.)

14 JULY. SHERMAN SILVER PURCHASE ACT. The Bland-Allison Act satisfied neither silverites nor gold standard advocates. Meanwhile, the steady decline in the market price of silver bullion (by 1890 it stood to gold at a ratio of 20 to 1), combined with the deepening economic depression, helped to increase the political strength of the silver and inflationist forces (reinforced by senators from the recently admitted Omnibus states [1889]). In the House, which still remained under the control of gold-standard men, the silverites gained new accessions from representatives voted into office by the Farmers' Alliances.

The prosilverite Senate passed a bill (June) for the free and unlimited coinage of silver, but the House blocked its passage. By threatening to vote against the McKinley tariff bill, Western interests were able to wrest a concession from conservative Easterners, and a compromise was arranged to permit a more liberal purchase policy. The Sherman Silver Purchase Act, while it did not provide for free silver, required the Treasury to purchase 4,500,000 ounces of silver each month at the prevailing market price and to issue in payment legal tender Treasury notes redeemable in gold or silver at the option of the Treasury. The amount of bullion specified was the currently estimated total U.S. production of silver.

The act had the effect of increasing the circulation of redeemable paper currency and weakening the federal gold reserve. Among Eastern business and financial groups it created a fear that the silver inflation might take the country off the gold standard. Nor did the act satisfy the demands of those who advocated free coinage and a bimetallic standard. Cleveland made his position clear. In a public letter (10 Feb. 1891) he attacked the "dangerous and reckless experiment of free, unlimited, and independent coinage."

4 Nov. Congressional elections in 39 states resulted in a Democratic landslide that cost the Republicans their control of the House. Public reaction against the McKinley Tariff of 1890 was blamed for the Republican defeat.

1892

PEOPLE'S (POPULIST) PARTY. The sectional struggle between debtor and creditor, intensified by the continuing agricultural depression, led the agrarian protest movement to take political action. Beginning in 1889–90, efforts were made to unite farmer and labor organizations on the basis of common objectives. The agrarian organizations of the West and South, together with labor, Granger, and Greenback representatives, held a meeting at St. Louis (Dec. 1889). In June 1890, the statewide People's party was formed in Kansas. In Dec. 1890, the Southern Alliance, the Farmers' Mutual Benefit Association, and the Colored Farmers' Alliance convened at Ocala, Fla., and drew up a list of grievances resembling the platform approved at St. Louis. These included cheap currency, the abolition of national banks, and the restriction of land ownership to American citizens. Labor men who at-

tended the Ocala meeting called for the establishment of a third party, but the Southern Alliance, fearing such a movement might bring the Negro into power, opposed independent action. The Alliance advised its members to support instead candidates of either major party who would pledge themselves to policies benefiting agriculture. In general, Southern agrarian leaders adopted the tactic of attempting to capture the Democratic machinery.

A national convention was held at Cincinnati (19 May 1891) to plan independent action. More than 1,400 delegates from 32 states adopted resolutions supporting a new party. The **People's Party of the U.S.A.** was formally organized at St. Louis (22 Feb.) and held its first national convention at Omaha (2 July). Present at Omaha were the outstanding leaders of the Populist movement, including **Ignatius Donnelly** (Minn.), **Thomas E. Watson** (p. 1178), **"Sockless Jerry" Simpson** (Kan.), **Mary Ellen Lease** (Kan.), **William A. Peffer** (Kan.), and **James Kyle** (S.D.). Only a small minority of the Southern Alliance backed the third-party movement.

The Populist convention nominated **James B. Weaver** (Iowa) for president and **James G. Field** (Va.) for vice-president. The Populist platform (4 July) demanded free and unlimited coinage of silver at 16 to 1, and an increase in the circulating medium of not less than $50 per capita; a national currency issued by the federal government only and without the use of banking corporations; government ownership and operation of all transportation and communication lines; a graduated income tax; establishment of a postal savings system; direct election of U.S. senators; adoption of the secret ballot, the initiative, and referendum; prohibition of the alien ownership of land; a shorter working day for industrial labor; and restrictions on immigration.

PRESIDENTIAL CAMPAIGN. The Republican National Convention met at Minneapolis (7 June) and on 10 June nominated President **Benjamin Harrison** for reelection and **Whitelaw Reid** (N.Y.) for vice-president. The party's chief plank was the high protective tariff. The Democratic National Convention met at Chicago (21 June) and nominated **Grover Cleveland** for president and **Adlai E. Stevenson** (Ill.) for vice-president. The straddling plank on the tariff, opposed by the radical wing of the Democratic party, was dropped in favor of a stronger declaration "that the federal government has no constitutional power to impose and collect tariff duties, except for purposes of revenue only." During the campaign, however, Cleveland took a moderate stand on the tariff. The national Prohibition Convention met at Cincinnati (29 June) and nominated John Bidwell (Calif.) for president and James B. Cranfill (Tex.) for vice-president. The Socialist Labor Convention met at New York and nominated Simon Wing (Mass.) for president and Charles H. Matchett (N.Y.) for vice-president.

Cleveland's unswerving position on the gold standard won him the heavy support of conservative Eastern financial and business groups. The Democrats kept the silver issue in the background except in those states where the inflationist forces were strong. Factors which militated against Republican success' included public reaction to the McKinley Tariff of 1890 and the labor disturbances of 1892.

8 Nov. PRESIDENTIAL ELECTION. Popular vote: **Cleveland,** 5,554,414; Harrison, 5,190,802; Weaver, 1,027,329; Bidwell, 271,058 (peak of popular vote in a presidential election for Prohibitionists); Wing, 21,164. Electoral vote: **Cleveland,** 277; Harrison, 145; Weaver, 22. The Democrats secured control of both houses of Congress.

SOUTHERN POPULISM IN DE-CLINE. Despite Weaver's relatively strong showing for a third-party candidate Southern Populists mainly remained loyal to the Democratic party on the issue of white supremacy. Populism's decline in the South was accelerated when the Democrats took over their money plank. Southern Populism's collapse paved the way for the rise of demagogues like **"Pitchfork Ben" Tillman** (1897–1918) of South Carolina and **James K. Vardaman** (1861–1930) of Mississippi, who wooed the votes of the poor whites with an agrarian program carrying white supremacy overtones.

1893

PANIC OF 1893: U.S. GOLD RE-SERVE. U.S. fiscal conditions were adversely affected by (1) failure (Nov. 1890) of the British banking house of Baring Bros., causing British investors to unload American securities, with a resultant drain of gold from the U.S.; (2) a sharp decrease in U.S. revenues attributed to the McKinley Tariff Act; (3) depletion of government surplus by pension grants of the Harrison administration. The decline of the U.S. gold reserve below the $100 million mark (21 Apr.) helped precipitate the panic. On 5 May stocks on the New York Stock Exchange dropped suddenly, crashing 27 June (see also p. 748). By 30 Dec. the gold reserve fell to $80 million.

1 Nov. REPEAL OF SHERMAN SILVER PURCHASE ACT. To stem the drain on the gold reserve Cleveland summoned (30 June) an extra session of Congress to convene 7 Aug., requesting repeal of the Sherman Silver Purchase Act. The struggle over repeal, centered in the Senate, proved the grimmest of Cleveland's presidential career. Repeal passed the House, 239–108 (28 Aug.), and the Senate, 48–37 (30 Oct.), but the administration's victory split the Democratic party.

1894

25 Mar.–1 May. "COXEY'S ARMY." Over the winter of 1893–94 growing economic distress and mass unemployment brought the formation of scattered groups of jobless men into "armies" whose leaders were known as "generals." Of these, the best known was "Coxey's Army," led by the Populist **Jacob S. Coxey** of Massillon, Ohio. Coxey called upon the unemployed to march upon Washington and deliver to Congress their demands for relief. Although many small detachments of the "army" started out from various points throughout the country, only 400 reached the national capital (30 Apr.). Coxey advocated a public works relief program of road construction and local improvements financed by a federal issue of $500 million in legal tender notes. The program had a 2-fold purpose: to provide jobs and to increase the amount of money in circulation. "Coxey's Army" disbanded after its 3 leaders (Coxey, Carl Browne, and Christopher Columbus Jones) were arrested for trespassing on the Capitol grounds.

FREE-SILVER PROPAGANDA. *Coin's Financial School* (1894), by William H. Harvey of Chicago, which soon became the infallible guide of the bimetallists, was followed by similar tracts, including *The American People's Money* (1895), by Ignatius Donnelly. Among the magazines that served as a platform for the silverites were the *Arena* and the *National Bimetallist*.

1895

5 Mar. APPEAL OF THE SILVER DEMOCRATS. The broadening cleavage in the Democratic party between gold and silver factions was indicated the "Appeal of the Silver Democrats" framed by **Richard P. Bland** (Mo.) and **William Jennings Bryan** (Neb., p. 992), leaders of the silver bloc in the House. The appeal, signed by a minority of House Democrats, called for the immediate restoration of the free and unlimited coinage of silver at the ratio of 16 to 1. During the year a number of free-silver conventions were held in the South and West.

GOLD RESERVE. Repeal of the Sherman Silver Act failed to halt depletion of the gold reserve. Confronted by declining government revenues, the Treasury was compelled to use the gold reserve not only for redemption but also for meeting operating expenses. After unsuccessfully attempting to win congressional authority to sell bonds, Secretary of the Treasury Carlisle took steps to maintain a normal gold reserve. Invoking the unrepealed provisions of the Resumption Act of 1875 for borowing gold, he invited bids for a bond issue of $50 million (Jan. 1894), and in Nov. 1894 asked for a similar loan; but owing to lack of public response to the offerings, had to place the loans with New York bankers. Successive withdrawals finally caused the gold reserve to fall to $41 million early in 1895. Cleveland moved to cope with the Treasury crisis by calling J. Pierpont Morgan, the New York banker, to a White House interview (7 Feb.). The result was a third loan placed with a banking syndicate headed by Morgan and August Belmont. The arrangement called for the purchase of 3,500,000 ounces of gold, to be paid for in bonds. One half of the gold was to be purchased abroad. It is estimated that the bankers realized a profit of some $1.5 million on the $62 million loan. While the loan succeeded in relieving the Treasury emergency for a time, it was demned by Populists and bimetallists. ...on the expiration of the Morgan-...elmont contract, the government was ...again compelled to resort to a loan when the reserve dipped to $79 million (Dec.), but this time the administration threw the $100 million loan open to the public (6 Jan 1896). Its quick subscription indicated a restoration of public confidence. But the Treasury had to resume withdrawal of gold to pay for bonds; consequently, by July 1896, the reserve fell below the $90 million mark. The situation was not serious because of the revival of business activity, but gold hoarding did not cease until after the election of 1896, when the future of the gold standard was assured.

1896

PRESIDENTIAL CAMPAIGN. The Prohibition National Convention met at Pittsburgh (27 May) and nominated Joshua Levering (Md.) for president and Hale Johnson (Ill.) for vice-president. A free-silver minority, organized as the National party, nominated Charles E. Bentley (Neb.) for president and J. H. Southgate (N.C.) for vice-president. The Republican National Convention met at St. Louis (16 June) and nominated **William McKinley** (Ohio, p. 1093) for president and **Garret A. Hobart** (N.J.) for vice-president on a platform upholding the single gold standard (although the Republicans promised to promote the free-silver policy by international agreement), the high protective tariff, and a vigorous foreign policy (calling for U.S. control of the Hawaiian Islands). The way for McKinley's nomination had been prepared by the maneuvers of the Cleveland industrialist and financier **Marcus A. Hanna** (p. 1049), named Republican party campaign manager. Adoption of the gold plank caused Western silver Republicans under Sen.

Henry M. Teller (Colo.) to bolt the party. Organized as the National Silver Republicans, they held a national convention at St. Louis (22 July) and endorsed the Democratic candidates. The Socialist Labor National Convention met at New York (4 July) and nominated Charles H. Matchett (N.Y.) for president and Matthew Maguire (N.J.) for vice-president.

When the Democratic National Convention met at Chicago (7 July), it was clear that the free-silver faction was in control of the party organization. The Democratic platform called for the free and unlimited coinage of silver at the 16 to 1 ratio; condemned trusts, monopolies, and the high protective tariff, as well as the use of injunctions against labor; and attacked the Supreme Court ruling in the income tax case. The dominant issue was the money question. In support of the adoption of the free-silver plan, William Jennings Bryan (Neb.) delivered his eloquent "Cross of Gold" speech (8 July), closing with this challenge to the advocates of the gold standard: "You shall not press down upon the brow of labor this crown of thorns, you shall not crucify mankind upon a cross of gold." **Bryan** was nominated for president and **Arthur Sewall** (Me.) for vice-president. The gold Democrats withdrew from the convention, organized the National Democratic party, and in convention at Indianapolis (2 Sept.) nominated **John M. Palmer** (Ill.) for president and **Simon B. Buckner** (Ky.) for vice-president on a platform supporting the gold standard. The People's (Populist) National Convention, meeting at St. Louis (22 July), endorsed Bryan's nomination and chose Thomas E. Watson (Ga.) for vice-president.

Supported by 3 parties, Bryan, the "Boy Orator of the Platte," waged a vigorous and strenuous campaign, traveling 13,000 miles in 14 weeks, making 600

1907

PANIC OF 1907. Stock market drop (beg. 13 Mar.) and business failures in mid-1907 were followed by the suspension (22 Oct.) of the Knickerbocker Trust Co. in New York. In order to avoid a more serious decline, Roosevelt permitted (4 Nov.) the U.S. Steel Corp. to acquire the Tennessee Coal and Iron Co., with the understanding that no antitrust action would be instituted. The panic revealed flaws in the currency and credit structure, and was directly responsible for the passage of the Aldrich-Vreeland Act.

1908

13 May. WHITE HOUSE CONSERVATION CONFERENCE. (p. 638).

30 May. ALDRICH-VREELAND ACT, passed as an emergency currency measure, authorized national banks for a period of 6 years to issue circulating notes based on commercial paper and state, county, and municipal bonds. In order to limit bank note emission based on securities other than federal bonds, a graduated tax up to 10% was levied on such notes. While the act introduced some elasticity into the national currency, it provided no safeguards for the credit supply. The most important provision was the establishment of a **National Monetary Commission** authorized to investigate and report upon the banking and currency systems of the U.S. and European countries. The commission, consisting of 9 senators and 9 representatives, was headed by Sen. **Nelson W. Aldrich** (R.I., 1841–1915). Its report, submitted to Congress on 8 Jan. 1912, contained legislative proposals (notably, a national reserve association with branches throughout the country) later incorporated in modified form in the Federal Reserve Act of 1913.

PRESIDENTIAL CAMPAIGN. The People's (Populist) National Convention met at St. Louis (2 April) and nominated **Thomas E. Watson** (Ga.) for president and Samuel W. Williams (Ind.) for vice-president. The United Christian National Convention met at Rock Island, Ill. (1 May), and nominated Daniel B. Turney (Ill.) for president and L. S. Coffin (Iowa) for vice-president. The Socialist National Convention met at Chicago (10 May) and nominated **Eugene V. Debs** (Ind.) for president and Benjamin Hanford (N.Y.) for vice-president. The Republican National Convention met at Chicago (16 June) and nominated **William H. Taft** (Ohio, p. 1165) for President and **James S. Sherman** (N.Y.) for vice-president. Taft was largely the personal choice of President Roosevelt, who had announced his intention not to serve for a second elective term. The Republican platform pledged tariff revision, stricter enforcement of antitrust legislation, and a furthering of Roosevelt's conservation program. The Democratic National Convention met at Denver (7 July) and nominated **William Jennings Bryan** (Neb.) for president and **John W. Kern** (Ind.) for vice-president on a platform that condemned monopolies and unequivocally pledged a reduction in tariff rates. The Prohibition National Convention met at Columbus, Ohio (15 July), and nominated Eugene W. Chafin (Ill.) for president and Aaron S. Watkins (Ohio) for vice-president. The Socialist Labor Convention met at New York (24 July) and nominated August Gillhaus (N.Y.) for president and Donald L. Munro (Va.) for vice-president. The Independence Party Convention met at Chicago (27 July) and nominated Thomas L. Hisgen (Mass.) for president and John Temple Graves (Ga.) for vice-president.

3 Nov. PRESIDENTIAL ELECTION. Popular vote: **Taft,** 7,679,006; Bryan,

6,409,106; Debs, 420,820; Chafin, 252,-
683; Hisgen, 83,562; Watson, 28,131;
Gillhaus, 13,825; Turney, 461. Electoral
vote: **Taft,** 321; Bryan, 162. The Republicans reained control of both houses of
Congress.

1910

TAFT'S TRUST POLICY. Under
Roosevelt, 44 antitrust suits were started;
under Taft, 90 proceedings were initiated
against monopolies. The Taft program
was carried out by Attorney General
George W. Wickersham (1858–1936).
Taft proposed requiring federal incorporation of companies engaged in interstate commerce, and the establishment
of a Federal Corporation Commission to
supervise companies holding national
charters, but Congress failed to act. The
2 major Supreme Court decisions of the
Taft administration were the **Standard
Oil Co.** case (1911, p. 674) and the
American Tobacco Co. case (1911, p.
674). The suit for dissolution against
the U.S. Steel Corp. (1911) had political
overtones. The bill filed by the government charged that the Steel Trust had
been strengthened by its absorption of
the Tennessee Coal and Iron Co. during
the panic of 1907, and alleged that the
corporation had used misleading statements in order to secure Roosevelt's consent. The implication that Roosevelt had
been hoodwinked served to widen the rift
between Taft and Roosevelt after the
latter's return from abroad in 1910.

**COMMISSION ON EFFICIENCY
AND ECONOMY.** In his first annual
message to Congress (1909), Taft
stressed "economy in expenditures" and
issued an executive order directing that
all estimates must first be submitted to
him. By this method the administration
succeeded in saving more than $42 mil-
lion during the fiscal year ending 30

June 1911 as compared to estimates for
the preceding year. In June 1910, Taft
secured a congressional appropriation of
$100,000 to investigate federal spending,
and appointed (Mar. 1911) a Commission on Efficiency and Economy to carry
out a survey of administrative organization. Its members included Frederick A.
Cleveland, William F. Willoughby, and
Frank J. Goodnow. The reports of the
commission pointed to outmoded business methods employed in numerous departments and recommended the establishment of a national budget. Partly
because of the Taft-Roosevelt schism,
partly because of patronage interests, the
commission failed to secure congressional
support and was finally dissolved. The
detailed budget that Taft transmitted to
Congress during his last year in office
was ignored. Although Taft's attempt to
establish a national budgetary system
failed, it encouraged similar fiscal innovations in state and local governments;
moreover, it paved the way for the Budget Act of 1921.

18 JUNE. MANN-ELKINS ACT, recommended by Taft, placed telephone,
telegraph, cable, and wireless companies
under the jurisdiction of the Interstate
Commerce Commission. It gave the commission authority to suspend new rates
pending a court decision and provided
for effective enforcement of the long and
short haul clause. The act created a
federal Court of Commerce to pass upon
appeals arising from rate disputes; this
tribunal, however, was abolished in
1912.

25 JUNE. POSTAL SAVINGS bank
system, recommended by Taft and established by act of Congress, authorized 2%
interest on funds deposited at specified
post offices.

25 JUNE. PUBLICITY ACT, recommended by Taft, required filing of statements concerning election campaign con-

tributions for representatives. Previously state corrupt practices acts had been passed (beg. N.Y. 1890).

25 JUNE. MANN ACT (WHITE SLAVE TRAFFIC ACT) prohibited interstate transportation of women for immoral purposes.

REPUBLICAN INSURGENCY. When Roosevelt left office, it was with the conviction that Taft, as his personally chosen successor, would carry forward the reform policies of the Roosevelt administration. Taft did not share Roosevelt's concept of the presidency as a stewardship of the public welfare, and early in his administration became involved in a party split that weakened his prestige and contributed to his break with Roosevelt.

During the Senate hearings and debates on the Payne-Aldrich Tariff (1909), open dissension within the Republican ranks emerged under the leadership of Sen. Robert M. La Follette (Wis.). Insurgent hostility toward Taft was hardened when he signed the tariff bill and then, in a speech at Winona, Minn. (17 Sept. 1909), termed it "the best bill that the Republican party ever passed." The Insurgents, most of whom came from the Midwest, later combined with the Democrats (1911–13) in enacting tariff revision measures which Taft vetoed.

19 MAR. REVOLT AGAINST "CANNONISM" in the form of an amendment (19 Mar.) to the House rules, offered as a resolution (17 Mar.) by George W. Norris (Neb.), deprived Speaker **Joseph G. Cannon** (Ill., 1836–1926) of his dictatorial power to appoint the Committee on Rules. This committee was made elective by the House itself and the speaker was barred from serving on it.

31 AUG. ROOSEVELT-TAFT SPLIT. In his "New Nationalism" speech at Osawatomie, Kan. (31 Aug.), Roosevelt, who had returned from Africa in June, attacked the Supreme Court's attitude toward social legislation and declared that the New Nationalism "maintains that every man holds his property subject to the general right of the community to regulate its use to whatever degree the public welfare may require it." The speech was interpeted as an assault upon the conservatism of the Taft administration.

BALLINGER-PINCHOT CONTROVERSY arose from charges made against the conservation policy pursued by Secretary of the Interior Richard A. Ballinger. Under the Roosevelt administration certain water-power sites in Wyoming and Montana had been withdrawn from sale by Secretary of the Interior James R. Garfield. Ballinger doubted the legality of the action and reopened the lands to public entry. Gifford Pinchot, chief of the U.S. Forest Service, publicly accused Ballinger of injuring the conservation program in order to aid corporation interests. Siding with Pinchot was **Louis R. Glavis,** a special agent of the Field Division of the Interior Department who, after being dismissed by order of Taft, charged in an article in *Collier's* (13 Nov. 1909) that Ballinger had favored the patenting of claims to Alaskan coal lands by interests alleged to include the Guggenheims. Taft upheld Ballinger. When a letter written by Pinchot in criticism of Ballinger's conduct was read to the Senate (6 Jan.) by Sen. Jonathan P. Dolliver (Iowa), an Insurgent Republican, Taft ordered Pinchot's removal from office (7 Jan.). A joint congressional committee was established (26 Jan.) to inquire into the administration of the Interior Department. While a majority of the committee exonerated Ballinger, the controversy had already become a major political issue that widened the breach between Taft and the Insurgent Republicans and ultimately contributed to the break between Taft and Roosevelt. Public feeling toward Ballinger was so unfavorable that he resigned (6 Mar. 1911) to relieve the Taft administration of political embarrassment.

8 Nov. MIDTERM ELECTIONS. The Democrats gained control of the House; the Senate, while nominally Republican, was actually under the control of a Democratic-Insurgent Republican bloc. In the state elections of 1910, the Democrats elected 26 governors, including **Woodrow Wilson** (N.J., p. 1187).

1911

21 JAN. National Progressive Republican League founded at Washington, D.C., by Insurgent Republicans under the leadership of Sen. Robert M. La Follette (Wis.). Sen. Jonathan Bourne (Ore.) was elected president of the organization, whose professed chief object was "the promotion of popular government and progressive legislation." Its platform: direct election of U.S. senators; direct primaries for the nomination of elective officers; direct election of delegates to national conventions; amendment of state constitutions to provide for the initiative, referendum, and recall; and a corrupt practices act. The Progressives sought to gain control of the Republican organization, block the nomination of Taft, and choose their own candidate, at this time, La Follette, whom they endorsed 16 Oct.

22 AUG. President Taft vetoed the joint resolution of Congress admitting Arizona to statehood, on the ground that the provision in its constitution authorizing the recall of judges was a blow at the independence of the judiciary. Arizona removed the offending clause and was

admitted to statehood (14 Feb. 1912), but afterward restored the article.

1912

SOCIAL LEGISLATION IN THE STATES. By 1912, height of the Progressive movement, there had been enacted in the states a considerable body of social legislation relating to wages and hours, the employment of women and children, and safety and health conditions in factories. A few landmarks among state laws: the adoption by Maryland (1902) of the first state workmen's compensation law; the adoption by Oregon (1903) of a 10-hour law for women in industry (upheld by the Supreme Court in 1908, in *Muller* v. *Oregon*); the enactment by Illinois (1911) of the first state law providing public assistance to mothers with dependent children; the first minimum wage law in the U.S., adopted by Massachusetts (1912), which established a commission to fix wage rates for women and children (this and similar legislation in other states invalidated by the Supreme Court, 1923, in *Adkins* v. *Children's Hospital*).

ROOSEVELT ENTERS THE RACE. Early in 1912 the La Follette boom among the Progressives began to weaken. At the same time Roosevelt, whose alienation from Taft and the conservative Republican leadership had brought him close to the Progressive camp, decided (letter to William B. Howland, 23 Dec. 1911) to oppose Taft for the Republican presidential nomination. A Chicago meeting (10 Feb.) of Republican leaders sent Roosevelt a letter (signed by 7 Republican governors) declaring "that a large majority of the Republican voters of the country favor your nomination, and a large majority of the people favor your election as the next President of the United States." In an address (21 Feb.)

New York, Philadelphia, Richmond, Atlanta, Dallas, Kansas City, St. Louis, Chicago, Cleveland, Minneapolis, and San Francisco). At the apex of the system was a Federal Reserve Board consisting of 7 members (subsequently increased to 8) including the Secretary of the Treasury and the Comptroller of the Currency. This central board was authorized to raise or lower the rediscount rate prevailing at the district reserve banks, thus giving it direct control over the credit supply.

The district banks were to serve as bankers' banks, i.e., as depositories for the cash reserves of the national banks (which were required to join the system) and of state banks (whose membership was optional). Each Federal Reserve bank was to be governed by a board of 9 directors, 6 of them appointed by the Federal Reserve Board. A member bank was required to subscribe to the capital stock of its district Federal Reserve bank in an amount equal to 6% of its own capital and surplus. The Federal Reserve banks were empowered to rediscount the commercial and agricultural paper of member banks, and the system's currency was to be based upon approved rediscounted paper deposited by member banks. Against such paper the reserve banks could issue Federal Reserve notes (accepted as government obligations) as part of the circulating money supply. The amount could be expanded and contracted in keeping with the changing requirements of business activity. Each reserve bank was required to maintain a gold reserve of 40% against Federal Reserve notes outstanding, although it was specified that this provision might be suspended in time of emergency.

1914

8 MAY. SMITH-LEVER ACT provided for a system of agricultural extension work based on cooperation between the Department of Agriculture and the land-grant colleges. Federal grants-in-aid were to be matched by state appropriations in carrying out the program.

26 SEPT. FEDERAL TRADE COMMISSION ACT, passed at Wilson's recommendation as part of his trust regulation program, was designed to prevent unfair methods of competition in interstate commerce. The Bureau of Corporations was eliminated, and in its place was established the Federal Trade Commission, a bipartisan body consisting of 5 members, authorized to demand annual and special reports from corporations, investigate the activities of persons and corporations (except banks and common carriers), publish reports on its findings, and issue cease and desist orders (subject to judicial review in the federal courts) to prevent unfair business practices. Among the practices which the commission subsequently singled out were trade boycotts, mislabeling and adulteration of commodities, combinations for maintaining resale prices, and false claims to patents.

15 OCT. CLAYTON ANTITRUST ACT, which supplemented and strengthened the Sherman Antitrust Act, was aimed at corporate methods hitherto not specified as illegal practices. It also contained provisions relating to labor and agricultural organizations. The act prohibited the following: price discriminations substantially tending to create a monopoly, tying contracts (i.e., contracts based on the condition that purchasers would not buy or handle the products of sellers' competitors), interlocking directorates in industrial aggregations capitalized at $1 million or more, and the acquisition of stockholdings tending to lessen competition. Officials of corporations violating antitrust statutes could be held individually responsible. The following remedies were provided whereby injured parties might secure relief: court injunctions, the issuance of cease and desist orders by the Federal Trade Commission, and civil suits for 3-fold damages in instances where the existence of price discrimination and tying contracts was established.

In regard to labor and agriculture, the act specified that "the labor of a human being is not a commodity or article of commerce; nothing contained in the antitrust laws shall be construed to forbid the existence and operation of labor, agricultural and horticultural organizations . . . nor shall such organizations or the members thereof be held or construed to be illegal combinations in restraint of trade under the antitrust laws." The act also forbade the use of the injunction in labor disputes unless the court decided that an injunction was necessary to prevent irreparable injury to property; made strikes, peaceful picketing, and boycotts legal under federal jurisdiction; and provided for trial by jury in contempt cases, except in instances where contempt was committed in presence of the court. Hailed by Samuel Gompers as labor's "Magna Carta," the act's labor provisions were substantially weakened by court interpretation.

1915

PREPAREDNESS MOVEMENT. Shortly after the beginning of World War I, the issue of military preparedness was introduced into public debate in the U.S. Private organizations and individuals pointed to occupied Belgium as an example of the fate in store for an unprepared nation, and undertook a campaign for strengthening the national defense. Among such organizations were the National Security League (est. Dec. 1914), the American Defense Society (est. Aug. 1915), the League to Enforce Peace (est. June 1915), and the Ameri-

can Rights Committee (est. Dec. 1915). Individuals prominent in the preparedness movement included **Theodore Roosevelt, Henry Cabot Lodge,** and **Henry L. Stimson.** The "Plattsburg idea" (military training camps for civilians) came into being at Plattsburg, N.Y., on 10 Aug. Preparedness was opposed by organized pacifist and antimilitarist groups who contended that the war did not involve vital U.S. interests. The most spectacular effort of the peace associations was Henry Ford's chartering of the "peace ship" *Oskar II,* which sailed for Europe (4 Dec.) in an ill-fated attempt to end the war by a negotiated peace. On 10 May Wilson in an address at Philadelphia declared: "There is such a thing as a man being too proud to fight. There is such a thing as a nation being so right that it does not need to convince others that it is right." But his opposition to a large standing army and advocacy of unarmed neutrality changed after the *Lusitania* incident (7 May, p. 359). On 7 Dec. he laid before Congress a comprehensive plan for national defense, and on 27 Jan. 1916 began a tour of the country to urge preparedness.

1916

10 Feb. Lindley M. Garrison resigned as Secretary of War. Garrison's advocacy of a volunteer force under direct national control, as opposed to the state-controlled National Guard units, was not accepted by Wilson, who feared loss of congressional support on the issue.

7 March. Newton D. Baker (Ohio, 1871–1937) appointed Secretary of War.

3 June. NATIONAL DEFENSE ACT, first major result of the administration's preparedness program, provided for expansion of the regular army to 175,000 men, and its further enlargement to 223,000 over a five-year period. It also authorized a National Guard of 450,000 men; established a Reserve Officers Training Corps at universities, colleges, and military camps; and made provisions for industrial preparedness.

17 July. FEDERAL FARM LOAN ACT provided farmers with long-term credit facilities similar to those made available to industry and commerce by the Federal Reserve Act. The country was divided into 12 districts under the general administration of a Federal Farm Loan Board consisting of the Secretary of Treasury and 4 members. In each district there was established a Farm Loan Bank (capitalized at $750,000) in which cooperative farm loan associations held membership. Farmers belonging to these associations could secure long-term loans (5–40 yrs.) on farm-mortgage security at interest rates (5%–6%) lower than those prevailing in commercial banks.

11 Aug. WAREHOUSE ACT authorized licensed and bonded warehouses to issue against specified agricultural commodities (including grain, cotton, tobacco, and wool) warehouse receipts negotiable as delivery orders or as collateral for loans. The measure assisted farmers in financing their crops.

29 Aug. COUNCIL OF NATIONAL DEFENSE established under the Army Appropriation Act. Organized (11 Oct.) under the chairmanship of Secretary of War Baker, this advisory body consisting of 6 cabinet members was charged with coordinating industry and resources for the national security and welfare. Its Advisory Commission, consisting of 7 civilian experts headed by Daniel Willard, was responsible for mapping preparedness plans in fields including transportation, munitions and manufacturing, labor, raw materials, supplies, engineering and education, and medicine and surgery.

7 Sept. SHIPPING ACT authorized the creation of the U.S. Shipping Board, a 5-man body empowered to build, purchase, lease, or requisition vessels through the agency of the Emergency Fleet Corporation, capitalized at $50 million.

PRESIDENTIAL CAMPAIGN. The Socialist Labor National Convention met at New York (23 Apr.) and nominated Arthur E. Reimer (Mass.) for president and August Gillhaus (N.Y.) for vice-president. The Socialist party held no convention; its candidates, nominated by a mail referendum, were Allen L. Benson (N.Y.) for president and George R. Kirkpatrick (N.J.) for vice-president. The Republican National Convention met at Chicago (7 June) and nominated Supreme Court Justice **Charles E. Hughes** (N.Y.) for president and **Charles W. Fairbanks** (Ind.) for vice-president. The Progressive National Convention, also meeting at Chicago (7 June), nominated Theodore Roosevelt for president and John M. Parker (La.) for vice-president. Roosevelt, however, declined the nomination, and gave his support to Hughes. Roosevelt's defection led to the rapid disintegration of the Progressive party. The national committee of the Progressive party endorsed (26 June) Hughes' nomination, but an Indianapolis conference of the Progressive party (3 Aug.) repudiated this step. The Democratic National Convention met at St. Louis (14 June) and renominated President **Woodrow Wilson** and Vice-President **Thomas R. Marshall**. The Prohibition National Convention met at St. Paul (19 July) and nominated J. Frank Hanly (Ind.) for president and Ira D. Landrith (Tenn.) for vice-president.

Wilson's supporters defended his record on neutrality and preparedness, waging the campaign with the slogan "He kept us out of war." The slogan was highly effective in attracting the support of women's groups, particularly in those Western states where the vote had been conferred on women. Some of the strongest opposition to Wilson came from Irish-American and German-American elements critical of his foreign policy. The Democrats, however, turned against Hughes his failure to repudiate (until late in the campaign) the support of these so-called hyphenate groups.

7 Nov. PRESIDENTIAL ELECTION. Popular vote: **Wilson,** 9,129,606; Hughes, 8,538,221; Benson, 585,113; Hanly, 220,506; Reimer, 13,403. Electoral vote: **Wilson,** 277; Hughes, 254. So close was the election that the final result was in doubt until it was definitely known that California had gone Democratic (by only 3,773 votes). The Democrats retained control of both houses of Congress.

1917

23 Feb. SMITH-HUGHES ACT provided for federal grants-in-aid, to be matched by the contributions of individual states, for promoting instruction in agriculture and the trades. It established a Federal Board for Vocational Education.

8 Mar. SENATE CLOTURE RULE, adopted by special session of Senate, permitted limitation of debate by two thirds of the senators present and voting. Rule 22 was amended (1949) to require two thirds of the entire Senate membership but modified (1959) to again require two thirds of the senators present. Cloture was successfully invoked to end filibusters only 8 times from 1919–70, and 5 times from 1971–3.

31 Mar. General Munitions Board established by Council of National Defense. Organized 9 Apr., it was responsible for coordinating the procurement of war materials for the War and Navy departments and for assisting them to acquire raw materials and manufacturing plants. Its purpose, however, was weakened by

conflicting authority and by the board's lack of power to enforce its decisions.

14 Apr. COMMITTEE ON PUBLIC INFORMATION, established by executive order of the president, was headed by the journalist **George Creel** (1876–1953) and consisted of the Secretaries of State, War, and Navy. Responsible for uniting American public opinion behind the war effort, the committee employed an elaborate nationwide publicity apparatus based on pamphlets, news releases, posters, motion pictures, and volunteer speakers.

24 Apr. LIBERTY LOAN ACT, a war finance measure, authorized the issue of bonds to be sold by public subscription and provided for loans to the Allied powers to enable them to purchase food and war supplies. The Liberty Loan drives were as follows: 1st, June 1917 ($2 billion); 2d, Nov. 1917 ($3.8 billion); 3d, May 1918 ($4.2 billion); 4th, Oct. 1918 ($6 billion); Victory Loan, Apr. 1919 ($4.5 billion).

18 May. SELECTIVE SERVICE ACT provided for the registration and classification for military service of all men between the ages of 21 and 30, inclusive; as amended by the Man Power Act (31 Aug. 1918) it required the registration of all men between the ages of 18 and 45. The 1st registration (5 June) enrolled 9,586,508 men; the 2d (5 June 1918) added well over a million who had come of age; and the 3d (12 Sept. 1918) enrolled 13,228,762. Of the 24,234,021 registered during the war, 2,810,296 were called up for service in the army.

15 June. ESPIONAGE ACT, aimed at treasonable and disloyal activities, provided severe penalties (up to $10,000 fine and 20 years' imprisonment) for persons found guilty of aiding the enemy, obstructing recruiting, or causing insubordination, disloyalty, or refusal of duty in the armed services. The act empowered the postmaster general to exclude from the mails newspapers, periodicals, and other material alleged to be treasonable or seditious. The constitutionality of the act was upheld in *Schenck* v. *U.S.* (1919).

28 July. WAR INDUSTRIES BOARD, established by the Council of National Defense as successor to the General Munitions Board, was directed to act as a clearing agency for the nation's war industries and to take steps to increase production and eliminate waste. A reorganization of the War Industries Board (4 Mar. 1918) placed at its head **Bernard M. Baruch** (1870–1965), who was given authority for all major controls. The board was endowed with wide powers over the determination of priorities, the conversion of existing facilities, the manufacture of war materials, price fixing, and the purchase of supplies for the U.S. and the Allies.

10 Aug. LEVER FOOD AND FUEL CONTROL ACT, effective for the duration of the war, empowered the president to make regulations and issue orders to stimulate and conserve the production, and control the distribution, of foods and fuels necessary to the war effort. The president was authorized to fix the price of wheat at not less than $2 a bushel (a provision effective until 1 May 1919; in practice, the guaranteed price was $2.20); to fix the price of coal, coke, and other commodities; to license producers and distributors; and to prohibit unfair trade practices. The act forbade the use of foodstuffs in the manufacture of distilled liquors, whose importation was also forbidden. **Herbert Hoover** was appointed Food Administrator (10 Aug.) and Harry A. Garfield named Fuel Administrator (23 Aug.). Among the other agencies employed in administering the act were the Grain Corporation (for the financing of wheat crops) and the Sugar Equalization Board (for stabilizing the price of sugar and regulating its distribution).

3 Oct. WAR REVENUE ACT, which made the income tax the chief source of revenue during the war, authorized a graduated income tax beginning at 4% on personal incomes of more than $1,000; raised the corporation tax to 6%; imposed a graduated excess profits tax of from 20% to 60% on corporations and persons; raised postal rates; and provided for sharp increases in excise taxes on luxuries, transportation, amusements, alcoholic beverages, and tobacco.

6 Oct. TRADING WITH THE ENEMY ACT forbade commerce with enemy nations or their associates and empowered the president to impose an embargo on imports and to establish censorship of material passing between the U.S. and any foreign nation. The War Trade Board assumed the task of licensing imports and halting commercial intercourse with the enemy. The act also created the Office of Alien Property Custodian to take possession and dispose of the property held in the U.S. by persons residing in enemy countries. **A. Mitchell Palmer** was named (12 Oct.) to the post.

18 Dec. PROHIBITION AMENDMENT. The war against Germany created wider support for the prohibition movement, which by the outset of 1917 had succeeded in establishing prohibition in 19 states. The **Woman's Christian Temperance Union** (est. 1874) spurred the founding (1893) of the **Anti-Saloon League,** which, along with spectacular crusaders like the hatchet-wielding Mrs. **Carrie A. Nation** (1846–1911), had long been agitating for a national prohibition amendment. With U.S. involvement in the war, there were added to the arguments of moral and social reformers the need for conserving food and the patriotic condemnation of individuals of German extraction prominent in the brewing and distilling industry. On 18 Dec. Congress adopted and submitted to the states an amendment to the Constitution prohibiting the manufacture, sale, or transportation of alcoholic liquors. This, the 18th Amendment, was declared ratified on 29 Jan. 1919 and went into operation on 16 Jan. 1920. It was repealed with the adoption of the 21st Amendment (1933).

26 Dec. U.S. RAILROAD ADMINISTRATION. An impending crisis in the national transportation system led President Wilson to place the railways under government operation. He named Secretary of the Treasury **William Gibbs McAdoo** (1863–1941) as director-general of the U.S. Railroad Administration, which controlled 397,014 miles of track operated by 2,905 companies. On 21 Mar. 1918 the **Railroad Control Act** provided for fixing compensation to the railroads during the period of government management (to end not later than 1 year and 9 months after ratification of a peace treaty), and established a regional system of administration. The U.S. Railroad Administration was subsequently authorized to control railway express companies and inland waterway systems.

1918

5 Apr. WAR FINANCE CORPORATION, created to finance war industries, was capitalized at $500 million and authorized to issue $3 billion in bonds and to make loans to financial institutions to cover commercial credits extended to war industries.

8 Apr. NATIONAL WAR LABOR BOARD appointed by President Wilson to act as court of last resort for labor disputes, Frank P. Walsh and ex-President Taft named cochairmen. On 8 June the **War Labor Policies Board** was constituted to standardize labor conditions, with Felix Frankfurter chairman.

10 Apr. WEBB-POMERENE ACT, authorized exporters to organize associations for export trade without becoming liable for violation of antitrust laws. Unfair methods of competition were prohibited.

16 May. SEDITION ACT, an amendment to the Espionage Act of 1917, provided severe penalties for persons found guilty of making or conveying false statements interfering with the prosecution of the war; willfully employing "disloyal, profane, scurrilous, or abusive language" about the American form of government, the Constitution, the flag, or the military and naval forces; urging the curtailed production of necessary war materials; or advocating, teaching, defending, or suggesting the doing of any such acts or things. The enforcement of the act was aimed chiefly at Socialists and pacifists, and resulted in the trial and imprisonment of the Socialist leaders Eugene V. Debs and Victor L. Berger. The case of *Abrams* v. *U.S.* (1919, p. 675) involved application of the Sedition Act.

20 May. OVERMAN ACT authorized the president to coordinate or consolidate executive bureaus, agencies, and offices in the interest of economy and the more efficient concentration of governmental operations in matters relating to the conduct of the war.

5 Nov. CONGRESSIONAL ELECTIONS gave the Republicans control of both houses of Congress. The result, coming after Wilson had appealed (25 Oct., p. 372) to the country to return a Democratic Congress, was interpreted as repudiation of the president.

THE UNITED STATES IN WORLD AFFAIRS, 1866-1918

★　★
★

The Treaty of Washington of 1871 marked an end of an era of strained relations with Great Britain. After a century of miscalculation the British welcomed the United States not only as a full-fledged member of the family of nations but into the small circle of great powers as well. While the acquisition of Alaska in 1867 completed the continental expansion of the United States, it by no means spelled finis to the aspirations of imperialist-minded groups for overseas dominion—in the Caribbean to the Danish West Indies, Santo Domingo, Cuba, and an isthmian canal, and in the Pacific to Samoa and Hawaii. Against the deep-rooted instincts of many traditionally isolationist and anti-imperialist Americans, the nation between 1898 and 1917 found itself involved, first, with the fragments of the Spanish Empire in America, then in Pacific and Asiatic adventures, and finally in Europe. If entry into the Spanish-American War set the United States on a new path in world affairs, the fruits of that victory prompted a clamorous demand for withdrawal. World War I involved America even more directly in world affairs, and it remained for Franklin D. Roosevelt's "Good Neighbor" policy to bring about fundamental changes in our relationships with Mexico, which President Wilson's well-meaning intervention had exacerbated, and finally to extricate America's military presence, with occasional later exceptions, from Caribbean lands, to achieve commonwealth status for Puerto Rico, a changing status for the Panama Canal, and independence for the Philippines.

Despite earnest attempts to remain neutral for some three years, the United States entered World War I as a full participant, an involvment which put American isolationism to its severest test. It was a test, too, of the Wilsonian vision of a new international order in which the United States would, it was hoped, assume a role commensurate with its power, prestige, and influence.

1866

31 May. FENIAN UPRISING. The Fenians, a secret Irish brotherhood organized in the 1850s to achieve independence for Ireland, crossed the Niag-

ara River with an army of several hundred and fought an engagement with Canadian militiamen ("Battle of Limestone Ridge") before fleeing back to New York. After the repulse of another Fenian attack (25 May 1870) under John

O'Neill, the leaders were arrested by the U.S. Marshal for Vermont.

1866–67

NAPOLEON III AND MEXICO. On 12 Feb. 1866 Secretary Seward delivered an ultimatum demanding French withdrawal from Mexico following the dispatch to the Mexican border under Gen. Sheridan of 50,000 U.S. troops. Napoleon withdrew his forces in the spring of 1867. Maximilian, Austrian Archduke, established on the Mexican throne as a result of the occupation of Mexico City by French forces (7 June 1863), was executed by Mexican partisans under Benito Juárez (19 June).

1867

ACQUISITION OF ALASKA. In Dec. 1866 Baron Edoard de Stoeckl, Russian minister to the U.S., was instructed to negotiate with Secretary Seward, an ardent expansionist, for the sale of Alaska, regarded by Russia as an economic liability. A treaty for the purchase of Alaska for $7,200,000 was submitted to the Senate (30 Mar.). With the aid of Sumner and a propaganda campaign, the treaty was ratified (9 Apr.), and formal transfer of "Seward's Folly" accomplished (18 Oct.). A similar campaign, aided by Stoeckl's judicious use of funds to buy votes, resulted in the adoption by the House of the necessary appropriation bill (14 July 1868).

24 Oct. DANISH WEST INDIES. Seward negotiated a treaty with Denmark for the acquisition of the Danish West Indies (now the Virgin Islands) for $7,500,000, but it died in the Senate.

1869–72

"ALABAMA" CLAIMS. The U.S. pressed claims against Great Britain for damage (estimated at 100,000 tons with cargoes) done to the Northern merchant marine by British-built Confederate raiders, including the *Alabama*. Seward negotiated the Johnson-Clarendon Convention (14 Jan. 1869) providing for adjudication of the claims, which the Senate, led by Sumner, rejected (13 Apr.). In the Grant administration Secretary Fish reopened negotiations. The Treaty of Washington (8 May 1871), which represented a triumph for Fish over Sumner, provided for the submission of all outstanding differences between the U.S. and Great Britain to an international arbitral tribunal (representatives from Italy, Switzerland, Brazil, and the interested parties). That tribunal decided (25 Aug. 1872) that Great Britain failed to use "due diligence" to prevent the Confederate raiders from going to sea, and awarded the U.S. $15,500,000. This amount was far below Sumner's demands (which included collateral damage, estimated at $2,125 million), but the tribunal refused to pass upon indirect claims.

1870

SANTO DOMINGO AFFAIR. Desirous of annexing Santo Domingo, Grant dispatched his secretary, Babcock, to survey the situation. On Babcock's return from the island Grant submitted a treaty of annexation to his cabinet, which was unanimously rejected. A more formal treaty was then drawn up and submitted to the Senate (10 Jan.). On 15 Mar. the Committee on Foreign Relations reported adversely on ratification and Sumner delivered his famous "Naboth's Vineyard" speech, a scathing denunciation of the Santo Domingo project, which cost him the chairmanship of that committee (deposed 9 Mar. 1871). Another opponent of ratification, Attorney General E. R. Hoar, was forced to resign from the cabinet. Despite Grant's insistence (31 May) that ratification would be "an adherence to the Monroe Doctrine," the treaty was defeated (30 June). On 14 July Secretary Fish submitted a memorandum upholding the no-transfer corollary (no territory shall be subject to transfer to a European power) as part of the Monroe Doctrine.

1873

CUBA AND THE "VIRGINIUS" INCIDENT. When revolt broke out in Cuba (1868) Fish persuaded Grant to abstain from recognition (1869). When Spanish authorities in Cuba captured (31 Oct. 1873) the arms-running ship *Virginius*, illegally flying the American flag, and summarily shot 53 of the crew (among them Americans) as pirates, Fish moderated U.S. demands and secured (29 Nov.) an indemnity of $80,000 for the families of the executed Americans.

1875

30 JAN. TREATY WITH HAWAII of commercial reciprocity signed, providing that no Hawaiian territory should be disposed to a third power. Senate approval 18 Mar.

1878

17 JAN. SAMOAN TREATY. U.S. interest in the Samoan Islands began as early as 1838 and was renewed after the Civil War. A U.S. naval officer, Commander Richard W. Meade, negotiated a treaty (17 Feb. 1872) with the Samoan chieftains giving the U.S. exclusive rights to a naval station at the strategic harbor of Pago Pago on the ilsand of Tutuila. The Senate failed to ratify the treaty. U.S. penetration was extended by Col. A. B. Steinberger, who, dispatched by President Grant as a special agent to the islands (1873), became prime minister. During the brief period of his ascendancy Steinberger was regarded by the Samoans as an American governor. The U.S. and the native chieftains had a mutual interest in confining German influence in Samoa. Accordingly, a treaty of amity and commerce was signed (17 Jan.) and approved (30 Jan.) by which the U.S. was given nonexclusive rights to a naval station at Pago Pago.

1880

3 JULY. MADRID CONVENTION. U.S. joined European powers in restricting extraterritorial rights of Moroccans. Senate approval 5 May 1881.

17 Nov. CHINESE TREATY. Anti-Chinese agitation, chiefly on the Pacific Coast, led to pressure by Western interests on President Hayes for abrogation of the Burlingame Treaty (1868) giving the Chinese the right of unlimited immigration to the U.S. Hayes vetoed (1 Mar. 1879) a congressional measure restricting the number of Chinese passengers aboard U.S.-bound ships on the ground that it was equivalent to exclusion and hence violative of the Burlingame Treaty. Hayes dispatched a mission to China to consider the revision of the treaty. The result was the Treaty of 1880, giving the U.S. the right to "regulate, limit or suspend" but not absolutely to prohibit entry of Chinese laborers. On 6 May 1882 the Exclusion Act restricted such immigration for a 10-year period.

1881

BLAINE'S FOREIGN POLICY. Secretary of State James G. Blaine, the most influential figure in the Garfield administration, advocated closer commercial and cultural ties with Latin America. His program had a dual aim: to strengthen the competitive position of the U.S. export trade, and to increase U.S. prestige by attempting to arbitrate Latin-American disputes threatening war or European intervention. Blaine failed to settle the War of the Pacific (begun by Chile against Bolivia and Peru in 1879), and made a fruitless attempt to intercede in the Costa Rica–Colombia and Mexico-Guatemala disputes.

He invited (22 Nov.) the Latin-American nations to a peace conference at Washington scheduled for 22 Nov. 1882. Invitations had already been accepted by 9 countries by the time Blaine left office (12 Dec.), but his successor, Frederick T. Frelinghuysen, revoked the invitations.

Blaine endeavored to secure British consent to modification of the Clayton-Bulwer Treaty. Hayes had asserted in a message to Congress (8 Mar. 1880) that since an isthmian canal would be virtually part of the U.S. coastline, it must on that account be under U.S. control. In Apr. 1880, the House adopted a resolution authorizing the president to "take immediate steps for the formal and final abrogation" of the treaty. When Blaine learned of reports that Colombia was sounding out several European nations on assuming the guarantee of an isthmian canal, he invoked (24 June) the U.S. "paramount interest" interpretation of the Monroe Doctrine. The British foreign secretary, Earl Granville, dispatched a note (10 Nov.) insisting on the finality of the Clayton-Bulwer Treaty. The Frelinghuysen-Zavala Treaty (1884), signed with Nicaragua, violated the Clayton-Bulwer Treaty, but died in the Senate.

1882

22 May. KOREAN–U.S. TREATY of Commerce and amity signed; recognized independence of Korea. Senate approval 13 Feb. 1883.

26 July. GENEVA CONVENTION OF 1862 for care of wounded proclaimed after Senate approval 16 Mar.

1884

1 Oct.–1 Nov. INTERNATIONAL PRIME MERIDIAN CONFERENCE, at Washington, recommended meridian of Greenwich as basis for counting longitude and mean time.

15 Nov.–26 Feb. 1885. CONGO CONFERENCE at Berlin, called by Germany to consider commerce and navigation in the Congo area and procedures for acquiring African territory, was participated in by the U.S., which had (22 Apr.) recognized the International Association of the Congo. The U.S. was instrumental in bringing conference agreement on freedom of trade and abolition of slave traffic in Central Africa, but declined to ratify the general act. On 2 July 1890 the U.S. signed an international agreement for suppression of the African slave trade; Senate approval 11 Jan. 1892.

1887

20 Jan. PEARL HARBOR. The Hawaiian Reciprocity Treaty of 1875, which had been renewed in 1884 but not approved by the Senate, was ratified when it was amended to give the U.S. the exclusive right to establish a fortified naval base at Pearl Harbor, near Honolulu.

RIVALRY IN SAMOA. Mutual suspicion and consular intrigues marked the activities of the U.S., Great Britain, and Germany in the Samoan Islands after 1879. A tripartite agreement reached in that year provided for a protectorate over the municipal government of Apia (an arrangement later extended to all of the islands), but it never received Senate approval. A German-instigated revolt brought the protest (19 June 1885) of Secretary of State Thomas F. Bayard, who proposed a 3-power meeting. Before discussions began at the Washington conference (25 June–26 July), the British and Germans came to an understanding whereby Britain supported Germany's ambition for a mandate over Samoa in return for German recognition of British interests in Africa and the Near East. The Washington conference terminated without reaching a decision. Germany then renewed her interference in Samoan affairs by deporting the resisting ruler and establishing a government under direct German influence. Tension rose after the new regime discriminated against U.S. and British commercial interests. By the close of 1888, warships of the 3 powers were stationed in Apia Harbor, and a conflict threatened.

1888

BAYARD-CHAMBERLAIN TREATY. Difficulties with Great Britain over the Canadian fisheries question arose after the U.S. served notice that beginning 1 July 1885 it would terminate the fishing clauses of the Treaty of Washington (1871). The Canadians then fell back on a narrow interpretation of the Treaty of 1818 and began seizing U.S. fishing vessels for technical violations. American resentment, especially in maritime New England, was aroused. On 2 Mar. 1887 Congress authorized President Cleveland to take retaliatory steps against Canada (by excluding her vessels from U.S. waters and halting the importation of Canadian products). A joint Anglo-American commission met at Washington (22 Nov. 1887). On 15 Feb. the Bayard-Chamberlain Treaty and a *modus vivendi* were concluded with Great Britain. The treaty was rejected (21 Aug.) by the Republican majority in the Senate, partly because it provided for a reciprocal tariff, partly because of anti-British feeling. But the *modus vivendi,* giving the U.S. privileges in Canadian ports, remained the basis for use of the fisheries until abrogated by Canada (1923) in retaliation against the Fordney-McCumber Tariff.

1889

BERLIN CONFERENCE ON SAMOA. Germany's policy of armed intervention in Samoa with the tacit approval of the British led President Cleveland to lay the question before Congress (15 Jan.). Terming the situation "delicate and critical," Cleveland asserted that the U.S. insisted upon the preservation of Samoan autonomy and independence. The threatened naval clash in Apia Harbor was averted by a hurricane (15–16 Mar.) that wrecked the U.S. warships *Trenton* and *Vandalia,* caused the *Nipsic* to be run ashore, and destroyed all of the German ships. Only the British *Calliope* escaped disaster. But even before the hurricane struck, President Harrison had already dispatched (14 Mar.) 3 American commissioners to the Berlin conference, which opened 29 Apr. The agreement, signed on 14 June, provided for the independence and autonomy of the Samoan Islands under a tripartite protectorate (the U.S., Great Britain, and Germany). The chief agents of the 3-power condominium were to be the chief justice and the president of the Apia municipal council. The agreement also provided for a foreign adviser to the Samoan king and a court for the settlement of land titles.

BLAINE'S LATIN-AMERICAN POLICY. Blaine's plan to call a Latin-American conference, which had been scrapped by his successor in the Department of State, finally won the approval of Congress, which on 24 May 1888 authorized President Cleveland to summon a conference for discussing measures for the promotion of the common peace and prosperity. Secretary of State Bayard issued invitations (13 July 1888); by the time the first International American Conference met at Washington (2 Oct. 1889–19 Apr. 1890), Blaine was again Secretary of State. Seventeen Latin-American nations were represented, Santo Domingo being the sole absentee. The major U.S. goal, to establish a customs union, was defeated by the opposition of the other delegates. The conference likewise failed to establish machinery for the arbitration of disputes, but set up the International Bureau of American Republics (later called the **Pan-American Union**), which served as a permanent agency for exchanging and disseminating information regarding each country; and paved the way for a U.S. policy of reciprocal tariff arrangements by executive agreement, as authorized by the McKinley Tariff Act of 1890.

1891

CONTROVERSIES WITH ITALY AND CHILE. Italy. The slaying (15 Oct. 1890) of the police chief at New Orleans, who had been investigating the activities of persons suspected of affiliation with the secret Mafia (Black Hand) Society, resulted in the trial and acquittal of the Italian suspects. A New Orleans mob broke into the jail (14 Mar.) and lynched 11 persons (3 of them Italian nationals). The Italian government demanded indemnity for the victims and punishment of the responsible parties. While Blaine deplored the action of the New Orleans mob, he refused to take action on the ground that the crime fell under state rather than federal jurisdiction. The Italian government withdrew its minister to the U.S. (31 Mar.),

and the U.S. took similar action, but there was no formal diplomatic break. President Harrison's annual message (9 Dec.) condemned the New Orleans lynching and assured the Italian government of the good faith of the U.S. government. The incident was closed with the offer (12 Apr. 1892) of a $25,-000 indemnity that was accepted by the Italian government.

Chile. Following the outbreak of civil war in Chile (1891), the rebel Congressionalist party sent a vessel, the *Itata*, to San Diego to take on a shipment of arms. The U.S.S. *Charleston* was ordered to pursue and seize the *Itata*. The rebel vessel was escorted back to San Diego but later released on the ground that there had been no violation of the neutrality laws. The incident gave the Congressionalists (who took over the Chilean government) reason for harboring resentment against the U.S. This hostility was brought to a head when a Valparaiso mob attacked (16 Oct.) sailors on shore leave from the U.S. cruiser *Baltimore*, killed 2, and injured 17. In his annual message to Congress (9 Dec.), President Harrison defended the conduct of the U.S. naval commanders. In reply, the Chilean foreign minister, M. A. Matte, sent a denunciatory telegram (11 Dec.), which aroused indignation in the U.S. Blaine's note to the Chilean government (21 Jan. 1892) stated that unless a retraction and apology were forthcoming, the U.S. would terminate diplomatic relations. In a special message to Congress (25 Jan. 1892) Harrison virtually asked for a declaration of war. The Chilean government submitted an official apology, and the incident was closed with the payment of an indemnity of $75,000.

1892

29 Feb. BERING SEA DISPUTE. The U.S. acquisition of the Pribilof Islands as a result of the Alaska purchase led to an Anglo-American controversy concerning jurisdiction over pelagic (i.e., ocean) sealing in the Bering Sea. The U.S., which exercised jurisdiction within the 3-mile limit, leased sealing rights to a private company. As the commercial value of sealskins rose, pelagic sealing vessels of other nations (principally Canada) began to operate in the waters beyond the 3-mile limit. The dispute was touched off when U.S. revenue cutters seized Canadian pelagic sealers in the Bering Sea (1886).

On 2 Mar. 1889 Congress empowered the president to take steps to protect U.S. rights and declared U.S. dominion over the waters of the Bering Sea. In a note to the British government (22 Jan. 1890), Secretary of State Blaine characterized its course as just short of piracy. In reply, British foreign secretary Lord Salisbury stated that Great Britain would hold the U.S. "responsible" for acts contrary to "established principles of international law." An Anglo-American arbitration treaty (29 Feb.) referred the question to a mixed international tribunal (French, Swedish, and Italian), whose decision (15 Aug. 1893) denied the U.S. claim to exclusive rights to a closed sea; provided for the assessment of damages against the U.S.; and prohibited pelagic sealing in a 60-mile zone around the Pribilof Islands for a specified period during each year. This protective regulation remained in force until 1908. The controversy was terminated with the payment (16 June 1898) of $473,151 by the U.S. to Great Britain.

1893

30 MAR. Senate confirmation of the appointment of Thomas F. Bayard as U.S. ambassador to Great Britain, first American to hold that rank.

HAWAIIAN QUESTION. The most vital links between the U.S. and Hawaii were the Hawaiian sugar planters, mostly Americans. The planters, ranged against native dynastic interests, brought off a revolution (1887) that succeeded in securing a liberal constitution and a government under their influence. However, they lost power in 1891. Meanwhile, the McKinley Tariff Act of 1890, which put imported sugar on the free list and authorized a bounty of 2 cts. a lb. for home-grown sugar cane, wiped out the reciprocity advantages hitherto enjoyed by Hawaiian sugar planters and broke sugar prices, with an estimated loss of $12 million.

Queen Liliuokalani, exponent of a firm pro-native policy, came to the Hawaiian throne in 1891. She revoked the liberal constitution of 1887 and by royal edict (14 Jan.) promulgated a new constitution giving her autocratic powers. The Americans under the leadership of **Sanford B. Dole** (p. 1014), had already established a revolutionary committee of safety to overthrow the native government, with the apparent support of the U.S. minister to Hawaii, the proannexationist **John L. Stevens** (1820–95). He ordered U.S. marines to be landed from the cruiser *Boston* (16 Jan.), ostensibly to protect American life and property. Aided by the marines, the committee of safety occupied the government buildings; and Stevens, without permission from the State Department, recognized the revolutionary regime (17 Jan.). On 1 Feb. Stevens raised the U.S. flag over the government buildings and proclaimed Hawaii a U.S. protectorate. Dole became president of the new government.

On 15 Feb. a treaty of annexation (signed 14 Feb.) drawn up by diplomatic commissioners of the Hawaiian provisional government was submitted to the U.S. Senate. Chiefly because of Democratic opposition, the Senate failed to act on the treaty by the time Harrison left office. President Cleveland withdrew the treaty (9 Mar.) and appointed ex-Cong. James H. Blount (Ga.) as special commissioner to Hawaii to conduct a thorough investigation. Blount ordered the withdrawal of the marines and the lowering of the American flag. After an inquiry lasting 4 months, he reported that Stevens' conduct had been improper; that the majority of Hawaiians were opposed to annexation; and that the Hawaiian sugar planters and their U.S. associates had been the chief force behind the revolution, hoping to secure the sugar bounty through annexation.

Independence of the provisional government was recognized when President Cleveland sent Albert S. Willis as the new minister to Hawaii. Willis was instructed to take steps to restore Queen Liliuokalani to power, with the proviso that she assume the obligations of the provisional government, grant amnesty to its leaders, and sustain the constitution of 1887. In return, the provisional regime was to abdicate. Queen Liliuokalani acceded to Cleveland's request on 18 Dec. President Dole, however, refused to surrender power, pointing out that the provisional government had received U.S. recognition and that the U.S. had no right to interfere in the internal affairs of Hawaii. Cleveland was unwilling to employ force to carry through his policy. In a special message to Congress (18 Dec.) he condemned the means by which the provisional government had been brought into power and stated he would not again submit the annexation treaty to the Senate. On 4 July 1894 the Republic of Hawaii was proclaimed, and on 7 Aug. 1894 Cleveland formally recognized the new government.

1895

VENEZUELAN BOUNDARY DISPUTE. The controversy between Venezuela and Great Britain over the boundary line of British Guiana went back to 1814 when the British took over that possession from the Dutch. In 1840 a survey made by Sir Robert Schomburgk, a British engineer, was rejected by Venezuela, and the dispute remained unsettled. With the discovery of gold in the contested region, Great Britain withdrew its offer of the Schomburgk line and claimed areas west of it. In 1887 Venezuela broke off diplomatic relations with Great Britain and asked the U.S. to arbitrate, but the U.S. offer to use its good offices was rejected by the British (1887). In his annual message to Congress in 1894 Cleveland declared that he would renew his attempt to bring about arbitration. A joint congressional resolution (20 Feb.) approved Cleveland's recommendation. Again Great Britain refused to arbitrate.

Largely under the influence of Secretary of State Richard Olney, Cleveland based the U.S. position on a broad construction of the Monroe Doctrine. Olney sent a note (20 July) to the British government stating that British pressure on Venezuela would be regarded by the U.S. as a violation of the Monroe Doctrine and that peaceful arbitration (with U.S. intercession toward that end) was the only way of settling the controversy. The belligerent tenor of the dispatch was evident in this: "Today the United States is practically sovereign on this continent, and its fiat is law upon the subjects to which it confines its interposition. Why? . . . It is because, in addition to all other grounds, its infinite resources combined with its isolated position render it master of the situation and practically invulnerable as against any or all other powers."

The reply (26 Nov.) of Lord Salisbury, the British prime minister and foreign secretary, asserted that the Monroe Doctrine was not applicable to the boundary dispute and rejected the U.S. offer of arbitration. The diplomatic correspondence was laid before Congress (17 Dec.) by President Cleveland, who affirmed the applicability of the Monroe Doctrine and recommended the creation of an independent commission to determine the boundary. "When such report is made and accepted," said Cleveland, "it will . . . be the duty of the United States to resist by every means in its power, as a wilful aggression upon its rights and interests, the appropriation by Great Britain of any lands or the exercise of governmental jurisdiction over any territory which after investigation we have determined of right belongs to Venezuela."

The American outburst caught the British off guard. In the eyes of Great Britain, whose imperial preoccupations lay· elsewhere, the Venezuelan dispute was a relatively minor matter. Furthermore, her rivalry with Germany and other powers in Africa and the Near East made American friendship desirable. This became doubly clear when Kaiser Wilhelm II sent to President Kruger of the Boer Republic an indiscreet congratulatory telegram (3 Jan. 1896) that offended the British. On 25 Jan. the British colonial secretary, Joseph Chamberlain, publicly asserted that war between the U.S. and Great Britain "would be an absurdity as well as a crime. . . . The two nations are allied and more closely allied in sentiment and interest than any other nations on the face of the earth."

The Venezuelan boundary commission (created by Congress in 1895) was appointed on 1 Jan. 1896. Presided over by Associate Justice **David J. Brewer** (1837–1910), and also including **Chief Justice Fuller** (p. 1035), it held its first meeting on 4 Jan. 1896. The British aided the U.S. authorities by furnishing data. A treaty signed by Great Britain and Venezuela (2 Feb. 1897) through the good offices of the U.S. provided for submitting the dispute to a board of arbitration, on which Brewer and Fuller also served. The awards (3 Oct. 1899) were in substantial accord with the original British claims and placed the boundary roughly along the Schomburgk line (Venezuela, however, being awarded the mouth of the Orinoco River).

CUBAN QUESTION. American interest in Cuba declined after the U.S. attempt (1875–76) to terminate the Cuban rebellion (1868–78), but was revived following the outbreak (24 Feb.) of the native insurrection against Spanish rule. Added to Spanish oppression as a cause of revolt was the severe impact upon the sugar economy of the panic of 1893 and the high protective Wilson-Gorman Tariff of 1894. American sympathy favored the rebels. Financial contributions from Americans aided Cuban juntas (committees of revolutionists) in organizing filibustering expeditions on American soil, but these ventures were blocked by the U.S. navy and revenue service.

The revolutionists followed a policy of widespread and thorough destruction of sugar plantations and mills (in which American interests had extensive holdings), hoping by this method to induce U.S. intervention and to break the will of the Spanish rulers. The task of suppressing the uprising was assigned to Gen. Valeriano ("Butcher") Weyler, who established (after 10 Feb. 1896) concentration camps where he indiscriminately confined revolutionists, sympathizers, and neutrals, including women and children, many of whom became victims of disease, semistarvation, and ruthless treatment. American sympathy for the rebels was fanned by the "yellow press" (William Randolph Hearst's New York *Journal* and Joseph Pulitzer's New York *World*).

By concurrent resolution, the Senate (28 Feb. 1896) and the House (6 Apr. 1896) called for the U.S. to accord belligerent rights to the Cuban revolutionists and offer its good offices to Spain for the recognition of an independent Cuba. Spain declined the U.S. offer (22 May 1896).

1898

RELATIONS WITH SPAIN. The liberal Sagasta ministry, which came into power at Madrid (Oct. 1897), made important concessions on Cuban policy (25 Nov. 1897), including the recall of Gen. Weyler, a measure of autonomy, release of imprisoned U.S. nationals, and reform of the concentration camp policy. These concessions satisfied neither the insurrectionists nor the loyalists in Cuba. Loyalists at Havana held a violent demonstration (12 Jan.) condemning Weyler's recall and the grant of autonomy. The yellow press in the U.S. renewed its attack on Spain. Within the Republican party a group of younger politicians (including Theodore Roosevelt and Henry Cabot Lodge), who regarded Cuba as the key to domination of the Caribbean and favored expansionism, called for a firm attitude.

9 FEB. DE LÔME LETTER, written by the Spanish minister to the U.S., Dupuy de Lôme, was published (9 Feb.) in Hearst's N.Y. *Journal.* This was a private communication that had been stolen from the mails in Havana and released to the Hearst press by Cuban revolutionists in the U.S. Dupuy de Lôme called President McKinley "weak and a bidder for the admiration of the crowd, besides being a would-be politician who tries to leave a door open be-

hind himself while keeping on good terms with the jingoes of his party." De Lôme immediately cabled his resignation to the Spanish government.

15 FEB. SINKING OF THE "MAINE." After the Havana riot of 12 Jan., the U.S. battleship *Maine* was ordered to Havana harbor, ostensibly to protect American life and property. On 15 Feb. at 9:40 P.M. the *Maine,* while at anchor in the harbor, was destroyed by an explosion which killed 260 officers and men. The Navy Department appointed a court of inquiry (17 Feb.). Although the government urged the public to reserve judgment, the yellow press attributed the disaster to enemy agents and demanded U.S. intervention in Cuba. "Remember the *Maine!*" became a popular slogan. Congress without dissent voted a $50 million defense appropriation (9 Mar.).

The naval court of inquiry reported (21 Mar.) that the *Maine* had been destroyed by the explosion of a submarine mine, but was "unable to obtain evidence fixing the responsibility . . . upon any person or persons." Despite strong pressure from the public, Congress, and a prowar group within the Republican party, the McKinley administration followed an antiwar policy. The U.S. minister to Spain, Stewart L. Woodford, was instructed (27 Mar.) to notify the Madrid government that the U.S. had no territorial ambitions in Cuba and that it sought the following: a Cuban armistice until 1 Oct. and the revocation of the concentration camp policy. On the latter point, Spanish agreement came on 5 Apr., and on 9 Apr. the Spanish yielded to the U.S. demand for an armistice. This information was cabled to McKinley on 10 Apr.

11 APR. McKINLEY'S WAR MESSAGE. Swayed by the powerful demand for war in and out of Congress, McKinley reversed his antiwar policy even before learning of the Spanish concessions. His message to Congress asked for the "forcible intervention" of the U.S. to establish peace in Cuba.

20 APR. WAR RESOLUTION. Congress adopted a joint resolution that (1) recognized the independence of Cuba; (2) demanded the withdrawal of the Spanish armed forces; (3) empowered the president to use the army and navy to carry out these demands; and (4) disclaimed any intention on the part of the U.S. to exercise sovereignty or control over Cuba, asserting that the government and control of the island would be left to its people after peace had been restored. (This last clause was the **Teller Amendment.**) McKinley signed the war resolution on 20 Apr.; and on the same day a formal ultimatum was served on Spain to the effect that if she did not grant Cuban independence and quit the island, the U.S. would take the necessary steps to carry the joint resolution into effect. On 21 Apr. Spain broke diplomatic relations with the U.S.; 22 Apr. the U.S. inaugurated blockade of Cuban ports; 24 Apr. Spain declared war against the U.S.; 25 Apr. formal U.S. declaration of war against Spain, made retroactive to 21 Apr.

The Spanish-American War, 1898

BALANCE SHEET. The opening of the war found the U.S. modern "steel navy" in an advanced state of readiness and efficiency. The navy consisted of about 2,000 officers and 24,000 men. The preparations of the Asiatic squadron, based at Hong Kong under the command of Commodore **George Dewey** (p. 1012), were enhanced by a secret order (25 Feb.) sent by Assistant Secretary of the Navy **Theodore Roosevelt,** who instructed Dewey to keep his fleet intact and to engage the Spanish fleet in the Philippines should war break out. In contrast, the U.S. army, consisting of about 2,100 officers and 28,000 men, was ill-prepared. Its high command, training, and equipment were inadequate, and it lacked proper supply and medical services for waging a tropical campaign. Congress authorized (22 Apr.) a volunteer force of 200,000 men, and approved (26 Apr.) an increase of the regular army to 60,000. The decisive battles of the war were naval engagements. On this score, the U.S. enjoyed the advantage, for the Spanish navy was outmoded in armament and had poorly trained crews.

1 MAY. BATTLE OF MANILA BAY. Dewey's Asiatic squadron at Hong Kong consisted of 4 cruisers (*Olympia, Boston, Baltimore,* and *Raleigh*) and 2 gunboats (*Petrel* and *Concord*). This force departed from Mirs Bay, China (27 Apr.), with orders to capture or destroy the Spanish squadron thought to be in Manila Bay under the command of Adm. Montojo. The U.S. squadron entered Manila Bay on the evening of 30 Apr. The Spanish fleet (consisting of 10 vessels, including cruisers and gunboats) lay off Cavite Point. Early on the morning of 1 May the U.S. fleet laid down a powerful broadside, methodically raking the Spanish line from end to end. The battle, beginning 5:40 A.M., was over in 7 hours. The Spanish suffered 381 men killed; all of the Spanish craft were destroyed, silenced, or captured. None of the American ships was damaged; U.S. casualties: 8 wounded.

13 AUG. FALL OF MANILA. Lacking the necessary support for land operations, Dewey imposed a blockade on

Manila Bay. Gen. Wesley Merritt was ordered (11 May) to the Philippines to support Dewey and take Manila. Merritt arrived at Manila Bay (25 July) with the final American contingent, bringing the total U.S. military strength there to 10,700 men. Dewey and Merritt sent (9 Aug.) the Spanish commander at Manila a formal demand for surrender. U.S. troops, reinforced by Filipino guerrillas under Gen. Emilio Aguinaldo, assaulted and occupied Manila (13 Aug.). On 14 Aug. Gen. Merritt received the Spanish capitulation and proclaimed the military occupation of the Philippines.

SPANISH FLEET IN CUBA. The blockade of Cuba was assigned to Rear Adm. **William T. Sampson** (along the northern shores) and Commodore **Winfield S. Schley** (along the southern shores). Sampson moved at once to hunt out the Spanish fleet; it was known that the enemy ships would have to recoal at Cuba or Puerto Rico after making the transatlantic voyage. Schley did not leave Key West until 19 May and did not arrive off Santiago de Cuba until 28 May. His delay gave the Spanish fleet its opportunity.

Commanded by Adm. Cervera, the Spanish force departed from the Cape Verde Islands (29 Apr.) and entered the harbor of Santiago de Cuba (19 May), where it lay under the protection of land batteries. Cervera's fleet of 4 cruisers and 3 destroyers was bottled up by Schley's force (29 May). Adm. Sampson arrived at Santiago (1 June) and assumed command of the blockading squadron. The capture or destruction of the Spanish fleet was the main task confronting the U.S. navy.

14 JUNE. CUBAN EXPEDITION. A land force of 17,000 regulars and volunteers, including the "Rough Riders" (the first U.S. Volunteer Cavalry Regiment under Col. **Leonard Wood** and Lt. Col. **Theodore Roosevelt**), was marshaled at Tampa, Fla., awaiting the end of the tropical rains before undertaking the invasion of Cuba. Commanded by Gen. **William Shafter,** this force was improperly trained, organized, and equipped. When the U.S. navy blockaded the enemy fleet at Santiago, Shafter was ordered to reinforce Sampson and seize the port. The expeditionary force sailed from Tampa on 14 June.

1 JULY. BATTLES OF EL CANEY AND SAN JUAN HILL. Shafter's force arrived off Santiago on 20 June and 2 days later began disembarking at Daiquiri and Siboney Bay, to the east of their main objective. Unloading operations were completed on 26 June; on 30 June the force began its march on Santiago. In the day-long battle of El Caney (1 July) about 7,000 U.S. troops took a strongly fortified village garrisoned by about 600 of the enemy. In the battle of San Juan Hill (1 July), in which the dismounted Rough Riders under Col. Theodore Roosevelt took part, the Americans seized the position under heavy fire. At a total cost of 1,572 casualties, the U.S. succeeded in winning command of the heights to the east and north of Santiago and were now in position to place the city and the Spanish fleet under artillery bombardment.

3 JULY. DESTRUCTION OF THE SPANISH FLEET. Sampson's blockading force outside Santiago harbor consisted of the battleships *Indiana, Iowa, Massachusetts, Oregon,* and *Texas,* and the cruisers *New York* and *Brooklyn.* Adm. Cervera, who was under orders not to surrender, decided to make an attempt to escape to the open sea. On the morning of 3 July the Spanish fleet left the harbor and tried to run the U.S. blockade. In a battle along the coast that lasted about 4 hours, the enemy fleet was destroyed by the superior fire of American guns. The Spanish losses, 474 killed and wounded, 1,750 taken prisoner; the

U.S. casualties, 1 killed, 1 wounded. The destruction of the Spanish fleet virtually terminated the war. Santiago and its garrison of 24,000 troops surrendered on 17 July.

7 JULY. ANNEXATION OF HAWAII. While Cleveland remained in the presidency, he checked all attempts to annex Hawaii. His successor, McKinley, favorably disposed to annexation, negotiated a new treaty of annexation (signed 16 June 1897), but Democratic and anti-imperialist Republican opposition in the Senate delayed its ratification. When the Japanese government protested against the treaty, McKinley pressed even harder for ratification. During the Spanish-American War Hawaii's use as a naval installation lent emphasis to its strategic value and brought increased demand for annexation. In order to preclude defeat under the rule requiring a two-thirds vote for ratification by the Senate, the treaty was accepted by a joint resolution of Congress, which required a simple majority vote (pp. 617, 1014).

4 AUG. Disease and food poisoning took such a high toll of U.S. troops in Cuba that the War Department instructed the Cuban expeditionary force to embark for Montauk Point, L.I. Such conditions, both in Cuba and in army camps in the U.S., were among those investigated by a commission appointed (8 Sept.) to inquire into the conduct of the war.

10 DEC. TREATY OF PARIS. On 26 July the Spanish government, making its approach through Jules Cambon, French ambassador at Washington, requested the U.S. to name peace terms. A protocol signed on 12 Aug. provided for a peace treaty to be concluded at Paris and terminated hostilities on the following terms: Spain was to relinquish Cuba, and cede Puerto Rico and one of the Ladrone Islands to the U.S.; and

the U.S. was to hold and occupy Manila pending the conclusion of a peace treaty that would determine the disposition and control of the Philippines.

When the peace commission met at Paris (1 Oct.), U.S. policy on the Philippines was vague and divided. Guided by economic, strategic, and humanitarian considerations, McKinley decided to demand the cession of the Philippines. The demand, made by the U.S. commissioners on 1 Nov., encountered strong Spanish opposition; but with the conclusion of the treaty (10 Dec.), the Spanish agreed to cede the Philippines to the U.S. for a payment of $20 million. Spain surrendered all claim and title to Cuba and agreed to assume the liability for the Cuban debt amounting to about $400 million. As indemnity, Spain ceded Puerto Rico and Guam to the U.S. (pp. 622, 624).

WAR COST. Of the more than 274,-000 officers and men who served in the army during the Spanish-American War and the period of demobilization, 5,462 died in the various theaters of operation and in camps in the U.S. Only 379 of the deaths were battle casualties, the remaining being attributed to disease and other causes. The total wounded was 1,604. The immediate cost of the war was about $250 million.

1899

TREATY FIGHT (pp. 619–620).

20 MAR. OPEN DOOR POLICY. Growing political and military weakness of China revealed during and after the Sino-Japanese War (1894–95) left her powerless to resist the demands of foreign powers for political and economic concessions in the form of leaseholds and spheres of influence. In 1898 and 1899 the British made overtures to the U.S. with a view to securing Anglo-American guarantees of equal commercial opportunity in China, but these proposals were rejected as contrary to the established U.S. policy of noninvolvement. But the U.S., despite the fact that its trade with China was relatively small, was disturbed by the possibility that the foreign powers might establish discriminatory tariffs and other commercial barriers in the Chinese regions under their influence.

The Open Door policy of securing equal commercial opportunity was more English than American in its origin. It was chiefly the work of Alfred E. Hippisley, a British citizen who had served in the Chinese customs service; and its fundamental idea had already been publicized in *The Break-up of China,* an influential book by Lord Charles Beresford, who visited the U.S. in 1899. Hippisley's views reached the U.S. administration through the offices of W. W. Rockhill, private adviser to Secretary of State John Hay (p.1054) on Far Eastern affairs. Hippisley drafted a memorandum (17 Aug.) that was revised by Rockhill (28 Aug.) and accepted by Hay (5 Sept.). In his circular letter of 6 Sept., Hay instructed the U.S. embassies at Berlin, St. Petersburg, and London (and subsequently those at Paris, Rome, and Tokyo) to request formal assurances from each power as regards their respective spheres of influence in China: (1) that each power would in no way interfere with any treaty port or vested interests; (2) that the existing Chinese treaty tariff would apply to such spheres of interest, and the duties would be collected by the Chinese government; and (3) that no power would discriminate in favor of its own subjects regarding railroad charges and harbor dues. The various powers gave evasive and qualified replies, but Hay saw fit to construe their answers as approval of his proposals. He announced (20 Mar. 1900) that the acceptance of the Open Door policy was "final and definitive."

18 MAY–29 JULY. 1st HAGUE CONFERENCE, called at the invitation of Czar Nicholas II of Russia (24 Aug. 1898) to consider disarmament, the limitation of methods of warfare, and the creation of machinery for the arbitration of international disputes, was participated in by 26 nations, including the U.S. The conference failed to enlist the support of most of the nations on the prohibition of certain instruments of war (e.g., poison gas and balloon-launched missiles) or disarmament, but established the **Permanent Court of International Arbitration.** The U.S., which lent its weight to securing such a body, signed a convention (29 July) providing for the peaceful settlement of international disputes by the following means: mediation by a third party, international commissions, and the international tribunal at The Hague. It was stipulated, however, that arbitration was not to be compulsory and was not to extend to any question involving national honor or integrity. In addition, the U.S. delegation insisted on a reservation concerning disputes involving application of the Monroe Doctrine.

2 DEC. PARTITION OF SAMOA. Continuing differences among the U.S., Germany, and Great Britain after 1889 created dissatisfaction with the tripartite protectorate over Samoa which did not survive the outbreak of native warfare over succession which followed the death of King Malietoa in 1898. In the disorder which ensued, U.S. and British naval vessels bombarded Apia, landed sailors, and suffered casualties. In 1899 Germany proposed the partition of the islands. By the Anglo-German treaty of 14 Nov., the Samoan Islands were divided between the U.S. and Germany, with Britain surrendering her claims in return for (1) rights in West Africa and elsewhere in the Pacific, and (2) relinquishment by Germany of rights in certain areas of Samoa. Several islands, including Tutuila (with its harbor of Pago Pago), went to the U.S.; the islands of Upolu and Savaii went to Germany. This agreement was confirmed by a treaty signed (2 Dec.) by the U.S., Germany, and Great Britain, and ratified (16 Jan. 1900) by the Senate. (See also p. 626.)

1900

BOXER REVOLT. In the spring of 1900 an aggressively antiforeign group of Chinese revolutionists known as Boxers rose in revolt to expel the "foreign devils" from China. The Boxers occupied Peking and laid the foreign legations under siege. An international expedition that included U.S. troops relieved Peking (14 Aug.). Secretary of State Hay, fearing that the foreign powers would use the Boxer incident as a pretext to abandon the Open Door policy and carve up China, dispatched a circular letter (3 July) stating it to be the policy of the U.S. "to seek a solution which may bring about permanent safety and peace to China, preserve Chinese territorial and administrative entity [an elaboration of the Open Door], protect all rights guaranteed to friendly powers by treaty and international law, and safeguard for the world the principle of equal and impartial trade with all parts of the Chinese Empire."

The **Boxer Protocol** (7 Sept. 1901) provided a total indemnity of $332 million. The U.S. share was set at $24,500,-000, but the U.S. subsequently accepted $4 million to satisfy private claims, eventually remitting the unpaid balance for the purpose of educating Chinese students in the U.S.

1901

2 Mar. PLATT AMENDMENT. At the end of the Spanish-American War Cuba remained under the control of a U.S. military administration headed by Gen. Leonard Wood. Cuban finances were reorganized and a public health and sanitation campaign (in which Dr. **Walter Reed** [p. 1136] and Maj. **William C. Gorgas** [p. 1043] figured) succeeded in exterminating the yellow-fever menace. While the U.S., by the Teller Amendment (1898), had disclaimed all intention of exercising sovereignty over Cuba, it feared that rapid and complete withdrawal might jeopardize Cuban political stability and threaten American strategic and financial interests.

Gen. Wood was instructed to authorize the Cubans to call a constitutional convention. The convention met on 5 Nov. 1900 and ultimately adopted a constitution based upon that of the U.S., but made no provisions for continuing future relations with the U.S. At the behest of Secretary of War Root, Wood informed the convention that the withdrawal of American control was conditional upon the adoption of such provisions. These provisions, known as the Platt Amendment, were incorporated in the Army Appropriation Bill and sponsored by Sen. Orville H. Platt (Conn.), though most of the clauses were drawn up by Secretary Root. Its more important provisions: (1) Cuba would never enter into any treaty with any foreign power impairing Cuban independence; (2) the Cuban government would not contract any public debt in excess of the capacity of its ordinary revenues to discharge; (3) the U.S. was authorized to intervene to preserve Cuban independence and maintain law and order; and (4) Cuba agreed to sell or lease to the U.S. lands necessary for naval or coaling stations. In effect, the amendment gave the U.S. a quasi-protectorate over Cuba.

The Cuban convention appended the amendment to the constitution (12 June); the U.S. withdrew from Cuba (20 May 1902); and, to preclude its elimination by the amending power, the Platt Amendment was incorporated into a treaty between the U.S. and Cuba (22 May 1903). The amendment was abrogated on 29 May 1934 (p. 386).

18 Nov. HAY-PAUNCEFOTE TREATY. U.S. pressure for the modification of the Clayton-Bulwer Treaty to secure exclusive control over an isthmian canal resulted in the signing (5 Feb. 1900) of the first Hay-Pauncefote Treaty. Great Britain agreed to renounce all joint rights to a canal which the U.S. was to construct, control, and maintain. The U.S. pledged to maintain the neutrality of the canal and was forbidden to fortify it. The treaty was ratified by the Senate (20 Dec. 1900); an amendment permitting U.S. fortification as well as other changes proved unacceptable to the British (Mar. 1901). Because of mounting difficulties with Germany and Russia, Great Britain was anxious to remain on friendly terms with the U.S. Following negotiations in Apr., the second Hay-Pauncefote Treaty was concluded (18 Nov.) and ratified by the Senate (16 Dec.). It abrogated the Clayton-Bulwer Treaty; permitted the U.S. to construct and control the canal; stipulated that neutrality would be maintained under U.S. auspices; and provided that the canal was to be free and open to ships of all nations on equal terms. In a memorandum of 3 Aug. the British conceded the right to fortify the canal.

1903

22 Jan. HAY-HERRAN CONVENTION. With the ratification of the Hay-Pauncefote Treaty, Congress had to choose between Panama (then a province of Colombia) and Nicaragua as the route for the isthmian canal. At first, on the recommendation of the Walker Commission (16 Nov. 1901) the Nicaraguan right of way was favored, chiefly because the New Panama Canal Co., successor to the bankrupt De Lesseps venture, asked the exorbitant price of more than $109 million for its holdings and franchises. But when the Panama Co. (4 Jan. 1902) lowered its price to $40 million, the commission recommended (18 Jan. 1902) the Panama rather than the Nicaragua route. Congress passed the Spooner Act (28 June 1902), stipulating 2 conditions for the construction of a Panama Canal: (1) purchase of the property and rights of the New Panama Canal Co. (for which Congress made an appropriation of $40 million), and (2) a Colombian grant to the U.S. of perpetual control over the right of way. The act, which also established the Isthmian Canal Commission, authorized the president, if negotiations for the Panama route failed, to purchase the Nicaraguan route.

It was now necessary to obtain an agreement whereby Colombia would relinquish sovereignty over the proposed Panama canal zone. The Hay-Herran Convention provided that in return for a payment of $10 million and an annual rental of $250,000 the U.S. would receive a 99-year lease (with option of renewal) over a canal zone 6 miles in width. Under this arrangement Colombia was not to receive any part of the money paid to the Panama Co. The convention was ratified by the U.S. Senate; after much delay, it was rejected by the Colombian Senate (12 Aug.). The Colombians, who wanted at least $25 million, believed that by deferring action until after Sept. 1904 (expiration date of the New Panama Canal Co.'s charter), they could then receive the full price offered by the U.S. The Colombian Senate adjourned (31 Oct.) without having taken further action.

PANAMA REVOLT. Colombia's effective rejection of the Hay-Herran Convention aroused the strong displeasure of President Roosevelt, who for a time contemplated recommending the forcible seizure of Panama. On 3 Nov. the province of Panama rose in revolt and declared itself independent of Colombia. The revolution was accomplished by native groups and foreign promoters linked to the Panama Co. who acted with the tacit approval of the Roosevelt administration. Even before the revolution broke out, Roosevelt ordered (2 Nov.) U.S. warships to Panama to maintain "free and uninterrupted transit" across the isthmus, guaranteed by the Treaty of New Granada (1846). On 6 Nov. the U.S. recognized the Republic of Panama and on 13 Nov. formally received Philippe Bunau-Varilla (a onetime associate of the New Panama Canal Co.) as minister from Panama.

18 Nov. HAY–BUNAU-VARILLA TREATY granted to the U.S. in perpetuity the use and control of a canal zone 10 miles wide across the Isthmus of Panama, giving it full sovereignty (including the right of fortification) over that zone as well as all rights to the holdings of the New Panama Canal Co. and the Panama R.R. Co. The neutrality of the zone was to be maintained in conformity with the Hay-Pauncefote Treaty. The U.S. guaranteed the independence of Panama and agreed to pay $10 million and an annual fee of $250,000 beginning 9 years after the exchange of ratifications. The treaty was ratified by the Senate on 23 Feb. 1904 (p. 627).

ALASKAN BOUNDARY DISPUTE arose after the Klondike gold rush of 1896 showed that the Alaskan Panhandle (lying in U.S. territory) commanded the water routes to the goldfields. The Canadians invoked the Anglo-Russian Treaty of 1825 to support their contention that the shoreline ran in such a fashion as to give them practical control of the important harbors of the Alaskan Panhandle (the Canadians maintained that the boundary followed the outer edges of the promontories; the U.S. claimed it followed the heads of the bays and inlets).

The U.S. and Great Britain signed (24 Jan.) a convention providing for a joint tribunal of 3 Americans and 3 Britons to arbitrate the questions. When the tribunal met at London, its U.S. membership comprised ex-Sen. George Turner (Wash.), Sen. Lodge, and War Secretary Root (hardly an impartial trio); its British representation consisted of 2 Canadians and Lord Alverstone, the Lord Chief Justice of England. During the tribunal's deliberations (3 Sept.–20 Oct.) President Roosevelt intimated that if the U.S. did not receive satisfaction, it would employ military force in the disputed area. This was among the first demonstrations of "big stick" diplomacy (a term derived from a statement made by Roosevelt in 1900: "I have always been fond of the West African proverb: 'Speak softly and carry a big stick, you will go far.'").

The U.S. claims were given a 4–2 majority when they were upheld by Lord Alverstone. The award ran a line excluding Canada from the ocean inlets of the Alaskan Panhandle.

1904

6 Dec. ROOSEVELT COROLLARY. During the rule of the dictator Cipriano Castro, Venezuela was plunged into heavy debt to European investors. Castro's unwillingness to meet these financial obligations led the European powers to consider taking forcible action, but they were mindful of the Monroe Doctrine, as indicated by the German memorandum to the State Department (Dec. 1901) disclaiming any intention of permanent occupation. At this time President Roosevelt did not regard such intervention as a violation of the Monroe Doctrine, for in his first annual message (1901) he observed that the U.S. did "not guarantee any State against punishment if it misconducts itself, provided that punishment does not take the form of acquisition of territory by any non-American power."

When Castro refused to submit the claims of the foreign powers to arbitration by the Hague Tribunal, Great Britain and Germany imposed a blockade (Dec., 1902) subsequently joined by Italian warships. Following the bombardment of Venezuelan ports and the destruction of Venezuelan naval craft, Castro asked Roosevelt to propose arbitration by the U.S. minister to Venezuela. This proposal was transmitted by Roosevelt (12 Dec. 1902) to Great Britain and Germany. Both powers accepted the principle of limited arbitration, and the matter was settled by the Hague Tribunal in 1904.

Similarly burdened by debts to European powers was the Dominican Republic, whose financial obligations were serviced chiefly by customhouse receipts pledged to various creditors (with the provision that default would permit the creditors to demand control of the customhouses). Political instability pointed to the likelihood of default by Santo Domingo. A proposal by Belgium (17 Oct. 1903) that the U.S. join in seizing all customhouses and provide for the governing of Santo Domingo by an international commission was refused by the U.S. A change in the Dominican regime brought into power a ruler (Gen. Morales) willing to accede to the U.S. administration of the customhouses.

The situation came to a head in 1904

when the debts payable to an American firm were given a preferred position over those owed to other creditors. The protests of European investors foreshadowed armed intervention, as in Venezuela. To forestall a threat to U.S. interest in the Caribbean, Roosevelt proclaimed in his annual message the dictum later known as the Roosevelt Corollary to the Monroe Doctrine (by which he transformed the doctrine from one of nonintervention by European powers to one of intervention by the U.S.): "Chronic wrongdoing, or an impotence which results in a general loosening of the ties of civilized society, may in America, as elsewhere, ultimately require intervention by some civilized nation, and in the Western Hemisphere the adherence of the United States to the Monroe Doctrine may force the United States, however reluctantly, in flagrant cases of such wrongdoing or impotence, to the exercise of an international police power."

The corollary was one of the outstanding examples of Roosevelt's "big stick" diplomacy. Santo Domingo signed an agreement with the U.S. (1905) providing for the U.S. administration of the customs and management of debt payments. Roosevelt carried out the protocol despite the fact that it was rejected by the Senate. A permanent treaty including the protocol in revised form was ratified (25 Feb. 1907) and on 31 July 1907 the U.S. withdrew from Santo Domingo.

1905

ROOSEVELT AND THE RUSSO-JAPANESE WAR. The Russo-Japanese War (10 Feb. 1904) jeopardized the Open Door policy. Roosevelt was perturbed by complaints of American commercial interests that the Russian advance into Manchuria endangered the Open Door. In a circular note (20 Feb. 1904) the U.S. asked the belligerents to respect "the neutrality" and "administrative entity" of China. However, each made its acceptance conditional upon the other's, and Russia went so far as to reject the proposed neutralization of Manchuria.

In Roosevelt's view, the complete defeat of either Russia or Japan was not desirable, since it would upset the balance of power in the Far East and endanger U.S. interests. On 25 Apr. Japan informed the U.S. that it would maintain the Open Door in Manchuria and restore that province to China. After the Japanese victory over the Russian fleet at the Battle of Tsushima Strait (27–29 May), the Japanese government formally asked Roosevelt (31 May) to take the initiative in acting as mediator. Roosevelt's proposal was accepted by Russia (6 June) and on 8 June he formally invited both powers to open joint negotiations.

In the interim, the secret Taft-Katsura Memorandum was concluded (29 July) by Secretary of War Taft, then on a mission to the Philippines, and the Japanese foreign minister. It stipulated that the U.S. would not interfere with Japanese ambitions in Korea in return for a Japanese promise to disclaim territorial conquest in the Philippines. This executive agreement was endorsed by Roosevelt (31 July) despite his earlier insistence on a Japanese pledge of support for the Open Door policy. The Japanese construed the Taft-Katsura Memorandum as U.S. approval of a Japanese protectorate over Korea (proclaimed 21 Dec.).

9 Aug. PORTSMOUTH PEACE CONFERENCE (held at the navy yard at Portsmouth, N.H.) was concluded by a Russo-Japanese peace treaty signed 5 Sept. Japan secured recognition of her dominant rights in Korea and, through the acquisition of Russia's Liaotung leasehold and the South Manchurian Ry.,

consolidated her economic and territorial position in Manchuria. Partly because of Roosevelt's opposition, the Japanese failed to obtain an indemnity and all of the island of Sakhalin (only its southern half was ceded to Japan). For his work as mediator, Roosevelt was awarded (1906) the Nobel peace prize.

1906

16 Jan. ROOSEVELT AND THE ALGECIRAS CONFERENCE. Since the turn of the century France had been engaged in securing agreements with Italy, Great Britain, and Spain looking toward the establishment of a French protectorate over Morocco, in return for recognizing the interests of these powers elsewhere in North Africa. German opposition to French ambitions and to the economic partition of North Africa grew stronger, particularly after the conclusion of the Anglo-French Entente (1904). Tension was heightened after Kaiser Wilhelm II made a speech at Tangier (31 Mar. 1905) proclaiming support of Moroccan independence.

Germany demanded an international conference on Morocco and asked Roosevelt to secure French participation. Although reluctant to intervene, Roosevelt feared that a Moroccan crisis might touch off a general European war. Through Roosevelt's efforts, France and Great Britain agreed to attend a conference at Algeciras, Spain, with U.S. delegates in attendance. Roosevelt was instrumental in securing German acceptance of the settlement (Act of Algeciras, 7 Apr.) affirming the independence and territorial integrity of Morocco, guaranteeing equality of commercial opportunity, establishing an international bank for the stabilization of Moroccan finances, and providing for the training and control of the Moroccan police by France and Spain. The Algeciras convention was ratified by the U.S. Senate (12 Dec. 1906) with the proviso that such approval was not to be construed as departure from the traditional U.S. policy of noninvolvement in purely European affairs.

RELATIONS WITH JAPAN. By the treaty of 1894 citizens of the U.S. and Japan were permitted mutual free entry, although both governments were empowered to protect domestic interests by legislating against excessive immigration of laborers. Because of American protests, Japan inaugurated a policy of voluntary limitation of emigration (Aug. 1900), but this move failed to halt the flow of emigrant laborers to Hawaii, Canada, or Mexico, whence entry to the U.S. could not be effectively controlled. The growth of anti-Japanese antagonism led West Coast labor to organize a Japanese and Korean Exclusion League (1905). Similar pressures, coinciding with the increasing fear of Japan as a military power ("the Yellow Peril"), resulted in a movement for the statutory exclusion of Japanese.

11 Oct. SAN FRANCISCO SCHOOL SEGREGATION. The San Francisco schools, disrupted by the earthquake and fire (18–19 Apr.), were reopened in July. On 11 Oct. the school board ordered the segregation of all Japanese, Chinese, and Korean children in a separate Oriental school. The Japanese government (25 Oct.) charged that the board's action violated the treaty of 1894. Faced with an impending international crisis, Roosevelt invited the San Francisco School Board to Washington for a conference (Feb. 1907), and effected an arrangement whereby the segregation order would be rescinded locally but the federal government take action on the immigration question. The result was an amendment to the Immigration Act of 1907 (20 Feb.) authorizing the president to exclude from the

U.S. immigrants holding passports to any country other than the U.S., any insular possession of the U.S., or the Canal Zone, and attempting to use such passports to enter the U.S. to the detriment of internal "labor conditions." By executive order (14 Mar.) Roosevelt put this authorization into effect.

"GENTLEMEN'S AGREEMENT" was embodied in a Japanese note (24 Feb. 1907) whereby Japan promised to withhold passports from laborers intending to migrate to the U.S., and recognized the American right to refuse admission to Japanese immigrants using passports originally issued for travel to any country other than the U.S. The San Francisco School Board order was formally rescinded 13 Mar. 1907. However, it was not until 18 Feb. 1908 that a Japanese note provided the basis for the effective restriction of immigration. To offset any Japanese surmises that the concessions extended by the U.S. in the Far East signified a fear of Japan, Roosevelt sent the bulk of the U.S. Navy on a world cruise (16 Dec. 1907–22 Feb. 1909) which demonstrated that the U.S. was now the 2d naval power in the world (Japan ranked 5th).

1907

15 June–15 Oct. 2D HAGUE PEACE CONFERENCE. Called by the Czar of Russia, this meeting, attended by 46 nations, was originally suggested by President Roosevelt in 1904 but had been postponed because of the Russo-Japanese War. The U.S. efforts for the establishment of a world court were unsuccessful. Of particular interest to the U.S. was the adoption by the conference of a revised version of the **Drago Doctrine** (reinforcing the Monroe Doctrine), which had been formulated (29 Dec. 1902) by Luis M. Drago, foreign minister of Argentina, during the dispute over the collection of the Venezuelan debts. The essence of the doctrine was that armed force must not be employed by a European power to collect national debts owed by American nations to foreign creditors.

PANAMA CANAL. Preliminary work on the Panama Canal was virtually halted in 1905 because of the heavy mortality rate caused by disease. In addition, opinion was divided over a sea-level canal as opposed to a lock canal. The sanitation program carried out under Col. **William C. Gorgas** of the U.S. Army Medical Department sharply reduced the deaths caused by malaria and yellow fever and enabled a long-term construction program under safe conditions. President Roosevelt signed a bill (29 June 1906) authorizing the construction of a lock canal. With the reorganization of the Canal Commission (1 Apr.), the entire project was placed under the direct authority of the Secretary of War. Appointed as chief engineer was Lt. Col. (later Col.) **George W. Goethals** (p. 1042) of the U.S. Army Corps of Engineers, under whose immediate direction the canal was built. The Panama Canal, 40.3 miles from shore to shore, links Cristobal, on the Caribbean, with Balboa, the Bay of Panama terminus. The total cost of original construction was more than $365 million. The canal was opened to traffic 15 Aug. 1914.

14 Nov.–20 Dec. CENTRAL AMERICAN PEACE CONFERENCE. The outbreak of war in Central America (19 Feb., involving Honduras, Nicaragua, and El Salvador, and dispatching of U.S. marines (Mar.) to protect American interests) prompted Secretary of State Root to propose, in conjunction with Mexico, the meeting of a peace conference in Washington under terms of treaty of peace signed by Central American nations 25 Sept. 1906. The participating powers were Costa Rica, Guatemala, Honduras, Nicaragua, and El Salvador. The U.S. was not a signatory party. The 8 conventions concluded by the conference included a general treaty of peace and amity and the establishment of a Central American Court of Justice (20 Dec.).

1908

30 Nov. ROOT-TAKAHIRA AGREEMENT, was an executive agreement concluded by an exchange of notes (30 Nov.) between Secretary of State Root and Ambassador Takahira. Carrying a step further the concession granted by the Taft-Katsura Memorandum, it provided that Japan and the U.S. would (1) maintain the "existing *status quo*" in the Pacific, (2) respect the territorial possessions belonging to each other in the Pacific, (3) uphold the Open Door policy in China, and (4) support by peaceful means the independence and integrity of China. The phrase "existing *status quo*," was interpreted by Japan as U.S. recognition of Japan's paramount imperialist influence in Korea and southern Manchuria.

1909

TAFT'S FAR EASTERN POLICY. President Taft and his Secretary of State, Philander C. Knox, reaffirmed the Open Door with a policy subsequently known as "**Dollar Diplomacy**"—increasing U.S. trade by supporting American enterprises abroad, and including Latin America as well as the Far East.

Shortly after Taft's inauguration an international consortium composed of French, British, and German bankers took steps to float a loan for building the Hukuang Railways in southern and central China. At the suggestion of the State Department an American banking group was organized to finance railroad concessions in China. The bankers' agent, Willard Straight, who played a dominant role in Far Eastern "Dollar Diplomacy," unsuccessfully asked the European interests for admission to the consortium. Only after Taft took the unprecedented step of making a personal appeal (15 July) to the Chinese regent, Prince Chun, was American participation permitted in a 4-power consortium agreement (signed on 20 May 1911). American bankers had already declined Straight's proposal (1909–10) to build a rail line in northern Manchuria. As a direct result of this attempted U.S. penetration of Manchuria, Russia and Japan concluded a treaty (4 July 1911) staking out spheres of influence in deliberate defiance of the Open Door. This treaty weakened U.S. prestige in the Far East. Japan's position in Manchuria was strengthened by the fact that France and Great Britain favored giving Japan a free hand there in order to safeguard their own spheres of influence elsewhere in the Far East.

Despite these setbacks, Secretary Knox encouraged the Chinese government to request (22 Sept. 1910) a large loan to underwrite currency reform in China and industrial development in Manchuria. Japan and Russia registered their opposition, and U.S. bankers announced that they would not be bound to participate in contracts objectionable to other powers. Although a 6-power consortium was established (20 June 1912), the final agreement was signed (26 Apr. 1913) without U.S. participation. Eager to avoid further commitments in China, American bankers informed President Wilson (5 Mar. 1913) that they would remain active there only under official pressure. Wilson withdrew U.S. support of the consortium (18 Mar. 1913) on the ground that its terms endangered China's "administrative independence." This step terminated the Taft-Knox pol-

icy in the Far East. The coming of World War I shifted U.S. interest to Europe and permitted Japan to expand at China's expense.

1910

7 Sept. NEWFOUNDLAND FISHERIES. The continuing controversy over the North Atlantic fisheries was finally resolved after the U.S. and Great Britain agreed (27 Jan. 1909) to submit the question to the Hague Tribunal. The decision was a compromise award upholding the Newfoundland claim to local regulation and authorizing the provisions of the rejected Bayard-Chamberlain Treaty (1888) pertaining to the definition of territorial bays. The award was confirmed by an Anglo-American convention (20 July 1912).

1911

U.S. INTERVENTION IN NICARAGUA. Nicaragua was the object of special U.S. interest because of the disturbing possibility that its canal route might fall under foreign control. In 1909 José S. Zelaya, an opponent of foreign penetration, was deposed as dictator of Nicaragua. The ensuing political turmoil brought to the presidency (1911) Adolfo Díaz, whose friendly policy toward the U.S. matured in the **Knox-Castrillo Convention** (6 June). This agreement gave the U.S. the right of intervention and provided for refunding of the national debt, payment to be secured by a customs receivership under U.S. protection. On 1 July the Nicaraguan government defaulted on a loan made by a British syndicate. Without waiting for the Senate to act, Knox persuaded a group of New York bankers to implement the treaty's provisions before formal ratification. The Senate adjourned without taking any action. Desperate for financial aid, the Nicaraguan government secured a loan of $1,500,000; in return, the U.S. bankers received control of the National Bank of Nicaragua and the government-owned railway. Customs receipts were pledged in payment, collection to be carried out under American auspices. The Knox-Castrillo Convention was rejected by the Senate, as was a similar one made with Honduras.

When native dissatisfaction with the agreement touched off a Nicaraguan revolt, the U.S. intervened. A force of marines was landed (14 Aug. 1912) to protect American interests. Knox then attempted to negotiate a treaty granting the U.S., in return for a payment of $3 million, the exclusive right of way for an interoceanic canal, a 90-year lease of the Great Corn and Little Corn Islands in the Caribbean, and a naval base on the Gulf of Fonseca. The Senate failed to act on this agreement. To insure the regular operation of the financial arrangements, a small detachment of marines remained in Nicaragua until 1925, and did not finally leave until 1933.

7 JULY. PELAGIC SEALING AGREEMENT. The controversy regarding pelagic sealing in the North Pacific persisted after Blaine's unsuccessful attempt to deal with it, and became acute as the steadily dwindling herds of seals were threatened with extinction. In 1911 a 4-power conference on the sealing industry was called at Washington and, participated in by the U.S., Great Britain, Russia, and Japan, agreed to a treaty, to continue in force subject to one year's notice, which outlawed for 15 years pelagic sealing north of the 30th parallel, established a U.S. monopoly of the catch, and authorized an allocation of profits to Great Britain and Japan in return for their withdrawal from pelagic sealing in the area. Japan abrogated the convention on 23 Oct. 1940.

CANADIAN RECIPROCITY. Anxious to forestall the breakup of trade with Canada, threatened in retaliation against the Payne-Aldrich Tariff of 1909, the Taft administration signed a reciprocity agreement (26 Jan.) providing for the reduction or elimination of duties on many Canadian items, chiefly agricultural commodities, and for reduced rates on U.S. manufactures. Because it involved fiscal matters, the agreement was subject to approval by both houses of Congress. The House approved, as did the Senate (22 July), despite opposition from Midwestern agricultural interests; but when Taft and several Congressmen publicly referred to the reciprocity agreement as a prelude to the U.S. annexation of Canada, national feeling was aroused in Canada. In the elections of 1911 the Liberal party, in favor of the agreement, was defeated by the antireciprocity Conservatives (21 Sept.), ending for the time being Canadian-American reciprocity.

ARBITRATION TREATIES. The arbitration treaties which Secretary of State Root negotiated (1908–09) with 25 nations, providing for the referral of controversies to the Hague Tribunal, were weakened by reservations concerning disputes involving national interests, honor, and independence. When Taft became president, he made efforts to obtain arbitration agreements of a more general character. The impetus was provided by the Anglo-Japanese Alliance, by which Great Britain was bound to aid Japan in the event of war. The U.S. was anxious to employ diplomatic means to restrain Japan. An opportunity arose with the renewal (13 July) of the Anglo-Japanese Alliance containing a proviso that neither nation would fight a third power with whom a general arbitration treaty was in force. The U.S. signed such treaties (3 Aug.) with Great Britain and France, but these agreements were vitiated by amendment in the Senate (which ratified them on 7 Mar. 1912), where Sen. Henry Cabot Lodge (Mass.) led the fight for reservations on matters involving Oriental exclusion and the Monroe Doctrine, and for determination by the Senate of the character of controversies before their submission to arbitration.

1912

2 Aug. LODGE COROLLARY. In 1911 it became known that a Japanese syndicate was conducting negotiations for the purchase of a large site near strategic Magdalena Bay, Lower California. The negotiations came to an end when the State Department registered its disapproval. A Senate resolution introduced by Lodge declared the U.S. viewed with "grave concern" the possession of strategically important areas "by any corporation or association which has such a relation to another Government, not American, as to give that Government practical power of control for national purposes." The Lodge Corollary extended the Monroe Doctrine's scope to non-European powers and to foreign companies as well as foreign nations.

1913

24 Apr. BRYAN'S "COOLING OFF" TREATIES. As early as 1905 William Jennings Bryan recommended that the U.S. take the initiative in establishing a system of arbitration providing for the referral of all international differences to a permanent court of arbitration. Shortly after becoming Secretary of State, he negotiated with 30 nations separate treaties (differing in detail, but similar in their broad features) providing for the referral of all international disputes, without exception, to a permanent investigating commission. Resort to armed conflict was prohibited until the commission submitted its report within a year. Twenty-one ratifications were finally exchanged.

MEXICAN REVOLUTION. Since 1877 Mexico had been almost without interruption under a dictatorship headed by President Porfirio Díaz, who had granted foreign investors liberal concessions for the development of Mexican resources including oil, mines, land, and railways. By 1913 a total of some $2 billion (of which more than half came from the U.S.) had been invested by foreign interests. A revolution led by the democratic reformer, Francisco I. Madero, broke out Nov. 1910. Americans were compelled to abandon their holdings and flee the country; some lost their lives. The revolution culminated in Díaz' resignation (25 May 1911) and the establishment of a liberal government.

The Taft administration recognized the Madero regime and embargoed the shipment of munitions to Madero's opponents; for the rest, the U.S. adhered to a policy of nonintervention. Madero was assassinated (22 Feb.) by agents of the reactionary Gen. Victoriano Huerta, who seized power and held it amid revolutionary upheaval. European powers recognized Huerta, but President Taft refused recognition despite pressure by American business interests.

When Wilson became president, he decided to follow a policy of cooperating with only such governments as rested upon the undoubted consent of the governed. In a speech (11 Mar.) he tacitly disapproved of Huerta and indicated the termination of Dollar Diplomacy with the announcement that the U.S. would not lend support to special interests. After a revolution headed by Venustiano Carranza gathered force, Wilson proposed an immediate armistice, to be fol-

lowed by a free election in which Huerta should not be a candidate. In return the U.S. would encourage American bankers to extend loans to the Mexican government.

Huerta's refusal (16 Aug.) evoked from Wilson a policy of "watchful waiting" and the application of a strict arms embargo. Huerta dissolved the Mexican Congress (10 Oct.) and was elected president (26 Oct.). American business interests renewed their demand for intervention, but Wilson, in a speech delivered at Mobile, Ala. (27 Oct.), asserted that the U.S. "will never again seek one additional foot of territory by conquest."

Wilson applied sharper pressure in a note (7 Nov.) requesting Huerta's retirement from power. The Mexican ruler was further notified (24 Nov.) that it was the policy of the U.S. to isolate him from material aid and foreign sympathy, and to force him out of office. Early in 1914 Wilson lifted the arms embargo to permit munitions to reach the opponents of Huerta and stationed U.S. naval units off Vera Cruz to block the entry of European shipments of war materials to the Huerta regime.

1914

9–21 Apr. TAMPICO AND VERA CRUZ INCIDENTS. An unarmed party from the U.S.S. *Dolphin*, one of the vessels stationed in Mexican waters, went ashore at Tampico (9 Apr.) to secure supplies, and by error entered a restricted area. Despite the cover of the U.S. flag, they were arrested by Huerta's troops on the charge of violating martial law. Although they were released promptly, with apologies from a superior officer, Adm. Henry T. Mayo peremptorily demanded that the port commander apologize formally, promise to punish the responsible officer, and hoist the American flag ashore, giving it a 21-gun salute. Mayo made these demands without consulting Washington, but the Wilson administration felt that he must be supported to preclude Huerta's exploitation of the incident. However, Huerta succeeded in evading the salute, despite a warning that a refusal would probably result in intervention.

Congress granted (22 Apr.) Wilson's request for permission to use force to uphold U.S. rights and secure redress of grievances. Meanwhile, U.S. forces had already landed on Mexican soil. Informed that a German ship was approaching with munitions, Bryan advised Wilson (21 Apr.) to use the navy to prevent delivery. On 21 Apr. the American forces bombarded Vera Cruz and occupied the city. Huerta promptly broke off diplomatic relations with the U.S. The incident united Mexican opinion behind Huerta and brought Mexico and the U.S. close to war.

20 May–30 June. ABC CONFERENCE. Wilson accepted the offer of the ABC Powers (Argentina, Brazil, and Chile) to mediate the dispute. At a meeting at Niagara Falls, Ontario, attended by representatives of the U.S., Mexico, and the ABC Powers, the mediators proposed the retirement of Huerta, establishment of a Mexican provisional government in favor of agrarian and political reforms, and no indemnity to the U.S. for occupation costs at Vera Cruz. This plan, agreed to 24 June, was rejected by Mexico, but its moral effect was instrumental in compelling Huerta to leave office (15 July). The U.S. occupation forces withdrew from Vera Cruz (23 Nov.) and on 19 Oct. 1915 the U.S. and several Latin-American nations recognized Carranza as *de facto* president.

15 June. PANAMA TOLLS ACT. On 24 Aug. 1912, Congress passed the Panama Canal Act, exempting U.S. coast-wise shipping from payment of tolls, in apparent contravention of the Hay-Pauncefote Treaty provision that the canal should be free and open to the vessels of commerce and of war of "all nations" on terms of entire equality. The British protested on the ground that "all nations" should include, rather than ex-clude, the U.S. American supporters of the act (which was approved by both major parties in the election of 1912) maintained that the equality provisions referred to uniformity of rates. Dis-turbed by the charges of bad faith brought against the U.S., Wilson rec-ommended (5 Mar.) repeal of the tolls exemption. Repeal passed the Senate on 11 June. Settlement of the controversy helped win British backing for the U.S. course in Mexico. The Panama Canal was officially opened to traffic on 15 Aug.

4 Aug. U.S. NEUTRALITY. With the outbreak of World War I (Germany de-clared war on Russia 1 Aug., on France 3 Aug., and invaded Belgium 3 Aug.; Britain declared war against Germany 4 Aug.), President Wilson issued a proc-lamation of neutrality. On 19 Aug. he publicly appealed to Americans to be "impartial in thought as well as in ac-tion."

6 Aug. CONTROVERSY OVER NEUTRAL RIGHTS. Great Brtain justi-fied her blockade of Germany by the "unusual" conditions of warfare. Secre-tary Bryan asked the belligerents (6 Aug. 1914) to accept the Declaration of London (drafted in 1909 and signed by the leading powers but not ratified) as a code of naval warfare. Because its guar-antees gave the Central Powers their only chance for large-scale trade with neutrals, they promptly accepted, condi-tional upon enemy agreement. France and Russia made acceptance conditional upon Great Britain, whose position was

clarified by an order in council (20 Aug. 1914). The order, setting the pattern of British trade regulation for the duration of the war, accepted the declaration but made exceptions to its contraband pro-visions, extending the list of conditional contraband beyond the categories speci-fied in the declaration.

A vigorous protest (26 Sept. 1914) by the State Department was withheld at the suggestion of Col. **Edward M. House** (p. 1061), private diplomatic adviser to President Wilson. The note sent instead (28 Sept. 1914) stressed the evil effects of British policy upon American public opinion rather than neutral rights. When the U.S. abandoned (22 Oct. 1914) its efforts to make the Declaration of Lon-don effective, the British, in successive orders in council (29 Oct., 23 Dec. 1914), further extended the contraband list and revived the **doctrine of the con-tinuous voyage** by proceeding to inter-cept neutral ships going to Germany and to neighboring countries (Holland, Den-mark, and the other Scandinavian nations, which lay in the Baltic area under the control of the German navy). This en-abled the British to seize many goods (especially foodstuffs) previously consid-ered fair trade for neutrals. The British declared (3 Nov. 1914) the North Sea a military area and presently mined it and proclaimed (11 Mar.) a blockade of all German ports, with all merchant ves-sels bound for or coming from a German port liable to seizure and confiscation.

15 Aug. LOANS TO BELLIGER-ENTS. The U.S. government announced that "loans by American bankers to any foreign nation which is at war are incon-sistent with the true spirit of neutrality." This policy was modified (Oct.) at the behest of **Robert Lansing** (1864–1928), then counselor for the State Department. Advised that the U.S. would not object to short-term credits, the National City Bank

(4 Nov.) advanced $10 million to the French government. In Sept. 1915 Wilson reluctantly agreed to the floating of general loans by the belligerents, and on 25 Sept. 1915 a group of American bankers completed negotiations for a loan of $500 million to France and Britain. By Apr. 1917 U.S. investors had purchased $2,300 million in bonds from the Allies in contrast with only about $20 million in German bonds. U.S. trade with the Allies rose from c.$800 million (1914) to c.$3 billion (1916), while direct exports to Germany and Austria-Hungary dropped from $169,289,775 to $1,159,-653.

1915

10 FEB. "STRICT ACCOUNTABILITY." The German government proclaimed (4 Feb.) the waters around the British Isles a war zone and announced that beginning 18 Feb. enemy merchant ships would be destroyed on sight in the forbidden area without provision for the safety of passengers and crew. Warning of the dangers resulting from the misuse of neutral flags and from the accidents of warfare, the German government declared that neutral craft entering the war zone would do so at their own risk. In contrast with the temporizing position on British interference with American rights on the high seas, the U.S. government registered a sharp protest (10 Feb.). The note stated that in the event American vessels or the lives of American citizens were destroyed by Germany on the high seas, the U.S. would view the act as "an indefensible violation of neutral rights" and hold Germany strictly answerable.

The German ambassador, Count Johann von Bernstorff, promptly urged the State Department to warn Americans against travel on belligerent ships, but his advice was not heeded. On 28 Mar. an American citizen perished in the sinking of the British liner *Falaba* in the Irish Sea. On 1 May the American tanker *Gulflight* was struck by a torpedo launched in a fight between a submarine and a British naval patrol off the Scilly Isles, causing the death of two Americans.

7 MAY. SINKING OF THE "LUSITANIA." The German embassy at Washington issued a warning (1 May) that Americans entering the war zone around the British Isles would do so at their own risk. On 7 May the British transatlantic steamer *Lusitania* was sunk off the Irish coast without warning by a submarine, with the loss of 1,198 lives, including 128 Americans. The ship's manifest subsequently revealed that the *Lusitania* carried some arms. The act precipitated a revulsion of public opinion against Germany.

13 MAY, 9 JUNE, 21 JULY. "LUSITANIA" NOTES. The first *Lusitania* note (13 May) was drafted by Wilson and signed by Bryan against his own inclination. It demanded that Germany abandon unrestricted submarine warfare, disavow the sinking of the *Lusitania,* and make reparation for the loss of U.S. lives. The note insisted upon the right of Americans to sail on the high seas and reiterated the "strict accountability" position. The German reply (28 May) excused the torpedoing on the ground that the *Lusitania* was armed and carried contraband (the vessel, in fact, was unarmed, but carried a shipment of rifles and cartridges). Wilson regarded the reply as evasive and unsatisfactory. A second note (also drafted by Wilson) took issue with the German contention that special circumstances imposed the necessity for unrestricted submarine warfare and demanded specific pledges. Bryan informed Wilson that he could not sign the note because he feared that it might involve the U.S. in war. His resignation, tendered on 7 June, was promptly accepted, and the second *Lusitania* note (9 June) was dispatched over the signature of Secretary Robert Lansing. The third note (21 July), virtually an ultimatum, warned Germany that a repetition of such acts would be regarded as "deliberately unfriendly."

24 July–1 Dec. GERMAN ESPIONAGE AND SABOTAGE. The U.S. Secret Service obtained possession of documents signed by Ambassador Bernstorff and Capt. Franz von Papen, revealing German sabotage activity in the U.S. Publication (beg. 15 Aug. in N.Y. *World*) led to the recall of the Austro-Hungarian Ambassador, Dr. Constantin Dumba (8 Sept.), and of the German attachés, Capts. Franz von Papen and Karl Boy-Ed (1 Dec.). On 30 July 1916 a munitions explosion on **Black Tom** Island, N.J., attributed to German sabotage, resulted in property loss of $22 million. On 11 Jan. 1917 an explosion wrecked the Canadian Car & Foundry plant at Kingsland, N.J. A Mixed Claims Commission (15 June 1939) found Germany guilty of both explosions, but Germany never paid the $55 million damage award.

19 Aug.–5 Oct. "ARABIC" CRISIS. Anxious to avoid the consequences of similar incidents, the German government privately instructed its submarine commanders (6 June) not to sink liners, even those under the enemy flag, without warning. When 2 American lives were lost in the sinking of the British steamer *Arabic* (19 Aug.), German Ambassador von Bernstorff rendered the so-called *Arabic* pledge (1 Sept.) on his own authority: "Liners will not be sunk by our submarines without warning and without safety of the lives of non-combatants, provided that the liners do not try to escape or offer resistance." During the remainder of 1915 the German U-boats concentrated on freighters in the Atlantic. The German government (5 Oct.) offered apologies and indemnity for the loss of American lives in the *Arabic* disaster, and this outcome was regarded as a diplomatic victory for the U.S.

INTERVENTION IN HAITI. A Haitian revolution raised Vibrun Guillaume Sam to power as president (5 Mar.), by which time Haiti's foreign debt had risen to c.$24 million. American financial interests held investments in the Haitian national bank and railroad, and the U.S., countering a Franco-German proposal (Mar. 1914) for joint customs, proposed a customs receivership. Following another revolution, resulting in the overthrow and assassination of President Sam (28 July), the U.S. marines, at Wilson's order, landed in Haiti (29 July) and imposed a military occupation. Sudre Dartiguenave, elected president (15 Aug.), signed a treaty (16 Sept.) by which Haiti became for all practical purposes a U.S. protectorate. The treaty, which went into effect for a 10-year period (with option of renewal) on 3 May 1916, stipulated that the Haitian public debt might not be increased, nor its tariff diminished, without U.S. consent.

1916

15 Mar. MEXICAN BORDER CAMPAIGN. Revolutionary opposition to Carranza was continued by a number of freebooting chieftains, particularly by **Pancho Villa** in northern Mexico. Villa was responsible for the deaths of Americans on both sides of the border. When 18 American engineers were invited by Carranza to return and operate the abandoned mines, Villa's band shot and killed them at Santa Ysabel (10 Jan.). Villa was also credited with repeated raids into Texas and New Mexico in the spring

of 1916. A raid on Columbus, N.M. (9 Mar.), resulted in 17 deaths. Congressional pressure for intervention mounted, and Wilson was compelled to abandon his policy of "watchful waiting."

With Carranza's reluctant consent, Gen. John J. Pershing was ordered to head a punitive expedition of 15,000 men and pursue Villa into Mexico. Wilson called out 150,000 militia and stationed this force along the border. The pursuit of Villa (begun 15 Mar.) aroused the antagonism of Carranza and intensified anti-American feeling. Carranza refused to accept a proposal signed (24 Nov.) by joint commissioners of Mexico and the U.S. for withdrawal of U.S. troops and joint but independent guarding of the border. As war with Germany became imminent, Wilson finally withdrew the U.S. expeditionary force (Jan.– 5 Feb. 1917). A new Mexican constitution was proclaimed (5 Feb. 1917), Carranza was elected president (11 Mar. 1917), and the U.S. extended *de jure* recognition to the new government.

LATIN-AMERICAN RELATIONS. Nicaragua: Bryan-Chamorro Treaty (signed 5 Aug. 1914) perpetuated the Taft-Knox policy of Dollar Diplomacy. An unsuccessful attempt to insert Platt Amendment provisions delayed Senate ratification until 18 Feb. 1916. Nicaragua received $3 million in return for granting the U.S. exclusive rights to a canal route and a naval base. The U.S. secured a 99-year lease (with option of renewal) to the Great Corn and Little Corn Islands and to the Gulf of Fonseca. The treaty evoked the protests of Costa Rica and Salvador, both claiming that it infringed upon their territorial rights. An adverse decision of the Central American Court of Justice was disregarded by the U.S. and Nicaragua.

Intervention in Santo Domingo. The financial protectorate set up in Santo Domingo in 1907 temporarily relieved that country of political instability. But renewal of domestic disorders led to a further increase in the public debt. By Sept. 1912, revolutionary forces had seized 2 customhouses and laid 2 others under siege. The Dominican Republic accepted (June 1914) the temporary appointment of a new American official who exercised a check on expenditures; but when the U.S. minister again demanded (Nov. 1915) the acceptance of a financial adviser, the Dominican president was reluctant to comply. Internal disorder forced his resignation (May); partial occupation of the country followed; and U.S. officials began collecting internal revenue, putting the financial advisership into practical operation. Secretary Lansing recommended (22 Nov.) full military occupation of Santo Domingo. The occupation was proclaimed on 29 Nov. and an internal administration was established under U.S. naval officers, who remained in charge until 1924 (p. 381).

22 FEB. HOUSE MISSION AND MEMORANDUM. President Wilson, anxious to avoid U.S. involvement in the European war and concerned with the necessity of a negotiated peace, dispatched (Dec. 1914) his private adviser and close friend, Col. Edward M. House, as an unofficial emissary on a secret mission to the foreign offices of the major belligerent powers. House arrived in London (6 Feb. 1915), where he conferred with the British foreign secretary, Sir Edward Grey. These discussions were inconclusive, as were those held (Mar.– Apr. 1915) at Paris and Berlin. House again went to Europe and conducted (Jan.–Feb.) another series of discussions with British, French, and German statesmen. House proposed an understanding by which Germany would be granted

wider scope in colonial areas and overseas markets in return for a pledge to
reduce her naval construction. While the
scheme lacked precise formulation, it
proposed the following peace terms: the
restoration of Belgium and Serbia, the
cession of Alsace-Lorraine to France, and
of Constantinople to Russia. House's
conversations at London resulted in the
House-Grey Memorandum (22 Feb.),
which promised on Wilson's behalf that,
"on hearing from France and England
that the moment was opportune," the
president would summon a peace conference. Should Allied acceptance be followed by German refusal, the U.S. "would
probably enter the war against Germany." Wilson's endorsement (6 Mar.)
of the memorandum was communicated
to Grey 8 Mar. However, the Allies and
the Central Powers still believed that
they could break the military deadlock
by force of arms; hence, the U.S. proposal for a negotiated peace fell on deaf
ears.

**3–7 MAR. GORE-McLEMORE RESO-
LUTIONS.** A German declaration (8
Feb.) to the effect that all armed enemy merchant vessels would be sunk
without warning after 1 Mar. raised fears
in Congress that the further loss of
American lives on the high seas would
draw the U.S. into war and touched off
a revolt within Democratic ranks.

Rep. Jeff McLemore (Tex.) introduced a resolution (17 Feb.) requesting
the president to warn Americans not to
travel on armed vessels. At a stormy
White House conference with party
leaders (21 Feb.), Wilson made it clear
that he was adamant in his interpretation of U.S. rights. Construing the Mc-
Lemore resolution as a challenge to U.S.
sovereignty and a test of his presidential
leadership, Wilson informed the Senate
Committee on Foreign Relations (24
Feb.) that he could not "consent to any

abridgement of the rights of American
citizens in any respect. . . ."

Sen. Thomas P. Gore (Okla.) introduced a resolution (25 Feb.) to deny
passports to Americans seeking passage
on armed belligerent vessels and demanded protection of American trade
in noncontraband from the Allied restrictions. (In a direct challenge to the administration, this resolution was later
modified to read that the loss of American life because of the sinking of an
armed merchant vessel by Germany
"would constitute a just and sufficient
cause of war between the United States
and the German Empire"; by such a
positive declaration, the opponents of
Wilson's position hoped to embarrass the
administration.) Wilson decided (29
Feb.) to bring the fight over the resolutions to a head. Under pressure from
the White House, the Gore resolution
was tabled in the Senate (3 Mar.), 68–
14, and the McLemore resolution tabled
in the House (7 Mar.), 276–142.

24 MAR. "SUSSEX" AFFAIR. A secret German order (21 Nov. 1915) authorized submarine commanders to regard as troop transports that could be
sunk without warning all ships plying
the English Channel. A German submarine torpedoed (24 Mar.) the *Sussex,*
an unarmed French cross-channel passenger ship, causing injury to several
Americans. The U.S. regarded the attack as a violation of the *Arabic* pledge.
Secretary Lansing called for drastic action, informing President Wilson (27
Mar.) that he favored an immediate
severance of diplomatic relations with
Germany. Wilson resisted the pressure
for a break, and substituted an ultimatum (18 Apr.) that unless Germany
immediately abandoned its present
methods of submarine warfare, the U.S.
would sever relations. Germany agreed
(4 May) to the U.S. demands, but laid

down the countercondition that the U.S. compel the Allies to respect the "rules of international law." Wilson accepted the pledge, but refused (8 May) to accept the condition.

18 July. BRITISH BLACKLIST of 85 American individuals and firms (30 commercial firms) which because of suspected dealings with the Central Powers were to be denied the use of British banking, shipping, and cable facilities. Responding to U.S. public opinion, Wilson considered asking Congress to prohibit loans and cut exports to the Allies. Two retaliatory laws were passed. The **Shipping Board Act** (7 Sept.) empowered the president to deny clearance papers to any ship refusing to accept cargo from blacklisted firms. The **Revenue Act** (8 Sept.) authorized the president to withhold clearance or port facilities from any ship guilty of unfair discrimination against American commerce. However, these discretionary powers were never exercised, partly because the British government, under the pressure of this legislation, began to make concessions, and partly because Secretary of Commerce William C. Redfield reported (23 Oct.) that retaliation would invite counter-reprisals without guaranteeing the desired concessions. In addition, the naval appropriation of 1916, the largest in U.S. peacetime history to date, served as an implied warning to Great Britain.

2 Sept.–12 Dec. GERMAN PEACE OVERTURES. At the behest (2 Sept.) of Chancellor Theobald von Bethmann Hollweg, the German ambassador to the U.S., Count Bernstorff, inquired whether the good offices of the U.S. would be offered if Germany guaranteed the restoration of Belgium. Bernstorff was informed that President Wilson would not take any steps toward mediation until after the fall elections. By 25 Nov. Wilson had completed the first draft of his

proposal for mediation and a program for an equitable peace, but the Allies were uncompromisingly hostile toward peace overtures. The fall of the Asquith cabinet in Great Britain (5 Dec.) and the accession of David Lloyd George as prime minister brought no change in policy. Before Wilson could release his peace proposal, the German government published a statement (12 Dec.) directed to all neutral powers announcing the willingness of Germany and the other Central Powers to enter immediately upon peace negotiations. The Allies declined the proposal because of the German refusal to state her peace terms.

18 Dec. WILSON'S PEACE NOTE to the belligerent powers was neither a peace proposal nor a mediation offer. It abandoned his proposed call for a general conference and put forward a simple request to both parties to state their war aims. The move was futile. The Germans refused a statement. An Allied joint reply (30 Dec.) rejected the German note of 12 Dec. In a joint note (10 Jan. 1917) to the U.S., the Allies outlined peace terms clearly unfavorable to the Central Powers: (1) the restoration of Belgium, Serbia, and Montenegro with appropriate indemnities; (2) the evacuation of the invaded territories of France, Russia, and Rumania with just reparations; (3) the restitution of territories or provinces taken from the Allies by force; (4) the liberation of Italians, Slavs, Rumanians, and Czecho-Slovaks from foreign domination; (5) the expulsion from Europe of the Ottoman Empire; and (6) the reorganization of Europe, guaranteed by a stable regime founded upon respect of nationalities and full security to all nations, great or small.

1917

17 Jan. PURCHASE OF THE VIRGIN ISLANDS. U.S. desire to annex the

Danish possessions in the Caribbean was heightened by fears that Germany had a long-standing ambition to use them as a naval base. By a treaty signed on 4 Aug. 1916, Denmark agreed to cede the Virgin Islands to the U.S. in return for $25 million (pp. 627–629).

22 JAN. "PEACE WITHOUT VICTORY." Shortly after receiving the Allied reply (10 Jan.) Wilson prepared his own program for a desirable peace settlement. In an address to the Senate (22 Jan.) he referred to the need for international organization as a guarantee of an enduring world peace and insisted upon "peace without victory."

1 FEB. RESUMPTION OF UNRESTRICTED SUBMARINE WARFARE. Early in 1917 the struggle between German civilian and military leaders over the unlimited use of the submarine came to a head. A conference at Pless (31 Aug. 1916) had agreed that the Supreme High Command of the German army should have the power to decide when the submarine campaign was to be opened. The leaders of the armed services agreed (Nov. 1916) that unless Germany's peace moves were successful, unrestricted U-boat warfare must be launched by the end of Jan. At a conference of political and military leaders, held (8–9 Jan.) at Pless, field headquarters of Gen. Paul von Hindenburg, Gen. Erich von Ludendorff supported the demand of the German admirals for resumption of unrestricted submarine warfare. Chancellor Bethmann Hollweg, spokesman of the civilian opposition, agreed reluctantly when it became apparent that the advantages likely to accrue (chiefly the destruction of the British means and will to fight) outweighed the dangers of U.S. entry into the war. Accordingly, Ambassador Bernstorff notified (31 Jan.) Secretary Lansing that, effective 1 Feb., submarine assaults against all neutral and belliger-

ent shipping would be renewed. The Germans specified that the U.S. would be permitted to send 1 ship to England each week, provided the vessel observed certain conditions set by the German government.

3 FEB. BREAK WITH GERMANY. The violation of the *Sussex* pledge made U.S. relations with Germany increasingly intolerable. On 3 Feb. U.S.S. *Housatonic* was sunk after warning. Wilson resisted (31 Jan.) Secretary Lansing's recommendation for a break, but soon made his own decision, and in an address to Congress (3 Feb.) announced the severance of diplomatic relations with Germany. He plainly implied that "actual overt acts" by the German government would bring positive steps by the U.S. A Senate resolution (7 Feb.) endorsed Wilson's action.

1 MAR. ZIMMERMAN NOTE was a code message (dated 19 Jan.) sent to Heinrich von Eckhardt, German minister in Mexico, by German foreign secretary Arthur Zimmermann. If war between Germany and the U.S. broke out, Eckhardt was to propose an alliance with Mexico on the following basis: "That we shall make war together and together make peace. We shall give generous financial support, and it is understood that Mexico is to reconquer the lost territory in New Mexico, Texas, and Arizona." Mexico was to urge Japan to switch to Germany's side. This message was intercepted and decoded by the British naval intelligence, and a copy given (24 Feb.) to **Walter Hines Page** (1855–1918), U.S. ambassador to Great Britain, who immediately transmitted it to the State Department, which, in turn, released it to the press (1 Mar.).

26 FEB.–13 MAR. ARMING OF U.S. MERCHANTMEN. Moving to prevent an overt act which would precipitate war with Germany, Wilson asked Congress (26 Feb.) for authority to arm American merchantmen in the hope of deterring submarines from attack. Publication of the Zimmermann note lent added force to his request. The House acted promptly (1 Mar.), passing the **Armed Ship Bill** by a vote of 403 to 13. In the Senate, however, a "little group of willful men" (as Wilson characterized these 7 Republicans and 5 Democrats) led by Robert M. La Follette filibustered the bill from 28 Feb. until the end of the session (4 Mar.). Wilson was then advised by Secretary Lansing (6, 8 Mar.) that under statute law he could arm merchant ships without the specific approval of Congress. The State Department announced (12 Mar.) that all American merchant vessels sailing through war zones would be armed. The Navy Department issued instructions (13 Mar.) authorizing such vessels to take action against submarines.

SUBMARINE TOLL. On 25 Feb., S.S. *Laconia* (British), with 2 U.S. dead, announced 26 Feb., day of Wilson's message to Congress; 12 Mar., S.S. *Algonquin*, unarmed, with warning; 16 Mar., sinkings reported of *City of Mem-*

phis, Illinois, and *Vigilancia;* 21 Mar., Standard Oil steamer *Healdton,* in safety zone off Dutch coast.

2 APR. WILSON'S WAR MESSAGE. Secretary Lansing favored war with Germany, maintaining that U.S. participation would encourage the democratic elements within Germany and lend support to the new democratic government in Russia, where the March Revolution brought a provisional regime into power on the 12th. Wilson delayed his commitment. The unanimous advice of his cabinet (20 Mar.) for war was influential, and on 21 Mar. Wilson issued a call for a special session of Congress to convene on 2 Apr. In a message asking for a declaration of war Wilson condemned the German submarine policy as "warfare against mankind," stated that the U.S. was joining the fight for ultimate world peace, and declared: "The world must be made safe for democracy."

4–6 APR. WAR RESOLUTION, which passed the Senate (4 Apr.), 82–6, was concurred in by the House (6 Apr.), 373–50.

The United States in World War I, 1917–18

6 APR. U.S. DECLARATION OF WAR ON GERMANY. The joint congressional resolution declaring a state of war was signed by President Wilson. War against Austria-Hungary was declared on 7 Dec. During World War I the U.S. was not formally a member nation of the Allies. To the end of that conflict she was known as an "Associated Power" in a group of "Allied and Associated Powers."

MILITARY SITUATION. The U.S. entry into the war came when the prospects for an Allied victory had taken

a decided turn for the worst. The peak of the German destruction of Allied shipping (chiefly British) was Apr., when 881,000 gross tons were lost. Although the monthly losses declined thereafter, averaging about 200,000 tons a month over the following year, they still exceeded the Allied capacity for replacement. French failure in the Aisne and Champagne offensives (Apr.) caused a sharp drop in morale and led to mutinies in the French army. The Flanders offensive (June–Nov.) by the British was indecisive, and won little ground at the cost of enormous casualties. Brusilov's offensive (July), launched by the Russians, was smashed by the Germans; the defeat contributed to an upsurge of peace sentiment in Russia. Following the November Revolution (6–7 Nov.) the Bolsheviks negotiated a separate peace (**Treaty of Brest-Litovsk,** 3 Mar. 1918). Not only was Russia lost as a military ally, her defection enabled the release of masses of German troops for use on the Western Front. At the close of the year (Oct.–Dec.) the Italians suffered a crushing disaster in the Caporetto campaign, which gave northeastern Italy above Venice to the enemy. The Allies were reduced to defensive tactics, and the winter of 1917–18 saw a lull in military operations on the Western Front. At the outset of 1918, the balance of strength on land appeared to lie with the Germans. U.S. participation gave the Allies fresh resources of manpower, finances, raw materials, and munitions, and offset depressed morale.

U.S. MILITARY CONTRIBUTION. When war was declared, there were about 200,000 men in the army. During the war this number was expanded to 4 million. A total of 4,791,172 men served in the armed forces of the U.S. during World War I; of these, about 2,800,000 were inducted through Selective Service; 32 camps and cantonments, with facilities for 1,800,000 men, were built to carry out the training program. The number of American soldiers who went to France was 2,084,000. By May 1918, the U.S. had 500,000 men in France, and the peak of overseas movement was reached in July 1918, when 313,410 troops arrived in France. In all, 42 infantry divisions were sent to France (each division consisting of about 1,000 officers and 27,000 men). Of these, 29 took part in active combat (7 regular army, 11 national guard, and 11 national army), bringing to 1,390,000 the

number of men who saw active combat service.

AMERICAN EXPEDITIONARY FORCE (A.E.F.) was commanded by Gen. **John J. Pershing** (p. 1127). From June 1917 until 11 Nov. 1918, more than 4,400,000 tons of cargo were shipped directly to France for the A.E.F. Adm. **William S. Sims** (1858–1936) commanded the U.S. naval forces abroad. The navy, which had a wartime strength of about 50,000, convoyed troop transports, chased submarines, and aided the British fleet in keeping German craft out of the North Sea.

When General Pershing arrived at Paris (14 June) as commander of the U.S. overseas forces, his army was nonexistent (the first U.S. troops, units of the 1st Division, did not arrive in France until 26 June). Pershing's orders for cooperation with the Allied forces in operations against the enemy specified that the U.S. forces "are a distinct and separate component of the combined forces, the identity of which must be preserved." Against Allied opposition, Pershing vigorously maintained his demand for an integral U.S. army and a U.S. sector on the Western Front. He received the full support of Wilson to use his forces according to his own judgment. In July Pershing won Allied consent for concentrating the U.S. forces in eastern France, in the area east of Verdun known as the Toul sector. General orders issued on 5 July created the general staff of the A.E.F. On 1 Sept. Pershing established his general headquarters at Chaumont.

The first U.S. troops to go to the front were units of the 1st Division. They moved (21 Oct.) into the Toul sector, relieving French units holding the line. Pershing did not participate in the conversations (Nov.) that resulted in the creation (27 Nov.) of the Supreme War Council, on which civilian and military leaders served. This group, an inadequate attempt to unify the Allied military command, left the conduct and control of each army to its respective government. The Supreme War Council decided that it would be inadvisable to undertake an offensive until a sufficient number of U.S. troops arrived in France.

2 Nov. LANSING-ISHII AGREEMENT. Japan joined (23 Aug. 1914) the Allies in the war against Germany and then attempted to expand her power in China and the North Pacific. Her policy of aggression was evident in the **21 Demands** on China (18 Jan. 1915). In revised form, these were embodied in a Sino-Japanese treaty (25 May 1915) by which Japan secured reluctant Chinese recognition of her position in South Manchuria and Shantung. This contributed to a renewal of U.S.-Japanese rivalry in the Far East and resulted in a U.S. note (11 May 1915) registering disapproval of the Japanese move and declaring that the U.S. would refuse to recognize any agreement impairing the political or territorial integrity of China, the Open Door policy, or the treaty rights of the U.S. in China.

The American position remained for some time the only foreign obstacle to Japan's realization of her objectives in China. To safeguard her territorial and economic ambitions, Japan took advantage of the submarine crisis and signed (1916–17) a number of secret treaties with the Allied powers designed to guarantee her succession to German rights in Shantung and the Northern Pacific islands. Her efforts to commit the U.S. to recognition of Japanese "paramount interests" in China resulted in the Lansing-Ishii Agreement.

Viscount Kikujiro Ishii was sent on a mission to Washington. Out of his discussions (6 Sept.–2 Nov.) with Secretary Lansing came an agreement by which the U.S. recognized that "territorial propinquity creates special relations between countries, and consequently, the Government of the United States recognizes that Japan has special interests in China, particularly in the part to which her possessions are contiguous." Japan affirmed respect for the Open Door policy and the independence and territorial integrity of China.

Lansing viewed the agreement as a stopgap measure designed to prevent full recognition of Japan's position in China. But the terms of the agreement were ambiguous. According to the U.S. interpretation, Japan was conceded only an economic hold on China. The Japanese, on the other hand, construed the agreement as a political concession. When translated into Chinese the world "special" appeared as "paramount." Yet the agreement left the U.S. at the end of World War I as the only important nation holding reservations of this kind.

1918

8 Jan. 14 POINTS. The year 1917 was marked in Europe by a growing demand for a statement of war aims and a negotiated peace. In May the Kerensky government took office in Russia with a pledge to promote a peace based on the self-determination of peoples and without annexation or indemnities. Pope Benedict XV circularized (1 Aug.) the leaders of the belligerent powers, suggesting the following as a basis for a just and durable peace: renunciation of indemnities; disarmament; the substitution of arbitration for war; the evacuation of Belgium, and a guarantee for its complete independence; the evacuation of occupied territories; freedom of the seas; and the examination of territorial claims in a "spirit of equity and justice." The U.S. reply (27 Aug.) expressed the desire for a just peace but asserted that the word of the German government could not be accepted as a guarantee.

When, following the November Revolution in Russia, the Bolsheviks published the secret treaties concluded by the Allies and condemned these arrangements as evidence of imperialist designs, the need for a statement of Allied war aims became exigent. When an Interallied Conference at Paris (29 Nov.–3 Dec. 1917) was unable to agree upon such a statement, Col. House urged Wilson to issue a formulation. Lloyd George, in a speech (5 Jan.) before British labor representatives, announced his nation's war aims.

Addressing Congress (8 Jan.), Wilson set forth 14 points "as the only possible program" for peace from the U.S. standpoint. The address was based upon consultations with Col. House and a report furnished by a group of academicians and publicists called The Inquiry. **The 14 Points** were as follows: (1) open covenants of peace openly arrived at; (2) absolute freedom of navigation of the seas alike in peace and war, except as the seas might be closed by international action for the enforcement of international covenants; (3) removal, so far as possible, of all economic barriers and the establishment of equality of trade; (4) adequate guarantees that national armaments would be reduced to the lowest point consistent with domestic safety; (5) an absolutely impartial adjustment of all colonial claims, based on the principle that the interests of the population must have equal weight with the equitable claims of the government; (6) evacuation of all Russian territory and the independent determination by Russia of her own political development and national policy; (7) evacuation and restoration of Belgium; (8) evacuation and restoration of all French territory and return to France of Alsace-Lorraine; (9) readjustment of the Italian frontiers along clearly recognizable lines of nationality; (10) opportunity of autonomous development for the peoples of Austria-Hungary; (11) evacuation of Rumania, Serbia, and Montenegro, restoration of occupied territories, and free access to the sea for Serbia; (12) the Turkish portions of the Ottoman Empire to be assured a secure sovereignty, but the other nationalities under Turkish rule to be given free opportunity of autonomous development, and the Dardanelles to be permanently opened as a free passage to the ships of all nations under international guarantees; (13) establishment of an independent Poland, to include territories having an indisputably Polish population, with free and secure access to the sea; and (14) a general association of nations to be formed under specific covenants for the purpose of affording mutual guarantees of political independence and territorial integrity to great and small states alike.

21 Mar. GERMAN SPRING OFFENSIVE. The growing effectiveness of the British blockade and the lessening force of the U-boat campaign led the German military leaders to undertake a series of great offensives on the Western Front in the hope of decisively crushing the Allies before U.S. troops could arrive in force. The Germans enjoyed superiority of numbers in the West. The German assault, under the command of Gen. Ludendorff, was launched (21 Mar.) along a 50-mile front on the Somme battlefield, with the immediate objective of splitting the French and British armies at their junction point and breaking through to the vital rail center of Amiens and, ultimately, to the Channel ports. By 6 Apr. the Germans had smashed the lines of the British 5th Army and had penetrated the Allied lines to a depth of about 35 miles, advancing beyond Noyon and Montdidier and coming within 12 miles of Amiens with its vast stores of British supplies. In this action (also known as the Picardy offensive), approximately 2,200 U.S. troops served with the British and French.

The critical situation led the Allied statesmen and military leaders to confer (26 Mar.) at Doullens-en-Picardie, where Gen. **Ferdinand Foch** was assigned the task of coordinating the Allied armies on the Western Front. Wilson gave his approval (29 Mar.) to the Doullens agreement and on 14 Apr. Foch was formally appointed supreme commander for the Western Front. Although Gen. Pershing never yielded his intention of having a separate U.S. army with its own front, American units, at his decision (28 Mar.), were placed at the disposal of Foch and thrown into action wherever needed during the enemy spring offensive. However, the Beauvais agreement (3 Apr.) concluded by an Interallied Conference contained a reference to a separate U.S. army, which was endorsed at the conference (1 May) of the Supreme War Council at Abbeville.

9–29 Apr. The attack upon Amiens had been only partly checked when the Germans struck again to the north in the Armentières sector and advanced for 17 miles up the Lys Valley; but the enemy was unable to exploit the wide gap in the British lines. About 500 Americans, serving with the British, participated in the Lys defensive.

27 May–5 June. The next German drive was directed against the French front along the Chemin des Dames north of the Aisne. In this, the third battle of the Aisne, the line from Rheims to a little east of Noyon was forced back. Soissons fell (29 May), and the Germans reached the Marne (31 May) on a 40-mile front about 50 miles from Paris. At this critical moment the U.S. 2d Division and elements of the 3rd and 28th Divisions were thrown into the line. By blocking (3–4 June) the German advance at

Château-Thierry, the Americans helped the French to stem the enemy drive.

6 June–1 July. BELLEAU WOOD. The first sizable U.S. action of the war was fought when the 2d Division recaptured **Vaux, Bouresches,** and **Belleau Wood,** with the 4th U.S. Marine Brigade attached to the 2d Division playing a notable role. About 27,500 Americans were engaged in the third battle of the Aisne.

9–15 June. The 3 enemy offensives established 2 salients threatening Paris, and the Germans now sought to convert them into one by a fourth massive blow delivered on a 27-mile front between Montdidier and Noyon. Even before the drive began the U.S. 1st Division demonstrated the fighting qualities of American troops by capturing (28 May) and holding the town of **Cantigny.** This first U.S. success reinforced the decision to permit Pershing to establish a separate army. In the Noyon-Montdidier offensive the French and Americans resisted firmly and the attack was halted after an initial German advance of about 6 miles. Throughout this operation the extreme left line of the salient was defended by the U.S. 1st Division. About 27,500 U.S. troops participated.

18 July–6 Aug. TURNING POINT: 2D BATTLE OF THE MARNE. On 15 July the Germans attacked simultaneously on both sides of Reims, the eastern point of the Aisne salient. To the east of Reims the Germans made slight gains; to the west they crossed the Marne, but made little progress. Stabilization of the Marne salient brought to an end the great German offensive. In this action some 85,000 American troops were engaged.

18 July–6 Aug. AISNE-MARNE OFFENSIVE. During the months of May and June more than 500,000 men were embarked from the U.S. for France, and in July the millionth American sol-

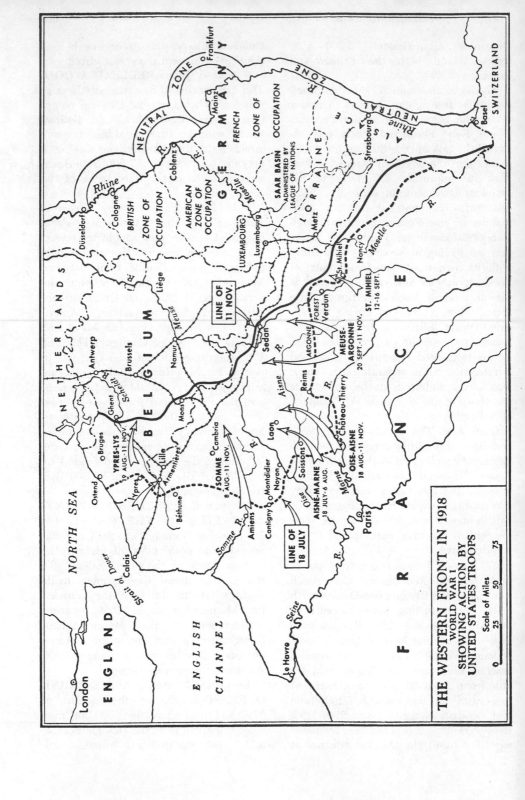

THE WESTERN FRONT IN 1918
WORLD WAR I
SHOWING ACTION BY
UNITED STATES TROOPS

Scale of Miles
0   25   50   75

dier arrived in France. The initiative passed from Ludendorff to Foch, who on 18 July launched his first counter-offensive, choosing as his point of attack the west flank of the German pocket from the Aisne to the Marne. About 270,000 U.S. troops, together with selected French units, were engaged in the Aisne-Marne offensive. When the operation was completed (6 Aug.), bringing to an end the 2d Battle of the Marne, the salient had been eliminated and the Allied line ran from Soissons to Rheims along the Vesle.

8 Aug. SOMME OFFENSIVE. The British, under Gen. Haig, struck at the Somme salient, initiating an offensive which, with intermittent lulls, lasted until 11 Nov. About 54,000 U.S. troops participated.

10 Aug. 1ST U.S. ARMY was organized, with Foch's consent, under the command of Gen. Pershing, who remained commander of the A.E.F.

18 Aug. OISE-AISNE OFFENSIVE was begun under Gen. Mangin, at the head of the French 10th Army. Starting from the Soissons-Rheims line, the French advanced by successive stages to the Aisne, to Laon, and on 11 Nov. were approaching the Belgian frontier. About 85,000 U.S. troops participated in the first stages of this advance, but by 15 Sept. all of these were withdrawn for the impending U.S. Meuse-Argonne offensive.

19 Aug. YPRES-LYS OFFENSIVE, launched by the British, lasted until 11 Nov. About 108,000 U.S. troops participated.

24 Oct.–4 Nov. BATTLE OF VITTORIO-VENETO on the Italian front ended in the rout of the Austrian army. About 1,200 U.S. troops participated.

12–16 Sept. ST. MIHIEL SALIENT. The first distinctively U.S. offensive was the reduction of the St. Mihiel salient, carried through largely by U.S. troops and wholly under the command of Gen. Pershing. The Americans were aided by French colonial troops and by British and French air squadrons. St. Mihiel, on the right bank of the Meuse, was at the tip of a salient below Verdun (in French hands) to the northwest and Metz (in German hands) to the northeast. Within 24 hours after the offensive began, the salient had been cut off, and the completion of the operation removed a German threat of long standing. About 550,000 American troops were engaged at St. Mihiel; U.S. casualties: about 7,000. The Americans captured 16,000 prisoners and 443 guns. The operation demonstrated the ability of U.S. commanders and troops to plan and execute a major military undertaking.

26 Sept.–11 Nov. MEUSE-ARGONNE OFFENSIVE. After the St. Mihiel victory, U.S. troops were removed from the line and largely concentrated along a sector between the Meuse River and the Argonne Forest. Every available American division was employed. The goal of the American attack was the Sedan-Mézières railroad, main line of supply for the German forces on the major segment of the Western Front. Cutting this line would force a general retirement that would include German evacuation of the Briey and Longwy iron fields, which the enemy had been using to supplement its iron supply. The U.S. offensive, part of a larger advance planned by Foch to compel a general withdrawal by the Germans, involved 1,200,000 U.S. troops. Its first and middle stages comprised a battle of attrition. The final phase of the offensive began 1 Nov. Within a week, the Americans were in hot pursuit of the enemy east of the Meuse, while toward the north they reached the outskirts of Sedan and cut the Sedan-Mézières railroad, making the German line untenable. The armistice (11 Nov.) brought the offensive to a halt. The operation cost 120,000 U.S. casualties and resulted in the capture of 16,000 prisoners and 468 guns.

29 Sept.–8 Nov. GERMAN PEACE MOVE. The rapid deterioration of the military position of the Central Powers during the summer of 1918 impelled Gen. Ludendorff, who foresaw imminent collapse, to press his government (29 Sept.) for an armistice. The situation became more critical with the surrender (30 Sept.) of Bulgaria. A new German regime headed by Prince Max of Baden took office on 2 Oct. and through Swiss auspices requested Wilson (6 Oct.) for an armistice preliminary to a conference which would use the 14 Points as a basis of peace. Austria made a similar request 7 Oct. Wilson spent about a month in negotiations. **Reasons for delay:** (1) Reluctance of the Allies to accept Wilson's war aims. The British pointed out that approval of the proposed armistice carried tacit acceptance of the 14 Points, and both the British and the French denied they had ever been asked to accept the 14 Points. However, a threat that the U.S. would take separate action finally compelled the Allies to accept (5 Nov.) the 14 Points as a basis for an armistice, but with 2 vital reservations. The Allies insisted upon reserving to themselves the unqualified right to discuss freedom of the seas in the peace conference, and they demanded that German restoration of evacuated territory include reparation for war damages to the civilian population. Wilson accepted these conditions and transmitted them to the German government (5 Nov.); thereafter responsibility for the truce was left to Gen. Foch. (2) Wilson's refusal to deal with a German government unless he was satisfied that it represented the German people. Following a mutiny in the German fleet that began at Kiel (3 Nov.), a revolution broke out (7 Nov.) in Bavaria. Austria had already

surrendered (4 Nov.). Kaiser Wilhelm II abdicated and fled from Germany (9 Nov.), and a German republic was proclaimed. Meanwhile, a German armistice commission met with General Foch in the Forest of Compiègne (8 Nov.).

11 Nov. ARMISTICE. Signing (5 A.M.) of the armistice brought the cessation of hostilities at 11 A.M.

The armistice terms were as follows: (1) German evacuation of occupied territory; (2) evacuation of the left bank of the Rhine and of the bridgeheads of Mainz, Cologne, and Coblenz; (3) reservation to the Allies and the U.S. of full right to make claim for damages; (4) surrender of submarines and internment of the German fleet; (5) abrogation of the treaties of Bucharest and Brest-Litovsk; (6) destruction of German aircraft, tanks, and heavy artillery; (7) maintenance of the Allied blockade until conclusion of the peace; (8) return of prisoners of war and deported civilians; and (9) 150,000 railway cars, 5,000 locomotives, and 5,000 trucks to be turned over to the Allies.

U.S. WAR COST. Total deaths for the U.S. armed forces (including army, navy, and marines) were 112,432—more than half caused by disease (chiefly the influenza-pneumonia pandemic that swept U.S. military camps). The battle casualties of the A.E.F. were 48,909 dead, 230,074 wounded. The total direct war expenditures (Apr. 1917–Apr. 1919), $21,850 million. (For loans to Allies, see pp. 379, 380, 383, 384.)

25 Oct. WILSON'S APPEAL TO THE ELECTORATE. Anxious that the position of the U.S. should not be weakened at the approaching peace conference, President Wilson decided to make the congressional elections a test of confidence in his policies. He issued an appeal to the voters to return a Democratic majority to both houses of Congress. The appeal evoked widespread disapproval, the Republicans condemning it as a violation of Wilson's declared wartime truce on politics. The election (5 Nov.) resulted in the Democratic loss of the House by 50 seats and of the Senate by 2 seats.

REPUBLICAN OPPOSITION. Wilson's announcement (18 Nov.) that he would attend the peace conference provoked a storm of Republican criticism, as did the announcement that in addition to Wilson the U.S. peace commission would consist of **Col. House, Secretary Lansing, Gen. Tasker Bliss,** and **Henry White.** No member of the Senate was included, and the only Republican member was White. Wilson sailed for Europe 4 Dec. on the *George Washington.*

1918–20. U.S.–ALLIED INTERVENTION IN RUSSIA. Complicating the Allied problems of war and peacemaking was the abdication of Czar Nicholas II (12 Mar. 1917), the overthrow of the successor Provisional Government under Alexander Kerensky by the October Revolution (which began 7 Nov., or 25 Oct. by the old calendar), which led to Bolshevik control under **Vladimir Ilich Ulyanov,** known as **Nikolai Lenin** (1870–1924). The Bolsheviks signed a separate peace with Germany at Brest-Litovsk (3 Mar. 1918). In the winter of 1917–18 counter-revolutionary White armies began to form in peripheral areas of the former Russian empire. Fourteen Allied nations, including the U.S., originally sent forces to secure Allied war stores and to protect northern ports from possible German attack but later assisted anti-Bolshevik resistance groups. U.S. troops dispatched to areas in northern Russia near Archangel (2 Aug.) and Murmansk and to eastern Siberia (Vladivostok, 16 Aug.) were withdrawn from the former region in June 1919 and from Siberia 1 Apr. 1920 (while Japanese forces remained until Oct. 1922). Although Wilson refused to recognize the Soviet government, he induced the Allies to abandon their interventionist attempt. The Paris peace conference never dealt adequately with the problems posed by the Russian Revolution and the temporary vacuum of power in East Asia.

AMERICA BETWEEN TWO WORLD WARS, 1919-39

The twelve years following the close of World War I proved an age of isolation, as well as one of disillusionment and normalcy. It was marked by withdrawal from the responsibilities of world order, from America's commitments in the Pacific, and from political experimentation and reform at home. Emerging from World War I as the leading world power, the United States proceeded to dissipate that power. It withdrew from participation in the postwar settlement, refusing to join not only the League of Nations but the World Court as well. The era of negativism was followed by one of positive and dynamic leadership under the presidency of Franklin Delano Roosevelt. Before the recovery to which the New Deal was dedicated had been achieved, the shadow of totalitarianism fell across the land and lengthened with every passing day. Although an instinctive isolationist like Wilson, F.D.R. came to recognize that isolation was no longer a meaningful concept, but that the posture of the totalitarian forces threatened the free world and America's security. Reluctantly, during his second administration, Roosevelt began to shift gears, to move from a posture of neutrality, which had functioned with deplorable partiality, to some kind of intervention both in Europe and in Asia.

If the Republican ascendancy of the 1920s had been pervasively negative, that of the New Deal was overwhelmingly positive. "This nation asks for action, and action now," F.D.R. declared in his first inaugural address, and, beginning with 4 March 1933, action came thick and fast. "The Roosevelt Revolution" contained far less novelty than improvisation, as its program borrowed heavily from Populist-Progressive tenets, but the speed of improvisation was geared to the necessities of economic crisis and unprecedented unemployment. In fact, the six years from 1933 through 1938 marked a greater upheaval in American institutions than any similar period in the nation's history, save perhaps for the impact of the Civil War on the South. If the New Deal was not a new game, it was a necessitous reshuffle of the cards, too long stacked against labor, the farmer, the small businessman, the consumer, and the aged. It is a tribute to the staying power of New Deal reform that both parties in subsequent administrations have built upon without repudiating the fundamentals of the New Deal.

Foreign Relations

1919

18 JAN. BEGINNING OF THE PEACE NEGOTIATIONS at Paris. All major decisions were made by the "Big Four," Wilson, Georges Clemenceau (for France), David Lloyd George (for Great Britain), and Vittorio Orlando (for Italy). Wilson's idealism was quickly challenged. France and Britain were determined to punish Germany. France wanted territorial concessions and reparations, as well as permanent military security against Germany. In addition, many of the provisions of the so-called **"Secret Treaties"** entered into by the Allies and known in broad outline to American leaders shortly after America's entry into the war ran counter to Wilsonian principles.

25 JAN.–14 FEB. DRAFT COVENANT OF THE LEAGUE OF NATIONS. Wilson insisted that the League must be central to the peace negotiations, a position which the other Allies accepted only after exacting serious concessions. On 25 Jan. the second plenary session voted to include the League in the peace settlement. Beginning on 3 Feb., a commission, presided over by Wilson, worked out a draft covenant submitted to the plenary session on 14 Feb., based upon the work of **David Hunter Miller** and **Lord Robert Cecil.** Wilson then returned to the U.S. on the *George Washington,* arriving at Boston on 24 Feb. Opposition was already mounting in the U.S. At a dinner meeting between Wilson and members of the Senate and House committees on foreign relations (26 Feb.) the president was grilled by his Republican critics. On 2 Mar., 37 Republican senators and 2 senators-elect signed a senatorial **Round Robin,** proposed by **Henry Cabot Lodge** (p. 1088) and **Frank B. Brandegee** (Conn.), and drafted by **Philander C. Knox,** which rejected the League in its existing form and opposed further consideration until after the final peace settlement; read in the Senate 2 days later. On 4 Mar. Wilson defiantly predicted in an address in New York that it would not be possible to "dissect the covenant from the treaty without destroying the whole vital structure."

MAR.–APR. WILSON'S RETURN TO EUROPE. French Demands. The president arrived at Brest on 13 Mar. The next day he was presented in Paris with a bill of particulars by Marshal Foch including (1) heavy but undefined reparations for German destruction of French property; (2) either an Allied occupation of Germany to the Rhine or the creation of a Rhineland buffer state. A bitter battle followed, in the midst of which Wilson became ill (3 Apr.). On 7 Apr. the president was reported to have ordered the *George Washington* to Europe, presumably to take him home unless a compromise could be worked out. The French yielded to Wilson's threat and agreed to a series of compromises. In return for a terminable occupation of German territory Wilson agreed to a treaty binding Britain and the U.S. to defend France against a future unprovoked German attack. This treaty was pigeonholed by the U.S. Senate.

Italian Demands. The Italians insisted on territorial commitments of the Treaty of London (26 Apr. 1915), by which Italy was promised a strategic boundary running to the Brenner Pass, including some 200,000 Germans, as well as territory on the head and eastern shore of the Adriatic. In addition, Italy now demanded the port of **Fiume.** Wilson agreed to the Brenner line before his own experts had clarified this violation of his own principle of self-determination, but on 19 Apr. he informed the American delegation that he would stand fast against Fiume. When Italy's peace delegates, **Vittorio Orlando** and **Sidney Sonnino,** continued to press their claims, Wilson appealed directly to the Italian people (23 Apr.) to desert their leaders in favor of a peace of justice. The Italians quit the conference at once, but returned on 6 May. They were unsuccessful in their demand for Fiume. That port did not pass under Italian control until 1924. Under the Italo-Jugoslav Treaty of Rapallo (1920) it had been nominally independent.

Japanese Demands. Japan insisted on recognition of her right to **Shantung,** which she had occupied during the war. Defeated, 11 Apr., in her effort to obtain the passage of a resolution on **race equality,** Japan on 15 Apr. refused to agree to have German rights in Shantung turned over to the Allied powers. She rested her claim on the Secret Treaties of 1917, on agreements with China of 25 May 1915 and 24 Sept. 1918, and on the **Lansing-Ishii** Agreement with the U.S. (see p. 367). On 28 Apr. Wilson surrendered to Japan, but exacted a promise that Shantung would be eventually returned to China, with Japan retaining only economic concessions in the province.

Compromises on the League Covenant. In response to proposals of such pro-League Republicans as William Howard Taft and A. Lawrence Lowell, Wilson proposed amendments to the Covenant to overcome opposition in the Senate. These included: (1) permission of the U.S. to refrain from participating in the mandate system established to administer the conquered colonies; (2) restraints upon League interference with such matters as tariffs and immigration; (3) granting permission to a state to withdraw from the League upon 2 years' notice; (4) excepting "regional understandings like the Monroe Doctrine" from the League's jurisdiction.

7 MAY–28 JUNE. TERMS OF THE VERSAILLES TREATY. The treaty was presented to the Germans on 7 May; they signed on 28 June. Wilson returned to the U.S. on 8 July, and presented the treaty to the Senate on 10 July. The final treaty (1) forced Germany to admit her **war guilt (Art. 231);** (2) stripped her of her **colonies, Alsace-Lorraine,** the **Saar Basin** (its final disposition to be determined by a plebiscite in 1935), **Posen,** and parts of **Schleswig** and **Silesia;** (3) exacted **reparations,** later fixed at $56 billion; (4) substantially **disarmed** her. Attached to the treaty was the **Covenant of the League of Nations,** which provided for: (1) an **Assembly** in which all member nations had an equal voice; (2) a **Council** made up of representatives from the U.S., Great Britain, France, Italy, Japan, and 4 other nations elected by the Assembly; (3) a **Secretariat,** permanently located at Geneva. Members pledged themselves to (1) respect and preserve against external aggression the territorial integrity and political independence of all member nations **(Art. X);** (2) submit to the League all disputes threatening war; (3) employ military and economic sanctions against nations resorting to war; (4) reduce armaments; and (5) cooperate in setting up a **Permanent Court of International Justice.**

10 JULY–19 Nov. SENATE OPPOSITION. The Senate divided on the League issue into 3 groups: (1) Democratic supporters of Wilson who favored immediate ratification, led by **Gilbert M. Hitchcock** (Neb., 1859–1934), who succeeded Thomas S. Martin as minority leader when the latter died during the course of the Senate debate on the issue; (2) moderates, headed by **Henry Cabot Lodge**, chairman of the Senate Committee on Foreign Relations, who favored participation in the League with reservations to protect American interests; and (3) "irreconcilables," including **Hiram W. Johnson** (Calif., 1866–1945), **William E. Borah** (p. 989), and **Robert La Follette** (p. 1079), who advocated complete rejection of the Covenant. On 19 Aug. Wilson at a luncheon conference with the Senate committee agreed to accept interpretative reservations not requiring consent of the other parties to the treaty nor embodied in the resolution of ratification. This failed to satisfy the irreconcilables, who now launched a nationwide propaganda campaign against ratification, financed by Andrew Mellon and Henry C. Frick. Since 6 of the 10 members of the Senate committee were irreconcilables, action was held up until 10 Sept., when the committee proposed 45 amendments and 4 reservations to protect traditional American policies. Wilson took the case to the people in a 9,500-mile tour of the West, commencing 4 Sept., in the course of which he delivered 37 speeches in 29 cities. On 10 Sept. Sens. Johnson and Borah began a tour in opposition to the League and the treaty. On 25 Sept. Wilson collapsed at **Pueblo**, Colo., and was rushed back to Washington, suffering a stroke on 2 Oct. which incapacitated him during this crucial period. (Invalided for more than 7 months, Wilson was cut off from developments outside his sickroom except for information communicated to him by his second wife, Mrs. Edith Bolling Galt Wilson, and the White House physician, Dr. Cary Crayson. He never fully regained his health.) A combination of Democrats and moderate Republicans voted down the reservations. On 6 Nov. Lodge reported a resolution of ratification accompanied by 14 reservations, which, while circumscribing somewhat American obligations under the Covenant, did not seriously impair the League. On 18 Nov. Wilson, in a letter to his supporters, expressed the view that the Lodge resolution "does not provide for ratification but, rather, for the nullification of the treaty," and urged its defeat. As a result, a combination of Wilson Democrats and irreconcilable Republicans defeated the resolution on 19 Nov. Had the Democrats voted for the Lodge resolution the League and the Treaty would have been carried, 81–13. Unconditional acceptance was defeated, by 38–53.

1920

JAN.–MAY. **SENATE AND THE TREATY.** A bipartisan approach to ratification was wrecked in January when Lodge yielded to threats by the irreconcilables and refused to modify his original reservations. On 9 Feb. the Senate voted to reconsider the treaty and referred it back to the committee, which reported it the following day with the reservations intact. Wilson remained adamant. In a message to the Jackson Day Dinner (8 Jan.) he insisted that the treaty must not be rewritten by the Senate, and again on 8 March reiterated his opposition to the Lodge reservations. On 19 March, 21 Democrats deserted Wilson to join the Republican reservationists in a vote on the Lodge resolution, which was again defeated, 49–35. When, on 20 May, Congress declared the war at an end by joint resolution, Wilson vetoed the action. Finally, on 2 July 1921, Congress, by a joint resolution, terminated war with Germany and Austria-Hungary, reserving for the U.S. any rights secured by the armistice, the Versailles Treaty, or as a result of the war. Separate treaties concluding peace with Germany, Austria, and Hungary were ratified 18 Oct.

JUNE–Nov. "SOLEMN REFEREN-DUM." Wilson urged the Democratic Convention which met in San Francisco on 28 June to endorse his views on the League. The party platform pledged unequivocal ratification of the Treaty of Versailles with only such reservations as should be found necessary under the U.S. Constitution. The party nominee, **James M. Cox,** publicly promised that as soon as possible after 4 Mar. 1921 the U.S. would enter the League. The Republicans were divided on the issue, Root, Taft, and Hughes, on the one hand, supporting the League, the irreconcilables opposing it. Hence, the Republican platform straddled the issue. It criticized the Covenant, but favored the formation of "an international association" to prevent war. Its candidate, **Warren G. Harding,** had no deep convictions either way. But when once in office, he promptly abandoned any attempt to bring the U.S. into the League, and retreated into what Wilson stigmatized as "sullen and selfish isolation." In his inaugural address Harding declared: "We seek no part in directing the destinies of the world." Again, in a special message to Congress on 2 Feb. 1923, he stated that the League "is not for us. Nothing could be more decisively stamped with finality."

1921

20 Apr. A settlement reached between the U.S. and Colombia regarding the Panama episode (p. 348) when the Senate advised ratification of a treaty authorizing payment to Colombia of $25 million and the granting of special land transportation privileges.

1921–22

12 Nov.–6 Feb. 1922. WASHINGTON ARMAMENT CONFERENCE. On 14 Dec. 1920 Sen. Borah introduced a resolution requesting the president to call an international conference for the reduction of naval armaments. The resolution was appended to the Naval Appropriations Bill for 1921. In accordance therewith President Harding (11 Aug.) invited the principal powers, except Russia, to a conference to consider not only naval disarmament, but questions concerning the Pacific and the Far East. The American delegation included Secretary of State **Charles Evans Hughes,** Elihu Root, Henry Cabot Lodge, and Oscar Underwood. Hughes, who was designated chairman of the conference, proposed at the first session (12 Nov.) not only a limitation upon future naval building but also a substantial scrapping of ships already built or in construction. The U.S. offered to scrap ships amounting to 845,000 tons; Great Britain was asked to scrap 583,000 tons; Japan, 480,000 tons. This program was immediately accepted in principle. It was further agreed to fix the tonnage of capital ships (over 10,000-tons displacement or having guns larger than 8-in. cal.) at a ratio of 5 (U.S.)–5 (Britain)–3 (Japan)–1.67 (France)–1.67 (Italy). France agreed to her ratio under pressure, but would not permit any limitation on cruisers, destroyers, or submarines, nor have land armaments placed on the agenda. As a result of the conference **9 treaties** were drafted and signed: (1) a **naval armaments** treaty between the 5 powers (U.S., Great Britain, Japan, France, and Italy) providing for a 10-year naval holiday during which no new capital ships were to be built, and establishing a ratio of capital ships (6 Feb. 1922); (2) a 5-power treaty between the same nations restricting the use of submarines in war by the accepted rules of naval warfare and outlawing asphyxiating gases; (3) a 4-power treaty (13 Dec.) between the U.S., Britain, France, and Japan, by which the signatories agreed to respect each other's rights over Pacific island possessions; (4) a 4-power treaty providing for consultation in the event of "aggressive action" in the Pacific (carrying with it the abrogation of the existing Anglo-Japanese alliance); (5) a 9-power treaty (6 Feb.) signed by all the states at the conference guaranteeing China's independence and territorial integrity, and reiterating the "Open Door" principle; (6) a similar treaty granting China greater control over her customs; (7) a treaty between Japan and China providing for the restoration of Kiachow and the Shantung peninsula to China (4 Feb.); (8) a treaty between Japan and the U.S. confirming American cable rights on the island of Yap; and (9) a 6-power treaty between the U.S., Britain, Japan, France, Italy, and China allocating the former German cable lines in the Pacific. The U.S. Senate ratified all the treaties, the 4-power treaty passing by the narrow margin of 4 votes, and with a reservation stating that "there is no commitment to armed force, no alliance, no obligation to join in any defense."

U.S. AND INTERALLIED WAR DEBTS. In addition to the war loans to the Allied governments, the U.S. also made loans after the armistice for relief purposes or as advances for the payment of surplus American war materials left in Europe at the close of the war:

To Allies	Total Indebtedness
Great Britain	$4,277,000,000.00
France	3,404,818,945.01
Italy	1,648,034,050.90
Belgium	379,087,200.43
Russia	192,601,297.37
Rumania	37,911,153.92
Greece	27,167,000.00
Cuba	10,000,000.00
Nicaragua	431,849.14
Liberia	26,000.00

To Countries Formed out of Allied Territory	
Estonia	13,999,145.60
Finland	8,281,926.17
Latvia	5,132,287.14
Lithuania	4,981,628.03

To Countries or Areas Formed Partially or Wholly Out of Enemy Territory	
Poland	159,666,972.39
Czechoslovakia	91,879,671.03
Yugoslavia	51,758,486.55
Austria	24,055,708.92
Armenia	11,959,917.49
Hungary	1,685,835.61

Total $10,350,479,074.70

As early as Dec. 1918 the British proposed to Wilson that they would agree to cancel debts due them from their Allies, virtually uncollectible claims approximating $10 billion, in return for the cancellation of British debts to the U.S. of about $4 billion. Wilson refused, insisting that the interallied debts were unrelated to German reparations. France also argued strongly for debt cancellation. To deal with this issue the World War Foreign Debt Commission, authorized by Act of Congress, 9 Feb. 1922, was set up to negotiate specific agreements. Based on their capacity to pay, the debtor nations accepted obligations of over $11.5 billion, payable over a 62-year period at an average interest rate of 2.135%. Under these agreements principal and interest totaled in excess of $22 billion. On 1 Aug. Great Britain (**Balfour Note**) agreed to remit, "as part of a satisfactory international settlement," both debts and reparations due herself, and in no case to ask more from her debtors than was necessary to pay her creditors. The U.S. remained adamant. President Coolidge continued the Harding policy. ("They hired the money, didn't they?") Finally, owing to the increasingly serious European financial situation, drastic reductions in principal were agreed to by the U.S. On 14 Nov. 1925 Italy's interest rate was reduced to .4% and 80.2% of the debt was canceled;

in Apr. 1926, the French interest rate was reduced to 1.6%, and 60.3% of the debt was canceled. Despite these concessions, the insistence by the U.S. on partial debt payments promoted anti-U.S. feeling in Europe, isolationism in America.

1922–23

1922, 4 DEC.–7 FEB. 1923. 2D CENTRAL AMERICAN CONFERENCE convened at Washington to settle issues between Nicaragua and Honduras. The U.S. and all Central American republics participated. The conference drew up a treaty of neutrality and provided for the establishment of a Central American court of justice and limitation of armaments.

1924

24 MAY. FOREIGN SERVICE ACT (Rogers Act) reorganized and consolidated the diplomatic and consular services and provided for initial appointment after examination, a period of probation, and promotion on merit.

15 DEC. 1923–9 APR. 1924. GERMAN REPARATIONS: THE DAWES PLAN. On 27 Apr. 1921 the Allied Reparations Commission set up under the Treaty of Versailles submitted a report fixing Germany's obligations at 132,000,000,000 gold marks. On 31 May 1922 the commission, to check the further collapse of the mark, granted Germany a moratorium for the remainder of the year despite protests from France. On 26 Dec. and, again, on 9 Jan. 1923, Germany was declared in default. Two days later French and Belgian troops began the occupation of the Ruhr. By 26 Sept., as a result of Germany's passive resistance, the mark had become worthless; the franc had depreciated 25%. On 15 Dec. 1923 President Coolidge announced that

Charles G. Dawes (1865–1951), Henry M. Robinson, and Owen D. Young would serve as experts on a commission to investigate German finances. The Dawes Plan, reported on 9 Apr. 1924, proposed (1) to stabilize German currency by reorganizing the Reichsbank under Allied supervision; (2) a schedule of payments for reparations, graduated from 1 billion gold marks in the first year (1924–25) to 2½ billion in the fifth year (1928–29). This plan was accepted by the Germans on 16 Apr. and adopted at a London conference (16 July–16 Aug.). Of a foreign loan totaling 800,000,000 gold marks to be advanced Germany under the plan, $110,000,000 was taken up in the U.S. To carry out the plan the Allied powers selected an American, S. Parker Gilbert (1892–1938), as Agent General of Reparations. At an Interallied Financial Conference at Paris (7–14 Jan. 1925) it was agreed that the U.S. should receive 2¼% of the annual payments made by Germany under the plan to satisfy American claims—$255,000,000 for American Army of Occupation costs, $350,000,000 for war damages.

U.S. AND THE LEAGUE. Although both Presidents Coolidge and Harding had favored entry into the League in 1920, neither took active measures to ratify the Covenant. On 11 Nov. 1929 Hoover declared that "public opinion will suffice to check violence" (similarly, on 14 Apr. 1930). Nevertheless, this period was marked by increasing U.S. participation in League affairs. On 17 Nov. 1924 U.S. delegates were represented at the International Opium Conference of the League, withdrawing on 6 Feb. 1925 when the U.S. proposal was not accepted. The U.S. participated in conferences on communication and transit (1926), in 3 conferences on the abolition of import and export prohibitions (1927), and in a conference on double taxation and fiscal evasion (1928). By 1931 212 persons had been officially appointed to represent the U.S. in more than 40 League conferences (Ellery C. Stowell), and the U.S. government maintained 5 permanent officials stationed at Geneva to represent American interests at the League (D. F. Fleming).

END OF DOMINICAN OCCUPATION. President Wilson directed (Dec. 1920) that preparations be made for ending military government in the Dominican Republic. An agreement on evacuation procedure was worked out by the State Department with a group of Dominican political leaders (30 June 1922). The military government delegated to a provisional president sufficient authority to permit the holding of elections. In July 1924 Gen. Horacio Vásquez was inaugurated as constitutional president and the U.S. marines withdrawn. A new treaty (27 Feb.) between the U.S. and the Dominican Republic superseded that of 1907.

1926

27 JAN.–JAN. 1935. U.S. AND THE WORLD COURT. The League Covenant provided for the establishment of a permanent Court of International Justice to consist of 15 members, to be elected by the Council and Assembly from a list of persons nominated by the Hague Court of Arbitration. The court was given jurisdiction over all international disputes submitted to it by states subscribing to the protocol, which was approved by the Council and Assembly in Dec. 1920. The U.S. had instructed its delegates to the 1st Hague Conference, 1899, and the 2d, 1907, to set up a permanent court of arbitration. On 17 Feb. 1923 Secretary of State Hughes wrote Harding urging U.S. membership in the World Court with the distinct under-

standing that such action would not involve any legal relation to the League. President Coolidge in 3 successive annual messages favored Senate action. On 3 Mar. 1925 the House supported a resolution of adherence by a vote of 303–28. Finally, on 27 Jan. 1926, the Senate approved adherence by 76–17, but attached reservations to safeguard U.S. interests. All were acceptable to members of the World Court except a reservation relating to advisory opinions. Since no agreement could be reached on this point, the U.S. did not join. In 1928 Hughes was chosen by the Council and Assembly to fill the vacancy in the World Court caused by the resignation of another American, **John Bassett Moore** (1860–1947). In Feb. 1929 Elihu Root sailed for Europe to join a commission to revise the statute of the court. His formula provided that the court shall not, without the consent of the U.S., render an advisory opinion touching any dispute to which the U.S. is a party, and reserved to the U.S. the right to withdraw from the court protocol if the interested parties insisted on an advisory opinion in the matter in which the U.S. claimed an interest. On 4 Mar. 1929 Hoover urged court membership in his inaugural address, and on 9 Dec. the U.S. chargé d'affaires in Switzerland, upon authorization of the president, signed the protocol of adherence with revisions agreed to both by the U.S. and the court members. Hoover submitted the protocol to the Senate on 10 Dec. 1930, but Sen. Borah blocked action. On 1 June the Senate Foreign Relations Committee finally came out for adherence. Involved in critical domestic affairs, President Roosevelt delayed risking debate on the issue until 16 Jan. 1935, when he urged ratification. Led by Huey P. Long (La.), the Senate rejected membership, 52–35. Although press opinion had favored the court, 3–1, the Hearst newspapers and the radio activities of Father Charles E. Coughlin kept the "irreconcilables" in line.

1927

20 JUNE–4 AUG. NAVAL DISARMAMENT: GENEVA CONFERENCE. On 10 Feb. President Coolidge called for a 5-power conference to be held at Geneva to consider limitations on the building of cruisers, destroyers, and submarines, not curbed at the Washington Conference. France and Italy refused to attend; Great Britain and the U.S. failed to agree on cruiser restrictions. The conference adjourned without accomplishment. In Feb. 1929 the U.S. authorized the construction of 15 cruisers of 10,000-ton displacement.

MAR.–27 AUG. 1928. OUTLAWRY OF WAR. As a result of conversations with Professor **James T. Shotwell** (1874–1965) of Columbia Univ. in Mar., French foreign minister **Aristide Briand** released 6 Apr. a proposal for the "outlawry of war" (a phrase attributed to Salmon O. Levinson). On 25 Apr. President **Nicholas Murray Butler** (p. 995) of Columbia Univ. revived the issue in a letter to *The New York Times*. On 11 June Secretary of State **Frank B. Kellogg** (1856–1937) made a formal acknowledgment. Briand submitted a draft treaty on 20 June. As a result of a conference with Sen. Borah, Kellogg substituted a **multinational** for a bilateral agreement in a note of 28 Dec. On 11 Jan. 1928 he published a draft treaty, which was brought to the attention of other powers on 13 Apr. On 27 Aug., 14 nations signed; eventually 62 nations signed. The sanctions of the **Kellogg-Briand Pact** rested on the moral force of world opinion.

31 JAN. 1917–26 DEC. 1927. MEXICAN-U.S. RELATIONS. The new Mexican Constitution of 1917 not only provided for radical political and social reforms but curbed foreign ownership of lands, mines, and oil fields. By a decree, 19 Feb. 1918, oil was declared an inalienable national resource, and titles to oil lands were to be converted into concessions. British and American companies promptly protested. Following the death of Carranza (21 May 1920) **Alvaro Obregón** was elected president (5 Sept.). He was recognized by the U.S., 31 Aug. 1923, upon an executive agreement (**Bucareli Agreement**) to respect subsoil rights acquired before 1917 and confirmed by some "positive act." After the election of **Plutarco Calles** in 1924, Secretary Kellogg warned Mexico (12 June) that the U.S. would continue its support "only so long" as Mexico "protects American lives and American rights." In retaliation the Mexican Congress passed 2 laws, to become effective 1 Jan. 1927, to implement the 1917 Constitution: the Petroleum Law, by which permanent foreign concessions were limited to 50 years and alien corporations required to waive their right of appeal to the home government (**Calvo Clause**); the Land Law, designed to break up the huge estates, restricted alien land ownership. A U.S. Senate resolution (27 Jan. 1927) unanimously recommended arbitration of the dispute with Mexico. In Sept. President Coolidge appointed **Dwight W. Morrow** (1873–1931) of J. P. Morgan & Co. as ambassador to Mexico. His conciliatory efforts quickly produced results. On 17 Nov. the Mexican Supreme Court declared the limitation on concessions under the Petroleum Law unconstitutional. On 25 Dec. the Mexican Congress granted unlimited confirmatory concessions to lands on which "positive" acts had been performed prior to 1 May 1917. Morrow's efforts to compose the differences between the Church and the Mexican government, growing

out of the act of 11 Feb. 1926 nationaliz-
ing church property, were interrupted by
the assassination of president-elect Obregón, 17 July 1928.

1927–28

NICARAGUAN RELATIONS. The
U.S. refused to recognize the government
of Emiliano Chamorro, which assumed
power after a revolt on 25 Oct. 1925.
After Chamorro became president (14
Jan. 1926), a Liberal insurrection was
started by Gen Augustino Sandino. The
U.S. landed troops and supported Adolfo
Díaz, Conservative, as president. On 4
May 1927 President Coolidge sent Henry
L. Stimson to bring the 2 factions together. Under an agreement Díaz was to
complete his term, the rebels were to disarm, and the U.S. was to supervise the
next election. When, 4 Nov. 1928, José
Moncada (Liberal) was elected president, Sandino left the country. Again, in
1931, he started a revolt, which was suppressed by 1933. Under President Hoover
U.S. troops were finally withdrawn from
Nicaragua in 1933. Meantime, the U.S.
had been impliedly criticized at the Havana Conference, opened by President
Coolidge, 16 Jan. 1928, in a proposed
resolution declaring that "no state has
the right to intervene in the internal affairs of another." Charles Evans Hughes,
heading the U.S. delegation, managed to
block its passage. Immediately after his
election on 6 Nov. Herbert Hoover embarked on a good-will tour (19 Nov.–6
Jan. 1929) of 11 Latin-American countries, where he received a cordial welcome.

17 Dec. 1928. CLARK MEMORAN-
DUM of the U.S. State Department,
drafted by J. Reuben Clark (1871–1961),
defined the Monroe Doctrine as stating
"a case of the U.S. v. Europe, and not
of the U.S. v. Latin America," in effect
repudiating the Roosevelt Corollary.

1929

YOUNG PLAN. German dissatisfaction with the operation of the reparations
program resulted in a new series of negotiations. On 19 Jan. Owen D. Young
(1874–1962) and J. P. Morgan were
named as American experts on a Committee on German Reparations, which
met in Paris (11 Feb.) to revise the
Dawes Plan, and designated Young as
chairman. The report aimed at a final
settlement of German reparations. It reduced the amount due from Germany to
$8,032,500,000, payable over 58½ years
at 5½% interest; set up a Bank for International Settlements from the profits
of which Germany's payments during the
final 22 years should be made; and provided for a further reduction should the
U.S. consent to scaling down the interallied war debts. In ratifying the debt
settlement agreement with the U.S. (21
July) the French Chamber of Deputies
resolved that the amounts paid to the
U.S. should be covered by German reparation payments. At the Lausanne Conference (16 June 1932) over 90% of the
reparations required to be paid under the
Young Plan were canceled.

1930

21 Jan.–22 Apr. LONDON NAVAL
CONFERENCE. On a visit to the U.S.
(4–6 Oct. 1929) Prime Minister Ramsay MacDonald of Great Britain discussed with President Hoover the issue
of naval disarmament. On 7 Oct. 1929
Great Britain issued a formal invitation
to the other 4 major naval powers. The
U.S. delegation was headed by Secretary
of State Stimson, and included Charles
Francis Adams, Secretary of the Navy,
Dwight W. Morrow, Hugh Gibson, and
Sens. David A. Reed (Rep.) and Joseph
T. Robinson (Dem.). France refused to
accept Italy's demands for parity with

any continental power, and neither nation signed the more important provisions of the treaty. The U.S., Great Britain, and Japan adopted a program of cruiser limitation; an "escalator" or escape clause permitted Britain to start construction should France or Italy threaten her traditional policy of a navy equal to both continental powers. In cruisers Japan was restricted to a 10–6 ratio, but in other auxiliaries except submarines received a 10–7 ratio. In submarines parity at an upper limit of 52,700 tons was adopted. The capital-ship ratio remained at 10–10–6, but no new ships were to be built until 1936 (except French and Italian battleships authorized at Washington but not yet begun). As a result, 5 British, 3 American, and 1 Japanese capital ship were scrapped. The treaty's expiration date was **31 Dec. 1936.** President Hoover called a special session to secure favorable action by the Senate (21 July). **Further disarmament efforts** were continued by the League's Preparatory Commission on Disarmament. A general disarmament conference assembled at **Geneva,** 2 Feb. 1932, with U.S. participation. When the U.S. proposal for **abolition of all offensive armaments** failed of adoption, President Hoover countered with a proposal for a 30% overall reduction. The conference adjourned in July, resumed negotiations in Feb. 1933, adjourned from June until Oct. (by which time Germany had announced her withdrawal from the League), and broke up without accomplishment in the spring of 1934.

1931

20 JUNE. HOOVER DEBT MORATORIUM. The deepening worldwide economic crisis made the payment of either reparations or war debts an impossibility. The repercussions of the New York stock market crash of Oct. 1929 were soon felt abroad. On 11 May 1931 the Austrian Credit-Anstalt failed. Foreign funds were hastily withdrawn from Germany. On 16 June the Bank of England, to stem the financial panic, advanced 150,000,000 schillings to the Austrian National Bank. On 20 June President Hoover proposed a **1-year moratorium** on both interallied debts and reparations. French opposition, delaying acceptance until 6 July, contributed to the closing of all the German banks by mid-July. The crisis seriously affected Great Britain, forcing the Bank of England off the gold standard on 21 Sept. The French position was presented to the U.S. by Premier Pierre Laval, who had a conference at the White House with the president, 23–25 Oct. As a result a statement was issued that, when the moratorium ended, some agreement on the interallied debts "covering the period of business depression," not merely the moratorium year, might be necessary.

1931–32

18 SEPT. JAPANESE AGGRESSION IN MANCHURIA. In violation of the Washington treaties, the Kellogg-Briand Pact, and the League Covenant Japanese army leaders occupied major Manchurian cities, in effect launching an unofficial war between Japan and China. Military control of South Manchuria was completed by 4 Jan. 1932. On 15 Sept. 1932 Japan formally recognized the new puppet state of **Manchukuo.**

7 JAN. 1932. STIMSON DOCTRINE. Secretary Stimson addressed an identical note to Japan and China declaring that the U.S. does not "intend to recognize any treaty or agreement . . . which may impair . . . the sovereignty, the independence, or the territorial and administrative integrity of the Republic of China . . . or the Open Door policy. . . ." Instead of supporting Stimson, the British Foreign Office on 11 Jan. professed its faith in Japan's assurances regarding the Open Door. On 29 Jan. naval and military intervention by the Japanese took place at Shanghai, where the Chinese forces were expelled, 3 Mar. Stimson proposed to **Sir John Simon,** British foreign secretary, that a joint protest be made on the basis of the 9-Power Treaty of 1922, but the British government, preferring to work within the League, was unresponsive. On 23 Feb. Stimson, in a letter to Sen. Borah, chairman of the Senate Foreign Relations Committee, declared that the U.S. would stand by its treaty rights in the Far East, and urged other nations to follow the Stimson Doctrine of nonrecognition. On 11 Mar. the League of Nations Assembly unanimously adopted a resolution incorporating this doctrine. On 31 May Japan, bowing to world opinion, withdrew from Shanghai.

10 Dec. 1931–27 Mar. 1933. LYTTON REPORT. The League attempted to end hostilities in the Far East, formally inviting the U.S. on 16 Oct. 1931 to appoint a representative to sit with the Council in considering the Manchurian crisis. The U.S. accepted. **Prentiss B. Gilbert,** consul at Geneva, was authorized to participate in such discussions as related to U.S. obligations under the Kellogg-Briand Pact; otherwise to act as an observer. Meantime, a ground swell was developing in the U.S. for an economic boycott of Japan, which President Hoover opposed. When it appeared that the League might impose sanctions, Stimson, on 19 Nov., told Charles G. Dawes, American ambassador to Great Britain: "We do not intend to get into war with Japan." On 10 Dec. the League appointed the Lytton Commission, including Gen. **Frank Ross McCoy** (1874–1954), an American, to investigate the Manchurian crisis. The **Lytton Report,** 4 Oct. 1932, condemned Japan, but proposed a settlement recognizing Japan's special interest in Manchuria, which was to become an **autonomous** state under Chinese sovereignty but Japanese control. The report was adopted by the League on 24 Feb. 1933, and on 27 Mar. Japan gave notice of withdrawal from the League.

1933

4 Mar. GOOD NEIGHBOR POLICY. In his first inaugural Franklin D. Roosevelt declared: "In the field of world policy I would dedicate this nation to the policy of the good neighbor—the neighbor who resolutely respects himself and, because he does so, respects the rights of others." The implementation of this policy meant a further improvement in relations with Latin America. At the **Montevideo Conference** Secretary of State **Cordell Hull** (1871–1955) supported declaration: "No state has the right to intervene in the internal or external affairs of another." This pact was unanimously adopted, 26 Dec. "The definite policy of the U.S. from now on is one opposed to armed intervention," declared F.D.R. on 28 Dec.

12 June–27 July. LONDON ECONOMIC CONFERENCE. President Hoover had pledged American participation in this conference called by the League at the request of the Lausanne Conference. Between 4 Mar. and 12 June the U.S. had abandoned the gold standard. Hence, Roosevelt was disinclined to support a currency-stabilizing program supported by the gold-bloc nations (France, Belgium, the Netherlands, Italy, and Switzerland). Secretary Hull received instructions en route to the conference to limit participation to negotiating bilateral tariff treaties. On 2 July President Roosevelt, in a radio message, rebuked the delegates for concentrating on currency stabilization. Since the other participating nations would not agree to consider tariff reductions until *after* currency stabilization, the conference broke up without substantial accomplishment. Its failure marked a blow at international cooperation and signalized the American drift toward isolation.

16 Nov. RECOGNITION OF SOVIET RUSSIA. Following the overthrow of the Kerensky regime in 1917, U.S. administrations had refused to recognize the Soviet Union on various grounds, including Russia's refusal to assume the obligations incurred by former governments as well as her revolutionary program for the overthrow of capitalist nations. Roosevelt's communication of 16 May addressed to 54 heads of states, urging military and economic disarmament, was sent, among others, to **Mikhail Kalinin,** titular head of the Russian government. On 10 Oct. the president requested Kalinin to send an envoy to the U.S. **Maxim Litvinov,** Commissar for Foreign Affairs, arrived in Washington on 7 Nov. In a formal exchange of notes (16 Nov.) Russia promised (1) not to interfere with the domestic affairs of the U.S., including abstaining from propaganda; (2) to extend religious freedom to American citizens in the Soviet Union and to negotiate an agreement to guarantee a fair trial to Americans accused of crime in Russia; (3) to negotiate a settlement of mutual claims (no specific agreement on debts outstanding was ever made). The expected increase in American foreign trade failed to materialize, and the Soviet Union violated her pledge on propaganda and interference in U.S. internal affairs.

1933–38

DECLINE OF DOLLAR DIPLO-MACY. Cuba. As a result of the collapse of sugar prices in the 1920s Cuban economic conditions deteriorated and were further damaged by the Hawley-Smoot Tariff (1930). In Aug. 1931 dictator **Gerardo Machado** suppressed a revolt against his regime. To stabilize Cuban internal conditions President Roosevelt sent **Sumner Welles** (1892–1961) as ambassador to Cuba. Arriving in Havana on 1 June 1933, Welles served as mediator between the Cuban administration and various opposition groups. A general strike and an army revolt forced Machado out of office (12 Aug.). On 5 Sept. another army coup forced out his successor, Carlos Manuel de Céspedes, and a practical dictatorship was established under **Fulgencio Batista.** The radical government of President **Grau San Martín** was not recognized by the U.S. On 20 Jan. 1934 this regime was overthrown by Carlos Mendieta, favored by the U.S., Batista, and Cuban conservatives, who successfully negotiated a treaty with the U.S. **abrogating the Platt Amendment** (29 May) and removing limitations previously imposed on Cuban sovereignty. Chief credit for these negotiations belongs to Sumner Welles. On 25 Aug. the U.S. and Cuba signed a reciprocal trade agreement by which duties on sugar were reduced from 2.5 cts. to .9 cts. per lb. Cuban sugar production was finally stabilized by the **Jones-Costigan Sugar Control Act** (in effect 8 June).

Haiti. As the result of the restoration of order and the stabilizing of finances with U.S. aid, U.S. troops were withdrawn on 6 Aug. 1934.

Panama. As a result of a conference in Washington between President **Harmodio Arías** and President Roosevelt, a declaration was issued (17 Oct. 1933) that Panama should be permitted the commercial rights of a sovereign state in the Canal Zone. Negotiations between the two nations were soon entered into to secure a modification of the Hay–

Bunau-Varilla Treaty of 1903. The new treaty signed 2 Mar. 1936 was not ratified by the U.S. Senate until 25 July 1939, owing in part to opposition from U.S. military and naval authorities. The treaty incorporated a pledge of joint action in case "of any threat of aggression which would endanger the security of the Republic of Panama or the neutrality or security of the Panama Canal," allowed the U.S. to expand its canal facilities or to begin new construction, and increased U.S. annual payments to Panama from $250,000 to $450,000.

HEMISPHERE SOLIDARITY. Early Phases. The rise of fascist and totalitarian regimes in Europe underscored the need for unity among the nations of the Western Hemisphere. Three Pan-American conferences prior to the outbreak of World War II dealt with this new world peril: (1) The **Montevideo Conference**, which denied the right of any state to intervene in the "internal or external affairs of another" (26 Dec. 1933); (2) the **Buenos Aires Conference**, opened by President Roosevelt (1 Dec. 1936) in a speech in which he declared that non-American states seeking "to commit acts of aggression against us will find a Hemisphere wholly prepared to consult together for our mutual safety and our mutual good," and which adopted a pact pledging consultation whenever war threatened; (3) the **Lima Conference** (24 Dec. 1938), which adopted the **Declaration of Lima,** not only reaffirming the absolute sovereignty of the American states but expressing their determination to resist "all foreign intervention or activities that may threaten them." It provided for consultation where the "peace, security, or territorial integrity" of any state should be threatened. Actually, the Argentina delegation blocked an even stronger declaration desired by Secretary Hull, who headed the U.S. delegation.

Closer Ties with Brazil. As a result of radical unrest in Brazil, President **Getulio Vargas** was granted almost dictatorial powers, which were enlarged by a new constitution proclaimed 10 Nov. 1937. The U.S. refused to label Vargas' government as fascist, and moved quickly to supplant German influence in that strategic area. Largely as a result of the efforts of Sumner Welles, Brazil concluded a series of agreements with the U.S., 9 Mar. 1939, by which it obtained financial aid for economic development.

SETTLEMENT OF THE MEXICAN EXPROPRIATION CONTROVERSY. Under a 6-Year Plan launched by President **Lázaro Cárdenas** (inaugurated 11 Nov. 1936) numerous social reforms were introduced. Acting under authority of a statute passed in 1936, Cárdenas nationalized most of the properties of British and U.S. oil companies, valued at $450 million (18 Mar. 1938). Secretary Hull admitted the right of expropriation, but insisted on fair compensation (30 Mar.). On 1 Apr. the U.S. discontinued purchasing Mexican silver at a price above the world level, an act which threatened Mexico's financial stability. Certain aspects of the controversy were settled by a joint commission, and payments by the Mexican government began in 1939; other aspects were settled by agreement between the U.S. and President **Avila Camacho** (19 Nov. 1941). Mexico agreed to pay $40 million in settlements of agrarian claims; the U.S. to establish a $40-million fund to support the peso, to resume purchase of Mexican silver at a price above the world market, and to issue through the Export-Import bank a $30-million credit for Mexican highway construction. Each party agreed to appoint an expert to arrive at an equitable valuation of the U.S.-owned oil properties. On 18 Apr. 1942 a figure of $23,995,991 for subsoil rights was announced, in addition to $9,600,000 paid by Mexico in individual settlements with 2 U.S. oil companies.

ISOLATION AND NEUTRALITY. As totalitarian regimes increasingly threatened the peace of Europe, the U.S. adopted a series of isolationist measures to avoid involvement in war. The **Johnson Debt Default Act** (13 Apr. 1934) prohibited loans to any foreign government in default to the U.S. Previously (June 1933) Britain, Czechoslovakia, Italy, Rumania, Latvia, and Lithuania had made token payments, their last on debts to the U.S. All formally defaulted on 15 June 1934. Only Finland continued to meet her payments in full. The new approach to neutrality, in part the result of the work of the **Nye Committee** (p. 411), sought to disentangle U.S. economic interests from foreign wars and constituted an abandonment of traditional concepts of neutral rights.

Neutrality Act of 1935. When Italy attacked Ethiopia (May 1935) the U.S. State Department drafted a bill which would have given the president power to embargo arms against one or all belligerents in future wars. Introduced in the House on 17 Aug., it was rejected by the Foreign Relations Committee, which substituted a resolution authorizing the president, after proclaiming the existence of a state of war, to prohibit all **arms** shipments and to forbid U.S. citizens from traveling on belligerent vessels except **at their own risk.** Yielding to the administration, Congress placed a 6-month limit on such embargo. Roosevelt signed the measure, 31 Aug., but characterized it as calculated to "drag us into war instead of keeping us out." The embargo did not include primary materials such as oil, steel, copper, easily converted to military use.

Neutrality Act of 1936. The Act of 1935 was extended on 29 Feb. 1936 to 1 May 1937, and forbade the extension of loans or credits to belligerents. On 14 Aug. 1936, in an address delivered at Chautauqua, N.Y., President Roosevelt pointed to the dangers of being drawn into war and declared: "I hate war."

Neutrality Acts of 1937. On 18 July 1936 the Spanish Civil War broke out, with a revolt of army chiefs in Spanish Morocco. Foreign powers soon intervened on both sides. Since the U.S. neutrality acts applied only to wars **between nations,** not to civil wars, new legislation was deemed necessary. On 6 Jan. 1937 Congress passed a joint resolution forbidding the export of munitions "for the use of either of the opposing forces in Spain." Under this act Roosevelt embargoed shipments to both sides. The embargo worked to the particular disadvantage of the Loyalist government in Madrid, as the rebels secured supplies from Italy and Germany. The deficiencies of each of the neutrality acts called for a more realistic and flexible measure, which was adopted on 1 May 1937. This act (1) authorized the president to list commodities **other than munitions** to be paid for on delivery (limited to 2 years); (2) made travel on belligerent vessels **unlawful.** Again, the ineffectiveness of the new act was demonstrated when, on 7 July 1937, fighting broke out between Japanese and Chinese troops near Peiping. The president declined to invoke the Neutrality Act of May 1937 on the ground that it would have worked to China's disadvantage. However, on 14 Sept. he forbade transport of munitions to China and Japan on U.S. government vessels, and notified private shippers that they acted at their own risk. Japan, with her large merchant marine, benefited by this ruling.

ROOSEVELT AND COLLECTIVE SECURITY: QUARANTINE SPEECH. In complete disagreement with the isolationist trend of the neutrality legislation, President Roosevelt, in a speech in Chicago, 5 Oct. 1937, urged an international quarantine of aggressors as the only means of preserving peace. Roosevelt soon recognized that he had moved ahead of public opinion, although his address undoubtedly encouraged a widespread U.S. boycott against Japanese goods.

NAVAL EXPANSION. Japan, on 29 Dec. 1934, denounced the Washington Naval Treaty of 1922. The U.S. refused to grand parity to Japan at the discussions preliminary to the 2d London Naval Conference, from which Japan withdrew, 15 Jan. 1936. Great Britain, the U.S., and France signed (25 Mar.) a treaty providing for minor limitations, largely made ineffective by numerous "escape clauses." In 1938 Congress voted a billion-dollar naval-building program (see p. 424).

DETERIORATING JAPANESE RELATIONS. Panay Incident. On 12 Dec. 1937 Japanese planes bombed a U.S. river gunboat, the *Panay*. The vessel sank with a loss of 2 killed, 30 wounded. (For the **Ludlow Amendment** [14 Dec.], see p. 423). On 14 Dec. the U.S. formally demanded apologies, reparations, and guarantees against further incidents. On the same day Japan formally apologized and gave the necessary assurances. On 25 Dec. Secretary Hull acknowledged the reply. On 6 Oct. 1938 U.S. ambassador **Joseph Clark Grew** (1880–1965) protested against Japanese violations of the Open Door in China. The Japanese note of 18 Nov. declared that the Open Door was "inapplicable" to the conditions "of today and tomorrow." The State Department, in its reply of 31 Dec., refused to recognize the "new order."

1938–39

DETERIORATING EUROPEAN CONDITIONS. On 11 Jan. 1938 President Roosevelt proposed to the government a program ~~ameliog~~ ~~war might~~ ference to ~~the~~ econo~~

break out. Prime Minister Neville Cham~~ berlain rejected this proposal. The **German war timetable:** 7 Mar. 1936, German reoccupation of the Rhineland; 17 Nov. 1936, Anti-Comintern Pact of Germany, Japan, and Italy against communism; Mar. 1938, annexation of Austria by Germany; Sept. 1938, the German-Czech crisis, which caused Chamberlain to intervene (at Berchtesgaden, 15 Sept.; at Godesberg, 22–23 Sept.). On 27 Sept. President Roosevelt appealed to Hitler and Mussolini for a peaceful solution of the issues. As a result of the **Munich Conference** and Agreement, 29 Sept., the Sudetenland and all vital Czech fortresses were yielded to Germany. Despite French and British guarantees of the new frontiers of Czechoslovakia, that nation came to an end in Mar. 1939, when Slovakia and Carpatho-Ukraine declared their independence, and Bohemia and Moravia became a German protectorate. On 23 Mar. Germany annexed Memel, and made stiff demands to Warsaw regarding Danzig and the Polish Corridor. On 31 Mar. Britain pledged Anglo-French aid to the Poles in case their independence was threatened, a pledge extended to Rumania and Greece on 13 Apr. Meantime, 7 Apr., Italy invaded Albania. On 15 Apr. President Roosevelt, in a letter to Hitler and Mussolini, asked assurances against attack on nations of Europe and the Near East. Denying warlike intentions, Hitler, in reply, restated German grievances. On 22 May, a military alliance was concluded between Germany and Italy. On a **Russo-German pact** was ~~signed~~ at Moscow. This provided ~~attacking~~ the other; (if either ~~were~~ would remain neutral if the other were attacked by a third party. The next day President Roosevelt addressed an appeal to President Ignacy Moscicki of Poland, to Hitler and King Victor Emmanuel proposing direct negotiations between Germany and Poland, arbitration or conciliation. Poland accepted concili-

ation. On 31 Aug. the Poles decreed partial mobilization.

Domestic Issues

1919

28 Oct. NATIONAL PROHIBITION ENFORCEMENT ACT (VOLSTEAD ACT) was passed over President Wilson's veto (27 Oct.). Designed to provide the enforcement apparatus for the 18th Amendment, the act went into effect on 16 Jan. 1920. It defined as intoxicating liquor any beverage containing more than ½ of 1% of alcohol and placed the administration of the law under the Bureau of Internal Revenue, in which the post of commissioner of prohibition was created. A supplementary act (23 Nov. 1921) limited the use of liquor by medical prescription and extended prohibition to the Hawaiian and Virgin Islands. The Jones Act (2 Mar. 1929) increased the penalties for violation. Widespread evasion of the Volstead Act was evidenced by the growth of bootlegging (i.e., the illicit liquor traffic) on a vast scale during the 1920s, when the organized distilling and distribution of liquor fell under the control of criminal elements.

24 Dec. President Wilson announced that on 1 Mar. 10 the railroads and express companies would be returned to private operation.

1920

13 Feb. Robert Lansing Secretary of State, but Wilson's ed as after the president charged him holding unauthorized meetings of cabinet following Wilson's physical collapse in 1919.

28 Feb. TRANSPORTATION ACT (ESCH-CUMMINS ACT) provided for the return of the railroads to private control on 1 Mar. and widened the powers of the Interstate Commerce Commission. The commission was authorized to draw up plans for the consolidation of all railroads into about a score of competing groups exempt from antitrust legislation; was empowered to make evaluations of the aggregate value of railroad properties, to set minimum and maximum rates, and to establish a fair return to stockholders; and was given jurisdiction over pooling, regulation of service and traffic, and new issues of securities. A recapture clause required carriers to turn over to the Interstate Commerce Commission one half of all net earnings in excess of 6%, these to be set aside as a revolving fund for the benefit of railroads handicapped by low income. **A Railroad Labor Board** was created for the adjustment of wage disputes.

5 June. MERCHANT MARINE ACT (JONES ACT) repealed emergency war legislation relating to shipping, reorganized the U.S. Shipping Board and extended its life, and authorized the sale of government-built ships to private operators, the proceeds up to $25 million to be used for loans to private owners for the construction of new craft. The Shipping Board was empowered to propose the establishment of shipping routes for the purpose of promoting mail and trade and to operate the shipping services interests took over. The coastwise commerce

was to be carried in U.S. vessels, as well as the mails where practicable.

10 JUNE. WATER POWER ACT established a **Federal Power Commission** consisting of the Secretaries of War, Interior, and Agriculture, with an executive secretary directly responsible for its administration. The act applied to water power reserves on public lands of the U.S. (except reservations) and to navigable streams, including falls, rapids, and shallows. The commission was empowered to issue licenses, limited to 50 years, for the construction and operation of facilities (e.g., power houses, dams, reservoirs, and transmission lines) for improving navigation and developing and utilizing power. Upon expiration of the lease, the government reserved the right to take over and operate these facilities. The commission was authorized to regulate rates and security issues of licensees under its jurisdiction.

26 AUG. 19TH AMENDMENT to the Constitution, providing for **woman suffrage,** was declared ratified.

PALMER RAIDS AND THE "RED SCARE." Following the Bolshevik Revolution in Russia, the Soviets carried out an intensive propaganda campaign against the Western nations. In 1919 the Workers' (later the Communist) party was established in the U.S. Beginning in the fall of 1919, ⟋ Department of Justice under A.⟋ Palmer made countrywide m⟋ litical and labor agitat⟋ ere arrested pe⟋ vere deporte⟋ S. trans⟋ ab⟋

vidual states, criminal syndicalist laws were invoked against radicals.

PRESIDENTIAL CAMPAIGN. The Socialist Labor Party Convention met at New York (5 May) and nominated W. W. Cox (Mo.) for president and August Gillhaus (N.Y.) for vice-president. The Socialist Party Convention met at New York (8 May) and unanimously nominated Eugene V. Debs (Ind.) for president. Debs was then serving a 10-year sentence in federal prison for having engaged in seditious activity in violation of the wartime Espionage Act. Seymour Stedman (Ohio) was chosen as the Socialist candidate for vice-president.

The Republican Convention met at Chicago (8 June) and on the 10th ballot nominated Sen. **Warren G. Harding** (Ohio, p. 1050) for president. Gov. **Calvin Coolidge** (Mass., p. 1005) was nominated for vice-president on the 1st ballot. The Republican platform rejected the Covenant of the League of Nations and made a vague declaration favoring an "agreement among the nations to preserve the peace of the world." Harding waged a front-porch campaign; in a well-calculated appeal to the postwar temper, he called for a "return to **normalcy.**"

The Democratic National Convention met at San Francisco (28 June) and on the 44th ballot nominated Governor **James M. Cox** (Ohio) for president. **Franklin D. Roosevelt** (N.Y., p. 1141), Assistant Secretary of the Navy, was nominated for vice-president by acclamation. The Democratic platform unequivocally endorsed the Versailles Treaty and the League of Nations, but did not "oppose the acceptance of any reservations ⟋king clearer or more specific the ob⟋s of the United States to the ⟋sociates."

⟋r Labor Party Conventio⟋ ⟋11 July) and nomin⟋ ⟋Utah) for pre⟋

and Max S. Hayes (Ohio) for vice-president. The Single Tax party convention met at Chicago (12 July) and nominated Robert C. Macauley (Pa.) for president and Richard Barnum (Ohio) for vice-president. The Prohibition Party Convention met at Lincoln, Neb. (21 July), and nominated A. S. Watkins for president.

2 Nov. PRESIDENTIAL ELECTION. Popular vote: **Harding**, 16,152,200; Cox (D), 9,147,353; Debs, 919,799; Watkins, 189,408; Cox (S.L.), 31,175; Christensen, 265,411; Macauley, 5,837. Electoral vote: **Harding**, 404; Cox (D.), 127.

1921

BUSINESS RECESSION. The sharp deflation, 1920–21 (p. 751), was the result of stringent credit, a glutted domestic market and heavy inventories, and a sharp drop in the export trade. Wages dropped; about 20,000 business failures occurred in 1921; and some 4,750,000 persons were unemployed. The recession's impact upon agriculture was more lasting (p. 694).

10 June. BUDGET AND ACCOUNTING ACT, the first material step in the reform of the national budget, created a Budget Bureau in the Treasury Department, with a director appointed by the president. At each regular session of Congress the president was to submit to the legislators a budget including estimates of expenditures and receipts for the following year together with estimates for the current and last fiscal years. The president was also to present a complete statement of the government's financial condition and, when deemed advisable, recommendations for loans, tax revision, and other financial measures. Except on special request of either house of Congress, no financial recommendation or quest for appropriations was to be by any government officer except

through the budget. The act also created a General Accounting Office, under the Comptroller General of the U.S., for carrying out an independent audit of government accounts. **Charles G. Dawes** (1865–1951) was named (21 June) as first director of the Bureau of the Budget.

9 Aug. VETERANS BUREAU was established as an independent unit, directly responsible to the president, for assuming the administration of all forms of veterans' relief. Col. **Charles R. Forbes** was named as its head.

15 Aug. PACKERS AND STOCKYARDS ACT related to livestock, livestock products, poultry, and dairy products. Its enforcement was vested in the Department of Agriculture. The act forbade unfair and discriminatory practices, the manipulation and control of prices, and other devices creating a monopoly and acting in restraint of trade. Operators of stockyards and other marketing facilities were required to register with the Department of Agriculture and to file their schedule of charges.

24 Aug. GRAIN FUTURES TRADING ACT was designed to regulate all contract markets authorized to sell grain for future delivery, in order to prevent market manipulation and monopoly practices. It discouraged speculative transactions by levying a prohibitive tax on grain sold for future delivery except by owners or certain authorized contract markets. The act was invalidated by the Supreme Court in 1922 and superseded by a second grain Futures Act (21 Sept. 1922) regulating trading under the interstate commerce power.

23 Nov. SHEPPARD-TOWNER ACT for the promotion of the welfare and health of maternity and infancy extended federal aid to states. The act authorized annual federal appropriations of $1 million. The act, which lapsed in 1 attacked as constituting ence in state affai

1922

18 FEB. COOPERATIVE MARKETING ACT (CAPER-VOLSTEAD ACT) exempted agricultural producers, cooperatives, or associations from the operations of antitrust laws and allowed cooperative buying and selling by farmers in interstate commerce. Administration of the act was vested in the Department of Agriculture.

22 SEPT. CABLE ACT granted married women U.S. citizenship independent of their husbands' status.

1923

KU KLUX KLAN EXPOSÉS. The Ku Klux Klan, a secret nativist organization patterned upon the rituals of its post-Civil War predecessor, and active against minority groups (Negroes, Catholics, Jews, and immigrants) as well as against certain tendencies in modern thought (e.g., birth control, pacifism, internationalism, Darwinism, and the repeal of prohibition), was revived at a meeting on Stone Mountain, Ga., Nov. 1915. At peak strength in the 1920s it was reported to have had 5 million members in the North, South, and Midwest, with political power in several states (including Ind., Okla., and Tex.). Exposés of its activities appeared in 1923. The Baltimore *Sun* (7 Jan.) exposed the reign of terror in Morehouse Parish, La., where despite evidence of torture and murder of marked victims, a grand jury refused to indict. Concurrently the N.Y. *World* exposed Klan activities in the North. In Vincennes, Ind., Grand Dragon David C. Stephenson was convicted on a charge of murder in the second degree (21 Nov. 1925). By 1926 Klan membership was on the decline. By 1930 it was estimated at only 9,000.

4 MAR. INTERMEDIATE CREDIT ACT was designed to facilitate loans for crop financing by means of an intermediate credit system that liberalized the use of short-term agricultural paper. It established 12 intermediate credit banks, 1 in each federal reserve bank district, under the jurisdiction of the Federal Farm Loan Board. Each bank, with a capital of $5 million subscribed by the government, was authorized to make loans (ranging from 6 months to 3 years) to cooperative producing and marketing associations. The act also authorized the creation of agricultural credit corporations by private interests.

2 AUG. DEATH OF PRESIDENT HARDING at San Francisco, while on a return trip from Alaska. Embolism was listed as the cause of death.

3 AUG. Vice-President Calvin Coolidge took the oath of office as president at Plymouth, Vt., becoming the 30th president of the U.S.

6 DEC. In his first annual message to Congress, President Coolidge voiced his support of U.S. adherence to a world court, the tax reduction plan of Secretary of the Treasury Andrew W. Mellon (1855–1937), and prohibition enforcement. He opposed the cancellation of Allied debts and the payment of a veterans' bonus. His program called for a scaling down of government expenditures, a minimum of government interference in business, and government aid to industry and commerce.

1924

HARDING ADMINISTRATION SCANDALS. Early in 1924 congressional committees, acting upon persistent rumors of graft and corruption in the Harding administration, brought to light scandals in the departments of Justice, Navy, and the Interior, and in the Veterans Bureau and the Office of the Alien Property Custodian. Col. Charles R.

Forbes, former chief of the Veterans Bureau, who had resigned in 1923, was indicted for fraud, conspiracy, and bribery, and sentenced (4 Feb. 1925) to 2 years in a federal penitentiary and a fine of $10,000. Col. Thomas W. Miller, the Alien Property Custodian, was also sent to prison (1927) on charges of conspiring to defraud the government.

The major scandals involved the lease of naval oil reserve lands by private interests and the influence over the Department of Justice wielded by the Ohio gang, a group of self-seeking politicians close to Harding. A Senate investigating committee disclosed that President Harding, acting with the approval of Secretary of the Navy Edwin Denby, had transferred (1921) to Secretary of the Interior **Albert B. Fall** (1861–1944) the administration of oil reserves at **Teapot Dome,** Wyo., and **Elk Hills,** Calif. During the Taft and Wilson administrations these reserves had been set aside for the use of the navy. The Teapot Dome reserve was secretly leased by Fall (7 Apr. 1922) to oil operator Harry F. Sinclair; the California fields were likewise leased (25 Apr., 11 Dec. 1922) to Edward L. Doheny.

The scandal came to light when a Senate committee headed by **Thomas J. Walsh** (Mont., 1859–1933) found that in 1921 Doheny had lent Fall $100,000 without interest or collateral, and that Fall, after retiring from the cabinet in March, 1923, had received a "loan" of $25,000 from Sinclair. A joint congressional resolution charged fraud and corruption. The government secured cancellation of the oil leases in 1927. Fall was indicted (30 June) for bribery and conspiracy, convicted of bribery, and sentenced to 1 year in prison and $100,000 fine. Sinclair and Doheny were acquitted of bribery; Sinclair sentenced to 9 months in prison and $1,000 fine for contempt of court.

An investigation revealed that Attorney General **Harry M. Daugherty** (1860–1941), acting in concert with members of the Ohio gang, had received payments from violators of the prohibition statutes. It was also disclosed that he had failed to prosecute for graft in the Veterans Bureau. Daugherty was tried for conspiracy, but acquitted (4 Mar. 1927). He resigned (Mar. 1924) at the request of President Coolidge.

The Supreme Court declared the Elk Hills lease invalid 28 Feb. 1927; the Teapot Dome lease, 10 Oct. 1927.

19 May. WORLD WAR ADJUSTED COMPENSATION ACT (SOLDIERS BONUS ACT). Shortly after the close of World War I organized veterans' groups, including the American Legion and the Veterans of Foreign Wars, initiated a demand for an ex-servicemen's bonus. The move was made on the assumption that veterans ought to be compensated for the differential between their service pay and the wages received by war workers who had remained in civilian life.

On 19 Sept. 1922 President Harding vetoed a bonus bill. Veterans' groups continued to exert pressure on Congress. On 18 Mar. a bonus bill was passed by the House, and on 23 Apr. it was approved by the Senate. It was vetoed (15 May) by President Coolidge, but was passed over his veto by the House (17 May) and Senate (19 May).

The act provided for the payment of adjusted compensation to all veterans (excluding officers above the rank of captain) on the basis of $1.25 a day for overseas service and $1 a day for service in the U.S. The bonus was made in the form of 20-year endowment policies on which ex-servicemen might borrow from the government up to about 25% of full value. Cash payment, which became a major issue in 1931–32, was finally authorized in 1936.

McNARY-HAUGEN BILL. The post-war depression in agriculture, deepened by a glutted market and a continuing slump in crop prices, and farm mortgages on expanded acreage, led spokesmen of farmer interests to consider basic legislation for coping with agricultural distress. The **Capper-Volstead Act** (1922) and the **Intermediate Credit Act** (1923) failed to satisfy agrarian discontent, mobilized by such organized groups as the American Farm Bureau Federation and the Farmers' National Council. A bipartisan agrarian bloc in Congress undertook to deal with the problem by 2 means: control of the surplus and stabilization of prices. The **McNary-Haugen Farm Relief Bill**, sponsored by Sen. **Charles L. McNary** (Ore., 1874–1944) and Rep. **Gilbert N. Haugen** (Iowa), was introduced in both houses of Congress (16 Jan.). The measure featured the equalization fee scheme, whereby a proposed federal farm board would purchase the annual surplus of specified commodities during years of large output and either keep it off the market until prices rose or sell it abroad at the prevailing world price. The equalization fee (i.e., the difference between the fixed domestic price and the free international price) was to be paid by producers of individual commodities in the event that the government suffered losses in selling at lower world prices. The bill was defeated in the House (3 June) when Western farm interests failed to muster adequate support. It suffered successive defeats in the House (21 May 1926) and Senate (24 June 1926). Passed by the Senate (11 Feb. 1927) and the House (17 Feb. 1927), it was vetoed by President Coolidge (25 Feb. 1927) on the ground that it incorporated a price-fixing principle and benefited special groups.

PRESIDENTIAL CAMPAIGN. The Commonwealth Land party (formerly the Single Tax party) met in convention (8 Feb.) and nominated W. J. Wallace (N.J.) for president and J. C. Lincoln (Ohio) for vice-president. The Socialist Labor Party Convention met at New York (11 May) and nominated Frank T. Johns (Ore.) for president and Verne L. Reynolds (Md.) for vice-president. The American Party Convention met at Columbus, Ohio (3 June) and nominated Judge Gilbert O. Nations (Washington, D.C.) for president and Charles H. Randall (Calif.) for vice-president. The Prohibition Party Convention met at Columbus, Ohio (5 June), and nominated Herman P. Faris (Mo.) for president and Miss Marie C. Brehm (Calif.) for vice-president.

The Republican Party Convention met at Cleveland (10 June) and nominated President **Coolidge** for reelection and Gen. **Charles C. Dawes** (Ill.) for vice-president. The Republican platform supported reduced taxes and retrenchment in government expenditures, the Fordney-McCumber tariff, the limitation of armaments, U.S. adherence to the World Court, and international action for the prevention of war.

The Democratic Party Convention met at New York (24 June) and, after a prolonged contest between the partisans William G. McAdoo (Tenn.) and Alfred E. Smith (N.Y., 1873–1944), nominated **John W. Davis** (W. Va., 1873–1955) for president on the 103rd ballot (9 July). Gov. **Charles W. Bryan** (Neb.) was nominated for vice-president. The Democratic platform favored a competitive tariff and endorsed disarmament and the League of Nations. It denounced the Ku Klux Klan and condemned the corruption of the Harding administration.

The Conference for Progressive Political Action, representing dissident agrarian and labor elements, met at Cleveland (4 July) and launched a new Progressive party that was endorsed by the Farmer Labor party, the Socialist party, and the American Federation of Labor. The Progressives nominated Sen. **Robert M. La Follette** (Wis.) for president and Sen. **Burton K. Wheeler** (Mont.) for vice-president. The Progressive platform called for government ownership of railroads and water power resources, the abolition of the use of the injunction in labor disputes, freedom for farmers and labor to organize and bargain collectively, ratification of the child labor amendment, limitation of judicial review, and tighter controls over futures trading in agricultural commodities. It denounced corruption in government, condemned the Mellon financial program, and attacked "the control of government and industry by private monopoly."

The Workers' (Communist) party met on 11 July and nominated William Z. Foster (Ill.) for president and Benjamin Gitlow (N.Y.) for vice-president.

4 Nov. PRESIDENTIAL ELECTION. Popular vote: **Coolidge,** 15,725,016; Davis, 8,385,586; La Follette, 4,822,856; Faris, 57,551; Johns, 38,958; Foster, 33,361; Nations, 23,867; Wallace, 2,778. Electoral vote: **Coolidge,** 382; Davis, 136; La Follette, 13. Both houses of Congress remained under Republican control.

1925

13 FEB. JUDGES' BILL. Continuing increase in the docket of the U.S. Supreme Court coupled with growing recognition of the value of the Circuit Courts of Appeals (created by Act of 3 Mar. 1891) led a committee of justices, Willis Van Devanter, James C. McReynolds, and George Sutherland, to draft a proposal for Congress. The bill became law, assisted by the lobbying of Chief Justice William Howard Taft, providing that most appeals from federal district courts would go directly to the Courts of Appeals. Appeals as of right by way of a Writ of Appeal from the Courts of Appeals and state courts to the Supreme Court were severely limited and the Supreme Court achieved substantial control of the cases it would hear through a *writ of certiorari* granted or denied at the discretion of the court.

10–21 JULY. SCOPES TRIAL (p. 829).

28 OCT.–17 DEC. "BILLY" MITCHELL TRIAL. Differences among military and naval authorities over the role of the airplane in warfare set the background for the court-martial of Col. William ("Billy") Mitchell (p. 1104) of the Army Air Service. A forthright critic of U.S. aviation policy, Mitchell publicly contended (5 Sept.) that the military high command was incompetent, criminally negligent, and almost treasonable in its administration of the national defense. An exponent of air power, he insisted that capital ships were vulnerable to air attack. Summoned to Washington, D.C., by the National Air Board, Mitchell advocated (29 Sept.) an independent department for aviation and a unified command of the armed services. A court-martial found him guilty of conduct prejudicial to good order and military discipline. He was suspended from the service for 5 years. Mitchell resigned from the service (29 Jan. 1926). He died in 1936. In 1942 he was posthumously restored to the service with the rank of major general.

1926

26 FEB. REVENUE ACT, in keeping with the Coolidge-Mellon fiscal program, reduced personal income and inheritance taxes and abolished a wide variety of excise imposts. It also repealed the publicity clause relating to income tax returns. Additional reductions were made in the Revenue Act of 29 May 1928.

2 Nov. CONGRESSIONAL ELECTIONS cut Republican majorities in both houses, with gains for Progressives.

1927

2 Aug. COOLIDGE'S WITH-DRAWAL. It was generally assumed that Coolidge would seek the presidential nomination in 1928. While on a vacation in the Black Hills of South Dakota, Coolidge issued the following statement to newspaper reporters at Rapid City, S.D.: "I do not choose to run for President in 1928."

SACCO-VANZETTI CASE. Nicola Sacco and Bartolomeo Vanzetti, 2 Italian anarchists, were arrested (5 May 1920) for having allegedly murdered (15 Apr.) a paymaster and guard at a shoe factory in South Braintree, Mass. They were convicted (14 July 1921) on what many regarded as insubstantial evidence. It was charged by liberals and radicals in the U.S. and abroad that Sacco and Vanzetti had been tried for their radical views rather than for any actual crime. During the 20s, when defense committees succeeded in securing a stay of the death sentence, the Sacco-Vanzetti case became a *cause célèbre*. Mass demonstrations for the convicted were held in the U.S., Latin America, and Europe. Under pressure of widespread protest that the convicted had not received a fair trial, Gov. Alvan T. Fuller (Mass.) appointed (1 July 1927) a commission (Pres. Abbott Lawrence Lowell of Harvard, chairman), which examined the evidence and conduct of the trial and sustained the verdict (27 July). Sacco and Vanzetti were put to death in the electric chair at the Charlestown State Prison (23 Aug.).

1928

FINAL DEFEAT OF THE McNARY-HAUGEN BILL. As the situation of the American farmer showed no sign of general improvement, agrarian spokesmen in Congress renewed efforts to enact the McNary-Haugen Farm Relief Bill. In a fifth attempt, the bill passed the Senate (12 Apr.), 53–23, and the House (3 May), 204–121, but was again vetoed by President Coolidge on the following grounds: that it sanctioned price fixing; was an improper delegation of the taxing power; would lead to overproduction and profiteering; and would antagonize overseas agricultural producers and thus invite retaliation. Coolidge's persistent opposition to this mode of farm relief was a leading issue in the presidential election of 1928.

15 May. FLOOD CONTROL ACT (p. 639).

22 May. MERCHANT MARINE ACT (JONES-WHITE ACT) was designed to encourage private shipping. It increased from $125 million to $250 million a ship construction loan fund from which private builders could borrow up to three quarters of the cost of constructing, reconditioning, or remodeling a vessel. It also permitted the sale of government-owned craft at low prices and liberalized long-term mail-carrying contracts.

PRESIDENTIAL CAMPAIGN. The Socialist Party Convention met at New York (13 Apr.) and nominated Norman Thomas (N.Y.) for president and James H. Maurer (Pa.) for vice-president. The Workers' (Communist) Party Convention met at New York (27 May) and nominated William Z. Foster (Ill.) for president and Benjamin Gitlow (N.Y.) for vice-president.

The Republican Party National Convention met at Kansas City, Mo. (12 June), and nominated Secretary of Commerce **Herbert C. Hoover** (Calif.) for president on the 1st ballot (14 June). Sen. **Charles Curtis** (Kan., 1860–1936) was nominated for vice-president. The Republican platform rejected the McNary-Haugen scheme for farm relief but supported the creation of a federal farm board authorized to promote the establishment of a farm marketing system and of farmer-owned and -controlled stabilization corporations or associations to prevent and control surpluses through orderly distribution. The platform upheld prohibition, the protective tariff, and the Coolidge foreign policy. During the campaign Hoover made his "rugged individualism" speech at New York (22 Oct.), in which he condemned the Democratic platform as state socialism and upheld free competition and private initiative as the traditional American way.

The Democratic Party Convention met at Houston, Tex. (26 June), and nominated Gov. **Alfred E. Smith** (N.Y.) for president on the 1st ballot (28 June) and Sen **Joseph T. Robinson** (Ark.) for vice-president. The Democratic platform, although not committed to the McNary-Haugen plan, pledged that "farm relief must rest on the basis of an economic equality of agriculture with other industries," and advocated the creation of a federal farm board with powers somewhat similar to those proposed in the McNary-Haugen Bill. The platform pledged enforcement of the prohibition laws; and while Smith supported this pledge, he called for repeal of the 18th Amendment. His position cost him the "dry" vote, particularly in the South. Also favored by the Democratic platform were collective bargaining for labor and the abolition of the use of the injunction in labor disputes, "except upon proof of threatened irreparable injury"; the stricter regulation of water power resources; and immediate independence for the Philippines. Republican foreign policy was condemned.

The Prohibition Party Convention met at Chicago (12 July) and nominated William F. Varney (N.Y.) for president and James A. Edgerton (Wash.) for vice-president. The Farmer Labor candidate for president was Frank E. Webb. The Socialist Labor party nominated Verne L. Reynolds for president.

6 Nov. PRESIDENTIAL ELECTION. Popular vote: **Hoover,** 21,392,190; Smith, 15,016,443; Thomas, 267,420; Foster, 48,770; Reynolds, 21,603; Varney, 20,106; Webb, 6,390. Electoral vote: **Hoover,** 444; Smith, 87. In part because of religious prejudice against Smith, a Roman Catholic, the electoral vote of 5 Southern states went to Hoover. The Republicans maintained control of both houses of Congress.

1929

15 APR. Special session of the 71st Congress convened at call of President Hoover to deal with farm relief and limited revision of the tariff.

EXPORT DEBENTURE PLAN. The agrarian relief scheme favored by the congressional farm bloc differed fundamentally from that advocated by President Hoover. Exponents of the subsidy principle, the farm bloc introduced in the Senate the export debenture plan initially advanced in 1926 and again in 1928. This scheme called for export bounties on specified commodities. Equal to one half of the tariff duties on such commodities, these bounties were to be added to the prevailing world price. Payment was to be made in the form of debentures receivable in payment of import duties. Thus the difference between the domestic and world price would be met by the government out of customs receipts. The proposal of this plan by the farm bloc touched off a heated contest between the Senate and House. The House 3 times (25 Apr., 17 May, 13 June) rejected the debenture plan passed by the Senate, and President Hoover made it clear that he would veto the measure. The Senate finally abandoned the scheme.

15 JUNE. AGRICULTURAL MARKETING ACT was an administration measure which eliminated the subsidy and price-fixing principle of the McNary-Haugen and export debenture plans. The act established a **Federal Farm Board** (consisting of 8 members and the Secretary of Agriculture) for promoting the marketing of farm commodities through agricultural cooperatives and stabilization corporations. It authorized a revolving fund of $500 million for low-interest loans to such agencies in the interest of the orderly purchasing, handling, and selling of surpluses of cotton, grain, livestock, and other specified commodities. The board was authorized to make agreements with cooperatives and stabilization corporations in order to prevent losses resulting from price fluctuations. As a means of maintaining an even level of staple prices, the Federal Farm Board created (1930 the **Cotton Stabilization Corps.**, the **Grain Stabilization Corp.**, the **Wool Marketing Corp.**, and similar bodies for the purpose of making purchases in the open market. However, the price support program did not succeed, partly because farmers were reluctant to reduce their acreage. In 1931 the board terminated its purchasing program; in 1933, after spending more than $180 million, it went out of existence.

PANIC OF 1929. (For the boom, 1922–29, fed by unprecedented securities speculation, see p. 751.) The Wall Street stock market crash (Oct.–Nov.) was the overt inception of the worldwide Great Depression. Severe breaks occurred on 24 Oct., when 13 million shares changed hands, and 29 Oct. (16 million shares traded). By 13 Nov. about $30 billion in the market value of listed stocks had been wiped out; by mid-1932 these losses had increased to c. $75 billion. (For the deepening depression, see p. 403.)

1930

3 JULY. VETERANS ADMINISTRATION ACT consolidated all federal functions for ex-servicemen's relief in a single agency known as the Veterans Administration.

4 Nov. CONGRESSIONAL ELECTIONS. In their first setback since 1916, the Republicans lost 8 seats in the Senate and their majority in the House. The vote on prohibition in states such as Rhode Island, Illinois, and Massachusetts pointed to lessening support for the 18th Amendment.

HOOVER RELIEF POLICY. Opposed to direct federal relief for unemployed persons suffering from genuine distress, President Hoover advocated a policy of decentralized work relief. In Oct. he formulated a relief program that called for federal leadership of a national voluntary effort by agencies operating on a self-help basis in state and local communities. His object was to "preserve the principles of individual and local responsibility." On 2 Dec. Hoover requested an appropriation of $100–$150 million for construction of public works. Hoover created national emergency relief organizations headed at various times by Walter S. Gifford, Newton D. Baker, and others. However, when early in 1932 unemployment rose to 10 million, Hoover approved the Relief and Construction Act (p. 400).

1931

19 JAN. WICKERSHAM REPORT. By 1929 it was clearly evident that the enforcement of the 18th Amendment had broken down, creating a set of serious social and political problems. An illegal traffic in liquor (rum running and bootlegging) fostered powerful crime syndicates and such racketeers as "Scarface" **Al Capone** (1899–1947) who ruled the beer traffic and other rackets in Chicago, but was jailed on income tax evasion (1931). In May 1929, President Hoover appointed a Law Observance and Enforcement Commission headed by former

Attorney General **George W. Wicker-sham** (1858–1936) to conduct a survey to serve as the basis for formulating public policy on the 18th Amendment. In its report the commission stated that effective enforcement was hindered by the lucrative returns of the illicit liquor traffic, by public antipathy or hostility, and by the belief that enforcement of the 18th Amendment ought to be the function of the federal government alone rather than a joint federal-state undertaking. The commission opposed repeal of the Prohibition Amendment; a majority of the commission, however, favored its revision. In submitting the report to Congress (20 Jan.), President Hoover stated that he did not favor repeal.

VETERANS' BONUS. As the depression deepened, veterans' groups demanded immediate enactment of a bill authorizing a loan of 50% on the adjusted compensation ("bonus") certificates provided for by the act of 1924. Congress passed such a bill but Hoover vetoed it (26 Feb.) on grounds that it would be a blow to government economy and benefit many veterans not actually in distress. Congress passed the bill (27 Feb.) over his veto. Later in the year Democratic congressional leaders proposed that the entire bonus be paid in cash. The pressure for legislative approval resulted in the "Bonus March" on Washington in 1932.

1932

2 Feb. **RECONSTRUCTION FINANCE CORP.** President Hoover advocated an economic recovery program based on the assumption that government loans to banks and railroads would check deflation in agriculture and industry and ultimately restore the levels of employment and purchasing power. He proposed to Congress (8 Dec. 1931) the creation of a government lending agency with authority to issue tax-exempt bonds and with wide powers to extend credit. The Senate (11 Jan.) and the House (15 Jan.) passed the measure establishing the Reconstruction Finance Corp., capitalized at $500 million and authorized to borrow to the extent of $2 billion to provide emergency financing for banking institutions, life insurance companies, building and loan societies, railroads, and farm mortgage associations. It was also empowered to subscribe the capital for government-owned corporations. The measure was signed by President Hoover on 22 Jan. The RFC was established on 2 Feb. with **Charles G. Dawes** as its head. Within 6 months it had authorized a total of $1.2 billion in loans to about 5,000 life insurance companies, agricultural credit corporations, and other financial institutions.

27 Feb. **GLASS-STEAGALL ACT,** a credit expansion measure, broadened the acceptability of commercial paper for rediscount by the Federal Reserve system and made available for industrial and business needs about $750 million of the government gold supply hitherto used to support the currency. This act was designed to counteract the contraction of credit due to foreign withdrawals and the domestic hoarding of gold and currency.

7 July. The House, 202–157, passed the Wagner-Garner Bill to extend the work of federal employment agencies to states which did not sponsor such units. The Senate passed it (9 July), 43–31. President Hoover vetoed the measure (11 July) on the ground that it would interfere with state control over unemployment problems.

21 July. **RELIEF AND CONSTRUCTION ACT** extended the scope and functions of the RFC and authorized it to incur a total indebtedness of $3 billion. The RFC was empowered to provide $1.5 billion in loans for the construction

by state and local agencies of public works of a self-liquidating character, and to furnish $300 million in temporary loans to states unable to finance the relief of economic distress. The act also broadened the powers of the RFC to assist agriculture.

22 July. FEDERAL HOME LOAN BANK ACT, a measure recommended to Congress by President Hoover (8 Dec. 1931), established a 5-man Home Loan Bank Board and created a series of discount banks for home mortgages that provided for homeowners a service similar to that performed for commercial interests by the Federal Reserve discount facilities. It authorized the establishment of 8 to 12 banks set up in different parts of the country with a total capital of $125 million. Eligible for membership in the system were building and loan associations, savings banks, and insurance companies. The measure was designed to reduce foreclosures, stimulate residential construction (and thus increase employment), and encourage home ownership by providing the facilities for long-term loans payable in installments.

28–29 July. "BONUS ARMY." The demand for the immediate cashing of adjusted compensation certificates in full provided the impetus behind the "Bonus March" on Washington, D.C. About 1,000 ex-servicemen descended on the national capital (29 May) with the avowed purpose of remaining there until Congress authorized the cash payment. Other groups of veterans who arrived in June from all parts of the country brought the total number in the "Bonus Expeditionary Force" to an estimated 17,000. Many camped on the Anacostia Flats, on the edge of the city, and others made their homes in shacks and unused government buildings near the Capitol.

The House (15 June) passed the **Patman Bonus Bill** providing for the issuance of $2.4 billion in fiat money to pay off the remainder of the soldiers' bonus certificates. The Senate (17 June) defeated the measure. The government then provided funds for returning the veterans to their homes. Most of the ex-servicemen departed, but about 2,000 refused to disband. An attempt by the Washington police to evict them forcibly resulted in the death of 2 veterans and 2 policemen. President Hoover called out federal troops (28 July), who completed the removel of the veterans with the use of infantry, cavalry, and tanks.

PRESIDENTIAL CAMPAIGN. The Socialist Labor Party Convention met at New York (30 Apr.) and nominated Verne L. Reynolds (N.Y.) for president and J. W. Aiken (Mass.) for vice-president. The Socialist Party Convention met at Milwaukee (21 May) and nominated Norman Thomas (N.Y.) for president and James H. Maurer (Pa.) for vice-president. The Communist Party Convention met at Chicago and nominated (28 May) William Z. Foster (N.Y.) for president and James W. Ford, a Negro and native of Alabama, for vice-president.

The Prohibition Party Convention met at Indianapolis (5 July) and nominated William D. Upshaw (Ga.) for president and Frank S. Regan (Ill.) for vice-president. The Farmer-Labor Party National Committee met at Omaha (9 July) and nominated Jacob S. Coxey (Ohio) for president. The Liberty Party Convention met at St. Louis and nominated (17 Aug.) W. H. Harvey (Ark.) for president and Frank B. Hemenway (Wash.) for vice-president.

The Republican Party Convention met at Chicago (14 June) and renominated President **Hoover** (on the 1st ballot) and Vice-President **Charles Curtis.** The Republican platform called for a sharp reduction in government expenditures, a balanced budget, the maintenance and

extension of the protective tariff to stabilize the home market, U.S. participation
in an international monetary conference,
the gold standard, restriction of immigration, revision of the Prohibition
Amendment, and veterans' pensions for
service-connected disabilities.

The Democratic Party Convention met
at Chicago (27 June) and nominated
Gov. **Franklin Delano Roosevelt** (N.Y.)
for president on the 4th ballot (30 June)
and **John Nance Garner** (Tex., 1868–
1967) for vice-president. Breaking the
tradition that a presidential nominee
must await formal notification of his
selection, Roosevelt flew from Albany to
Chicago (2 July) and delivered an
acceptance speech stressing the need
for the reconstruction of the nation's
economy. "I pledge you, I pledge myself," he told the convention, "to a **new
deal** for the American people."

The Democratic platform advocated a
drastic cut in government spending, a
balanced budget, a competitive tariff for
revenue, unemployment and old-age insurance under state laws, a sound currency, U.S. participation in an international monetary conference, repeal of
the Prohibition Amendment, and veterans' pensions for service-connected
disabilities. It called for the "enactment
of every constitutional measure that will
aid the farmer to receive for basic farm
commodities prices in excess of the cost
of production." The platform advocated
banking and financial reforms including
the federal regulation of holding companies, of exchanges trading in securities
and commodities, and of the rates of
interstate utility companies. It supported protection of the investing public
by requiring full publicity and filing with
the government of all offerings of foreign
and domestic stocks and bonds.

During the campaign Roosevelt delivered numerous speeches in which he
set forth a program of economic nationalism and social reconstruction shaped by
him with the aid of a group of assistants
(including **Rexford G. Tugwell, Ray-
mond Moley,** and **Adolf A. Berle, Jr.**)
known as the "**Brains Trust.**" Roosevelt's
appeal was made to the "forgotten man
at the bottom of the economic pyramid"
(a phrase he first used on 7 Apr., before
his nomination). In an address delivered
(23 Sept.) at the Commonwealth Club
of California, at San Francisco, he said
that the function of government was to
meet "the problem of underconsumption,
of adjusting production to consumption,
of distributing wealth and products more
equitably, of adapting existing economic
organizations to the service of the people.
. . ." However, such economic regulation was to be assumed "only as a last
resort."

Hoover condemned Roosevelt's philosophy of government as a "radical departure" from the American way of life
and called for the decentralization of
government to permit the free expansion
of private enterprise. Should the New
Deal come to power, Hoover warned (31
Oct.), "the grass will grow in streets of
a hundred cities, a thousand towns; the
weeds will overrun the fields of millions
of farms. . . ."

8 Nov. PRESIDENTIAL ELECTION.
Popular vote: **Roosevelt,** 22,809,638;
Hoover, 15,758,901; Thomas, 881,951;
Foster, 102,785; Upshaw, 81,869; Har-
vey, 53,425; Reynolds, 33,276; Coxey,
7,309. Electoral vote: **Roosevelt,** 472;
Hoover, 59. Roosevelt carried 42 states;
Hoover carried Maine, Vermont, New
Hampshire, Connecticut, Pennsylvania,
and Delaware. The Democrats secured
majority control of both branches of Con-
gress. The composition of the 73rd Con-
gress was as follows: in the Senate, 60
Democrats, 35 Republicans, and 1
Farmer-Laborite; in the House, 310
Democrats, 117 Republicans, and 5
Farmer-Laborites.

1933

6 FEB. 20TH AMENDMENT to the Constitution, sponsored by George W. Norris (Neb.) and proposed on 2 Mar. 1932, was declared ratified. This so-called "**Lame Duck**" Amendment provided that effective 15 Oct. 1933 Congress would convene each year on 3 Jan. and that the terms of the president and vice-president would begin on 20 Jan. following the national elections.

15 FEB. At Miami, Fla., an assassin, Giuseppe Zangara, fired 6 shots at close range at president-elect Roosevelt and the party in the latter's open touring car. Roosevelt was uninjured, but several others were wounded, including Mayor **Anton Cermak** of Chicago, who died on 6 Mar. Zangara was put to death in the electric chair at Raiford, Fla. (20 Mar.).

ECONOMIC CRISIS. In the interim between the presidential election and the inauguration of President Roosevelt economic conditions reached gravely critical proportions. From Dec. 1932 to Mar. 1933 the index of industrial production dropped from 64 to an all-time low of 56. The nation's banking system revealed signs of alarming weakness as runs on banks became increasingly frequent and the hoarding of currency set in on a large scale. From 1930 until the eve of Roosevelt's inauguration, a total of 5,504 banks shut down. These banks had total deposits of $3,432,000,000. On 4 Feb. Louisiana declared a 1-day bank holiday. In Michigan, Gov. W. A. Comstock issued a proclamation (14 Feb.) calling for an 8-day bank holiday. By 2 Mar., 21 other states had suspended or drastically restricted banking operations. In New York, Gov. Herbert H. Lehman proclaimed (4 Mar.) a 2-day bank holiday. By Inauguration Day virtually every bank in the Union had been closed or placed under restriction by state proclamations.

4 MAR. In his inaugural address, Roosevelt affirmed that "the only thing we have to fear is fear itself," and called for vigorous national leadership.

5 MAR. President Roosevelt summoned the 73rd Congress to convene in special session on 9 Mar. Invoking powers granted by the Trading with the Enemy Act of 1917, Roosevelt prepared a proclamation, effective 6 Mar., declaring a 4-day national banking holiday suspending all transactions in the Federal Reserve and other banks, trust companies, credit unions, and building and loan associations. In order to permit the continuance of business operations, the use of scrip was allowed (e.g., clearing house certificates or other evidence of claims against the assets of banks). The proclamation also placed an embargo for a like period (6–9 Mar.) on the export of gold, silver, and currency, and ordered that gold and silver could be exported or withdrawn only on a license from the Treasury Department. During the first 3 days after the banking holiday, 4,507 national banks and 567 state member banks were opened (i.e., about 75% of all the member banks of the Federal Reserve system). Within 2 weeks stock prices rose 15%, with a return flow of hoarded currency and a rapid return of gold and gold certificates to the Treasury and the Reserve banks.

12 MAR. FIRST "FIRESIDE CHAT." Initiating a practice that became customary during his administration, President Roosevelt addressed the American people by nationwide radio broadcast. On this occasion he explained the steps he had taken to meet the financial emergency.

The New Deal

INAUGURATION OF THE NEW DEAL. The special session of the 73rd Congress that met on 9 Mar. was called by the president to deal with the banking crisis, but Roosevelt decided to hold Congress in session to deal with unemployment and farm relief. By the time this session (later known as the "Hundred Days") ended its deliberations (16 June), it had enacted a comprehensive body of legislation affecting banking, industry, agriculture, labor, and unemployment relief. This was the initial phase of the "First New Deal" (1933–35), aimed primarily at **relief and recovery.**

9 Mar.–16 June. "HUNDRED DAYS" produced the following body of legislation:

9 Mar. EMERGENCY BANKING RELIEF ACT, introduced, passed, and approved on the same day, confirmed all of the emergency steps taken by the president and the Secretary of the Treasury since 4 Mar. The Senate vote was 73–7; the House vote was unanimous. The act, affecting all national banks and Federal Reserve banks, gave the president broad discretionary powers over transactions in credit, currency, gold, and silver, including foreign exchange. Gold hoarding and export were forbidden. A maximum penalty of $10,000 fine and 10 years in prison was provided. The act permitted sound banks in the Federal Reserve system to open only under licenses from the Treasury Department; gave the Comptroller of the Currency authority to appoint conservators to care for the assets of insolvent national banks; authorized the Secretary of the Treasury to call in all gold and gold certificates in the country; enlarged the open-market operations of the Federal Reserve banks; and empowered the RFC to subscribe to the preferred stock of national banks and trust companies. This act, combined with the proclamation of 6 Mar., succeeded in checking the money panic.

20 Mar. ECONOMY ACT, requested by President Roosevelt on 10 Mar., was passed by the House (11 Mar.), 266–138, and by the Senate (15 Mar.), 62–13. It was designed to balance the budget of normal expenditures through (1) reductions of up to 15% in the salaries of government employees; (2) cuts in veterans' pensions and other allowances, particularly pension payments based on nonservice-connected disabilities; and (3) the reorganization of government agencies with a view to economy. Roosevelt estimated that the savings effected under this act would total $500 million. The amount actually saved was about $243 million.

22 Mar. BEER-WINE REVENUE ACT, aimed at securing additional revenue, amended the Volstead Act to legalize wine, beer, lager beer, ale, and porter of 3.2% maximum alcoholic content by weight, or 4% by volume, and levied a tax of $5 per barrel of 31 gallons. The act left to the states all regulatory and control measures, especially those relating to sale and distribution, and incorporated safeguards for states whose prohibition laws stipulated a lesser alcoholic content. The measure took effect on 7 Apr.

31 Mar. CIVILIAN CONSERVATION CORPS REFORESTATION RELIEF ACT, passed as an unemployment relief measure, established the Civilian Conservation Corps (CCC), authorized to provide work for 250,000 jobless male citizens between the ages of 18 to 25 in reforestation, road construction, the prevention of soil erosion, and national park and flood control projects under the direction of army officers. Work camps were established for those enrolled in the CCC; the youths received $30 per month, part of which went to dependents. Four government departments (War, Interior, Agriculture, Labor) cooperated in carrying out the program. CCC had as many as 500,000 on its rolls at one time; by end of 1941 had employed over 2 million youths.

APR.–MAY. BLACK-CONNERY-PERKINS WAGES AND HOURS BILL was displaced on the legislative program by the NIRA (p. 407).

19 APR. The U.S. officially abandoned the gold standard, causing a decline in the exchange value of the dollar abroad and an increase in the prices of commodities, silver, and stocks on American exchanges.

12 MAY. FEDERAL EMERGENCY RELIEF ACT created the Federal Emergency Relief Administration (FERA) and authorized an appropriation of $500 million, allotting half this amount as direct relief to the states and the balance for distribution on the basis of $1 of federal aid for every $3 of state and local funds spent for relief. The FERA was based on the system of outright grants to states and municipalities, as differentiated from the loan policy initiated under the Hoover administration. The act left the establishment of work relief projects for employables to state and local bodies and authorized the RFC to supply the funds for distribution to the states through a relief administrator. Harry L. Hopkins (p. 1061) was appointed Federal Relief Administrator.

12 MAY. AGRICULTURAL ADJUSTMENT ACT was designed to restore the purchasing power of agricultural producers. The drastic decline of farm income between 1929 and 1932 had prompted a farmers' strike in the summer of 1932 organized by the Farmers' Holiday Assn., led by Milo Reno of Iowa, and reinforced by warnings in Jan. 1933 from the conservative American Farm Bureau Federation. The chief objects of the AAA were the elimination of surplus crops of basic commodities through curtailed production and the establishment of parity prices for enumerated basic commodities. Parity price was based on the purchasing power of the farmers' dollar at the level of 100 cts. during the base period of 1909–14 for corn, cotton, wheat, rice, hogs, and dairy products; and the base period of 1919–29 for tobacco. The act incorporated the subsidy principle: in return for voluntarily reducing acreage or crops, farmers were to be granted direct benefit or rental payments. The funds for such payments were to be derived from levies on the processors of specified farm products. The act established the Agricultural Adjustment Administration (AAA). In 1934 the list of enumerated commodities was extended by the Jones-Connally Farm Relief Act and the Jones-Costigan Sugar Act.

The act relieved the credit situation by providing for the refinancing of farm mortgages through the agency of the Federal Land Banks. In addition, the Thomas Amendment to this act permitted the president to inflate the currency by the following means: devaluation of the gold content of the dollar, free coinage of silver at a ratio to gold determined by the president, and the issuance of paper currency to the amount of $3 billion. This last provision was never implemented by Roosevelt. The devaluation provision, however, enabled the president to make attempts to raise prices through control of the so-called "commodity dollar."

The processing tax and production control features of the Agricultural Adjustment Act were declared unconstitutional by the Supreme Court in U.S. v. Butler (1936, p. 677).

18 MAY. TENNESSEE VALLEY AUTHORITY. During World War I the national government, at a cost of $145 million, built a large hydroelectric power plant and two munitions plants at Muscle Shoals, on the Tennessee River in Alabama. During the 1920s the government unsuccessfully attempted to dispose of

the Muscle Shoals facilities to private interests. Sen. **George W. Norris** (Neb., p. 1117) conducted a campaign to place the power resources of the Tennessee River at the service of the watershed's inhabitants, and to devote the World War I plants to the manufacture of fertilizer. On 25 May 1928 and again on 3 Mar. 1931 a group of legislators headed by Norris secured the passage of bills providing for government operation of Muscle Shoals, but the measures were vetoed by Presidents Coolidge and Hoover, respectively, on the ground that government operation would constitute governor of New York, Roosevelt sponsored and executed a statewide planning movement and helped to establish a state competition with private enterprise. As power authority. In Jan. 1933, he visited Muscle Shoals with a group of officials and experts. Before his accession to the presidency, Roosevelt envisioned for the Tennessee River drainage basin and adjoining territory a program embracing not merely power development but a plan of regional development based on the control and use of water resources. Aimed at furthering the general social and economic welfare of the region, the program contemplated flood control, land reclamation, the prevention of soil erosion, afforestation, the elimination of marginal lands from cultivation, and the distribution and diversification of industry.

The aims of Roosevelt and Norris were embodied in the act establishing the **Tennessee Valley Authority** (TVA), an independent public corporation with a board of three directors (the initial board consisted of Arthur E. Morgan, chairman; Harcourt A. Morgan, and David E. Lilienthal). The TVA was authorized to construct dams and power plants and to develop the economic and social well-being of the Tennessee Valley region (covering the states of Tenn.,

N.C., Ky., Va., Miss., Ga., and Ala.). It was authorized to produce, distribute, and sell electric power and nitrogen fertilizers to the industry and people of the region, and to sell explosives to the federal government. A "yardstick" for public utilities was embodied in the provisions for the construction of transmission lines to farms and villages not supplied with electricity at rates that were reasonable and fair, and for the selling of power to municipalities and other public bodies.

Between 1933 and 1944 9 main-river dams and many subsidiary ones were built along the water system. During World War II, TVA supplied the power facilities for the manufacture of munitions and aluminum and for the atom bomb plant at Oak Ridge, Tenn.

27 MAY. FEDERAL SECURITIES ACT was designed to compel full disclosure to investors of information relating to new securities issues publicly offered or sold through the mails or in interstate commerce. It required that with certain exceptions (e.g., federal, state, and municipal bonds; railroad securities; securities of religious, charitable, and educational bodies) all new issues were to be registered with the Federal Trade Commission by the filing of sworn statements placed on public file (in 1934 this function was transferred to the Securities and Exchange Commission).

5 JUNE. GOLD REPEAL JOINT RESOLUTION, another move for making the abandonment of the gold standard effective, canceled the gold clause in all federal and private obligations and made contracts and debts payable in legal tender.

6 JUNE. NATIONAL EMPLOYMENT SYSTEM ACT authorized a national employment system, established as the U.S. Employment Service, based on cooperation with states maintaining such agencies. It required matching of state appropriations for employment services.

13 June. HOME OWNERS REFINANCING ACT created the Home Owners Loan Corporation (HOLC), with a capital stock of $200 million and an authorized issue of $2 billion in bonds, to refinance home mortgage debts for nonfarm owners. Refinancing was accomplished by the exchange of HOLC bonds for mortgages and all other obligations (up to a total of $14,000), which were then converted into a single first mortgage. The HOLC was also empowered to furnish cash advances for taxes, repair, and maintenance up to 50% of appraised values on unencumbered properties. By the time the HOLC terminated its activities in June 1936, it had made loans covering 1 million mortgages.

16 June. BANKING ACT OF 1933 (GLASS-STEAGALL ACT) created the **Federal Bank Deposit Insurance Corporation** for guaranteeing individual bank deposits under $5,000. It also extended the open-market activities of the Federal Reserve Board to enable it to prevent excessive speculation on credit; permitted branch banking; divorced deposit from investment affiliates; and widened the membership of the Federal Reserve system to include savings and industrial banks.

16 June. FARM CREDIT ACT was designed to facilitate short-term and medium-term credits for agricultural production and marketing, thereby refinancing farm mortgages on long terms at low interest. On 27 Mar. President Roosevelt had by executive decree consolidated in a single agency, the Farm Credit Administration (FCA), the functions of all federal units dealing with agricultural credit (e.g., the Federal Farm Board, the Federal Farm Loan Board).

16 June. EMERGENCY RAILROAD TRANSPORTATION ACT, applying to carriers and subsidiaries subject to the Interstate Commerce Act, was designed to avoid unnecessary duplication of services and facilities; to promote financial reorganization of the carriers; and to provide for the study of other means of improving conditions pertaining to rail transportation. The act repealed the "recapture" clause of the Transportation Act of 1920, placed railroad holding companies under the supervision of the Interstate Commerce Commission, provided for a simpler rule of rate making, and created the office of Federal Coordinator of Transportation (a post to which **Joseph B. Eastman** was appointed).

16 June. NATIONAL INDUSTRIAL RECOVERY ACT (called the NIRA) was designed to revive industrial and business activity and to reduce unemployment. It was based on the principle of industrial self-regulation, operating under government supervision through a system of fair competition codes. The act created the National Recovery Administration (NRA) and formalized the fair trade codes that had been used by many industrial and trade associations in the period after World War I. Under the NIRA, fair competition codes drawn up by such associations and approved by the president were enforceable by law. The president was also empowered to prescribe codes for industries and to make agreements or approve voluntary agreements. Actions under codes and agreements were exempt from the operations of the antitrust laws. The courts could issue injunctions agains violators. When business pressure compelled the administration to abandon the Black-Connery-Perkins Bill, provision for labor was made in Section 7a of the NIRA guaranteeing labor's right "to organize and bargain collectively through representatives of their own choosing." Gen. **Hugh S. Johnson** (1882–1942) was appointed (16 June) head of the NRA, an

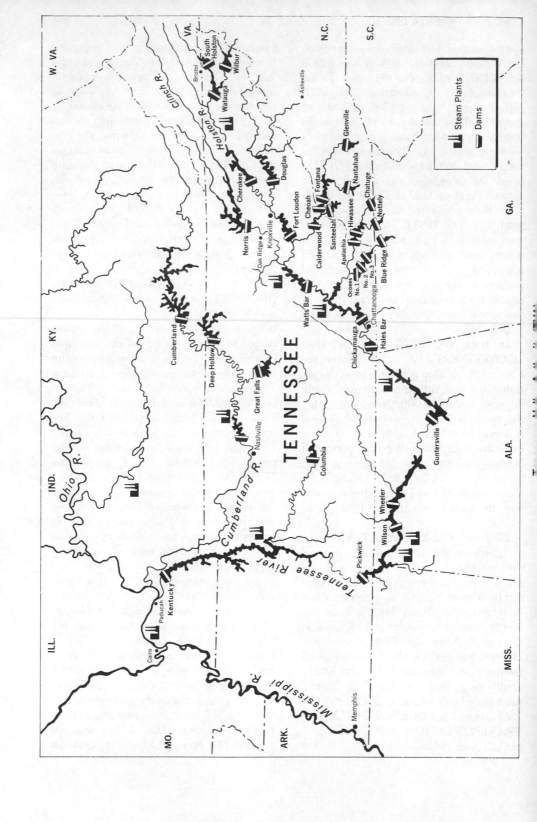

agency which ultimately affected about 500 fields and a total of 22 million employees. Sen. Robert F. Wagner (N.Y.) was appointed chairman of the **National Labor Board,** established (5 Aug.) by the president under NIRA to enforce the right of collective bargaining.

While the NRA was initially successful, code violations soon became increasingly frequent; complaints of cutthroat competition and unfair price fixing became numerous. The National Recovery Review Board, established on 19 Feb. 1934, reported (21 May 1934) that the NRA was encouraging monopoly and cartelization to the detriment of the small businessman. The Supreme Court held the NIRA unconstitutional in *Schechter Poultry Corp.* v. *U.S.* (1935, p. 676).

Title II of the NIRA established the **Public Works Administration** (PWA) for the construction of roads, public buildings, and other projects, for which a fund of $3,300 million was authorized. Secretary of the Interior **Harold L. Ickes** (p. 1065) was named (16 June) to head the agency. The PWA was created for the purpose of increasing employment and business activity by means of "pump priming" (i.e., the raising of popular consuming power). During its recovery phase, the PWA spent a total of more than $4,250 million on some 34,000 public projects.

16 JUNE. Special session of the 73rd Congress adjourned.

18 OCT. COMMODITY CREDIT CORPORATION, an agency organized under the AAA with a capitalization of $3 million (increased in 1936 to $100 million), was authorized to use RFC funds for extending loans to farmers on their crops. Its purpose was to support farm prices by enabling producers to retain commodities. At the outset, loans were extended chiefly to cotton farmers; as a result cotton prices were bolstered.

22 OCT. "COMMODITY DOLLAR." President Roosevelt announced that he had authorized the RFC to establish a government market for gold newly mined in the U.S. and to buy and sell gold on the world market if necessary in order to enable the government to take "in its own hands the control of the gold value of our dollar."

The new gold policy was put into effect on 25 Oct., when the government set the price at $31.36 an ounce (as compared with $29.01 an ounce on the world market on 21 Oct.). The price was subsequently increased until it reached $34.06 on 18 Dec. The gold value of the dollar was set at 66 cts. This forced devaluation of the dollar, however, did not accomplish its object of raising farm commodity prices above the world level. Moreover, the measure provoked complaints from foreign nations (which feared that cheaper American goods gave U.S. exporters an unfair advantage in world trade); brought "sound money" elements in the Democratic party into open conflict with the administration; and ultimately led inflationist groups to increase their pressure for silver legislation.

8 Nov. CIVIL WORKS ADMINISTRATION (CWA) was established as an emergency unemployment relief program for the purpose of putting 4 million jobless persons to work on federal, state, and local make-work projects. **Harry L. Hopkins** was appointed (8 Nov.) as its administrator. Funds were allocated from FERA and PWA appropriations supplemented by local governments. The CWA was created to offset a drop in the business revival of mid-1933 and to cushion economic distress over the winter of 1933–34. The CWA was terminated in Mar. 1934, and transferred its functions to the FERA. Of the more than $933 million spent on 180,000 work projects,

more than $740 million went directly into wages and salaries.

5 Dec. 21ST AMENDMENT to the Constitution, proposed on 20 Feb. 1933 and providing for the **repeal of the 18th (Prohibition) Amendment,** was declared ratified.

21 Dec. Acting under the Thomas Amendment to the Agricultural Adjustment Act, President Roosevelt ordered the Treasury to buy at 64½ cts. an ounce (21½ cts. above the prevailing market price) all the silver mined in the U.S. during the ensuing 4-year period.

1934

30 Jan. GOLD RESERVE ACT OF 1934 was designed to give the government full control over dollar devaluation and to increase commodity prices without relying on inflationary measures. The act empowered the president to do the following: to set the limits for devaluation of the dollar at from 50 to 60 cts. in relation to its gold content; to change the value within these limits from time to time, as deemed necessary by him; to impound in the Treasury the gold stocks held by the Federal Reserve banks; to assure to the government any profit that might accrue to the Treasury from an increase in the value of gold; and to use part of this profit to set up a fund (the Exchange Stabilization Fund) of $2 billion with which to stabilize the dollar. By proclamation (31 Jan.) Roosevelt fixed the value of the dollar at 59.06 cts.

31 Jan. FARM MORTGAGE REFINANCING ACT established the Federal Farm Mortgage Corporation (FFMC) under the Farm Credit Administration and authorized it to issue up to $2 billion in bonds guaranteed in principal and interest. The purpose of the FFMC was to further the refinancing of farm debts by exchanging its bonds for con-

solidated farm loan bonds and investing them directly in mortgage loans.

2 Feb. EXPORT-IMPORT BANK, established by President Roosevelt under powers granted to the RFC and NRA, was created to encourage the flow of overseas commerce by financing trade with foreign nations in the following ways: short-term credits in connection with the exportation of agricultural commodities, extension of longer-term credit to American firms desiring to export industrial manufactures, and loans to American exporters where foreign governments failed to provide their own nationals with sufficient exchange to permit them to meet dollar obligations. Two banks were set up, one to provide credits for trading with the Soviet Union, which had recently received formal diplomatic recognition by the U.S.; another (12 Mar.) to provide credit facilities for trading with Cuba and ultimately other foreign nations. Both banks were consolidated in a single bank in 1936.

15 Feb. CIVIL WORKS EMERGENCY RELIEF ACT authorized $950 million for use by the FERA until the end of the fiscal year 1935 for operating the program of civil works and direct relief. This program emerged (1935) as the Works Progress Administration (WPA). Under the Emergency Work Relief Program authorized by the Act of 15 Feb., a total of 2,500,000 unemployed were on the rolls by Jan. 1935, when direct relief was returned to state and local governments.

23 Feb. CROP LOAN ACT authorized the Farm Credit Administration to extend loans to agricultural producers in 1934 for crop production and harvesting. A fund of $40 million was set up for this purpose. Approximately $37,900,000 was loaned.

27 Mar. VINSON NAVAL PARITY ACT authorized the building of a full-treaty-strength navy within the limits set by the Washington Naval Limitations Treaty of 1922 and the London Naval Limitation Treaty of 1930. It provided for the construction of 100 warships and more than 1,000 airplanes over a 5-year period. Congress, however, did not appropriate sufficient funds, and until 1938 naval construction was carried out chiefly on a replacement basis.

28 Mar. INDEPENDENT OFFICES APPROPRIATIONS ACT represented the first defeat President Roosevelt sustained at the hands of Congress. The Senate and House passed (26 Mar.) the Independent Offices Bill restoring the cuts made under the Economy Act of 1933. It increased salaries of government employees by $125 million and the allowances of World War I veterans by $228 million. President Roosevelt vetoed the bill (27 Mar.) on the ground of economy. The House (310–72, 27 Mar.) and the Senate (63–27, 28 Mar.) overrode the veto.

7 Apr. JONES-CONNALLY FARM RELIEF ACT extended the list of enumerated basic agricultural commodities subject to the Agricultural Adjustment Act, adding barley, flax, peanuts, grain sorghums, rye, and beef and dairy cattle.

21 Apr. COTTON CONTROL ACT (BANKHEAD ACT) provided for the compulsory reduction of surplus cotton crops through the licensing of individual producers who in turn received benefit payments. The act, a departure from the voluntary principle of the AAA, authorized the fixing of a national limitation on the cotton crop and provided for the allocation of crops and marketing quotas for cotton-growing states, counties, and farmers. A tax of not less than 5 cts. a pound was authorized for production in excess of stipulated quotas.

27 Apr. HOME OWNERS LOAN ACT guaranteed the principal and interest of the $2 billion in bonds authorized for the refinancing of home mortgages. From the funds made available as a result of the guarantee, the HOLC was enabled to extend further assistance for the repair and maintenance of homes and to provide funds to savings and loans associations operating under federal sponsorship.

9 May. JONES-COSTIGAN SUGAR ACT extended the list of enumerated basic crops subject to the Agricultural Adjustment Act to include sugar cane and sugar beets, and authorized benefit payments allocated from funds derived from a processing tax on sugar. It sought to stabilize the price of sugar by authorizing limitation on the national production of these sugar crops and empowered the Secretary of Agriculture to put all sugar imports on a quota basis. The decision of the Supreme Court in *U.S.* v. *Butler* (1936) invalidated the tax features of this act.

NYE MUNITIONS INVESTIGATION. The Senate voted (12 Apr.) an inquiry into the manufacture and traffic in arms in the U.S. Sen. **Gerald P. Nye** (N.D.) was appointed (23 Apr.) chairman of the Senate Munitions Investigating Committee, whose public hearings stressed the heavy profits made by American financiers and armament makers during World War I and sought to show, although without conclusive evidence, that the U.S. entry in World War I was due to the covert pressures they exerted. The activities of the Nye Committee, which continued until 1936, strengthened isolationist sentiment and set the domestic background for the neutrality legislation of 1935, 1936, and 1937 (see p. 388).

18 May. CRIME CONTROL ACTS. To counteract the widespread rise of racketeering, kidnaping, and other forms of crime, 6 new crime laws were enacted, among others empowering the federal government to punish persons assaulting, resisting, killing, or interfering with federal agents performing their law-enforcement duties and authorizing the death penalty for kidnapers taking their victims across state lines (the last as a result of the kidnaping and murder of the son of Charles A. and Anne Morrow Lindbergh (1 Mar. 1932). The federal criminal code was further strengthened by the Crime Prevention Compact Act (16 June) which permitted the states to enter into compacts for the prevention of crime and the enforcement of criminal laws.

24 MAY. MUNICIPAL BANK-RUPTCY ACT permitted cities and other local government units to petition the federal courts for the ensuing 2 years to approve plans for readjusting their debt burden, providing that holders of 51% of outstanding obligations gave their consent.

6 JUNE. SECURITIES EXCHANGE ACT provided for federal regulation of the operations of exchanges dealing in securities and for the correction of unfair practices in the securities markets. It established the **Securities and Exchange Commission** (SEC) and authorized that unit to license stock exchanges. It made trading in securities subject to the regulations of the SEC and prohibited price manipulation. It empowered the Federal Reserve Board to regulate the use of credit in financing trading in securities by prescribing regulations governing margin requirements (a move designed to curb speculation).

7 JUNE. CORPORATE BANK-RUPTCY ACT permitted the reorganization of corporations, provided that at least two thirds of their creditors consented, and stipulated that a petition for reorganization might be filed in court by a creditor or stockholder if approved by at least one fourth of other stockhold-

ers (10% where the corporation was not insolvent but unable to meet maturing obligations).

12 JUNE. FARM MORTGAGE FORE-CLOSURE ACT authorized the Land Bank Commissioner to extend loans to farmers to enable the recovery of farm properties owned by them prior to foreclosure.

15 JUNE. NATIONAL GUARD ACT made that military organization a part of the Army of the U.S. in time of war or during a national emergency declared by Congress.

19 JUNE. COMMUNICATIONS ACT abolished the Federal Radio Commission and established the **Federal Communications Commission** (FCC) for the regulation of interstate and foreign communications by telegraph, cable, and radio. The act transferred to the FCC the authority of the Interstate Commerce Commission for control of communications, and imposed new regulations for the control of radio broadcasting.

19 JUNE. SILVER PURCHASE ACT, a compromise measure passed to meet the demands for additional inflation voiced by farmer and silver interests in Congress, empowered the president to increase the monetary value of the Treasury's silver holdings until they should reach one third the value of its gold stocks; to nationalize silver stocks and purchases of domestic and foreign silver; and to impose a 50% profits tax on certain transfers of silver in order to preclude a windfall for silver speculators. By presidential order (9 Aug.) the Treasury was directed to buy all silver in the U.S. at 50 cts. an ounce, all newly mined silver at 64.64 cts. an ounce, and to pay for it with silver certificates at the rate of $1.29 an ounce (thereby placing silver on a 27–1 ratio with gold). This move benefited U.S. silver producers.

19 JUNE. **LABOR DISPUTES JOINT RESOLUTION** established the National Labor Relations Board, replacing the National Labor Board, 1933.

27 JUNE. **RAILROAD RETIREMENT ACT OF 1934** was declared unconstitutional in *Railroad Retirement Board* v. *Alton R.R. Co.* (1935, p. 676).

27 JUNE. **CROSSER-DILL RAILWAY LABOR ACT** (p. 768).

28 JUNE. **FEDERAL FARM BANKRUPTCY ACT (FRAZIER-LEMKE FARM BANKRUPTCY ACT)**, designed to prevent foreclosures, provided additional relief to farmers by enabling them to secure credit extensions. Provision was made whereby farmers could repurchase their properties at a newly appraised value with small annual payments, at an interest rate of 1%, distributed over a 6-year period. In the event creditors opposed such a settlement, farmers could retain possession on fair and reasonable terms for **5 years**, during which time bankruptcy proceedings were suspended. This act was declared unconstitutional in the case of *Louisville Joint Stock Land Bank* v. *Radford* (1935, 295 U.S. 555).

28 JUNE. **NATIONAL HOUSING ACT** was designed to stimulate residential construction, promote improvement in housing standards, and create a sound system of home financing. It established the **Federal Housing Administration** (FHA) for the purpose of insuring loans made by banks, trust companies, building and loan associations, and other private lending institutions for new construction, repairs, alterations, and improvements. The act, which enabled the modernization of farm properties and of small business plants and equipment, increased the borrowing power of the HOLC to $3 billion.

28 JUNE. **TOBACCO CONTROL ACT** (similar to the Cotton Control Act of 1934) authorized a compulsory production quota system for tobacco planters and subjected to an ad valorem tax producers who did not agree to crop reduction.

6 Nov. **CONGRESSIONAL ELECTIONS** gave the Democrats a gain of 9 seats in the Senate and 9 seats in the House. The 74th Congress was the first to convene (3 Jan. 1935) under the provisions of the 20th Amendment.

1935

4 JAN. **SECOND NEW DEAL.** In his annual message to Congress, President Roosevelt outlined a program of **social reform** that signalized the launching of the second New Deal, designating 3 major goals: security of livelihood through the better use of national resources; security against unemployment, old age, illness, and dependency; and slum clearance and better housing. He also recommended a national works program for absorbing the needy unemployed. The chief beneficiaries of the second New Deal were labor and the smaller farmers.

8 APR. **EMERGENCY RELIEF APPROPRIATION ACT** signalized the withdrawal of the federal government from the arena of direct relief, which was left to the states and local communities, and provided for the establishment of a large-scale national works program for jobless employables, who were required to meet a means test in order to qualify for work relief. Established as the major agency of the program was the **Works Progress Administration** (WPA), which beginning in 1939 was called the **Works Projects Administration. Harry L. Hopkins** was appointed (6 May) administrator of the WPA. About 85% of the funds spent on WPA projects went directly into wages and salaries. Beginning in 1936 the "security wage" of WPA

workers was based on the prevailing hourly rate, at reduced hours of work (the average monthly maximum schedule ranging between 120 and 140 hours). By Mar. 1936, the WPA rolls reached a total of more than 3,400,000 persons; after initial cuts in June 1939, it averaged 2,300,000 monthly; and by 30 June 1943, when it was officially terminated, the WPA had employed more than 8,500,000 different persons on 1,410,-000 individual projects, and had spent about $11 billion. While most of the projects were geared to the employment of manual labor, provision was made by way of arts projects for writers, actors, artists, and musicians. In addition to the WPA, other participating agencies in the national works program included the Public Works Administration, the Civilian Conservation Corps, and the National Youth Administration. During its 8-year history, the WPA built 651,087 miles of highways, roads, and streets; and constructed, repaired, or improved 124,031 bridges, 125,110 public buildings, 8,192 parks, and 853 airport landing fields. It operated community recreation and educational centers and carried out numerous surveys of federal, state, and local archives. The WPA was attacked on the grounds of inefficiency, extravagance, waste, and political corruption. Defenders pointed to its constructive achievements and to the rise in national purchasing power.

27 Apr. SOIL CONSERVATION ACT established the Soil Conservation Service as a permanent unit of the Department of Agriculture for the control and prevention of soil erosion.

1 May. RESETTLEMENT ADMINISTRATION (known as the RA) was established by executive order under powers granted by the Emergency Relief Appropriation Act of 1935. Undersecretary of Agriculture **Rexford G. Tugwell** was appointed administrator. The gen-

eral objectives of the RA included the improvement of the conditions of impoverished farm families that had not been materially aided by the AAA, and the prevention of waste due to unprofitable farming operations and improper land use. The RA was authorized to administer projects involving resettlement of destitute or low-income families from rural and urban areas, or soil erosion, flood control, stream pollution, and reforestation; and to grant loans to enable the purchase of farm lands and equipment by smaller farmers, farm tenants, sharecroppers, or farm laborers. Among the activities of the RA were the establishment of subsistence homestead communities and the construction of suburban communities for low-income city workers—"Greenbelt towns," including Greenbelt (near Washington, D.C.), Greenhills (near Cincinnati), and Greendale (near Milwaukee). The functions of the RA were absorbed by the Farm Security Administration in 1937.

11 May. RURAL ELECTRIFICATION ADMINISTRATION (called the REA) was established by executive order under powers granted by the Emergency Relief Appropriation Act of 1935. Its purpose was to formulate and administer a program of generating and distributing electricity in isolated rural areas which were not served by private utilities. The REA was authorized to lend the entire cost of constructing light and power lines in such areas, on liberal terms of 3% interest, with amortization extended over a 20-year period. Priority was given to publicly owned plants distributing electricity.

22 May. VETO OF THE PATMAN BONUS BILL. The Patman Bill provided for the full and immediate payment in cash by issuance of $2,200 million greenbacks of the adjusted compensation certificates held by World War I veterans, which, under the act of 1924, were not due to mature until 1945. President Roosevelt, establishing a precedent by appearing before a joint session of Congress to deliver a veto message in person, rejected the bill, chiefly on the grounds that enactment of the measure would spur inflation and increase the national deficit. The House (322–98, 22 May) overrode the veto, but the Senate (54–40, 23 May) sustained it.

27 May. The NIRA was invalidated by the Supreme Court decision in the case of *Schechter Poultry Corp.* v. *U.S.* (p. 676).

7 June. NATIONAL RESOURCES COMMITTEE was created by executive order under powers granted by the Emergency Relief Appropriation Act of 1935 for the purpose of collecting and preparing plans, data, and information relating to the planned development and use of land, water, and other national resources. The successor to the National Resources Board set up on 30 June 1934, it later became known as the National Resources Planning Board and was entrusted with the preparation of long-range plans for the development of national resources and the stabilization of employment. It was terminated on 1 July 1943 upon failure of Congress to appropriate further funds.

26 June. NATIONAL YOUTH ADMINISTRATION (called the NYA) was established by executive order under powers granted by the Emergency Relief Appropriation Act of 1935. It was created as a part of the WPA and was placed under the direction of **Aubrey Williams.** The purpose of the NYA was to administer a work-relief and employment program for persons between the ages of 16 and 25, chiefly from relief families and no longer in regular full-time attendance at school, and to provide part-time employment for needy school, college, and graduate students to help them continue their education. By

1936, some 600,000 persons were engaged in NYA activities, with a peak in 1939–40 when about 750,000 students in 1,700 colleges and universities and more than 28,000 secondary schools received NYA benefits. In 1939 the NYA was transferred to the Federal Security Agency, and in 1942 became part of the War Manpower Commission. During 1941–43 it trained workers for national defense activities at an average rate of 30,000 a month. The NYA was terminated Sept. 1943.

5 July. NATIONAL LABOR RELATIONS ACT (WAGNER-CONNERY ACT) created a new National Labor Relations Board (NLRB) with power to determine appropriate collective bargaining units subject to elections it supervised at the request of the workers, to certify the duly chosen trade union, and to take testimony about unfair employer practices and issue cease and desist orders. Section 7 upheld the right of employees to join labor organizations and to bargain collectively through representatives of their own choosing. Section 8 defines unfair labor practices on the employers' part. The constitutionality of the act was upheld by the Supreme Court (Mar. 1937, p. 677). This legislation was soon complemented by state "Wagner Acts."

9 Aug. MOTOR CARRIER ACT placed buses and trucks engaged in interstate commerce under the authority of the Interstate Commerce Commission, which was empowered to regulate finances, labor, and minimum and maximum rates.

ANTI-NEW DEAL COALITION. Dissatisfaction with the social, fiscal, and other aspects of the New Deal led to the emergence of several organized antiadministration groups during 1934–35. The **Liberty League** (est. Aug. 1934), which drew its following from industrialists, financiers, corporation lawyers, conservative Democrats, and others, attacked the New Deal as a departure from the Constitution and actively opposed the passage of such measures as the Wagner-Connery Labor Relations Bill and the Wealth Tax Bill. The **Old Age Revolving Pension** scheme proposed by Dr. **Francis E. Townsend** of Long Beach, Calif., called for payments of $200 a month to persons 60 years of age and over, the pensions to be drawn from a national 2% tax on commercial transactions. The **Share-Our-Wealth** movement inspired by Sen. **Huey P. Long** (La., p. 1088) demanded that the federal government make "Every Man a King" by guaranteeing a minimum annual income of $5,000 to every family. Rev. **Gerald L. K. Smith** succeeded to Long's leadership of the Share-Our-Wealth clubs and formed an alliance with the Townsend movement, later to include Rev. **Charles E. Coughlin,** of Royal Oak, Mich., who in 1934 organized the **National Union for Social Justice.** Coughlin advocated a program of social reform that was specific in its support of silver inflation but vague on most other points. His radio speeches, directed against international bankers, Communists, labor unions, and the Roosevelt administration, attracted a national audience. The Smith-Townsend-Coughlin coalition gained in strength during 1935 and in 1936 emerged as a third-party movement. However, it never succeeded in uniting under a single and continuous leadership.

14 Aug. SOCIAL SECURITY ACT (an administration measure motivated in part by an attempt to win over the Townsend-Long following) created the Social Security Board as a general administrative agency and provided for the following in relation to unemployment compensation, old-age security, and various social services: (1) Establishment of a cooperative federal-state system of **unemployment compensation** designed to promote substantial uniformity of unemployment insurance plans among the various states and to invite the states to legislate in this field. The act levied a federal tax on total payrolls of employers of 8 or more workers (with certain exceptions, including agricultural laborers) equal to 1% in 1936, 2% in 1937, and 3% thereafter. Each state was to administer its own insurance system, and was to receive credit up to 90% of the federal tax. The act authorized grants to the states to enable them to meet administrative costs in providing unemployment insurance. (2) A tax for **old-age and survivors' insurance** to be levied in equal amounts upon all employers and employees (with specified exceptions) commencing at 1% in 1937 and gradually increasing to 3% in 1949. This part of the act was exclusively federal in scope and character. Out of the national fund created by these taxes the federal government was to pay to retired individuals 65 years of age and over a retirement pension (beg. 1 Jan. 1942) ranging from a minimum of $10 to a maximum of $85 per month, depending upon the number of working years during which the employee contributed. (3) Authorized money grants to states to help them meet the cost of **old-age pensions allowed under state laws** to aged persons in need of relief, the grants to match the amount contributed by the state, with a maximum federal contribution of $15 per month for each individual plus a small amount for administrative purposes. (4) Authorized money grants to the states to assist them in relief of the destitute blind and of homeless, crippled, dependent, and delinquent children, and in services such as public health work, vocational rehabilitation, and maternity and infant care. The tax features of the act were upheld by the Supreme Court in *Steward Machine Co.* v. *Davis* and *Helvering et al.* v. *Davis* (1937).

23 Aug. BANKING ACT OF 1935 included the following provisions: (1) The title of the Federal Reserve Board changed to the Board of Governors of the Federal Reserve System, the board's ex-officio members were eliminated, and its membership increased from 6 to 7, with 1 member to serve as chairman for 4 years; (2) control over the regulation of credit vested in an Open Market Committee consisting of the Board of Governors and 5 representatives of the Federal Reserve banks; (3) purchase of government securities by the Federal Reserve banks confined to open-market operations; (4) Board of Governors empowered to increase the reserve requirements of member banks up to a limit of twice existing maximums; (5) Federal Reserve banks permitted to lend to member banks on time or demand notes with maturities not exceeding 4 months; (6) national banks authorized to make real estate loans.

28 Aug. PUBLIC UTILITY HOLDING COMPANY ACT (WHEELER-RAYBURN ACT), designed to counteract the monopolistic public utility holding company device for controlling gas and electric operating companies, vested in the Federal Power Commission authority to regulate interstate transmission of electric power; in the Federal Trade Commission authority over gas; in the SEC authority over financial practices of such holding companies. The act restricted electric and gas holding companies to operations as single and concentrated systems confined to a single area, and called for simplification of the corporate structure of utility holding companies in order to eliminate pyramiding. The "death sentence" clause set a term of 5 years, at the end of which any holding company which could not demonstrate its localized, useful, and efficient character would be dissolved. In compliance public utility holding companies

had by 1952 divested 753 affiliates, with assets of $10.3 billion.

29 Aug. FARM MORTGAGE MORATORIUM ACT OF 1935 (FRAZIER-LEMKE ACT OF 1935) was passed following the Supreme Court decision invalidating the Federal Farm Bankruptcy Act of 1934. It provided for a 3-year moratorium against seizure for farmers who secured court permission, thus enabling debt-burdened farmers to keep possession of their properties by paying a fair and reasonable rental determined by the court.

29 Aug. WAGNER-CROSSER RAILROAD RETIREMENT ACT provided pensions for railroad employees after retirement and established a Railroad Retirement Board of 3 members appointed by the president to administer the law; amended and incorporated in the Railroad Retirement Act of 1937 (24 June).

30 Aug. GUFFEY-SNYDER BITUMINOUS COAL STABILIZATION (or CONSERVATION) ACT, popularly known as the "little NRA," created the Bituminous Coal Labor Board and the National Bituminous Coal Commission to administer production quota, price-fixing, and labor regulations based on the NRA soft coal code. The act sought to stabilize the bituminous coal-mining industry. A 15% tax based on the market value of coal was levied on producers, with 90% of the tax being remitted to producers complying with the code. The act was invalidated by the Supreme Court decision in the case of Carter v. Carter Coal Co. et al. (1936) and was succeeded by the Guffey-Vinson Act (1937).

30 Aug. REVENUE ACT OF 1935 (WEALTH TAX ACT). In his message to Congress on tax revision (19 June), President Roosevelt declared: "Our revenue laws have operated in many ways to the unfair advantage of the few, and they have done little to prevent an un-

just concentration of wealth and economic power." His recommendations were embodied in the Revenue Act, which increased the surtax rate on individual incomes over $50,000 and affected individual estates of decedents over $40,000. Taxes on individual incomes above $1 million were graduated steeply to 75% on income in excess of $5 million. Although an inheritance tax feature proposed by the president was eliminated from the bill, estate and gift tax rates were increased. In place of the existing uniform tax of 13¾%, income tax rates for small corporations were lowered to 12½%; rates on all corporation incomes above $50,000 raised to 15%; additional taxes of 6% were levied on profits in excess of 10%, graduated to 12% on profits in excess of 15%.

1936

6 JAN. The Agricultural Adjustment Act was invalidated by the Supreme Court in *U.S.* v. *Butler* (p. 677).

24 JAN. ADJUSTED COMPENSATION ACT. A bill calling for full and immediate cash payment of adjusted service (bonus) certificates held by World War I veterans demanding payment before the maturity date (1945) was passed by the Senate (20 Jan.) and the House (22 Jan.), but was vetoed by President Roosevelt (24 Jan.). Both branches of Congress immediately overrode his veto. The act authorized the issuance of 9-year interest-bearing bonds convertible into cash at any time. On 15 June more than $1,500 million in bonus bonds were distributed to some 3 million World War I veterans.

29 FEB. SOIL CONSERVATION AND DOMESTIC ALLOTMENT ACT, designed to replace the invalidated AAA, enabled the continued restriction of agricultural output, not by contracts with farmers for the control of crop production, but by **benefit payments** to growers who practiced soil conservation in cooperation with the government program. Farmers participating in the program through their county agricultural associations leased to the government land withdrawn from use for soil-depleting crops (such as corn, cotton, tobacco, wheat, and oats), and in return received compensation for their efforts to check wastage of fertility and erosion. Payments depended upon acreage withdrawn from soil-depleting crop production and turned over to soil-conserving crops. Provision was made whereby sharecroppers and tenants received part of the payments.

20 JUNE. FEDERAL ANTI-PRICE DISCRIMINATION ACT (ROBINSON-PATMAN ACT), aimed primarily at chain stores engaged in interstate commerce, made illegal unreasonably low prices tending to destroy competition and empowered the Federal Trade Commission to abolish price discrimination tending to promote monopoly or reduce competition.

22 JUNE. REVENUE ACT OF 1936 included among its provisions an undistributed profits tax on corporate income that added to the normal corporation income tax a scale of surtaxes ranging from 7% to 27%—attacked by business groups as penalizing the setting aside of corporate profits for expansion or as reserves for slack periods.

22 JUNE. FLOOD CONTROL ACT (p. 639).

26 JUNE. MERCHANT MARINE ACT OF 1936, substituted for the U.S. Shipping Board the **U.S. Maritime Commission,** an independent regulatory agency empowered to carry out a program to develop an American merchant marine through government aid. The act eliminated subsidies in the form of ocean mail contracts and provided instead outright subsidies based on differentials between foreign and domestic operating and construction costs. Other provisions of the act related to labor standards for seamen. As amended 23 June 1938 a **Maritime Labor Board** was established, primarily as a mediatory agency. In 1941 the board was shorn of its mediatory functions.

30 JUNE. **WALSH-HEALY GOVERNMENT CONTRACTS ACT** provided that all persons employed by a contractor dealing with the U.S. goverment shall be paid not less than the prevailing minimum wages as determined by the Secretary of Labor and shall not be permitted to work in excess of 8 hours a day or 40 hours a week; child labor (boys under 16, girls under 18) and convict labor barred in government contracts.

PRESIDENTIAL CAMPAIGN. The Socialist Labor Party Convention met at New York City (26 Apr.) and nominated John W. Aiken (Mass.) for president and Emil F. Teichert (N.Y.) for vice-president. The Prohibition Party Convention met at Niagara Falls, N.Y. (5 May), and nominated Dr. D. Leigh Colvin (N.Y.) for president and Claude A. Watson (Calif.) for vice-president. The Socialist Party National Convention met at Cleveland (23 May) and nominated Norman Thomas (N.Y.) for president and George Nelson (Wis.) for vice-president.

The Republican National Convention met at Cleveland (9 June) and on 11 June nominated Gov. **Alfred M. Landon** (Kan., 1887–   ) for president; on 12 June Col. **Frank Knox** (Ill.) was chosen for vice-president. The Republican platform condemned the New Deal, accused President Roosevelt of usurping the powers of Congress, and charged that regulated monopoly had displaced free en-

terprise and unconstitutional laws been passed. The platform called for return of responsibility for relief administration to nonpolitical local agencies, the protection of the rights of labor to organize and to bargain collectively, a balanced budget, farm subsidies, a revamped system of social security, opposed further devaluation of the dollar; but made no specific proposals for repealing New Deal legislation except for revising corporate and personal income taxation policies. During the campaign the Republicans were supported by conservative Democrats (including Alfred E. Smith, Bainbridge Colby, and John W. Davis) active in the Liberty League.

Rep. **William Lemke** (N.D.), a Republican, announced (19 June) that he would be presidential candidate on the Union party ticket and that the vice-presidential candidate would be Thomas C. O'Brien (Mass.). Lemke's candidacy was endorsed by Rev. Charles E. Coughlin, whose organization, the National Union for Social Justice, backed the endorsement at its first national convention, held at Cleveland (14 Aug.). The Union party platform, which denounced the New Deal, was drawn up with an eye to attracting the supporters of Coughlin, Townsend, and Gerald L. K. Smith.

The Democratic National Convention met at Philadelphia (23 June) and renominated President **Roosevelt** on 26 June and Vice-President **John N. Garner** on 27 June. The convention **abolished the two-thirds rule** for choosing candidates, in force since 1832, and restored the simple majority rule. In his acceptance speech (27 June), President Roosevelt attacked "economic royalists" who, he claimed, had "created a new despotism and wrapped it in the robes of legal sanction." The Democratic platform took its stand on the administration's record.

Labor's Nonpartisan League (which included the American Labor party in New York State) and the National Progressive Conference endorsed Roosevelt's candidacy.

The Communist Party National Convention met at New York City (24 June) and nominated Earl Browder (Kan.) for president and James W. Ford (N.Y.) for vice-president.

The campaign ranked among the most bitterly waged in U.S. political history. The Republicans attacked the New Deal as a bureaucratic, planned economy. About 80% of the press opposed Roosevelt. In defense, Roosevelt declared in his opening speech of the campaign (Syracuse, N.Y., 29 Sept.): "The true conservative seeks to protect the system of private property and free enterprise by correcting such injustices and inequalities as arise from it."

3 Nov. PRESIDENTIAL ELECTION. Popular vote: Roosevelt, 27,751,-612; Landon, 16,681,913; Lemke, 891,-858; Thomas, 187,342; Browder, 80,181; Colvin, 37,609; Aiken, 12,729. Electoral vote: Roosevelt, 523; Landon, 8. Roosevelt carried every state but Maine and Vermont, winning the most overwhelming electoral majority since Monroe's victory in 1820 and the greatest in any national contest in which there were 2 or more separate tickets. The election gave the Democrats majorities of 76–16 in the Senate and 331–89 in the House.

1937

20 JAN. Inauguration of President Franklin D. Roosevelt, serving his 2d term; John N. Garner, vice-president. Roosevelt was the first president inaugurated on this day, set by the 20th Amendment. In his inaugural address, Roosevelt reemphasized his objectives of social justice. The challenge to American democracy, he said, is the "tens of millions of its citizens . . . who at this very moment are denied the greater part of what the very lowest standards of today call the necessities of life. . . . I see one-third of a nation ill-housed, ill-clad, ill-nourished. . . ."

5 FEB.–22 JULY. SUPREME COURT FIGHT. The continued invalidation by the Supreme Court of major New Deal economic and social legislation led to the severest test of President Roosevelt's political leadership. On 5 Feb. Roosevelt submitted to Congress a plan for reorganizing the federal judiciary. His proposal included the following: (1) an increase in the membership of the Supreme Court from 9 to a maximum of 15 if judges reaching the age of 70 declined to retire; (2) addition of a total of not more than 50 judges to all levels of the federal courts; (3) sending of appeals from lower-court decisions on constitutional questions directly to the Supreme Court; (4) requiring that government attorneys be heard before any lower court issued an injunction against the enforcement of any act of Congress where the question of constitutionality was involved; and (5) assigning district judges to congested areas in order to expedite court business.

Announcement of the plan aroused widespread and bitter debate. The opposition concentrated on the proposal for increasing the Supreme Court membership. Roosevelt was accused of perverting the Constitution, and of attempting to "pack" the Supreme Court, to destroy judicial independence and integrity, and to aggrandize the power of the executive. Even administration adherents in and out of Congress who believed that the court plan had its merits insisted that the proper mode of making the change lay in a constitutional amendment. By early Mar. the bill had produced serious disunity in Democratic ranks in Congress. Sen. Burton K.

Wheeler (Mon.), a New Dealer, took the lead in campaigning against the measure. At the hearings which the Senate Judiciary Committee conducted on the proposal the weight of recorded opinion was against the plan. The opposition took heart from a personal letter (21 Mar.) which Chief Justice Charles E. Hughes sent to Sen. Wheeler pointing out that the Supreme Court was fully abreast of its work and needed no new justices.

When it became clear that the drift of congressional opinion was against the Judiciary Reorganization Bill, President Roosevelt took personal command of the campaign for the measure. In an address at the Democratic Victory Dinner held at Washington, D.C. (4 Mar.), he asserted that the "Personal economic predilections" of the court majority had rendered the national and state governments powerless to deal with pressing problems. In a fireside chat to the nation (9 Mar.), he declared that the courts had "cast doubts on the ability of the elected Congress to protect us against catastrophe by meeting squarely our modern social and economic conditions," and maintained that the purpose of the bill was to restore that balance of power among the 3 major branches of the federal government intended by the framers of the Constitution.

A number of developments contributed to the weakening of the claims for the urgency of the bill. The Supreme Court Retirement Act (1 Mar.), approved by Roosevelt, permitted Supreme Court justices to retire at the age of 70. The impending retirement of Justice Willis Van Devanter, a foe of the New Deal, was announced on 18 May. The death (14 July) of Sen. Joseph T. Robinson (Ark.), majority leader of the ate fight for the reorganiz weakened further th forces. But even

Supreme Court in a number of leading decisions (29 Mar.–24 May) sustained important New Deal and state legislation, including the Washington state minimum-wage law for women, the Frazier-Lemke Farm Mortgage Moratorium Act of 1935, the Social Security Act, and the Wagner Labor Relations Act. These decisions, tantamount to judicial approval of the second New Deal, indicated that the court personnel was responsive to the national temper, and induced the administration to compromise. On 22 July the Senate (70–20) recommitted the original reorganization bill to the Judiciary Committee, where it died. On 26 Aug. President Roosevelt signed the **Judicial Procedure Reform Act,** a modified measure that reformed the procedure of the lower courts but made no provision for the appointment of new justices and judges.

Political costs of the court battle: (1) brought into the open a break on domestic policy in the Democratic ranks that, except for the liberal wing of the party, was never fully repaired and became especially evident in the congressional elections of 1938; (2) enabled Republicans and conservative Democrats to block other administration-sponsored legislation, such as the Executive Reorganization Bill (finally passed in 1939), whose merits were overlooked in the heat of feeling against the proposal for revamping the courts.

Although Roosevelt failed to secure provisions for adding new judgeries on the Supreme Court, he filled ng 4 years. the court within a.) in 1937, Stan-Among the 938, Felix Frankfur-were 939, William O. Douglas 939, Frank Murphy (Mich.) Robert H. Jackson (N.Y.) in and James F. Byrnes (S.C.) in

26 APR. GUFFEY-VINSON BITU-MINOUS COAL ACT reenacted all of the chief provisions of the outlawed Guffey-Snyder Act of 1935 with the exception of the wages-and-hours clause. It authorized the promulgation of a new code of fair competition for the bituminous coal industry (promulgated on 21 June), placed the output of soft coal under federal regulation, laid a revenue tax of 1 ct. a ton on soft coal, and imposed on noncode producers a penalty tax of 19½% of the sales price.

22 JULY. BANKHEAD-JONES FARM TENANT ACT, designed to cope with the steady decline in U.S. farm ownership and the rise of farm tenancy and sharecropping, established the **Farm Security Administration** (FSA), under which the Resettlement Administration was placed. The act authorized low-interest loans repayable in small installments over a 40-year period to farm tenants, sharecroppers, and farm laborers whose applications for the purchase of farms were approved by committees of local farmers. The act also authorized rehabilitation loans for operating expenses and educational assistance. The FSA, often against heavy opposition from Southern conservatives, developed a program of regulating the supply and wages and hours of migrant workers, of aid to migrants by way of sanitary camps and medical services, and of cooperative homestead communities.

18 AUG. MILLER-TYDINGS EN-ABLING ACT, reluctantly signed by President Roosevelt as a "rider" to an appropriation bill for the District of Columbia, amended the federal antitrust laws so as to exempt resale price maintenance contracts made by producers or distributors of branded or advertised goods traded in interstate commerce in states where the resale price was authorized by state laws, occasionally under existing federal statutes. The number of states immediately affected was 42. The act was supported by influential trade associations on the ground it would end destructive competition brought on by price cutting.

26 AUG. REVENUE ACT OF 1937 was aimed at closing loopholes in the income-tax laws which permitted evasion of tax payments.

1 SEPT. NATIONAL HOUSING ACT (commonly known as the WAGNER-STEAGALL ACT), designed to alleviate housing conditions in low-income groups, established the **U.S. Housing Authority** (USHA) under the Department of the Interior, authorized to extend low-interest 60-year loans to local public agencies meeting at least 10% of the cost of low-cost slum clearance and housing projects, and to grant subsidies for setting rents geared to low-income levels in areas where local agencies provided an amount equal to 25% of the federal grant. By 1 Jan. 1941 the USHA had made loan contracts for 511 low-rent public housing projects containing a total of 161,162 dwelling units whose estimated development cost was $767,526,-000. During World War II the USHA was active in planning, constructing, and operating defense housing facilities.

15 NOV.–21 DEC. SPECIAL SESSION OF CONGRESS. On 12 Oct. President Roosevelt issued a proclamation calling Congress to convene in extra session on 15 Nov. On that date he submitted a message recommending the passage of legislation including a new agricultural program, wages-and-hours standards, reorganization of the executive branch, and planning for the conservation and development of national resources. During the 5-week session, Congress failed to enact any of the recommended measures, largely owing to the defection of Southern Democratic conservatives who joined with Republicans in blocking the administration's program.

1938

3 JAN. Although his annual message to Congress was for the most part concerned with domestic issues, President Roosevelt opened it with a reference to unsettled world conditions, declaring: "We must keep ourselves adequately strong in self-defense." On 28 Jan. he submitted to Congress recommendations for increased expenditures for armaments, including $8,800,000 for antiaircraft matériel, $6,080,000 for defense industry tools, and a 220% increase in the authorized naval construction program.

10 JAN. LUDLOW RESOLUTION. Beginning in 1935, the Ludlow Resolution for a national referendum on a declaration of war, sponsored by Rep. **Louis Ludlow** (Ind.), was introduced several times but failed of passage. The proposed resolution, in the form of a constitutional amendment, stated that except in the event of an invasion of the U.S. or its territorial possessions, the authority of Congress to declare war should not become effective until confirmed by a majority vote in a nationwide referendum. After the amendment was reintroduced in 1937, a national poll revealed that 73% of those polled favored a popular referendum of this type (however, the poll also showed that majority opinion favored a larger army and navy for defense). With the convening of the 2d session of the 75th Congress passage seemed assured. President Roosevelt sent a letter (6 Jan.) to Speaker William B. Bankhead asserting: "Such an amendment to the Constitution as that proposed would cripple any President in his conduct of our foreign relations, and it would encourage other nations to believe that they could violate American rights with impunity." The House (209–188) returned the resolution to committee. The vote for consideration of the resolution came from most Republican members and from most Democratic members from Western areas; opposed were representatives from the South and Northeast.

16 FEB. AGRICULTURAL ADJUSTMENT ACT OF 1938. When it became apparent that the Soil Conservation and Domestic Allotment Act of 1936 had proved unable to curb farm surpluses and price declines during the recession of 1937–38, that act was superseded by an administration-sponsored measure which revived the Agricultural Adjustment Act of 1933 in modified form. The processing taxes of the original AAA were eliminated, and financing provided out of the federal treasury. The act (1) empowered the Secretary of Agriculture to fix a marketing quota whenever it was determined that a surplus of any export farm commodity (such as cotton, wheat, rice, tobacco, and corn) threatened the price level; (2) authorized acreage allotments to each grower after two thirds of the farmers had by referendum expressed their approval of the marketing quota; (3) incorporated the **"parity payment"** principle and established the **"ever-normal granary"** arrangement by the following means: the Commodity Credit Corporation was authorized to make loans to farmers on their surplus crops at a level slightly below "parity" (a price based on the Aug. 1909–July 1914 level of farm purchasing power). Such excess crops were to be stored under government auspices, and the farmer was to repay the loan and market the surplus during crop failure years when the price was at "parity" or above. Since such disposal of surpluses would prevent the market price from rising too high above "parity," this arrangement stabilized agricultural prices and stored surplus crops without loss to individual farmer income.

The act also established the **Federal Crop Insurance Corporation** (FCIC) as an agency of the Department of Agriculture with a capitalization of $100 million, authorized to insure wheat crops only, beginning with the harvest of 1939, by accepting wheat in payment of premiums on insurance policies taken out against crop losses from unavoidable causes (such as drought, flood, hail, and plant diseases) ranging from 50% to 75% of the average yield.

14 APR. ROOSEVELT AND BUSINESS RECESSION. To combat the business recession under way since Aug. 1937, President Roosevelt sent to Congress a series of recommendations, which he outlined to the nation in a fireside chat the same day. They involved a reversal of the administration's deflationary policy, the expansion of WPA rolls from 1,500,000 to 3 million, a $3-billion recovery and relief program, "desterilizing" more than $3 billion in idle gold in the Treasury, "pump-priming" through RFC loans, and a "loose money" policy authorized by the Board of Governors of the Federal Reserve System. On 21 June the Emergency Relief Appropriation Act became law.

17 MAY. NAVAL EXPANSION ACT OF 1938 (also known as **VINSON NAVAL ACT**) authorized a $1,090,656,000 expansion of a "2-ocean" navy over the ensuing 10 years and provided for a maximum increase of 135,000 tons in capital ships up to a tonnage of 660,000, a maximum increase of 68,754 tons in cruisers up to a tonnage of 412,500, and an increase of 40,000 tons in aircraft carriers up to a tonnage of 175,000.

26 MAY. HOUSE COMMITTEE TO INVESTIGATE UN-AMERICAN ACTIVITIES, popularly known as the Dies Committee after its chairman, **Martin Dies** (Tex.), was established for the purpose of conducting investigations into Nazi, Fascist, Communist and other organizations termed "un-American" in character.

27 MAY. REVENUE ACT OF 1938, supported by Democratic and Republican opponents of the New Deal on the ground that tax concessions to business were necessary for the stimulation of the national economy, was passed by Congress on 11 May and became law without the signature of President Roosevelt. It repealed the progressive normal tax and undistributed profits tax authorized in 1936 and substituted a tax of 19% on corporations whose income exceeded $25,000, with the tax being reduced by a flat 2½% of dividends paid out of income subject to the tax (in effect it reduced taxes on large corporations and increased them on smaller firms). The measure also drastically modified the progressive tax provisions applicable to capital gains and losses.

16 JUNE. TEMPORARY NATIONAL ECONOMIC COMMITTEE (TNEC) was a joint legislative-executive body authorized by joint congressional resolution and established under the chairmanship of Sen. **Joseph C. O'Mahoney** (Wyo.), with **Leon Henderson** serving as executive secretary. Earlier, 29 Apr., President Roosevelt had submitted to Congress recommendations for curbing monopolies and the growing concentration of economic power. The TNEC conducted public hearings (1 Dec. 1938–26 Apr. 1940) to determine the effects of monopoly on prices, wages, profits, consumption, investment, cartels, patents, and many other aspects of the national economy with a view to improving federal antitrust policy and procedure. In its final report (31 Mar. 1941) the committee included the following among its recommendations: (1) amendment of the patent laws and revision of Patent Office procedure; (2) amendment of the Clayton Antitrust Act to lessen centralization of corporate resources; (3) prohibition of specified activities of trade associations tending to violate the antitrust laws; (4) legislation authorizing the Federal Trade Commission to forbid corporations from acquiring the assets of competing corporations over a certain size, unless it could be shown that such acquisition was in the public interest; (5) legislation to deal with the control exercised by foreign governments and their industry over American concerns through patent laws; (6) repeal of the Miller-Tydings Act of 1937; (7) allocation of defense funds in such a way as to eliminate monopoly control of basic products; (8) legislation prohibiting the use of "basing point" and other industrial pricing systems resulting in the elimination of competition; and (9) additional appropriations to strengthen the machinery for enforcing the antitrust laws by the Department of Justice and the Federal Trade Commission. Some antitrust suits initiated as a direct result of the TNEC's activities were suspended during World War II.

22 June. Chandler Act, amending **Federal Bankruptcy Act of 1898,** providing under Chapter XI procedures available to persons, partnerships, or corporations in financial distress, to voluntarily petition for the settlement, satisfaction, or extension of time of payment of unsecured debts, if acceptable to majority of creditors of each class affected, so as to avoid liquidation.

24 June. FOOD, DRUG, AND COSMETIC ACT, following enactment (21 Mar.) of **Wheeler-Lea Act** (broadening Federal Trade Commission's control over advertising of food, drugs, and cosmetics), superseded Pure Food Act of 1906. It prohibited misbranding of products; required manufacturers of foods, drugs, and cosmetics to list on their products' labels the ingredients used in processing; and forbade the use of false and misleading advertising claims dis-

seminated in more than 1 state. Enforcement of misbranding was left to the Food and Drug Administration; of advertising, to FTC, also given extended powers over unfair trade practices.

25 June. FAIR LABOR STANDARDS ACT (WAGES AND HOURS LAW), applied to enterprises which engaged in, or which affected, interstate commerce, with many occupations exempted (including farm laborers, domestic servants, and professional workers); established (1) a minimum wage of 40 cts. an hour (amended to 75 cts. an hour, 1949; to, most recently, $2.25, 1974) and (2) a maximum work week of 40 hours, to be put into effect, for wages, within 8 years beginning at 25 cts. an hour, and for hours, at 3 years beginning at 44 hours per week, with time and a half for overtime (750,000 workers received wage increases when the law went into effect in Aug.); (3) forbade labor by children under 16, and restricted to nonhazardous occupations those under 18. Constitutionality upheld by the Supreme Court in *U.S.* v. *Darby Lumber Co.* (1941, p. 678).

4 July. "THE NATION'S NO. 1 ECONOMIC PROBLEM." As a result of a request by President Roosevelt (22 June) to the National Emergency Council to prepare a report on the problems and needs of the South, the Conference on Economic Conditions in the South met at Washington. In a message (4 July) to the conference, Roosevelt declared: "It is my conviction that the South presents right now the nation's No. 1 economic problem." The findings of the conference, set forth in the comprehensive *Report on Economic Conditions of the South,* issued 12 Aug., pointed out that despite the South's good natural and human resources and potential untapped market, its people suffered from inadequate living standards.

8 Nov. CONGRESSIONAL ELECTIONS. To lessen the dependence of the New Deal domestic and foreign program on conservative Democrats (alienated from the administration over such issues as the Fair Labor Standards Act, the Anti-Lynching Bill [defeated by a Southern filibuster], and appropriations for the Farm Security Administration), President Roosevelt decided to participate actively in the Democratic primary campaign in order to effect the nomination of party liberals, with a fireside chat (24 June). The primary campaigns in selected districts in which Roosevelt made direct appeals included New York City, Georgia, Maryland, and Kentucky. Roosevelt's personal intervention fell far short of its intended goal. He failed to defeat Walter F. George (Ga.) and Millard F. Tydings (Md.), but scored a victory over Rep. John J. O'Connor of New York City. Although the Democrats retained control of both branches of Congress, the elections indicated the first Republican gains since 1928. The Democrats lost 7 seats in the Senate, 80 in the House. The composition of the 76th Congress was as follows: Senate, 69 Democrats, 23 Republicans, 2 Farmer-Laborites, 1 Progressive, 1 Independent; House, 261 Democrats, 164 Republicans, 4 others.

1939

4 JAN. In his annual message to Congress, President Roosevelt for the first time since taking office proposed no new domestic reforms, but stressed the dangers posed to democracy and international peace by the forces of aggression.

5 JAN. The $9-billion budget submitted to Congress by President Roosevelt for the fiscal year 1940 included $1,319,558,000 for national defense.

12 JAN. President Roosevelt urged Congress to pass additional appropriations, amounting to $525 million, for an emergency program of national defense. He proposed that $300 million of this sum be used for military aviation to strengthen the air defenses of the continental U.S. and outlying possessions and territories, and suggested that the balance be devoted to the "2-ocean" navy, the training of civilian air pilots, the facilitating of matériel procurement, and the improvement and strengthening of the seacoast defenses of Panama, Hawaii, and the continental U.S. On 4 Mar. he requested further appropriations to increase the national defense, and on 26 Apr. signed an appropriations bill for $549 million. On 29 Apr. he submitted an additional request for defense appropriations.

3 APR. ADMINISTRATIVE REORGANIZATION ACT OF 1939. On 12 Jan. 1937 the report of the President's Committee on Administrative Management was submitted to Congress with President Roosevelt's recommendation for the enactment of most of its proposals. The Executive Reorganization Bill aimed to increase government efficiency by regrouping and simplifying the many federal agencies, boards, commissions, and other units that had come into existence since the turn of the century, and thereby reduce or eliminate overlapping and waste. In 1937, and again in 1938, the measure was not passed, largely owing to the fight over the reorganization of the judiciary and to opposition from conservative Democrats and Republicans, who charged that the bill would make Roosevelt a "dictator." Following the 1938 elections, there was little opposition to the measure, and the bill, in modified form, was approved.

Plans I and II for the regrouping of 50 government units were submitted to Congress by President Roosevelt on 25 Apr. and 9 May, respectively, and went into effect by presidential order on 1 July failing the passage of concurrent resolutions nullifying these plans. Under Plans I and II the president set up a **Federal Security Agency,** a **Federal Works Agency,** and a **Federal Loan Agency,** under all of which a total of 24 units was placed; and by transfer, consolidation, or abolition distributed among these 3 new agencies and the Executive Department the major independent establishments of the government. The Bureau of the Budget was transferred to the Executive Office of the President from the Treasury Department. By presidential order (8 Sept.) the reorganization of the Executive Office of the President established the following principal divisions: the White House Office, the Bureau of the Budget, the National Resources Planning Board, the Liaison Office for Personnel Management, the Office of Government Reports, and an optional office for emergency management (established 25 May 1940 as the Office for Emergency Management). The president was provided with 6 administrative assistants. Three additional reorganization plans were submitted in 1940 and became effective that year.

16 MAY. FOOD STAMP PLAN, a New Deal scheme established for the purpose of disposing of surpluses of agricultural commodities to persons on relief, was inaugurated in Rochester, N.Y. Recipients of relief were permitted to buy each week between $1 and $1.50 worth of "orange stamps" for each member of the family unit. For each $1 worth of these stamps the purchaser received gratis 50 cts. worth of "blue stamps" redeemable for foods officially designated as surplus commodities. By the end of 1940 the plan had been adopted in more than 100 cities. World War II forced its discontinuance (resumed 21 Sept. 1959 under "surplus food" plan).

CUT IN RELIEF EXPENDITURES. Although employment began to increase in Sept. 1938, it failed to reach the level of Sept. 1937. President Roosevelt requested (5 Jan.) a deficiency appropriation of $875 million for the Works Progress Administration. Congress reduced this to $725 million. Further requests by Roosevelt (7 Feb., 14 Mar.) for $150 million to avoid drastic reduction of WPA employment were scaled down by Congress (11 Apr.) to $100 million. The lack of sufficient funds necessitated a reduction of WPA rolls to 2,578,000 in June, 1939. On 27 Apr. Roosevelt recommended an appropriation of $1,477 million for the WPA for the fiscal year 1940. Although the Emergency Relief Appropriation Act of 1939 (30 June) allotted this sum, it abolished the Federal Theater Project, reduced the security wage, and set an 18-month limit for continuous WPA employment. (The act also changed the name of the Works Progress Administration to the Works Projects Administration.) The measure brought a nationwide strike of WPA workers and resulted in the dismissal of many.

2 AUG. HATCH ACT was passed chiefly as a direct result of alleged political malpractices involving the votes of WPA workers in the border states of Kentucky, Tennessee, and Maryland during the elections of 1938. The act prohibited federal officeholders below the policy-making echelon in the executive branch of the government to participate actively in political campaigns, to solicit or accept contributions from work relief employees, and to make use of official authority or favors in order to interfere with or influence the outcome of presidential or congressional elections. On 19 July 1940 an amendment to the act extended its scope to state and local government workers whose salaries were drawn in whole or in part from

federal funds, and limited the annual expenditures of political parties to
$3 million and individual campaign con-
tributions to a maximum of $5,000. The
constitutionality of the act was upheld
in *United Public Workers* v. *Mitchell*
(330 U.S. 75, 1947) and, after another
challenge, again by the Supreme Court
in *United States Civil Service Commission* v. *National Association of Letter
Carriers* (413 U.S. 548, 1974).

**4 Aug. RECLAMATION PROJECT
ACT** (p. 639).

**10 Aug. SOCIAL SECURITY
AMENDMENTS.** Most of the improvements proposed by the Social Security
Board in its report transmitted to Congress (16 Jan.) by President Roosevelt
were embodied in amendments to the Social Security Act passed by the House
(10 June) and the Senate (13 July). The
amendments included the following provisions: (1) the date for starting monthly
old-age benefit payments was advanced
to 1 Jan. 1940; (2) supplementary old-
age benefits provided for aged wives;
(3) average wages replaced total wages
as the basis for computing old-age benefits; (4) old-age insurance coverage extended to maritime workers, persons
earning wages after they reached 65,
and employees of federal instrumentali-
ties, e.g., member banks in the Federal Reserve System; (5) the increased
taxes to be paid by employers and em-

ployees postponed until 1943; (6) the
maximum federal grant for each aged
or blind person increased by $15 to $20
per month; and (7) the federal contribution toward state aid to dependent
children increased from one third to
one half the amount granted each individual. The **Social Security Act of 1950**
raised employers' and employees' 1¼%
payroll tax to 2% in 1954, 2½% in 1960,
3% in 1965, 3¼% in 1970, and extended
coverage. By the **Social Security Act of
1952** (signed by President Truman, effective 1 Sept.) old-age and survivor
insurance benefits were increased $5 per
month or 12½% (whichever is greater),
and beneficiaries permitted to earn $75
a month instead of $50. Liberalized and
expanded by **Act of 1954** (1 Sept.), extending benefits to 7 million additional
workers, including farm workers and
household domestics, permitting retired
persons over 65 to receive benefits while
earning up to $1,200 per year; and by
Act of 1956 (1 Aug.), providing old-
age and survivors' insurance benefits for
totally and permanently disabled workers beginning at age 50 and reducing
from 65 to 62 the age at which women
are eligible for OASI benefits. **Act of
1958** (29 Aug.) increased benefits c.7%
and raised earnings from $4,200 to
$4,800; further liberalizations provided
under **Acts of 1960, 1961, 1965, 1967,
1968, 1969, 1972,** and **1974.**

THE UNITED STATES
IN WORLD WAR II

The Nazi *Blitzkrieg* and Pearl Harbor together destroyed the myth that America could be insulated from European catastrophe or from the domination of Asia and the Pacific by a single nation. World War II committed the country to intervention in world affairs and a postwar isolationist reaction made less than expected headway. Unlike World War I, there never for a moment was any question where American sympathies lay in World War II: Hitler and Pearl Harbor had taken care of that.

World War II differed from all previous wars in its truly total character. With a few notable exceptions, it involved every great nation and most of the smaller ones as well. It was total in that it was fought in every quarter of the globe, even South America not being spared naval engagements, and on a dozen different fronts, on land, in the air, and at sea. It was total in that it affected every segment of society and the economy, making no distinction between combatants and civilians. It was almost total in its destructive character, ending with the first use of a terrible new weapon, the atomic bomb.

In contrast to World War I, the United States assumed leadership in building a grand alliance dedicated to victory and to the establishment of a postwar international organization for maintaining world peace and security. Especially close was the cooperation between the Americans and the British, but the relations between the Anglo-Americans and the Soviet Union must be viewed against a background of almost a generation of mutual mistrust and the paranoid leadership of the Soviet chieftain Joseph Stalin. For the most part the larger need of maintaining an unbroken Allied front against the common enemy prevailed, and only toward the very close of the war was it evident to Franklin D. Roosevelt that the wartime unity of the grand alliance was unlikely to survive the strains of postwar reconstruction and bitter ideological competition.

Prelude to Global War, 1939–41

1939

1 SEPT.–5 OCT. WAR BEGINS: PO-
LAND CRUSHED. Germany invaded
Poland (1 Sept.). Great Britain and
France declared war on Germany; Bel-
gium proclaimed its neutrality (3 Sept.).
The Germans crossed the Vistula (11
Sept.), the San (16 Sept.), and de-
manded the surrender of Warsaw (17
Sept.). Soviet forces invaded Poland
17 Sept.). With the fall of Warsaw (27
Sept.) main organized resistance in Po-
land ended. Soviet-German partition of
Poland (28 Sept.). Polish government-
in-exile formed in Paris (30 Sept.). Last
Polish forces east of the Vistula surren-
dered (5 Oct.).

3–21 SEPT. U.S. POSITION. In a fireside chat (3 Sept.) President Roosevelt
declared: "This nation will remain a
neutral nation, but I cannot ask that
every American remain neutral in
thought as well." On 5 Sept. the U.S.
proclaimed its neutrality. Under the
Neutrality Act of 1937 President Roosevelt prohibited the export of arms and
munitions to belligerent powers. On 8
Sept. he proclaimed a limited national
emergency, and on 21 Sept. urged a
special session of Congress to repeal the
arms embargo.

3 OCT. DECLARATION OF PAN-
AMA, issued by the Inter-American Conference, announced sea safety zones in
the Western Hemisphere, south of Canada. Belligerent powers were warned to
refrain from naval action within these
zones.

11 OCT. President Roosevelt was informed by Albert Einstein and other
scientists of the possibilities of developing an atomic bomb.

14 OCT.–12 MAR. 1940. RUSSO-FIN-
NISH WAR. On 14 Oct. Russia presented
Finland with demands for military and
territorial concessions, and invaded Finland 30 Nov. The war terminated with
the signing of a treaty at Moscow 12
Mar. 1940.

4 Nov. NEUTRALITY ACT OF 1939
repealed the arms embargo and authorized "cash and carry" exports of arms
and munitions to belligerent powers. The
bill passed the Senate, 63–30 (27 Oct.),
and the House, 243–181 (2 Nov.).

1940

26 JAN. U.S.-Japanese commercial
treaty of 1911 expired. Secretary Hull
notified the Japanese government that
trade between the two nations would rest
on a day-to-day basis.

9 FEB. WELLES MISSION. President
Roosevelt announced that Under Secretary of State Sumner Welles would leave
for Europe to gather information concerning the war aims of the belligerent
powers and the possibility of a just and
lasting peace. He reported to Roosevelt
28 Mar.

30 MAR. A Japanese-dominated government in China was established at
Nanking under Wang Ching-wei.

9 APR.–11 JUNE. INVASION OF
NORWAY. German troops invaded Denmark and Norway by sea and air 9 Apr.
An Anglo-French expeditionary force
which came (18–20 Apr.) to the aid of
the resisting Norwegian troops was evacuated on 2 May. On 9 May British troops
occupied Iceland. On 29 May the British
announced the capture of Narvik, but
withdrew on 11 June. A puppet regime

under Vidkun Quisling was established in Norway on 1 Feb. 1942.

17 APR. Secretary Hull announced that any change in the *status quo* of the Netherlands East Indies would be prejudicial to the peace and security of the Pacific area.

10 MAY–4 JUNE. FALL OF THE NETHERLANDS AND BELGIUM. Germany invaded Luxembourg, the Netherlands, and Belgium by land and air (10 May). British Prime Minister Neville Chamberlain resigned, and was succeeded (11 May) by **Winston Churchill,** who headed a coalition government. The Netherlands government fled to Great Britain (14 May) and the army capitulated on the 15th. On 27–28 May King Leopold III ordered the Belgian army to capitulate, thus forcing the withdrawal of the Anglo-French expeditionary force from Belgium. The **Evacuation from Dunkirk** of 338,226 British and French troops (28 May–4 June) was completed with the use of 861 vessels of all types.

16 MAY–3 JUNE. U.S. PREPAREDNESS AND AID TO BRITAIN. President Roosevelt, who in his annual budget message (3 Jan.) had requested $1,800 million for national defense, asked for new appropriations of $1,182 million and called for a production program of 50,-000 planes a year. On 31 May he requested an additional $1,277,741,170 for the acceleration and development of military and naval requirements. In response to Prime Minister Churchill's appeal for military supplies, the War Department (3 June) released to Great Britain surplus or outdated stocks of arms, munitions, and aircraft. More than $43 million worth was sent in the month of June alone.

5 JUNE.–10 JULY. FALL OF FRANCE. Battle of France opened (5 June) with German crossings of the Somme and the Aisne-Oise canal. Italy declared war on France and Great Britain (10 June) and Italian forces penetrated southern France. On 13 June Premier Paul Reynaud of France appealed to President Roosevelt for aid. Following a breakthrough at Sedan, German troops entered Paris (14 June), compelling transfer of the French government to Bordeaux. On 16 June France requested release from obligations under the Anglo-French agreement barring a separate peace, and Marshal Henri-Philippe Pétain succeeded Reynaud as head of the French government. On 17 June he asked for armistice terms. An armistice with Germany was signed at Compiègne (22 June); with Italy on 24 June. In London the French National Committee under Gen. Charles de Gaulle pledged (18 June) continued French resistance against Germany. On 2 July the Pétain government established its headquarters at Vichy; on 10 July Pétain was granted dictatorial powers.

15–22 JUNE. U.S. DEFENSE MEASURES. On 15 June President Roosevelt established the **National Defense Research Committee,** with Dr. **Vannevar Bush** (1890–1974) as chairman. In May 1941 this body was supplanted by the Office of Scientific Research and Development. The **Pittman Resolution** (16 June), designed to strengthen the military defenses of the Latin-American republics, authorized the sale of munitions to the governments of the republics of the Western Hemisphere. The U.S. notified Germany and Italy that it would refuse to recognize transfer of title from one non-American power to another of any geographic region of the Western Hemisphere. On 20 June **Henry L. Stimson** (N.Y., p. 1159) was named Secretary of War; **Frank Knox** (Ill., 1874–1944) Secretary of the Navy. On 22 June Congress adopted national-defense tax measures designed to yield $994,300,000 a year. The national debt limit was raised from $45 billion to $49 billion.

17 JUNE. Soviet forces completed the occupation of Lithuania, Latvia, and Estonia, which were incorporated into the Soviet Union 25 Aug.

28 JUNE. ALIEN REGISTRATION ACT (commonly called the **SMITH ACT**) strengthened existing laws governing the admission and deportation of aliens and required the fingerprinting of all aliens in the U.S. The measure, however, was designed primarily to check subversive activities. The act made it unlawful for any person to advocate or teach the overthrow or destruction of any government in the U.S. by force or violence, and to organize or become a member of any group dedicated to teaching such doctrine.

30 JULY. ACT OF HAVANA was unanimously approved by delegates of the 21 republics of the Pan-American Union gathered at an Inter-American Conference. It provided that the American republics, collectively or individually, might in the interest of the common defense take over and administer any European possession in the New World endangered by aggression. The measure was designed to prevent the transfer to Germany of European colonies in the Western Hemisphere.

4 AUG. Italian troops invaded British Somaliland and completed its occupation on 19 Aug.

8 AUG.–31 OCT. BATTLE OF BRITAIN. The Luftwaffe, with more than 2,600 operational fighters and bombers at its disposal, opened a vast air offensive against British shipping, RAF installations, factories, land transportation, and cities in the British Isles. The Nazi objective was to soften Great Britain in preparation for an invasion of England by sea and air. The Battle of Britain came to a climax on 15 Sept. when 56 German aircraft were destroyed (the original British claim was 185). Aircraft losses, 10 July–31 Oct.:

British fighters lost by RAF..... 915
Enemy aircraft actually destroyed
  (according to German records) 1,733
Enemy aircraft claimed by British 2,698

Defeat in this crucial battle compelled the Germans to abandon plans for the invasion of the British Isles.

18 AUG.–29 OCT. U.S. DEFENSE MEASURES. Meeting at Ogdensburg, N.Y. (18 Aug.), to discuss defense problems common to Canada and the U.S., Prime Minister W. L. Mackenzie King and President Roosevelt agreed to establish a **Permanent Joint Board on Defense.** On 27 Aug. Congress authorized induction of the National Guard into federal service. Initial units were called out 31 Aug. On 3 Sept. a defense agreement between the U.S. and Great Britain provided for the transfer of 50 U.S. overage destroyers to the British; in exchange, the U.S. acquired the right to take 99-year leases on naval and air bases in Newfoundland, Bermuda, the Bahamas, Jamaica, St. Lucia, Trinidad, Antigua, and British Guiana. On 16 Sept. the **Selective Training and Service Act** (the **Burke-Wadsworth Bill**) was approved. The first peacetime program of compulsory military service in the U.S., it provided for the registration of all men between 21 and 35, and for the training over a 1-year period of 1,200,000 troops and 800,000 reserves. The first registration (16 Oct.) resulted in a listing of 16,400,000 men; the first draft numbers were selected on 29 Oct.

MAY–JULY. PUBLIC OPINION IN THE UNDECLARED WAR. The policy of aiding the democracies set off a protracted debate. An important force in marshalling sentiment favorable to aid short of war was the Committee to Defend America by Aiding the Allies (est. mid-May), whose first chairman was a Republican editor from Kansas, William Allen White. To counter the interventionists Gen. Robert E. Wood, a Middle Western executive, organized in July the America First Committee, with its first public statement issued 4 Sept., one day after the president informed Congress of the Destroyer-Bases Agreement. Isolationists drew upon a wide spectrum of public opinion, including extreme reactionaries, moderate conservatives, and left-leaning pacifists.

4–27 Sept. JAPANESE AGGRESSION. Secretary Hull advised the Japanese government (4 Sept.) that aggression against French Indochina would bring adverse reaction in the U.S. On 12 Sept. Joseph C. Grew, U.S. ambassador to Japan, warned Secretary Hull that Japan might interpret a drastic embargo on oil as sanctions and retaliate. On 22 Sept. Japan concluded with Vichy France an agreement giving the former air and troop maintenance bases in Indochina. On 27 Sept. Japan signed at Berlin a 3-power pact with Germany and Italy providing for a 10-year military and economic alliance. By this pact, which made Japan a member of the Axis, each of the signatories pledged mutual assistance in the event of war with a nation not then a belligerent. The pact was subsequently signed by other nations, including Bulgaria, Rumania, Hungary, and Yugoslavia. On 26 Sept. President Roosevelt proclaimed an embargo, effective 16 Oct., on exports of scrap iron and steel to all countries outside the Western Hemisphere except Great Britain. The ban was aimed at Japan. Ambassador Horinouchi protested the move as an "unfriendly act" (8 Oct.).

8–28 Oct. AXIS MOVES IN THE BALKANS. On 8 Oct. German troops began occupation of Rumania. On 28 Oct. Italy invaded Greece from Albania. British forces were landed on Crete and other Greek islands. Fighting between Greeks and Italians continued through the winter and spring.

PRESIDENTIAL CAMPAIGN. The Republican National Convention met at Philadelphia (28 June) and nominated **Wendell L. Willkie** (N.Y., 1892–1944) for president and Sen. **Charles L. McNary** (Ore.) for vice-president on a platform that attacked the New Deal administration but supported most of its major reforms. The Democratic National Convention met at Chicago (15 July) and received a message (16 July) from President Roosevelt stating that he had no desire to be a candidate for a 3d term. On 18 July **Roosevelt** was nominated for a 3d term; Secretary of Agriculture **Henry A. Wallace** (Iowa) was nominated for vice-president. Both major parties supported the national defense program, aid to Britain, and hemispherical defense, but opposed participation in foreign wars. Other presidential candidates: Norman Thomas (N.Y.), Socialist; Roger Babson (Mass.), Prohibition party; Earl Browder (N.Y.), Communist; and John W. Aiken, Socialist Labor.

5 Nov. PRESIDENTIAL ELECTION. Popular vote: **Roosevelt,** 27,244,160; Willkie, 22,305,198; Thomas, 100,264; Babson, 57,812; Browder, 48,579; Aiken, 14,861. Electoral vote: **Roosevelt, 449** (38 states); Willkie, 82 (10 states).

20 July. President Roosevelt approved a bill authorizing a 2-ocean navy for the defense of the U.S. and the Western Hemisphere at a cost of $4 billion. The measure increased the authorized U.S. warship tonnage by 70% to a level of 3,500,000, and provided for the construction of about 200 warships, including 7 battleships of 55,000 tons each.

13 Nov.–8 Feb. 1941. BRITISH MEDITERRANEAN OFFENSIVE. British naval aircraft dealt a severe blow to the Italian fleet at Taranto (13 Nov.). Wavell's offensive began 9 Dec., with a surprise attack around the Italians' southern flank in North Africa. By 8 Feb. the British had occupied El Agheila, 500 miles from Matrûh, their starting point, and destroyed Marshal Rodolfo Graziani's army, capturing 133,000 prisoners.

20–29 Dec. U.S. DEFENSE PRODUCTION. The Office of Production Management, with **William S. Knudsen** (1879–1948) as director, was set up by President Roosevelt (20 Dec.) to coordinate defense production and speed all material aid "short of war" to Great Britain and other anti-Axis nations. On 21 Dec. Germany asserted U.S. aid to Great Britain was "moral aggression." In a fireside chat on national security (29 Dec.) Roosevelt stressed the Axis threat to the U.S. and called for an immense production effort that would make the U.S. "the great arsenal of democracy."

1941

6 Jan. "FOUR FREEDOMS." In his annual message to Congress President Roosevelt recommended Lend-Lease for the Allies and enunciated the "Four-Freedoms": freedom of speech and expression, freedom of worship, freedom from want, and freedom from fear.

27 Jan.–29 Mar. SECRET U.S.-BRITISH STAFF TALKS, held in Washington, produced a plan known as ABC-1, suggesting the strategy for war. In the event of Anglo-U.S. involvements in war with both Germany and Japan the concentration of force should be on **Germany first.**

Feb.–27 May. BATTLE OF THE ATLANTIC. Although the battle had assumed grim proportions as early as Nov. 1940, when the pocket battleship *Scheer* attacked a convoy and sank the *Jervis Bay,* it was at a critical stage at the time of the secret U.S.-British staff talks. In Feb.-Mar. the *Scharnhorst* and *Gneisenau* sank or captured 22 ships (115,000 tons). U-boats, using "wolf-pack" tactics, reached great effectiveness. To 9 Apr. 1940 total Allied and neutral shipping

losses had amounted to 688,000 gross tons. Between 10 Apr. 1940 and 17 Mar. 1941 losses amounted to 2,314,000 gross tons. On 11 Apr. Roosevelt informed Churchill that the U.S. would extend security zone and patrol areas to a line covering all North Atlantic waters west of about West Long. 26° (thereafter "the sea frontier of the U.S."). On 21 May the *Robin Moor,* an American merchant ship, was sunk by a German submarine in the South Atlantic, off the coast of Brazil. On 24 May the British warship *Hood* was sunk by the German battleship *Bismarck* in the North Atlantic. The *Bismarck* was sunk (27 May) while attempting to return to port.

5 Mar. The Republic of Panama agreed to permit the U.S. to extend air defenses beyond the limits of the Canal Zone. The agreement was limited to the duration of the war.

11 Mar. LEND-LEASE ACT approved by President Roosevelt. It was drawn up primarily to offset the exhaustion of British credits for the purchase of war supplies. The measure passed the Senate, 60–31 (8 Mar.), and the House, 317–71 (11 Mar.). Lend-Lease enabled any country whose defense the president deemed vital to that of the U.S. to receive arms and other equipment and supplies by sale, transfer, exchange, or lease. An initial appropriation of $7 billion was authorized. Total Lend-Lease aid during the course of the war amounted to $50,226,845,387. On 15 Mar. President Roosevelt promised increasing aid to the Allies for a total victory. Lend-Lease was terminated 21 Aug. 1945. Total Lend-Lease aid by U.S. (Mar. 1941–Sept. 1946) amounted to $50.6 billion; reverse Lend-Lease received by U.S., $7.8 billion.

24 Mar.–15 Apr. ROMMEL'S COUNTEROFFENSIVE. A North African offensive by German and Italian forces under Gen. Erwin Rommel compelled the British (whose strength was drained by the dispatch of 60,000 troops to help Greece resist the Germans) to evacuate Bengasi and to withdraw to Egypt by the end of May. British troops aided by the Royal Navy held out at Tobruk.

6 APR.–1 JUNE. Germany invaded Greece and Yugoslavia (6 Apr.). The Yugoslavian army surrendered on 17 Apr.; Greek resistance ended on 23 Apr. The British withdrew from the Greek mainland (29 Apr.). German airborne troops landed in Crete (20 May) and by 1 June had conquered the island.

9 APR. GREENLAND. Signing of U.S.-Danish agreement pledging the U.S. to defend Greenland against invasion. In return, the U.S. was granted the right to construct, maintain, and operate in Greenland air, naval, radio, and other defense installations. President Roosevelt announced that the defense of Greenland was essential to the security of the Western Hemisphere.

13 APR. Mutual nonaggression pact signed at Moscow by Japan and Russia.

21–27 APR. U.S., Dutch, and British military planning officers met at Singapore and drew up a strategic plan for combined operations against Japan should the latter commit aggression against the U.S.

27 MAY–16 JUNE. President Roosevelt proclaimed (27 May) an unlimited national emergency and ordered (16 June) the closing of German and Italian consulates in the U.S. by 10 July. In retaliation, the German and Italian governments ordered the closing of U.S. consulates in European areas under Axis control.

22 JUNE. INVASION OF RUSSIA. Germany invaded the Soviet Union. Together with Finnish and Rumanian troops, the German forces penetrated Russia along a 2,000-mile front extending from the Arctic to the Ukraine. By mid-Aug. the Germans had overrun most

of the Ukraine; by early Sept. they reached Leningrad; by mid-Nov. they had laid Sevastopol under siege and reached the outskirts of Moscow. Rostov fell on 22 Nov., but was retaken by the Russians on 29 Nov. In Dec. the Russians launched a counteroffensive.

24 JUNE–6 Nov. AID TO RUSSIA. On 24 June President Roosevelt promised U.S. aid to the Soviet Union. On 12 July Great Britain and Russia signed a mutual assistance pact at Moscow barring a separate peace with Germany. British and Soviet forces occupied Iran (25–29 Aug.). U.S.-British missions conferred in Moscow (29 Sept.) to determine Russian defense needs, and on 1 Oct. decided to grant Russian requests for matériel. The U.S. granted Lend-Lease credit of $1 billion to the Soviet Union (6 Nov.).

28 JUNE. OFFICE OF SCIENTIFIC RESEARCH AND DEVELOPMENT established by executive order, with **Vannevar Bush** (1890–1974), chairman, and **James B. Conant** (p. 1004) deputy. The OSRD became the principal agency for coordinating U.S. scientific effort, including radar, proximity fuse, sonar (antisubmarine warfare), and the **atomic bomb,** whose development was transferred to the army on 1 May 1943 and placed in charge of an administrative unit known for security reasons as the **"Manhattan District" project.** See also pp. 443, 452, 801.

7 JULY. ICELAND. By agreement with the Icelandic government, the U.S. landed forces in Iceland to prevent its occupation by Germany for use as a naval or air base against the Western Hemisphere. The agreement stipulated that the U.S. would withdraw following the close of the European war.

24 JULY–24 AUG. U.S.-JAPANESE RELATIONS. Japan occupied French Indochina (24 July). Two days later President Roosevelt froze all Japanese credits in the U.S., thus bringing Japanese-American trade to a virtual halt. Simultaneous action was taken by Great Britain. Japan ordered freezing of all U.S. and British funds. Roosevelt nationalized (26 July) the armed forces of the Philippines for the duration of the emergency, placing them under the command of Gen. **Douglas MacArthur** (p. 1090), who was named commander in chief of U.S. forces in the Far East. The Japanese ambassador to the U.S., Adm. Kichisaburo Nomura, was informed by Roosevelt that additional attempts to extend Japanese military control in the Far East would compel the U.S. to take immediate steps to protect American rights and interests. On 24 Aug. Prime Minister Churchill promised that Great Britain would come to the aid of the U.S. should the negotiations with Japan break down.

14 Aug. ATLANTIC CHARTER, a joint statement of principles issued by President Roosevelt and Prime Minister Churchill, formulated the broad postwar aims of the U.S. and Great Britain. The charter was not an alliance nor a binding legal commitment. It was drawn up at secret meetings (9–12 Aug.) that took place aboard the U.S. cruiser *Augusta* and the British battleship *Prince of Wales* at Argentia Bay off Newfoundland. Drafted by Roosevelt and Churchill with the aid of Sumner Welles and Sir Alexander Cadogan, the document included the following points: (1) renunciation of territorial or other aggrandizement; (2) opposition to territorial changes contrary to the wishes of the people immediately concerned; (3) support of the right of peoples to choose their own form of government; (4) support, with due respect for existing obligations, of the easing of restrictions on trade, and access to raw materials on equal terms; (5) support of cooperative efforts to improve the economic position

and social security of the peoples of the world; (6) freedom from want and fear; (7) freedom of the seas; and (8) disarmament of aggressor nations pending the establishment of a permanent peace structure. On 24 Sept. it was announced that 15 anti-Axis nations, among them the Soviet Union, had endorsed the Atlantic Charter.

18 Aug. SELECTIVE SERVICE EXTENSION. President Roosevelt approved a bill extending for 18 months the army service of draftees. The House vote (12 Aug.) on the extension of Selective Service was 203–202.

4 Sept.–30 Oct. WARFARE IN THE ATLANTIC. A German submarine attacked the U.S.S. *Greer*, a destroyer on duty in waters off Iceland (4 Sept.). On 11 Sept. President Roosevelt announced a "shoot-on-sight" order to U.S. naval forces in U.S. defensive waters, stating that German and Italian vessels would enter these areas at their own risk. Five days later the U.S. navy undertook merchant convoy duty as far as Iceland. On 9 Oct. President Roosevelt asked Congress to modify the Neutrality Act of 1939 to permit arming of U.S. merchantmen engaged in overseas commerce and their passage through combat zones. The U.S. destroyer *Kearny* was torpedoed and damaged by a German submarine in waters west of Iceland (17 Oct.), causing the loss of 11 American lives. On 30 Oct. the U.S. destroyer *Reuben James*, on convoy duty in waters off Iceland, was attacked and sunk by a German submarine, with about 100 American lives lost. The Senate, 50–37, approved repeal of restrictive sections in the 1939 Neutrality Act (7 Nov.), and the House followed (13 Nov.), 212–94. The measure, which became law on 17 Nov., authorized the arming of U.S. merchant vessels and permitted them to carry cargoes to belligerent ports.

18 Oct.–6 Dec. JAPANESE ATTITUDE HARDENS. On 18 Oct. the Japanese cabinet headed by Prince Fumimaro Konoye resigned. Gen. Hideki Tojo became prime minister. U.S. ambassador Grew warned Washington (17 Nov.) of the possibility of a sudden attack by the Japanese. On 20 Nov. discussions in Washington were opened between Secretary Hull and the 2 Japanese negotiators, Ambassador Nomura and a special envoy, Saburo Kurusu. Japan demanded that the U.S. abandon China; lift the orders freezing Japanese credits in the U.S.; resume full trade relations with Japan; exert pressure to aid Japan in securing supplies from the Netherlands East Indies; and bring a halt to U.S. naval expansion in the Western Pacific. On 26 Nov. Hull countered with a set of proposals that included the withdrawal of Japanese troops from China and Indochina and the conclusion of a multilateral nonaggression pact. The U.S. proposals restated the following principles: respect for the territorial integrity and sovereignty of all nations; support of the principle of noninterference in the internal affairs of other countries; support of the principle of equality, including equality of commercial opportunity; nondisturbance of the *status quo* in the Pacific except by peaceful means. In return, Hull promised to free frozen Japanese assets and to resume treaty based commercial relations. Asking for 2 weeks in which to study the proposals, Japan in the meantime, while recognizing the great danger in directly attacking U.S. territory, stepped up military and naval preparations in Asia and the Pacific. On 25 Nov. (Washington time) the carrier force that attacked Pearl Harbor left the Kurile Islands. The next day U.S. warned Great Britain of an impending Japanese attack. War and Navy Departments, believing it likely that the Japanese would strike in the Philippines or Southeast Asia, sent (27 Nov.) warnings of imminent war to commanders of U.S. forces in the Pacific. On 29 Nov. Premier Tojo publicly asserted that U.S. and British influence must be eliminated from Asia, and on 1 Dec. Japan publicly rejected the Hull proposals. The next day the U.S. requested an explanation by Japan for increasing its forces in Indochina, and on 6 Dec. President Roosevelt made a direct appeal to Emperor Hirohito, asking him to use his influence to preserve the peace and to withdraw troops from French Indochina.

7 Dec. ATTACK ON PEARL HARBOR. On the morning of Sunday, 7 Dec., Japanese naval and air forces made a sneak attack on the U.S. fleet at the Pearl Harbor naval base in Hawaii. On the same day (8 Dec., Far Eastern time) the Japanese launched assaults on the Philippines, Guam, and Midway Island, and on British forces at Hong Kong and in the Malay Peninsula. The air attack at Pearl Harbor began at 7:55 A.M. (local time; 1:20 P.M. Washington time) and continued until 9:45 A.M. Of the 8 battleships at Pearl Harbor, the *Arizona, California* and *West Virginia* were sunk; the *Nevada* was grounded; the *Oklahoma* capsized; others were damaged. Altogether 19 ships were sunk or disabled; 5 battleships were later raised; 4 restored to the fleet. About 150 U.S. planes were destroyed, 2,335 soldiers and sailors and 68 civilians were killed, and 1,178 were wounded. During the morning of 7 Dec., the official Japanese reply to the U.S. proposals of 26 Nov. arrived at Washington, with instructions to the Japanese envoys to present it to Secretary Hull at 1 P.M. (Washington time). Nomura and Kurusu, however, did not appear in Hull's office until 2:05 P.M., just as Hull received reports of the attack on Pearl

Harbor. On 24 Jan. 1942 a presidential commission headed by Supreme Court Justice Owen J. Roberts attributed the effectiveness of the Japanese attack to the failure of the naval and military commanders at Hawaii (Rear Adm. Husband Kimmel and Lt. Gen. Walter Short) to adopt adequate defense measures. Previously (17 Dec. 1941) **Chester W. Nimitz** (p. 1115) had succeeded Kimmel in command of the Pacific fleet.

8 Dec. With only 1 dissenting vote, the U.S. Congress declared war on Japan.

11 Dec. Germany and Italy declared war on the U.S., which then recognized a state of war with these nations.

19 Dec. Congress extended military conscription to men between the ages of 20 and 44.

The War in the Pacific and the Far East, 1941–45

1941

8–25 Dec. JAPANESE GAINS. Thailand and Malaya were invaded by the Japanese (8 Dec.). On 10 Dec. the British battleship *Prince of Wales* and the battle cruiser *Repulse* were sunk by Japanese torpedo planes in the South China Sea. This blow to Allied naval strength enabled the Japanese capture of Singapore and other enemy successes in Southeast Asia. The Japanese made landings on the Philippines (10–23 Dec.); took Guam (13 Dec.), Wake Island (22 Dec.), and Hong Kong (25 Dec.).

2 Jan. Supreme command for American, British, Dutch, and Australian forces in the Far East (ABDACOM), headed by Gen. Sir Archibald P. Wavell, with Maj. Gen. George P. Brett, deputy, was announced following a meeting at Washington.

1942

2 Jan.–6 May. BATAAN AND CORREGIDOR. Manila and Cavite fell to the Japanese (2 Jan.). Gen. MacArthur's forces retired to Bataan Peninsula, where MacArthur established headquarters at the fortress of Corregidor ("The Rock") in Manila Bay. On 17 Mar. MacArthur arrived in Australia after secretly leaving Bataan Peninsula, and took command of the Allied forces in the Southwest Pacific. After resisting a siege of more than 3 months, Bataan fell 9 Apr. American forces under Gen. **Jonathan M. Wainwright** withdrew to Corregidor Island in Manila Bay. On 6 May Wainwright surrendered Corregidor and its garrison of 11,500 to the Japanese.

11 Jan.–3 May. JAPAN'S ADVANCE. Japanese forces occupied the Netherlands East Indies (11–31 Jan.). In the first major sea battle between the Allies and Japan, the Battle of **Macassar Strait** (between Borneo and Celebes), Allied sea and air forces inflicted severe damage on a large Japanese invasion convoy (24–27 Jan.). On 31 Jan. British troops withdrew from Malaya to Singapore and on the same day Vice-Adm. **William F. Halsey, Jr.,** carried out a bombardment of the Marshall and Gilbert Islands. Singapore and its British garrison unconditionally surrendered (15 Feb.). A naval battle was fought in Badoeng Strait (19–20 Feb.). On 24 Feb. the British withdrew from Rangoon, in Burma. Its occupation by the Japanese (9 Mar.) cut off supplies from the Burma Road. Mandalay fell 3 May. The **Battle of the Java Sea** (27 Feb.–1 Mar.), fought as a delaying action by the U.S. fleet under

Adm. **Thomas C. Hart**, resulted in the most severe U.S. naval losses since Pearl Harbor. On 6 Mar. Batavia, capital of the Netherlands East Indies, fell. By 9 Mar. the Japanese conquest of Java had been completed. On 8 Mar. Japanese troops landed at Lae and Salamaua in New Guinea. On 10 Mar. Lt. Gen. **Joseph W. Stilwell** ("Vinegar Joe") was made chief of staff of Allied armies in the Chinese theater of operations.

18 APR.–6 JUNE. STIFFENING ALLIED RESISTANCE. On 18 Apr. carrier-based U.S. army bombers (B-25s) led by Maj. Gen. **James H. Doolittle** raided Tokyo. On 7–8 May was fought the **Battle of the Coral Sea**, the first naval engagement in history in which surface ships did not engage enemy ships (all fighting was done by carrier-based planes). One Japanese carrier was sunk, 2 damaged, as well as a number of other ships. The U.S. carrier *Lexington* was lost in this engagement, which halted the enemy advance upon Australia by frustrating the Japanese attempt to seize Port Moresby in southern New Guinea in order to cut the Australian supply line. The naval and air **Battle of Midway** (3–6 June), in the Central Pacific, resulted in the first major defeat of Japanese naval forces. The attempted enemy seizure of Midway Island ended in failure, with the loss of 4 aircraft carriers and 275 planes. This action checked the Japanese advance across the Central Pacific, eliminated the threat to Hawaii, and restored the balance of naval power in the Pacific.

3–21 JUNE. The Japanese bombed Dutch Harbor and Ft. Mears, Alaska (3–4 June), and occupied the islands of Attu and Kiska in the westernmost Aleutians (12–21 June). On 21 June the Oregon coast was shelled. Previously (23 Feb.) an oil refinery near Santa Barbara, Calif., had been shelled by a Japanese submarine.

22 JULY. Japanese forces in northern New Guinea began an overland push against Port Moresby on the southern coast. After crossing the Owen Stanley Mountains they were halted by Australian forces who counterattacked from Port Moresby (29 Sept.) and crossed the Owen Stanley Range (10 Oct.).

7 AUG.–9 FEB. 1943. GUADALCANAL, 1ST MAJOR OFFENSIVE. Countering Japanese advances in the Solomons, U.S. marines landed at Guadalcanal (7 Aug.) and seized the airport, renaming it Henderson Field. Marines also landed on Tulagi, Florida, and other nearby islands. Two days later occurred the naval **Battle of Savo Island,** north of Guadalcanal, resulting in the loss of 4 heavy cruisers (3 U.S., 1 Australian), a Japanese victory which temporarily deprived U.S. forces on Guadalcanal of air and naval support. A 6-month fight for the island followed. A naval battle of the Eastern Solomons (23–25 Aug.) resulted in damage to Japanese carriers and cruisers by aircraft from the U.S. carriers *Enterprise* and *Saratoga*. On 26 Aug. Japanese landed at Milne Bay in New Guinea, but were defeated after a 2-week battle. The naval **Battle of Cape Esperance** (11–12 Oct.), in the Solomons, resulted in a U.S. victory over the Japanese, who lost 1 carrier and 4 destroyers. Strong Japanese attacks (21–25 Oct.) failed to take Henderson Field. The naval **Battle of Santa Cruz** (26–27 Oct.), in the Solomons, resulted in the sinking of 2 Japanese destroyers and damage to 8 other enemy warships. The naval **Battle of Guadalcanal** (12–15 Nov.), a decisive U.S. victory, prevented the Japanese from landing substantial reinforcements and made possible the conquest of Guadalcanal by U.S. troops. This action cost the U.S. 2 cruisers and 7 destroyers. The Japanese lost 2 battleships, 1 cruiser, 2 destroyers, and 10 transports. By 9 Feb. 1943 Japanese forces completed the abandonment of Guadalcanal.

1943

23 JAN.–16 SEPT. **GAINS IN NEW GUINEA.** Ground fighting ended in Papua (23 Jan.), with the Japanese cleared out. The air **Battle of the Bismarck Sea** (2–3 Mar.), in the New Guinea area, resulted in the destruction of 12 Japanese troop convoys and 10 warships and the death of Adm. Yamamoto. On 16 Sept. U.S. forces under Gen. MacArthur took Lae in New Guinea, completing reconquest of Lae-Salamaua area.

24 MAR.–15 AUG. **STRUGGLE FOR THE ALEUTIANS.** Naval battle of the Komandorski Islands in the western Aleutians resulted in a U.S. victory. U.S. forces landed on Attu (11 May), in the western Aleutians. By 3 June all organized enemy resistance on Attu had ended. On 15 Aug. U.S. and Canadian troops reoccupied Kiska without resistance, the Japanese having already left the island.

30 JUNE–26 DEC. **U.S. SOUTH PACIFIC OFFENSIVE** began 30 June with the landing of U.S. troops on Rendova Island, in New Georgia. The naval **Battle of Kula Gulf** (6 July) was followed by other U.S. naval victories (Aug.–Oct.) which gave the Allies control of the waters adjacent to the central Solomons. On 1 Nov. U.S. marines landed at Bougainville, in the northern Solomons, in a thrust toward the bastion of Rabaul. The Japanese struck back, but naval **Battle of Empress Augusta Bay** (2 Nov.), off Bougainville, resulted in a decisive Japanese defeat and enabled the Allies to cut the supply lines to Rabaul, thus isolating all enemy forces remaining in the Solomons and securing the U.S. flank for an advance toward the Philippines. The next steps were landings by U.S. forces at Arawe (15 Dec.) and Cape Gloucester (26 Dec.) in New Britain.

21 Nov. **U.S. CENTRAL PACIFIC OFFENSIVE,** under Adm. **Chester W. Nimitz,** commander in chief, Pacific fleet, aimed at capturing islands "up the ladder" of the Solomons, the Gilberts and Marshalls, the Marianas, and the Bonin Islands to within effective bombing distance of Japan, began with landings on **Tarawa** and **Makin** in the Gilbert Islands. At Tarawa, which was not secured until 24 Nov., the direct assault on heavily fortified positions cost the U.S. 2nd Marine Division 913 killed and missing, and 2,037 wounded.

25 AUG.–21 DEC. Lord Louis Mountbatten was appointed (25 Aug.) supreme Allied commander, Southeast Asia. On 21 Dec. Gen. Stilwell began his campaign in northern Burma.

1944

31 JAN.–25 Nov. **CENTRAL PACIFIC ADVANCE.** U.S. forces invaded (31 Jan.) the Marshall Islands, taking Roi and Namur (3 Feb.), Kwajalein (6 Feb.), and Eniwetok (17–22 Feb.); landed on the air and naval base of Saipan (15 June), in the Mariana Islands, completing its conquest 9 July, on Guam (21 July), completing its reoccupation 9 Aug. The invasion of the Palaus began with the landing of U.S. marines on Peleliu (15–17 Sept.), finally taken on 25 Nov.

1 MAR.–22 APR. **SOUTHWEST PACIFIC GAINS.** U.S. troops invaded the Admiralty Islands (1 Mar.), completing their occupation on 25 Mar., and landed at Hollandia (22 Apr.), Dutch New Guinea, seizing enemy airfields.

17 MAY–3 AUG. **BURMA CAMPAIGN.** The capture (17 May) by Allied forces of Myitkyina airstrip in northern Burma gave them an air route to China. After

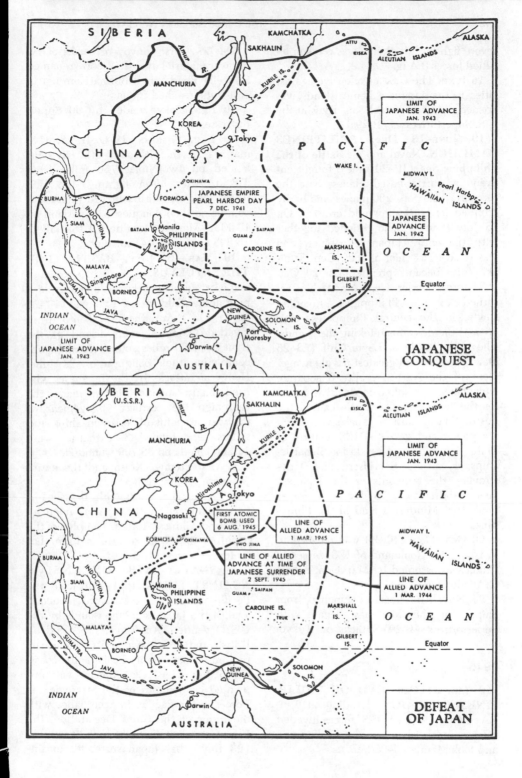

severe fighting Myitkyina was retaken by Allied forces 3 Aug.

16 June. The U.S. air offensive against cities in the Japanese home islands was opened with an attack on Kyushu by U.S. Superfortresses (B-29s).

19 June–15 Dec. PHILIPPINES CAMPAIGN. Naval and air **Battle of the Philippine Sea** (19–20 June), fought entirely by carrier-based planes, cost the Japanese 3 carriers, 200 planes, and badly crippled its battleships and cruisers. On 18 July Premier Tojo resigned together with the entire Japanese cabinet, and was relieved as chief of staff. Gen. Kuniaki Koiso became premier. On 20 Oct. U.S. forces under Gen. MacArthur returned to the Philippines. Invading Leyte, in the central Philpines, they opened the drive for retaking the islands. The naval **Battle of Leyte Gulf** (23–25 Oct.), the last and greatest naval engagement of the war—in reality 3 separate engagements—resulted in decisive defeat for the Japanese. The battle caused the destruction of most of Japan's remaining sea power and gave the U.S. control of Philippine waters. After losing 2 battleships, 4 carriers, 9 cruisers, and 9 destroyers, the remnants of the Japanese fleet withdrew. On 15 Dec. U.S. forces landed on Mindoro Island in the Philippines.

28 Oct. Gen. Stilwell was recalled to Washington. Command of U.S. forces in China was assumed by Maj. Gen. **Albert C. Wedemeyer.**

24 Nov. Air offensive launched from Saipan in the Marianas began with Superfortress (B-29) attacks on Tokyo.

1945

9 Jan.–23 Feb. END OF PHILIPPINES CAMPAIGN. Landing at Lingayen Gulf (9 Jan.), U.S. forces invaded Luzon, main island of the Philippines, and took Manila (5–23 Feb.).

28. Jan. First convoy of trucks carrying war matériel over the Ledo (renamed Stilwell) Road across Burma from northeast India reached China.

10 Feb. Tokyo raided by 90 Superfortresses (B-29s).

19 Feb.–17 Mar. IWO JIMA. U.S. marines of the 4th and 5th Divisions landed on Iwo Jima, 750 miles from Tokyo. After bitter fighting, the U.S. forces took Mt. Suribachi (23 Feb.) and completed their conquest of the island on 17 Mar. Marine casualties: 4,189 killed, 15,308 wounded, 441 missing.

19 Mar.–21 June. BATTLE FOR THE RYUKYUS. U.S. carrier planes made extensive attacks on Japanese shipping and airfields in the Ryukyus (19–21 Mar.). On 1 Apr. the U.S. Tenth Army invaded **Okinawa,** main island of the Ryukyus, 360 miles southwest of Japan, completing their conquest on 21 June. Heavy air attacks by the Japanese, who used many suicide planes, made the campaign the costliest engagement of the war in point of losses in ships and sailors. The total U.S. casualties were 11,260 killed and 33,769 wounded.

5 Apr. Premier Koiso and the entire Japanese cabinet resigned.

30 Apr. The Fourteenth British Imperial Army in Southeast Asia, aided by U.S. and Chinese forces, completed the expulsion of Japanese armies from that sector.

May–Aug. AIR OFFENSIVE AGAINST JAPAN, the greatest in the Pacific and Far East war, was launched against the Japanese home islands by the U.S. Twentieth Air Force, supported by British and U.S. naval units which carried out attacks along the Japanese coast. On 5 July Gen. **Carl Spaatz** was appointed commander of the Strategic Air Forces in the Pacific. In accordance with the terms of the Cairo Declaration, the U.S., Great Britain, and China demanded (26 July) that Japan surrender unconditionally. Japan formally rejected the Potsdam surrender ultimatum on 29 July. An **atomic bomb** with an explosive force of 20,000 tons of TNT was dropped (6 Aug.) on the Japanese city and military base of **Hiroshima,** the first time this weapon, until then held secret, was used for a military purpose. The bomb destroyed over 4 square miles of the city and brought death or injury to over 160,000 persons.

8 Aug. Russia declared war on Japan. Soviet armies invaded Manchuria.

9–15 Aug. An **atomic bomb** was dropped on the Japanese city and naval base of **Nagasaki.** On 10 Aug. the Japanese cabinet under Premier Suzuki offered to surrender on condition that Emperor Hirohito keep his throne. The Japanese accepted the Allied terms on 14 Aug. **V-J Day** (15 Aug.).

15 Aug. U.S. CASUALTIES (in the Pacific theater: 41,322 dead out of total casualties 170,596); in all theaters by 15 Aug.: 321,999 dead; 800,000 wounded, captured, or missing; 111,426 of the 124,079 captured returned to U.S. control. The ratio of fatalities per 100 wounded in World War II was less than one half the ratio of World War I, owing, among other reasons, to **penicillin,** the **sulfa** drugs, early use of **blood plasma,** and an efficient system of evacuation (much of it by air). Total maximum **enrollment** in all U.S. forces was 12,-466,000 (army, 8,300,000; navy, 3,500,-000; marine corps, 486,000; coast guard, 180,000).

27 Aug.–9 Sept. U.S. forces began occupation of Japan (27 Aug.). The Japanese foreign minister and chief of staff signed the formal surrender on board the U.S.S. *Missouri* in Tokyo Bay, whereby home islands were to be under U.S. army of occupation, while the Emperor was to remain as head of state (2 Sept.). Surrender terms for Japanese forces in China were signed at Nanking (9 Sept.).

European and Mediterranean Theaters of War, 1942–45

1942

7 Jan.–29 June. BRITISH VS. ROMMEL IN AFRICA. On 18 Nov. 1941 the British Eighth Army had opened its offensive in Libya, reached Agheila (7 Jan.), but held it for only 2 weeks. On 21 Jan. Rommel struck against the British and pressed them back in the neighborhood of Tobruk. A new offensive was launched in Libya by Rommel (26 May). Axis troops took Tobruk and Bardia (21 June), and Matrûh, in Egypt (29 June). The Axis advance was checked at El Alamein (29 June), 7 miles west of Alexandria.

20 Jan.–12 May. RUSSIAN COUNTERATTACK. The Russians retook Mozhaisk (20 Jan.), claimed Dorogobuzh (23 Feb.), advanced near Kursk (29 Apr.), and attacked near Kharkov (12 May).

26 Jan. U.S. forces arrived in Northern Ireland.

27 Feb.–19 Aug. COMMANDO RAIDS. Allied paratroopers raided Bruneval, France (27 Feb.); British commandos raided St. Nazaire (28 Mar.); and on 19 Aug. Dieppe was raided by about 6,000 British and Canadian troops and a small force of U.S. Rangers. About 3,350 invaders were killed, wounded, or taken prisoner.

30 May–17 Aug. ALLIED AIR WAR. First 1,000-bomber raid carried out by the British on Cologne (30 May), fol-

lowed the next day by a 1,000-bomber raid on Essen and the Ruhr, and a 1,000-plane raid on Bremen (25 June). The first independent U.S. bombing attack in Europe was carried out (17 Aug.) by Eighth Air Force Flying Fortresses (B-17s) in raids on railroad yards near Rouen.

10 JUNE. LIDICE, town in Czechoslovakia, laid waste by the Germans in reprisal for the assassination (27 May) of Reinhard Heydrich, Gestapo official.

28 JUNE–13 SEPT. GERMAN SUMMER OFFENSIVE AGAINST RUSSIA started from Kirsh (28 June). Sevastopol fell to the Germans (1 July) after an 8-month siege. The Germans took Voronezh (7 July), Rostov (24 July), Markov (9 Aug.), crossed the Don River (20 Aug.), and opened the siege of Stalingrad (22 Aug.). On 1 Sept. they crossed the Kerch Straits from the Crimea and invaded the south Caucasus. They entered Stalingrad (13 Sept.).

23 OCT.–24 DEC. ALLIED CAMPAIGNS IN NORTH AFRICA. British Eighth Army under Gen. Bernard L. Montgomery launched (23 Oct.) third Allied offensive in North Africa. British victory at **El Alamein** (4 Nov.) forced Rommel's forces to make a full retreat from Egypt by 12 Nov. The British took Bardia (12 Nov.), Tobruk (13 Nov.), Bengasi (20 Nov.).

8 Nov.–1 DEC. OPERATION TORCH. In the first major Allied amphibious operation in this theater, commanded by Gen. **Dwight D. Eisenhower,** with Adm. Sir Andrew Cunningham, naval commander, U.S. and British forces landed (8 Nov.) in North Africa. The main landings were made at Casablanca, Oran, and Algiers. On 10 Nov. fighting ceased at Oran. On 15 Nov. Allied troops advanced into Tunisia. Earlier, on 11 Nov., an armistice was arranged with Adm. Jean-François Darlan, Vichy representative in French North Africa, and the same day German

forces entered Unoccupied France. Final agreement with Darlan was reached 13 Nov. On 27 Nov. the French fleet at Toulon was scuttled by its crews to prevent seizure of warships by Germans. With U.S. and British approval, Darlan became chief of state in French North Africa (1 Dec.), but he was assassinated in Algiers (24 Dec.), and Gen. Henri Giraud was appointed temporary administrator of North Africa.

19 Nov.–3 MAR. 1943. RUSSIAN COUNTEROFFENSIVE began on the Stalingrad front (19 Nov.), on Velikie Luki-Rzhev front (25 Nov.), and on Middle Don River (16 Dec.). On 18 Jan. 1943 the Russians raised the 17-month siege of Leningrad, the Germans at **Stalingrad** surrendered (2 Feb.), and the Russians retook Rostov (14 Feb.), Kharkov (16 Feb.), and Rzhev (9 Mar.).

1943

24 JAN.–13 May. END OF THE AFRICAN WAR. Tripoli fell to the British Eighth Army (24 Jan.). On 6 Feb. Gen. Eisenhower was appointed commander in chief of all Allied forces in North Africa. On 14 Feb. U.S. II Corps, commanded by Maj. Gen. Lloyd R. Fredendall, was thrown back by Rommel's Afrika Korps at **Kasserine Pass.** The Americans retook the position on 19 Feb. and by 23 Feb. had checked Rommel's drive. In March Fredendall was replaced by Maj. Gen. **George S. Patton, Jr.** (p. 1122). On 19 Mar. U.S. forces took El Guettar in Tunisia. On 21 Mar., from the east, Gen. Montgomery launched an offensive against Axis forces on the Mareth Line in Tunisia. The British breakthrough took place on 29 Mar. On 7 Apr. U.S. First Army and British Eighth Army joined lines near Gafsa, thus encircling the Axis forces in Tunisia. Tunis fell to the British, and Bizerte to the Americans (7 May). The main Axis forces under Gen. Jurgen

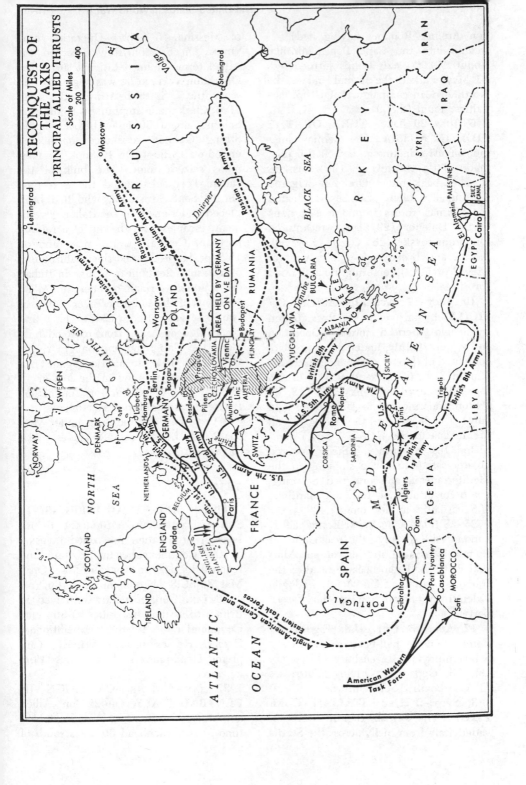

RECONQUEST OF
THE AXIS
PRINCIPAL ALLIED THRUSTS

Scale of Miles

0   200   400

von Arnim (Rommel having fled) retreated into the Cape Bon peninsula.
About 250,000 Axis troops surrendered.
13 May marked the formal end of the
North African campaign. Total U.S. casualties: about 18,500.

**5 July–29 Dec. TURN OF THE
TIDE IN RUSSIA.** The German summer offensive in Russia, launched 5 July,
made little headway. The Russians
smashed back, retook Orel and Belgorod
(4 Aug.), Smolensk (25 Sept.), cleared
the German forces from the east bank
of the Dnieper (29 Sept.), recaptured
Dnepropetrovsk (26 Oct.), Kiev (7
Nov.), and broke enemy lines west of
Kiev (29 Dec.), entering Poland on 3
Jan. 1944.

**10 July–17 Aug. INVASION OF
SICILY** by air and sea was begun
by Anglo-American forces (Operation
HUSKY) on 10 July, under the immediate
command of deputy commander Gen. Sir
Harold R. L. G. Alexander, with British
forces led by Montgomery and U.S. by
Patton. Palermo fell to U.S. troops (24
July), Catania to British (5 Aug.). Fall
of Messina to the U.S. (17 Aug.) completed the conquest of Sicily, assured
greater safety to Allied shipping in the
Mediterranean, and provided a spring-
board for attacks on Italy and Sardinia.
U.S. casualties totaled about 7,400.

25–28 July. King Victor Emmanuel II
announced (25 July) the resignation of
Premier Mussolini and his cabinet. Marshal Pietro Badoglio became head of the
Italian government. On 28 July Badoglio
ordered the dissolution of the Fascist
party.

17 Aug.–15 Oct. U.S. Eighth Air
Force raided ball-bearing works at
Schweinfurt and Regensburg (17 Aug.).
On 15 Oct. U.S. Flying Fortresses
(B-17s) bombed Schweinfurt.

**3 Sept.–2 Dec. ITALIAN CAM-
PAIGN.** The British Eighth Army in-
vaded Italy from Sicily across the Straits
of Messina (3 Sept.)—Operation BAY-
TOWN. On 8 Sept. Italy accepted the
Allied terms of unconditional surrender.
Operation AVALANCHE was begun 9 Sept.
when the U.S. Fifth Army under Gen.
Mark Clark made amphibious landings at
Salerno, about 30 miles below Naples.
Strong German resistance at Salerno
ended on 18 Sept. On 10 Sept. the Germans seized Rome. The bulk of the
Italian fleet surrendered the next day.
On 12 Sept. Mussolini, who had been
placed under arrest by the Italian government, escaped with the aid of a raiding
party of German paratroopers, and on
15 Sept. he proclaimed the establishment
of a Fascist Republican regime in Italian
areas under German domination. Allied
crossings of the Volturno River (north of
Naples) took place (12–14 Oct.) and
by 25 Dec. an Allied front bisected Italy
along the Garigliano and Sangro rivers.
On 2 Dec. 1943 an air raid against Al-
lied-held Bari resulted in the loss of 16
vessels. An Allied Control Commission
for Italy was established 10 Nov.

9 Oct. Yugoslav partisans under Marshal Tito began assault against Axis
forces near Trieste.

1944

11 Jan. ALLIED AIR OFFENSIVE.
Strategic air offensive from the British
Isles in preparation for Allied invasion
of the Continent began 11 Jan., and
reached its peak in Apr. and May. On 6
Mar. 800 U.S. planes bombed Berlin.

16 Jan. Gen. Eisenhower arrived in
Britain to assume his duties as Supreme
Commander, Allied Expeditionary
Forces. He established **SHAEF** (Su-
preme Headquarters, Allied Expedition-
ary forces).

**22 Jan.–4 June. CAMPAIGN IN
CENTRAL ITALY.** On 22 Jan. Allied
amphibious landings were made at Net-
tuno-Anzio beachhead 30 miles south of

Rome. The successful Allied assault on Cassino, in central Italy, a key position in the German Gustav Line, begun 15 Mar., ended 18 May. On 4 June Rome was liberated by the U.S. Fifth Army.

29 JAN.–9 MAY. FURTHER SOVIET GAINS. On 29 Jan. the Russians announced the Moscow-Leningrad area had been cleared of German troops. The Russians recaptured Odessa (10 Apr.) and Sevastopol (9 May).

22 MAR. German forces occupied Hungary.

6 JUNE. OPERATION OVERLORD. Allied forces concentrated in southern England invaded Europe on a 60-mile line along the coast of Normandy, from the mouth of the river Orne to the beaches near Ste-Mère-Église on the Cotentin Peninsula. The spearhead assault by a force of 176,000 troops was made with 4,000 invasion craft supported by 600 warships and an air cover of 11,000 planes, and was preceded by the descent of U.S. and British parachute and glider troops. The entire action was under the unified command of Gen. Eisenhower and was the largest amphibious operation of the war and all history. The ground forces (21st Army Group) were under the command of Gen. Montgomery. The American land contingent (U.S. First Army) was commanded by Gen. **Omar N. Bradley** (p. 991). The Germans countered (14 June) by initiating the bombing of southern England with jet-propelled pilotless aircraft (V-1s), launched across the Channel from special sites in France and Belgium, with London as chief target. The U.S. forces reached the west shore of the Cotentin Peninsula (18 June). On 27 June Cherbourg and its demolished harbor works were captured by U.S. forces. By 2 July the Allies had landed in Normandy about 1 million troops, 566,648 tons of supplies, and 171,532 vehicles. The British forces captured Caen (9

July); the U.S. forces took St. Lô (18 July), road center linking Normandy with Brittany. U.S. "breakout" from St. Lô (25 July) enabled powerful armored thrust toward Avranches and into Brittany, which by 10 Aug. had been overrun and cut off by the U.S. Third Army under Gen. Patton. The St. Lô action concluded the Allied offensive in Normandy and opened the **Battle of France.**

23 JUNE. The Russians opened their summer offensive along an 800-mile line south of Leningrad.

19 JULY. Leghorn taken by the U.S. Fifth Army.

20 JULY. Attempted assassination of Hitler and plot to overthrow the Nazi regime ended in failure.

2 AUG. Polish underground army in Warsaw area commanded by General Bor (Komorowski) opened fight against the Germans. The Polish forces surrendered on 2 Oct.

3–23 AUG. Allies closed the Falaise-Argentan pocket, causing heavy German losses.

12 AUG. Florence fell to British forces. German troops in Italy pulled back to the Gothic Line.

15 AUG. OPERATION DRAGOON. Allied forces, including the U.S. Seventh Army under Gen. **Alexander M. Patch,** landed in southern France, between Marseilles and Nice, and drove up the Rhône Valley.

25 AUG.–11 SEPT. LIBERATION OF FRANCE, BELGIUM, AND LUXEMBOURG. On 25 Aug. Paris was liberated. On 28 Aug. the U.S. Third Army reached the Marne. Brussels and Antwerp were liberated by British and Canadian troops (4 Sept.). By 5 Sept. the Allies had landed 2,086,000 men and 3,466,000 tons of supplies in Western Europe. Luxembourg was liberated 11 Sept.

7 SEPT. Germans fired first V-2 (p. 800) on London.

8 Sept. Bulgaria surrendered to the Allies.

12 Sept.–3 Dec. BATTLE FOR GERMANY. U.S. forces entered Germany near Eupen and Trier (12 Sept.). In an attempt to turn the flank of the Westwall and gain a bridgehead on the Rhine, the Allies landed 34,000 airborne troops in Holland (17–28 Sept.). The U.S. forces took Eindhoven and Nijmegen. The British were defeated at Arnhem. The Canadian First Army cleared the Scheldt Estuary (9 Oct.–9 Nov.), thus enabling the Allies to use the urgently needed port facilities of Antwerp. The U.S. First Army took Aachen (21 Oct.) after a battle that began on 2 Oct. and required penetration of the Siegfried Line. Aachen was the first large German city taken by the Allies. The U.S. Third Army entered Metz (22 Nov.) and Strasbourg (23 Nov.), and U.S. forces reached the Roer River (3 Dec.).

22 Sept.–29 Dec. SOVIET ADVANCES. Russians took Tallinn (22 Sept.) and entered East Prussia (20 Oct.). Russian and Yugoslav forces seized Belgrade (20 Oct.), and the Russians entered Budapest 29 Dec.

3 Dec. Civil war broke out in Greece and lasted until 12 Jan. 1945).

16–26 Dec. BATTLE OF THE BULGE. A German counteroffensive under the command of Gen. Karl von Rundstedt was launched in the Ardennes along an 80-mile front held by an inadequate number of U.S. troops, many of whom lacked battle experience. By this surprise attack the Germans hoped to split the Allied Armies and take Liège and Antwerp. After advancing 50 miles to a point near Dinant, within 4 miles of the Meuse, the German drive was checked, largely owing to the defense of ringed Bastogne, which was relieved on 26 Dec. The original Allied line in the Ardennes was not restored until 21 Jan. 1945. The Battle of the Bulge resulted

in about 77,000 U.S. casualties, including 8,000 killed, 48,000 wounded, and 21,-000 captured or missing.

1945

12–23 Jan. Russians launched general offensive in Poland (12–15 Jan.), took Warsaw (17 Jan.), Lodz (19 Jan.), and reached the Oder River (23 Jan.).

8 Feb.–26 Apr. GERMANY CRUSHED. British offensive launched in Holland (8 Feb.); U.S. Third Army crossed the Saar River (22 Feb.). The Saar-Palatinate area was cleared of German troops by 25 Mar. U.S. forces penetrated the Ruhr Valley (23 Feb.) and reached the Rhine near Düsseldorf (2 Mar.). Cologne and Düsseldorf fell on 7 Mar.; on the same day U.S. forces captured the **Remagen Bridge** across the Rhine before the Germans could demolish it, and secured a bridgehead on the east bank. On 23 Mar. Allied forces crossed the Rhine between Rees and Wesel by water and air. The Ruhr was enveloped and reduced (24 Mar.–18 Apr.), with the surrender of 325,000 German troops. On 27 Mar. U.S. forces took Mannheim and Frankfurt am Main. The U.S. Ninth Army reached the Elbe (11 Apr.). The Russians launched (13 Apr.) a drive on Berlin, entering the city on 24 Apr. U.S. forces took Nuremburg (21 Apr.). U.S. and Russian troops met at Torgau, on the Elbe (25 Apr.). On 26 Apr. the British took Bremen.

3 Mar. Finland, which had quit the war against Russia 4 Sept. 1941, declared war against Germany.

28 Apr. Mussolini and his mistress, Clara Petacci, captured and killed by Italian partisans in the town of Dongo, on Lake Como, as he tried to flee to Switzerland. Allied forces invaded the Po Valley.

1 May–5 June. GERMAN CAPITULATION. On 1 May the provisional German government under Adm. Karl Doenitz announced Hitler's death. It was reported that he had committed suicide in Berlin. On 2 May Berlin fell and the German forces in Italy surrendered. The German forces in the Netherlands, Denmark, and northwest Germany surrendered 4 May. Field Marshal Jodl signed (7 May, 2:41 A.M. French time) the instrument of unconditional surrender of Germany in the Allied headquarters at Reims. 8 May, **V-E Day**—formal end of the war in Europe. The German surrender was formally ratified at Berlin (9 May). On 5 June Germany was placed under an Allied Control Council and divided into four occupation zones.

The United States and the Western Hemisphere, 1942–45

HEMISPHERE SOLIDARITY. On 12 Jan. 1942 the U.S. and Mexico established a joint defense commission. At the **Rio de Janeiro Conference** (15–28 Jan.) of American foreign ministers, delegates of all 21 American republics, under the leadership of Sumner Welles and Oswaldo Aranha, chairman, voted to recommend to their respective governments a break in diplomatic relations with the Axis powers. All of the governments involved, with the exception of Chile and Argentina, severed relations. Chile broke off relations with the Axis (20 Jan. 1943); Argentina not until 26 Jan. 1944. The U.S. revealed (19 Mar. 1942) establishment of air bases in Guatemala to defend the Panama Canal Zone. On 30 Mar. the Inter-American Defense Board held its first session at Washington, D.C. President Roosevelt and President Getulio Vargas of Brazil, in conference aboard a U.S. destroyer off Natal, Brazil, announced (28 Jan.) agreement on common defense aims. The friendly relations between the U.S. and Mexico were stressed at a meeting (21 Apr.) of Roosevelt and President Avila Camacho. On 16 Aug. 1944 the U.S. government froze Argentina's gold assets in the U.S. in retaliation against the Argentine government's refusal to cooperate fully against the Axis. On 29 Sept. Roosevelt expressed concern over the continuing spread of Nazi and Fascist influence in Argentina and accused its government of having failed to fulfill its "solemn inter-American obligations." The Inter-American Conference on Problems of War and Peace met (21 Feb.–8 Mar. 1945) at Chapultepec Castle, Mexico City. All of the American republics except Argentina were represented. The conference adopted (3 Mar.) the **Act of Chapultepec**, a regional security agreement binding for the duration of the war. It provided that aggression upon one American state by another would be regarded as aggression against all and specified the "use of armed force to prevent or repel aggression." On 27 Mar. 1945 Argentina declared war on Germany and Japan, was admitted to the Pan-American Union (4 Apr.), and recognized (9 Apr.) by U.S., other American republics, and Great Britain.

WAR MOBILIZATION. By executive order the 9-man **War Manpower Commission** (WMC) was established (18 Apr. 1942) for the more effective utilization of manpower resources. Federal Security Administrator **Paul V. McNutt** was named chairman. Later that year its powers were extended to include jurisdiction over Selective Service, the U.S. Employment Service, and other war recruiting and training agencies. Voluntary male enlistments in the military services were ended. All males 18–38 became subject to Selective Service (draft age lowered to 18, 13 Nov. 1942), with deferments limited to war industries, agriculture, hardship cases, and the clergy. After a trial, drafting of 38–45 was ended, but all males between 45 and 64 were registered (25 Apr.). Women were enlisted for noncombat duties in the Women's Auxiliary Army Corps (WAACS, by act of 15 May 1942), Women Appointed for Voluntary Emergency Service (WAVES), Women's Auxiliary Ferrying Squadron (WAFS), *Semper Paratus* Always Ready Service (SPARS), and the Women's Reserve of the Marine Corps. To deal with the labor shortage, President Roosevelt decreed (9 Feb. 1943) for the duration of the war a minimum work week of 48 hours, applicable immediately in U.S. areas where labor shortages prevailed, but specified time-and-a-half for the extra 8 hours. Following Roosevelt's "hold-the-line" order (8 Apr. 1943), the WMC adopted regulations to "freeze" 27 million workers in war jobs.

WAR PRODUCTION. On 13 Jan. President Roosevelt appointed **Donald M. Nelson** chairman of the **War Production Board** (WPB) with authority to mobilize the nation's resources for a total war effort. WPB was the principal agency in the field of production and supply. On 21 Jan. Nelson abolished the Office of Production Management, whose functions were absorbed by the WPB. On 8 Apr. the WPB halted nonessential residential and highway construction in a move to conserve materials for the war effort. On 14 Aug. 1944 Nelson issued orders permitting limited reconversion of industry from war to civilian output. Nelson resigned (30 Sept.) and was succeeded by Julius A. Krug. On 2 Nov. President Roosevelt appointed Nelson his "personal representative" and requested

him to organize war production in China. The WPB was terminated 4 Oct. 1945, and its functions transferred to the Civilian Production Administration. On 3 Oct. 1944 **James F. Byrnes** was named head of the newly established Office of War Mobilization and Reconversion.

STRATEGIC AND CRITICAL WAR MATERIALS. In June 1942 the WPB substituted for general priorities a classified system of specific allocations of all strategic materials. The problem was also tackled by other officials and war agencies. On 7 Jan. 1942 Federal Loan Administrator Jesse H. Jones announced a $4-billion program for increasing production of synthetic rubber. On 14 Apr. control of the U.S. stockpile of critical and essential materials was transferred to the **Board of Economic Warfare** headed by Vice-President Henry A. Wallace. On 15 Sept. William M. Jeffers, president of the Union Pacific R.R., was appointed **Rubber Administrator** with full authority over the entire U.S. rubber program. On 15 July 1943 President Roosevelt abolished the Board of Economic Warfare and created the Office of Economic Warfare (OEW), headed by Leo T. Crowley, which absorbed its predecessor's functions as well as the foreign subsidiaries of the RFC on 25 Oct. Other war agencies concerned with war materials included **Petroleum Administrator for War** (executive order, 2 Dec. 1942, preceded, 28 May 1941, by Office of Petroleum Coordinator for War, with the Secretary of the Interior as coordinator); **Solid Fuels Administrator for War** (established in the Department of the Interior by executive order, 19 Apr. 1943, with power over coal and certain other solid fuels, including supervision of operations when mines were placed under government control). Financing for war industries was facilitated by the RFC and the **Smaller War Plants Corp.,** established by act of Congress, 11 June 1942 and terminated 27 Dec. 1945, when its functions were transferred to the RFC.

PRICE CONTROL AND RATIONING. The Emergency Price Control Act (30 Jan. 1942) established the **Office of Price Administration** (OPA) to fix price ceilings on all commodities (except farm products) and to control rents in defense areas. This federal agency was originally created (11 Apr. 1941) as the Office of Price Administration and Civilian Supply, with **Leon Henderson** as first Federal Price Administrator; succeeded (Jan. 1943) by Prentiss M. Brown, in turn by Chester Bowles (Oct. 1943), and by Paul A. Porter (Feb. 1946). **Rationing** began 27 Dec. 1941, with auto tires. The first war ration book (1942) provided coupons for sugar, then coffee, with separate books for gasoline (1 Dec.), and coupon sheets for fuel oil. Point rationing was started early in 1943 with meat, fats and oils, butter, cheese, and processed foods. Shoes were later added. At its peak 13 rationing programs were administered. Before the close of Nov. 1945 all rationing programs were ended except for sugar and rubber tires. Tire rationing ended 31 Dec. 1945; sugar, 11 June 1947. As compared with World War I considerable price stabilization was obtained. By V-J Day consumer prices had risen 31% as against 62% by the Armistice of 1918. (See also p. 751.)

LABOR CONTROLS. In Mar. 1941 the National Defense Mediation Board, a tripartite body, with **William H. Davis** as chairman, was given investigatory and mediatory powers to deal with labor disputes in defense industries. In Nov. 1941 it rejected the United Mine Workers' demand for a union shop in the steel companies' "captive mines." CIO members resigned and the board's usefulness was destroyed. It was replaced (12 Jan.

1942) by a 12-man **National War Labor Board** (NWLB), equally divided among public, employers, and labor representatives, with Davis as chairman (to 8 Mar. 1945), with authority to settle disputes by mediation and arbitration. In the **International Harvester Case** (15 Apr.) the board granted the union **maintenance of membership** on condition that a majority of union employees, voting in a secret election, approved; modified in June to provide a 15-day period when employees could resign from union membership, after which maintenance of membership would go into effect. The board tied wage increases to the rise in the cost of living since 1 Jan. 1941 ("**Little Steel**" formula, 16 July). On 8 Apr. 1943 President Roosevelt issued his "hold-the-line" order freezing prices, wages, and salaries; modified in effect (12 May). Because of a strike involving 450,000 soft-coal miners and 80,000 anthracite miners, Roosevelt ordered (1 May) Secretary of the Interior Harold L. Ickes to take over all coal mines in the Eastern U.S. Roosevelt placed responsibility for the stoppage upon **John L. Lewis** (p. 1083), who called off the strike on 2 May. The war **Labor Disputes Act** (**Smith-Connally Anti-Strike Act**), passed over Roosevelt's veto (25 June), broadened presidential power to seize plants where interference with war production was threatened by a labor disturbance; made illegal the instigation of strikes in plants seized by the government; and made unions liable for damage suits for failure to give 30 days' notice of intention to strike in war industries. By order of President Roosevelt (27 Dec.) the U.S. Army took temporary possession of all railroads in the U.S. in order to prevent a strike of railway workers. The railroads were returned to private management on 18 Jan. 1944. On 28 Dec. 1944 the U.S. army took possession of

Montgomery Ward establishments in Chicago and elsewhere following the firm's refusal to obey NWLB directives.

FEPC. The migration of Negroes from rural sections to industrial areas led to a demand for ending racial discrimination in war industries and the armed services. The **Fair Employment Practice Committee,** originally established (25 June 1941) to curb discrimination in war production and government employment, was strengthened by an executive order (27 May 1943) calling for the mandatory incorporation of nondiscrimination clauses in war contracts and subcontracts. Race riots broke out in Detroit (20–21 June). President Roosevelt ordered out federal troops to quell the disturbance. A strike in the transportation field in protest against the upgrading of Negroes occurred in Philadelphia 1 Aug. 1944, and the U.S. army quickly restored order and normal transportation facilities. In Feb. 1946 a bill for a permanent FEPC was killed in the Senate by a filibuster. Again in 1950 the Senate blocked passage, and a modified plan was blocked in 1952. By the end of 1946 5 states (N.Y., N.J., Mass., Conn., and Wash.) had enacted Fair Employment Practice acts.

OTHER WAR AGENCIES. Office of Civilian Defense (28 Jan. 1942), with Mayor **Fiorello H. La Guardia** (N.Y.) director; succeeded by James N. Landis. **Director of Economic Stabilization,** filled (4 Oct. 1942) by Supreme Court Justice **James F. Byrnes** (S.C.), who (28 May 1943) headed the **Office of War Mobilization** (OWM), established to unify the activities of federal agencies engaged in the production or distribution of civilian supplies. **Office of Scientific Research and Development** (28 June 1941). **Office of Lend-Lease Administration** (executive order 8 Oct. 1941). **Office of Censorship** (executive order 19 Dec. 1941), with Byron Price director until Nov. 1945.

Office of Defense Transportation (executive order 18 Dec. 1941). **War Shipping Administration** (executive order 7 Feb. 1942), with Rear Adm. **Emory S. Land** as administrator. **National Housing Agency** (executive order 24 Feb. 1942). **Office of Alien Property Custodian** (executive order 11 Mar. 1942). **Office of Foreign Relief and Rehabilitation** (by State Department order 4 Dec. 1942). **Office of Coordinator of Inter-American Affairs** (executive order 30 July 1941), **Nelson A. Rockefeller,** coordinator (1940–44). **Office of War Information** (OWI, executive order 13 June 1942), to consolidate in one agency the information activities, both foreign and domestic, of the government (Office of Facts and Figures, Office of Government Reports, Division of Information of the Office of Emergency Management, and the Foreign Information Service), **Elmer Davis,** director. **Office of Strategic Services** (executive order 13 June 1942), placed under the jurisdiction of the Joint Chiefs of Staff, to engage in intelligence operations abroad and in the analysis of strategic information; **William J. Donovan,** director.

ATOMIC BOMB PROJECT. The Manhattan Engineer District for the development of the atomic bomb was placed under the command of Brig. Gen. **Leslie R. Groves** (13 Aug. 1942). Construction was begun (Sept.–Dec.) on the 3 chief installations of the Manhattan District: the U-235 separation plant (Oak Ridge, Tenn.), the bomb development laboratory (Los Alamos, N.M.), and the plutonium production works (Hanford, Wash.). Scientists working on the Argonne Project at the Univ. of Chicago effected the first self-sustaining nuclear reaction (2 Dec.). The first atomic bomb was exploded (16 July 1945) in a test at Alamogordo, N.M.

GI LEGISLATION. The "state rights" soldier vote bill became law (31 Mar.

1944) without President Roosevelt's signature. Roosevelt approved (22 June) the "GI Bill of Rights" authorizing educational and other benefits for World War II veterans.

1942 ELECTION TREND. Congressional, state, and local elections (3 Nov.) indicated a swing toward the Republicans, who gained 46 seats in the House, 9 in the Senate. The Democrats, however, retained control of both houses.

RELOCATION AND ENEMY ALIENS. By order of President Roosevelt (19 Feb. 1942), the Secretary of War was authorized to prescribe restricted military areas from which persons might be excluded. About 110,000 Japanese-Americans living in California, Oregon, Washington, and Arizona were by 29 Mar. transferred to relocation camps in the U.S. interior. On 12 Oct. Attorney General Francis Biddle announced that, effective 19 Oct., 600,000 unnaturalized Italians in the U.S. would no longer be considered as enemy aliens. On 17 Dec. 1944 the U.S. army announced the termination, effective 2 Jan. 1945, of the mass exclusion from the West Coast of persons of Japanese ancestry.

INTERNAL SECURITY MEASURES. On 27 June 1942 J. Edgar Hoover, director of the FBI, announced the arrest of 8 Nazi saboteurs who had been landed from submarines on the Long Island and Florida coasts. Convicted by a secret military tribunal appointed by the president, 6 were electrocuted and the other 2 given long prison terms. On 23 July, 28 persons, including George Sylvester Viereck, William Dudley Pelley, and Gerald Winrod, were indicted as seditionists. In the course of their trial in 1944 Judge Edward C. Eichers died, and the indictments were dismissed (1946) by Chief Justice Bolitha L. Laws of the District Court for the District of Columbia, who rebuked the Department of Justice for "lack of diligence" in prosecution. On 15 May 1943 the third International (Comintern) was dissolved in Moscow. On 20 May 1944 the Communist party of the U.S. dissolved as a political party but was reconstituted as a supposedly nonparty group under the name of the Communist Political Association, headed by Earl Browder. Congressman Martin Dies' **Committee on Un-American Activities** was given permanent status by a House vote, 207–186 (3 Jan. 1945). The Dies Committee recommended dismissal of some 3,800 government employees; but after a Department of Justice investigation, only 36 were found to warrant dismissal. On 27 July 1945 the Communist Political Association voted to disband and to reconstitute the Communist Party of the U.S. On 29 July William Z. Foster replaced Earl Browder as head of the Communist organization.

PLANNING FOR PEACE: CONNALLY-FULBRIGHT RESOLUTION. On 16 Mar. 1943 Sens. Joseph Ball (Rep., Minn.), Harold Burton (Rep., Ohio), Carl Hatch (Dem., N.M.), and Lister Hill (Dem., Ala.) began a bipartisan movement to commit the U.S. Senate to participation in an international organization. On 21 Sept. the House of Representatives adopted the Fulbright Resolution (introduced by J. W. Fulbright [Ark.]) favoring "the creation of appropriate international machinery with power adequate to establish and to maintain a just and lasting peace," and U.S. participation "through its constitutional process." A similar resolution (introduced by Tom Connally [Tex.] was adopted in the Senate, 85–5 (5 Nov.), with the express stipulation that any treaty made to carry out its purpose would require a vote of two thirds of the Senate. On 21 July 1945 the Senate approved U.S.

membership in the United Nations Food and Agriculture Organization. On 28 July the Senate ratified the United Nations Charter by a vote of 89 to 2. President Truman signed the charter (8 Aug.).

PRESIDENTIAL CAMPAIGN OF 1944. The Republican National Convention met at Chicago (26 June) and nominated (27 June) Gov. **Thomas E. Dewey** (N.Y.) for president and Gov. **John W. Bricker** (Ohio) for vice-president. The Democratic National Convention met at Chicago (19 July) and on 20 July renominated President **Roosevelt.** Sen. **Harry S. Truman** (Mo.) was chosen as vice-presidential candidate. Minor party candidates: Norman Thomas (N.Y.), Socialist; Claude A. Watson (Calif.), National Prohibition; and Edward A. Teichert (Pa.), Socialist Labor. Both major parties backed U.S. participation in some form of postwar international organization to maintain world peace and security. Organized labor took part in the campaign through the agency of the C.I.O. Political Action Committee (PAC), which claimed that its support helped to elect 17 candidates for the Senate and 120 for the House.

7 Nov. PRESIDENTIAL ELECTION. Included in the national vote were 2,691,160 soldiers' ballots. Popular vote: Roosevelt, 25,602,505; Dewey, 22,006,278; Thomas, 80,158; Watson, 74,758; and Teichert, 45,336. Electoral vote: Roosevelt, 432 (36 states); Dewey, 99 (12 states). The Democrats retained control of both houses of Congress.

1945, 12 Apr. DEATH OF PRESIDENT ROOSEVELT. President Roosevelt died suddenly of a cerebral hemorrhage at Warm Springs, Ga. Vice-President **Harry S. Truman** took the oath of office as 33rd president of the U.S.

International Conferences, Declarations, and Agreements, 1941–45

1941

22 Dec. Prime Minister Winston Churchill arrived in Washington for a series of conferences with President Roosevelt. The fundamental basis of joint strategy was affirmed: to concentrate upon the defeat of the Axis in Europe (which was viewed as the decisive theater of war), and to follow a policy of containment in the Far East until military successes in Europe or mounting Allied resources permitted stronger blows against Japan. The last of this series of conferences was held on 14 Jan. 1942. The Declaration of the United Nations was drafted and the Combined Chiefs of Staff and the Munitions Assignment Board were set up.

1942

1 Jan. UNITED NATIONS DECLARATION was signed at Washington. Twenty-six nations, including the U.S., Great Britain, the Soviet Union, and China, affirmed the principles of the Atlantic Charter, pledged the employment of their full military and economic resources against the Axis, and promised not to make a separate armistice or peace with the common enemy.

27 Jan. Anglo-American Combined Raw Materials Board established at Washington.

6 Feb. Joint Anglo-American War Council established at Washington.

23 Feb. Master Mutual Lend-Lease

Agreement signed by the U.S. and Great Britain, Australia, and New Zealand.

29 Apr. Hitler and Mussolini conferred at Salzburg.

26 May. Great Britain and Russia signed a 20-year mutual aid pact.

29 May. The Soviet foreign minister, Vyacheslav M. Molotov, arrived in Washington for conferences with President Roosevelt and other high U.S. officials. Among the results of the meetings was a new Lend-Lease protocol with Russia. The agreement provided that materials or data received from the U.S. would not be transferred to other parties without U.S. consent and that materials still available at the end of the war would be returned to the U.S. The new agreement went into effect on 1 July.

9 June. U.S. and Great Britain established a Combined Production Resources Board and a Combined Food Board.

18–27 June. Anglo-American conference at Washington discussed strategy problems. Roosevelt and Churchill participated, as did Russian and Chinese representatives.

July. The Combined Chiefs of Staff, meeting in London, decided to invade North Africa and to postpone a second front in Europe as well as the Pacific offensive.

12–15 Aug. 1ST MOSCOW CONFERENCE. Principal participants were Soviet Premier Joseph V. Stalin, Prime Minister Churchill, and W. Averell Harriman, who represented President Roosevelt. Churchill, with the support of Harriman, informed Stalin that it was not possible to open a second front in Europe in 1942.

9 Oct. U.S. and Great Britain announced they would abandon extraterritorial rights in China. A treaty incorporating this provision was signed by the U.S. and China on 11 Jan. 1943.

1943

14–24 Jan. CASABLANCA CONFERENCE was held in French Morocco. President Roosevelt and Prime Minister Churchill declared that the war would be fought until the "**unconditional surrender**" of the enemy had been secured. Agreement in principle was reached on a second front, but not on its location. U.S. officials favored an invasion of the Continent through France. The British urged an assault on the "soft underbelly" of Europe (i.e., Italy and the Balkans). A compromise was reached on the invasion of Sicily and Italy without prejudice to the ultimate invasion of Europe from the west. No agreement was worked out on the conflicting claims for leadership of Gens. Charles de Gaulle and Henri Giraud, who also attended the conference. Gen. Dwight D. Eisenhower was placed in supreme command of the North African theater.

25 Apr. The Soviet Union broke off relations with the Polish government-in-exile.

12–25 May. ANGLO-AMERICAN CONFERENCE (trident) at Washington planned global strategy and the opening of a second front in Europe. President Roosevelt, Prime Minister Churchill, the Combined Chiefs of Staff, and many U.S. and British officials took part. The date (1 May 1944) for the Normandy invasion was definitely set and the seizure of the Azores authorized unless Portugal could be persuaded by negotiation to grant the use of bases on the islands. The conference also agreed to step up the quantity of aviation gasoline being flown over "the hump" from India to China.

18 May–3 June. The United Nations Conference on Food and Agriculture met at Hot Springs, Va. It established the Food and Agriculture Organization (FAO) of the United Nations.

22 May. Moscow announced the dissolution 15 May of the Third International (Comintern).

31 May. In French Algiers, Gens. Charles de Gaulle and Henri Giraud announced their agreement on the formation of a French Committee of National Liberation, of which they were copresidents. The committee, which became (2 June 1944) the French Provisional Government-in-Exile, promised full support to the war against the Axis. On 23 Oct. 1944 the U.S., Great Britain, and Russia recognized the committee as the French provisional regime.

11–24 Aug. 1ST QUEBEC CONFERENCE (QUADRANT) attended by President Roosevelt, Prime Minister Churchill, and top-ranking advisers including the Combined Chiefs of Staff, reaffirmed 1 May 1944 as the target date for the Normandy invasion (OVERLORD), which was to be supplemented by landings in Southern France (ANVIL, later DRAGOON). Agreement was reached on stepping up military operations in the Far East, particularly in Burma, and a Southeast Asia Command was established, with Lord Louis Mountbatten as Supreme Allied Commander. The Chiefs of the Naval Staffs reported that the Battle of the Atlantic against the U-boat had turned in favor of the Allies.

19–30 Oct. MOSCOW CONFERENCE OF FOREIGN MINISTERS was the first Allied 3-power meeting of World War II. It was attended by Secretary of State Cordell Hull, Foreign Minister Anthony Eden, and Foreign Minister V. M. Molotov, together with U.S., British, and Soviet military officials. The most controversial point in the discussions involved the status of the Polish government-in-exile at London, which the Soviet Union refused to recognize. The U.S. and Great Britain assured the Russians that preparations for opening a second front in Europe were under way.

Stalin made an unconditional promise that after Germany's defeat Russia would enter the war against Japan. The conference established a European Advisory Commission for the purpose of formulating a postwar policy for Germany. The Moscow Declaration issued at the close of the conference recognized "the necessity of establishing at the earliest practicable date a general international organization, based on the principle of the sovereign equality of all peace-loving states, and open to membership by all such states, large and small, for the maintenance of international peace and security."

9 Nov. The United Nations Relief and Rehabilitation Administration (UNRRA) was established with the signing of an agreement at Washington by 44 nations. Its purpose was to aid liberated populations in war-devastated areas of Europe and the Far East. **Herbert H. Lehman** (1878–1963), former governor of New York, was named director general of UNRRA. By agreements of Mar. 1944 and Dec. 1945 the member countries contributed $4 billion. The U.S. paid 72% of UNRRA's operating expenses; 90% of all food and other supplies distributed were products of U.S. farms or factories.

22–26 Nov. 1ST CAIRO CONFERENCE. President Roosevelt and Prime Minister Churchill conferred with Generalissimo and Madame Chiang Kai-shek regarding the war in the Far East. The **Declaration of Cairo** (1 Dec.) affirmed that the 3 powers would prosecute the war against Japan until her unconditional surrender and that they had no desire for territorial expansion; that Japan should be deprived of all Pacific islands acquired since 1914, whether by capture or League of Nations mandate; that all territories which Japan had taken from the Chinese, such as Manchuria, Formosa, and the Pescadores, should be restored to China; and that the 3 powers were "determined that in due course Korea shall become free and independent."

At the **2d Cairo Conference** (4–6 Dec.) Roosevelt and Churchill held discussions with the president of Turkey, Ismet Inönü. This conference affirmed the alliance between Great Britain and Turkey and noted "the firm friendship existing between the Turkish people," the U.S., and the Soviet Union. As a result of military decisions taken at the second Cairo Conference, the command of the invasion of Western Europe was conferred on Gen. **Dwight D. Eisenhower.**

28 Nov.–1 Dec. TEHERAN CONFERENCE, held at the capital of Iran, was attended by President Roosevelt, Prime Minister Churchill, and Premier Stalin. It was the first 3-power war conference in which Stalin took a personal part. The chief subject of the meeting was the projected Anglo-American invasion of Western Europe, supported by a flanking invasion through Southern France, and the timing of this assault with the Soviet offensive against Germany. Stalin reaffirmed his promise to enter the war against Japan. The conference formulated a plan for an international organization to keep the peace.

1944

1–22 July. UNITED NATIONS MONETARY AND FINANCIAL CONFERENCE (BRETTON WOODS CONFERENCE), held at Bretton Woods, N.H., was attended by representatives of 44 nations. The conference established an International Monetary Fund of $8.8 billion (of which about 25% was contributed by the U.S.) for the stabilization of national currencies (it effected a general evaluation of the currencies of Western Europe late in 1949) and the

fostering of world trade. It also set up an International Bank for Reconstruction and Development with a capitalization of $9.1 billion (of which about 35% was supplied by the U.S.) for extending loans to nations requiring economic rehabilitation. By 1950 the bank had made loans of only $700 million. Russia refused to participate in these financial arrangements.

27 July. The Polish Committee of National Liberation, organized at Moscow, was recognized by the Soviet government. The committee, which later transferred its headquarters to Lublin, was entrusted with administrative control of Polish areas taken by the Red Army.

21 Aug.–7 Oct. DUMBARTON OAKS CONFERENCE, held near Washington, D.C., was attended by representatives of the U.S., Great Britain, the Soviet Union, and China (with the last 2 meeting separately, since Russia was still at peace with Japan). The conference discussed the draft of a charter for a permanent postwar international organization for maintaining world peace and security. The tentative proposals (known as the Dumbarton Oaks Plan) served as the basis for the Charter of the United Nations. Agreement on the veto issue could not be reached, Russia refusing to agree to bar a member of the Security Council from voting on a question to which it was itself a party.

11–16 Sept. 2D QUEBEC CONFERENCE, attended by President Roosevelt and Prime Minister Churchill, considered strategic plans for final victory over Germany and Japan. The chief subjects of the conference were the demarcation of the zones of occupation following the conquest of Germany and the policy governing the postwar treatment of that nation. The **Morgenthau plan** (sponsored by Secretary of the Treasury Henry Morgenthau, Jr.) for reducing Germany to an agrarian economy was tentatively approved at this conference, but was rejected by President Roosevelt a month later.

9–18 Oct. 2D MOSCOW CONFERENCE, attended by Prime Minister Churchill and Premier Joseph Stalin, divided the Balkans into spheres, Russia to predominate in Rumania, Bulgaria, and Hungary, Great Britain in Greece, with Yugoslavia to be shared. It was generally agreed that the Curzon Line should bound Poland on the east and the Oder River on the west. Roosevelt, who was not a party to these arrangements, let it be known that he would not be bound by them.

1945

Jan. Malta Conference. Combined Chiefs of Staff planned final campaign against Hitler.

4–11 Feb. YALTA CONFERENCE, held in the Crimea, was attended by President Roosevelt, Prime Minister Churchill, and Premier Stalin, together with their top diplomatic and military advisers. Most of the important agreements remained secret until the postwar period. In exchange for her pledge to enter the war in the Far East, Russia was given the Kurile Islands, the southern half of Sakhalin, and an occupation zone in Korea, and was granted privileged rights in Manchuria and in the Chinese cities of Dairen and Port Arthur. In addition, the U.S. and Great Britain agreed to recognize the autonomy of Outer Mongolia, which had severed its connections with China and come under Soviet influence. The U.S. and Great Britain also agreed to award eastern Poland to the Soviet Union. Poland's eastern border was fixed on the Curzon Line; and that nation was to receive territorial compensation in the north and west at the expense of Germany. Agreement was reached for reorganizing the Polish (Lublin) government on a broader democratic basis. The Russian demand of $20 billion in reparation payments from Germany, to be taken out of current production, was referred to a reparations commission. The 3 powers reaffirmed the "unconditional surrender" formula and issued a Declaration of Liberated Europe pledging the Big Three to support postwar governments in the liberated states which would be representative of the popular will through free elections. The conferees announced they had worked out a formula for voting procedure in the Security Council and that a conference to elaborate the United Nations Charter would convene at San Francisco on 25 Apr. It was secretly agreed that the Ukraine and Byelorussia would be accorded full and equal membership in the United Nations organization on the footing of independent nations.

5 Apr. The Soviet Union denounced its 5-year nonaggression pact with Japan.

21 Apr. The Soviet Union concluded a 20-year mutual assistance pact with the Polish Provisional Government (the Lublin regime).

25 Apr.–26 June. UNITED NATIONS CONFERENCE ON INTERNATIONAL ORGANIZATION, attended by delegates of 50 nations, assembled at San Francisco to draft the Charter of the United Nations Organization (UNO). The Russians at San Francisco interpreted the Yalta voting formula to mean that a nation could use the veto to forbid the Security Council from even discussing questions which might require force in their settlement. Secretary of State Edward R. Stettinius, Jr., threatened that the U.S. would not participate in the organization unless the Russians yielded. The deadlock was broken when President Truman directed Harry L. Hopkins, then in Moscow, to take the issue to Stalin. The latter agreed that the veto should not be used to prevent discussion. Following the announcement (7 June) of this compromise, a draft charter was worked out. The charter of the United Nations provided for 6 chief organs: (1) a **General Assembly** of all member nations as the policy-making body, each nation to have a single vote; (2) a **Security Council** of 11 members in continuous session for deciding diplomatic, political, or military disputes, the Big Five (the U.S., Great Britain, the Soviet Union, France, and China) to have permanent seats, the other 6 to be held for 2-year terms; (3) an **Economic and Social Council** of 18 members elected by the General Assembly for the purpose of dealing with human welfare and fundamental rights and freedoms; (4) an **International Court of Justice** (sitting at The Hague) for dealing with international legal disputes, its 15 judges to be elected by the General Assembly and the Security Council; (5) a **Trusteeship Council** made up of states administering trust territories, the permanent members of the Security Council, and members elected by the General Assembly for a 3-year term; and (6) a **Secretariat,** headed by the Secretary-General, for performing the routine administrative work of the UNO, the staff to be selected from nations holding membership in the UN. The charter was unanimously approved on 25 June and signed on the following day. By charter amendments effective 31 Aug. 1965, Security Council membership was increased to 15; Economic and Social Council membership was increased to 27, and voting procedures were changed accordingly.

5 JUNE. **EUROPEAN ADVISORY COMMISSION** established German occupation zones, assigning eastern Germany to Russia, dividing the south between the U.S. and France, and placing Great Britain in charge of the west.

Berlin, situated in the heart of the Soviet zone, was shared among the occupying powers, leaving all ground approaches dominated by the Russians. The administration of Berlin was entrusted to a military Kommandatura.

17 JULY–2 AUG. **POTSDAM CONFERENCE,** held near Berlin, was attended by President Harry S. Truman, Prime Minister Churchill (who after 28 July was replaced by the newly chosen British prime minister, Clement R. Attlee, head of the Labour government), and Premier Stalin. Also present, in addition to other top-ranking officials, were Secretary of State James F. Byrnes, Foreign Secretary Anthony Eden (who after 28 July was replaced by Ernest Bevin), and Foreign Secretary V. M. Molotov. The first declaration issued by the conference was the "unconditional surrender" ultimatum (26 July) presented to Japan. The chief questions before the conference were the plan for the occupation and control of Germany and the settlement of various European problems. A Council of Foreign Ministers, its members drawn from the Big Five, was established and entrusted with the preparation of draft treaties with Austria, Hungary, Bulgaria, Rumania, and Finland, and with the proposal of settlements of outstanding territorial questions. The council was also authorized to negotiate an agreement with a central German government whenever the latter should come into being. The occupation authorities were to conduct programs designed to denazify, decentralize, disarm, and democratize Germany, which was to be treated during the ocupation period as a single economic unit. Provision was made for the trial of war criminals (shortly after the conference an International Military Tribunal was set up). Final delimitation of the Polish-German frontier was left to the peace treaty. The Soviet Union abandoned its $20-billion reparations de-

FRENCH
BRITISH
RUSSIAN
U.S.
GREATER BERLIN

DENMARK

OCCUPIED by U.S.S.R.

OCCUPIED by POLAND

U.S. Hamburg
Bremen ZONES.
Berlin
INTERNATIONAL
ZONE

NETHERLANDS

POLAND

BRITISH ZONE

RUSSIAN ZONE

Bonn

BELGIUM

Frankfort

OCCUPIED by POLAND

LUX

U.S. ZONE

CZECHOSLOVAKIA

SAAR FRENCH

ZONE

FRANCE

Munich

SWITZERLAND   AUSTRIA

**FOUR-POWER OCCUPATION
of GERMANY**

0   50   100   150   200 MILES

mand in exchange for a reparations schedule based on a percentage of useful capital equipment in the Western zone and materials in the Eastern zone. The conference agreed that Germany should make good for losses suffered at its hands by the United Nations. Provision was made for the mandatory transfer of 6,500,000 Germans from Hungary, Czechoslovakia, and Poland to Germany. Economic agreements were reached concerning German industry, foreign trade, finance, communications, and transpor-

tation. At the earliest practicable date the German economy was to be decentralized for the purpose of eliminating excessive centralization of economic power as exemplified by cartels, syndicates, and trusts. Primary emphasis in the German economy was to be given to the development of agriculture and peaceful domestic industries.

14 Aug. The Sino-Soviet treaty signed at Moscow formalized China's consent to the concessions granted to the Soviet at the Yalta Conference.

THE UNITED STATES AND THE BALANCE OF WORLD POWER, 1945-74

★ ★
★

With the close of World War II, the preponderance of power had moved to the periphery; the U.S. and the U.S.S.R. emerged as the two "superpowers" of the postwar era. Each interpreted the actions of the other as aggressive. Each championed an ideology antithetical to the other. Once the dynamic of the Cold War—the continuous confrontation between the "Free World" and the "Communist Bloc"—was set in motion, it tended to feed upon itself. The postwar era differed from all the others in one crucial respect—the power of the atom had been tapped. Although man could now destroy himself, paradoxically, the "balance of terror" kept conflict at conventional levels.

After nearly thirty years, the U.S. and the U.S.S.R. remain the two superpowers, but the bipolarity and the venomous climate of the Cold War era are slowly fading. The force of nationalism has exposed a degree of fragmentation in the Communist world; a huge number of uncommitted nations have emerged; other powers—Japan, China, West Germany—increasingly must be reckoned with by the U.S. and the U.S.S.R., along with the oil-rich states of the Middle East. In response, the United States did not retreat into isolation as it had after World War I, but the Vietnam War underscored the limits of power and the need to be more prudently selective in commitments overseas.

The Cold War: Opening Phases, 1945–52

1945

11 SEPT.–2 OCT. LONDON CONFERENCE. The first meeting of the Council of Foreign Ministers failed to bring agreement on treaties with Italy, Bulgaria, Hungary, and Rumania. The conference broke up over the issue of Chinese and French participation and revealed a cleavage between Russia and the West.

16–26 DEC. MOSCOW CONFERENCE. The second meeting of the Council of Foreign Ministers considered international control of atomic energy, a new 4-power control commission for Japan, trusteeship for Korea, and the drafting of European peace treaties by a 5-power conference for submission to a peace conference of the 21 Allied nations.

1945–49

WAR CRIMES TRIALS. Nazis. Acting under a charter adopted in London (Aug. 1945) to bring to trial the German and Japanese war criminals for crimes against (1) peace, (2) humanity, and (3) the laws of war, an International Military Tribunal at Nuremburg, Germany, tried 24 principal Nazi offenders (20 Nov. 1945–1 Oct. 1946). U.S. prosecutor was Associate Justice **Robert H. Jackson** (1892–1954). Twelve Nazis were sentenced to be hanged: Reichsmarschall Hermann Göring (committed suicide by poisoning on the eve of his execution), Martin Bormann, *in absentia,* and the 10 who were hanged 16 Oct. 1946: Joachim Ribbentrop, Field Marshal Wilhelm Keitel, Col. Gen. Alfred Jodl, Ernst Kaltenbrunner, Alfred Rosenberg, Hans Frank, Wilhelm Frick, Arthur Seyss-Inquart, Julius Streicher, and Fritz Sauckel; 3 were acquitted: Franz von Papen, Hjalmar Schacht, Hans Fritsche; 3 escaped trial: Martin Bormann, whereabouts unknown, Gustav Krupp because of advanced age and ill health, and Robert Ley, who committed suicide after indictment. In addition, the U.S. conducted a series of 12 trials, each centered on an occupation group. In all, 836,000 former Nazis were tried in the U.S. zone, of whom 503,360 were convicted, 430,890 fined less than 1,000 Rm., 27,413 sentenced to perform some community work, 7,768 given short terms in labor camps, 18,503 pronounced ineligible to hold office, and 20,865 suffered partial property confiscation.

Japanese war leaders were tried by an International Military Tribunal for the Far East (est. 19 Jan. 1946). Trials (3 June 1946–12 Nov. 1948) resulted in death sentences being meted out to former Premier Hideki Tojo and Gens. Seishiro Itagaki, Kenji Doihara, Heitaro Kimura, Iwane Matsui, and Akira Muto; on appeal the U.S. Supreme Court denied jurisdiction 20 Dec. 1948; the 7 were hanged in Tokyo 23 Dec. Adm. Shigetaro Shimada and Army Chief of Staff Yoshijiro Umezu and 14 others were given life sentences, former Foreign Minister Shigenoi Togo sentenced to 20 years, and former Foreign Minister Mamoru Shigemitsu 7 years (paroled Nov. 1950). In addition, a large number of high-ranking Japanese army and navy officers were tried before special tribunals in Japan and throughout the areas of Japanese military operations for offenses against the laws of war. As of 19 Oct. 1949, 4,200 Japanese had been convicted, 720 executed.

1947. "The MacArthur Constitution," originally drafted by the Occupation authorities, was subsequently redrafted, debated, and approved by the Japanese, and went into effect 3 May 1947. It launched a program of democratic reform, including dissolution of trusts (*zaibatsu*), support for the formation of political parties, labor unions, agrarian reform, and the emancipation of women.

1945–52

INDOCHINA. While criticizing French colonial policy in Indochina and advocating some kind of international trusteeship arrangement for the region, President Franklin D. Roosevelt was reluctant to risk a confrontation with the French—and the British—over the French desire to reclaim the area after the war. Upon Roosevelt's death U.S. policy toward Indochina was in a state of disarray. In Mar. 1945 the Japanese allowed Emperor Bao Dai to proclaim Vietnam's independence but when the Japanese occupation collapsed (Aug. 1945) Bao Dai abdicated, going into exile in France. The Viet Minh (the nationalist resistance organization, including the Indochinese Communist Party, established May 1941), led by Ho Chi Minh, set up its capital in Hanoi and proclaimed (2 Sept. 1945) Vietnam an independent democratic republic. By the end of 1945 the French army, which had returned to launch a campaign to reconquer Vietnam, had gained control of the south. Ho Chi Minh received no reply to a series of letters written (Oct. 1945–Feb. 1946) to President Harry S. Truman or the Secretary of State James F. Byrnes, appealing for U.S. and UN intervention against French colonialism. Large-scale hostilities erupted in North Vietnam in Dec. 1946. Driven out of Hanoi, Ho Chi Minh went underground to lead a guerrilla war. On 8 Mar. 1949 France and Bao Dai concluded an agreement by which France acknowledged the "independence" within the "French Union" of a unified, non-Communist state of Vietnam. Ho Chi Minh's Democratic Republic of Vietnam, which controlled a large part of the country, was recognized by Peking and Moscow in Jan. 1950. Fearful that Bao Dai was weak and tainted with French colonialism, the U.S. delayed recognizing Bao Dai's Saigon regime until 7 Feb. 1950. In response to a French request, the U.S. announced (8 May) it would provide economic and military aid to the French in Indochina, beginning with a grant of $10 million. On 27 June President Truman announced the dispatch of a 35-man military mission to Vietnam, followed the next month by an economic aid mission. On 23 Dec. the U.S., France, Vietnam, Cambodia, and Laos (the last 2, like Vietnam, "associated states" within the French Union) signed an agreement which "recognized the common interest" of the states in defending "the principles of freedom" and provided for U.S. aid. U.S. aid to the French effort in Indochina jumped to some $500 million in 1951 and increased annually thereafter. In the north, after the fall of major French outposts, French forces defended the Red River Delta while within France opposition to the war grew and within Vietnam Bao Dai's political support evaporated, leading to his withdrawal from the scene in Oct. 1952.

1946

INAUGURATION OF UNITED NATIONS ORGANIZATION. On 10 Jan. the first session of the UN General Assembly began in London. Trygve H. Lie of Norway was elected (1 Feb.) Secretary General. The Security Council convened the same month. The first complaint considered by the Security Council was raised (19 Jan.) by Iran and was directed against the U.S.S.R., alleging Soviet refusal to withdraw its troops from Iranian soil and interference in Iranian internal affairs. The Security Council considered the complaint despite Soviet abstention, but the issue was eventually resolved without official UN action (p. 465). In apparent retaliation, the U.S.S.R. complained (21 Jan.) of interference by British troops in the internal affairs of Greece. The developing cleavage between the West and the U.S.S.R., which would significantly affect the functioning of the UN, dimming hopes that the international organization would secure peace in the postwar world, soon became even more apparent.

The U.S.S.R. used the veto power for the first time 16 Feb., rejecting a U.S. proposal that Britain and France negotiate the withdrawal of their troops from Syria and Lebanon. Both the U.S. and the U.S.S.R. used the UN as a forum to propagandize against each other.

28 Feb. Secretary Byrnes declared that the U.S. would not and could not "stand aloof if force or the threat of force is used contrary to the purposes and principles" of the UN Charter.

15 Mar. "IRON CURTAIN" SPEECH. President Truman was in the audience when Sir Winston Churchill, in a speech at Fulton, Mo., observed that "from Stettin in the Baltic to Trieste in the Adriatic, an Iron Curtain has descended across the Continent." Noting the end of an era of hopeful wartime collaboration between the Western Allies and the U.S.S.R., Churchill called for closer Anglo-American cooperation to meet the new situation.

25 Apr.–16 May, 15 June–12 July, 29 July–15 Oct. PARIS PEACE CONFERENCE, attended by foreign minister of Great Britain, France, the Soviet Union, and the U.S., considered peace treaties for the Axis satellites, agreed (1 July) on terms of the treaties, and called a 21-nation conference to study the drafts. The 21-nation conference revealed increasing disagreement between Russia and the West, and the conference broke down when the Soviet Union objected to participation by the smaller powers.

4 Nov.–12 Dec. The Council of Foreign Ministers, at New York, completed **peace treaties** with minor Axis nations. Secretary Byrnes, supported in his firmer stand against the U.S.S.R. by President Truman's dismissal (20 Sept.) of Secretary of Commerce Wallace, who had opposed a "get tough with Russia" policy, succeeded in reaching agreement with Soviet Foreign Minister Molotov.

The treaties were signed for the U.S. in Washington by Secretary Byrnes (20 Jan. 1947), for the other powers in Paris (10 Feb.), and were ratified by the U.S. Senate on 4 June. **Italy.** The Republic of Italy (formed 14 July 1946) agreed to make reparations in kind to Yugoslavia ($125 million), the U.S.S.R. ($100 million), Greece ($105 million), Ethiopia ($25 million), and Albania ($5 million); to restrict its armed forces; to cede the Dodecanese Islands to Greece; to cede Fiume, the Istrian peninsula, and much of Venezia Giulia to Yugoslavia; and to set up Trieste provisionally as a free territory under UN guarantee. Italy renounced all claims to its former colonies. A UN Assembly resolution provided for a united and independent Libya (Cyrenaica, Tripolitania, and Fezzan), and Italian Somaliland was placed under Italian trusteeship for 10 years. **Hungary** agreed to pay reparations in kind to the Soviet Union of $200 million and $50 million each to Czechoslovakia and Yugoslavia. Northern Transylvania was returned to Rumania and the Carpatho-Ukraine became part of the Soviet Ukraine. **Rumania** agreed to make reparations to the U.S.S.R. ($300 million) and confirmed the cession of Bessarabia and northern Bucovina to the Soviet Ukraine and of southern Dobruja to Bulgaria. **Bulgaria** was required to pay in reparations $25 million to Czechoslovakia and $45 million to Greece. **Finland** agreed to pay reparations to Russia of $300 million and to cede to the Soviet Union the Arctic port of Petsamo, her part of the Rybachi peninsula west of Murmansk, and the Karelian peninsula, including the port of Viipuri. The U.S.S.R. gave up its lease on Hangö but took a 50-year lease on a naval base at Parkkala on the Gulf of Finland.

27 Dec. President Truman reported to Congress that settlements had been made with 7 nations (representing 70%

of U.S. Lend-Lease aid) including Great Britain (27 Mar.), but as yet not with the Soviet Union (received $11.1 billion; supplied about $2.2 million as reciprocal Lend-Lease). Coincident with settlement of the British agreement the U.S. granted Britain an additional loan of $3.75 billion payable at 2% in 50 annual installments beginning 31 Dec. 1951.

GERMANY. The U.S. announced 27 May it would suspend dismantling in its German zone, thus ending this mode of reparations payment in its occupation area. On 2 Dec. the U.S. and Great Britain agreed to merge their occupation zones.

IRAN. To prevent Nazi penetration of Iran and to protect a supply route from the Persian Gulf to the U.S.S.R., an Anglo-Soviet agreement (1941) provided for the stationing of British troops in the south and Soviet troops in the north. Under the agreement all troops were to be withdrawn within 6 months of the end of hostilities. The U.S.S.R. promoted the separatist revolts in the northern provinces of Azerbaijan and Kurdistan which began late in 1945. While British and U.S. troops—which had arrived after U.S. entry in the war to help move supplies to the U.S.S.R.—began to withdraw, Soviet troops remained (Dec. 1945), blocking the attempts of Iranian troops to put down the rebellion in Azerbaijan. After the U.S.S.R. announced (25 Feb. 1946) that its troops would stay beyond the 2 Mar. deadline set for evacuation, the U.S. sent (6 Mar.) a protest note to the U.S.S.R. calling for "immediate" withdrawal and repeated the demand in the UN Security Council. A Soviet-Iranian agreement was announced on 5 Apr., and on 4 May Iran reported that the withdrawal was complete. Since the first major crisis of the postwar period took place in the Near East, that region began to assume a larger place in U.S. foreign policy. By

Nov. 1946 the U.S. was preparing to supply Iran with arms.

TURKEY. During 1945 the U.S.S.R. had begun to apply pressure on Turkey, demanding: (1) cession of several Turkish districts on the Turkish-Soviet frontier; (2) revision of the 1936 Montreux Convention, which provided for exclusive Turkish supervision of the Dardanelles, to provide instead for joint Soviet-Turkish administration; and (3) the leasing to the U.S.S.R. of naval and land bases in the strait to provide for the "joint defense" of Turkey and the U.S.S.R. U.S. responses designed to demonstrate support for Turkey included: (1) President Truman's warning, in an Army Day speech (6 Apr. 1946), that the U.S. would aid the UN with military power to protect nations in the Near East from "coercion or penetration"; (2) protest notes (21 Aug. and 11 Oct. 1946) rejecting Soviet demands; and (3) naval movements in the Mediterranean. Soviet pressure appeared to ease late in 1946.

GREECE. In Aug. 1946 a Communist-led rebellion against the right-wing government, elected 31 Mar., broke out in Greece, a continuation of the civil war which erupted after termination of the German occupation and was halted when the British effected a truce (p. 448). With their major activities in the north, the guerrillas gained support and sanctuaries from the neighboring Communist states of Albania, Bulgaria, and Yugoslavia. In Sept. the British, who had informed the U.S. in April of their desire to disengage their troops from Greece in the fall, confirmed their intention to begin at least partial withdrawals. Largely blaming the Athens regime for the political and economic chaos, the report (10 Oct.) of the Parliamentary Delegation that had surveyed conditions in Greece attached severe restrictions to future British economic aid.

In an initial move to support the Greek government, the U.S. granted Greece (11 Oct. 1946) $25 million in credits to purchase surplus U.S. military equipment in Europe.

INTERNATIONAL CONTROL OF ATOMIC ENERGY. On 24 Jan. 1946 the UN General Assembly created the UN Atomic Energy Commission (UNAEC), to study the international control of atomic energy. The State Department issued (28 Feb.) the **Acheson-Lilienthal Report** which, with some modifications, became the official U.S. proposal to the UNAEC. Presented (14 June) to the UNAEC by **Bernard M. Baruch** (1870–1965) and hence dubbed the "**Baruch Plan,**" the proposal provided for an International Atomic Development Authority which would carry out its responsibilities (1) for ensuring the full exploitation of the peaceful potentialities of atomic energy; (2) for providing states with security against surprise attack by violators of the ban on atomic weapons by fully exercising—uninhibited by the veto power of any state —its capacities for ownership, management, research, licensing, and inspection. The plan was to be put into effect in stages, the crucial point being that the agency's control mechanisms should become fully operative and demonstrate their effectiveness *before* the U.S. would carry out its obligation to dispose of its atomic weapons, accept the prohibition on the manufacture or use of such weapons, and turn over to the agency all of its scientific and technological knowledge concerning atomic energy. The U.S.S.R. responded first (19 June) with a plan involving no international machinery for control or enforcement and later (11 June 1947) with a scheme which, like the first, embodied a reversal of U.S. priorities. The U.S.S.R. proposed that the U.S. abandon its monopolistic position in atomic energy by destroying its weapons and accepting the prohibition of the manufacture or use of such weapons before establishing a system of international supervision, such international agency to function in subordination to the UN Security Council (hence the veto would be operative) and would lack the authority to own, operate, or license atomic facilities, possessing only limited inspection powers. The Baruch Plan was essentially accepted by the UNAEC in its first report (30 Dec. 1946), which was approved (4 Nov. 1948) by the General Assembly, but Soviet opposition prevented any progress toward its realization, and the UNAEC suspended its meetings 29 July 1949.

1 Aug. ATOMIC ENERGY ACT OF 1946. Sponsored by Sen. Brian McMahon (Conn., 1903–52), the act transferred full control over all materials, facilities, production, research, and information relating to nuclear fission from the War Department to an **Atomic Energy Commission** to be composed of 5 civilians nominated by the president and confirmed by the Senate.

1946–52

KEY ATOMIC EXPLOSIONS: fourth U.S. atomic explosion in tests with warships at Bikini Atoll, 1 July 1946; fifth, 25 July. New and improved bomb exploded in 3 tests at Eniwetok Atoll, Apr.–May 1948. On 24 Sept. 1949 it was disclosed that the U.S.S.R. had exploded its first atomic weapon. On 31 Jan. 1950 President Truman announced that the U.S. would undertake development of the **hydrogen bomb.** On 6 Apr. 1952 it was announced that the U.S. was manufacturing the H-bomb. On 3 Oct. Great Britain exploded its first atomic weapon in the Monte Bello Islands, off Australia.

On 1 Nov. 1952 the U.S. exploded its first hydrogen bomb, the most powerful bomb yet made.

1947

GERMANY. 10 MAR.–24 APR. MOSCOW CONFERENCE. Secretary Marshall and British Foreign Minister Ernest Bevin advocated a federal form of government for Germany, as opposed to Russia's demand for a centralized state, and rejected the Soviet claim for $10 billion reparations.

29 MAY. Secretary Marshall instructed Gen. **Lucius D. Clay** (1897–   ); military governor, U.S. Zone, to strengthen the bizonal organization in Germany and expedite upward revision of the level of bizonal industry. A directive of the Joint Chiefs of Staff to Gen. Clay (11 July) urged him to work toward "an increasing standard of living in Germany" and "a self sustaining German economy." Under orders of U.S. and British commanders (29 Aug.) the maximum production was fixed at the 1936 level of German industry, thus increasing Germany's potential by one third over the 4-power level of Mar. 1946. A new level was introduced by the Allied powers on 3 Apr. 1951, and restrictions further relaxed.

25 NOV.–16 DEC. LONDON CONFERENCE. The fifth session of the Council of Foreign Ministers was marked by Soviet charges that the Allies had violated the Potsdam Agreement. The meeting adjourned without fixing a time or place for another meeting.

12 MAR. TRUMAN DOCTRINE. The British government informed the U.S. (21 Feb.) that because of Britain's economic crisis it could give no further financial aid to Greece or Turkey after 31 Mar. The U.S. moved into the breach, a pattern that had already begun to establish itself. Addressing a joint session of Congress to request authorization of a program of economic and military aid to Greece and Turkey, President Truman declared that U.S. policy must "support free peoples who are resisting attempted subjugation by armed minorities or outside pressures" and that U.S. assistance should be "primarily through economic and financial aid." Such a U.S. policy was deemed necessary because "the free peoples of the world look to us for support in maintaining their freedoms. If we falter in our leadership, we may endanger the peace of the world." Opponents argued that the Truman Doctrine would undercut the UN and could provoke a clash with the U.S.S.R. The Senate formally endorsed the Truman Doctrine 23 Apr. in a vote (67–23) on a bill to strengthen Greece and Turkey; the House followed 9 May (287–107). On 22 May President Truman approved an initial appropriation of $400 million in aid to Greece and Turkey—$250 million for Greece and $150 million for Turkey. U.S. military missions left for Greece and Turkey, 20 and 23 May, respectively.

Soviet Reaction. On 18 Sept. Andrei Y. Vishinsky, Soviet deputy foreign minister, attacked U.S. "warmongers" in the UN Assembly. On 5 Oct. Moscow announced formation of the Cominform, successor to the Comintern dissolved in 1943, and proclaimed its determination to block the Marshall Plan (p. 468). A *coup d'état* (25 Feb. 1948) gave the Communists control of the government of Czechoslovakia. The new regime was headed by Klement Gottwald. On 10 Mar. Czech Foreign Minister Jan Masaryk committed suicide in Prague.

In a report (28 Nov. 1949) to Congress, President Truman hailed the results of U.S. aid, indicating that the Truman Doctrine had led to "containment" of the Communists in Greece and "close cooperation between Turkey and the Western world."

18 July. President Truman signed an agreement naming the U.S. administering authority, within the UN Trusteeship System, of the Trust Territory of the Pacific Islands (p. 629).

July. CONTAINMENT policy concept articulated in "The Sources of Soviet Conduct," an article by "X" (**George F. Kennan,** 1904–) in the quarterly *Foreign Affairs.* Representing the newly formulated position of the U.S. government, the article stated: "It is clear that the main element of any United States policy towards the Soviet Union must be that of a long-term, patient but firm and vigilant containment of Russian expansive tendencies. . . . Soviet pressure against the free institutions of the Western world is something that can be contained by the adroit and vigilant application of counter-force at a series of constantly shifting geographical and political points."

2 Sept. THE INTER-AMERICAN TREATY OF RECIPROCAL ASSISTANCE, signed in Rio de Janeiro by representatives of the U.S. and the states of Latin America, was the realization of a recommendation included in the Act of Chapultepec (p. 449). The first postwar defense system entered into by the U.S., it provides that "an armed attack by any State shall be considered as an attack against all American states." The treaty set up no machinery to implement its obligations but is complementary to the Charter of Bogotá (30 Apr. 1948), creating an organization of 21 American republics (p. 470).

1948

EUROPEAN RECOVERY PROGRAM. From V-E Day to the spring of 1947 the U.S. provided Europe with over $11 billion in the form of UNRRA aid, loans, etc. Opposition to UNRRA arose from the fact that the bulk of its relief supplies were distributed in Eastern Europe (ex-enemy countries were outside its functions; liberated countries in Western Europe had refused UNRRA assistance). A post-UNRRA Relief Bill (31 May 1947) appropriated $350 million relief for Austria, Greece, Italy, Hungary, and Poland.

On 8 May 1947, Under Secretary of State Dean Acheson speaking at Cleveland, Miss., revealed a "prologue to the Marshall Plan," outlining the rationale for U.S. participation in a European recovery program. The **Marshall Plan** was launched when, in an address at Harvard on 5 June, Secretary of State George E. Marshall proposed that the Europeans take the initiative in jointly drawing up a comprehensive recovery program for which U.S. support would then be provided. Marshall declared that U.S. policy was directed "not against any country or doctrine but against hunger, poverty, desperation, and chaos. Its purpose would be the revival of a working economy in the world so as to permit the emergence of political and social conditions in which free institutions can exist." Key participants in the formulation of the basic proposal included, in addition to Marshall and Acheson, Will L. Clayton, Under Secretary of State for Economic Affairs; Charles E. Bohlen, Special Assistant to the Secretary of State; George F. Kennan, director of the Department of State Policy Planning Staff.

The foreign ministers of Great Britain, France, and the Soviet Union met at Paris (27 June–2 July 1947) to consider Marshall's proposal of U.S. economic aid. On 2 July Soviet Foreign Minister Molotov walked out of the preliminary meeting, charging that the Marshall Plan was an "imperialist" plot for the enslavement of Europe. Great Britain and France invited 22 nations to join a Committee for European Economic Cooperation to draft plans for reconstruction.

The U.S.S.R. and its satellites did not attend the Marshall Plan Conference, which convened 12 July in Paris. Representatives of the 16 European nations which participated set up a Committee for European Economic Cooperation, which drew up a master plan for European reconstruction based on massive U.S. financial assistance. Its report (22 Sept.) estimated dollar aid needed for the next 4 years between $16.4 and $22.4 billion.

On basis of reports of the Krug Committee (9 Oct.), the House Select Committee on Foreign Aid (Herter Committee, 10 Oct.), the Nourse Committee (28 Oct.), and the Harriman Committee (7 Nov.), a special session of Congress convened 17 Dec. to deal with aid to Europe as well as inflation, and enacted the Foreign Aid Act of 1947 providing interim relief for France, Italy, and Austria ($540 million), part to go to China. On 19 Dec. President Truman submitted to Congress a European Recovery Program which called for $17 billion in U.S. grants and loans over a 4-year period. Congress authorized the program 2 Apr. 1948 and **Paul G. Hoffman** (1891–1974) was confirmed (7 Apr.) as administrator of the Economic Cooperation Administration (ECA) which, independent of the State Department, ran the program. Inaugurated in mid-1948 with a virtually unmatched degree of bipartisan public support, the European Recovery Program, unlike earlier and subsequent aid programs, achieved its objectives at less cost and in less time than anticipated.

FOREIGN ECONOMIC AND MILITARY AID PROGRAMS: 1946–1973
[In millions of dollars. For years ending June 30]
(Source: *Statistical Abstract, 1974*)

Year	Total Economic and Military Aid[1]	ECONOMIC AID			MILITARY AID		
		Total	Loans	Grants	Total	Loans	Grants
1946–1973, total	163,694	101,520	34,313	67,207	62,175	3,698	58,477
1946–1952	34,670	31,186	8,519	22,668	3,483	—	3,483
1953–1961	47,411	24,054	5,850	18,203	23,358	165	23,193
1962	7,157	4,469	2,128	2,341	2,688	151	2,537
1963	7,234	4,372	2,124	2,248	2,862	123	2,739
1964	5,253	4,076	2,036	2,040	1,177	75	1,102
1965	5,373	4,121	2,059	2,063	1,251	110	1,141
1966	7,074	4,784	2,238	2,546	2,290	317	1,973
1967	6,883	3,942	1,662	2,281	2,941	323	2,618
1968	6,920	4,103	1,835	2,267	2,817	263	2,554
1969	6,772	3,524	1,340	2,185	3,248	281	2,968
1970	6,647	3,676	1,389	2,288	2,971	70	2,901
1971	7,705	3,442	1,299	2,143	4,263	743	3,520
1972	8,538	3,941	1,639	2,301	4,597	550	4,047
1973	8,363	4,118	1,391	2,726	4,245	550	3,695

— Represents zero.
[1] The figures for Economic Aid shown in this table represents total U.S. Economic Aid—not just the Aid under the Foreign Assistance Act.

17 Mar. BRUSSELS TREATY of collective self-defense signed by Britain, France, Belgium, Luxembourg, and the Netherlands. The treaty provided that if one of the signatories were attacked in Europe the other parties would come to its aid with "all military and other aid and assistance in their power." The signatories of the Brussels Pact hoped that their alliance would attract U.S. backing. President Truman, addressing a joint session of Congress on the same date, hailed the 50-year defense pact and termed it "deserving of our full support."

2 MAY. ORGANIZATION OF AMERICAN STATES (OAS) established with the signing of the **Charter of Bogotá.** A regional association for the purpose of general cooperation and the promotion of peace, the OAS includes the U.S. and all the states of Latin America. The Charter of Bogotá, which complements the Rio Treaty of Reciprocal Assistance (p. 468), gave a permanent institutional framework to the loosely knit agencies, committees, and procedures of the Pan-American Union, which the OAS superseded, providing for: (1) an Inter-American Conference, to meet every 5 years; (2) consultative conferences of foreign ministers; (3) a Council, an executive body composed of 1 delegate from each state; (4) a Secretariat; and (5) various commissions. OAS headquarters were established in Washington, D.C.

CREATION OF ISRAEL. A special session of the UN General Assembly convened (28 Apr. 1947) to determine the future of the Palestine mandate. Largely because of U.S. influence, the General Assembly adopted (29 Nov.) a plan for Palestine's partition into Arab and Jewish states. When Israel proclaimed its independence, on 14 May 1948, the U.S. was the first country to recognize the new state, doing so within minutes. The Arabs rejected the partition and went to war against Israel. After UN mediator Count Folke Bernadotte of Sweden was assassinated in Jerusalem (17 Sept.), **Ralph J. Bunche** (1904–71) of the U.S. succeeded him as mediator and effected armistice agreements between Israel and its Arab neighbors. Israel was admitted to the UN, 11 May 1949. Attempting to bring stability to

the Middle East, the U.S. joined Britain and France in issuing a **Tripartite Declaration** (25 May 1950) in which they pledged that if either Israel or the Arabs broke the terms of the UN armistice they would act at once "both within and outside the United Nations to prevent such a violation." The declaration also opposed the development of an arms race between the Arab states and Israel.

11 JUNE. VANDENBERG RESOLUTION adopted (64–4) by the Senate. Sen. Arthur H. Vandenberg (Mich., 1884–1951), with the encouragement of the Truman administration, framed a declaration of U.S. foreign policy, introduced as S Res 239, supporting the principle of U.S. association with "regional and other collective arrangements" affecting national security, as permitted under Article 51 of the UN Charter. While having no legal force, the Vandenberg Resolution led to the opening of negotiations with the nations of Europe to construct a defense alliance on an Atlantic basis.

24 JUNE. BEGINNING OF BERLIN BLOCKADE AND AIRLIFT. Ministerial level 4-Power discussions on Germany having broken down (p. 467), the Western Powers continued to discuss the future of Germany without the U.S.S.R. The Soviets withdrew their representative from the Allied Control Council in Berlin 20 Mar. 1948. On 30 Mar. the Soviets refused to allow American, British, and French troop trains to go to Berlin without their inspection, beginning a graduated process of closing off various means of ground transportation to that city. On 7 June the Western Powers announced their intention to create a federal state in their zones, which would be consolidated. Currency reform, a major step in the economic rehabilitation of a unified West Germany, was inaugurated 18 June and extended to West Berlin when the Soviets introduced (23 June) a new mark in their own zone, including all of Berlin. On 24 June the Soviets clamped a total blockade on all land traffic between Berlin and West Germany (these land routes not having been guaranteed by the Potsdam Agreement or the Allied Control Council), charging that the Western Powers had violated the Potsdam Agreement. The Western Powers began the Berlin Airlift to supply 2,100,-000 residents of the blockaded area. The U.S.S.R. announced (1 July) that it would no longer participate in the meetings of the Berlin Kommandatura. Diplomatic discussions between the West and the Soviets (31 July–2 Sept.) proved fruitless and the Western Powers took the blockade issue to the UN Security Council (4 Oct.), where the U.S.S.R. vetoed a compromise proposal (25 Oct.) and boycotted discussions. In Feb. 1949 the U.S. and British forces set up a blockade to halt all traffic across the eastern boundaries of their respective zones. Secret and informal talks between the U.S. ambassador to the U.N., Philip Jessup, and the U.S.S.R. ambassador to the UN, Jacob Malik, begun in Feb. 1949, preceded the U.S.S.R.'s agreement to lift the blockade, the only condition being that the Council of Foreign Ministers convene to discuss questions relating to Berlin and Germany. A 4-Power communiqué (5 May) announced that the blockade would be lifted, effective 12 May, and the Council of Foreign Ministers would convene in Paris 23 May. During the Berlin Airlift, which lasted 321 days, American and British airmen made 272,264 flights and transported 2.3 million tons of food and other supplies. The Soviet blockade of Berlin not only failed to alter the direction of U.S. policy in Germany (and Europe) but accelerated its thrust.

1949

20 Jan. Point IV. In the fourth section of his inaugural address—hence the name Point IV—President Truman called for a "bold new program" of U.S. technical and capital assistance to the underdeveloped areas of the world. The president asked Congress (24 June) for authority to guarantee U.S. private investment in less developed areas and $45 million to start the program. On 27 Sept. 1950 $26.9 million were appropriated ($35 million had been authorized) to inaugurate the program.

4 Apr. FOUNDING OF NATO. Following passage of the Vandenberg Resolution (p. 470), President Truman directed the State Department to discuss the question of regional security with Canada and the signatories of the Brussels Treaty (p. 469). Tentative agreement on a collective defense arrangement had been reached by Oct. 1948 when Denmark, Iceland, Italy, Norway, and Portugal were invited to join the negotiations. The 12 nations signed the North Atlantic Treaty in Washington, 4 Apr. 1949. Ratified by the Senate 21 July, the treaty became effective 24 Aug. By Article 5 of the treaty, each party agreed that an attack on any one of them would be considered an attack against them all, to be followed by the taking "individually and in concert with the other Parties, such action as it deems necessary, including the use of armed force, to restore and maintain the security of the North Atlantic area." The pact also provided for the establishment of a North Atlantic Treaty Organization (NATO), headed by a North Atlantic Council, to draw up plans for concerted action; called for intensified military self-help and mutual aid measures; and provided for the admission of new members by unanimous invitation. The U.S. was

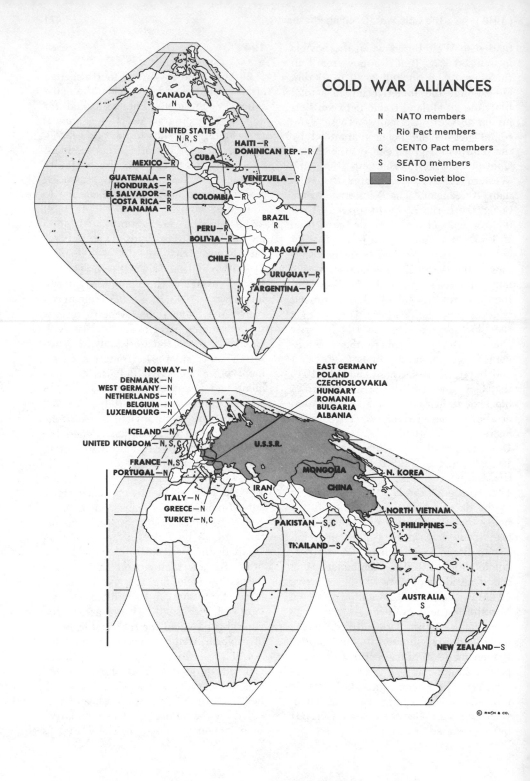

COLD WAR ALLIANCES

N NATO members
R Rio Pact members
C CENTO Pact members
S SEATO members
▨ Sino-Soviet bloc

CANADA
N

UNITED STATES
N, R, S

HAITI—R
DOMINICAN REP.—R

MEXICO—R

CUBA

VENEZUELA—R

GUATEMALA—R
HONDURAS—R
EL SALVADOR—R
COSTA RICA—R
PANAMA—R

COLOMBIA—R

PERU—R
BOLIVIA—R

BRAZIL
R

PARAGUAY—R

CHILE—R

URUGUAY—R

ARGENTINA—R

NORWAY—N
DENMARK—N
WEST GERMANY—N
NETHERLANDS—N
BELGIUM—N
LUXEMBOURG—N

ICELAND—N
UNITED KINGDOM—N, S, C

FRANCE—N, S
PORTUGAL—N

ITALY—N
GREECE—N
TURKEY—N, C

EAST GERMANY
POLAND
CZECHOSLOVAKIA
HUNGARY
ROMANIA
BULGARIA
ALBANIA

U.S.S.R.

MONGOLIA

CHINA

N. KOREA

IRAN
C

PAKISTAN—S, C

THAILAND—S

NORTH VIETNAM

PHILIPPINES—S

AUSTRALIA
S

NEW ZEALAND—S

© RM⁞N & CO.

for the first time committed to a European alliance in peacetime. Greece and Turkey joined NATO in Feb. 1952.

23 MAY–20 JUNE. PARIS CONFERENCE. The sixth session of the Council of Foreign Ministers failed to reach agreement on the German question. Russian proposals for German unification and withdrawal of Allied troops were unacceptable to the West. In turn, Russia rejected Western proposals for the extension of the Bonn Constitution to East Germany.

8 DEC. FLIGHT OF CHINESE NATIONALISTS TO FORMOSA. After the defeat of Japan, the U.S. took steps to reinforce the Nationalists under Chiang Kai-shek. Although by late 1945 the Nationalists controlled strategic cities in eastern and southern China, the Communists held large sections of the north, with full-scale civil war imminent. In Dec. 1945 Gen. **George C. Marshall** was sent to China as a special U.S. ambassador to promote a truce and the formation of a coalition government. Discussions between the 2 factions were undertaken and an uneasy cease-fire established (10 Jan. 1946). Mao Tse-tung, head of the Chinese Communists, demanded (24 June 1946) that the U.S. halt military aid to the Nationalists and that all U.S. forces leave. Abandoning his frustrating mission, officially terminated 7 Jan. 1947, Marshall returned to the U.S., denouncing both sides. Full-scale civil war ensued. Lt. Gen. **Albert C. Wedemeyer,** named (11 July 1947) to appraise the situation in China and Korea, condemned (24 Aug.) the use of force by the Chinese Communists and stressed the need for thoroughgoing political and economic reforms on the part of the Nationalists. Wedemeyer's recommendation that the U.S. provide the Nationalists with a comprehensive program of moral and material support was not accepted. While the Truman administration re-

fused fully to commit the U.S. to the Nationalists, the president signed (3 Apr. 1948) a foreign aid bill which earmarked $463 million, $125 million of which could be allocated for military purposes, to the Nationalist regime. Chiang requested (18 Nov. 1948) an immediate increase in material aid but Secretary of State George C. Marshall declared (24 Nov. 1948) that a large U.S. aid program might directly involve the U.S. in the civil war. With the war going decisively in favor of the Communists, who had taken control of Peking (Jan. 1949) and made it their capital, Congress authorized (14 Apr. 1949) the president to use unobligated funds until 15 Feb. 1950 to aid areas of China not controlled by the Communists.

A State Department white paper on China (*United States Relations with China; With Special Reference to the Period 1944–1949*), released 6 Aug. 1949, made the point that the Nationalists were on the verge of collapse because of the political, economic, and military deficiencies of the Chiang regime and that no greater amount of U.S. aid would have prevented the ultimate victory of the Communists. Secretary of State Dean Acheson observed in an accompanying letter that "the only alternative open to the United States was full-scale intervention on behalf of a government which had lost the confidence of its own troops and its own people." Powerful critics branded the white paper a "whitewash" of a policy by which the U.S. had "sold China down the river" and "lost" it to the Communists, allowing it to "pass into the Soviet orbit."

The Communist Chinese arrest (27 Oct. 1949) of U.S. Consul General Angus Ward in Mukden raised a storm of official and unofficial U.S. protest, making even less likely U.S. recognition of the Communist regime in the near future. Ward was released and deported with his staff in Dec. 1949.

The Communists challenged the right of the Nationalists to represent China in the UN and demanded (18 Nov. 1949) their ouster. The Soviet delegate boycotted (13 Jan.–1 Aug., 1950) the Security Council in protest of the continued presence of the Nationalists. U.S. policy toward China was ambivalent. While Britain, France, the U.S.S.R., and several other nations recognized the Chinese Communist government, the People's Republic of China, the U.S. continued to recognize the Nationalist regime on Formosa as China's legal government and to oppose any immediate change in China's UN representation. Yet in Jan. 1950 the U.S. refused to commit forces to Formosa's defense.

1950

11–14 May. LONDON CONFERENCE of foreign ministers of Great Britain, France, and the U.S. considered mutual defense problems and declared that Germany should "reenter progressively the community of free peoples of Europe."

1950–52

NATO DEFENSE PLANNING. The general strategic plan developed by NATO military planners, who began to meet Oct. 1949, was based on the following propositions: (1) the U.S. would assume responsibility, in case of hostilities, to use the atomic bomb in an air offensive against the aggressor; (2) ground forces on the Continent would blunt the enemy offensive; (3) U.S., British, and French fleets would secure control of the seas; and (4) Western European aircraft would be assigned to air defense and short-range tactical bombardment. While it was believed that

U.S. superiority in nuclear weapons— NATO's "sword"—would deter Soviet aggression for several years, NATO discussions began to focus on Europe's military capacity—NATO's "shield." This raised 2 crucial and interrelated problems: how to increase NATO's military strength in Europe and how to effect Germany's rearmament.

9 Sept. 1950. President Truman announced approval of "substantial increases" of U.S. forces in Europe (then consisting of 2 divisions in Germany) contingent upon European contributions to "our common defense."

15–20 Sept. 1950. The North Atlantic Council, meeting at New York, agreed to adopt a **"Forward Strategy."** In order to ensure the defense of all European members, any aggression was to be resisted as far to the east as possible. Such a strategy implied the defense of Europe on German soil and demanded forces far exceeding those available to NATO at the time (about 14 divisions on the European continent, compared to some 210 Soviet divisions). The council requested the NATO Defense Committee to plan for an integrated force, under a centralized command, adequate to deter aggression. The U.S. urged that Germany be rearmed while France insisted that German military participation in NATO be deferred until after the NATO allies had rearmed and an integrated defense force had been established.

26 Oct. 1950. In an effort to prevent creation of an autonomous German army, the French proposed the Pleven Plan, creation of a special, integrated European force of some 100,000 men in which German contingents at the battalion level would participate.

6 Dec. 1950. Under great pressure from the U.S., the French accepted a compromise on German rearmament. Under restricted conditions German forces would participate in Europe's defense under NATO and European planning for a European Army based on the Pleven Plan could go forward.

18 Dec. 1950. BRUSSELS CONFERENCE of foreign ministers of North Atlantic Pact nations approved plan for arming Western Europe. On 19 Dec. the conference agreed on Gen. **Dwight D. Eisenhower** as supreme commander of the North Atlantic Pact forces. He took formal command of SHAPE (Supreme Headquarters, Allied Powers in Europe) at Paris on 2 Apr. 1951, but resigned in the spring of 1952 to campaign for the Republican nomination for the presidency, and was replaced by Gen. **Matthew B. Ridgway** (1895–   ).

The "**Great Debate.**" Prior to the dispatch of 4 additional U.S. divisions to Europe, signaled in President Truman's statement of 9 Sept., Republicans, led by former President **Herbert Hoover** and Sen. **Robert A. Taft** (Ohio, p. 1165), attacked the administration's military policies, opening the "Great Debate" of 1951. In a nationwide broadcast (20 Dec.) Hoover denounced the "rash involvement" of U.S. forces in "hopeless campaigns," arguing that the U.S. should cut off aid to Europe until those nations demonstrated a will to defend themselves. Meanwhile the U.S. should build up its own air and naval power, reinforce its Pacific bases and rearm Japan, thereby creating a "Gibraltar of Western Civilization." Taft, in a Senate speech (5 Jan. 1951), embraced Hoover's thesis, also charging the administration with having formulated policy since 1945 "without consulting Congress or the people." A fiery partisan debate ensued with the introduction (8 Jan.) by Senate Minority Leader **Kenneth S. Wherry** (Neb., 1892–1951) of a sense of the Senate resolution that no U.S. ground forces be sent to Europe "pending the adoption of a policy with respect thereto by the Congress." Gen. Eisenhower, ad-

dressing an informal joint session of Congress (1 Feb.), declared that because there was "no acceptable alternative" the U.S. had to assist Europe with troops as well as armaments. During public hearings of the Senate Foreign Relations Committee and Armed Services Committee in Feb., Secretary of Defense George C. Marshall disclosed that it was planned during 1951 to add 4 U.S. divisions to the 2 already in Europe and both he and the Joint Chiefs of Staff testified against any congressional limitation on U.S. troops for NATO. Govs. Thomas E. Dewey and Harold E. Stassen supported the administration's plans as being an "Eisenhower program." The Senate passed (4 Apr.) resolutions approving a "fair share" contribution of U.S. troops to NATO, asking the president to consult with Congress before sending troops abroad and declaring that no more than 4 divisions should be sent to Europe without Senate approval. Truman hailed the Senate's action as a "clear endorsement" of his troop plans but ignored the Senate's claim to a voice in future troop commitments—an issue which did not really arise again until the Vietnam War. The "Great Debate" served to confirm both the U.S. decision to defend Western Europe on the ground and the president's power to commit U.S. forces abroad without prior congressional approval.

20 Feb. 1952. The NATO Council in Lisbon agreed upon West Germany's financial and military contribution to mutual defense and set up permanent council headquarters in Paris.

27 May 1952. An agreement to create a **European Defense Community (EDC)** with a joint European army was signed in Bonn by France, Germany, Italy, and the Benelux countries. The EDC command would report directly to NATO. While Germany would remain outside NATO membership, her defense was guaranteed by NATO members in a protocol, signed the same day, which extended NATO defense commitments to Germany. In a separate "peace contract," consisting of 4 conventions signed by the U.S., Britain, France, and West Germany, the latter gained virtually complete sovereignty, the Allied occupation was ended, Allied military rights in Germany were reserved, and provision was made for German contributions to the cost of maintaining Allied forces in Germany. In addition, the U.S. and Britain gave France a separate pledge that their troops would remain in Europe indefinitely. The Senate ratified the peace contract and NATO protocol 1 July, 1952. The "peace contract" remained suspended pending French approval of EDC (p. 484).

1951

8 SEPT. JAPANESE PEACE TREATY, signed at San Francisco by 49 nations (not including the U.S.S.R.), provided for withdrawal of occupation forces not later than 90 days after a majority of the signatories ratified and recognized Japan's "full sovereignty." Japan in turn acknowledged the independence of Korea and renounced all claims to Formosa, the Pescadores, the Kuriles, Sakhalin, and the Pacific islands formerly under her mandate, and agreed to UN trusteeship over the Ryukyu and Bonin Islands. By the **U.S.-Japanese Treaty** signed the same day at San Francisco Japan granted the U.S. the right to maintain armed forces in Japan. Previously, on 1 Sept., a **Tripartite Security Treaty** (U.S., Australia, and New Zealand) provided for mutual assistance. A similar pact was signed between the U.S. and the Philippines (30 Aug.), implementing the Philippines Trade Act (continuing free trade between the U.S. and the Philippines until 1954, with gradual imposition of tariff duties over a 20-year period thereafter), the Philippines Rehabilitation Act (both acts, 30 Apr. 1946), and the Philippines Military Assistance Act (26 June 1946).

1952

5–8 JAN. President Truman and Prime Minister Churchill reviewed the world situation in a conference at Washington and reported (9 Jan.) an agreement by which U.S. airbases in Britain would not be used for atomic bombing of Communist Europe without British consent.

The Korean War

1945–49. PREWAR CONDITIONS. As a result of the Second World War, Korea was "temporarily" divided at the 38th parallel into 2 zones, one occupied by the U.S. and the other by the U.S.S.R. On 1 Oct. 1946 Under Secretary of State Acheson reasserted U.S. intention to stay in Korea until it was united and free. On 17 Sept. 1947 the U.S. informed the Soviet Union of its intention to refer the question of Korean independence to the UN, which passed a resolution proposing free elections in the spring of 1948 in order to create a provisional government for the entire country. On 23 Jan. 1948 the Soviet government informed the UN that the UN Temporary Commission on Korea would not be permitted to visit North Korea. On 22 Mar. the U.S. military governor in Korea announced an extensive land-reform program. On 1 May the North Koreans announced adoption by a "North and South Korean Conference" at Pyongyang of a constitution for the "People's Democratic Republic of Korea" with jurisdiction over all Korea. On 10 May elections held in U.S.-occupied South Korea under the observation of the UN Temporary Commission were boycotted in North Korea. On 15 Aug. the Republic of Korea was proclaimed at Seoul, South Korea, with Syngman Rhee as president. On 9 Sept. a "People's Republic" claiming authority over the entire country was set up in North Korea. On 10 Dec. the Rhee government signed an agreement with the U.S. providing for a program of economic assistance to be carried out by the ECA and the War Department. In a speech on 12 Jan. 1949 Secretary Acheson omitted Korea from the U.S. defense perimeter, but added that the military security of other areas in the Pacific would be "the commitment of the entire civilized world" under the UN Charter. A Soviet veto (19 Apr.) blocked admission of the Republic of Korea into the UN. The U.S. completed withdrawal of its forces from Korea 29 June 1949, leaving only an American military advisory group numbering 500 men. The UN Commission on Korea reported 2 Sept. failure to settle differences between the Korean Republic and the North Korean Communist regime and stressed the danger of civil war. Both sides indicated their intention to achieve unification by force, if necessary.

25 June 1950. NORTH KOREAN AGGRESSION. North Korean Communist forces equipped with Soviet-made weapons invaded South Korea. The absence of a Soviet representative at the Security Council (p. 474) facilitated action. On 25 June the council ordered an immediate cease-fire and the withdrawal of North Korean forces. On the evening of 26 June President Truman decided to order the air force and navy to give support to the Korean forces, authorizing missions south of the 38th parallel, to order the 7th Fleet to prevent an attack on Formosa, and to increase aid to Indochina. On the next day the Security Council (27 June) called upon UN members to "furnish such assistance as may be necessary to the Republic of Korea to repel the armed attack and to restore international peace and security in the area." Truman the same day ordered U.S. air and sea forces to give the Korean government troops cover and support. Seoul fell to the North Koreans 28 June. On 30 June U.S. ground forces were ordered into the fighting and authorized to conduct missions above the 38th parallel. On 7 July the U.S. government announced that the draft would be employed to enlarge the army. The same day the UN voted for a unified UN command in Korea under a commander to be designated by the U.S. Gen. **Douglas MacArthur** was so designated 8 July. On 20 July President Truman proposed partial mobilization of U.S. resources to meet the Korean crisis and urged Congress to enact a $10 billion rearmament program. Future Security Council action was blocked by the return (1 Aug.) of Yakov A. Malik, Soviet representative.

MILITARY OPERATIONS. Battle of the **Pusan Beachhead** (6 Aug.–15 Sept.) in Southern Korea. Red offensive, which captured Pohang 6 Sept., failed to drive UN forces off the peninsula. Launching a counteroffensive (15 Sept.), UN forces made an amphibious landing at **Inchon** and began an eastward sweep across the peninsula. The operation was timed with the breakout of UN forces from the beachhead in southeastern Korea. On 26 Sept. Gen. MacArthur announced the capture of Seoul.

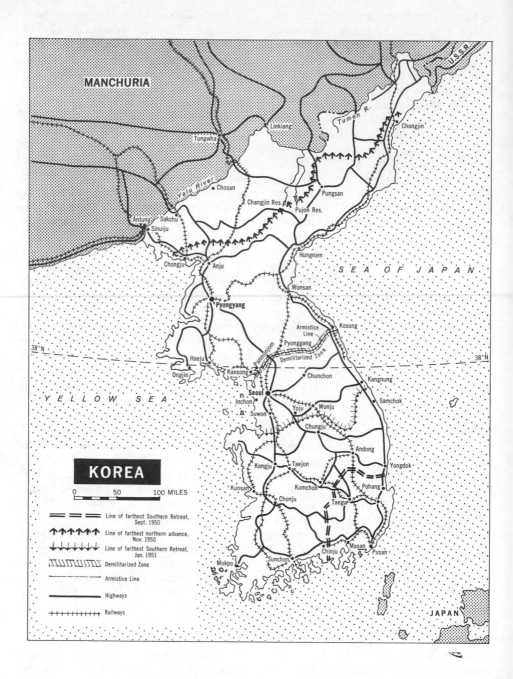

MANCHURIA

Tungwha

Linkiang

Tumen R.

Chongjin

U.S.S.R.

Yalu River

Chosan

Antung Sakchu

Sinuiju

Chongju Anju

Changjin Res.

Pujon Res.

Pungsan

Hungnam

SEA OF JAPAN

Pyongyang

Wonsan

Armistice Line

Kosong

Pyonggang

38° N

Haeju

Kaesong

Panmunjom

Demilitarized Zone

38° N

Ongjin

Chunchon

Kangnung

Seoul

Inchon

Yoju

Wonju

Samchok

YELLOW SEA

Suwon

Chungju

Andong

Yongdok

Kongju

Taejon

Kumchon

Pohang

KOREA

0   50   100 MILES

Kunsan

Chonju

Taegu

Mokpo

Sunchon

Chinju

Masan

Pusan

JAPAN

═ ═ ═   Line of farthest Southern Retreat, Sept. 1950

↑↑↑↑↑   Line of farthest northern advance, Nov. 1950

↓↓↓↓↓   Line of farthest Southern Retreat, Jan. 1951

⊥⊥⊥⊥⊥   Demilitarized Zone

────────   Armistice Line

━━━━   Highways

+++++++   Railways

Chinese Communist Intervention. On 30 Sept. Foreign Minister Chou En-lai implied that the Chinese government might intervene. U.S. forces crossed the 38th parallel, 1 Oct. On 7 Oct. the General Assembly laid down the objectives of the UN action in Korea as to "ensure conditions of stability throughout Korea" and called for "a unified, independent and democratic government" of Korea. On 11 Oct. Peking denounced the crossing of the 38th parallel and declared that China "cannot stand idly by." On 20–21 Oct. UN troops captured Pyongyang, capital of North Korea, and advanced toward the Manchurian border, reaching Chosan on the Yalu, 26 Oct. From 26 Oct.–24 Nov., troops identified as Chinese were fighting alongside the North Koreans. On 24 Nov. Gen. MacArthur ordered an "end-the-war" offensive. On 26 Nov. Chinese Communist forces opened a massive counteroffensive against UN troops in the Yalu Valley. The operation ended in a general UN retreat toward the 38th parallel and the abandonment (5 Dec.) of Pyongyang. A UN Security Council resolution (30 Nov.) calling for withdrawal of Chinese Communists and promising to safeguard Chinese border interests was vetoed by the Soviet delegate. On 3 Nov. the UN General Assembly adopted the "Uniting for Peace" Resolution, asserting its right to deal with any threat to the peace where failure of the permanent members of the Security Council to agree prevented the council from functioning. U.S. forces retreated (4 Jan. 1951) south of Seoul to the Han River. A counteroffensive (25 Jan.–21 Apr.) led to the retaking of Seoul (14–15 Mar.) and the recrossing of the 38th parallel (1 Mar.). On 1 Feb. the General Assembly passed a resolution condemning Communist China as an aggressor, but limiting UN objectives to a cease-fire and return to the status quo. A North Korean–Chinese offensive (22 Apr.–8 July) was turned back.

11 Apr. 1951. REMOVAL OF MAC-ARTHUR. Disagreements over strategy between President Truman and Gen. MacArthur led to a meeting on Wake Island (15 Oct. 1950) which produced surface unity. But disagreements grew with Truman's refusal to accede to MacArthur's requests to expand the war by employing Nationalist Chinese troops to attack mainland China and by strategic bombing of China. Advised (Mar. 1951) that Truman intended to invite truce talks, MacArthur torpedoed the plan by publicly threatening the Chinese with expansion of the war. In a letter to House Minority Leader Joseph W. Martin (Mass.), disclosed 5 Apr., MacArthur declared that "there is no substitute for victory." Truman removed MacArthur from command (11 Apr.) but MacArthur was invited to address a joint session of Congress (19 Apr.). Closed hearings of the Senate Armed Services and Foreign Relations Committees began 3 May. No report was issued.

10 JULY 1951–26 JULY 1953. ARMISTICE NEGOTIATIONS. With U.S. troops just north of the 38th Parallel, Soviet representative Malik proposed a cease-fire and armistice along the parallel (23 June 1951). Acheson accepted in principle on 26 June. Truce talks began 10 July at Kaesong but were broken off 22 Aug. They resumed 25 Oct. at Panmunjom. During the following 2 years a stalemate prevailed, with heavy but limited military engagements. Eisenhower visited Korea (2–5 Dec. 1952) following his election. Stalin died 5 Mar. 1953, and a breakthrough in the armistice negotiations occurred 3 weeks later. On 17–18 June, South Korean guards allowed 25,000 North Korean prisoners to escape but the armistice was signed by the truce delegates in Panmunjom on

26 July 1953 and hostilities halted at 10 P.M. Under its terms a demilitarized zone of 4 kilometers separating the Communists from the Allies was set up; a neutral repatriation committee was to control the remaining prisoners, including those refusing repatriation, the strength of both sides was to be frozen, and the administration of the truce was to be entrusted to a military armistice commission consisting of 5 from each side. The armistice gave South Korea about 1,500 square miles more territory than it had before the fighting began, when the 38th parallel was the dividing line.

19 JAN. 1954. The Senate Foreign Relations Committee approved a U.S.–South Korean mutual defense treaty, with the stipulation that armed aid should be provided only in the case of "external armed attack" against the Republic of Korea. Ratifications were exchanged, 17 Nov., and the U.S., on the same day, agreed to expand its military and economic aid to Korea in 1955. On Oct. 26, 1958, China announced the withdrawal of the "Chinese People's Volunteers" from North Korea.

U.S. Casualties: 33,629 battle dead; 20,617 dead from other causes; 103,284 wounded.

Foreign Policy: Eisenhower-Dulles Years, 1953–60

1953

"CAPTIVE PEOPLES" RESOLUTION. On 27 Jan. Secretary of State John Foster Dulles (p. 1018) in a radio-TV talk held out to "captive" people behind the Iron Curtain a promise that "you can count on us." A resolution drafted by Dulles was introduced into both houses of Congress, 20 Feb., deploring "the forcible absorption of free peoples into an aggressive despotism" and denouncing Soviet interpretations of wartime agreements to "bring about the subjugation of free peoples." After the death of Stalin (5 Mar.), the administration, uncertain as to the future direction of Soviet policy, persuaded congressional leaders to shelve the resolution (HJ Res 200). The administration's essentially propagandistic intent was underscored, when, 18–24 June, strikes, arson, and rioting broke out in numerous East German cities, including Berlin, and Russian and East German

troops restored order only after shooting, but the U.S. made no move to intervene. Eisenhower told the press (1 July) that the U.S. planned no physical intervention in East Europe. However, on 30 Nov. Secretary Dulles declared the U.S. would not "confirm their captivity" by recognizing Russia's incorporation of Lithuania, Estonia, and Latvia.

26 SEPT. MUTUAL DEFENSE ASSISTANCE AGREEMENT WITH SPAIN signed, providing for development and maintenance of U.S. air and naval installations in Spain in return for U.S. military and economic aid. When the executive agreement, originally concluded for 10 years, was extended for 5 years (26 Sept. 1963), a joint declaration was issued which in effect committed the U.S. to Spain's defense. While favoring Spain's admission to NATO, the U.S. has not pressed the issue in view of opposition of other members to the Franco regime. From 1953–68 Spain received $1.2 billion in various forms of U.S.

military aid. The agreement was extended for 2 years (20 June 1969) and again for 5 years (6 Aug. 1971), providing Spain with an additional $385 million in various forms of military assistance in exchange for continuation of U.S. base rights.

8 Dec. "ATOMS FOR PEACE" proposal. The deadlock which had developed over international control of atomic energy, as well as the broader disarmament issue to which it was linked, prompted President Eisenhower to take a new tack and to stress new ways of devoting the atom to peaceful uses. Addressing the UN General Assembly, he proposed (8 Dec.) that the governments "principally involved" make contributions of uranium and fissionable materials from their stockpiles to an International Atomic Energy Agency (IAEA) which would be responsible for the protection and storage of these materials and would devise methods for their allocation to serve peaceful purposes. From 19 Mar.– 23 Sept. 1954 the U.S.-proposed draft statute for the projected agency was rejected by the U.S.S.R., which stressed that the issues of disarmament and peaceful uses of atomic energy were inseparable. As the U.S.-Soviet impasse became apparent, the U.S. decided to proceed with the negotiation of a draft statute without the U.S.S.R., but without closing the door to Soviet participation. An 8-nation group (the U.S., Australia, Belgium, Canada, France, Portugal, South Africa, and Britain), meeting in Washington during the summer of 1954, prepared a first draft for the IAEA. Late in Sept. the U.S.S.R., in a sudden reversal, indicated its willingness to separate the issues of disarmament and the peaceful uses of atomic energy. The UN General Assembly unanimously adopted (8 Dec. 1954) a resolution calling for early establishment of an IAEA

to promote the peaceful uses of atomic power. In Aug. 1955, the first draft statute was circulated to all UN members and specialized agencies and the efforts of the negotiating group were endorsed (3 Dec. 1955) by the General Assembly. Responding to pressure from the General Assembly, the U.S. decided to make the draft statute the subject of multilateral negotiations. Brazil, Czechoslovakia, India, and the U.S.S.R. were invited to join the original 8 in negotiations (27 Feb.–18 Apr. 1956), which produced a revised draft statute submitted in Oct. to a conference consisting of all members of the UN and the specialized agencies. This conference prepared and approved the **Statute of the IAEA,** signed (26 Oct.) by the representatives of 70 governments and entered into force 30 July 1957. The statute provides for an IAEA with a wide range of functions bearing on the peaceful use of atomic energy but it has not supplanted bilateral arrangements for making fissionable materials available for peaceful uses. On 30 Aug. 1954 President Eisenhower had signed the Atomic Energy Act of 1954, authorizing the exchange with other countries of information and material for the peaceful use of atomic energy.

1953–60

INDOCHINA. In Nov. 1953 the French occupied the key northern outpost, Dien Bien Phu. With the French military position in Vietnam deteriorating, a conference of the Big-4 foreign ministers met in Berlin, proposing (18 Feb. 1954) that a broader conference be convened 26 Apr. in Geneva to discuss the situations in Korea and Indochina.

Spring 1954. U.S. Twice at the Brink of Military Intervention. U.S. military aid had accounted for the bulk of the cost of the French war in Vietnam— 78%, according to a report (16 Mar. 1954) of the French National Assembly. The U.S. government was opposed to a negotiated settlement in Indochina under current conditions, projecting it would lead to the loss to Communism not only of Vietnam but of the whole of Southeast Asia: the "falling row of dominoes" theory, publicly supported (7 Apr.) by President Eisenhower. Secretary of State Dulles was among those urging a U.S. air strike to prevent the fall of Dien Bien Phu. After serious consideration such action was tentatively rejected on 4 Apr., when consultations (3 Apr.) suggested that the congressional support deemed necessary would not be forthcoming unless other nations, especially Britain, participated. Despite firm British opposition, after the fall of Dien Bien Phu (7 May) the U.S. again prepared for military intervention, but the French government became reluctant to initiate further military operations and, after continued deterioration of the French military position, the U.S. notified (15 June) the French that the time for intervention had passed.

26 Apr.–20 July. The Geneva Conference. The first plenary session concerning Indochina was held on 8 May. (The 19 nations failed to agree on a Korean settlement, ending their talks 19 June.) The U.S., France, Britain, U.S.S.R., Communist China, Cambodia, Laos, and the 2 Vietnam regimes participated in the discussions which led to the **Geneva Agreements** on Indochina of 20 July. These *inter alia* provided for: (1) armistices in Laos, Cambodia, and Vietnam; (2) partition of Vietnam by the fixing of a provisional military demarcation line at the 17th parallel with a 5-kilometer demilitarized zone (DMZ) on either side —Viet Minh forces to withdraw to the north and French Union forces to the south; (3) freedom of Vietnamese civil-

ians to choose whether to live in the North or the South; (4) prohibition of foreign bases in Indochina or of entry of any of the Indochinese states into military alliances; (5) establishment of an International Control Commission composed of Indian, Canadian, and Polish representatives; and (6) the holding of general elections throughout Vietnam in July 1956. Not associating itself with the Geneva Agreements, the U.S. took note of them and unilaterally declared that it would refrain from the threat or use of force to disturb them.

Aug. 1954–1960. Despite pessimistic U.S. intelligence estimates of the probability of a stable, civilian regime in South Vietnam, the National Security Council recommended direct U.S. military, economic, and political support for the government headed by Ngo Dinh Diem (became premier, June 1954). President Eisenhower approved (20 Aug.) the NSC policy paper by which the U.S. assumed the burden of defending South Vietnam. Even before this policy decision was taken, a CIA team headed by Col. Edward G. Lansdale began (June) covert operations against the Viet Minh. In a protocol to the SEATO pact (p. 484) the signatories extended their protection to Vietnam, Cambodia, and Laos. President Eisenhower promised Diem, in a letter 23 Oct., U.S. aid "in developing and maintaining a strong, viable state capable of resisting attempted subversion or aggression through military means." The first U.S. military advisers were dispatched to train the South Vietnamese army on 23 Feb. 1955. On 16 July, Diem, with U.S. backing, rejected the reunification elections provided for in the Geneva Agreements and on 26 Oct. he declared South Vietnam a republic with himself as president. In May 1956 the U.S. sent 350 additional military personnel to Vietnam on a "temporary" mission—lifting the number of

U.S. forces in South Vietnam above the 342 limit provided in the Geneva Agreements. In response to stepped-up Viet Cong (Vietnamese Communists) insurgency, the U.S. increased (May 1960) its military advisers in Vietnam to 685.

1954

JAN. 12. "MASSIVE RETALIATION" DOCTRINE ARTICULATED. Prompted by the Eisenhower administration's commitment to the reduction of federal spending and by advances in atomic weapons technology, the "New Look" in national security policy emphasized reductions in army manpower, the development of tactical nuclear weapons, and the buildup of strategic air power employing nuclear weapons—a "bigger bang for the buck." The complementary strategic doctrine was articulated 12 Jan. by Secretary of State John Foster Dulles. The capacity of the Strategic Air Command (SAC) to inflict "instant, massive retaliation"—always the primary deterrent against direct Soviet attack—would now serve "at times and places of our own choosing" as an explicit deterrent of lesser aggression. The doctrine of "massive retaliation" drew sharp criticism, both domestic and foreign; only after lengthy negotiations did Britain, Turkey, and Italy agree to the stationing of intermediate-range nuclear weapons on their soil (France refused, choosing instead to develop her own atomic force; and one of its major objectives, the withdrawal of U.S. troops from Europe, was never carried out, out of respect for America's NATO partners).

25 JAN.–18 FEB. BERLIN CONFERENCE OF FOREIGN MINISTERS. Agreement between East and West could not be reached on the reunification of Germany. The U.S.S.R. proposed a 50-year all-European security treaty, which would exclude the U.S. from the defense of Europe and make Red China and the U.S. equal "observers" of the pact's application. This proposal was rejected by Great Britain and France.

13 MAY. ST. LAWRENCE SEAWAY. The Wiley-Dondero Act authorized the U.S. to join Canada in construction of a 27-foot deep channel between Montreal and Lake Erie and established the St. Lawrence Seaway Development Corp. to finance and construct navigational improvements along the St. Lawrence in U.S. territory. This action reflected growing dependence of Midwestern steel mills on iron ore of the Quebec-Labrador region. St. Lawrence Seaway and St. Lawrence power project formally opened 26–27 June 1959. Seaway made possible the navigation of ships of 27-foot draft from Montreal to Lake Superior except in winter months.

GUATEMALA COUP. By the end of 1953 the U.S. regarded as threatening the spread of Communist influence in the regime of Guatemala's Jacob Arbenz Guzmán, elected president in 1950. At a meeting of the OAS in Caracas in Mar. 1954 the U.S. secured the adoption of a resolution calling for consultation on moves to head off Communist penetration in the Western Hemisphere. The arrival 15 May at Puerto Barrios of a vessel containing arms from Czechoslovakia was regarded (17 May) by the U.S. State Department as "a development of gravity." On 18 June an insurgent force under Col. Carlos Castillo Armas and, as later revealed, supported by the CIA, invaded Guatemala from Honduras. The UN Security Council (20 June) called for termination of the invasion and requested states to refrain from assisting the attackers. On 29 June the Arbenz Guzmán government was overthrown and an anti-Communist military junta installed. The meeting of OAS foreign ministers called for (26 June) by the OAS Council and projected for 7 July was canceled. On 1 Sept., with dissolution of the junta, Col. Castillo Armas became president. On 30 Oct. the U.S. promised Guatemala $6,425,000 in economic aid and on 18 June 1956 the U.S. and Guatemala signed a military assistance pact.

8 Sept. The SEATO Pact, a U.S.-sponsored Southeast Asian collective defense treaty, was signed in Manila by the delegates of 8 nations: Australia, Great Britain, France, New Zealand, Pakistan, the Philippines, Thailand, and the U.S. The pact pledged joint action against aggression upon any member nation but, unlike NATO (p. 471), created no unified military command. Taiwan was excluded from the treaty region which was defined as "the general area of Southeast Asia . . . and the Southwest Pacific not including the Pacific areas north" of 21° 30′ N lat. In an addendum insisted upon by Secretary of State Dulles, the U.S. specified that America's agreement to "act to meet the common danger" applied "only to Communist aggression" and that in the event of "other aggression or armed attack" the U.S. would merely consult its allies. In a separate protocol, the signatories extended their protection to South Vietnam, Cambodia, and Laos—which the **Geneva Agreements** (p. 482) barred from joining any military alliance. The Senate ratified (82–1) the SEATO treaty 1 Feb. 1955.

27 Sept. "DEW LINE." Supplementing the Pinetree Chain of radar stations extending across the continent north of the U.S.-Canadian border (work begun 1950) and the "Mid-Canada Line" 500 miles farther north (1953), the U.S. and Canada agreed in principle on establishing a third radar line, "Distant Early Warning" (DEW) Line, across Arctic Canada from Alaska to Greenland. DEW Line went into operation 1 July 1957.

TAIWAN STRAITS CRISIS. On 2 Feb. 1953, President Eisenhower announced his decision to lift the U.S. 7th Fleet's blockade of Taiwan, making possible Nationalist attacks against the Red Chinese mainland. On 11 Aug. 1954 Chou En-lai declared that Taiwan must be liquidated. President Eisenhower rejoined (17 Aug.) that "any invasion of Formosa would have to run over the 7th Fleet." Red China then turned attention to the Nationalist-held offshore islands, launching, 3 Sept., a bombardment of Quemoy and Little Quemoy. The Nationalists retaliated 7 Sept. against Amoy. At a meeting of the National Security Council on 12 Sept. the president rejected proposals for military action against Communist China because of the dangers of atomic war. On 2 Dec. 1954 the U.S. and Nationalist China signed a mutual defense treaty. While the treaty, which did not apply to islands along the Chinese mainland, was before the Senate, Communist China increased pressure on Nationalist China by seizing (18 Jan. 1955) Ichiang, 210 miles north of Formosa, and increasing attacks on Quemoy and Matsu. This situation led to the **Formosa Resolution**—requested by President Eisenhower in a special message (24 Jan.), passed by both houses and signed by the president 29 Jan. The Formosa Resolution authorized the president to employ the armed forces of the U.S. "as he deems necessary to defend Formosa and the Pescadores against armed attack, this authority to include the securing and protection of such related positions and territories . . . as he judges to be required or appropriate in assuring the defense of Formosa and the Pescadores." The imprecision regarding the offshore islands was intended to convey to the Communist Chinese the implication that U.S. forces might be used to repulse an invasion of Quemoy or Matsu while conveying to the Nationalist Chinese that the U.S. was not specifically committed to defending the islands, as such a commitment might encourage the Nationalist Chinese to attempt to regain the mainland. The **U.S.-Nationalist Chinese mutual security pact** was ratified by the Senate (65–6) on 9 Feb. 1955. The U.S. 7th Fleet helped the Nationalist Chinese evacuate 17,000 civilians and 25,000 troops from the Tachen islands during Feb. without Communist interference. On 1 Aug. Communist China released the 11 U.S. airmen (but not the 2 civilians) sentenced as spies Nov. 1954. Simultaneously, U.S. and Communist Chinese ambassadors began a series of secret talks, first in Geneva and then in Warsaw, which were to extend into the early 1970s.

1955

25 JAN. U.S. and the Republic of Panama signed a treaty of cooperation concerning the Panama Canal (p. 627).

AUSTRIAN PEACE TREATY. At the Moscow conference of foreign ministers (1947; p. 467) it was agreed to continue discussion of Austrian problems through a Treaty Commission. Agreement on a treaty, nearly completed by Dec. 1949, was blocked by the Soviets. Suddenly, in the spring of 1955 the U.S.S.R. invited the Austrian chancellor to discussions 11–16 Apr. in Moscow, where agreement was reached on a draft treaty. Accord was rapidly reached, and the U.S., Britain, France, the U.S.S.R., and Austria signed the Austrian State Treaty in Vienna 15 May. The pact reestablished Austria as a sovereign, independent, and democratic state with its pre-1938 borders, barred any economic or political union with Germany, provided no reparations would be paid but gave the U.S.S.R. certain oil concessions and refineries, provided for the withdrawal of all occupation troops by the end of 1955, barred Austria from owning or making atomic weapons or guided missiles, and declared Austria's military neutrality in perpetuity. The treaty was ratified (63–3) by the Senate 17 June.

BAGHDAD PACT. In an effort to block Soviet pressures on the northern tier of Middle Eastern states, the U.S. promoted formation of what became the Baghdad Pact—a mutual defense treaty which, by Apr. 1955, included Turkey, Pakistan, Iran, Iraq, and Britain. The U.S. declined to join formally, to avoid alienating Egypt by creating formal ties with Iraq. Egyptian President Gamal Abdel Nasser denounced Iraq for allying with the West and, in the fall of 1955, turned to the Soviets for military equipment in an attempt to gain a decisive military advantage over Israel. On 21–22 Nov. 1955 the Baghdad Pact Council held its first meeting in Baghdad with U.S. observers present. U.S. officials also participated in the defense and antisubversion committees of the pact, formally joining the military committee June 1957. The U.S. provided military and economic aid to the members of the pact and (29 Nov. 1956) issued a declaration of support for the pact and the independence and territorial integrity of its members. On 5 Mar. 1959 the U.S. signed bilateral cooperation agreements with Turkey, Iran, and Pakistan in Ankara. On 24 Mar. Iraq announced its withdrawal from the Baghdad Pact, and canceled its military and economic agreements with the U.S. (30 May). The Baghdad Pact was officially changed to **Central Treaty Organization** (CENTO), 18 Aug.

5 MAY. OCCUPATION OF WEST GERMANY ENDED. Despite the U.S. decision to proceed with German rearmament with or without French cooperation, the French National Assembly rejected (30 Aug. 1954) ratification of EDC (p. 475). On 3 Oct. agreement was reached in London on a new formula, devised by Prime Minister Anthony Eden, for meeting the problem of German rearmament and integration in NATO. With a protocol to the Brussels Treaty (p. 475) a new alliance, to be known as the Western European Union (WEU), comprising the 5 Brussels Treaty members plus Italy and West Germany, was created. The same protocol permitted German rearmament, with restrictions to reassure France. Adjoining the protocol establishing WEU was a revised "peace contract" giving the Federal Republic of Germany "the full authority of a sovereign state over its internal and external affairs" and in other ways somewhat more advantageous to the Germans than the original 1952 "peace contract" (p. 476). A protocol to the NATO pact authorized West Germany to join the organization once the other agreements were ratified. The various documents of the interlocking accord were signed in Paris (23 Oct.) and the Western deadlock on Germany was broken 30 Dec. 1954, when the French National Assembly approved the Brussels protocol and the other agreements. The protocols to the 1952 "peace contract" and the North Atlantic Treaty admitting Germany to the alliance were ratified (76–2) by the U.S. Senate 29 Mar. 1955. On 5 May the U.S., Britain, and France ended the occupation of West Germany and the Federal Republic of Germany formally joined NATO the next day. German rearmament proceeded slowly; the last of the 12 authorized divisions committed to NATO in 1965.

18–23 July. "SUMMIT" MEETING AT GENEVA. British Prime Minister Winston Churchill first suggested a "summit" conference of the heads of government of the U.S., Britain, France, and the U.S.S.R. in May 1953, but the Eisenhower administration, fearful that such a conference would interfere with plans to tie West Germany into NATO, was unresponsive. During 1954 British, French, and Soviet interest in such a meeting mounted but the U.S. insisted upon prior ratification of the Austrian treaty (p. 485) and progress on accords on Germany (23 Oct.). These conditions met, the 3 Western Powers proposed to the U.S.S.R. (10 May) that the 4 Powers meet soon to attempt to "remove sources of conflict between us." Attending the conference in Geneva were **President Eisenhower, British Prime Minister Anthony Eden, French Premier Edgar Faure,** and **Soviet Premier N. A. Bulganin.** Also present was **Nikita S. Khrushchev,** First Secretary of the Communist Party, who was emerging as the key figure in the Soviet hierarchy. On the agenda were 4 items: reunification of Germany, European security, disarmament, and improvement of East-West relations. The Western Powers gave first priority to German reunification, proposing that 3 safeguards surround a Germany reunited on the basis of free elections: a 5-Power mutual defense pact, an agreement as to the total forces and armaments permitted in Germany, and the setting up of a demilitarized zone between East and West. The Soviet Union gave first priority to European security, proposing again, as it had at the Berlin Conference of 1954 (p. 483), an all-European treaty of mutual defense, excluding the U.S. except as an "observer." On 21 July President Eisenhower made his "Open Skies" proposal: that each nation give the other "a complete blueprint" of its military establishments and that each permit the other freedom of photographic reconnaissance over its national territory. Although the conference ended with no agreements other than upon a directive to the foreign ministers of the 4 Powers to pursue matters on the agenda in Oct., it produced "the spirit of Geneva"—generally interpreted as a desire on both sides to avoid confrontation and seek accommodation. The foreign ministers of the 4 Powers met 27 Oct.–16 Nov. in Paris without reaching any agreement.

1956

SUEZ CRISIS. In response to Soviet arms shipments to Egypt in 1955–56, Israel stepped up military preparations. Israel's request to buy arms from the U.S. was rejected by President Eisenhower (7 Mar. 1956) on the ground that such sales would lead to an "Arab-Israeli arms race." On 17 Dec. 1955 the U.S. offered Egypt a loan of $56 million for construction of the Aswan High Dam, intended to increase Egypt's arable land and supply electric power. Britain followed with an offer of $14 million and the World Bank indicated willingness to lend another $200 million. Egypt accepted the offers (17 July), but Secretary of State Dulles, disturbed by Nasser's deepening ties with the U.S.S.R., announced (19 July) that the U.S. was withdrawing its Aswan loan offer. Britain withdrew its loan offer and the World Bank offer, contingent upon the others, automatically lapsed. In retaliation, President Gamal Abdel Nasser on 26 July announced that he was nationalizing the Suez Canal and would use the tolls to defray the expenses of constructing the dam. Nasser also refused to guarantee the safety of Israeli shipping. Conflicts over control of the canal were not resolved during 3 months of intensive negotiations, which included an international conference in London 16–23 Aug. On Oct. 29 the armed forces of Israel (whose borders with Syria, Jordan, and Egypt had been the scene of almost continuous fighting) invaded the Gaza strip and the Sinai peninsula, completing occupation of the Sinai peninsula to within 10 miles of the Suez Canal by

5 Nov. British and French aircraft attacked Egypt 31 Oct.–5 Nov. and an Anglo-French paratrooper force was dropped at the northern end of the canal 5 Nov. By 6 Nov. British and French forces controlled the canal. On 31 Oct. President Eisenhower declared himself opposed to the use of force as an instrument for settling international disputes. Yielding to U.S. pressure and Soviet threats of intervention (5 Nov.), the British, French, and Israelis accepted a cease-fire to become effective midnight 6 Nov. British, French, and Israeli troops withdrew as a UN Emergency Force (UNEF) was installed to act as a buffer between Egypt and Israel.

HUNGARIAN REVOLT. Antigovernment demonstrations in Budapest 23 Oct. 1956 forced a reshuffling of the government. Revolutionaries demanded that the government denounce the Warsaw Pact as well as seek the complete liberation of the country from Soviet troops. On 30 Oct. Moscow promised major concessions. The next day President Eisenhower hailed these developments as "the dawning of a new day" in Eastern Europe, but earlier, on 21 Oct., in connection with Polish uprisings, Secretary Dulles had made it clear that the U.S. would not give military aid. On 4 Nov. Soviet troops and tanks opened a violent assault on Budapest, and a new all-Communist government was set up. The revolt was crushed. It was revealed on 16 June 1958 that ex-premier Imre Nagy was executed following a secret trial. While making no effort directly to intervene in Hungary, the U.S. mounted a massive propaganda attack, in the UN and elsewhere, upon the Soviet actions.

1957

EISENHOWER DOCTRINE. After the Suez Crisis (1956), Secretary of State Dulles, concerned lest the Franco-

British setback prompt the U.S.S.R. to fill the Middle East vacuum, sought congressional support for presidential discretion in order to deter the Soviets. On 5 Jan. 1957, President Eisenhower, before a joint session of Congress, urged support for a declaration, immediately dubbed the Eisenhower Doctrine. The Eisenhower Doctrine, embodied in H J Res 117, introduced 5 Jan. and passed by Congress 7 Mar., authorized the president to extend economic and military aid to any Middle East nation requesting it, authorized the use of $200 million in Mutual Security funds for fiscal 1957, and declared that "if the President determines the necessity" the U.S. was "prepared to use armed forces to assist" any nation or group of nations in the Middle East "requesting assistance against armed aggression from any country controlled by international communism." The resolution failed to specify the nations to which it applied.

1958

27 APR.–15 MAY. Vice-President Richard M. Nixon made a goodwill tour of 8 South American countries, but encountered hostile demonstrations, particularly in Peru (7–8 May) and Venezuela (13 May). A precautionary movement of U.S. forces into Caribbean bases was ordered by President Eisenhower in view of the virulence of the demonstrations in Venezuela.

3 MAY. ANTARCTICA. The U.S. proposed to the other 11 involved nations that a treaty be formulated to preserve the present legal status of the continent. Political claims would be frozen, and the continent would remain a scientific laboratory for an indefinite period. At a conference in Washington (15 Oct.–1 Dec. 1959) attended by 12 nations (7 of which had made territorial claims in Antarctica; the remainder had conducted scientific work there), a treaty was adopted and signed which reserved that continent exclusively for peaceful purposes and froze territorial claims for the duration of the treaty (34 years).

LEBANON. On 14 July a leftist coup, believed inspired by Nasser (heading the United Arab Republic, created by a merger of Egypt and Syria 1 Feb. 1958) and the U.S.S.R., ousted the pro-Western government of Iraq. Ongoing internal strife in Lebanon led President Camille Chamoun, fearing the effects of the Iraq coup, to appeal to the U.S. for support. President Eisenhower immediately ordered 5,000 U.S. marines from the 6th Fleet to land (15 July) in Lebanon to protect the Chamoun government while British troops were flown into neighboring Jordan (also under pressure from pro-Nasser elements) at King Hussein's behest. Citing the Eisenhower Doctrine (p. 487), the President in a message to Congress (15 July) declared Lebanon's territorial integrity and independence as "vital to U.S. interests" and found "indirect aggression from without." He also pledged to withdraw U.S. forces as soon as the UN was prepared to assume responsibility. Called into emergency session, the UN General Assembly approved a resolution putting the Lebanon-Jordan problem in the hands of Secretary General Dag Hammarskjold. As the political situation became more stable, U.S. forces —which had reached 15,000 but participated in no combat activities—were reduced and by 25 Oct. their withdrawal from Lebanon was completed.

TAIWAN STRAITS CRISIS. Following Soviet–Red Chinese discussions in Peking 31 July–3 Aug. 1958, bombardment of Quemoy and Matsu was renewed 23 Aug. In Sept. the U.S. 7th Fleet began to furnish naval escort to Nationalist convoys to the beleaguered garrison of Quemoy, but stopped 3 miles short of the objective to remain outside

Chinese territorial waters. A more cautious policy on both sides became evident. After Secretary Dulles criticized the concentration of large military forces on the off-shore islands, President Eisenhower (1 Oct.) noted that a cease-fire would provide "an opportunity to negotiate in good faith." A brief cease-fire was ordered by the Red Chinese on 6 Oct., and on 25 Oct. Red China announced that it would reserve the right to bombard the islands on alternate days of the month. This signaled the end of the acute phase of the Taiwan crisis.

BERLIN CRISIS. From 1949, when records began to be kept, to the end of 1958, some 2.9 million East Germans had fled into West Germany. Although by 1958 East German authorities had virtually sealed off the long frontier between the 2 Germanys, passage from East to West Berlin remained open. Meanwhile West Berlin had become a prosperous "showplace of democracy" and a symbol of Western commitment to resist Soviet pressure. The U.S., Britain, and France, refusing to recognize the German Democratic Republic (the Communist regime in East Germany), insisted on dealing with the U.S.S.R. in maintaining their positions in and access to West Berlin under the 4-Power occupation agreements. Accusing the West of violating those agreements by making Berlin a base for "subversive activity," Premier Khrushchev threatened on 10 Nov. 1958 to transfer Soviet responsibilities in Berlin to the East German regime, implying that the West would either deal with the German Democratic Republic or risk a land, water, and air blockade of West Berlin, and possible further escalation. The White House declared (21 Nov.) the intention of the West to "maintain the integrity" of West Berlin. On 27 Nov. the U.S.S.R. put a 6-month deadline on its transfer of authority to the German Democratic Re-

public, at the same time proposing that Berlin become a "free city." The U.S., Britain, and France, in similar notes to Moscow 31 Dec., formally rejected the Soviet position. While not leading to any forceful military gestures, the Berlin crisis dominated East-West relations in 1959, precipitating a flurry of diplomatic activity and travel by world leaders. Visiting the U.S. in Jan., Soviet Deputy Premier Anastas I. Mikoyan urged East-West talks on Berlin and related issues while playing down the ultimatum of Nov. President Eisenhower announced (3 Aug.) that he and Khrushchev would exchange visits that fall, after his own meetings with Chancellor Adenauer, Prime Minister Macmillan, and President de Gaulle in their respective capitals. Premier Khrushchev arrived in Washington 15 Sept., visiting New York, Los Angeles, San Francisco, Des Moines, and Pittsburgh before meeting with Eisenhower (25–27 Sept.) at the presidential retreat at Camp David, Md. It was agreed to hold a 4-Power summit conference soon to discuss Berlin and the problem of German reunification, and the Berlin ultimatum, in effect, was withdrawn.

1959–60

DETERIORATION OF U.S. RELATIONS WITH CUBA. After 3 years of guerrilla warfare, the resistance movement headed by **Fidel Castro** provoked the resignation (1 Jan 1959) and flight of the dictator Fulgencio Batista. As Castro proceeded to organize a broadly based social and economic revolution, anti-American in its nationalist assertions, relations with the U.S. rapidly deteriorated. At a meeting of OAS foreign ministers (Aug. 1959) the U.S. denounced Cuba as contributing to tensions in the Caribbean and urged an investigation by the Inter-American Peace Committee.

The final rupture between Cuba and the U.S. was precipitated when the Cuban government seized (29 June 1960) 3 U.S.- and British-owned oil refineries in Cuba after they refused to process 2 barge-loads of Soviet oil. Acting under a congressional authorization granted 3 July, President Eisenhower cut (6 July) the quota of Cuban sugar imported to the U.S. by 700,000 tons. Accusing the U.S. of attempting "to strangle the economy of Cuba," Premier Khrushchev warned (9 July) that any U.S. military intervention would confront Soviet rockets. Eisenhower replied (9 July) that the U.S. would not "permit the establishment of a regime dominated by international Communism in the Western Hemisphere." By decrees of July and Oct., the Castro government nationalized all big foreign and Cuban businesses. Spurred by the U.S., the OAS conference of foreign ministers condemned (28 Aug.) Communist intervention in the hemisphere. Further U.S. purchases of Cuban sugar were suspended and an embargo placed (20 Oct.) on most exports to Cuba. Threats made by Castro and members of his government against the continued U.S. occupation of the naval base at Guantanamo, held under the U.S.-Cuban treaty of 1903, prompted a White House announcement that it was "firm administration policy" to fight to defend the base. President Eisenhower ordered (17 Nov.) U.S. naval units to patrol Central American waters and shoot if necessary to prevent any Communist-led invasion of Guatemala or Nicaragua. On 2 Dec. Eisenhower announced that he had authorized the use of $1 million for the relief and resettlement in the U.S. of refugees from the "Communist-controlled" Castro regime. Beginning in July 1960, in various UN forums Cuba charged the U.S. with carrying on an interventionist policy and conspiring to commit aggression. In one of his last official acts, President Eisenhower broke off U.S. diplomatic relations with Cuba (3 Jan. 1961) in protest against "a long series of harassments, baseless accusations, and vilifications."

1960

19 JAN. NEW U.S.–JAPAN SECURITY PACT signed in Washington. The U.S.-Japan defense treaty of 8 Sept. 1951, signed along with the Japanese Peace Treaty (p. 476), allowed the U.S. virtually a free hand in disposing of its armed forces in and about Japan. A Mutual Defense Assistance Agreement (8 Mar. 1954) provided for U.S. aid in developing Japan's self-defense forces. Negotiations looking toward a revision of the 1951 treaty to give Japan a larger voice in military arrangements on its territory began in Tokyo in Oct. 1958 and continued through 1959 with Ambassador Douglas MacArthur II representing the U.S. Removing remaining residues of Japan's postwar occupation status, the new treaty dropped old provisions forbidding Japan to grant military rights to a third power without U.S. consent and permitting the use of U.S. troops to put down disorders in Japan. The new pact committed the 2 parties to come to each other's defense only if either were attacked "in the territories under the administration of Japan," and affirmed U.S. rights to land, air, and naval bases in Japan, while making use of these bases for combat operations or any shifts in the deployment or equipment of U.S. forces conditional upon "prior consultation." Massive demonstrations and student riots failed to prevent ratification of the treaty (19 May) by the Japanese House of Representatives but renewal of anti-American demonstrations forced the Japanese government, on 16 June, to withdraw its invitation to President Eisenhower, who was in Manila

preparatory to flying to Japan. His "good-will" tour aborted, Eisenhower returned to the U.S. On 18 June Japan's ratification became effective and Prime Minister Nobusuke Kishi, at whom the demonstrations had also been aimed, resigned. On 22 June the U.S. Senate ratified (90–2) the treaty, which was extended automatically and indefinitely on 23 June 1970 unless at any time thereafter either party wished to negotiate a revision or gave one-year notice that it wished to dissolve the pact.

MAY. U-2 INCIDENT. On 5 May the U.S.S.R. announced that an American U-2 (Lockheed high-altitude) plane used for photographic reconnaissance had been brought down (1 May) 1,200 miles inside the U.S.S.R. Previously, on 3 May, NASA released a CIA cover story of a lost weather research plane which might have been forced down inside the Soviet border owing to mechanical failure. On 7 May Premier Khrushchev announced that the pilot, Francis Gary Powers, was alive and had confessed to being a CIA agent. Secretary of State Christian Herter announced (9 May) that, at the president's direction, the U.S. had engaged in "extensive aerial surveillance" over the U.S.S.R. (the flights had begun in 1956), and President Eisenhower stated (11 May) that he himself had authorized the U-2 flights—an unprecedented avowal of espionage activities by a head of state. At the opening of the long-planned, 4-Power Summit Conference in Paris, Khrushchev censured (16 May) the "spy flight," demanded that the U.S. renounce flights over the U.S.S.R., called for postponement of the Summit Conference for "approximately 6 to 8 months," by which date a new U.S. president would have assumed office, and withdrew his invitation to Eisenhower to visit the U.S.S.R. The Summit Conference broke up 17 May. Powers

was tried (17–19 Aug.), found guilty of espionage, and sentenced to 10 years' loss of liberty. He was released (10 Feb. 1962) in exchange for the convicted Soviet spy Rudolf Abel. On 1 July the U.S.S.R. shot down a U.S. RB-47, a reconnaissance plane, on a flight to the Barents Sea; 2 surviving U.S. airmen were imprisoned, but released by the Soviet government 25 Jan. 1961.

14 DEC. UN DECLARATION ON COLONIALISM adopted by the 15th Session of the UN General Assembly. Virtually amending the UN Charter, Resolution 1514 proclaimed the rights of all peoples to self-determination and independence, calling for a "speedy and unconditional end" to colonialism "in all its forms and manifestations." The Declaration on Colonialism was passed 90–0 with 9 abstentions. The U.S.— along with Australia, Belgium, the Dominican Republic, France, Portugal, the Union of South Africa, and the United Kingdom—abstained. That U.S. policy toward the "Third World" was altered by the succeeding administration was dramatized by UN Ambassador Adlai E. Stevenson's statement (15 Mar. 1961) in the Security Council endorsing steps toward "full self-determination" in Angola, Portugal's African "province," and supporting creation of a UN committee to investigate disorders in that colony. The U.S. associated itself with the Declaration on Colonialism and (27 Nov.) voted for the establishment of a committee to implement it.

CONGO CRISIS. Following proclamation of the Congo's independence from Belgium (30 June), the army mutinied and the province of Katanga seceded. The U.S. refused to respond unilaterally to the Congo government's request for military aid. Subsequently the 14 July resolution of the UN Security Council directed the Secretary General, Dag Hammarskjold, to establish a UN force to restore order—which became known as ONUC (Force de l'Organisation des Nations Unies au Congo). During the 4 years of ONUC involvement, ending 30 June 1964, UN troops from a number of countries were involved in an anarchical situation of civil and tribal war. The U.S. supplied planes flown by ONUC and half of ONUC's financial support, promoting the cause of unity of the Congo. After the UN involvement ended, rebellion was renewed and Prime Minister Moise Tshombe (formerly leader of secessionist Katanga) requested U.S. military assistance, receiving (13 Aug. 1964) 4 transport planes, 3 helicopters, and 105 military personnel. U.S. planes also aided in the rescue of hostages from leftist rebels in Stanleyville (24 Nov.

1964). When the U.S.S.R. and other nations refused to pay special assessments for ONUC, the U.S. pressed for denial of the Soviet vote in the UN General Assembly, as specified in Article 19 of the UN Charter. At the 1964 General Assembly session potential dissolution was avoided by taking actions only by unanimous consent. A compromise arranged by the General Assembly's Special Committee on Peacekeeping Operations (18 Feb. 1965) provided that budget deficits would be made up by voluntary contributions. In 1967 3 U.S. planes were dispatched to the Congo again to aid the government of Joseph Mobutu against an uprising led by former Prime Minister Tshombe.

Foreign Policy: The Kennedy Years, 1961–63

1961

1 MAR. PEACE CORPS established on a temporary basis by executive order. On the same date President Kennedy requested legislation giving permanent status to the program which would send young American volunteers to other nations where, as educators, health workers, and technicians, they would help implement human resource and economic development programs. More than 13,000 Americans had already offered their services when the enabling legislation was signed 22 Sept. By executive order (effective 1 July 1971) the Peace Corps, VISTA (p. 529), and other volunteer programs were merged in a new agency, Action.

13 MAR. ALLIANCE FOR PROGRESS. Calling for a "decade of democratic progress" in Latin America, President Kennedy spelled out a 10-point program of Inter-American cooperation. Chartered (17 Aug.) at the Inter-American Conference in Punta del Este, Uruguay, the Alliance for Progress program committed OAS members to a 10-year, $100 billion program, to which the U.S. pledged $20 billion (at least $1 billion per year in various forms of public spending). The *Alianza's* goals included: a 2.5% annual increase in GNP, a more equitable distribution of national income, industrial growth and increased agricultural productivity, price stability, agrarian and tax reforms, extension of education, improvement of public health and medical services, and increased low-cost housing. The uneven results have served in large part as testimony to the ambitiousness of the *Alianza's* proclaimed objectives. Despite the creation (Jan. 1964) of an Inter-American Committee for the Alliance, and the announced support of Presidents Johnson and Nixon for

continued pursuit of the goals articulated at Punta del Este, from the U.S. standpoint the *Alianza* quickly became a foreign aid program based upon traditional bilateral negotiations between the U.S. and individual Latin-American nations.

17 APR. BAY OF PIGS INVASION. On 17 Mar. 1960 President Eisenhower had approved a CIA project involving the training and supplying of anti-Castro refugees to infiltrate Cuba. By Nov. the plans had escalated to a direct amphibious assault, in anticipation that such a landing would touch off a mass uprising against Castro. In spite of his own doubts about the operation, President Kennedy yielded to the combined advice of the CIA, the Joint Chiefs of Staff, and Secretary of Defense Robert McNamara, approving it early in April. Having ruled out any direct involvement of U.S. forces and confronted by persistent reports that the U.S. would furnish support for the expedition—an ill-kept secret—Kennedy publicly disclaimed (12 Apr.) "intervention in Cuba by the United States Armed Forces." Air strikes against Cuban airfields Apr. 15 by B-26 fighter-bombers piloted by Cuban exiles from bases in Nicaragua were perceived by Castro as "a prelude to invasion." A force of some 1,500 men, mostly Cuban exiles, landed 90 miles south of Havana at the *Bahía de Cochinos* (Bay of Pigs) on 17 Apr. As the result of faulty assumptions and poor planning, the invasion was crushed within 3 days. President Kennedy assumed responsibility for the fiasco, which resulted in worldwide denunciation of the U.S., while ordering an intensive review of CIA operations. Castro offered to exchange his 1,200 prisoners for 500 bulldozers, then demanded an "indemnity" of $28 million. The prisoners were finally exchanged for $52 million (privately raised) in food and medical supplies in Dec. 1962. The Bay of Pigs episode strengthened Castro—who pro-

claimed (2 Dec.), "I am a Marxist-Leninist and will be one until the day I die"—and increased U.S. concern about his efforts to "export revolution." At a meeting of OAS foreign ministers (22–31 Jan. 1962), at which Marxism-Leninism, alignment with the Communist bloc, and conduct of subversive activities were condemned, it was declared that by its acts the Cuban government had "voluntarily placed itself outside the inter-American system." Cuba's participation in the activities of the OAS (from which no state may be expelled) was thus suspended.

BERLIN WALL. Responding to the friendly overtures from the Soviets which followed the advent of his administration, President Kennedy agreed to meet Premier Khrushchev in Vienna, 3–4 June, for exploratory talks, after first meeting with Prime Minister Macmillan, Chancellor Adenauer, and President de Gaulle. At Vienna Khrushchev asserted that if the Western Powers failed to come to terms on a final German settlement he was determined to sign a separate treaty with East Germany "this year"—an ultimatum repeated (15 June) in an address in Moscow. Convinced that a demonstration of firmness was required, President Kennedy made statements (28 June and 19 July) indicating that the "real intent" of the Soviets was to force the Western Powers out of Berlin and then, on 25 July, he called for an extra $3.5 billion in defense spending—approximately one-half for immediate procurement of weapons and equipment—and an increase in U.S. and NATO forces. At the same time plans to more than double draft calls and call up reserve and National Guard units were announced. In response, Khrushchev threatened mobilization (7 Aug.) and, beginning 13 Aug., the Communists sealed off the border between East and West Berlin—first with a fence and then with a concrete wall topped with barbed wire. Kennedy ordered 1,500 troops to West Berlin to bolster the permanent U.S. contingent of 5,000 and sent Gen. Lucius Clay and Vice-President Lyndon B. Johnson to the scene as further symbols of U.S. commitment. An official end to the crisis came 17 Oct., when Premier Khrushchev, addressing the 23rd Communist Party Congress, backed away from his ultimatum by suggesting that the question of a deadline was of little significance if the West showed readiness to settle the German problem. While refraining from delivering another ultimatum, the Soviets continued to assert their intention of signing a separate pact with East Germany unless the West came to terms on a new regime for Berlin. The Berlin Wall was a scene of perpetual incident as East Germans risked Communist fire attempting to cross into West Berlin. With H Con Res 570 (10 Oct. 1962), Congress reaffirmed Western rights in Berlin and declared that the U.S. was determined to prevent "by whatever means may be necessary, including the use of arms, any violation of those rights by the Soviet Union directly or through others." Standing near the Berlin Wall, President Kennedy told a cheering crowd (26 June 1963) that the U.S. "will risk its cities to defend yours because we need your freedom to protect ours." He concluded by saying, *"Ich bin ein Berliner."*

FLEXIBLE RESPONSE DOCTRINE. At the time President Kennedy took office, NATO "shield" forces, though increasingly armed with tactical nuclear weapons, still fell short of goals. In military terms, NATO's combat forces stationed in Europe, not considered an effective "shield," had become a "trip wire" which would warn of, or precipitate, a full nuclear "exchange." President Kennedy and his advisers developed an alternative strategic theory based on a policy of "flexible response" to varying levels of pressure. As flexible response required greater reliance on conventional forces, the U.S. urged that NATO forces in West Germany be increased to the level of 30 divisions (there were then 24) and be equipped to fight with both conventional and nuclear weapons. Strongly opposed to the proliferation of independent nuclear forces and concerned with the need to promote greater unity within the NATO alliance (the Summit Conference of 1955 [p. 486], by raising hopes of East-West detente, had opened an era of discord within NATO), the Kennedy administration advocated creation of a NATO nuclear force (approved in principle Dec. 1957 by the NATO Council). Most prominently discussed was the **multilateral nuclear force (MLF)**—a fleet of Polaris-armed vessels to be manned by mixed crews and integrated into the NATO command. However, the flexible response doctrine, as elaborated, necessitated a strategy of "controlled" or "graduated" nuclear response, which required a central command—meaning effective U.S. control over the firing of nuclear weapons. U.S. efforts to promote the controversial MLF concept were pressed during 1963–64, but lapsed thereafter. NATO officially accepted the flexible response doctrine in 1967. U.S. adoption of flexible response involved strengthening both U.S. strategic programs, to provide an invulnerable second strike capacity in the form of underground and mobile missiles, and conventional forces equipped to deal with a wide variety of contingencies.

1961–62

LAOS. After the Geneva Conference of 1954 (p. 482), indigenous Communists (Pathet Lao) continued to harass the neutralist government. In the developing triangular struggle between neutralist, Pathet Lao, and rightist elements, the Eisenhower administration supported the latter which, led by Boun Oum, regained control of the government on 16 Dec. 1960. In early 1961 the Boun Oum government was under fire by the other 2 factions. President Kennedy chose to press for a compromise. At the reconvened Geneva Conference the U.S. proposed (17 May) a revised neutrality program for Laos, involving a cease-fire and formation of a coalition government. When matters in Laos reached a head (Apr.–May 1962) Kennedy ordered 5,000 U.S. troops to Thailand to underscore U.S. concern while at the same time increasing pressures on Boun Oum to accede to a tripartite coalition. The 3 Laotian factions agreed (11 June) on the formation of a coalition government, paving the way for the signing, on 23 July, by 14 participants in the Geneva Conference, of agreements guaranteeing the neutrality, territorial integrity, and independence of Laos and specifying procedures for the withdrawal from the country of all foreign forces.

1962

22 Oct.–20 Nov. CUBAN MISSILE CRISIS. The increasing flow of Soviet military and economic aid, evident since midsummer, prompted increasing pressures on the Kennedy administration to take some direct action against Cuba. A new treaty, under which Cuba was to receive from the U.S.S.R. arms and technicians "to resist the imperialists' threats," was announced 1 Sept. President Kennedy, acknowledging Soviet missile deliveries to Cuba, described the weapons as short-range and defensive in nature but warned (13 Sept.) that if Cuba became an offensive military base "of significant capacity for the Soviet Union" the U.S. would do "whatever

must be done" to protect its security. Congress, modeling S J Res 230 (3 Oct.) after Kennedy's statement of 13 Sept., declared U.S. determination to prevent, with arms if necessary, the Cuban regime from extending its subversive activities to other parts of the hemisphere or the establishment in Cuba of an externally supported military capability threatening U.S. security. First shown "hard" evidence on 16 Oct. that the U.S.S.R. was building missile bases in Cuba with offensive capabilities against the U.S., President Kennedy announced on 22 Oct. that U.S. policy demanded their withdrawal, imposed "a strict quarantine of all offensive military equipment under shipment to Cuba," warned the armed forces to be prepared for any eventuality, and reinforced U.S. forces at Guantanamo. Calling for emergency meetings of the OAS Council and the UN Security Council, Kennedy appealed to Premier Khrushchev to eliminate the "reckless and provocative threat to world peace." Having secured (23 Oct.) the endorsement of the OAS Council to take action under the Rio Treaty of Reciprocal Assistance, Kennedy ordered the quarantine to take effect 24 Oct. As the first Soviet ship stopped (25 Oct.) was carrying only oil, it was allowed to proceed. By that time several Soviet-bloc ships heading toward Cuba 22 Oct. had reversed course. On 26–27 Oct. Kennedy received 2 communications from Khrushchev: one proposing removal of the missiles in exchange for a U.S. guarantee against Cuban invasion, another proposing removal of the missiles in exchange for U.S. dismantling of missile bases in Turkey. Choosing to ignore the more formal, second note, Kennedy responded (27 Oct.) to the first, proposing removal of the U.S. quarantine and a guarantee against invasion of Cuba in exchange for the withdrawal of Soviet missiles under appropriate UN supervision. With Khrushchev's letter of 28 Oct., agreement was reached on these terms. President Kennedy announced (20 Nov.) that the missile bases had been dismantled and lifted the quarantine.

21 DEC. President Kennedy and British Prime Minister Macmillan, meeting in Nassau, agreed that the U.S. would supply Britain with Polaris missiles—to replace the recently cancelled British Skybolt missiles—for which the British would supply both nuclear warheads and submarines. The resulting British nuclear force was, along with a comparable U.S. force, to be assigned to a NATO nuclear force if and when such a force were established. After the Nassau Agreement was published it was transmitted to French President Charles de Gaulle with an accompanying memorandum containing a U.S. offer to sell Polaris missiles to France on the same terms. France rejected the offer. The Nassau Agreement, underlining Britain's "special relationship" with the U.S., exacerbated problems involved in British entry into the European Common Market (EEC).

1963

20 JUNE. "HOT LINE" agreement signed by the U.S. and U.S.S.R. in Geneva—a result of the Cuban missile crisis' demonstration of the need for a rapid communication line directly linking Moscow and Washington to avoid miscalculations during an emergency. Operative 30 Aug., the Hot Line was not used until the Six-Day War of 1967 (p. 506).

LIMITED NUCLEAR TEST BAN TREATY. Following a period of total stalemate, brought on by the Korean conflict and intensification of the Cold War, the UN Atomic Energy Commission (p. 466) merged with the UN Commission for Conventional Armaments (est. 13 Feb. 1947) to form (11 Jan.

1952) the UN Disarmament Commission. Thereafter disarmament talks were carried on in a variety of forums, most under the aegis of the UN, ranging in size from the full membership of the UN General Assembly to private talks of the U.S., U.S.S.R., and Britain. A 5-member (U.S., U.S.S.R., Britain, France, Canada) subcommittee of the UN Disarmament Commission, established 19 Apr. 1954 to conduct negotiations in private, separated from earlier package proposals for comprehensive disarmament certain partial, though usually interrelated, steps toward disarmament. Measures discussed in this context included: a nuclear test ban as a first step toward suspension of production of nuclear arms, establishment of inspection zones to guard against surprise attack, and agreed ceilings on conventional forces. These talks collapsed 6 Sept. 1957.

In the meantime, atomic weapons tests continued, accompanied by mounting fears of the dangers of atomic fallout and radioactive contamination. The detonation of an H-bomb "within the last few days," announced by the U.S.S.R. 20 Aug. 1953, was confirmed by the U.S. Atomic Energy Commission (AEC). The U.S. detonated its second H-bomb on 1 Mar. 1954 at Bikini Atoll in the Marshall Islands. The blast, in the megaton range, starkly revealed the peril of atomic fallout: of the 23 men on the Japanese fishing boat *Fukuryu Maru (Fortunate Dragon)*, which was 80 miles away from the explosion, 1 died and the others all suffered serious injury from the radioactive ash, several Japanese fishing vessels, many of which had not come within 1,000 miles of Bikini, brought in radioactively contaminated catches. Widespread fallout was also reported from the Soviet nuclear weapons test series begun in mid-Sept. 1954. The UN Scientific Committee on the Effects of Atomic Radiation reported (10 Aug.

1958) that, while the relative danger from fallout varied from region to region, "even the smallest amounts of radiation are liable to cause deleterious genetic, and perhaps also, somatic effects."

On 31 Mar. 1958 the U.S.S.R. announced suspension of nuclear testing, reserving the right to renew if other nations failed to follow suit. The U.S. conducted an extensive nuclear weapons test series in the Marshall Islands Apr.–July 1958 and tested smaller-magnitude weapons in Nevada until 31 Oct. The U.S. AEC reported (7 Nov.) that the U.S.S.R. had exploded nuclear devices 1 and 3 Nov. President Eisenhower declared that, while the Soviet tests relieved the U.S. of any obligation to refrain from testing, it would observe a voluntary suspension for the time being. A voluntary moratorium on atomic testing was observed by the U.S., U.S.S.R., and Britain (France began tests in 1960) until 1 Sept. 1961, when the U.S.S.R. resumed atmospheric nuclear testing. The U.S. announced (5 Sept. 1961) resumption of underground and laboratory nuclear tests (begun 15 Sept.) and 25 Apr.–4 Nov. 1962 the U.S. conducted atmospheric nuclear weapons tests in the Pacific.

The Conference of Experts to Study the Possibility of Detecting Violations of a Possible Agreement on Suspension of Nuclear Tests met 1 July–21 Aug. 1958 in Geneva. The U.S.S.R. accepted (30 Aug.) the report of the technical experts and previously (22 Aug.) the U.S. invitation to negotiate a test ban under international controls. The U.S., U.S.S.R., and Britain began test ban talks in Geneva 31 Oct. 1958, which continued intermittently until 29 Jan. 1962. On 14 Jan. 1963 the U.S. and the U.S.S.R. began private talks in New York on a test ban treaty with the use of automatic recording devices to monitor underground tests—a system requiring "very few" on-site inspections. Britain joined these talks (22 Jan.), but an impasse was reached and the talks ended 31 Jan. The U.S., Britain, and the U.S.S.R. announced 10 June that high-level talks would be held in Moscow in July to seek agreement on a nuclear test ban. Opening 15 July, the 3-Power discussions of an uninspected test ban led to the Limited Nuclear Test Ban Treaty, signed in Moscow 5 Aug. The signatories pledged not to conduct nuclear weapons tests in the atmosphere, in outer space, or under water but were permitted to continue underground testing. When ratified (80–19) by the Senate (24 Sept.), 99 nations had already subscribed to the treaty, which went into effect 10 Oct.

The Vietnam War

U.S. TROOP LEVELS IN VIETNAM 1960-72
(Source: Department of Defense)

U.S. troop levels as of 31 Dec. of each year:

1960	900	1967	485,600
1961	3,200	1968	536,100
1962	11,300	1969	475,200
1963	16,300	1970	334,600
1964	23,300	1971	156,800
1965	184,300	1972	24,200
1966	385,300		

1961–63. BROADENING OF U.S. COMMITMENT. While U.S. involvement in Vietnam dated back to the Truman administration (p. 462), and, as the French withdrew, the U.S. government began directly to support the anti-Communist Saigon regime (p. 481), the U.S. commitment expanded markedly in

1961. On 11 May President John F. Kennedy dispatched to Vietnam 400 Special Forces soldiers (counterinsurgency specialists) and 100 additional military advisers, and authorized a campaign of clandestine warfare against North Vietnam to be conducted by South Vietnamese personnel trained and directed by the CIA and some Special Forces personnel. It was decided in Nov. to enlarge greatly the U.S. military advisory mission in Vietnam and, for the first time, to assign U.S. forces to combat support missions. The latter decision led to U.S. involvement in actual fighting and an increase in American casualties—from 14 in 1961 to 489 in 1963.

During 1963 Buddhist demonstrations became the focus for widespread Vietnamese political opposition to the Diem regime. In a TV interview (2 Sept. 1963) President Kennedy criticized the Saigon government and observed that the U.S. could play only a supportive role in Vietnam: it was "their war" to win or lose. With tacit U.S. approval, a military coup was launched 1 Nov., leading to Diem's assassination and a succession of military coups. Immediately following the Diem coup Viet Cong (South Vietnamese Communists) activity increased.

The Johnson Years

7 AUG. 1964. TONKIN GULF RESO-LUTION. During the first 6 months of 1964, U.S. officials seriously considered and planned toward escalation of the war, focusing especially on initiation of bombing of North Vietnam. Major policy planners argued that a congressional resolution was needed before such action could be taken. On 1 Feb. Operation Plan 34A was inaugurated—a program of clandestine operations against North Vietnam significantly different from pre-viously covert operations: larger in scale and military in nature, controlled in Saigon by the U.S. Military Assistance Command. South Vietnamese naval commandos on a 34A mission raided, 31 July, 2 North Vietnamese islands, passing on their return the northbound U.S. destroyer *Maddox*. The *Maddox* was on a separate 34A mission, an intelligence-gathering patrol of the Gulf of Tonkin, but the North Vietnamese assumed it was part of the assault mission and, on 2 Aug., 3 North Vietnamese PT boats attacked her. On 3 Aug. 2 more 34A assaults took place and intelligence patrols were resumed by the *Maddox* and a companion ship, the *Turner Joy*. During the night of 4 Aug. the *Maddox* and *Turner Joy* radioed reports of combat—received in Washington, because of the time difference, starting at 9:20 A.M. Despite confusion as to whether an attack had actually taken place, President Lyndon B. Johnson informed congressional leaders (6:45 P.M.) that he had ordered reprisal air strikes against the North and would ask the next day for a congressional resolution. After brief hearings, in which the provocative nature of U.S. operations in the area was concealed, the Tonkin Gulf Resolution, declaring support for "the determination of the President, as Commander-in-Chief, to take all necessary measures to repel any armed attack against forces of the United States and to prevent further aggression," and affirming U.S. intentions to aid any member or protocol state of the SEATO pact "requesting assistance in the defense of its freedom," passed the House (414–0) and the Senate (88–2) on 7 Aug. Only Sens. Wayne Morse (Ore., 1900–74) and Ernest Gruening (Alas., 1887–1974) were opposed. Under Secretary of State Nicholas deB. Katzenbach testified before the Senate Foreign Relations Com-

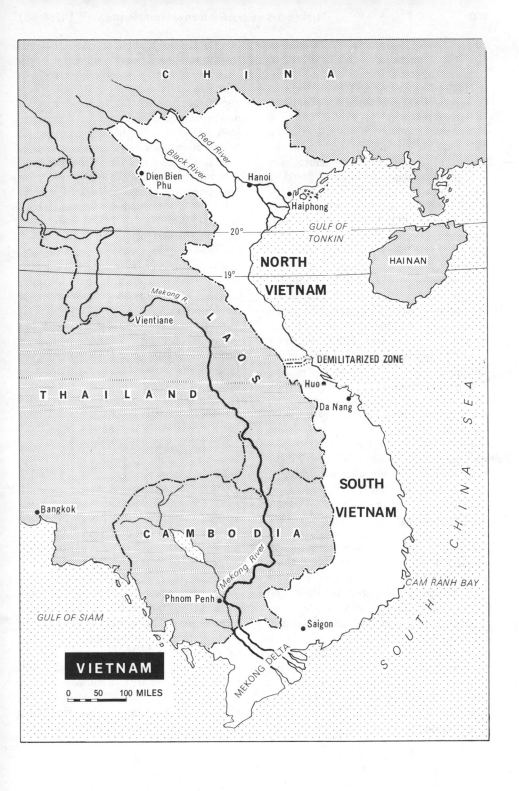

mittee (Apr. 1967) that the resolution was the "functional equivalent" of a "declaration of war."

1965–67. ESCALATION. A Viet Cong attack 7 Feb. on a U.S. military advisers' compound at **Pleiku,** killing 8 Americans, triggered a presidential decision which for months had been the subject of serious planning efforts. On 8 Feb. President Johnson ordered a heavy reprisal air strike against the North and on 13 Feb.–after a Viet Cong attack (11 Feb.) on U.S. barracks at Qui Nhon had evoked a similar U.S. reprisal–Johnson ordered sustained bombing of the North, begun on 2 Mar.

The buildup of formal U.S. military units began (8 Mar.) when 2 battalions of Marines landed at Da Nang. On 1 Apr. Johnson, recognizing that sustained bombing had failed to move Hanoi to negotiate, decided to increase both U.S. military support forces and Marine combat forces, and to permit use of U.S. ground troops for offensive actions. There was no public acknowledgment of the crucial change of mission until it was admitted by the State Department on 8 June. The 13–19 May U.S. bombing pause was, according to the authors of the *Pentagon Papers* (p. 537), used to deliver to Hanoi a "demand for their surrender"–but appeared to be a peaceful gesture the failure of which could justify subsequent escalation. In late May the Viet Cong summer offensive began and in June U.S. troops participated in their first major "search and destroy" mission–the typical operation of the war, which usually lacked established battle lines. President Johnson announced on 28 July his decision greatly to increase U.S. combat forces–the U.S. commitment to an Asian land war had been made. The first major confrontation between U.S. and North Vietnamese forces, in the Ia Drang Val-

ley (Oct.–Nov.), demonstrated that, although they took heavy losses, the North Vietnamese army could maneuver in hostile country despite U.S. helicopters and planes and led the U.S. commander in Vietnam, Gen. William C. Westmoreland (1919–   ), to request vast increases in manpower.

A week after Ho Chi Minh declared that acceptance of Hanoi's peace plan was necessary to end the war, the U.S., ending a 37-day pause, resumed bombing (31 Jan. 1966). The 8 Feb. communiqué issued after the 2-day Honolulu meeting of President Johnson and South Vietnamese Premier Nguyen Cao Ky affirmed U.S. commitments to South Vietnam and stressed a new plan of combining military progress and civil reform. In Apr. the U.S. began using B-52s for raids on North Vietnam and, in a major escalation of the air war, on 29 June began strikes against oil installations in the Hanoi and Haiphong area. President Johnson met Premier Ky and the heads of the 5 other nations participating in the war–South Korea, Thailand, Philippines, Australia, New Zealand–in Manila (24–25 Oct.), where joint determination was pledged and a 4-point "Declaration of Peace" was issued. Escalation of the air war continued as B-52 sorties in the North increased from 60 to 800 per month in Feb. 1967. Sorties were aimed at lines of communications as well as such fixed targets as bridges, rail yards, troop barracks, petroleum storage tanks, and, for the first time, urban power plants–one located 1 mile from the center of Hanoi. On 3 Aug. Johnson announced U.S. forces in Vietnam would be increased to 525,000 by June 1968 and requested a 10% income tax surcharge to finance the war –estimated (17 Jan. 1968) to be costing the U.S. $25 billion a year. In South Vietnam Nguyen Van Thieu was elected

(3 Sept. 1967) president—an office which the new constitution (effective 1 Apr.) granted sweeping powers.

1965–68. DOMESTIC DISSENT ESCALATES. While the Johnson administration stated that U.S. involvement in the Vietnam War was necessary to demonstrate that the U.S. kept its commitments, to halt Communist aggression, to assure the independence of South Vietnam, and to contain China; as U.S. participation in the war grew so did domestic opposition. In 1965–66 the war came under increasing congressional criticism from both "doves" who wanted to deescalate the war and "hawks" who wanted greater military effort. Sen. **J. William Fulbright** (p. 1034), a leading "dove," used televised hearings (Jan.–Feb. 1966) of the Senate Foreign Relations Committee to call attention to the weaknesses of U.S. policy. Public dissent expanded rapidly from university "teach-ins" (1965) to massive demonstrations, notably the antiwar parades (15 Apr. 1967) sponsored by the Spring Mobilization Committee (New York City crowds—estim. 125,000–350,000; San Francisco—approx. 50,000); and the march (21–22 Oct.) from the Lincoln Memorial to the Pentagon, where some 55,000 protesters were met by solid lines of troops with fixed bayonets. After Secretary of Defense Robert S. McNamara reported (14 Oct. 1966) to the president that neither the "pacification" program (the drive to extend the South Vietnamese government's control to the countryside) nor the air war against the North was succeeding, doubts began to erode the administration's basic internal consensus. Sen. **Eugene F. McCarthy** (Minn., 1916–   ), a major antiwar critic, announced (30 Nov. 1967) his candidacy for the Democratic presidential nomination. In 1968, while protest demonstrations were widespread, debate over the war became a major issue in the Democratic primaries (p. 533).

1968. TURNING POINT.

Tet Offensive. Ignoring the week-long truce proclaimed for Tet (Lunar New Year), Viet Cong and North Vietnamese forces launched, on 30 Jan., a major 3-pronged offensive directed against: Saigon and all major cities and most important towns; U.S. forces at Khesanh and other outlying outposts; the countryside evacuated by government troops drawn back to defend the cities. Heavy fighting continued in Saigon through 20 Feb., and Hue, captured by North Vietnamese forces 31 Jan., was not retaken by U.S. and South Vietnamese (ARVN) forces until 24 Feb., when over 80% of Vietnam's cultural and religious center had been reduced to rubble. The 76-day siege of Khesanh was lifted 5 Apr. In the ferocious fighting U.S. forces sustained record casualties, though far less than Communist losses. The Communists suffered a military defeat but they demonstrated they could move at will, devastate major population centers, and disrupt the pacification program. The Tet offensive raised questions about the capacity of U.S. military force to end the war. Gen. Westmoreland's request (27 Feb.) for 206,000 new troops (to raise U.S. forces in Vietnam to 731,000) roughly half before 1 May, required a major call-up of reserves, which until then had been avoided, and vastly increased expenditures. President Johnson's decision (13 Mar.) that, in addition to the 10,500-man reinforcement already made, 30,000 more soldiers (reservists) would be sent to Vietnam, signaled an upper limit to the U.S. military commitment.

Peace Moves. Previously during the Johnson administration, U.S. bombing pauses, temporary truces, public and secret efforts by the U.S., other nations, and organizations—all had failed to bring about negotiations. President Johnson announced on 31 Mar., a unilateral halt of all U.S. air and naval bombardment of the North except in the area adjacent to the DMZ (effectively, up to the 20th parallel), and called upon Hanoi, which had indicated that a cessation of U.S. bombing was a precondition for peace talks, to begin negotiations. Hanoi agreed (3 Apr.) to the opening of a conference in Paris. On 7 Apr. bombing was stopped above the 19th parallel. Preliminary peace talks between the U.S. and North Vietnam began (10 May) in Paris. President Johnson announced (31 Oct.) U.S. cessation of "all air, naval and artillery bombardment of North Vietnam" as of 1 Nov. On 16 Jan. 1969 agreement was reached on the physical arrangements for expanded peace talks—to include the National Liberation Front (Viet Cong) and the Saigon regime.

The Nixon-Ford-Kissinger Years

1969. On 23 Feb. Communist forces launched a new general offensive in which U.S. troops—in Mar. at their peak level of the war, 541,500—took heavy casualties. President Richard M. Nixon secretly authorized intensive bombing raids over Cambodia (begun Mar.) to hinder Communist operations in Vietnam. After meeting (8 June) with President Thieu on Midway Island, Nixon announced the first U.S. troop withdrawal —25,000 men to leave Vietnam by the end of Aug. In a TV speech (3 Nov.) Nixon explained his administration's plan for the gradual withdrawal of all U.S. combat forces from Vietnam on a flexible timetable related to: (1) progress of the **"Vietnamization"** program— the intensified U.S. effort, launched in Mar., to train and equip South Vietnamese forces to assume major combat responsibilities; (2) progress in the Paris

negotiations; and (3) levels of enemy activity.

Massive antiwar demonstrations resumed: millions, in cities and towns across the country, participated in "Moratorium Day" demonstrations on 15 Oct. and more than 250,000 gathered in Washington on 15 Nov. for a "March against Death."

16 Nov. My Lai Massacre first reported in the press. U.S. infantrymen gunned down (16 Mar. 1968) at least 450 unarmed South Vietnamese civilians —women, children, and old men. Lt. William L. Calley, Jr. was court-martialed (24 Nov.) and convicted, Mar. 1971, for premeditated murder of at least 22 Vietnamese civilians.

3 Sept. Ho Chi Minh died and control of North Vietnam was assumed by a group of Communist party leaders.

1970. On 18 Mar. Prince Norodom Sihanouk, Cambodia's neutralist chief of state, was overthrown by pro-West Lon Nol, who, alarmed by movements of Communist forces, appealed to President Nixon for extensive military supplies. Nixon announced 30 Apr. the **Cambodian Incursion**—a joint U.S.–South Vietnamese attack against Communist border sanctuaries in Cambodia, justified as "indispensable" for success of the U.S. troop withdrawal program in the context of the situation in Cambodia. Large caches of supplies were taken in the operation, which involved 32,000 U.S. and 48,000 ARVN troops and ended 30 June, but, alerted by military activities prior to 30 Apr., the Communists had already withdrawn most of their forces and some supplies from the sanctuaries. The operation spurred expansion of Communist-controlled areas in Cambodia.

May. Cambodia–Kent State Dissent. Demonstrations opposing the Cambodian Incursion took place on college campuses throughout the nation. Protests intensified after National Guardsmen shot to death (4 May) 4 students on the campus of Kent State Univ. (Kent, Ohio) during an antiwar demonstration and 2 students were killed by state police at Jackson State College, Miss. (14 May). A demonstration (9 May) attracted 60,000–100,000 to Washington. An intensive antiwar lobbying campaign focused on Congress. Counterdemonstrations by construction workers ("hard hats") occurred in New York City (8 May).

31 Dec. Congress repealed the **Tonkin Gulf Resolution** (p. 498) in a foreign military sales bill signed (13 Jan. 1971) by President Nixon, who did not view the resolution as necessary to justify U.S. involvement. Lengthy senatorial debate of measures to limit or end U.S. military involvement in Indochina (1969–72) demonstrated growing disillusionment with the war but, by approving each year the various defense and supplementary Vietnam appropriations, Congress set no effective limits on U.S. actions.

1971. On 8 Feb. the ARVN, with U.S. air support, launched a major drive into **Laos** aimed at North Vietnamese supply bases along the Ho Chi Minh trail, the main infiltration route into South Vietnam. The operation ended 24 Mar., earlier than projected, as the South Vietnamese took heavy losses. The operation fanned concern over a widening of the war. The heavily censored transcript of a Senate foreign relations subcommittee investigation (released 20 Apr. 1970) indicated the growth of U.S. involvement in Laos since the Geneva Agreements of 1962 (p. 495). Those activities brought to light included: covert military assistance of the Royal Laotian government in its war in northern Laos against Pathet Lao and North Vietnamese forces and the shift, after the cessation (1 Nov. 1968) of bomb-

ing North Vietnam, of U.S. air strikes to targets in Laos—both in the north and along the Ho Chi Minh trail in the southeast.

June. Publication of the **Pentagon Papers** (p. 537) helped further erode confidence in the government's conduct of the war.

3 Oct. President Nguyen Van Thieu was reelected in a controversial 1-man election in South Vietnam.

1972–73. ENDING OF AMERICAN INVOLVEMENT. On 25 Jan. 1972 President Nixon revealed that his National Security Adviser Henry A. Kissinger (p. 1077) had, since 4 Aug. 1969, held 12 secret negotiating sessions in Paris with Le Duc Tho, a member of Hanoi's Politburo, and/or Xuan Thuy, Hanoi's chief delegate to the formal Paris peace talks; disclosed the U.S. settlement proposal privately presented to Hanoi on 11 Oct. 1971; and accused Hanoi of refusing to continue the secret sessions which, unlike the formal talks, had "until recently . . . showed signs of yielding some progress." North Vietnamese troops launched a major offensive across the DMZ and from the west on 30 Mar. 1972. The U.S. provided heavy air support for the ARVN and resumed intensive bombing of the North —on 16 Apr. raiding Haiphong and Hanoi for the first time since 1968—as North Vietnamese troops advanced, gaining control of Quang Tri province by 2 May. On 8 May Nixon announced that to prevent delivery of war supplies to North Vietnam he had ordered: (1) the mining of Haiphong Harbor and all other North Vietnamese ports (mines to be activated 11 May); (2) a blockade of North Vietnam; (3) intensified bombing of rail and other lines of communication; and (4) continuation of air and naval strikes against military targets in the North. Cessation of these actions was linked to acceptance of a cease-fire and release of American prisoners of war (POWs) but, significantly, not to North Vietnamese withdrawal from the South. Despite continuing success of the North Vietnamese offensive, U.S. troop withdrawals continued—the last U.S. combat units left South Vietnam 13 Aug. Intensive U.S. air operations continued in both North and South and by the fall Communist military fortunes were beginning to decline. A breakthrough in peace negotiations occurred during private Kissinger–Le Duc Tho meetings 8–11 Oct. Kissinger met with President Thieu in Saigon (19–23 Oct.), unsuccessfully attempting to persuade him to accept the draft settlement upon which the U.S. and Hanoi were close to final agreement. President Nixon ordered (23 Oct.) a temporary halt of all bombing north of the 20th parallel. On 26 Oct. Kissinger announced that the U.S. and Hanoi were in substantial agreement on the 9-point settlement disclosed earlier the same day in a Hanoi broadcast. By the end of Nov. emergency deliveries to South Vietnam of some $1 billion of military equipment were completed. Private discussions between Kissinger and Le Duc Tho (20–25 Nov. and 4–14 Dec.) recessed with no final agreement reached. On 18 Dec. the U.S. resumed bombing attacks above the 20th parallel, including round-the-clock B-52 raids in the Hanoi-Haiphong area—the heaviest bombing of North Vietnam of the war. The White House announced 30 Dec. cessation of bombing north of the 20th parallel and resumption (8 Jan. 1973) of Kissinger–Le Duc Tho discussions. Negotiations concluded 13 Jan. and on 27 Jan. in Paris the U.S., North Vietnam, South Vietnam, and the Viet Cong's Provisional Revolutionary Government signed a 4-party "Agreement on Ending the War and Restoring Peace in Vietnam." In the afternoon the U.S. and North Vietnam signed the 2-party version of the agreement, acknowledging the Provisional Revolutionary Government. The agreement *inter alia* provided for: release of all American POWs; withdrawal from South Vietnam of all U.S. forces and military personnel within 60 days; a cease-fire in status quo effective 27 Jan. to be supervised by a 4-nation International Commission of Control and Supervision; an end to foreign military activities in Laos and Cambodia and cessation of the use of the territory of either for military operations directed at Vietnam; receipt of military replacement aid and unlimited economic aid by the Saigon regime; formation of a tripartite National Council of National Reconciliation and Concord composed equally of members named by the Saigon regime and the Viet Cong, to promote implementation of the agreement and national reconciliation, and to organize elections in South Vietnam. By 29 Mar. 587 American POWs had been released and 23,500 U.S. troops withdrawn from South Vietnam.

1973–75. THE FALL OF SOUTH VIETNAM. The fragility of the Paris accords was revealed as the Control Commission was unable to prevent the continuation of hostilities and acrimonious disagreements blocked formation of the National Council of National Reconciliation and Concord. The number of North Vietnamese troops in the South increased. The Thieu government continued to receive substantial U.S. military (fiscal years 1973–74: $3,179.2 million) and economic aid. Two years of attacks by Communist and ARVN forces produced no major changes in territory.

The collapse of the Saigon regime began with the fall (9 Jan. 1975) of Phuoc Binh, capital of Phuoc Long Province. The capture (13 Mar.) of Ban Me Thuot (capital of Darlac Province) in the central highlands, 160 miles north of Saigon, prompted President Thieu to order a withdrawal of all forces from Pleiku and Kontum, bastions of the northern highlands, and a retirement to the coast of forces farther north. In the ensuing hasty retreat, which precipitated panic and refugee flights, Hue (26 Mar.), Da Nang (31 Mar.), and the coastal regions as far as the approaches to Saigon were abandoned. After fighting for 2 weeks at Xuan Loc, 40 miles east of Saigon, ARVN troops withdrew on 22 Apr. The Viet Cong announced their capture of the huge air base at Bien Hoa, 15 miles northeast of Saigon on 30 Apr.

On 21 Apr., in a speech carried on radio and TV, in which he accused the U.S. of breaking its promises of support and blamed the military debacle on U.S. cuts in aid, President Thieu resigned. Vice President Tran Van Huong took over, but on 27 Apr., with the concurrence of the National Assembly, he named General Duong Van Minh to become president and end the war. On 28 Apr. President Gerald Ford ordered the emergency helicopter evacuation of all Americans remaining in South Vietnam. U.S. helicopters removed (29 Apr.) approx. 1,000 Americans and 5,500 Vietnamese. (During the last 2 weeks of the war approx. 120,000 Vietnamese fled and were taken to the U.S.) On 30 Apr. President Minh announced the unconditional surrender of the Saigon government to the Provisional Revolutionary Government of South Vietnam.

1973–75. FALL OF CAMBODIA. By the time U.S. bombing in Cambodia ceased (p. 511), the Communist-led Khmer Rouge insurgents claimed approx. 90% of Cambodia's territory. Assisted by U.S. military (fiscal years 1973–74: approx. $519.3 million) and economic aid, the Lon Nol forces held until 1975, when Khmer Rouge forces blockaded the Mekong River, cut off all land access to Phnom-Penh and began closing in on the capital. Premier Lon Nol and his family left Cambodia on 1 Apr. and, Phnom-Penh's airport having been overrun, remaining U.S. citizens and American embassy personnel were evacuated (11 Apr.) by helicopter. On 17 Apr. the Phnom-Penh government surrendered to the Khmer Rouge forces.

MILITARY CASUALTIES (from 1 Jan. 1961)	KILLED	WOUNDED
United States	46,079	303,640
South Vietnam	184,546	495,931
Communist	927,124	unavailable
CIVILIAN CASUALTIES		
South Vietnam	451,000	935,000
REFUGEES		
South Vietnam		over 6.5 million
Cambodia		over 2 million
Laos		over 1 million
North Vietnam		unavailable

Foreign Policy: The Johnson Years, 1964–68

1965

DOMINICAN REPUBLIC INTERVENTION. A popular revolt, headed by civilian supporters of Juan Bosch (a liberal deposed by a military coup, 25 Sept. 1963) and some junior military officers, broke out 24 Apr. against the conservative, military-backed, civilian government of Donald Reid Cabral. Following Reid Cabral's resignation (25 Apr.), conflict between the military and the rebels escalated. On 27 Apr. President Johnson announced he had ordered the evacuation of U.S. citizens from Santo Domingo. A contingent of 400 U.S. marines landed (28 Apr.) and, as the result of decisions taken that day, heavy reinforcements of U.S. troops followed immediately, reaching by 17 May a total of 22,000. On 2 May President Johnson justified the U.S. military intervention on the ground that a popular revolution had been "taken over" by a "band of Communist conspirators." According to the **"Johnson Doctrine"** then enunciated, domestic revolution in the Western Hemisphere ceases to be of purely local concern when "the object is the establishment of a Communist dictatorship." U.S. action was widely criticized in the U.S. and Latin America both on grounds of the slim evidence of Communist involvement in the rebellion and because the U.S. had, contrary to key provisions of the constituent documents of the OAS (the Rio Treaty of Reciprocal Assistance and the Charter of Bogotá), acted unilaterally. The Council of the OAS was first convened on the Dominican Republic situation the evening of 28 Apr. and U.S. efforts to "internationalize" its intervention resulted in an OAS resolution (6 May) authorizing creation of an Inter-American Peace Force (IAPF). The IAPF (established 23 May and composed primarily of U.S. troops, joined by small contingents from Brazil, Costa Rica, El Salvador, Honduras, and Nicaragua) remained in the Dominican Republic until 22 Sept. 1966. The state of civil war ended with the establishment of a U.S.-supported provisional government (31 Aug. 1965) which conducted free elections (1 Mar. 1966), in which Joaquin Balaguer, a supposed moderate who had served as premier during the dictatorial regime of Rafael Trujillo, was elected president.

1967

16 MAR. U.S.–SOVIET CONSULAR TREATY ratified (66–28) by the Senate. Signed 1 June 1964, the consular convention was the first bilateral treaty between the U.S. and U.S.S.R. since 1917. Detailing the legal framework and procedures for the operation of consulates in each country, it contained 2 key provisions, novel to such conventions, assuring full diplomatic immunity to all consular officials and employees of each country and prompt notification of detainment of a citizen of either country and access to him by his own consular authorities. Because of Vietnam the Johnson administration did not press for ratification until 1967. Approval of the pact, despite Vietnam War tensions, was the first legislative endorsement of the administration's policy of "building bridges" to the U.S.S.R. and Eastern Europe. President Johnson signed the convention 21 Mar. and the U.S.S.R. ratified it 26 Apr. 1968.

25 APR. OUTER SPACE TREATY unanimously approved by the Senate. Besides establishing general principles for the peaceful international exploration of outer space (including the moon and other celestial bodies), the treaty banned weapons of mass destruction, weapons tests, and military bases in outer space; suspended claims of national ownership or sovereignty in outer space; and established measures for the protection of astronauts. The treaty was signed 27 Jan. 1967 by the U.S., U.S.S.R., Britain, and 57 other countries.

5–10 JUNE. SIX-DAY WAR. War broke out between Israel and the Arab states as Israel reacted to removal of the UN peace-keeping force, at Egypt's request, to Arab troop movements, and to the closure of the Gulf of Aqaba to Israeli ships. Administration spokesmen indicated (5 June) that the U.S. was "neutral," in the sense of not being a belligerent, but this was "not an expression of indifference." The same day the U.S. 6th Fleet was put on alert and 2 aircraft carriers and other vessels moved east from Crete. Soviet Premier Aleksei N. Kosygin used the Hot Line (5 June) to inform the U.S. that the U.S.S.R. did not intend to intervene unless the U.S. did. By 10 June, when all parties had responded to the cease-fire called for (6 June) by the UN Security Council, Israel had driven 12 miles into Syria, seizing the Golan Heights; taken all of Egypt's Sinai peninsula and Gaza strip; and captured from Jordan the Old City of Jerusalem and all Jordanian territory adjoining Israel west of the Jordan River. Soviet efforts to have the UN Security Council and, later in June, the UN General Assembly adopt resolutions condemning Israel as an aggressor and ordering its withdrawal from all captured territories were rejected by the U.S. and failed to be adopted.

After the Six-Day War France, Israel's main supplier of jet aircraft, imposed an embargo on all arms sales to Middle East combatants, blocking delivery to Israel of 50 Mirages on order and already paid for. The U.S.S.R. decided immediately to reequip the devastated Arab air forces. Israel sought a new supplier of sophisticated combat aircraft and for the first time a U.S. administration was faced with the choice of either supplying Israel with aircraft or accepting at home the political responsibility for allowing Israel to lose military superiority. Israel had previously obtained U.S. surface-to-air Hawk antiaircraft missiles in 1962, Patton tanks in 1965, and, early in 1966, agreement was reached for the first sale of U.S. combat aircraft to Israel 48 A-4 Skyhawks (light fighter-bombers), to be delivered in 1968. After the Six-Day War the U.S. became Israel's chief supplier of sophisticated weaponry. The sale to Israel of 50 Phantom F-4s (supersonic jet fighter-

bombers) was announced 27 Dec. 1968.

23–25 June. GLASSBORO CONFERENCE. President Lyndon B. Johnson and Soviet Premier Aleksei N. Kosygin met at the end of Kosygin's visit to the UN to present Soviet views on the Middle East crisis to the General Assembly. The impromptu "summit" held at Glassboro State College, N.J., a site midway between New York City and Washington, had nebulous results.

1968

23 Jan. "PUEBLO" SEIZURE. The 906-ton U.S. Navy intelligence-gathering ship which, according to U.S. officials, was in international waters 25 miles off North Korea was captured, along with its 83-man crew, by North Korea. North Korean officials contended that the "armed spy ship" had "intruded way into" their territorial waters. After the failure of initial U.S. diplomatic efforts to recover the *Pueblo* and its crew, President Johnson ordered (25 Jan.) the call-up of some 14,000 men in Air Force and Navy Air Reserve and Air National Guard. At that time U.S. military forces stationed in South Korea numbered approximately 56,000. U.S. and North Korean negotiators discussed the *Pueblo* incident at Panmunjom throughout the year. On 22 Dec. North Korea released the 82 surviving crew members and returned the body of the 83rd, who had died during the ship's capture, but retained possession of the ship. A North Korean draft statement assigning guilt in the incident to the U.S. was signed by a U.S. military officer, although U.S. officials rejected its "official" character, deeming it an expedient to secure release of the crewmen.

Foreign Policy: The Nixon-Kissinger Years, 1969–74

1969

13 Mar. NUCLEAR NONPROLIF-ERATION TREATY ratified (83–15) by the Senate. The product of more than 4 years of negotiations at the 18-Nation Disarmament Conference in Geneva, the treaty was signed (1 July 1968) by the U.S., U.S.S.R., and 60 other nations (not including France or the People's Republic of China) and submitted (9 July) to the Senate, but ratification was delayed in reaction to the Soviet invasion (20–21 Aug.) of Czechoslovakia. The treaty banned the spread of nuclear weapons (nuclear-weapons states pledged not to transfer them to non-nuclear states and states not possessing nuclear weapons pledged not to receive such devices); established safeguard procedures; and insured nondiscriminatory access to nuclear energy for peaceful uses. On 24 Nov. 1969 the treaty was signed by both President Nixon and Soviet President Nikolai V. Podgorny.

21 Nov. REVERSION OF OKINAWA TO JAPANESE ADMINISTRATION announced. Six months of intensive negotiations culminated in Premier Eisaku Sato's visit (19–21 Nov.) to Washington and the announcement that by the end of 1972 administration of the Okinawa (Ryukyu) and Bonin Islands would revert to Japan. Under the terms of the arrangement agreed upon, the provisions of the 1960 U.S.-Japan security pact (p. 490) would extend to U.S. bases on Okinawa. Both parties agreed on the need to retain extensive U.S. military facilities—a $2 billion complex, covering about 110 square miles

had been established—on Okinawa but in response to Japanese antinuclear sentiments the U.S. agreed to remove its nuclear weapons prior to reversion and to reintroduce them only after prior consultation with the Japanese government, as the 1960 pact provided. Prior to the reversion, completed 15 May 1972, Okinawa was the only U.S. base in Asia of which the U.S. had entirely free use.

1971

3 Sept. BERLIN ACCORD signed by envoys of the U.S., U.S.S.R., Britain, and France, the first such settlement since the end of World War II. Endorsed by both Germanys, the accord, designed to improve communications between sections of the divided city and between West Germany and Berlin, became part of a comprehensive Berlin agreement signed 3 June 1972 in Berlin by the foreign ministers of the 4 Powers. The 1972 Berlin agreement, while not changing the city's legal status, recognized the existence of separate East and West German nations. On 4 Sept. 1974 the U.S. and East Germany established formal diplomatic relations.

1972

15 Feb. SEABED ARMS TREATY ratified (83–0) by the Senate. Prohibiting deployment of nuclear weapons on the ocean floor outside the 12-mile territorial limit, but not applicable to submarines anchored or resting on the seabed, the treaty had already been signed by 85 other nations, including the

U.S.S.R. and Britain, but not France or the People's Republic of China.

21–28 FEB. NIXON'S VISIT TO CHINA. After a week of private conferences, public banquets, and sightseeing tours, President Richard M. Nixon, the first U.S. President to visit China, and Premier Chou En-lai issued (27 Feb.) a joint communiqué indicating agreement on the need for increased contacts between the 2 nations. In the most controversial segment of the communiqué, the U.S. accepted Peking's contention that Taiwan was part of China, conceded that Taiwan's fate should be decided by the Chinese, and pledged ultimate withdrawal of U.S. military forces from Taiwan. In the same document the People's Republic of China claimed sovereignty over Taiwan and asserted that settlement of the Taiwan question was crucial to normal relations with the U.S. Nixon's visit, given heavy live coverage on U.S. television, dramatically marked the momentous change in U.S.-China policy set in motion by the Nixon administration. This reversal in policy had been foreshadowed in 1969 when, unilaterally and unconditionally, the U.S.: eased travel and trade restrictions (21 July), suspended the regular 2-destroyer patrol (7th Fleet) of the Taiwan Straits (Nov.), lifted the $100 limit on purchases of Chinese goods, and permitted foreign subsidiaries of U.S. companies to trade in nonstrategic goods with mainland China (19 Dec.). After a 2-year lapse, U.S.-Chinese ambassadorial talks in Warsaw, the only official contacts between the 2 countries since 1955, resumed (20 Jan. 1970). The termination of all restrictions on the use of U.S. passports for travel to the People's Republic of China (15 Mar. 1971) and the lifting of the 20-year-old total embargo on U.S. trade with Communist China (14 Apr.) coincided with a Chinese invitation (6 Apr.) to the U.S. table tennis team to visit the mainland and their warm reception (14 Apr.) by Premier Chou En-lai in Peking. Following the secret meeting in Peking (9–11 July) between Chou En-lai and Dr. Henry Kissinger, Presidential Assistant for National Security Affairs, President Nixon announced (15 July) he would visit China before May 1972 "to seek normalization of relations between the two countries" and to exchange views on questions of mutual concern.

In a policy shift signaled (2 Aug. 1971) by Secretary of State **William P. Rogers** (1913–   ), the U.S. submitted (27 Sept.) a resolution to the UN General Assembly recommending that the Peking regime represent China in the Security Council while noting that Taiwan had a continued right to representation in the General Assembly. Despite U.S. efforts on behalf of the "2 China" policy, after a week of intense UN debate the General Assembly on 25 Oct. voted (76–35 with 17 abstentions) to admit Peking, seat it in the Security Council, and expel Taiwan from all UN bodies. The general thrust of U.S. China policy and the timing of Dr. Kissinger's second visit to Peking (20–26 Oct.) undercut the U.S. position in the UN.

The U.S. and China announced, 22 Feb. 1973, that they would set up liaison offices, not having embassy or mission status but with full diplomatic immunity, in each other's capitals. The U.S. office in Peking opened officially with the arrival (14 May) of veteran diplomat **David K. E. Bruce** (1898–   ).

22–30 MAY. MOSCOW SUMMIT. Richard M. Nixon, the first U.S. president to visit Moscow, returned to Washington (1 June) with 7 agreements he had signed with Soviet leaders, providing for: (1) the prevention of incidents between vessels and aircraft of the U.S. and Soviet navies at sea and in the air space over it; (2) cooperation in the fields of science and technology; (3) cooperation in health research; (4) cooperation in environmental protection; (5) cooperation in the exploration of outer space, with a joint-docking experiment contemplated for 1975; (6) the development of commercial and economic relations; and (7) arms control. Although the Johnson administration had begun to explore with the U.S.S.R. the possibility of some sort of freeze on strategic nuclear delivery systems, real progress on the question did not begin until the preliminary U.S.-U.S.S.R. **Strategic Arms Limitation Talks (SALT)** in Helsinki 17 Nov.–22 Dec. 1969. These established the framework for the full-scale SALT negotiations which opened 16 Apr. 1970 in Vienna and led to the 2 agreements signed in Moscow. The accords were based on 3 premises: (1) because the development of offensive weapons systems was markedly more advanced than that of defensive weapons systems, a freeze on both offensive and defensive systems would leave each side vulnerable to a first strike; (2) each side was confident that it could survive a first strike with sufficient capacity to destroy the other; and (3) the threat of nuclear obliteration—the "balance of terror" that had prevailed for a quarter century—was an adequate deterrent to all-out war. Signed in Moscow were: (1) a treaty limiting the deployment of antiballistic missile systems

(ABMs) to 2 for each country—one to protect the capital and one to protect an ICBM field; and (2) an executive agreement, to run for 5 years, limiting the number of offensive weapons to those already under construction or deployed. The Senate (88–2) ratified the ABM treaty (3 Aug.). The overwhelming majority reflected in part the reluctance with which the Senate had approved construction of the Safeguard ABM system to be located in North Dakota (key vote 6 Aug. 1969, when an amendment to block work on Safeguard was defeated 50–50). The offensive arms agreement did not require congressional action but was submitted (13 June) to both houses in the form of a resolution. After adopting amendments which, while not affecting the accord itself, indicated the uneasiness of Senate hard-liners, Congress completed action 25 Sept.

At Moscow U.S. and Soviet leaders professed a shared belief that the 2 nations should develop closer commercial and economic ties. The first major result was the Soviet agreement to buy at least $750 million in American grains over a 3-year period (p. 708).

13 July. $42.5 million were appropriated to the State Department for use by the president to help other nations and international organizations control narcotics traffic. The bulk of the funds was used for payments to Turkish farmers for ceasing opium poppy production and for enforcement of that effort. By the summer of 1974 the Turks had resumed opium poppy production.

1973

15 Feb. U.S.–CUBA ANTI-HIJACK PACT signed by Secretary of State William P. Rogers and Foreign Minister Raúl Roa. In the 5-year "memorandum of understanding" to curb hijacking of

OPERATIONAL U.S. AND SOVIET MISSILES

	1965 (Mid-Year)	1970 (Projected, End of Year)
Intercontinental Ballistic Missiles (ICBMs)		
U.S.	934	1,054
U.S.S.R.	224	1,290
Submarine Launched Ballistic Missiles		
U.S.	464	656
U.S.S.R.	107	300

aircraft and ships between the 2 countries, each agreed either to try hijackers for the offense or to extradite them. U.S. officials asserted that the agreement did not foreshadow improved U.S.-Cuba relations.

17–25 June. BREZHNEV-NIXON SUMMIT II. Leonid I. Brezhnev, Secretary General of the Soviet Communist Party, repaid President Nixon's 1972 visit to Moscow. After his stay in Washington, where he met also with members of Congress and business executives, Brezhnev spent 2 days at the president's home in San Clemente, Calif. While several agreements were signed during the week, the main significance of the visit was symbolic: to demonstrate that the 2 superpowers had moved from a period of peaceful coexistence to one of détente. In addition to a declaration of principles intended to accelerate SALT and an agreement pledging each nation to avoid actions which could provoke a nuclear confrontation, the 2 leaders signed pacts initiating or extending cooperation in various scientific, cultural, and commercial fields.

CAMBODIA. Reacting against heavy U.S. bombing of Cambodia, where hostilities (p. 505) continued, Congress passed a $3.3 billion supplemental appropriations bill including an immediate cutoff of funds for the Cambodia bombing (vetoed 27 June by President Nixon). A compromise was reached when President Nixon assured Congress (29 June) that U.S. military activity in Cambodia would cease by 15 Aug. Legislation stipulating an end to all combat activities in Indochina by 15 Aug. was signed by the president, 1 July.

YOM KIPPUR WAR. War broke out 6 Oct. when Egyptian and Syrian troops crossed into Israeli-occupied territory in the Sinai peninsula and the Golan Heights. The U.S. announced 15 Oct. that it was resupplying Israel with military equipment to counterbalance the U.S.S.R.'s "massive airlift" to Egypt. On 17 Oct. 11 Arab oil-producing nations agreed to reduce their production and export of crude oil by 5% and to embargo its sale to nations deemed friendly to Israel. Saudi Arabia announced (20 Oct.) it was halting all oil supplies to the U.S. and all other Arab Persian Gulf producers followed suit (21 Oct.). A UN Security Council resolution (22 Oct.) calling for a cease-fire was accepted by Israel and Egypt (22 Oct.) and by Syria (24 Oct.), although sporadic fighting continued. What appeared to be a near confrontation between the U.S. and the U.S.S.R. was averted 25 Oct. when, reportedly in response to a Soviet threat unilaterally to move troops into the Middle East to supervise the truce, U.S. armed forces were placed on a worldwide alert in the early morning hours as a "precautionary" measure and, that afternoon, the U.S.S.R. agreed to creation of a UN peacekeeping force (UNEF) in which no big power would participate. On 7 Nov. Secretary of State Henry Kissinger met with Egyptian President Anwar el-Sadat in Cairo and the 2 countries announced that diplomatic relations, broken off during the Six-Day War of June 1967, would be resumed (resumption 28 Feb. 1974). A 6-point cease-fire agreement worked out by Kissinger was signed 11 Nov. by Egypt and Israel, leading to an exchange of prisoners of war and the lifting of the Israeli sieges of the city of Suez and of the Egyptian 3d Army, which after crossing the Suez Canal had had its supply lines broken by Israeli forces. The diplomatic efforts of Secretary of State Kissinger also led to the inauguration (21 Dec.) of Middle East peace talks in Geneva—participants including the U.S., U.S.S.R., and the UN. An Egyptian-Israeli accord (signed 18 Jan. 1974) providing for a mutual disengagement and pullback of forces along the Suez Canal and the establishment of a UNEF buffer zone was negotiated through the mediation of Kissinger, who shuttled (11–17 Jan.) between meetings with Egyptian and Israeli officials. On 18 Mar. 7 of 9 Arab oil-producing countries (all but Libya and Syria) agreed in Vienna to lift the embargo against the U.S.—an action explained as a response to a U.S. policy shift away from Israel.

1974

28 APR.–31 MAY. KISSINGER'S MIDDLE EAST "SHUTTLE" DIPLOMACY. Traveling back and forth between Middle Eastern capitals, Secretary of State Kissinger promoted a cease-fire and complex troop disengagement agreement between Israel and Syria, whose forces had regularly engaged in artillery duels on the Golan Heights since the end of the Yom Kippur War. The accords were signed (31 May) by Israeli and Syrian representatives in Geneva.

12–18 JUNE. NIXON'S MIDDLE EAST TOUR, including visits to Egypt, Saudi Arabia, Syria, Israel, and Jordan, symbolized recent changes in U.S. policy in the area and the success of Secretary of State Kissinger's efforts to bring greater stability to the region.

27 JUNE–3 JULY. NIXON–BREZHNEV SUMMIT III indicated the commitment of the 2 superpowers to détente. Only 2 minor accords on arms control were signed, underscoring the failure of SALT to produce agreement on terms limiting offensive nuclear arms. Several accords were signed promoting closer cooperation in technological and commercial areas.

DOMESTIC ISSUES AND NATIONAL POLITICS FROM TRUMAN TO NIXON, 1945-74

★ ★
★

The postwar years brought Americans a continuing succession of problems. The nation's mood ran the gamut of hysterical suspicion, political apathy, bitter disillusionment, and exacerbated social and political divisiveness. The end of World War II, with its special problems of economic readjustment, was quickly followed by the Cold War, which on the domestic front fed a paranoiac search for traitors within. If the 1950s proved a time of complacency and political apathy, with such pressing problems as race relations largely deferred, the Thousand Days of Kennedy brought renewed vitality to the national government, a mood brutally shattered in Dallas. Although the U.S. attained its greatest degree of prosperity in the mid- and late 1960s, and achieved as well a series of notable reforms, both political and social, the Vietnam War cruelly divided the nation. Its conduct raised disturbing doubts about the credibility of the government and contributed to that revolution in mores and values which was sweeping the Western world. The Nixon administration assumed office in 1969 with the professed intention of "bringing us together," but a combination of misdirected leadership, double-digit inflation, and a cluster of high-level scandals revealed its incapacity to achieve its goals.

1945

WARTIME AGENCIES abolished by executive order included the Office of Censorship, Office of War Information, the Foreign Economic Administration, and War Production Board.

6 SEPT. RECOVERY PROGRAM recommended to Congress by President Truman consisted of 21 points, among them legislation toward full employment,

an increase in the minimum wage, construction of 1–1.5 million homes annually, and a single federal research agency.

28 SEPT. TRUMAN PROCLAMATION asserted authority over the subsoil and seabed of the Continental Shelf (confirmed by international Convention on the Continental Shelf, 29 Apr. 1951).

19 Nov. COMPREHENSIVE MEDICAL INSURANCE proposed by President Truman in message to Congress.

1946

1946–53 ANTI-INFLATION MEAS-URES. On 31 Dec. 1945 the National War Labor Board was abolished and replaced by the Wage Stabilization Board (WSB), which in turn was replaced (29 July 1952) by a new board with circumscribed powers. On 21 Feb. 1946 the Office of Economic Stabilization was established by executive order. **Chester Bowles** (1901–   ) was named director. Price control ended 30 June after President Truman vetoed a new measure, but was revived in modified form 25 July. On 15 Oct. meat price controls were ended and all other price and wage controls save on rents, sugar, and rice terminated 9 Nov. On 26 July 1948 Truman urged a special session of Congress to enact an inflation-control program calling for revival of excess profits taxes, priorities, and rationing. On 16 Aug. the **Anti-Inflation Act,** a compromise bill became law; on 17 Aug. the Board of Governors of the Federal Reserve System ordered curbs on installment buying. The **Defense Production Act of 1950** (8 Sept.) gave the president broad economic powers, including authority to stabilize wages and prices. On 21 Dec. **Charles E. Wilson** (1886–1961) was named director of the newly established Office of Economic Stabilization (26 Jan. 1951). On 30 June 1952 a compromise 1-year extension of the Defense Production Act with economic controls weakened was signed by Truman. Last price controls ended 17 Mar. 1953.

20 FEB. EMPLOYMENT ACT OF 1946 required the president to submit an annual economic report, created a 3-member Council of Economic Advisers to assist the president, a Joint Economic Committee of the Congress, and declared the continuing policy of the federal government to promote maximum em-ployment, production, and purchasing power. The act did not endorse deficit spending and deliberately unbalanced budgets, but it was clear that this instrument of economic policy would be adopted.

2 AUG. LEGISLATIVE REORGANIZATION ACT cut the number of standing committees from 48 to 19 in the House, from 33 to 15 in the Senate, and required regular meetings and records. The act provided for an annual legislative budget to complement the presidential budget and established the Legislative Reference Service as a special branch of the Library of Congress to provide Congress with information bearing on legislation. Title III, the **Federal Regulation of Lobbying Act,** required lobbyists to register and report their lobbying expenses. The legislative budget was abandoned in 1949. The elimination of standing committees led to proliferation of subcommittees of the Congress.

5 Nov. CONGRESSIONAL ELECTIONS were marked by Republican victories, picking up 13 Senate seats, 56 House seats, thereby controlling the entire Congress for the first time in 14 years.

21 MAR. LOYALTY PROGRAM established by Executive Order 9835 required the investigation of all government employees and all applicants for government jobs.

23 JUNE. TAFT-HARTLEY ACT, passed by Congress over President Truman's veto of 20 June: (1) banned the closed shop, which forbade the hiring of nonunion men; (2) permitted employers to sue unions for broken contracts or damages inflicted during strikes; (3) established a Federal Mediation and Conciliation Service, and required employers to submit a 60 day notice ("cooling-off" period) for termination of contract; (4) authorized the U.S. government to obtain injunctions imposing a cooling-off period of 80 days on any strike imperilling the national health or safety; (5) required unions to make public their financial statements; (6) forbade union contributions to political campaigns; (7) ended the "check-off system," in which the employer collected union dues; (8) required union leaders to take an oath that they were not members of the Communist party. The act was amended 22 Oct. 1951 to permit union-shop contracts without first polling employees.

7 JULY. HOOVER COMMISSION. Commission on Organization of the Executive Branch of the government was established with Herbert Hoover as chairman. The final reports (1949) proved influential: 116 of 273 recommendations were fully accepted, 35 mostly accepted, 45 partially accepted.

18 JULY. PRESIDENTIAL SUCCESSION ACT revised the law of 1886 and made the speaker of the House first and the president *pro tempore* of the Senate second in line of succession of president and vice-president, followed by the Secretary of State and other cabinet members according to rank.

26 JULY. NATIONAL SECURITY ACT coordinated the army, navy, and air force into a single national military establishment under the **Secretary of Defense** with cabinet status. Act also established a **National Security Council** and under it the **Central Intelligence Agency** (CIA) to correlate and evaluate intelligence activity relating to national security. Agency was denied internal security functions. Directors: Rear Adm. Roscoe Hillenkoeter (1947–50), Gen. Walter Bedell Smith (1950–53), Allen W. Dulles (1953–61), John A. McCone (1961–65), William A. Radford (1965–66), Richard Helms (1966–72), James R. Schlesinger (1973), William E. Colby (1973–   ).

1948

24 JUNE. SELECTIVE SERVICE ACT, passed after earlier act expired 31 Mar. 1947, provided for registration of all men between 18 and 25, with induction restricted to those between 19 and 25, for 21 months' service. On 30 June 1950 the draft was extended by law to 9 July 1951 and the president authorized to call out the National Guard and organized reserves for 21 months' active service. The draft was further extended (19 June 1951) to 1 July 1955 and the draft age lowered to 18½, paving the way for possible institution of universal military training.

30 JULY. EQUALITY IN THE ARMED SERVICES ordered by President Truman, following congressional failure to include ban in Selective Service Act of 1948. Truman established the President's Committee on Equality of Treatment and Opportunity in the Armed Services, whose report, *Freedom to Serve* (1950), coupled with the exigencies of the Korean War, largely wiped out segregation and discrimination in the armed forces. The report, *To Secure these Rights* (1947), of the President's Committee on Civil Rights, established by executive order (5 Dec. 1946), led to Truman message to Congress (2 Feb. 1948) recommending permanent civil rights commission, congressional committee on civil rights, a civil rights division of the Justice Department, federal antilynching law, a permanent FEPC, laws against discrimination in interstate transportation, and laws for protection of the right to vote. Truman banned discrimination in hiring of federal employees by executive order (26 July 1948) and established the Committee on Government Contract Compliance to effectuate nondiscrimination clauses in government contracts (3 Dec. 1951).

3 Aug. HISS CASE. Whittaker Chambers, admitted former Communist courier, testified at hearing of the House Un-American Activities Committee that Alger Hiss had been a member of the prewar Communist apparatus in Washington. A slander suit brought by Hiss against his accuser led to the production by Chambers of State Department classified documents or copies thereof allegedly turned over to him by Hiss. Rep. **Richard M. Nixon** (p. 1115) of the House Committee charged (6 Dec.) that the administration was more interested in concealing "embarrassing facts than in finding out who stole the documents." On 15 Dec. Hiss was indicted on 2 counts of perjury by a federal grand jury in New York. His first trial ended 8 July 1949 in a hung jury; he was found guilty at his second trial and sentenced (17 Nov.) to 5 years in prison.

PRESIDENTIAL CAMPAIGN. The Republican National Convention met at Philadelphia (21 June) and on 24 June nominated Gov. **Thomas E. Dewey** (N.Y.) for president and Gov. **Earl Warren** (Calif., p. 1077) for vice-president. The Democratic National Convention met at Philadelphia (12 July) and on 15 July renominated President **Harry S. Truman** and chose Sen. **Alben W. Barkley** (Ky., p. 979) for vice-president. Several Southern delegations walked out of the convention in protest against the strong civil rights plank and nominated Gov. **J. Strom Thurmond** (S.C.) for president on a States' Rights ("Dixiecrat") ticket. Other minor-party presidential candidates: Henry A. Wallace (N.Y.), Progressive; Norman Thomas (N.Y.), Socialist; Claude A. Watson (Calif.), National Prohibition; Edward A. Teichert (Pa.), Socialist Labor. Truman conducted his campaign against the "do-nothing" 80th Congress, which he called back into session (26 July). He rallied support on a 31,000-mile "whistle-stop"

barnstorming campaign to overcome divisions within his party and a large early Dewey lead.

2 Nov. PRESIDENTIAL ELECTION. Popular vote: **Truman,** 24,105,812; Dewey, 21,970,065; Thurmond, 1,169,-063; Wallace, 1,157,172; Thomas, 139,-414; Watson, 103,224; Teichert, 29,244; Dobbs, 13,613. Electoral vote: **Truman** 303; Dewey 189; Thurmond 39. The Democrats regained control of Congress, securing a majority of 12 in the Senate and 93 in the House.

1949

17 Jan. The trial began of 11 top leaders of the U.S. Communist party on charges of violating the Smith Act of 1940. They were convicted 14 Oct. and sentenced 21 Oct. to prison terms. Their conviction was affirmed by the Supreme Court in 1951 (*Dennis* v. *U.S.*, p. 679).

19 Jan. The president's salary was increased by act of Congress to $100,000 with a tax-free expense allowance of $50,000; salaries of vice-president and speaker of the House raised to $30,000.

20 June. REORGANIZATION ACT authorized the president to reorganize the executive branch of the government subject to veto by a majority of the full membership of either the House or Senate. In 1957 the act was amended to provide that plans could be vetoed by simple majority of either house. Act expired (1 June 1959), was reinstated early in 1961, and expired 1 June 1963.

10 Aug. NATIONAL SECURITY ACT renamed the National Military Establishment of the Department of Defense and reorganized it. A nonvoting chairman of the Joint Chiefs of Staff was set up, to which post President Truman named Gen. Omar N. Bradley (p. 991).

26 Oct. MINIMUM WAGE raised from 40 cts. to 75 cts. effective Jan. 1950.

1950

9 FEB. Sen. Joseph R. McCarthy (p. 1091) charged in a speech at Wheeling, W. Va., that 205 Communists (later revised to 57) were working in the State Department. McCarthy's charges gained wide public attention and led to investigation by special subcommittee of Senate Foreign Relations Committee, whose report (20 July) found the charges false.

7 MAR. Judith Coplon and Valentin Gubitchev, a Soviet consular official, were found guilty of conspiracy and attempted espionage against the U.S. Gubitchev was expelled from the U.S.

KEFAUVER INVESTIGATIONS. The Senate Special Committee to Investigate Interstate Crime, headed by Sen. Estes Kefauver (Tenn., 1903–62), attracted nationwide attention (1950–51) when its hearings were televised.

TRUMAN ADMINISTRATION CORRUPTION. Evidence of corruption among federal officials occurred during probe of Investigations Subcommittee of Senate Committee on Expenditures in the executive departments (Aug. 1949), where testimony suggested that officials were securing government contracts in return for a 5% commission ("five-percenters"). Truman aide Maj. Gen. Harry Vaughan admitted to accepting gift of a deep freeze (13 Aug. 1949). Secretary of the Treasury Snyder demanded the resignation of James P. Finnegan, St. Louis Collector of Internal Revenue (Aug. 1950), Finnegan finally resigning 24 Apr. 1951. On 31 July 1951 George J. Schoeneman, Commissioner of Internal Revenue, resigned. Collectors of Internal Revenue at Boston, San Francisco, and Brooklyn were removed along with 31 other Revenue Bureau officials as well as T. Lamar Caudle, Assistant Attorney General in charge of the Justice Department's Tax Division, and Charles Oliphant, chief counsel of the Revenue Bureau. President Truman appointed Newbold Morris (N.Y.) to investigate corruption among federal officials (1 Feb. 1952) but Morris was removed by Attorney General J. Howard McGrath (3 Apr.), who in turn was replaced (4 Apr.) by James P. McGranery.

28 AUG. SOCIAL SECURITY AMENDMENTS raised wage base to $3,600 per year with new payroll tax schedule, increased benefits approximately 70%, eased eligibility requirements for the aged, and extended system to bring in some 9.2 million workers—self-employed, domestic, agricultural, and in state and local government. Social security benefits were raised slightly in 1952.

23 SEPT. INTERNAL SECURITY ACT OF 1950 (McCARRAN ACT), passed over President Truman's veto, provided for registration of Communist and Communist-front organizations, and for the internment of Communists during national emergencies, and prohibited employment of Communists in national defense work. The act prohibited from entry into the U.S. anyone who had been a member of a totalitarian organization; but by amendment, 28 Mar. 1951, anyone who was under 16 when forced into such a group, or who joined to maintain his livelihood was not banned for that reason alone.

1 Nov. ASSASSINATION ATTEMPT. Two Puerto Rican Nationalists, Oscar Collazo and Griselio Torresola, attempted to assassinate President Truman at Blair House, Washington, D.C. Torresola was killed instantly; Collazo was tried and sentenced to death for the killing of a guard, but on 24 July 1952, the same day that Truman signed an act enlarging the self-government of Puerto Rico, he commuted the sentence to life imprisonment.

7 Nov. MIDTERM ELECTIONS. After a campaign during which a major issue was "softness on Communism,"

Republicans made wide gains in congressional and state elections, increasing their representation by 5 seats in the Senate and 28 in the House. The Democrats, however, maintained control of both houses.

29 DEC. CELLER-KEFAUVER ACT OF 1950 amended Section 7 of Clayton Act to prohibit corporate acquisitions where the effect may be to substantially lessen competition, thus granting power to cope with monopolistic tendencies in their incipiency.

1951

26 FEB. 22ND AMENDMENT made 2 terms the maximum for the presidency and barred election for more than 1 term of a person who held that office for more than 2 years of a term to which some other person was elected. The amendment did not apply to President Truman.

1952

8 APR. STEEL SEIZURE. President Truman seized steel mills to avoid strike by steel workers. After Supreme Court ruled the seizure unconstitutional (2 June; *Youngstown Sheet and Tube* v. *Sawyer,* p. 679), Truman returned mills to owners. Ensuing strike was settled with wage and price increases (24 July).

30 JUNE. McCARRAN-WALTER ACT codifying immigration laws (p. 658).

16 JULY. KOREAN GI BILL OF RIGHTS provided veterans with educational benefits, mustering-out pay, housing, business and home-loan guarantees, similar to those given to World War II veterans.

PRESIDENTIAL CAMPAIGN. The Republican National Convention convened at Chicago (7–11 July). Preceding the convention the National Committee ruled on disputed credentials of delegates from the Southern states, awarding most of the delegates from the crucial states of Georgia, Louisiana, Mississippi, and Texas to Sen. **Robert A. Taft** despite the claims of Gen. **Dwight D. Eisenhower,** whose backers carried the fight to the floor of the convention. In an initial test of strength the Eisenhower forces (658–548) secured adoption of a rule barring disputed delegates from voting on contested seats until their own credentials had been decided. Thereafter the convention sustained Eisenhower delegates in Georgia and Texas, and the General was the victor over Taft on the 1st ballot as a result of switch by Minnesota from Harold E. Stassen to Eisenhower. Vice-Presidential nominee was Sen. **Richard M. Nixon** (Calif.). The Republican platform attacked the stands of the Truman administration on China and Korea, advocated a balanced budget, reduced national debt, "progressive tax relief," retention of the Taft-Hartley Act, and federal legislation in the matter of discriminatory employment practices while conceding the right of "each state to order and control its own domestic institutions."

On 30 Mar. President Truman announced: "I shall *not* be a candidate for reelection," leaving the race for a Democratic nominee wide open for the first time since 1932. At the Democratic National Convention at Chicago (21–26 July) Gov. **Adlai E. Stevenson** (Ill., p. 1158), Truman's own choice, was nominated on the 3d ballot after trailing Sen. Estes Kefauver on the first 2. Stevenson, who did not seek the nomination, was the first presidential nominee to be drafted since Garfield (1880). A Southern bolt failed to develop after the convention permitted delegations from Virginia, South Carolina, and Louisiana to vote despite their refusal to take an oath to support the party's candidates. Sen. **John J. Sparkman** (Ala.) was nominated for vice-president. The platform endorsed the domestic and foreign policy of the New and Fair Deals; advocated repeal of the Taft-Hartley Act and federal legislation to secure civil rights.

Minor-party candidates: Progressive (and American Labor): Vincent W. Hallinan; Socialist Worker, Farrell Dobbs; Socialist, Darlington Hoopes; Christian Nationalist (in 5 states) and Constitution (2 states), Gen. Douglas MacArthur; Prohibition, Stuart Hamblen.

After disclosures that Sen. Nixon had been the beneficiary of a secret fund from California businessmen, Nixon defended his conduct in the emotional and effective "Checkers" speech on TV (23 Sept.). Eisenhower announced the following day that Nixon would remain on the ticket.

Eisenhower announced (24 Oct.) that he would make a personal trip to Korea after the election to try to facilitate the end of the war. He visited Korea 2–5 Dec.

4 Nov. PRESIDENTIAL ELECTION. Gen. **Eisenhower** scored a sweeping personal victory, with 442 electoral votes to Stevenson's 89. The Republican candidate carried 4 Southern states: Tennessee, Virginia, Florida, and Texas. Both candidates received the highest popular vote for a winner and loser respectively in U.S. history: Eisenhower, 33.9 million; Stevenson, 27.3 million; Hallinan, 140,-123; Hoopes, 20,203; Dobbs, 10,312; Hamblen, 72,949; MacArthur, 17,205. The Republicans captured both houses by a slim majority: Senate, 48 Rep., 47 Dem., 1 Ind. (Wayne L. Morse, Ore.).

1953

7 Jan. BRICKER AMENDMENT. An amendment to the Constitution to limit the scope of international treaties to which the U.S. could be a party and to impose novel controls on the power of the president to negotiate treaties and executive agreements was proposed by Sen. John W. Bricker (Ohio). The amendment was opposed on 6 Apr. by Secretary of State John Foster Dulles as "dangerous to our peace and security." After extended debate the Senate (26 Feb. 1954) rejected the amendment, 60–31, one vote short of the two-thirds majority required.

25 Mar. McCARTHY ALLEGATIONS that Charles E. Bohlen, nominated ambassador to the U.S.S.R., ought to be disqualified from that position because of his close association with the foreign policies of F.D.R. and Truman did not succeed in blocking Bohlen, who was confirmed by the Senate 74–13 (27 Mar. 1953). McCarthy, chairman of the Senate Permanent Investigating Subcommittee of the Government Operations Committee, conducted (1953–54) a long series of hearings, public and secret, on the role of Communism in government and in other areas of American life. During the same period the Senate Internal Security Subcommittee under Sen. William Jenner (Ind.) investigated Communism in education, and the House Un-American Activities Committee, under the chairmanship of Rep. Harold R. Velde (Ill.), looked into Communist activities in the entertainment field. On 4 Feb. 1954 McCarthy set off on a Lincoln Week speech-making tour, whose theme, he announced, was the Democratic party's "twenty years of treason." McCarthy's tactics were denounced by President Eisenhower, who on 14 June 1953 assailed "the book burners," on 23 Nov. 1953 asserted the right of everybody to meet his "accuser face to face," and on 31 May 1954 attacked "demagogues thirsty for personal power and public notice."

After McCarthy's investigation (Dec. 1953–Jan. 1954) of alleged subversion in the Signal Corps Engineering Laboratories at Ft. Monmouth, N.J., the McCarthy subcommittee, with McCarthy appearing as a party rather than a member, held hearings on a controversy between Army Secretary Robert T. Stevens and 2 associates, and McCarthy and 2 aides. At issue were Army charges that McCarthy had attempted to secure preferential treatment for a former consultant, Private G. David Schine, and McCarthy charged that the army had tried to pressure him into calling off his Ft. Monmouth investigation; 35 days of televised hearings (22 Apr.–17 June) featured McCarthy and special army counsel Joseph N. Welch. McCarthy's attack (9 June) on a member of Welch's Boston law firm, Hale and Dorr, produced Welch's emotional reply, "Little did I dream you could be so reckless and so cruel as to do an injury to that lad. . . . Have you left no sense of decency?" The majority report of the 7-man subcommittee largely exonerated McCarthy from charges of "improper influence," although the 3 Democrats disagreed, and 1 Republican stated that he was convinced the principal accusation of each side was borne out.

On 2 Aug. the Senate established a select committee to study charges against McCarthy, with Sen. Arthur V. Watkins (Utah) as chairman. On 2 Dec. the Senate "condemned" by a vote of 67–22 McCarthy for contemptuous conduct toward the Senate Subcommittee on Privileges and Elections and for abuse of the Select Committee.

11 APR. DEPARTMENT OF HEALTH, EDUCATION, AND WELFARE was created to take over functions of Federal Security Agency, by means of a presidential reorganization plan and a joint resolution of the Congress making it effective 10 days after presidential signature. Mrs. Oveta Culp

Hobby was sworn in as first Secretary (11 Apr.).

22 MAY. SUBMERGED LANDS ACT (p. 640).

19 JUNE. ROSENBERGS EXECUTED in Sing Sing Prison. Klaus Fuchs, a German-born physicist, was sentenced 1 Mar. 1950 by a British court to a 14-year term in prison after being convicted of atomic espionage for the Soviet Union. His trial was followed by the arrest in the U.S. of his confederate, Harry Gold, sentenced to 30 years in prison (9 Dec. 1950), and by the trial and conviction (29 Mar. 1951) for atomic espionage of Julius and Ethel Rosenberg, who were sentenced to death, and of Morton Sobell, to a 30-year term.

1954

11 JAN. REPUBLICAN FARM PROGRAM. President Eisenhower in a message to Congress proposed to replace rigid, mandatory farm price supports with flexible supports based on "modernized parity" instead of the "old" parity (the 1910–14 relationship between prices farmers received for their products and prices they paid for the articles they bought). The bill finally enacted by Congress substituted 82½–90% of parity for rigid 90% props for wheat, cotton, rice, and peanuts; 75–90% for dairy products instead of prevailing 75% level; and gave the Department of Agriculture authority to barter surplus crops to foreign nations for strategic goods. Eisenhower signed the bill 28 Aug.

1 MAR. 5 Congressmen were shot on the floor of the House of Representatives by Puerto Rican nationalists; all recovered.

1 APR. AIR FORCE ACADEMY. President Eisenhower signed a bill authorizing the establishment of an Air Force Academy, similar to West Point and

Annapolis; first class sworn in at Lowry Air Force Base, Denver, Colo., 11 July 1955, and academy moved 1958 to permanent site near Colorado Springs.

13 MAY. ST. LAWRENCE SEAWAY (p. 483).

17 MAY. *BROWN* v. *BOARD OF EDUCATION OF TOPEKA* (347 U.S. 483) reversed *Plessy* v. *Ferguson* (1896), with its "separate but equal" doctrine. In 1950 *McLaurin* v. *Okla. State Regents* (339 U.S. 637) and *Sweatt* v. *Painter* (339 U.S. 629) had struck down state laws for the higher or professional education of Negroes as failing to meet the requirements of equality. In the Brown case, involving elementary education, the Supreme Court (Earl Warren, Chief Justice) held unanimously that segregation in public education was a denial of the equal protection of the laws. The court (349 U.S. 294, 1955) directed the lower courts to admit Negroes to public schools on a racially nondiscriminatory basis "with all deliberate speed." Reactions ranged from compliance in some border states to hostile gestures toward the court. In response to the desegregation decisions of the Supreme Court, White Citizens' Councils, originating in Mississippi, 1954, spread to much of the South. This prosegregationist movement used economic pressures against proponents of desegregation, including mortgage foreclosures, withdrawal of credit, job dismissals, and business boycotts. On 19 Jan. 1956, the Alabama Senate passed a "nullification" resolution; the Virginia legislature adopted (1 Feb.) an "interposition" resolution asserting the right of the state to "interpose its sovereignty" against the decision of the court. On 11 Mar., 19 U.S. senators and 81 representatives issued a **"Southern Manifesto"** declaring their purpose to use "all lawful means" to reverse the desegregation decision. Spearheading the drive for de-

segregation was the National Association for the Advancement of Colored People (NAACP) with a membership of some 310,000 in 1956.

29 JUNE. OPPENHEIMER CASE. Atomic Energy Commission upheld by vote of 4–1 the decision of a 3-man review board (1 June), which had voted 2–1, refusing to reinstate the security clearance of **J. Robert Oppenheimer** (p. 1119), wartime head of Los Alamos atomic laboratory.

2 AUG. HOUSING LEGISLATION. The Housing Act of 1954 authorized the construction over a 1-year period of 35,-000 houses to serve families displaced by programs of urban redevelopment, slum clearance, or urban renewal, increased the amount of the maximum mortgage on both sale and rental housing, lowered down payments, and lengthened amortization periods. Provisions were included to curb future abuses under FHA operations as a result of disclosures of irregularities in the administration of the FHA home-loan insurance program. An additional 45,000 public housing units for the next 2 years were authorized by the Housing Act of 1955 (11 Aug.). The Housing Act of 1957 (12 July) raised maximum permissible mortgage amounts in a number of FHA programs and cut required cash payments. As a result of the increase under the act of existing $900-million capital-grant authorization for urban renewal by another $350 million, urban renewal programs were sharply stepped up. The Housing Act of 1958 (1 Apr.) further liberalized minimum down payments and increased the funds available for home mortgages. Another housing bill providing $650 million for slum clearance and urban renewal was signed by President Eisenhower on 24 Sept. 1959 after his veto of 2 other bills had been sustained. A stopgap housing bill extending the FHA loan improvement program 1 year was signed 14 Sept. 1960.

16 Aug. INTERNAL REVENUE CODE OF 1954, a major tax reform, permitted (1) dividend credit and exclusion; (2) retirement income credit; (3) accelerated depreciation; (4) deductions for medical expenses; and (5) increased the maximum charitable deduction.

24 Aug. COMMUNIST CONTROL ACT deprived the Communist party of rights, privileges, and immunities, subjected Communists to penalties under the Internal Security Act, and provided that Communist-infiltrated organizations lose their rights under the National Labor Relations Act. On 11 Oct. the Civil Service Commission reported that 2,611 security risks had been dismissed from federal positions in the period 28 May 1953–30 June 1954, and 4,315 other civilian employees had resigned before determination was completed about "unfavorable" information in their files.

30 Aug. ATOMIC ENERGY ACT permitted private power companies to own reactors for production of electric power, to own nuclear materials, and to obtain patents on their own atomic inventions, which had to be shared with others for 5 years. In addition, the law authorized the release of certain information on atomic weapons to European allies and the sharing of information on the peaceful use of atomic energy with friendly nations.

1 Sept. SOCIAL SECURITY ACT AMENDMENTS raised benefits, raised the wage base to $4,200, created a new tax schedule, and added approximately 7.5 million workers to the program's coverage, largely self-employed farmers. Further Social Security amendments during the Eisenhower administration include those of 1 Aug. 1956, lowering the minimum age for benefits to women to 62, creating disability insurance for

those 50–64 years of age who were permanently disabled, and slightly extending program's coverage; 28 Aug. 1958, increasing benefits and wage base to $4,800, and providing a new tax schedule; 13 Sept. 1960, eliminating the minimum age of 50 years for disability coverage.

2 Nov. CONGRESSIONAL ELECTIONS. Election marked by controversial role of Vice-President Nixon, who charged that Democrats were unfit to govern because of their record on Communism. Democrats narrowly regained control of Congress, with a 29-seat margin in the House, and a 1-seat margin in the Senate. The Democrats won 19 of the 36 gubernatorial contests, including the Maine election (13 Sept.) of Edmund S. Muskie.

1955

30 June. SECOND HOOVER COMMISSION on Organization of the Executive Branch of the Government (created 10 July 1953) filed final report with Congress with basic theme, "get government out of business."

11 July. DIXON-YATES CONTRACT. On 5 Oct. 1954 the AEC approved a contract under which the Middle South Utilities, Inc., and the Southern Co. (Dixon-Yates group) were to build a generating plant at West Memphis to feed power into the TVA system to supply Memphis, Tenn. The contract was an issue during the congressional elections of 1954, when the Democrats raised the cry of "Nixon, Dixon and Yates." In Feb. 1955 the Joint Congressional Atomic Energy Committee disclosed that Adolph H. Wenzell, Bureau of the Budget consultant, had participated in the Dixon-Yates negotiations, although he was also vice-president of the First Boston Corp., Dixon-Yates' financial agent. Following an announcement that the city of Memphis had voted to build its own steam-generating plant, the contract was canceled by President Eisenhower 11 July. Generating capacity of TVA system rose from 2.9 million kilowatts (1950) to 11.3 million kilowatts (1960). On 15 Nov. 1960, TVA sold publicly an initial issue of $50 million bonds to be secured by net power revenues. TVA's expansion brought steam-generating projects of great magnitude, accounting in 1960 for 10% of all power production by the nation's utility systems, and servicing an area of 80,000 square miles in 7 states.

4 Aug. HELL'S CANYON. Proponents of public power were unable to secure passage in 1955 and 1957 of a bill providing for a single high federal dam at Hell's Canyon in the Snake River, about 100 miles below Weiser, Ida. The Federal Power Commission awarded, 4 Aug. 1955, a license to the Idaho Power Co. to build 3 small dams.

24 Sept. EISENHOWER'S ILLNESSES. President Eisenhower suffered a coronary thrombosis in the early hours of 24 Sept. on vacation in Colorado. He entered Fitzsimons Army Hospital near Denver, began to resume limited official activities 30 Sept., and returned East in Nov. On 10 June 1957 the president was seized by an attack of ileitis, was operated upon for removal of part of the intestinal tract, and entered a period of convalescence. In his 2d term he suffered a slight stroke on 25 Nov. 1957.

1 Dec. MONTGOMERY BUS BOYCOTT. A boycott by blacks of buses in Montgomery, Ala., began when Mrs. Rosa Parks, a 43-year-old seamstress, refused to relinquish her seat to white man. Mrs. Parks was arrested and fined $10 (5 Dec.). Under the leadership of Rev. Dr. **Martin Luther King, Jr.** (p. 1076) the boycott resulted in the bus company's loss of 65% of its normal income. Following a Supreme Court decision of 13 Nov.

1956 the boycott was ended and unsegregated bus service began (21 Dec.).

1956

17 Feb. NATURAL GAS BILL VETO. President Eisenhower vetoed bill to exempt independent producers of natural gas from federal utility rate control after Sen. Francis Case (S.D.) revealed he had been offered $2,500 campaign contribution by the oil interests.

11 Apr. UPPER COLORADO PROJECT (p. 641).

29 June. HIGHWAY ACT (p. 617).

PRESIDENTIAL CAMPAIGN. The Democratic National Convention convened at Chicago (13–17 Aug.). **Adlai E. Stevenson** was nominated on the 1st ballot with 905½ votes to 200 for Gov. Averell Harriman of N. Y., supported by ex-President Truman. Prior to the balloting Sen. **Estes Kefauver** (Tenn.) withdrew his name and asked his 200 delegates to support Stevenson. Sen. Kefauver was named for second place on the ticket, defeating Sen. John F. Kennedy (Mass.) by a narrow margin. The Republican National Convention, opening in San Francisco on 20 Aug., renominated **Dwight D. Eisenhower** and **Richard M. Nixon.**

Platform differences were not sharp. The Democrats asserted the right of all citizens to "equal opportunities for education"; the Republicans declared their approval of the Superior Court decision that segregation must be "progressively eliminated." The Democrats favored public as opposed to private development of water power; the Republicans advocated partnership among federal agencies, the states, and private enterprise. The Democrats supported 90–100% parity payments to farmers; the Republicans, the flexible parity payments.

In the ensuing campaign Stevenson proposed an international ban on the testing of H-bombs. Late in Oct. Marshal Bulganin impliedly endorsed Stevenson's position and was rebuked by Eisenhower. The latter stages of the campaign were marked by serious international crises in the Middle East and Hungary (p. 487).

6 Nov. PRESIDENTIAL ELECTION. Eisenhower scored a personal victory but the Republican party lost ground in Congress. Eisenhower secured a landslide electoral vote of 457–73, and a popular vote of 35,590,472 to 26,029,752 for Stevenson. Minor-party vote: T. Coleman Andrews (Constitution), 107,929; Enoch A. Holtwick (Prohibition) 41,973, Eric Haas (Socialist Labor), 44,300; Darlington Hoopes (Socialist), 1,763. One Democratic elector in Alabama voted for Walter P. Jones. The Democrats carried both the House, 232–199, and the Senate, 49–47, presaging 4 years of divided rule in Washington.

1957

21 Aug. NIAGARA POWER ACT authorized N.Y. State Power Authority to build a $532 million power project at Niagara Falls, N.Y. The Niagara project was put into operation in 1961. By 1963, the Niagara plant was the nation's second greatest hydroelectric generating plant, trailing only the Grand Coulee Dam on the Columbia River.

30 Aug. JENCKS ACT. In response to the decision in *Jencks* v. *U.S.* (353 U.S. 675; 1957), which had given the defendant in a federal trial the right to see all evidence in government files, new law provided that only material in FBI files relating to the subject of a witness' testimony at a trial might be produced in court after his direct examination.

9 Sept. CIVIL RIGHTS ACT OF 1957, first civil rights legislation since Reconstruction, established a 6-man Civil Rights Commission and a Civil Rights Division in the Department of Justice. Although an 1866 Civil Rights Law giving the president power to use troops to enforce civil rights laws was repealed, the new act prohibited attempts to intimidate or prevent persons from voting, and authorized the attorney general to seek injunctions in district court if a person was deprived of his right to vote. The longest personal senatorial filibuster on record, 24 hours 18 minutes, by Sen. J. Strom Thurmond (S.C.) on 28–29 Aug. failed to stop passage of the law.

24 Sept. LITTLE ROCK. Sporadic violence broke out in 1956 at such places as the Univ. of Ala., Mansfield, Tex., and Clinton, Tenn., when Negro students sought admission to all-white schools. In 1957, with the start of the fall term, the school integration issue erupted at Little Rock, Ark. A federal district judge nullified a state court injunction forbidding the school board to start integration beginning with the upper grades of high school. Gov. Orval E. Faubus on the eve of the school opening called out the National Guard to maintain order, although not a single case of interracial violence had been reported to the police. As a result the 9 Negro students were prevented from entering the high school. Despite a meeting of Gov. Faubus with President Eisenhower at Newport 14 Sept., the governor did not withdraw the troops until the federal court issued an injunction barring him from obstructing the Negro students' entry. Rioting broke out on 23 Sept. after the National Guard was withdrawn. On 24 Sept. the president dispatched 1,000 U.S. paratroopers of the 101st Airborne Division to Little Rock and put the Arkansas National Guard under federal command. The Negroes entered the guarded school 25 Sept. Gradually the troops were reduced. Elsewhere in the South integration made slow progress. A start was made in Sept. in North Carolina at Charlotte, Greensboro, and Winston-Salem, but in the lower South there was massive resistance. Of the border states, West Virginia, Maryland, Missouri, and Oklahoma had made the most progress by the fall of 1957; Kentucky, Delaware, Arkansas, and Tennessee the least. Token integration, begun in New Orleans schools 14 Nov. 1960, sparked rioting and heavy absenteeism. On 1 Dec. the U.S. Circuit Court of Appeals declared unconstitutional a series of segregation laws and interposition resolutions adopted by the Louisiana legislature.

1958

10 FEB. REGULATORY AGENCY SCANDALS. Investigations by the House Interstate and Foreign Commerce Legislative Oversight Subcommitee led to hearings about the firing (30 Jan.) of its own counsel, Prof. Bernard Schwartz, who had been discharged after he accused the committee of potential whitewash of FCC scandals. Hearings unveiled improper conduct of FCC Commissioner Richard A. Mack over award of Miami's Channel 10. Mack resigned 3 Mar. Later hearings revealed that Boston industrialist Bernard Goldfine had given Chief Presidential Assistant Sherman Adams a vicuna coat and an oriental rug and had in turn received preferential treatment before the FTC and the SEC. Adams resigned 22 Sept.

29 JULY. NASA. Soviet space achievements of 1957 (p. 801) inaugurated space race. Congressional hearings before Senate Preparedness Subcommittee, chaired by Lyndon B. Johnson, revealed agreement on need for larger and better coordinated research and development program. The National Aeronautics and Space Administration was established for this purpose, while the Department of Defense remained responsible for military activities in outer space.

6 AUG. DEFENSE REORGANIZATION ACT affirmed direction, authority, and control of Secretary of Defense over 3 "separately organized departments."

20–21 AUG. DEFEAT OF JENNER-BUTLER BILL and other bills attempting to limit aspects of jurisdiction of the Supreme Court and reverse or modify results of decisions in cases of *Watkins* v. *U.S.* (p. 680), *Pennsylvania* v. *Nelson* (p. 679), and *Yates* v. *U.S.* (p. 680) by the Senate by close votes.

25 AUG. A law granting pensions to ex-presidents of the U.S. became effective, the first ever enacted to provide pensions for former chief executives.

28 AUG. AGRICULTURE ACT modified price supports on basic crops for 1959 and 1960, giving farmers choice between modified price supports and increase of crop allotments. Supports on dairy products were raised 31 Aug. 1960.

28 AUG. LABOR PENSION REPORTING ACT required the reporting and disclosure of employee welfare and pension plans covering more than 25 employees, whether operated by unions, employers, or both in combination.

2 SEPT. NATIONAL DEFENSE EDUCATION ACT provided $295-million loan fund to lend college students $1,000 at 3% interest over 10 years with 50% reduction if the student later teaches in an elementary or secondary school for 5 years after graduation. In addition, $280 million was voted for grants to state schools for facilities in sciences or modern foreign languages, with matching grants by states, 5,500 fellowships for graduate students planning to go into college or university teaching, c. $28 million for language study in higher institutions, and $18 million for utilization of TV, radio, motion pictures, and related media for educational purposes.

4 Nov. CONGRESSIONAL ELECTIONS strengthened the Democratic party's control of Congress by 15 seats

in the Senate and 48 in the House, with a net gain of 6 governorships (including Alaska). Accountable in part for Democratic victories were the 1958 recession, farm opposition to the administration policy of lowered price supports for farm products, labor opposition to state right-to-work laws prohibiting union membership as a condition of employment, and dissatisfaction with administration leadership in foreign affairs. Sen. **John F. Kennedy** (Mass.) gained in political stature as a result of his re-election by a record margin of 860,000 votes.

1959

27 JUNE. **STRAUSS NOMINATION DEFEATED.** The Senate refused by a vote of 49–46 to confirm **Lewis L. Strauss** (1896–1974) as Secretary of Commerce, the first cabinet nominee since 1925 to be rejected. Opposition to Strauss was based upon his role in denying J. Robert Oppenheimer security clearance, his involvement in the Dixon-Yates contract, and accusations that he had withheld information from the Congress while chairman of the AEC.

29 AUG. **VETERANS PENSION ACT** made major revisions in benefits of needy veterans for nonservice-connected disabilities, or of their widows and children.

14 SEPT. **LANDRUM-GRIFFIN ACT** (Labor Management Reporting and Disclosure Act), designed to suppress gangsterism, racketeering, and blackmail in labor organizations, enacted a cluster of proposals, including the anticorruption, fair election, and trusteeship guarantees proposed by Sen. John F. Kennedy (Mass.), 15 Apr.; the "Bill of Rights" of Sen. Thomas H. Kuchel (Calif.), 22 Apr., setting criminal penalties to protect union members against unfair actions by their unions; and the amendment of Sen. John L. McClellan (Ark.), 24 Apr., revising the ban on secondary boycotts

under the Taft-Hartley Act to prohibit unions from inducing or coercing an employer or employee to stop doing business with another firm or handling its goods, and to extend the secondary boycott prohibitions to all unions.

1960

1 FEB. **SIT-IN MOVEMENT** began in Greensboro, N.C., where 4 black college students took lunch-counter seats in a Woolworth store in peaceful protest against "local custom" of refusing to serve a seated black person.

6 MAY. **CIVIL RIGHTS ACT OF 1960** strengthened provisions of the 1957 Act for court enforcement of voting rights. Judges were authorized to appoint referees to help Negroes register and vote; voting and registration records were required to be preserved; criminal penalties were prescribed for bombing and bomb threats.

PRESIDENTIAL CAMPAIGN. The Democratic National Convention convened at Los Angeles (11 July). Sen. **John F. Kennedy** was nominated (13 July) on the 1st ballot, 806 to 409 votes for his nearest rival, Sen. **Lyndon B. Johnson** (Tex.), who won the nomination for vice-president. Despite a strong civil rights plank, the Southern delegates failed to walk out. The platform favored placing medical care for the aged under social security and criticized the administration's tight-money policy. At the Republican National Convention in Chicago **Richard M. Nixon** was nominated (27 July) on the 1st ballot, after Gov. Nelson A. Rockefeller had eliminated himself for consideration on the ticket. **Henry Cabot Lodge** (Mass.) was nominated for vice-president. Reaffirming the Eisenhower foreign policy, the platform pledged a health program "on a sound fiscal basis and through a contributory system," an expanded national defense program, and a strong civil rights bill, including enforcement of the right to vote and desegregation in the public schools.

PRESIDENTIAL DEBATES. Kennedy and Nixon appeared on 4 nationally televised hour-long programs (26 Sept.; 7, 13, 21 Oct.) in which newsmen questioned them and they were permitted to rebut each other's remarks. The debates were made possible by suspension by Congress of the "equal time" provision of the **Communications Act of 1934.** Result of debates was inconclusive, although probably of slight benefit to Kennedy.

8 Nov. PRESIDENTIAL ELECTION. In the closest presidential election since 1884, **Kennedy** was elected by just over 100,000 out of a record 68.8 million votes cast. Kennedy received 34,226,731 votes and Nixon 34,108,157. Minor-party candidates: Eric Haas (Socialist Labor), 47,522; Farrell Dobbs (Socialist Workers), 40,165; Dr. Rutherford B. Decker (Prohibition), 46,203; Gov. Orval Faubus (National States Rights), 40,165. Because of demands for recount in some of the close states, such as Illinois and Texas, and the role of unpledged electors from Mississippi, the final issue was in some doubt until the electoral college vote, 19 Dec., which gave **Kennedy** 300 (22 states); Nixon, 219 (26 states); Sen. Harry F. Byrd, 15 (unpledged electors in Ala. and Miss. and 1 Nixon vote in Okla.). Hawaii's vote was withheld at that time as a recount was still in progress. Official count, 6 Jan. 1961, gave Kennedy 303 (including Hawaii), Nixon 219.

1961

17 Jan. EISENHOWER FAREWELL message warned nation of military-industrial complex.

DEFENSE BUDGETS
Fiscal Years 1950–1973
(Source: House Appropriations Committee, 1960–1973; Congressional Quarterly, 1950–1959.)

Fiscal Year	[In Billions] Appropriation[1]
1950	$12.9
1951	13.3
1952	56.9
1953	46.6
1954	34.4
1955	28.8
1956	31.9
1957	34.7
1958	33.8
1959	39.6
1960	39.2
1961	40.0
1962	46.7
1963	48.1
1964	47.2
1965	46.8
1966	46.9
1967	58.1
1968	69.9
1969	71.2
1970	69.6
1971	66.6
1972	70.5
1973	74.3

[1] Above amounts exclude appropriations not made in the regular annual Defense Appropriation Acts.

20 Jan. KENNEDY'S INAUGURAL ADDRESS called for "a grand and global alliance" to combat tyranny, poverty, disease, and war, served notice on the world that the U.S. was ready to "pay any price" to assure survival and "the success of liberty," but also to resume negotiations with the Soviet Union to ease world tensions. "Let us never negotiate out of fear. But let us never fear to negotiate," the president declared. Kennedy urged his fellow Americans: "ask not what your country can do for you—ask what you can do for your country."

29 Mar. 23RD AMENDMENT gave citizens of the District of Columbia the right to vote in presidential elections with the number of electors equivalent to those possible if the District had Congressional representation. Amendment had cleared Congress 16 June 1960.

1 May. AREA REDEVELOPMENT ACT authorized loans, grants, technical assistance to industrial and rural redevelopment areas ("depressed areas").

5 MAY. MINIMUM WAGE increased in stages to $1.25/hour. Previous increase to $1/hour effective 1 Mar. 1956. The 1961 law brought the 23.9 million workers then covered to a wage of $1.14 (Sept. 1961), and $1.25 (Sept. 1963). For the 3.6 million newly covered workers, wages of $1/hour (Sept. 1961) increased to $1.14 (Sept. 1964), and $1.25 (Sept. 1965).

25 MAY. MOON COMMITMENT. In message to Congress Kennedy urged commitment to goal of "landing a man on the moon and returning him safely to earth" before end of decade.

30 JUNE. HOUSING ACT OF 1961, most comprehensive since 1958, attempted to reduce urban blight, improve low- and moderate-income housing, and stimulate economy through increase in construction.

1962

26 MAR. *BAKER* v. *CARR* (p. 681).

10 APR. STEEL PRICE INCREASES resisted vigorously by President Kennedy, who charged that they constituted "a wholly unjustified and irresponsible defiance of our public interest." Beginning 13 Apr. the companies responded by canceling their price increases.

31 AUG. COMMUNICATIONS SATELLITE (p. 802).

30 SEPT.–10 OCT. MEREDITH CRISIS. Over the "interposition" of Gov. Ross Barnett, James Meredith, a black, was admitted under federal court order to the Univ. of Mississippi, not, however, without a riot in which 2 died and federal troops, along with the federalized National Guard, were called up. Meredith received his degree 18 Aug. 1963. On 11 Sept. 1963 Gov. George C. Wallace backed down from refusal to allow integration of Univ. of Alabama, after

President Kennedy federalized the National Guard.

11 OCT. TRADE EXPANSION ACT removed bars to world trade by giving the president authority to cut tariffs up to 50% below the 1962 level or raise them 50% above the 1934 level within the next 5 years, and to remove tariffs on products in which the U.S. and Western Europe account for 80% of free world trade.

6 Nov. CONGRESSIONAL ELECTIONS. The Democrats reversed the usual midterm trend by picking up 4 seats in the Senate, with minimal losses in the House. The Republicans won several important gubernatorial contests, including the reelection of Nelson Rockefeller in New York and the election of George W. Romney in Michigan, but former vice-president Richard M. Nixon was beaten in his campaign to unseat Gov. Edmund G. Brown of California.

1963

14 AUG. HIGHER EDUCATION FACILITIES ACT authorized 5-year program of federal grants and loans for construction or improvement of public and private higher educational facilities.

CIVIL RIGHTS. The Kennedy administration witnessed the most massive demonstrations by civil rights groups since Reconstruction and achieved a notable breakthrough in that area. Among the major accomplishments were the presidential support given to the *Brown* v. *Board of Education of Topeka* ruling and presidential commitment to integration of public facilities. Major administration efforts went into enforcement of the voting rights provisions of the 1957 and 1960 Civil Rights Laws. The Civil Rights Division of the Department of Justice, with the support of the president and his brother, Attorney General Robert Kennedy, and under the direction of Assistant

Attorney General Burke Marshall and his deputy, John Doar, brought over 50 suits in 4 states to secure the right to vote for the Negro. Among the most significant executive orders to end discrimination was that of 20 Nov. 1962, prohibiting racial and religious discrimination in housing built or purchased with federal aid.

THE 1,000 DAYS. The "New Frontier" brought to the public service a distinctive style together with some of the enthusiasm and intellectual vigor of "The Hundred Days" (9 Mar.–16 June 1932) without achieving a comparable legislative record. Able appointees, notably Secretary of Defense **Rober S. McNamara,** Secretary of Labor **Arthur J. Goldberg,** Secretary of the Interior **Stewart L. Udall,** and FCC head **Newton N. Minow,** revitalized their departments and agencies. On the legislative front, however, the results were modest. Congress defeated proposals for a Department of Urban Affairs, along with bills for housing, medical care for the aged, and federal grants for public school construction and teachers' salaries.

22 Nov. ASSASSINATION OF KENNEDY. While riding in a motorcade on a visit to Dallas, where he was seeking to heal a rift in the Texas Democratic party, the president was shot by **Lee Harvey Oswald,** a former marine and leftist. He was pronounced dead at 1 P.M., one-half hour after the shooting. Gov. John B. Connally (Tex.) was also shot. **Lyndon B. Johnson,** who also had been riding in the motorcade, took the oath of office from Federal District Judge Sarah T. Hughes in the presidential plane 2 hours after the assassination. Oswald, while in police custody, was shot and killed by **Jack Ruby,** Dallas nightclub owner (24 Nov.), an event which was recorded by TV coverage. Ruby was convicted of murder 14 Mar. 1964, and sentenced to death. On 27 Sept. the 888-page report of the 7-man Presidential Commission, headed by Chief Justice Earl Warren, held Oswald to be the sole assassin.

1964

8 JAN. WAR ON POVERTY called for by President Lyndon B. Johnson in State of the Union Address. Subsequently the **Economic Opportunity Act** (30 Aug.) and other legislation was enacted for a coordinated attack on multiple causes of poverty—illiteracy, unemployment, and inadequate public services. $947.7 million authorized for 10 separate programs conducted by Office of Economic Opportunity including Job Corps, VISTA (Volunteers in Service to America), work-training programs, work-study programs, and small-business incentives.

23 JAN. 24TH AMENDMENT ratified banning the poll tax as a prerequisite for voting in federal elections. Submitted to the states by Congress 27 Aug. 1962.

26 FEB. TAX REDUCTION ACT. Personal income tax rates were reduced from 20–91% scale to 14–70% over 2-year period; corporate rates from 52% to 48%.

2 JULY. CIVIL RIGHTS LAW OF 1964. Mass civil rights demonstrations for equality in Birmingham, Ala. (beginning 3 Apr. 1963) attracted wide attention focused upon harsh treatment of demonstrators. President Kennedy announced commitment to equality in public accommodations (11 June 1963); 200,000 marched in Washington, D.C. (28 Aug. 1963) "for jobs and freedom." After a long legislative fight, the House passed the bill (10 Feb. 1964). Cloture was enforced by a vote of 71–29 to end a Senate filibuster (10 June 1964), the first time a filibuster had been ended on a civil rights bill. Senate passed bill 73–27 (19 June) and House the revised version (2 July, date of the president's signature).

Omnibus bill included provisions (1) to bar discrimination in public accommodations; (2) authorizing the attorney general to institute suits to desegregate schools or other public facilities; (3) outlawing discrimination in employment on the basis of race, color, religion, sex, or national origin; and (4) gave added protection to voting rights by making a 6th-grade education a rebuttable presumption of literacy and by prohibiting denial of registration due to immaterial errors in filling out registration forms. The public accommodations sections were upheld by the Supreme Court in *Heart of Atlanta Motel* v. *U.S.* (p. 681).

8 JULY. Senate Rules and Administration Committee Report on Robert ("Bobby") G. Baker, former Secretary to the Senate Majority Leader Lyndon B. Johnson, found him "guilty of many gross improprieties" but cited no specific violations of law.

9 JULY. URBAN MASS TRANSPORTATION ACT OF 1964 provided financial aid up to $375 million.

3 SEPT. WILDERNESS PRESERVATION ACT (p. 642).

PRESIDENTIAL CAMPAIGN. The Republican National Convention, opening in San Francisco 13 July, nominated Sen. **Barry M. Goldwater** (Ariz.) for president and Rep. **William E. Miller** (N.Y.) for vice-president on the 1st ballot, in a triumph for the conservative wing of the Republican party. The platform pledged enforcement of the Civil Rights Law of 1964, affirmed presidential control over nuclear weapons, but the convention rejected a proposal denouncing the right-wing John Birch Society.

The Democratic Convention, held in Atlantic City 24–27 Aug., nominated **Lyndon B. Johnson** for president and Sen. **Hubert H. Humphrey** (Minn.) for vice-president, by acclamation. The latter was Johnson's declared choice.

3 Nov. PRESIDENTIAL ELECTION. In the biggest landslide of the century **Johnson** was elected, with 486 electoral votes (44 states and the District of Columbia) and 43.1 million votes (61%) to Goldwater's 6 states and 27.1 million votes (38.8%). Minor-party candidates: Eric Haas (Socialist Labor), 21,390; Clifton DeBerry (Socialist Worker), 10,934; Earle H. Munn (Prohibition), 18,227; John Kasper (National States Rights), 11,204. The Democrats strengthened their hold on Congress and lost but one governorship, retaining 33.

1965

4 JAN. STATE OF THE UNION. The president called for a vast program to achieve the "Great Society," including a massive attack on crippling and killing diseases, a doubling of the war on poverty in 1965, enforcement of the Civil Rights Law and elimination of barriers to the right to vote, reform of the immigration laws, an education program of scholarships and loans with a first-year authorization of $1.5 billion, and a "massive effort" to establish more recreational and open space areas. The Johnson budget (25 Jan.) called for an expenditure of $97.7 billion, less than 15% of the gross national product, the lowest ratio in 15 years, with an anticipated deficit of $5.3 billion.

JOHNSON'S LEGISLATIVE ACCOMPLISHMENTS. At the urging of the president the 1st session of the 89th Congress passed the most significant amount of legislation since the New Deal including:

11 APR. Elementary and Secondary School Act, the first large-scale program of aid to elementary and secondary schools, granting $1.3 billion to school districts on the basis of number of needy children, including funds for parochial

and private pupils disbursed under public school supervision.

30 July. Medicare providing medical care for the aged financed through the Social Security System (p. 816). Social security benefits were increased by 7%, the social security tax raised to 5.65%, and the income based to $6,600. Widows aged 62 became eligible for benefits. The tax and income base rose to 5.9% and $7,800 by law in 1967 and benefits were increased 13% by law, 2 Jan. 1968.

6 Aug. Voting Rights Act of 1965 suspended literacy and other voter tests and authorized federal supervision of registration in states and individual voting districts where tests had been used and where fewer than half of voting-age residents were registered or had voted. The Justice Department suspended literacy tests in 7 states (7 Aug.).

10 Aug. Omnibus Housing Act established new programs of rent supplements to low-income families and authorized federal funds to place low-income individuals into private housing.

9 Sept. Department of Housing and Urban Development (HUD) was established, absorbing functions and programs of Housing and Home Finance Agency (HHFA), and administering and coordinating federal programs. Robert C. Weaver was chosen first Secretary of HUD.

29 Sept. National Foundation of the Arts and Humanities established to provide financial assistance for painters, actors, dancers, musicians, and others in the arts.

2 Oct. Water Quality Act of 1965 (p. 640).

3 Oct. Immigration Laws were revised (p. 658), setting annual quotas of 120,000 for immigrants from the Western Hemisphere with no national quotas, and 170,000 from the rest of the world with a maximum of 20,000 from any one nation.

20 Oct. Air Quality Act amendments of 1965 (p. 641).

20 Oct. Higher Education Act provided the first federal scholarships to college undergraduates and other assistance. Other legislation passed during the session included a reduction of excise taxes by $4.7 billion over a 4-year period (21 June).

1965–66 RACIAL DEMONSTRATIONS. Rev. Martin Luther King, Jr., led a 5-day, 54-mile march from Selma to Montgomery, Ala. (21–25 March 1965). Stokely Carmichael, chairman of Student Non-Violent Coordinating Committee (SNCC), popularized "Black Power" as a slogan (14 May 1966); the slogan endorsed at the Congress of Racial Equality (CORE) National Convention (4 July) but rejected at the NAACP Convention (4–9 July). Dr. King's first Southern Christian Leadership Conference drive in the North was launched in Chicago (29 July 1966) for open housing. After violent opposition from lower-class whites, an agreement to end de facto housing segregation was reached with civic leaders and Mayor Richard J. Daley (26 Aug.).

1965–68. URBAN RACIAL RIOTING. Racial violence occurred in the "ghettoes" of almost all the nation's large cities. Among those affected were Los Angeles (11–16 Aug. 1965), where riots in the Watts area took 28 Negro lives and $200 million damages; Chicago (12–15 July 1966); Newark (12–17 July 1967); Detroit (23–30 July 1967), where 40 persons died, 2,000 were injured, and 5,000 left homeless by rioting, looting, and burning until 4,700 paratroopers dispatched by the president arrived. The **assassination of Martin Luther King, Jr.,** set off a wave of riots (4–11 April 1968) in 125 cities in 29 states.

"Poor People's Campaign" for reforms in welfare, employment, and housing policies, led in Washington, D.C. (29

Apr.–23 June 1968) by Dr. King's successor, **Dr. Ralph Abernathy,** as head of Southern Christian Leadership Conference. The president's 11-member National Advisory Commission on Civil Disorders headed by Gov. Otto Kerner (Ill.) stated, in a 1,400-page report on the 1967 riots (released 29 Feb. 1968) that: (1) the U.S. is "moving" toward separate and unequal societies, black and white, but it is possible to head off the division; (2) white racism is the chief cause of Negro violence and riots; (3) to reverse the situation calls for unprecedented levels of funding and performance.

1965–68. VIETNAM WAR DISSENT (p. 501).

1966

3 Mar. VETERANS EDUCATIONAL BENEFITS granted for all who served 180 days on active duty after 1955. Veterans pensions and educational allowances increased, 1967.

9 Sept. NATIONAL TRAFFIC AND MOTOR VEHICLE SAFETY ACT required federal establishment of safety standards on all vehicles from 1968 model year and on used cars within 2 years, as well as federal standards for tires. The **Highway Safety Act,** enacted the same day, required each state to set up federally approved highway safety programs by 31 Dec. 1968 or face the loss of 10% of federal-aid construction funds. Impetus for the legislation came from the efforts of **Ralph Nader** (p. 1112).

23 Sept. MINIMUM WAGE was raised for 30 million workers already covered from $1.25/hour to $1.40, effective 1 Feb. 1967, and to $1.60 effective 1 Feb. 1968. Coverage was extended to 9.1 additional workers in retail stores, restaurants, and hotels, as well as one third of nation's 1.2 million farm workers, and some service workers. Their minimum wage was to become $1 (1967) and rise to $1.60/hour by 1971 except for the farm workers ($1.30 by 1971).

15 Oct. DEPARTMENT OF TRANSPORTATION was created, including federal agencies dealing with air, rail, and highway transportation but not Maritime Administration nor the Corps of Engineers nor urban mass transit. The independent regulatory bureaus were left with their rate-making and regulatory functions. Alan S. Boyd was confirmed as first secretary 12 Jan. 1967; department began operation 1 Apr. 1967.

3 Nov. CLEAN WATER RESTORATION ACT OF 1966. (p. 640).

3 Nov. MODEL CITIES. Demonstration Cities and Metropolitan Area Redevelopment Act encouraged rehabilitation of slums, financed metropolitan area planning, provided land-development mortgage insurance over a 3-year period: 63 "model" or demonstration cities were chosen by HUD to draw up plans for the program (16 Nov. 1967).

8 Nov. CONGRESSIONAL ELECTIONS. The Republican party gained 3 Senate and 47 House seats, enabling a revived conservative coalition to slow down the Johnson legislative program in Congress. Republicans also won 8 additional governorships. **Black voting** increased from 28.6% of the 5 million persons of voting age in the South to 47.5% as registrations rose from 687,000 to 1,150,000 after the 1965 Voting Rights Act.

1967

10 Feb. 25TH AMENDMENT ratified, providing procedures for presidental succession and disability. Amendment had been proposed by Congress 6 July 1965.

17 Oct. UNIFIED BUDGET recommended by Presidential Commission on the Federal Budget to replace existing multiplicity of budgets, including administrative, consolidated cash, and national income accounts budget. The Unified Budget, which was adopted by President Johnson for the remaining years of his term, included in addition to previous items, transactions of federally administered trust funds, an accrual account system, and government loan operations.

7 Nov. PUBLIC BROADCASTING CORPORATION established to provide financial assistance for noncommercial educational TV and radio broadcasting.

1968

1 Apr. OPEN HOUSING LAW to prohibit discrimination in the sale or rental of 80% of all housing when fully in effect; not applicable to privately owned homes sold without the services of a real-estate agent. Act also included provisions making it a crime to cross interstate lines with intent to incite or take part in riot.

23–30 Apr. COLUMBIA UNIVERSITY student demonstrations paralyzed the campus. Student demonstrations occurred in May in many other institutions.

29 May. TRUTH-IN-LENDING ACT required disclosure to consumer of information about credit transactions in terms of the annual rate calculated under specified procedures.

19 June. OMNIBUS CRIME CONTROL AND SAFE STREETS ACT established Law Enforcement Assistance Administration (LEAA) in the Justice Department to administer program of grants to states to be spent for upgrading law-enforcement and criminal-justice operations. $100 million was authorized for fiscal 1969 and $300 million for fiscal 1970. In addition the act (1) permitted broad wiretapping by all levels of government while banning private wire-

tapping or electronic eavesdropping; (2) attempted to overturn by legislation Supreme Court decisions in *Mallory* v. *U.S.* (1957), *Miranda* v. *Ariz.* (p. 681), and *U.S.* v. *Wade* (p. 685) by providing that a confession would not be inadmissible solely because of a delay no more than 6 hours after arrest in bringing defendant before commissioner, nor because he was not informed of his constitutional rights, nor would testimony of eyewitness at lineup be inadmissible because defendant was denied counsel.

26 June. FORTAS NOMINATION. President Johnson nominated Justice Abe Fortas (26 June) as Chief Justice after Earl Warren had informed Johnson of his intention to retire, contingent upon the qualifications of a successor. Circuit Court of Appeals Judge Homer Thornberry was nominated to fill the Fortas vacancy. The Fortas nomination was withdrawn (4 Oct.) by the president at his request after the Senate refused to invoke cloture (45 for, 43 against; 59 votes needed) to end a filibuster.

28 June. TAX SURCHARGE of 10% on personal and corporate income taxes enacted.

1 Aug. HOUSING. A $5.3-billion, 3-year program designed to provide more than 1.7 million units of new and rehabilitated housing for low-income families including federal subsidies to help the poor buy their houses and rent apartments.

2 Oct. CONSERVATION measures included (1) scenic rivers bill to preserve stretches of wild and scenic rivers in their natural state; (2) law establishing a national system of trails; (3) the 58,000-acre Redwood National Park; and (4) the 1.2-million-acre North Cascades National Park.

PRESIDENTIAL CAMPAIGN. Following the unexpected success of antiwar candidate Sen. Eugene F. McCarthy (Minn.) in the New Hampshire primary

(12 Mar.) where he polled 42% of the vote against 48% for the yet unannounced candidate Johnson, Sen. Robert F. Kennedy (N.Y., p. 1075) also a major critic of U.S. involvement in Vietnam, announced his candidacy (16 Mar.). President Lyndon B. Johnson declared in a TV address: "I shall not seek, and I will not accept, the nomination of my party for another term as President" (31 Mar.). Vice-President Hubert H. Humphrey entered the race (27 Apr.). Sen. Kennedy was assassinated (5 June), the night of his victory in the California primary. His death (6 June) cast a shadow over the election year. Humphrey easily won renomination at the Democratic National Convention in Chicago (26–29 Aug.) after Sen. Edward M. Kennedy (Mass.), the brother of John F. and Robert F. Kennedy, refused to seek the nomination. The convention was marred by dramatic clashes between police and peace demonstrators in the streets of Chicago. Sen. Edmund S. Muskie (Me.) was nominated for vice-president.

Richard M. Nixon and Gov. Spiro T. Agnew (Md.) were nominated by the Republican Convention in Miami (8 Aug.). George C. Wallace and Gen. Curtis E. LeMay were the candidates of the American Independent Party.

5 Nov. PRESIDENTIAL ELECTION. In a dramatically close election, **Richard M. Nixon** was elected president with 302 electoral votes (1 elector later voted for George C. Wallace) and 31,785,480 (43.4%) votes to 191 electoral votes and 31,275,166 (42.7%) for Humphrey, and 45 (later 46) and 9,906,473 (13.5%) for Wallace.

Minor-party candidates: Hennings Blomen (Socialist-Labor), 52,588; Dick Gregory (New) 47,097; Fred Halstead (Socialist Worker), 41,300; Eldridge Cleaver (Peace and Freedom), 36,385; E. Harold Munn, Sr. (Prohibition), 14,-519; Charlene Mitchell (Communist and

Free Ballot), 1,075. The antiwar New Party placed Sen. Eugene McCarthy on the ballot in some states without his consent, receiving 25,858 votes, and received 1,480 votes in 3 states where no candidate was listed.

The Democrats maintained control of the Congress, 243–192 in the House, 58–42 in the Senate (later 57–43 due to a death). The Republicans gained a net of 5 governorships to dominate 31 of 50 statehouses (later 30, due to the resignation of Spiro Agnew as governor).

1969

17 JAN. Presidential salary increased to $200,000 annually; travel allowance of $40,000 (untaxable) and official allowance of $50,000 (taxable) remained. Vice-president's salary raised to $62,500, 7 Aug. Presidential retirement allowance increased from $25,000 to $60,000 and widow's pension from $10,000 to $20,000 (1970).

20 JAN. NIXON'S INAUGURAL ADDRESS stated that Americans "cannot learn from one another until we stop shouting at one another" and announced that the government "will strive to listen in new ways."

18 FEB. HOUSE COMMITTEE ON UN-AMERICAN ACTIVITIES changed to House Committee on Internal Security with mandate modified to authorize committee to investigate groups seeking to overthrow or change the form of the federal government by violence or obstruct the execution of internal security laws.

3 JULY. CIVIL RIGHTS POLICIES. Statement by Attorney General John N. Mitchell and Secretary of HEW, Robert H. Finch, on school desegregation guidelines insisted that dual school systems must end by Sept. unless "bona fide educational and administrative problems warrant delay." HEW and Department

of Justice argued in court (19 Aug.) that HEW-approved desegregation plans should be withdrawn and desegregation delayed. While Nixon administration efforts to secure compliance switched from lawsuits to HEW fund cutoffs, attorneys in the Civil Rights Division of the Department of Justice drafted protests against decision to delay desegregation in 33 Mississippi counties (26 Aug.). U.S. Supreme Court ordered end to all school segregation at once (29 Oct.; *Alexander* v. *Holmes Co.*, p. 682). Leon E. Panetta, chief of Civil Rights Office of HEW, strong advocate of desegregation, resigned because of political pressures (17 Feb. 1970) triggering letter to the president from over 100 members of the office expressing disappointment, as well as a memorandum from 1,800 members of the staffs of HEW offices to Secretary Robert H. Finch asking for an explanation of HEW's civil rights policy.

HAYNSWORTH-CARSWELL NOMINATIONS. Justice Abe Fortas resigned (14 May) after disclosure that he had accepted and belatedly returned installment on lifetime retainer from family foundation of convicted stock manipulator. Warren Burger, judge of the U.S. Court of Appeals for the D.C. Circuit (1956–69), nominated to succeed retiring Chief Justice Earl Warren, was confirmed by vote of 74–3 (9 June). The nomination of Clement Haynsworth, chief judge of the U.S. Court of Appeals for the 4th Circuit, to succeed Fortas was defeated 55–45 (21 Nov.) by the Senate, after debate over Haynsworth's sensitivity to the appearance of ethical improprieties, following disclosures that he had participated in cases where he held stock interests. A second Nixon nomination, G. Harrold Carswell, judge of the U.S. Court of Appeals for the 5th Circuit, was defeated 51–45 (8 Apr.

1970) after a debate over his racial views and intellectual caliber. Harry A. Blackmun, judge of the U.S. Court of Appeals for the 8th Circuit, was confirmed unanimously by the Senate (12 May 1970).

20 JULY. MOON LANDING (p. 803). Cost of civilian space program through 1969–$24.6 billion.

3 Nov. PRESS ATTACKS by Nixon administration gained wide attention with Des Moines, Iowa, speech of vice-president Spiro T. Agnew deploring the power of a "small band of network commentators." Agnew attacked the *New York Times* and *Washington Post* at Montgomery, Ala., 20 Nov. Later pressures on press encompassed federal and state subpoenas requiring reporters to testify before grand juries to disclose sources for stories about criminal activities, upheld by Supreme Court in *Branzburg* v. *Hayes* (p. 684); *Pentagon Papers* litigation (p. 537, 541, 684); and FBI investigation of CBS correspondent Daniel Schorr (1971).

4 Nov. Defense Department dismissed A. Ernest Fitzgerald, deputy for management systems in Office of Assistant Secretary of the Air Force, for disclosure of cost overruns on C-5A by Lockheed Aircraft (13 Nov. 1968). On 1 Aug. 1971 federal government guaranteed up to $250 million in bank loans for Lockheed Aircraft Corp., apparently near bankruptcy. Fitzgerald was reinstated in 1973.

1970

1 JAN. NATIONAL ENVIRONMENTAL POLICY ACT OF 1969 (NEPA) made the protection of the environment a national commitment (p. 642).

JAN. MILITARY SURVEILLANCE of civilian political activity during late 1960s described in *Washington Monthly* article by former Army Intelligence Capt.

Christopher H. Pyle. Hearings of Subcommittee on Constitutional Rights of Senate Judiciary Committee (Feb.–Mar. 1971) further explored army intelligence program which army announced had been abandoned.

3 Apr. WATER QUALITY IMPROVEMENT ACT OF 1970 (p. 640).

May. CAMBODIA-KENT-STATE DISSENT (p. 502).

1 July. WHITE HOUSE REORGANIZATION PLAN created Office of Management and Budget, absorbing existing Bureau of the Budget (p. 392), with authority to oversee and evaluate all federal programs in 12 cabinet departments. A Domestic Council was created to evaluate and tie together interagency planning with presidential adviser John R. Ehrlichman chosen as executive director.

CRIMINAL LAWS recommended by Nixon administration enacted during 1970 included (1) **Organized Crime Control Act of 1970** providing for immunity for witnesses for use of testimony, special grand juries to investigate organized criminal activities, and limited disclosure of electronic surveillance evidence; (2) **District of Columbia Court Reorganization and Criminal Procedure Act of 1970** (29 July) modernizing the D.C. court system, and depriving the liberal U.S. Court of Appeals for the D.C. Circuit of jurisdiction over local criminal cases, as well as providing for stiff law-enforcement measures such as selective preventive detention, no-knock search and arrest warrants, and elimination of jury trials for juveniles; (3) **Omnibus Crime Control Act of 1970,** authorizing $3.55 billion federal aid to state and local law-enforcement agencies over a 3-year period: (4) **Drug Abuse Prevention and Control Act of 1970** unifying and revising federal narcotics laws, and providing expanded programs of rehabilitation.

12 Aug. POSTAL REFORM. Postal Reorganization Act replaced Post Office Department with an independent governmental agency and removed the Postmaster General from the cabinet.

5 Oct. URBAN MASS TRANSIT grants and loans up to $3.1 billion approved.

26 Oct. LEGISLATIVE REORGANIZATION ACT provided for public recording of roll-call votes in congressional committees and House committee of the whole, as well as liberalization of committee procedures.

3 Nov. CONGRESSIONAL ELECTIONS. Republicans suffered net loss, losing 9 House seats and 11 governorships (giving Democrats control of 29) but picking up 2 Senate seats. Basic campaign strategy of Republicans was to appeal to "silent majority" of "middle America" on issues such as the Vietnam War ("peace with honor") and "law and order." Vice-President Agnew's attacks on "radical-liberals" and vigorous rhetoric ("nattering nabobs of negativism") and tough presidential address of 2 Nov., were apparently answered effectively by televised reply for Democrats of Sen. Edmund Muskie (Me.).

25 Nov. Secretary of the Interior Walter J. Hickel was fired by President Nixon because "essentials of confidence" did not exist. Nixon and Hickel differed on approaches to the environment and the young.

30 Nov. AGRICULTURE ACT OF 1970 (p. 695).

29 Dec. OCCUPATIONAL SAFETY AND HEALTH ACT mandated that employers shall provide employment "free from recognized hazards to employees," provided for federal establishment and enforcement of safety and health standards for the protection of workers.

31 Dec. 1970 CLEAN AIR ACT (p. 641).

1971

22 JAN. NEW AMERICAN REVO-LUTION called for by President Nixon in State of the Union Address asking Congress to enact legislation to secure 5 of 6 great goals: (1) welfare reform, (2) environmental initiatives, (3) health insurance reform, (4) revenue sharing, (5) government reorganization. The 6th goal was full prosperity in peacetime.

1 MAR. Bomb exploded in restroom of Capitol, 30 minutes after a telephone warning in which the action was proclaimed a protest against U.S. involvement in Laos (p. 503), causing $200,000 damage.

23 MAR. D.C. NONVOTING CONGRESSIONAL DELEGATE, Walter E. Fauntroy, first since 1875 elected by citizens of Washington.

24 MAR. SST PROGRAM DEFEATED. The Senate by vote of 51–46 eliminated funding for 1,800 mph supersonic transport plane following a similar vote (18 Mar.) by the House.

1 MAY. AMTRAK began service (p. 618).

1 JULY. PENTAGON PAPERS, classified history of the policy decisions which led to U.S. involvement in Vietnam commissioned by Secretary of Defense Robert S. McNamara (1967), were first published in *New York Times.* Injunctions by Justice Department sought against *New York Times* (15 June), *Washington Post,* and other newspapers denied by U.S. Supreme Court 30 June (p. 684). Daniel Ellsberg, former Defense Department aide, was indicted (28 June) for theft of government property and violation of the espionage act in leaking classified documents (also p. 541).

30 JUNE. 26TH AMENDMENT. After the Supreme Court declared unconstitutional (21 Dec. 1970, *Oregon* v. *Mitchell,* p. 683) a section of the **Voting Rights Extension Act** (22 June 1970), which lowered the voting age to 18 in state and local as well as federal elections, Congress proposed 26th Amendment (23 Mar. 1971) lowering franchise to 18 in all elections. The court had early upheld the voting act as applicable to presidential and congressional elections. The amendment was quickly ratified. In addition, the **Voting Rights Extension Act** extended the **Voting Rights Act of 1965** and prohibited literacy tests as a qualification for voting, established uniform residence requirements for voting in presidential elections, and applied the act to Northern cities or counties where literacy tests had previously been required.

11 JUNE. PHASE 1 of Nixon Economic Policy (p. 752).

21 SEPT. SELECTIVE SERVICE extended draft for 2 years and increased military pay and benefits, a step toward all-volunteer army. The draft, based upon the **Universal Military Training and Service Act of 1951** had previously been extended in 1955, 1959, 1963, and 1967. With the expiration of the Act (30 June 1973), the armed forces were on an all-volunteer basis for the 1st time since 1948.

10 DEC. REVENUE ACT OF 1971 (p. 737).

12 DEC. DEVALUATION OF DOLLAR (p. 711).

1972

22 MAR. WOMEN'S RIGHTS AMENDMENT proposed by Congress and sent to states, providing "Equality of rights under the law shall not be denied or abridged by the United States or by any state on account of sex."

7 APR. FEDERAL ELECTION CAMPAIGN ACT effective. Signed 7 Feb., the act repealed the **Corrupt Practices Act of 1925** and limited the amount a candidate or his family could contribute to his own campaign. In addition, the act limited to 10 cts. per voter the amount that could be spent by candidates for Congress and the presidency for media advertising, strengthened the requirements for reporting of campaign receipts and expenditures, including names and addresses of all persons who made contributions or loans in excess of $100.

17 June. WATERGATE BREAK-IN (p. 539).

17 Oct. SUPPLEMENTAL SECURITY INCOME program established by 1972 Social Security Act Amendments replacing existing federal-state programs of assistance to the aged, blind, and disabled with a program fully financed and administered by the federal government, effective 1 Jan. 1974. Social security benefits continued to increase but so did the social security tax and the wage base for the tax.

18 Oct. FEDERAL WATER POLLUTION ACT, enacted into law as Congress overrode President Nixon's veto (p. 640).

20 Oct. REVENUE SHARING, a 5-year program to distribute $30,236,-400,000 of federal tax revenues to state and local governments as supplements to their own revenues, to use generally as they saw fit.

PRESIDENTIAL CAMPAIGN. Operating under reforms in delegate selection processes and convention procedures made by the Commission on Party Structure and Delegate Selection, headed first by Sen. **George McGovern** (1922–   ), the Democratic party held more primaries accounting for more convention votes than hitherto. Primaries were generally not "winner-take-all." Among other reforms were the opening of the delegate selection process to all enrolled party members, and the proportionate representation of minorities, women, and young persons.

Basing his campaign for the nomination primarily upon opposition to the Vietnam War, Sen. McGovern (S.D.) did unexpectedly well in primaries and profited by the new convention guidelines. **McGovern** captured the Democratic presidential nomination on the 1st ballot at the Democratic National Convention, Miami Beach, Fla. (10–13 July). The Democratic platform called for immediate withdrawl from Indochina, abolition of the draft, amnesty for war resisters, and guaranteed income above the poverty line.

Sen. **Thomas F. Eagleton** (Mo.), chosen by McGovern and the convention for the vice-presidential nomination, withdrew from the ticket (31 July) at McGovern's request after discovery by reporters that he had been hospitalized 3 times for psychiatric disorders. Nomination of **R. Sargent Shriver** (Md.), former director of the Peace Corps, apparently McGovern's 7th choice, was agreed to at a special meeting of the Democratic National Committee (8 Aug.).

The Republican National Convention, also meeting in Miami Beach (21–23 Aug.), renominated **Richard M. Nixon** and **Spiro T. Agnew.** The Republican platform supported presidential foreign policies, welfare reform, revenue sharing, governmental reorganization, national health insurance, and opposed amnesty for war resisters and the busing of children to correct racial imbalance in schools.

The American Independent Party nominated John G. Schmitz (Calif.) for president after potential nominee Gov. George C. Wallace, paralyzed as a result of gunshot wounds inflicted by Arthur Bremer at a political rally in Laurel, Md. (15 May), withdrew from the Presidential race after an impressive showing in Northern primaries.

Minor-party candidates included Benjamin Spock (People's Party), Earl H.

Munn (Prohibition), John Hospers (Libertarian), Louis Fisher (Socialist Labor), Linda Jenness (Evelyn Reed in some states) (Socialist Worker), Gus Hall (Communist).

Campaign was marked by a minimum of personal appearances by Nixon, who relied instead upon heavy expenditures, estimated at well over $50 million, and upon "surrogate campaigners," including cabinet officials. McGovern, whose campaign was poorly organized, assailed the Nixon regime as "the most corrupt administration in history," but failed to lure the president into debating the issue.

7 Nov. PRESIDENTIAL ELECTION. Nixon, 47,169,911 (60.8%); McGovern, 29,170,383 (37.5%).

Minor-party candidates: Schmitz (American), 1,099,482; Spock (People's), 78,-756; Munn (Prohibition), 13,505; Hall (Communist), 25,595; Fisher (Socialist Labor), 53,814; Jenness or Reed (Socialist Workers), 66,677.

Electoral vote: **Nixon,** 520 (49 states), McGovern, 17 (Mass., D.C.); 1 elector in Virginia voted for John Hospers (Calif.) and Theordora Nathan (Ore.). The Republicans, however, made a net gain of only 13 seats in the House, losing 2 Senate seats and one governorship.

1973

PRESIDENTIAL IMPOUNDMENTS. After Congress denied President Nixon's request for a $250 billion ceiling in fiscal 1973 outlays, Nixon impounded $12 billion in funds for the Department of Transportation ($2.9 billion, largely for highway construction), the Department of Defense ($1.9 billion), Agriculture Department (food stamp, REA loans), and other federal programs. In 1973–74 federal courts almost uniformly ruled that the actions were illegal; Congress est. procedures (12 July 1974) to override impounding.

12 Feb. DEVALUATION OF DOLLAR (p. 711).

10 Aug. AGRICULTURAL ACT ended farm subsidy system, setting target prices for wheat, feed grain, cotton. If farmers' average sales price fell below target, government to pay difference.

10 Oct. RESIGNATION OF SPIRO AGNEW as vice-president was followed within hours by his pleading *nolo contendere* to a single charge of federal income-tax invasion. As part of the plea bargain, publication of grand-jury criminal information against Agnew cited acceptance of payoffs from construction company executives while governor of Maryland and vice-president. Under the procedures of the 25th Amendment President Nixon nominated House Minority Leader Gerald R. Ford to succeed Agnew, 12 Oct. Senate confirmed Ford 27 Nov. by a vote of 92–3, and House of Representatives on 6 Dec., 387–5. Ford took oath of office the same day.

7 Nov. WAR POWERS ACT veto overridden by Congress. Act set 60-day limit on presidential commitment of troops to hostilities abroad or into situations where hostilities appeared imminent, unless Congress authorized continued action; 30 days more are permissible for safe withdrawal of troops.

Watergate Chronology, 1972–75

17 June 1972. WATERGATE BREAK-IN. On the eve of the '72 presidential campaign the first glimmer of what would prove an unprecedented series of scandals reaching into the White House occurred when 5 men were apprehended in the act of burglarizing the offices of the Democratic National Committee located in Watergate, an apartment-hotel complex in Washington, D.C. Links between the accused and E. Howard Hunt, Jr., White House consultant (revealed 19 June), and G. Gordon Liddy, counsel to the Committee to Reelect the President (CRP, disclosed 22 July), coupled with evidence that the accused carried money traceable to CRP's finance committee, implied a tie-in between the burglary and the president's reelection campaign (1 Aug.).

19 JUNE. EARLY WHITE HOUSE DENIALS. Press Secretary Ronald L. Ziegler referred to the break-in as a "third-rate burglary." President Nixon stated (29 Aug.) that no one in the administration was involved and that "technical violations" of the election law had occurred on both sides. Ex-Attorney General John N. Mitchell resigned as campaign chairman (1 July), citing family problems.

JUNE–JULY. COVERUP. Early attempts at covering up the burglary included (1) destruction of documents in offices of H. R. Haldeman, White House Chief of Staff; (2) emptying Hunt's White House safe; (3) pressures on FBI to limit investigation to avoid compromising the CIA; (4) money raised to support burglary defendants (indicted 15 Sept.); (5) perjury before grand jury committed by Jeb Stuart Magruder, deputy director of CRP.

29 SEPT. WASHINGTON POST reporters Bob Woodward and Carl Bernstein reported that John Mitchell, while attorney general, had personally controlled a secret fund to finance intelligence operations against Democrats. Woodward and Bernstein revealed (10 Oct.) that a secret fund had financed spying and sabotaging of Democratic primary campaigns encompassing such activities as (1) forgery of correspon-dence, (2) false leaks to the press, and (3) seizure of confidential campaign files. President Nixon's appointments secretary, Dwight L. Chapin, was accused of hiring Donald H. Segretti, who recruited agents. Ziegler accused the *Washington Post* of "character assassination" and of "the shoddiest kind of journalism."

8–30 JAN. 1973. TRIAL OF WATERGATE 7. Although Attorney General Richard G. Kleindienst indicated (28 Aug.) that the investigation would be the "most extensive, thorough and comprehensive since the assassination of President Kennedy," only the original 7 men stood trial. At the trial, **Judge John J. Sirica** (1904–   ), chief judge of the U.S. District Court for the District of Columbia, expressed dissatisfaction with the questioning of the prosecution and personally interrogated defense witnesses in order to get to the bottom of the scandal. Five defendants pleaded guilty and 2 were convicted by a jury. At sentencing (23 Mar.) Sirica read a letter from James W. McCord, a defendant and former security coordinator of CRP, charging that others had been involved, that defendants had been pressured to plead guilty, and that perjury had been committed at the trial.

28 FEB. GRAY CONFIRMATION HEARINGS before Senate Judiciary Committee. L. Patrick Gray, acting director of the FBI, nominee for director, produced FBI recordings indicating that John Dean, the president's counsel, had sat in on all FBI interviews and received FBI files, evidence suggesting a coverup by White House aides. Dean claimed executive privilege and refused to testify. Gray asked the president (5 Apr.) to withdraw his nomination and resigned 27 April.

30 APR. HALDEMAN-EHRLICHMAN RESIGNATIONS. After the president announced (17 Apr.) that he had begun extensive new inquiries on 21 March, Ziegler indicated that all previous

White House statements were "inoperative." The president announced (30 Apr.) the resignations of Haldeman, Ehrlichman (his adviser on domestic affairs), and Kleindienst, praising all 3 men, while dismissing Dean. In a later statement (22 May), Nixon conceded a White House coverup, but pleaded innocent of planning or knowledge thereof.

11 MAY. ELLSBERG CHARGES DISMISSED by Federal Judge W. Matthew Bryne, Jr. (Calif.) after receiving information that there had been a wiretap from late 1969 to early 1970 on Ellsberg's telephone, and that the government could not find the tape transcripts. Ellsberg and Anthony J. Russo were charged with espionage, theft, and conspiracy in connection with the Pentagon Papers (p. 537). It had been previously reported (27 Apr.) that Hunt and Liddy had burglarized the files of Ellsberg's former psychiatrist (3 Sept. 1971) with some assistance from the CIA. On 30 Apr. it was reported that Ehrlichman had met with Judge Byrne at the Western White House, San Clemente (5 Apr.), and again in Santa Monica (7 Apr.), to inform him that he was being considered for the post of director of the FBI.

17 MAY–7 AUG.; 24 SEPT.–15 NOV. ERVIN COMMITTEE HEARINGS. By a vote of 70–0 (7 Feb.) the Senate established a 7-man Select Committee on Presidential Campaign Activities with Sen. **Sam J. Ervin, Jr.** of North Carolina (1896–) as chairman, and Prof. **Samuel Dash** as chief counsel. Televised public hearings brought the Watergate scandal high public visibility. Among the most significant testimony: (1) Magruder confessed to having committed perjury before the grand jury (14 June) and implicated Mitchell in planning the burglary; (2) Dean (25–29 June) asserted that the president had been party to the coverup for 8 months, implicated the president in offers of executive clemency

to the burglary defendants and Haldeman and Ehrlichman in the coverup; he revealed the existence of a White House "Enemies List" of politicians, journalists, academicians, entertainers, and others, for potential harassment, including audits by the IRS, as well as information about the "Plumbers," a special White House program of wiretaps and other activities under a Special Investigations Unit, begun originally to plug press leaks; (3) Mitchell's statement (10–12 July) that "White House horrors" encompassed an attempt to forge State Department cables to implicate President John F. Kennedy in the assassination of Ngo Dinh Diem and therefore to besmirch his brother, Sen. Edward M. Kennedy; (4) Alexander Butterfield, former deputy presidential assistant, disclosed (16 July) that Nixon had tape recorded all his conversations in the White House and Executive Office Building; (5) Herbert W. Kalmbach, formerly Nixon's personal attorney, admitted (16 July) to having raised $220,000 for the defendants; (6) Ehrlichman asserted (24–30 July) that the Ellsberg psychiatrist's burglary had been within the constitutional powers of the president.

APR.–OCT. COX INVESTIGATIONS. After Kleindienst resigned, **Elliot L. Richardson** was appointed attorney general (30 Apr.) and Prof. **Archibald Cox** (1912–) special prosecutor (18 May). Butterfield's revelations prompted Nixon to assert executive privilege and to refuse to release the tapes to either Cox (23 July) or to the Ervin Committee (17 July). Both then served subpoenas upon the president 23 July. Judge Sirica ordered Nixon to turn over the tapes to him (29 Aug.) (p. 685). After Sirica's decision was upheld by the U.S. Court of Appeals for the District of Columbia Circuit (12 Oct.), the president decided not to appeal to the Supreme Court. Nixon offered a "compromise," written summaries of tapes whose accuracy would be verified by Sen. John C. Stennis (Miss.), but with Cox enjoined to seek no further presidential documents through the judicial process.

20 Oct. "SATURDAY NIGHT MASSACRE." After Cox turned down the compromise, Nixon ordered both Attorney General Richardson and William D. Ruckelshaus, deputy attorney general, to dismiss him. Both refused and resigned. Solicitor General Robert H. Bork, becoming acting attorney general, then fired Cox, and FBI agents sealed off the offices of Richardson, Ruckelshaus, and the special prosecutor. Adverse public reaction led (1) the president to agree (23 Oct.) to obey Sirica's order for the tapes; (2) to the introduction of 16 impeachment resolutions in the House of Representatives, sponsored by 84 representatives; (3) to the appointment of Sen. William Saxbe (Ohio) as attorney general (1 Nov.), and Leon Jaworski (1905–   ), Houston attorney, as special prosecutor (1 Nov.). Of 9 tapes included in Sirica's order, 2 were asserted by the White House (31 Oct.) never to have existed, and an 18-minute gap appeared on a third (26 Nov.). Court-appointed experts later found the gap to be the result of multiple manual erasures (4 June 1974).

RELATED WATERGATE "SCANDALS" included (1) ITT, suggesting a possible presidential involvement in settlement of an antitrust suit in 1971 favorable to International Telephone and Telegraph Corp., which later pledged to defer the cost of the Republican National Convention; (2) campaign contributions by major corporations made under CRP pressure; (3) Milk Fund, suggesting a connection between the president's decision to approve higher milk price supports (Mar. 1971) and a pledge from the dairy industry of large campaign contributions; (4) Hughes gifts—whether the president knew about large and secret gifts of cash, allegedly campaign donations (1969–70), from Howard Hughes, financier, to Charles G. "Bebe" Rebozo, the president's close friend; (5) San Clemente-Key Biscayne—whether the method by which the president bought his 2 estates was improper and whether he had profited illegally from government expenditures of above $10 million to secure the grounds; (6) president's taxes —whether the president committed fraud in the preparation of his 1969–72 tax returns; the Joint Committee on Internal Revenue Taxation of the Congress, reviewing the president's taxes at his request, reported (3 Apr. 1974) that he owed $476,531 in back taxes and interest, which the president announced he would pay. The report drew no conclusions as to fraud; (7) Vesco case—John Mitchell and Maurice H. Stans, the latter former Secretary of Commerce and finance chairman of CRP, were found innocent (28 Apr. 1974) after jury trial of conspiracy in soliciting a gift of $200,000 to the president's campaign fund from financier Robert Vesco in exchange for interceding with the SEC on his behalf. Stans and Mitchell were also acquitted of perjury and obstruction of justice.

IMPEACHMENT PROCEEDINGS. Impeachment resolutions were turned over to the House Judiciary Committee, which began preliminary investigations, 30 Oct. 1973, by granting broad subpoena power to the chairman, Peter Rodino (N.J.; 1909–   ). Closed hearings, directed by staff counsel John Doar commenced 9 May 1974. Although the president refused to comply with a committee subpoena for tapes (4 Apr.), the president released 1,200 pages of edited transcripts of 42 taped conversations (30 Apr.). Judge Sirica turned over to the Judiciary Committee, 26 Mar., the sealed grand jury report (1 Mar.), apparently citing the president as a co-conspirator in the Watergate coverup. Judge Sirica ordered Nixon (20 May) to turn over 64 tapes to Jaworski. The Supreme Court agreed on 31 May to bypass the Court of Appeals and hear the appeal from Sirica's order.

NIXON RESIGNATION. After televised debate, the House Judiciary Committee voted 3 articles of impeachment. On 27 July the committee voted 27–11 to recommend impeachment of Nixon on the ground that he "engaged personally and through his subordinates and agents in a course of conduct designed to delay, impede, and obstruct the investigation" of the Watergate break-in; "to cover up, conceal, and protect those responsible"; and to "conceal the existence and scope of other unlawful covert activities." A second article passed (29 July) by a vote of 28–10 charging Nixon with a persistent effort to abuse his authority in violation of his constitutional oath. The president was accused of engaging in conduct "violating the constitutional rights of citizens, impairing the due and proper administration of justice in the conduct of lawful inquiries, of contravening the law of governing agencies of the executive branch and the purposes of these agencies." The committee passed (30 July) 21–17 a third article charging the president with unconstitutional defiance of committee subpoenas, thus impeding the impeachment process. That day the committee voted down by 26–12 articles accusing Nixon of usurping congressional war powers by the secret bombing of Cambodia and of demeaning his office by misconduct of personal financial affairs. Nixon released (5 Aug) the transcript of 3 tapes of 23 June 1972 which revealed that he had been aware of a "coverup" long before 21 Mar. 1973, and that he personally had ordered a halt to the FBI investigation. Most of Nixon's remaining defenders in the Congress, including all 11 Republicans who had voted against the first article of impeachment, considered this the "smoking gun," evidence sufficient to support the first article. Nixon announced his resignation 8 Aug., stating that he "no longer had a strong enough political base" to persevere. The resignation took effect 11:35 A.M. on 9 Aug. when delivered to Secretary of State Kissinger.

9 AUG. FORD ACCESSION. Ford took the oath of office from Chief Justice Warren E. Burger at 12:03 P.M. in a ceremony in the East Room of the White House and delivered "not an inaugural address, not a fireside chat, not a campaign speech" but "just a little straight talk among friends." Ford nominated **Nelson A. Rockefeller** (p. 1139) to be vice-president on 20 Aug.

8 SEPT. NIXON PARDON. Ford gave Nixon an unconditional pardon for all federal crimes that he committed or may have committed or taken part in. Nixon did not confess guilt but in a statement admitted to "mistakes." A concurrent agreement recognized Nixon's title to the tape recordings and ultimate right to destroy them but preserved them for a 3-year period for use in court. The pardon and agreement on the tapes were widely criticized. By statute, Congress placed the tapes and Nixon administration papers in the custody and control of the federal government, requiring explicit Congressional authorization for destruction of any materials. President Ford testified personally (17 Oct.) before the House Judiciary Subcommittee on Criminal Justice stating, "There was no deal, period."

1 JAN.–17 APR. 1975. CONVICTION OF NIXON AIDES. Haldeman, Ehrlichman, Mitchell and former Assistant Attorney General Robert Mardian were convicted on all counts and Kenneth W. Parkinson, former lawyer for CRP, acquitted after a 64-day jury trial. Mitchell,

Haldeman, and Ehrlichman were convicted of conspiracy, obstruction of justice, and perjury; Mardian of the conspiracy to obstruct justice in the original investigation of the Watergate break-in. Haldeman, Ehrlichman, and Mitchell were sentenced to 2½ to 8 years in prison by Judge Sirica (21 Feb.) and Mardian to 10 months to 3 years. Ehrlichman had previously been convicted (12 July 1974) with G. Gordon Liddy, Bernard Barker, and Eugenio Martinez, of conspiring to violate the civil rights of Daniel Ellsberg's former psychiatrist, Lewis J. Fielding, and of making false statements to the FBI and grand juries.

In a separate case, former Secretary of Commerce Maurice Stans was fined $5,000 (14 May) after having pleaded guilty to 5 misdemeanor violations of federal campaign laws, including 2 counts of "nonwillful acceptance" of illegal corporate campaign contributions. Three members of the Nixon cabinet were sentenced for crime, Mitchell, Stans, and former Attorney General Richard G. Kleindienst, who had pleaded guilty to a misdemeanor charge involving the withholding of information and received a suspended sentence. Former Secretary of the Treasury John B. Connally, Jr., was acquitted of bribery charges (17 Apr.).

PRESIDENTS
AND THEIR CABINETS

Dates given below are when each individual assumed office

1st President	**George Washington**	**1789, 1793**
Vice President	John Adams	1789, 1793
State[1]	John Jay	1789*
	Thomas Jefferson	1790
	Edmund Randolph	1794
	Timothy Pickering	1795
War[2]	Henry Knox	1789
	Timothy Pickering	1795*
	James McHenry	1796
Treasury[3]	Alexander Hamilton	1789
	Oliver Wolcott, Jr.	1795
Post. General[4]	Samuel Osgood	1789
	Timothy Pickering	1791
	Joseph Habersham	1795
Atty. General[5]	Edmund Randolph	1790
	William Bradford	1794
	Charles Lee	1795

* ad interim.
[1] Dept. of Foreign Affairs est. 27 July 1789; redesignated Dept. of State 15 Sept. 1789.
[2] Est. 7 Aug. 1789.
[3] Est. 2 Sept. 1789.
[4] Est. 22 Sept. 1789.
[5] Est. 24 Sept. 1789, Dept. of Justice created 22 June 1870.

2d President	**John Adams**	**1797**
Vice President	Thomas Jefferson	1797
State	Timothy Pickering	1797
	Charles Lee	1800*
	John Marshall	1800, 1801*
War	James McHenry	1797
	Benjamin Stoddert	1800
	Samuel Dexter	1800, 1801*
Treasury	Oliver Wolcott, Jr.	1797
	Samuel Dexter	1801
Post. General	Joseph Habersham	1797
Atty. General	Charles Lee	1797
Navy[1]	Benjamin Stoddert	1798

* ad interim.

3d President	**Thomas Jefferson**	**1801, 1805**
Vice President	Aaron Burr	1801
	George Clinton	1805
State	John Marshall	1801*
	Levi Lincoln	1801*
	James Madison	1801

War	Henry Dearborn	1801
	John Smith	1809*
Treasury	Samuel Dexter	1801
	Albert Gallatin	1801, 1805
Post. General	Joseph Habersham	1801
	Gideon Granger	1801, 1805
Atty. General	Levi Lincoln	1801
	John C. Breckinridge	1805
	Caesar A. Rodney	1807
Navy	Benjamin Stoddert	1801
	Henry Dearborn	1801*
	Robert Smith	1801

* ad interim.
[1] Est. 3 May 1797.

4th President	**James Madison**	**1809, 1813**
Vice President	George Clinton	1809
	Elbridge Gerry	1813
State	Robert Smith	1809
	James Monroe	1811, 1813, 1814,* 1815
War	John Smith	1809*
	William Eustis	1809
	James Monroe	1813, 1814, 1815*
	John Armstrong	1813
	Alexander J. Dallas	1815*
	William H. Crawford	1815
	George Graham	1816*
Treasury	Albert Gallatin	1809, 1813
	George W. Campbell	1814
	Alexander J. Dallas	1814
	William H. Crawford	1816
Post. General	Gideon Granger	1809, 1813
	Return J. Meigs, Jr.	1814
Atty. General	Caesar A. Rodney	1809
	William Pinkney	1812, 1813
	Richard Rush	1814
Navy	Robert Smith	1809
	Charles W. Goldsborough	1809,* 1813*
	Paul Hamilton	1809
	William Jones	1813
	Benjamin Homans	1814*
	Benjamin W. Crowninshield	1814

* ad interim.

5th President	**James Monroe**	**1817, 1821**
Vice President	Daniel D. Tompkins	1817, 1821
State	John Graham	1817*
	Richard Rush	1817*
	John Quincy Adams	1817, 1821
War	George Graham	1817*
	John C. Calhoun	1817, 1821
Treasury	William H. Crawford	1817, 1821
Post. General	Return J. Meigs, Jr.	1817, 1821
	John McLean	1823
Atty. General	Richard Rush	1817
	William Wirt	1817, 1821
Navy	Benjamin W. Crowninshield	1817
	John C. Calhoun	1818*
	Smith Thompson	1818, 1821
	John Rodgers	1823*
	Samuel L. Southard	1823

* ad interim.

	6th President	**John Quincy Adams**	1825
Vice President		John C. Calhoun	1825
State		Daniel Brent	1825*
		Henry Clay	1825
War		James Barbour	1825
		Samuel L. Southard	1828*
		Peter B. Porter	1828
Treasury		Samuel L. Southard	1825*
		Richard Rush	1825
Post. General		John McLean	1825
Atty. General		William Wirt	1825
Navy		Samuel L. Southard	1825

* ad interim.

	7th President	**Andrew Jackson**	**1829, 1833**
Vice President		John C. Calhoun	1829
		Martin Van Buren	1833
State		James A. Hamilton	1829*
		Martin Van Buren	1829
		Edward Livingston	1831, 1833
		Louis McLane	1833
		John Forsyth	1834
War		John H. Eaton	1829
		Philip G. Randolph	1831*
		Roger B. Taney	1831*
		Lewis Cass	1831, 1833
		Carey A. Harris	1836*
		Benjamin F. Butler	1836,* 1837*
Treasury		Samuel D. Ingham	1829
		Asbury Dickins	1831*
		Louis McLane	1831, 1833
		William J. Duane	1833
		Roger B. Taney	1833
		McClintock Young	1834*
		Levi Woodbury	1834
Post. General		John McLean	1829
		William T. Barry	1829, 1833
		Amos Kendall	1835
Atty. General		John M. Berrien	1829
		Roger B. Taney	1831, 1833
		Benjamin F. Butler	1833
Navy		Charles Hay	1829*
		John Branch	1829
		John Boyle	1831*
		Levi Woodbury	1831, 1833
		Mahlon Dickerson	1834

* ad interim.

	8th President	**Martin Van Buren**	**1837**
Vice President		Richard M. Johnson	1837
State		John Forsyth	1837
War		Benjamin F. Butler	1837*
		Joel R. Poinsett	1837
Treasury		Levi Woodbury	1837
Post. General		Amos Kendall	1837
		John M. Niles	1840
Atty. General		Benjamin F. Butler	1837
		Felix Grundy	1838
		Henry D. Gilpin	1840
Navy		Mahlon Dickerson	1837
		James K. Paulding	1838

* ad interim.

9th President	**William Henry Harrison**	**1841**
Vice President	John Tyler	1841
State	J. L. Martin	1841*
	Daniel Webster	1841
War	John Bell	1841
Treasury	McClintock Young	1841*
	Thomas Ewing	1841
Post. General	Selah R. Hobbie	1841*
	Francis Granger	1841
Atty. General	John J. Crittenden	1841
Navy	John D. Simms	1841*
	George E. Badger	1841

* ad interim.

10th President	**John Tyler**	**1841**
Vice President	———	
State	Daniel Webster	1841
	Hugh S. Legaré	1843*
	William S. Derrick	1843*
	Abel P. Upshur	1843,* 1843
	John Nelson	1844*
	John C. Calhoun	1844
War	John Bell	1841
	Albert M. Lea	1841*
	John C. Spencer	1841
	John M. Porter	1843
	William Wilkins	1844
Treasury	Thomas Ewing	1841
	McClintock Young	1841, 1843,* 1844*
	Walter Forward	1841
	John C. Spencer	1843
	George M. Bibb	1844
Post. General	Francis Granger	1841
	Selah R. Hobbie	1841*
	Charles A. Wickliffe	1841
Atty. General	John J. Crittenden	1841
	Hugh S. Legaré	1841
	John Nelson	1843
Navy	George E. Badger	1841
	John D. Simms	1841*
	Abel P. Upshur	1841
	David Henshaw	1843
	Thomas W. Gilmer	1844
	Lewis Washington	1844*
	John Y. Mason	1844

* ad interim.

11th President	**James K. Polk**	**1845**
Vice President	George M. Dallas	1845
State	John C. Calhoun	1845
	James Buchanan	1845
War	William Wilkins	1845
	William L. Marcy	1845
Treasury	George M. Bibb	1845
	Robert J. Walker	1845
Post. General	Charles A. Wickliffe	1845
	Cave Johnson	1845
Atty. General	John Nelson	1845
	John Y. Mason	1845
	Nathan Clifford	1846
	Isaac Toucey	1848
Navy	John Y. Mason	1845, 1846
	George Bancroft	1845
	John Y. Mason	1846

* ad interim.

12th President	Zachary Taylor	1849
Vice President	Millard Fillmore	1849
State	James Buchanan	1849
	John M. Clayton	1849
War	William L. Marcy	1849
	Reverdy Johnson	1849*
	George W. Crawford	1849
Treasury	Robert J. Walker	1849
	McClintock Young	1849*
	William M. Meredith	1849
Post. General	Cave Johnson	1849
	Selah R. Hobbie	1849*
	Jacob Collamer	1849
Atty. General	Isaac Toucey	1849
	Reverdy Johnson	1849
Navy	John Y. Mason	1849
	William B. Preston	1849
Interior[1]	Thomas Ewing	1849

* ad interim.
[1] Est. 3 Mar. 1849.

13th President	Millard Fillmore	1850
Vice President	———	
State	John M. Clayton	1850
	Daniel Webster	1850
	Charles M. Conrad	1852*
	Edward Everett	1852
War	George W. Crawford	1850
	Samuel J. Anderson	1850*
	Winfield Scott	1850*
	Charles M. Conrad	1850
Treasury	William M. Meredith	1850
	Thomas Corwin	1850
Post. General	Jacob Collamer	1850
	Nathan K. Hall	1850
	Samuel D. Hubbard	1852
Atty. General	Reverdy Johnson	1850
	John J. Crittenden	1850
Navy	William B. Preston	1850
	Lewis Warrington	1850*
	William A. Graham	1850
	John P. Kennedy	1852
Interior	Thomas Ewing	1850
	Daniel C. Goddard	1850, 1850*
	Thomas M.T. McKennan	1850
	Alexander H.H. Stuart	1850

* ad interim.

14th President	Franklin Pierce	1853
Vice President	William R. King	1853
State	William Hunter	1853*
	William L. Marcy	1853
War	Charles M. Conrad	1853
	Jefferson Davis	1853
	Samuel Cooper	1857*
Treasury	Thomas Corwin	1853
	James Guthrie	1853
Post. General	Samuel D. Hubbard	1853
	James Campbell	1853
Atty. General	John J. Crittenden	1853
	Caleb Cushing	1853
Navy	John P. Kennedy	1853
	James C. Dobbin	1853
Interior	Alexander H.H. Stuart	1853
	Robert McClelland	1853

* ad interim.

15th President	James Buchanan	1857
Vice President	John C. Breckinridge	1857
State	William L. Marcy	1857
	Lewis Cass	1857
	William Hunter	1860*
	Jeremiah S. Black	1860
War	Samuel Cooper	1857*
	John B. Floyd	1857
	Joseph Holt	1861,* 1861
Treasury	James Guthrie	1857
	Howell Cobb	1857
	Isaac Toucey	1860*
	Philip F. Thomas	1860
	John A. Dix	1861
Post. General	James Campbell	1857
	Aaron V. Brown	1857
	Horatio King	1859,* 1861,* 1861
	Joseph Holt	1859
Atty. General	Caleb Cushing	1857
	Jeremiah S. Black	1857
	Edwin M. Stanton	1860
Navy	James C. Dobbin	1857
	Isaac Toucey	1857
Interior	Robert McClelland	1857
	Jacob Thompson	1857
	Moses Kelly	1861*

* ad interim.

16th President	Abraham Lincoln	1861, 1865
Vice President	Hannibal Hamlin	1861
	Andrew Johnson	1865
State	Jeremiah S. Black	1861
	William H. Seward	1861, 1865
War	Joseph Holt	1861
	Simon Cameron	1861
	Edwin M. Stanton	1862, 1865
Treasury	John A. Dix	1861
	Salmon P. Chase	1861
	George Harrington	1864,* 1865*
	William P. Fessenden	1864
	Hugh McCulloch	1865
Post. General	Horatio King	1861
	Montgomery Blair	1861
	William Dennison	1864, 1865
Atty. General	Edwin M. Stanton	1861
	Edward Bates	1861
	James Speed	1864, 1865
Navy	Isaac Toucey	1861
	Gideon Welles	1861, 1865
Interior	Moses Kelly	1861*
	Caleb B. Smith	1861
	John P. Usher	1863,* 1863, 1865

* ad interim.

17th President	Andrew Johnson	1865
Vice President	———	
State	William H. Seward	1865
War	Edwin M. Stanton	1865, 1868
	Ulysses S. Grant	1867*
	John M. Schofield	1868
Treasury	Hugh McCulloch	1865
Post. General	William Dennison	1865
	Alexander W. Randall	1866,* 1866

* ad interim.

Atty. General	James Speed	1865
	J. Hubley Ashton	1866*
	Henry Stanbery	1866
	Orville H. Browning	1868*
	William M. Evarts	1868
Navy	Gideon Welles	1865
Interior	John P. Usher	1865
	James Harlan	1865
	Orville H. Browning	1866

* ad interim.

18th President	**Ulysses S. Grant**	**1869, 1873**
Vice President	Schuyler Colfax	1869
	Henry Wilson	1875
State	William H. Seward	1869
	Elihu B. Washburne	1869
	Hamilton Fish	1869, 1873
War	John M. Schofield	1869
	John A. Rawlins	1869
	William T. Sherman	1869
	William W. Belknap	1869, 1873
	George M. Robeson	1876*
	Alphonso Taft	1876
	James D. Cameron	1876
Treasury	Hugh McCulloch	1869
	John F. Hartley	1869*
	George S. Boutwell	1869, 1873
	William A. Richardson	1873
	Benjamin H. Bristow	1874
	Charles F. Conant	1876*
	Lot M. Morrill	1876
Post. General	St. John B.L. Skinner	1869*
	John A.J. Creswell	1869, 1873
	James W. Marshall	1874
	Marshall Jewell	1874
	James N. Tyner	1876
Atty. General	William M. Evarts	1869
	J. Hubley Ashton	1869*
	Ebenezer R. Hoar	1869
	Amos T. Akerman	1870
	George H. Williams	1872, 1873
	Edwards Pierrepont	1875
	Alphonso Taft	1876
Navy	William Faxon	1869*
	Adolph E. Borie	1869
	George Robeson	1869, 1873
Interior	William T. Otto	1869*
	Jacob D. Cox	1869
	Columbus Delano	1870, 1873
	Benjamin R. Cowen	1875*
	Zachariah Chandler	1875

* ad intorim.

19th President	**Rutherford B. Hayes**	**1877**
Vice President	William A. Wheeler	1877
State	Hamilton Fish	1877
	William M. Evarts	1877
War	James D. Cameron	1877
	George W. McCrary	1877
	Alexander Ramsey	1879
Treasury	Lot M. Morrill	1877
	John Sherman	1877

Post. General	James N. Tyner	1877
	David M. Key	1877
	Horace Maynard	1880
Atty. General	Alphonso Taft	1877
	Charles Devens	1877
Navy	George M. Robeson	1877
	Richard W. Thompson	1877
	Alexander Ramsey	1880*
	Nathan Goff, Jr.	1881
Interior	Zachariah Chandler	1877
	Carl Schurz	1877

* ad interim.

20th President	**James A. Garfield**	**1881**
Vice President	Chester A. Arthur	1881
State	William M. Evarts	1881
	James G. Blaine	1881
War	Alexander Ramsey	1881
	Robert T. Lincoln	1881
Treasury	Henry F. French	1881*
	William Windom	1881
Post. General	Horace Maynard	1881
	Thomas L. James	1881
Atty. General	Charles Devens	1881
	Wayne MacVeagh	1881
Navy	Nathan Goff, Jr.	1881
	William H. Hunt	1881
Interior	Carl Schurz	1881
	Samuel J. Kirkwood	1881

* ad interim.

21st President	**Chester A. Arthur**	**1881**
Vice President	——	
State	James G. Blaine	1881
	Frederick T. Frelinghuysen	1881
War	Robert T. Lincoln	1881
Treasury	William Windom	1881
	Charles J. Folger	1881
	Charles E. Coon	1884*
	Henry F. French	1884*
	Walter Q. Gresham	1884
	Hugh McCulloch	1884
Post. General	Thomas L. James	1881
	Timothy O. Howe	1882
	Frank Hatton	1883,* 1884*
	Walter Q. Gresham	1883
Atty. General	Wayne MacVeagh	1881
	Samuel F. Phillips	1881*
	Benjamin H. Brewster	1882
Navy	William H. Hunt	1881
	William E. Chandler	1882
Interior	Samuel J. Kirkwood	1881
	Henry M. Teller	1882

* ad interim.

22nd President	**Grover Cleveland**	**1885**
Vice President	Thomas A. Hendricks	1885
State	Frederick T. Frelinghuysen	1885
	Thomas F. Bayard	1885
War	Robert T. Lincoln	1885
	William C. Endicott	1885
Treasury	Hugh McCulloch	1885
	Daniel Manning	1885
	Charles S. Fairchild	1887
Post. General	Frank Hatton	1885

	William F. Vilas	1885
	Don M. Dickinson	1888
Atty. General	Benjamin H. Brewster	1885
	Augustus H. Garland	1885
Navy	William E. Chandler	1885
	William C. Whitney	1885
Interior	Merritt L. Joslyn	1885*
	Lucius Q. C. Lamar	1885
	Henry L. Muldrow	1888*
	William F. Vilas	1888
Agriculture[1]	Norman J. Colman	1889

* ad interim.
[1] Est. 11 Feb. 1889.

23rd President	**Benjamin Harrison**	**1889**
Vice President	Levi P. Morton	1889
State	Thomas F. Bayard	1889
	James G. Blaine	1889
	William F. Wharton	1892,* 1893*
	John W. Foster	1892
War	William C. Endicott	1889
	Redfield Proctor	1889
	Lewis A. Grant	1891*
	Stephen B. Elkins	1891
Treasury	Charles S. Fairchild	1889
	William Windom	1889
	Allured B. Nettleton	1891*
	Charles Foster	1891
Post. General	Don M. Dickinson	1889
	John Wanamaker	1889
Atty. General	Augustus H. Garland	1889
	William H. H. Miller	1889
Navy	William C. Whitney	1889
	Benjamin F. Tracy	1889
Interior	William F. Vilas	1889
	John W. Noble	1889
Agriculture	Norman J. Colman	1889
	Jeremiah M. Rusk	1889

* ad interim.

24th President	**Grover Cleveland**	**1893**
Vice President	Adlai E. Stevenson	1893
State	William F. Wharton	1893
	Walter Q. Gresham	1893
	Edwin F. Uhl	1895*
	Alvey A. Adee	1895*
	Richard Olney	1895
War	Stephen B. Elkins	1893
	Daniel S. Lamont	1893
Treasury	Charles Foster	1893
	John G. Carlisle	1893
Post. General	John Wanamaker	1893
	Wilson S. Bissell	1893
	William L. Wilson	1895
Atty. General	William H.H. Miller	1893
	Richard Olney	1893
	Judson Harmon	1895
Navy	Benjamin F. Tracy	1893
	Hilary A. Herbert	1893
Interior	John W. Noble	1893
	Hoke Smith	1893
	John M. Reynolds	1896*
	David R. Francis	1896
Agriculture	Jeremiah M. Rusk	1893
	Julius Sterling Morton	1893

* ad interim.

25th President	**William McKinley**	**1897, 1901**
Vice President	Garret Hobart	1897
	Theodore Roosevelt	1901
State	Richard Olney	1897
	John Sherman	1897
	William R. Day	1898
	Alvey A. Adee	1898*
	John M. Hay	1898, 1901
War	Daniel S. Lamont	1897
	Russell A. Alger	1897
	Elihu Root	1899, 1901
Treasury	John G. Carlisle	1897
	Lyman J. Gage	1897, 1901
Post. General	William L. Wilson	1897
	James A. Gary	1897
	Charles Emory Smith	1898, 1901
Atty. General	Judson Harmon	1897
	Joseph McKenna	1897
	John K. Richards	1898,* 1901*
	John W. Griggs	1898, 1901
	Philander C. Knox	1901
Navy	Hilary A. Herbert	1897
	John D. Long	1897
Interior	David R. Francis	1897
	Cornelius N. Bliss	1897
	Ethan A. Hitchcock	1899, 1901
Agriculture	Julius Sterling Morton	1897
	James Wilson	1897

* ad interim.

26th President	**Theodore Roosevelt**	**1901, 1905**
Vice President	Charles Warren Fairbanks	1905
State	John M. Hay	1901, 1905
	Francis B. Loomis	1905*
	Elihu Root	1905
	Robert Bacon	1909
War	Elihu Root	1901
	William Howard Taft	1904, 1905
	Luke E. Wright	1908
Treasury	Lyman J. Gage	1902
	Leslie M. Shaw	1902, 1905
	George B. Cortelyou	1907
Post. General	Charles Emory Smith	1901
	Harry C. Payne	1902
	Robert J. Wynne	1904, 1905
	George B. Cortelyou	1905
	George von L. Meyer	1907
Atty. General	Philander C. Knox	1901
	William H. Moody	1904, 1905
	Charles J. Bonaparte	1906
Navy	John D. Long	1901
	William H. Moody	1902
	Paul Morton	1904, 1905
	Charles J. Bonaparte	1905
	Victor H. Metcalf	1906
	Truman H. Newberry	1908
Interior	Ethan A. Hitchcock	1901, 1905
	James R. Garfield	1907
Agriculture	James Wilson	1901, 1905
Comm. & Labor[1]	George B. Cortelyou	1903
	Victor H. Metcalf	1904, 1905
	Oscar S. Straus	1906

* ad interim.
[1] Est. 14 Feb. 1903.

27th President	**William Howard Taft**	**1909**
Vice President	James S. Sherman	1909
State	Robert Bacon	1909
	Philander C. Knox	1909
War	Luke E. Wright	1909
	Jacob M. Dickinson	1909
	Henry L. Stimson	1911
Treasury	George B. Cortelyou	1909
	Franklin MacVeagh	1909
Post. General	George von L. Meyer	1909
	Frank H. Hitchcock	1909
Atty. General	Charles J. Bonaparte	1909
	George W. Wickersham	1909
Navy	Truman H. Newberry	1909
	George von L. Meyer	1909
Interior	James R. Garfield	1909
	Richard A. Ballinger	1909
	Walter Lowrie Fisher	1911
Agriculture	James Wilson	1909
Comm. & Labor	Oscar S. Straus	1909
	Charles Nagel	1909

* ad interim.

28th President	**Woodrow Wilson**	**1913, 1917**
Vice President	Thomas R. Marshall	1913, 1917
State	Philander C. Knox	1913
	Wm. Jennings Bryan	1913
	Robert Lansing	1915,* 1915, 1917
	Frank L. Polk	1920*
	Bainbridge Colby	1920
War	Henry L. Stimson	1913
	Lindley M. Garrison	1913
	Hugh L. Scott	1916*
	Newton D. Baker	1916, 1917
Treasury	Franklin MacVeagh	1913
	William Gibbs McAdoo	1913, 1917
	Carter Glass	1918
	David F. Houston	1920
Post. General	Frank H. Hitchcock	1913
	Albert Sidney Burleson	1913, 1917, 1918
Atty. General	George W. Wickersham	1913
	James Clark McReynolds	1913
	Thomas Watt Gregory	1914, 1917
	A. Mitchell Palmer	1919
Navy	George von L. Meyer	1913
	Josephus Daniels	1913, 1917
Interior	Walter Lowrie Fisher	1913
	Franklin Knight Lane	1913, 1917
	John Barton Payne	1920
Agriculture	James Wilson	1913
	David Franklin Houston	1913, 1917
	Edwin T. Meredith	1920
Commerce[1]	Charles Nagel	1913
	William C. Redfield	1913
Labor[2]	Charles Nagel	1913
	William Bauchop Wilson	1913

* ad interim.
[1] Est. 4 Mar. 1913, divided from Labor.
[2] Est. 4 Mar. 1913, divided from Commerce.

29th President	**Warren G. Harding**	**1921**
Vice President	Calvin Coolidge	1921
State	Bainbridge Colby	1921
	Charles Evans Hughes	1921

War	Newton D. Baker	1921
	John W. Weeks	1921
Treasury	David F. Houston	1921
	Andrew W. Mellon	1921
Post. General	Albert Sidney Burleson	1921
	Will H. Hays	1921
	Hubert Work	1922
	Harry S. New	1923
Atty. General	A. Mitchell Palmer	1921
	Harry M. Dougherty	1921
Navy	Josephus Daniels	1921
	Edwin Denby	1921
Interior	John Barton Payne	1921
	Albert B. Fall	1921
	Hubert Work	1923
Agriculture	Edwin T. Meredith	1921
	Henry C. Wallace	1921
Commerce	Joshua Willis Alexander	1921
	Herbert C. Hoover	1921
Labor	William Bauchop Wilson	1921
	James J. Davis	1921

* ad interim.

30th President	**Calvin Coolidge**	**1923, 1925**
Vice President	Charles G. Dawes	1925
State	Charles Evans Hughes	1923, 1925
	Frank B. Kellogg	1925
War	John W. Weeks	1923, 1925
	Dwight F. Davis	1925
Treasury	Andrew W. Mellon	1923, 1925
Post. General	Harry S. New	1923, 1925
Atty. General	Harry M. Dougherty	1923
	Harlan Fiske Stone	1924
Navy	Edwin Denby	1923
	Curtis D. Wilbur	1924, 1925
Interior	Hubert Work	1923, 1925
	Roy O. West	1929
Agriculture	Henry C. Wallace	1923
	Howard M. Gore	1924,* 1924, 1925
	William M. Jardine	1925
Commerce	Herbert C. Hoover	1923, 1925
	William F. Whiting	1928,* 1928
Labor	James J. Davis	1923, 1925

* ad interim.

31st President	**Herbert C. Hoover**	**1929**
Vice President	Charles Curtis	1929
State	Frank B. Kellogg	1929
	Henry L. Stimson	1929
War	Dwight F. Davis	1929
	James W. Good	1929
	Patrick J. Hurley	1929
Treasury	Andrew W. Mellon	1929
	Ogden L. Mills	1932
Post. General	Harry S. New	1929
	Walter F. Brown	1929
Atty. General	John G. Sargent	1929
	James DeWitt Mitchell	1929
Navy	Curtis D. Wilbur	1929
	Charles F. Adams	1929
Interior	Roy O. West	1929
	Ray L. Wilbur	1929

Agriculture	William M. Jardine	1929
	Arthur M. Hyde	1929
Commerce	William F. Whiting	1929
	Robert P. Lamont	1929
	Roy D. Chapin	1932,* 1932
Labor	James J. Davis	1929
	William N. Doak	1930

* ad interim.

32d President	**Franklin D. Roosevelt**	**1933, 1937, 1941, 1945**
Vice President	John N. Garner	1933, 1937
	Henry A. Wallace	1941
	Harry S. Truman	1945
State	Cordell Hull	1933, 1937, 1941
	Edward R. Stettinius	1944, 1945
War	George H. Dern	1933, 1937
	Harry H. Woodring	1936,* 1937
	Henry L. Stimson	1940, 1941, 1945
Treasury	William H. Woodin	1933
	Henry Morgenthau, Jr.	1934,* 1934, 1937, 1941, 1945
Post. General	James A. Farley	1933, 1937
	Frank C. Walker	1940, 1941, 1945
Atty. General	Homer S. Cummings	1933, 1937
	Frank Murphy	1939,* 1939
	Robert H. Jackson	1940, 1941
	Francis Biddle	1941, 1945
Navy	Claude A. Swanson	1933, 1937
	Charles Edison	1939,* 1940,* 1940
	Frank Knox	1940, 1941
	James V. Forrestal	1944, 1945
Interior	Harold L. Ickes	1933, 1937, 1941, 1945
Agriculture	Henry A. Wallace	1933, 1937
	Claude R. Wickard	1940, 1941, 1945
Commerce	Daniel C. Roper	1933, 1937
	Harry L. Hopkins	1938,* 1939
	Jesse H. Jones	1940, 1941, 1945
	Henry A. Wallace	1945
Labor	Frances Perkins	1933, 1937, 1941, 1945

* ad interim.

33d President	**Harry S. Truman**	**1945, 1949**
Vice President	Alben W. Barkley	1949
State	Edward R. Stettinius	1945
	James F. Byrnes	1945
	George C. Marshall	1947
	Dean G. Acheson	1949
War[1]	Henry L. Stimson	1945
	Robert P. Patterson	1945
	Kenneth C. Royall	1947
Treasury	Henry Morgenthau, Jr.	1945
	Fred M. Vinson	1945
	John W. Snyder	1946, 1949
Post. General	Frank C. Walker	1945
	Robert E. Hannegan	1945
	Jesse M. Donaldson	1947, 1949
Atty. General	Francis Biddle	1945
	Tom C. Clark	1945, 1949
	J. Howard McGrath	1949
	James P. McGranery	1952
Navy[1]	James V. Forrestal	1945
Interior	Harold L. Ickes	1945
	Julius A. Krug	1946, 1949
	Oscar L. Chapman	1949,* 1950,* 1950

Agriculture	Claude R. Wickard	1945
	Clinton P. Anderson	1945
	Charles F. Brennan	1948
Commerce	Henry A. Wallace	1945
	W. Averall Harriman	1946,* 1947,* 1947
	Charles Sawyer	1948, 1949
Labor	Frances Perkins	1945
	Lewis B. Schwellenbach	1945
	Maurice J. Tobin	1948,* 1949,* 1949
Defense[1]	James Forrestal	1947
	Louis A. Johnson	1949
	George C. Marshall	1950
	Robert A. Lovett	1951

* ad interim.
[1] Dept. of Defense est. 26 July 1947, incorporating Dept. of War and Dept. of Navy.

34th President	**Dwight D. Eisenhower**	**1953, 1957**
Vice President	Richard M. Nixon	1953, 1957
State	John Foster Dulles	1953, 1957
	Christian A. Herter	1959
Treasury	George M. Humphrey	1953, 1957
	Robert A. Anderson	1957
Post. General	Arthur E. Summerfield	1953, 1957
Atty. General	Herbert Brownell, Jr.	1953, 1957
	William P. Rogers	1958,* 1958
Interior	Douglas McKay	1953
	Frederick A. Seaton	1956, 1957
Agriculture	Ezra Taft Benson	1953, 1957
Commerce	Sinclair Weeks	1953, 1957
	Lewis L. Strauss	1958*
	Frederick H. Mueller	1959,* 1959
Labor	Martin P. Durkin	1953
	James P. Mitchell	1953,* 1954,* 1954, 1957
Defense	Charles E. Wilson	1953, 1957
	Neil H. McElroy	1957
	Thomas S. Gates, Jr.	1959,* 1960,* 1960
H.E.W.[1]	Oveta Culp Hobby	1953
	Marion B. Folsom	1955, 1957
	Arthur S. Flemming	1958

* ad interim.
[1] Est. 1 Apr. 1953.

35th President	**John F. Kennedy**	**1961**
Vice President	Lyndon B. Johnson	1961
State	Dean Rusk	1961
Treasury	C. Douglas Dillon	1961
Post. General	J. Edward Day	1961
	John A. Gronouski	1963
Atty. General	Robert F. Kennedy	1961
Interior	Stewart L. Udall	1961
Agriculture	Orville L. Freeman	1961
Commerce	Luther H. Hodges	1961
Labor	Arthur J. Goldberg	1961
	W. Willard Wirtz	1962
Defense	Robert S. McNamara	1961
H.E.W.	Abraham A. Ribicoff	1961
	Anthony J. Celebrezze	1962

36th President	**Lyndon B. Johnson**	**1963, 1965**
Vice President	Hubert H. Humphrey	1965
State	Dean Rusk	1963, 1965
Treasury	C. Douglas Dillon	1963, 1965
	Henry H. Fowler	1965

Post. General	John S. Gronouski	1963, 1965
	Lawrence O'Brien	1965
Atty. General	Robert F. Kennedy	1963
	Nicholas Katzenbach	1965
	Ramsey Clark	1967
Interior	Stewart L. Udall	1963, 1965
Agriculture	Orville L. Freeman	1963, 1965
Commerce	Luther H. Hodges	1963
	John T. Conner	1965
	Alexander B. Trowbridge	1967
	C. R. Smith	1968
Labor	W. Willard Wirtz	1963, 1965
Defense	Robert S. McNamara	1963, 1965
	Clark Clifford	1968
H.E.W.	Anthony J. Celebrezze	1963, 1965
	John W. Gardner	1965
	Wilbur J. Cohen	1968
H.U.D.[1]	Robert C. Weaver	1966
Transport.[2]	Alan S. Boyd	1967

[1] Est. 9 Sept. 1965.
[2] Est. 1 Apr. 1967.

37th President	**Richard M. Nixon**	**1969, 1973**
Vice President	Spiro T. Agnew	1969, 1973
	Gerald R. Ford	1973
State	William P. Rogers	1969
	Henry A. Kissinger	1973
Treasury	David M. Kennedy	1969
	John B. Connally	1971
	George F. Shultz	1972
	William E. Simon	1974
Post. General[1]	Winton M. Blount	1969
Atty. General	John N. Mitchell	1969
	Richard G. Kleindienst	1972
	Elliot L. Richardson	1973
	William B. Saxbe	1973
Interior	Walter J. Hickel	1969
	Rogers C.B. Morton	1971
Agriculture	Clifford M. Hardin	1969
	Earl L. Butz	1971
Commerce	Maurice H. Stans	1969
	Peter G. Peterson	1972
	Frederick B. Dent	1973
Labor	George P. Shultz	1969
	James D. Hodgson	1970
	Peter J. Brennan	1973
Defense	Melvin R. Laird	1969
	Elliot L. Richardson	1973
	James R. Schlesinger	1973
H.E.W.	Robert H. Finch	1969
	Elliot L. Richardson	1970
	Casper W. Weinberger	1973
H.U.D.	George W. Romney	1969
	James T. Lynn	1973
Transport.	John A. Volpe	1969
	Claude S. Brinegar	1973

[1] On 1 July 1971 the Post Office Department because the semi-independent U.S. Postal Service with non-Cabinet status.

38th President	**Gerald R. Ford**	**1974**
Vice President	Nelson A. Rockefeller	1974
State	Henry A. Kissinger	1974
Treasury	William E. Simon	1974

Atty. General	William B. Saxbe	1974
	Edward H. Levi	1975
Interior	Rogers C.B. Morton	1974
	Stanley K. Hathaway	1975
Agriculture	Earl L. Butz	1974
Commerce	Frederick B. Dent	1974
	Rogers C.B. Morton	1975
Labor	Peter J. Brennan	1974
	John T. Dunlop	1975
Defense	James R. Schlesinger	1974
H.E.W.	Casper W. Weinberger	1974
	F. David Mathews	1975
H.U.D.	James T. Lynn	1974
	Carla Anderson Hills	1975
Transport.	Claude S. Brinegar	1974
	William T. Coleman, Jr.	1975

* ad interim.

PARTY STRENGTH IN CONGRESS

[Ad-Administration; AM-Anti-Masonic; C-Coalition; D-Democratic; DR-Democratic-Republican; F-Federalist; J-Jacksonian; NR-National Republican; Op-Opposition; R-Republican; U-Unionist; W-Whig]

Congress	Year	President	Senate						House					
			Majority Party		Principal Minority Party		Others		Majority Party		Principal Minority Party		Others	
1	1789–91	F	(Washington)	Ad	17	Op	9	0	Ad	38	Op	26	0
2	1791–93	F	(Washington)	F	16	DR	13	0	F	37	DR	33	0
3	1793–95	F	(Washington)	F	17	DR	13	0	DR	57	F	48	0
4	1795–97	F	(Washington)	F	19	DR	13	0	F	54	DR	52	0
5	1797–99	F	(J. Adams)	F	20	DR	12	0	F	58	DR	48	0
6	1799–01	F	(J. Adams)	F	19	DR	13	0	F	64	DR	42	0
7	1801–03	DR	(Jefferson)	DR	18	F	14	0	DR	69	F	36	0
8	1803–05	DR	(Jefferson)	DR	25	F	9	0	DR	102	F	39	0
9	1805–07	DR	(Jefferson)	DR	27	F	7	0	DR	116	F	25	0
10	1807–09	DR	(Jefferson)	DR	28	F	6	0	DR	118	F	24	0
11	1809–11	DR	(Madison)	DR	28	F	6	0	DR	94	F	48	0
12	1811–13	DR	(Madison)	DR	30	F	6	0	DR	108	F	36	0
13	1813–15	DR	(Madison)	DR	27	F	9	0	DR	112	F	68	0
14	1815–17	DR	(Madison)	DR	25	F	11	0	DR	117	F	65	0
15	1817–19	DR	(Monroe)	DR	34	F	10	0	DR	141	F	42	0
16	1819–21	DR	(Monroe)	DR	35	F	7	0	DR	156	F	27	0
17	1821–23	DR	(Monroe)	DR	44	F	4	0	DR	158	F	25	0
18	1823–25	DR	(Monroe)	DR	44	F	4	0	DR	187	F	26	0
19	1825–27	C	(J. Q. Adams)	Ad	26	J	20	0	Ad	105	J	97	0
20	1827–29	C	(J. Q. Adams)	J	28	Ad	20	0	J	119	Ad	94	0
21	1829–31	D	(Jackson)	D	26	NR	22	0	D	139	NR	74	0
22	1831–33	D	(Jackson)	D	25	NR	21	2	D	141	NR	58	14
23	1833–35	D	(Jackson)	D	20	NR	20	8	D	147	AM	53	60
24	1835–37	D	(Jackson)	D	27	W	25	0	D	145	W	98	0
25	1837–39	D	(Van Buren)	D	30	W	18	4	D	108	W	107	24
26	1839–41	D	(Van Buren)	D	28	W	22	0	D	124	W	118	0
27	1841–43	W	(W. Harrison)										
		W	(Tyler)	W	28	D	22	2	W	133	D	102	6
28	1843–45	W	(Tyler)	W	28	D	25	1	D	142	W	79	1
29	1845–47	D	(Polk)	D	31	W	25	0	D	143	W	77	6
30	1847–49	D	(Polk)	D	36	W	21	1	W	115	D	108	4
31	1849–51	W	(Taylor)										
		W	(Filmore)	D	35	W	25	2	D	112	W	109	9
32	1851–53	W	(Filmore)	D	35	W	24	3	D	140	W	88	5
33	1853–55	D	(Pierce)	D	38	W	22	2	D	159	W	71	4
34	1855–57	D	(Pierce)	D	40	R	15	5	R	108	D	83	43
35	1857–59	D	(Buchanan)	D	36	R	20	8	D	118	R	92	26
36	1859–61	D	(Buchanan)	D	36	R	26	4	R	114	D	92	31

PARTY STRENGTH IN CONGRESS

[Ad-Administration; AM-Anti-Masonic; C-Coalition; D-Democratic; DR-Democratic-Republican; F-Federalist; J-Jacksonian; NR-National Republican; Op-Opposition; R-Republican; U-Unionist; W-Whig]

Congress	Year	President	Senate			House		
			Majority Party	Principal Minority Party	Others	Majority Party	Principal Minority Party	Others
37	1861–63	R (Lincoln)	R 31	D 10	8	R 105	D 43	30
38	1863–65	R (Lincoln)	R 36	D 9	5	R 102	D 75	9
39	1865–67	R (Lincoln)						
		R (Johnson)	U 42	D 10	0	U 149	D 42	0
40	1867–69	R (Johnson)	R 42	D 11	0	R 143	D 49	0
41	1869–71	R (Grant)	R 56	D 11	0	R 149	D 63	0
42	1871–73	R (Grant)	R 52	D 17	5	D 134	R 104	5
43	1873–75	R (Grant)	R 49	D 19	5	R 194	D 92	14
44	1875–77	R (Grant)	R 45	D 29	2	D 169	R 109	14
45	1877–79	R (Hayes)	R 39	D 36	1	D 153	R 140	0
46	1879–81	R (Hayes)	D 42	R 33	1	D 149	R 130	14
47	1881–83	R (Garfield)						
		R (Arthur)	R 37	D 37	1	R 147	D 135	11
48	1883–85	R (Arthur)	R 38	D 36	2	R 197	D 118	10
49	1885–87	D (Cleveland)	R 43	D 34	0	D 183	R 140	2
50	1887–89	D (Cleveland)	R 39	D 37	0	D 169	R 152	4
51	1889–91	R (B. Harrison)	R 39	D 37	0	R 166	D 159	0
52	1891–93	R (B. Harrison)	R 47	D 39	2	D 235	R 88	9
53	1893–95	D (Cleveland)	D 44	R 38	3	D 218	R 127	11
54	1895–97	D (Cleveland)	R 43	D 39	6	R 244	D 105	7
55	1897–99	R (McKinley)	R 47	D 34	7	R 204	D 113	40
56	1899–01	R (McKinley)	R 53	D 26	8	R 185	D 163	9
57	1901–03	R (McKinley)						
		R (T. Roosevelt)	R 55	D 31	4	R 197	D 151	9
58	1903–05	R (T. Roosevelt)	R 57	D 33	0	R 208	D 178	0
59	1905–07	R (T. Roosevelt)	R 57	D 33	0	R 250	D 136	0
60	1907–09	R (T. Roosevelt)	R 61	D 31	0	R 222	D 164	0
61	1909–11	R (Taft)	R 61	D 32	0	R 219	D 172	0
62	1911–13	R (Taft)	R 51	D 41	0	D 228	R 161	1
63	1913–15	D (Wilson)	D 51	R 44	1	D 291	R 127	17
64	1915–17	D (Wilson)	D 56	R 40	0	D 230	R 196	9
65	1917–19	D (Wilson)	D 53	R 42	0	D 216	R 210	6
66	1919–21	D (Wilson)	R 49	D 47	0	R 240	D 190	3
67	1921–23	R (Harding)	R 59	D 37	0	R 303	D 131	1
68	1923–25	R (Coolidge)	R 51	D 43	2	R 225	D 205	5
69	1925–27	R (Coolidge)	R 56	D 39	1	R 247	D 183	4
70	1927–29	R (Coolidge)	R 49	D 46	1	R 237	D 195	3
71	1929–31	R (Hoover)	R 56	D 39	1	R 267	D 167	1
72	1931–33	R (Hoover)	R 48	D 47	1	D 220	R 214	1
73	1933–35	D (F. Roosevelt)	D 60	R 35	1	D 310	R 117	5
74	1935–37	D (F. Roosevelt)	D 69	R 25	2	D 319	R 103	10
75	1937–39	D (F. Roosevelt)	D 76	R 16	4	D 331	R 89	13
76	1939–41	D (F. Roosevelt)	D 69	R 23	4	D 261	R 164	4
77	1941–43	D (F. Roosevelt)	D 66	R 28	2	D 268	R 162	5
78	1943–45	D (F. Roosevelt)	D 58	R 37	1	D 218	R 208	4
79	1945–47	D (F. Roosevelt)						
		D (Truman)	D 56	R 38	1	D 242	R 190	2
80	1947–49	D (Truman)	D 45	R 51	0	D 188	R 246	1
81	1949–51	D (Truman)	D 54	R 42	0	D 263	R 171	1
82	1951–53	D (Truman)	D 49	R 47	0	D 235	R 199	1
83	1953–55	R (Eisenhower)	R 48	D 47	1	R 221	D 212	1
84	1955–57	R (Eisenhower)	D 48	R 47	1	D 232	R 203	0
85	1957–59	R (Eisenhower)	D 49	R 47	0	D 232	R 199	0
86	1959–61	R (Eisenhower)	D 62	R 34	0	D 280	R 152	0
87	1961–63	D (Kennedy)	D 65	R 35	0	D 261	R 176	0
88	1963–65	D (Kennedy)	D 67	R 33	0	D 258	R 174	0
		D (Johnson)						
89	1965–67	D (Johnson)	D 68	R 32	0	D 295	R 140	0
90	1967–69	D (Johnson)	D 64	R 36	0	D 248	R 187	0
91	1969–71	R (Nixon)	D 57	R 43	0	D 243	R 192	0
92	1971–73	R (Nixon)	D 55	R 45	0	D 255	R 180	0
93	1973–75	R (Nixon)	D 57	R 43	0	D 244	R 191	0
94	1975–77	R (Ford)	D 61	R 38	0	D 289	R 144	0

JUSTICES OF THE UNITED STATES SUPREME COURT

Name Chief Justices in italics	Service Term	Yrs.	Name Chief Justices in italics	Service Term	Yrs.
John Jay, N.Y	1789–1795	6	David J. Brewer, Kan.	1889–1910	21
John Rutledge, S.C.	1789–1791	2	Henry B. Brown, Mich.	1890–1906	16
William Cushing, Mass.	1789–1810	21	George Shiras, Jr., Pa.	1892–1903	11
James Wilson, Pa.	1789–1798	9	Howell E. Jackson, Tenn.	1893–1895	2
John Blair, Va.	1789–1796	7	Edward D. White, La.	1894–1910	16
Robert H. Harrison, Md.	1789–1790	1	Rufus W. Peckham, N.Y.	1895–1910	14
James Iredell, N.C.	1790–1799	9	Joseph McKenna, Cal.	1898–1925	27
Thomas Johnson, Md.	1791–1793	2	Oliver W. Holmes, Jr., Mass.	1902–1932	29
William Paterson, N.J.	1793–1806	13	William R. Day, Ohio	1903–1922	19
John Rutledge, S.C.*	1795–1795	..	William H. Moody, Mass.	1906–1910	4
Samuel Chase, Md.	1796–1811	15	Horace H. Lurton, Tenn.	1910–1914	5
Oliver Ellsworth, Conn.	1796–1799	4	Charles E. Hughes, N.Y.	1910–1916	6
Bushrod Washington, Va.	1798–1829	31	Willis Van Devanter, Wyo.	1911–1937	26
Alfred Moore, N.C.	1799–1804	5	Joseph R. Lamar, Ga.	1911–1916	6
John Marshall, Va.	1801–1835	34	*Edward D. White*, La.	1910–1921	11
William Johnson, S.C.	1804–1834	30	Mahlon Pitney, N.J.	1912–1922	12
Henry B. Livingston, N.Y.	1806–1823	17	Jas. C. McReynolds, Tenn.	1914–1941	27
Thomas Todd, Ky.	1807–1826	19	Louis D. Brandeis, Mass.	1916–1939	23
Joseph Story, Mass.	1811–1845	34	John H. Clarke, Ohio	1916–1922	6
Gabriel Duval, Md.	1811–1836	25	*William H. Taft*, Conn.	1921–1930	9
Smith Thompson, N.Y.	1823–1843	20	George Sutherland, Utah	1922–1938	16
Robert Trimble, Ky.	1826–1828	2	Pierce Butler, Minn.	1922–1939	17
John McLean, Ohio	1829–1861	32	Edward T. Sanford, Tenn.	1923–1930	7
Henry Baldwin, Pa.	1830–1844	14	Harlan F. Stone, N.Y.	1925–1941	16
James M. Wayne, Ga.	1835–1867	32	*Charles E. Hughes*, N.Y.	1930–1941	11
Roger B. Taney, Md.	1836–1864	28	Owen J. Roberts, Penn.	1930–1945	15
Philip P. Barbour, Va.	1836–1841	5	Benjamin N. Cardozo, N.Y.	1932–1938	6
John Catron, Tenn.	1837–1865	28	Hugo Black, Ala.	1937–1971	34
John McKinley, Ala.	1837–1852	15	Stanley Reed, Ky.	1938–1957	19
Peter V. Daniel, Va.	1841–1860	19	Felix Frankfurter, Mass.	1939–1962	23
Samuel Nelson, N.Y.	1845–1872	27	William O. Douglas, Conn.	1939–....	..
Levi Woodbury, N.H.	1845–1851	6	Frank Murphy, Mich.	1940–1949	9
Robert C. Grier, Pa.	1846–1870	24	*Harlan F. Stone*, N.Y.	1941–1946	5
Benj. R. Curtis, Mass.	1851–1857	6	James F. Byrnes, S.C.	1941–1942	2
John A. Campbell, Ala.	1853–1861	8	Robert H. Jackson, N.Y.	1941–1954	13
Nathan Clifford, Me.	1858–1881	23	Wiley B. Rutledge, Iowa	1943–1949	6
Noah H. Swayne, Ohio	1862–1881	20	Harold H. Burton, Ohio	1945–1958	13
Samuel F. Miller, Iowa	1862–1890	28	*Fred M. Vinson*, Ky.	1946–1953	7
David Davis, Ill.	1862–1877	15	Thomas C. Clark, Tex.	1949–1967	18
Stephen J. Field, Cal.	1863–1897	34	Sherman Minton, Ind.	1949–1956	7
Salmon P. Chase, Ohio	1864–1873	9	*Earl Warren*, Calif.	1953–1969	16
William Strong, Pa.	1870–1880	10	John Marshall Harlan, N.Y.	1955–1971	16
Joseph P. Bradley, N.J.	1870–1892	22	William J. Brennan, Jr., N.J.	1956–....	..
Ward Hunt, N.Y.	1872–1882	10	Charles E. Whittaker, Mo.	1957–1962	5
Morrison R. Waite, Ohio	1874–1888	14	Potter Stewart, Ohio	1958–....	..
John M. Harlan, Ky.	1877–1911	34	Byron R. White, Colo.	1962–....	..
William B. Woods, Ga.	1880–1887	7	Arthur J. Goldberg, Ill.	1962–1965	3
Stanley Matthews, Ohio	1881–1889	8	Abe Fortas, Tenn.	1965–1969	4
Horace Gray, Mass.	1881–1902	21	Thurgood Marshall, N.Y.	1967–....	..
Samuel Blatchford, N.Y.	1882–1893	11	*Warren E. Burger*, D.C.	1969–....	..
Lucius Q. C. Lamar, Miss.	1888–1893	5	Harry A. Blackmun, Minn.	1970–....	..
Melville W. Fuller, Ill.	1888–1910	22	Lewis F. Powell, Jr., Va.	1971–....	..
			William H. Rehnquist, Ariz.	1971–....	..

* Acting chief justice; the Senate refused to confirm nomination.

[1] The *First Judiciary Act* (Sept. 24, 1789) made provision for a Supreme Court to consist of 1 Chief Justice and 5 Associate Justices. The size of the court was decreased to 5 by the *Judiciary Act of 1801* (13 Feb.) but restored to 6 by their repeal of that Act (*Act of 8 Mar. 1802*). The size of the Supreme Court increased to 7 (*Act of 24 Feb. 1807*), to 9 (*Act of 3 Mar. 1837*), and to 10 (*Act of 3 Mar. 1863*). It was reduced to 7 (*Act of July 23, 1866*) but restored to its present size of 9 by the *Act of 10 Apr. 1869*.

THE DECLARATION OF INDEPENDENCE

The unanimous Declaration of the thirteen United States of America.

WHEN, in the Course of human events, it becomes necessary for one people to dissolve the political bands which have connected them with another, and to assume, among the Powers of the earth, the separate and equal station to which the Laws of Nature and of Nature's God entitle them, a decent respect to the opinions of mankind requires that they should declare the causes which impel them to the separation.

We hold these truths to be self-evident, that all men are created equal, that they are endowed by their Creator with certain unalienable Rights, that among these, are Life, Liberty, and the pursuit of Happiness. That, to secure these rights, Governments are instituted among Men, deriving their just Powers from the consent of the governed. That, whenever any form of Government becomes destructive of these ends, it is the Right of the People to alter or to abolish it, and to institute new Government, laying its foundation on such Principles, and organizing its Powers in such form, as to them shall seem most likely to effect their Safety and Happiness. Prudence, indeed, will dictate that Governments long established should not be changed for light and transient causes; and, accordingly, all experience hath shewn, that mankind are more disposed to suffer, while evils are sufferable, than to right themselves by abolishing the forms to which they are accustomed. But, when a long train of abuses and usurpations, pursuing invariably the same Object, evinces a design to reduce them under absolute Despotism, it is their right, it is their duty, to throw off such Government, and to provide new Guards for their future Security. Such has been the patient sufferance of these Colonies; and such is now the necessity which constrains them to alter their former Systems of Government. The history of the present King of Great Britain is a history of repeated injuries and usurpations, all having in direct object the establishment of an absolute Tyranny over these States. To prove this, let Facts be submitted to a candid world.

He has refused his Assent to Laws the most wholesome and necessary for the public good.

He has forbidden his Governors to pass Laws of immediate and pressing importance, unless suspended in their operation till his Assent should be obtained; and when so suspended, he has utterly neglected to attend to them.

He has refused to pass other Laws for the accommodation of large districts of People, unless those People would relinquish the right of Representation in the legislature; a right inestimable to them and formidable to tyrants only.

He has called together legislative bodies at places unusual, uncomfortable, and distant from the depository of their Public Records, for the sole Purpose of fatiguing them into compliance with his measures.

He has dissolved Representative Houses repeatedly, for opposing, with manly firmness, his invasions on the rights of the People.

He has refused for a long time, after such dissolutions, to cause others to be elected; whereby the Legislative Powers, incapable of Annihilation, have returned to the People at large for their exercise; the State remaining in the mean time exposed to all the dangers of invasion from without, and convulsions within.

He has endeavoured to prevent the Population of these States; for that purpose obstructing the Laws for Naturalization of Foreigners; refusing to pass others to encourage their migrations hither, and raising the conditions of new Appropriations of Lands.

He has obstructed the Administration of Justice, by refusing his Assent to Laws for establishing Judiciary Powers.

He has made Judges dependent on his Will alone, for the tenure of their offices, and the amount and payment of their salaries.

He has erected a multitude of New Offices, and sent hither swarms of Officers to harass our People, and eat out their substance.

He has kept among us, in times of Peace, Standing Armies, without the Consent of our legislatures.

He has affected to render the Military independent of and superior to the Civil Power.

He has combined with others to subject us to a jurisdiction foreign to our constitution, and unacknowledged by our laws; giving his Assent to their Acts of pretended Legislation:

For quartering large bodies of armed troops among us:

For protecting them, by a mock Trial, from Punishment for any Murders which they should commit on the Inhabitants of these States:

For cutting off our Trade with all parts of the world:

For imposing Taxes on us without our Consent:

For depriving us, in many cases, of the benefits of Trial by Jury:

For transporting us beyond Seas to be tried for pretended offences:

For abolishing the free System of English Laws in a neighbouring province, establishing therein an Arbitrary government, and enlarging its Boundaries, so as to render it at once an example and fit instrument for introducing the same absolute rule into these Colonies:

For taking away our Charters, abolishing our most valuable Laws, and altering fundamentally the Forms of our Governments:

For suspending our own Legislatures, and declaring themselves invested with Power to legislate for us in all cases whatsoever.

He has abdicated Government here, by declaring us out of his protection, and waging War against us.

He has plundered our seas, ravaged our Coasts, burnt our towns, and destroyed the Lives of our People.

He is at this time transporting large Armies of foreign Mercenaries to compleat the works of death, desolation and tyranny, already begun with circumstances of Cruelty and perfidy scarcely paralleled in the most barbarous ages, and totally unworthy the Head of a civilized nation.

He has constrained our fellow Citizens, taken Captive on the high Seas, to bear Arms against their Country, to become the executioners of their friends and Brethren, or to fall themselves by their Hands.

He has excited domestic insurrections amongst us, and has endeavoured to bring on the inhabitants of our frontiers, the merciless Indian Savages, whose known rule of warfare, is an undistinguished destruction of all ages, sexes and conditions.

In every stage of these Oppressions, We have Petitioned for Redress, in the most humble terms: Our repeated Petitions, have been answered only by repeated injury. A Prince, whose character is thus marked by every act which may define a Tyrant, is unfit to be the ruler of a free People.

Nor have We been wanting in attentions to our Brittish brethren. We have warned them from time to time of attempts by their legislature to extend an unwarrantable jurisdiction over us. We have reminded them of the circumstances of our emigration and settlement here. We have appealed to their native justice and magnanimity, and we have conjured them by the ties of our common kindred, to disavow these usurpations, which, would inevitably interrupt our connexions and correspondence. They too have been deaf to the voice of justice and of consanguinity. We must, therefore, acquiesce in the necessity, which denounces our Separation, and hold them, as we hold the rest of mankind, Enemies in War, in Peace Friends.

We, therefore, the Representatives of the *united States of America,* in GENERAL CONGRESS assembled, appealing to the Supreme Judge of the World for the rectitude of our intentions, DO, in the Name, and by Authority of the good People of these Colonies, solemnly PUBLISH and DECLARE, That these United Colonies are, and of Right, ought to be *free and Independent States;* that they are

Absolved from all Allegiance to the British Crown, and that all political connexion between them and the State of Great Britain, is and ought to be totally dissolved; and that, as FREE and INDEPENDENT STATES, they have full Power to levy War, conclude Peace, contract Alliances, establish Commerce, and to do all other Acts and Things which INDEPENDENT STATES may of right do. AND for the support of this Declaration, with a firm reliance on the protection of divine Providence, we mutually pledge to each other our Lives, our Fortunes, and our sacred Honour.

John Hancock,

Josiah Bartlett, Wm Whipple, Saml Adams, John Adams, Robt Treat Paine, Elbridge Gerry, Steph. Hopkins, William Ellery, Roger Sherman, Samel Huntington, Wm Williams, Oliver Wolcott, Matthew Thornton, Wm Floyd, Phil Livingston, Frans Lewis, Lewis Morris, Richd Stockton, Jno Witherspoon, Fras Hopkinson, John Hart, Abra Clark, Robt Morris, Benjamin Rush, Benja Franklin, John Morton, Geo Clymer, Jas Smith, Geo. Taylor, James Wilson, Geo. Ross, Caesar Rodney, Geo Read, Thos M:Kean, Samuel Chase, Wm Paca, Thos Stone, Charles Carroll of Carrollton, George Wythe, Richard Henry Lee, Th. Jefferson, Benja Harrison, Thos Nelson, Jr., Francis Lightfoot Lee, Carter Braxton, Wm Hooper, Joseph Hewes, John Penn, Edward Rutledge, Thos Heyward, Junr., Thomas Lynch, Junor., Arthur Middleton, Button Gwinnett, Lyman Hall, Geo Walton.

THE CONSTITUTION OF THE UNITED STATES

Preamble

We the People of the United States, in Order to form a more perfect Union, establish Justice, insure domestic Tranquility, provide for the common defence, promote the general Welfare, and secure the Blessings of Liberty to ourselves and our Posterity, do ordain and establish this Constitution for the United States of America.

Article I

Section 1. All legislative Powers herein granted shall be vested in a Congress of the United States, which shall consist of a Senate and House of Representatives.

Section 2. The House of Representatives shall be composed of Members chosen every second Year by the People of the several States, and the Electors in each State shall have the Qualifications requisite for Electors of the most numerous Branch of the State Legislature.

No Person shall be a Representative who shall not have attained to the Age of twenty five Years, and been seven Years a Citizen of the United States, and who shall not, when elected, be an inhabitant of that State in which he shall be chosen.

Representatives and direct Taxes shall be apportioned among the several States which may be included within this Union, according to their respective Numbers, [which shall be determined by adding to the whole Number of free Persons, including those bound to Service for a Term of Years, and excluding Indians not taxed, three fifths of all other Persons.]¹ The actual Enumeration shall be made within three Years after the first Meeting of the Congress of the United States, and within every subsequent Term of ten Years, in such Manner as they shall by law direct. The Number of Representatives shall not exceed one for every thirty Thousand, but each State shall have at Least one Representative; and until such enumeration shall be made, the State of New Hampshire shall be entitled to chuse three, Massachusetts eight, Rhode-Island and Providence Plantations one, Connecticut five, New-York six, New Jersey four, Pennsylvania eight, Delaware one, Maryland six, Virginia ten, North Carolina five, South Carolina five, and Georgia three.

When vacancies happen in the Representation from any State, the Executive Authority thereof shall issue Writs of Election to fill such Vacancies.

The House of Representatives shall chuse their Speaker and other Officers; and shall have the sole Power of Impeachment.

Section 3. The Senate of the United States shall be composed of two Senators from each State, [chosen by the Legisla-

¹ Superseded by the Fourteenth Amendment.

ture thereof,][2] for six Years; and each Senator shall have one Vote.

Immediately after they shall be assembled in Consequence of the first Election, they shall be divided as equally as may be into three Classes. The Seats of the Senators of the first Class shall be vacated at the Expiration of the second Year, of the second Class at the Expiration of the fourth Year, and of the third Class at the Expiration of the sixth Year, so that one third may be chosen every second Year; [and if Vacancies happen by Resignation, or otherwise, during the Recess of the Legislature of any State, the Executive thereof may make temporary Appointments until the next Meeting of the Legislature, which shall then fill such Vacancies.][3]

No Person shall be a Senator who shall not have attained to the Age of thirty Years, and been nine Years a Citizen of the United States, and who shall not, when elected, be an Inhabitant of that State for which he shall be chosen.

The Vice President of the United States shall be President of the Senate, but shall have no Vote, unless they be equally divided.

The Senate shall chuse their other Officers, and also a President pro tempore, in the Absence of the Vice President, or when he shall exercise the Office of President of the United States.

The Senate shall have the sole Power to try all Impeachments. When sitting for that Purpose, they shall be on Oath or Affirmation. When the President of the United States is tried, the Chief Justice shall preside: and no Person shall be convicted without the Concurrence of two thirds of the Members present.

Judgment in Cases of Impeachment shall not extend further than to removal from Office, and disqualification to hold and enjoy any Office of honor, Trust or Profit under the United States: but the Party convicted shall nevertheless be liable and subject to Indictment, Trial, Judgment and Punishment, according to Law.

Section 4. The Times, Places and Manner of holding Elections for Senators and Representatives, shall be prescribed in each State by the Legislature thereof; but the Congress may at any time by Law make or alter such Regulations, except as to the Places of chusing Senators.

[The Congress shall assemble at least once in every Year, and such Meeting shall be on the first Monday in December, unless they shall by Law appoint a different Day.][4]

Section 5. Each House shall be the Judge of the Elections, Returns and Qualifications of its own Members, and a Majority of each shall constitute a Quorum to do Business; but a smaller Number may adjourn from day to day, and may be authorized to compel the Attendance of absent Members, in such Manner, and under such Penalties as each House may provide.

Each House may determine the Rules of its Proceedings, punish its Members for disorderly Behaviour, and, with the Concurrence of two thirds, expel a Member.

Each House shall keep a Journal of its Proceedings, and from time to time publish the same, excepting such Parts as may in their Judgment require Secrecy; and the Yeas and Nays of the Members of either House on any question shall, at the Desire of one fifth of those Present, be entered on the Journal.

Neither House, during the Session of Congress, shall, without the Consent of the other, adjourn for more than three days, nor to any other Place than that in which the two Houses shall be sitting.

Section 6. The Senators and Repre-

2 Superseded by the Seventeenth Amendment.
3 Modified by the Seventeenth Amendment.

4 Superseded by the Twentieth Amendment.

sentatives shall receive a Compensation for their Services, to be ascertained by Law, and paid out of the Treasury of the United States. They shall in all Cases, except Treason, Felony and Breach of the Peace, be privileged from Arrest during their Attendance at the Session of their respective Houses, and in going to and returning from the same; and for any Speech or Debate in either House, they shall not be questioned in any other Place.

No Senator or Representative shall, during the Time for which he was elected, be appointed to any civil Office under the Authority of the United States, which shall have been created, or the Emoluments whereof shall have been encreased during such time; and no Person holding any Office under the United States, shall be a Member of either House during his Continuance in Office.

Section 7. All bills for raising Revenue shall originate in the House of Representatives; but the Senate may propose or concur with Amendments as on other Bills.

Every Bill which shall have passed the House of Representatives and the Senate, shall, before it become a Law, be presented to the President of the United States. If he approve he shall sign it, but if not he shall return it, with his Objections to that House in which it shall have originated, who shall enter the Objections at large on their Journal, and proceed to reconsider it. If after such Reconsideration two thirds of that House shall agree to pass the Bill, it shall be sent, together with the Objections, to the other House, by which it shall likewise be reconsidered, and if approved by two thirds of that House, it shall become a Law. But in all such Cases the Votes of both Houses shall be determined by yeas and Nays, and the Names of the Persons voting for and against the Bill shall be entered on the Journal of each House respectively. If any Bill shall not be returned by the President within ten Days (Sundays excepted) after it shall have been presented to him, the Same shall be a Law, in like Manner as if he had signed it, unless the Congress by their Adjournment prevent its Return, in which Case it shall not be a Law.

Every Order, Resolution, or Vote to which the Concurrence of the Senate and House of Representatives may be necessary (except on a question of Adjournment) shall be presented to the President of the United States; and before the Same shall take Effect, shall be approved by him, or being disapproved by him, shall be repassed by two thirds of the Senate and House of Representatives, according to the Rules and Limitations prescribed in the Case of a Bill.

Section 8. The Congress shall have Power To lay and collect Taxes, Duties, Imposts and Excises, to pay the Debts and provide for the common Defence and general Welfare of the United States; but all Duties, Imposts and Excises shall be uniform throughout the United States;

To borrow Money on the credit of the United States;

To regulate Commerce with foreign Nations, and among the several States, and with the Indian Tribes;

To establish a uniform Rule of Naturalization, and uniform Laws on the subject of Bankruptcies throughout the United States;

To coin Money, regulate the Value thereof, and of foreign Coin, and fix the Standard of Weights and Measures;

To provide for the Punishment of counterfeiting the Securities and current Coin of the United States;

To establish Post Offices and post Roads;

To promote the Progress of Science and useful Arts, by securing for limited

Times to Authors and Inventors the exclusive Right to their respective Writings and Discoveries;

To constitute Tribunals inferior to the supreme Court;

To define and punish Piracies and Felonies committed on the high Seas, and Offences against the Law of Nations;

To declare War, grant Letters of Marque and Reprisal, and make Rules concerning Captures on Land and Water;

To raise and support Armies, but no Appropriation of Money to that Use shall be for a longer Term than two Years;

To provide and maintain a Navy;

To make Rules for the Government and Regulation of the land and naval Forces;

To provide for calling forth the Militia to execute the Laws of the Union, suppress Insurrections and repel Invasions;

To provide for organizing, arming, and disciplining, the Militia, and for governing such Part of them as may be employed in the Service of the United States, reserving to the States respectively, the Appointment of the Officers, and the Authority of training the Militia according to the discipline prescribed by Congress;

To exercise exclusive Legislation in all Cases whatsoever, over such District (not exceeding ten Miles square) as may, by Cession of particular States, and the Acceptance of Congress, become the Seat of the Government of the United States, and to exercise like Authority over all Places purchased by the Consent of the Legislature of the State in which the Same shall be, for the Erection of Forts, Magazines, Arsenals, dock-Yards, and other needful Buildings;—And

To make all Laws which shall be necessary and proper for carrying into Execution the foregoing Powers, and all other Powers vested by this Constitution in the Government of the United States, or in any Department or Officer thereof.

Section 9. The Migration or Importation of such Persons as any of the States now existing shall think proper to admit, shall not be prohibited by the Congress prior to the Year one thousand eight hundred and eight, but a Tax or duty may be imposed on such Importation, not exceeding ten dollars for each Person.

The Privilege of the Writ of Habeas Corpus shall not be suspended, unless when in Cases of Rebellion or Invasion the public safety may require it.

No Bill of Attainder or ex post facto Law shall be passed.

No Capitation, or other direct, Tax shall be laid, unless in Proportion to the Census or Enumeration herein before directed to be taken.[5]

No Tax or Duty shall be laid on Articles exported from any State.

No Preference shall be given by any Regulation of Commerce or Revenue to the Ports of one State over those of another; nor shall Vessels bound to, or from, one State, be obliged to enter, clear, or pay Duties in another.

No money shall be drawn from the Treasury, but in Consequence of Appropriations made by Law; and a regular Statement and Account of the Receipts and Expenditures of all public Money shall be published from time to time.

No Title of Nobility shall be granted by the United States: And no Person holding any Office of Profit or Trust under them, shall, without the Consent of the Congress, accept any present, Emolument, Office, or Title, of any kind whatever, from any King, Prince, or foreign State.

Section 10. No State shall enter into any Treaty, Alliance, or Confederation;

[5] Modified by the Sixteenth Amendment.

grant Letters of Marque and Reprisal; coin Money; emit Bills of Credit; make any Thing but gold and silver Coin a Tender in Payment of Debts; pass any Bill of Attainder, ex post facto Law, or Law impairing the Obligation of Contracts, or grant any Title of Nobility.

No State shall, without the Consent of the Congress, lay any Imposts or Duties on Imports or Exports, except what may be absolutely necessary for executing it's inspection laws; and the net Produce of all Duties and Imposts, laid by any State on Imports or Exports, shall be for the Use of the Treasury of the United States; and all such Laws shall be subject to the Revision, and Control of the Congress.

No State shall, without the Consent of Congress, lay any Duty of Tonnage, keep Troops, or Ships of War in time of Peace, enter into any Agreement or Compact with another State, or with a foreign Power, or engage in War, unless actually invaded, or in such imminent Danger as will not admit of delay.

Article II

Section 1. The executive Power shall be vested in a President of the United States of America. He shall hold his Office during the Term of four Years, and, together with the Vice President, chosen for the same Term, be elected, as follows.

Each State shall appoint, in such Manner as the Legislature thereof may direct, a Number of Electors, equal to the whole Number of Senators and Representatives to which the State may be entitled in the Congress: but no Senator or Representative, or Person holding an Office of Trust or Profit under the United States, shall be appointed an Elector.

[The Electors shall meet in their respective States, and vote by Ballot for two Persons, of whom one at least shall not be an Inhabitant of the same State with themselves. And they shall make a List of all the Persons voted for, and the Number of Votes for each; which list they shall sign and certify, and transmit sealed to the Seat of the Government of the United States, directed to the President of the Senate. The President of the Senate shall, in the Presence of the Senate and House of Representatives, open all the Certificates, and the Votes shall then be counted. The person having the greatest Number of Votes shall be the President, if such Number be a Majority of the whole Number of Electors appointed; and if there be more than one who have such Majority, and have an equal Number of Votes, then the House of Representatives shall immediately chuse by Ballot one of them for President; and if no Person have a Majority, then from the five highest on the List the said House shall in like Manner chuse the President. But in chusing the President, the Votes shall be taken by States, the Representation from each State having one Vote; A quorum for this purpose shall consist of a Member or Members from two thirds of the States, and a Majority of all the States shall be necessary to a Choice. In every Case, after the Choice of the President, the Person having the greatest Number of Votes of the Electors shall be the Vice President. But if there should remain two or more who have equal Votes, the Senate chuse from them by Ballot the Vice President.][6]

The Congress may determine the Time of chusing the Electors, and the Day on which they shall give their Votes; which Day shall be the same throughout the United States.

No Person except a natural born Citizen, or a Citizen of the United States,

[6] Superseded by the Twelfth Amendment.

at the time of the Adoption of this Constitution, shall be eligible to the Office of President; neither shall any Person be eligible to that Office who shall not have attained to the Age of thirty five Years, and been fourteen Years a Resident within the United States.

In Case of the Removal of the President from Office, or of his Death, Resignation, or Inability to discharge the Powers and Duties of the said Office,[7] the Same shall devolve on the Vice President, and the Congress may by Law provide for the Case of Removal, Death, Resignation or Inability, both of the President and Vice President, declaring what Officer shall then act as President, and such Officer shall act accordingly, until the Disability be removed, or a President shall be elected.

The President shall, at stated Times receive for his Services, a Compensation, which shall neither be encreased nor diminished during the Period for which he shall have been elected, and he shall not receive within that Period any other Emolument from the United States, or any of them.

Before he enter on the Execution of his Office, he shall take the following Oath or Affirmation:—"I do solemnly swear (or affirm) that I will faithfully execute the Office of President of the United States, and will to the best of my Ability, preserve, protect and defend the Constitution of the United States."

Section 2. The President shall be Commander in Chief of the Army and Navy of the United States, and of the Militia of the several States, when called into the actual Service of the United States; he may require the Opinion, in writing, of the principal Officer in each of the executive Departments, upon any Subject relating to the Duties of their respective Offices, and he shall have Power

[7] Modified by the Twenty-fifth Amendment.

to grant Reprieves and Pardons for Offenses against the United States, except in Cases of Impeachment.

He shall have Power, by and with the Advice and Consent of the Senate, to make Treaties, provided two thirds of the Senators present concur; and he shall nominate, and by and with the Advice and Consent of the Senate, shall appoint Ambassadors, other public Ministers and Consuls, Judges of the supreme Court, and all other Officers of the United States, whose Appointments are not herein otherwise provided for, and which shall be established by Law: but the Congress may by Law vest the Appointment of such inferior Officers, as they think proper, in the President alone, in the Courts of Law, or in the Heads of Departments.

The President shall have Power to fill up all Vacancies that may happen during the Recess of the Senate, by granting Commissions which shall expire at the End of their next Session.

Section 3. He shall from time to time give to the Congress Information of the State of the Union, and recommend to their Consideration such Measures as he shall judge necessary and expedient; he may, on extraordinary Occasions, convene both Houses, or either of them, and in Case of Disagreement between them, with Respect to the Time of Adjournment, he may adjourn them to such Time as he shall think proper; he shall receive Ambassadors and other public Ministers; he shall take Care that the Laws be faithfully executed, and shall Commission all Officers of the United States.

Section 4. The President, Vice President and all civil Officers of the United States, shall be removed from Office on Impeachment for, and Conviction of, Treason, Bribery, or other high Crimes and Misdemeanors.

Article III

Section 1. The judicial Power of the United States, shall be vested in one supreme Court, and in such inferior Courts as the Congress may from time to time ordain and establish. The Judges, both of the supreme and inferior Courts, shall hold their Offices during good Behaviour, and shall, at stated Times, receive for their Services, a Compensation, which shall not be diminished during their Continuance in Office.

Section 2. The judicial Power shall extend to all Cases, in Law and Equity, arising under this Constitution, the Laws of the United States, and Treaties made, or which shall be made, under their authority;—to all Cases affecting Ambassadors, other public Ministers and Consuls;—to all Cases of admiralty and maritime Jurisdiction;—to Controversies to which the United States shall be a Party;—to Controversies between two or more States;—between a State and Citizens of another State;[8]—between Citizens of different States,—between Citizens of the same State claiming Lands under Grants of different States, and between a State, or the Citizens thereof, and foreign States, Citizens or Subjects.

In all cases affecting Ambassadors, other public Ministers and Consuls, and those in which a State shall be Party, the supreme Court shall have original Jurisdiction. In all the other Cases before mentioned, the supreme Court shall have appellate Jurisdiction, both as to Law and Fact, with such Exceptions, and under such Regulations as the Congress shall make.

The Trial of all Crimes, except in Cases of Impeachment, shall be by Jury; and such Trial shall be held in the State where the said Crimes shall have been committed; but when not committed within any State, the Trial shall be at such Place or Places as the Congress may by Law have directed.

Section 3. Treason against the United States, shall consist only in levying War against them, or in adhering to their Enemies, giving them Aid and Comfort. No Person shall be convicted of Treason unless on the Testimony of two Witnesses to the same overt Act, or on Confession in open Court.

The Congress shall have Power to declare the Punishment of Treason, but no Attainder of Treason shall work Corruption of Blood, or Forfeiture except during the Life of the Person attainted.

Article IV

Section 1. Full Faith and Credit shall be given in each State to the public Acts, Records, and judicial Proceedings of every other State. And the Congress may by general Laws prescribe the Manner in which such Acts, Records and Proceedings shall be proved, and the Effect thereof.

Section 2. The Citizens of each State shall be entitled to all Privileges and Immunities of Citizens in the several States.

A Person charged in any State with Treason, Felony, or other Crime, who shall flee from Justice, and be found in another State, shall on Demand of the executive Authority of the State from which he fled, be delivered up, to be removed to the State having Jurisdiction of the Crime.

[No Person held to Service or Labour in one State, under the Laws thereof, escaping into another, shall, in Consequence of any Law or Regulation therein, be discharged from such Service or Labour, but shall be delivered up on Claim of the Party to whom such Service or Labour may be due.][9]

Section 3. New States may be admitted by the Congress into this Union;

---

[8] Modified by the Eleventh Amendment.

[9] Superseded by the Thirteenth Amendment.

but no new State shall be formed or erected within the Jurisdiction of any other State; nor any State be formed by the Junction of two or more States, or Parts of States, without the Consent of the Legislatures of the States concerned as well as of the Congress.

The Congress shall have Power to dispose of and make all needful Rules and Regulations respecting the Territory or other Property belonging to the United States; and nothing in this Constitution shall be so construed as to Prejudice any Claims of the United States, or of any particular State.

Section 4. The United States shall guarantee to every State in this Union a Republican Form of Government, and shall protect each of them against Invasion; and on Application of the Legislature, or of the Executive (when the Legislature cannot be convened) against domestic Violence.

Article V

The Congress, whenever two thirds of both Houses shall deem it necessary, shall propose Amendments to this Constitution, or, on the Application of the Legislatures of two thirds of the several States, shall call a Convention for proposing Amendments, which, in either Case, shall be valid to all Intents and Purposes, as Part of this Constitution, when ratified by the Legislatures of three fourths of the several States, or by Conventions in three fourths thereof, as the one or the other Mode of Ratification may be proposed by the Congress; Provided that no Amendment which may be made prior to the Year One thousand eight hundred and eight shall in any Manner affect the first and fourth Clauses in the Ninth Section of the first Article; and that no State, without its Consent, shall be deprived of its equal Suffrage in the Senate.

Article VI

All Debts contracted and Engagements entered into, before the Adoption of this Constitution, shall be as valid against the United States under this Constitution, as under the Confederation.

This Constitution, and the Laws of the United States which shall be made in Pursuance thereof; and all Treaties made, or which shall be made, under the Authority of the United States, shall be the supreme Law of the Land; and the Judges in every State shall be bound thereby, any Thing in the Constitution or Laws of any State to the Contrary notwithstanding.

The Senators and Representatives before mentioned, and the Members of the several State Legislatures, and all executive and judicial Officers, both of the United States and of the several States, shall be bound by Oath or Affirmation, to support this Constitution; but no religious Test shall ever be required as a Qualification to any Office or public Trust under the United States.

Article VII

The Ratification of the Conventions of nine States, shall be sufficient for the Establishment of this Constitution between the States so ratifying the Same.

done in Convention by the Unanimous Consent of the States present the Seventeenth Day of September in the Year of our Lord one thousand seven hundred and Eighty seven and of the Independence of the United States of America the Twelfth.

In witness whereof We have hereunto subscribed our Names.

Go. Washington, *President and deputy from Virginia; Attest* William Jackson, *Secretary; Delaware:* Geo. Read, Gunning Bedford, jr., John Dickinson, Richard Bassett, Jaco. Broom; *Maryland:* James McHenry, Daniel of St. Thomas Jenifer, Daniel Carroll; *Virginia:* John Blair, James Madison, Jr.; *North Carolina:* Wm. Blount, Richd. Dobbs Spaight, Hu Williamson; *South Carolina:* J. Rutledge, Charles Cotesworth Pinckney, Charles Pinckney, Pierce Butler; *Georgia:* William Few, Abr. Baldwin; *New Hampshire:* John Langdon, Nicholas Gilman; *Massachusetts:* Nathaniel Gorham, Rufus King; *Connecticut:* Wm. Saml. Johnson, Roger Sherman; *New York:* Alexander Hamilton; *New Jersey:* Wil. Livingston, David Brearley, Wm. Paterson, Jona. Dayton; *Pennsylvania:* B. Franklin, Thomas Mifflin, Robt. Morris, Geo. Clymer, Thos. FitzSimons, Jared Ingersoll, James Wilson, Gouv. Morris.

[AMENDMENTS]

A R T I C L E S in addition to, and Amendment of the Constitution of the United States of America, proposed by Congress, and ratified by the Legislatures of the several States, pursuant to the fifth Article of the original Constitution.

[The first ten articles proposed 25 Sept. 1789; declared in force 15 Dec. 1791]

Article I

Congress shall make no law respecting an establishment of religion, or prohibiting the free exercise thereof; or abridging the freedom of speech, or of the press; or the right of the people peaceably to assemble, and to petition the Government for a redress of grievances.

Article II

A well regulated Militia, being necessary to the security of a free State, the right of the people to keep and bear Arms, shall not be infringed.

Article III

No Soldier shall, in time of peace, be quartered in any house, without the consent of the Owner, nor in time of war, but in a manner to be prescribed by law.

Article IV

The right of the people to be secure in their persons, houses, papers, and effects, against unreasonable searches and seizures, shall not be violated, and no Warrants shall issue, but upon probable cause, supported by Oath or affirmation, and particularly describing the place to be searched, and the persons or things to be seized.

Article V

No person shall be held to answer for a capital, or otherwise infamous crime, unless on a presentment or indictment of a Grand Jury, except in cases arising in the land or naval forces, or in the Militia, when in actual service in time of War or public danger; nor shall any person be subject for the same offense to be twice put in jeopardy of life or limb; nor shall be compelled in any criminal case to be a witness against himself, nor be deprived of life, liberty, or property, without due process of law; nor shall private property be taken for public use, without just compensation.

Article VI

In all criminal prosecutions, the accused shall enjoy the right to a speedy and public trial, by an impartial jury of the State and district wherein the crime shall have been committed, which district shall have been previously ascertained by law, and to be informed of the nature and cause of the accusation; to be confronted with the witnesses against him; to have compulsory process for obtaining witnesses in his favor, and to have the Assistance of Counsel for his defense.

Article VII

In Suits at common law, where the value in controversy shall exceed twenty dollars, the right of trial by jury shall be preserved, and no fact tried by a jury, shall be otherwise re-examined in any Court of the United States, than according to the rules of the common law.

Article VIII

Excessive bail shall not be required, nor excessive fines imposed, nor cruel and unusual punishments inflicted.

Article IX

The enumeration in the Constitution, of certain rights, shall not be construed to deny or disparage others retained by the people.

Article X

The powers not delegated to the United States by the Constitution, nor prohibited by it to the States, are reserved to the States respectively, or to the people.

Article XI [proposed 5 Mar. 1794; declared ratified 8 Jan. 1798]

The Judicial power of the United States shall not be construed to extend to any suit in law or equity, commenced or prosecuted against one of the United States by Citizens of another State, or by Citizens or Subjects of any Foreign State.

Article XII [proposed 12 Dec. 1803; declared ratified 25 Sept. 1804]

The Electors shall meet in their respective states, and vote by ballot for President and Vice-President, one of whom, at least, shall not be an inhabitant of the same state with themselves; they shall name in their ballots the person voted for as President, and in distinct ballots the person voted for as Vice-President, and they shall make distinct lists of all persons voted for as President, and of all persons voted for as Vice-President, and of the number of votes for each, which lists they shall sign and certify, and transmit sealed to the seat of the government of the United States, directed to the President of the Senate;—The President of the Senate shall, in the presence of the Senate and House of Representatives, open all certificates and the votes shall then be counted;—The person having the greatest number of votes for President, shall be the President, if such number be a majority of the whole number of Electors appointed; and if no person have such majority, then from the persons having the highest numbers not exceeding three on the list of those voted for as President, the House of Representatives shall choose immediately, by ballot, the President. But in choosing the President, the votes shall be taken by states, the representation from each state having one vote; a quorum for this purpose shall consist of a member or members from two-thirds of the states, and a majority of all the states shall be necessary to a choice. [And if the House of Representatives shall not choose a President whenever the right of choice shall devolve upon them, before the fourth day of March next following, then the Vice-President shall act as President, as in the case of the death or other constitutional disability of the President.][10] The person having the greatest number of votes as Vice-President, shall be the Vice-President, if such number be a majority of the whole number of Electors appointed, and if no person have a majority, then from the two highest numbers on the list, the Senate shall choose the Vice-President; a quorum for the purpose shall consist of two-thirds of the whole number of Senators, and a majority of the whole number shall be necessary to a choice. But no person constitutionally ineligible to the office of President shall be eligible to that of Vice-President of the United States.

Article XIII [proposed 1 Feb. 1865; declared ratified 18 Dec. 1865]

Section 1. Neither slavery nor involuntary servitude, except as a punishment for crime whereof the party shall have been duly convicted, shall exist within the United States, or any place subject to their jurisdiction.

Section 2. Congress shall have power to enforce this article by appropriate legislation.

Article XIV [proposed 16 June 1866; declared ratified 28 July 1868]

Section 1. All persons born or naturalized in the United States, and subject to the jurisdiction thereof, are citizens of the United States and of the State wherein they reside. No State shall make or enforce any law which shall abridge the privileges or immunities of citizens of the United States; nor shall any State deprive any person of life, liberty, or property, without due process of law; nor deny to any person within

[10] Superseded by the Twentieth Amendment.

its jurisdiction the equal protection of the laws.

Section 2. Representatives shall be apportioned among the several States according to their respective numbers, counting the whole number of persons in each State, excluding Indians not taxed. But when the right to vote at any election for the choice of electors for President and Vice President of the United States, Representatives in Congress, the Executive and Judicial officers of a State, or the members of the Legislature thereof, is denied to any of the male inhabitants of such State, being twenty-one years of age, and citizens of the United States, or in any way abridged, except for participation in rebellion, or other crime, the basis of representation therein shall be reduced in the proportion which the number of such male citizens shall bear to the whole number of male citizens twenty-one years of age in such State.

Section 3. No person shall be a Senator or Representative in Congress, or elector of President and Vice President, or hold any office, civil or military, under the United States, or under any State, who, having previously taken an oath, as a member of Congress, or as an officer of the United States, or as a member of any State legislature, or as an executive or judicial officer of any State, to support the Constitution of the United States, shall have engaged in insurrection or rebellion against the same, or given aid and comfort to the enemies thereof. But Congress may by a vote of two-thirds of each House, remove such disability.

Section 4. The validity of the public debt of the United States authorized by law, including debts incurred for payment of pensions and bounties for services in suppressing insurrection or rebellion, shall not be questioned. But neither the United States nor any state shall assume or pay any debt or obligation incurred in aid of insurrection or rebellion against the United States, or any claim for the loss or emancipation of any slave; but all such debts, obligations, and claims shall be held illegal and void.

Section 5. The Congress shall have power to enforce, by appropriate legislation, the provisions of this article.

Article XV [proposed 27 Feb. 1869; declared ratified 30 Mar. 1870]

Section 1. The right of citizens of the United States to vote shall not be denied or abridged by the United States or by any State on account of race, color, or previous condition of servitude.

Section 2. The Congress shall have power to enforce this article by appropriate legislation.

Article XVI [proposed 12 July 1909; declared ratified 25 Feb. 1913]

The Congress shall have power to lay and collect taxes on incomes, from whatever source derived, without apportionment among the several States, and without regard to any census or enumeration.

Article XVII [proposed 16 May 1912; declared ratified 31 May 1913]

The Senate of the United States shall be composed of two Senators from each State, elected by the people thereof, for six years; and each Senator shall have one vote. The electors in each State shall have the qualifications requisite for electors of the most numerous branch of the State legislatures.

When vacancies happen in the representation of any State in the Senate, the executive authority of such State shall issue writs of election to fill such vacancies: *Provided,* That the legislature of any State may empower the executive thereof to make temporary appointments until the people fill the vacancies by election as the legislature may direct.

This amendment shall not be so construed as to affect the election or term of any Senator chosen before it becomes valid as part of the Constitution.

Article XVIII [proposed 18 Dec. 1917; declared ratified 29 Jan. 1919; repealed by the 21st Amendment]

Section 1. After one year from the ratification of this article the manufacture, sale, or transportation of intoxicating liquors within, the importation thereof into, or the exportation thereof from the United States and all territory subject to the jurisdiction thereof for beverage purposes is hereby prohibited.

Section 2. The Congress and the several States shall have concurrent power to enforce this article by appropriate legislation.

Section 3. This article shall be inoperative unless it shall have been ratified as an amendment to the Constitution by the legislatures of the several States, as provided in the Constitution, within seven years from the date of the submission hereof to the States by the Congress.[11]

Article XIX [proposed 4 June 1919; declared ratified 26 Aug. 1920]

The right of citizens of the United States to vote shall not be denied or abridged by the United States or by any State on account of sex.

Congress shall have power to enforce this article by appropriate legislation.

Article XX [proposed 2 Mar. 1932; declared ratified 6 Feb. 1933]

Section 1. The terms of the President and Vice President shall end at noon on the 20th day of January, and the terms of Senators and Representatives at noon

---

[11] Superseded by the Twenty-first Amendment.

on the 3d day of January, of the years in which such terms would have ended if this article had not been ratified; and the terms of their successors shall then begin.

Section 2. The Congress shall assemble at least once in every year, and such meeting shall begin at noon on the 3d day of January, unless they shall by law appoint a different day.

Section 3. If, at the time fixed for the beginning of the term of the President, the President elect shall have died, the Vice President elect shall become President. If a President shall not have been chosen before the time fixed for the beginning of his term, or if the President elect shall have failed to qualify, then the Vice President elect shall act as President until a President shall have qualified; and the Congress may by law provide for the case wherein neither a President elect nor a Vice President elect shall have qualified, declaring who shall then act as President, or the manner in which one who is to act shall be selected, and such person shall act accordingly until a President or Vice President shall have qualified.

Section 4. The Congress may by law provide for the case of the death of any of the persons from whom the House of Representatives may choose a President whenever the right of choice shall have devolved upon them, and for the case of the death of any of the persons from whom the Senate may choose a Vice President whenever the right of choice shall have devolved upon them.

Section 5. Sections 1 and 2 shall take effect on the 15th day of October following the ratification of this article.

Section 6. This article shall be inoperative unless it shall have been ratified as an amendment to the Constitution by the legislatures of three-fourths of the several States within seven years from the date of its submission.

Article XXI [proposed 20 Feb. 1933; declared ratified 5 Dec. 1933]

Section 1. The Eighteenth article of amendment to the Constitution of the United States is hereby repealed.

Section 2. The transportation or importation into any State, Territory, or possession of the United States for delivery or use therein of intoxicating liquors, in violation of the laws thereof, is hereby prohibited.

Section 3. This article shall be inoperative unless it shall have been ratified as an amendment to the Constitution by conventions in the several States, as provided in the Constitution, within seven years from the date of the submission hereof to the States by the Congress.

Article XXII [proposed 24 Mar. 1947; declared ratified 26 Feb. 1951]

Section 1. No person shall be elected to the office of the President more than twice, and no person who has held the office of president, or acted as President, for more than two years of a term to which some other person was elected President shall be elected to the office of the President more than once. But this Article shall not apply to any person holding the office of President when this Article was proposed by the Congress, and shall not prevent any person who may be holding the office of President, or acting as President, during the term within which this Article becomes operative from holding the office of President or acting as President during the remainder of such term.

Section 2. This article shall be inoperative unless it shall have been ratified as an amendment to the Constitution by the legislatures of three-fourths of the several States within seven years from the date of its submission to the States by the Congress.

Article XXIII [proposed 16 June 1960; ratified 29 Mar. 1961]

Section 1. The district constituting the seat of government of the United States shall appoint in such manner as the Congress may direct:

A number of electors of President and Vice President equal to the whole number of Senators and Representatives in Congress to which the District would be entitled if it were a State, but in no event more than the least populous state; they shall be in addition to those appointed by the States, but they shall be considered, for the purpose of the election of President and Vice President, to be electors appointed by a State; and they shall meet in the District and perform such duties as provided by the twelfth article of amendment.

Section 2. The Congress shall have power to enforce this article by appropriate legislation.

Article XXIV [proposed 27 Aug. 1962; ratified 23 Jan. 1964]

Section 1. The right of citizens of the United States to vote in any primary or other election for President or Vice President, for electors for President or Vice President, or for Senator or Representative in Congress, shall not be denied or abridged by the United States or any State by reason of failure to pay any poll tax or other tax.

Section 2. The Congress shall have power to enforce this article by appropriate legislation.

Article XXV [proposed 6 July 1965; ratified 10 Feb. 1967]

Section 1. In case of the removal of the President from office or of his death or resignation, the Vice President shall become President.

Section 2. Whenever there is a vacancy in the office of the Vice President, the President shall nominate a Vice President who shall take office upon confirmation by a majority vote of both Houses of Congress.

Section 3. Whenever the President transmits to the President pro tempore of the Senate and the Speaker of the House of Representatives his written declaration that he is unable to discharge the powers and duties of his office, and until he transmits to them a written declaration to the contrary, such powers and duties shall be discharged by the Vice President as Acting President.

Section 4. Whenever the Vice President and a majority of either the principal officers of the executive departments or of such other body as Congress may by law provide, transmit to the President pro tempore of the Senate and the Speaker of the House of Representatives their written declaration that the President is unable to discharge the powers and duties of his office, the Vice President shall immediately assume the powers and duties of the office as Acting President.

Thereafter, when the President transmits to the President pro tempore of the Senate and the Speaker of the House of Representatives his written declaration that no inability exists, he shall resume the powers and duties of his office unless the Vice President and a majority of either the principal officers of the executive department or of such other body as Congress may by law provide, transmit within four days to the President pro tempore of the Senate and the Speaker of the House of Representatives their written declaration that the President is unable to discharge the powers and duties of his office. Thereupon Congress shall decide the issue, assembling within forty-eight hours for that purpose if not in session. If the Congress, within twenty-one days after receipt of the latter written declaration, or, if Congress is not in session, within twenty-one days after Congress is required to assemble, determines by two-thirds vote of both Houses that the President is unable to discharge the powers and duties of his office, the Vice President shall continue to discharge the same as Acting President; otherwise, the President shall resume the powers and duties of his office.

Article XXVI [proposed 23 Mar. 1971; ratified 1 July 1971]

Section 1. The right of citizens of the United States, who are eighteen years of age or older, to vote shall not be denied or abridged by the United States or by any State on account of age.

Section 2. The Congress shall have power to enforce this article by appropriate legislation.

2
Topical
Chronology

THE EXPANSION OF THE NATION

★　★
★

America's abundant natural resources made it possible to create almost from the start a society with few of the carryovers of European feudalism, one based upon freeholding farmers. These abundant resources were hospitable to population growth, rapid interior settlement, and an optimistic economic climate favoring investment and development. A nation of freeholding farmers was promoted by federal land policy. Initially intended for gradual sale at high prices to provide federal revenue, land was made available for credit on increasingly liberal terms. When the Panic of 1819 plunged the credit of farmers into disarray, cash payments were required instead, an action which spurred a reduction of land prices, culminating in the demand for free land and, finally, in the Homestead Act of 1862. Closely related to the revenue secured from the public domain was the movement for national programs for internal improvements, a movement which in the 1830s culminated in a program for the distribution of the revenues to the states, the precedent for the recent Revenue-Sharing program.

Down through 1867 (the Pacific island of Midway excepted) territorial expansion, acquired by purchase, conquest, or diplomacy, and fostered by notions of "manifest destiny," created a continental domain. In the decades that followed the argument was increasingly pressed that overseas expansion was needed for expanding markets, for enhancing national prestige, and for national security, aside from religious and humanitarian considerations. Whether or not broadening markets to slake the appetite of ever-expanding industrial capitalism proved the predominant consideration, the United States did by the turn of the twentieth century find itself in possession of an overseas empire. Imperialism, however, never sat easily on the American conscience. Cuba quickly acquired full sovereignty, the Philippines its independence after a much longer interval, and Alaska and Hawaii became states of the Union. The path that Puerto Rico, the Virgin Islands, Guam, and the Trust Territories will take is as yet unclear, although a third road is offered by Puerto Rico's Commonwealth status, to which some Indian groups are also aspiring.

The civil rights struggle of the 1960s brought with it a retrospective look at the immense costs by which the North American continent had been tamed, including the decimation of American Indian society through disease, war, and maladministration, and the long and shameful chapter of black slavery. Almost from the beginning the federal government exercised some degree of control over private land acquisition by providing lands for the support of educational and charitable institutions. The post-Civil War period saw the burgeoning of a conservation movement and the growth of a national park system. Recent decades have brought a growing awareness that the era of limitless abundance was rapidly drawing to a close, that, beyond the early conservation measures, orderly future growth, prosperity, and even survival dictated far sterner conservation measures than had been adopted in the past, and that ecological considerations be given a high priority in national planning.

Territorial Expansion, Transportation, and Communications

GEOGRAPHICAL FACTORS. English settlement was favored by a heavily forested coastal area abounding in good ports and river systems leading into the interior. For the first 150 years the English colonists were largely confined within a strip running from the Atlantic coast inland to the Appalachian Mountains. First to be settled was the southern Tidewater region and the northern coastal lowlands; second, the Piedmont area above the fall line, a rolling elevation extending to the mountain barrier. The French ascended the St. Lawrence and the Great Lakes, and by easy portages were able to settle the interior as far as the upper Mississippi long before the English. For the English colonists the chief natural passages across the mountain barrier were: **To Canada**— Hudson–Lake George–Lake Champlain– Richelieu River. **To the Ohio Valley**— (1) Mohawk–Lake Ontario; (2) Susquehanna-Monongahela; (3) Potomac-Monongahela; (4) Roanoke-Kanawha. **To the South**—Valley of Virginia–upper Tennessee–Cumberland.

STAGES OF FRONTIER EXPANSION. The **frontier** (usually defined as an area containing not less than 2 nor more than 6 inhabitants to the square mile, and actually a plurality of zones) was constantly pushing into the interior, and generally according to the following stages: (1) initial zone—hunters, trappers, fur traders; (2) cattlemen; (3) miners (less significant in the colonial period than later); (4) farmers; (5) town dwellers.

EARLY NORTHERN FRONTIER EXPANSION: 1630–77. Advancing New England settlements spread over the coastal lowlands and up river valleys, thus isolating Indian tribes that occupied the highlands of the interior. The natives struck back in 2 wars—the Pequot War (1636–37, p. 43) and King Philip's War (1675–77, pp. 46–47). In the latter the Wampanoags (east of Narragansett Bay), Narragansetts, and Nipmucks (between coast and Connecticut Valley) were virtually exterminated.

1677–1704. Indian defeat allowed peaceful expansion over the remaining river valleys and into the highlands of Massachusetts and Connecticut. When wars with French Canada (pp. 74–75) brought new Indian attacks (1689–

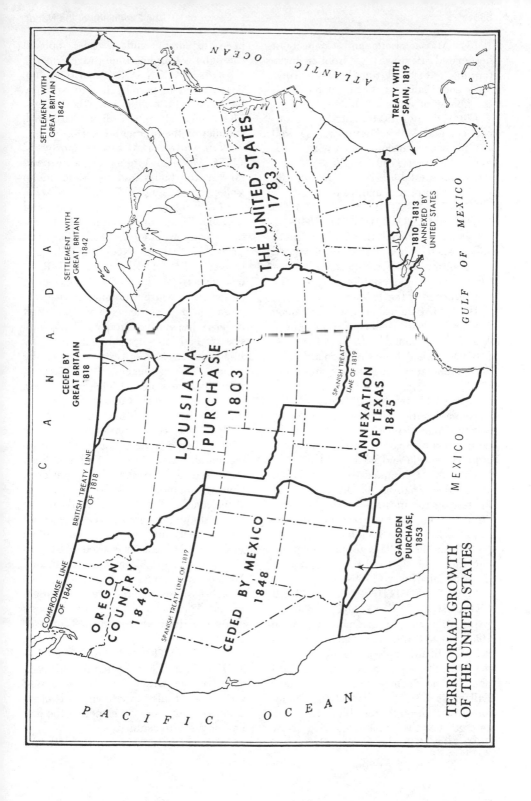

TERRITORIAL GROWTH
OF THE UNITED STATES

PACIFIC OCEAN

ATLANTIC OCEAN

GULF OF MEXICO

CANADA

MEXICO

THE UNITED STATES
1783

LOUISIANA
PURCHASE
1803

OREGON
COUNTRY
1846

CEDED BY MEXICO
1848

ANNEXATION
OF TEXAS
1845

SETTLEMENT WITH
GREAT BRITAIN
1842

SETTLEMENT WITH
GREAT BRITAIN
1842

TREATY WITH
SPAIN, 1819

1810–1813
ANNEXED BY
UNITED STATES

CEDED BY
GREAT BRITAIN
1818

BRITISH TREATY LINE
OF 1818

COMPROMISE LINE
OF 1846

SPANISH TREATY LINE OF 1819

SPANISH TREATY
LINE OF 1819

GADSDEN
PURCHASE,
1853

1713), Massachusetts and Connecticut designated 19 towns as frontier forts, forming a fortified ring between York, Me., and Plainfield, Conn. Behind this the frontier advanced steadily.

1704–76. By 1750 the interior of Connecticut and Massachusetts was so well settled that expansion turned northward, where between 1750 and 1776 74 new towns were established in Vermont, 100 in New Hampshire, and 94 in Maine.

EARLY SOUTHERN FRONTIER EXPANSION SOUTHWARD: 1646–76. Settlement followed river valleys south and west. Indian attacks were prevented by granting 600-acre plots to adventurers who would establish forts on the western edge of the Tidewater.

1663–90. Establishment of the colony of Carolina, with centers of settlement at Albemarle Sound and Charleston (1670), pushed back the Spaniards who had been advancing northward from Florida.

1689–1713. Border warfare along the **Carolina frontier,** as part of the Intercolonial Wars (p. 75), resulted in the destruction of Spanish missions in southeastern Georgia and western Florida.

1713–32. Continued Indian warfare along the Spanish borderland, highlighted by the massacre of several hundred Carolinians by Yamassee Indians (1715), led to the founding of Georgia (p. 76) in 1732. This resulted in pushing the Spanish frontier back beyond the Altamaha River (1739–42).

EARLY SOUTHERN FRONTIER EXPANSION WESTWARD: 1650–76. Exploration of the Piedmont began in 1650 when Capt. Abraham Wood and Edward Bland explored to the forks of the Roanoke. A more important expedition under Thomas Batts and Robert Fallam (1671–73) followed the Staunton River through the Blue Ridge to emerge on the westerly-flowing New River. By 1673 the Yadkin River had

been explored, and a pass opened through the Carolina Blue Ridge.

1676. BACON'S REBELLION (p. 33), caused in part by failure to maintain a peaceful frontier with the Indians. The defeated rebels fled westward, stimulating the frontier advance.

1716. Governor Alexander Spotswood (1676–1740) of Virginia led an expedition up the James into the Shenandoah Valley, advertising the West.

1750. Engrossment of the Virginia and Carolina Piedmont by the mid-18th century, with 2 huge grants: (1) Lord Fairfax—"Northern Neck" of Virginia between the Rappahannock and Potomac rivers; (2) Earl of Granville—most of northern North Carolina. Hence, exploration and settlement of the West deemed imperative. In New York land system had discouraged settlement by small farmers in the western part of the colony. The settlement, Oct. 1710, of 3,000 Palatines near Livingston Manor, to produce naval stores, soon failed, some settlers moved into the Schoharie Valley, but could not get title. By 1750 all the river valleys and principal arable areas in New York had been engrossed by speculators and insiders, causing immigration to be deflected to Pennsylvania. But cheaper lands to the south drew immigrants (Germans and Scotch-Irish) into the Valley of Virginia (by 1727; Winchester settled 1731). In 1751 German Moravians purchased 100,000 acres near Yadkin River, N.C. Scotch-Irish settled the western fringes of the Appalachians and built outposts along the rivers of the upper Tennessee system.

EARLY INTERIOR TRANSPORTATION. River systems preferred to overland passage. Original roads were based on Indian trails. Intertown and intercolonial roads were developed in the first half of the 18th century.

1732. First stagecoach line for the

conveyance of the public opened between Burlington and Amboy, N.J. Connections made by boat from Amboy to New York and from Burlington to Philadelphia.

1756. Through stage, Philadelphia to New York, took 3 days (coach traveling 18 hours a day).

1760–76. Three roads to the West through western Pennsylvania had now been opened: **Forbes Road** (from Ft. Loudoun to Ft. Pitt), **Braddock's Road** (from Ft. Cumberland on the Potomac to Ft. Pitt), and **Gist's Road** (from Ft. Cumberland to the upper Monongahela).

c.1776. A continuous system of highways extended from Boston to Savannah, but no hard-surfaced turnpike existed, except for a hard-graveled road leading out from Portsmouth, Me. (c.1760).

1672–83. ORIGINS OF THE POSTAL SYSTEM. Temporary mail route opened between New York and Boston, 1672; discontinued upon recapture of New York by the Dutch, 1673. No organized postal system in early period. Massachusetts (1673) and Connecticut (1674) provided for transmission of official documents by riders. Massachusetts, by act of 1677, fixed a price for private letters and appointed a postmaster; similarly, Pennsylvania, 1683.

1691–1706. Colonial Postal System Under Proprietary Management. Thomas Neale granted a monopoly for 21 years; operation proved profitless, and Neale gave up patent before expiration date.

1707–75. Colonial Postal System Linked with Imperial System. By act of Parliament, 1710, the postmaster general of London was made postmaster general for the whole empire. Plan to extend postal system to Southern colonies blocked by Virginia until 1732 when ex-Governor Spotswood became postmaster general. The appointment in 1753 of Benjamin Franklin and William Hunter as joint postmasters general resulted in improving efficiency and increasing revenues. By 1758 newspapers were admitted to the mails at fixed rates. Franklin was removed from office in 1774 as a result of his release of the Hutchinson letters (pp. 96–97). In 1764 a second postal district was set up south of Virginia, including the Floridas and Bahamas, with headquarters at Charleston. Regular monthly packets were running to both New York and Charleston (by 10 Jan. 1769), and Suffolk, Va., was established as the transfer point between the 2 districts.

1774–75. William Goddard, publisher of the *Maryland Journal,* proposed (2 June 1774) that a "Constitutional Post Office" be set up to replace the "unconstitutional" British system. By 18 May 1775 all colonies to the north of the Carolinas had established their own postal systems. On recommendation of a committee headed by Franklin the Continental Congress approved a plan (26 July) establishing a postal system for the United Colonies with Franklin as postmaster general. All inland service of the British system came to a halt (25 Dec.). Plagued by wartime inflation, postal rates by 1779 rose to 20 times the '75 level. Rates again revised (12 Dec. 1780, 24 Feb. 1781). System reorganized in 1782; franking privileges curtailed. Within a year the service was flourishing, although foreign mails continued to be carried by British and French packets.

1745–49. LAND COMPANY RIVALRY. To contest the claims of Lord Fairfax, Virginia granted lands beyond the first ridge of mountains to such Tidewater families as the Carters, Beverleys, Pages, and Robinsons. By 1754 grants totaled 2.8 million acres. The latter phases of the Intercolonial Wars were marked by ambitious efforts of land

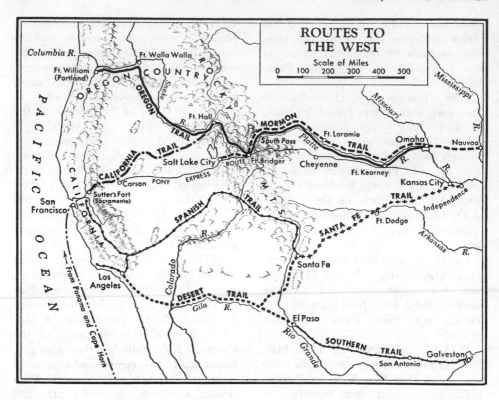

ROUTES TO
THE WEST
Scale of Miles
0   100   200   300   400   500

speculators to exploit the trans-Appalachian area and by the formation of grandiose land companies. Early in 1747 the **Ohio Co.** was organized by Thomas Lee. Its traders under Hugh Parker and Thomas Cresap (c.1702–90) reached the Ohio country (by 20 Oct. 1748). On 16 Mar. 1749 the Privy Council granted the company 200,000 acres in the area bounded by the Ohio and Great Kanawha rivers and the Allegheny Mts., on condition they be settled and a fort built. Opposing crown grants of her territory Virginia granted (12 July) 800,000 acres to run west from the Va.-N.C. border to the **Loyal Co.**, formed by John Lewis (d. 1753) and Dr. Thomas Walker (1715–94), with the support of John Robinson (1704–66), president of Virginia Council, and son, John, speaker of the Burgesses. (See also p. 79.)

1750–53. Ohio Co. Developments. Christopher Gist (c.1706–59) explored the Ohio country as far west as Pickawillany for the company (31 Oct. 1750–51). The **Treaty of Logstown** between Virginia and the Iroquois and Delaware Indians (13 June 1752) ceded to Virginia lands south of the Ohio and authorized the Ohio Co. to build a fort and settle that area. Cutting a road over an old Indian route from the mouth of Wills Creek to the mouth of Red Stone Creek on the Monongahela (1753), Gist persuaded 11 families to settle near him on Red Stone Creek.

1744–54. ADVANCE OF PENNSYLVANIA TRADERS. The French who occupied the Ohio Valley resented the Ohio Co. intrusion, but were more alarmed by an influx of Pennsylvania traders under George Croghan and others. To protect the interior from this invasion, they decided to throw a line of forts across the back country of Pennsylvania. Ft. Le Boeuf at the French Creek portage and Ft. Venango at the junction of that stream with the Allegheny were built in 1753. **George Washington** was sent by Lt. Gov. Dinwiddie of Virginia (a member of the Ohio Co.) to warn away the French (p. 79). At the Winchester Conference (10 Sept.) the Indians abrogated the Treaty of Logstown and moved into the French camp.

1754–63. FRENCH AND INDIAN WAR (pp. 79–82) at its outset brought a cessation of land grants as well as settlement in the West. French seizure of the forks of the Ohio (17 Apr. 1754) and the defeat of Washington at Ft. Necessity (3 July) and of Braddock at Ft. Duquesne (9 July 1755) drove the earliest settlers on the Monongahela back to the Atlantic watershed. To the north, the fall of Oswego (14 Aug. 1756) and the abandonment of the Mohawk by Gen. Webb (c.31 Aug.) forced the settlers to flee toward Schenectady and Albany. To the south, after suffering raids from Indians operating out of Ft. Duquesne (winter, spring 1755–56), the colonies, largely through the prodding of Washington, built a string of forts running from the mouth of Wills Creek on the Potomac (Ft. Cumberland) south along the south branch of the Potomac and the headwaters of the James and Roanoke rivers to Ft. Prince George in South Carolina. Ft. Loudoun on the Little Tennessee (completed summer 1757) served as an advance base to secure friendship of the Cherokee and Creeks. Cherokee raids on the Virginia frontier (spring 1758–Sept. 1759) and the retaliations of the frontiersmen led Gov. Lyttleton of South Carolina to make a treaty with the Cherokee (26 Dec. 1759) whereby the Indians agreed to surrender those guilty of disorders.

Lyttleton held some of the negotiators hostage at Ft. Prince George. Cherokee attacked the fort (19 Jan. 1760) unsuccessfully and turned to the westernmost settlements for vengeance. The slaying of the hostages (16 Feb.) brought a full-scale attack on the western forts, and Ft. Loudoun, isolated and reduced to starvation, surrendered (7 Aug.); its garrison slaughtered en route to Ft. Prince George (10 Aug.). The relief sent by Amherst (1 Apr. 1760) was ineffective, and war continued until Col. Grant, after a series of destructive raids, forced all the tribes to sue for peace (1761). After the abandonment of Ft. Duquesne by the French (24 Nov. 1758), settlers poured into the Monongahela and Youghiogheny valleys over roads built by Braddock and Forbes (p. 81) in spite of the Treaty of Easton (1758) and Col. Bouquet's proclamation (1761) forbidding settlement. By 1763 over 200 houses had been erected around Ft. Pitt alone. The recapture of Oswego and the fall of Ft. Niagara (1759) had a similar effect on the Mohawk Valley.

1755–62. Other Land Projects. Samuel Hazard, Philadelphia merchant, and Lewis Evans (c.1700–56), surveyor and mapmaker, proposed a new trans-Appalachian colony to include the Ohio and part of the Mississippi valleys. Franklin requested the crown to create two new colonies, one along the Scioto, the other south of Lake Erie (1756).

1762. Route for a canal from the Susquehanna at Middletown to the Schuylkill at Reading surveyed by Pennsylvania to prevent diversion of Western trade to Baltimore (settled, 1730); project postponed until 1791.

SUSQUEHANNA CO., under a charter from Connecticut, began the settlement of the Wyoming Valley over the protests of Pennsylvania.

1763. MISSISSIPPI CO., headed by **George Washington,** which had purchased military-bounty grants to the Virginia militia for a fraction of their value, petitioned the crown (9 Sept.) for 2.5 million acres at the junction of the Ohio and Mississippi to satisfy their claims.

7 May. Beginning of **Pontiac's Rebellion** (pp. 84, 85).

7 OCT. ROYAL PROCLAMATION OF 1763.

DEC. "**Suffering Traders,**" including **George Croghan** (c.1718–82), Sir William Johnson's deputy, and 2 Pennsylvania mercantile firms, Byanton, Wharton & Morgan and Simon, Trent, Levy & Franks, organized to seek compensation for losses suffered at the hands of the Indians. **Illinois Co.** (Mar. 1766) and **Indiana Co.** (1763–67) resulted from this group's activities.

1764, 10 JULY. Adoption by the Board of Trade of a plan by Croghan, Johnson, and Col. John Stuart (1718–98), Indian commissioner for the southern district, for subdividing the northern and southern districts and placing trade under the supervision of the commissioners. The plan broke down in the South owing to the refusal of the governors to curb illicit trade; in the North as a result of Johnson's order that all Great Lakes' trade be transacted at Detroit and Mackinac. Result: New York and Montreal traders and Frenchmen operating from beyond the Mississippi captured the fur trade. Peltry exports declined from £28,067 (1764) to £18,923 (1768).

20 JULY. Order in Council placed region west of the Connecticut River and north of Massachusetts (Vermont) within boundaries of New York. Patents had been issued (since 1750) by Gov. **Benning Wentworth** (1696–1770) of New Hampshire for 119 townships, or about one half the region.

1765. By a preliminary agreement

with the Choctaw and Chickasaw, Stuart secured acceptance of the high-tide line as the boundary of the Floridas.

1766, 17 APR. Opinion of R. Cholmondely, Auditor General of North America, that the Proclamation of 1763 did not void prior land grants encouraged speculators to press their claims both in England and the colonies.

1767, 11 SEPT. Lord Shelburne (Secretary of State for the Southern Department) proposed abolition of the Indian Department, withdrawal of most troops from Indian territory, and creation of 3 new colonies (Upper Ohio, Illinois country, Detroit district) to be open for settlement. No action taken.

Fall. All licensed traders permitted by Johnson to operate north of Lake Superior and the Ottawa River.

1767–68. EXPLORATION OF KENTUCKY. Daniel Boone (p. 988), a frontiersman from the Upper Yadkin Valley, on his first trip into trans-Appalachian country (winter) proceeded along the present border of Kentucky and West Virginia without entering the bluegrass region. At least 4 parties of hunters had preceded him (1766), including **Benjamin Cutbird,** who had traveled along the Tenn.-Ky. border to the Mississippi, and thence south to New Orleans to market furs.

1768, MAR. Lord Hillsborough, first Secretary of State for the Colonies (since Jan.), secured cabinet acceptance of a new plan for the West: (1) Indian superintendents restricted to imperial affairs; (2) fur trade reverted to the colonies; (3) Proclamation Line to be moved west by treaties with the Indians.

MODIFICATIONS OF THE PROCLAMATION LINE. By the **Treaty of Hard Labor** (14 Oct.) between Stuart and the Cherokee the Virginia border was pushed west to a line running from Chiswell's mine to the mouth of the Big Kanawha on the Ohio. The Creeks agreed at Pensacola (Nov.) to have the South Carolina border run from Ft. Tryon south to the Savannah; Georgia's western border fixed at the Ogeechee River. By the **Treaty of Ft. Stanwix** (5 Nov.) between Johnson and the Iroquois the crown secured all land east of a line drawn near Ft. Stanwix, south to the Unadilla River, along that stream to the town of Unadilla, thence south to the Delaware near Hancock, N.Y., westward to Oswego, southwest to the west branch of the Susequehanna near Williamsport and along that river to its head, thence west to Kittanning on the Allegheny, and along that river and the Ohio west to the mouth of the Tennessee—including much of western New York, the region between the branches of the Susquehanna, and the area west of the Big Kanawha—beyond what the British ministry had proposed. Meanwhile, on 3 Nov. the Indiana Co., with Johnson's aid, purchased from the Iroquois 1,800,-000 acres southeast of the Ohio from an extension of the Mason-Dixon Line (southern boundary line of Pa.) to the Little Kanawha.

1769. VANDALIA. Samuel Wharton formed "Walpole group" (including Thomas Walpole, British banker; Lord Hertford, Lord Chancellor; and George Grenville), organized as **Grand Ohio Co.** (27 Dec.), to obtain a crown grant of 20 million acres under the Treaty of Ft. Stanwix. On 4 Jan. 1770 the Lords of the Treasury approved the grant, to be organized as the proprietary colony of **Vandalia.**

1769–73. SETTLEMENT AND SPECULATION. Pittsburgh land office stormed by purchasers (Apr. 1769). Population of western Pennsylvania, end of 1769, 5,000 families; 1771, 10,000 families. Other Western settlements: Lewisburg and Peterstown (W. Va.), 1769–70; along the Watauga (1768), Holston, and Nolichucky lower

rivers (1769). Judge **Richard Henderson** (N.C., 1735–85) sponsored a hunting expedition led by **Daniel Boone** (with John Stuart and John Finley) which used the Cumberland Gap and crossed the Licking, Kentucky, Green, and Cumberland river valleys before returning (spring 1771). In Aug. 1771 a proprietary force failed to oust the Connecticut settlers from the Wyoming Valley, Pa.

PROCLAMATION LINE CHANGES. The **Treaty of Lochaber** between Stuart and the Cherokee (18 Oct. 1770) modified the line by pushing the border westward to a line running from a point near the forks of the Holston to the mouth of the Great Kanawha, adding 9,000 square miles to Virginia, including most of the lands claimed by the Greenbrier and Loyal Cos. In surveying this line John Donelson tripled the acreage acquired under the treaty by running it along the Kentucky River to its mouth (with the connivance of Indian companions). In addition, the transmission to Croghan (9 Apr. 1772) of the **Camden-Yorke opinion** (1757, by the British Attorney General and Solicitor General), with the omission of the word "Grand Mogul," encouraged land companies to interpret crown authorization of the purchase of lands from Indian princes without crown patents (applicable originally to India) as being applicable to America. Pennsylvania speculators immediately made capital of this interpretation: Wabash and Illinois land companies organized 1774, and the George Croghan-William Trent interests accumulated 6 million acres, chiefly in western Pennsylvania. **Watauga Association** was a squatters' agreement, 1772, to obtain from the Indians by lease a tract embracing the northeast corner of Tennessee, south and east of the south fork of the Holston River, and a second tract including the headwaters of the Nolichucky River and

Lick Creek. On 14 Aug. 1772 the crown approved the **Vandalia** grant in payment of £10,460 7s 3d; Board of Trade fixed boundaries and drafted charter (3 Apr. 1773), but actual title never conferred. The coming of the Revolution killed this project. By a treaty with the Creeks (1 June 1773) Georgia's boundary was moved west from the Ogeechee to the Oconee River.

1774, JAN.–10 OCT. LORD DUNMORE'S WAR. In an effort to control the northwest, Virginia's royal governor, **John Murray, Earl of Dunmore** (1732–1809), seized western Pennsylvania, appointing John Connolly governor at Pittsburgh. This action, combined with the entry of colonial hunters into Kentucky, goaded the Shawnee and Ottawa into war (by 10 June). Neutralization of Cherokee, Choctaw, Chickasaw, and Creeks in South obtained by manipulations of Stuart and **James Robertson** (1742–1814), negotiator of Watauga lease; in the North by Johnson and Croghan. On 24 July Maj. Angus McDonald marched into the Muskingum Valley. In a 2-pronged attack, Col. Andrew Lewis descended the Great Kanawha while Dunmore led a column down the Ohio. **Chief Cornstalk,** Shawnee leader, attacked Lewis at Point Pleasant (W. Va.) and was defeated (10 Oct.) at the **Battle of Point Pleasant.** By the **Treaty of Camp Charlotte** the Indians yielded hunting rights in Kentucky and agreed to allow unmolested transportation on the Ohio.

20 MAY, Quebec Act (p. 97), which extended the boundaries of Quebec to the Ohio and Mississippi, antagonized colonies claiming Western lands under charters (notably Virginia) as well as speculators who had made purchases under the Camden-Yorke opinion (e.g., Wabash-Illinois and Croghan-Trent interests).

16 JUNE. Harrodsburg, Ky., founded by **James Harrod** (1742–93). Burned during Lord Dunmore's War, it was rebuilt the following year.

1775. Transylvania Co. under Judge Richard Henderson (Jan.) sent out **Daniel Boone** (10 Mar.) to blaze a trail through Cumberland Gap to the bluegrass country of Kentucky (**Wilderness Road**). By the **Treaty of Sycamore Shoals** (17 Mar.) the Cherokee for £10,000 conveyed an area between the Kentucky River and the southern border of the Cumberland Valley, as well as a strip through Cumberland Gap. At the same conference the Watauga settlers converted their lease into a purchase (19 Mar.). **Boonesborough** founded by Boone (6 Apr.), where he was joined by Henderson (20 Apr.) and the first settlers. A second group under **Benjamin Logan** (c.1743–1802) founded St. Asaph's Station (Apr.). An offshoot of Henderson's emigrants settled at Boiling Springs Station (Mercer Co., Ky.). Delegates from these new settlements met at Boonesborough (23 May) under Henderson and set up a proprietary government for **Transylvania.** Delegates to Continental Congress were rejected (25 Sept.). Population, back country, Maryland-Georgia, est. 250,000.

1776–83. THE WEST IN THE AMERICAN REVOLUTION. In the early phases of the war British advantages in the West stemmed from (1) loyalty of the Indian commissioners, Stuart and Guy Johnson (succeeded his uncle, Sir William, 1774) to the crown; (2) traditional seaboard-frontier animosities; (3) superiority of British goods. American military achievements had sufficiently overcome these handicaps to permit (by 1779–80) a resumption of migration into Kentucky and Tennessee over the Wilderness Road. Land companies continued their activities and the states engaged in a struggle for control of the West. **Frontier Military Incidents:** The Watauga settlements, forewarned by Stuart, withstood Cherokee attacks at Eaton's Station at the forks of the Holston (20 July **1776**) and at Ft. Watauga (21 July). North Carolina troops retaliated by burning the Middle Cherokee towns and, acting with South Carolinians, attacked the Lower Cherokee (Sept.–Oct.). In Nov. the Watauga settlements were incorporated into North Carolina. Dissatisfied with Transylvania Co. domination, Kentucky settlers at a conference (6 June) called by **George Rogers Clark** (p. 1001) petitioned Virginia for annexation. The area was organized as a county (6 Dec.) and formally incorporated into Virginia (early 1777). By the end of 1776 Kentucky settlers, as a result of Shawnee and Delaware raids, were concentrated in three main centers—Harrodsburg, St. Asaph's, and Boonesborough. George Rogers Clark, appointed (2 Jan. **1778**) by Gov. **Patrick Henry** of Virginia, surprised the British and captured their base at **Kaskaskia** (4 July) and **Vincennes** (20 July). By the middle of Aug. he was in control of the Illinois country; established as Illinois Co. by Virginia (9 Dec.), Vincennes was retaken by the British under Capt. Henry Hamilton (Dec.). Boonesborough withstood a Shawnee siege (7–16 Sept.) after being warned by Boone, who escaped captivity (winter to 16 June). **Joseph Brant** (1742–1807), a Mohawk chief, with 300 Iroquois, destroyed Cobleskill (30 May) and continued depredations down the Mohawk Valley. A second column under Col. **John Butler** (1728–96), moving farther south, slew 360 settlers in the **Wyoming Massacre** (3 June). Joining Brant, they raided **Cherry Valley,** N.Y. (11 Nov.), costing the defenders 30 killed, 71 wounded. For the Sullivan campaign, see p. 119. On 29 Jan. **1779** George Rogers Clark captured Hamilton's force at Vincennes. The neutralization of the southern Indians for the remainder of the war resulted from a combined Virginia–North Carolina attack under Col. Evan Shelby which destroyed 11 Chickamauga villages in the Tennessee Valley (Apr.) and the destruction of 6 more villages by a South Carolina force in the fall. Settlers now moved into the Tennessee and Kentucky area over the Wilderness Road and down the Ohio. Nashville founded by Judge Henderson and James Robertson (1779–80); Louisville now assumed an urban character. Population of Kentucky, 1780: 20,000. **Further Frontier Raids:** British force attacked the Illinois country; repulsed at Cahokia and St. Louis (May, **1780**). Marching over the Maumee-Miami route, Henry Bird captured the Kentucky posts of Riddle's Station (20 June) and Martin's Station (27 June) along the Licking River. **Battle of King's Mountain** (7 Oct., p. 121) ended Loyalist raids in the Carolina back country. Retaliatory raids upon the Cherokee conducted by the Watauga settlers under Col. **John Sevier** (1745–1815) led to further land cessions by the second **Treaty of Long Island** (26 July **1781**). The Mohawk Valley, virtually in British hands as far east as Schenectady (as late as Aug.) was cleared (Aug.–Oct.) by a force under Col. **Marinus Willett** (1740–1830). Open conflict between the Delaware Indians and frontiersmen broke out in May **1782** as a result of the unprovoked slaughter of 96 Christian Delawares at Gnadenhutten (early spring). Marching into the Ohio country to bolster the frontier, William Crawford was defeated on the Upper Sandusky (4 June). During 1782 Brant's raiders penetrated Pennsylvania as far east as Hannastown; others, operating from Detroit, pushed into Kentucky as far south as Bryant's Station, defeating a Kentucky force at the **Battle of Blue Licks** (19 Aug.). The situation was critical when news of peace talks reached the West (c.Nov.).

1776–83. CONTROVERSY OVER WESTERN LANDS. John Dickinson's draft of the Articles of Confederation (12 July **1776**) proposed limiting the western boundaries of the states; rejected by committee. **Land Bounties:** Congress granted land to British military deserters (12, 27 Aug.) and 100–500 acres, depending on rank, to all soldiers up to the rank of colonel who would serve in the Continental Army for the duration of the war or until discharged (7, 18 Sept.). Land bounties were granted generals under the same conditions (12 Aug. 1780; 850–1,100 acres). Larger grants were offered by the states (N.Y., 600 acres; Pa., 200–2,000; Va., 100–1,500; N.C., 640–12,000). Continental and state grants underscored the need for political organization of the West. In Aug. **1777** states whose charters gave them no western lands (Pa., N.J., Del., Md., N.H., R.I.) proposed that Congress be empowered to limit the western boundaries of the states. The motion failed, but over their protests, a clause was added to the Articles of Confederation (27 Oct.) providing that no state be deprived of western lands for the benefit of the U.S. By the **Treaty of DeWitts Corner** (20 May) the Lower Cherokee ceded their remaining land in South Carolina, and by the **Treaty of Long Island** (20 July) the Overhill Cherokee surrendered lands east of the Blue Ridge and the Watauga-Nolichucky region. On 4 Nov. **1778** the Virginia assembly voided all Indian sales within its charter limits, in effect curbing land engrossment under the Camden-Yorke opinion. On 15 Dec. Maryland, spurred on by speculators eager for western lands claimed by Virginia, announced its refusal to ratify the Articles of Confederation until western lands were ceded to Congress by the states. On 17 Dec. Virginia offered to provide western lands for soldiers of the Revolution, but Maryland remained adamant (6 Jan. **1779**). As a result of the activities of the Illinois and Wabash Cos., the Virginia assembly nullified all Indian purchases in the Northwest (May, June). On 14 Sept. the Indiana and Vandalia cos. petitioned Congress for a confirmation of land grants. In Nov. a committee of Congress recommended that Virginia make no further grants until the end of the war. On 1 Feb. **1780** the New York legislature ceded to the U.S. all claims to western lands (based on her overlordship of the Iroquois). Connecticut followed (10 Oct.), excepting a 3-million-acre tract in Ohio (the Western Reserve). On 2 Jan. **1781** Virginia ceded her claims north of the Ohio River (p. 123). On 30 Dec. **1782** the commissioners appointed under the Articles of Confederation awarded to Pennsylvania all lands claimed by Connecticut within the charter limits of the former colony. The conditional offer of land cession by Virginia was rejected by Congress (13 Sept. **1783**); a revised offer (20 Oct.) was accepted 1 Mar. **1784**, Congress agreeing to reserve as bounty land for Virginia a tract between the Scioto and Little Miami, along with a small tract opposite Louisville. By the **Treaty of Augusta** with the Creeks (1 Nov.) Georgia extended her northern boundary west from the Tugaloo to the Oconee River. As a result of dissatisfaction with this treaty the Creeks raised to "kingship" **Alexander McGillivray** (c.1759–93), a half-breed and implacable foe of land cessions, who (June 1784) accepted a Spanish colonelcy.

1784–86. INLAND NAVIGATION. Potomac Co. (organized, 1784, with charters from both Md. and Va. and a grant of £6,666 by each state; **George Washington,** first president) publicly raised £40,300 to build a route from the headquarters of the Potomac to the Cheat or Monongahela rivers (connecting the Potomac Valley with the West); constructed a canal by 1808 along the Potomac with the first water locks in the U.S., although the project was not a paying one. (For steamboat franchise to John Fitch, 1786, see p. 792; for **Annapolis Convention,** 11–14 Sept. 1786, p. 137.)

1784–88. ORGANIZATION OF THE WEST. On 20 Feb. **1784** Georgia created Tennessee Co. to include the region of the big bend of the Tennessee, with authority to grant land entrusted to 3 commissioners associated with a land-engrossing project launched (1783) by **William Blount** (1749–1800) of North Carolina. On 2 June the North Carolina legislature ceded its western lands (most of which had been disposed of to speculators, 1783–84), with the proviso that Congress accept within 12 months. Under the leadership of **John Sevier** the trans-Allegheny settlers, in convention at Jonesboro (Tenn., 23 Aug.), set up the independent state of **Franklin** (including a southwest fringe of Va.) and continued down to 1787 to seek admission to the Union. On 20 Nov. North Carolina repealed its cession law and attempted to reestablish control over Franklin. By the **2d Treaty of Ft. Stanwix** (22 Oct.) the Six Nations of the Iroquois ceded to the U.S. all lands west of the Niagara River (rejected by the Ohio tribes). On 21 Jan. **1785** the Wyandot, Chippewa, Delawares, and Ottawa at Ft. McIntosh ceded to the U.S. all the present state of Ohio except for a strip south of Lake Erie between the Maumee River and a line drawn along the Cuyahoga and Tuscarawas rivers. On 7 Feb. Georgia created the county of Bourbon on land ceded by the Indians between the 31st parallel and the Yazoo, but in control of Spain, which ordered the Georgia commissioners to leave (10 Oct.). In 1788 Georgia repealed the act. Led by Col. McGillivray, the Creeks were defeated in a short war with Georgia (May–Nov.) and signed the **Treaty of Galphinton** (12 Nov.), recognizing the cession of the Treaty of Augusta and yielding a strip on the coast from the Altamaha to the St. Mary's. **Massachusetts–New York Controversy:** Massachusetts cession of western lands completed (19 Apr.), excepting claims in New York. By agreement with New York (**1786**) the western part of the state was divided by a line running north and south through Sodus Bay. New York retained sovereignty over the whole region, but Massachusetts was awarded land west of the line.

Land Ordinance of 1785 (20 May, p. 134).

Treaty of Dumpling Creek (May 1785) between "State of Franklin" and the Cherokee extended the former's borders south and west along the Holston to the watershed of the Little River; disallowed by U.S. commissioners at the **Treaty of Hopewell** (28 Nov.), which confirmed Cherokee rights to most of the land held in 1777. Dissatisfied with the Treaties of Augusta and Galphinton, the Creeks resumed hostilities (summer 1786). On 28 Feb. the British government notified the U.S. that it would refuse to comply with the Treaty of Paris (Art. 7) and give up posts in the Great Lakes region which were centers of Indian unrest (notably in Ohio) until the U.S. honored British debts (Art. 4). On 8 Mar. **1787** South Carolina ceded its narrow strip of western claim to the U.S., leaving only North Carolina and Georgia with western claims. On 15 July **1788** Congress rejected the Georgia cession of its western lands (1 Feb.). Such cessions were not completed until the acceptance (2 Apr. 1790) of the second North Carolina act of cession (22 Dec. 1789) and the ratification by the Georgia legislature (16 June 1802) of the Articles of Agreement and Cession (24 Apr. 1802) between U.S. and Georgia. On 20 June 1788 Congress granted 4,000 acres to each head of a family settling the Illinois country before 1783 (c.150 French families), a privilege extended to those at Vincennes and along the Wabash (1790), although, for the most part, the grants were not actually made. By making bounty warrants transferable (9 July), Congress eased operations for the big land companies.

1786–88. SETTLEMENTS IN OHIO. Formation in Boston (1 Mar. 1786) of a new **Ohio Co.**, organized by Gens. **Benjamin Tupper** (1738–92) and **Rufus Putnam** (1738–1824), to dispose of $1 million worth of stock in exchange for Continental certificates redeemable at par in exchange for public lands. In behalf of the company Rev. **Manasseh Cutler** (1742–1823) petitioned Congress (5–14 July 1787) for 1½ million acres at $.66⅔ an acre. In a deal with Col. **William Duer** (1747–99), secretary of the Board of Treasury, the Ohio Co. was authorized to act for a group of insiders with whom Cutler organized the **Scioto Co.** Under authority of Congress (23 July) the board sold (27 July) to Cutler 1,500,000 (actually 1,781,760) acres for $1 million with an option on another 5 million acres. The lands lay between the first 7 ranges of townships (already surveyed) and the Scioto River. By agreement the option was assigned to the Scioto Co. In Oct. **John Cleve Symmes** (1742–1814) of New Jersey petitioned Congress for land on similar terms; granted (1788) a 20-mile strip east of the Great Miami. The first auctions of land surveyed in Ohio (the 7

Ranges) brought in only $176,090 in inflated currency (Sept.–Oct.). To offset lawlessness and "facilitate the surveying and selling" of public lands Congress resolved (3 Oct.) to station troops on the frontier. On 7 Apr. 1788 **Marietta, Ohio,** was founded by settlers sent out by the Ohio Co.

1786–90. JAY-GARDOQUI TREATY (29 Aug. 1787) between Spain and U.S. (p. 135), while never ratified, aroused such discontent in the West that "Spanish Conspiracy" spread through Kentucky and Tennessee, led by **James Wilkinson** and **John Sevier**. Purpose: to separate lower Mississippi Valley from U.S. under Spanish protection. Separatism threat remained in the West until Pinckney's Treaty (1795, p. 153).

1787, 13 JULY. NORTHWEST ORDINANCE (p. 139).

1789. First Yazoo land grant (25,400,-000 acres) to a group of speculating companies authorized by Georgia legislature; additional grant made in 1795; immediate settlement impeded by Indian wars and Spanish diplomatic intrigues.

1789–1829. EXTENSION OF POSTAL SERVICE. As late as 1792 Vermont, Kentucky, Tennessee, and the entire West had no post office, but the federal government rapidly expanded the mail routes. The Act of 1794 established additional post roads and provided for stage transportation; the Act of 1814 provided that mail service be arranged from the nearest post office to the courthouse of any county in any state or territory. As a result, many new mail lines were extended to outlying regions. Miles of post roads in operation: 1790–94, 5,001; 1825–29, 104,521. Postal rates, 1825–38 (about half the rate prevailing in 1815): up to 30 mi., 6 cts.; 30–80 mi., 10 cts.; 80–150 mi., 12½ cts.; 150–400 mi., 18¾ cts.; over 400 mi., 25 cts.

1790. Southwest Territory organized.

ACQUISITION OF THE TERRITORY AND PUBLIC DOMAIN OF THE CONTINENTAL U.S., 1781–1867

Year and How Acquired	Total Area (Acres)
1781–1802 State cessions	236,825,600
1783 Treaty of Paris with Gt. Britain	541,364,480
1803 Louisiana Purchase[1]	529,911,680
1803 Red River Basin[2]	29,601,920
1819 Cession from Spain	46,144,640
1845 Annexation of Texas	249,066,240
1846 Oregon Compromise	183,386,240
1848 Mexican Cession	338,680,960
1850 Purchase from Texas	78,926,720
1853 Gadsden Purchase	18,988,800
1867 Alaska Purchase	375,296,000

[1] Data exclude areas eliminated by the Treaty of 1819 with Spain. Such areas are included in figures for annexation of Texas and the Mexican Cession.
[2] Drainage basin of the Red River of the North, south of the 49th parallel, sometimes considered part of the Louisiana Purchase.

Settlement of Gallipolis, in the Ohio country, by French immigrants on lands fraudulently claimed by Scioto Co. promoters; some eventually resettled on the "French Grant" authorized by Congress (1795).

1790–95. EARLY TURNPIKES. Opening of the **Philadelphia-Lancaster Turnpike** (1790), completed, 1794. Its financial success encouraged considerable building of toll roads, especially in New England and the Middle States. Construction of the **Knoxville Road** (1791–95), linking the Wilderness Road to the Cumberland settlements. **Wilderness Road** opened to wagon traffic (1795), facilitating settlement in the lower Ohio Valley. In the same year the **Old Walton Road** was opened, connecting Knoxville and Nashville, serving as route for settlers in the Tennessee interior.

1791, 4 Nov. A mixed force of regulars and militia led by Gen. **Arthur St. Clair** (1736–1818), governor of the Northwest Territory, was defeated by Indians of the Maumee and Wabash rivers. St. Clair was replaced (5 Mar. 1792) by Gen. **Anthony Wayne** as commander of troops in the Ohio country.

Vermont admitted to the Union.

1792. Kentucky admitted to the Union.

Capt. **Robert Gray** (1755–1806), of the ship *Columbia* out of Boston, discovered and named the Columbia River.

1792–1800. EARLY CANALS. Western Inland Lock Navigation Co., chartered in New York, 1792, opened canal (1796) around the Little Falls in the Mohawk River. Santee Canal constructed (1792–1800), joining the Cooper and Santee rivers in South Carolina. Middlesex Canal constructed (1793), linking Boston with the Merrimack River.

1794, 20 Aug. BATTLE OF FALLEN TIMBERS, won by Gen. Anthony Wayne at the rapids of the Maumee, in northwest Ohio, hastened to a close Indian resistance in the area, secured the Northwest frontier, and gave added proof of the national government's stability.

19 Nov. By **Jay's Treaty** (p. 152) the British agreed to evacuate the Northwest posts by 1 June 1796. The securing of the military frontier encouraged steady settlement of the upper Ohio Valley and freed the Old Northwest from diplomatic intrigues and Indian threats until shortly before the War of 1812.

1795, 3 Aug. TREATY OF GREENVILLE, signed by 12 Indian tribes, set up a definite boundary in the Northwest Territory between Indian lands and those available to U.S. settlers.

27 Oct. Treaty of San Lorenzo, also called **Pinckney's Treaty** (p. 153), signed with Spain; its favorable commercial and boundary provisions allayed Western discontent and separatist feeling.

Organization of the Connecticut Land Co., which purchased the **Western Reserve** in northeast Ohio. Its general agent was **Moses Cleaveland** (1754–1806), who laid out and named the city of Cleveland (1796).

1796. Tennessee admitted to the Union.

U.S. Military Reserve laid out in the Ohio country; set apart for land bounties to Revolutionary veterans.

Congress authorized construction of **Zane's Trace,** first road running through Ohio. Connecting Wheeling and Limestone (later Maysville), it was one of the main routes taken by emigrants.

1796–1803. **Holland Land Co.** organized by Dutch bankers, to whom Robert Morris sold in 1792–93 the greater part of a tract west of the Genesee River, helped to advance the settlement of western New York and Pennsylvania.

1798. Establishment of the **Mississippi Territory** opened the Old Southwest to settlement, but large-scale colonization came only after the pacification of the Georgia Indians and the elimination of Spanish control of the West Florida ports.

1800. Liberal provisions of the Land Act of 1800 (p. 633) stimulated settlement of the Old Northwest.

Establishment of the Indiana Territory.

1803, 30 APR. LOUISIANA PURCHASE (p. 158) secured the Mississippi Valley against foreign economic and diplomatic pressures, ushered in period of Western settlement temporarily halted by the War of 1812.

7 JUNE. Treaty of Vincennes, signed by 9 Indian tribes of the Old Northwest, gave the U.S. title to disputed lands along the Wabash River, beyond the line established by the Treaty of Greenville.

Ohio admitted to the Union.

1803–06. LEWIS AND CLARK overland expedition to the Far Northwest (p. 160).

1804–05. Lower Red River and Ouachita River explored by government scientific expedition under **William Dunbar** (1749–1810).

1805. Creation of the territories of Louisiana and Michigan.

1805–06. Government expedition to the upper Mississippi led by Lt. **Zebulon M. Pike** (p. 1128), who also conducted an expedition to the Southwest (1806–07).

1806. Government expedition led by Thomas Freeman (d. 1821) produced first accurate map of the lower Red River.

1807. John Colter (c.1775–1813), one of the pioneer fur traders in the Far West, traveled through the country south of the Yellowstone River, penetrating the valley of the Big Horn.

17–21 AUG. New York-to-Albany and return voyage of the *Clermont,* designed by **Robert Fulton** (p. 1036); inaugurated era of successful steamboat navigation on a commercial basis.

1807–08. Encouraged by the achievements of the Lewis and Clark expedition, parties of trappers and traders penetrated the region of the Missouri and Yellowstone rivers; led to the organization of the Rocky Mountain fur trade, active until c.1840.

1808. Incorporation of the **American Fur Co.,** organized by **John Jacob Astor** (p. 976).

1809. Establishment of Illinois Territory.

Treaty of Ft. Wayne, signed with Indians of the Old Northwest, gave the U.S. title to large tract in southern Indiana.

Formation of the Missouri Fur Co.; declined after c.1812.

First successful sea voyage (New York to Philadelphia) by a steamboat made by the *Phoenix,* designed by **John Stevens** (1749–1838).

1809–11. Exploration of the Missouri River beyond the Mandan villages made by **Thomas Nuttall** (1786–1859), natural scientist, who later carried out explorations along the Arkansas and Red rivers (1818–20).

1811. Fur trading post of **Astoria** established at the mouth of the Columbia River by Astor's Pacific Fur Co. (1810).

7 Nov. BATTLE OF TIPPECANOE (p. 167).

Construction at Pittsburgh of the sidewheeler *New Orleans*, the first steamboat used on western waters; made voyage between Louisville and New Orleans. First voyage on the upper rivers made in 1815 by the *Enterprise*, from Brownsville on the Monongahela to New Orleans and return.

1811–18. TURNPIKES (or toll roads) rapidly proliferated. Construction of the **Cumberland Road** (also called the **Old National Road**), a paved highway connecting Cumberland, Md., with Wheeling on the Ohio River. Subsequent extensions brought it to Columbus, Ohio, and to its final terminus at Vandalia, Ill. One of the chief arteries of western colonization, it was later neglected, only to become a part of U.S. Highway No. 40 in the era of the motorcar. As early as 1810 some 300 turnpike corporations had been chartered in New England, New York, and Pennsylvania, but The **Turnpike boom** came to an end in the mid-1820s. By that date all major cities in the eastern and northern states were interconnected by surfaced roads, while the South lagged behind.

1812. Louisiana admitted to the Union.

Creation of the Missouri Territory.

1812–13. Expedition under the fur trader **Robert Stuart** (1785–1848) made eastward journey from Astoria to St. Louis over route virtually unknown to white men; discovered **South Pass,** later used by California and Oregon immigrants.

1812–14. War of 1812 (pp. 169–182) brought Western expansion to a tempo-

rary halt. The war has been attributed by some historians to have been in part a result of frontier expansionist sentiment (Southern ambitions to secure East and West Florida; Western "land hunger" for Canadian territory) and of Western desire for security against Indian attacks. In fact, political and nationalist considerations are now deemed the chief motives for U.S. entry.

1813. West Florida seized by the U.S. British and Indians defeated at **Battle of the Thames** (5 Oct.), breaking power of Indians of the Old Northwest and opening region to settlement.

1814. Battle of Horseshoe Bend (27 Mar.) ended in defeat of Creek Indians by force under Andrew Jackson, and led to drafting of **Treaty of Ft. Jackson** (9 Aug.) in which Creeks ceded large tracts in Mississippi Territory. These events ended Indian resistance in Southwest and opened region to pioneers after War of 1812.

1815. Treaties of Portage des Sioux terminated virtually all Indian resistance in the Old Northwest; enabled rapid settlement of the westernmost part of the upper tier of trans-Appalachia.

c.1815–50. End of the War of 1812 brought resumption of westward expansion and large-scale settlement of the Lake Plains, the Mississippi Valley frontier, the Gulf Plains, and the Southwest. The northern areas were settled chiefly by emigrants from the Northeast (although many Southerners emigrated to the lower tiers of Ohio, Indiana, and Illinois) and, after 1848, by immigrants from Northern Europe. The Gulf Plains and Southwest were settled mostly by emigrants from the Southern seaboard and Piedmont. This period witnessed the rapid expansion of the "Cotton Kingdom" in the deep South.

1816. Indiana admitted to the Union.

1816–18. First Seminole War ended

in defeat of Florida Indians by expedition under Gen. **Andrew Jackson** (p. 1068).

1816–21. Series of treaties with Indians of the Southwest encouraged settlement in middle Georgia and in western Alabama and Tennessee.

1817. Mississippi admitted to the Union.

Creation of Alabama Territory.

STEAMBOAT. The *Washington,* designed by Henry M. Shreve (1785–1851) and launched at Wheeling, made return voyage between Louisville and New Orleans, initiating successful commercial steam navigation on the Ohio-Mississippi route. Quickly following was the inauguration of steam navigation on Lakes Ontario and Erie. Technical developments, such as a more efficient high-pressure engine (by 1825), stimulated steamboat building and operation. **Rates of speed** of fastest steamboats: On Hudson, 30 miles an hour; on Mississippi, 25 miles downstream, 16 upstream. **Passenger fares** fell rapidly from high initial levels: New Orleans to Louisville before 1818, $100–$125; 1825, $50; 1830s, $25–$30. Pittsburgh to Cincinnati, 1825, $12; 1840s, $5. Middle Western cities served by the Mississippi steamboat system outdistanced others before 1850. **Population,** 1850: Cincinnati, 115,000; St. Louis, 78,000; Louisville, 43,000; New Orleans, 116,000. Great Lakes ports: Chicago, 30,000; Buffalo, 42,000.

1817–18. Exploration of southern Missouri and Arkansas by **Henry R. Schoolcraft** (1793–1864), geologist and ethnologist, who made pioneer studies of the North American Indians.

1817–25. Construction of the **Erie Canal,** extending from Albany to Buffalo and linking the Hudson River with Lake Erie; was authorized by an act of the New York legislature of 1817, and vigorously pushed by **De Witt Clinton** (1769–1828). Formally opened in Oct.

1825, the canal made Buffalo and New York entrepôts of Western commerce, quickly became the chief route for emigrants from New England to the Great Lakes country, and was instrumental in creating an agricultural boom in the West. Its success set off a **canal-building boom.**

1818. Illinois admitted to the Union.

1819. **ADAMS-ONÍS TREATY** (p. 188) provided for cession of **East Florida** to the U.S. and defined western borders of Louisiana Purchase.

Alabama admitted to the Union.

Creation of Arkansas Territory.

24 MAY–20 JUNE. The *Savannah,* first steamship to cross the Atlantic, made voyage from Savannah to Liverpool.

1820. Maine admitted to the Union.

Moses Austin (1761–1821) granted Spanish charter to settle 300 families in Texas; colonization scheme carried out by his son, **Stephen F. Austin** (p. 977).

Army expedition under Maj. Stephen H. Long (1784–1864) explored the region between the Missouri River and the Rocky Mountains. Its report strengthened the myth of the "Great American Desert," a misnomer for the Great Plains but originating with Pike's report (p. 1128).

Completion of **Jackson's Military Road,** connecting Florence, Ala., and the Gulf region near New Orleans.

1821. Missouri admitted to the Union.

1821–22. Opening of the **Santa Fe Trail** to the commerce of the Southwest. Although parts of the trail had been in use, it remained for **William Becknell** (c.1790–c.1832), a Missouri trader, to define the route that was soon plied by trade caravans.

1822. Organization of the trapping and trading business that later became known (1830) as the **Rocky Mountain Fur Co.,** which originated the rendezvous method (as distinguished from trading posts). It dominated the trade in

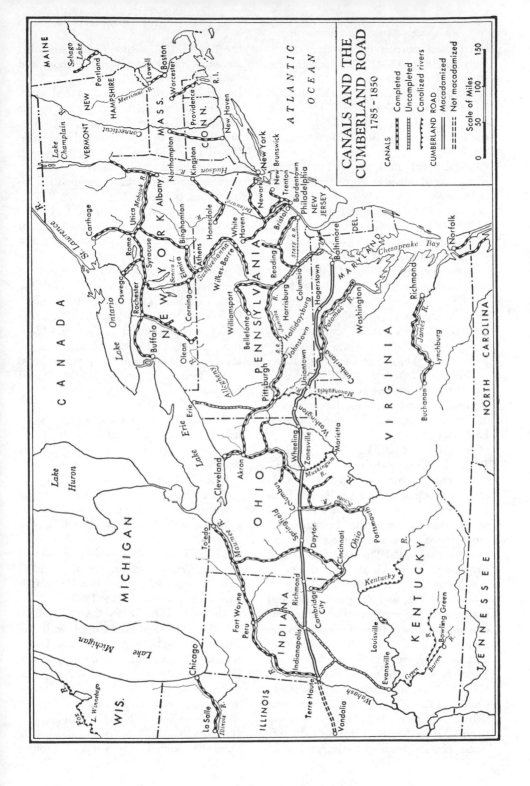

CANALS AND THE
CUMBERLAND ROAD
1785 – 1850

CANALS
Completed
Uncompleted
Canalized rivers

CUMBERLAND ROAD
Macadamized
Not macadamized

Scale of Miles
0   50   100   150

the central portion of the Rockies, finally yielding (1834) to the superior resources of the American Fur Co.

1822–23. Expeditions up the Missouri River to the Yellowstone led by **William H. Ashley** (c.1778–1838), one of the founders of the Rocky Mountain Fur Co.

1824. South Pass, at the lower point of the Wind River range of the Rockies, rediscovered by Thomas Fitzpatrick (c.1799–1854) and Jedediah Smith (1798–1831), active in the Rocky Mountain fur trade. It was later used by emigrants taking the Oregon Trail.

James Bridger (1804–81), fur trader and guide, credited with discovery of the Great Salt Lake. Another fur trader, **Peter S. Ogden** (1794–1854), for whom Ogden, Utah, is named, credited with being one of the first white men to explore the region of the Great Salt Lake.

Gibbons v. Ogden (p. 665), by ending private monopolies in interstate shipping, contributed to the expansion of steam navigation on Eastern rivers, harbors, and bays.

1824–50. CANALS TO TIDEWATER. Construction of the **Morris Co. Canal** across New Jersey (1824–32), connecting New York Harbor with the mouth of the Lehigh River, served as important route for Lehigh coal. Other canals between upcountry and tidewater included the **New Haven and Northampton** (1835, abandoned 1847); the **Delaware and Hudson,** connecting Honesdale, Pa., and Kingston, N.Y., and used chiefly for transportation of anthracite coal, reaching peak traffic, 1872; the **Lehigh** and the **Morris** in Pennsylvania and New Jersey; the **James River and Kanawha** from Richmond to Buchanan, Va., 1832–51; the **Chesapeake and Ohio Canal** (1828–50), linking Georgetown with Cumberland, Md., based on a route begun earlier by the Potomac Co., suffered heavily from the competition of

the B. & O. R.R., whose tracks paralleled its route; the **Pennsylvania Portage and Canal System** (Philadelphia to Pittsburgh, 1826–40), the eastern and western sections of which were joined by the **Allegheny Portage Railway** (1831–35), projected as a competitor of the Erie Canal in a bid for Western commerce, but burdened with high construction costs and strong railroad competition almost from the beginning.

1825. Definite adoption by U.S. government of **removal policy** providing for transfer of eastern Indians to trans-Mississippi regions in order to facilitate advance of white settlement and to fix a permanent Indian frontier beyond the 95th meridian. Originated by Secretary of War John C. Calhoun in 1823, the policy was announced by President Monroe (1825), and carried out on an extensive scale by President Jackson. Most of the Indians of the Old Northwest and Southwest were resettled in present-day Kansas and Oklahoma.

Treaties of Prairie du Chien established boundaries of Indian lands in Old Northwest. This division of tribal lands enabled the U.S. government to make individual treaties for land cessions.

Establishment of Ft. Vancouver by Hudson's Bay Co. on Columbia River solidified British control of the Oregon country.

1826. Treaty of Washington, signed by the Creek Indians, whose removal from Georgia to beyond the Mississippi was accomplished during 1827–29.

1825–56. WESTERN CANALS, linking the Ohio and Mississippi with the Great Lakes. The original **Welland Canal** around Niagara Falls, connecting Lakes Erie and Ontario, was built by Canada, 1829–33. Other interior canals included the Ohio Canal, connecting Portsmouth and Cleveland, 1825–32; Miami Canal (Cincinnati and Toledo, 1825–45); Louisville and Portland Canal around

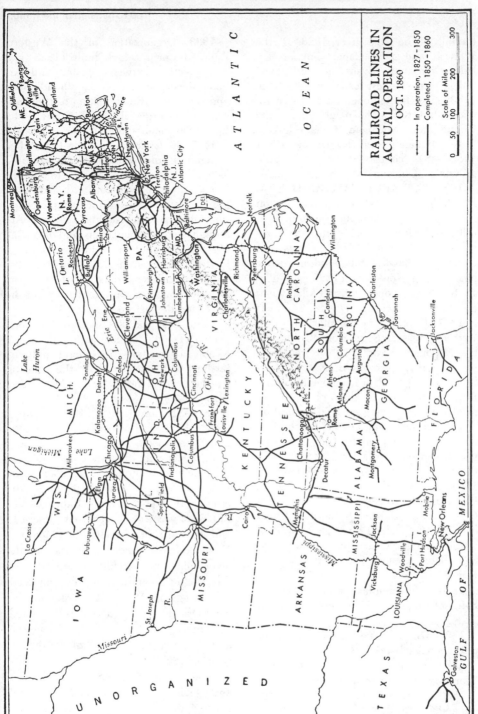

RAILROAD LINES IN
ACTUAL OPERATION
OCT. 1860

In operation, 1827–1850
Completed, 1850–1860

Scale of Miles
0   50   100   200   300

The gauge of all the principal Southern railroads was changed, June 1886, to 4 ft. 9 in. to conform to Northern railroads; previously it was generally 5 ft.

the falls of the Ohio River, 1826–31; the **Wabash and Erie Canal,** linking Toledo, Ohio, with Evansville, Ind. (452 miles), the longest canal in the U.S. (1832–56), helped open up northern Indiana, but was a financial failure; the **Illinois and Michigan Canal,** linking Lake Michigan and the Illinois River (1836–48), contributed to the rapid growth of Chicago (still in active use).

1826–40. EARLY RAILROAD ERA. In 1825 the Stockton and Darlington R.R. began operations in England. U.S. railroad building quickly rivaled European construction. Early efforts included **Mohawk and Hudson R.R.,** chartered in New York (1826), built in 1830; began operations (Albany to Schenectady) in 1831.

1827. Construction of short-line railway in Massachusetts from Quincy to the Neponset River, used for transporting granite; construction of the short-line Mauch Chunk R.R. in Pennsylvania from Carbondale to the Lehigh River, used for transporting coal; incorporation of the **Baltimore and Ohio R.R.,** the first passenger railway in the U.S. Construction began on 4 July 1828, lagged after the Panic of 1837, and was resumed in 1848. In 1853 the connection between Baltimore and Wheeling was completed. Chartering of the South Carolina Canal and R.R. Co., which by 1833 completed a rail link from Charleston to Hamburg, S.C.; later became the South Carolina R.R. Co.

1828. Philadelphia and Columbia R.R., chartered in New Jersey, opened 1834.

1829–57. Construction of the Memphis and Charleston R.R.

1830. Incorporation of the Boston and Worcester R.R., opened in 1835.

1830–32. Construction of the Lexington and Ohio R.R.

1832–52. Construction of the **New York and Harlem R.R.**

1833. Organization of the Western Railroad Corp., which built (1835–42) a connection between **Boston and Albany;** incorporation of the **Philadelphia and Reading R.R.;** formation of the **Central of Georgia R.R.,** which by 1843 linked Savannah and Macon.

1835–36. Chartering of the **Louisville, Cincinnati and Charleston R.R.,** projected by Southern interests to enable local centers to compete with Northern ports as entrepôts for the commerce of the Ohio and Mississippi valleys. Although state particularism and financial obstacles brought the venture to an end in 1839, the separate state roads built by local interests served as the foundation for the Southern rail network built in the 2 decades before the Civil War.

1836. Erie and Kalamazoo R.R. connected Toledo, Ohio, with Adrian in Michigan Territory; Richmond and Petersburg R.R. chartered by the state of Virginia, later the **Atlantic Coast Line R.R.** (1900).

1836–51. Construction of the Western and Atlantic R.R., connecting Atlanta and Chattanooga.

1837. As part of a state internal improvements program, Michigan projected 3 railroads: the Michigan Northern (Port Huron–Grand Rapids), the **Michigan Central** (Detroit–St. Joseph), and the Michigan Southern (Monroe–New Buffalo). Under separate private ownership, the Michigan Central and the Michigan Southern were completed to Chicago in 1852. Chartering of the **New Orleans and Nashville R.R.,** aimed at tapping the trade of the Tennessee and Cumberland regions; failed after the panic of 1837.

1840. Completion of the **Vicksburg and Jackson R.R.,** traversing central Mississippi.

U.S. had 3,328 miles of railroad; all Europe only 1,818.

1826–30. Explorations of California and the Pacific Northwest by **Jedediah Smith** (1798–1831).

1827. American Fur Co. absorbed the Columbia Fur Co.; thereafter dominated the upper Missouri trade.

1830. Congressional enactment of the **Removal Bill** empowering the president to transfer any eastern Indian tribe to trans-Mississippi areas.

Maysville Road Bill vetoed by President Jackson (p. 201).

1831–32. Expedition to the upper Mississippi led by **Henry R. Schoolcraft,** who discovered the source of that river to be a lake, which he named Itasca.

1832. Black Hawk War in the upper Mississippi Valley. The defeat of the Sauk and Fox led by the chieftain Black Hawk ushered in an active period (1832–37) of Indian removal to trans-Mississippi areas. By 1846 Indian removal from the Old Northwest had been completed.

Completion of the **Chicago Road,** a military highway facilitating the settlement of southern Michigan and upper Indiana.

1832–33. Treaties of Payne's Landing and **Ft. Gibson,** authorizing removal of the Seminoles from Florida to beyond the Mississippi, led to resistance culminating in the **Second Seminole War.**

1832–35. Rocky Mountain trapping and hunting expedition led by Capt. **Benjamin L. E. Bonneville** (1796–1878), subject of Washington Irving's *The Adventures of Captain Bonneville* (1837).

1833. Opening of the Black Hawk Purchase on the west bank of the Mississippi inaugurated large-scale settlement of Iowa country.

Organization of the village of **Chicago;** incorporated as a city in 1837.

1833–34. Expedition under the Rocky Mountain fur trader **Joseph R. Walker** (1798–1876) climbed the Sierra Nevada (believed to be the first ascent from the east made by white men), penetrated the Yosemite Valley, and on the return journey crossed the Sierra through the gap later called Walker Pass.

1834. With others, Rev. **Jason Lee** (1803–45), a Methodist missionary, explored the Willamette Valley and established the first mission and the first American agricultural settlement (near present-day Salem, Ore.) in the Oregon country.

Overland expedition to Oregon led by **Nathaniel J. Wyeth** (1802–56) from Independence, Mo., to Fort Vancouver. A member of this expedition was the ornithologist John K. Townsend (1809–51), who wrote *Narrative of a Journey across the Rocky Mountains to the Columbia River* (1839). Wyeth attempted to establish in the Pacific Northwest a project for exploiting the natural resources of the Columbia River region. His venture, the Columbia River Fishing and Trading Co. (1834–37), was unsuccessful due to the opposition of the Hudson's Bay Co.

The **Territorial Road,** a land route facilitating settlement in southern Michigan, opened to traffic.

1835. Treaty of New Echota ceded to the U.S. all Cherokee lands and provided for the transportation of the Cherokee Indians to areas beyond the Mississippi; removal completed by 1838.

Completion of the removal of Alabama Creek Indians to beyond the Mississippi.

Overland journey from St. Louis to the Green River under the leadership of Dr. **Marcus Whitman** (1802–47) and Rev. Samuel Parker (1779–1866), sponsored by the American Board of Commissioners for Foreign Missions. Whitman's next expedition from St. Louis (1836), the first party with women to cross the Rockies, reached Oregon, where Whitman established the Walla Walla mission.

1835–40. Final period of the Rocky Mountain fur trade.

1835–42. Second Seminole War ended with removal of most of the Seminole Indians from Florida to beyond the Mississippi.

c.1835–c.1841. State-assisted internal improvement programs in the states of the Old Northwest stimulated a **Transportation Boom,** particularly in Western canal building, resulting in heavy speculation in both lands and transportation facilities, many of the latter being built with funds from British investors. These elaborate programs collapsed after the **Panic of 1837,** burdening the states with heavy indebtedness. Between 1816 and 1840, about $125,000,000 was spent on canal projects alone. In the following decade some of the uncompleted projects were resumed by private interests, but railroad competition ultimately made canal operations unprofitable.

1836. Establishment of the independent **Republic of Texas** (pp. 210–211); recognized by the U.S. in 1837.

Arkansas admitted to the Union.

Territories of Iowa and Wisconsin organized.

1837. Michigan admitted to the Union.

1837–40. Opening of the **Lumbering Frontier** in northern Wisconsin and Minnesota, which in turn attracted farmers by creating a demand for foodstuffs.

1840–46. Father Pierre-Jean De Smet (1801–73), Jesuit missionary, founded Catholic missions in the Oregon country and the Great Plains.

1841, 4 SEPT. Distribution-Preemption Act (p. 635).

Bidwell-Bartleson party inaugurated overland migration to California, opening California Trail through South Pass and across Humboldt region of Nevada; followed by numerous emigrants in next years.

1842. Exploring expedition to the Wind River range of the Rockies led by **John C. Frémont.** Second expedition (1843–44) took Frémont from the Missouri River to the Oregon country, thence to Pyramid Lake, into present-day Nevada, and across the Sierra into California. He returned to St. Louis by way of Nevada and Utah. The expeditions contributed valuable scientific observations and stimulated popular interest in the Far West, although Frémont saw no territory not previously explored by fur traders.

1842–43. Beginning of the "great migration" to the Oregon country as the "Oregon fever" spread throughout the Midwest, bringing settlers from Missouri, Ohio, Kentucky, and other states. The **Oregon Trail,** parts of which had been used by fur traders and explorers, became the main route for emigrants. The trail extended from **Independence, Mo.,** to **Astoria,** at the mouth of the Columbia River.

1844. First successful transmission of message by telegraph (pp. 794–795).

1845. ANNEXATION OF TEXAS (p. 225).

Texas and Florida admitted to the Union.

3 MAR. Postal Act reduced postage to 5 cts. a ½ oz. for 300 mi. and authorized mail subsidies for transatlantic steamers; discontinued in 1859.

1846. OREGON TREATY gave U.S. undisputed claim to Pacific Northwest south of 49th parallel (p. 232); stimulated migration to region.

Bear Flag Revolt in the Sacramento Valley; conquest of California by the Americans (p. 238).

Iowa admitted to the Union.

Pennsylvania R.R. chartered. Under the direction of **John Edgar Thomson** (1808–74) a link between Pittsburgh and Philadelphia was built; opened to passenger traffic, 18 July 1858, but the road's major expansion came after the Civil War.

1846–47. Donner party, a group of emigrants bound for California, suffered extreme hardships during winter at Donner Lake and Prosser Creek.

1847. First Mormon settlers arrived in the Salt Lake Valley after overland trek from Kanesville (now Council Bluffs, Iowa). Under the leadership of **Brigham Young** (p. 1190), Salt Lake City was founded (1847) and the State of Deseret established (Mar., 1849) with Young as governor.

Collins Line opened transatlantic steamship service between New York and Liverpool. Ocean Steam Navigation Co. opened similar service between New York and Bremen. These routes were abandoned after the reduction of federal mail subsidies in 1857–58.

Formation of the railway company later known (1851) as the Chicago and Rock Island R.R., the first to reach the Mississippi River (1854), across which it constructed the first bridge (1856).

Mobile and Ohio R.R. chartered; projected by Southern interests, it later received land-grant subsidies from Alabama and Mississippi.

Hannibal and St. Joseph R.R. (built 1851–59) incorporated in Missouri.

1847–51. Construction of the Hudson River R.R., connecting New York and Albany.

1848, 24 Jan. DISCOVERY OF GOLD in California by James W. Marshall on property of **Johann Augustus Sutter** (1803–80); announced by President Polk in farewell message to Congress (Dec.), starting **gold rush** (1849).

2 Feb. TREATY OF GUADALUPE HIDALGO gave U.S. large domain in the Southwest (p. 247).

Wisconsin admitted to the Union.

Oregon Territory established.

1848–49. Frémont's expedition explored railroad route across the Rockies; followed by similar venture in 1853–54.

1848–56. As part of a state program of internal improvements, the North Carolina R.R. was built from Charlotte to Goldsboro.

1849. Minnesota Territory established.

Pacific R.R. Co. (later the **Missouri Pacific R.R.**) chartered in Missouri. Built during 1851–56, it eventually linked St. Louis with Kansas City, and was the first railroad west of the Mississippi River.

Incorporation in Pennsylvania of the railway later known (1853) as the Delaware, Lackawanna and Western R.R.

1849–55. Consolidation of 4 railways in Illinois resulted in creation (1855) of the **Chicago, Burlington and Quincy R.R.**; furnished the Midwest with important connections to Eastern markets.

1850, 9 Sept. California admitted to the Union.

TEXAS CESSION of all claims to New Mexico territory for $10 million (also p. 253).

Territories of Utah and New Mexico established.

20 Sept. Congressional Act authorized land grants to Illinois, Mississippi, and Alabama, for railroad construction between Chicago and Mobile; permitted state grants to railways of tracts in the public domain in alternate sections not exceeding 6 miles. Between 1850–57 some 21 million acres were granted to subsidize the construction of railroads in the Mississippi Valley.

Louisville and Nashville R.R. chartered; completed in 1859.

1851. Chartering of the **Illinois Central R.R.**, the first land-grant railway. Completed in 1856, it linked Chicago, Galena, and Cairo. It received more than 2.5 million acres and, in the course of selling these lands in order to provide for construction costs, carried out extensive colonization work.

1853. Washington Territory organized.

GADSDEN PURCHASE (p. 257).

Consolidation of 3 New York railways connecting New York with Buffalo brought creation of the **New York Central Co.,** which in 1867 came under the control of Commodore **Cornelius Vanderbilt** (p. 1173).

The Cleveland, Columbus and Cincinnati R.R. joined with the Pittsburgh, Ft. Wayne and Chicago R.R. at Crestline, Ohio, to form the first rail connection between Pittsburgh and Cincinnati.

Opening of the Cleveland and Erie R.R.

1854. Territories of Kansas and Nebraska organized; "popular sovereignty" principle inflamed issue of slavery in the territories (p. 258).

Assassination of James King, editor of *San Francisco Bulletin,* marked the apogee of desperado activity in California; led to setting up of **Vigilance Committee** utilizing quasi-legal process to restore order.

1854–57. War Department explorations for a railroad route to the Pacific constituted the federal government's first attempt at a comprehensive and systematic geographical examination of the West.

1855. Opening of the St. Marys Falls Ship Canal, linking Lake Huron with Lake Superior.

1857–58. Conflict of authority with the federal government resulted in dispatch of U.S. troops to Utah Territory; virtually bloodless "Mormon War" ended in compromise.

1858. Minnesota admitted to the Union.

Inauguration of mail service to California by the **Butterfield Overland Mail,** until 1861 active between St. Louis-Memphis and the Pacific coast.

Opening of the **mining frontier** following the discovery of gold in **Colorado, Nevada,** and **British Columbia; Pikes Peak gold rush** (1858–59). **Comstock Lode** (Virginia City) yielded $300 million in gold and silver in 20 years; continuous and profitable mining made possible by **Sutro Tunnel** (1869–79), built by **Adolph Sutro** (1830–98). Leadville, Colo., silver production peak 1880–93.

1859. Oregon admitted to the Union.

Establishment of the Leavenworth and Pikes Peak Express, a stage-line company operating between Leavenworth and Denver.

1860. Kansas territorial legislature chartered the Central Overland, California and Pikes Peak Express, to operate over the "Central Route" through South Pass between St. Joseph and Salt Lake City.

Establishment of the **Pony Express,** relay mail service between St. Joseph, Mo., and San Francisco; first run inaugurated on 3 Apr. 1860.

RAIL TRANSPORTATION ON THE EVE OF THE CIVIL WAR. Between 1840–60 an additional 28,000 miles were added to the U.S. railroad system, representing capital expenditures of close to a billion dollars. Originally, most of the railroads were extensions of existing lines of water transportation, but by 1855 New York was joined by a continuous line of rails to Chicago. The rapid expansion of East-West rail connections outpaced direct rail connections between North and South. As yet no direct rail connection existed along the coast between Washington, Charleston, and Savannah. However, the trunk lines from Chicago to New Orleans linked the South with the Middle West. The farthest western extension of the railroads by 1860 was to **St. Joseph** on the Missouri, but on the Pacific coast a short road near **Sacramento,** Calif., had already been built, signalizing the beginning of West-East construction.

Rail vs. Water-Turnpike Transportation by 1860: Rates per ton-mile ranged from about 15 cts. for turnpikes, 2 cts. for railroads, and from ¼ ct. to 1 ct. for canals.

TIME REQUIRED FOR FREIGHT SHIPMENTS FROM CINCINNATI TO NEW YORK CITY, 1815–1860, BY VARIOUS ROUTES AND METHODS*

Date	Route	Average Time Elapsed
1817	Ohio River keelboat to Pittsburgh, wagon to Philadelphia, wagon or wagon and river to N.Y.	52 days
1843–51	Ohio River steamboat to Pittsburgh, canal to Philadelphia, railroad to N.Y.	18–20 days
1852	Canal across Ohio, Lake Erie, Erie Canal, and Hudson River	18 days
1850's	Steamboat to New Orleans and packet to N.Y.	28 days
1852	All rail via Erie R.R. and connecting lines	6–8 days

* By permission of George R. Taylor, *The Transportation Revolution* (N.Y., Rinehart, 1951).

1860–64. MINING FRONTIER. Gold discovered (1860), in Humboldt and Esmeralda, Nev., intensified rush to mining areas. Government over these areas evolved through (1) mining camps; (2) vigilance committees providing a speedy trial for law-and-order offenders; (3) permanent government, territorial and state. In 1861–64 gold was discovered in Snake River Valley, **Idaho** (Clearwater and Salmon River gold fields; pop. Idaho City, 1863, 6,000). **Montana** gold rush (1863). Main camps: **Virginia City, Helena** (1864). Gang terrorism led by **Henry Plummer** put down by vigilantes, 1864.

1860–66. Pacific Telegraph Act, 16 June 1860, authorized the U.S. to construct a telegraph line from Missouri to San Francisco. The first telegraph message, San Francisco–Washington, D.C., was transmitted 24 Oct. 1861. The merger in 1866 of the **Western Union Telegraph Co.** (1856), controlling Western lines, with the American Telegraph Co. (1855) in control of the East, led to rapid expansion of telegraph service. **Postal Telegraph** organized, 1881.

1861. Kansas admitted to the Union. Colorado, Dakota, and Nevada organized as territories.

Merchandise admitted to the U.S. mails.

Beginning of the **Cheyenne-Arapaho War,** caused by the influx of miners into Colorado; climax in 1864 when Denver was isolated. On 28 Nov. the **Chivington Massacre** of 450 Indians took place, when Colorado militia under Col. J. M. Chivington attacked the main Indian encampment; submission of Indians by Oct., 1865.

1862–93. WESTERN RAILROAD BUILDING. (1) **Central Route:** Chicago to San Francisco via lowlands near South Pass. Pacific Railroad Act (1 July 1862) authorized the **Union Pacific R.R.** to build a line from Nebraska to Utah, where it was to meet the **Central Pacific** (organized, 1861, and directed by **Collis P. Huntington** [1821–1900] and **Leland Stanford** [p. 1155]) building east from California. Land grants of 10 alternate sections per mile on both sides of the entire distance were made (also p. 636). The route was completed, 10 May 1869, by a junction of the 2 lines at **Promontory,** Utah. Corrupt practices of **Crédit Mobilier,** Union Pacific's construction company, came into the open in Dec. 1867; scandal also attached to the operations of the **Crocker Corp.,** responsible for Central Pacific building. The latter used Chinese labor; the Union, Irish. In 1880 U.P. absorbed the Kansas Pacific and Denver Pacific, giving it access to Kansas City. By 1893 it had over 8,000 miles of track.

(2) **Northern Route: Northern Pacific R.R.** (chartered, 1864), to utilize route from Lake Superior to Portland, Ore., financed by **Jay Cooke** (p. 1005); reorganized, 1881, by **Henry Villard** (1835–1900); route completed, 1883. An additional northern route was started in 1878 by the St. Paul, Minneapolis, and Manitoba R.R. (reorganized, 1889 as **Great Northern R.R.**), as a result of the seizure of control of the bankrupt St. Paul and Pacific R.R. by **James J. Hill** (1838–1916). By 1893 the line reached the Pacific at Seattle, Wash. To compensate for the lack of a land grant Hill promoted farm settlement along the entire route to create traffic.

(3) **35th Parallel Route: Atchison, Topeka and Santa Fe R.R.**, promoted by **Cyrus K. Holliday** (1826–1900), received a land grant from Congress in 1863 of 3 million acres in alternate sections in Kansas. By 1872 the line reached Colorado. Over a combination of its own and leased tracks it ran to Los Angeles via Needles and Yuma by 1883, by which date the line had 7,100 miles of track, from Kansas City to the West Coast.

(4) **Southern Route** (32nd parallel) was granted the **Texas & Pacific R.R.** (organized, 1871), to build to California and meet the tracks of the **Southern Pacific R.R.**, a line operated by the controllers of the Central Pacific. Acquired by Jay Gould, 1879, T. & P. later shared track privileges with S.P. east of El Paso, which the latter railroad had reached in 1881, joining eastern lines in 1882 to complete a route to New Orleans.

1863. West Virginia admitted to the Union. Arizona and Idaho territories organized, the latter being separated from the Oregon Territory.

1863–73. Congress authorized, 1863, free-carrier mail service direct to ad-

dressee. By 1871, 51 cities had carrier service. In 1873 the **postal card** was introduced from Europe.

1864. Nevada admitted to the Union to ensure the ratification of the 13th Amendment.

Montana Territory organized.

Railway mail service, proposed by George B. Armstrong in 1862, inaugurated by Postmaster General Montgomery Blair (1813–83). **Money order** system went into operation 1864.

1865. Submission of the Indians marked the end of the **Apache and Navajo** wars and the establishment of reservations (1866–67). **First Sioux War,** caused in part by U.S. project to construct a road from Fort Laramie, Wyo., to Bozeman, Mont., ended on 29 April 1868, when Sioux agreed to accept permanent reservation in Dakota Territory.

CATTLE KINGDOM. Beginning of the "Long Drive" of cattle from Texas to railroads of Kansas and Nebraska. The transfer of cattle was caused by (1) a price decline in Texas, (2) scarcity and price rise in the Middle West, (3) the Civil War. Between 1865 and 1879, 4 million head of cattle were thus transported. A byproduct of the Long Drive was the "cattle towns"—**Abilene** (1867), Ellsworth, Newton (after 1872), and **Dodge City,** Kansas (after 1875). From these centers live cattle were shipped to slaughterhouses in Chicago. The **refrigerator car** (by 1875) delivered Western dressed beef to the East.

1867. Nebraska admitted to the Union.

30 Mar. ALASKA PURCHASE (p. 334).

Establishment by Congress of the **Oklahoma Reservation** for members of the Five Civilized Tribes (eventually settled by 75,000 Indians), of the Black Hills Reservation for the Sioux, and 5 smaller reservations.

Beginning of the extermination of the

buffalo. Hides worth $1 to $3 per head. By 1883, about 13 million buffalo had been killed.

1867–69. 4 GREAT WESTERN SURVEYS by the federal government: (1) by **Clarence King** (1842–1901), of 40th parallel (1867–78); (2) by Dr. **Ferdinand V. Hayden** (1829–87) of a geological survey of Nebraska and Wyoming (1867–78); (3) by Lt. **George M. Wheeler,** of the 100th meridian (1872–79); (4) by Maj. **John W. Powell** (p. 1132) of Utah, Nevada and Arizona (1869–78).

1867–1910. EASTERN RAILROAD CONSOLIDATION. Organization, 1867, of the **New York Central & Hudson River R.R.** by **Cornelius Vanderbilt** (p. 1173), subsequently adding the N.Y., West Shore, and Buffalo R.R. By 1885 control over the Michigan Central and the "Big Four" system (connecting Cleveland, Cincinnati, Chicago, and St. Louis) had been obtained. In 1898 the Boston and Albany R.R. was leased. The **Pennsylvania Co.,** a pioneer holding company (1870), was organized by the Pennsylvania R.R. for rail lines leased or controlled. Rapid expansion of lines to Pittsburgh, Cincinnati, Chicago, St. Louis, and to Baltimore and Washington followed. Having acquired terminal facilities on the west shore of the Hudson, it constructed a tunnel under the river and opened a terminal in New York City in 1910. By 1866 **Erie R.R.** was in control of stock manipulator **Daniel Drew** (1797–1879), who was associated with **Jay Gould** (1836–92) and **James Fisk** ("Jubilee Jim," 1834–72) in stock manipulations at the expense of Cornelius Vanderbilt, operations which threw the line into bankruptcy in 1875; reorganized by J. P. Morgan, 1894.

1868. Wyoming Territory organized. Beginning of first **Dakota boom.** By 1873, population of the Dakotas rose to 20,000.

1870. Beginning of the **Texas boom.** During the next decade the number of Texas farms increased from 61,125 to 174,184.

23 May. Start of the first transcontinental railroad trip from Boston to Oakland.

1871–86. Apache War in New Mexico and Arizona began 30 Apr. 1871 with the massacre of over 100 Apaches at Camp Grant, Ariz. The conflict ended with the capture of the Apache leader, Geronimo, in 1886, and the remnants of the tribe were assigned small reservations in the Southwest. Yeoman service in this and other campaigns was rendered by the "Buffalo Soldiers," the 9th and 10th Cavalry regiments authorized by Congress in 1866 to be formed of Negro troops.

1873. Passage of the **Timber Culture Act** (p. 637).

Panic of 1873 interrupted railroad construction. By that date the Rock Island R.R. extended to Council Bluffs (1869); the Chicago, Burlington & Quincy to south-central Nebraska; the Illinois Central to Sioux City; the Chicago, Milwaukee & St. Paul into Iowa; the Chicago & Northwestern across Minnesota and into the Dakotas; the Northern Pacific had reached Bismarck, N.D.; the Lake Superior & Mississippi had extended to Duluth; and the Santa Fe had completed the trans-Kansas line.

1873–1907. SOUTHERN RAILROAD EXPANSION. The Baltimore & Ohio completed its line to Cincinnati (1873); later extended its lines north to Lake Erie and west to Chicago, Cincinnati, and St. Louis. Chesapeake and Ohio crossed the Appalachians, reaching Asheville, N.C., 1892; Norfolk and Western extended to the Ohio Valley, 1892. In 1900 the Clinchfield completed crossing from North Carolina to Tennessee; in 1907 the Virginian completed the last Appalachian route. The main north-south route of the Southern Railway was completed to Atlanta, 1873; the Atlantic Coast Line consolidated more than 100 smaller lines, 1898–1900; Seaboard Airline, 1900. By the 1890s southern Florida was reached by the Florida East Coast. Another line from Atlanta to Cincinnati had been completed in 1880.

1874. The worst grasshopper plague in U.S. history spread devastation among Great Plains farmers from the Dakotas to northern Texas.

Joseph F. Glidden (1813–1906) marketed his first **barbed wire** and solved the problem of fencing the cattle range. Ultimately the American Steel and Wire Co. (U.S. Steel subsidiary) established a virtual monopoly of barbed wire based on the Glidden patents.

1875. Opening of the **Black Hills area** in South Dakota to gold seekers, after gold was reported (Aug.) by U.S. military expedition headed by Gen. **George A. Custer** (1839–76). By fall over 15,000 prospectors entered the region. Main camps: **Custer City** and **Deadwood** (the latter the scene of legendary lawlessness created by such residents as **James Butler** ["Wild Bill"] **Hickok;** actually only 4 murders and no lynchings marred its pioneer years). Ultimately the **Homestake Mining Co.** assumed control of operations in this area.

1875–76. Second Sioux War caused by (1) the gold rush into the Black Hills reservation; (2) extension of the route of the Northern Pacific R.R.; (3) corruption in the Department of the Interior. U.S. troops finally defeated Chiefs **Sitting Bull** and **Crazy Horse** (31 Oct. 1876), but not before Custer and a contingent of 264 men were annihilated at the **Battle of the Little Big Horn** (25–26 June).

1876. Colorado admitted to the Union.

1877. Passage of the **Desert Land Act** (p. 637).

Nez Percé War, fought in the Pacific Northwest. Nez Percé Indians under **Chief Joseph** were defeated (Oct.) and assigned a reservation in Oklahoma.

1877–1915. EARLY TELEPHONE EXPANSION. Operation in 1877 of the first practical intercity telephone lines— Salem to Boston (Bell), Chicago to Milwaukee (Gray)—led to establishment by 1880 of 148 telephone companies operating 34,305 miles of wire. These systems were ultimately consolidated by the **American Telephone & Telegraph Co.** By 1895 long-distance telephone lines were in operation between New York and Chicago; connections extended to Denver, 1911; to San Francisco, 1915. Number of telephones in the U.S.: 1900, 1,355,900; 1932, 17,424,406; 1952, 43,003,800; 1970, 120,155,000.

1878. Timber and Stone Act (p. 637).

1878–85. Second Dakota boom, promoted by entry of Northern Pacific R.R. and Great Northern into territory by 1882, followed by other lines. Peak in homestead grants in the Dakotas was reached in 1884 when 11,083,000 acres were granted to settlers. Population, 1890, 539,583; Montana, 142,924.

1879. "EXODUS OF 1879" in which between 20,000 and 40,000 Negroes from South sought homesteads in Kansas when word spread they would be welcome there, only to be turned back by lack of capital, inexperience, and white hostility.

1883. Four standard time zones established, facilitating railroad operations.

1883–86. Coeur d'Alene gold rush to northern Idaho. In 1885 the **Bunker Hill** and **Sullivan Mines** were discovered, eventually yielding $250 million in silver and lead.

1883–87. END OF THE CATTLE BOOM marked by big business control of ranching. In Wyoming 23 stock-raising corporations were organized with a total capital of $12 million. Overstocking the range was followed by serious drought, 1885–86, and a cold winter, 1886–87. Prices crashed in 1885. Result: the end of the open range and the introduction of fenced pastures and better cattle breeding.

1884. RAILROAD LAND GRANTS. Estimate of all public lands granted to railroads: 155,504,994 acres (Donaldson), almost the area of Texas (Union Pacific, 20 million; Santa Fe, 17 million; Central and Southern Pacific, 24 million; Northern Pacific, 44 million, sales of which by 1917 had brought the last-named railroad over $136 million). Western states also granted roads 49 million acres. Because of noncompletion of a number of projected roads, the final federal total: **131,350,534 acres** (U.S. General Land Office, *Ann. Rep.,* 1943). In addition, loans totaling $64,623,512 were advanced to 6 companies to build the Pacific routes, which were repaid with interest by 1898–99. In return, the land-grant railroads agreed to transport U.S. property and troops "free," a clause which was adjusted to **50%** of normal commercial rates. In 1940 Congress eliminated reductions on U.S. government's civilian passenger and freight traffic, but low rates continued during World War II for U.S. army and navy freight and personnel; discontinued 1 Oct. 1946.

17 May. Organic Act applied the laws of Oregon to Alaska after a period of government by the War Department.

1887. Dawes Severalty Act (p. 645). Interstate Commerce Act (p. 309).

1889. North Dakota, South Dakota, Montana, and Washington admitted to the Union (with Idaho and Wyoming admitted, 1890)—known as the **Omnibus States.**

22 Apr. Since 1884 "Sooners" led by **David L. Payne** and **W. L. Couch** had been entering the **Oklahoma District,** a triangle of rich land in the center of Indian Territory owned by no one tribe, only to be dispersed by troops. Constant pressure led to the opening of the district to homesteaders, or "Boomers" as they were called, at noon. Within a few hours, 1,920,000 acres were settled under bedlam conditions (Oklahoma City by nightfall—population, 10,000).

1890, 2 May. Oklahoma Territory organized.

U.S. Census Director, in his report, announced that **"there can hardly be said to be a frontier line."**

The **Ghost Dance War** on the Black Hills Reservation arose when U.S. Army authorities sought to curb religious rites of the Teton Sioux; came to an end with an Indian massacre at the **Battle of Wounded Knee** (29 Dec.).

1891, 22 Sept. Lands of the Sauk, Fox, and Pottawatomie in Oklahoma Territory (900,000 acres) opened to settlement.

1892. Opening of the Cheyenne-Arapaho Reservation of 3 million acres.

1893, 16 Sept. Second major "Boomer" invasion of Oklahoma on 6 million acres of the **Cherokee Outlet.**

1896. KLONDIKE GOLD RUSH. Gold discovered 16 Aug. 1896 on Bonanza Creek, near Dawson, Canada, 50 miles east of Alaska border; followed by gold rush. Peak production, 1900, $22 million; total production, 1885–1929, exceeded $175 million.

Utah admitted to the Union.

Rural free delivery established.

1898. 7 July. Annexation of **Hawaii** (pp. 339–340, 345). On 30 Apr. 1900 Congress granted territorial status to Hawaii, the new government defined in the Organic Act becoming effective 14 June 1900.

1900. LAND SETTLEMENT. In the 30 years ending 1900, 430 million acres had been occupied; 225 million placed under cultivation. For the entire period,

1607–1870, 407 million acres occupied; 189 million improved.

1900–52. HIGHWAY CONSTRUCTION AND MOTOR TRANSPORTATION. Twentieth-century highway construction augmented the use of the automobile, the motor truck, and the bus as formidable competitors to railroad transportation. Asphalt roads had been introduced in New York City in the 1870s; Portland cement in the U.S. in 1894. Surface roads increased in mileage from 161,000 (1905) to 521,000 (1925), and 1,527,000 (1945). Most notable of numerous highway projects was the **Alaskan Highway (Alcan)**, work upon which was started on 12 Mar. 1942 and completed 1 Dec., 1,523 miles from Dawson Creek, B.C., through Canada and the Yukon Territory to Fairbanks, Ala. Constructed as a military supply route during World War II at a cost of $138 million, it was opened to tourists, summer 1948. **Passenger car registrations:** 1900, 8,000; 1913, 1,258,062; 1930, 26,545,281; 1951, 42,700,000. **Motor truck registrations:** 1904, 700; 1913, 67,667; 1952, 9,116,000. Regular route intercity passengers carried by **intercity bus** averaged 425 million (1944–48).

1906. Alaska permitted to elect a delegate to Congress.

1907. Oklahoma and Indian Territory admitted to the Union as 1 state.

1911–52. AIRPLANE TRANSPORTATION, following the first successful airplane flight by the **Wright brothers,** 1903, at Kitty Hawk (p. 797), made rapid strides in the U.S. The first air-mail service, New York to Washington, 1918; across the continent, 8 Sept. 1920. 15 Oct., first contracts for international air mail (Western Hemisphere) awarded to private operators. By the **Kelly Act** (1925) air-mail contracts were to be awarded on the basis of private bidding.

Factors promoting air transport in this period include (1) inauguration of regular night flying (Chicago to Cheyenne), 1923; (2) installation of radio beacons for aerial navigation (Washington, D.C.), 1925; (3) passage of the **Air Commerce Act,** 1926, which inaugurated a government program of aid to civil air transport and navigation, including the establishment of airports. Rapid expansion followed.

1927, 21 MAY. First nonstop flight, New York to Paris, by **Charles A. Lindbergh, Jr.** (1902–1974).

1 SEPT. Air express established by arrangement between American Railway Express Agency and airlines.

1934, 19 FEB. All domestic air-mail contracts canceled by Postmaster General **James A. Farley** (1888–   ) on the ground of collusion. U.S. Army Air Corps assumed operations pending new arrangements with private operators, who began to handle air mail by 8 May. The **Air Mail Act** of 12 June provided that the ICC was to determine "fair and reasonable" air-mail rates and to review them periodically, and reduced air-mail postage to 6 cts. an oz.

1935. Inauguration of transpacific air service (San Francisco to Manila) by Pan American Airways.

1938, 23 JUNE. Civil Aeronautics Act created **Civil Aeronautics Authority (CAA)** empowered to regulate rates of air transport and foster stability in the field.

1939. Inauguration of transatlantic air service (New York–Southampton) by Pan American Airways and Imperial Airways.

1947. First fully automatic (without pilot control) transport flight (U.S. Army C-54), Newfoundland to England. Airlines carried 12,890,208 **revenue passengers** that year as against 5,782 in 1926 and 1,365,706 in 1938.

1948–52. First U.S. jet-propelled commercial air transport—Consolidated Vultee Convair; first British DeHaviland Comet (1949); revised version ordered by several U.S. airlines (1952).

Domestic air routes in operation: 139,030 miles (1948) as compared with 8,252 miles in 1926 and 35,492 in 1938. **Domestic cargo,** exclusive of mail (estimated), 30,637,879 (ton-miles) for express, 69,023,000 for freight.

1912. New Mexico and Arizona admitted to the Union, completing the political organization of the West. Alaska given territorial status (population: 1920, 55,000, as against 30,000 in 1867).

1913. Establishment of **domestic parcel post** by Act of 24 Aug. 1912. Parcel post arrangements between the U.S. and the United Kingdom had been in existence since 1902

1919–50. EXPANSION OF RADIO COMMUNICATION SYSTEMS (pp. 798, 954–956).

1954, 13 MAY. ST. LAWRENCE SEAWAY (p. 483).

27 SEPT. "DEW LINE" (p. 484).

1956–72. HIGHWAY CONSTRUCTION AND MOTOR TRANSPORTATION.

29 June, the **Highway Act of 1956** authorized $32 billion over the next 13 years for construction of a 41,000-mile interstate system of highways and for completing construction of the federal-aid system of highways, the federal government to contribute 90% of construction costs for the interstate and 50% for the federal-aid system. The act also provided for new taxes on gasoline and other highway-user items for a **Highway Trust Fund** to finance the programs. By 1972 cost estimates has risen to $76.3 billion for a 42,500-mile interstate system and 1980 was considered a possible completion date; 33,796 miles of the interstate system were open to traffic.

Passenger car registrations 1972: 96,-397,000 as compared with 61,682,000 in 1960.

Truck and bus registrations 1972: 21,-209,000 as compared with 12,187,000 in 1960.

Intercity bus lines carried 401 million passengers in 1970 as compared with 366 million in 1960.

Motor vehicles transported 412 billion ton-miles of freight, 21.3% of domestic freight traffic in 1970, as compared with 285 billion ton-miles, 21.5% in 1960.

1958, 3 MAY. ANTARCTICA (p. 488).

1959, 3 JAN. ALASKA admitted to the Union as the 49th state. The first bill for Alaskan statehood was introduced in 1916 but the drive for statehood did not become sustained and serious until 1943. Partisan and sectional considerations figured importantly in congressional debates on statehood for the Democratic and pro-civil-rights territory. In order to demonstrate their readiness, Alaskans drafted and approved (24 Apr. 1956) a state constitution and elected (9 Oct.) to Congress 2 "senators" and a "representative." For Alaska to become a viable state it was considered necessary to give it an endowment of federal lands, which comprised more than 99% of its area. The Alaskan Statehood Act (7 July 1958) granted the state the right to select 102,-550,000 acres of vacant unreserved public lands and an additional 800,000 acres adjacent to communities.

21 AUG. HAWAII admitted to the Union as the 50th state. In 1903 the popularly elected Hawaii legislature petitioned for statehood, a request repeated at least 17 times. The first of a long series of Hawaiian statehood bills was introduced in 1919. The drive for statehood became significant in 1934 when it gained the support of the territory's economic leadership. Opposition in Congress to Hawaii's admission was based upon doubts about the wisdom of admitting a noncontiguous state, concern of Southerners as to the admission of pro-civil-rights congressmen, and fears of excessive Communist influence among unionized longshoremen and plantation workers.

1966, 15 Oct. DEPARTMENT OF TRANSPORTATION created (p. 532).

1968–74. RAILROAD REORGANI-ZATIONS. Pennsylvania and New York Central R.R. merger forming Penn Central R.R. was upheld by the Supreme Court 15 Jan. 1968 (p. 682). The New York, New Haven, and Hartford R.R. was absorbed into the Penn Central system (Dec. 1968). The Penn Central filed a petition in bankruptcy, 22 June 1970, but was the beneficiary of a law authorizing $125 million in federal loan guarantees (8 Jan. 1971). **AMTRAK,** a semipublic corporation created by the **Rail Passenger Service Act of 1970** to operate a nationwide passenger system,

began service on 1 May 1971. The act enabled those railroads that wished to transfer all intercity passenger operations to the new corporation to do so. Travel was up 11% (1973) on AMTRAK, whose showpiece was the Washington, D.C. to New York City **Metroliner,** developed under the **High-Speed Ground Transportation Act of 1965,** which made its first run 16 Jan. 1969. Under the Rail Reorganization Act of 2 Jan. 1974 Congress provided for the reorganization of the Penn Central and 6 other bankrupt railroads in the Northeast and Midwest, established a federal agency to design a new rail system as a profit-making enterprise, a corporation to run it and to issue up to $1.5 billion in guaranteed loans. The legislation also authorized the expenditure of $585 million and required construction of new electrified high-speed rail service in the Northeast Corridor.

Chronology of the States of the Union

1.	Delaware	7 Dec. 1787	26.	Michigan	26 Jan. 1837
2.	Pennsylvania	12 Dec. 1787	27.	Florida	3 Mar. 1845
3.	New Jersey	18 Dec. 1787	28.	Texas	29 Dec. 1845
4.	Georgia	2 Jan. 1788	29.	Iowa	28 Dec. 1846
5.	Connecticut	9 Jan. 1788	30.	Wisconsin	29 May 1848
6.	Massachusetts	6 Feb. 1788	31.	California	9 Sept. 1850
7.	Maryland	28 Apr. 1788	32.	Minnesota	11 May 1858
8.	South Carolina	23 May 1788	33.	Oregon	14 Feb. 1859
9.	New Hampshire	21 June 1788	34.	Kansas	29 Jan. 1861
10.	Virginia	25 June 1788	35.	West Virginia	20 June 1863
11.	New York	26 July 1788	36.	Nevada	31 Oct. 1864
12.	North Carolina	21 Nov. 1789	37.	Nebraska	1 Mar. 1867
13.	Rhode Island	29 May 1790	38.	Colorado	1 Aug. 1876
14.	Vermont	4 Mar. 1791	39.	North Dakota	2 Nov. 1889
15.	Kentucky	1 June 1792	40.	South Dakota	2 Nov. 1889
16.	Tennessee	1 June 1796	41.	Montana	8 Nov. 1889
17.	Ohio	1 Mar. 1803	42.	Washington	11 Nov. 1889
18.	Louisiana	30 Apr. 1812	43.	Idaho	3 July 1890
19.	Indiana	11 Dec. 1816	44.	Wyoming	10 July 1890
20.	Mississippi	10 Dec. 1817	45.	Utah	4 Jan. 1896
21.	Illinois	3 Dec. 1818	46.	Oklahoma	16 Nov. 1907
22.	Alabama	14 Dec. 1819	47.	New Mexico	6 Jan. 1912
23.	Maine	15 Mar. 1820	48.	Arizona	14 Feb. 1912
24.	Missouri	10 Aug. 1821	49.	Alaska	3 Jan. 1959
25.	Arkansas	15 June 1836	50.	Hawaii	29 Aug. 1959

1970, 12 Aug. POSTAL REORGANI-ZATION ACT (p. 536). Pieces of mail handled 1970 (estimated): 84.9 billion as compared with 7.1 billion in 1900 and 27.7 billion in 1940.

1970. AIRPLANE TRANSPORTA-TION. On 22 Jan. a Boeing 747 carried 362 passengers on its first commercial flight, New York–London. By year's end more than 100 of these "jumbo jets," capable of carrying up to 500 tourist-class passengers, were in service on domestic and international routes. Capable of carrying up to 400, the Mc-Donnell Douglas DC-10 and Lockheed 10–11 followed the 747 into commercial service.

Domestic revenue passengers carried 1970: 153 million as compared with 38 million in 1955 and 92 million in 1965.

Domestic ton-miles flown, express and freight 1970: 2.216 billion as compared with 228 million in 1955 and 943 million in 1965.

Domestic ton-miles flown, mail 1970: 715 million as compared with 87 million in 1955 and 226 million in 1965.

The American Empire

1858–1947 OVERSEAS EXPANSION OF THE U.S.

Year	Accession	Area, sq. mi.
1858	Johnston Atoll (Johnston and Sand Islands)	1
1863	Swan Islands[1]	3
1867	Alaska	586,412
1898	Midway Islands	2
1898	Wake Island	3
1898	Hawaii	6,450
1898	Palmyra Atoll	4
1898	Philippines[2]	115,600
1898	Puerto Rico	3,435
1898	Guam	212
1899	American Samoa	76
1903	Panama Canal Zone[3]	553
1914	Corn Islands[4]	4
1916	Navassa Island	2
1917	U.S. Virgin Islands	133
1928	Roncador Cay, Serrano Bank, Serranilla Bank[5]	.4
1934	Howland, Baker, and Jarvis Islands	3
1934	Kingman Reef	.5
1939	Canton and Enderbury Islands[6]	27
1947	Trust Territory of the Pacific Islands (Micronesia)[7]	716

[1] Turned over to Honduras in accordance with treaty signed 22 Nov. 1971.
[2] Ceded by Spain in 1898, the Philippines constituted a territorial possession of the U.S. until granted independence 4 July 1946.
[3] Under U.S. jurisdiction in accordance with treaty of 18 Nov. 1903, with the Republic of Panama.
[4] Leased from the Republic of Nicaragua for 99 years but returned to Nicaragua 25 Apr. 1971.
[5] Turned over to Colombia in 1973 under an agreement reached 8 Sept. 1972.
[6] Administered by the U.S. under a joint control agreement with the United Kingdom.
[7] Former Japanese mandated islands, under UN trusteeship with the U.S. as administering authority. Ocean area approx. 3 million sq. mi.

1898–1946. The Philippines.

1899. TREATY FIGHT. As a result of the Treaty of Paris (10 Dec. 1898; p. 345), Spain ceded to the U.S. the Philippines, as well as Puerto Rico and Guam. Senate debate on the treaty focused upon the Philippines—whose acquisition represented a major departure from previous American experience—and revealed the sharp division between the imperialists and anti-imperialists. The former, notably **Henry Cabot Lodge** (p. 1088) and **Albert Beveridge** (p. 985), stressed national prestige, the civilizing mission of the U.S., economic and strategic advantages, and the contention that foreign powers active in the Far East would establish a foothold in the Philippines if the U.S. withdrew. The anti-imperialists, among them **George F. Hoar, John Sherman, Thomas B. Reed, Charles Francis Adams** (1835–1915), **Carl Schurz,** and **E. L. Godkin,** maintained that the acquisition of noncontiguous areas peopled by alien stocks incapable of assimilation was contrary to the traditional U.S. isolationism, inimical to the Monroe Doctrine, and contrary to U.S.

principles of self-government. Democrats and Populists were generally opposed to the treaty, and were joined by a minority group of New England Republicans. The leader of the Democratic party, William Jennings Bryan, succeeded in influencing a sufficient number of opponents of the treaty to vote for it on the ground that it would end the war. The question of the independence of the Philippines, Bryan pointed out, could be left to the national election of 1900. The treaty was ratified (6 Feb.) by the close vote of 57–27 (thus securing confirmation by a 2-vote margin).

1899–1901. COLONIAL STATUS ISSUE. Imperialists contended that acquisition did not automatically incorporate the new possessions—including also Puerto Rico (p. 622) and Guam (p. 624) —into the U.S. and endow them with the constitutional privileges of U.S. citizens. Anti-imperialists argued that the "Constitution followed the flag," i.e., that territorial acquisition made these dependencies an organic part of the U.S., entitled to all constitutonal guarantees— a position based on legal arguments which tended to justify their position that annexation was an error. A middle group held that only "fundamental" constitutional guarantees, as distinguished from "formal" privileges, were applicable to the insular possessions. The anti-imperialists suffered another defeat when the constitutional status issue was settled by the Supreme Court in the so-called **Insular Cases** (1901 *et seq.*, p. 673).

1899–1902. PHILIPPINE INSURRECTION. At the outbreak of the Spanish American War the U.S. returned the insurrectionist leader **Emilio Aguinaldo** to the Philippines to direct the native uprising against the Spanish. Aguinaldo organized a Filipino army and on 12 June 1898 established a provisional government, proclaiming its independence of Spain. The Filipino rebels be-

lieved that the U.S. would grant freedom and independence to the islands. When Aguinaldo learned (4 Jan. 1899) that the Treaty of Paris gave the U.S. control of the Philippines, he called upon the people (5 Jan.) to declare their independence. On 4 Feb. the Filipinos broke out in armed revolt against U.S. rule. To suppress the uprising the U.S. employed a force of 70,000 men against a Filipino army almost as large. Organized Filipino resistance came to an end by the close of 1899 but guerrilla warfare that led to ruthless measures on both sides continued until mid-1902, despite the earlier capture (23 Mar. 1901) of Aguinaldo. Scattered resistance continued until 1906. The administration's Philippine policy was condemned by the Anti-Imperialist League, an organization established in June 1898 that included many influential citizens among its numbers.

1899. SCHURMAN COMMISSION. President McKinley appointed (20 Jan.) a Philippine Commission headed by Jacob G. Schurman, president of Cornell Univ., to study the situation in the islands and to submit a report to serve as a basis for setting up a civil government. In June the Schurman Commission recommended ultimate independence for the islands, but suggested the continuation of U.S. rule for an indefinite period, until the Filipinos were ready for self-government.

1900. TAFT COMMISSION. On 7 Apr. President McKinley appointed a second Philippine Commission, headed by Federal Circuit Judge William Howard Taft. The 5-man commission which, in accord with the Schurman Commission's recommendations, was directed to establish a civil government in the islands began to exercise legislative powers on 1 Sept. and, with the termination of military government (except in areas where rebellion persisted) became the civil government on 4 July 1901. (All military government was ended a year later.) As president of the commission, Taft became civil governor of the Philippines. Guided by specific instructions written by Secretary of War Elihu Root, the commission proclaimed guarantees essentially those of the U.S. Bill of Rights, organized municipal administrations, and by progressive steps created a government for the Philippines. Taft encouraged Filipino participation, ultimately adding 3 Filipinos to the commission.

1 JULY 1902. PHILIPPINE GOVERNMENT ACT (also known as the Organic Act) passed by Congress constituted the Philippine Islands an unorganized territory. It confirmed the president's appointment of the Taft Commission, ratified the commission's reforms, and assured increased self-government—providing for establishment of a popular assembly (after peace was established and a census taken). The commission would then become the upper house of the bicameral legislature, its members retaining also their executive and ministerial functions. In the first general elections (1907) the Nationalist party, which stood for immediate independence, gained 58 of 80 assembly seats.

29 AUG. 1916. JONES ACT reaffirmed the U.S. intention to withdraw its sovereignty over the islands and to recognize their independence as soon as a stable government should be established. The act provided for male suffrage, established an elective Senate in place of the Philippine Commission, and vested executive power in the governor, to be appointed by the U.S. president. The governor was given veto power, subject to review by the president, but all appointments made by the governor were subject to confirmation by the Philippine Senate. From this time onward the Filipinos effectively controlled their domestic affairs. The Jones Act also provided for free trade between the Philippines and the U.S. (most U.S. duties and quotas on Philippine exports had already been removed). The U.S. maintained a virtual monopoly of Philippine trade as Philippine exports expanded.

PHILIPPINE INDEPENDENCE. Following the election of 1932 a movement gained ground to implement the promise of independence for the Philippines contained in the Jones Act. Joining forces to promote independence were U.S. beet-sugar and dairy interests seeking to bar Philippine cane sugar and coconut oil, respectively; organized labor favoring immigration curbs; and anti-imperialists. The immediate result was the **Hawes-Cutting Act,** passed by a Democratic Congress over the president's veto in the closing days of the Hoover administration, 13 Jan. 1933. The act provided for independence after 12 years, but reserved to the U.S. the right to military and naval bases, and to the U.S. Supreme Court the right to review the decisions of the Philippine courts. The Philippine legislature rejected the measure in Oct. on the ground that its real aim was to exclude Philippine products and labor from the U.S. To meet some of these criticisms, Congress (24 Mar. 1934) passed the **Tydings-McDuffie Act,** which substantially reenacted the Hawes-Cutting bill, but provided for the removal of U.S. military posts and the settlement by negotiation of the future status of U.S. naval bases. This act was unanimously accepted by the Philippine legislature (1 May). Under its authority a convention met on 30 July to frame a constitution, which President Roosevelt approved on 8 Feb. 1935. The constitution was ratified, 14 May, and the first president, **Manuel Quezon,** elected on 17 Sept. On 14 Apr. 1937 President Roosevelt appointed the Joint Preparatory

Commission on Philippine Affairs to recommend a program for economic adjustment. The committee proposed that the 75% of preferences existing on 4 July 1946 (the date when Philippine independence was to go into effect) be gradually eliminated by 31 Dec. 1960.

The Philippines became independent on the projected date, 4 July 1946. By an executive agreement embodying provisions of the Philippine Trade Act of 1946 (30 Apr. 1946), signed on that date, the Philippines received tariff concessions (duty-free entry until 1954 with duties to be gradually imposed over the following 20 years) but in return had to treat U.S. exports to the Philippines similarly and accept a "parity clause" guaranteeing U.S. businessmen equal rights with Filipinos to exploit Philippine natural resources and operate public utilities. The "parity clause" necessitated amendment (Mar. 1947) of the Philippine Constitution, which the U.S. had approved in 1935.

1898–1973. Puerto Rico.

After the outcome of the war with Spain had been decided in Cuba (p. 345), a U.S. force of some 3,500 under Gen. Nelson A. Miles landed in Puerto Rico—meeting only token military resistance and general popular acceptance (25 July 1898). After evacuation of the Spanish governor-general (18 Oct.) the U.S. took over complete authority. Spain's cession of Puerto Rico to the U.S. by the Treaty of Paris (10 Dec.; p. 345) was recognition of an accomplished fact. Puerto Rico was controlled by the military pending congressional establishment of civil government.

12 Apr. 1900. THE FORAKER ACT provided for the establishment of a temporary civil government in Puerto Rico, effective 1 May. The president was empowered to appoint, with senatorial consent, the governor and the 11 members (at least 5 of whom were to be natives of Puerto Rico) of the executive council, which was to serve as the upper house of the legislature. Popular elections were provided for the lower house and a Resident Commissioner to speak for Puerto Rico in the U.S. House of Representatives (he could vote only in committee). Federal tariffs, at reduced rates, were applied to products of Puerto Rico—with the provision that their proceeds were to be returned to the insular treasury. (Taxes collected in the U.S. on Puerto Rican products were not actually paid to Puerto Rico until the provision was clarified in the Jones Act of 1917). Puerto Rico was also exempted from federal internal revenue taxes. Puerto Rican politicians were unwilling to undergo an indefinite period of tutelage under the Foraker Act—a majority demanding full territorial status and U.S. citizenship. A split began to emerge about 1909 between those who spoke of ultimate statehood and those who looked toward independence.

2 Mar. 1917. THE JONES ACT (also known as the Organic Act for Puerto Rico) made Puerto Rico an "organized but unincorporated" territory of the U.S. and granted Puerto Ricans U.S. citizenship. Regulation of the suffrage was left to the Puerto Rican government (male suffrage had become universal under the local discretion permitted by the Foraker Act) and a bill of rights essentially similar to that of the U.S. was established. The upper house of the legislature was made elective. The governor and the supreme court were to be appointed by the president, who would also appoint 4 of the 6 department heads.

1899–1952. ECONOMIC SITUATION AND MOVEMENT FOR REFORM. Included within U.S. tariff walls, Puerto Rico found a ready market for its agricultural products, particularly sugar.

Adoption of U.S. currency and unobstructed financial movement between the island and the U.S. mainland facilitated large capital investment—some $120 million during the first 3 decades of U.S. rule—which revolutionized sugar production. As sugar corporations absorbed the limited productive land which had sustained small farmers producing for local consumption, Puerto Rico was forced to import its foodstuffs. By the 1930s sugar production had expanded to more than 16 times what it had been under Spain but few Puerto Ricans lived above the subsistence level; poverty was widespread and unemployment high. Population pressure increased as the application of modern medical knowledge radically cut the island's death rate, causing the population nearly to double between 1899 and 1940 (1899: 953,000; 1940: 1,869,000).

In 1934 a commission of Puerto Ricans produced the first serious proposals for reform and development, the Chardón Plan, which stressed distribution of land to the cultivators and development of industry by essentially restrictive and protective measures. Established in 1935, the Puerto Rican Reconstruction Administration (PRRA)—successor to the New Deal Puerto Rican Emergency Relief Administration (PRERA)—was to have implemented the Chardón Plan but, to a large extent a victim of the politics of a colonial situation, the PRRA accomplished little. In answer to Nationalist violence (1935–36), the U.S. government fanned the status issue as serious consideration was given the Tydings Bill (1936). This punitive offer of independence under adverse economic conditions realigned Puerto Rico's political parties into pro- and anti-independence groups. The victorious pro-statehood coalition generally coincided with the forces opposed to economic and social reform.

Only temporarily sidetracked, the incipient political movement for reform took the form of the new Popular Democratic Party (PPD) led by **Luis Muñoz Marín** (p. 1097). Muñoz argued that immediate economic and social problems took precedence over the status issue. Appealing to the lower classes, the PPD won tenuous control over the legislature in 1940. The PPD's electoral success brought **Rexford G. Tugwell** (1891–   ) —a vigorous advocate of democratic planning—to Puerto Rico as governor in 1941. Tugwell and Muñoz established a cooperative relationship and the PPD undertook such reforms as land redistribution and establishment of an economic development program. Popular approval of the Muñoz-Tugwell program resulted in an overwhelming victory for the PPD in the 1944 elections. Gathering momentum after 1945, **"Operation Bootstrap"** gave marked impetus to industrial development by providing various incentives to investors in new or expanded industry and construction—notably 10-year tax exemptions (increased up to 17 years in 1963).

1952. ESTABLISHMENT OF THE COMMONWEALTH. In 1946 President Truman named Jesús T. Piñero as the first Puerto Rican governor. The Organic Act was amended (5 Aug. 1947) to provide for popular election of the governor. Advocating a commonwealth status (estado libre asociado), Muñoz was elected governor (2 Nov. 1948), decisively defeating advocates of both statehood and independence. U.S. sanction of a self-governing status for Puerto Rico was given with Puerto Rican Federal Relations Act of 1950, adopted "in the nature of a compact" and affirmed by a special election (4 June 1951). Accordingly, the Commonwealth of Puerto Rico was established by a constitution, drawn up by a Puerto Rican convention; approved in a referendum (3 Mar. 1952);

accepted with minor amendments in the Commonwealth Act (3 July); and, after acceptance of the U.S. amendments, proclaimed by Puerto Rico on 25 July 1952. The Puerto Ricans are free to modify the constitution so long as such changes do not conflict with the U.S. Constitution, the Puerto Rican Federal Relations Act, or the Commonwealth Act. The Puerto Rican constitution provides for popular election of a governor every 4 years with unlimited reelection permitted and a bicameral legislature in which the representation of minority parties is guaranteed. The judicial power is vested in one supreme court and lower courts but appeal to the federal court system is possible. Puerto Ricans elect a Resident Commissioner to the U.S. Congress. Puerto Ricans do not vote in U.S. presidential elections although emigrants on the U.S. mainland may do so.

1952–73. ECONOMIC DEVELOPMENT. In 1956 a milestone was passed when income derived from industry began to surpass that derived from agriculture. By the 1970s income from manufacturing (textiles, apparel, leather goods, electrical and electronic equipment, chemicals, etc.) was more than 4 times that from agriculture—although sugar, tobacco, and rum were still produced and exported. The bulk of Puerto Rico's trade has been with the U.S. (80–90% of imports; approx. 95% of exports). San Juan became the center of an important tourism industry. After 1968 more than 1 million people visited Puerto Rico annually. By 1972 per capita income had increased to $1,713—the highest in Latin America but far below that of the U.S. Unemployment rarely dropped below 13%.

REEXAMINATION OF COMMONWEALTH STATUS. The U.S.–Puerto Rican Commission on Status (estab. 24 Feb. 1964) reported that commonwealth, statehood, and independence were all theoretically open to Puerto Rico and urged a plebiscite. With statehood and independence advocates urging a boycott, 709,293 of the 1,067,349 eligible voted in the plebiscite of 23 July 1967. Results: commonwealth, 60%; statehood, 39%; independence, .06%. In the elections of 5 Nov. 1968 the New Progressive Party (PNP), which advocated statehood, won control of the House and the governorship (Luis A. Ferré). In the 1970s expressions of dissatisfaction with commonwealth status increased, taking the form of demonstrations and terrorist fires and bombings. A significant irritant was the navy's use of Culebra (a small island 22 miles off Puerto Rico, with a population of some 900) for bombing and target practice. On 24 May 1973 Secretary of Defense Elliot Richardson ordered such operations shifted, effective mid-1975, to 2 uninhabited islands off Puerto Rico. Leaders of the PPD, which regained control of the government in the elections of 7 Nov. 1972 (Rafael Hernández Colón, governor), argued that the commonwealth relationship needed to be improved and self-government broadened.

1898–1973. Guam.

During the Spanish-American War (pp. 343–345) the cruiser *Charleston,* convoying American troops en route to the Philippines, was ordered to stop and capture the Spanish island of Guam. This was accomplished (20 June 1898) without difficulty as the garrison did not know that Spain was at war. Spain ceded Guam to the U.S. (10 Dec. 1898) by the Treaty of Paris (p. 345).

By executive order (23 Dec. 1898) President McKinley made the Navy Department responsible for Guam's administration. In the absence of congressional action, the procession of navy governors assigned to Guam had virtually unlimited powers—which were usually exercised in the manner of a paternalistic caretaker. Through World War II indigenous Guamanians—an admixture of Chamorro, Spanish, and Filipino—played no important role in their own government. The Guam Congress was established as an appointive, advisory council in 1917 and became elective in 1931; but its development was not encouraged.

Guam was occupied by the Japanese from 13 Dec. 1941 to 9 July 1944 (pp. 438, 440). During the later stages of the War in the Pacific some 200,000 U.S. servicemen came to Guam and roughly 40% of the land was preempted for military purposes.

POST WORLD WAR II. At the request of President Truman, planning began (May 1949) for the transfer of administrative authority in Guam from the navy to the Department of the Interior. The transfer became effective 1 Aug. 1950.

Despite the change to civilian administration, the life and economy of Guam were dominated by the presence of the U.S. navy and air force. A tight security clearance system—established during the Korean War under the authority of the Guam Naval and Airspace Reservations (Executive Order 8683, 14 Feb. 1941) —inhibiting economic development by making it extremely difficult for any transpacific travelers (including Americans) to stay in Guam and by usually preventing reentry of aliens, was not lifted until 21 Aug. 1962 (Executive Order 11045). Guam became increasingly significant as a U.S. strategic military outpost. The Guam naval base became an important haven for Polaris submarines. During the Vietnam War Anderson Air Force Base served as a key takeoff point for American B-52s. U.S. military personnel and their dependents combined with resident "statesiders" and Filipinos outnumbered the indigenous Guamanians through 1970. The presence of the U.S. military transformed Guam's economy. Agriculture decreased in importance as a wage and service economy grew. As of 1970 the island imported approx. 96% of its essential goods, including foodstuffs.

Typhoon Karen (11–12 Nov. 1962) caused damages estimated at $60–$100 million. Designated a disaster area, Guam was allocated $16 million by the Office of Emergency Planning. Under the Guam Rehabilitation Act of 1963, as amended, Guam was authorized to receive $75 million in loans and grants to restore and improve public facilities—providing the basic infrastructure for economic development. Beginning in 1967, when regular commercial air service between Guam and Japan was first established, a substantial tourist industry began to be developed. In 1973 more than 90,000 tourists, mostly Japanese, visited Guam.

After World War II Guamanians requested U.S. citizenship, an Organic Act, and greater self-government. The Guam Congress was granted legislative authority in August 1947. Under the terms of the **Organic Act of 1950** (1 Aug.) those born in Guam became U.S. citizens, although not permitted to vote in national elections. The Organic Act provided for an appointive governor and a unicameral legislature. The act was amended (11 Sept. 1968) to make the governorship elective, beginning in 1970. As a result of local legislation, from 1965 to 1971, Guamanians elected a Washington representative who served as a liaison between Guam and the U.S. Congress. A U.S. law (10 Apr. 1972) gave Guam one delegate to the U.S. House of Representatives. The delegate could vote in committee but not on the floor of the House.

Population (1970): 84,996.

Status: organized, unincorporated territory of the U.S.

1899–1974. American Samoa.

U.S. interest in establishing a naval base and way station for ships trading with the Orient led to embroilment in struggles for authority in Samoa (pp. 335–337). With the partition of Samoa (2 Dec. 1899; p. 346), the U.S. acquired the island of Tutuila (with Pago Pago, one of the finest harbors in the Pacific) and all other islands of the Samoan group east of 171° W. Although the high chiefs of Tutuila and Aunuu ceded those islands to the U.S. on 17 Apr. 1900; the high chiefs of Tau, Olosega and Ofu ceded their islands to the U.S. on 14 June 1904; and U.S. jurisdiction was extended to Swain's Island (more than 200 miles north of Tutuila) in 1925; Congress did not formalize U.S. possession of American Samoa until 1929, when the islanders were granted the status of "nationals" of the U.S.

By executive order (19 Feb. 1900) President McKinley placed the Samoan islands assigned to the U.S. under control of the navy. While Pago Pago was developed as a naval station, the navy maintained a caretaker regime. Under a system of indirect rule village, county, and district councils continued to meet to manage local affairs and an assembly (*fono*) of chiefs (*matai*) from all of American Samoa, presided over by the naval governor, met annually, beginning in 1905. By executive order (effective 1 July 1951) administrative responsibility for American Samoa was transferred from the navy to the Department of the Interior. Since that time the Secretary of the Interior has appointed the territory's governor. In Dec. 1952 the territory's first general elections were held—for a reorganized House of Representatives. The new upper house, the Senate, was selected in accordance with Samoan custom. *Matai* continued to do well under the election system, but not to the exclusion of others. The first constitution of American Samoa—drawn up by a committee chaired by the governor and ratified (27 Apr. 1960) by a convention of traditionally elected chiefs, became effective Oct. 1960. A bicameral legislature having a measure of competence (previous assemblies were solely advisory) was established. A new constitution, drafted by a constitutional convention, was approved in a territory-wide election (19 Nov. 1966). Powers of the legislature increased; e.g. for the first time it could appropriate funds raised from local revenues. Like its predecessor, the new constitution embodied various provisions designed to protect traditional customs and patterns of authority. In Nov. 1972 a proposal that the governor be elected was rejected by a 4 to 1 margin in a controversial referendum— the territory's governor, John Haydon, was found guilty of violating the Hatch Act (p. 427) but his removal from office was not demanded. A new constitution, providing for local election of the governor and lieutenant governor, was rejected by American Samoa's voters in Nov. 1973.

ECONOMIC DEVELOPMENT. In 1961 U.S. efforts to promote American Samoa's economic development began markedly to accelerate. **H. Rex Lee** (governor, 1961–67) inaugurated a 3-year "rehabilitation" program at the outset of his administration. Federal funding rose from $2.6 million in fiscal 1961 to $9.6 million in 1962. Programs were adopted to foster commerce and industry (e.g. tourism, tuna canning, watch assembly); improve education (educational TV system operative since 1964); and upgrade other public services. By fiscal 1973 the territory's budget was $27.5 million, of which $7.6 million were derived from local revenues. Subsistence farming and fishing remain major facets of economic life.

POPULATION (1970): 27,159.

STATUS: unincorporated, unorganized territory.

1903–74. Panama Canal Zone.

Since the signing of the Hay-Bunau-Varilla Treaty in 1903 (p. 349), the Panama Canal Zone has been in effect a U.S. government reservation. The Canal Zone Government and the Panama Canal Co. are the 2 operating agencies in the area (extending 5 miles on each side of the axis of the Panama Canal) in which the U.S. was granted perpetual sovereignty by the 1903 treaty with the Republic of Panama. Both agencies are headed by a single individual, appointed by the president. As governor of the Canal Zone he reports directly to the Secretary of the Army while as president of the Panama Canal Co., which operates the Canal and the Panama R.R., he reports to a board of directors appointed by the Secretary of the Army.

By a treaty signed 25 Jan. 1955, the U.S. agreed: (1) to increase from $430,-000 to $1.93 million the annuity paid to the Republic of Panama; (2) to give Panama $28 million worth of buildings and real estate no longer required by the Canal Zone administration; (3) to guarantee equality of pay and opportunity to U.S. citizens and noncitizen employees in the Canal Zone; and (4) to construct a bridge over the Pacific entrance to the Canal to serve as a link in the Inter-American Highway. The bridge opened 12 Oct. 1962.

On 3 Nov. 1959 mobs attacked the U.S. embassy in Panama City and attempted to invade the Canal Zone. To allay Panamanian ill feeling, President Eisenhower ordered (7 Sept. 1960) that the Panamanian as well as the U.S. flag should henceforth be flown at certain sites. A later order (30 Dec. 1963) banned the flying of any flags in front of Canal Zone schools. Clashes (9–10 Jan. 1964) between U.S. troops and Panamanians were provoked when U.S. students attempted to raise the American flag over the Canal Zone high school. This outbreak of violence, which caused the deaths of 21 Panamanians and 4 U.S. soldiers, led to attempts to renegotiate the Canal Zone's status. After a change of government, Panama in 1970 rejected preliminary agreements reached in 1967 providing for the termination of exclusive U.S. sovereignty in the Canal Zone. At a UN Security Council meeting held in Panama (Mar. 1973), the U.S. vetoed a resolution calling upon the U.S. and Panama to negotiate a new treaty to "guarantee full respect for Panama's effective sovereignty over all its territory." On 7 Feb. 1974 the U.S. and Panama concluded an agreement on basic principles to guide the negotiation of a new Panama Canal treaty which would provide for the eventual transfer of sovereignty over the Canal Zone to the Republic of Panama.

POPULATION (1970): 44,189.

NOTE: normally some 11,000 U.S. military personnel are stationed in the Canal Zone.

1917–73. American Virgin Islands.

By a treaty signed on 4 Aug. 1916, Denmark agreed to cede to the U.S. St. Thomas, St. Croix, St. John, and approximately 50 small islets and cays in the Caribbean (p. 363). The U.S. took official possession on 31 Mar. 1917. The Act of 3 Mar., authorizing payment of $25 million for the Virgin Islands, also sanctioned the continuation of existing governmental institutions with only minor changes. In the governor, to be appointed by the president, were vested "all military, civil and judicial powers necessary to govern" the islands. The authority of the 2 local councils (St.

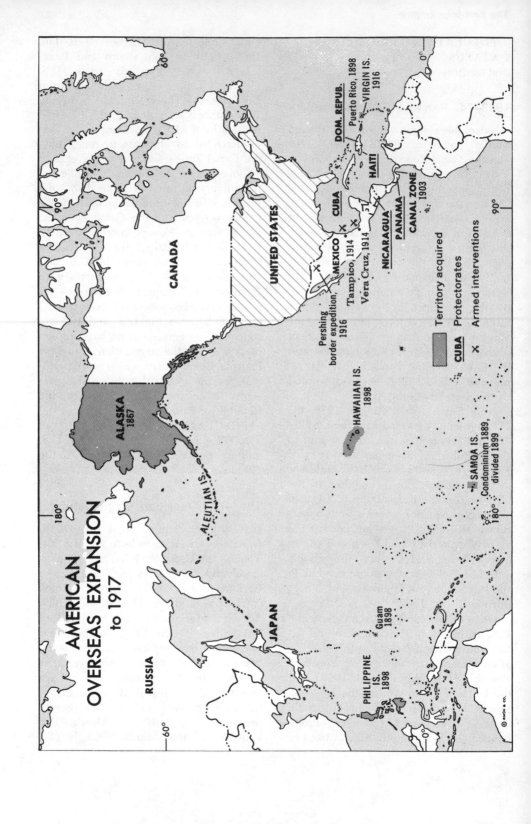

AMERICAN
OVERSEAS EXPANSION
to 1917

Legend:
- Territory acquired
- Protectorates (CUBA)
- X Armed interventions

RUSSIA

JAPAN

CANADA

UNITED STATES

ALASKA 1867

ALEUTIAN IS.

HAWAIIAN IS. 1898

PHILIPPINE IS. 1898

Guam 1898

SAMOA IS. Condominium 1889, divided 1899

MEXICO
Tampico, 1914
Vera Cruz, 1914
Pershing border expedition, 1916

DOM. REPUB.
Puerto Rico, 1898
VIRGIN IS. 1916
CUBA
HAITI
NICARAGUA
PANAMA
CANAL ZONE 1903

© RAND & CO.

Thomas and St. Croix) was limited and property or income requirements restricted the electorate to about 5.5% of the population, which was about 80% black. Naval governors administered the Virgin Islands until Feb. 1931, when administrative authority was transferred to the Department of the Interior.

The Virgin Islanders were granted U.S. citizenship by congressional acts of 1927 and 1932. The Organic Act of 22 June 1936 altered the political structure of the islands. Nearly universal suffrage was put into effect. The 2 local councils were to meet at least once a year as a territorial legislature. The governor was deprived of an absolute veto. The Revised Organic Act of 1954 designated the Virgin Islands an unincorporated territory (instead of an "island possession"); replaced the 2 local councils with a single, unicameral legislature; and provided for return of U.S. revenue collections on products of the Virgin Islands. A reform long sought by the Virgin Islanders was achieved in 1968 when the Organic Act was amended to provide for local election of the governor. Melvin Herbert Evans, a black physician, was elected to a 4-year term as governor in Nov. 1970. In 1972 a U.S. law gave the Virgin Islands one delegate to the U.S. House of Representatives; the delegate could vote in committee but not on the floor of the House. Tensions increased in 1972–73 with several murders which, apparently, were racially motivated.

ECONOMIC DEVELOPMENT. During the first 4 decades of U.S. administration, the economy of the Virgin Islands languished. In 1961, with the advent of the Kennedy administration and the appointment as governor of Ralph Paiewonsky (a white born in the Virgin Islands and an accomplished lobbyist and fund-raiser), a massive infusion of capital began. Increased federal development aid, much of it channeled through the Virgin Islands Corporation (a public body established in 30 June 1949 with a broad mandate to promote economic development), was accompanied by heavy private investment. The infrastructure for tourism was built and by 1969 over 1 million tourists per year were visiting the islands. St. Thomas was given over almost completely to tourism. The previously sugar-based economy of St. Croix was diversified to include—in addition to the production of rum—tourism, oil refining, aluminum and watch making.

POPULATION (1970): 62,468.

STATUS: unincorporated territory.

1945–74. Micronesia.

In the course of World War II the U.S. gained control of the Pacific Islands formerly mandated to Japan—the Marshalls, Carolines, and Marianas (p. 440): 2,203 islands or islets, approximately 716 square miles of land, scattered over an ocean area of 3 million square miles. After the Japanese surrender a navy military government of Micronesia was established. Conflict between those proposing outright U.S. annexation of Micronesia, to protect perceived U.S. defense interests, and proponents of U.S. support for creation of a strong UN trusteeship system led to development of the "strategic area" trust concept. A slot for Micronesia in the trusteeship system acceptable to the U.S. was provided by incorporating in the UN Charter drawn up at the San Francisco Conference in 1945 (p. 458) specifications that in the case of trust areas designated strategic ultimate UN authority would reside in the Security Council (where the U.S. would have a veto), rather than the General Assembly. Despite continued pressure for Micronesia's annexation, the U.S. submitted (26 Feb. 1947) a draft trusteeship agreement to the UN Security Council. With minor amendments

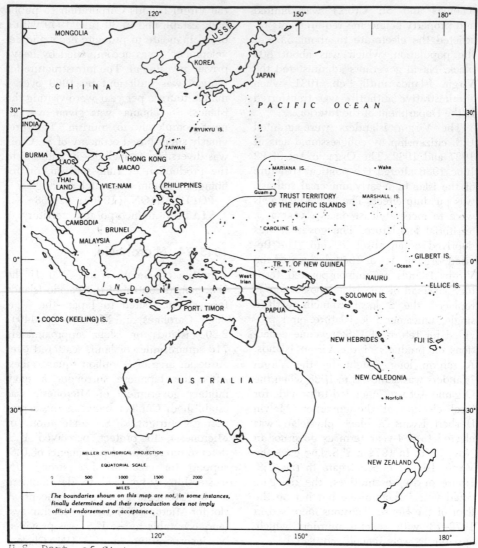

U.S. Dept. of State

Trust Territory of the Pacific Islands

the U.S. proposal was unanimously accepted (2 Apr.) by the Security Council, approved by joint resolution of Congress and signed by President Truman on 18 July. Besides designating all of Micronesia—become officially the Trust Territory of the Pacific Islands (TTPI)—a strategic area, the agreement included provisions designed further to safeguard U.S. security interests—e.g. Article 13 provided that any part of the TTPI could be "closed for security reasons" by unilateral action of the U.S. and thus be excepted from the prescribed UN oversight procedures. The agreement also committed the U.S. to promote the educational, social, and economic advancement of the Micronesians and their development toward self-government or independence.

U.S. SECURITY OPERATIONS IN MICRONESIA. U.S. use of sites in the Marshall Islands for the testing of atomic weapons, begun in July 1946 at Bikini Atoll (p. 466), continued under the trusteeship administration. The Pacific Proving Grounds, established at Eniwetok Atoll (1947) and enlarged to include Bikini (1953), were closed to UN inspection. Experiments involving the explosion of nuclear and thermonuclear weapons were conducted in the Marshalls through 1958. The testing of nuclear weapons caused the displacement of more than 300 Marshallese from their ancestral homes. Fallout from the hydrogen bomb explosion of 1 Mar. 1954 caused significant short- and long-term medical problems for the 82 inhabitants of Rongelap. President Kennedy announced (8 Feb. 1962) that future atmospheric nuclear tests would be removed to sites outside the TTPI. Beginning in the 1950s Kwajalein Atoll (Marshall Islands) was developed from a naval station into a major facility for the testing of ballistic missiles.

CIVIL ADMINISTRATION. By executive order (18 July 1947) Micronesia's military government was succeeded by a civil administration under the temporary jurisdiction of the navy. President Truman transferred administrative responsibility for the TTPI to the Department of the Interior by executive order effective 1 July 1951. During the 1950s the TTPI was administered as a low-budget, caretaker operation. Cautious steps were taken to promote the development of Western democratic forms of local self-government. Partially in response to a severely critical UN Trusteeship Council report (27 July 1961), the Kennedy administration began to accelerate Micro-

nesian development programs. The $7.5 million ceiling on annual appropriations for civil administration (estab. 30 June 1954) was raised (19 July 1962) to $15 million for fiscal 1963 and $17.5 million thereafter. Federal subsidies for civil operations in the TTPI continued to increase, in 1972 reaching the level of approx. $68 million (compared to approx. $5 million in local revenues). Beginning in late 1966 Peace Corps Volunteers (p. 492) were sent to the TTPI, the only time they served in a U.S.-administered area. By the early 1970s efforts to improve education, public health, and other social services had met with greater success than those to foster a viable economy. A successor to earlier advisory councils, the Congress of Micronesia was established (12 July 1965) as a bicameral legislature with restricted powers—e.g. the U.S. Congress retained the power of appropriation of federal funds.

POLITICAL STATUS NEGOTIATIONS. Formal negotiations between U.S. officials and representatives of the Congress of Micronesia, led by Sen. Lazarus Salii, concerning Micronesian self-determination and the nature of Micronesia's political status after termination of the Trusteeship Agreement, began in Sept. 1969. By 1973 an impasse had been reached in attempts to define a relationship of "free association" between the U.S. and a self-governing Micronesia. Key problems related to: (1) U.S. security requirements; (2) possible Micronesian independence; and (3) the level of U.S. financial support under a free-association arrangement. Micronesia's potential for internal fragmentation became more salient as separate status negotiations between the U.S. and representatives of the Marianas District were opened (13 Dec. 1972). After their fourth round of negotiations (15–31 May 1974), agreement on a Commonwealth of the Northern Marianas was close to completion—an arrangement which would allow for U.S. development of a major air-naval base on the island of Tinian.

WAR CLAIMS. Impending Micronesian self-determination spurred U.S. action on an issue long of major concern to the Micronesians—war damage claims against both Japan and the U.S. The Micronesian Claim Act of 1971 (1 July) authorized: (1) payment of $5 million, to comprise the U.S. half of $10 million which the U.S. and Japan had agreed

(18 Apr. 1969) would be made available to the Micronesians as an *ex gratia* compensation for damages resulting from the hostilities of World War II; (2) payment of an additional $20 million to settle Micronesian claims against the U.S. for damages sustained after the U.S. secured the islands—the post-secure period ending 1 July 1951; and (3) creation of a Micronesian Claims Commission to handle both sets of claims.

POPULATION (1970): 102,250.

Land, Natural Resources, and the Environment

With the establishment of the national government, the disposal of the public domain was regulated under the Ordinance of 1785, which was accepted by the federal Congress but not recognized as binding. In practice, this conservative and orderly land policy favored the speculator at the expense of the actual settler.

New land legislation became urgent to meet both Treasury needs and the prospect of large-scale Western settlement. Wayne's defeat of the Northwest Indians

(1794) and the signing of the **Treaty of Greenville** (1795) gave the U.S. secure occupancy of the lands northwest of the Ohio River and encouraged Western pioneering.

Alexander Hamilton's "Report of a Uniform System for the Disposition of the Lands" (1790–91) had ignored the accurate and uniform survey procedure of the Ordinance of 1785 in favor of a modified system of indiscriminate location. His policy reflected the conservative

PUBLIC LANDS OF THE UNITED STATES
Disposition of Public Lands 1781 to 1970 (In acres)

Disposition by methods not elsewhere classified[1]	303,500,000	Granted to States for:	
		Support of common schools	77,600,000
Granted or sold to homesteaders	287,500,000	Reclamation of swampland	64,900,000
Granted to railroad corporations	94,300,000	Construction of railroads	37,100,000
Granted to veterans as military bounties	61,000,000	Support of misc. institutions[6]	21,700,000
Confirmed as private land claims[2]	34,000,000	Purposes not elsewhere classified[7]	117,500,000
Sold under timber and stone law[3]	13,900,000	Canals and rivers	6,100,000
Granted or sold under timber culture law[4]	10,900,000	Construction of wagon roads	3,400,000
Sold under desert land law[5]	10,700,000	**Total granted to States**	**328,300,000**
		Grand Total	**1,144,100,000**

[1] Chiefly public, private, and preemption sales, but includes mineral entries, script locations, sales of townsites and townlots.
[2] The Government has confirmed title to lands claimed under valid grants made by foreign governments prior to the acquisition of the public domain by the United States.
[3] The law provided for the sale of lands valuable for timber or stone and unfit for cultivation.
[4] The law provided for the granting of public lands to settlers on condition that they plant and cultivate trees on the lands granted.
[5] The law provided for the sale of arid agricultural public lands to settlers who irrigate them and bring them under cultivation.
[6] Universities, hospitals, asylums, etc.
[7] For construction of various public improvements (individual items not specified in the granting act) reclamation of desert lands, construction of water reservoirs, etc.

Land Owned by the Federal Government (In acres)

Agency (June 30, 1971)	Public Domain	Acquired	Total
Bureau of Land Management	471,680,093.0	2,364,892.1	474,044,985.1
U.S. Forest Service	160,176,950.0	26,637,350.4	186,814,300.4
U.S. Fish and Wildlife Service	24,401,982.7	3,505,275.9	27,907,258.6
U.S. Park Service	19,587,492.2	4,883,982.8	24,471,475.0
U.S. Army	7,051,453.0	3,998,858.0	11,050,311.0
Bureau of Reclamation	5,829,133.1	1,749,102.4	7,578,235.0
U.S. Air Force	6,941,946.0	1,383,762.0	8,325,708.0
Corps of Engineers	787,232.7	6,599,510.2	7,386,742.9
Bureau of Indian Affairs	4,204,809.2	781,155.9	4,985,965.1
U.S. Navy	2,155,750.0	1,431,366.7	3,587,116.7
Atomic Energy Commission	1,446,299.6	678,684.5	2,124,984.1
Other Agencies	530,489.5	1,395,991.4	1,926,480.9
Totals	**704,793,631.0**	**55,409,932.3**	**760,203,563.3**

(Source: Bureau of Land Management, U.S. Dept. of the Interior)

views of Eastern business interests desiring a check on the agricultural class and the systematic regulation of the labor supply. Its complete adoption would have meant the priority of revenue from sales to large speculators over actual settlement by cultivators.

1796, 18 MAY. After a lengthy House debate on land policy, Congress passed the **Land Act of 1796.** It provided for rectangular survey and public auction sales, but raised the minimum price from **$1 to $2 an acre,** payable within a year. The lands were to be divided into township units 6 miles square, and half of these were to be divided into single sections of **640 acres.** Intervening townships were to be disposed of in single sections, alternate townships in units of 8 sections. Land offices were established at Cincinnati and Pittsburgh. The attempt of frontier interests to secure an amendment for the sale of half of the 640-acre tracts in quarter sections (160 acres) was defeated in the Senate. Because of poor administrative machinery and inadequate credit provisions, only 48,566 acres were sold by 1800.

1800, 10 MAY. The needs of Western interests led to the adoption of a more liberal policy under the **Land Act of 1800** (also known as the **Harrison Land Act**). It retained the minimum price of **$2 an acre,** but authorized minimum purchases of **320 acres, a 4-year credit,** and a discount of 8% for cash payment. A fron-

tier demand for the incorporation of the preemption principle was defeated. Land offices were established at Cincinnati, Chillicothe, Marietta, and Steubenville. This act served as the model for similar legislation until 1820. Sales under it began in Apr. 1800; by 1 Nov. 1801, 398,466 acres had been sold. Although its provisions were calculated to favor revenue rather than actual settlement, in practice the system encouraged the latter. The more important modifications of the act were:

OHIO ENABLING ACT (30 Apr. 1802). With the admission of the first public-land state, the federal government adopted the policy of retaining title to all ungranted tracts within state boundaries, except 1 section in each township set aside for educational purposes.

ACT OF 3 MAR. 1803. Provided for the survey and sale of ungranted lands in the Mississippi Territory.

LAND ACT OF 1804 (26 Mar.). Reduced the minimum cash payment to **$1.64 per acre** and authorized minimum sales of **160 acres.**

ACT OF 2 MAR. 1805. Provided for the determination and confirmation of Spanish and French land grants in Louisiana, extended the U.S. land surveys over the Louisiana Purchase, and authorized penalties for squatters illegal settlers).

INTRUSION ACT (3 May 1807). Authorized penalties for unregistered squatters; poorly enforced.

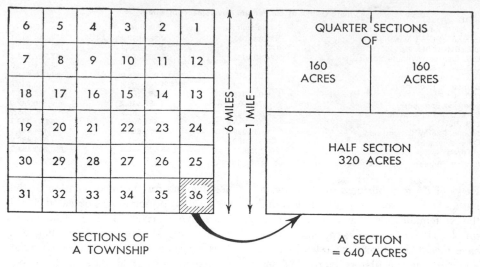

Public Land Survey System

SECTIONS OF
A TOWNSHIP

A SECTION
= 640 ACRES

ACT OF 25 APR. 1812. Established the General Land Office as a bureau of the Treasury Department. The central executive and administrative duties pertaining to public lands were transferred from the Secretary of the Treasury to a commissioner. In 1849 the Land Office was transferred to the Department of the Interior.

The liberal credit provisions of the Act of 1800 stimulated **widespread speculation,** weakened the national land system, and contributed to the Panic of 1819. Secretary of the Treasury W. H. Crawford reported that since 1789 the government had disposed of $44 million worth of land, but up to 30 Sept. 1819 had been paid only half that amount. By 1820 Congress had passed 12 relief acts for land purchasers. The precarious financial condition of the government after the War of 1812 made reform imperative.

1820, 24 APR. Under the **Land Act of 1820,** the **credit system was abolished,** but the minimum price was reduced to **$1.25 an acre** and minimum purchases were fixed at **80 acres.** In principle, this benefited the pioneer, but heavy and almost universal indebtedness made the full cash payment stipulation a hindrance to the actual settler and benefited the speculator.

1821–32. Eleven relief acts were passed by Congress to meet Western demands for (1) cheap land; (2) **preemption** (the legal confirmation of squatter claims on public lands as opposed to engrossment by nonresident purchasers). Except for some special instances, the national government had since its foundation opposed demands for granting preemption or donations to actual settlers.

After 1820 public-land policy was linked to (1) the maneuvering of North and South for sectional balance, and (2) the rise of the West as a distinctive section, with its own special interests. Sen. **Thomas Hart Benton** (Mo., p. 983), champion of the West, introduced (1824) his first bill providing for grading the price of land, whereby public lands would be sold at less than $1.25 an acre or even given away, after such tracts had failed to draw purchasers at the legal minimum price.

Western demands were echoed in urban areas. The Jacksonian era witnessed the rise in Northeastern centers of workingmen's groups supporting the agrarian program for more land. In New York City, labor publicists such as **Thomas Skidmore** denounced land monopoly, while another, **George Henry Evans** (1805–56, later the leader of the Land Reform movement), advocated free homesteads for Eastern surplus labor.

1829, 29 Dec. The Eastern conservative viewpoint was reflected in the resolution introduced by Sen. **Samuel A. Foot** (Conn., 1780–1846) proposing an inquiry into the advisability of temporarily restricting the sale of public lands (a proposal that touched off the **Webster-Hayne** debate, p. 200)—a resolution denounced by Western spokesmen.

1830. An alliance of South and West enabled the Senate to pass Benton's **Graduation Bill** (May), but the measure was tabled in the House. This sectional alliance, however, effected the passage of the **Pre-emption Act of 1830** (29 May), authorizing settlers who had cultivated land on the public domain in 1829 to enter as many as **160 acres** at the minimum price of **$1.25 an acre.** Although the act was adopted as a temporary measure, its substance was renewed at regular intervals (1832–40), and it remained in force until 22 June 1842.

1836, 23 June. HENRY CLAY'S SURPLUS REVENUE ACT provided for the distribution of the Treasury surplus in excess of $5 million as a **loan** to the states according to population. This was a modification of Clay's earlier proposals to distribute the proceeds of land sales to the states. However, the surplus disappeared in the Panic of 1837 and payments were discontinued. Western pressure caused the passage of further legislation combining the ideas of **Benton** (**preemption**) and **Clay** (**distribution**).

1841, 4 Sept. DISTRIBUTION-PRE-EMPTION ACT authorized settlers to stake claims on most surveyed lands and to purchase up to **160 acres** at the minimum price of **$1.25 an acre** (except for alternate sections of land grants to canals and railroads, which could be preempted at $2.50 an acre). The act, constituting a signal victory for the West, recognized (1) settlement before purchase was not illegal (making **permanent** the preemption feature of the Act of 1830); (2) actual settlement was now given priority in official policy over revenue. The distribution provisions authorized the grant of 500,000 acres to each new state for the construction of internal improvements; 10% of the proceeds of land sales were apportioned to the states in which the lands were located, and the remainder, minus administrative costs, to be divided among the states according to their representation in Congress. At the behest of the South, a stipulation was included that such apportionment was to be repealed in the event that the tariff should exceed the 20% level. The distribution provisions were repealed in Aug. 1842.

1854, 3 Aug. GRADUATION ACT marked the emerging sectional alliance of the Northeast and the West (against Southern opposition). It provided that all unsold lands on the market for **10 years or more** were to be sold at **$1 an acre;** 15 years or more, 75 cts. an acre; 20 years or more, 25 cts. an acre; **30 years or more, 12½ cts. an acre.** The provisions applied preemption to graduated lands but did not cover mineral lands and grants for internal improvements and railroads. As a result, 30 to 40 million acres were sold a year. Repealed, 2 June 1862.

1860. Land Reform movement (1840–60) gained ground with Eastern labor and by support from **Horace Greeley.** The program included free homesteads of 160 acres, homestead exemption from attachment for debts, and limitation on land grants to large interests. A Homestead Act that finally passed both houses was vetoed (22 June 1860) by President Buchanan. The Republican platform of 1860 included a homestead plank.

1862, 20 MAY. HOMESTEAD ACT offered any citizen or intending citizen who was the head of a family and over 21 years of age **160 acres** of surveyed public domain **after 5 years** of continuous residence and payment of registration fee ranging from $26–$34. As an alternative, land under the act could be acquired **after 6 months** residence at **$1.25 an acre**. Such homesteads were to be exempt from attachment for debt.

2 JULY. MORRILL ACT granted to each loyal state 30,000 acres for each senator and representative then in Congress for the purpose of endowing at least 1 agricultural college. Under its provisions **69 land-grant** colleges have been established.

1862–64. PACIFIC RAILWAY ACTS. By Act of 1 July 1862 a central transcontinental railroad was authorized with rights of way and 10 alternate sections per mile of public domain on both sides of the railway granted. A second act (2 July 1864) doubled the land grants and gave the government a second instead of a first mortgage on railroad property. The Northern Pacific, chartered by Congress 1864, was granted 20 sections per mile in the states, 40 sections per mile in the territories.

1862–1904. DISTRIBUTION OF PUBLIC DOMAIN. During this period 610,763,183 acres were acquired **by purchase** as against only **147,351,370** acquired **free** (except for fees). More acreage was patented under the Homestead Act **after 1904** than before that date, although most of these newer lands were inferior.

1864, 21 MAR. A homestead bonus provided for soldiers with 2 years' service, subject to a year's residence.

1866. Mining lands on public domain opened to occupation.

21 JUNE. SOUTHERN HOMESTEAD ACT, designed to provide free 160-acre farms in 5 Southwestern states to freed slaves. High costs of farm-planting and deliberate sabotage by plantation owners seeking to retain labor supply by keeping free Negroes at home made act ineffective; by 1872, when repealed, only 4,000 black families had received lands.

1870, 9 JULY. Congress authorized a survey of mineral lands to be sold at **$2.50 per acre.** Later amendment raised the price of land with lodes to $5 an acre, and reduced iron areas to the usual $1.25.

1871. Termination of land grants to railroads (also p. 611).

1872, 1 MAR. MINING LAW authorized prospectors who discovered gold, silver, iron, and certain other ores on public land to stake a claim for the land, mine it, and ultimately to obtain a patent (document of title) giving them the land and all its surface and subsurface resources in fee simple.

1872–1974. DEVELOPMENT OF THE NATIONAL PARK SYSTEM. Yellowstone was established (1 Mar. 1872) as the first National Park when Congress set aside a large tract of federally owned land in what became Montana, Idaho, and Wyoming, indicating that National Parks were to be created for the public's benefit and enjoyment, to preserve in as natural a state as possible areas of outstanding value in terms of natural scenery, recreation, and wildlife conservation. By 1974 Congress had established 38 National Parks, encompassing some 15 million acres. By the **Antiquities Act** (8 June 1906) the president was authorized to create National Monuments by withdrawing from the public domain and setting aside for preservation any lands with great natural or historic interest. By 1974 there were 85 National Monuments, encompassing some 9 million acres. The **National Park Service** was established by statute (25 Aug. 1916) to administer these areas. The National Park system has come also to include historical and commemorative areas—National Historic Parks, National Battlefields, National Military Parks, National Historic Sites, National Memorials, and National Cemeteries—and primarily recreational areas: National Seashores, National Lakeshores, National Recreation Areas, National Parkways, and National Scenic Riverways.

1873, 3 MAR. TIMBER CULTURE ACT authorized any person who kept 40 acres of timber land in good condition to acquire title to 160 acres thereof. The minimum tree-growing requirement was reduced in 1878 to 10 acres.

Coal Lands Act provided for sale of coal lands belonging to the U.S. Individuals could acquire up to 160 acres, associations, 320 acres, at $10–$20 an acre, depending on the distance of the land from railroads.

1877, 3 MAR. DESERT LAND ACT authorized individuals to acquire 640 acres at 25 cts. an acre, provided the land was irrigated within 3 years.

1878, 3 JUNE. TIMBER CUTTING ACT allowed bona fide settlers and miners to cut timber on the public domain, free of charge, for their own use. **Timber and Stone Act,** applicable to California, Oregon, Nevada, Washington, and later extended to all public-land states, provided for the sale of timber and stone lands unfit for cultivation at $2.50 an acre, with a limit of 160 acres.

1879, 3 MAR. Establishment of the U.S. Geological Survey, with **Clarence King** (1842–1901) as first director.

1885, 3 APR. Suspension by **William Andrew Jackson Sparks,** Land Commissioner, of all entries of titles where fraud was suspected, by this action preserving 2,750,000 acres for bona fide settlers. Sparks was dismissed in Nov. 1887, and the reforms were revoked.

1887–94. BEGINNINGS OF CONSERVATION. Early conservation measures included the establishment of the **Division of Forestry** (1887) in the Department of Agriculture and, shortly afterward, the survey of irrigation sites by Maj. **John W. Powell** (p. 1132) of the U.S. Geological Survey. The **Forest Reserve Act** (3 Mar. 1891) repealed the Timber Culture Act of 1873 and Timber Cutting Act of 1878 and authorized the president to set apart forest reserve lands in any part of the public domain. During Harrison's administration 13 million acres were set aside. The Pre-emption Act was repealed (3 Mar. 1891). The **Carey Act** (18 Aug. 1894) authorized the president to grant to each public-land state a maximum of 1 million acres within its boundaries for irrigation, reclamation, settlement, and cultivation. The surplus funds accruing to each state from this program were to be used for reclaiming other lands in the state.

1897. Publication of Capt. **Hiram Martin Chittenden's** (1858–1917) report on irrigation (*Reservoirs in Arid Regions*) served as the basis of later legislation, particularly the National Reclamation Act (1902).

The Pettigrew Amendment, a rider on an appropriation bill, permitted the president to change or revoke land reservations and excluded agricultural and mineral lands from reservations. Passed by the Senate and defeated by the House, a compromise was finally reached. The delegation of power to the president was held unconstitutional in *U.S.* v. *Grimond,* 1911.

1901–09. THEODORE ROOSEVELT'S CONSERVATION POLICY. In 1901, at the outset of his administration,

Roosevelt announced that the conservation of forest and water resources was a national problem of vital importance. The conservation program carried out under his leadership was instrumental in educating the country in the need for the planned protection and development of physical resources. During his incumbency more than 148 million acres were set aside as national forest lands and more than 80 million acres of mineral lands withdrawn from public sale. Also withdrawn were some 1,500,000 acres of water-power sites.

An important step in the conservation program was initiated with the appointment (14 Mar. 1907) of the **Inland Waterways Commission** for the study of such routes with a view to relieving transportation congestion. When the commission's first report indicated that water transportation was related to the general problem of natural resources, Roosevelt summoned the **White House Conservation Conference** (13 May 1908). Among those in attendance were members of the cabinet, the justices of the Supreme Court, congressmen, and the governors of 34 states. The conference succeeded in bringing wide public attention to the problem.

A direct outgrowth of the conference was the **National Conservation Commission** (8 June), of which **Gifford Pinchot** (1865–1946) was named chairman. The commission's systematic study of mineral, water, forest, and soil resources was supplemented by the work of local conservation commissions in 41 states. The commission's first report, submitted to President Roosevelt on 11 Jan. 1909, was the first attempt to inventory U.S. natural resources. The Commission urged repeal of the Timber and Stone Act of 1878, the valuation of land at title value instead of $1.25, and the repeal of the Desert Land Act. Organized later in 1909 was the National Conservation Association, a private body (Charles W. Eliot, president).

1901, 15 Feb. Congress passed an act establishing a licensing system for the use of water power on public lands.

1902, 17 June. NATIONAL RECLAMATION ACT (NEWLANDS ACT) set aside almost the entire amount of proceeds of public-land sales in 16 Western and Southwestern states to finance construction and maintenance of irrigation projects in arid states.

1904. KINKAID HOME ACT provided for grants of 640 acres of desert land in Nebraska after 5 years' residence and improvements valued at $800; extended, 1909, to the rest of the public domain.

1906, 11 June. FOREST HOMESTEAD ACT provided for the opening, at the discretion of the Secretary of Interior, of forest lands of agricultural value under the provisions of the Homestead Acts.

29 June. By executive order all coal lands were withdrawn from entry to permit their appraisal; later opened to buyers at from $35–$100 an acre.

1907, 19 June. A protest meeting against the land reservation policy, led by Western grazing interests, convened in Denver. A rider on an appropriation bill repealed the Forest Reserve Act of 1891. Before signing the bill, President Roosevelt added 21 reserves.

1909, 19 Feb. ENLARGED HOMESTEAD ACT, to satisfy Western cattle interests, increased the maximum permissible homesteads to 320 acres in portions of Colorado, Montana, Nevada, Oregon, Utah, Washington, Wyoming, and Arizona. Of these, 80 acres were to be cultivated. Timber and mineral lands were specifically excepted.

25 Aug. First National Conservation Congress convened in Seattle under the leadership of lumber interests.

1910, 25 June. An act of Congress

authorized the president to withdraw public lands subject to further legislation and prohibited the creation of further reserves in Oregon, Washington, Idaho, Colorado and Wyoming.

1916, 29 Dec. STOCK-RAISING HOMESTEAD ACT enlarged the maximum permissible homestead to 640-acre tracts of grazing or forage land not suitable for irrigation, and reserved mines and coal deposits.

1920, 25 Feb. MINERAL LEASING ACT, with later amendments, removed from the scope of the Mining Law of 1872 certain minerals—including oil, gas, coal, phosphate, and sulfur—making them available only on a discretionary leasing basis. The act required the Interior Department to use a system of competitive bidding for mineral leases for areas known to contain oil and gas and required the bidder to pay a royalty on his production in addition to the amount bid to obtain the lease.

1928, 15 May. FLOOD CONTROL ACT authorized $325 million for levee work in the Mississippi Valley over a 10-year period.

21 Dec. BOULDER CANYON PROJECT ACT, authorizing construction of Hoover (Boulder) Dam, marked effective beginning of federal government construction of large, multipurpose (water supply, irrigation, hydroelectric power, flood control, navigation) water projects. The **Reclamation Project Act of 1939** (4 Aug.) formalized this trend in planning of Reclamation Bureau (in Department of the Interior; established under Reclamation Act of 1902) water projects established during the New Deal, including giant Grand Coulee Dam (built 1933–42) on the Columbia River.

1933–36. NEW DEAL CONSERVATION PROGRAM, TVA, p. 405; Soil Conservation program of AAA, p. 423; Civilian Conservation Corps, p. 404; Conservation programs of FERA, CWA,

PWA, pp. 405, 409, 410; Soil Conservation Service, p. 414; Resettlement Administration, p. 414. The **Taylor Grazing Act** (28 June 1934) provided for the segregation of up to 8 million acres (later raised to 142 million) for grazing purposes under the jurisdiction of the newly established Grazing Service in the Interior Department.

1935. President Roosevelt withdrew the remainder of the public domain for purposes of conservation. As of 1949, 455 million out of 1.9 billion acres were under federal ownership, or 23.89% of the total U.S. land area. By 1950 no less than 181.2 million acres were reserved in national forests. Mineral, water power, and oil reserves (mostly subsoil rights) affected another 47,948,454 acres; about 20 million acres under irrigation.

1936, 22 June, FLOOD CONTROL ACT, for the first time asserted federal government responsibility for controlling floods in river basins all over the country. Major responsibility was assigned to the Army Corps of Engineers.

1946, 16 July. BUREAU OF LAND MANAGEMENT (BLM) created, uniting the functions of the former General Land Office and the former Grazing Service. The BLM was given responsibility for control and management of all the public lands of the U.S. and Alaska, including their surface and subsurface resources.

1947, 31 July. MATERIALS ACT, for the first time made it possible for the Secretary of the Interior to sell timber, sand, stone, gravel, clay, and certain related resources located on public lands without transferring title to the lands on which the materials were found. The materials had to be sold by competitive bidding where the appraised value exceeded $1,000.

1948–73. WATER POLLUTION became a cause of increasing public concern. The first major **Water Pollution**

Control Act (30 June 1948): (1) provided funding for sewage plant construction; (2) permitted the Justice Department to file suits to require cessation of polluting practices; (3) set up a Water Pollution Control Advisory Board; and (4) authorized pollution studies and research. The 1948 Act was amended (9 July 1956), authorizing $500 million over the next 10 years in federal grants for construction of sewage treatment works. As amended (20 July 1961) the act provided for higher grants and gave the Secretary of HEW authority to prosecute polluters without state government permission. Federal antipollution laws were significantly strengthened by the Water Quality Act of 1965 (2 Oct.), requiring states to establish by 30 June 1967, and enforce, water quality standards for all interstate waters within their boundaries. If states failed to take action or set standards considered too weak by HEW then the latter would set federal standards. The Clean Waters Restoration Act (3 Nov. 1966): (1) authorized $3.55 billion during fiscal 1967–71 for construction of sewage treatment plants, eliminating dollar ceilings on individual grants and permitting federal payment of up to 50% of construction costs if states contributed funds and set water quality standards for noninterstate waters; (2) authorized new programs of federal grants for research on industrial water pollution and advanced waste treatment and water purification measures; and (3) authorized federal grants to assist river basin planning organizations. According to a General Accounting Office report (4 Nov. 1969) the expenditure of $5.4 billion since 1957 on waste treatment facilities had accomplished little: efforts to combat pollution were inadequately financed, badly organized, poorly planned, and undermined by industrial and municipal pollution. The Water Quality Improvement Act of 1970 (3 Apr.), spurred by the Santa Barbara oil spills of 1969: (1) authorized the federal government to clean up disastrous oil spills with the polluter responsible for costs up to $14 million; (2) provided for absolute liability in cases of willful negligence or misconduct; (3) required compliance with water quality standards and the purposes of the act by all federal agencies engaged in any kind of public works activities; and (4) required builders of nuclear power plants to comply with state water pollution standards. The Federal Water Pollution Control Act Amendments of 1972 (enacted 18 Oct. over President Nixon's veto) initiated a major change in basic approach to water pollution control by limiting effluent discharges as well as setting water quality standards. The measure: (1) set a national goal of eliminating all pollutant discharges into U.S. waters by 1985; (2) made the discharge of any pollutant by any person unlawful except as authorized by a discharge permit; (3) authorized expenditure of $24.7 billion, including more than $18 billion in grants to states for construction of waste treatment plants; and (4) allowed citizens to sue polluters, the federal government, or the EPA (p. 642).

1953, 22 MAY. SUBMERGED LANDS ACT granted to the coastal states the rights then held by the federal government to a maximum distance of 3 geographical miles, subject to an exception for historic boundaries not over 3 leagues from the coast in the Gulf of Mexico. This exception has been ruled applicable only to Texas and Florida. U.S. v. Louisiana, 363 U.S. 1 (1960) and U.S. v. Florida, 363 U.S. 121 (1960). The Outer Continental Shelf Lands Act, 7 Aug. 1953, provided for federal administration of the Continental Shelf.

1955, 1 AUG. Repeal of the Timber and Stone Act of 1878.

1955–74. AIR POLLUTION became an increasing source of national concern as emissions from motor vehicles, basic industries (especially petroleum refineries, smelters, and iron foundries), power plants, home and office heating systems, and refuse incinerators caused health hazards and discomfort. Federal government involvement began (14 July 1955) with authorization of $25 million for fiscal 1956–60 for Public Health Service air pollution research. The **Clean Air Act of 1963** (17 Dec.) authorized $95 million for fiscal 1964–67 in matching grants to state, local, and interstate agencies to develop air pollution prevention and control programs and provided for a series of steps, culminating in legal action, which a state, locality, or the federal government could take to arrest air pollution. The **Clean Air Act Amendments of 1965** (20 Oct.): (1) directed the Secretary of HEW to establish emission standards for new motor vehicles; (2) authorized accelerated research to reduce sulfur oxide emissions from fuel combustion sources such as electric generating plants; and (3) initiated national research programs to develop new methods of solid waste disposal. The first standards for hydrocarbon and carbon monoxide exhaust emissions, published 29 Mar. 1966, were applicable to most new gasoline-powered motor vehicles beginning with the model year 1968. The **Air Quality Act of 1967** (21 Nov.) substantially enlarged federal responsibility: (1) authorizing $428.3 million for federal air pollution control efforts in fiscal 1968–70, $125 million earmarked for research on pollution caused by fuels combustion; (2) authorizing the Secretary of HEW to designate air quality control regions; (3) providing full federal financing for regional control commissions to be established by state governors; and (4) empowering the Secretary of HEW to enforce air quality standards in the control regions if the regional commissions failed to enforce an air pollution plan conforming to HEW guidelines. The **Clean Air Act of 1970** (31 Dec.) established a 3-year, $1.1 billion, comprehensive air pollution control program, including provisions requiring model year 1975 cars to emit 90% less carbon monoxide and hydrocarbons than did 1970 cars and specifying that 1976 cars must emit 90% less nitrogen oxides than 1971 cars. After twice refusing, EPA (p. 642) Administrator William D. Ruckelshaus granted (11 Apr. 1973) auto manufacturers the additional year they requested to meet the 1975 emission standards but imposed interim standards far stricter than the industry contended were feasible.

1956, 11 Apr. UPPER COLORADO PROJECT ACT authorized $760 million in initial costs for one of the largest and most controversial Reclamation Bureau multipurpose water projects.

1959, 23 June. RECREATION AND PUBLIC PURPOSES ACT AMENDMENTS, substantially increasing the acreage limitations of the 1954 Act (which had broadened the Recreation Act of 1926), authorized the sale or lease—to federal, state, and local agencies and nonprofit groups—of public lands to be used for recreational or other public purposes. Each state could receive up to 6,400 acres annually to establish state parks, and other agencies could receive up to 640 acres annually for recreation purposes. For nonrecreation purposes each state or other agency could receive an additional 640 acres annually.

1961, 23 Feb. PRESIDENT KENNEDY'S LAND POLICY. In his natural resources message, Kennedy, reflecting the basic development of public-land policy indicated by the Taylor Grazing Act of 1934 and evident in the postwar period, set forth the principle of **retention and multiple use:** public land was to be regarded as a potentially valuable natural resource which, rather than being disposed of, should be retained in federal ownership and administered under the principle of multiple use and sustained yield of surface resources. Kennedy's statement, together with Secretary of the Interior **Stewart L. Udall's** policy statement of 14 Feb., indicated that the BLM would not classify areas as open to homestead entry if they were especially valuable for some other public purpose, such as recreational development, and that the BLM would attempt to assure that all public lands, whether disposed of or retained by the government, would be used in a manner producing substantial benefits for the nation.

1964, 3 SEPT. NATIONAL WILDERNESS PRESERVATION SYSTEM established. 9.1 million acres of national forest lands which had been classified by administrative action as "wild," "wilderness," or "canoe" areas were immediately designated part of the system, to be safeguarded permanently (subject to existing rights) against commercial use and construction of permanent roads and buildings. However, new mining claims and mineral leases were allowed until 31 Dec. 1983 but not thereafter. Other federal lands were to be added after review by the executive branch and approval of Congress. Opposition from commercial mining, lumbering, and cattle-grazing interests slowed expansion of the system. By 1973 another 1.9 million acres had been added.

3 SEPT. LAND AND WATER CONSERVATION FUND ACT set up a special federal fund to help finance accelerated acquisition of outdoor recreation areas by federal and state agencies.

1970, 1 JAN. NATIONAL ENVIRONMENTAL POLICY ACT OF 1969 (NEPA) made protection of the environment a matter of national policy. NEPA also: (1) required all federal agencies to consider the effects on the environment of all major activities and to include in every recommendation for legislation or other significant actions an **impact statement**—a written analysis of those effects as well as alternatives to the proposal; (2) established in the Office of the President a 3-member Council on Environmental Quality; and (3) directed that the president submit to Congress an annual environmental quality report.

22 APR. "EARTH DAY" observed. In the late 1960s the warnings of such well-known environmentalists as Dr. Barry Commoner that industrial man was doing broad and perhaps irreversible damage to his surroundings began to evoke a wide popular response. Suggested by Sen. Gaylord Nelson (Wis.) as a means to focus national attention on ecological problems, Earth Day—when millions of Americans participated in environmental teach-ins, antipollution protests and various clean-up projects—marked the peak of national harmony on environmental issues. Thereafter enthusiasm for "saving the earth" began to diminish somewhat with realization of the multifarious economic costs of cleaning up the environment.

2 OCT. ENVIRONMENTAL PROTECTION AGENCY (EPA) created through executive reorganization. The EPA consolidated in a single agency, independent of existing departments, all major programs to combat pollution.

1971, 23 JUNE. The Public Land Law Review Commission (estab. 1964) in its 343-page report, *One Third of the Nation's Land,* recommended to the president and Congress that stringent controls over the environment be put into effect without delay on the 755 million acres of federally owned public land. The 19-member commission, headed by Rep. Wayne N. Aspinall (Colo.), in its more than 350 recommendations provided guidelines to aid Congress in overhauling outmoded laws and unsnarling often conflicting regulations governing the use and sale of federal lands.

1972, 21 Oct. FEDERAL ENVIRON-MENTAL PESTICIDE CONTROL ACT. A controversy over the dangers of pesticides was touched off by publication of *The Silent Spring* (1962) by **Rachel Carson** (1907–64). A study (1968) by the General Accounting Office showed that federal agencies took little action to enforce the Federal Fungicide, Insecticide and Rodenticide Act of 1947 requiring registration and proper labeling of pesticides. The 1972 act required that all pesticides be registered with the EPA (p. 642), which would control their manufacture, distribution, and use, and facilitated the banning of hazardous pesticides and the imposition of penalties for their improper use. On 14 June EPA Administrator William D. Ruckelshaus announced a ban (effective 31 Dec.) on almost all remaining uses of the pesticide DDT.

1973, 16 Nov. ALASKAN PIPELINE ACT. After 5 years of controversy between environmental groups and elements of the oil industry and their allies, construction of the huge pipeline—which ultimately could carry up to 2 million barrels of crude oil per day from Alaska's North Slope to the ice-free port of Valdez on the Gulf of Alaska, to be transported by tanker to the U.S.—was authorized. To prevent further court challenges by environmentalists—a ruling (9 Feb.) of the U.S. Court of Appeals, District of Columbia Circuit, blocking pipeline construction had been upheld (2 Apr.) by the Supreme Court—the act provided that all actions necessary for completion of the pipeline be taken without further delay under the National Environmental Policy Act of 1969 and restricted judicial review to constitutional grounds. The Aleyeska consortium, builders and operators of the pipeline, were held liable for the full costs of controlling and removing any pollution caused by the pipeline.

Indian Land Policy and Reform
Since the Civil War

1869–94. INDIAN LAND CESSIONS. In less than a century following American independence the Indians, by a long series of treaties, ceded enormous tracts of land to the U.S. The old Indian Country on the Great Plains was reduced to the Indian Territory (later the state of Oklahoma) while the extinguishment of Indian titles proceeded rapidly from the Rockies to the Pacific coast. In 1869 a Board of Indian Affairs was created to exercise joint control with Interior Department officials over appropriations for Indian land cessions, to control the ceded trust lands not a part of the public domain, along with the reservations with

their valuable natural resources. In 1871 Congress ordered a cessation of treaty-making with Indian tribes. Between 1784 and 1894 a total of 720 Indian land cessions (often overlapping) were made (Royce), and up to 1880 the U.S. government had expended in excess of $187 million in goods or money to extinguish Indian titles, but huge amounts were quickly diverted to creditor traders.

1871, 3 Mar. INDIAN APPROPRIATIONS ACT rider declared no Indian tribe or nation to be recognized thereafter as an independent power with whom the U.S. could contract by treaty and established the policy that tribal

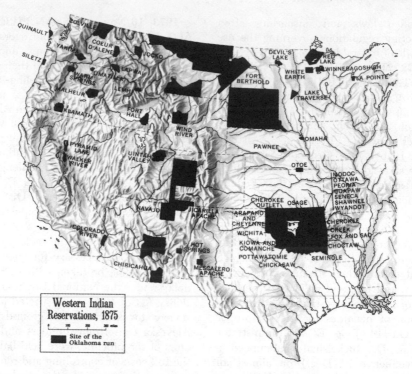

Western Indian Reservations, 1875

0   100   200   300 miles

■ Site of the Oklahoma run

affairs could be managed by the U.S. government without tribal consent.

1881. Publication of Helen Hunt Jackson's *A Century of Dishonor* (1881) aroused new concern over Indian problems and sparked agitation by the Indian Rights Association, organized within a year.

1887, 8 FEB. DAWES GENERAL ALLOTMENT (SEVERALTY) ACT passed in response to reformers who believed reservation life fostered indolence and perpetuated customs which hindered assimilation. The act provided for the dissolution of Indian tribes as legal entities and the division of tribal lands among individual members—160 acres to each head of family and 80 acres to each adult single person. The government retained a 25-year trust patent; upon its expiration full ownership would devolve upon the individual and U.S. citizenship would be conferred. Reservation land

remaining after distribution of allotments to living tribe members was declared surplus and could be opened to non-Indian homesteaders. The **Burke Act** (8 May 1906) speeded up allotment of lands to individual Indians by authorizing the Secretary of the Interior to waive the 25-year trustee period and issue patents in fee to Indians deemed competent to manage their own affairs. This procedure was further liberalized by the Commissioner of Indian Affairs in Apr. 1917. 118 reservations were thus allotted; Indians lost 86 million acres (62%) of land in Indian ownership prior to 1887. The undermining of Indian culture which resulted from the assault on communal organization basic to tribal organization did not automatically produce assimilation.

1924, 2 JUNE. INDIANS AS CITIZENS. Defined by the Supreme Court, 1831 (p. 667), as "domestic dependent" nations, the Indians received piecemeal U.S. citizenship (Wyandots, 1855, Potawatomi, 1861, Kickapoos, 1862), a practice liberalized by the Dawes Act and extended, 1901, to all Indians in Indian Territory. By the **Snyder Act of 1924** all Indians born in the U.S. were admitted to full U.S. citizenship.

1924–34. INDIAN REFORMS. As a result of strong Indian protests, the **Fall Indian Omnibus Bill (Bursum Bill)** was defeated. In effect the bill would have transferred Pueblo title to white settlers. Under Act of 1924 a Pueblo Land Board was set up to fix compensation for lands; such compensation was awarded in 1933. Publication of Brookings Institution report *The Problem of Indian Administration* (1928) revealed deficiencies in federal administration. The **Indian Reorganization (Wheeler-Howard) Act (18 June 1934)** ended land allotments in severalty and provided for revestment to tribal ownership of surplus lands hitherto open to sale. Other provisions of the act encouraged tribal self-government and sought to improve Indian economic conditions.

1946, 13 Aug. INDIAN CLAIMS COMMISSION established to settle all outstanding Indian claims against the U.S. from the beginning of the nation until the date of the act (the U.S. Court of Claims to have original jurisdiction over Indian claims arising after 13 Aug. 1946 as well as appellate jurisdiction over the Indian Claims Commission). It was estimated that the commission's work would take 30 years with a final cost to the government of over $1 billion.

1953, 1 Aug. TERMINATION RESOLUTION. By concurrent resolution Congress adopted the policy of promoting termination: discontinuance of federal controls, restrictions, and benefits for Indians under federal jurisdiction. The withdrawal of federal services or trust supervision from 61 tribes or other Indian groups took place 1954–60, before opposition caused deceleration of the program—Indian tribes and such Indian organizations as the National Congress of American Indians condemned termination, advocating instead self-determination and a review of federal policies. During the 1960s federal aid greatly expanded and reservation governments were made eligible as sponsoring agencies for numerous federal economic opportunity programs.

1969, 20 Nov. CAPTURE OF ALCATRAZ ISLAND by 78 Indians, demanding that it be made available as a cultural center, signaled the rise of Indian activism. (The occupation, which had succumbed to media overexposure and indecision, was ended 11 June 1971 when the 15 remaining holdouts were removed without resistance by U.S. marshals.) The American Indian Movement (AIM), founded in 1970, soon emerged as the most militant spokesman for radical reform of federal-Indian relations—focusing public attention on the problems of the American Indian by occupying (2–8 Nov. 1972) the Washington, D.C. offices of the Bureau of Indian Affairs, demanding the rights and property guaranteed Indians by treaties with the U.S., and by occupying (27 Feb.–8 May 1973) the village of Wounded Knee, S. Dak., challenging the locally elected Oglala Sioux government and demanding general reform in Indian tribal government.

1970–72. LAND RESTORATIONS. By the Act of 15 Dec. 1970, 48,000 acres in the Blue Lake area of New Mexico were returned to the **Taos Pueblo Indians,** who considered the area a shrine whose religious value was destroyed when it was put to multiple use after being taken from them by the U.S. Forest Service in 1906. The **Alaska Native Land Claims Act (18 Dec. 1971)** granted to the 53,000 native Eskimos, Indians, and

Aleuts title to 40 million acres of federal lands and $962.5 million divided among native villages and regional corporations. The act was in answer to native claims that land had been illegally taken from them by the federal government through provisions of the Statehood Act (p. 617). By executive order (20 May 1972) some 21,000 acres of land in Washington were returned to the **Yakima Indian** tribe, for whom the area has religious significance.

The land had been incorporated in the Mt. Rainier Forest Reserve in 1908 on the mistaken belief it was public land.

1970, 8 JULY. TERMINATION POLICY REPUDIATED expressly in President Nixon's message to Congress. Rejecting assimilation as a goal of federal policy and paternalistic approaches to federal support, the administration endorsed a policy of Indian self-determination.

POPULATION, IMMIGRATION, AND ETHNIC STOCKS

Despite a population expansion from 1790 to 1900 running at a rate of from 25% to 35% per decade (slightly lower during the Civil War years), an increase in part the result of a constant flow of immigration, in part from large family formations, and in part the result of improved public health statistics, the United States never fulfilled Malthusian prophecies of population growth outrunning available food supply. Down to the end of the nineteenth century large tracts still awaited settlement, while revolutionary improvements in farm technology kept food production abreast of population. The deceleration of that earlier extraordinary growth rate is largely a twentieth-century phenomenon, traceable to the immigration restriction laws of the 1920s and to a decline in the birth rate, both in the depression years of the 1930s and again in the 1960s and 1970s. Starting with a large nucleus of settlers from England, the colonies and then the United States quickly became multi-ethnic. The character of non-English immigration shifted from Northern Europe in pre-Civil War days to Central-Eastern and Southern Europe after 1885, with Latin-American immigration playing an increasingly significant role beginning with the depression years of the 1930s. Accompanying this relative decline of migration from English-speaking countries was an increasing emphasis upon the values of cultural pluralism.

Internal migration has been associated in the public mind with the westward movement, but equally dramatic has been the shift of population from an overwhelmingly rural America of 1790 to the urban society of the 1970s. Notable in the movement has been the vast migration of blacks from the rural South to the urban North and West.

The civil rights movement of the 1960s not only reinforced black pride but also stimulated ethnic feelings among Mexican-Americans and led many different ethnic groups to a reexamination of their heritage.

Population

Figures prior to the first Census, 1790, are computed on the basis of militia, polls, taxables, families, and houses (Greene and Harrington).

1790. Regional Distribution of Population: New England, 25.7%; Middle states, 25.9%; Southern states, 48.5%.

AREA OF THE 13 COLONIES

1625	1,980	(Va., 1,800, Plymouth, 180)
1641	50,000	(English settlers)
1688	200,000	
1715	434,600	
1754	1,485,634	
1774	2,600,000	(Bancroft; 3,016,678, informal Congress poll)
1783	2,389,300	(Continental Congress)
1790	3,929,625	

ORIGINAL THIRTEEN STATES IN ORDER OF POPULATION

Virginia	747,610	(inc. W. Va.)
Massachusetts	475,199	(inc. Maine)
Pennsylvania	434,373	
North Carolina	393,751	
New York	340,120	
Maryland	319,728	(inc. Dist. of Columbia)
South Carolina	249,073	
Connecticut	237,655	
New Jersey	184,139	
New Hampshire	141,885	
Georgia	82,548	
Rhode Island	68,825	
Delaware	59,096	

URBAN POPULATION TRENDS TO 1790

	Phila. (1682)	N.Y. (1624)	Boston (1630)	Charleston (1680)	Baltimore (1730)
1730	8,500	8,500	13,000	c.4,000	
1750	13,400	13,300	15,731	8,000	c.100
1770	28,000	21,000	15,520	10,863	c.5,000
1790	42,444	33,131	18,038	16,359	13,503

URBAN POPULATION (8,000 INHABITANTS OR MORE) COMPARED WITH TOTAL POPULATION, 1710–1900 (A Century of Population Growth)

Year	% of Total
1710	2.5
1740	4.3
1790	3.3
1860	16.1
1900	32.9

Using the more recent reclassification of the Census Bureau (Urban Population, 2,500 inhabitants or more), the urban percentage, **1790**, was 5.4% as against 56%, **1940**.

LEADING U.S. CITIES SINCE 1790

	1820 (De Bow, Statistical View)		1860 (8th Census)
New York	123,700	New York	1,080,330
Philadelphia	112,800	Philadelphia	565,529
Baltimore	62,700	Baltimore	212,418
Boston	43,300	Boston	177,840
New Orleans	27,200	New Orleans	168,675

	1900		1970
New York	3,437,202	New York	7,895,000
Chicago	1,698,575	Chicago	3,367,000
Philadelphia	1,293,697	Los Angeles	2,816,000
St. Louis	575,238	Philadelphia	1,949,000
Boston	560,892	Detroit	1,511,000

CENTER OF POPULATION, 1790–1970
(Stat. Abstr. of the U.S., 1973)

1790:	23 mi. E. of Baltimore, Md.
1850:	23 mi. S.E. of Parkersburg, W. Va.
1900:	6 mi. S.E. of Columbus, Ind.
1950:	8 mi. N.–N.W. of Olney, Richland Co., III.
1970:	5.3 mi. E.–S.E. Mascoutah City Hall, St. Clair Co., III.

POPULATION OF THE U.S. SINCE 1790

Year	Population (in thousands)	% Increase over Preceding Census
1790	3,929	....
1800	5,308	35.1
1810	7,239	36.4
1820	9,638	33.1
1830	12,866	33.5
1840	17,069	32.7
1850	23,191	35.9
1860	31,443	35.6
1870	38,558	22.6
1880	50,155	30.1
1890	62,947	25.5
1900	75,994	20.7
1910	91,972	21.0
1920	105,710	14.9
1930	122,775	16.1
1940	131,409	7.3
1950	150,697	14.5
1960	179,323	18.5
1970	203,235[1]	13.3

[1] Population of U.S., Puerto Rico, and outlying areas was 183,285,009 (1960) up 22.1%, and 207,976, 452 (1970) up 13.5%.

The 15-year period 1941–55 marked reversal of downward birth rate trend (*Stat. Abstr. of the U.S., 1949, 1951, 1969, 1973*). After that time the down trend set in again, accelerating during the decade 1961–70. Total yearly population growth (1961–70) was 1.3% compared with 2.2% for 1951–60.

	Birth Rate (per 1,000 population)	Death Rate (per 1,000 population)
1915	30.1	13.2
1936	16.7	11.6
1950	24.1	9.6
1960	23.7	9.5
1970	18.4	9.5

LIFE EXPECTANCY, 1789–1970
(Historical Statistics of the U.S., to 1971)

	At Birth		Age 20		Age 40		Age 60	
	Male	Female	Male	Female	Male	Female	Male	Female
1789 (Mass.)	34.5	36.5	34.2	34.3	25.2	26.9	14.8	16.1
1900–02	48.23	51.08	42.19	43.77	27.74	29.17	14.35	14.23
1945	64.4	69.5	48.6	52.9	30.6	34.4	15.4	17.8
1970	68.1	75.4	50.3	57.1	32.0	38.0	13.2[1]	16.8[1]

[1] 1970 life expectancy for both males and females at age 65.

INTERNAL MIGRATION WITHIN THE U.S., 1870–1940

	East-West Movement (Net gain of states west of Mississippi River)[1]	North-South Movement (Net gain of the North)[2]
1870	2,298,952	752,455
1880	3,300,378	639,018
1890	4,078,157	500,026
1900	3,993,554	274,403
1910	4,592,106	77,878
1920	4,188,945	430,200
1930	3,497,090	1,419,137
1940	2,731,002	1,381,500

[1] Excess of persons born east and living west of the Mississippi over persons born west and living east.
[2] Excess of persons born in the South and living in the North over persons born in the North and living in the South.

1951–60. POPULATION SHIFTS. Final 1960 census returns brought the loss of 3 House of Representative seats for Pa.; 2 for N.Y., Mass., and Ark.; and 1 each for 12 other states. Chief gainers: Calif., 8; Fla., 4. Largest percentage population gains scored by Fla., 78.7; Nev., 78.2; Alaska, 75.8; Ariz., 73.7; Calif., 48.5; Del., 40.3. Losses: Ark., 6.5; W. Va., 7.2; D.C., 4.8.

1960–66. MIGRATION TRENDS. The movement west continued. California gained more than 3.1 million. Reversing 60 years of out-migration, the Northeast gained 450,000 persons while the South experienced a net gain of 800,000, although 3.7 million Negroes left the South.

1960–70. METROPOLITAN, URBAN AND RURAL POPULATION
(Stat. Abstr. of the U.S., 1973)

	Rural (millions)	Urban	Metropolitan[1]
1960	54.1	125.3	119.6
1970	53.9	149.3	139.4

[1] 243 SMSA's (Standard Metropolitan Statistical Areas) defined by Office of Management and Budget, generally conceived as an integrated economic and social unit with a large population nucleus. Each SMA contains one central city of 50,000 inhabitants or more, or a city of at least 25,000 which together with the population of contiguous places constitutes for general economic and social purposes a single community with combined population of at least 50,000.

1920–70. NATIVE BORN POPULATION

1920:	86.8%
1930:	88.4%
1940:	91.2%
1950:	92.8%
1960:	94.6%
1970:	95.3%

1967. 200 MILLION. The "population clock" of the U.S. Census indicated the presence of the 200-millionth American at 11 A.M., 20 Nov., although most demographers believed this figure had been achieved earlier.

1970. COMMISSION ON POPULATION GROWTH AND THE AMERICAN FUTURE, established by law (16 Mar.). Commission report received 5 May 1972.

1970. CENSUS UNDERCOUNT of about 5.3 million, 1.9 million of whom were black. The rate of underenumeration, 2.5% (1970) compared with 2.7% (1960), 3.3% (1950).

Indian Population: 793,000.

1970–75. POPULATION SHIFTS highlighted by new rural growth with nonmetropolitan areas growing faster than metropolitan areas, due in part to decentralization of manufacturing, growth of recreation and retirement areas located in warm climates, the environmental movement, and a leveling off of the loss of farm population.

1970. FAMILY PLANNING SERVICES AND POPULATION RESEARCH ACT (26 Dec.) established goal of making family planning sources and information available to every woman in U.S., creating Federal Office of Population Affairs in Dept. of Health, Education, and Welfare to administer HEW responsibilities and authorizing $382 million for new and expanded sources and research programs for fiscal years 1971–73.

1972. ZERO POPULATION GROWTH. During first quarter of 1972 birth rate dropped below level of replacement rate, reflecting readier access to contraceptive services, changing sexual mores, later marriages, changing concepts of family size, changes in the economy, and the liberalization of state abortion laws (pp. 685, 817), the first being Colorado (effective 25 Apr. 1967).

1935–70. SOCIAL WELFARE EXPENDITURES UNDER PUBLIC PROGRAMS
(Federal, State, Local)
(Stat. Abstr. of the U.S., 1973)

	Total ($ millions)	Social Insurance	Public Aid	Health & Medical Programs
1935	6,548	406	2,998	427
1940	8,795	1,272	3,597	616
1950	23,508	4,947	2,496	2,064
1960	52,293	19,307	4,101	4,464
1970	145,965	54,756	16,488	9,750

1940–68. ILLEGITIMATE LIVE BIRTHS
(Stat. Abstr. of the U.S., 1973)

Year	Total	% All Births	Rate Per 1,000 Unmarried Age 15–44
1940	89,500	3.5%	7.1
1950	141,600	3.9%	14.1
1960	224,300	5.3%	21.8
1968	339,200	9.7%	24.1

1940–70. DIVORCES (inc. annulments) PER 1,000
(Stat. Abstr. of the U.S., 1973)

Year	Total (in thousands)	Rate per 1,000
1940	264	2.0
1950	385	2.6
1960	393	2.2
1970 (prel.)	715	3.5

1960–70. CRIME RATE PER 100,000 INHABITANTS
(Stat. Abstr. of the U.S., 1973)

	Total	Murder & Nonnegligent Manslaughter	Robbery	Burglary
1960	1,126	5	60	502
1965	1,516	5	71	653
1970	2,747	8	171	1,071

Immigration of Non-English Stock

1624. Walloon settlement of New Amsterdam (p. 49).

1624–64. Dutch settlement of New Netherland (pp. 49–50); on the Delaware 1657–64 (pp. 51–53). Dutch cultural decline in New York City noted by 1763, when an invitation was extended to Rev. Archibald Laidlie, English-speaking Scottish minister, to preach in the Dutch Reformed Church. In Hudson and Hackensack valleys Dutch language persisted until 1835–41.

1637–55. Swedish settlement on the Delaware (p. 52).

1682. First Welsh settlement near Philadelphia.

1683–84. Settlement of **Germantown** (13 families from Crefeld, Germany) by Rhinelanders and Palatines under **Francis Daniel Pastorius** (1651–c.1720) and **Johann Kelpius** stamped Pennsylvania-Dutch settlement with cultural and linguistic persistence down to the 20th century.

1685. FRENCH HUGUENOT settlement following the revocation of the Edict of Nantes (18 Oct.), chiefly to New York (New York City and New Rochelle), Massachusetts (Boston, Salem, and Oxford), and South Carolina (Charleston and along Santee River).

1689. Beginning of sizable emigration from Scotland of Covenanters (opposing Anglican Church rule) and Jacobites (supporters of Stuart cause), and from Northern Ireland (Ulster) of Scotch-Irish Presbyterians (est., 1607–09); especially significant after Act of Parliament, 1704, barring Presbyterians from public office. English Navigation Act caused economic deterioration in Ireland and the exaction of tithes for the support of the Church of England was resented.

1709. Passage of Parliamentary Act of 1709 (Whig) extended the privilege of natural-born subjects to strangers who took the oath of allegiance and partook of the Sacrament (naturalizing German Protestant refugees); repealed by Tories, 1711. More liberal naturalization laws had been passed in the colonies beginning with the 17th century.

1710. GERMAN PALATINES, numbering over 3,000, given temporary refuge in England (1709) from devastations of War of Spanish Succession and severe winter, 1708–09, were transported to New York to produce naval stores in Hudson Valley. Unfavorable economic conditions caused their migration under **Conrad Weiser** (1696–1760) to Schoharie Valley (1713), then to the Mohawk Valley, and ultimately in some instances to Bucks (1723) and Berks counties, Pa. (1728–29).

Settlement of 650 Palatines by **Baron de Graffenried** at New Bern, N.C.; attacked and nearly destroyed by Indians in Tuscarora War, 1712, and colonists scattered throughout southeastern North Carolina.

1714–20. MAIN EXODUS OF SCOTCH-IRISH (including Jacobites after suppression of revolts of 1715 and 1745 on behalf of the 2 Stuart Pretenders) started, spurred by expiration, beginning 1717, of leases and increased rent demands by landlords in Ireland. A small portion went to New England but the bulk settled the counties of western Pennsylvania, between the Susquehanna and the Allegheny Mts., moving down the Shenandoah Valley (1732) into Virginia, the Carolinas, and Georgia. The famines, 1740–41, and the decline of the Irish linen industry, c.1771, assured the continuance of this emigration momentum.

1727–75. HEAVY GERMAN MIGRATION continued, including settlers from the German-Swiss cantons of Bern and Zurich, with substantial Pietist representation.

1735–53. MORAVIAN COLLECTIVIST EXPERIMENTS, under the leadership of **Augustus Gottlieb Spangenberg** (1704–92), at Savannah (1735), Bethlehem, Pa. (1744), and vicinity of Winston-Salem, N.C. (1753).

1740. Act of Parliament specifically provided for naturalization in the colonies, with 7-year residence provision, and the usual oaths not to be required of Jews or Quakers.

1768. 1,400 settlers from **Minorca, Leghorn,** and **Greece** established by Dr. **Andrew Turnbull** at New Smyrna, East Florida, the second-largest mass migration to the colonies. After an insurrection (p. 760), the colony was eventually abandoned (by 1777), and Turnbull lost his holdings.

IMMIGRATION TO U.S., 1790–1820 (8th Census, 1860, Prelim. Report, based upon a "survey of the irregular data previous to 1819"—a deduction of 14.5% for transients should be made from the following approximations): 1790–1800, 50,000; 1800–10, 70,000; 1810–20, 114,000.

1798. Alien and Sedition Laws (p. 155) providing for the deportation of subversive aliens.

1819–60. IMMIGRATION LAWS. State immigration laws, continuing colonial practices (Pa., head tax, 1729), generally required a bond upon entry of passengers deemed likely to be a public charge. Federal laws, 1819, 1847, 1848, 1855, were designed to protect immigrants from overcrowding and unsanitary conditions of the Atlantic crossing which had led to heavy mortality rate; largely ineffective.

1827–38. GREAT IRISH AND GERMAN MIGRATION to the U.S. began.

NATIONAL OR LINGUISTIC STOCKS IN THE U.S., 1790
(Based upon nomenclature, Census of 1790, as computed in Amer. Hist. Assn., *Ann. Rep., 1931,* I).[1]

State	Eng-lish	Scotch	Ulster	Irish Free State	German	Dutch	French	Swed-ish	Span-ish	Unas-signed	Total
Maine	60.0	4.5	8.0	3.7	1.3	0.1	1.3	....	....	21.1	100.0
New Hampshire	61.0	6.2	4.6	2.9	.4	.1	.7	....	....	24.1	100.0
Vermont	76.0	5.1	3.2	1.9	.2	.6	.4	....	....	12.6	100.0
Massachusetts	82.0	4.4	2.6	1.3	.3	.2	.8	....	....	8.4	100.0
Rhode Island	71.0	5.8	2.0	.8	.5	.4	.8	0.1	....	18.6	100.0
Connecticut	67.0	2.2	1.8	1.1	.3	.3	.9	....	....	26.4	100.0
New York	52.0	7.0	5.1	3.0	8.2	17.5	3.8	.5	....	2.9	100.0
New Jersey	47.0	7.7	6.3	3.2	9.2	16.6	2.4	3.9	....	3.7	100.0
Pennsylvania	35.3	8.6	11.0	3.5	33.3	1.8	1.8	.8	....	3.9	100.0
Delaware	60.0	8.0	6.3	5.4	1.1	4.3	1.6	8.9	....	4.1	100.0
Maryland and District of Columbia	64.5	7.6	5.8	6.5	11.7	.5	1.2	.5	....	1.7	100.0
Virginia and West Virginia	68.5	10.2	6.2	5.5	6.3	.3	1.5	.6	....	.9	100.0
North Carolina	66.0	14.8	5.7	5.4	4.7	.3	1.7	.2	....	1.2	100.0
South Carolina	60.2	15.1	9.4	4.4	5.0	.4	3.9	.2	....	1.4	100.0
Georgia	57.4	15.5	11.5	3.8	7.6	.2	2.3	.6	....	1.1	100.0
Kentucky and Tennessee	57.9	10.0	7.0	5.2	14.0	1.3	2.2	.5	....	1.9	100.0
Area enumerated	60.9	8.3	6.0	3.7	8.7	3.4	1.7	.7	....	6.6	100.0
Northwest Territory	29.8	4.1	2.9	1.8	4.3	....	57.1	....	....	....	100.0
Spanish, United States	2.5	.3	.2	.1	.4	....	....	....	96.5	....	100.0
French, United States	11.2	1.6	1.1	.7	8.7	....	64.2	....	12.5	....	100.0
Continental United States	60.1	8.1	5.9	3.6	8.6	3.1	2.3	0.7	0.8	6.8	100.0

[1] W. S. Rossiter, *A Century of Population Growth* (1909), had previously estimated English and Welsh stock at 82.1% of total; Scotch and Irish, 8.9%, and the Germans, 5.6% (1790).

Causes included (1) cold winter, 1829–30; (2) restrictive legislation against German Jews; (3) economic distress in Northern Ireland; (4) increasing factionalism in Southern Ireland.

1843–82. "OLD IMMIGRATION": Scandinavian, Irish, and German. (1) **Scandinavian:** Although the settlement of 53 Scandinavians in western New York, 1825, marked the beginning of the inflow to the U.S., a more substantial Swedish inflow began c.1841 with a settlement of a small group at Pine Lake, Wis., and the main Scandinavian migration setting in, 1843, with a total of 1,777 in that year. The number rose to 4,106, 1852, and then leveled off until the post-Civil War period, with peak immigration, 1868–83 (1882, 105,326), again leveling off to 29,391 by 1914. Settlement primarily in Wisconsin and Minnesota. (2) **Irish:** Although substantial Irish immigration began in 1809 and was resumed at the close of the War of 1812, the main flow started in the 1820s,

representing 44% of the total immigration, 1830–40. Irish immigration (largely Roman Catholic) reached its peak after the great famine of 1846, constituting 49% of the total, 1841–50. Such emigration was in part assisted by British and Irish authorities. The immigrants were employed on canal and railroad construction projects. All-time peak year, 1851, 221,253. Highest post-Civil War year, 1883, 81,486. (3) **German** immigration amounting to 30% of the total, 1830–40, was augmented by bad farm conditions in the 1840s and by political refugees from the Revolution of 1848 (e.g., **Carl Schurz**), with German colonies formed in New York, Baltimore, Cincinnati, St. Louis, and a completely Germanized Milwaukee (by 1850). Peak German migration, 1853–54, 356,955 for the two years, with revival beginning 1866, reaching 149,671 in 1873, and setting a pre-World War I peak in 1882 of 250,630.

IMMIGRATION TO THE U.S., 1820–1972
(U.S. Bureau of the Census, *Historical Statistics of the U.S. to 1957; Statistical Abstract, 1958–73.*)

Year	No. of Persons[1]	Year	No. of Persons[1]	Year	No. of Persons[1]
1820	8,385	1871	321,500	1922	309,556
1821	9,127	1872	404,806	1923	522,919
1822	6,911	1873	459,803	1924	706,896
1823	6,354	1874	313,339	1925	294,314
1824	7,912	1875	227,498	1926	304,488
1825	10,199	1876	169,986	1927	335,175
1826	10,837	1877	141,857	1928	307,255
1827	18,875	1878	138,469	1929	279,678
1828	27,332	1879	177,826	1930	241,700
1829	22,520	1880	457,257	1931	97,139
1830	23,322	1881	669,431	1932	35,576
1831	22,633	1882	788,992	1933	23,068
1832	60,482	1883	603,322	1934	29,470
1833	58,640	1884	518,592	1935	34,956
1834	65,365	1885	395,346	1936	36,329
1835	45,374	1886	334,203	1937	50,244
1836	76,242	1887	490,109	1938	67,895
1837	79,340	1888	546,889	1939	82,998
1838	38,914	1889	444,427	1940	70,756
1839	68,069	1890	455,302	1941	51,776
1840	84,066	1891	560,319	1942	28,781
1841	80,289	1892	579,663	1943	23,725
1842	104,565	1893	439,730	1944	28,551
1843	52,496	1894	285,631	1945	38,119
1844	78,615	1895	258,536	1946	108,721
1845	114,371	1896	343,267	1947	147,292
1846	154,416	1897	230,832	1948	170,570
1847	234,968	1898	229,299	1949	188,317
1848	226,527	1899	311,715	1950	249,187
1849	297,024	1900	448,572	1951	205,717
1850	369,980	1901	487,918	1952	265,520
1851	379,466	1902	648,743	1953	170,434
1852	371,603	1903	857,046	1954	208,177
1853	368,645	1904	812,870	1955	237,790
1854	427,833	1905	1,026,499	1956	321,625
1855	200,877	1906	1,100,735	1957	326,867
1856	200,436	1907	1,285,349	1958	253,265
1857	251,306	1908	782,870	1959	260,686
1858	123,126	1909	751,786	1960	318,000
1859	121,282	1910	1,041,570	1961	271,000
1860	153,640	1911	878,587	1962	284,000
1861	91,918	1912	838,172	1963	306,000
1862	91,985	1913	1,197,802	1964	292,000
1863	176,282	1914	1,218,480	1965	297,000
1864	193,418	1915	326,700	1966	323,000
1865	248,120	1916	298,826	1967	362,000
1866	318,568	1917	295,403	1968	454,448
1867	315,722	1918	110,618	1969	358,579
1868	138,840	1919	141,132	1970	373,326
1869	352,768	1920	430,001	1971	370,478
1870	387,203	1921	805,228	1972	384,685

[1] From 1820–67, figures represent alien passengers arrived; 1868–91 and 1895–97, immigrant aliens arrived; 1892–94 and 1898 to present, immigrant aliens admitted.

1849–1950. MEXICAN-AMERICANS IN THE U.S. The Treaty of Guadalupe Hidalgo (2 Feb. 1848) permitted Mexicans to continue to reside in the territories acquired thereunder by the U.S., including the right to acquire U.S. citizenship, guaranteed their property and the rights of U.S. citizens "according to the principles of the Constitution" (Articles VIII, IX). The period down to 1910 was marred by innumerable controversies over conflicting land grants and serious discrimination against Mexican-Americans, who served as the core of the labor force in the Southwest. After 1890 hundreds of thousands of Mexicans entered the U.S. illegally ("**wetbacks**"), enticed by American farm, railroad, and mining interests. Segregation was long practiced in California public schools under the law of 1885, amended 1893 (abolished since the 1950s), and ethnic clashes occurred sporadically—most notorious example the anti "Zoot-Suit" rioting in Los Angeles (June, 1943).

1854–68. Chinese immigrant labor (largely employed on transcontinental railroad projects, but in at least 1 case in a New England textile mill) totaled 75,000 in this period.

1865–85. CONTRACT LABOR. Office of Commissioner of Immigration established 4 July 1864; authorized to admit contract laborers under agreements based on a maximum of 12 months' labor for the immigrant's passage to the U.S.

1866. Most Southern states, notably South Carolina, attempted to attract European immigrants to take the place of Negro workers, but without success.

1868–82. CHINESE EXCLUSION. The Burlingame Treaty, 1868, gave Chinese the right to immigrate to the U.S., but anti-Chinese sentiment on the Pacific coast ("Sandlot Riots," San Francisco, July 1877) resulted in the enactment by Congress, 1879, of a bill abrogating the provision; vetoed by President Hayes, who appointed a commission to negotiate a new treaty. The result was the Treaty of 17 Nov. 1880 permitting the U.S. to "regulate, limit or suspend" but not to prohibit the entry of Chinese laborers. Chinese immigration in this period, 160,000, with 1882 the peak year,

IMMIGRATION BY COUNTRY OF ORIGIN, 1820–1950

(U.S. Bureau of the Census, Hist. Stat. of the U.S., 1789–1945; Statistical Abstract, 1946–50.)

(Figures are totals, not annual averages, and were tabulated as follows: 1820–67, alien passengers arrived; 1868–91 and 1895–97, immigrant aliens arrived; 1892–94 and 1898 to present, immigrant aliens admitted. Data below 1906 relate to country whence alien came; since 1906, to country of last permanent residence.)

Countries	1820–1900	1901–1910	1911–1920	1921–1930	1931–1940	1941–1950	1820–1950
Europe: Albania[1]	....	....	....	1,663	2,040	85	3,788
Austria[2]	1,027,195	2,145,266	453,649	32,868	3,563	24,860	4,172,104
Belgium	62,161	41,635	33,746	15,846	4,817	12,189	170,394
Bulgaria[3]	160	39,280	22,533	2,945	938	375	66,231
Czechoslovakia[1]	....	....	3,426	102,194	14,393	8,347	128,360
Denmark	192,768	65,285	41,983	32,430	2,559	5,393	340,418
Estonia[1]	....	....	....	1,576	506	212	2,294
Finland[1]	....	....	756	16,691	2,146	2,503	22,096
France	397,489	73,379	61,897	49,610	12,623	38,809	633,807
Germany[2]	5,010,248	341,498	143,945	412,202	114,058	226,578	6,248,529
Great Britain: England	1,824,054	388,017	249,944	157,420	21,756	112,252	2,753,443
Scotland	368,280	120,469	78,357	159,781	6,887	16,131	749,905
Wales	42,076	17,464	13,107	13,012	735	3,209	89,603
Not specified[4]	793,741	....	....	....	....	....	793,741
Greece	18,685	167,519	184,201	51,084	9,119	8,973	439,581
Hungary[2]	....	....	442,693	30,680	7,861	3,469	4,172,104
Ireland	3,873,104	339,065	146,181	220,591	13,167	25,377	4,617,485
Italy	1,040,479	2,045,877	1,109,524	455,315	68,028	57,661	4,776,884
Latvia[1]	....	....	....	3,999	1,192	361	4,952
Lithuania[1]	....	....	....	6,015	2,201	683	8,899
Luxembourg[1]	....	....	....	727	565	820	2,112
Netherlands	127,681	48,262	43,718	26,948	7,150	14,860	268,619
Norway[5]	474,684	190,505	66,395	68,531	4,740	10,100	814,955
Poland[6]	165,182	....	4,813	227,734	17,026	7,571	422,326
Portugal	63,840	69,149	89,732	29,994	3,329	7,423	263,467
Rumania[7]	19,109	53,008	13,311	67,646	3,871	1,076	158,021
Spain	41,361	27,935	68,611	28,958	3,258	2,898	173,021
Sweden[5]	771,631	249,534	95,074	97,249	3,960	10,665	1,228,113
Switzerland	202,479	34,922	23,091	29,676	5,512	10,547	306,227
Turkey in Europe	5,824	79,976	54,677	14,659	737	580	150,453
U.S.S.R.[8]	761,742	1,597,306	921,201	61,742	1,356	548	3,343,895
Yugoslavia[3]	....	....	1,888	49,064	5,835	1,576	58,363
Other Europe	1,940	665	8,111	9,603	2,361	5,573	28,253
Total Europe	17,285,913	8,136,016	4,376,564	2,477,853	348,289	621,704	33,246,339
Asia: China	305,455	20,605	21,278	29,907	4,928	16,709	398,882
India	696	4,713	2,082	1,886	496	1,761	11,634
Japan[9]	28,547	129,797	83,837	33,462	1,948	1,555	279,146
Turkey in Asia[10]	29,088	77,393	79,389	19,165	328	218	205,581
Other Asia	5,883	11,059	5,973	12,980	7,644	11,537	55,076
Total Asia	369,669	243,567	192,559	97,400	15,344	31,780	950,319
America: Canada & Newfoundland[11]	1,051,275	179,226	742,185	924,515	108,527	171,718	3,177,446
Central America	2,173	8,192	17,159	15,769	5,861	21,665	70,819
Mexico[12]	28,003	49,642	219,004	459,287	22,319	60,589	838,844
South America	12,105	17,280	41,899	42,215	7,803	21,831	143,133
West Indies	125,598	107,548	123,424	74,899	15,502	43,725	496,696
Other America[13]	....	....	....	31	25	29,276	29,332
Total America	1,219,154	361,888	1,143,671	1,516,716	160,037	354,804	4,756,270
Africa	2,213	7,368	8,443	6,286	1,750	7,367	33,427
Australia & New Zealand	19,679	11,975	12,348	8,299	2,231	13,805	68,337
Pacific Islands	7,810	1,049	1,079	427	780	5,437	16,582
Countries not specified	219,168	33,523[14]	1,147	228	....	142	254,208
Total all countries	19,123,606	8,795,386	5,735,811	4,107,209	528,431	1,035,039	39,325,482

[1] Countries added to list since beginning of World War I are theretofore included with countries to which they belonged. [2] Data for Austria-Hungary not reported until 1861. Austria and Hungary recorded separately after 1905. Austria included with Germany 1938–45. [3] Bulgaria, Serbia, Montenegro first reported in 1899. Bulgaria reported separately since 1920. In 1920, separate enumeration for Kingdom of Serbs, Croats, Slovenes; since 1922, recorded as Yugoslavia. [4] For United Kingdom. [5] Norway included with Sweden 1820–68. [6] Included with Austria-Hungary, Germany, and Russia 1899–1919. [7] No record of immigration until 1880. [8] Since 1931, U.S.S.R. has been broken down into European Russia and Siberia (Asiatic Russia). [9] No record of immigration until 1861. [10] No record of immigration until 1869. [11] Includes all British North American possession 1820–98. [12] No record of immigration 1886–93. [13] Included with "Countries not specified" prior to 1925. [14] Includes 32,897 persons returning in 1906 to their homes in U.S.

39,579. In 1882 a bill to prohibit the immigration of Chinese laborers for a period of 10 years received the signature of President Arthur. New treaty, 1894, recognized a 10-year exclusion period. Upon China's termination of this agreement, 1904, an exclusion act of 1902 was reenacted without terminal date. By Act of Congress, 17 Dec. 1943, Chinese immigration was permitted within the strict limitations of the quota system, with an annual quota of 105.

1882, 18 Aug. Federal act excluded criminals, paupers, the insane, and other undesirables, and imposed a head tax of 50 cts. upon those entering; subsequently raised to $2 (1903) and to $4 (1907).

1885, 26 Feb. CONTRACT LABOR ACT forbade the importation of contract laborers, but exempted professional, skilled, and domestic labor; modified, 1891, with respect to certain professional categories; again in 1907 and 1917.

1885–1914. "NEW IMMIGRATION" from Eastern and Southern Europe developed in the middle and late 1880s as prosperity dried up the source of German immigration. Heavy inflow now developed from Russia, Russian Poland, Austria-Hungary, the Balkans, and Italy. The periodic persecution of the Jews in Russia also contributed to large migrations.

1901–05: from Italy, 959,763; Russia, 658,735; Austria-Hungary, 944,239; Germany, 176,995; Great Britain and Ireland, 385,469. Concentration of sizable foreign-born blocs appeared in the larger cities: Chicago (Poles, Bohemians, Hungarians), New York (Italians and Jews), Boston (Irish). **1905–14:** zenith of U.S. immigration, with the million mark exceeded in 6 separate years. In the peak year, 1914, 73.4% of the total immigrants came from Southern and Eastern Europe as against 13.4% from Northern and Western Europe.

1887. AMERICAN PROTECTIVE ASSOCIATION founded at Clinton, La. An anti-Catholic, anti-immigrant organization, peaking in 1896.

1903, 3 Mar. Act providing for U.S. inspection of immigrants at European ports of departure, with the U.S. government given the right to deport any

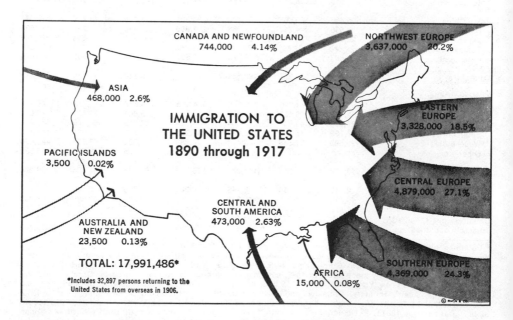

CANADA AND NEWFOUNDLAND
744,000   4.14%

NORTHWEST EUROPE
3,637,000   20.2%

ASIA
468,000   2.6%

**IMMIGRATION TO
THE UNITED STATES
1890 through 1917**

EASTERN EUROPE
3,328,000   18.5%

PACIFIC ISLANDS
3,500   0.02%

CENTRAL EUROPE
4,879,000   27.1%

CENTRAL AND
SOUTH AMERICA
473,000   2.63%

AUSTRALIA AND
NEW ZEALAND
23,500   0.13%

SOUTHERN EUROPE
4,369,000   24.3%

TOTAL: 17,991,486*

*Includes 32,897 persons returning to the
United States from overseas in 1906.

AFRICA
15,000   0.08%